DICTIONNAIRE ECONOMIQUE ET JURIDIQUE

FRANÇAIS-ANGLAIS
ANGLAIS-FRANÇAIS

ECONOMIC AND LEGAL DICTIONARY

FRENCH-ENGLISH
ENGLISH-FRENCH

Jean Baleyte
Professeur Agrégé d'Anglais
Chargé de cours au Centre d'Enseignement et de Recherche Appliqués au Management
(C.E.R.A.M., Sophia Antipolis)

Alexandre Kurgansky
Diplômé d'Études Supérieures de Droit Public
Chargé de cours à l'Université de Nice – Sophia Antipolis
Notaire

Christian Laroche
Docteur en Droit
Diplômé de l'Université de Cambridge (C.P.E.)
Maître de conférences à l'Université de Nice – Sophia Antipolis

Jacques Spindler
Docteur ès Sciences Économiques
Maître de conférences à l'Université de Nice – Sophia Antipolis
Directeur du Centre de Finances Publiques et d'Ingénierie Financière

DICTIONNAIRE ECONOMIQUE ET JURIDIQUE

ECONOMIC AND LEGAL DICTIONARY

3ᵉ édition
revue et augmentée

Préfaces de

René-Jean Dupuy
Professeur au Collège de France

et de

A.I. McEwan
K.C.H.S., Q.C., M.A., L.L.B.

L·G·D·J

© 1992 L.G.D.J.
ISBN 2-775-00643-5
Tous droits de reproduction, de traduction et d'exécution réservés pour tous pays

Avant-propos

Le Dictionnaire juridique, économique et fiscal français-anglais/anglais-français dont nous présentons la troisième édition est le résultat d'un travail collectif. Des activités complémentaires exercées dans des domaines différents et des préoccupations convergentes nous ont amenés à confronter et à partager des informations recueillies et des connaissances acquises séparément dans la poursuite de nos recherches au sein de l'Université de Nice. Ces dernières nous ont conduits à consulter un nombre considérable de documents anglais ou américains, non traduits ou, au mieux, traduits de manière infidèle. Des difficultés majeures ont surgi, que les dictionnaires existants ne permettent que trop rarement de résoudre et auxquelles il a fallu, par conséquent, apporter des solutions appropriées. Nous avons ainsi pris conscience des problèmes d'interprétation, au premier chef linguistiques, qui peuvent se poser aux utilisateurs français, même avertis, d'ouvrages spécialisés en langue anglaise, et notre propre expérience nous a, en même temps, rendu plus évidente, s'il est possible, la nécessité de l'interdisciplinarité.

Il était impérieux, par ailleurs, de mettre les résultats de la recherche au service des praticiens : exportateurs et importateurs, cadres de l'industrie et du commerce et, en général, de tous ceux qui, par leur fonction, ont à traiter de questions juridiques, économiques et fiscales dans le cadre des relations internationales et tout particulièrement dans la perspective du grand marché intérieur sans frontières promis aux européens pour le 1er janvier 1993. C'est donc un vaste public d'usagers éclairés que nous avons formé le dessein de servir ; il nous est, dès lors, apparu éminemment utile de réunir dans un même volume, sous une forme synthétique, l'essentiel du vocabulaire des affaires utilisé dans les pays de langue française et de langue anglaise.

Nous avons composé un dictionnaire qui sera, nous l'espérons, un instrument de travail efficace. Il ne peut s'agir, toutefois, que d'une œuvre imparfaite : l'exemple de Quemner, notre regretté prédécesseur dans la collection des dictionnaires bilingues des Éditions de Navarre, nous a appris qu'elle demeure sous la menace d'un vieillissement certain à plus ou moins long terme. Nous nous sommes donc efforcés de serrer au plus près l'actualité. Il n'était pas question, cependant, d'accepter des formes trop ésotériques ou des néologismes promis à un rapide oubli. De même, a été résolument exclu le « franglais » dont l'usage, révélateur d'une réelle et regrettable paresse de l'esprit ou d'un snobisme passager, se montre à l'occasion si dangereux.

Nous n'avons pas davantage donné asile à un grand nombre de termes et locutions d'argot de métier, presque tous américains, dont le pittoresque séduit mais qui n'en suscitent pas moins la méfiance. Seuls ont été retenus les plus usités, sur les conseils de nos amis d'Outre-Manche et d'Outre-Atlantique, parmi lesquels nous nous permettons de citer seulement Richard B. Tupper, de New York, si parfaitement informé, de par sa profession, du parler de la Bourse. En outre, il nous a semblé parfois nécessaire d'éclairer le sens de certaines expressions par un bref commentaire, mais en nous abstenant d'expliciter longuement les concepts.

Que cette nouvelle édition de l'ouvrage, fruit de recherches ininterrompues, soit maintenant à la disposition des lecteurs est une satisfaction dont il nous est agréable, pour conclure, de remercier les Éditions de Navarre.

J.B., A.K., C.L., J.S.
(Nice)

P.S. — Tout travail contenant nécessairement une part d'incertitude, nous serions reconnaissants au lecteur de bien vouloir signaler à l'éditeur les inexactitudes ou omissions qu'il aurait relevées en vue de rectifications ultérieures.

Première préface

« C'est une belle langue que l'anglais ; il en faut peu pour aller loin. Avec god dam, *en Angleterre, on ne manque de rien nulle part... Les Anglais, à la vérité, ajoutent par-ci par-là quelques autres mots en conversant ; mais il est bien aisé de voir que* god dam *est le fond de la langue. »*

Il semble que depuis cette boutade du Barbier de Séville, les Anglais n'aient cessé d'augmenter un vocabulaire que Beaumarchais feignait de croire superfétatoire. L'extraordinaire richesse de la langue anglaise et son extrême souplesse, si admirables en littérature, se retrouvent aussi dans l'écriture juridique et économique, encore que la technicité des domaines circonscrive la pensée et les mots dans l'ordre de la spécialité.

Celle-ci connaît une extension considérable du fait du buissonnement des relations d'affaires au plan international. Or celui-ci fait à l'anglais et au français une place dominante. Si du point de vue quantitatif le premier a aujourd'hui supplanté le second, la langue française reste très utilisée et l'on pourrait presque dire que, dans les rapports internationaux, l'anglais est aujourd'hui la langue de ceux qui ignorent le français. Tel est le cas des Nations Unies ou des Communautés Européennes, en dépit de la diversité des langues reconnues comme officielles. Mais il faut aussi et surtout compter avec les relations privées commerciales, toujours plus complexes.

L'utilisation du présent dictionnaire devrait justifier sa réussite. Il fallait pour en entreprendre l'élaboration un réel courage, les auteurs n'entendant pas se limiter au domaine juridique. A cet égard, le champ de cet ouvrage est singulièrement plus vaste que celui couvert par ses prédécesseurs.

L'élargissement du dictionnaire à l'économie et à la fiscalité était inévitable. Il serait artificiel de méconnaître que, de nos jours, le juridique et l'économique sont malaisément dissociables, comme d'ignorer l'importance croissante des questions fiscales dans les rapports transnationaux. On ne saurait dès lors se borner au vocabulaire juridique au sens étriqué du terme, sous peine de réduire considérablement la valeur pratique de l'ouvrage.

Certes le présent dictionnaire ne porte pas en principe sur les concepts, mais sur le vocabulaire, il n'en reste pas moins que la dialectique des mots et des choses est subtile, mouvante, riche d'ambiguïtés, accrues par les disparités de régime juridique existant entre les pays concernés.

Cette observation imposait un travail interdisciplinaire ; il a été rendu possible par le Professeur Jean Baleyte dont les qualifications techniques de linguiste éminent se doublent d'une personnalité attachante, aimée de générations d'étudiants et qui fait de lui un remarquable animateur. Il a su constituer une équipe de haute valeur et d'un singulier dynamisme. Avec M. Jacques Spindler, aussi savant économiste et fiscaliste qu'angliciste consommé, il a fait appel à deux juristes linguistes, M. Alexandre Kurgansky, notaire, et M. Christian Laroche, également fiscaliste, qui se sont lancés avec enthousiasme et compétence dans la tâche commune.

Le résultat nous paraît excellent. Il répond d'abord essentiellement aux besoins de la pratique. Elle dispose désormais d'un instrument de travail dont elle ne saurait se passer. Pour être avant tout conçu pour servir aux praticiens, ce dictionnaire ne s'adresse pas moins aux chercheurs qui travaillent sur un plan scientifique, notamment dans l'ordre du droit comparé.

Il faut voir que pour les uns comme pour les autres, le temps n'est plus où le recours au dictionnaire se bornait à faciliter la lecture. Il est de plus en plus fréquent d'écrire en anglais, devenu instrument quasi universel de communication.

On songe à l'observation de Charles Dickens : « La difficulté d'écrire l'anglais m'est extrêmement ennuyeuse. Ah, mon Dieu ! Si l'on pouvait toujours écrire cette belle langue de France ! »

Il semble que chacun éprouve pour sa propre langue le sentiment de ses difficultés intimes : « C'est une langue bien difficile que le français, disait Colette. A peine écrit-on depuis quarante-cinq ans qu'on commence à s'en apercevoir. »

Aussi bien ce dictionnaire ne saurait avoir la prétention de faire de ses utilisateurs des écrivains anglais ou français dans une langue qui n'est pas la leur, mais il permettra sûrement aux uns d'exprimer avec rigueur et précision leur pensée comme aux autres d'en saisir fidèlement la portée.

Il faut pour rédiger un tel dictionnaire avoir en tête non seulement l'exigence du sens du mot, usuel ou exceptionnel, mais encore des nuances qu'il peut permettre.

Cet ouvrage, dû à la conjonction de l'expérience, du savoir et de la probité, constitue un outil précieux. Seul un travail conduit avec une rigueur scientifique indiscutable pouvait satisfaire les impératifs de la pratique.

René Jean DUPUY
Professeur au Collège de France
(Paris)

Seconde préface

Given the extraordinary degree of erudition, ingenuity, judgment and the other qualities required on the part of those who collaborate to produce a dictionary, and in particular a bi-lingual dictionary, one might be pardoned perhaps for supposing that only a lexicographer should presume to write a preface to the finished work. However, in these days, when consumers boldly make their voices heard in the market-place, the views of users, even of dictionaries, may be not without relevance.

One of the many consequences or at any rate concomitants of McLuhan's concept of the global village in the electronic era is the ever-accelerating pace of change in all areas of human endeavour. Even to-day's vocabulary will be obsolescent to-morrow. At the same time, ours is an era of national interdependence quite as much as of national independence. Industrialists, businessmen and professionals of every country are and must be in daily communication with each other if they are to fulfil their obligations to society. It is not surprising, therefore, that translation bureaus are mushrooming in every major city and that there is a pressing demand for up-to-date bilingual and multi-lingual dictionaries oriented towards serving the needs of the business and professional communities of the major linguistic groups.

As a practising lawyer in the field of corporate and commercial law, I regard a dictionary such as this as an invaluable tool which I must have to hand if I am to respond to the exigencies of my practice.

In no dictionary can the word list ever be complete. Consequently, an important part of the high art of the lexicographer lies in his capacity to be selective. Having had an opportunity to review some of the proofs of this dictionary, I have been greatly impressed by the layout, the clear type and, above all, the combination of erudition and the sense of practicality which have gone into the selection of the word list.

In my submission, the authors have rendered a signal service to us all in producing a work which possesses such useful physical attributes and at the same time evinces a scholarly concern to help the user find rapidly "le mot juste".

I.A. McEWAN, K.C.H.S. Q.C., M.A., LLB.
(Toronto, Ont., Canada)

FRANÇAIS-ANGLAIS

ABRÉVIATIONS

A.	Administration	Administration
a.	adjectif	adjective
A.A.	Anglo-américain	Anglo-american
adv.	adverbe	adverb
ASS.	Assurance	Insurance
B.	Bourse	Stock Exchange
C.	Commerce, droit commercial	Commerce, commercial law
C.E.E.	Communauté Économique Européenne	European Economic Community
cf.	confer	confer
civ.	civil	civil
C.L.	Common Law	Common Law
conj.	conjonction	conjunction
cr.	criminel	criminal
D.	Douanes	Customs
Eco.	Économie	Economy
E.	Exportation	Export
e.g.	par exemple	exempli gratia
Engl.	Angleterre	England
Eq.	Equity	Equity
esp.	spécialement	especially
etc.	et caetera	et cetera
F.	Finance, fiscalité	Finance, taxation
f.	substantif féminin	feminine noun
Fam.	Familier	colloquial
fig.	au figuré	figuratively
hist.	historique	historic
i.e.	par exemple	id est
inform.	informatique	data processing
inv.	invariable	invariable
journ.	journalisme	journalism
J.	Juridique	Juridical
m.	substantif masculin	masculine noun
milit.	militaire	military
M.P.	Membre du Parlement	Member of Parliament
n.b.	nota bene	nota bene
N.Y.	New York	New York
opp.	opposé	opposed
part.	participe	participle
pej.	péjoratif	pejorative
p.ex.	par exemple	for example
pol.	politique	political
pl.	pluriel	plural
pr.	procédure	procedure
prep.	préposition	preposition
qch.	quelque chose	something
qfs.	quelquefois	sometimes
qn.	quelqu'un	some one
q.v.	se reporter à (ce mot)	see (this word)
r.	relatif	relative
s.	substantif	substantive
Scot.	Ecosse	Scotland
sg.	singulier	singular
s.o.	quelqu'un	some one
sp.	spécialement	especially
sth.	quelque chose	something
syn.	synonyme	synonymous
U.K.	Royaume-Uni	United Kingdom
U.S.	États-Unis	United States
v.	verbe	verb

Le signe = veut dire égal à.
Le signe # indique la plus proche correspondance d'un terme ou d'une notion dans l'autre langue.

The symbol = means equal to.
The symbol # shows the nearest meaning of a term or notion in the other language.

A

à *(30 jours) de date* : (30 days) after date.

à l'abandon : in utter neglect.
— (m) *de possession* : abandonment of property.

à l'amiable : amiably.
[J] by private contract.

abondance (f) : plenty.
année d'— : bonanza.
société d'— (la) : the affluent society.

à bon droit : lawfully, rightfully.

à la condition que : provided that.

a contrario : to the contrary.

à l'encontre de : in opposition, to the contrary.
aller à l'— : to go against.

à fonds perdus : without security.

à juste titre : as it should be, as was only fair.

à peine de : under penalty of.

à qui de droit : to whom it may concern.
transmis, renvoyé — : referred to the party concerned, to the competent authority.

à tant de date : maturing... days after date.

à valoir sur : on account of.

à vie : lifelong.

ab intestat : [J] intestate.
décéder — : to die intestate.
hériter — : to succeed to an intestate estate.
succession — : intestacy.

ab ovo : from the very beginning.

abaissement *(des prix)* (m) : lowering (of prices).

abaisser *(prix, taux, etc.)* (v) : to bring down, to lessen, to reduce (prices, rates, etc.).

abandon *(de famille, de droits, de biens...)* (m) : abandonment (of family), cession, renunciation, surrender (of rights, property...).
— *d'actif* : composition between merchant (debtor) and creditors by surrender of property, yielding up of assets.
— *(d'enfant, de foyer)* : desertion (of child, of home).
— *de biens d'un failli à ses créanciers* : surrender of a bankrupt's property.
— *des poursuites* : abandonment of action, nolle prosequi, discontinuance, voluntary nonsuit.
biens à l'— : ownerless property.
faire — : to make over.
abandonnataire (m) : [J] releasee, [ASS] abandonee.
abandonnateur (m) : [J] releasor.

abandonner (v) : to give up, to renounce, to surrender.
— *des droits* : to surrender rights.
— *des poursuites judiciaires contre un débiteur* : to surrender suing a debtor.
— *une police d'assurance sur la vie par rachat* : to surrender a life insurance (assurance) policy.
— *ses prétentions* : to renounce one's claims.
enfant **abandonné**, *femme abandonnée* : deserted child, wife.
objet abandonné : derelict.

abattement *(d'impôts)* (m) : abatement, allowance, deduction, exemption, remission, [U.S.] tax break.
— *à la base* : basic abatement, personal allowance.
— *forfaitaire* : standard deduction.

abdication (f) : abdication.

abdiquer (v) : *(renoncer au trône)* to abdicate, to renounce the throne, *(renoncer à des droits)* to renounce (rights).

aberration (f) : aberration.
— *mentale* : insanity.

abjurer (v) : to forswear.

abolir (v) : to suppress, to abolish.

abolition (f) : abolishment, abolition.
— *(d'un arrêté ou décret)* : annulment, repeal (of a decree).

abonnement (m) : subscribing, subscription.
[D] composition for dues.
[F] *payer par* — : to pay by instalments.
[ASS] *police d'*— : floating policy.
s'abonner (v) : *(à un journal)* to subscribe to a newspaper, *(aux chemins de fer)* to take a season-ticket.

aborder *(l'affaire au fond)* (v) : to take up the main issue.

aborner (v) : to mark out (field, etc.), to delimit.
abornement *d'un champ* (m) : marking out a field.

aboutissant (m) : abutting, adjacent, bordering.
(m pl) [J] *les tenants et* —*(s)* : fronting and abutting parts (of an estate), abutalls.
les tenants et —*(s) d'une affaire* : full details of an affair.

abréger (v) : *(un texte)* to epitomize (a text), *(des débats)* to summarize (proceedings, hearings).
— *l'exposé des faits* : to state the facts briefly.

abréviation (f) : shortening, contraction, abbreviation.

abri (m) : shelter.
sans-— : homeless.

abrogatif (a) : abrogative.

abrogation (f) : abrogation, cancellation, rescission.
[J] — *d'une loi* : repeal of a law.
clause **abrogatoire** : annulling, rescinding clause.

abroger *(loi, article)* (v) : to repeal (law, section).

absence (f) : absence.
— *de l'une des parties à un procès* : nonappearance of a party to an action.
— *de contrepartie (dans un contrat)* : absence of consideration (in a contract).
absent *(personne dont on est sans nouvelles depuis sept ans, ce qui constitue une présomption de décès)* : an individual unheard of for seven years (a presumption of death).
absent (a) *(contribuable)* : absent (taxpayer).

absolu (a) : absolute.
règle —*(e)* : hard and fast rule.

absolutoire (a) : absolving.
[J] *décision* — : acquittal.

excuse — : excuse involving acquittal.

absorber (v) : to absorb.
société **absorbée** *par une nouvelle société* : company incorporated in a new company.

absorption *(d'une société)* (f) : amalgation merger (of a company).

(s') abstenir de (v) : to abstain from.
— *une succession (ne pas faire acte d'héritier)* : to forgo an inheritance (abstention).

abstention (f) : abstention, disclaimer.
— *fautive* : nonfeasance, punishable abstention.

abus (m) : [J] abuse, infringement, misuse, violation.
— *d'autorité* : misuse of authority.
— *de confiance* : breach of trust, fraudulent misuse of funds.
— *de droit* : abuse of right, misuse of law.
— *de droits* : infringement of rights.
— *de jouissance* : infringement (abuse) of ownership, disturbance of possession.
— *de pouvoir* : abuse of discretion, ultra vires.
commettre un — *de pouvoir* : to override one's commission.
— *de la puissance paternelle* : misuse of parental authority.
réformer un — : to redress an abuse.

abuser (v) : to misuse, to deceive, to act improperly.
— *de la bonne foi de quelqu'un* : to take advantage of s.o.'s good faith.
— *d'une fille* : to rape a girl.

abusif (a) : improper, unauthorized.
[F] *réserves* **abusives** : improper accumulations.

abusivement (adv) : improperly.

accaparement (m) : coemption, buying out, monopolizing.

accaparer (v) : to corner, to hoard, to buy up stocks, to monopolize.

accapareur (m) : buyer up, (U.S.) cornerer, monopolist.

accéder (v) : [J] *(à une requête)* to comply with a request, *(à un pacte)* to accede to a covenant.

accéléré (a) : accelerated.
[J] *procédure* —*(e)* : expeditious procedure.

acceptation (f): acceptance.
[J] [C] — *bénéficiaire, sous bénéfice d'inventaire*: acceptance without liability beyond the assets descended.
— *de banque*: banker's acceptance.
crédit par —: acceptance facility.
— *(s) croisées*: acceptance cross-facilities.
— *de donation, de succession*: acceptance of a donation, an estate.
— *tacite*: tacit acceptance.
à défaut d'—: in case of non-acceptance.
— *sous condition, sous réserve*: qualified acceptance.
— *par honneur, par intervention*: acceptance supra protest, act of honour.
défaut d'—: non-acceptance.
maison d'—: accepting house.
refuser l'—: to dishonour a bill.
accepter: to accept, to agree (to do).
accepter une lettre de change: to meet, to honour a bill.
faire accepter une traite: to get (have) a draft (bill, effect) met (honoured, accepted).
accepté (a): accepted.

accepteur (m): [C] acceptor, drawee.

acception (f): acception, favouring, partiality.
[J] *la loi ne fait — de personne*: equal protection of law.

accès (m): access, approach.
voies d'—: approaches.
[J] *droit d'—*: right of access.

accessible à (a): accessible, available to, open to.

accession (f): *(au pouvoir)* accession (to power), *(à un contrat)* adherence (to a contract), *(à un traité)* accession (to a treaty), *(à une charge publique)* entry (to an office).

accessoire (a et m): (a) accessory, incidental.
[J] *droits —(s)*: appurtenances.
garantie —: collateral security.
[F] *avantages —(s)*: [U.S.] fringe benefits.
frais —(s): incidental expenses.
revenus —(s): additional (extra) earnings.
[A] *règlement — à l'application d'une loi*: regulation incidental to the administration of an act.
(m) *l'— suit le principal*: the decision on the main issue applies to accessory matters.
les —(s): fittings, appurtenances.

accident (m): accident.
— *de la circulation*: street, road accident.
— *mortel*: fatality, fatal accident.
— *de personne*: casualty.
— *du travail*: work-injury, industrial accident, occupational accident (injury).
assurance individuelle-—: casualty insurance.
constat d'—: report on accident.
par —: fortuitously.
[F] — *de parcours (dans la marche normale du marché)*: hiccup.

accidenté (a et m): *(personne)* the victim of an accident, *(automobile)* damaged (car).
les accidentés (m pl): the casualties, the injured.

accidentel (a): accidental.

accipiens (m): the beneficiary.

accise (f): [F] excise.
droits d'—: excise duties.

accommodement (m): [C] composition.
en venir à un — avec qqn: to come to terms with s.o.
faire un —: to compose.
par voie d'—: by way of composition.
un mauvais — vaut mieux qu'un bon procès: an indifferent settlement is better than a good case in court.

accompli *(fait)* (a): accomplished (fact).

accomplir (v): *(promesse, commandement)* to fulfil (promise, order), *(réussir à)* to achieve, to carry out.

accomplissement (m): accomplishment, achievement, carrying out.
dans l'— de ses devoirs: while on duty, in the performance of one's duties.
— *d'une condition*: fulfilment of a condition.

acconage (m): lighterage.

acconier (m): lighterage contractor.

accord (m): agreement, consent, settlement.
[A] — *(= règlement)*: settlement.
— *général sur les tarifs douaniers et le commerce*: General Agreement on Tariffs and Trade (G.A.T.T.).
— *sectoriel conclu entre le personnel d'une seule usine d'une société et cette société*: factory agreement.
[J] (C) *conclure, passer un —*: to enter into an agreement.
d'un commun —: by common consent.
en parfait —: in perfect understanding.
si un — intervient: if an agreement is reached.
se mettre d'— (avec): to come to an agreement (with).

accorder (v) : to allow, to grant.
[F] — *un dégrèvement* : to allow a deduction.
déduction **accordée** *aux personnes âgées* : age allowance.
[J] (C) — *un délai* : to allow time, respite.
— *un différend* : to settle a difference.
— *des dommages intérêts* : to award damages.
[A] — *une autorisation* : to license.

(s') accorder (v) : to settle for (sth).

accoutumé (a) : customary.

accréditation (f) : accreditation.

accrédité (m) : agent. [F] holder of a letter of credit.
presse —(e) : journalistic establishment.

accréditer (v) : to give standing to s.o.
— *un ambassadeur (accréditation)* : to accredit an ambassador.

accréditeur (m) : [F] surety, guarantor.

accréditif (m) : [F] letter of credit (also *lettre accréditive*).
loger un — : to open a credit with a bank.

accroissement (m) : increase.
taux d'— : rate of growth, increase.
[J] *droit d'*— : accretion (of legacy, of rights of survivors, through death of co-legatee or interested party).
[F] — *de valeur* : appreciation.

accroître (v) : to increase.
— *la circulation fiduciaire* : to inflate currency.

accueillir (v) : to receive, to greet.
— *une requête* : to accede to a request.

acculer à la faillite (v) : to squeeze, [U.S.] to corner.

accumulation (f) : accumulation (of income, of interests).
— *des impôts* : pyramiding-taxes.
accumuler *(thésauriser)* : to accumulate, to hoard money.

accusateur (m).
[J] — *privé* : plaintiff.
— *public (Ministère public)* : public prosecutor.

accusation (f) : [J] accusation, charge, prosecution.
acte d'— : indictment, charge.
chef d'— : count of indictment, specification, particulars of charge.
mise en — : arraignment, committal for trial.

chambre des mises en — # grand jury.
l'— : the case for the Crown, [U.S.] the State.

accusé (a et m) : (a) — *de complicité* : indicted on a charge of complicity.
(m) (cr.) accused, defendant, prisoner at the bar.

accuser (v) : to accuse, to charge (with).
[C] — *réception de* : to acknowledge receipt of.

achalandage (m) : goodwill, custom.

achat (m) : purchase, buying ; thing bought.
— *au comptant* : purchase for ready money, for cash.
— *à crédit* : purchase on credit.
— *à découvert* : bull purchase.
— *de fournitures* : procurement.
[B] — *de soutien d'une devise nationale sur le marché des changes* : support buying.
— *à tempérament* : instalment buying.
— *à terme* : purchase for the account.
facture d'— : invoice.
ordre d'— : indent.
pouvoir d'— : purchasing (spending) power.
prix d'— : prime cost, actual cost, cost price, purchase price.
promesse d'— : promise to buy.
service des —(s) : buying department.

acheminer *(marchandises)* (v) : to forward, to dispatch (goods).

acheter (v) : to buy, to purchase.
[B] — *à découvert* : to bull the market.
— *à la baisse (hausse)* : to buy for a fall (rise).
— *à terme* : to buy for cash.
— *à 30 jours* : to buy at 30 days after date.
[C] — *à crédit* : to buy on credit.
— *au détail* : to buy by retail.
— *en gros* : to buy wholesale (in bulk).
— *ferme* : to make a firm purchase.

acheteur (m) : buyer, purchaser.
[J] vendee.
solde — : buyer's balance.
[C] *obligations des* —(s) : buyers' obligations.
obligations d'un — : agreement binding upon a buyer.

achèvement *(d'un travail)* (m) : completion (of work).
vente en l'état futur d'— : sale for possession on completion.

aciérie (f) : steel works.

acolyte (m): accomplice.

acompte (m): instalment, payment on account.
— *sur dividende*: interim dividend.
— *de préférence*: option money.
en — : on account.
recevoir un — : to receive money on account.
vente par — *(s)*: sale on the deferred payment (instalment) scheme, hirepurchase.
verser un — : to pay in an instalment.
[F] — *provisionnel*: provisional instalment.
— *provisionnel de base*: instalment base.
— *trimestriel*: provisional quarterly instalment.

(les) à-côtés d'une question : the side-issue of a question.

acquéreur (m): purchaser.
[J] one who acquires title, particularly to immovable property, by purchase.
— *en vertu d'un droit de préemption*: [U.S.] pre-emptor.

acquérir (v): to acquire, to secure.
— *force de la chose jugée*: indisputable rights acquired after a judgement at law (res judicata).
— *la personnalité morale*: to acquire the legal status of an artificial person.

acquêt (m): [J] acquired property (property acquired in common by husband and wife).
communauté réduite aux — *(s)*: joint estate of husband and wife comprising only property acquired after their marriage.

acquiescement *(à un jugement)* (m): [J] acceptance of a judgement.

acquiescer (v): to acquiesce in, to assent to.
— *à une demande, requête*: to meet a demand, a request.

acquis (a): acquired.
droits — : vested interests.

acquisition (f): acquisition, purchase.

acquit (m): [J] acquittal.
ordonnance d' — : order of acquittal.
[D] clearance certificate *(navire, aéronef)*.
— *-à-caution*: permit, transire, excise-bond, bond-note.
— *de franchise*: clearance inwards duty free.
— *de sortie*: exeat, clearance outwards.
[C] receipt, acquittance.
donner — *de qch.*: to give receipt for sth.
payer le solde à l' — *de qn*: to pay the balance on s.o.'s behalf.

« *pour* — » : « received with thanks », « paid », « settled ».

acquittement (m): [J] acquittal, verdict of not guilty, dismissal, discharge.
[C] *(d'une dette, d'un paiement)*: discharge (of a debt, of a payment).
en — *d'une dette*: in satisfaction of a debt.

acquitter (v): to acquit, to discharge, to dismiss (a prisoner), to pay off, to settle.
— *une dette*: to discharge a debt.
— *une facture, une lettre de change*: to receipt an invoice, a bill.
— *qn d'une obligation*: to release s.o. from an obligation.
s' — *d'une obligation*: to fulfil, to carry out, to discharge an obligation.
[D] — *les droits*: to pay the duties.

acte (m): outward act.
— *délictueux, criminel*: misdemeanour, felony.
— *frauduleux*: fraudulent action.
— *illicite*: illicit, forbidden action.
— *licite*: lawful, permissible action.
— *de présence*: appearance.
— *punissable*: punishable action.
— *sexuel*: sexual intercourse.
— *de soumission*: surrender.
— *d'usage*: normal, customary action.
[J] 1. **acte juridique**: legal transaction.
— *d'aliénation*: transfer of property or rights, conveyance.
— *d'attribution*: assignment.
— *bilatéral*: bilateral act.
— *à cause de mort*: statement of last wishes.
— *de commerce*: act of merchant.
— *de complaisance*: act of accommodation.
— *pour le compte de qui il appartiendra, pour le nommable, par élection d'ami (de command)*: action on behalf of the interested party.
— *consensuel*: contract by mutual assent (whatever the form).
— *constitutif*: incorporation.
— *de crédit*: opening of credit.
— *déclaratif*: adjudicative decree, declaration of legal status.
— *de dépôt*: bailment.
— *en double*: act in duplicate.
— *extrajudiciaire*: extrajudicial act, act out of court.
— *fictif, simulé*: fictitious, sham transaction.
— *fiduciaire*: fiduciary agreement, contract of trusteeship.
— *d'héritier*: claim of inheritance.
— *interruptif d'instance*: stay of proceedings.
— *interruptif de prescription*: interruption of prescription, [U.S.] toll of the statute (of limitations).
— *de nantissement*: hypothecation certificate.
— *nul*: deed null and void.

— *du palais* : act between two counsels, [U.S.] attorneys at law.
— *de possession* : assumption of ownership.
— *préparatoire* : preparatory action.
— *de procédure* : legal proceedings.
— *recognitif* : recognizance, recognitory act.
— *résolutoire* : resolutory action, rescission, defeasance.
— *de société* : deed of partnership.
— *solennel* : act in solemn form.
— *en suspens* : transaction in abeyance.
— *suspensif* : suspensive action.
— *à titre gratuit* : deed-poll.
— *à titre onéreux* : contract for valuable consideration.
— *translatif du droit de propriété* : assignment of title, conveyance.
— *unilatéral* : act of benevolence.
— *de vente* : agreement for sale.
— *entre vifs* : res inter vivos acta.
— *de dernière volonté* : last will and testament.
2. **écrit rédigé en vue de constater un acte juridique** : proof in writing of a legal transaction.
— *d'accusation* : bill of indictment.
— *additionnel* : rider.
— *d'adhésion* : accession, adhesion.
— *authentique* : instrument executed, drawn up by a notary or by a public authority.
— *en brevet* : instrument, the original of which is not kept by the notary but handed over to the parties.
— *de cautionnement* : surety bond, guaranty.
— *de cession* : conveyance, deed of transfer, assignment.
— *de concession* : concession, licence, franchise, charter, grant.
— *constitutif de gage* : mortgage bond, debenture bond.
— *de donation entre vifs* : deed of gift.
— *de fondation* : deed of foundation.
— *instrumentaire* : process.
— *judiciaire* : writ.
— *en minute* : act, the original of which is kept by the authorities or by a notary.
— *notarié, passé devant notaire* : deed executed and authenticated by a notary.
— *de notoriété* : certificate, affidavit.
— *officiel* : official document.
— *de partage* : act of partition of real property.
prendre — *de* : to take legal cognizance.
— *probant, probatoire* : cogent evidence.
— *de procédure* : writ, process, summons.
— *public* : official document.
— *privé, sous seing privé* : simple contract, private agreement made in writing but not sealed and witnessed.
demander, donner — *de* : to have sth. certified, confirmed in writing, recorded in a minute-book.
« *donner* — *de... que* » : « to give official notice of... that... ».
— *en double* : public or private instrument drawn up in two originals.
dresser, passer un — : to draw up, to execute an act.
[A] — *d'administration* : administrative act (action).
— *anticonstitutionnel* : unconstitutional action.
— *arbitraire* : arbitrary action.
faire — *d'autorité* : to act with full powers.
— *de baptême* : christening certificate.
— *de bonne vie et mœurs* : certificate of good character.
— *constitutionnel* : constitutional act (action).
— *de décès* : death certificate.
— *diplomatique* : diplomatic instrument.
— *de gouvernement* : act of state.
— *juridictionnel, de juridiction contentieuse* : sentence, judgement in disputed matters.
— *de juridiction gracieuse* : act of voluntary jurisdiction.
— *législatif* : legislative act (action).
— *de mariage* : marriage certificate.
— *de naissance* : birth certificate.
— *de nationalité* : ship's certificate of registry.
— *officiel, public* : official act (action).
— *de poursuite* : (civ.) proceedings, (cr.) prosecution.
[D] — *de francisation* : certificate of registry.
(m pl) records, transactions.
— (s) *de l'état civil* : birth, marriage and death certificates.
Acte unique européen (A.U.E.) : Single European Act (SEA).

actif (a et m) : (a) active, brisk.
population active : working population, gainfully employed population.
(m) assets, credit account.
[C] *commerce* — : brisk business (trade).
[J] — *successoral* : net estate.
[F] — *disponible* : available assets, liquid assets.
— (s) *douteux* : doubtful assets.
— (s) *engagés* : pledged assets.
— *immobilisé* : capital assets, fixed assets, tied up capital.
— *net* : net assets.
— *net rectifié* : adjusted net book value.
— *réalisable* : realizable assets.
— *social* : company's assets.
apport partiel d' — : partial business transfer.
insuffisance d' — : insufficiency of assets.
plus-value d' — : capital gains on fixed assets.
rendement des — (s) : return on investment (R.O.I.).
sous-estimation de l' — : undervaluation of assets.

action (f) : 1° **action**.
[J] action, claim, complaint, lawsuit, prosecution.

— *aquilienne*: action for compensation with respect to wrongful damage done to property.
— *en cessation de trouble de jouissance*: action for disturbance of possession.
— *de change*, — *cambiaire*: claim based on a bill of exchange.
— *civile*: action for damage caused by an agent.
— *confessoire*: affirmative, petitory action for the enforcement of an encumbrance on real estate.
— *en constatation d'un droit*: affirmative action for a right.
— *en contestation d'état*: action to dispute a legal status.
— *en contestation de l'état de collocation*: action for modification of collocation of the established order of priority of creditors in bankruptcy.
— *en contrefaçon*: action for infringement of patent.
— *en déchéance de brevet*: action for forfeiture of patent.
— *en désaveu de paternité*: action for disavowal, for repudiation, bastardy case.
— *directe*: direct action.
— *en divorce*: divorce suit.
— *en dommages-intérêts*: claim for damages.
— *pour cause d'enrichissement sans cause*: action for money had and received, equitable action for mistake.
— *en exécution de contrat*: action for specific performance.
— *immobilière*: real action.
— *en indemnité*: claim for compensation.
— *en libération de dette*: action for discharge of debt.
— *en liquidation de l'actif social*: action for liquidation of the company's assets.
— *en mainlevée*: action for replevin, for restoration of rights.
— *mixte*: mixed action (for the recovery of a thing or for damages, and also for the payment of a penalty, i.e. an action both real and personal).
— *mobilière*: personal action.
— *négatoire*: negatory action (to establish the non-encumbrance of an estate).
— *en nullité*: action for avoidance of contract.
— *oblique*: indirect action of the creditor, availing himself of the rights of his negligent debtor (also called *action indirecte* or *action subrogatoire*).
— *en paiement*: action for payment.
— *en partage*: action for distribution.
— *de la partie civile, conclusions civiles*: action instituted by a private person for damages, parallel to prosecution in a criminal case.
— *en recherche de paternité*: action of bastard for affiliation.
— *en réclamation d'état*: claim of legitimate child to affirm his status.

— *paulienne*: revocatory action.
— *pénale*: criminal action.
— *en pétition d'hérédité*: claim to succeed to an estate held by a third party.
— *pétitoire*: petitory, affirmative action, claim of ownership.
— *possessoire*: possessory action, claim for possession of real estate.
— *principale*: main issue.
— *publique*: prosecution.
— *en radiation de marque, de brevet*: action for annulment of trade-mark, of patent rights.
— *en reconnaissance de dette*: action for acknowledgement of debt.
— *reconventionnelle*: counter-claim, cross-action.
— *en rectification de l'état civil*: action for rectifying civil status (in public registers of birth, marriage and death).
— *en rectification de cadastre*: action for rectifying the data of a cadastral survey.
— *en reddition de compte*: action for an (involuntary) account.
— *en réduction des dispositions du défunt*: action in abatement.
— *en réduction du prix*: (quanti minoris) action for goods sold and delivered.
— *réelle*: (actio in rem) real action.
— *en réintégration (réintégrande)*: action for reinstatement, restoration.
— *en réparation du préjudice*: action for legal redress.
— *en réparation du préjudice moral*: action for vindictive damages, smart-money, heart-balm action.
— *en répétition de l'indu*: (condictio indebiti) action for the recovery of payment made by mistake.
— *rescisoire, résolutoire*: rescissory action.
— *en responsabilité*: vicarious liability action.
— *en restitution*: action for restitution, rehabilitation.
— *en revendication*: (condictio possessionis) action for recovery of property.
— *en revendication immobilière*: action for declaration of title to land.
— *révocatoire*: revocatory action (of will, etc.).
— *en séparation de biens*: action for separate maintenance, for separation of estate.
— *en séparation de corps*: (a mensa et thoro) action for separation from bed and board.
intenter une — *à qn*: to institute proceedings, to bring a lawsuit against s.o., to sue s.o., to go to law.
mandat d'— : receiving order (in bankrupcy).
2° **part du capital social** [F] [C] share, [U.S.] stock.
—(s) *qui priment en matière de dividendes*: shares that rank first in dividend rights.
—(s) *qui prendront part à la distribution des dividendes du mois*: shares that will rank for

this month dividends.
— *d'apport* : initial share.
— *cotée* : listed share.
— *non cotée* : unlisted share.
— *différée* : deferred share.
— *ne donnant pas droit à dividende* : exrights share.
— *émise* : issued share, outstanding share.
— *de fondation* : founder's share.
— *de garantie* : qualification share.
— *gratuite* : bonus share.
— *indivise* : joint share.
— *à l'introduction* : shop share.
— *de jouissance* : dividend share.
— *libérée* : fully paid share.
— *non libérée* : partly paid share.
— *nominative* : registered share.
— *de numéraire* : share paid in money *(opp. action d'apport).*
— *ordinaire* : ordinary share, [U.S.] common stock, equity security. *(le terme « equity » qui s'applique en fait à ce qui reste à un emprunteur après qu'il se soit libéré d'une hypothèque est aussi communément employé dans le sens d'action ordinaire* : the word « equity » which actually applies to what is left for a borrower after he has redeemed a mortgage on an asset is also commonly used with the meaning of ordinary share).
— *au-dessous du pair* : share at discount.
— *au porteur* : bearer share, transferable share.
— *prioritaire* : preferred share.
— *à la souche* : unissued share.
cession d'— (s) : disposal (transfer) of shares.
détenir des actions : to hold shares.
distribution d'actions gratuites : distribution of bonus shares.
droit d'enregistrement de cession d'— (s) : registration dues on transfer of shares.
émettre des — (s) (au pair, au-dessus du pair) : to issue shares (at par, at a premium).
option de souscription (ou d'achat) d'— (s) : option on (for) application for shares (or purchase of shares).
répartition d'— (s) : allotment of shares.
société par — (s) : joint stock company.
souscrire une — : to subscribe, to buy a share.
titre d'— : share certificate.

actionnaire (m) : shareholder, stockholder.
— *principal* : leading shareholder.
registre des — (s) : stock-ledger.

actionnariat *(des salariés)* (m) : industrial co-partnership.

actionner *(en justice)* (v) : to take, to open, to institute proceedings against s.o., to go to law.
— *en dommages-intérêts* : to sue for damages.

activation *(des droits de tirages spéciaux du F.M.I.)* (f) : activation (of special drawing rights I.M.F.).

activité (f) : activity.
— *(s)* : strategy.
— *bancaire* : banking.
être en —, de service : to be in service.
société exerçant une — commerciale : trading company.
[B] *marché sans —* : dull market.

actualisation *(coefficient, taux d')* (f) : discount (coefficient, rate), hurdle rate (coefficient) present rate.

actualité *(l')* (f) : current events.

actuel (a) : current, existing at the present time.
la loi — (le) : the current law.
paiement — : actual payment.

ad litem : concerning a specified lawsuit.
provision — : security for costs.

ad valorem : corresponding to the value.

addenda (m) : addendum.

addition (f) : adding up, aggregation, accretion.
— *de revenus* : income aggregation.
faire une — à un bâtiment : to add to a building.

additionnel (a) : additional.
centimes — (s) : additional part of a tax paid over and above the assessment (mostly for local purposes).
clause — (le) (d'un projet de loi) : rider (of a bill).
taxe — (le) : tax supplement.

adéquation (f) : relevance.

adhérer (v) : to adhere.
— *à un concordat* : to accept a composition in bankruptcy.
— *à un traité* : to adhere to a treaty.
donner son **adhésion** *à un pacte* : to accede to a covenant.

adhésion *aux Communautés Européennes* : accession to the European Communities.

adiré (a) : lost, mislaid.
titre —, pièce — (e) : act gone astray.

adition *(d'hérédité)* (f) : acceptance of an inheritance.

adjoint (m) : assistant, deputy.

adjudicataire (m) : successful tenderer for a contract, contractor, purchaser at auction (highest bidder).

adjudication (f) : adjudication, allocation, award, giving out, allocation of contract.
— *des bons du trésor* : bill auction.
— *à l'éteinte de chandelle* : auction by inch of candle.
— *publique* : formal public sale, public auction.
— *au rabais* : adjudication to the lowest bidder.
— *à la surenchère* : adjudication to the highest bidder.
par voie d' — : by auction, by tender.
— *par voie d'arbitrage* : award.
mettre qch. en — : to invite tenders, to put up for sale by auction.

adjuger (v) : to adjudge, to allocate, to knock off (down).
— *au demandeur le bénéfice de ses conclusions* : to find for the plaintiff.
— *les dépens* : to award the costs.

admettre (v) : to admit, to hear.
— *qn à se justifier* : to give s.o. a hearing.
— *qn au barreau* : to call s.o. to the bar.

administrateur (m) : administrator, director, manager, trustee.
[J] — *judiciaire en matière de faillite* : receiver, inspector, trustee in bankruptcy.
— *judiciaire en matière de succession (curateur)* : executor *(succession réglée par testament)*, administrator *(succession ab intestat)*.
— *-séquestre* : sequestrator, assignee, depositary, trustee of sequestrated property, official receiver.
— *-délégué* : managing director, [U.S.] president.
— *-gérant d'un journal* : managing editor.
— *à temps plein* : executive director.
[A] — *civil* : senior civil servant.
— *foncier, de biens* : estate, house agent, steward.

administration (f) : administration, direction, management, trusteeship, receivership, [U.S.] agency.
l' — : the Civil Service, the Authorities, [U.S.] the Administration.
l' — *fiscale* : [U.K.] the Inland Revenue, the Revenue Authorities, [U.S.] the Internal Revenue.
l' — *des douanes* : [U.K.] the Customs Authorities, the Board of Customs.
conseil d' — : governing body, board of directors.

administrer (v) : to administer, to manage, to conduct, to dispense.
[J] — *la justice* : to render justice.
— *des preuves* : to produce proofs.

admissible (a) : allowable, eligible.
[J] *excuse* — : allowable excuse.
[F] *montant* — : eligible capital amount.

admission (f) : [D] — *en douane* : entry of goods.
[B] — *à la cote* : stocks admitted for quotation on the official share list.

adoption (f) : adoption.
— *d'une loi* : passing, carrying of a bill.
adoptant : adoptive parent.
adopté *(enfant adoptif)* : adopted child.

adoucir *(peine)* (v) : to mitigate (penalty).

adresse (f) : 1° address, petition, request; 2° domicile.
[C] — *au besoin (un « au besoin »)* : referee in case of need (mentioned on a bill of exchange).
adresser *(une déclaration d'impôt)* : to send in, to file (a return).
la déclaration doit, sans avis ni mise en demeure, être adressée à l'Inspecteur, pas plus tard que... : the return shall, without notice or demand, be filed with the Inspector, no later than...
s'adresser à *(qqn)* : to apply to (s.o.).

adultère (m) : adultery.
commerce **adultérin** : adulterous intercourse.
[J] criminal conversation, « Crim. Con. ».

advenant : [J] *le cas advenant que* : in the event of sth happening.

adversaire (m) : adversary, opponent.
[J] *la partie* — : the opposing party, the other side.

affacturage (m) : factoring.
— *à forfait* : forfaiting.

affaire (f) : case, lawsuit, deal, business.
[J] — *classée* : unsolved case definitely disposed of.
instruire une — : to investigate a case, to get up the case against s.o.
[C] 1° *transaction* : deal, transaction, business.
— *(s) imposables* : taxable transactions.
— *(s) non payées* : unpaid (dishonoured) transactions.
— *(s) résiliées* : cancelled transactions.
2° *entreprise* : business concern.
une — *qui marche bien* : a paying concern, a business that is doing well.

une — véreuse : a doubtful business.
bureau d'—(s) : agency office.
chiffre d'—(s) : turnover.
homme d'—(s) : businessman, agent.
relations d'—(s) : business connections.
être en —(s) avec (qqn) : to deal with (s.o.).

affectation (f) : [F] allocation, allotment, appropriation, assignment.
— *d'une somme d'argent (à une destination) :* allotment of an amount of money (to a purpose).
— *de crédits, de fonds :* appropriation of credit, of funds.
— *d'un emprunt :* allotment of a loan.
— *à un poste :* assignment to an item.
— *aux réserves :* allocation to reserve funds.
compte d'— (*montrant la façon dont le bénéfice net est réparti entre les réserves, les dividendes, etc.*) : appropriation account (showing how net profit is distributed between reserves, dividends, etc.).

affecter (v) : to allocate, to appropriate, to assign, to concern, to ear-mark.
[F] — *des fonds à :* to ear-mark funds for.
— *aux réserves :* [U.S.] to place to reserves.
impôts **affectés** : ear-marked taxes.
[J] *domaine affecté d'une hypothèque :* burdened, mortgaged estate.
ladite disposition affecte... : the said provision concerns...

afférent à (a) : accruing to, falling to, relating to.
bénéfices —(s) à une activité : profits accruing to an activity.
— *à un emploi :* attaching to a position.
— *à une période donnée :* in respect of a given period.
— *à une transaction :* relating to a transaction.
portion —(e) à qqn : portion (share) accruing to s.o.

affermage (m) : lease-farming.
— *de créances :* factoring.

affermataire (m) : tenant farmer.

affermateur (m) : lessor.

affichage (m) : bill-sticking.
droit d'— : fee for the right to post bills.

affiche (f) : poster, bill.
— *sur papier libre (exemple de droit de timbre) :* public notice (exempt from stamp duty).
timbre pour —(s) : poster stamp.

afficher *(une vente)* (v) : to advertise, to bill (a sale).

affidavit (m) : affidavit.

affiliation (f) : 1° affiliation, 2° branch of a firm.

affilier *(à)* (v) : to affiliate (to).
s'affilier à un syndicat : to join a union.

affirmation (f) : [F] [J] affidavit, solemn affimation.
— *de créance :* proof of indebtedness.

afflictif (a) : [J] *peine afflictive :* punishment involving death, personal restraint or penal servitude.

affluence (f) (d'acheteurs) : out-turn (of buyers).

afflux de fonds (m) : capital inflow.

affouage (m) : [J] *droit d'— :* common of estovers.

affranchir (v) : to stamp, to frank.

affranchissement (m) : postage, franking, stamping.

affrètement (m) : affreightment, chartering of ship.
[E] — *au voyage :* trip charter.
— *à temps :* time charter.
contrat d'—, charte-partie : charter-party.

affréter *(un avion)* : to charter (a plane).

âge (m) : age.
— *légal :* coming of age, majority.
âgées *(personnes) :* the aged.
déduction accordée aux personnes âgées : age allowance.
contribuable d'un certain — : elderly tax payer.
tranche d'— : age bracket (range).

agence (f) : agency, bureau.
— *pour l'emploi :* employment bureau.
— *immobilière :* estate agency.
— *de location :* house agency.
— *de presse :* press agency.
— *de publicité :* advertising agency.
— *de renseignements :* enquiry (information) agency.
— *de voyages :* tourist (travel) agency.
— *Internationale de l'Aviation Civile :* Civil Aviation Authority (C.A.A.).
— *internationale de l'énergie atomique (A.I.E.A.) :* International Atomic Energy Association (I.A.E.A.).

agencement (m) : layout, [C] fittings.

agent (m) : agent, representative of a firm, officer.
— *d'affaires* : general agent.
— *d'assurances* : insurance agent.
— *de change* : stock broker.
— *des contributions directes* : tax officer.
— *des contributions indirectes* : excise officer.
— *de l'Etat* : officer.
— *exclusif* : sole agent.
— *d'exécution* : lower management.
— *immobilier* : real estate agent, [U.S.] realtor.
— *de la force publique* : member of the police force, of the armed forces.
— *maritime* : shipping agent.
— *de renseignements* : informer.

agglomération (f) : built-up area.

aggravation (f) : increase, augmentation.
[F] — *de la pression fiscale* : increase of the tax burden.
[J] — *d'une peine* : augmentation of penalty.
circonstances **aggravantes** : aggravation.

agio (m) : agio.
[B] **agiotage** : agiotage, gambling on premium (on gold).
agioteur : jobber.

agir (v) : to act.
— *d'autorité* : to act with full powers.
— *contre qn (en justice)* : to sue s.o., to go law, to open proceedings.
— *és qualités* : to act in one's capacity.
— *d'office* : to act ex officio.
avoir qualité pour — : to have the necessary powers to act.

agissements *(frauduleux)* (m pl) : (fraudulent) dealings.

agitation (f) sociale : social unrest.

agnat (m) : agnate, relation on the father's side.

agraire (a) : agrarian.
loi — : agrarian law.
mesures — *(s)* : land measures.

agrandir (v) *(magasin, clientèle, etc.)* : to enlarge, to extend, to increase.

agrégats (m pl) monétaires *(constituant les disponibilités monétaires)* : monetary aggregates.

agrément (m) : consent, approbation, acceptance, assent.
— *fiscal* : ministerial approval.
donner son — : to give one's consent.
lettre — : letter of acceptance.

agréer : to accept, to approve, to recognize.

agresseur (m) : agressor.

agression (f) : aggression.
[J] unprovoked assault.

agro-alimentaire *(l')* (m) : agribusiness, agrofoods.

aide (f) : aid, assistance, relief.
[F] *(les)* — *(s)* *(hist.)* : aids.

aïeul (m) : grandfather.
aïeux : ancestors.

aîné *(l')* (m) : the elder (of two), the eldest (of more than two).
*droit d'***aînesse** *(hist.)* : birth-right.

ainsi *(adv.)* : so.
si le contribuable choisit d'en faire —... : if the taxpayer so elects...

ajournement (m) : postponement, adjournment, putting off of proceedings.
[J] 1° summons to appear ; 2° stay.

ajourner (v) : to defer, to postpone.

ajouter (v) : to add.
— *foi à* : to credit.
— *des notes marginales* : to append marginal notes.
s'ajouter : to be aggregated.
les gains s'ajoutent : gains are aggregated.

ajustement (m) : adjustement.
[F] — *des comptes* : balancing item.
— *résultant du coût de la vie* : cost of living adjustment.

alcool (m) : alcohol.
taxes et droits sur les — *(s)* : taxes and duties on spirituous liquors.

aléa (m) : hazard, risk.

aléatoire (a) : aleatory, problematical, risky.
[J] *contrat* — : aleatory contract (depending upon an uncertain event).

alibi (m) : alibi.
invoquer, plaider, fournir, prouver l' — : to set up, to plead, to establish, to produce an alibi.

aliénabilité (f) : alienability.

aliénable (a) : alienable, transferable.

aliénation (f) : alienation, transfer, assignment (of property, rights).
— *mentale, d'esprit* : derangement of mind.

aliéné (m) : insane person, lunatic.
[J] non compos (mentis).
— *interdit* : certified lunatic.
— *biens* — *(s)* : disposed property.
curateur d'un — : committee for a lunatic.

alignement *(sur les conditions de la concurrence en matière de crédit)* (m) : matching.

aliments (m pl) : [J] alimony.
créance alimentaire : claim for alimony.
obligation alimentaire : obligation to support.
pension alimentaire : allowance for necessaries.

alinéa (m) : paragraph.

allégation (f) : averment, allegation, plea.
— *(s) des parties* : assertions of the parties.

allègement *(fiscal)* (m) : (tax) break, concession, mitigation.
alléger *(charges)* (v) : to alleviate (charges).

alléguer (v) : to plead, to put up a plea, to bring forward a proof, to pretend, to assert, to claim.
— *d'un prétexte* : to advance a pretext.

alliance (f) : alliance.
[J] *(rapports existant entre un époux et la famille de l'autre)* : affinity.
(parents et) **alliés** : relations by marriage, connection.

allocataire (m) : recipient of an allowance.

allocation (f) : allocation, apportionment, assignment, allowance, grant ; allotment of shares.
— *de cherté de vie* : cost of living bonus.
— *de chômage* : unemployment benefit.
— *(s) familiales* : family allowance.
— *forfaitaire* : standard allowance.
— *de logement* : housing allowance.
— *de maladie* : sick allowance, sick pay.
— *de salaire unique* : special allowance for families with one wage-earner.
— *aux vieux travailleurs salariés* : aged wage-earners allowance.

allonge (f) : allonge.
[J] rider.

allouer (v) : to allow, to grant, to apportion.
— *une somme à titre de dommages-intérêts* : to award an amount of money as damages.

allotissement (m) : [J] apportionment, allotment.

alternative (f) : option.

amarrage *(droits d')* (m) : berthage, berth duties.

ambulant (a) : itinerant.
marchant — : itinerant merchant.
receveur — : [U.K.] itinerant collector of taxes.

amélioration (f) : improvement.
— *(s) apportées à un immeuble, impenses* : leasehold improvements.
— *de l'équipement* : betterment, improving of plant.

aménagement (m) : improvement, development.
frais d' — : development expenses.
— *du territoire* : town and country planning, [U.S.] zoning.
aménager *(maison, magasin)* (v) : to arrange, to dispose, to convert into (house, shop).

amende (f) : [J] *(imposée par le tribunal)* fine, *(imposée par le jury)* amercement.
— *fiscale* : tax penalty.

amendement (m) : [A] amendment.
— *du sol* : amelioration of land.
amender *un projet de loi* : to amend a bill.

amener (v) : to bring.
— *le pavillon* : to strike colours.
[J] *mandat d'* — : order to offender or witness to appear, writ of capias.

ameublissement (m) : [J] 1° conversion of realty into personalty (species of agreement which by fiction gives to immovable property the quality of movable) ; 2° inclusion of realty in the communal estate.

amiable (a) : friendly, conciliatory, amicable.
— *compositeur* : arbitrator, referee.
règlement à l' — : amicable arrangement.
vente à l' — : private sale.
liquider une affaire à l' — : to settle a difference out of court.

amnistie (f) : amnesty.

amnistier (v) : to amnesty, to pardon.

amodiation (f) : leasing (land, berth or fishing...).
amodiateur, amodiataire : lessor, lessee.

amorti (a) : amortized, written off.
dette — (e) : debt written off.

amortir (v) : to amortize, to write off, to redeem, to depreciate.
amortissable (a) : depreciable, redeemable.

amortissement (m) : amortization, depreciation, redemption, sinking, wiping out, writing off.
1° *diminution de la valeur d'un bien par usure ou obsolescence. (Il est tenu compte de l'amortissement aux fins d'établissement de l'impôt, mais il est calculé d'après certaines règles qui ne sont pas nécessairement en rapport avec l'amortissement 'de l'entreprise)* : the reduction of the value of an asset through wear and tear or obsolescence. (Depreciation is taken into account for tax assessment purposes, but it is calculated according to certain rules which do no necessarily bear any relation with the depreciation calculated by the accounting department of the business.)
— *accéléré* : accelerated depreciation.
— *dégressif* : declining balance depreciation, amount written off.
— *sur immeubles* : depreciation on premises.
— *financier* : amortization.
— *linéaire* : straight-line depreciation.
méthode d'— par annuités : annuity method of depreciation.
provision par — : allowance for depreciation.
tableau d'— : redemption table.
2° *remboursement progressif d'une dette grâce à un fonds ou caisse d'amortissement auquel des sommes sont versées périodiquement. (A ces sommes s'ajoutent les intérêts qu'elles produisent de sorte qu'elles permettent de liquider la dette par versements échelonnés ou en bloc)* : the gradual repayment of a debt to a « sinking fund » into which sums are put periodically. (The interests these sums bring accumulate and are added to them so that they eventually allow to settle the debt in instalments or in a lump sum.)
— *d'un emprunt* : sinking of a loan.
caisse d'— : redemption fund, sinking fund.
méthode progressive d'— : compound interest method.
plan d'— : terms of redemption.

ampliation (f) : exemplification, duplicate, copy of an act, of a receipt.
« *pour —* » : « certified true copy ».

analogie (f) : analogy.
par — avec : on the analogy of.
analogique *(raisonnement)* : analogical (argument).

analyse (f) : analysis.
— *comparative de la publicité selon les media* : media analysis.
— *coûts-avantages* : cost-benefit analysis.
— *critique méthodique* : critical path.
— *prévisionnelle par analogie avec une situation passée* : regression analysis.
— *du rapport coûts/profits* : cost/benefit analysis.
— *de sensibilité (c.à d. de la rentabilité d'un investissement aux changements de ses variables)* : sensitivity analysis.

analyser (v) : to analyse, [U.S.] to analyze.
— *des états financiers* : to analyse financial statements.

anatocisme (m) : anatocism, compound interest.

ancien (a) : former.
les — (s) règlements : the former regulations.
les — (s) combattants : the war veterans.

ancienneté (f) : seniority, length of service.
[A] *avancement à l'—* : promotion by seniority (opp. *avancement au choix* : promotion by selection).

angarie (f) : [J] angary.

animé (a) *(commerce, marché)* : (voir « actif »).

annales *(officielles)* (f pl) : annals, public records.

année (f) : year.
— *bissextile* : leap year.
— *civile* : legal year, calendar year.
— *comptable* : accounting year.
— *échue* : expired year.
— *fiscale* : fiscal year.
— *d'imposition* : year of assessment, taxable year, year of taxation.
payer à l'— : to pay by the year.

annexe (a et f) :
(a) supplementary.
activité — : sideline.
budget — : supplementary funds.
documents — (s) : enclosures.
lettre — : covering letter.
revenus — (s) : supplementary income.
taxes — (s) à une contribution : taxes ancillary to a contribution.
(f) — *d'un document* : rider.
— *à une loi* : schedule.

annexer *(un document à un dossier)* : to append (a document to a file).

annonce (f) : advertissement, ad.
faire passer une — : to run an ad.
— pleine page : full page spread.
annoncer : to advertise, to announce.
annoncer (un prix, par un vendeur) : to ask, to offer (a price).
annoncier : advertiser, advertising agent.

annoter (v) : to annotate.
code — : annotated text of a code.

annuaire (m) : directory, trade directory.

annuel (a) : yearly, annual.
amortissement — : annual depreciation.
principe de l'annualité de l'impôt : concept of an annual tax.

annuitaire *(dette)* (a) : (debt) payable by instalments.

annuité (f) : annuity, annual instalment.
— d'amortissement : depreciation allowance, deduction.
— constante de capital : annual value.
méthode de l'— : annual capital charge method.

annulation (f) : annulment.
[J] *(d'un jugement)* repeal, quashing, rescision, *(d'un acte judiciaire)* abatement, *(d'un contrat)* cancellation, avoidance, *(d'un droit)* defeasance, *(d'un testament)* setting aside, invalidation.
arrêt d'— : reversal.

annuler (v) : *— un arrêté :* to overrule (an order).
— une commande : to withdraw an order.
— un contrat : to cancel a contract.
— une loi : to repeal, to rescind, to revocate a law.
— un marché : to call off a deal.

anonyme (a) : anonymous.
compte — : impersonal account.
société — : joint-stock company, [U.S.] business corporation.

antécédents (m pl) : antecedents, record.
[J] *— d'un accusé :* past record of the accused.

antérieur *(à)* (a) : former, prior, previous (to).
antérieurement à l'année où le revenu a été perçu : previous to the year when the income was received.

antériorité (f) : anteriority.
droit d'— : right of priority.

antichrèse (f) : [J] (vivum vadium) living pledge (of real estate).

anticipation (f) : anticipation.
paiement par —, paiement anticipé : prepayment.
accepter une traite par — : to accept a bill in advance.
remboursement anticipé : redemption before due date, maturity.

anticonstitutionnel (a) : anticonstitutionnal.

antidate (f) : antedate.
acte antidaté : antedated act.

anti-trust *(législation)* : antitrust (legislation).

apatride (m) : stateless person.

aperçu (m) : glimpse.
[J] *un — de la cause :* a summary of the case.
[C] *un — de la dépense :* a rough estimate of the cost.

apparent (a) : visible, conspicuous, apparent, obvious.
mort —(e) : apparent (not real) death.
servitude —(e) : apparent, patent, conspicuous easement (with structures, outward works, etc.).
vice — : obvious defect, [J] flaw.
entreprises apparentées : associated companies.

appartement (m) : flat.
— meublé : furnished flat.
— occupé à titre gratuit : rentfree flat.

appartenance (f) : appurtenance.

appartenir (v) : to belong, to be owned by.
— de droit : to belong rightfully.
— en propre : to possess sth. in one's own right.
ainsi qu'il appartiendra : as befitting.
à tous ceux qu'il appartiendra : to all whom it may concern.
le bien appartenait au contribuable à la date à laquelle... : the property was owned by the taxpayer at the time when...

appel (m) : appeal, call, roll-call.
— aux créanciers : call-up of creditors in bankruptcy.
— nominal : (d'une assemblée) call-over, (du jury) array.
— des témoins : roll-call of witnesses.
vote par — nominatif : to take a vote by calling over the names of members.
[J] 1° appeal at law :

— *devant le Conseil d'Etat français* : appeal to the French Conseil d'Etat.
— *d'une décision* : appeal against a decision.
— *joint, incident* : appeal on a point of law.
— *a minima* : public prosecutor's appeal against too mild a sentence.
— *tardif* : appeal lodged after expiry of time-limit.
avis d'—, intimation : notice of appeal.
casser un jugement en — : to quash a sentence on appeal, to set sentence aside and order a new trial, to remand the case, to modify judgment on the law and on the facts.
cour d'— : court of appeals.
délai d'— : time-limit for lodging an appeal.
demandeur en — (appelant) : plaintiff in appeal.
défendeur en — (intimé) : defendant in appeal (respondent).
fol — : unfounded appeal.
jugement frappé d'— : judgment under appeal.
juger en — : to hear an appeal.
relief d'— : prolongation of time-limit for appeal.
faire —, de, interjeter — : to lodge, to lay, to take an appeal.
un — n'est pas suspensif : an appeal is not a stay.
2° *appel (évocation) en garantie (litis denunciatio)* : introduction of third parties (approximately an impleader).
[F] — *de fonds* : calling up of capital, call for funds.
— *aux souscripteurs* : call to subscribers, call for payment on stocks.
[B] — *de marge* : request for additional cover in forward deals.
[C] — *d'offres* : invitation of tenders, appeal for tenders, bid invitation.

appelable (a) : [J] appealable (action).

appelant (m) : [J] plaintiff in appeal, appellant.
l'— et l'intimé : appellant and respondent.
— *d'un jugement* : appellant against a judgment.
se porter — : to appeal.

appelé (m) : [J] substitutional heir, reversioner, heir in remainder.

appeler (v) : to call.
— *une cause* : to call the cause (on the roll).
— *en garantie* # to implead.
— *d'un jugement* : to appeal against a judgment.
— *en justice* : to summon, to sue s.o.
— *en témoignage* : to call s.o. to witness.
être appelé à une charge (un emploi), à exercer des fonctions : to be entrusted with an office, an employ, duties.
être appelé dans une instance : to be implicated in a suit.
[F] *capital appelé* : called-up capital.

appellation (f) : appelation.
— *contrôlée* : guaranteed vintage.
— *injurieuse* : abusive terms.
— *d'origine* : caption.

appert (il appert) (v. apparoir) : it appears.

application (f) : application.
— *de la loi* : enforcement of law.
— *matérielle (absolue)* : application (of law) ratione materiae.
— *d'une peine* : determination of penalty.
— *des règlements* : administration of regulations.
— *d'une somme d'argent* : employment of a sum of money.
— *temporaire* : temporary application.
— *territoriale (relative)* : application (of law) ratione loci.
arrêté d'— : decree stating measures for the enforcement of a law.
en — de : in pursuance of.
appliquer les dispositions de la loi : to bring, to put the law into operation, to enforce the law.
appliquer le maximum de la peine : to inflict the heaviest penalty provided.
appliquer une politique : to implement a policy.
s'appliquer à : to apply to.
l'alinéa suivant s'applique au cas où... : the following paragraph applies to the case when...

appoint (*activité d'*) (m) : side-line (activity).
faire l'— : to make up the even money.

appointé (a) : salaried (person), referred (cause).

appointements (m pl) : emoluments, pays, salary.
toucher des — : to draw a salary.

apport (m) : contribution.
[J] — *dotal* : marriage portion.
— *des pièces* (dans un procès) : depositing of documents (in a suit).
biens d'— : estate brought in.
clause de reprise d'—(s) : clause providing for withdrawal of the marriage portion.
— *de preuves* : induction of facts.
[F] —, *action d'—* : initial share.
— *de fonds dans une entreprise* : capital brought into a business.
— *de biens* (dans une société) : contribution of property (to a partnership).
— *en espèces* : allowance in cash.

— *en nature :* allowance (contribution) in kind.
— *(s) partiels d'actif :* partial business transfer.
capital d'— : initial capital.
remboursement d'— (s) : refunding, repayment of contribution.

apporter (v) : to bring, to provide, to cause.
— *des preuves à l'appui de ce qu'on avance :* to substantiate one's assertions.

apporteur *(de capitaux)* (m) : contributor (of capital).

apposer (v) : to affix, to place, to put.
— *une affiche :* to stick a bill.
— *sa signature, son sceau :* to set, to append one's hand, seal.
[J] — *les scellés :* to imprint, to affix the seals (by a public officer).

appréciation (f) : evaluation, valuation, estimation, appraisement.
[J] — *du juge :* the judge's comment, summing up.
— *des preuves :* appraising the truth of the evidence.
[ASS] — *des risques :* estimation of risks.
[C] — *d'un bien :* rise in value of a possession.
faire l'— des marchandises : to value (appraise) goods.
apprécier *(dégâts, etc.) :* to assess.

appréhender (v) : to dread, to fear, to apprehend sth.
[J] — *qn :* to seize, to arrest, to apprehend s.o.

apprentissage (m) : apprenticeship *(stage des professions libérales)* articles ; learning.
engager qn par un brevet d'— : to indent s.o.
contrat d'— : indenture, articles of apprenticeship.
faire son — : to serve one's apprenticeship with s.o.
taxe d'— : apprenticeship tax (in France).
apprenti : apprentice.

approbation (f) : 1° approval, approbation.
[J] — *de l'autorité de tutelle :* approval, commendation of the board of guardians.
— *maritale :* husband's consent (to wife's legal transactions).
— *des comptes :* passing of accounts.
avec l'— de : with the agreement of.
2° authentication of document, certifying, reconcilement.

appropriation (f) : appropriation (of property).
— *frauduleuse d'objets trouvés :* fraudulent appropriation of lost property.

approprié (a) : proper, suitable, appropriate.
indemnité — (e) : suitable compensation.

approuver (v) : 1° to approve of ; 2° to agree, to sanction, to consent to, to back.
— *un dividende, une facture :* to pass a dividend, an invoice.
— *un contrat :* to ratify a contract.
— *une décision :* to be in agreement with a decision.
— *une nomination :* to confirm an appointment.
— *qch. officiellement :* to agree formally (to sth).
être **approuvé** : to receive approval.
« *Lu et approuvé* » : « read and approved » (elliptic and invariable formula).

approvisionnement (m) : supply(ing).
approvisionner : to supply (with).

appui (m) : support.
documents, pièces, preuves à l'— d'une cause : documents, proofs in support of a case.
accusation avec preuves à l'— : accusation supported by proofs.

appuyer (v) : to support, to second.
— *une demande :* to support a request.
— *une proposition :* to back, to second a motion.
— *son opinion sur :* to base one's opinion on.

après (prép) : after.
— *impôt :* after tax.
(d') **après** : according to, from.
d'après la loi, le testament : under the law, according to the will.

apte (a) : fit, suited, qualified to do sth., for sth.
— *aux fonctions :* fit for the office.
— *à posséder :* qualified to possess.
— *à succéder :* entitled to inherit.
— *à tester :* capable of making a will.

aptitude (f) : aptitude, natural disposition, ability, qualification.
— *au travail :* fitness for work.
brevet, certificat d'— : qualifying title, certificate of capacity (to fill a position).

apurement (m) : auditing, checking, reconciliation.
— *d'une dette :* wiping out of a debt.

apurer (v) : to audit, to check, to pass *(des comptes)*, to discharge, to wipe off *(des engagements)*.

aquilienne *(responsabilité)* (a) : [J] liability for wrongful damage done to property.

arbitrage (m) : [J] arbitration, award.
– *international* : international arbitration.
– *obligatoire* : compulsory arbitration.
traité d'– *permanent* : permanent arbitration treaty.
[B] – *de change* : arbitration of exchange.
– *de place à place* : shunting.
– *en reports* : jobbing in contangoes.

arbitraire (a) : arbitrary (choice), discretionary (punishment).
laissé à l'– *de* : left to the discretion of.

arbitral (a) : [J] arbitral.
commission –*(e)* : board of referees.
compromis – : compromise.
jugement, règlement –, *solution, sentence* – *(e)* : award, settlement by arbitration.
juridiction – *(e), tribunal* – : court of arbitration.

arbitre (m) : 1° *(amiable compositeur)* arbiter, 2° *(tiers-arbitre)* arbitrator.
– *-rapporteur* : referee in a commercial suit.
surarbitre : umpire.

arbitrer (v) : to arbitrate, to value, to decide as judge, arbitrator or expert.
– *une défense, des frais, des dommages* : to value, to fix, to determine the amount of expenses, of costs, the damage.
– *un différend* : to settle a difference by arbitration.
– *rendre une sentence* **arbitrale** : to make an award.

arbre (m) **de décision** : decision tree, game tree.

archiviste (m) : recorder.

argent (m) : 1° silver :
– *de bon aloi* : genuine, sterling quality silver.
– *fin* : fine, pure silver.
pièces d'– : silver coin.
2° money, property, wealth :
– *avancé au jour le jour* : call money.
– *frais* : fresh funds.
– *mort* : dead capital.
– *de poche* : pocket money.
avancer de l'– : to advance funds.
être en embarras d'– : to be short of money, to be in financial straits.
marché de l'– : money market.
payer – *comptant,* – *sur table* : to pay cash.
placer de l'– : to invest funds.
réparation d'un dommage en – : compensation for damage in money.

arguer (v) : to infer, to assert, to deduce ; to argue.
– *un acte de faux* : to assert a deed to be forged.
– *de sa bonne foi* : to plead bona fide.

argument (m) : 1° argument.
– *concluant* : conclusive argument.
– *faux, captieux* : fallacious, specious argument.
réfuter, rétorquer un – : to refute, to cast back an argument.
2° outline, summary, synopsis.

argumentation (f) : argumentation.

argutie (f) : quibble, cavilling.

armateur (m) : ship-owner, fitter-out of ship, expedition.

armement (m) : commissioning, lifting-out a ship.
entreprise d'– : shipping company.
mettre un navire en – : to put a ship in commission.
port d'– : port of registry.
l'– *français* : the french shipping.

armes (f pl) : arms, weapons.
commerce des – : traffic in weapons.
permis de port d'– : licence to carry firearms.

arpentage (m) : land survey.

arpenteur (m) : surveyor.

arracher (v) : to tear, to pull out.
– *des aveux* : to extort a confession.

arraisonner *(un vaisseau)* (v) : to hail, to speak a vessel ; to stop and examine a ship.

arrangement (m) : arrangement.
– *à l'amiable* : coming to terms.
– *avec ses créanciers* : composition with one's creditors.
– *international* : international arrangement.
en vertu d'–*(s) antérieurs* : under previous understandings.
sauf – *contraire* : unless otherwise agreed.
terminer un procès par – : to settle amicably a lawsuit.

arrérages (m pl) : arrears (of salary, pension, shares...) interest.
– *prescrits* : statute-barred interest.
coupon d'– : interest, dividend warrant.
laisser courir ses – : not to draw one's pension or dividends.
payer le principal et les – : to pay the capital

— 29 —

sum and the outstanding interests thereon.

arrestation (f) : arrest, caption.
- *arbitraire* : false arrest.
- *illégale* : illegal arrest.
- *préventive* : detention on suspicion, being in custody awaiting trial.
ordre, mandat d'— : warrant for arrest, writ of capias.
mettre en état d'— : to take into custody.

arrêt (m) : stop, stoppage.
[J] 1° *— des poursuites* : nolle prosequi.
— de la procédure : abatement.
2° arrest, attachment, embargo, impounding, seizure :
mandat d'— : warrant for arrest, writ of capias.
saisie-— : attachment, garnishment.
garder les —(s) : to be under arrest.
lancer un mandat d'— : to issue a warrant for arrest.
mettre — sur un navire : to put an embargo on a ship.
faire — sur des marchandises : to seize goods.
3° judgment delivered by a superior court (*Cour de cassation, Cour d'assises, Conseil d'Etat*), decree.
— d'accusation : indictment.
— par adoption de motifs : judgment taking up the grounds of the lower court.
— civil : judgment in civil matters.
— par contumace : sentence in absence (contumacy).
— par défaut : judgment by default.
— de doctrine, de principe : judgment of a superior court involving an important decision on matters of principle.
— d'espèce : judgment based on practical motives pertaining to a specific case rather than on legal grounds.
— de mort : death sentence.
— pénal : judgment in a criminal case.
— provisoire : provisional remedy, interlocutory decree, decree nisi.
— de renvoi : a) remand, b) nonsuit.
— de suspension, un « avant faire droit » : injunction.
— de suspension provisoire : restraint.
prononcer, rendre un — : to pronounce, to deliver, to give a judgment ; to issue, to pronounce a decree.
se pourvoir, recourir contre un — : to lay, to lodge an appeal.
3° [C] *— des affaires* : slow business.
arrêt du travail : cessation from work.

arrêté (m) : [A] decree, order, decision of an administrative authority.
— d'exécution : decree providing for the enforcement of a law.
— ministériel : decree, order in council, [U.S.]

Departmental order.
— municipal : by(e)-law.
prendre un — : to pass a decree.
[C] *— de compte* : settlement of an account.

arrêter (v) : to stop, to delay, to detain :
[J] to arrest, to attach, to take s.o. in charge, to distrain (goods).
— les poursuites : nolle prosequi, to quash an action.
[F] to settle, to fix, to determine :
— un compte : to draw up an account.
— un compte de frais : to draw up costs.
— un marché : to make a contract.
— un solde : to draw up a balance.
— les termes, un texte : to settle the wording, the terms, to draw up, to draft a text.
— un programme : to draw up a program(me).
[A] *— des dispositions générales* : to lay down general rules.

arrhes (f pl) : earnest money, deposit.

arriéré (m et a) : [F] (m) arrears.
— de dettes : [U.S.] past due.
— d'impôt : tax arrears.
— de loyer : arrears of rent.
avoir de l'arriéré : to be in arrears (behindhand).
(a) overdue, outstanding.
intérêts —(s) : outstanding interest.

arrimer (v) : to stow.

arriviste (m) : careerist.

arriver (v) **à un accord** : to reach a settlement.

(s')arroger (*un droit, un privilège*) (v) : to arrogate to oneself a right, a privilege, to assume a right.

arrondir (v) : to round up, (off).
— (au chiffre inférieur) : to round down.
somme **arrondie** *au franc le plus proche* : amount rounded up to the nearest franc.

arrondissement (m) # [A] district.

arsenal (m) : body.
l'— législatif : the body of the law.

article (m) : [J] provision, section, paragraph, (of a code, a law...).
interrogatoire sur faits et —(s) : (civ.) questions put by one party to the other,
(# affidavit of discovery of documents).
[C] item, article, commodity.
—(s) de choc : (U.S.) a blockbuster.
—(s) coûteux : big-ticket items.
— de dépense : item of expenditure.

mélange d'—(s) (bons et mauvais) : mixed bag.
— *d'occasion* : second-hand article.
— *(s) de première nécessité* : necessities.
— *promotionnel vendu à part pour « appâter » la clientèle* : loss leader.
— *rectificatif d'erreur (dans un compte)* : balancing item.
— *(s) soldés* : odd lots.
faire l'— : to puff one's goods.

articulation (f) : [J] written enumeration of facts.
articuler *un fait* : to state a fact.
articuler des conclusions : to set forth the pleas.

artifice (m) : artifice.
— *de procédure* : trick of procedure.

artisan (m) : artisan, craftsman, [U.S.] operative.

artisanat (m) : handicrafts, cottage industry.

ascendance (f) : ancestry.
ascendants : ancestors, relatives in the ascending line.
ascendants par alliance : ancestors by marriage.
ligne ascendante : line of ascent.
pension d'ascendants (directs) : pension to parents.

asile (m) : shelter, home, refuge, retreat.
— *d'aliénés* : mental hospital.
[J] *droit d'—* : right of sanctuary.
lieu d'— : place of refuge.

assassin (m) : assassin, murderer.
[J] person guilty of murder.

assassinat (m) : assassination.
[J] murder with malice aforethought, [U.S.] murder in the first degree.

assassiner (v) : to assassinate, to murder deliberately.

(il est fait) assavoir : let it be known that.

assemblée (f) : 1° meeting.
— *d'actionnaires* : shareholders' meeting.
— *des créanciers* : creditors' meeting (in bankruptcy).
— *extraordinaire* : extraordinary meeting.
— *générale* : general meeting.
— *ordinaire* : ordinary meeting.
— *plénière* : plenary meeting.
— *(réunion) privée* : private meeting.
— *publique* : public meeting.

2° assembly *(corps constitué)* (public body).
— *constituante* : constituent assembly.
— *législative* : legislative assembly.
— *générale de l'O.N.U.* : general assembly of the U.N.

assentiment (m) : assent, concurrence, consent.
— *du représentant légal* : consent of the legal representative.
avec l'— de : with the concurrence of.

asseoir (v) : to establish, to found, to ground.
— *une assurance, une pension sur une tête déterminée* : to settle an insurance, a pension on s.o.
— *un impôt sur qch.* : to put a tax on sth, to base a tax on sth.
— *une rente, une hypothèque sur un bien qui en assure le paiement* : to encumber an estate with an annuity, a mortgage.

assermentation (f) : administration of oaths.
faire prêter serment (**assermenter**) : to administer an oath (the oath).
assermenté *(fonctionnaire)* : sworn (official).

assertion (f) : assertion.

assesseur (m) : assessor.
juge-— : associate judge.

assiette (f) : basis.
— *de l'impôt sur le revenu* : basis of taxation on income.
— *d'un impôt* : basis of a tax.
— *d'une rente* : property on which an annuity is secured.

assignable à (a) : assignable to, liable to be summoned to.

assignation (f) : [J] serving of a writ, summons or process, writ of summons, subpoena.
signifier, envoyer une — : to serve a writ, to subpoena a witness.
[F] assignment, allotment.

assigner (v) : to assign, to allot, to fix.
— *une tâche (à qqn)* : to apportion a task (to s.o.).
[J] to summon, to subpoena, to cite *(un témoin, etc.)*, to issue a writ against s.o., to serve a writ on s.o. *(en justice)*.
— *en contrefaçon* : to bring an action for infringement of patent.
[A] — *à résidence* : to require to reside, to assign a forced residence.
[F] — *un fonds à un usage particulier* : to earmark a fund for a special use.

assis (a) : seated.
la magistrature — (e) : the judges as a body, the Bench (opp. *la magistrature debout* : the law-officers of the State).
[F] *fortune — (e)* : well established fortune.

assises (f pl) : [J] the assizes.
cour d'— : assize court.
renvoi devant la cour d'— : committal for trial.
— d'un congrès : sittings of a congress.
tenir ses — (annuelles) : to hold one's (annual) meeting(s).

assistance (f) : aid, assistance, relief, help.
— judiciaire : (gratuitous) legal aid.
— maritime : salvage.
— publique # National Assistance, Poor relief.
— sociale : welfare work.
— aux vieillards : relief of old people.

assister (v) : 1° *(aider)* to help, to aid, to assist.
— qn de (ses) conseils : to help s.o. with advice.
2° *(être présent)* to attend.
— à un conseil d'administration : to attend a meeting of the board of directors.

association (f) : association, society, company, fellowship, partnership.
— de bienfaisance : charity, charitable corporation, institution.
— à but non lucratif : non-profit making association, not for profit organization.
— commerciale : trading company, commercial partnership.
— cultuelle, diocésaine, paroissiale, consistoriale : church, diocesan, parochial, consistorial association.
— d'intérêts : pooling, pursuit of common interests.
— internationale des courtiers : association of international bond dealers.
— ouvrière : workmen's association, trade-union.
— de malfaiteurs : conspiracy, [U.S.] combination.
— patronale : employers' association.
— en participation : special partnership.
— professionnelle : professional association.
— religieuse : religious fellow-ship.
— savante : scientific society, body.
— secrète : secret society, organization.
— de sociétés appartenant à une même industrie : horizontal integration.
— syndicale : trade-union.
— reconnue d'utilité publique : association officially acknowledged to serve public purposes.
(d') — : associative.
droit d'— : right of combination.

entrer en — : to enter into partnership.

associé (a et m) :
(a) associate, associated.
(m) partner.
— commanditaire : sleeping partner, secret partner.
dernier — : junior partner.
— gérant : managing partner.
— en nom : active partner.
— principal : senior partner.
porteurs — (s) : joint holders of stock.
compte courant d'— : shareholder's loan account.

associer (v) : to associate.

assortiment (m) : [C] matching, assortment, set, varied stock-in-trade.
— d'échantillons : range of patterns.

assouplir (v) *(les règlements sur...)* : to deregulate.

assujetti (m et a) : subject to.
(m) *— à l'impôt* : taxpayer.
(a) *acte — au timbre* : act liable to stamp duty.

assujettissement *à l'impôt* (m) : liability to tax.

assumer (v) : to assume.
— une responsabilité : to assume a responsability.
— une charge : to assume a burden, to take office.

assurance (f) : assurance, insurance (*en principe, assurance s'appliquerait plutôt aux personnes et insurance aux biens, mais, en fait, assurance est tombé en désuétude*), coverage, covering.
agent d'— (s) : insurance agent.
— abonnement : floating policy.
— individuelle-accidents : (personal) accident insurance, casualty insurance.
— automobile (tous risques ou aux tiers) : motor-car insurance (comprehensive, all-in or third party).
— pour compte d'autrui : insurance on account of a third party.
— -bâtiment : builder's risk insurance.
— contre le bris des glaces : plate glass insurance.
— à capital différé, à dotation, à terme fixe : endowment insurance.
— de cautionnement et de crédit : bail and credit insurance.
— chômage : unemployment insurance (compensation).
— collective : group insurance.
— complémentaire : complementary insurance.
— conjointe : joint insurance.

— *cumulative* : double insurance.
— *en cas de décès* : insurance in case of death.
— *contre les dégâts des eaux* : water-damage insurance.
— *de l'employeur contre les accidents du travail* : employer's liability insurance, workmen's compensation insurance.
— *facultative* : voluntary insurance.
— *sur fret* : freight insurance.
— *contre la grêle* : hail insurance.
— *hors cargaison* (mar.) : hull insurance.
— *contre l'incendie* : fire insurance.
— *invalidité* : disablement insurance.
— *libérée* : paid-up insurance.
— *-maladie* : sickness, [U.S.] health insurance.
— *maritime* : marine (maritime, sea) insurance.
— *contre les mauvaises créances* : credit insurance.
— *multirisque* : comprehensive insurance.
— *mutuelle* : mutual insurance.
— *obligatoire* : compulsory insurance.
— *avec (sans) participation aux bénéfices* : insurance with (without) profit-sharing.
— *« pertes d'exploitation »* : insurance against business interruption.
— *à primes (non) restituables* : insurance with redeemable (or irredeemable) premiums.
— *(s) sociales, sécurité sociale* : national insurance, [Engl] contributive insurance scheme.
— *de rentes différées* : deferred annuities insurance.
— *de rente d'invalidité* : disablement pension insurance.
— *de rente d'orphelin* : orphan's pension insurance.
— *de rente de veuve* : widow's pension insurance.
— *de rente viagère* : life annuity insurance.
— *de rente viagère avec remboursement de capital en cas de décès, sous déduction des rentes payées* : life annuity insurance with, in case of death, refund of capital remaining after deduction of paid annuities.
— *de rente viagère reversible* : revertible life annuity insurance.
— *de rente de vieillesse* : old age pension insurance.
— *de la responsabilité civile* : vicarious liability insurance (for damage caused by an agent).
— *tous risques* : all-in insurance, insurance against all risks.
— *contre les risques professionnels* : professional risks insurance.
— *à terme* : time insurance.
— *au tiers* : third party or public liability insurance.
— *transports* : transport insurance (goods and person).
— *sur la vie* : life insurance.
— *vieillesse* : old age insurance.
— *contre le vol avec effraction* : burglary insurance.
attestation d'— : certificate of insurance.
compagnie d'— : insurance (assurance) company.
contracter une — : to take out an insurance policy.
contrat d'— : insurance contract, policy.
contre-— (ré-assurance) : reinsurance.
courtier d'—(s) : insurance broker.
fonds d'— : insurance fund.
police d'— : insurance (assurance) policy.
preneur d'— : placer.
prestation d'— : indemnity benefit.
prime d'— : insurance premium, rate.
rachat d'— : redemption of a policy.
report des primes d'— : carry-over of rates.
tarif d'— : insurance rate (tariff).
valeur d'— : insurance value.
valeurs d'—(s) : insurance shares.

assurer (v) : to assure, to insure, to fixe, to secure, to fasten.
— *une rente à qn* : to settle an annuity upon s.o.
assuré (a) : assured, insured, secured.
assuré (m) : insured person, insurant.
assureur (m) : insurer.
assureur maritime (de Lloyd's) : underwriter.

astreinte (f) : [J] daily fine for delay in performance of contract or in payment of debt.

atelier (m) : workshop, machine shop.
chef d'— : shop-foreman, overseer.

atermoiement (m) : [J] attermining, [C] composition, arrangement with creditors for extension of time of payment, letter of respite.
— *d'une lettre de change* : renewal of a bill.
atermoyer *un paiement* (v) : to defer, to put off a payment.

atout (m) *(avantage)* : asset.

attaché (m) : [A] — *d'administration* : junior civil servant.
— *d'ambassade* : attaché in the diplomatic service.

attaquer (v) : to attack, to assail, to tackle, to impugn.
— *en justice* : to go to law, to institute proceedings.
— *un jugement* : to dispute the validity of a judgment.
[C] — *un nouveau marché* : to tap a new market.

atteinte (f) : 1° reach.
2° hit, blow, stroke, attack.

— 33 —

porter — aux conditions de la concurrence: to interfere with conditions of competition.
porter — au crédit de...: to undermine the credit of...
porter — à l'honneur de qn: to reflect, to cast a slur on s.o.
porter — aux intérêts de qn: to interfere with s.o.'s interests.
— au droit de propriété: trespass.

attenant (a): adjoining.
fonds —: bordering real estate.

attendu que...: whereas...
les —(s) d'un jugement: reasons adduced for a judgment.

attentat (m): outrage, criminal attempt.
— à la sûreté de l'Etat: high-treason, treason-felony.
— aux mœurs: immoral offence.
— public à la pudeur: indecent exposure.
attenter *à ses jours:* to lay violent hands on oneself.

attentatoire (a): challenging.
action — à l'autorité: action in contempt of authority.
mesure — à la liberté, aux droits: measure involving undue restraint of personal liberty, of rights.

attente (f): expectation.
valeur d'—: expectation value.

atténuation (f): mitigation.
[J] *— de peine:* mitigation of punishment or sentence.
circonstances **atténuantes**: extenuation, extenuating circumstances.

atténuer (v): to mitigate.

attestation (f): testimonial, certificate.
— sous serment: affidavit.
— de bonne vie et mœurs: certificate of good character.
— de paiement d'impôt: tax voucher.
attester: to attest, to certify sth., to bear testimony, to bear witness, to testify to sth.
— qn (de qch.): to call s.o. to witness (to sth.).
attesté: proven.

attitré (a): appointed.
agent attitré: appointed agent.

attribuer (v): to distribute, to appropriate, to allot, to allocate, to attribute.
— des actions: to allot shares.

attributaire (m): beneficiary of an attribution, allottee.

attributif (a): attributing, assigning.
[J] *acte —:* attribution, assigning.
arrêt — de compétence: judgment assigning jurisdiction to court.
clause **attributive** *de juridiction:* clause (in contract, etc.) determining the competent jurisdiction.

attribution (f): 1° attribution, assigning, attributing, ascription, allocation, prerogative.
[J] *— abstraite:* attribution valid with no cause.
— causale: attribution, the validity of which is conditional upon the existence of a cause.
— des enfants à l'un des époux: assigning wardship of children to father or mother (in separation, divorce).
— fiduciaire: assignment in trust.
— indirecte: indirect attribution.
— de juridiction: prerogative, power of jurisdiction.
— pour cause de mort: assignment for cause of death.
— sans cause: unlawful attribution.
acte d'—: deed of attribution.
cause de l'—: legal ground of attribution.
mobiles de l'—: reasons for attribution.
[F] allocation of parts or shares.
2° (f pl) competency, obligations, scope of activity, powers.
—(s) du juge en matière de...: competency of a judge in matters pertaining to...
il n'entre pas dans les —(s) du percepteur de...: it does not lie within the competence of the tax-collector to...

au-dessous, au-dessus
— du pair: below, above the par.

au porteur: to bearer.
action au —: bearer-stock, share.
titre au —: bearer-bond.

audience (f): [J] day in court, hearing by the court, sitting, session, court.
lever l'—: to close the session, the sitting.
plaider en — publique: to plead in open court.
suspendre l'—: to adjourn.

(huissier) audiencier (m): [J] court crier, usher.

auditeur (m): hearer, listener.
[A] *— au Conseil:* junior civil servant at the Council.
— à la Cour des comptes: Commissioner of Audit (in France).

audition (f) : [J] hearing.
 − *des témoins :* hearing of witnesses.
 − *contradictoire :* cross-examination.
 − *sur commission rogatoire :* hearing in virtue of letters rogatory.
 [F] − *de compte :* audit.

augmentation (f) : increase, augmentation, [U.S.] raise, increment, increasing.
 − *des immobilisations :* capital formation.
 − *d'impôt :* increase of taxation.
 − *de prix :* increase of price.
 − *de salaire :* increase of wages, [U.S.] salary raise.
 en − : increasing, on the increase.
 augmenter : to go up, to increase, to rise, to advance.

auréole (f) *(effet d')* : halo effect (voir ce mot).

auriculaire (a) : *(confession, témoignage) :* auricular.
 témoin − : ear-witness.

aurifères (a) **(valeurs)** : golds.

austérité (f) *(politique d')* : austerity (policy).

autarcie (f) : self-sufficiency.

auteur (m) : 1° *(d'un crime)* author, perpetrator ; *(d'un plan)* promoter.
 − *d'un procédé :* originator of a process.
 − *d'un accident :* party at fault in an accident.
 2° *(d'un livre)* author, writer ; *(de musique)* composer ; *(d'un tableau)* painter.
 droit d'− : copyright.
 droits d'− : copyright royalties.
 abandon définitif des droits d'− : outright assignment of copyright.

authentifier (v) : to certify, to legalise.

authentique (a et m) : (a) authentic, genuine.
 acte − : instrument drawn up by a notary or by a public authority.
 copie − : authentic copy.
 document − : authentic deed.
 en forme − : duly certified.
 texte − : official wording.
 titre − : valid document.
 (m) *l'* − *d'une pièce :* the original.

autofinancement (m) : self-financing, ploughing back.
 − *par bénéfices reversés dans l'affaire :* ploughing back of profits into a business.

autographe (a) : *lettre* − : autographic letter.

automatique (a) : automated, automatic.

automatisation (f) : automation.

autonome (a) : self-contained, autonomous, self sustaining.

autonomie (f) : autonomy, self-government.

autopsie (f) : autopsy, post mortem (examination).

autorisation (f) : 1° authorization, authority, permit :
 − *d'établissement :* permit to take up permanent residence (domicile).
 − *du juge :* authorization by judge.
 − *de justice :* authorization by court.
 donner à qn l'− *de faire quelque chose :* to give s.o. authority to do something.
 2° licence :
 accorder une − : to licence.
 − *d'exploiter un débit de tabac, une salle de spectacle :* tobacco, theatre licence.
 avoir l'− : to be licensed.

autorité (f) : authority, power.
 faire − *en matière de :* to be an authority on.
 [J] *agir de pleine* − : to act with full powers.
 − *de la chose jugée :* resjudicata.
 par − *de justice :* under a writ of execution.
 [J] *les* −*(s) constituées :* the powers that be, the Authorities.
 −*(s) d'exécution :* executive authorities.
 − *fiscale :* the Inland Revenue, [U.S.] the Internal Revenue.
 − *judiciaire :* judiciary power.
 − *de tutelle :* guardianship.

auxiliaire (a et m) : (a) auxiliary ; (m) aid, assistant.

autrui : others, other people, third party, person.
 droits, biens d'− : another's rights, property.

aval (m) : lower part of a stream.
 en − : down-stream.
 [C] guaranty of a bill of exchange (« at the bottom » of the bill).
 − *de banque :* bank bill.
 donner son − *à,* **avaliser** *un billet :* to endorse, to back a bill.
 donneur d'− **(avaliste)** : guarantor, backer (of a bill).
 effet **avalisé** : backed bill.

avance (m) : advance, lead.
 − *de fonds :* loan.
 − *sur contrat :* advance on a contract.
 − *sur garanties :* advance against securities.

– *d'hoirie*: advancement.
– *sur marchandises*: advance loan on goods.
– *sur nantissement*: advance against security.
– *sur titres*: loan on stock.
compte d'—(s): working capital fund.
d'avance: beforehand, in advance.
en — sur (programme): ahead of (schedule).
avancer de l'argent: to advance, to lend, money.

avancement (m): advancing, hastening, furtherance, promotion.
[J] – *d'hoirie*: advancement.
[A] – *à l'ancienneté*: promotion by seniority.
– *au choix*: promotion by selection.

avantage(s) (m): benefit(s), facilities.
– *(s) accessoires*: perquisites, [U.S.] fringe benefits.
– *accordé à employé*: employee benefits, (U.S.) employee compensation.
– *(s) en argent*: extra payments, benefits in cash.
accorder des —(s) financiers compensatoires à un employé rétrogradé à un poste inférieur: to kick an employee upstairs (« he was kicked upstairs »).
– *(s) en nature*: benefits in kind.
– *(s) offerts aux acheteurs par des sociétés concurrentes*: competitive claims.
il y a — à...: it is best to...
avantageux: advantageous, favourable.

avant dire droit, *avant faire droit (jugement)*: injunction, provisional, interlocutory judgment.

avant-projet (m): draft.

avarie (f): injury, damage (to ship, engine, etc.).
[ASS] average.
– *(s) communes, grosses*: general average.
– *simple, particulière*: particular average.
compromis d'—: average bond.
franc d'—(s): free from average.
règlement d'—(s) (dispache): adjustment of average.
répartiteur d'—(s) (dispacheur): averager, average adjuster, stater.

avenant (m) (*à un contrat d'assurance*): additional clause (to an insurance policy).
– *additionnel*: supplementary protocol.

avenir (m): [J] writ of summons to opposing counsel.

aventure (f): adventure, chance, luck, venture.
[E] *grosse —*: bottomry, respondentia.
contrat, lettre, de grosse —: bottomry bond.

prêt à la grosse —: bottomry loan, (*sur la cargaison du navire*) respondentia.

avertissement (m): notice, warning.
[J] *billet d'—*: summons to appear before a magistrate.
lettre d'—: admonitory (warning) letter.
[F] tax-bill, reminder, notification.

aveu (m): avowal, confession.
de l'— de tous: by common consent.
[J] – *judiciaire*: (cognovit actionem) admission, acknowledgment by record, confession of defence.
faire des —(x) complets: to make a full confession.

avilissement (m): debasement.
– *des prix*: fall in prices.

avis (m): opinion, judgment, decision, advice, councel.
un —: a piece of advice.
– *consultatif*: advisory opinion.
– *d'échéance*: expiry notice.
– *d'expert*: expert opinion.
– *au lecteur*: foreword.
lettre d'— (descriptive d'un envoi): advice note.
– *de réception*: delivery note.
– *officiel*: official notice.
– *au public*: notice to the public.
jusqu'à nouvel avis: until further notice, orders.
sauf — contraire: unless (we, you...) hear of the contrary.
suivant —: as per advice.
sur — motivé: stated opinion (concerning...).
[J] announcement, intimation, notice, warning.
de l'— du tribunal: in the court's opinion.
– *de crédit*: bank credit advice.
– *d'exécution*: contract note.
[E] – *d'expédition*: shipping advice.
[F] – *de mise en recouvrement*: notice of assessment.
– *de remise*: [U.S.] remittance advice.
– *de répartition*: letter of allotment.

avocat (m): barrister-at-law, counsel, [Scot.] advocate.
[U.S.] attorney at law.
– *conseil*: consulting barrister, legal expert.
– *général* # deputy Director of Public Prosecution at a court of appeals.
– *(s) généraux à la Cour de Justice de la CEE*: Advocates-General of the EEC Court of Justice.
– *d'office*: counsel ex officio to assist a poor person.
– *à la Cour*: barrister allowed to plead at a court of appeals.

être reçu — au barreau: to be called to the bar, [U.S.] to become member of the Bar Association *(# l'ordre des —(s)).*

avoir (m) : property, credit, assets.
(m) **avoir** *(opposé à « doit » en comptabilité) :* credit (as opposed to « debit » in accountancy and bookkeeping).
avoir fiscal concernant les revenus mobiliers : tax credit on income from movable property (in France).
avoir social : registered capital.
compte avoir (bilan) : creditor side of a balance.
(m pl) **avoirs** : assets, property, holding.
avoirs en banque : property lodged with a bank.
avoirs financiers : financial assets.
avoirs à l'étranger : external (foreign) assets.

avortement (m) : 1° *(expulsion spontanée, fausse couche) :* miscarriage.
2° [J] *(expulsion provoquée) :* abortion.
3° [C] *entreprise qui a avorté :* venture which has come to nothing.

avoué (m) : # solicitor.
étude d'— : office of solicitor.

avouer (v) : to acknowledge, to admit, to confess.
— *sa faute, son crime :* to confess one's offence, crime.
— *une dette :* to acknowledge a debt.

avulsion (f) : [J] avulsion.

ayant cause (m) (pl **ayants cause**) : [J] assign, cessionary (esp. in inheritance matters), trustee, executor.
— *à titre particulier :* particular, specific, devisee and/or legatee.
— *à titre universel :* residuary devisee and legatee (see *légataire*).

ayant droit (m) (pl **ayants droit**) : eligible person.
[J] assign, rightful claimant or owner, interested party, beneficiary.

NOTES

B

bafouer (v) : to scoff, to jeer at (s.o.).
bafouer la justice : to flout justice.

bagarre (f) : scuffle *(entre une foule et la police)*, affray, brawl, free fight.

bagne (m) : convict prison.

bail (m) (pl baux) : [J] lease (to tenant).
— *à cheptel* : agist, lease of live-stock.
— *à colonat partiaire (métayage)* : farming lease with rent payable in kind, [U.S.] share-crop system.
— *à construction* : building lease.
— *emphytéotique (emphytéose)* # long lease (up to ninety-nine years).
— *en cours* : operating lease.
— *à ferme* : lease of a farm, of ground, of land, farming lease.
— *à loyer* : house-letting lease.
— *à long terme* : long lease.
— *à vie* : lease for life.
donner à — : to lease out.
louer une ferme à — : to lease out a farm.
passer un — : to draw up, to sign a lease (an agreement).
prendre à — : to lease.
prêt- — : hire-purchase, leasing.
renouveler un — : to renew a lease, to take a new lease.
résilier un — : to avoid a lease.
terres louées à — : lands out on lease.

bailleur (m) : lessor.
[J] — *de fonds* : money-lender, capitalist, sleeping partner.

baisse (f) : fall.
actions en — : falling, going down shares.
être en — (Bourse) : to be off (Stock Exchange), to be down.
[C] [B] — *de la demande* : fall (off) in demande.
— *des prix* : drop in prices.
marché orienté à la — : falling market.
spéculation à la — : bear speculation.
spéculer à la — : to go (to speculate) for a fall, to go a bear.

baisser (v) : to go down, to fall, to durease.
la valeur de ce terrain a baissé : the value of this ground (land) has gone down.
— *le prix de* : to lower the price of, to cheapen.
— *le prix d'un produit au-dessous du prix habituel* : to mark down.
faire — les cours, les prix : to bear down quotations, prices.

baissier (m) : bear, short in stock.

balance (f) : [C] balance (of an account).
— *commerciale* : balance of trade.
— *commerciale déficitaire (excédentaire)* : passive (active) balance of trade.
— *d'inventaire* : balance sheet.
— *des opérations courantes (d'un pays)* : current account.
— *des paiements excédentaire, déficitaire* : balance of payments surplus, deficit.
— *de vérification* : trial balance.
balancer *un compte, faire la balance* : to settle an account.

balisage (m) : beaconing (sea), ground-lighting (airport).
droit de — : beaconage.

ballottage (m) : ballotage, voting by white or black balls ; second ballot at parliamentary election.

ban (m) : public proclamation.
publier les —(s) : to publish the banns (of marriage).
rompre son — (hist.) : to break a prohibition from entering certain towns or areas.

banc (m) : bench, seat.
— *du jury* : jury-box.
— *des magistrats* : the bench.
— *des ministres* : the Treasury Bench.
— *des prévenus* : dock.

bancable *(effet)* (a) : bankable (bill), negotiable in a bank.

bande (f) : [J] party, gang.
[C] — *publicitaire* : advertising streamer.
[B] — *d'enregistrement des cours* : tape.

bannissement (m) : banishment, exile.

banque (f) : bank.
— *d'affaires, de dépôt* : business bank, merchant bank.
— *commerciale* : commercial bank.
(la) haute — : high finance.
— *d'émission* : bank of issue.
— *d'entreprise* : corporate banking.
— *de détail* : retail banking.
— *à domicile* : home banking.

— *de données :* data bank.
— *foncière :* land bank.
— *hypothécaire :* mortgage bank.
— *Internationale pour la Reconstruction et le Développement (la « Banque Mondiale ») :* International Bank for Reconstruction and Development (B.I.R.D.).
carnet, livret de banque : pass-book, bankbook.
compte en — *:* bank account.
employé de — *:* bank-clerk.
frais de — *:* bank charges.
opérations de — *:* banking transactions.
— *des Règlements Internationaux (B.R.I.) :* Bank for International Settlements (B.I.S. ou B.I.Z.).
relevé de compte en — *:* bank statement.
solde en — *:* bank balance.
succursale d'une — *:* bank-branch.
taux d'escompte de la Banque de France (d'Angleterre) : Bank of France (of England) rate.
verser de l'argent à un compte en — *:* to bank.
— *de virement :* clearing bank.
chèque **bancaire** : bank cheque, [U.S.] check.
crédit bancaire : bank credit.
effet bancaire : bank bill.
secret bancaire : bank secret.

banquier (m) : banker.

banqueroute (f) : bankruptcy.
[J] — *simple :* bankruptcy with irregularities deemed a breach of the law.
— *frauduleuse :* fraudulent bankruptcy, amounting to crime.

banqueroutier (m) : (fraudulent) bankrupt.

baptême (m) : baptism, christening.
nom de — *:* christian name, first name.

baraterie (f) : barratry.

barème (m) : schedule, tariff, table, scale *(des salaires, etc.)*, assize *(des prix)*, price list.

barrage *(d'un chèque)* (m) : crossing of a cheque.

barre (f) : [J] — *de tribunal :* bar of a court of justice.
— *des témoins :* witness-box.
paraître à la — *:* to appear before the court.
mander, traduire à la — *:* to summon, to prosecute s.o.
entendre à la — *:* to give a hearing (in trial).

barré *(chèque)* (a) : crossed (cheque).
barrer un chèque : to cross a cheque.

barreau (m) : [J] bar.
être admis au — *:* to be called to the bar, [U.S.] to become member of the Bar Association.

rayer du — *:* to disbar.

barrières douanières (f pl) : tariff walls, tariff barriers, customs barriers, customs duties.

bas (a) : low.
être au — *de l'échelle (dans une profession) :* to be on the ground-floor.

base (f) : base, basis.
abattement à la — *:* basic abatement.
année de — *:* base year.
— *fixe :* fixed base.
— *d'imposition :* taxable base, basis of assessment.
salaire de — *:* basic pay (wage).
« la base » (dans une organisation syndicale) : the grass-roots, the rank and file (Trade Unions).

baser (v) : to base.
(se) — *sur :* to found upon.

bataille (f) *de procurations* : proxy contest.

batellerie (f) : inland water transport, river shipping, lighterage.

bâtiment (m) : building, edifice, structure, ship.
— *de commerce, marchand :* freighter, merchant ship, merchantman, trading vessel.
— *de servitude :* harbour craft.
[C] *le* — *:* the building trade, the constructional trades.
terrain à **bâtir** : building site, land.

bâtonnier (m) : leader, president of the bar.

« battage » (m) (fam.) : booming.
faire du battage (en faveur de) : to boom (for).

beau-fils (m) : stepson, son-in-law.

beau-frère (m) : brother-in-law.

beau-père (m) : stepfather, father-in-law.

beaux-parents (m pl) : parents-in-law.

belle-fille (f) : stepdaughter, daughter-in-law.

belle-mère (f) : stepmother, mother-in-law.

belle-sœur (f) : sister-in-law.

belligérant (m et a) : belligerent.

bénéfice (m) : profit, gain, benefit, privilege, advantage.
— *de l'âge :* prerogative of age.
sous — *de... :* under reservation of...
[F] (C) : profit, gain.

— *par action (BPA)* : earnings per share.
— *actualisé net* : premium, cumulative cash surplus, excess profit.
— *actualisé unitaire* : cumulative present value cash.
— *annuel* : yearly profit.
— *brut* : gross profit, [U.S.] mark up.
— *(s) commerciaux* : business (trading) profits.
— *comptable* : book profit.
— *(s) distribués (non distribués)* : distributed (undistributed) profits.
— *escompté* : anticipated profit.
— *d'exploitation* : operating profit, trading profit.
— *après impôt* : earned surplus, after-tax profit, earnings, yield.
— *avant impôt* : pretax profit.
— *imposable* : taxable profit.
— *net* : clear, net profit.
— *net plus amortissements* : cash flow (the net cash flow is retained earnings and depreciation provisions before or after tax).
réaliser des — (s) : (U.S.) to chalk up.
— *(s) reportés* : profits carried forward.
faire apparaître un — : to show a profit.
part de — : bonus.
participation aux — (s) : profit sharing.
participation des salariés aux — (s) de l'entreprise (de l'expansion) : industrial co-partnership.
répartition des — (s) : allotment of profits.
super — (s) : excess profits.
[E] — *d'affrètement* : profit on charter.
[J] benefit, privilege, advantage.
— *de l'assistance judiciaire* : grant of legal aid.
— *des circonstances atténuantes* : grant of extenuating circumstances.
— *du concordat* : acceptance of a composition with bankrupt (by creditors).
— *de discussion* : (beneficium excussionis) lawful claim of a surety for a preliminary distraint upon the principal debtor.
— *de division* : (beneficium divisionis) right of sureties to go bail each for his part only.
— *du doute* : benefit of the doubt.
— *d'inventaire* : (beneficium inventarii) acceptance of an estate without liability beyond the assets descended.
— *de la subrogation légale dans les droits du créancier* : privilege of entering into the rights of a creditor.

bénéficiaire (m et a) : beneficiary, payee.
(a) [J] *héritier —* : heir accepting succession cum beneficium inventarii.
[ASS] *tiers —* : the third party beneficiary.
[F] *capacité —* : earning power.
compte — : account showing a credit balance.
solde — : profit balance.

bénéficier (v) : to benefit, to profit (by).
[J] — *d'un non-lieu* : to be discharged.
[C] — *d'une remise* : to be subject to a discount.

faire — d'une remise : to allow a discount.

bénévole (a) : benevolent.
[J] *mandataire —* : unpaid agent.

besoin (m) : need, necessity, occasion.
au — : when required, if necessary.
[J] *en tant que de —* : as may be required, as occasion shall require.
— *(s) d'emprunt du gouvernement* : (U.K.) Government Borrowing Requirements (G.B.R.).
— *(s) d'emprunt du secteur public non couverts par des rentrées fiscales* : Public Sector Borrowing Requirements.

bien (m) : 1° good, weal, welfare.
le — public : the common welfare.
économie du bien-être : welfare economics.
bien-fondé : [J] the merits of a case or claim, the grounds for.
établir le bien-fondé de sa demande : to substantiate one's claim.
2° **bien(s)** *(concept patrimonial)* estate, property, assets, goods and chattels.
ameublissement d'un bien : conversion of realty into personalty.
— *(s) d'apport* : estate brought in, (civ.) contribution of husband and wife to joint resources upon marriage.
— *(s) collectifs* : collective property, public goods.
— *(s) composant la masse de la faillite* : bankrupt's total estate.
— *(s) communaux* : commons.
— *(s) communs, de communauté* : communal estate, joint estate of husband and wife, [U.S.] community property.
— *(s) de consommation* : consumer goods.
— *(s) corporels* : tangible property.
— *(s) disponibles (quotité disponible par testament)* : disposable portion of property.
— *(s) domaniaux* : state property, public domain.
— *(s) d'équipement* : capital goods, [U.S.] equipment.
— *(s) de famille* : family estate, [U.S.] homestead.
— *(s) fonciers* : landed property.
— *-fonds* : real estate, landed property, tenement.
— *(s) gagés* : pledged assets.
— *(s) hypothéqués* : mortgaged property, encumbered estate.
— *(s) immeubles, immobiliers* : immovable property, real estate.
— *(s) incorporels* : intangible property.
— *(s) indivis* : indivisum, coparceny, undivided, joint estate.
— *jacent* : land in abeyance.
— *(s) libres* : available assets.
— *(s) libres d'hypothèque* : estate free from

encumberance.
— *(s) de mainmorte* : property in mortmain.
— *(s) matrimoniaux* : property acquired by married couple.
— *(s) meubles, mobiliers* : personal estate, personalty, chattels, movables.
— *(s) oisifs* : unproductive property.
— *(s) paraphernaux* : separate property of wife.
— *(s) patrimoniaux* : patrimony.
— *(s) présents* : actual assets.
— *(s) privatifs* : private goods.
— *(s) de production* : producer's good.
— *(s) propres du mari, de la femme* : husband's, wife's separate estate.
— *(s) en rentes* : funded property.
— *(s) réservés* : separate property of husband and wife.
— *(s) d'une société* : company's assets.
— *(s) de la succession* : hereditaments, estate.
— *tenant* : land bordering on an estate.
— *(s) sous tutelle #* merit goods.
— *(s) vacants, sans maître, à l'abandon* : ownerless property, derelict.
— *(s) à venir* : future estate.
— *(s) en viager* : life estate.
cession de — *(s)* : assignment of property.
communauté de — *(s)* : intercommunity.
prendre une hypothèque sur un — : to raise a mortgage on property.
reprise de — *(s)* : recovery of property.
séparation de — *(s)* : separate estate.

bienfaisance (f) : charity.
bureau de — : relief committee.

biffer (v) : *(un mot)* to erase a word, *(un nom)* to strike off a name, *(un procès)* to strike an action off the roll.

biffure (f) : cancellation.
[J] striking off the roll.

bigamie (f) : bigamy.

bilan (m) : balance, balance-sheet, statement.
— *d'activité d'une agence publicitaire* : billing.
— *consolidé* : consolidated balance.
haut de — : patrimonial accounts.
— *hebdomadaire* : weekly statement.
— *de liquidation (dans une faillite)* : statement of affairs (in bankruptcy).
dresser, établir le — : to draw up, to strike the balance-sheet.
déposer son — : to file up a petition in bankruptcy.
faux — : fraudulent balance-sheet.
méthode du — : balance method.

bilatéral (a) : bilateral, two-sided.
[J] *contrat* — *parfait* : (contractus bilateralis aequalis) bilateral contract, the parties assuming corresponding obligations (sale, exchange, lease, etc.).
contrat — *imparfait* : (contractus bilateralis inaequalis) bilateral contract, the parties assuming obligations of a different kind (loan, deposit, etc.).

billet (m) : note, ticket.
— *d'abonnement* : season ticket.
— *de chemin de fer* : railway ticket.
[C] — *à ordre* : promissory note, bill.
— *à présentation* : bill payable on demand.
— *à vue* : bill payable at sight.
— *au porteur* : bill payable to the bearer.
— *simple* : promissory note of hand.
— *de trésorerie* : commercial paper.
[E] — *de santé (patente)* : certificate of health.
[F] — *de banque* : banknote, [U.S.] bill.
— *(s) émis et en circulation à l'intérieur du pays* : home currency.

bisaïeuls (m pl) : great-grandparents.

blame (m) : blame, disapproval, reprimand.

blanc (a et m) : (a) blank.
acceptation en — : blank acceptance.
— *-seing* : signature to a blank document, paper signed in blank.
bulletin de vote — : blank voting-paper.
crédit en — : blank credit.
donner — *-seing à qn* : to give s.o. a free hand.
endos en — : blank endorsement.
chèque en — : blank cheque.
mariage — : unconsummated marriage.
quittance en — : uncomplete receipt.
donner carte blanche : to give full power.
signer un document en — : to sign an uncompleted document.
sortir — *d'une affaire* : to come out of a business without a stain.
opération **blanche** : profitless deal.
(m) *les blancs* : blank spaces in a document.

blanchir (v) **de l'argent** : to launder money.

blesser les intérêts (v) : to be prejudicial to.

blessure (f) : wound, hurt, injury.
[J] *coups et* — *(s)* : assault and battery.

bloc (m) : block, lump, coalition *(de partis)*.
acheter, vendre en — : to buy, to sell, the whole stock.
adjuger en — : to adjudicate the whole lot.

blocage (m) : blocking-up, clamping.
— *(s) des prix et des salaires* : prices and salaries freeze.
[F] *compte* **bloqué** : blocked account.
[C] **bloquer** *(les prix)* : to freeze, to clamp

(prices).

blocus (m) : blockade.
forcer le — : to run the blockade.
lever le — : to raise the blockade.

boisson (f) : drink, liquor.
taxes et droits sur les — (s) alcoolisées : taxes and duties on spirituous liquors.

bon (m et a) :
(m) : voucher, bill, note of hand, bond.
[C] *— de caisse* : cash voucher.
— de commande : order form.
— de commission : commission note.
— de livraison : delivery order.
— à vue : sight draft.
bonne affaire : bargain.
[F] *adjudication des — (s) du Trésor* : bill auction.
— du Trésor : treasury bill, (U.K.) exchequer bill.
— du Trésor à court terme : (U.S.) bill.
— des P.T.T. : bond issued by the postal administration.
— au porteur : bearer bond.
— nominatif : registered bond.
porteur de — (s) : bondholder.
(a) : good, proper, sound.
aux — (s) soins de : care of (c/ö).
« *— pour...* » : « good for... » (written by the debtor over his signature showing amount or thing due or the purpose of the document, e.g. :
— pour autorisation, aval, pouvoir).
— sens : common sense.
en — état : in a good state.
— (s) offices : good offices.
[ASS] **bonne** *arrivée* (« *sous réverse de bonne arrivée du navire au port de destination, sans avarie* ») : safe arrival (of ship).
[J] *bonne foi* : good faith.
de bonne foi : bona fide.
acquéreur, possesseur, tiers de bonne foi : bona fide purchaser, possessor, third party.
témoin de bonne foi : reliable, trustful witness.
bonnes mœurs : morality.
certificat de bonne vie et mœurs : certificate of good character.
en bonne et due forme : in due form.

boni (m) : surplus, bonus.

bonification (f) : allowance, backwardation, bonus, rebate.
— sur les actions : bonus on shares.

bonifier (v) : to improve (land), to allow a discount, to credit, to make good (up) (shortage).

boniment (m) : sales talk.

bord (m) : board, side (of ship), edge, border, brink, hem, brim, rim, shore, bank ; ex ship.
charger à — : to ship.
journal de navigation, de — : logbook.
[E] *franco —* : free on board (F.O.B.).
bord à bord (BAB) : free in and out (FIO).

bordereau (m) : memorandum, detailed statement, docket *(de marchandises, de l'encaisse, etc.)*, consignment note, abstract, schedule, bordereau, voucher.
— (x) des achats et ventes : bought and sold notes.
— de crédit, de débit : credit, debit note.
[D] *— descriptif* : bill of entry, air consignment, air waybill.
— d'escompte : list of bills for discount.
— d'expédition : dispatch note.
— de livraison : issue voucher.
— de paye : wages docket, payroll.
— des pièces d'un dossier : docket.
— des prix : price-list.

bornage (m) : demarcation, marking out of land.

borne (f) : boundary-mark, stone, post, milestone.

« **bouche-trou** »(m) *(mesures d'urgence)* : stop-gap measures.

bouilleur de cru (m) : farmer who distils for his own consumption, home distiller.

bourgeois (m) : burgess, burgher, citizen.

bourse (f) : the Exchange.
— d'entretien : maintenance grant.
— du travail : Labour Exchange.
[B] *à la Bourse* : on the Stock Exchange (on' Change).
— animée : lively market.
— calme : quiet market.
— de commerce : Commodities Exchange # the Royal Exchange.
— des grains : Corn Exchange.
— de marchandises : Products Exchange, commodity exchange.
— des valeurs : Stock Exchange.
Commission des Opérations de Bourse (C.O.B.) # Securities and Exchange Commission.
coup de — : deal on the Stock Exchange.
cours de la — : share list.
courtier en — : share-broker, jobber, [U.S.] commissions broker, dealer, specialist.
jouer à la — : to speculate on the Stock Exchange.
jour de liquidation en — : pay-day, settlement day, call option day.
— de New York : New York stock exchange (NYSE).

deuxième — (New York) : New York curb exchange.
opérations de — : Stock Exchange business.
tenue de la — : Stock Exchange tone.
titres admis à la — : listed stock.

boursicoter (v) : to dabble in stocks, to punt.
boursicoteur (m) : dabbler.

boursier (a) : market.
valeur boursière : market value.

boycotter (v) : to boycott.

braconnage (m) : poaching.

branche (f) : branch, limb, bough *(d'arbre)*.
— de l'administration : branch of the civil service.
— du commerce : branch of trade.
— d'une famille (aînée, cadette) : branch of a family (older, younger).

brasser des affaires (v) : to handle big business.
brasseur *d'affaires* : big businessman.

brevet (m) : (letters) patent, (royal) warrant.
1° [J] *acte en —* : contract delivered by a notary in the original.
2° diploma, certificate.
— de capitaine (de la marine marchande) : master's certificate.
3° *— d'invention* : patent.
agent en — (s) d'invention : patent-agent.
bureau des — (s) (Office de la propriété industrielle) # Patent Office.
contrefaçon d'une invention ou fabrication faisant l'objet d'un — : infringement of a patent.
déchéance de — : forfeiture of patent.
demandeur d'un — : claimant for a patent.
titulaire d'un — : patentee.
faire **breveter** : to take out a patent.

bris (m) : [J] breaking *(de scellés, etc.)*, wreck *(de navire)*.
— de prison : prison breaking.
— de clôture : breach of close.
droit de — : escheat (of sea wreck washed ashore).
[ASS] *assurance contre le — des glaces* : plate-glass insurance.

brocard (m) : 1° gibe, lampoon.
2° any legal term in current use among lay persons.

brochure *(publicitaire)* (f) : (advertising) booklet, brochure.

brouillard *(comptabilité)* (m) : (accounting) waste-book, counter cash-book.

brouillon *(d'un document)* (m) : draft (of a document).

bru (f) : daughter-in-law.

bruit (m) : 1. noise. 2. report, rumour.
le — court : it is rumoured.
— et tapage nocturne : disturbance of the peace at night.

brut (m) *(pétrole)* : crude (oil).

brut (a) : gross (profit, value, weight).
[C] *vendre — pour net* : to sell goods with packing included in the weight.

budget (m) : budget, estimates.
les articles du — : the appropriations.
— d'annonceur : account.
commission du — : # (U.S.) Committee of Ways and Means.
— domestique : household budget.
— de fonctionnement : operational budget.
— d'investissement : capital budgeting.
— ordinaire de publicité : above the line advertising expenditure.
budget prévisionnel principal (d'une entreprise, pour une période ordinairement de 6 à 12 mois) : master budget.
équilibrer le — : to balance the budget.
inscrire au — : to budget for.

budgétaire (a) : budgetary.
collectif — : deficiency bill, (U.K.) bill of supply.
excédent — : budgetary surplus.
rationalisation des choix — (s) (R.C.B.) : Planning, Programming, Budgeting System (P.P.B.S.).
situation — : budgetary statement.

bulletin (m) : bulletin, report, paper, form.
— d'adhésion : membership form.
[E] *— de chargement* : shipping documents, consignment note.
[J] *— législatif* : publication of laws and statutes.
[C] *— de commande* : order form.
[B] *— de la cote* : stock list.

bureau (m) : office, bureau, board of directors, officers of a meeting, a company, etc., committee.
— de bienfaisance : relief committee.
— des brevets (Office de la propriété industrielle) # Patent Office.
— de change : exchange bureau office.
— de douane : customs office, station.
— d'Etudes : design office, research department.
— d'information : public relations, information desk, service.
— international du travail (B.I.T.) : International Labour Office (I.L.O.).

– *de placement* : employment bureau, labour exchange.
– *de police* : police station.
– *de poste* : post office.
– *de tabac* : tobacconist's shop.
– *de vote* : polling station.

but (m) : aim, intent, object.
– *à –* : without (any) davantage to either.

dans le – de (frauder) : with the intent (to defraud).
dans un – lucratif : for pecuniary gain.
organisme à – non lucratif : non-profit organization.

butoir *(financier, fiscal)* (m) : (financial, fiscal) buffer.

NOTES

C

cabinet (m): closet, small room.
— *juridique*: law firm.
— *de travail*: study, office, room, consulting room.
[J] Government, the cabinet.
conseil de — : cabinet council.
— *ministériel*: minister's departmental staff.
chef de — : principal private secretary.

cabotage (m): coastwise trade, traffic.
grand, petit — : off-shore, inshore coastal traffic.
capitaine au — : master of a coasting vessel.

cachet (m): *(de la poste)* post-mark, *(d'un fabricant)* maker's trade-mark.

cadastre (m): [A] cadastral survey, land registry, [U.S.] Real Estate Register.

cadeaux (m. pl.) **publicitaires**: [C] advertising give aways.

cadence *(de production)* (f): rate of output, [U.S.] effort.

cadet (a et m): younger, junior.
(a) *branche* **cadette**: younger branch (of a family).
(m) *le* — : the youngest.

cadre (m): 1° *(supérieur d'entreprise)*: executive, [U.S.] high, senior executive, senior staff, top executives.
cadres d'exécution: first line management.
retraite des — *(s)*: [U.S.] executive retirement plan.
2° *(d'activité)*: frame.
dans le cadre de...: within the framework of...
dans le — *de l'exploitation d'une entreprise*: in the course of a business.
sortir du — *de (ses) fonctions*: to go beyond (one's) duties.

caduc, caduque (a): *(legs)* null and void, *(contrat)* lapsed, *(dette)* statute-barred.

c.a.f. *(coût, assurances, fret)*: C.I.F. (cost, insurance, freight).

cahier *(des charges)* (m): conditions of a contract, specifications, articles and conditions (of sale, public works contract, etc.), particulars of sales.

caisse (f): 1° cash-box, counting house, cash in hand, fund, pay-desk, till, box, chest, packing case, check-out counter (supermarché).
— *enregistreuse*: cash register.
faire la — : to balance up the takings.
livre de — : cash-book.
petite — : petty cash.
2° fund.
— *d'amortissement*: a) sinking fund, redemption fund; b) office for the redemption of the national debt.
— *de crédit agricole*: co-operative farm credit bank.
— *des dépôts et consignations*: deposit and consignment office.
— *d'épargne*: savings bank.
— *noire*: slushfund.
— *des retraites*: pension fund.
— *de retraites vieillesse*: old age pension fund.
— *de sécurité sociale*: social security fund(s).
livret de — *d'épargne*: savings bank book.

caissier (m): cashier, cash clerk, collecting clerk, [U.S.] teller (in a bank).

calcul *des revenus* (m): computation of income.
1° *selon la méthode « d'augmentation »*: accrual basis method.
2° *par un système de comptabilisation ne tenant compte que des recettes réellement encaissées et des dépenses effectivement payées par le contribuable*: cash basis method (which only includes the amounts actually received and the expenses paid by the taxpayer).

calcul (m) **des probabilités**: theory of probability.

calculatrice (f): calculator, calculating machine.

calculer (v): *(valeur)* to reckon the value of, *(revenu)* to calculate, to compute.

calamité (f): disaster.

calomnie (f): calumny, defamation.
— *écrite*: libel.
— *orale*: slander.
dénonciation **calomnieuse**: false accusation.

cambiste (a et m): (a) *place cambiste*: exchange centre; (m) [B] exchange broker, foreign exchange dealer.

— *agréé* : authorized dealer.

cambriolage (m) : housebreaking, burglary, breaking and entering.

camelote (f) : trash, shoddy articles.

camionnage (m) : cartage, haulage.
   camionneur : carrier, carman.

campagne *(publicitaire)* (f) : advertising campaign, [U.S.] drive.

camisole *(de force)* (f) : strait-waist-coat, jacket.

canal (m) : *(maritime)* ship-canal, *(d'irrigation)* irrigation canal.

« **canards boîteux** » *(entreprises en difficulté)* : lame ducks.

candidat (m) : candidate, applicant.
   candidature : candidacy, application.
   faire acte de — : to apply for, (fam.) to put in for a job.

canon (m) : canon, rule of the ecclesiastical authority.
   droit — : canon law.

canton (m) : [A] smallest administrative district, subdivision of an *arrondissement* ; sovereign Swiss canton (e.g. *république et* — *de Genève*).

(se) **cantonner** (v) : to confine oneself to...

capacité (f) : ability, legal ability, capacity, competence, qualification.
   [J] — *d'ester en jugement* : capacity to appear.
   — *d'ester en justice* : capacity to sue.
   — *d'exercer* : capacity to practise.
   — *de s'obliger* : capacity to contract and convey.
   — *de tester* : testamentary capacity.
   [F] — *d'autofinancement* : self financing flow.
   — *bénéficiaire* : earning power.
   — *d'imposition* : taxability, taxable capacity.
   — *de payer* : ability to pay.
   — *de production* : productive capacity (powers), production capacity, [U.S.] plant capacity.
   avoir — *de faire qch* : to be entitled (qualified) to do sth.
   — *de traitement (informatique)* : data-handling capacity.

capitaine (m) **de port** : harbour master.

capital (m et a) : capital.
   1° — *(d'une société)* : assets.
   — *actions* : equity, share capital, capital stock.
   — *appelé* : called-up capital.
   — *d'apport* : initial capital.
   — *déclaré* : stated capital.
   — *effectif (libéré, réel, versé)* : (fully) paid-up capital.
   — *d'emprunt* : loan capital.
   — *d'établissement* : opening (initial) capital.
   — *et intérêts* : principal and interests.
   — *liquide* : money (liquid) capital.
   — *nominal* : nominal (subscribed) capital.
   — *non libéré* : uncalled capital.
   — *en numéraire* : cash capital.
   — *social* : authorized capital, registered capital, nominal capital, joint stock (assets), capital base, capital funds.
   gains en — : capital gains.
   plus-value en — : capital profits, gains.
   prélèvement sur le — : capital levy.
   — *de roulement* : trading capital, working capital.
   valeur en — : capital value.
   compte (de) — : capital account.
   capitaux *circulants* : circulating (floating) capital (assets), revenue assets.
   — *flottants* : hot money.
   capitaux immobilisés : fixed assets, money tied up.
   capitaux investis : funded capital.
   capitaux mobilisables : capital that can be made available.
   capitaux propres : stockholder's equity.
   capital souscrit : subscribed capital.
   capitaux versés : paid-in (paid-up) capital.
   augmentation des capitaux (de capital) : increase of capital.
   fuite des capitaux : flight (exodus) of capital.
   mettre des capitaux dans une affaire : to put (to invest) capital into a business.
   mouvements de capitaux : capital movements.
   2° *crime* — : capital crime.
   peine — *(e)* : capital punishment, death sentence.
   3° *question* — *(e)* : essential (main) issue.

capitalisation *(d'intérêts)* (f) : capitalization (of interests).
   — *boursière* : market capitalization.

capitaliser (v) : to capitalize.

capitalisme (m) : capitalism.
   — *dynamique* : stream-lined capitalism.

capitaliste (m) : capitalist, investor.

capitalistique *(entreprise)* (a) : capitalistic (firm, concern).

captation *(d'héritage)* (f) : [J] obtaining succession by insidious means, captation.

caractère (m) : character, disposition, nature.
— (s) spécifiques d'un délit : the facts of the case (also called éléments constitutifs de délit).
agir en — de : to act in the capacity of.

carambouiller (v) : to convert (property) fraudulently.

carence (f) : default.
[J] insolvency.
procès-verbal de — : statement of insolvency, default.

cargaison (f) : cargo, freight, lading.

carnet (m) : note book.
— de commandes : order book.
— d'échéances : bills payable book.
— à souches : counterfoil book, [U.S.] stub book.
[F] — de banque : pass book.
— de chèques : cheque book.
— de versements : pay-in-book.

carte (f) : card, sheet of paper.
— d'affaires : business card.
— de crédit : credit card, charge card.
— d'identité : identity card.
— grise : car licence.
— de séjour : permission to reside.
— perforée : punched card.
— blanche : full warrant to act for the best.
« — blanche » : blanket authority.
donner — blanche (à qn) : to give (s.o.) a free hand.

cartel (m) : cartel.

cas (m) : case, instance.
— concret : case history.
— d'espèce : concrete case.
— de force majeure : irresistible circumstances outside one's control, act of God.
— fortuit : accident, accidental case.
— imprévu : emergency.
— de nécessité : urgency.
en — de mort : in case of death.
le — échéant : eventually, should the occasion arise, in case of need.
hormis le — de : barring the case of.
au — où : in the event of.
en aucun — : on non account.
— (juridique) : (legal) case, cause.
étude de — de situation : case study.

cascade (taxes en) (f) : cascade taxes.

case (f) : box.
mettre une croix dans la — : to put a cross in the box.

casier (m) : [J] — judiciaire : criminal record.
— judiciaire vierge : clean record.
extrait de — judiciaire : certificate of non-punishment or of penalties incurred, delivered by the Ministry of Justice.
— fiscal : tax record.

cassation (f) : [J] cassation, annulment, repeal, quashing, rescission of judgment.
Cour de — : supreme court of appeals (entertaining jurisdiction in matters of form and procedure).

casser (v) : 1° to annul, to quash ; 2° to dismiss.
— un arrêt : to annul a judgement.
— un testament : to set aside a will.
— un fonctionnaire : to cashier a civil servant.

casuel (a et m) : fortuitous.
[J] condition casuelle : contingent condition.
[F] le — : perquisites, fees in addition to salary.

catastrophe (f) : disaster.
— financière : crash.

catégorie (de revenu) (f) : category, rating, [U.S.] schedule of income.
— (s) socio-professionnelles : social and economic (professional) categories.

cause (f) : [J] cause, suit, action ; ground, consideration (in contracts), cause of action.
— célèbres : famous cases, trials.
avocat sans — : briefless barrister.
être chargé d'une — : to hold a brief.
appel des — (s) : calling the roll.
agir en connaissance de — : to act with... (in) full knowledge of the facts.
en tout état de — : whatever the circumstances, in any case, at all events.
— en état : issue joined.
gain de — : recovery of judgment.
donner gain de — au requérant : to find for the plaintiff.
mettre (qn) en — : to implicate (s.o.), to involve (s.o.) in.
mettre en — l'honnêteté de qn : to question the honesty of s.o.
mettre qn hors de — : to exonerate s.o., to rule out of court.
partie en — : party to a suit.
perdre sa — : to lose one's case.
les personnes en — : the persons involved.
questions hors de — : irrelevant questions.
entendre une — : to hear a case.
la — est entendue : the matter is decided.
cause (= provision) : consideration.

caution (f) : 1° (garantie) security, safety, deposit, qualification, guarantee, caution

money, indemnity, bail, surety, [U.S.] suretyship.
mettre en liberté sous — : to admit s.o. to bail, to allow bail.
verser une — : to pay a deposit.
— *bancaire* : guarantee facility.
— *judiciaire* : (cautio judicatum solvi) security for costs and eventual penalty by foreign plaintiff not possessing real property in France.
— *juratoire* : guaranty given by oath.
— *légale* : legal (compulsory) guaranty.
contre- — : additional security.
tierce- — : contingent liability.
2° *(personne)* surety, security, guarantor.
— *bourgeoise* : surety of recognized standing.
—*(s) conjointes et solidaires* : sureties liable jointly and severally.
donner, fournir, se porter, — *pour qn* : to go bail, to stand security, to be surety for s.o., to be s.o.'s guarantor, to enter into recognizance.
acquit à — : excise-note, bond-note.
sujet à — : unreliable.

cautionnement (m) : [J] surety-bon, guaranty.
— *judiciaire* : bail.
— *solidaire* : joint guaranty, bond.
— *commercial* : caution-money, suretyship.
déposer un — : to pay in caution-money.
cautionner *(quelqu'un)* (v) : to stand surety, to go bail, to stand as a guarantor, (for s.o.).
obligations cautionnées : hypothecated bonds.

cavalerie *(d'effets de change)* (f) : [C] accommodation bills (credit).

cédant (m) : alienator, assignor, conveyor.

céder (v) : to give up, to part with yield to, to surrender (right).
— *un bail* : to transfer a lease.
— *un fonds de commerce* : to sell the goodwill of a business.
— *(des points)* : to give up (points).

cédule (f) : [F] schedule (of taxes).
impôt **cédulaire** : scheduled tax.
méthode cédulaire d'imposition : schedular method of taxation.

célibat (m) : celibacy.
célibataire : *(homme)* bachelor, *(femme)* spinster.

celui, celle qui : whichever.
des deux méthodes (d'imposition), celle qui... : whichever of the two methods...

cellule (f) : cell (of prison).
voiture **cellulaire** : police-van, the Black Maria.

cens (m) : quota (of taxes payable), rating.

censeur (m) : censor, auditor (in joint stock companies).

centième (m) **de point** *(0,01 %)* : basis point.

centimes additionnels (m) : county (borough) rates, additional percentages.

central *(siège)* (a) : head office.

central (m) **téléphonique** : telephone exchange.

centraliser (v) : to centralize.

centre (m) : centre, [U.S.] center.
— -*auto* : autocentre.
— *commercial* : shopping centre, center.
— *d'affaires international* : world trade center.
— *des affaires* : business centre, centre of business.
— *de magasins d'usine* : factory outlet center.
principal — *d'affaires* : regular and established place of business.
[F] — *d'intérêts* : centre of attraction.

cercle (m) : club, gaming house.
[A] (hist.) territorial division, district (in former French colonies).

certain (a) : certain, sure, unquestionable.
date —*(e)* : fixed date.
à jour — : on stated day ne varietur.
preuve —*(e)* : irrefutable evidence.
un — *M. Untel* : one So-and-so.
témoin — : reliable witness.

certificat (m) : certificate.
[A] — *de bonne vie et mœurs* : certificate of good character.
— *consulaire de conformité* : consular invoice.
— *médical* : medical certificate.
[D] — *d'entrepôt* : warrant.
— *de drawback* : drawback, debenture, certificate of acknowledgement.
— *d'origine* : certificate of origin.
[F] — *provisoire* : share certificate.
— *de dépôt (entraînant des exonérations fiscales)* : (U.S.) all savers certificate.

certification *(des signatures)* (f) : witnessing of signatures (by notary or stock broker on transfer of stocks and shares).

certifier (v) : to certify.
copie **certifiée** *conforme* : certified true copy.

cessation (f) : 1° *(fin d'activité)* cessation, cessing.
après — *de l'exploitation d'une entreprise* : after ceasing to carry on a business.

— *de bail :* expiry of lease.
— *de commerce :* winding-up.
2° *(paiements)* discontinuance, suspension (of payments).
état de — *de paiements :* default.
3° *(d'application)* termination.
— *de relations d'affaires :* termination of business relations.
4° [J] *action en* — *de trouble de jouissance :* action for disturbance of possession.
— *de poursuites :* nonsuit, discontinuance.

cesser (v) : to cease.
— *le travail :* to cease work.
— *les affaires :* to give up business.
— *de fabriquer :* to discontinue (a line).
— *les paiements :* to suspend (stop) payments.

cessibilité (f) : transferability.
[A] *arrêté de* — : decree of transferability.

cessible (a) : transferable.
droits — *(s) :* transferable rights.

cession (f) : cession, transfer, conveyance, alienation, assignation (assignment), disposal, surrender.
acte de — : deed of conveyance.
— *d'actifs :* disvertment.
— *d'actions :* sale of shares.
— *-bail :* lease-back.
— *de biens :* disposition.
— *de droits d'auteur :* assignation (of a copyright).
— *de terre :* release.

cessionnaire (m) : transferee, assignee.
(d'une licence) licensee, *(d'un chèque)* endorser of cheque, *(d'un titre)* holder of a bill.

chaîne (f) :
— *du froid :* cold chain.
— *de montage :* assembly line.
production à la — : line production.
travail à la — : work on the assembly line, flow production.
— *de magasins, d'hôtels :* chain-stores, chain of hotels.

chaland (m) : customer, buyer.
chalandage (m) d'opinion : opinion shopping
— *fiscal :* treaty shopping.

chambardement (m) : shake-out.

chambre (f) : chamber, house.
— *des mises en accusation* # grand jury.
— *d'agriculture :* chamber of agriculture.
— *civile :* civil division of a court of justice.
— *de commerce et d'industrie :* chamber of commerce and industry, [U.S.] board of trade.
— *de compensation :* clearing-house.
— *du conseil :* court chambers.
— *correctionnelle :* division of a court of justice judging minor offences.
— *criminelle :* criminal division of a court of justice.
— *des métiers :* guild chamber of trade.
— *des référés, des requêtes :* division of the *Cour de cassation* entrusted with the preliminary examination of cases.
— *syndicale :* employers federation.
— *syndicale des agents de change :* stock exchange committee.
juger une affaire toutes — *(s) réunies :* sitting in banc (of all divisions of a court of justice).

champ (m) **d'activité** : range of action.

champ (m) **d'application** *(de l'impôt)* : the scope (of tax).

chandelle (f) : candle.
[J] *vente à* — *éteinte :* candel auction, auction by inch of candle.

change (m) : 1° change, exchange. 2° (rate of) exchange. 3° *(= lettre de* —*)*.
action de — : claim based on a bill of exchange.
agent de — : stock-broker.
billet de — : promissory change.
bureau de — : (foreign) exchange office.
— *du jour :* current exchange rate.
— *effectif :* real exchange.
contrôle des — *(s) :* (foreign) exchange control.
cours du — : rate of exchange, exchange rate.
cours du — *sur l'étranger, (sur l'intérieur) :* foreign (inland) rate of exchange.
— *au pair :* exchange at par.
opérations de — : exchange transactions.

changeur (m) : money changer.

changement (m) : change, alteration.
— *à une clause :* alteration in a clause.
— *d'hypothèque :* transfer of mortgage.

changer *(des devises)* (v) : to (ex)change (currency).

chantage (m) : blackmail, extortion.
— *à la protection contre le gangstérisme :* protection racket.
faire **chanter** *qn :* to blackmail s.o.

chantier (m) : site, yard, [U.S.] location.
— *de construction :* building (construction) yard, [U.S.] job site.
— *naval :* shipyard.

chaparder (v) : to pilfer.

chapitre (m) : chapter, section.
chapitre des dépenses : item of expenses.

charge (f) : 1° burden, charge, responsibility, trust, office.
– *de l'exercice :* expense of the year.
– *(s) d'entretien :* outlays for upkeep.
– *(s) d'exploitation :* working expenses.
– *(s) de famille :* dependents (dependants).
– *fiscale :* taxation (tax) burden, burden of taxation.
– *(s) incompressibles :* incompressible expenses (costs).
– *(s) salariales :* wage costs, wage outlays.
– *(s) sociales :* social costs.
cahier des – *(s) :* specifications, articles and conditions (of sale, of public works contract, etc.).
personnes à – : dependents (dependants), dependent persons (child, relative).
frais à la – *de :* expenses (costs) chargeable to, taxable to, payable by.
impôts à la – *d'un locataire :* taxes payable by a tenant.
être mis à la – *de qn :* to be taxed to s.o.
la partie du salaire qui dépasse une certaine limite) peut être mise à la – *de l'employé :* [U.K.] the portion (of the pay that exceeds a certain limit) may be taxed to the employee.
libre de – *(s) :* free from encumbrances.
2° – *de la preuve :* burden of proof (onus probandi).
fait de – : breach of trust.
témoin à – : witness for the prosecution.
[A] – *d'officier public ou ministériel :* office of notary *(notaire)*, of bailiff *(huissier)*.
se démettre d'une – : to resign an office.
– *(s) publiques :* public offices.
3° load, burden.
– *d'un navire :* lading of a ship.
– *utile :* carrying capacity.

chargement (m) : *(de navire)* lading, *(de wagon)* loading-up, *(de lettre)* registration ; cargo, freight, load ; registered letter or parcel.
lettre, police de – : consignment note.

charger (v) : to entrust, to instruct (to do sth.).
se – *des intérêts de qn :* to take charge of the interests of s.o.

charte (f) : charter, (ancient) title.
– *des Nations Unies :* charter of the United Nations.
la Grande – : Magna Carta (of Engl.).

charte-partie (f) : charter-party.

chasse (f) : hunting, game-shooting.
– *aux bonnes occasions :* bargain hunting.
– *gardée :* (game) preserves.
permis de – : hunting permit.
louer une – : to rent a shoot.
« **chasseur** *de têtes* » *(personne qui recrute des cadres supérieurs particulièrement compétents) :* headhunter.

châtiment (m) : punishment, chastisement.

chef (m) : head, chief, leader, principal.
1° – *de bureau (ou de service technique) :* head clerk, [U.S.] staffman.
– *caissier :* head cashier.
– *de la comptabilité :* chief accountant.
– *d'entreprise :* head of a business, entrepreneur.
chef de famille : head of a family (of a household).
– *de gare :* station master.
– *de produit :* product manager.
– *de publicité :* account executive.
– *de rayon :* head of department, buyer, shopwalker, [U.S.] floor manager.
– *de service :* departmental manager.
– *des services fiscaux : (Administration Centrale)* chief of tax services, *(Direction Régionale)* tax commissioner.
– *du protocole :* head of the protocol (section of the Foreign Office).
2° – *de dépense :* expense item.
– *d'accusation :* count of an indictment.
3° *(posséder) de son* – : (to own) in one's own right.
faire qch. de son propre – : to do sth. on one's own authority (account).

cheptel (m) : live stock of a country or belonging to a landlord.
[J] – *vif :* live stock leased.
– *mort :* agricultural implements and farm buildings leased.

chèque (m) : cheque, [U.S.] check, voucher.
– *bancaire :* banker's draft.
– *barré :* crossed cheque.
– *non barré (ouvert) :* open cheque.
– *en blanc :* blank cheque.
– *certifié, visé :* certified cheque.
– *au porteur :* bearer cheque.
– *prescrit :* stale cheque.
– *postal :* giro cheque.
– *sans provision :* bad worthless, dud cheque, [U.S.] bouncing, flash check.
– *de voyage :* travel(l)er's cheque.
faux – : forged cheque.
bénéficiaire d'un – : payee of a cheque.
compte de – *(s) :* [U.S.] checking account.
C.C.P. (compte – *postal) :* giro account.
formule de – : cheque form.
toucher un – : to cash a cheque.

chéquier (m) : cheque book.

chiffrage (m) : ciphering.

chiffre (m): figure, cipher.
baisse du – d'affaires : downspring.
– d'affaires : sales, turnover, [U.S.] billing.
– d'affaires à l'exportation : export sales.
– d'affaires hors taxe : turnover excluding taxes.
impôt (taxe) sur le – d'affaires : turnover tax, sales tax.

chirographaire (a): [J] depending on a simple contract.
créance – : unsecured debt.
créancier – : simple contract creditor.
obligation – : simple contract.

choc (m): shock.
– pétrolier : oil shock.
– monétaires : monetary shocks.

choisir (v): to elect.
un contribuable peut – de payer... : a taxpayer may elect to pay...

choix (m): option, election.
au – du contribuable : at the option of the taxpayer.
– des investissements entre des portefeuilles : portfolio selection.
[C] *au choix :* all at the same price.

chômage (m): 1° abstention from work (on feast days, etc.).
– du dimanche : sunday closing.
fête chômée : feast day kept as holiday.
2° *– (involontaire) :* unemployment.
– conjoncturel : short-term unemployment.
– déguisé : disguised unemployment.
– frictionnel : frictional unemployment.
– technique : technical (technological) unemployment.
ouvriers en – : unemployed (workers).
allocation, indemnité, secours de – : unemployment benefit, dole.
fonds de – : unemployment fund.
le taux de – : the unemployed figure, (U.S.) the jobless rate.

chômeur (m): unemployed workman, out-of-work.

chose (f): thing.
– d'autrui : another's property.
– (s) fongibles : (fungibiles res) fungible things.
– jugée : res judicata.
– litigieuse : property disputable at law.
– publique : the commonweal, the state.
– saisie : attached, distrained thing.
– sans maître : (bona vacantia) derelict.

chute (f): fall.
– brutale : collapse.

– des prix, des cours : drop in prices, quotations.

ci-après : hereafter.

ci-dessous : hereinafter.

ci-inclus : enclosed.

ci-joint : herewith.

circonstance (f): circumstance.
[J] *– (s) et dépendances :* appurtenances.
– (s) atténuantes, aggravantes : extenuating circumstances, aggravation.
circonstancié (rapport) : detailed (account).

circuit (m):
– d'actions : circuity of actions.
– (s) économiques : (cyclical) economic channels.

circulaire (f): circular (letter), memorandum.

circulant *(capital)* (a): circulating, working (capital).

circulation (f): circulation, traffic-circulation (journaux).
(actions) en – : outstanding (shares).
(billets) en – : (bank-notes) in circulation.
– fiduciaire : credit (currency, fiduciary) circulation.
– routière : road traffic.
libre – de la main-d'œuvre : free movement of labour (of workers).
libre – des marchandises : free movement of goods.
retirer de la – : to withdraw from circulation.

citation (f): quotation, citation.
[J] writ of summons.
– de témoins : subpoena of witnesses.
signifier, notifier une – : to serve a summons on s.o., to subpoena s.o.
citer qqn en justice : to have the law on s.o.

cité (f): city, town, township.
droit de – : freedom of the city, citizenship.

citoyen (m): citizen.
droits de – : civic rights.

civil (a): civil (rights, etc.).
action – (e) : civil action.
année – (e) : calendar, legal year.
capacité – (e) : (legal) capacity.
code – : code of civil law.
droit – : civil law.
droits – (s) : civil rights.
état – : a) civil status, b) registry office in

charge of civil statuts.
jour — : 24 hours.
liste — *(e)* : civil list.
maison — *(e)* # secretariat of the President of the Republic.
mariage — : marriage without religious ceremony.
partie — *(e), conclusions* — *(es)* : action instituted by a private person for damages, parallel to prosecution in a criminal case.
procédure — *(e)* : procedure in civil law.
procès civil : civil case.
responsabilité — *(e)* : vicarious liability (for damage caused by an agent).
société — *(e) immobilière* : real property company.
tribunal — : court entertaining jurisdiction in civil matters.

civiliser (v) : to try a case in civil law (when the criminal proceedings are closed).

civiques *(droits)* (a) : civic (rights).

clair (a) : clear.
bénéfice — *et net* : clear profit.

clairvoyance (f) **en affaires** : business acumen.

classe *(sociale)* (f) : (social) class.
les — *(s) moyennes* : the middle classes.
la — *ouvrière* : the working class.

classement général (m) : general arrangement.

classer (v) : to class(ify), to file, to docket.
affaire **classée** : [J] unsolved case, definitely disposed of, dismissed, [C] charged, written off books.
[F] *valeurs classées* : investment stock.

classeur (m) : file.

classification (f) : demarcation.

clause (f) : clause, provision.
— *abrogatoire* : rescinding clause.
— *additionnelle* : rider.
— *annexe* : supplementary clause.
— *compromissoire* : arbitration clause.
— *de juridiction* : competence clause.
— *comminatoire* : comminatory clause.
— *d'un contrat* : article.
— *dérogative* : derogatory clause.
— *d'exclusivité* : exclusive, « sole rights » clause.
— *discriminatoire* : discriminative (discriminatory) clause.
— *léonine* : leonine convention, unconscionable bargain, oppressive agreement.

— *de la nation la plus favorisée* : the most favoured nation clause.
— *à ordre* : clause to order.
— *pénale* : penalty clause.
— *de préciput* : clause providing for a part of an estate or inheritance to be set aside for one of the coheirs and devolving upon him in addition to his portion.
— *de préemption* : pre-emptive clause.
— *de régularisation* : clause in policy to the effect that insurance starts after payment of first premium.
— *résolutoire* : resolutive, avoidance amendment, defeasance clause, condition.
— *de retour sans frais* : « no expenses », no protest notice (on bill).
— *rouge* : red clause.
— *de sauvegarde* : saving clause.
— *de style* : formal clause.
— *d'usage* : customary clause.
sauf — *contraire* : unless there be any (unknown) clause to the contrary, unless otherwise provided, failing any stipulation to the contrary.

clearing *(accord de)* (m) : clearing agreement.

clerc (m) : clerk (in lawyer's office).
premier clerc : head clerk.

client (m) : client, customer, patron, buyer.
— *-type (profil du)* : customer profile.
— *(s) blasés* : jaded customers.
— *(s) potentiels* : prospects, prospective customers.

clientèle (f) : custom, goodwill.
— *aisée (achetant des produits hauts de gamme)* : upmarket customers.
belle — : wide connexion.

climat (m) **social agité** : social unrest.

clos *(exercice)* (a) : (financing period) ending on.

clôture (f) : 1° enclosure, fence, fencing.
mur de — : enclosing wall.
[J] *bris de* — : breach of close.
2° conclusion, end, closure, closing.
[F] [J] [C] — *d'un compte* : winding up of an account.
— *d'un débat* : closure of a hearing.
— *de l'exercice* : closing of the business, fiscal, etc. year.
— *de la faillite (pour insuffisance d'actif)* : closing of bankruptcy proceedings (when assets are inadequate to defray legal expenses).
— *des inscriptions* : registration deadline.
— *de la souscription* : closing of the application list.

cours de — : closing price.
prononcer la — des débats : to declare the discussion (the hearing) closed.
demander la — : to move the closure, to motion for the adjournment.
clôturer : to close, to end, to finish.

coaccusé (m) : [J] co-defendant.

coaction (f) : coercion, compulsion.

coaliser (v) : to combine, to unite.

coalition (f) : coalition, league.

coassocié (m) : joint partner, co-partner.

coassurance (f) : [ASS] joint insurance.

coauteur (m) : [J] (civ.) joint author, maker, (cr.) accomplice.

cocaution (f) : collateral security.

cocréancier (m) : joint creditor.

code (m) : code, statute book (most French legislation is codified).
— *civil* : code of civil law.
— *de commerce* : code of mercantile law, commercial law.
— *postal* : (U.S.) postal code, zip code.
— *de procédure civile, — de procédure pénale* : rules of civil, criminal procedure.
— *de justice militaire* : articles of war.
— *maritime* : admiralty law, law of navigation, maritime law.
— *pénal* : code of criminal law.
— *de la route* : highway code, road regulations.
— *du travail, de la sécurité sociale* : labour, social welfare laws.
—(s) *des douanes* : customs code.
— *général des impôts* : general tax code.

codébiteur (m) : joint debtor.
—(s) *solidaires* : debtors liable jointly and severally.

codéfendeur (m) : co-defendant, *(en appel, en* Eq., en divorce) co-respondent.

codemandeur (m) : joint plaintiff.

codétenteur (m) : joint holder.
— *d'un héritage* : joint heir.

codétenu (m) fellow-prisoner.

codicille (m) : codicil.

codification (f) : codification, classification of laws.

codirecteur (m) : joint manager.

coefficient (m) : coefficient, coefficient ratio.
— *de capital* : incremental capital, output ratio.
— *de capitalisation des résultats (CCR)* : price earning ratio.
— *de liquidité* : current ratio.
— *de majoration* : grossing up ratio.
— *de trésorerie* : cash ratio.

coercition (f) : coercion, duress.
mesures **coercitives** : coercive measures.

coffre-fort (m) : safe.

cogérance (f) : joint management.
cogérant : co-administrator, joint manager.
co-gérer : to manage jointly.

cognat (m) : cognate, relation on the mother's side.

cohabitation (f) : cohabitation, living together of unmarried couple, [U.S.] companionate marriage.

cohéritier (m) : joint heir, coheir.
— *indivis* : heir in indivisum.

colégataire (m) : joint legatee.

colicitant (m) : [J] co-vendor.

colis (m) : packet, parcel.
par — postal : by parcel post.

collaborateur (m) : collaborator, fellow-worker.

collatéral (a) : collateral, relative.
[J] *héritier —* : collateral heir.

collation (f) : collation (of documents).

collationner (v) : to collate, to compare (two copies).

collectivité (f) : community, common ownership.

collège (m) : college, secondary school.
— *électoral* : electorate.

collocation (f) : order in which creditors in bankruptcy are placed and paid.
[J] collocation.

collusion (f) : collusion.

collusoire *(pratique)* (a) : collusive (practice).

co-locataire (m et f) : cotenant.

colonage (m) : **colonat** *partiaire* farming leasehold whereby the farmer shares the produce of the farm with the landlord (syn. *métayage, bail à mi-fruit*), [U.S.] share-crop system.

colporteur (m) : door-to-door salesman, hawker.

comestibles (m pl) *(denrées)* : consumables.

comité (m) : board, committee.
— *consultatif* : advisory board.
— *de contrôle des créanciers* : committee of inspection (in bankruptcy).
— *de direction* : board of management, steering committee, [U.S.] executive committee.
— *d'entreprise* : work council, joint consultative (production) committee.
— *de restructuration* : steering committee, advisory committee.

command (m) : [J] [C] principal in purchase.
déclaration de — : declaration by buyer in sale of land that he is acting for a third party.

commande (f) : [C] order, purchase order.
fait sur — : made to order.
livre de — : order-book.
enregistrer une — : to book an order.
passer une — : to order an article.
— *passée par un acheteur d'outre-mer à un exportateur* : indent.
payable à la — : cash with order.
— *en souffrance* : order in the pipe-line.

commandement (m) : command.
[J] summons to pay before execution.
[C] *agir en vertu d'un* — : to act in purchase by procuration.

commander (v) : 1° **(ordonner)** to command, 2° **(faire une commande)** to order.

commanditaire (m) : limited sleeping partner, [U.S.] silent partner, *(publicité)* sponsor.

commandite (m) : capital invested by sleeping partner.
société en — : company limited by shares, limited liability company, limited partnership company, limited sleeping partnership.

commandité (m) : active partner.
commanditer : to finance, to support as a sleeping partner, [U.S.] to stake, *(publicité)* to sponsor.

commencement (m) : beginning, commencement.
— *d'un délai* : commencement of term, bar period.
— *d'exécution* : (cr.) attempt to commit a crime (showing felonious intent coupled with an over act), (pr.) to open proceedings.
— *de prescription* : starting date of bar, prescription.
— *de preuve* : prima facie evidence.

commerçant (a et m) : (m) merchant, tradesman, businessman.
les — *(s)* : the trade.
(femme) commerçante : married woman engaged in business.
— *forain* : itinerant vendor, booth keeper.
— *indépendant* : indépendant retailer.
(a) business-like, commercial, mercantile.
quartier — : trading centre, shopping centre.
rue — *(e)* : shopping street, very busy street.
ville — *(e)* : trading town.

commerce (m) : commerce, trade, business.
— *de détail* : retail trade.
— *en gros* : wholesale trade.
— *d'exportation* : export trade.
— *d'importation* : import trade.
— *extérieur* : foreign trade.
— *sur la base de la réciprocité* : reciprocal trading.
— *intérieur* : home trade.
— *intra-branche* : intra-industry trade.
— *de luxe* : luxury trade.
le — : the commercial world.
bourse de — : Commodities Exchange (= Royal Exchange).
chambre de — : chamber of commerce.
code de — : mercantile laws.
effets de — : negotiable instruments.
le haut — : big business.
hors — : for private circulation.
livres de — : ledgers (as prescribed by law).
maison de — : business firm.
Ministère du — : the Board of Trade, [U.S.] Department of Commerce.
naviguer au — : to be in the merchant-service.
marine de — : mercantile marine.
navire de — : merchant ship.
le petit — : small tradespeople.
registre du — : register of commercial firms.
société de — : trading company.
tribunal de — : commercial court.
voyageur de — : commercial traveller.
acte de — : act of merchant.
fonds de — : stock-in-trade, business, goodwill.
représentant de — : trade representative.

commercer (v) : to trade, to deal in.

commercial (a) : commercial.
balance — (e) : trade balance.
locaux **commerciaux** : business premises.
transaction — (e) : deal, commercial transaction.

commercialisation (f) : marketing, commercialising.

commercialité *(d'un billet à ordre)* (f) : negotiability (of a bill).

commettant (m) : [J] principal to a deal, actual purchaser or vendor represented by an agent.
— *et préposé* : principal and agent.

commettre (v) : to commit, to perpetrate, to entrust, to make.
— *un crime* : to perpetrate a crime.
— *un expert* : to appoint an expert.
— *une faute* : to make a mistake, an error, to act wrongfully.
— *qch. aux soins de qn* : to entrust s.o. with sth.
avocat **commis** *d'office* : counsel appointed ex officio (by the *bâtonnier*).

comminatoire (a) : comminatory (decree, clause, etc.).

commis (m) : clerk, book-keeper, shop assistant.
— *principal* : head clerk.
[J] agent (of merchant).
— *-greffier* : assistant of the clerk of the court.
[C] — *-voyageur* : commercial traveller, [U.S.] drummer.

commissaire (m) : commissioner.
— *du Gouvernement* : expert in administrative law, generally a civil servant, at the « Conseil d'Etat » (in France).
— *de la marine* : paymaster.
— *de navire* : purser.
— *de police* : police superintendent.
— *-priseur* : auctioneer, official valuer, appraiser.
— *-répartiteur* : assessor of taxes.
— *de transport* : forwarding agent.
[F] — *aux comptes* : auditor, [U.S.] statutory auditor.

commissariat (m) : 1° *(de police)* police station, 2° *(aux comptes)* auditorship, 3° *(à l'énergie atomique)* [U.S.] Atomic Energy Commission.

commission (f) : commission, order, allowance.
1° [J] warrant, charge.

— *rogatoire* : rogatory commission, letters rogatory, written interrogatories.
avoir la — *de faire quelque chose* : to be empowered, commissioned to do sth.
2° [C]
— *d'engagement* : commitment fee.
— *de chef de file* : management fee.
— *de garantie, de placement* : underwriting fee.
— *de gestion* : agency fee.
— *immédiate* : flat fee.
vente à — : sale on commission.
droits de — : factorage.
maison de — : commission agency.
[F] brokerage, factorage, commission business.
3° commission, committee.
— *du budget* : budget committee, [U.S.] Committee of Ways and Means.
— *d'enquête parlementaire* : board, court of inquiry, select committee, royal commission, [U.S.] congressional investigation committee.
— *d'examen* : board of examiners.
— *arbitrale* : board of referees.
— *de conciliation* : conciliatory board.
— *paritaire (mixte)* : (joint) committee in which both sides are represented (on an equal footing).
— *de révision de l'impôt* : tax review board.

commissionnaire (m) : 1° *(mercantile)* agent, broker, buyer, factor.
— *d'achat* : buyer.
— *en banque* : outside broker.
— *en douane* : customs agent, custom house broker.
— *en marchandises* : commission-agent.
— *en gros* : factor.
— *de transport, expéditeur* : forwarding agent, shipping agent.
2° carrier, messenger, porter.

commissoire *(clause)* (a) : [J] resolutive clause in a contract of sale in case of non-payment within a stipulated time.

commodant (m) : [J] lender in a *commodat* loan (see : *commodat*).

commodat (m) : [J] loan of anything but money, to be return unimpaired, (Scot.) commodatum.

commodataire (m) : [J] borrower in a *commodat* loan (sse : *commodat*).

commodité *(à votre)* (f) : to (your) convenience.

commodo & incommodo *(enquête de)* : administrative inquiry in a neighbourhood, before giving permit to start a noisy or obnoxious trade, or to erect buildings to that purpose.

commuer (v) : [J] to commute (penalty).

commun (a) : common.
  le bien — : the public weal.
  biens —(s) : communal estate.
  chose commune: common property.
  en droit — : in ordinary law.
  fonds — : (joint) common fund.
  l'intérêt — : the public interest.
  jugement, arrêt — : judgment, decree, enforceable against a defaulter as well as against the appearing party.
  la maison —(e) : townhall.
  tare **commune** : average tare.
  en — : joint.
  exploitation en — : joint operation.
  mettre en — *(ressources, etc.)* : to pool (resources...).
  (conditions acceptées) d'un — *accord* : (conditions agreed upon) with one accord (by mutual agreement).
  les **communs** *(m pl) (d'un domaine)* the outbuildings.

communal (a) : [J] common.
  conseil — : communal council.
  école —(e) : elementary school.
  terrains **communaux** : commons.

communauté (f) : community, society.
  [J] — *de biens, entre époux, universelle* : communal estate, joint estate of husband and wife comprising all property, present and future, [U.S.] community property, regime.
  — *de biens réduite aux acquêts* : communal estate comprising only property acquired after marriage.
  — *conventionnelle* : agreement modifying the rules of the standard (legal) antenuptial settlement.
  biens exclus de la : — separate property of wife, not included in the communal estate.
  — *Européenne du Charbon et de l'Acier (CECA)* : European Coal and Steel Community (ECSC).
  C— *Economique Européenne (CEE)* : European Economic Community (EEC).
  — *d'intérêts* : community of interests.
  — *légale* : in absence of an antenuptial settlement, the legal regime is in France the *communauté réduite aux acquêts*.

communicable (a) : communicable.
  [J] *droit* — : transferable right.

communication (f) : communication.
  — *interurbaine* : trunk call.
  — *téléphonique* : phone call.

[J] — *de pièces* : discovery.

commutation (f) : [J] commutation.
  contrat **commutatif** : commutative contract (calling for an equivalent performance from each of the parties).
  [ASS] *nombres de* — *(tables de mortalité)* : basic numbers.
  commuter (v), **commuer** *une peine* : to commute a penalty.

comourants (m pl) : [J] commorientes.

compagne (f) : (female) companion, wife.
  [J] unmarried partner in life, [U.S.] companionate marriage.

compagnie (f) : company, association, [U.S.] corporation.
  — *d'assurances* : insurance company.
  — *d'assurances agréée par l'Etat* : approved society.
  — *d'aviation* : air (line) company.
  — *des chemins de fer* : railway company.
  — *maritime* : shipping company.
  et — : and C°.

comparaître (v) : [J] to appear before a court, to stand one's trial.
  être cité à — : to be summoned to appear.

comparution (f) :
  mandat de — : summons.
  non- — : default, failure to appear.

comparse (m) : [J] minor accomplice in lawbreaking or crime.

compatible (a) : consistent with.

compensateur (-trice) (a) : countervailing.
  taxe — : countervailing duty.

compensation (f) : compensation, set-off, offset, clearing, recoupment.
  [J] settlement per contra.
  [A] *caisse de* — : equalization fund for family allowances, etc.
  [F] *chambre de* — : clearing house.
  opération de — : barter deal.
  [B] *cours de* — : making-up price.

compensatoire (a) : compensatory.
  solde — : compensing cash balance.

compenser (v) : to compensate, to counterbalance.
  — *les dépenses* : to tax each party for its own costs, to share, to divide out the costs.
  — *une dette par une autre* : to set off a debt against another.

— *des chèques :* to clear cheques.

compétence (f) : [J] competence, competency, jurisdiction, powers of a court.
— *matérielle, quant au fond, absolue :* competence of a court ratione materiae.
— *du lieu, locale, territoriale :* competence of a court ratione loci.
— *relative :* competence of a court ratione personae.
conflit de — : conflict or concurrence of jurisdiction of powers of administrative authorities.
décliner la — *du tribunal :* to disclaim the jurisdiction of the court.
rentrer dans la — *du tribunal :* to fall within the competence of the court.
sortir de sa — : to exceed one's powers.
cela n'est pas de sa — : this is beyond (outside) his scope.
— *fiscale :* fiscal jurisdiction.
clause de — : domiciliary clause.
gestion des —(s) *et de la connaissance :* skills and knowledge management.

compétent (a) : 1° concerned, relevant.
transmettre au service — : to pass on to the department concerned, 2° *(personne) :* competent, qualified.
3° [J] *le tribunal est* — : the court entertains jurisdiction.

compéter (v) : to belong rightfully.
ce qui peut lui — *dans la succession :* part which may be his in the succession.
exceptions compétant au débiteur : objections in law raised by the debtor.
cette affaire compète au tribunal de... : this case falls within the jurisdiction of the court of...

compétiteur (m) : competitor, contender.

complaignant (m) : [J] plaintiff in matter of possession (see *complainte*).

complainte (f) : [J] possessory action which may be instituted by a person after one year of adverse possession of real estate or rights.

complaisance (f) : complaisance.
[C] *effet de* — (familiar *cavalerie*) : accommodation bill.

complément (m) : completion, complement.
ordonner un — *d'instruction :* to require a fuller preliminary investigation (of a case).
— *de provision :* additional fee.

complémentaire (a) : complementary.
renseignements —(s) : further information.
taxe — : complementary tax.

complet (a) : full.
adresse —(e) : full address.
compléter *(un formulaire) :* to fill in, up, out (a form).

complice (m) : accomplice, abettor, accessory (to), confederate.
[J] — *par assistance :* accessory after the fact.
— *par instigation :* accessory before the fact.
— *d'adultère :* avowterer *(cité en procès de divorce)* co-respondent.
être — *d'un crime :* to be party to a crime.

complicité (f) : complicity.
[J] aiding and abetting.
agir de — *avec qn :* to act in complicity (collusion) with s.o.

complot (m) : conspiracy, plot, [U.S.] combination.
[J] — *contre la sûreté de l'Etat :* high-treason, treason-felony.

comportement (m) : behaviour.
— *collusifs :* collusive behaviour.

comporter (v) : to include.

composer (v) :
— *avec ses créanciers :* to come to terms with one's creditors.
composés (intérêts) : compound (interests).

compositeur *(amiable)* (m) : arbitrator.

composition (f) : arrangement, compromise, settlement.
[J] compensation.

comprendre (v) : 1° *(inclure)* to include, to cover, 2° *(interpréter)* to read.
le paragraphe doit être compris comme se rapportant à : the subsection must be read as referring to.

compression *(de crédits)* (f) : (credit) squeeze, curtailment.
— *de personnel :* cutback.

compris *(tout)* : inclusive (of).

compromis *(arbitral)* (m) : [J] compromise, composition.
mettre en — : to submit for arbitration.
obtenir un — : to compound (with creditors).
passer un — *(avec) :* to come to an arrangement (with).

compromissoire (a) : [J] *clause* — : reference, arbitration clause in agreement.

COM

comptabilisé *(non-)* : (un)accounted.

comptabiliser (v) : to carry.

comptabilité (f) : 1° *(science)* accountancy, 2° *(d'une entreprise)* the accounts of a firm, accounting, the books of a firm, 3° *(tenue des livres)* bookkeeping (book-keeping).
— *analytique (des prix de revient, industrielle)* : cost accounting.
— *par fabrication* : [U.S.] process costing.
— *nationale* : national accounting.
— *en partie simple, (double, à double entrée)* : single (double entry) bookkeeping.
— *publique* : public accounts.
service de la — : account department.
tenir la — *(de)* : to keep the accounts (the books) (of).

comptable (a et m) :
(a) *exercice* — : accounting period.
pièce — : bookkeeping voucher, original document, accountable receipt.
quittance — : formal receipt.
valeur — : book value, written down value.
— *(d'une somme d'argent)* : accountable for, answerable for, responsible for.
(m) 1° accountant, 2° bookkeeper.
— *agréé* : certified public accountant (CPA).
expert- — : chartered accountant [U.S] certified (public) accountant.

comptant (a et m) : spot, [F] for delivery.
argent — : cash.
acheter, vendre au — : to buy, sell for ready money, cash.
— *contre documents* : cash against documents.
— *sans escompte* : net prompt cash.
valeurs au — : securities dealt in for cash.
le marché du — : the spot market.

compte (m) : 1° account ; 2° reckoning, calculation.
arrêté de — : account stated (settled).
— *d'achat* : account of goods purchased.
— *(s) approuvés* : certified accounts.
— *d'attente* : provisional, proforma, suspens account.
— *d'avance* : loan account.
— *de chèques* : banking, drawing account.
— *de chèques postaux* : postal drawing account.
— *clients* : details accounts, receivable ledger.
— *courant* : current, running account, [U.S.] drawing account.
— *courant postal* : [U.S.] postal checking account.
— *courant portant intérêt placé chez un agent de change* : cash management account.
— *créditeur* : credit account.
— *débiteur* : a) *(solde débiteur)* debit account, overdraft, balance due, balance of indebtness,
b) blank credit.
— *de débours* : disbursement account.
— *de dépôt* : deposit account.
— *à découvert* : overdrawn account.
— *enregistré sous numéro confidentiel* : numbered account (e.g. in a Swiss bank).
— *d'exercice d'exploitation* : balance sheet.
— *d'exploitation* : operating statement.
— *des frais* : expense account.
— *de fournitures à crédit* : credit account.
— *indivis* : joint account.
— *joint* : joint account.
— *justificatif* : income and expenditure account.
— *matière* : property account.
— *de prêt* : credit loan.
— *de profits et pertes* : profit and loss account.
— *de recettes et dépenses* : in and out account.
— *(s) à recevoir* : receivables.
— *rendu* : report.
— *(s) pour lesquels des réserves sont exprimées* : qualified accounts.
— *spécifié* : detailed account.
— *de tutelle* : account (of guardianship).
— *de virements* : clearing account.
— *à vue* : call deposit account.
livre (registre) de — *(s)* : account book, ledger.
payer, verser à — : to pay in account.
avoir un — *ouvert avec qn* : to have credit with s.o.
être de — *à demi avec qn* : to go halves with, to do business on a 50-50 % basis.
porter en — : to put on account.
faire une opération pour le — *de tiers* : to carry out a transaction on a third party's account.
arrêter un — : to strike a balance.
tenir les —*(s)* : to keep the accounts.
donner son — *à qn* : to pay off s.o. (on dismissal).
être en — *avec qn* : to have an account with s.o.
s'établir à son — : to set up in business on one's own account.
laisser une marchandise pour — : to leave goods on a merchant's hands.
règlement des —*(s)* : settlement, adjustment of accounts, of difference, of dispute, etc.
rendre — *de qch* : to render an account of sth.
solde de compte : balance (of account).
Cour des —*(s)* # [U.S.] State Audit Office.
2° reckoning, calculation.
faire le — *des dépenses* : to add up expenses.
être loin de — : to be out of one's reckoning.
pour le — *de* : on behalf of.
— *tenu (des circonstances)* : having regard to (circumstances).

compter (v) : to count, to compute, to reckon.
— *(un article, tant...)* : to charge (so much, for an item).

à — de... : from...
— sur qqn : to rely on (s.o.).
— sur qqch : to bank on (sthg).

comptoir (m) : counter, factory, warehouse.
comptoir d'escompte : discount bank.

concédant d'une licence (m) : licensor.

concéder (v) : 1° *(un droit, une licence)* to grant (a right, a licence).
— *un contrat (à)* : to place a contract (with).
2° — *(admettre)* : to admit, to allow, [U.S.] to franchise.

concentration *(horizontale, verticale)* (f) : (horizontal, vertical) concentration, merger.

conception (f) : conception.
enfant conçu : child unborn, [J] en ventre sa mère, person en venter, unborn person.
période légale de — : period of time during which the parents should have lived together to beget a legitimate child.
— *d'un produit* : styling.

concernant : re.
restriction — les déductions pour dépenses afférentes à un emploi : limitation re employment expense deduction.
en ce qui concerne : in (with) regard to.

concession (f) : concession, grant, franchise, licence, permit, charter.
[A] — *minière* : mining concession, [U.S.] claim.
— *de services publics* : concession of public services (to private companies).
— *de sépulture* : grant of grave.
— *de terres* : grand of land, [U.S.] franchise.
— *de travaux publics* : contract for public works.
— *exclusive de vente (ou de fabrication)* : [U.S.] franchise.

concessionnaire (m et a) :
(m) 1° *(agent exclusif)* sole agent, distributor.
2° *(locataire)* lessee.
(a) *compagnie —* : statutory company.

concevoir (v) : to design.

conciliation (f) : conciliation.
[J] reconciliation.
ordonnance de non- — : order pendete lite in divorce suit, regarding wife's domicile and alimony as well as wardship of children.

conciliatoire (a) : conciliatory.

concilier un différend (v) : to bring about an agreement.

concluant(e) *(preuve)* (a) : conclusive (evidence).

conclure (v) : 1° *(contrat d'assurance)* to conclude (a contract of insurance), 2° *(marché)* to enter into a bargain.
— *(mettre un point final à) des accords* : to finalise agreements.

conclusions (f pl) : [J] findings, decision, pleadings brief, pleas.
accepter les — : to join issue.
adjuger ses — au demandeur : to find for the plaintiff.
— *des parties* : bill of complaint, of particulars, [U.S.] brief.
— *civiles* : action instituted by a private person for damages, parallel to prosecution in a criminal case.
— *en matière de dommages-intérêts* : statement of claims.
déposer des — : to deliver statements.
le jury a conclu au meurtre : the jury returned a verdict of homicide.

concordat (m) : composition to creditors, bankrupt's certificate, discharge in bankruptcy.
— *par abandon d'actif* : legal settlement between merchant and creditors by surrender of property, scheme of composition.

concordataire (m) : certified (certificated) bankrupt.

concourir à prouver (v) : to go to prove.

concours (m) : concourse, concurrence, coming together.
[J] equality of rank and rights.
— *de plusieurs actes punissables* : concurrent punishable offences.
— *de droits* : concurrent rights, equality of rank and rights (between creditors, etc.).
— *de lois* : concurrence of legal provisions.
[A] competitive entrance examination.
marché sur — : contract concluded by a public authority after free choice among competitive tenders.

concubinage (m) : concubinage.
concubinaire : concubinary.
concubine : concubine.
concubins : concubines.

concurremment *(venir)* (adv) : to rank equally.
— *avec* : in conjunction with.

concurrence (f) : concurrence, coincidence (of events).
jusqu'à — de... : to the amount of, to the extent of, not exceeding.

actions libérées à − de leur valeur nominale : fully paid-up shares.
[J] see *concours.*
[C] competition, rivalry.
− *acharnée :* keen competition, cut-throat competition.
− *basée sur la qualité (et non sur les prix de vente) :* non-price competition.
− *déloyale :* unfair competition.
− *illicite :* fraudulent competition.
− *impitoyable :* cut-throat competition.
libre − : free competition.
− *monopolistique :* monopolistic competition.
− *parfaite :* perfect competition.
à des conditions normales de − : at arm's length.
faire − *à qn :* to compete with s.o.
formes de la − : competition patterns.

concurrent (m) : competitor.

concurrentiel (a) : *(prix, ...)* competitive (prices, ...).

concussion (f) : extortion (by public official), peculation.

condamnation (f) : condemnation.
[J] conviction, judgment, sentence.
− *par contumace :* sentence in absence.
− *aux dépens :* order to pay costs.
− *à mort, à la peine capitale :* death sentence.
− *à vie :* life sentence.
passer − : to admit that one is wrong.
prononcer − : to pass judgment.
purger une − : to serve one's time.

condamné (m) : convict, condemned man (or woman).

condition (f) : condition.
1° state, status.
la − *des personnes (état civil) :* civil status.
− *juridique :* legal status.
la − *du mineur, de l'enfant naturel, de l'étranger :* status of minor, bastard, alien.
changer de − : to change one's station in life.
2° stipulation, terms.
satisfaire aux −*(s) légales requises :* to meet, to fulfil the legal requirements.
−*(s) essentielles :* essential requirements.
les −*(s) essentielles des contrats, des obligations :* the essential terms of a contract, an agreement.
les −*(s) d'application d'une loi :* rules governing the application of a law.
les −*(s) de capacité :* legal title, qualification (to do sth.).
être dans les −*(s) requises pour agir :* to be entitled to act.
−*(s) de faveur :* preferential terms.
les −*(s) de travail :* a) conditions of employment, b) working conditions.
les −*(s) de validité :* conditions of validity.
marchandise qui n'a pas les −*(s) requises :* goods non-conform.
offre sans − : unconditional offer.
3° clause, obligation, charge, terms (of an agreement, etc.).
−*(s) de crédit :* credit terms.
− *expresse :* express clause.
les conditions générales (du contrat) d'assurance : general clauses (terms) of an insurance (contract).
les conditions d'un legs : the terms of a legacy.
−*(s) d'usage (les) :* usual terms.
faire ses −*(s) :* to submit one's conditions.
4° future event.
− *accomplie :* condition fulfilled.
à cette − : on this understanding.
− *casuelle :* (condicio causalis) fortuitous condition.
− *illicite :* illicit condition.
− *impossible :* impossible condition.
− *légale :* (condicio juris) legal condition.
− *mixte :* (condicio mixta) condition depending for fulfilment upon the will of one of the contracting parties and that of a third party.
− *négative :* contract valid provided that a certain event shall not occur.
− *nulle :* null and void condition.
− *positive :* contract valid provided that a certain event shall occur.
− *potestative :* (condicio potestativa) condition depending upon the will of one of the contracting parties, which may bring to pass an event making the contract valid.
− *résolutoire :* condition of avoidance in contract, defeasance clause, condition subsequent.
− *suspensive :* suspensive condition, condition precedent.
− *en suspens :* outstanding condition.
actes ne souffrant pas de − : acts to be performed unconditionally.
force rétroactive de la − : ex post facto effect of the condition.
marchandises à − : goods a) on sale or return, b) on approval.
obligation sous − : conditional agreement.
sous − *que :* provided that.
5° rank, station.
de − *modeste :* in humble circumstance.

conditionnel (a) : conditional.
acceptation − *(le) :* conditional (qualified) acceptance.
prêt − : loan made on condition.

conditionnement (m) : packaging.

conduction (f) : [J] leasing.

conduite (f) d'une affaire : management.

confédération (f) : confederation, confederacy.

confessoire *(action)* (a) : [J] affirmative petitory action for the enforcement of an encumbrance on real estate.

confiance (f) : confidence, trust, reliance.
de — *(affaire)* : (business) trustworthy, reliable.
avec — : confidently.
abus de — : breach of confidence, of trust.
digne de — : reliable, trustworthy.
homme de — : confidential clerk.

confidentiel *(à titre)* : in (strict) confidence.

confirmation (f) : [J] affirmative judgment by appellate jurisdiction.

confirmer (v) : 1° *(une déposition)* to corroborate (evidence), 2° *(une assertion)* to bear out (an assertion).

confiscation (f) : confiscation, seizure of real property, forfeiture.
perdre qch. par — : to forfeit sth.

confisquer (v) : to confiscate, to seize.

conflit (m) : conflict, clash, struggle, dispute.
être en — : to be in conflict.
[J] concurrence.
— *d'attribution* : concurrence of jurisdiction between the judiciary and the administration.
— *d'autorité* : overlapping of authority.
— *de compétence* : concurrence of jurisdiction.
— *de juridiction* : concurrence of jurisdiction between two courts.
— *d'opinions* : disagreement.
— *positif* : two courts claiming jurisdiction.
— *négatif* : two courts disclaiming jurisdiction.
— *de lois* : adversity, conflict of laws.
— *du travail* : industrial dispute, labour dispute.
tribunal des — *(s)* : french jurisdictional court deciding if a given question shall be disposed of by administrative court or by civil court.
opinions en — : conflicting opinions.

conforme (a) : conform.
[J] *« pour copie* — *»* : certified true copy.
[C] *passer écritures* — *(s)* : to agree entries.
— *à l'échantillon* : up to, true to sample.
— *à la demande* : as per order.
conformément à : in accordance with, pursuant to, consistent with.
conformément à la loi : according to (the) law.
conformément aux ordres : in compliance with orders.
en conformité *(avec la présente loi)* : as required (by this act).
se conformer à : to comply with.

confrontation (f) : *(de l'accusé et des témoins)* confrontation, *(de manuscrits)* collation.

confronter (v) : to confront.

confusion (f) : confusion.
[J] merger in ownership (in easement, usufruct, by extinguishment of a debt through succession of creditor to debtor or vice-versa, etc.).
— *de droits* : merger of rights.
— *de parts* : uncertainty as to the father of a child born in the first months of a second marriage concluded before the expiry of the legal time of waiting (see *viduité*).
— *de peines* : merger in criminal law (two or more sentences to run concurrently).
— *de pouvoirs* : reciprocal encroachment of the legislative, judiciary or executive powers.

congé (m) : holiday, leave, dismissal.
[E] — *maritime (lettre de mer)* : clearance of a ship (sea-letter).
[A] — *pour le transport des alcools* : release of spirits from bond.
— *(s) payés* : holidays with pays, [U.S.] paid vacations, vacations with pay.
être en — *de maladie (de convalescence)* : to be on sick-leave.
demander son — : to give notice.
donner son — *à un employé* : to discharge an employee.
donner — *à un locataire* : to give notice to quit.
— *à un propriétaire* : to give notice of leaving.

congédiement (m) : dismissal.

congédier (v) : to dismiss.

conjecturer (v) : to surmise.

conjoint (a et m) : (a) joint.
[J] *cautions* — *(es) et solidaires* : sureties jointly and severally liable.
légataires — *(s)* : co-legatees.
legs — : joint legacy.
[F] *compte courant* — : joint current account.
(m) one's husband, wife, spouse.

conjointement (adv) : jointly.
— *et solidairement* : jointlyl and severally.

conjoncture (f) : conjuncture, circumstances, (economic) conditions, present economic trends, present state of the economy.

conjoncturel (a) : cyclical, short-term.
prélèvement — : temporary levy.

conjugal (a) : conjugal.
[J] *devoir, droit,* — : conjugal right (s), marital intercourse.
domicile — : legal abode of a married couple.

connaissance (f) : knowledge.
porter à la — *de qn :* to inform s.o., to bring to s.o.'s knowledge.
être de la — *d'un tribunal :* to be within the cognizance of a court.
en — *de cause :* with full knowledge of the facts.

connaissement (m) : [E] bill of lading.

connaître (v) : to know.
[J] — *de :* to hear, to have competency, to deal with.

connexe (a) : connected with, related to.

connivence (f) : connivence, complicity.
agir de — *avec qn :* to act in collusion, to be in league with s.o.

consanguinité (f) : consanguinity.
frère **consanguin**, *sœur consanguine :* halfbrother, half-sister, on the father's side.
mariage consanguin : intermarriage.

consécutif à (a) : subsequent to.

conseil (m) : 1° council, board, 2° counsellor, counsel, 3° advice.
[J] — *de famille :* board of guardians.
— *judiciaire :* guardian, administrator of estate of young spendthrift.
pourvu d'un — *judiciaire :* under guardianship.
— *fiscal :* tax adviser, tax lawyer, [U.S.] tax consultant.
— *juridique :* consulting lawyer, legal expert.
— *de justice :* court of justice held aboard ships at sea.
— *des prud'hommes :* conciliation board in industrial disputes.
— *en organisation :* management consultant.
ingénieur- — : consulting engineer, engineering consultant.
[A] — *de la Banque de France :* board of directors *(régents)* of the Bank of France.
— *d'Etat :* (in France) highest administrative jurisdiction and advisory body to the Government in matters of legislation.
— *des ministres :* the cabinet.
— *municipal :* town-council.

— *de l'Ordre des Juristes :* (England, Wales) Law Society.
[C] — *d'administration :* board of directors.
— *de surveillance :* board of trustees, supervisory Board.
— *d'administration d'une œuvre de bienfaisance :* board of trustees.

conseiller (m) : councillor, counsellor.
— *à la Cour d'appel, de Cassation :* judge of appeal.
— *municipal :* town counsellor, alderman.
— *référendaire à la Cour des comptes #* Commissioner of Audit.

consentement (m) : consent, assent.
— *tacite :* acquiescence.
par — *mutuel :* by mutual consent.
donner son — : to consent to.

consentir (v) : to consent.
— *un prêt :* to grant a loan.
— *une remise :* to allow a discount.
— *une vente :* to authorize a sale.
prêt **consenti** : current loan.

(en) conséquence de : in pursuance of, in consequence of.

conservation (f) : conservation.
— *des forêts :* conservancy of forests.
[B] *coût de* — *des titres :* carrying costs.
[J] — *des hypothèques :* mortgage registry.
conservateur *des hypothèques :* registrar of mortgages.

conservatoire (a) :
mesures — (s) : measures of conservation, protective measures, urgent measures.
saisie — : sequester, arrestation.

conserve(s) (f pl) : canned, tinned, preserved food.

considérant que... : whereas...

considérants (m pl) : [J] *(d'une loi)* preamble, *(d'un jugement)* grounds.

considération (f) :
sans — *de :* without regard to.
prendre en — *(demande, proposition) :* to entertain (request, proposal).

considérer (v) : to consider, to regard as.
considéré : regarded as.
être — *comme :* to be deemed to be.

consignataire (m) : [J] depositary, trustee.
[C] consignee.

consignateur (m) : consignor, shipper.

consignation (f) : *(d'argent)* consignation, lodging, deposit.
— *d'amende* : deposit of the amount of an eventual penalty in case of non-performance, previous to certain transactions.
— *en justice, au greffe* : deposit of a sum with the clerk to the court.
— *en guise de paiement* : deposit of the sum due as payment.
marchandises en — : consignment of goods.
[J] *contrat de* — *de marchandises* : contractus aestimatorius.

consigne (f) : instructions, detention.
[D] *marchandises en* — *à la douane* : goods held up at the custom house.

consigner par écrit (v) : to write down.

consilium fraudis [J] : fraudulent intention, intention to inflict loss on one's creditors.

consolidation (f) : [J] merger in ownership.
[F] funding of floating debt;
— *du bilan* : (see : *bilan*).

consolider (v) :
dette **consolidée** : funded debt, consols.
— *des arrérages* : to fund interests.

consommateur (m) : consumer.
(mouvement de) défense des —*(s)* : consumerism.
préférence des —*(s)* : consumer's preference.

consommation (f) : accomplishment, consumption.
[J] — *du mariage, d'un crime* : consummation of marriage, of a crime.
[A] *droits de* — : excise duties.
[C] *société de* — : co-operative supply stores.
la société de — : the consumer society.
biens de — : consumer goods.
biens de — *d'un prix unitaire élevé* : big ticket goods, items.
— *déterminable, ostentatoire* : conspicuous consumption.
— *des ménages* : household consumption.
— *privée* : private consumption.
dépenses de — : consumption expenditure.

consomptible (a) : consumptible, consumable.
choses qui se consomment par l'usage (—*s*) : consumptible things.

consortium *(bancaire)* (m) : (bank) pool.

consorts (m pl) : [J] jointly interested parties, confederates.

conspiration (f) : conspiracy, plot.
conspirer *la mort de qn* : to plot s.o.'s death.

constant *(taux)* (a) : fixed (rate).

constant *(francs)* (a) : constant.

constat (m) : (or *procès-verbal de* —) : official report, record, statement of fact, certified statement.
dresser un — : to draw up a report, to record.
[J] — *d'huissier* : affidavit made out by a bailiff.
[A] — *de décès* : death certificate.

constatation (f) : verification, establishment (of fact).
— *d'un décès* : proof of death.
—*(s) d'une enquête* : findings of an investigation.
— *d'identité* : proof of identity.
procéder aux —*(s)* : to proceed to an official inquiry.

constater (v) : *(des faits)* to ascertain, to establish (facts).

constituant (a) : constituent, *(partie d'un tout)* component.
pouvoir — : constituent power.
titre **constitutif** *de propriété* : title deed.

constituer (v) : to constitute, to set up, to make.
1° — *avocat, arbitre, mandataire, fondé de procuration* : to brief a barrister, (a solicitor), an arbitrator, an attorney, a proxy.
— *un capital en viager* : to settle a life annuity.
— *une dot, une rente à qn* : to settle a dowry, an annuity on s.o.
— *constituer une fondation* : to make an endowment.
— *qn en frais* : to put s.o. to expenses.
— *un gage* : to pawn, to pledge (sth).
— *des garanties* : to offer security.
— *qn son héritier* : to make s.o. one's heir.
— *une hypothèque* : to create a mortgage.
— *le jury* : to impanel the jury.
— *qn prisonnier* : to take s.o. into custody.
— *des réserves* : to set apart a reserve fund.
— *une servitude* : to institute an easement, to set a charge on, to encumber real estate.
— *une société* : to incorporate a company.
2° *se* — *demandeur* : to institute proceedings.
se — *partie civile* to claim for damages by a private individual (parallel to prosecution).
se — *prisonnier* : to give oneself up (to justice).
ils se **constituèrent** *en commission* : they resolved themselves into a committee.
3° *les autorités* **constituées** : the legal authorities, the powers that be.

les corps constitués : the official bodies.

constituteur de rente (m) : settlor, grantor of an annuity.

constitution (f) : 1° constituting, establishing.
— *d'avoué :* briefing of lawyer.
— *de dot, de rente, etc. :* settlement, settling, of a dowry, of an annuity, etc. (see *constituer*).
— *d'un comité :* institution of a committee.
— *de pension :* pension planning.
— *d'une société :* incorporation of a company.
lieu de — : place of incorporation.
frais de — : preliminary expenses (in the formation of a company).
2° constitution, organic law.
— *républicaine, monarchique :* republican, monarchic constitution.

constitutionnel (a) : constitutional.
le droit — : constitutional law.
les droits —(s) : civic rights guaranteed by the constitution.
les lois —(les) : the organic laws.

consulaire (a) : consular.
le **consul** *de France :* the French consul.
[J] *juge* — : tradesman sitting as judge in a commercial court.

consultatif (a) : consultative, advisory (committee, etc.).
avoir une voix **consultative** : to be present in an advisory capacity.
avocat **consultant** : counsel in chambers.

consultation (f) : consultation, conference, legal opinion, medical advice.
cabinet de — : consulting-room.
consulter *un avocat :* to take counsel's opinion.

contentieux (a et m) : contentious matter.
[A] — *administratif :* contentious business falling within the competence of the administrative courts.
— *des fonctionnaires :* matters in dispute concerning civil servants.
[C] *bureau de* — : private office dealing with legal matters, legal department.
service du — : disputed claims, legal department, office of a firm.
— *fiscal :* tax suit.
section du — *au Conseil d'Etat :* judicial section of the « Conseil d'Etat ».

contenu (m) :
— *d'un bien assuré :* contents.
— *habituel :* usual contents.

contestation (f) : contestation, dispute, protest.
matières en — : matters at issue.
sans — *possible :* beyond all question.
[J] — *administrative :* contentious matter falling within the competence of administrative jurisdiction.
action en — *d'état :* action to dispute a civil status.
action en — *de l'état de collaboration :* action for modification of collocation.
— *en cause :* litio contestatio.
— *de droit civil, privé, public :* dispute on interpretation of civil, private, public law.
— *du droit du bénéficiaire dans l'assurance :* contestation of the right of the beneficiary of an insurance.
— *judiciaire :* lawsuit.
— *de légitimité :* bastardy procedure.
contester *une créance :* to reject a claim.
contester à qn le droit de faire qch : to challenge s.o.'s right to do sth.

contester un dommage (v) : to put a loss at issue.

contexte (m) : *(d'un acte)* text (of a deed).

contingent (m) : contingent, quota.
[J] *réclamer son* — : to claim one's proportionate share.

contingentement (m) : curtailment, quantitative restrictions, fixing of quotas.

contingenter (v) : to curtail.

contractant (a) : contracting.

contracter une dette (v) : to incur a debt.

contractuel (a) : contractual (obligation, debt, etc.).
[J] *action* —(le) : action for breach of contract.
obligation —(le), *rapport contractuel :* privity.
date —(le) : date of agreement.
peine —(le) : penalty for non-fulfilment of contract.
[A] *agent* — : temporary official.

contradicteur (m) : adversary, opposing counsel.

contradictoire (a) :
[J] *jugement* — : judgment after trial.
arrêt rendu **contradictoirement** : judgment given after full argument on both sides.
examen — : cross-examination.
contradiction *dans les termes :* (contradictio in adjecto) contradiction in terms.
les contradictions de l'accusé : the inconsis-

tency of the defendant.

contraindre (v) : *(en justice)* to sue s.o.

contrainte (f) : constraint.
[J] a) restraint, b) duress.
— *par corps*: attachment, body execution, imprisonment for debts.
— *morale*: vis compulsiva, implied coercion, intimidation.
— *personnelle*: personal restraint.
— *physique*: vis absoluta, actual coercion.
— *par saisie des biens*: distraint.
agir sous — : to act under duress.
mesures de — : compulsory measures.
[A] writ served after two reminders to recalcitrant tax-payer by the Inland Revenue, followed by immediate execution, notwithstanding opposition.
porteur de — *(s)*: process server, serving-officer, bailiff.

contraire (a) : contrary (to).
[J] *défense au* — : counterclaim.
sauf disposition, clause — : except as otherwise agreed, unless otherwise provided for, unless there be a provision, clause to the contrary.

contrairement à : contrary to, as opposed to.

contrat (m) : [J] contract, agreement, deed of covenant.
1° *les formes de* — *(s)* : contracts in law.
— *accessoire*: accessory contract.
— *administratif*: contract concluded by public services.
— *aléatoire*: aleatory contract.
— *en forme authentique*: contract drawn up by notary or public authority.
— *de bienfaisance*: contract of benevolence.
— *bilatéral parfait*: (contractus bilateralis aequalis) entire contract, bilateral contract, the parties assuming corresponding obligations (sale, exchange, lease, etc.).
— *bilatéral imparfait*: (contractus bilateralis inaequalis) bilateral contract, the parties assuming obligations of a different kind (loan, deposit, etc.).
— *certain*: executory contract.
— *collectif*: collective agreement.
— *collectif de travail*: collective labour bargain.
— *commutatif*: commutative contract.
— *consensuel*: consensual contract.
— *désintéressé*: contract without a consideration (loan without interest, etc.).
— *écrit*: writtent contract.
— *exigible*: debt due.
— *de fait*: implied contract.
— *fictif*: fictitious, sham contract.

— *fiduciaire*: fiduciary agreement, contract of trusteeship.
— *de gage*: bailment.
— *de garantie*: secured debt, underwriting contract.
— *illicite*: illegal contract.
— *incertain*: hazardous agreement.
— *sui generis*: contract not provided for by law.
— *judiciaire*: contract of record.
— *léonin*: leonine convention, unconscionable bargain, oppressive agreement.
— *mixte*: mixed contract (public and private).
— *notarié*: deed of agreement drawn up and authenticated by a notary.
— *nul*: contract null and void.
— *pignoratif*: pignorative contract, loan in form of sale, with privilege of repurchase.
— *réel*: real contract (contract in rem).
— *résolutoire*: (countrarius consensus) resolutory, terminable contract.
— *sous seing privé*: private deed (private agreement made in writing, but not sealed and witnessed).
— *simple*: simple or parol contract.
— *solennel*: specialities.
— *successif*: agreement for periodically renewable performance or services (lease, employment, etc.).
— *synallagmatique*: synallagmatical, bilateral contract, indenture.
— *à titre gratuit*: gratuitous contract.
— *à titre onéreux*: contract for a valuable consideration.
— *type*: contract in standard form.
— *unilatéral*: (contractus unilateralis) contract of benevolence, deed-poll (gift, surety-bond, negotiable instrument, etc.).
2° *divers* — *(s)* : some contracts.
— *(marché) à forfait*: outright sale.
— *à la grosse (aventure)*: bottomry, respondentia.
— *d'abandonnement*: surrender of property to creditor by insolvent debtor.
— *d'abonnement*: sale upon previous order, subscription.
— *(acte) d'adoption*: adoption of a child.
— *d'affermage*: farming lease.
— *d'affrètement*: affreightment, charterparty.
— *d'association-gestion*: venture nurturing.
— *d'assurance*: insurance.
— *de commission*: commission.
— *de courtage*: brokerage agreement.
— *de dépôt*: deposit agreement.
— *d'édition*: contract for publishing.
— *d'emploi*: engagement.
— *d'engagement à bord*: ship's articles.
— *entre époux*: legal transaction between man and wife.
— *de fourniture*: contract of supply.
— *de garantie*: agreement for collateral security.

— *de livraison:* contract of delivery.
— *de louage:* (locatio rei) hiring, letting, contract of hire, lease.
— *de louage d'ouvrage:* (locatio operis) work by contract agreement.
— *de louage de service, de travail:* (locatio operarum) engagement (of workmen, servants).
— *« en mains »:* conveyance of real estate, providing that costs shall be included in the price.
— *clefs en main:* turnkey contract.
— *de mariage:* antenuptial settlement for the purpose of regulating the enjoyment and devolution of real or personal property.
— *de nantissement:* contract for cover, pledge, collateral security.
— *de rente:* annuity contract.
— *de rente viagère:* life annuity contract.
— *fait au nom d'une autre personne par un représentant autorisé:* contract by attorney.
— *de société:* partnership deed.
— *entre une société et un administrateur (convention):* contract of service.
— *(s) à terme de taux d'intérêt:* interest rate futures.
— *à terme d'instrument financier:* financial futures.
— *en faveur d'un tiers:* contract for the benefit of a third party.
— *translatif de propriété:* conveyance.
— *de transport:* shipping contract.
— *de travail:* (locatio operarum) engagement (of workmen, servants).
— *d'union:* agreement on the part of creditors in bankruptcy to take concerted action.
— *de vente:* bill of sale.
3° *action en exécution de — :* action for specific performance of a contract.
passer un — : to conclude an agreement.
résilier un — : to cancel an agreement.
rupture de — : breach of contract.
[A] [C] enterprise, submission, adjudication.

contravention (f): minor (petty) offence, breach of police regulations.
dresser — : to take s.o.'s name and address.

contre: against.
[C] *règlement par — :* settlement per contra.
[J] *Jones — Smith:* Jones versus Smith.

contre-accusation (f): [J] counter-charge.

contre-analyse (f): counter analysis, check analysis.

contrebande (f): contraband, smuggling.
— *d'armes:* smuggling of weapons.
— *de guerre:* war contraband.
faire la — : to engage in smuggling.
marchandises de — : smuggled goods.

contrebandier (m): smuggler, smuggling ship.

contrecarrer *(un enquêteur)* (v): to interfere with (an investigator).

contre-caution (f): [J] additional security, counter surety.

contre-coup (m) *(d'une décision)*: backlash.

contre-dater (v): to change the date (of a letter).

contre-dénonciation (f): [J] notification by the distraining party to garnishee of the execution writ served to the distrained party.

contredit (m): rejoinder.
sans — : unquestionably.

contre-écriture (f): [C] contra-entry in books.

contre-enquête (f): [F] counter-inquiry, new hearing of witnesses (ordered upon a motion by a party denying direct evidence submitted by the other party).

contre-épreuve (f): repetition test.

contre-expertise (f): [J] second expert appraisement ordered to check the first one.

contrefaçon (f): 1° counterfeiting, forging; fraudulenty copying or imitating.
2° counterfeit, forgery, fraudulent imitation; pirated edition.
[J] — *d'un objet breveté, de la propriété littéraire:* infringement of patent, of copyright.
poursuites en — : action for infringement of patent, of copyright.

contrefaire (v): to counterfeit, to forge.

contre-gage (m): [J] counter-pledge.

contre-incendie (f): feed-back.

contre-lettre (f): [J] 1° counter-deed, defeasance, pocket-agreement.
2° deed drawn up in the same from as the antenuptial settlement between the parties to the marriage, setting forth the modifications brought to the latter as drafted originally and as finally adopted on the wedding-day.

contremaître (m): foreman, overseer.

contremarque (f): counter-mark (on gold plate, etc.).

contre-mémoire (m) : counter-statement.

contre-ordre (m) : counter-order, countermand.
sauf —, *à moins de* — : unless (I) hear to the contrary.

contrepartie (f) : [J] 1° the other party (in transaction).
2° counterpart, duplicate (of document, etc.).
[C] contra (in books).
3° consideration (of a contract), proceeds.
en — : per contra.
— *en argent* : consideration in money.
prêt sans — : [U.S.] unrequited lending.

contre-passer (v) : [C] 1° to return, to endorse back bill of drawer. 2° to reverse, to contra-transfer (items, entry).

contre-plainte (f) : [J] counter-charge.

contre-prétention (f) : counter-claim.

contre-preuve (f) : [J] counter-evidence.

contreseing (m) : counter-signature.
avoir le — *de qn* : to sign for s.o.

contresigner (v) : to countersign.

contrestarie (f) : [E] increased compensation to owner for protracted delay in lading or unlading ship, if the time is determined by contract.

contre-valeur (f) : [F] value in exchange.

contrevenant (m) : offender, delinquent, contravener, infringer (of regulations), trespasser.
les —(*s*) *seront poursuivis* : trespassers will be prosecuted.

contrevenir (v) : to contravene, to infringe (an order).
— *au règlement* : to contravene the regulations.

contre-vérité (f) : untruth.

contribuable (m) : taxpayer, ratepayer.
(a) : taxpaying.

contribuer (v) : to contribute.
— *financièrement* : to contribute (funds to...).
— *à* : to make a contribution to.

contributif (a) : contributive.
facultés **contributives** : taxability, ability to pay, taxpaying ability, taxpaying capacity.

contribution (f) : 1° contribution.
— *alimentaire* : allowance for necessaries.
— *patronale, ouvrière* : employer's, employee's contribution to the national (contributive) insurance scheme.
2° tax, rate.
— (*s*) *directes* : direct taxation, direct taxes, assessed taxes.
— (*s*) *indirectes* : indirect taxation, indirect taxes, excise.
— *des patentes* (hist.) : business licence tax.
— *personnelle* : levy per capita.
percevoir des — (*s*) : to collect taxes.
receveur des — (*s*) : tax-collector.

contrôle (m) : 1° roll, list.
— *nominatif* : nominal roll.
— *de service* : duty roster.
porter qch. sur les — (*s*) : to take sth. on charge.
porter qn sur les — (*s*) : to take s.o. on the strength.
2° (or, argent) testing, assaying, assay office.
cachet de — : hallmark.
3° checking, verification, control.
[A] inspection, supervision.
— *de présence* : time-keeping.
[C] [F] auditing, checking, of accounts.
— « *a posteriori* » *de la rentabilité* : post completion audit.
— *budgétaire* : budgetary control.
— *des changes* : foreign exchange control.
— *de comptabilité* : auditing, checking of accounts.
— *interne* : internal control.
sous — *étranger* : foreign owned.
prise de — *majoritaire* : acquisition.
contrôler *une information* : to check a piece of information.

contrôleur (m) : inspector, supervisor, controller (of Government department), assessor, examiner, time-keeper.
[J] — *aux liquidations* : assignee, representative of creditors in bankruptcy (to assist receiver).
[A] — *des contributions directes* : assessor of direct taxes, inspector of taxes.
[C] — *aux comptes* : auditor of company's accounts.
— *interne* : internal auditor.

controuvé (*fait*) (a) : false, of pure imagination.

controverse (f) : controversy.
question de droit **controversée** : moot point, debated point of law.

contumace (f) : refusal to appear in court when legally summoned or disobedience to the rules and orders of court. [J] contumacy.

condamné par — : sentenced in his, her absence.
purger sa — : to surrender to law, after being sentenced in absence.

contumax (m) : [J] defaulter.

convaincre *(de)* (v) : to convince (of).
[J] to convict (of), to prove (s.o.) guilty (of).
atteint et **convaincu** *d'un crime* : guilty of crime in fact and law.
être convaincu que : to be satisfied that.

convenir (v) : 1° *(admettre)* to acknowledge, 2° *(convenir de)* to agree about (on) sth to settle (a price).
convenu : agreed.
langage convenu : code language.

convention (f) : convention.
1° covenant, agreement.
— *internationale* : international convention, treaty.
2° [J] articles, clauses (of deed, etc.)
sauf — *contraire* : unless there be any (unknown) clause to the contrary, unless otherwise provided.
— *authentique* : convention drawn up by notary or public authority.
— *collective (de travail)* : collective (labour) bargain, labour agreement.
— *consulaire* : consular convention.
— *matrimoniale* : antenuptial agreement.
— *de partage* : partition agreement.
— *à l'amiable* : amicable arrangement.
projet de — : draft agreement.

conversion *(en)* (f) : conversion, change (into).
[J] — *d'un procès civil en procès criminel* : conversion of a civil lawsuit into criminal proceedings.
— *de saisie immobilière en vente volontaire* : sale of attached estate by auction authorized by court.
[F] — *d'un emprunt, de rente* : conversion of Government interest bearing stocks into a lower denomination, redemption being offered to unwilling holders.
— *d'obligations en actions* : debenture conversion.
— *des parts sociales en actions* : conversion of partnership shares into stocks.
— *au pair* : conversion at par.
convertible *(en)* : convertible (into).
convertir *des capitaux (à l'étranger)* : to translate.

conviction (f) : *(pièces à)* exhibits (in criminal case).

convocation (f) : convocation, convening *(du parlement, des électeurs, des actionnaires, des créanciers, etc.)*, calling up *(des réservistes)*, letter fixing an appointment.
[A] summons, invitation to an interview by the police, etc.

convoquer (v) : *(les actionnaires)* to call the shareholders, to call together.

co-obligation

coopération (f) : co-operation.
société de — : association of workmen exploiting in common their work and savings.

coopérative (a et f)
(a) *société* — : co-operative society.
(f) co-operative stores.
— *de consommation* : consumer co-operative.
— *de placement* : investment trust, securities trust.
— *de vente* : marketing co-operative.

coopter (v) : to co-opt.

coordonner (v) : to liaise.

copartageant (m) : joint heir.

copie (f) : duplicate, copy.

copropriétaire (m) : co-owner, joint owner, part owner.

copropriété (f) : joint ownership.
société immobilière de — : real property corporation.

corbeille (f) : [B] the ring.

corporation (f) : corporation, public body, trade-guild.

corporel (a) : bodily, tangible.
biens —*(s)* : tangible property.

corps (m) : body.
1° simple body, element.
[J] — *du délit* : corpus delicti.
2° human body, corpse.
perdu — *et biens* : (ship) lost with all hands.
[J] *contrainte par* — : body execution, attachment for contempt of court.
prise de — : apprehension.
séparation de — : a mensa et thoro, separation from bed and board.
3° main part.
— *de l'acte* : body of an instrument.
— *de bâtiment* : main building.
4° whole, entirety, group, organized body, profession.

— *constitués* : official bodies.
— *diplomatique* : diplomatic corps [C.D.].
en — : in corpore.
— *législatif* : legislative body.
— *des lois* : corpus juris, body of the law.
— *médical* : the medical profession.
— *de métier* : corporation, trade guild.
— *de preuves* : body of evidence.

correcteur (m) : proof-reader.

correction (f) : chastisement, reproof, punishment.
[J] — *paternelle* : (hist.) a father's right to have his child locked-up for a certain time.

correctionnel (a) : [J] *délit correctionnel* : minor offence.
chambre — *(le)* : division of court judging minor offences.
tribunal de police — : court of summary jurisdiction (# petty sessions, magistrate's courts).
correctionnaliser *une affaire* # to send a case before a court of summary jurisdiction.

correspondance (f) : correspondence.
achat et vente par — : mail order business.

correspondancier (m) : [C] corresponding clerk.

correspondant (m) *en valeurs du Trésor* : reporting dealer.

corriger (v) : to adjust.
chiffres **corrigés** *des variations saisonnières* : seasonally adjusted figures.

corroborer (v) : to corroborate.
preuve **corroborante** : confirming proof, [J] adminicle.

corrompre (v) : to corrupt.
— *les juges* : to corrupt, to bribe the judges.
essayer de — *un témoin* : to tamper with a witness.
— *un texte* : to adulterate a text.

corruption *(de mineurs)* (f) : suborning (of minors).

corvée (f) : forced labour, statute labour ; fatigue task.

cosignataire (m) : co-signatory.

cotation en bourse (f) : fixing.

cote (f) : 1° proportion, quota, share.
[A] assessment.
[B] quotation (Stock Exchange).
— *des prix* : list of prices, share list.
bulletin de la — *boursière* : Stock Exchange daily official list.
actions admises à la — : listed shares.
marché hors — : curb, over the counter market.

2° classification of documents by numbers or letters, reference.

coter (v) : to quote.
— *à l'ouverture* : to begin the day's trading session, to open.

cotisation (f) : contribution, subscription, quota, share.
[A] assessment of taxpayer.
assurance à — *(s)* : contributory insurance.
— *patronale* : employer's share.
— *à une association, un club* : membership dues.
— *syndicale* : political levy.
— *retraite* : old age benefit.

cotiser *(à tant)* (v) : to assess (at so much), to contribute.

cotutelle (f) : [J] co-guardianship (especially of the husband of a woman appointed as guardian).

coulage (m) : leakage, waste.

coulisse (f) : [B] outside market.

coulissier (f) : outside broker.

coup (m) : knock, blow.
tomber sous le — *de la loi* : to fall within the provisions of, to fall foul of the law.
être sous le — *d'une accusation* : to lie under an accusation.
[J] —*(s) et blessures* : assault and battery.

coupable (a, m et f) : (a) guilty (person).
— *de vol* : guilty of theft.
[J] *s'avouer* — : to plead guilty.
déclarer quelqu'un — : to find s.o. guilty.
(m et f) culprit.
[J] delinquent.

coupes (f pl) *sombres (dans le budget de l'Etat)* : « the axe ».

coupon (m) : cutting.
[F] coupon.
— *de dividende* : dividend-warrant.
— *détaché* : ex-dividend coupon.
— *-réponse* : international reply coupon.

couponnage (m) : couponing.
— *croisé* : cross couponing.

coupure *(billet de banque)* (f) : denomination.
— *de presse* : newspaper cutting, [U.S.] clipping.

cour (f) : [J] court.
— *d'Appel* : court of appeal.
— *d'assises* : assizes.

– *de Cassation* # judiciary committee of the House of Lords, [U.S.] Supreme Court.
– *des Comptes*: State Audit Office.
– *Internationale de Justice*: International Court of Justice.
la Haute – *de justice*: political court elected by the legislative bodies, competent in impeachment cases.
– *martiale*: a) *(juge le personnel militaire)* court-martial ; b) *(juge les civils selon la loi martiale)* military commission.
– *de renvoi*: court of appeals to which a case is referred by the *Cour de cassation* after quashing judgment previously given by another court of appeals. (See also *conseil* [J] , *tribunal, organisation judiciaire*).

courant (a et m) : current, ordinary, present, running, going.
(a) *affaires* – *(es)*: current (affairs) matters.
année – *(e)* : present year.
besoins – *(s)* : current wants (requirement).
compte – : current account, running account, open account.
compte – *postal* : post office current account.
dette – *(e)* : floating debt.
prix – : running (going) price.
(m) *le* – *du marché* : current market prices.
tenir au – : to keep informed.

courbe (f) : curve.
– *des prix* : graph, schedule of prices.
– *en forme de J (de Laffer)* : J (Laffer) curve.
– *prévisionnelle de la demande* : demand curve.

courrier *(par retour de)* (m) : by return of post, [U.S.] by return mail.

cours (m) : course, flow, path, price.
affaire en –, *affaire en* – *d'instance, de procédure, d'instruction* : proceedings in progress, started.
affaires en – : outstanding business.
l'année en – : the current year.
la transaction en – : the deal in progress.
[C] *long* – : foreign trade.
– *du marché* : market price, quotation.
[F] circulation, currency (of money).
– *forcé* : compulsory legal tender.
– *d'achat* : cost.
[B] – *acheteur et vendeur* : bild-and-offer price.
– *de la Bourse* : Stock Exchange quotations.
– *du change* : rate of exchange.
– *de clôture* : closing price.
– *de compensation* : making-up price.
– *au comptant* : cash price.
– *d'émission* : subscription rate.
– *extrêmes* : highest and lowest prices.
– *du ferme* (opp. *cours de prime*) : price of firm stock.
– *du jour*: to-day's rate, price of the day.
– *limité* : limited price.
– *moyen* : average, middle price.
– *d'ouverture, du début* : opening price.
– *pratiqués* : bargains done, ruling prices.
prêt en – : current loan.
– *de prime* : option price, price of call, put.
– *de rachat* : buying in price.
– *à terme* : settlement price, price for the account.
les derniers – : the latest quotations.
hors du – : out of the money.
le – *du sucre est de...* : sugar is quoted at.
avoir – *(monnaie)* : to be legal tender (currency), to be current.

court (a) : short.
(à) – *terme* : short-term.
crédit à – *terme* : short credit.
dépôt à – *terme* : deposit at short notice.
placement à – *terme* : short-term investment, short-dated investment.
prêt à – *terme* : short loan, short-notice loan, short-term loan.
effet à – *(e) échéance* : short bill, short-dated bill.

courtage (m) : brokerage, commission, percentage.

courtier (m) : broker.
– *assermenté* : broker on oath.
– *de change* : bill-broker, jobber, dealer, stockbroker.
– *de commerce, de marchandises* : general, commercial broker.
– *maritime* : ship-broker.
– *marron* : swindler, [B] sharepusher, unlicensed broker.
– *en immeubles* : land-agent, estate agent, [U.S.] realtor.

cousin (m) : cousin.
– *germain* : first cousin.
– *issu de germain* : second cousin.

coût (m) : cost.
– *d'acquisition* : book value.
– *en augmentation rapide* : spiraling costs.
– *du capital* : cost of capital.
– *différentiel* : increment cost.
– *d'exploitation* : operating (running) cost.
– *de fabrication* : manufacturing cost.
– *fictif* : [U.S.] shadow cost.
– *initial* : historical cost.
– *marginal* : marginal cost.
– *moyen* : average (mean) cost.
– *normal* : standard cost.
– *d'opportunité* : opportunity cost.
– *d'option* : option cost.
– *de production* : production costs.
– *du travail* : labour cost.

— *de vente* : selling cost.
— *(s) sociaux* : social costs.
— *-assurance-fret (CAF)* : cost insurance freight (CIF).
— *et fret (C et F)* : cost and freight (CF).
le — de la vie : the cost of living.
loi des — comparatifs : law of comparative costs.

coûtant *(au prix)* (a) : at cost price.

coûter (v) : to cost.

coûteux (a) : expensive.

coutume (f) : custom, habit.
[J] customary or common law (also called *droit* **coutumier**).
pays de —, de droit coutumier : provinces to the north of the river Loire (opp. *pays de droit écrit*, of statutory, roman law, to the south).

couvert *(prêt, dépense)* (a) : met (loan, expenses).

couverture (f) : covering, cover, coverage.
[C] [B] margin, cover.
— *de billets de banque* : cover (in gold) of paper currency.
sans — : without security, cover.
— *à terme* : forward cover.

couvrir (v) : to cover.
— *le dommage* : to indemnify for damages.
— *une enchère* : to outbid in auction, to bid a higher price.
— *ses subordonnés* : to be responsible for subordinates acting upon orders.
— *la prescription, la péremption, le vice d'un contrat* : to annul the effects of prescription, time-limitation, flaw, in a contract.
— *une nullité* : to annul a voidance.
[B] **se couvrir** : to hedge.
— *(dépenses)* : to remit (a sum), to refund.

covendeur (m) : [J] covendor.

créance (f) : claim, debt, credence, indebtedness.
lettres de — : credentials (of diplomatic agents), letter of credit (commerce).
[J] chose in action.
— *alimentaire* : claim of alimony.
— *résultant d'un cautionnement* : claim out of bail-bond.
— *certaine* : unquestionable claim.
— *cessible* : transferable, assignable claim.
— *chirographaire* : unsecured debt.
— *compensable* : debt liable to be off-set.
— *conditionnelle* : qualified debt.
— *(s) douteuses* : bad debts.
— *de droit public* : debt to the community, incurred under the law.
— *exigible* : debt due, outstanding, claimable debt.
— *non exigible* : accruing debt.
— *fiscale* : revenue claim.
— *garantie* : secured debt.
— *garantie par gage* : pledged debt.
— *(s) gelées* : frozen credits.
— *hypothécaire* : debt secured by a mortgage, mortgage claim.
— *irrécouvrable* : bad debt.
— *litigieuse* : litigious claim.
— *dans la masse* : claims of creditors in bankruptcy.
— *naturelle* : rightful claim but prescribed or voidable.
— *privilégiée* : preferential debt, privileged debt.
— *saisie* : attached debt.
— *véreuse* : doubtful claim.
titre de — : evidence of debt.

créancier (m) : creditor, obligee.
— *chirographaire* : simple contract creditor.
— *gagiste* : pledgee.
— *hypothécaire* : mortgagee.
— *dans la masse* : creditor in bankruptcy.
— *privilégié* : chargee.
— *putatif* : presumed creditor.
être — *(d'une maison)* : to hold a claim (against a firm).

crédirentier (m) : [J] recipient of an allowance, life annuitant.

crédit (m) : credit, repute, influence, prestige.
— *(prêt)* : loan.
— *public* : financial standing of the State.
[J] — *imaginaire* : misdemeanour of obtaining credit by fraud.
[A] — *budgétaire* : appropriation.
— *(s) de droits* : postponement of payments due to the Inland Revenue.
— *municipal* : Municipal Pawn Office.
[C] — *et débit* : credit and debit.
— *documentaire* : advance on warrant, on bill of lading, etc.
société mutuelle de — : mutual credit society, friendly society.
[F] *établissement, société de —* : bank, loan society.
lettre de — : letter of credit, accreditation.
— *-bail* : leasing.
— *à la consommation* : consumer credit.
— *croisé* : swap.
— *à découvert* : uncovered credit.
— *différé* : deferred credit.
— *passerelle, relais* : bridging loan.
— *ponctuel* : spot credit.
— *de soutien* : standby credit.

— *(s) supplémentaires*: supplementary estimates.
— *à taux révisable*: rollover credit.
— *de restructuration*: new-money.
facilités de — *:* line of credit.
acheter (vendre) à — *:* to buy (sell) on credit (on trust).
— *d'impôt*: tax credit.
— *d'impôt fictif*: matching credit.

créditer *(un compte)* (v): to credit an account.

créditeur (m et a): creditor, credit.
(a) *compte* — *:* credit account.
solde — *:* credit balance.
(m) — *(s) divers*: sundry creditors.
— *obligataire*: bond creditor.

créer (v) *(une société)* to float, to found, to launch, to set up (a company).

crémaillère *(parité à)* (f): crawling peg, crawling peg system.

creux, creuse (a): [F] sagging.
heures — *(s)*: slack hours.
mois — *:* lean month.

criée (f): [J] auction.
audience des — *(s)*: forced sale of real estate in court.
vente à la — *:* sale by auction (of produce).

crieur (m): auctioneer.

crime (m): crime.
[J] felony, crime.
— *capital*: capital offence.
— *d'État*: treason.
— *de faux*: forgery.
— *d'incendie*: arson.
tentative de — *:* attempted felony.
convaincre de — *:* to return a verdict of guilty, to find a true bill.
commettre un — *:* to commit, to perpetrate a crime.

criminaliser *(un délit)* (v): to qualify a malfeasance as a criminal offence and transfer the case from the *tribunal correctionnel* to the *Cour d'assises*.

criminel (m et a): (m) criminal, felon, guilty of crime.
poursuivre au — *:* to take criminal proceedings.
« *le* — *tient le civil en état* »: a case may not be tried in civil law so long as the criminal proceedings are not closed.

grand — *:* offender liable for trial in assizes.
(a) *attentat* — *:* criminal attempt.
droit — *:* criminal, crown law.

crise (f): crisis, emergency.
— *économique*: slump.
— *de l'énergie*: energy crisis.
— *du pétrole*: shortage of oil.
— *cyclique*: cyclic, cyclical crisis.

critère (m): criterion, standard, test.

croissance (f): growth.
— *circulaire (diversification par introduction de produits apparentés)*: product extension (development).
— *économique*: economic growth.
— *équilibrée*: balanced growth.
— *déséquilibrée*: unbalanced growth.
— *durable*: sustainable growth.
— *de la firme*: business growth.
taux de — *:* rate of growth.

croissant (a): growing, increasing.
rendement — *:* increasing return.

croupier (m): sleeping partner.

culture (f): cultivation.
en — *:* under crop.

cumul *des fonctions* (m): plurality of offices.
[J] — *des peines*: cumulative sentence, concurrence of penalties.
— *juridique*: sentences to run consecutively.

cumulatif (a): cumulative.
montant des immobilisations **cumulatives**: cumulative capital amount.
cumulé *(intérêts, revenu)*: accrued (interest, income).

curatelle (f): guardianship, wardship.

curateur (m): *(d'une succession ab intestat)* trustee, administrator, *(d'un mineur émancipé)* guardian.
— *d'un aliéné*: committee for a lunatic, [Scot.] curator.
— *au ventre*: guardian to child unborn.

curriculum vitae (m): id; data sheet.

cycle (m): cycle.
— *du commerce*: trade cycle.
— *économique*: business cycle.
— *de vie d'un produit*: product life cycle.

cyclique (a): cyclic, cyclical.
maxima — *(s)*: cyclical peaks.

NOTES

NOTES

D

dans *(un délai de deux mois)* : within (two months,...).

date (f) : date, time of the year.
[J] *− authentique* : certified date.
− certaine : legal date of a private agreement for a third party.
− d'échéance : maturity, due date.
[C] *effet à trente jours de −* : bill maturing thirty days after date.
− de fin d'exercice (société) : date of the end of the company's fiscal year.
− limite : deadline.
− limite d'utilisation d'un produit : sell-by date.
− de livraison : delivery date.
à la − donnée : at the particular time.
en − du : dated from, under date of.
à **dater** *du* : from.

datif (a) : sth. established by a will or by a judge (opp. *légal* : provided by law).
[J] *tuteur −* : guardian appointed by the family council or by court.
curatelle, tutelle, **dative** : trusteeship, guardianship, established by court.

dation (f) : [J] act of giving in judiciary form (not to be confused with *donation*).
dation en paiement : datio insolutum.
− d'arrhes : paying of earnest money.
− de tuteur, de tutelle : providing of tutor, of tutorship, by court.

de commodo et incommodo : [A] administrative inquiry in a neighbourhood, before giving permit to start a noisy or obnoxious trade, or to erect buildings to that purpose.

de cujus *(successione or bonis agitur)* : [J] the deceased, [U.S.] decedent.

de droit : de jure (opp. de facto).

de gré à gré : amiably, [J] by simple contract.
vente − : free market transaction.

de plein droit : [J] ipso jure.
les héritiers acquièrent − l'universalité de la succession dès que celle-ci est ouverte : the entire succession descends to the heirs immediately upon the owner's death.

débats judiciaires (m pl) : [J] hearing, proceedings, trial.
− à huis-clos : hearing in camera.
diriger les − : to conduct the proceedings.
réouverture des − : new trial (if the judges are equally divided, a further judge is called in and a new trial begins).
résumé (des −) : summing up bill.
trancher un − : to settle a dispute.
débattre : to be at issue.
les faits **débattus** : the facts at issue.

débauchage (m) : discharging (of workmen), [U.S.] laying off.

débauche (f) : debauchery.
1° [J] *excitation de mineur à la −* : inducing a minor to lead a dissolute life.
2° **débaucher** *les ouvriers* : a) to induce workmen to strike, b) to discharge, to turn off hands, to reduce one's staff.

débet (m) :
[J] *acte enregistré en −* : deed exceptionally recorded duty-free by registry office.
[A] *arrêt de −* : decree by the French «Cour des Comptes» to enforce restitution by civil servant of public moneys.
[C] [F] debit.
être en − : to settle an account partially.

débirentier (m) : [J] payee of an allowance.

débit (m) : debit.
débiter : to charge against, to debit.
[C] [F] *débiter un compte de* : to debit an account to the amount of.
débiter une somme d'un compte : to debit an account by a sum.
note de − : debit memo.
somme à porter au − de : to debit s.o. with (a sum), to charge a sum to s.o.

débitant (m) : retailer.

débiteur (m) : debtor, obligor.
[C] [F] *compte −* : debit account, blank credit.
solde − : debit balance, overdraft, balance due, balance of indebtedness.

débloquer des fonds (v) : to release funds.

débouché (m) : outlet, opening, channels for trade.
[C] *trouver de nouveaux* — *(s)* : to find new markets.

débours (m) : expenses, outlay.

débouter (v) : [J] to cast, to dismiss, to reject (a suit).
être **débouté** *de sa demande :* to be non-suited.
(m) *jugement de débouté :* billa cassetur, non-suit.

débrayer (v) *(cesser le travail)* : to walk out.
organiser un **débrayage** : to stage a walk-out.

décaissement (m) : withdrawal, outward payment, cash outflow, cash outlay.

décaisser (v) : to pay out, to withdraw.
— *une somme :* to withdraw a sum of money.

décalage horaire (m) : time gap.

décentralisation (f) : devolution, decentralisation.

décentraliser (v) : to decentralise.

décéder (v) : to die, to decease.

décerner (v) : to decree, to award, to assign.
[J] — *un mandat d'arrêt contre Untel :* to issue a warrant for the arrest of So-and-so, a writ of capias.

décès (m) : death.
[J] *acte de* — : death certificate.
jugement déclaratif de — : finding of presumed death.

décharge (f) : [J] release, acquittal, of accused person.
témoin à — : witness for the defence.
failli **déchargé**, *non déchargé :* discharged, undischarged bankrupt.
[C] — *d'un impôt :* relief of tax.
[C] [F] (bank) letter of indemnity.
porter une somme en — : to book an amount in reduction of debt.
— *sans réserve :* clean signature.
— *de 50 % :* composition of half the amount due.

décharger (*qn d'une dette*) (v) : to remit, to discharge of, to exonerate of (a debt).
— *(d'une tâche, d'une obligation) :* to release.

déchéance (f) : downfall, forfeiture.
[J] loss, withdrawal, cancelling, of rights (as a penalty), foreclosure, lapse, forfeiture.

— *d'un administrateur :* disqualification of a director.
— *de nationalité :* loss, withdrawal of nationality.
— *de la puissance paternelle :* loss of parental authority.
— *de la propriété littéraire :* lapse of copyright.
— *quadriennale :* lapse of all claims against the State after four years.
action en — *de brevet :* action for forfeiture of patent.
[F] — *de titres :* forfeiture of shares.
— *du terme :* event of default.
[ASS] — *d'une police :* running out, expiration of a policy.
déchu *de (ses) droits :* having forfeited (one's) right.

déchets (m pl) : waste.
— *(s) nucléaires :* nuclear waste.

décider (v) : to decide, to settle.
— *en faveur de qn :* to give a ruling in favour of s.o.

décision (f) : decision.
[J] ruling, award.
preuve **décisive** : conclusive evidence.
serment **décisoire** : decisive oath.
une — *rendue en faveur d'un contribuable n'engage pas l'administration dans son traitement d'autres contribuables :* a ruling given to one taxpayer does not bind the tax administration in its treatment of other taxpayers.
— *(s) d'une assemblée :* conclusions of an assembly.
porter une — : to make a decision known.
prendre une — *(sens général) :* to make (take) a decision, to reach a decision.
prise de — : decision making.
[C] — *de désinvestir :* abandonment decision.
— *d'investir :* investment decision.
prise de — : decision making.
arbre **décisionnel** : decision tree.

déclarant (m) : the declarant, *(contribuable)* the taxpayer.

déclaratif (a) : *acte* — : probate of legal status.
jugement — : adjudicate, declaratory judgment.
jugement — *de faillite :* adjudication of bankruptcy.

déclaration (f) : declaration, statement.
[J] — *du jury :* the findings of a jury.
fausse — : misrepresentation.
— *de naissance, de décès :* notification of birth, death.
— *de naturalisation :* letters of naturalization.
— *sous serment :* sworn statement, affidavit.

— *de succession* : statement by heir concerning the estate of the deceased liable to taxation.
— *estimative, définitive (d'impôts)* : [U.S.] tax declaration, return.
— *de consommation* : entry for home use.
— *d'entrée (de sortie)* : clearance inwards (outwards).
— *d'intention* : statement of intent.
— *pour marchandises en franchise* : entry for duty-free goods.
— *en douane* : bill of entry, declaring (dutiable goods).
— *de mise en entrepôt* : warehousing entry.
— *patronale* : employers' return.
— *de réexportation* : shipping bill.
— *de solvabilité* : declaration of solvency.
— *de soumission* : declaration for bond.
— *de revenu* : income-tax return, tax return.
— *sous serment* : affidavit.
— *de versement* : receipt.

déclaré (a) :
revenu — : reported income.
sans valeur —*(e) (colis)* : uninsured (parcel).
— *coupable de vol* : convicted of theft.

déclarer (v) : to declare, to certify, to report, to return.

déclencher (v) : to trigger off.

déclinatoire (a et m) : [J] (a) declinatory (plea, etc.) ; (m) plea in bar of trial.

décliner *(responsabilité)* (v) : to decline (responsability).
— *toute obligation* : to disclaim any obligation.

décommander (v) : to cancel, to call off.

décompte (m) : deduction from sum to be paid.
[A] working out of charges.
[C] detailed account.

déconcentration (f) : [A] disconcentration.

déconfiture (f) :
[J] insolvency (of non-trader).
tomber en — : to fail to meet one's liabilities.

décote (f) : marginal relief (reduction).
— *dégressive* : wanishing exemption.

découler (v) : to be derived from, to follow.
— *d'un accord* : to arise out of an agreement.
la perte en capital en **découlant** : the capital loss therefrom.

décourager *(les investissements)* (v) : to discourage (investments).

découvert (m) : deficit.
[F] overdraft, uncovered balance.
crédit à — : unsecured credit.
— *d'une banque* : uncovered balance.
— *budgétaire* : budgetary deficit.
avances à — : unsecured (uncovered) advances.
mettre (un compte) à — : to overdraw an account.
faire la chasse au — : to squeeze the bears.
[B] *acheter, vendre à* — : to bull, to bear the market.
[ASS] the uninsured part of a thing, the real value exceeding the insured value.

décret (m) : decree, fiat, edict, order.
— *présidentiel* : edict by the President of the Republic eventually countersigned by one or more ministers.
— *-loi* : decree-law (deemed a legal enactment), executive order, order in council.
— *portant règlement d'administration publique* : edict outlining practical measures for the application of a law.

décréter (v) : to enact, to decree.

dédit (m) : [C] forfeit clause, penalty for breaking a contract.

dédommagement (m) : indemnification, compensation, offset.
recevoir une somme en — *de qch.* : to receive a sum as (in) compensation for sth.

dédommager (v) : to compensate.

dédouané (a) : out of bond, cleared.
marchandises —*(es)* : duty-paid goods.

dédouanement (m) : [D] clearance of goods at the custom house.

dédouaner (v) : *(marchandises)* to clear, to take out of bonds (goods).

déductible (a) : deductible, allowable, to be deducted.
(frais, perte) —*(s)* : allowable (expenses, loss).

déduction (f) : abatement, allowance, deduction, relief.
— *pour frais* : allowance for expenses.
— *avant impôt* : taxable base allowance.
— *d'investissement* : capital (investment) allowance.
— *spéciale d'amortissement (pouvant être accordée avant l'amortissement normal)* : initial allowance (that may be granted before normal amortization or depreciation).
— *supplémentaire (amortissement)* : additional (first year) depreciation, bonus depreciation.

— *pour épuisement (mine)* : depletion allowance.
admis en — : allowed.
sans — : net cash payment.
sous — *de* : less.
sous — *d'escompte, d'impôt, (escompte, impôt) déduit* : less discount, less tax.

déduire (v) : to write off, to deduct, to strike off, to substract.
à — : net out.

défaillance (f) : [J] default, defaulting (in contracto).
[ASS] protracted default.

défaillant (m et a) : (m) defaulter, absconder.
(a) defaulting.

défalcation (f) : deduction, abatement (of taxes).

défalquer (v) : to write off.

défaut (m) : absence, failure.
[J] default, non appearance.
— *de comparution* : failure to appear.
— *de déclaration* : failure to make a return.
— *de paiement* : failure to pay.
faire — : to fail to appear, to lack.
jugement par — : judgment by default.
— *-congé* : non appearance of plaintiff.
donner — : record of default by court.
[C] — *d'acceptation* : non-acceptance (of bill), failure to accept.
[F] — *de provision* : « no funds », « no effects ».
— *croisé* : cross default.
à — *de* : failing, for want of, in default of.
à — *d'un accord entre les parties* : failing agreement between the parties.

défavorable (a) : adverse.
fluctuations —*(s) des prix* : adverse price movements.

défectueux (a) : faulty, unsound, defective.
[J] *acte* —, *jugement* — : deed, judgment with flaw.
endos — : incorrect endorsement.

défendeur (m), **défenderesse** (f) :
[J] (*en* C.L.) defendant, (*en* Eq. *et en appel*) respondent, *(en instance de divorce)* respondent, *(complice d'adultère, co-—)* co-respondent.
— *reconventionnel* : counter-claimant.

défense (f) : [J] defence, plea.
—*(s) à exécution* : order of court of appeals forbidding the enforcement of a judgment.
légitime — : self-defence.

moyens de la — : plea of the defendant.
présenter la — : to put the case.
— *du consommateur (mouvement de)* : consumerism.
— *nationale* : national defence.

défenseur (m) : [J] counsel for the defence.
— *d'office* : counsel for the defence appointed by the Court.
[A] — *(s) de l'environnement* : conservationists, environmentalists.

déférer (v) : [J] to submit, to refer a case to a court; to transfer a case from a lower instance to a court of appeals.
— *qn à la justice* : to hand over, to give up s.o. to justice.
— *le serment à qn* : to administer, to tender the oath to s.o., to swear *(témoin)*, to swear in *(jury)*.

déficit (m) : deficiency, loss, shortage.
— *de caisse (d'encaisse)* : shortage in the cash.
— *de la balance des paiements* : balance of payments deficit.
en — **(déficitaire)** : adverse.
balance des paiements — : adverse balance of payments.
— *commercial* : trade gap.
budget en — : adverse budget.
compte déficitaire : account showing a debit.
combler le — : to make up the deficit.
— *très supérieur aux prévisions* : deficit overshoot.

défini (a) : defined.

définitif *(jugement)* (a) : legally binding (judgment).

définition (f) *de poste* : job description.

déflation (f) : deflation.

défraîchi (a) : shop-spoiled.

défunt (m) : deceased.

dégagement (m) : redemption of mortgage or pledge, of stocks lodged as security *(titres en nantissement)*, taking out of pawn.
—, *vente en masse* : unwinding.

dégager (v) :
— *qn d'une obligation* : to relieve (absolve) s.o. from an obligation.
— *des titres* : to release securities.
[B] « *la place est* **dégagée** » : « the market is all bears (all takers) ».
être **dégagé** *d'une responsabilité* : to be relieved of responsibility.

dégât: damage.
expertise de — (s): damage survey.

dégradation (f): degradation, (wrongful) waste, wear and terar, *(milit.)* loss of rank.

degré (m): degree.
— de parenté: degree of relationship.
— de précision: accuracy.

dégressif (a): decreasing, degressive, tapering.
amortissement — : depreciation on diminishing values.
méthode de calcul de l'amortissement — : declining balance method.
système — : diminishing instalment system.
système — de taxation: regressive tax system.
tarifs — (s): decreasing rates, grade rates.
taux — (s): tapering rates.

dégressivité (f): degression.

dégrèvement (m): reduction.
[J] disencumbering of an estate (see *purge*).
[F] abatement of taxes, relief from taxation, tax relief, tax cut, reduction of taxes.
— pour charges de famille: allowance for dependent relatives.

dégrever (v): to relieve (s.o.) of a tax, to derate (income), to reduce taxes on.

déguerpissement (m): [J] moving out of tenant (to elude payment of ground rent).

délai (m): delay, respite, notice, time, time-limit.
[J] *— de grâce*: days of grace, respite.
— de congé: term of notice from and to employer or employee.
— de prescription: prescription period, term of limitation.
— de protection littéraire: term of copyright.
demander un — : to ask for time.
demande de prolongation du — d'opposition (ou d'appel): application to extend the time for objecting (or appealing).
[C] *— de paiement*: term of payment.
— de livraison: term of delivery, lead time.
— de préavis: notice (period of).
— de réflexion: cooling off period.
accorder un — : to allow respite.
octroyer un — : to grant time.
dans un — de (dix) jours: at (ten) day's notice.
à bref — : in the near future, at short notice.

délaissement (m): desertion, abandonment.
[J] renunciation of rights (esp. abandonment by third party holding a mortgaged property to a creditor, to avoid being a defendant in attachment proceedings).
— de poursuites: abandon of prosecution.
[ASS] abandonment.

délaisser (v): to forgo, to relinquish, to abandon, to neglect.
les valeurs (x.) sont délaissées: the (x.) stocks are neglected.

délégation (f): denouncement, informing.

délégataire (m): delegatee.

délégation (f): delegation (of authority), transfer, assignment of debt.
par — : on the authority of.
[J] *— judiciaire*: delegation of powers to a police official by the *parquet* (public prosecutor's office).

délégatoire *(pouvoir)* (a): delegatory (power).

délégué syndical (m): shop steward, union representative.

délibération (f): [J] proceedings.

délibéré (m): [J] consultation of judges.
vider un — : to make an award, to give a verdict after consultation.
— sur le siège: consultation of judges sotto voce during the sitting.
— sur rapport: consultation of judges after hearing the report of one of them.
affaire mise en — : judgment adjourned for further consultation.

délictuel (a): ex delicto, intentional.
[J] *responsabilité — (le)*: aquilian responsibility (opp. *responsabilité contractuelle*).

délictueux (a): punishable.
[J] *acte —* or *délit*: misdemeanour, offence.

délier (v): to undo.
— d'un serment: to release from oath.

délinquant (m et a): [J] (m) delinquent, offender, trespasser.
— primaire: first time offender.
— d'habitude: recidivist, habitual criminal, « old lag » *(« cheval de retour »)*.
(a) *l'enfance — (e)*: juvenile offenders, delinquency.

délit (m): [J] misdemeanour, offence, indictable offence.
quasi-— : technical offence.
pris en flagrant — : caught in the act, red-handed.

déloyal (a) : unfair.

demande (f) : request, question, petition, application (for).
— *de renseignements :* inquiry.
[J] claim, action.
— *en garantie :* impleader.
— *en grâce :* petition for a reprieve.
— *introductive d'instance :* writ of summons, first process.
— *faite sur le barreau :* plaintiff's declaration made verbally to the court, superseding written procedure.
— *reconventionnelle :* counterclaim, cross action, set-off.
— *en divorce :* action for divorce.
— *de déduction :* claim to allowances.
formulaire de — : form for claiming.
[A] indent.
— *de renseignements :* inquiry.
[C] [F] demand.
sur — : on request, upon application.
— *d'achat :* [U.S.] purchase requisition.
— *composite (d'un produit servant à divers usages) :* composite demand.
— *d'emploi :* [U.S.] employment application.
— *globale :* aggregate demand.
argent payable sur — : call money.
la loi de l'offre et de la — : the law of supply and demand.

demander (v) : to apply for, to request.
— *le remboursement (d'une dette, d'un emprunt) :* to call a loan.

demandeur (m), **demanderesse** (f) :
[J] plaintiff, appellant, applicant.

démarchage (m) : canvassing, door-to-door selling.

démarcheur (m) : agent, canvasser, tout, door-to-door salesman.

démarrage *(économique)* (m) : start, take off (of an economy).

démembrement (m) : [J] division (of land). [F] stripping.

demeure (f) : tarrying, stay, sojourn.
[J] *meubles à fixe — :* (landlord's) fixtures.
mise en — : formal notice, summons to do sth.

déménagement (m) : removal, (re)-moving.
frais de — : removal, moving expenses.

demi-tarif (m) : half-rate (transport), half-fare.

demi-terme *(de loyer)* (m) : half-quarter's rent.

démonstrateur (m) : demonstrator.

démontrer *(un droit)* (v) : to evidence (a right).

dénationalisation (f) : denationalisation.
dénationaliser : to denationalise.

dénégation (f) : denial.
[J] traverse.
— *de responsabilité :* disclaimer of responsibility.

déni (m) : denial, refusal.
[J] — *de justice :* miscarriage of justice.

dénonciation (f) : declaration, denunciation, information against s.o.
[J] — *d'instance :* instituting proceeding.
— *de nouvel œuvre :* action for disturbance of possession, esp. against erecting structures forbidden by law (easement, etc.).
— *d'un traité :* denunciation.
dénonciateur (a) : denunciative, denunciatory.
dénonciateur (m) : contact.
[C] notice of termination of agreement, of partnership.

denrée (f) : commodity, foodstuff, produce.
— *(s) alimentaires :* foodstuffs, food products, articles of food and drink.
— *(s) périssables :* perishables, perishable goods.
— *(s) de première nécessité :* essential goods (products).

densité de (f) (la) population : population density.
— *de probabilités :* risk profile.

dépareillé (a) : unmatched.

départ usine (m) : ex-works.

dépassement (m) : exceeding.
— *des crédits :* overstepping appropriations.

dépendance (f) : dependence.
[J] —(s) : outbuildings, messuage.
avoir un lien de — avec (une société) : not to deal at arm's length with a corporation.

dépendant(es) *(profession)* (a) : dependent (personal services).

dépens (m pl) : [J] costs.
être condamné aux — : to be ordered to pay costs.
taxe des — : taxation of costs.

dépense(s) (f) : expenditure, expenses, outgoings, outlays, charge.
— *budgétaires* : budgetary expenditure.
— *de consommation* : consumption expenditures.
— *courantes* : running (current) expenses.
— *diverses* : general (sundry) expenses.
— *d'équipement (en immobilisations)* : capital expenses (expenditure), capital outlay.
— *d'exploitation* : 1° business expenses, operating expenses, working expenses. 2° operating costs.
— *fiscales* : tax expenditures.
— *imprévues* : contingent expenses.
— *indirectes ou fixes* : indirect charges, indirect expenses, fixed charges.
— *préférentielles* : expense preference.
— *de publicité* : advertising expenses.
— *destinées à financer la publicité (par des moyens autres que médiatiques)* : below the line expenditure.
— *renouvelables (périodiques)* : recurring expenses.
excédent des — *(sur les recettes)* : excess of expenditure (over receipts).
réduire les — : to reduce (to cut down) expenditure.
dépenser *sans compter* : to splurge.

déplacement (m) : displacement, shifting, movement.
— *de fonds* : displacement of funds.
— *de l'offre et de la demande* : shift in supply and demand.
frais de — : travelling expenses.

déplacer *(la charge fiscale)* (v) : to shift the tax burden.

dépliant *(publicitaire)* (m) : (advertising) folder.

déport (m) : [B] backwardation, forward discount.

déposant (m) : [J] bailor, witness.
[F] depositor.

déposer (v) : to deposit, to lodge, to file, to register, to lay.
[J] — *en justice* : to give evidence, to depose.
— *une plainte contre qn* : to prefer a charge, to lay, to lodge a complaint, against s.o., [U.S.] to file a claim.
— *son bilan* : to file a petition in bankruptcy, to declare bankruptcy.
— *une demande de brevet* : to file an application for a patent.
— *une marque de fabrique* : to register a trade mark.
marque **déposée** : registered trade-mark.
— *un projet de loi* : to table, to bring in a bill.

[F] — *son argent, ses titres, à la banque* : to deposit one's money, stocks, at the bank; to bank.
— *sa charge* : to resign, to give up office.
— *une déclaration de revenus* : to file a tax return.

dépositaire (m) : [C] [F] trustee, bailee.
— *de l'autorité publique* : public servant.
[C] — *exclusif (de)* : sole agent (for).

déposition (f) : [J] deposition, evidence, testimony, statement by witness.
recueillir une — : to take s.o.'s evidence.

dépossession (f) : dispossession.
[J] eviction, disseizin, ouster of rightful owner.

déposséder *(de)* : to oust (of).

dépôt (m) : depositing, deposit, depository, store.
[J] bailment of goods.
— *de garantie entre mains de tiers* : escrow.
— *légal d'un livre* : copyrighting of a book (by depositing duty copies).
— *de titres en nantissement (hypothèque des titres)* : lodging stock as a security.
mandat de — : committal order.
écroué au — : committed to the cells.
[D] goods in bond.
[C] goods on sale and return.
— *de marchandises* : warehouse.
— *de bois* : timber yard.
— *de charbon* : coal yard.
— *d'essence* : petrol station.
[F] — *en banque* : bank deposit.
certificat de — : certificate of deposit.
compte de — *à vue* : drawing account.
compte de — : deposit account.
— *de garantie* : earnest money, deposit.
— *en garde* : safe custody.
— *à terme ou à échéance fixe* : deposit for a fixed period.
— *à court terme* : call money.
frais de — : custody charge.
récépissé de — : custody receipt.
société de — : joint-stock bank.

dépouillement *(des dividendes)* (m) : (dividend) stripping.

dépouiller *(un compte)* (v) : to analyse, [U.S.] analyze (an account), to look into (an account).
— *un scrutin* : to tally votes.
système des **dépouilles** : [U.S.] spoil system.

dépréciation (f) : *(de la monnaie)* depreciation, *(d'un équipement)* wear and tear, debasement.

dérangement (en) : out of order.

déréglementation (f) : deregulation.

dernier entré, premier sorti (DEPS) : last in, first out (LIFO).

dérober (v) : to steal, to snatch away, to rob.

dérogation (f) : derogation.
— *à une loi* : impairment of a law.
par — *aux dispositions en vigueur* : notwithstanding the legal provisions in force.
clause **dérogatoire** : derogatory clause.

désaccord (m) : disagreement.

désaffectation (f) : [J] putting of public building to another purpose.

désamorcer (v) *(un conflit)* : to defuse a conflict.

désarmer (v) *(un navire)* : to lay up, to pay off (a ship).

désarrimer (v) : to break bulk.

désaveu (m) : abnegation, disavowal, denial, repudiation.
[J] — *d'un agent* : disowning of an agent.
— *de paternité* : disowning of offspring.
action en — *de la paternité* : bastardy case.

descendance (f) : descendants, lineage, issue.

descente (f) : descent.
[J] — *de justice,* — *sur les lieux* : visit of experts, officials, etc., to the scene of the occurrence.

description *(du mobilier)* (f) : inventory (of furniture).

déséquilibre (m) : disequilibrium, imbalance.
— *des échanges* : imbalance of exchanges.

deshérence (f) : [J] default of heirs.
tomber en — : to escheat.

désignation (f) : designation.
[A] — *de qn pour un poste* : appointment, nomination of s.o. to a post.

désigner (v) : *(un arbitre, un expert, un mandataire)* to nominate, to appoint (arbitrator, expert, proxy), *(cataloguer)* to list.
les biens personnels **désignés** : listed personal property.

désinflation (f) : disinflation.

désintéressé (a) : 1° *(personne)* disinterested (person).
2° *(avis)* unbiased, unprejudiced (advice).

désintéressement *(d'un associé)* (m) : buying out, paying off (a partner).

désintéresser *(des créanciers)* (v) : to buy out, to pay off, to satisfy (creditors).

désintermédiation (f) : disintermediation.

désistement (m) : nolle prosequi, desistance, nonsuit.
[J] — *d'action* : confession of defence, of plea, withdrawal of suit, abandonment of action.
— *de demande* : waiver of claim.

(se) désister (v) : to withdraw (one's candidature).
— *d'une plainte* : to withdraw a charge.

dessaisir (v) : to disseize, to dispossess.
le tribunal s'est **dessaisi** *de l'affaire* : the court decided not to proceed with the case.

dessaisissement (m) : handing over.
[J] disseizin, dispossession.

dessous : under.
— *de table* : bribe.
au - — *de la normale* : below standard.
au - — *du taux d'intérêt préférentiel sur découvert* : off-prime.
au - — *de la valeur nominale* : « premium ».

destinataire (m) : addressee, consignee, payee, recipient.
— *d'un envoi de fonds* : remittee.

destination (f) : destination.
[J] — *du père de famille* : easements, charges on real property, set up by the previous owner.
immeuble par — : (landlord's) fixtures.

destituer (v) : to dismiss.

destitution (f) : dismissal.

désuétude (f) : disuse, desuetude, obsolescence.
[J] *loi tombée en* — : law fallen into abeyance, obsolete.

détacher (v) : to cut off, to detach, to tear out.
coupon **détaché** : ex coupon.

détail (m) : detail, particular.
[A] internal economy.
[C] *commerce de* − : retail trade.
les − *(s) d'un compte* : the items of an account.
indiquer tous les − *(s)* : to give full particulars.

détaillant (m) : retailer.

détaxation (f) : reduction, remission of tax.

détaxe (f) : remission, drawback of tax.

détaxé (a) : free of tax, duty free.

détaxer (v) : to take the duty (tax) off.

détenir (v) : to hold, to detain.
− *des titres (en garantie)* : to hold securities, stock (as security).
− *une part du marché* : to hold a shave of the market.

détenteur (m) : holder, custodian, owner of copyright.
[J] *tiers* − : third party holding disputed property, mortgaged land, etc.
[C] − *d'un compte* : account holder.

détention (f) : [J] 1° precarious possession, tenure.
2° detention, imprisonment, confinement.
− *arbitraire* : illegal detention.
− *provisoire (préventive)* : detention under remand.

détenu (m) : prisoner.
[J] − *condamné* : condemned prisoner.
− *préventif* : prisoner under remand.

déterminer (v) : to ascertain, to determine.
− *le revenu imposable* : to assess taxable income.

détournement (m) : embezzlement, misappropriation of funds.
− *d'avion* : hijacking.
[J] − *de fonds* : wrongful conversion, embezzlement, misappropriation of funds.
− *de fonds publics* : fraudulent misuse of public funds.
− *de mineurs* : abduction of minors.
− *de pièces* : diversion of documents.
détourner *des fonds* : to convert funds to one's own use, to embezzle funds.

détriment (m) : detriment.
au − *de* : at the expense of, to the detriment of.

dette (f) : debt.
[J] − *propre* : debt recoverable on the personal property of husband or wife.
[C] − *(s) actives* : debts owed to us, book debts ranking as assets, accounts receivable.
− *à court (long) terme* : short (long)-term debt.
− *amortissable* : redeemable debt.
− *(s) exigibles* : claimable, due, outstanding, debts.
− *d'honneur* : debt of honour.
− *liquide* : liquid debt.
− *(s) passives* : debts owed by us, liabilities.
− *viagère* : life annuity (debt).
acquitter une − : to pay off a debt.
contracter une − : to incur a debt.
réclamer une − : to press for a debt.
reconnaître une − : to acknowledge a debt.
une reconnaissance de − : an I.O.U. (I owe you).
[F] *la* − *flottante* : the floating debt.
la − *inscrite, perpétuelle, consolidée* : the funded, consolidated debt.
le grand livre de la − *publique* : the national debt register.

dévalorisation (f) : 1° *(d'une monnaie)* : devaluation.
2° *(d'un bien quelconque)* : fall in value (of an asset).

développement (m) : development.
plan de − *à long terme* : corporate planning.

devers : *(garder qch. par devers soi)* to keep (sth.) in one's possession.

devis (m) : estimate, specification, tender, bill of quantities.
− *approximatif* : rough estimate.

devise *(étrangère)* (f) : (foreign) currency.
− *qui s'échange librement* : free currency.

devoir (v) *[forme d'insistance et tournure impersonnelle]* : *les sommes suivantes* **doivent** *être incluses* : there shall be included the following amounts.

dévolution (f) : [J] devolution, transmission of rights or property.
− *d'un héritage à l'Etat* : escheat.

diagramme (m) *comparatif des ventes nouvelles* : bar chart.

dichotomie *(des honoraires)* (f) : feesplitting (between doctors, lawyers, ...).

diffamation (f) : defamation.
− *orale* : slander.
écrit **diffamatoire**, *libelle* : libel.

différend (m) : difference, dispute, disagreement.
partager le − : to split the difference.
vider, trancher un − : to settle a difference.

différentiel (a) : différentiel.
− *d'intérêt* : interest rate differential.
− *de rendement* : yield differential.

différer (v) : *(un jugement)* to defer, to postpone, *(un paiement)* to put off, to hold over.
− *l'échéance d'un effet* : to let a bill lie over.
frais, paiements **différés** : deferred charges, payments.

difficulté (f) : difficulty, trouble.
entreprise en − : ailing firm.

dilatoire (a et m) : (a) dilatory.
manœuvre − : delaying trick.
[J] *exception* −, *(m)* − : dilatory exception.
moyen − : sham plea.

diligence (f) : diligence, industry, application, despatch.
faire − : to hurry, to make haste.
[J] proceedings.
faire ses −*(s) contre qn* : to institute proceedings against s.o.
à la − *des parties* : action to be taken by anyone of the contending parties.

diligenter *(une enquête)* (v) : to examine witnesses.

diminution (f) : 1° *(de valeur)* decrease (in value), lessening.
2° *(rabais)* reduction, allowance, rebate.
accorder une − : to allow a rebate.
diminuer : to decrease.

diplômé (m) : graduate.

dire (m et v) : statement, assertion.
[J] allegation.
− *le droit* : to state the legal position, to pass a judgment.
−*(s) et observations* : statements and remarks.
selon les −*(s) du témoin* : according to witness.
à − *d'expert* : according to expert opinion, at a valuation.

direct (a) : direct.
descendant en ligne −*(e)* : direct descendant.
émission en − *(radio, T.V.)* : live broadcast (radio, T.V.).
impôts −*(s)* : assessed taxes, direct taxes.
investissements −*(s)* : direct investment.

directeur (m) : director, manager, leader, *(d'une affaire commerciale, d'une administration, etc.)* head, *(d'une prison)* governor, warden, *(d'un journal)* editor.
− *général de société* : chief executive.
−*-gérant* : managing director.
− *technique* : technical manager.
[J] − *des créanciers (syndic de faillite)* : receiver, inspector, trustee in bankruptcy.

direction (f) : 1° *(d'une entreprise etc.)* management.
2° *(administration)* administration.
− *du budget* : Budget Division.
comité de − *(d'une entreprise)* : managing committee (of a firm).
− *de la comptabilité publique* : Division of Public Account.
− *des douanes* : Division of Customs.
− *générale des impôts (D.G.I.)* : General Tax Division.

directive (f) : [E.E.C.] directive.

directives (f pl) : directions.

dirigeants (m et a) : (m) *(d'une entreprise)* manager, executive, leader.
(a) *les classes* −*(es)* : the ruling classes, [U.K.] the establishment.

diriger (v) : 1° *(sens général)* to direct.
2° *(une entreprise)* to manage (an enterprise, a firm), to operate.

dirigisme (m) : planned economy, planning.

dirimant (a) : [J] nullifying (circumstances, clauses).

disagio (m) : depreciation, diminution, drop in value (opp. *agio*).

discontinu (a) : discontinuous.
possession −*(e)* : discontinuous possession.

discontinuation de poursuites (f) : cessation from prosecution.

discontinuer (v) : to discontinue.

discrétion (f) : discretion, prudence, circumspection, secrecy.
à la − *de (qn)* : at (s.o.'s) disposal.
à − : unconditionally.

discrétionnaire (a) : discretionary.
[J] *pouvoir* − : full powers to act (see also *pouvoir*).
[A] discretionary (power).

discrimination *(fiscale)* (f) : (tax) discrimination.
sans − : indiscriminate.

discriminatoire (a) : discriminatory.

disculpation (f) : exculpation, exoneration.
se disculper de : to clear oneself of.

discussion (f) : discussion, debate.
[J] — *de biens* : enquiry into the assets of a debtor.
— *(s) salariales à l'échelle nationale* : national pay bargaining.
document servant de base à une — : discussion paper.
sans division ni — : jointly and severally.

discutable (a) : arguable, debatable.

discuter *(un débiteur)* (v) : to discuss, to sell up (a debtor).
— *sérieusement d'une affaire* : to get down to brass and tacks.

disjoindre *(affaires)* (v) : to sever (cases).

disjonction (f) : separation.
[J] severance (of causes).

dispache (f) : [ASS] average, adjustment.

dispacheur (m) : averager, average, adjuster, stater (also *commissaire-répartiteur*).

dispense (f) : exemption, waiver.
— *d'âge* : waiving of age limit.

disponible (a) : available.
[J] *biens* —(s), *portion* — *par testament, quotité* — *de la succession* : disposable portion of property.
[F] *capital* — : spare capital.
[B] *marché du* — : spot market.
le — *(actif* —*)* : available (liquid) assets.

disponibilité (f) : ready money, abilities.
être en — : to be unattached, on half-pay.

disposant *(d'une rente)* (m) : settlor (of an annuity).

disposer (v) : 1° *(de)* to have at one's command (disposal).
2° *(que)* to prescribe, to enjoin, to provide (that), to provide for.

dispositif (m) : disposition, order of things.
[J] — *du jugement, de la loi* : enacting terms of a judgment, of a statute.
— *de jugement* : terms of judgment submitted to court by agreement of the parties.
— *des statuts* : purview.

disposition (f) : 1° disposal, disposition, arrangement, design.
mettre à la — *de qn* : to put at the disposal of s.o., to make available to s.o.
2° *(d'une loi, etc.)* provisions (of an act, etc.) order, prescription.
— *(s) du Code des Impôts* : provisions of the Tax Code.
— *(s) diverses* : miscellaneous provisions.
— *(s) générales* : general rules.
— *du droit de propriété d'un bien* : settlement.
— *à vue* : sight draft.
les — *(s) du marché* : the tone of the market.
— *(s) d'un testament* : dispositions, clauses, devises of a will.
sauf — *contraire* : unless provided otherwise, unless I hear to the contrary.
prendre des — *(s)* : to make arrangements, to provide for.

dissimulation *(d'actif, de bénéfices)* (f) : concealment (of assets, of profits).

dissolution *(d'une société)* (f) : dissolution, winding up (of a company), *(de mariage)* annulment (of marriage), *(du Parlement)* dissolution (of Parliament).

dissoudre (v) : to dissolve, to wind up.

distinct (a) : distinct, separate.
imposition —*(e)* : separate taxation.

distraction (f) : 1° division, severance.
2° misappropriation of funds, supplies.
[J] — *des dépens* : award of costs to the solicitor of the winning party.
demande en — *de biens saisis* : request to divert from execution some of the attached property.
— *par contribution* : adjudication of dividend to creditors in bankruptcy.

distribution (f) : apportioning, delivery.
[J] adjudication of bankrupt's debts.
[C] — *de probabilités* : risk profile.
distribuer : to distribute, to market (food).

dit (m) : [J] written assertion of facts.
ledit, ladite : the said.

divergence (f) : divergence.
indicateur des —*(s) des monnaies (par rapport à l'ECU)* : divergence indicator.
limite de — *à partir de laquelle l'intervention devient obligatoire* : divergence limit.

divers *(droits)* (a) : miscellaneous (duties).

diversification (f) *brutale* : drastic diversification.

divertissement (m) : [J] misappropriation by a coheir (or a spouse) of property belonging to a succession or to the communal estate.

dividende (m) : dividend.
[J] — *concordataire :* dividend amount payable upon each franc of a bankrupt's-liabilities.
— *cumulatif :* cumulative dividend.
— *(s) disbribués :* distributed dividends.
[F] — *provisoire :* interim dividend.
second — *:* superdividend.
solde de — *:* final dividend.
action de — *(de jouissance) :* dividend share, junior stock.

diviser (v) : 1° *(sens général)* to divide (into). 2° *(en parts)* to split, to share.

division (f) : division, partition, splitting.

divorce (m) : divorce.
demande en — *:* petition for divorce.
demander le — *:* to sue for divorce.
intenter une action en — *:* to take divorce proceedings.

dock (m) : dock.
[A] *droits de* — *:* dock dues.
[D] [C] warehouse.

document (m) : document, bill of lading, invoice, insurance policy, attestation, bill, share, material.
— *d'achat :* purchase vouchers.
— *(s) contre paiement :* documents against payment.
— *probant :* conclusive evidence in writing.
— *(s) remis sous réserve d'acceptation :* documents against acceptance.
— *(s) de bord :* ship's papers.

documentaire *(crédit)* (a) : banker's credit for payment against documents.
effet, traite — *:* draft with documents attached.

doit (m) : [C] debit, liability.
— *et avoir :* debit and credit.

dol (m) : [J] (dolus) deceit, deception, fraud, false representation, fraudulent misrepresentation.
— *éventuel :* (dolus eventualis) intended scheme, action whose results may knowingly prove illicit.
— *incident :* (dolus incidens) fraud pertaining to accessories of a contract, without which the victim would not have contracted under the same conditions.
— *principal :* inducing the victim to contract under false pretences.

dollar (m) : dollar.
pénurie de —*(s) :* dollar gap.
surabondance de — *(s) :* dollar glut.

dolosif (a) : fraudulent.
intention **dolosive** : (civ.) intention to wrong s.o. (cr.) intention to injure interests protected by law.

doléances (f) : grievances.
exprimer des — *:* to state (one's) grievances.

domaine (m) : domain, real estate, property.
— *public, domaine de l'Etat :* public property.
— *forestier :* national forest.
revenu des —*(s) :* revenue from state-owned property.
chose dans le — *public :* thing in common use and not coverable by patent.
ouvrage tombé dans le — *public :* work out of copyright, work in public domain.
[J] demesne.

domicile (m) : dwelling place, home.
[J] domicile (place of principal establishment, not of actual residence as in A.A. law).
— *d'affaires :* business centre.
— *civil :* place where a person exercices his civil rights.
— *conjugal :* domicile of a married couple (the husband's).
— *de droit, légal :* domicile assigned by law to certain persons not in full possession of civil rights (minor, prodigal, lunatic, convict under judicial disability).
— *élu :* address for service.
— *réel (personnel) :* place of abode, residence.
— *social :* registered office.
élire — *(dans un endroit) :* to elect (for legal purposes) one's domicile (somewhere).
réintégrer son — *:* to resume possession of one's domicile, to return home.
sans — *fixe :* with no fixed abode.
violation de — *:* trespass quod clausum fregit, violation of the privacy of a person's home.
franco à — *:* carriage paid.
payable à — *:* at address of payer.
travailler à — *:* home worker.
visite **domiciliaire** : search of a house by a magistrate.

domiciliation (f) : [C] domiciliation (bill at banker's, etc.).
domiciliataire : person, bank, etc. where a bill is domiciliated.

domicilié (a) : domiciled, established.

dommage (m) : damage, injury.
—*(s)-intérêts, dommages et intérêts :* damages, award.
— *(s) de guerre :* war damages.
actionner, poursuivre, en —*(s)-intérêts :* to sue for damages.

obtenir des − *(s)-intérêts* : to recover damages, award.
− *corporel* : bodily injury.
− *(s) matériels* : damages to property, material damages.
être passible, tenu de − *(s)-intérêts* : to be liable for damages.
− *(s) d'ordre mental ou physique subis par X.* : mental or physical injury to So and so.
réparer les − *(s)* : to repair the damages.

dommageable (a) : prejudicial.
acte − : tort.

donation (f) : [J] donation, bequest.
− *entre vifs* : disposition inter vivos.
acte de − *entre vifs* : deed of gift.
− *par personne interposée* : donation through an intermediary.

donataire (m) : donee.

donateur (m) : donor.

donnée (f) : datum, (pl) data.
traitement des − *(s)* : data processing.

donneur *(de caution)* (m) : guarantor.
− *d'ordre (d'achat ou de vente) en bourse* : principal (stock exchange).

dont : from.
[B] option rate.

dormant *(capital)* (a) : improductive (capital).

dos (m) : back.
renvoyer les parties − *à* − : to dismiss both parties unsuited.

dossier (m) : documents, file (relating to an affair), record (of official, prisoner, etc.).
avoir un − *lourdement chargé* : to have a very bad record.
[J] − *d'une procédure* : brief, demurrerbook.
réunir le − *d'une affaire* : to brief a case.
joindre une pièce au − : to file a document.
− *permanent* : continuing audit file (C.A.F.).
[F] holding.

dot (f) : dowry, dower, marriage-portion.
[J] *régime* **dotal** *(abrogé en France)* : antenuptial settlement in trust for the married woman.
apport dotal : dowry brought by a spouse.

dotation (f) : *(fondation)* foundation, *(de fonds)* appropriation.
[F] − *aux amortissements* : capital allowance.

doter (v) : 1° *(de moyens)* to endow (with means).
2° *(de matériel)* to equip (with plant).
− *une fondation (d'une somme)* : to appropriate (a sum) to a fund, to endow an institution.

douaire (m) : [J] widow's dower, marriage settlement in favour of wife.

douane (f) : [D] customs.
Administration des − *(s)* : Customs Administration, the Board of Customs, the Customs Authorities.
bureau de − : custom-house, station.
carnet de passage en − : international customs pass.
déclaration en − : bill of entry.
déclaration en − *à la sortie* : clearance.
droits de − : duties.
exempt des droits de − : duty-free.
franc de − : duty paid.
marchandises en − : bonded goods.
passer des marchandises en −, *remplir les formalités de la* − : to effect custom clearance.
visite de la − : custom's examination.

douanier (m) : custom-house officer, customs officer.

douanier *(tarif)* (a) : customs, tariff.
barrières **douanières** : tariff walls.
union douanière : customs union.

double (a) : double.
− *étalon monétaire* : double monetary standard.
− *imposition* : double taxation.
− *option (* − *prime)* : put and call.
comptabilité en partie − : double entry bookkeeping.
− *emploi* : duplication.
en − *exemplaire* : in duplicata.
faire − *emploi* : to overlap.

doute (m) : doubt, misgiving, uncertainty.
[J] *acquittement au bénéfice du* − : acquittal on benefit of the doubt.
le − *profite à l'accusé* : in dubio pro reo.

douteux (a) : doubtful.
créances **douteuses** : bad (doubtful) debts.

Dow Jones *(indice)* : [B] Dow Jones Industrial Average.

dresser *(procès verbal)* (v) : to draw up (a report).

droit (m) : 1° law.
− *administratif* : administrative law (law governing the relations between public authorities and citizens or private body corporates).

— *aérien* : air law.
— *de change, cambiaire* : law on negotiable instruments.
— *civil* : civil law.
— *coercitif* : coercive law.
— *commercial* : business, commercial, mercantile law, law merchant.
— *commun* : ordinary law, rule.
— *comparé* : comparative law.
— *constitutionnel* : constitutional law.
— *conventionnel* : contractual provisions.
— *coutumier* : common law.
— *criminel, pénal* : criminal law, Crown law.
— *dispositif* : yielding law.
— *écrit* : statutory law.
— *électoral* : election law.
— *fiscal* : fiscal law.
— *foncier* : ground law.
— *des gens* : law of nations.
— *international privé* : private international law, law of conflicts.
— *international public* : public international law.
— *judiciaire* : adjective law.
— *maritime* : maritime law, admiralty law, navigation law.
— *militaire* : military law.
— *des obligations* : law of contract.
— *positif* : substantive law.
— *public* : public law.
— *romain* : roman law.
— *rural* : rural law.
— *des sociétés* : corporation law.

2° right (mostly in pl).
— *d'accès* : right of access.
— *(s) accessoires* : appurtenances.
— *d'accroissement* : accretion, right of a heir to the lapsed portion of a coheir.
— *acquis* : vested interests.
— *d'affouage* : common of estovers.
— *d'aînesse* : birthright.
— *d'asile* : privilege of sanctuary.
— *d'association* : right of association.
— *attaché* : cum dividend, (security) cum coupon.
— *d'auteur* : copyright.
— *des belligérants* : right of belligerents.
— *(s) de cité* : freedom of a city.
— *(s) civils* : civil, civic right.
— *(s) civiques* : political rights.
— *de communication* : right (of litigants) to discovery.
— *(s) compensateurs* : countervailing duties.
— *(s) constitutionnels* : rights under the constitution.
— *corporel* : chose in possession.
— *de la défense* : rights of the defendant, of counsel for defence.
— *de deshérence, d'épave, de naufrage* : escheat.
— *détaché* : ex dividend, (security) ex-coupon.
— *de distraction* : right to division, severance.

— *d'émission* : exclusive right of note issue (of the Bank of France).
— *d'emption* : right of emption.
— *d'ester en jugement* : capacity to appear (in court).
— *d'ester en justice* : capacity to sue.
— *d'établissement* : permission to establish oneself in a foreign country.
— *d'évocation* : right of a higher court to summon a case pending below, writ of certiorari.
— *de gage* : possessory lien.
— *de grâce* : right of free pardon (exercised by the President of the Republic).
— *(s) de l'homme* : human rights.
— *de jouissance* : a) right of undisturbed possession, b) right (on a date) to dividends and interests (see *droit attaché, détaché*).
— *de la masse* : right of the general body of creditors in bankruptcy.
— *(s) mobiliers* : intangible property, assets, choses in action.
— *de pacage* : grazing rights.
— *de passage* : right of way.
— *de préemption* : right of pre-emption.
— *de préférence, priorité* : preferential, priority right.
— *de prise* : right of warlike capture.
— *de rachat, réméré* : right of repurchase.
— *(s) réels (à l'exception du droit de propriété)* : chattels real.
— *régalien, de souveraineté* : sovereign rights.
— *de regard* : right of inspection.
— *de reproduction* : copyright.
— *résolutoire* : resolutory right, right to enter an action for defeasance.
— *de rétention* : possessory lien.
— *de réunion* : right of assembly.
— *de suite* : indefeasible rights of mortgagee pertaining to mortgaged estate, even if ownership changes.
— *(s) de tirage spéciaux* : special drawing rights.
— *d'usage* : user.
— *de vaine pâture, de pâturage* : right of common, commonage.
— *(s) de vente exclusifs* : sole selling rights.
— *de visite* : right of visit and search.
— *de vote* : franchise (a right to elect a M.P.).

3° charge, dues, duty, fee (mostly in pl).
— *d'auteur* : royalties.
— *de bassin* : dock dues.
— *de chancellerie* : chancellery dues.
— *de consommation* : excise duties.
— *de commission* : brokerage, commission.
— *de douane* : custom duties, customs (duties).
— *(s) d'émission* : tax on issues.
— *(s) d'exécution* : performing rights (in music).

— *d'enregistrement* : registry fee.
— *d'entrée* : import duty.
— *de garde, de dépôt* : custody charge.
— *de greffe* : clerk of the court's dues.
— *de recommandation* : registration fee.
— *d'inscription* : entrance fee.
— *(s) (frais) judiciaires, de justice* : court-costs.
— *de magasinage* : storage, warehouse dues.
— *de mouillage* : berthage, keelage.
— *de mutation* : transfer taxes.
— *de mutation entre vifs* (inter vivos) :
a) *à titre onéreux* : (for valuable consideration) estate duty.
b) *à titre gracieux* : (by deed-poll) gift tax.
— *de mutation après décès* (after death) : inheritance tax, estate duty, legacy tax, probate duty.
— *de navigation* : shipping dues.
— *de passage* : ferry dues.
— *des pauvres* : entertainment tax.
— *de péage* : toll tax.
— *de port* : harbour rates, wharfage, port dues.
— *de rachat* : equity of redemption.
— *(s) de représentation* : dramatic fees, performing rights (in dramatic or dramatico-musical work).
— *de sortie* : export duty.
— *de succession* : succession duty.
— *de succession par testament* : probate duty.
— *de surestarie* : demurrage.
— *de timbre* : stamp duty.
— *de voirie* # Road Fund tax.
— *(s) voisins (des droits d'auteur)* : fees of performers, record manufacturers and broadcasting organisations.

4° *abus de* — : misuse of law, of process.
avoir — *à qch* : to have a right to sth.
pour avoir — *(au paiement)* : to qualify (for payment).
avoir le —, *être en* — *de faire qch.* : to be entitled to do sth.
à bon — : with good reason.
à qui de — : to whom it may concern.
conférer un — *à qn* : to bestow a right on s.o.
de plein — : ipso jure.
donner — : to confer title.
être dans son — : to be within one's rights.
exercer un — : to exercice a right.
faire — *à une demande* : to accede to a request, to allow a claim.
faire valoir son — : to put in a claim, to enforce one's right.
grevé d'un — : encumbered.
justifier son — : to show title.
liquider des —*(s)* : to indemnify s.o. for his rights.

marchandises passibles, assujetties aux —*(s), exemptes de* —*(s)* : dutiable goods, duty-free goods.
outrepasser ses —*(s)* : to go beyond one's rights.
s'adresser à qui de — : to apply to the proper quarter.
règle de — *strict* : unescapable legal rule, law, provision.
responsable en — : legally responsible.
sans — : unlawfully.
sauvegarder un — : to protect a right.
sous les peines de — : encurring penalties, under pains, provided, stipulated by law.
taux des —*(s)* : rate of duties, taxes.
par voies de — : by legal process.

5° *droit de vote (dans une société)* : the voting power (in a company).

dû, due (a et m) : due, owing.
en port — : carriage forward.
en temps — : in due time.
exiger son — : to claim one's due.
contrat en bonne et — *forme* : contract drawn up in due form, formal contract.
somme — : amount due.

ducroire (m) : [C] del credere, guarantee-commission or agent.

dudit : thereof.

duplicata (m) : duplicata, double.
[J] second exemplar of a deed which, unlike a *copie*, is accepted as an original draft.
[C] *(deuxième de change)* : second of exchange.

duplique (f) : [J] (defendant's) rejoinder.

durable (a) : durable, lasting, standing.
biens de consommation — : durables, durable goods, consumer durable goods.
accord — : standing agreement.

durant : 1° during ; 2° *(d'un bout à l'autre de l'année)* throughout the year.

durée (f) : *(sens général)* duration, *(d'un séjour)* period of (a) stay, *(d'un bail)* term of (a) lease, *(du travail)* hours of labour.
— *moyenne d'investissement* : average period of investment.
— *d'utilisation d'un bien* : useful line, guideline life.
tableau de — *d'utilisation des biens (amortissement)* : guideline.

dynamique (a et f) : (a) dynamic.
économie – : dynamic economics.
fixation – *du cours du change* : dynamic peg of the exchange rate.
(f) dynamics.

NOTES

NOTES

E

eau (f) : water.
[A] *(administration des) − (x) et forêts* : waterways and forestry department.
service des − (x) : water supply.

écart *(inflationniste)* (m) : (inflationary) gap.
− *d'inflation, différentiel d'inflation* : inflation gap.
− *minimum des cours du marché* : tick.
− *des primes* : [B] difference between the price for firm and option stock.
− *des prix* : cost variance.
− *(qui se creuse) entre le taux d'inflation et les tranches d'imposition* : bracket creep.

échange (m) : exchange, (troc) barter.
− *de monnaies différentes* : swap, back-to-back loans.
en − : in exchange.
libre − : free trade.
valeur d'− : exchange value.
échangiste : exchanger.

échantillon (m) : *(de vin)* sample, *(de tissu,* etc.) pattern, *(d'un travail)* specimen.
[C] *conforme à l'−* : up to sample.
− *aléatoire* : probability (random) sample.
− *témoin* : check sample.
échantillonnage : sampling.

échéance (f) : *(de paiement)* date, *(d'un effet)* term, falling due, maturity, maturity date.
[C] *billet, à longue, à courte −* : long-dated, short-dated, bill.
échu : outstanding, past date.
billets échus : bills overdue.
intérêts échus : outstanding interests.
intérêts à échoir : accruing interests.
papier à − : bill to mature.
[F] *emprunt à courte, à longue −* : short-term, long-term loan.
faire face à une − : to meet a bill.

échéancier (m) : [C] bill-book.

échéant (a) : falling due.

échelle (f) : ladder, scale.
− *des prix* : scale of prices.
− *mobile des salaires, des traitements* : sliding scale of wages, of salaries, cost of living adjustment, [U.S.] escalator clause.
− *sociale* : social ladder (scale).
économie d'− : economics of scale (of mass production).

échelonner (v) : to spread out, to stagger.
− *des paiements, sur un certain nombre de mois* : to spread out payments over a certain number of months.
versements échelonnés : payments by instalments.
s'− (de... à) : to range (from... to).

échoir (v) : to fall due, to mature.
billets échus : bills overdue.
intérêts échus : outstanding interest.
intérêts à − : accruing interest.

éclaircissement (m) : elucidation.
[F] *demande d'−(s)* : elucidation question, inquiry.

éconduction d'instance (f) : [J] non suit, billa cassetur.

économie (f) : 1° saving(s), thrift, sparingness, 2° economy, 3° *(science)* Economics.
1° − *de temps* : saving of time.
2° − *dirigée* : controlled economy.
− *dirigiste (planifiée)* : planned economy.
− *de marché* : market economy.
3° − *en voie de développement* : developing economics.
− *appliquée, mathématique* : (applied, mathematical) economics.
− *de l'environnement* : environmental economics.
− *de la santé* : health economics.
micro-(macro)- − : micro-(macro)-economics.

économique (a) : 1° *(peu cher)* cheap, economical, inexpensive, 2° economic.
analyse, pensée, politique, théorie − : economic analysis, thought, policy, theory.
prévision − : business forecasting.
reprise − : industrial, trade recovery.
économiquement *faible* : poor person.
[J] pauper.

économiser (v) : to save.

économiste (m) : economist.

écrit (a et m) : document, writing.
par − : in writing.
[J] *droit −* : statute law.

écriture (f) : legal, commercial, paper, document, record.
[J] *faux en −(s)* : forged deed, tampering

with registers, false entry.
[C] entry, item.
— (s) comptables: books.
— (s) en partie double: double entry.
commis aux — (s), aide-comptable: bookkeeper.
passer les — (s): to post the books.

écrou (m): [J] entry on prison calendar of receipt of prisoner into custody.
levée d'— : discharge from prison, release of prisoner.
livre d'— : prison calendar, [U.S.] blotter.
ordre d'— : committal to gaol.
écrouer qn: to commit, to consign s.o. to prison.
écroué au dépôt: run in.

écu (unité monétaire européenne): European Currency Unit.

édicter (v): to enact, to decree.

édifice (m) social (l'): social structure (the).

édile (m): town counsellor.

éditeur (m): publisher.
[J] — responsable: person responsible at law for the contents of publications (for newspapers: gérant responsable).
droits d'**édition**: publishing rights.
le juge ordonne l'édition des pièces: order by judge to discover documents.
éditorial: leading article in a newspaper.

effectif (a et m): (a) effective, actual, (m) staff, personnel, manpower, (m pl), [U.S.] manning.
(m) — au complet: full force (of men).
(a) bénéfice — : effective income.
coût — : actual cost.
francs — (s): cash.
résidence **effective**: actual residence.
valeur effective: actual value.

effectivement (adv): actually.

effectuer (v): (un calcul) to make a calculation, (des dépenses) to incur expenses, (des réparations) to make repairs, (des transactions commerciales) to carry on business dealings.
s'effectuer (paiement): to be effected, made (payment).

effet (m): effect, result.
[J] 1° — (s) de droit: legal effects.
— constitutif: constituting effect (e.g. registration of a mortgage).
— déclaratif: stating the legal position (e.g. affiliation of a bastard).
— libératoire: release from a liability (e.g. paying a debt).
— pécuniaire: pecuniary effect.
— quant au fond: fact having a bearing on the merits of a case.
— quant à la forme: formal effect.
— réel: material effect.
— rétroactif: ex post facto, retrospective effect.
— résolutoire: resolutive effect.
— de revenu: income effect.
— de snobisme: snob effect.
— suspensif: suspensive effect.
— transitoire: transient, temporary, transitory effect.
avoir, porter, produire — : to come into force, effect, operation, to become operative.
donner — : to give effect.
mettre à — : to carry into effect.
de nul — : of no effect.
prendre — : to take effect, to become operative, to be put into force.
sans — : ineffective, of no avail.
2° — (s), — (s) mobiliers: possessions, belongings, personal effects, clothes; goods and chattels.
[C] —, — de commerce: negotiable instrument, bill, trade paper.
— bancable: bill discountable.
— (traite) de cavalerie, de complaisance: accommodation bill.
— (s) de change: bills of exchange.
— déplacé (opp. effet bancable): bill undiscountable.
— (s) à payer: bills payable.
— (s) personnels laissés par testament: effects left by bequest.
— (s) à recevoir: receivables, bills receivable.
— à renouvellement (de complaisance): kite, windmill.
— à vue: sight draft, draft at sight.
[F] — (s) publics: gilt-edged securities, Government or public corporation stock, public bonds.
— au porteur: bearer stock, bearer securities.
— nominatif: registered stock.
avaliser, cautionner un — : to guarantee, to back a bill.
créer, tirer un — : to draw a bill.
endosser un — : to indorse a bill.
protester un —, lever protêt d'un — : to protest a bill.
renouveler un — : to renew a bill.
signer un — : to sign a bill.
(see alsol lettre de change, traite).

efficacité (f): efficiency.

efficience (f): effectiveness.

effondrement (m) (des prix, etc.): collapse (of prices, etc.).
s'**effondrer**: to collapse.

le marché s'est effondré : the bottom has fallen out of the market.

effraction (f) : house-breaking.
[J] trespass quod clausum fregit, breach of close, breaking and entering.
vol avec — : burglary.

égal à (a) : equal to.

égalisation (f) : equalization.
fonds d'— des changes : currency equalization fund.

égalité (f) : par, parity.
— *devant l'impôt :* equality before taxation.

(eu) égard à : taking into account, consistent with.

élargissement (m) : [J] release (of prisoner).

élasticité *(de la demande)* (f) : elasticity (of demand).

élection (f) : election, polling.
[J] *droit électoral (actif) :* franchise.
faire — de domicile : to elect domicile.

élément (m) : element, datum.
[J] —*(s) constitutifs de délit :* factors that constitute an offence : 1° — *matériel :* the facts of the case (So-and-so has been a party to the offence), 2° — *moral :* moral factor (exitence of malice), 3° — *légal :* legal factor (So-and-so's action is deemed an offence and punishable in law), 4° — *injuste :* unjust handling (So-and-so's action is not justified by a right. If so, it might be only a technical offence : e.g. killing a human being in self-defence).
[F] — *de l'actif immobilisé :* capital assets.
—*(s) d'actif incorporel :* intangible assets.
—*(s) déductibles :* deductions, deductions allowed.
— *indirect du prix de revient (ex. loyer, entretien des locaux...) :* indirect cost.
— *du revenu :* item of income.
—*(s) du train de vie :* elements of the standard of living.

élevage (m) **intensif** : battery farming.

élever (v) : *(un enfant)* to bring up, to foster, to rear, *(du bétail)* to raise, to breed, *(des protestations)* to raise.
1° *les difficultés se sont élevées :* difficulties arose.
2° *le compte s'élève à 10 000 F :* the bill amounts to, come to 10 000 F.

éligible (a) : eligible.

élire (v) : to elect.

éluder (v) :
— *le paiement de l'impôt :* to evade payment of tax.

émancipation (f) : emancipation.
[J] — *de mineur :* emancipation of a minor.

émargement (m) : *(d'un compte)* initialling, statement, return, etc., *(donner reçu du salaire)* signing pay-roll, *(attester sa présence)* signing time-sheet.
feuille d'— : pay sheet, time sheet.
émarger au budget de l'Etat : to be on Government pay, to be an official.

emballage (m) : packing.
— *non consigné :* non-returnable packing.
— *vide :* empty packing material, empties.
— *publicitaire :* flash pack.

embargo (m) : embargo.
mettre l'— sur un navire : to lay an embargo on a ship.

embauche (f) : engaging of workmen, hiring.
embaucher : to engage, to hire, to take on (workers).

émetteur *(d'actions)* (m) : issuer (of shares).

émettre (v) : to issue.
— *un chèque :* to issue (make out) a cheque.
— *un emprunt :* to float a loan.

émission (f) : emission.
[J] — *de fausse monnaie :* uttering.
[F] *(de billets de banque, etc.)* issue, issuing, *(un emprunt)* floating.
cours, prix d'— : floating price.
droit d'— : privilege of the Bank of France to issue banknotes.
droits d'— : tax on issues.
— *entièrement souscrite :* entirely subscribed issue (loan).
[C] — *publicitaire :* commercial.

emmagasiner (v) : to store, to warehouse.

émolument (m) : [J] portion of inheritance.
[A] perquisites of officials.
émoluments (m pl) : emoluments, salary, remuneration, fees.
[J] taxed charges, as distinct from fees, of *officiers ministériels,* for acting in their official capacity, conduct-money of witness, fees of experts.

empêchement (m) : hindrance, impediment, prevention.
en cas d' — : in case of prevention.
[J] — *au mariage :* diriment impediment.
empêcher *(entraver) :* to impede.

emphytéose (f) **ou bail emphytéotique :** [J] long lease (up to 99 years).
redevance **emphytéotique :** long lease rent.
emphytéote : lessee, holder of a long lease.

empiéter (v) : to encroach upon, to overlap.
— *sur le terrain, l'autorité de qn :* to encroach upon (on) s.o.'s land, authority.
— *sur les droits de qn :* to infringe s.o.'s rights.

emploi (m) : *(de qch.)* use, employment, *(de qn)* appointment, assignment, employment, job, occupation, post.
au titre d'un — *antérieur :* in consideration of past employment.
employé : employee.
employé, employée de magasin : shop-assistant, shop-girl.
—, — *(e), à la vente :* salesman, saleswoman.
— *de banque :* bank clerk.
— *des chemins de fer :* railway servant.
— *chargé du contrôle à la caisse :* checker.
employeur : employer.

empreinte (f) : impression, imprint, stamp.
— *digitale :* finger-print.

emprise (f) : emprise.
[J] land or ground acquired for public purposes.

emprisonnement (m) : imprisonment.

emprunt (m) : loan.
[F] *amortir un* — : to sink a loan.
— *amortissable :* redeemable loan.
— *consolidé :* funded debt.
— *à court moyen, long terme :* short, medium, long term loan.
— *extérieur :* foreign loan.
— *non garanti :* loan without security.
— *garanti par gage :* pledged loan.
— *hypothécaire :* mortgaged loan.
— *intérieur :* inland loan.
— *national :* national loan.
— *avec option de change :* loan redeemable in optional currency.
— *à primes :* loan with premium.
— *privé :* private loan.
— *d'Etat :* Government loan, (U.K.) British funds.
— *d'Etat réservé aux personnes du 3ᵉ âge (indexé) :* granny bond.
— *remboursable sur demande :* call loan, money.
— *sur titres :* loan on stocks (securities).
contracter un — : to raise a loan.
émettre, lancer un — : to float a loan.
rembourser un — : to return a loan.
souscrire à un — : to apply for debentures, to subscribe to a loan.
titre d'un — : loan bond, certificate.

emprunter (v) : to borrow.
— *à court terme :* to borrow short, at short term.

emprunteur (m et a) : (m) borrower, (a) borrowing.
l'Etat — : the borrowing State.

en : therefrom.
le revenu qu'un contribuable perçoit venant d'une entreprise ou d'un bien est le bénéfice qu'il en tire : a taxpayer's income from a business or a property is his profit therefrom.

encadrement (m) du crédit : credit squeeze, tightening of credit, credit rationing.

encaisse (f) : ready cash, cash in hand.
— *or de la Banque de France :* gold bullion and coin held by the Bank of France, gold reserve.
— *en devises insuffisante pour couvrir les emprunts en devises :* foreign exchange mismatching.
processus d'ajustement d' —(s) : stock adjustment mechanisms.

encaissement (m) : collection, cashing in, cash inflow.
donner un chèque à l'— : to have a cheque collected (by bank).
revenus **encaissés** *en France :* income received in France.

encaisser (v) : to collect.
— *un chèque :* to cash a cheque.

encaisseur (m) : collector, payee ; bank cashier, bank messenger.

encan (m) : public auction of movables.
mettre qch. à l'— : to put sth. up for auction.

enchères (f) : bid.
mettre, porter une — : to make a bid.
vente aux —(s) : sale by auction.
—(s) *forcées :* forced sale (by auction).
— *au rabais :* dutch auction.
aller d'— *en* — : to run up the bids.
folle — : irresponsible bit that cannot be made good.
procédure de vente sur folle — : resale at an

auction when the purchaser or highest bidder has either been unable to pay for it, or otherwise failed to fulfil the conditions.
enchérir *sur qn* : to outbid s.o.
enchérisseur : bidder.
au dernier enchérisseur : to the highest bidder.

enclore *(terrain)* (v) : to fence in (a plot of ground).

encombré *(marché)* (a) : glutted (market).

encouragements (m pl) : incentives.
– *(s) fiscaux* : tax incentives, stimuli.
– *à la production* : incentive payments.

encourir (v) : to incur.
– *un risque* : to take a chance.
– *des sanctions* : to be liable to penalties.

encours (m) *des bons du Trésor à court terme* : volume of bank bills available for exchange on the market.

endettement (m) **extérieur** : foreign indebtedness.

endommager (v) : to damage.

endos (m), **endossement** : endorsement on bill or cheque.
[J] [C] – *en blanc* : blank endorsement.
– *de complaisance* : accommodation endorsement.
– *conditionnel* : qualified endorsement.
– *de garantie*, – *pignoratif* : endorsement giving the endorsee the right of a pledge with regard to the endorsed bill.
– *restreint* : restrictive endorsement.
– *translatif* : endorsement transferring the ownership of a bill to order to the endorsee (special endorsement).
– *mandataire* : endorsee by proxy.
endossataire, endossé : endorsee.
endosser *(un effet, un chèque)* : to back (a bill, a cheque).
endosseur : endorser.

enfant (m et f) : child.
– *abandonné* : deserted, forsaken child.
– *adoptif* : adopted child.
– *assisté, trouvé* : foundling.
– *en bas âge* : infant (approximately under eight years).
– *conçu* : child unborn, en ventre sa mère, person en enter, unborn person.
– *légitime* : legitimate child.
– *mineur* : minor, under age.
– *naturel* : bastard, illegitimate child.
– *à naître* : nasciturus, future child.
– *né viable* : viable infant.
– *posthume* : posthumous child.

– *putatif* : putative child.
– *reconnu* : affiliated child.
– *supposé* : supposititious, set-up child (to displace the real heir).
[J] infant.
enfance *délinquante* : juvenile offenders, delinquency.
maison de correction, d'éducation, pour – (s) : reformatory.
rapt d' – : abduction of a minor.
sans – : childless.
suppression de part ou d' – : concealment of birth, offence by a woman concealing her pregnancy and making away with the child in order to suppress his claim to an inheritance.
traite des – (s) et des femmes : white slave traffic.

enfreindre (v) : [J] to break, to infringe, to breach, to transgress.
– *un traité* : to violate a treaty.

engagement (m) : 1° *(mise en gage)* pawning, pledging, 2° *(obligation consentie)* commitment, engagement, obligation, liability, promise, contract agreement.
– *à acheter ou à vendre à un prix fixé, à une date ultérieure* : forward contract.
– *sans réserve et sans faille* : water-tight commitment.
faire face à ses – (s) : to meet one's commitments, to carry out one's engagements, to fulfil one's obligations.
– *écrit* : written pledge.
3° *(de personnel)* engagement, indenture.
4° [J] – *d'immeuble* : temporary assignment of real property.
5° [A] – *de dépenses publiques* : expenditure for public purposes on account of future budgets, i.e. not yet appropriated, involving Government responsibility (e.g. for the five years equipment plan, budgeted yearly).
6° [F] – *de capitaux* : tying-up of capital.
(opération) qui exige l' – d'importants capitaux : capital intensive (business).
7° voluntary enlistment in the armed forces.

engager (v) : to engage, *(mettre en gage)* to pawn.
[J] *accord qui* **engage** : binding agreement.
– *des poursuites* : to institute proceedings.
– *des poursuites* : to take legal action, to sue.
[F] – *des capitaux dans une affaire* : to engage (put) capital in a business.
– *des frais* : to incur expenses.
s'engager (a) : to agree (to), to bind oneself (to).
votre réponse ne vous engage pas : your answer does not bind you.
s'engager par contrat (à faire) : to contract (to do).

enjoindre *(à qn de faire qch.)* (v) : to require (s.o. to sth.).

enlèvement (m) : removal, kidnapping, taking away.
[J] — *de mineur :* abduction.
— *à main armée :* abduction by force of arms.

en propre : in one's own right.

enquête (f) : inquiry, investigation.
— *par circulaires :* written requests for information to persons outside a company.
faire procéder à, une — sur qch. : to hold an inquiry, to inquire into sth.
[J] hearing of witnesses before trial.
— *judiciaire après mort d'homme :* inquest post mortem.
commission d'— parlementaire : board, court of inquiry, select committee. Royal commission, [U.S.] congressional investigation committee.
[A] — *de commodo et incommodo :* administrative inquiry in a neighbourhood, before giving permit to start a noisy or obnoxious trade, or to erect buildings to that purpose.
[F] —*(s) et Vérifications Nationales :* National Audit Service.
enquêter (v) : to investigate.

enrayer (v) *l'inflation* : to curb inflation.

enregistrement (m) : registration, registry; booking, entering. [J] record.
société enregistrée : incorporated company.
[A] *bureau d'— :* registry office for stamp and duties # Wills and Probate Department.
receveur de l'— : registrar.
enregistrer : to fill, to list, to register (luggage).
enregistrer une commande : to book an order.
enregistrer une perte : to carry a loss.

enrichissement (m) : enrichment.
[J] *action pour cause d'— illégitime :* action for money had and received.

enrôlement (m) : 1° [J] enrolment (on the cause-list).
2° enlistment.
enrôler *de force :* to press.

enseigne (f) : [C] sign.
— *lumineuse :* advertising lights.

ensemble (m) *des coûts à la production :* factory costs.
— (m) *des nouvelles (journaux) :* news covering.

entacher (v) : to blemish, to sully.
[J] to vitiate.
acte **entaché** *d'un vice de forme ou de fond :* act vitiated by a formal or fundamental flaw.
transaction entachée de dol : fraudulent transaction.

entamer (v) : to cut into, to open.
— *son capital :* to break into one's capital.
— *le crédit de qn :* to deal a blow to s.o.'s credit.
— *des négociations :* to open negotiations.
— *des poursuites :* to institute proceedings.

entendre (v) : to hear, to intend, to mean, to listen, to understand.
[J] *l'affaire sera entendue le... :* the case will come up for hearing on the...
« *les parties entendues* » : « the parties having stated their case ».
s'entendre avec : to agree with.

entente (f) : agreement, understanding.
— *industrielle :* cartel, combine.

entérinement (m) : [J] ratification, confirmation, by court (of an expert's report, etc.).
entériner (v) : to ratify, to confirm.

entier (a) : entire, whole.
[J] *restitution en — :* restitutio in integrum.
responsabilité —(e) : full responsability.

entièrement (adv) : wholly.
personne — à charge : wholly dependent person.

entité (f) : entity.
[J] — *de droit public :* public corporation.

entorse (f) : sprain, twist.
faire une — à la loi : to stretch the law.

en tout état de cause : whatever the situation, the legal position.

en tout temps : at any time.
mandat révocable — : mandate revocable at any time.
prêt dénonçable — : loan returnable at call.

entrave (f) : shackle, fetter.
[J] — *à la liberté de travail :* impeding of the liberty to work.
entraver *le cours de la justice :* to impede the action of law.
entraver la circulation : to hold up the traffic.
entraver une enquête : to hinder an enquiry.

entrée (f) : entry, entering, admission, admittance, way in, entrance, input.
— *en fonctions :* taking up duties.

— *en jouissance*: taking possession.
— *en séance*: opening of a meeting.
— *en vigueur*: coming into force, effect, operation, becoming enforceable, effective, operative.
[D] *droit d'—*: import duty, lease premium.
[C] *livre des —(s)*: entry-book.
— *de capitaux*: capital inflow.
« *— libre* » *(magasin)*: walk-round shop, no obligation to buy.

entrer (v): to enter.
[F] *premier entré, premier sorti* (P.E.P.S.): first in first out (F.I.F.O.).
dernier entré, premier sorti (D.E.P.S.): last in first out (L.I.F.O.).

entremetteur (m), **entremetteuse** (f): intermediary, go-between; procurer, procuress.

entreposeur (m): [A] bonder entrusted with the sale of commodities under Government monopoly (tobacco, matches and salt).

entrepositaire (m): bonder, warehouse man.

entrepôt (m): warehouse, store.
[D] *— de douane*: bonded warehouse.
— *maritime*: wharf.
marchandises en —: bonded goods.
entreposer: to bond goods.

entrepreneur (m): contractor, entrepreneur.
— *en bâtiment*: building contractor.
— *de déménagements*: furniture remover.
— *de pompes funèbres*: undertaker.
— *de transports*: carrier, forwarding agent.
fonction de l'—: firm, business entrepreneurial function.
[J] *hypothèque légale de l'—*: statutory lien of a contractor.

entreprise (f): undertaking, venture.
1° — *agricole*: farm business.
— *commerciale*: business concern.
— *concessionnaire*: concessionary company (of public services).
— *déjà installée*: on-going business.
— *en difficulté*: ailing firm.
— *industrielle*: industrial concern.
— *de navigation*: shipping company.
— *de navigation aérienne*: air transport company.
petite et moyenne — (P.M.E.): small and medium sized enterprises (SMEs).
— *en régie*: state managed industry.
— *subventionnée*: subsidized company.
— *de transports*: carrying business, forwarding company.
2° — *contre les droits de*: attempt upon the rights of.

entretien (m): *(des choses)* upkeep, maintenance, keeping in repair, in good order.
(de la famille) support, maintenance.
frais d'—: cost of maintenance.
gagner son —: to earn one's keep.
— *et réparations*: maintenance and repairs.
réparations d'—: maintenance repairs.

énumérer (v): to list.

enveloppe (f): envelope.
— *de paye*: pay envelope, packet.
— *timbrée à l'adresse (du candidat)*: stamped addressed envelope (S.A.E.).

environnement (m): environment.

envoi (m): sending, dispatch, forwarding, consignment, shipment.
date d'— par la poste: mailing date.
— *en nombre*: bulk mail.
[J] *— en possession*: vesting order, writ of possession.
[C] *lettre d'—*: covering note, letter of advice.
— *de fonds*: remittance.
envoyer *des fonds*: to remit.

envoyé (m): messenger, representative, *(du gouvernement)* envoy.
notre — spécial à: our reporter in.

épargne (f): saving(s), economy, thrift, lay-by.
bon d'—: National savings certificate, savings bond.
caisse d'—: savings bank.
dépôts d'—: savings, saving deposits.
— *forcée*: forced saving.
— *liquide*: liquid saving.
— *de précaution*: precautionary saving.
— *privée*: private saving.
esprit d'—: thrift.
livret de caisse d'—: savings bank book.
rapport — -revenu: saving-to-income ratio.

épave (f): wreck, derelict.
—*(s) d'un naufrage*: wreckage.
[J] unclaimed object, ownerless animal.
—*(s) flottantes*: flotsam.
—*(s) rejetées*: jetsam.
droit d'—: escheat.

époux (m et pl), **épouse** (f): husband, wife, consort.
[J] spouse.
les — Untel: Mr. So-and-so and wife.
communauté entre —, — communs en biens: communal estate, joint estate of husband and wife, [U.S.] community property.
— *séparés de biens*: separate estates of mar-

ried couple.

éprouver *(une perte)* (v) : to suffer (a loss).

épuisement (m) : exhaustion.
— *des ressources minières* : depletion of mineral ressources.
épuisé *(article)* : sold out, out of stock.

équilibre (m) : balance, equilibrium.
— *financier des entreprises publiques* : financial balance of public firms.
budget **équilibré** : balanced budget.
équilibrer : to balance.
— *(s')* : to balance, to poise.
le marché (s')est équilibré : the market is poised.

équipe (f) de créateurs en publicité : creative department.

équipement (m) : equipment, plant.
biens d'— : capital goods.
— *lourd* : heavy plant.
s'équiper en machines : to tool up.

équité (f) : equity.

équivalent à : equivalent to.

équivoque (sans) (f) : unequivocally.

errata (m pl) : errata (corrigenda).

errements (m pl) : erring ways, mistaken ideas.
[A] usual administrative procedure, [U.S.] action « through channels ».

erreur (f) : error, mistake, blunder.
[J] — *judiciaire* : miscarriage of justice (esp. cr., involving unjust condemnation).
— *de droit* : mistake in law.
— *de fait* : mistake in fact.
— *légère* : slight error of no account in legal matters.
— *manifeste* : unmistakable error.
— *de personne* : error in involving a wrong person in the act.
— *radicale* : fundamental error, making an act null and void.
— *sur la chose* : error incorpore.
— *sur le contrat* : error in negotio.
— *sur la personne* : diversity.
— *sur la quantité* : error in quantity.
— *sur la substance* : error in substantia.
par — : by mistake.

erroné (a) : faulty.

escale (f) : port, airport of call.

escompte (m) : [C] rebate, discount.
— *au comptant,* — *de caisse* : discount for cash.
[F] — *de banque,* — *dehors* : bank discount.
— *de facture* : trade discount.
— *officiel, le taux d'*— : bank (of France) rate (of discount).
— *en dedans* : true discount.
prendre un effet à l'— : to discount a bill of exchange.
taux d'— *pour crédits à découvert* : [U.S.] prime rate.
[B] call for delivery of securities before settlement.
escompter *un effet* : to discount a bill, to discount a draft.

escroc (m) : sharper, swindler.
— *« à l'américaine »* : con-man.

escroquerie (f) : swindle, fraud, obtaining sth. under false pretences, fraudulent representation.

espace (m) : space.
Administration pour l'Aéronautique et l'— : [U.S.] National Aeronautics and Space Administration.
— *(s) économique(s)* : economic spaces.

espèce (f) : kind, sort.
[A] *arrêt d'*— : judgment based on practical motives pertaining to a specific case, rather than on legal grounds.
un cas d'— : a specific, a concrete case.
en l'— : in this particular case.
loi applicable en l'— : law applicable to the case in point.
[F] — *(s) (monnayées)* : specie, cash, coin, hard cash.
contre — *(s)* : for a consideration, for cash.

espérance (f) mathématique : expected value.

espionnage (m) : spying.
— *industriel* : industrial spying (espionage).

essai (m) : test.
prendre à l'— : to take on trial.
vente à l'— : sale on approval.

essentiel (a) : essential.
activités — *(les) (d'une société)* : core activities, mainstream activities.

essieu (m) : axel.
taxe à l'essieu : axel tax.

essor (m) : boom.
— *économique* : trade boom.

estampille (f) : official stamp.
[C] trade-mark.
estampiller *des actions* : to stamp shares.

estarie (jours d') : [E] lay days.

ester en jugement (v) : capacity to appear.

ester en justice (v) : to go to law.
capacité d'— en justice : capacity to sue.

estimatif (a) : estimative (cost, etc.).
devis — : estimate.
état — : inventory and valuation of chattels (in view of a legal transaction).
valeur **estimative** : estimated value.

estimation (f) : *(valeur)* estimate, estimation (price, value), *(de marchandises)* appraising, valuing (of goods), *(de dommages)* assessment (of damage), rating.
— *de l'endettement possible d'un client* (de l'importance du prêt que l'on peut lui accorder) : credit rating.
— *de l'importance de l'écoute* (T.V., radio) : ratings.

estimer (v) : *(des marchandises)* to estimate, to value, to appraise, *(des dommages)* to assess, to rate.
estimateur : valuer, appraiser.

établir (v) : 1° *(s'assurer de)* to ascertain, 2° *(un compte, un bilan)* to draw up (an account, a balance-sheet).
— *une accusation* : to substantiate a charge.
— *un budget* : to draw up a budget.
— *son droit* : to establish one's rights.
— *un enfant* : to provide for one's child.
— *une facture* : to make out an invoice.
— *un fait* : to prove a fact.
— *l'identité de qn* : to establish the identity of s.o.
— *l'innocence de qn* : to establish (to prove) the innocence of s.o.
— *un plan* : to work out a plan.
— *un prix* : to fix a price.
— *une quittance* : to give a receipt in full.
— *une règle, une servitude* : to set up a rule, an easement.
— *le revenu d'un contribuable* : to ascertain a taxpayer's income.
s'établir (v) : to establish oneself, to take up one's abode in a place, to settle in business.
contribuable étranger **établi** *en France* : foreign taxpayer domiciled (established) in France.

établissement (m) : establishment, premises.
1° setting up, installing, building up, instituting, creating, forming, founding.
dépenses d'— : capital expenditure.
— *des prix de revient* : costing.
frais de premier — : initial expenses of business, organisation expenses, capital outlay.
2° institution.
— *de crédit* : bank, loan society.
— *de charité* : charity, charitable corporation, establishment.
— *pénitentiaire* : prison, [U.S.] penitentiary.
— *(reconnu) d'utilité publique* : institution officially recognized as serving the public interest.
3° taking up an abode, settling down.
[F] *lieu du principal —* : regular and established place of business.
[J] *droit d'—* : right granted to an alien to fix his residence in the country (mostly under a treaty).
4° — *(d'un formulaire)* : completion of a form.

étalage (m) : display, show (of goods).
— *destiné à faire impression* : window-dressing.
étalagiste : window-dresser.

étalement *(paiements, vacances)* (m) : spreading out.
étaler *(vacances, paiements)* : to stagger.

étalon (m) : standard (of weights, measures, make, value, etc.).
[F] — *-or lingot* : gold bullion standard.
— *de change-or* : gold exchange standard.

Etat (m) : the State.
les —(s) contractants : Contracting States.
— *monarchique, républicain* : monarchic, republican form of government.
confédération d'—(s) : confederation of sovereign States.
affaire d'— : affair of State, of the highest political importance.
le chef de l'— : the head of the State.
le Conseil d'— : the Council of State (see *Conseil* [A]).
coup d'— : coup d'état.
homme d'— : statesman.
raison d'— : the national interest (overriding moral considerations).
secrétaire d'Etat # under-secretary in the British an American Governments.
les —(s)-Unis de l'Amérique du Nord : the United States of America.
— — *providence* : Welfare State.

état (m) : 1° condition, state.
en bon — : in good repair (condition).
en tout — de cause : whatever the circumstances.
être en — (de faire) : to be in a position to do.
hors d'— (de faire) : unable, not in a position to do.

– *des choses* : state of things, circumstances.
– *de fait* : actual position.
– *de fortune* : financial standing.
– *de guerre* : state of war, war footing.
– *d'indisponibilité* : unavailability.
– *d'ivresse* : intoxication.
– *juridique* : legal status.
– *de paix* : peace.
– *de prévention* : imprisonment on suspicion, being in custody, committed for trial.
– *de siège* : (under) martial law.
2° profession, position, social status.
– *de famille* : family status (as defined by marriage, relationship, relationship by marriage).
– *militaire* : service with the armed forces.
– *de fonctionnaire* : status of a civil servant.
– *de mariage* : marital status.
[J] *affaire en état* : issue joined.
3° civil status.
– *civil* : a) civil status, as defined by birth, marriage, divorce, death, b) registry office in charge of civil status.
officier de l'– civil : official entitled to draw up records of civil status : magistrate, mayor, consul, captain at sea.
actes de l'– civil : certificates of civil status delivered at the registry office.
4° [hist.] *les trois –(s)* : the three estates of the realm of France : clergy, nobility, commonalty *(tiers-état)*.
5° statement, report, list, return, record, [U.S.] schedule.
– *des bénéfices* : statement of earned surplus.
état des biens : list of times belonging to an estate, inventory.
– *de cessation des paiements* : default.
– *des charges* : statement of charges, of incumbrances.
– *des comptes, de dépenses* : statement of accounts, of expenses, account status.
– *des cotes irrécouvrables* : return of bad debts.
– *de collocation* : collocation, order of priority of creditors in bankruptcy.
– *descriptif des immeubles* : description of real estate.
– *estimatif* : inventory and valuation of chattels (in view of a legal transaction).
– *de frais* : bill of costs.
– *des immeubles* : list of items of a real estate.
– *des lieux* : inventory of fixtures as between landlord and tenant.
– *mensuel* : monthly return.
– *de paiements* : schedule of payments.
– *de répartition* : allotment.
– *des rémunérations successives* : salary record.
– *des salaires* : pay-sheet, roll.
– *de services* : statement of positions held successively by a soldier or civilian.
– *(s) de service* : description of services performed by a soldier or civilian.
– *de situation* : financial position (of a bank, a ward, etc.).
rayer des –(s) : to strike off the roll.

éteindre (v) : to extinguish.
– *une dette* : to pay off a debt.
– *une obligation* : to discharge an obligation.

(s')étendre *(de - à)* (v) : to run (from - to).
exercice s'étendant de - à : period running from - to.
étendues (relations) : wide acquaintanceship.

étendue (f) de la couverture *(sociale)* : extent of (social) cover.

étiquette (f) : label.
– *de prix* : price-tag.

étranger (a et m) : (m) alien, (a) foreign.
biens –(s) : foreign property.
sous contrôle – : foreign-owned.
impôt – : foreign tax.

étrangler *(une maison de commerce concurrente)* (v) : to freeze out (a firm).

être (m) : being, creature.
– *moral (personne morale)* : juridical person.

étude (f) : survey, report ; office of notary, solicitor, chambers of barrister, attorney-at-law.
bureau d'–(s) : engineering department.
– *sur les besoins des consommateurs* : consumer research.
– *du comportement* (ex. ce que les acheteurs pensent d'un produit, ce que les ouvriers pensent de leurs conditions de travail) : attitude survey.
– *critique des méthodes de travail* : method study.
– *de marché* : market survey.
– *du marché d'après des documents déjà publiés* : (market) desk research.
– *des mouvements de fonds (entrée-sortie)* : funds flow.
– *des temps et ordonnancement* : time and notion study.
vendre son – : to sell one's practice (by lawyer).

étudier *(un cas, une question)* : to investigate, to look into (a question), to study (a case).

Euratom : Euratom.

eurodevises (f pl) : eurocurrencies.

euro-*obligation, -crédit, -devise, -dollar, -marché* : euro-bond, -credit, -currency, -dollar, -market.

évaluation (f) : *(de biens)* appraisal, appraisement, valuation, *(de dommages)* assessment, *(de poids)* estimate, *(d'impôts)* rating, *(prévision)* projection.
[F] — *administrative* : administrative rating.
[F] — *des coûts par absorption* : absorption casting.
— *de police d'assurance* : valuation of policy.
— *réelle* : actual rating.
— *des stocks au prix de vente* : adjusted selling price.
évaluer une propriété en vue d'imposition : to assess a property for purposes to tax.
évaluateur : valuer, appraiser.

évasion (f) : escape, absconding.
— *de capitaux* : flight, exodus of capital.
— *fiscale* : tax avoidance.
— *de prison* : flight from prison.

événement (m) : event.
à tout — : as a measure of precaution.
[J] — *de la condition* : occurrence of the condition.
[A] issue, outcome.

éventail (m) : fan.
— *de produits* : range of products.
— *des salaires* : salary range, income spread.

éventuel (a) : incidental, contingent.

éviction (f) : eviction.
[J] dispossession, ejectment of tenant.

évincer (v) : to oust.

évocation (f) : [J] *droit d'* — : right of a higher court to summon a case pending before the court below.
— *(appel) en garantie* : (litis denunciatio) introduction of third partie (approximately an impleader).

évolution (f) *d'une situation dans l'entreprise* : change.

exactitude *(d'une déclaration, d'une comptabilité)* (f) : accuracy, reliability (of a statement, of accounting records).
avec — : accurately.

examiner (v) : to examine, to review.
— *une affaire* : to investigate a matter.

excédent (m) : excess, surplus.
— *de l'actif sur les dettes (le passif)* : excess of assets over liabilities.
— *de caisse* : surplus in cash, « overs ».
— *de dépenses* : deficit.
— *des dépenses sur les recettes* : excess of expenditure over receipts.

— *de recettes* : surplus.
somme en — : sum in excess.

exception (f) : [J] objection in law, plea in bar, demurrer, plea in confession and avoidance, incidental plea of defence.
— *de bonne foi* : plea of (having acted) bona fide.
— *de caution contre l'étranger* : plea of non compliance with the rule of cautio judicatum solvi.
— *de chose jugée* : plea of res judicata.
— *de communication de pièces* : plea of non-discovery.
— *déclinatoire, exception d'incompétence* : declinatory plea.
— *de défaut de qualité pour agir ou pour défendre* : plea of incapacity.
— *dilatoire* : dilatory plea.
— *de discussion* : (beneficio excussionis) petition for preliminary distraint upon the principal debtor.
— *de division* : (beneficio divisionis) claiming the privilege of sureties to a debt to go bail each for his part only.
— *de dol* : (exceptio dolis generalis) plea of fraud.
— *d'enrichissement* : plea of money had and received.
— *de fond* : exceptio in rem.
— *de forme* : exceptio in formam.
— *de garantie* : introduction of third parties (approximately an impleader).
— *de jeu* : plea of gambling debts (not recoverable in law).
— *libératoire, péremptoire* : peremptory plea (e.g. a plea based on the statute of limitations).
— *de litispendance* : (lis alibi pendens) plea of suit pending elsewhere.
— *de nullité* : plea of voidance.
— *de péremption de l'action* : plea based on the statute of limitations.
— *personnelle* : exceptio in personam.
— *préjudicielle* : interlocutory plea.
— *de renvoi* : a) plea for nonsuit, b) jurisdictional plea.
— *de simulation* : plea of simulation.
— *tirée de l'abus d'un droit* : plea based on the misuse of a right.
concours d' — *(s)* : concurrent demurrers.
former, opposer une — : to demur.
juridiction d' — : jurisdiction of an exceptional court.
soulever une — : to raise an objection.
à titre d' — : by way of an exception.

exceptionnel (a) : exceptional.
ressources — *(les)* : non recurring income.

excès (m) : excess.
commettre un — *de vitesse* : to exceed the

speed limit.
[J] — *de pouvoir*: action ultra vires.

exciper de (v) : to plead sth.
— *l'autorité de la chose jugée*: to plead res judicata.
— *sa bonne foi*: to allege one's good faith.
— *l'incompétence du tribunal*: to disclaim the jurisdiction of the court.
— *une quittance*: to plead that receipt in full has been given.

excitation (f) : instigation.
[J] — *de mineur à la débauche*: inducing a minor to lead a dissolute life.
— *à la révolte*: incitement to rebellion.

exclure (v) : to exclude, to leave out, to debar (from).
sommes **exclues** *du calcul du revenu*: amounts not included (excluded) in computing income.

exclusif (a) : exclusive.
agent — : sole agent.
droit — : exclusive right.

exclusion (f) : exclusion.
à l' — *de*: exclusive of, to the exclusion of.

exclusive (f) : debarment.

exclusivité (f) : sole rights, exclusive rights.
en — *(film)*: exclusive (film).

excusable (a) : excusable.

excuse (f) : excuse.
[J] — *absolutoire*: excuse involving acquittal.
— *atténuante*: extenuation, extenuating, excuse.
— *légale*: legal excuse (e.g. killing in self-defence).

ex-dividende

exécuteur (m), **exécutrice** (f) : executor, executrix, performer.
[J] — *testamentaire*: executor, executrix.

exécution (f) : [J] 1° performance, levy, enforcement, carrying out.
en — *de*: in pursuance of.
— *d'un acte*: drawing up of a deed.
— *de la compensation*: operating a set-off.
— *effective de la prestation*: actual performance of dues.
— *intégrale d'un contrat*: specific performance.
— *de jugement*: enforcement of a judgment.
— *des lois*: enforcement of law.
— *de mesures conservatoires*: application of measures of conservation, of protective,
urgent, measures.
— *des obligations*: fulfilment of obligations.
— *par voie de contrainte*: compulsory levy under attachment.
ordonnance d'—, *titre exécutoire*: writ of execution.
défenses à — : order of court of appeals forbidding enforcement of a judgment.
arrêté d' — : administrative decree stating executory measures for the enforcement of a law.
donnant lieu à — *provisoire*: immediately enforceable.
mettre à — : to carry into effect.
2° distraint, distress, levy by sale of debtor's chattels.
3° putting to death.
— *capitale*: (cr.) execution.
— *militaire*: to court-martial and shoot s.o.
ordre d' — : death warrant.
exécuter : to distrain upon a debtor.
exécuter un contrat, une obligation: to execute a contract.
exécuter un ordre: to carry out an order.
exécuter un testament: to execute a will.
s'exécuter: to decide to pay one's debt, to fulfil a promise.
[B] hammering a defaulter.

exécutoire (a et m) : [J] (a) enforceable.
— *par provision*: for provisional enforcement.
acte en forme — : instrument ready for enforcement.
force — : enforceable.
formule — : executory formula, clause.
jugement — : enforceable judgment (i.e. provided with the executory formula).
titre — : proof of indebtness calling for enforceable payment, i.e. writ of execution.
(m) writ of execution.
— *de dépens*: order to pay costs.
délivrer un — *pour le montant des dépens*: to issue execution to recover costs.

exemplaire, en double, en triple : in duplicate, in triplicate.

exemption (f) : exemption.
[F] — *fiscale, d'impôts*: immunity from taxation.
— *de service militaire*: exemption from military service.
lettre d'exemption: bill of sufferance.
exempter *le prévenu de toute peine*: to declare the prisoner innocent.
[D] **exempt** *des droits de douane*: duty free.
exempt de frais: « no expenses ».
[F] *exempt d'impôt*: free of tax.

exequatur (m) : exequatur.
[J] 1° judicial or administrative authorization to enforce a foreign judgment (extension of judgments).

2° confirmation of an arbitration award by court.
[A] exequatur in favour of consuls.

exercer (v) : *(un choix)* to exercise (an option), *(une action sur)* to act upon, *(une activité)* to be engaged in, *(une emprise)* to exert, *(des poursuites contre qn)* to bring an action against s.o., *(une pression sur qn)* to exert a pressure on s.o.

exercice (m) : exercise.
en − : in office.
[F] − *financier, commercial, social :* financial, commercial, business year, twelvemonth.
− *budgétaire :* budgetary year, fiscal period ; balance-sheet.
− *1989 attaché, détaché :* cum, ex, dividend 1989.
l' − *écoulé :* the year under review.
exercer *un chantage :* to blackmail.
exercer un métier : to carry out a trade.

exhibition (f) : presentation.
[J] (civ.) exhibition, production of documents, (cr.) indecent exposure.

exiger (v) : to require.

exigible (a) : exigible, claimable, due, demandable.
[C] *paiement* − : payment due.
passif − : current liabilities.
exigibilité : payability.
les exigibilités : current liabilities.

existant (a) : existent.
les lois − (s) : the existing laws, the laws in force.

existence (f) : existence.
moyens d' − : means of subsistence.

exode (m) rural : rural depopulation, drift from the land.

exonération (f) : exoneration.
[F] − *de l'impôt :* exemption from tax.
[B] **exonérer** *une marchandise :* to take duty off goods.

expansion (f) : boom.
un marché en pleine − : a booming market.

expédient (a et m) : (a) advisable, expedient, (m) shift.
avoir recours à des − (s) : to resort to shifts.

expéditeur (m) : shipper, consigner ; sender, consignor of goods, forwarding agent (also : **expéditionnaire**).

expédition (f) : expedition, consignment, shipping, shipment ; dispatch (of business).
− *en douane :* clearance.
bulletin d' − : way-bill.
maison d' − : forwarding firm.
[J] copy.
première − : first authentic copy.
en double, triple − : in duplicate, in triplicate.
expédier : to send, to forward, to dispatch, to consign (goods).
expédier un acte : to draw up an instrument.

expérimenter (v) : to experiment.

expert (m) : expert, valuer, appraiser.
− *-comptable :* chartered accountant, [U.S.] certified public accountant.
− *en écritures :* handwriting expert.
− *judiciaire :* expert appointed by court.
à dire d' − : at a valuation, according to expert advice.
rapport d' − : see *expertise.*

expertise (f) : expert appraisement, valuation, opinion, testimony.
− *médico-légale :* medico-legal report.
contre- − : second expert appraisement ordered to check the first one.
[ASS] − *d'avarie :* damage-survey.
faire l' − : to appraise, to value.
expertiser : to examine, to survey, to value.

expiration (f) : expiration, end, term of payment.
[J] expiry, termination.
− *du délai pour dépôt des conclusions du défendeur :* expiration of the time to answer.

exploit (m) : [J] writ, process, summons, notice.
− *d'ajournement :* summons to appear.
− *-demande :* indictment, complaint.
− *introductif d'instance :* first process.
− *de saisie :* writ of attachment.
signifier un −, **exploiter** : to serve a writ.
huissier, **exploitant** : writ-serving officer.

exploitable (a) : distrainable (goods), workable (quarry).
[J] liable to execution after service of writ.

exploitant *agricole* (m) : farmer.

exploitation (f) : exploitation, working (of mine, railroad, farm, etc.).
− *étalée :* continuous output investment.
− *d'une invention :* utilization of a patent.
− *patronale :* sweating system.
− *ponctuelle :* point output investment.
frais d' − : working expenses.
matériel d' − : working plant.
société d' − : development company.

expomarché (m) : trade mart.

exponse (m) (also *déguerpissement*) : [J] moving out of tenant to elude payment of ground rent.

exportateur (m) : exporter.

exportation (f) : exportation (of goods).
[C] *les — (s)* : the export trade, exports.
articles d'— : exports.
permis d'— : export licence.
prime d'— : bounty, drawback.
[F] *— de capitaux* : flight, exodus of capital.

exposant (m) : exhibitor.
(organiser une) exposition (f) : to stage an exhibition.

exposé (m) : account (of facts, etc.).
[J] *— des motifs (d'une loi)* : explanatory statement (to a bill).
— des faits : finding.
— des motifs (pour une réclamation) : statement of a claimant's argument.
— de la procédure à suivre : sketch of procedure to be adopted.
faire l'— de la situation : to give an account of the state of affairs.
exposer *un projet* : to sketch out a plan.

(à la condition) expresse que : on the distinct understanding that.

expressément *(stipuler)* (adv) : (to provide) specifically.

expression (f) : term.

expropriation (f) : expropriation, compulsory surrender of real estate, purchase under compulsion.
[J] taking land by the power of eminent domain.
— pour cause d'utilité publique : taking over of real estate for a public purpose.

exproprier (v) : to expropriate.

expulser (v) : to evict.

expulsion (f) : expulsion, deportation (of alien).
[J] eviction of tenant.
[A] *ordre, arrêté d'—* : deportation order, warrant.

extensif (a) : extensive.

extension (f) : extension, augmentation (of industry).
donner de l'— : to extend.
par — : in a wider sense.

prendre de l'— : to grow, to increase, to spread, to be booming.

extérieur (a et m) : (a) exterior, outer, foreign.
affaires — (es) : foreign relations.
commerce — : foreign trade.
(m) *à l'—* : abroad.

exterritorialité (f) : [J] extraterritoriality, exterritoriality.

exterritorial (a) : off-shore.

extinction (f) : extinction.
adjudication à l'éteinte de chandelle, à l'— des feux : auction by inch of candle.
— de l'hypothèque : extinguishment of a mortgage (see also *hypothèque*).
— des obligations : termination of contract, of indebtness.
éteindre *une dette* : to extinguish, to pay off, to wipe out a debt.
éteindre *un droit* : to extinguish a right, to quiet title.
éteindre *une pension, une rente* : to redeem a life annuity.
laisser s'éteindre une servitude : to allow an easement, to lapse through disuse.

extorquer (v) : to extort.

extorsion (f) : extortion (of promise, etc.).
[J] *— de fonds, de signature* : obtaining money, signature (by swindle, blackmail, under false pretences).

extrader (v) : to extradite.

extradition (f) : [J] extradition.

extrait (m) : *(d'un livre, registre)* extract, excerpt, *(d'un acte, compte)* abstract.
— d'acte d'état civil (acte de naissance, de mariage, de décès) : birth, marriage, death, certificate.
— du casier judiciaire : certificate of non-punishment or of penalties incurred (delivered by the Ministry of Justice, extract from police records).
— certifié conforme : authenticated abstract.
— de compte : statement of account.

extrajudiciaire (a) : extrajudicial, done out of court.
serment — : voluntary oath.

extralégal (a) : extralegal, not legally authorized.

extra muros : outside the town.

extranéité (f) : [J] foreign origin, alien status.

extraordinaire (a) : extraordinary.
assemblée — : special meeting.
frais —(s) : extras, non recurring expenditure.

extraterritorialité (f) : see *exterritorialité*.

extrinsèque (a) : extrinsic.
[J] *éléments* —(s) *d'un acte :* conditions not accounted for in an instrument.
[F] *valeur* — : legal (fictitious) value (of currency).

NOTES

F

fabricant (m): manufacturer, maker.

fabrication (f): 1° manufacture, manufacturing, making.
coûts de — : manufacturing costs.
2° in a disparaging sense : adulteration.
vin **fabriqué** : wine that has been tampered with.
[J] — *de fausse-monnaie* : coinage offence.
— *de faux en écriture* : forging of documents.

fabrique (f): manufacture.
marque de — : trade-mark, brand.
prix de — : manufacturer's price.
secret de — : manufacturing secret.
valeur en — : cost price.
« **fabriquer** *ou acheter* » *(des pièces détachées)* : make or buy.

façade (f): (ASS) fronting.

facilité (f): facility.
accorder des — *(s)* : to grant facilities for payment (terms).
— *(s) de caisse* : overdraft facilities.
— *(s) de paiement* : facilities for payment, easy terms, deferred payment.

F.A.C.O.B. *(traité facultatif obligatoire de réassurance)* : open cover.

façon (f): making, fashioning.
artisan à — : jobbing, craftsman.
[C] *matière et* — : material and labour.

fac-similé (m): facsimile, exact copy of signature, writing, etc.

factage (m): carriage and delivery, transport of goods.

facteur (m): 1° carrier, transport agent, postman, railway porter.
2° factor.
— *(s) aléatoires* : random factors.
— *(s) économiques* : economic factors.
— *humain* : personal element (factor).
— *de mise en valeur de la créativité* : characteristics of creativity.
— *de production* : factor of production, input.
— *de récupération* : capital recovery factor.
revenu national au coût des — *(s)* : national income at factor costs.

factice (a): factitious, sham.
opérations — *(s)* : artificial transactions.
valeur — : factitious value.

factorage (m): [C] commission.

factum (m): scurrilous pamphlet.
[J] statement of the facts of a case, brief (also *mémoire*).

facturation (f): invoicing, [U.S.] billing.

facture (f): [C] invoice, bill of sale.
— *d'avoir* : credit note.
— *provisoire* : pro forma invoice.
suivant — : as per invoice.
facturer : to invoice.
facturier : invoice-clerk, sales book.

facultatif (a): optional, permissive.
réserves **facultatives** : optional, voluntary reserves.

faculté (f): option, right, faculty, leave, liberty option.
l'accusé jouit de toutes ses — *(s)* : the accused is of sound mind, in possession of all his faculties.
avec — *d'achat ou de vente* : with the option of purchase and sale.
facultés contributives : ability to pay.
— *de remboursement anticipé* : put back.
[B] — *du double* : call of more.

faillite (f): insolvency.
[J] bankruptcy (see *liquidations de biens* and *règlement judiciaire*), (*la loi du 13 juillet 1967 a profondément modifié la notion de* —. *Un certain nombre d'expressions qui n'ont plus de valeur juridique sont cependant restées d'usage courant ; c'est pourquoi elles ont été conservées ici*: the bankruptcy law of july 13th 1967 has deeply altered the very concept of bankruptcy ; however a number of phrases, though void of « legal » meaning, are still in almost everyday use : that is why they are mentioned here).
administrateur judiciaire (en matière de —*)*
syndic (de la — *)* : inspector, official receiver, trustee in bankruptcy.
concordat après — : bankrupt's certificate, [U.S.] discharge in bankruptcy.
concordat préventif à la — (*p. ex. par abandon d'actif*) : composition (e.g. by cession).
dividende de — : dividend, (equal) distribution

in bankruptcy.
faire — : [U.S.] to go into litigation.
— *frauduleuse, banqueroute* : fraudulent bankruptcy.
jugement déclaratif de — : decree of bankruptcy.
liquidation de la — : final settlement in bankruptcy proceedings.
masse des biens de la — : bankrupt's (total) estate.
masse active, passive : bankrupt's assets, liabilities.
masse des créanciers de la — : general body of creditors.
révocation de la — : repeal of bankruptcy.
déclarer, mettre qn en —, *prononcer la faillite de qn* : to adjudge, to adjudicate s.o. bankrupt.
se mettre en —, *déposer son bilan* : to file a petition in bankruptcy.
tomber en —, *faire* — : to go bankrupt.
failli : bankrupt.
failli frauduleux, banqueroutier : fraudulent bankrupt.

faire (v) : to do, [B] to call.
— *des affaires avec (qqn)* : to do business with (s.o.).
— *de la cavalerie* : to bring accommodation bills into circulation.
— *un chèque (de)* : to make out a cheque (for).
— *diligence* : to institute proceedings.
— *état de qch.* : to take sth. into account, to note a fact, to depend on sth.
— *face à* : to face, to meet, to cope with.
— *face à la demande* : to meet the demand.
— *les fonds* : to put up the money for an undertaking.
— *jurisprudence* : to create an authoritative precedent (in case law).
— *justice* : a) to deliver a just sentence, b) to carry out death sentence.
— *opposition* : to appeal against a decision, to ask for an injunction against sth.
— *de la prison* : to be in jail.
— *un procès à qn* : to institute proceedings against s.o.
— *le procès de qn* : to criticize s.o.
— *une rente (à qn)* : to allow (s.o.) an income.
— *savoir, assavoir* : to notify.
— *valoir qch.* : to set off sth., to advantage.
— *valoir un droit en justice* : a) to put in, to assert a claim, b) to have a right enforced by court.
obligation de —, *de ne pas* — : legal obligation to act, to abstain from action.
[J] mandatory, restrictive injunction.
se — *justice* : a) to take the law in one's own hands, b) to commit suicide.

fait (m) : fact, act, deed, achievement.
— *accompli* : accomplished fact.
être au — *de qch.* : to be fully informed about sth.
— *d'autrui* : act of a stranger.
— *concluant* : conclusive evidence.
— *(s) constitutifs de délit* : see *éléments constitutifs de délit.*
— *générateur de l'impôt* : tax point.
— *non pertinent* : non-relevant fact.
— *notable* : important item.
— *notoire* : fact of common knowledge.
— *nouveau* : novum.
— *du prince* : action by Government unhampered by legal considerations (mostly reversible).
constatation de — : vérification (of facts).
en — *et en droit* : in fact and in law.
mettre qn au — *de qch.* : to give s.o. information about sth.
au moment des — *(s)* : at the time of the occurrences.
moyens de — : practical grounds put forward for a claim (opp. *moyens de droit*).
point, question, de — : matter, question, issue, of fact (opp. *question de droit*).
possession de — : actual adverse possession.
prendre qn sur le — : to catch s.o. red-handed.
prendre — *et cause pour* : to side wholeheartedly with.
un — *nouveau s'est produit* : a new development occurred.
en venir au — : to come to the point.
voie de — : act of violence, assault and battery (opp. *voies de droit*).

fallacieux (a) : deceptive, fallacious.
arguments — : special pleading.

falsification (f) : *(de documents)* falsification, forging, *(d'aliments)* adulteration, *(de monnaie)* counterfeiting.
[J] — *des registres* : tampering with registers.
falsifier *des comptes* : to falsify, to tamper with accounts.

famé (bien, mal) (a) : of good repute, ill-famed.

famille (f) : family.
[J] *biens de* — : patrimony.
bien de — *insaisissable* : homestead immune from attachment.
gérer des biens en bon père de — : to administer prudently an estate.
livret de — : booklet delivered by mayor to married couple for registration of births and deaths in the family.
prévenir la — *(accident, décès)* : to inform the next of kin.
soutien de — : bread-winner.
[F] *valeurs de père de* — : giltedged stock.

fantaisie (f): imagination, fancy.
[C] *articles, prix, de* — : fancy goods, prices.
marque de fabrique de — : imaginary trade mark.

fantôme (a): shadow.
société — : bogus company.

fardeau (m): burden.
[J] — *de la preuve*: burden of proof.
[F] — *fiscal*: tax burden.

faussaire (m): forger (of a document).

fausser (v): to falsify, to alter.
fausse déclaration: false statement, misstatement.
— *les comptes*: to falsify the books.
— *les faits*: to alter the facts.

faute (f): fault, mistake, error; transgression, delinquency, offence, misconduct, miscarriage.
[J] wrongful act.
— *par abstention*: affirmative negligence.
— *délictuelle*: transgression committed with the intention to harm s.o.
— *d'impression*: misprint.
— *quasi-délictuelle*: technical offence.
— *grave*: serious offence.
— *intentionnelle*: deliberate transgression of duty.
— *légère*: peccadillo.
— *professionnelle*: offence against professional standards.
fauteur: abettor, supporter, instigator.
fauteur de troubles: agitator.
être fauteur et complice d'un crime: to have art and part in a felony.
fautif: faulty.

faux (a): false, untrue, wrong, mistaken.
[J] forgery.
— *incident civil, inscription de (en) faux*: plea of forgery.
arguer une pièce de — : to put in a plea of forgery.
s'inscrire en — *contre qch.*: to deny sth.
acte — : forged deed.
— *bilan*: fraudulent balance-sheet.
— *chèque*: forged cheque.
fausse déclaration: misrepresentation.
— *fret*: dead weight.
— *-fuyant*: untrue excuses.
fausse monnaie: counterfeit money.
crime de fausse monnaie: coinage offence.
— *-monnayeur*: coiner.
— *en œuvre d'art*: fake.
— *serment*: perjury.
— *témoignage*: false witness, false evidence, perjury.
— *témoin*: false witness.
inscription en — : plea of forgery.

faveur (f): favour.
billet de — : complimentary ticket.
en — *de*: on behalf of.
jours de — : days of grace.
[J] *majorité de* — : unqualified majority of a jury insufficient for conviction.
minorité de — : qualified minority of a jury sufficient for acquittal.
prix de faveur: preferential price.

fédéral (a): federal.
impôt — : federal tax.
Etat — : federal State.

fédération (f): union.
— *syndicale ouvrière*: trade union.

feint (a): sham.

femme (f): woman, wife.
[J] — *célibataire*: feme discovert, sole, spinster.
— *commune en biens*: wife having a common estate with her husband.
— *divorcée*: divorced woman.
— *en puissance de mari*: married woman, (sp. eu égard à ses incapacités légales) feme covert (hist.).
— *(fille) publique*: prostitute.
la — *Untel*: the married woman So-and-so.

férié (*jour*) (a): holiday, [U.K.] bank holiday.

fermage (m): rent-leasehold system.
— *brut moyen*: the average sum considered due as rent.

ferme (a et f): (f) farm.
[J] 1° farming lease.
— *à colonage* (or *colonat*) *partiaire, métairie*: farming lease whereby the farmer shares the produce of the farm with the landlord, [U.S.] share-crop system.
— *à moitié fruit*: farmer and landlord sharing the produce of the farm by halves.
bail à — : farming leasehold.
prendre une terre à — : to rent, to take a lease of a piece of land.
fermier: tenant of farm.
fermier général (Hist.): tax farmer.
2° concession, exclusive licence.
ferme des jeux: gaming house licence.
compagnie **fermière**: company to which State property is farmed out (e.g. *compagnie fermière de Vichy*).
fermier d'entreprise: contractor.
(a) [C] *acheter, vendre,* — : to buy, to sell firm, to make a firm sale.
[B] firm sale.
cours — : firm quotation.
valeur — : firm stock.

fermer (v) : to close.
société d'investissement **fermée** : closed-end investment fund.

fermeture (f) : closing, shutting.
heure de — : closing time.
[F] — *d'un compte* : closing, shut down of an account.

feu (a) : late.
[J] *fils de* — *Untel* : son of So-and-so deceased, of the late So-and-so.
— *vert (donner le) (pour des négociations)* : to give the go-ahead.

feuille (f) : leaf.
— *d'audience* : court minutes.
— *de chargement* : consignment note, [U.S.] bill of lading.
— *d'émargement* : pay-roll.
— *d'impôt* : tax return.
— *de paye* : pay-roll, pay-sheet, wage sheet.
— *de présence* : time-sheet, register of attendances.
— *de route* : military transport ticket.
— *de séance* : summary record of a meeting.
— *de versement* : paying-in slip.

fiançailles (f pl) : betrothal, engagement.
contrat de — : promise of marriage, marriage contract.
rupture de — : breach of promise (of marriage).
fiancé, fiancée : the betrothed, affianced.
les fiancés : the affianced couple.

fiche (f) : peg, card, voucher.
[A] — *de police* : hotel registration form.
fichier, *jeu de fiches* : card-index, file, card box.

fictif (a) : fictitious, sham, pro forma.
action **fictive** : feigned stock.
associé — : nominal partner.
compte — *(anonyme)* : impersonal account.
dividende — : sham dividend.
crédit — : fictitious credit.
crédit d'impôt — : matching, notional credit.
prix — : nominal price.
vente — : [U.S.] washed sale.

fiction juridique (f) : legal fiction, fiction of law.

fidéicommis (a et m) : (m) [J] trust, trusteeship, deposit.
[J] *acte de* — : trust deed.
auteur de — : assignor in trust (cestui que trust).
(m) **fidéicommissaire** : trustee.
(a) *héritier fidéicommissaire* : heir in trust.
substitution fidéicommissaire : substitution of heir, reversion remainder (see *appelé*).

fidéjussion (f) : [J] security, surety.
fidéjusseur : fidejussor, surety, warranter.

fidélité (f) : faithfulness.
[J] — *conjugale* : carnal faithfulness of married couple.
serment de — : oath of allegiance.

fiduciaire (m et a) : fiduciary.
(m) [J] beneficiary of a trust, trustee.
(a) *contrat* — : fiduciary agreement, contract of trusteeship.
certificat — : trustee's certificate.
héritier — *(appelé)* : heir in trust, substituted heir.
propriété — : property held in trust.
société — : trust company.
[F] *circulation* — : fiduciary currency, fiat money, paper money.
fiduciant : assignor in trust (cestui que trust).
fiducie : trusteeship, trust deed, assignment, (Scot.) assignation, in trust.

filature (f) : shadowing by a detective.

filiale (f) : [C] affiliated, subsidiary company ; field organization.
— *intégralement contrôlée* : wholly owned subsidiary.

filiation (f) : consanguinity in lineal descent, descendants.
recherche de la — : research for affiliation.

filière (f) : stock and die.
[A] — *administrative* : the usual official channels.
[C] [B] trace.
— *(s) industrielles* : industrial channels.

fille (f) : girl, daughter.
— *-mère* : unmarried mother.
belle- — : daughter-in-law.
petite- — : grand-daughter.
— *(femme) publique* : prostitute.
[J] — *nom de jeune* — : maiden name.
la — *Untel* : the unmarried woman, spinster So-and-so.

filleul (m), **filleule** (f) : god-child.

filou (m) : pickpocket, thief, cheat.

fils (m) : son.
beau- — : son-in-law.
petit- — : grand-son.
M. Untel — : Mr. So-and-so junior.

fin (f) : end, close, finish, termination, purpose.
à toutes — *(s) utiles* : to all purposes.

aux — *(s) de :* for the purpose of.
aux seules — *de :* solely for.
— *de la journée de travail :* knocking off time (fam.).
[J] aim, object, end, of a procedure (mostly in pl.).
— *(s) civiles en matière pénale :* (private) civil action parallel to prosecution and aiming at pecuniary compensation.
— *(s) de non-payer :* untrue excuses offered by a debtor to avoid payment.
— *(s) de non-procéder :* dilatory demurrer.
— *(s) de non-recevoir :* a) *(dénégation)* traverse, b) *(exception)* demurrer, c) *(forclusion)* estoppel, d) *(irrecevabilité)* plea in bar, e) *(rejet)* dismissal.
adjuger les — *(s) de la requête :* to find for the plaintiff.
sauf bonne — *:* under reserve.
prendre — *:* to end, to expire.
renvoyer qn des — *(s) de sa plainte :* to nonsuit s.o.
rendre une — *de non-recevoir :* nolle prosequi, to dismiss a case.
[C] end of the month.
payable — *courant, fin prochain :* payable at the end of the current month, of next month.
— *(s) de séries :* oddments.

finance(s) (f) : finances, resources, ready money.
assainir les — *:* to purge the finances.
faire qch. moyennant — *:* to do sth. for a (valuable) consideration.
— *publiques :* public finance.
loi de — *:* appropriation bill, finance act.
loi de — *rectificative :* special amending act.
receveur de — *:* tax-collector.
la haute — *:* high finance.
[A] *Ministre des* — *:* Minister of Finance, # Chancellor of the Exchequer, [U.S.] Secretary of the Treasury.
le Ministère des — *#* the Exchequer, [U.S.] Department of the Treasury.

financement (m) : financing.
— *basé sur les actifs :* asset-based financing.
— *d'emprunts à long terme par dépôts à court terme :* maturity mismatching.
— *par augmentation de capital :* equity financing.

financier (a et m) : (a) financial, (m) financier.
le marché — *:* the money-market, the stock-market.

firme (f) : [C] firm, business concern.

fisc (m), (**fiscal** (a), **fiscalité** (f)) : the Exchequer, the Treasury, the Inland Revenue, [U.S.] the Internal Revenue.

les agents du — *:* collectors of taxes, of customs and excise, revenue officials or authorities, commissioners of Inland Revenue.
l'administration **fiscale** : the tax(ation) authorities.
année — *(e) :* fiscal year, period.
dans un but **fiscal** : for the purposes of revenue.
charge — *(e) :* tax burden.
conseil — *:* tax adviser.
droit — *:* fiscal legislation, law.
droits **fiscaux** : State dues, taxes, customs and excise duties, the Inland Revenue.
évasion — *(e) :* tax avoidance.
exemption — *(e) :* tax exemption.
fraude — *(e) :* tax evasion.
incitations — *(es) :* tax incentives.
loi — *(e) :* taxation law.
pression — *(e) :* tax burden.
puissance — *(e) :* Treasury rating of an automobile.
recettes — *(es) :* revenue from taxes, (Inland) revenue taxes.
système — *:* fiscal system.
timbre — *:* revenue stamp.
volet — *:* tax volet.
fiscalité : financial system.

fixage (m) : [B] fixing.

fixation (f) : fixing.
[J] — *des dommages-intérêts :* assessment of damages.
— *des indemnités :* determination of compensation.
— *de la peine :* determination of penalty.
action en — *de droit :* affirmative action for a right.
intérêt **fixe** : fixed interest.
meuble à fixe demeure : (landlord's) fixtures.
résidence fixe : permanent abode.
[F] — *des impôts :* assessment (of taxes).
[C] *prix fixe :* fixed price.
[B] *cours fixe :* firm quotation.
— *des cours :* fixing.

fixer (v) : to fix.
— *le montant de :* to assess the amount of.
— *des objectifs :* to set objectives.
— *les règles (pour une procédure) :* to regulate.
— *un prix :* to arrive at a price.

flagrant (a) : flagrant.
[J] *pris en* — *délit :* in flagrante delicto, caught red-handed, in the act.

flambée *(des prix)* (f) : jump (in prices).

flèche (f) : arrow, shot.
montée en — *des prix et salaires :* wage-price spiral.

prix qui montent en — : rocketing prices.

fléchir (v) : *(le marché)* to sag, to weaken, *(les prix)* to chop.

flot (m) : wave.
[J] *choses de* — *et de mer :* flotsam and jetsam.
[F] *la dette* **flottante** : the floating debt.
flottement *concerté des monnaies :* joint float.
flottement « impur » (marché des changes) : dirty float.
[B] **flottant** (a) : float.

fluctuation (f) : fluctuation, variation.
— *des cours (en plus ou moins) :* swings and roundabouts.
—(s) *des changes :* fluctuations in exchange.
—(s) *du marché :* market fluctuations.
—(s) *défavorables des prix :* adverse price movements.

flux (m) : flow.
— *économique :* economic flow.
— *monétaire :* flow of money, monetary flow.
— *de trésorerie* # cash flow.

foi (f) : faith.
— *conjugale :* carnal faithfulness of married couple.
la bonne — : good faith.
de bonne — : bona fide.
de mauvaise — : mala fide.
en — *de quoi :* in witness whereof.
profession de — : profession of faith, political platform.
sous la — *du serment :* on oath, affidavit.
texte qui fait — : authentic text.
[J] *acheteur de bonne* — : bona fide purchaser.

foire (f) *d'empoigne :* rat race.

fomenter (v) : to foment.
— *des troubles :* to stir up unrest.

foncier (a) : of the land.
administrateur — : land agent, steward.
amélioration —(e) : land improvement, betterment.
bien — : real estate.
charge —(e) : praedial encumbrance.
dette —(e) : debt secured on landed property.
droit — : ground law.
impôt, contribution —(e) : land tax.
obligation —(e), *titre* — : debenture secured on landed property (issued by the Land Bank).
propriétaire — : ground landlord, landowner.
propriété —(e) : landed property.
registre — : land register, terrier, cadastal survey.
rente —(e) : ground rent.

servitude —(e) : servitude, easement covenant running with the land.

fonction (f) : 1° function, office.
la — *publique :* the civil service.
2° duty, function.
— *de l'entrepreneur :* entrepreneurial function.
voiture de — : company car.
— *actuelle (dans un questionnaire) :* present position.

fonctionnaire (m) : civil, public servant, officer, official.
— *d'autorité :* official entitled to give orders.
— *de droit :* regular official.
— *de fait :* official de facto.
— *de gestion :* managing official (in charge of public moneys, etc.).
— *d'occasion :* occasional official.

fonctionnement (m) : operation.
coût de — : operating costs.

fonctionner (v) : to function, to act, to work, to operate.

fond (m) : substance, essential features.
[J] main issue (of a suit, of a problem, etc.).
le — *de la cause est en état :* the case is at issue upon its merits.
exception de — : exceptio in rem.
juger, statuer sur le — : to pronounce judgment on the merits.
le — *emporte la forme :* the substance is more important than the form.
[F] — *de réserve :* legal reserve.

fondamental (a) : basic.
règles —(es) : basic rules.

fondateur (m) : founder.
[F] *(d'une entreprise)* promoter.
part de — : founder's share.

fondation (f) : founding, foundation, endowment fund.
[J] endowment, endowed establishment, institution.
le **bien-fondé** *d'une demande :* the merits of a case.
créance **fondée** : legal claim.
dette fondée : funded debt (opp. floating debt).
fondé *de pouvoirs, fondé de procuration spéciale et authentique :* [J] attorney in fact, [C] manager, managing director, signing clerk.

fondement (m) : basis.
sans fondement : groundless.

fonder (v) : to fund.
— *une dette :* to fund a debt.
— *l'impôt sur :* to base taxation on.

— *une société* : to float a company, to form a company.
en se **fondant** *sur l'hypothèse que* : on the assumption that.

fonds (m) [J] 1° : real estate (esp. lands).
— *dominant* : dominant tenement.
— *servant, grevé* : servient tenement, encumbered estate.
— *indivis* : joint estate.
bien- — : landed property.
2° means, resources, patrimony.
— *de commerce* : business, goodwill.
— *dotal* : dowry.
— *de magasin, de marchandises* : stock-in-trade.
— *de terre* : tenement.
[F] fund (for special purpose).
affecter des — : to earnmark funds.
appel de — : call for funds, call up of capital.
bailleur de — : silent, sleeping partner.
détournement de — : embezzlement, misappropriation of funds, [J] wrongful conversion.
détourner des — : to divert money.
faire les — : to supply the capital, to provide for a bill of exchange.
— *d'amortissement* : sinking fund.
— *des assurances* : insurance fund.
— *de bienfaisance* : charity fund.
— *bloqués* : frozen assets.
— *de chômage* : unemployment fund.
— *consolidés* : funded debt.
— *d'Etat,* — *publics* : Government, public corporations stocks.
— *de l'Etat, fonds publics* : public money, funds.
— *Monétaire International* : International Monetary Fund (I.M.F.).
— *de pensions, de prévoyance, de réserve* : pension, provident, reserve fund.
— *de placement sur marché monétaire* : money market fund.
— *propres* : equity capital.
— *de roulement* : working capital, operating capital.
— *sans affectation déterminée* : unappropriated funds.
— *social* : registered capital.
— *de stabilisation des changes* : exchange stabilization fund.
mise de — : paid-in capital.
placer son argent à — *perdu* : to purchase a life annuity.
prêt à — *perdu* : loan without security.
rentrer dans ses — : to recover outlay, to get one's money back.
virer des — : to transfer funds.

fongible (a) : fungible.

forage (m) : drilling.

forain (a et m) : from outside, foreign, itinerant.
(a) [J] *saisie* — *(e)* : distraint upon the goods of a person living in furnished rooms.
(m) *marchand* — : stall keeper (at a fair), pedlar.

force (f) : force, strength, power.
— *armée* : the military.
— *de chose jugée* : res judicata, (judgement) possessing force of law.
— *est demeurée à la loi* : the right has been vindicated.
— *exécutoire* : enforceable.
avoir — *libératoire* : to be legal tender.
— *de loi* : force of law.
— *majeure* : force majeure, circumstances outside one's control, act of God.
— *obligatoire* : binding power, force.
— *probante* : convincingness.
— *publique* : armed forces, police force.
— *résolutoire* : resolutive effect.
— *rétroactive* : ex post facto, retrospective effect.
— *suspensive* : suspensive effect.
— *(s) de terre, de mer et de l'air* : land, sea and air forces.
— *de vente* : sales force.
agent de la — *publique* : constable.
maison de — : prison.
forcé : forced.
liquidation forcée : compulsory winding up.
[J] *vente forcée* : execution.
travaux forcés : hard labour.
[F] *cours forcé de la monnaie* : compulsory legal tender.
emprunt forcé : compulsory loan.

forclusion (f) : [J] preclusion, estoppel, barring; foreclosure of mortgage.

forestier (a) : forest.
fonds — : forest fund.
produits — *(s)* : forestry products.

forfait (m) : 1° [J] heinous crime.
2° [C] contract, composition, agreement, agreed consideration.
prix à — *(forfaitaire)* : lump price, flat rate.
travail à — : contract work, job work.
vente à — : a) outright sale, b) selling of futures.
3° [F] estimated income.

forfaitaire (a) : contractual, agreed.
déduction — : standard deduction.
impôt — : empirical, notional assessment, [U.S.] presumptive assessment.
marché — : transaction by contract.
(règlement, paiement) — : lump sum (settlement, payment).
versement — *à la charge des employeurs* :

payroll tax.

forfaitairement (adv.) : contractually, for an agreed consideration.

forfaiture (f) : abuse of authority, maladministration, prevarication.
[J] misprision.
forfaire à l'honneur : to lapse from honour.
forfaire à son devoir : to fail in one's duty.

formalité (f) : formality, formal procedure.
c'est une — : it's a matter of form.
remplir les — (s) : to act according to prescribed forms, to comply with formalities.
[D] *— (s) en douane :* customs clearance.

formation *(de la main d'œuvre)* (f) : (manpower) training.
— professionnelle : vocational training.

forme (f) : form, method of procedure.
[J] *— authentique :* duly certified.
— juridique : legal form.
en bonne et due — : regular.
en — exécutoire : enforceable.
vice de — : (inopérant) defect, (entraînant nullité) substantial flaw.
avertissement dans les —(s) : due warning.
pour la — : for form's sake, as a matter of form.

formule (f) : 1° [J] prescribed wording (of contract, clause, oath, etc.).
2° printed form to be filled up (bill of exchange, cheque, claim, questionnaire, receipt, etc.).
formuler : *(doctrine)* to formulate, *(document)* to draw up, *(proposition)* to enonciate, to frame, *(règle)* to lay down.
[J] *formuler une plainte :* to lodge, to bring forward a complaint.
formuler des griefs : to set forth grievances.

forte *(devise)* : hard (currency).

fortuit (a) : fortuitous, by change.
cas — : accidental case, accident, [J] act of God.

fortune (f) : fortune, resources, estate ; chance, luck, wealth.
[ASS] *— de mer :* perils of the sea.
[F] *impôt sur la — :* taxation of capital, property tax.

fossé *(fiscal)* (m) : (tax) moat.

fou (m), **folle** (f) : madman, madwoman.

fouille *(policière)* : bodily search.

fourchette (f) : bracket.
calculer la — : to bracket, to determine the range of.

fournir (v) : to complete, to fill ; to supply, to furnish, to provide.
— des renseignements à qn : to provide s.o. with information.
— une déclaration fiscale : to file a tax return.
fournisseur : supplier, purveyor.
fournisseur maritime : ship-chandler.

fourniture(s) (f) : supplies of goods, [U.S.] findings.
— de bureau : office stationery.
passer un marché pour la — de : to make a contract for the supply of.

fourrière (mise en) (f) : poundage.

foyer (m) : home, household.
— permanent : permanent home.

fraction (f) : fraction, splitting, percentage.
— d'une prestation : proportion of a benefit.
fractionnement d'un titre : stock-split.

fractionner (v) : to split.

frais (m pl) : expenses, costs, disbursement.
— accessoires : fringe expenses.
— d'administration et de gestion : administrative expenses.
— d'aménagement : development expenses.
— de bureau : office allowance (expenses).
— de chancellerie : chancellery dues.
compte de — : sundries account.
compte de — généraux : charges account.
— de déplacement (de route) : travelling (per diem) expenses.
— de déplacement de témoin : conduct money.
— de dépôt : deposit fee.
— divers : sundries, sundry expenses.
— de douane : customs duties.
— d'émission d'actions : expense of issuing shares.
— d'expertise : expert's fees, [U.S.] consultancy fees.
— d'exploitation exprimés en numéraire : financial costs.
faux — : incidentals, incidental expenses, untaxable costs.
faux — divers : contingencies.
— de garde : custody expenses.
— de garde d'enfant : child care expenses.
— généraux : general expenses, standing expenses, overheads, overhead expenses.
— généraux fixes : fixed overheads.
— de gérance : administrative expenses, management expenses.
— d'installation (de premier établissement) : initial expenses, first outlay, initial outlay.

— *judiciaires (de justice)*: legal expenses, court costs.
— *et loyaux coûts*: costs and (notary's) fee for drawing up a deed.
— *de magasinage*: warehousing, storage.
menus — : petty expenses.
— *médicaux*: medical expenses.
— *à payer*: outstanding expenses.
— *de procès*: costs of a lawsuit.
indemnité pour — *professionnels*: expenses account.
— *de publicité*: advertising expenses.
— *de publicité partagés* (entre fabricant et commerçant): cooperative advertising.
— *de représentation*: entertainment expenses.
— *de scolarité*: tuition fees.
— *taxés*: taxed costs.
— *de transport*: freight charges, carriage.
— *de transport à la charge du destinataire*: carriage inwards, freight forward.
— *de transport à la charge de l'expéditeur*: carriage outwards.
adjucation des — : award of costs.
sans — : free of charge.
effet « sans — »: « no expenses ».
total des — : total expenses incurred, [U.S.] overall expenses.
être condamnés aux — : to be ordered to pay costs.
les — *suivent le principal*: costs abide the event.

franc (m et a): (m) French monetary unit, (a) free.
[E] — *d'avarie*: free of average.
— *de coulage*: free of leakage.
[F] — *de droits, d'impôt*: duty, taxfree.
avoir part **franche** *dans une affaire*: to share in the profits of a business without contributing to the expenses.
bien — *d'hypothèque*: clear estate.
jour — : clear day.
— *de tous impôts présents et futurs*: immune from all present and future taxation.

franchisage (m): franchising.

franchise (f): exemption, freedom of a city.
en — : duty free, free of duty.
— *diplomatique*: diplomatic privilege (exterritoriality).
— *douanière*: duty-free import.
lieu de — : sanctuary, asylum.
importation en — : free import.

francisation (f): [D] registry as a French ship.
[J] — *de nom*: right of a person under naturalization process to have his foreign sounding name frenchified.

franco (adv): free, carriage free, postage paid.
[E] — *le long du navire*: free alongside ship (F.A.S.).
— *bord*: free on board (F.O.B.).
— *camion*: free on truck (F.O.T.).
— *de port*: carriage free (paid), free of charge.
— *wagon*: free on rail (F.O.R.).
[C] — *sur la demande*: free on request.
livré — : delivered free.

frapper (v): to strike, to hit.
— *des marchandises d'un droit*: to impose, to levy a duty on goods.
— *d'un impôt*: to tax.
— *de la monnaie*: to coin money.
— *d'une peine*: to inflict a penalty.
immeuble **frappé** *d'hypothèque*: mortgaged real estate.

fratricide (m): [J] crime of fratricide; the fratricide, brother-slayer.

fraude (f): fraud, deception, fraudulence, deceit, fiddling.
— *commerciale*: cheating in commercial transactions (on weight, quantity, etc.).
— *douanière*: smuggling.
— *fiscale*: tax evasion.
en — *des créanciers*: to the detriment of creditors.
en — *de la loi*: against the law.
par — : under false pretences.
passer en — : to smuggle through the customs.
[J] — *civile*: false representation.
— *pénale*: fraudulent representation, cheating.
banqueroute **frauduleuse**: fraudulent bankruptcy.
fraudeur: defrauder, cheat, smuggler.
fraudeur fiscal: tax dodger.
frauder *le fisc*: to defraud the Revenue.

freiner (v): *(les prix)* to curb, *(la production)* to check.

frelater (v): to adulterate, to sophisticate (food, wine, etc.).

frénésie (f) *d'achats*: buying space.

frère (m): brother.
— *par adoption*: adoptive brother.
— *aîné*: eldest, elder brother.
— *cadet*: younger, youngest brother.
— *consanguin*: frater consanguineus, half-brother on the father's side.
— *germain*: german, own brother.
— *légitime*: legitimate brother.
— *naturel*: half-brother born out of parental wedlock.

— *puîné*: brother born after the first-born child.
— *utérin*: frater uterinus, half-brother on the mother's side.
beau- — : brother-in-law.
demi- — : half-brother.
— *de lait*: foster brother.

fret (m) : 1° freight, freightage, chartering.
prendre un navire à — : to charter a ship.
fréter: a) to freight out (ship), b) (also *affréter*) : to charter (ship).
fréteur: ship-owner.
2° load, cargo.
faux — : dead weight.

frontal (m) : facing.

frontalier (a et m) : (a) of the frontier.
carte — *(e)*: pass for borderers.
trafic — : local traffic and trade on both sides of the border.
(m) frontiersman, borderer.

frontière (f) : border, frontier.
— *maritime*: sea border.

frôler (v) *(ex. le record des ventes)*: to nudge.

fructifier (v) : to bear interest.

fruit (m) : fruit, income, profit, produce.
[J] — *(s) casuels*: perquisites.
— *(s) civils*: income of capital.
— *(s) industriels*: earnings.
— *(s) naturels*: praedial, natural produce.
ferme, culture, à mi- — : farming lease whereby the farmer and the landlord share equally the produce of the farm, [U.S.] sharecrop system.

frustratoire (a) : frustratory.
[J] *acte* —, *frais* — *(s)*: unnecessary, frivolous proceedings or acts by a law official *(officier ministériel)* in order to increase his fees.
appel — *(fol appel)*: ungrounded appeal as a delaying trick.

fuite (f) : flight.
[J] *danger de* — : danger of absconding (of suspect).
délit de — : taking to flight after a car accident.
préparatifs de — : taking steps to run away.
présomption de — : presumption of flight.
tentative de — : attempt to escape.
[F] — *des capitaux*: flight, outflow of capital.
contribuable en — : asbsconder.

fusion (f) : fusion, melting.
[C] [J] merger of corporations.
— *-absorption*: merger-acquisition.
— *par absorption d'une société par une autre*: merger by amalgamation.
— *par création d'une nouvelle société par la* — *de plusieurs autres*: merger by consolidation.

fusionner (v) : to amalgamate, [U.S.] to merge.
sociétés **fusionnées** : amalgamated companies.

NOTES

NOTES

G

gabarit (m) : template.

gabegie (f) : underhand dealings, trickery.

gage (m) : 1° pledge, lien, pawn.
[J] pledged chattels, security.
créance garantie par — : secured debt.
droit de — : possessory lien.
lettre, titre de — : mortgage, security, bond.
meubles **gagés** : furniture under distraint.
mise en — : pawning, pledging.
réalisation du — : execution.
*saisie-***gagerie** : writ of execution on tenant's furniture and chattels.
titres en — : securities in pawn.
*créancier-***gagiste** : pledgee.
prêteur sur —(s) : pawnbroker.
2° token, sign.
3° forfeit.
4° wages, pay.
être aux —(s) *de qn* : to be in the pay of s.o.
gagiste : pledger, pawner.

gagner (v) : *(jeu, procès)* to win, *(par son travail)* to earn.
— *des points* : to gain points.
revenu **gagné** : earned income.
revenu non **gagné** : unearned income.
valeur qui **gagne** *du terrain* : gainer.

gain (m) : gain, profit, earnings, [U.S.] avails.
— *de temps* : saving of time.
[F] — *en capital* : capital gains.
— *(à la loterie)* : winnings (from the lottery).
enregistrer de légers —(s) : to add a fraction.
[J] — *de cause* : recovery (of judgment).

gala (m) *au profit d'une œuvre de bienfaisance* : charity performance.

gamme (f) : scale, range.
— *d'opérations* : lay out sheet.
— *des prix* : scale of prices.
— *de production* : production range.

garant (m) : guarantor, surety, bail.
se porter — *pour qn* : to bail s.o. out, to stand security for s.o.

garantie (f) : *(de paiement)* guaranty, security, surety, *(d'exécution de contrat)* pledge.
(En principe, surety *s'applique aux obligations de droit civil, tandis que* guaranty *a un sens proprement commercial.)*

[J] — *accessoire* : collateral security.
— *de banque* : bank guarantee.
—(s) *constitutionnelles* : personal rights under the constitution.
— *de bonne exécution* : performance bond.
— *de l'emploi (ou de la propriété)* : security of tenure.
— *étendue* : comprehensive guarantee.
— *prioritaire d'un emprunt* : prior charge.
— *réelle* : corporeal security.
appel, évocation en —, *exception de* — : introduction of third parties (approximately an impleader).
dépôt de — : earnest money.
dépôt de — *entre mains de tiers* : escrow.
laisse en — : to leave on deposit.
lettre de — : letter of indemnity.
prendre des —(s) : to insure against risks.
sans — : unwarranted.
s'entourer de —(s) : to obtain safeguards.
verser une somme en — : to leave, to pay a deposit.

garantir (v) : to guarantee, to underwrite.
— *une émission d'actions* : to underwrite an issue of shares.
— *qn* : to go bail, to stand security for s.o.
créance **garantie** : secured debt.

garde (m et f) : (m) keeper, watchman.
— *-chasse* : gamekeeper.
— *-forestier* : ranger, forester.
— *-frontière* : frontier guard.
— *-magasin* : warehouseman.
— *-meuble* : storage (furniture).
(navire) — *-pêche* : ship for the protection of fisheries.
le — *des sceaux* : the Keeper of the Seals (the Minister of Justice).
(f) *(de personnes)* guardianship, care, custody, *(de choses)* care.
[J] *attribution de la* — *d'un enfant* : custody procedure.

garder (v) : to keep, to retain.

gardien (m) : keeper, caretaker.
— *de la paix* : police officer.
— *de prison* : warder.
gardiennage : guarding (of parking lots, etc.).

gare (f) : railway station.
— *de marchandises* : goods station, [U.S.] freight yard.
— *maritime* : harbour station.

— 123 —

– *de triage*: marshalling yard.
[E] *franco* – : free on rail.

garni (m): furnished room.

gaspillage (m): waste.

gaspiller (v): to waste, to squander.

gel (m) du crédit: credit freeze, credit squeeze.

gendarme (m): constable, policeman.

gendre (m): son-in-law.

gêne (f): want, embarrassment.
– *financière*: pecuniary difficulties, financial pressure.
– *de trésorerie*: shortness of cash.

général *(impôt, etc.)* (a): general (tax, etc.).
hausse – (e) des prix: general advance in prices.
niveau – des prix: general level of prices.
théorie – (e): general theory.

gens (m pl): people, folk(s), men and women.
– *d'affaires*: businessmen.
– *d'église*: clergy(-men), church(y) people.
– *de justice*: law officials (of the lower order).
– *de maison*: servants.
– *de mer*: sailors.
– *du monde*: society people.
– *de robe*: the Robe, the legal profession.
[J] *droit des* – : law of nations.

geôle (f): [A] gaol, jail, prison.
geôlier: gaoler, jailer, turnkey.

gérance (f): management (of business, newspaper, real estate, etc.).
avoir la – d'un dépôt: to be in charge of a chain store.
frais de – : costs of management.
– *libre*: franchise.
gérant: manager, managing director, director, administrator, house agent.
– *responsable*: managing editor.
gérer *un bien en bon père de famille*: to administer an estate with due diligence.
– *une affaire*: to run a company.
– *un compte*: to operate an account.
– *un portefeuille*: to manage s.o.'s financial affairs.
– *une tutelle*: to administer the estate of a ward.

gestion (f): management (of works, etc.), care (of public monies), administratorship, stewardship.
– *du personnel*: manning arrangements.

– *de portefeuille*: [U.S.] financial administration.
– *des stocks*: stock management, inventory management.
– *des stocks par ordinateur*: computerized stock management.
– *de trésorerie*: cash management.
mauvaise – : mismanagement.
rendre compte de sa – : to render an account of one's stewardship.
[J] – *d'affaires*: business management.
approbation de la – de l'autorité de tutelle: approval, commendation of the board of guardians.
ordonner une – : to give an administration order.

gisement *(de pétrole, de charbon)* (m): (oil, coal) field.

global (a): total, inclusive.
impôt – : inclusive tax.
indemnité, somme – (e): lump, compensation sum.
globalement: in the lump, in the aggregate.

les **gnomes** (m pl) de Zurich : the Zurich gnomes.

gonflement (m): bulge.
– *des besoins en main-d'œuvre*: featherbedding.
– *des stocks*: bulging inventories (stocks).

gonfler (v): to inflate, [U.S.] to pad.
– *artificiellement afin de prendre des commissions plus élevées*: to churn.

goulot *(d'étranglement)* (m): bottleneck.

gouvernant (m): governor.
les – (s) et les **gouvernés**: the governors and the governed.

gouvernante (f): housekeeper.

gouvernement (m): the powers that be, the Authorities, [U.S.] the Administration.
gouvernemental (a): governmental, public.

gouverner (v): to govern, to rule.

gouverneur (m): governor.
– *de la Banque de France*: Governor of the Bank of France.

grâce (f): grace.
délai, jours, de – : grace period, days of grace, respite, time allowed.
recours en – : petition for a reprieve.
[J] *droit de* – : prerogative of the President of the Republic to grant free pardon *(– présidentielle)*.

gracier (v) : to pardon, to reprieve.

gracieux (a) : gratuitous, free.
juridiction **gracieuse** : voluntary jurisdiction.

grand (a) : — *livre* : ledger.
— *livre de la dette publique* : the national debt register.
— *livre des titres* : share ledger (register), securities ledger.
— *livre des ventes, des achats* : sales, purchases ledger.
— *magasin* : department store.
— *-mère* : grandmother.
— *(s)-parents* : grandparents.
— *-père* : grandfather.
— *-route* : highway.

« **grande** surface » (f) : large store.

graphique (m) : diagram, graph, chart.
— *descriptif des diverses phases d'une fabrication* : process chart.
— *de progressivité* : flow-chart diagram.

gratification (f) : bonus, bounty, gratuity, *(pourboire)* tip.

« **gratte** » (f) *(profit malhonnête)* : rake-off.

gratuit (a) : free, gratuitous.
à titre — : free of charge, as a gift.
accusation — *(e)* : ungrounded accusation.
action — *(e)* : bonus share.
aide, assistance judiciaire (—(e)) : (in forma pauperis) (free) legal aid.

gratuité (f) : gratuitousness.

(de) **gré à gré** : by mutual consent.

greffe (m) : registry.
[J] clerk of the court's office.
[F] registry of joint-stock company.
droits de — : registry dues.
greffier : clerk of the court.

grève (f) : strike.
— *générale* : general strike.
— *de la faim* : hunger-strike.
— *patronale* : lock-out, turn-out.
— *perlée* : canny strike, go-slow strike.
— *de solidarité* : sympathetic strike.
— *surprise* : snap, lightning strike.
— *sur le tas* : strike and occupation of premises by the strikers, sit-in strike.
— *tournante* : strike by turns.
— *du zèle* : working to rule.
allocation de — : strike pay.
briseur de — : blackleg, yellow labour.
clause pour cas de — : strike clause.
faire la grève, se mettre en — : to go on strike, to walk out.
meneur de — : strike-leader.
ordonner une — : to call a strike.
piquet de — : strike picket.
gréviste : striker.

grever (v) : to burden ; [J] *(un patrimoine)* to encumber, to entail, *(un bien)* to mortgage.
biens **grevé** *d'hypothèques* : burdened estate.
grevé d'un impôt : subjected to a tax, tax-burdened.
[A] to lay a rate on *(un immeuble)*.

grief (m) : grievance, ground for complaint.
— *d'appel* : statement of grounds of an appeal.

griffe (f) : stamped signature, stamp.

grille *(des salaires)* (f) : scale (of salaries), wage differential(s).

grippage *(dans la marche d'une entreprise)* : bind.

grivèlerie (f) : (or filouterie d'aliments) eating a meal and slipping away without paying : [J] misdemeanour of obtaining credit by false pretences.

gros (a, adv, m) : (a).
[C] — *(se) affaire* : big concern.
[E] — *(se) aventure* : bottomry.
[F] — *bénéfice* : substantial benefit.
— *intérêt* : high interest.
— *(se) somme* : large sum.
(adv) *acheter en* — : to buy wholesale, to buy in bulk.
commerçant en — **(grossiste)** : wholesaler.
gagner — : to earn a lot.
(m) *commerce de* — : wholesale trade.
maison de — : firm.
prix de — : wholesale price.

grosse (f) : [J] engrossed document, first authentic copy of judgment (bearing the executory formula), title or agreement.
grossoyer : to engross *(document)*.

groupage (m) : bulking, grouping.

groupe (m) : group ; task force.
— *de pression* : [U.S.] pressure group (lobbying).
— *de réflexion* : decision-making unit.
— *de travail* : task group.
[F] *fiscalité de* — : group income taxation.

groupement (m) : pool, group.
— *d'achat* : purchasing group.
— *d'achat de matières premières (en vue de la spéculation)* : commodities pool.

— *financier :* financial pool.
— *de personnes :* body of persons.
grouper : to collect.

guelte (f) : [C] commission, percentage on sales.

guérir (v) : to cure.
[J] — *un vice de contrat :* to cure a defect.

guerre (f) : war.
conseil de — : a) war council, b) court-martial.
contribution de — : war levy.
dommages de — : war damage.
droit de la — : the laws of war.

guet-apens (m) : ambush.
[J] *meurtre par — :* murder with felonious intent.

guichet (m) : window of booking office, box office, pay desk.
— *automatique (banque) :* automatic telling machine (A.T.M.).
[F] *payer à —(s) ouverts :* all comers paid.

NOTES

NOTES

H

habile (a) : clever, handy.

habillage (m) de bilan : window-dressing.

habiliter (v) : to enable, to entitle, to empower.
avoir **habilité** *à succéder* : to be entitled to succeed.
être habilité à ester en justice : to have capacity to institute proceedings.
être habilité à recueillir des signatures : to be empowered to collect signatures.
habiliter un mineur, un incapable : to confer legal capacity on a minor, on a person disqualified by law or judgment.
lettres **habilitantes** : enabling letters.
*loi d'***habilitation** : enabling act, statute.

habitation (f) : habitation, dwelling place.
[J] house, tenement, domicile, residence.
− à loyer modéré (H.L.M.) : moderate rent house (housing).
société H.L.M. : moderate rent housing cooperative.

habitude (f) : habit, custom, practice, use.
[J] *délinquant d'−* : recidivist, habitual criminal, « old lag » *(« cheval de retour »)*.
d'habitude : usually.

habituel *(domicile)* (a) : usual, customary (domicile, abode).

halage (m) : *(de bateau)* warping, hauling, *(de chaland)* towing.
[J] *servitude de chemin de −* : freedom of tow-path as condition attaching to the ownership of riparian lands.

hall (m) *(d'accueil) (gare, aéroport)* : concourse.

halle (f) : covered market.

harmonisation *(fiscale)* (f) : (tax) harmonization.

hasard (m) : chance, luck, venture.
échantillon au − : random sample.
jeux de − : game of chance, gambling.
hasardeux (a) : risky.
spéculation hasardeuse : risky speculation (venture).

hausse (f) : rise.
[C] [F] [B] *hausse des prix* : advance, inflation of prices, appreciation.
− générale des prix : general advance in prices.
− illicite des prix : illegal rise of prices.
− de valeur : appreciation.
− d'une valeur : rise in a stock.
en − : *(prix)* rising, on the rise, up, *(bourse)* rising.
jouer à la − : to speculate on a rise, to bull the market.
les prix sont à la − : the prices are hardening.
opération à la − : dealing for a rise.
spéculateur à la −, haussier : bull.
tendance à la − : upward tendency (trend).
valeurs en − : advance.
réviser (les prévisions) à la − : to revise (forecasts) upwards.
marché **haussier** : bullish, bull market.

haut (a, adv et m) : high, tap.
[J] *la − (e) Cour (de justice)* : political court elected by the legislative bodies, competent in impeachment cases.
− fonctionnaire : high official.
− (e) trahison : high treason, treasonfelony.
les − (es) parties contractantes : the high contracting parties.
− de gamme (article) : upscale (item).

havre (m) : haven.
− fiscal : tax haven.

hebdomadaire (a) : weekly.
bilan − : weekly return.

héberge (f) : [J] line above which a party wall between two buildings of different heights belongs exclusively to the owner of the higher building; line on a wall separating two buildings formed by the roof-ridge of the lower building.

héberger (v) : to shelter and feed.

héritage (m) : [J] heirdom, inheritance, *(biens-fonds)* hereditaments.
acceptation, addition d'− : acceptance of an estate.
acceptation bénéficiaire, sous bénéfice d'inventaire : acceptance without liability beyond the assets descended.
captation d'− : captation, obtaining succession by insidious means.
dévolution de l'− : devolution of an estate.
masse des biens, actif de l'− : gross, net, estate.

part d'—: the portion.
(action en) pétition d'— (or *d'hérédité*) : claim of succession to an estate held by a third party.
recueillir un —: to come into a legacy.
renoncer à l'—, répudier un —: to forgo, to relinquish a succession.
liquidation d'un —: settlement of a succession.
héréditaire: hereditary.
pétition d'hérédité: claim, right of inheritance.

héritier (m) : [J] *(héritier ab intestat, légitime)* heir, next-of-kin.
— *antérieur:* prior heir.
— *apparent:* heir apparent, supposed heir.
— *bénéficiaire:* see *héritage, acceptation bénéficiaire*.
— *de biens immobiliers:* heir-at-law, rightful heir, devisee.
— *de biens mobiliers:* distributee.
— *collatéral:* collateral heir.
— *institué:* testamentary heir (see *légataire, léguer*).
— *présomptif:* presumptive, expectant heir, next-of-kin.
— *réservataire:* heir who cannot be totally disinherited. (Louisiana : forced heir).
— *substitué, appelé:* substitutional heir, remainder-man, reversioner.
— *à titre particulier:* see *légataire*.
— *à titre universel:* see *légataire*.
— *du trône:* the heir apparent.
— *universel:* see *légataire*.
biens **héritables**: heritable property, hereditaments.
indigne d'hériter: debarred from succession.

heure (f) : hour, time.
—*(s) de bureau:* open for business, office hours.
— *légale:* civil time.
—*(s) de grande écoute (radio, T.V.):* prime time.
— *de pointe:* peak hour, rush hours.
—*(s) ouvrables, de travail:* working time.
faire des —(s) supplémentaires: to work overtime.
travail à l'—: time work, casual labour.
être payé à l'—: to be paid by time, by the hour.

hiérarchie (f) : hierarchy, chain of command.
— *des objectifs* (« *de haut en bas* ») : hierarchy of objectives.

hiérarchique (a) : hierarchical.
chaîne — verticale de direction: vertical chain of command.

historique (a) : historic(al).
la Bourse japonaise a atteint son plus haut niveau —: the Japanese Market peaked to a new all-time high.

hoirie (f) : [J] inheritance, succession.
avance d'—: advancement.

homicide (a, m et f) : (a) homicidal, (m) homicide.
[J] a) the crime of homicide, b) the murderer, the murderess.
— *intentionnel, prémédité, volontaire:* felonious homicide, murder, voluntary manslaughter, wilful homicide, [U.S.] murder in the first degree.
— *excusable:* excusable homicide.
— *involontaire, par imprudence, par négligence:* manslaughter, murder in chancemedley, [U.S.] murder in the second degree.

« **hommage** *de l'éditeur* » : with the publisher's compliments.

homme (m) : man.
— *d'affaires:* businessman.
— *d'état:* statesman.
— *de loi:* lawyer, legal practitioner.
— *de paille:* man of straw, dummy.
— *à procès:* litigious man.
— *de robe:* lawyer.

homogène (a) : homogenenous.
comptabilité par sections —(s): burden center accounting.

homologation (f) : [J] confirmation, ratification (by court or competent authority), probate.
— *judiciaire:* confirmation by the court.
homologuer *un testament:* to prove, to grant probate of a will.

honneur (m) : honour.
[J] [C] *acceptation par —:* acceptance (of a bill) for honour.
intervention, paiement par —: payment on behalf of a third party for honour.
prêt d'—: loan on trust.
honorer, *faire — à une traite:* to honour, to meet a bill.
ne pas honorer une traite: to dishonour a bill.
maison **honorable**: firm of high standing.

honoraires (m pl) : *(des professions libérales, sauf les avocats)* fee, *(des avocats)* retainer, refresher, *(droits d'auteur)* royalties.
— *d'engagement:* commitment fee.
— *précomptés:* front end fee.
verser des —: to pay in a fee.

horaire (m) : time-table.
– *(s) flexibles* : flextime (flexible time).

horizon (m) économique : planning horizon.

hors (prép) : out of, outside.
[J] *mettre qn – la loi* : to outlaw s.o.
mettre qn – de cause : to exonerate s.o.
mettre un associé – d'intérêt : to buy out a partner.
prononcer un – de cour : to dismiss s.o.'s case, to nonsuit s.o.
questions – de cause : irrelevant questions.
[C] *– concours* : non competing (on account of acknowledged excellence).
– saison : off season.
– de vente : unsaleable.
[F] *– taxes* : net of taxes.
– T.V.A. : outgoing V.A.T.
[B] *marché – cote* : curb market.
– Bourse (– séance : transactions menées par téléphone après la fermeture de la Bourse) : after hours.

hôte (m) : *(qui reçoit)* host, *(logeur)* landlord, landlady, *(invité)* guest, visitor.
hôtesse (f) : *(qui reçoit)* hostess.

hôtel (m) : hotel, hostelry.
– des ventes : auction room.
– de ville : town hall.
hôtelier : hotel-keeper.

hui (adv) : to-day.
[J] *ce jour d'–* : this day.

huis (m) : door.
[J] *demander le – clos* : to ask for a trial in camera.
entendre une cause à – clos : to hear a case in camera.
ordonner le – clos : to clear the court, to order a case to be heard in camera.
séance à – clos : private sitting.

huissier (m) : 1° (gentleman) usher.
2° [J] (process server) sheriff's officer, bailiff, [U.S.] marshal.
– -audiencier : court usher.
acte signifié par ministère d'– : process served by bailiff.

huitaine (f) : some eight units.
[J] *– franche* : eight clear days.
jugement (remis) à – : case deferred for a week.

hypothécable (a) : mortgageable.

hypothécaire (a) : pertaining to mortgage.
affectation – : mortgage charge.
contrat – : mortgage deed.
créancier, débiteur – : mortgagee, mortgagor.
marché – : mortgage market.
obligations – (s), nominatives, au porteur : mortgage bonds (debentures) registered, to bearer.
prêt – : loan on a mortgage, mortgage loan.
taxe – : mortgage duty.
titre – : mortgage bond.

hypothèque (f) : [J] mortgage.
– conventionnelle : mortgage by contract.
– générale : blanket mortgage.
– judiciaire : mortgage ordered by court.
– légale : statutory lien.
– maritime : mortgage of ships.
– prépostère : mortgage securing a future claim.
– en premier rang : first mortgage.
– subsidaire : subsidiary mortgage (securing another and enforceable only if the latter does not operate).
– du vendeur : vendor's lien.
biens affectés, grevés d'– : encumbered, mortgaged estate.
biens francs d'– : clear estate.
conservateur des – (s) : registrar of mortgages.
conservation des – (s) : mortgage registry.
constituer une – : to create a mortgage.
extinction d'une – : extinguishment of mortgage (redemption of mortgage by mortgagor).
lever, prendre une – : to raise a mortgage.
libération judiciaire d'une – : removal of mortgage by court.
mainlevée d'– : release of mortgage.
première – : first mortgage.
privilège d'– : mortgage charge.
purge d'une – : satisfaction of mortgage (redemption of mortgage by mortgagee).
purger une – : to disencumber an estate, to redeem, to pay off a mortgage.
radiation d'– : entry of satisfaction of mortgage.
relevé d'– (s) : search of encumbrances.
saisie d'une – : foreclosure.
sur – : on mortgage.
titre de première – : first-mortgage bond.
hypothéquer *une créance* : to secure a debt by mortgage.
hypothéquer des titres (déposer des titres en nantissement) : hypothecation (lodging stock as a security).

hypothèse (f) : hypothesis, assumption.
– de base : basic assumption.
en se fondant sur l'– que : on the assumption that.

NOTES

I

idéal (a) : [J] *concours − (formel)* : perfect concurrence (several offences in one action).

identification (f) : identification.
[J] **identifier** : to establish the identity of s.o.

identité (f) : identity.
[A] *établir son −* : to prove one's identity.
carte, pièce, papiers d'− : identity card, papers.
[J] *− de l'action judiciaire* : eadem personae, eadem res, eadem causa petendi.
service de l'− judiciaire : the Criminal Records Office.

idéologie (f) : ideology ; theorizing.

idéologique (a) : ideologic(al).

ignorance (f) : ignorance, lack of knowledge.
par − : through ignorance.

ignorer (v) : to ignore, to be ignorant of.
[J] *nul n'est censé − la loi* : (nemo censitur ignorance legem) ignorance of law is no excuse.

illégal (a) : illegal, unlawful.
absence −(e) : absence without leave.
exercice − d'une profession : unlawful practice of a profession, trade.
commettre une **illégalité** : to commit an unlawful act.

illégitime (a) : illegitimate, undue, illegal.
[J] *enfant − (naturel)* : illegitimate child, bastard.
mariage − : unlawful marriage.
[F] *enrichissement −* : illegal enrichment.

illicite (a) : illicit, unlawful.
concurrence − (déloyale) : unfair competition.
profits −(s) : illicit profits.

illimité (a) : unlimited.
congé − : indefinite leave.
responsabilité −(e) : unlimited liability.

illisible (a) : illegible (signature, etc.).

image *(de marque)* (f) : brand, public image.

imbécile (a) : imbecile.
(a cause for *interdiction*).

imitation (f) : imitation, copy, forgery, counterfeit.
− de signature : forging of signature.

immatériel (a) : unsubstantial.
[J] *biens, droits −(s)* : intangible rights, assets.
dommage − : moral prejudice.

immatriculation (f) : registering, registration, enrolment, enrolling.
− d'un navire : registry of a ship.
plaque d'− (minéralogique) d'une automobile : registration plate of a motor-car.

immédiat(e) *(cause, successeur)* (a) : direct, (cause, successor).
voisinage − : immediate vicinity.

immeuble (a et m) : house, premises, building, estate, property.
[J] real, fixed.
biens −(s) : real estate, realty.
− agricole, rural : landed property.
− par déclaration du propriétaire (immobilisation) : conversion of personal property into real by declaration of owner (such as Government stock, shares of the Bank of France, etc.).
− par destination : fixtures.
− fictif : thing fictitiously considered as real property.
− hypothéqué : encumbered, [U.S.] affected, property.
− par nature : tangible real property.
− par l'objet auquel il s'applique : chattels real, intangible real property.
− de rapport : building erected for letting out, *(péjoratif)* tenement.
− urbain : urban property.
− à usage commercial : business premises.
− à usage de bureaux : office building.
impôt **immobilier** : land tax, tax on realty.
agence **immobilière** : estate agency.
placements immobiliers : investments in real estate.
propriété immobilière : real estate.
saisie immobilière : attachment of real property.
société immobilière : building society.
vente immobilière : sale of real property.

(s')immiscer dans (v) : *(une affaire)* to interfere with (an affair).
− une succession : to assume a succession.
immixtion *d'un commanditaire dans la gestion*

d'une société : interference of a sleeping partner in the management of a company.

immobilisation (f) : [F] tie-up of capital, immobilization, capitalisation of expenditure.
immobilisations, actif **immobilisé** : fixed assets, capital expenditure.
capital immobilisé : locked-up capital.
immobiliser : to tie up.

immoralité (f) : immorality.

immunité (f) : immunity.
– *diplomatique :* exterritoriality (of diplomatic personnel).
– *fiscale :* tax immunity, exemption from taxation, franchise.
– *parlementaire :* parliamentary immunity of members of legislative bodies against prosecution and arrest (may be lifted by the assemblies and not operative when the member is taken in flagrante delicto).
– *totale :* unqualified immunity.

immutabilité (f) : immutability.

impact *(de l'impôt)* (m) : impact (of taxation).

impartial (a) : unbiased, unprejudiced.

impartir (v) : [J] to grant (right, favour), to allow.
– *un délai :* to allow time.
– *des pouvoirs :* to allow powers.

impasse (f) : deadlock.
– *budgétaire :* « impasse », budgetary deficit.
négociations dans l'– : negotiations in a deadlock.
se trouver dans une – : to be, to find oneself in a dilemma.

impayé (a et m) : (a) unpaid.
(m) [C] bill dishonoured, unpaid on term unsettled.

impense (f) : [F] [J] expense.

impératif *(loi, mandat)* (a) : imperative (law, mandate).
décision **impérative** : binding decision.

impéritie (f) : incompetence.

imperfection (f) : [J] defect (of contract).

impertinent (a) : [J] irrelevant.

impétrant (m) : grantee (of degree, title), plaintiff.

implantation (f) : setting up, location.

implicite (a) : absolute, implicite, implied.
accord – : implied agreement.

impliquer *(dans)* (v) : to involve (in).

(les) impondérables (m pl) : intangible factors.

importance (f) : importance, import, extent.
sans – : unimportant, petty.
– *d'une maison :* standing of a firm.

importateur (a et m) : (a) importing.
pays – : importing country.
(m) importer.

importation (f) : importation, importing, import.
commerce d'– : import trade.
droits d'– : import duties.
– (s) invisibles (visibles) : invisible (visible) imports.
harmonisation des prix à l'– avec les prix intérieurs américains : American selling price.

importer (v) : to import.

imposable (a) : taxable, rateable, assessable.
revenu – : taxable income.

imposer (v) : to lay on.
[J] **imposé** *par la loi :* statutory.
– *une charge à qn :* to lay a charge on s.o.
charges imposées au successeur : charges on an estate.
[F] – *qn :* to tax s.o., to rate s.o.
– *un immeuble :* to assess a building, to levy a rate on a building.
– *qch. :* to make sth. taxable.
contribuable imposé à : taxpayer subject to.
[C] *marchandises imposées :* goods rated.
prix imposé : retail price fixed by manufacturer.

imposition (f) : [F] 1° imposition, taxing, taxation ; assessment (of property).
2° tax, duty ; rates.
année d'– : tax year.
capacité d'– : taxability, ability to pay, taxpaying ability, taxpaying capacity.

impôt (m) : (also *contribution* or *taxe*) [A] tax, duty, rate.
1° – *(s) (par leur nature) :* kinds of taxation.
– *additionnel :* additional tax.
– *sur le capital :* capital levy, capital tax, property tax.
– *de capitation :* head tax.
– *cédulaire :* scheduled tax.
– *dégressif :* degressive taxation, tax on des-

cending scale.
— *direct* : direct taxation, assessed taxes.
— *forfaitaire* : composition tax.
—, *contribution de guerre (hist.)* : war levy.
— *indiciaire* : tax rated on outward signs of wealth (servants, cars, etc.).
— *indirect* : indirect taxation, indirect taxes, excise taxes.
— *sur la fortune* : capital tax, property tax, taxes on wealth.
— *mobilier* : tax on personalty.
— *personnel* : capitation.
— *progressif* : graduated tax.
— *proportionnel* : flat rate tax.
— *réel* : property tax.
— *sur le produit de qch.* : tax on the proceeds of sth.
— *de quotité* : tax calculated by application of a flat rate to all the property taxable (the total product of the tax is not stated in advance unlike the *impôt de répartition*).
— *de répartition* : tax resulting from the apportionment of a global figure stated in the appropriation bill *(loi de finances)*.
— *retenu à la source* : withholding of tax, deduction at source.
— *sur les superbénéfices* : excess profits tax.
— *de superposition* : supertax, surtax.
2° — *(s) (par leur application)* : levied taxes.
a) — *direct* : assessed, direct, taxes.
— *sur les bénéfices agricoles* : tax on agricultural profits, farmer's tax.
— *sur les bénéfices industriels et commerciaux* : tax on industrial and commercial profits.
— *sur les bénéfices des professions non commerciales* : tax on professionnal earnings.
— *sur le chiffre d'affaires* : turnover tax, sales tax.
— *des centimes additionnels* : additional tax paid over and above the assessment (mostly for local purposes).
— *(s) communaux* : rates, borough rates.
— *foncier* : land tax.
— *sur le revenu (des personnes physiques)* : income-tax.
surtaxe progressive sur le revenu : supertax, surtax.
contribution mobilière : occupancy tax.
— *sur les mutations* : death and gift duty.
contribution des patentes (taxe professionnelle) : licence and franchise duties.
— *sur la plus-value, sur la valeur ajoutée, sur l'augmentation de valeur* : betterment tax, tax on unearned increment.
— *sur la plus-value (en capital) réalisée* : capital gains tax.
— *sur la propriété bâtie, non bâtie* : tax on structures, on ground plots.
— *sur les traitements, salaires, pensions et rentes viagères* : tax on salaries, wages and life annuities.

— *sur les sociétés* : corporation tax, corporate duty, [U.K.] advanced corporation tax (A.C.T.).
— *sur les salaires à la charge des employeurs* : pay-roll tax, tax on salaries.
— *de voirie* : Road Fund tax.
b) — *indirect* : indirect taxes, excise.
— *de consommation, à la consommation* : excise duties, tax on commodities, consumption tax.
— *des jeux* : tax levied on gaming in clubs, on race bettings, etc.
— *sur le luxe* : luxury taxe.
l'Enregistrement : registry fees.
le Timbre : stamp duties, stamp tax.
— *sur les opérations de Bourse* : tax on Stock Exchange transactions.
— *sur le revenu des capitaux mobiliers* : tax on stocks and shares.
taxe sur les transactions : sales tax.
— *(taxe) sur les spectacles* : entertainment tax.
3° *action en répétition de l'*— : claim for refund of tax.
arrérages d'— : outstanding tax.
asseoir l'— *sur qch.* : to lay, to levy a tax on sth.
assiette de l'— : subject-matter of taxation, basis of tax.
assujetti à l'— *(contribuable)* : taxpayer.
assujettissement à l'— : liability for (to) tax.
congé en matière d'— *indirect* : release from bond.
dégrèvement d'— : tax reduction.
dégrèvement partiel d'— : reduced assessment.
dégrever partiellement : to reduce the tax.
déclaration d'— : tax return.
évasion en matière d'— : tax avoidance.
exempt d'— : immune from tax, tax-free, duty-free.
exonéré d'— : exempt from tax.
frapper d'un — : to tax, to lay a tax on.
fraude en matière d'— *(fraude fiscale)* : tax evasion.
majorer les —*(s)* : to increase taxes.
percevoir un — : to collect a tax.
percepteur des contributions directes : tax collector, tax gatherer.
péréquation des —*(s)* : equalization of taxes.
provision pour — : reserve for taxation.
rappel de l'— : calling in of additional or outstanding tax.
receveur des contributions indirectes : collector of excise.
réduction avant — : tax allowance.
remettre un — : to remit a tax.
remise de l'— : remission of tax.
rôle de l'— : assessment roll.
taux de l'— : rate of taxation.
théorie de l'— : theory of taxation.

imprescriptible (a) : [J] imprescriptible, indefeasible (right, etc.).

imprévision (f) : want of foresight.

imprévu (a) : unforeseen, unexpected, contingent.
cas — : contingency.
dépenses — (es) : contingent expenses.
événements — (s) : (unexpected) contingent events.

imprimé (m) : form.
— (s) : printed matter.

improductif *(placement)* (a) : unproductive (investment).

imprudence (f) : imprudence, rashness.
[J] misfeasance.
— *professionnelle* : imprudent act.
homicide par — : manslaughter through negligence.

impubère (m et f) : [J] under the age of puberty (minor).

impuissance (f) : [J] impotentia cœundi.
impuissant : impotent.

impur (a) : dirty.
flottement — (sur le marché des changes) : dirty float.

imputation (f) : imputation, appropriation.
[J] (civ.) a) (collatio bonorum) deduction of a payment, a gift, etc., from a sum or a portion, b) application of a partial payment to one of several outstanding debts to the same creditor (debtor's privilege).
(cr.) charge.
— *calomnieuse* : slanderous charges.
[F] — *intégrale* : full credit.
— *des paiements* : application of payments.
méthode de l'— : credit method, tax credit method.

imputer (v) : to impute, to apply, to charge.
[J] — *un crime à un innocent* : to impute a crime to an innocent person.
[F] — *qch. sur qch.* : to deduct sth. from sth., to charge sth. to sth.
— *des frais à, sur, un compte* : to charge expenses to an account.

inacceptation *(d'une traite)* (f) : non-acceptance (of a draft).

inaccordable(s) *(intérêts)* (a) : irreconciliable (interests).

inacquitté (a) : undischarged.
facture — (e) : unreceipted bill.

inactif (a) : dull.

inaction *(du marché)* (f) : dullness (of the market).

inactivité (f) : dullness.
être en — (personne) : out of work, unemployed (person).

inadmissible (a) : inadmissible, out of the question.

inaliénabilité (f) : [J] inalienability.

inaliénable (a) : untransferable.
le domaine public est — : public property may not be assigned.

inamovibilité (f) : [J] fixity of tenure, irremovability of judge (holding appointment for life), [U.S.] « appointment for good behavior ».
agencements **inamovibles** *(meubles à fixe demeure)* : fixtures.

inapplicable (a) : inapplicable, unenforceable.

inapte (a) : unfit for, unsuited for (to).

inattaquable *(raisonnement, droit)* (a) : unquestionable (argument, right).

inauguration (f) : inauguration, (U.S.) opening dedication.

incapable (a) : incapacitated, disqualified.
— *d'engendrer* : impotent.
— *de contracter, de tester* : incompetent to make, disqualified from making a contract, a will.
— *de travailler* : unfit to work, disabled.

incapacité (f) : *(physique)* unfitness, disablement.
[J] disability, disqualification, legal incapacity.
frappé d'— : incapacited, disqualified by law (minor, married woman) or judgment (convict, prodigal, lunatic).
— *électorale* : disfranchissement.
— *d'ester en justice* : incapacity to sue.
— *permanente* : permanent disablement.
— *temporaire* : temporary disablement.
— *de travail* : incapacitation for work.

incarcération (f) : imprisonment.

incertitude (f) : uncertainty.
— *sur le comportement des consommateurs* : consumer uncertainty.

incessible (a): inalienable, unalienable, untransferable.
droit — : inalienable right.

incessibilité (f): [J] intransferability, inalienability (of right).

inceste (m): incest.

inchangé (a): unaltered, unchanged.

incidemment (adv.): incidentally.

incidence *(de l'impôt)* (f): incidence (of tax), tax effect.

incident (m et a): (m) [J] point of law, incidental plea.
faux — civil (inscription de, en, faux): plea of forgery.
soulever un — : to raise a point of law.
(a) *appel* — *(joint), recours* — : appeal on a point of law.
jugement — : interlocutory judgment.

incitation (f): incitement, instigation.
[J] — *de mineur à la débauche*: inducing a minor to lead a dissolute life.
[F] —*(s) fiscales*: tax incentives.
incitation à investir: investment incentive, stimulus.

inclure (v): to include.
ci-inclus: enclosed herewith.
[J] to insert.
éléments à — *(dans une déclaration d'impôt)*: inclusions (in a tax return).

inclusion (f): inclusion, insertion.
— *d'une clause nouvelle dans un contrat*: insertion of a new clause in an agreement.

incomber (v): (impersonal) incumbent.
il **incombe** *au demandeur d'apporter la preuve de ses allégations* (actori incumbat probatio): it rests with the plaintiff to substantiate his allegations.

incommode (a): inconvenient.
[A] *établissements* —*(s)*: business premises of noisy or obnoxious trades (see *enquête* de commodo et incommodo).

incommutabilité (f): [J] indefeasibility of right or property.
— *de la possession*: absolute ownership.
propriétaire **incommutable**: absolute owner, owner who cannot be dispossessed.
biens incommutables: non-transferable property.

incompatibilité (f): incompatibility.
[J] — *de fonctions*: incompatibility of offices.
— *d'humeur*: incompatibility (cause put forward in divorce cases).
incompatible *avec*: incompatible with, inconsistent with.

incompétence (f): incompetence, lack of authority to do sth.
[J] lack of jurisdiction.
— *absolue*: complete lack of jurisdiction of a court (not the one provided by law in a specific case).
— *matérielle*: incompetency ratione materiae.
— *personnelle*: incompetency ratione personae.
— *relative*: relative incompetency (the court is qualified, but the case should be submitted to another tribunal of the same order and degree).
— *territoriale*: incompetency ratione loci.
exception d'— *(déclinatoire)*: declinatory plea.
jugement d'— : disclaimer of jurisdiction.
incompétent *(à)*: unqualified, not qualified (to).
tribunal incompétent: unqualified court.

incompressible (a) *(frais généraux)*: fixed (charges, expenses).

inconciliable (a): incompatible (theories, etc.).

inconditionnel (a): unconditional.
[J] *responsabilité* —*(le)*: absolute liability.

inconduite (f): [J] misconduct.

inconsommable (a): permanent.
[J] *capital* — : indestructible capital (land, etc.).

incontestable (a): undeniable, unquestionable.
argument — : cogent.
les faits sont —*(s)*: the facts are indisputable.
incontesté: uncontested, unquestioned.

inconvénient (m): drawback.

inconvertible (a): unconvertible.

incorporation (f): incorporation.
— *des réserves*: incorporation of reserves.

incorporel (a): incorporeal, intangible.
[J] *biens* —*(s)*: intangible property, choses in action.

incorruptible (a): [J] unbribable, incorruptible.

incriminer (v): [J] to accuse, to charge, to indict.

inculpation (f): [J] indictment, charge, inculpation (for misdemeanour).
— *(arrêté) sous l'— de meurtre:* (arrested) on a charge of murder.
inculpé de complicité: charged with complicity.
inculpé: the accused (of a misdemeanour).
inculpé défaillant: defaulting defendant.

incurie (f): slackness, careless negligence.

indéchiffrable (a): unintelligible, illegible (writing).

indélicat (a): indelicate, dishonest, unscrupulous.
procédés — (s): sharp practices.

indemnisation (f): indemnification.

indemnité (f): *(pour pertes subies)* indemnity, indemnification, compensation, *(pour retard)* penalty; allowance, grant, benefit.
— *pour accident de travail:* injury benefit.
— *d'assurance:* insured amount.
— *de cherté de vie:* cost of living allowance, bonus.
— *de chômage:* unemployment benefit, dole.
— *de congédiement:* dismissal allowance.
— *de départ:* « golden handshake » payment.
— *en cas de décès:* death benefit.
— *de déplacement, indemnité journalière:* per diem allowance, travelling allowance.
— *de déplacement de témoin:* conduct money.
— *d'éviction:* compensation for ejection.
— *d'expert:* expert's fees.
— *d'expropriation:* indemnity for expropriation.
— *fixée par accord:* penalty agreed beforehand.
— *familiale, de charges de famille:* family allowance, child bounty.
— *(s) de fonctionnaires:* special grants, allowances to officials.
— *de fonction:* entertainment allowance.
— *forfaitaire:* indemnification by a lump sum.
— *de guerre:* war indemnity.
— *de licenciement:* dismissal allowance.
— *de liquidation:* final settlement.
— *de logement:* rent allowance.
— *de résidence, de nourriture:* board-wages.
— *parlementaire:* Member's emoluments.
— *de route:* travelling expenses, mileage.
— *de sauvetage:* salvage.
— *supplémentaire:* weighting allowance.
— *(droits) de surestarie:* demurrage.
— *pour incapacité de travail temporaire, pour invalidité:* partial, permanent, disablement allowance, pension.

— *de vie chère:* cost-of-living allowance.
action en — : claim for compensation.
droit à une — : right to compensation.

indépendamment *(de)* (adv): regardless (of), without regard to.

indépendance (f): independence.

indépendante *(activité)* (a): independent (activity).
circonstances — (s) de la volonté de qn: circumstances beyond s.o.'s control.

indésirable (a): undesirable.

index (m): *(table des matières)* topical index.

indexation (f): pegging of prices, indexation, indexing.
indexer: to index-link, to gear (salaries) to.
indexer les prix: to peg prices.
indexé: index-linked.
valeurs indexées: index-linked stock.

indication (f): indication, piece of indication.
— *d'origine:* caption.
[F] *fausse — de revenu:* false declaration of income, untrue income return.
indicateur: informer, police spy.
— *économique:* indicator.
indicateurs des activités économiques (au cours d'une courte période précédente): (U.S.) coincident indicator.
des activités économiques avancées (courte période): leading indicators.
des activités économiques retardées (longue période): lagging indicators.
à (court, long) terme: (shorter, longer) indicators.
indicateur des divergences (des monnaies européennes par rapport à l'ECU): divergence indicator.

indice (m): indication, sign, index, (statistics), figure.
— *boursier:* Stock Exchange index.
— *du coût de la vie:* index numbers of the cost of living, cost-of-living index.
— *Dow-Jones:* Dow-Jones index.
— *d'écoute:* T.V. rating (T.V.R.).
— *(s) pondérés:* weighted indexes.
— *des prix compte tenu de l'impôt:* tax and price index.
— *des prix de détail:* consumer (retail) price index.
— *de profitabilité* (d'enrichissement relatif): probability index (P.I.).
— *de rentabilité interne:* internal rate of return.
— *des valeurs en Bourse:* stock average.
— *de valeur d'échange:* exponent of exchan-

geable value.
nombres −(s) du coût de la vie : index numbers of the cost of living.

indifférent (a) : indifferent, immaterial.
la façon dont est déterminé le montant est − (e) : the manner in which the amount is determined is immaterial.

indigent (m) : (now **économiquement faible**) poor, needy.
[A] poor person.

indignité (f) : indignity.
exclu de la succession pour cause d'− : debarred from succession.

indirect (a) : indirect.
avantage − : unfair advantage.
impôt − : indirect tax, excise duty.
ligne −(e) (de parenté) : collateral relationship.
[J] *preuve −(e) :* circumstancial evidence.

indisponibilité (f) : [J] inalienability.
biens **indisponibles** : inalienable property, entailed estate.
quotité indisponible de l'héritage : entailed portion.
[F] *fonds indisponibles :* unavailable capital.

indissolubilité (f) : [J] indissolubility (of marriage).

individuel (a) : individual, personal, private, single.
[J] several *(chacun pour le tout).*
droits −(s) : personal rights.
entreprise −(le) : sole proprietorship.
responsabilité conjointe et solidaire (−(le)) : joint and several liability.

indivis (a) : joint.
bénéficiaires − : joint beneficiaries.
biens − : undivided, joint, estate.
propriétaires − : joint owners.
succession −(e) : inheritance in indivisum.

indivisibilité *(des co-auteurs d'un dommage, etc.)* (f) : joint liability of those responsible for (an injury, etc.).

indivision (f) : [J] co-ownership, joint tenancy, indivisum, (hist.) coparcenary.
indivisaire : co-owner, (hist.) coparcener.
indivisément, *par indivis :* jointly.

indu (a) : [J] not owed, not due (money), *action en répétition de l'− :* (condictio indebiti) action for the recovery of payment made by mistake.
[A] against the regulations.

induire en erreur (v) : to delude, to mislead.

indûment (adv.) : unduly.
impôt − perçu : tax unduly collected.

industrie (f) : industry, manufacture, trade.
− (aéronautique, artisanale, automobile, chimique, etc.) : (aircraft, cottage, motor-car, chemical, etc.) industry.
− du bâtiment : building (constructional) trade.
− clé : key industry.
− pharmaceutique : [US] ethical drug industry.
− de pointe : high-tech.
− principale : staple industry.
− de transformation : processing industry.
− qui emploie une main-d'œuvre nombreuse : labour intensive industry.
les −(s) lourdes : the heavy industries.
les −(s) légères : the light industries.

industriel (a et m) : (m) manufacturer, industrialist.
(a) industrial.
centre − : industrial centre.
« *−(les)* » *(valeurs industrielles) :* industrials, industrial shares.
établissement − : manufacturing firm.
logistique −(le) : engineering.

inégalité (f) : inequality.
les inégalités sociales : social inequalities.

inéligibilité (f) : ineligibility.

inéligible (a) : ineligible.

inemployé *(capital)* (a) : unemployed (capital).

inexact(e) *(déclaration, évaluation)* (a) : inaccurate, incorrect, wrong (statement, valuation).

inexactitude (f) : inaccuracy, incorrectness.

inexécution (f) : non performance, non-fulfiment, breach (of...).
inexécutable *(projet)* : unworkable (scheme).

inexistence *(de preuve)* (f) : non-existence (of a proof).

inexigible (a) : not-due, not payable.

infamant (a) : defamatory, ignominious.
[J] *peine infamante :* penalty involving loss of civil rights.

infanticide (a, m et f) : [J] infanticide, child murder, child murderer, murderess.

inférieur (à) (a) : below, inferior (to).
si le revenu est — à une somme donnée, il n'est pas imposable : if income is below a given amount, it is not taxable.

infirmer (v) : to cancel, to annul, [U.S.] to vacate.
[J] to annul, to quash a judgment, to set verdict aside, to weaken evidence, to invalidate a claim.
— un jugement en appel : (pour erreur de droit) to reverse, *(pour erreur de fait)* to recall a judgment.

infirmité (f) : disablement.

inflation (f) : inflation.
— à deux chiffres : two digit inflation.
— anticipée : expected inflation.
— galopante : galloping inflation.
— monétaire : inflated currency.
— par poussée des coûts : cost-push inflation.
— provoquée par excès de la demande : excess demand inflation.
— provoquée par une pression de la demande : demand-pull inflation.
— rampante : creeping inflation.
— structurelle : built-in inflation.
juguler l'— : to control inflation.
taux d'— : rate of inflation.
politique d'expansion par — : feed the cold theory.

infliction (f) : [J] infliction (of penalty).
infliger *une amende :* to impose a fine.

information (f) : 1° [J] enquiry.
ouverture d'une — : (cr.) opening of a preliminary investigation.
2° *(nouvelles) :* news, [U.S.] news coverage.
3° *(données) :* data.
informer *contre qn :* to inform, to lay information against s.o.
renvoyer une cause à plus ample informé : to defer a case for further enquiry.
s'informer *de qch. :* to enquire about, to make enquiries about (sth.)
pour plus ample **informé** : for further inquiry.

informatiser (v) : to computerize.

informatique (f) : data processing, electronic D.P., computer science.
— de gestion : business data processing.

informe (a) : formless, not complying with the requirements of law.

infraction (f) : [J] infraction, offence, trespass.
— au devoir : breach of duty.
— des droits : infringement of rights, trespass.
— à la loi : infraction of, trespassing against the law.
— à la paix publique : breach of the peace.
— au règlement : breach of the rules, the regulations.
être en — avec les règlements : to infringe regulations.

infrastructure (f) : facilities (v. installations).

ingérence (f) : interference.
s'ingérer *dans les affaires d'autrui :* to interfere with somebody else's business.

ingratitude (f) : ungratefulness.
[J] cause of revocation of a bounty inter vivos or in will.

inhabilité (f) : [J] legal incapacity.
inhabile *à tester :* incompetent to make a will.

inhibition (f) : prohibition.
[J] « *— (s) et défenses sont faites de...* » : « the parties are prohibited from... ».

inimitié (f) : hostility.
[J] *— capitale :* bias, partiality, fundamental ill-feeling (motive for challenge of judge or arbitrator, exception to witness).

initiative (f) : initiative.
— privée : free enterprise.
syndicat d'— : local association for the encouragement of touring.
[J] *— législative :* right of the Government and of the *Assemblée Nationale* and the *Sénat* to propose legislation. Bills tabled by the Government are known as *projets de loi,* those tabled by Members as *propositions de loi* (≠ Government bills, private Member's bills).

initié (m) : [B] insider.
délit d'— : insider dealings offence.

injonction (f) : [J] injunction.
arrêt portant — : order of the court.
— de payer : order, injunction to pay.

injure (f) : wrong, injury, insult, abuse, public slandler.
[J] tort.
— grave : injury or slander so serious as to give ground for divorce.
— par correspondance postale ou télégraphique circulant à découvert : abuse in telegram or open letter, semi-public injury, (a minor offence : *délit correctionnel*).
écrits **injurieux** : libel.
discours injurieux : derogatory speech.

injustifié (a): [J] unwarrantable.
[F] *enrichissement* − : unexplained, unaccountable, enrichment.

innocence (f): innocence.

innocent(e) (m et f): innocent, *(non coupable)* not guilty.
innocenter *qn*: to clear s.o. of a charge, to declare not guilty.

innomé (a): unnamed, nameless.
[J] *contrat* − : innominate contract.

inofficiel (a): unofficial.

inofficieux (a): [J] inofficious.
testament − : inofficious will, testament.

inopérant (a): [J] inoperative.
mesures − *(es)*: inoperative measures.

inquisition (f): inquisition.
[A] − *fiscale*: ruthless fiscal measures.

insaisissable (a): [J] not attachable, not distrainable.
bien de famille − : homestead immune from attachment.
insaisissabilité *des salaires*: immunity from distraint (attachment).

insalubre *(immeuble, industrie)* (a): unhealthy (building, industry).

inscription (f): inscribing, registration, enrolment, entry.
[J] [F] − *de (en) faux*: plea of forgery.
− *en compte*: putting in.
− *à un compte courant*: credit to a current account.
− *sur le grand livre (de la Dette publique)*: Treasury scrip.
− *hypothécaire*: registration of mortgage.
− *d'un marin au rôle d'équipage*: signing ship's articles.
− *maritime*: seaboard conscription, conscription among the coastal population for the navy.
− *au rôle*: enrolment on causelist.
être **inscrit** *au barreau*: to be called to the bar.
la dette inscrite: the consolidated debt.
droit d'− : registration, entrance fee.
feuille d'− : entry form.
inscrire une question à l'ordre du jour: to put an item on the agenda.
[B] *valeur inscrite, non inscrite à la cote officielle*: listed, unlisted stock.
inscrire *un nom*: to enter a name.

insertion (f): insertion.

insolvabilité (f): [C] insolvency.
débiteur notoirement **insolvable**: debtor notoriously insolvent.
[J] state of bankruptcy of non-merchants.

insoumis (m): [J] absentee conscript or reservist.

inspecteur (m): inspector.
− *des impôts*: inspector of taxes.
− *de police*: police inspector.
− *du travail*: factory inspector.

inspection (f): inspection, inspectorate.
[A] − *du travail*: labour inspectorate, inspection.

instabilité *(économique)* (f): (economic) instability.

installations (f pl): equipping, fittings.
− *industrielles*: industrial facilities.
− *portuaires*: harbour facilities.

instance (f): [J] process, suit, instance.
− *d'appel*: court of appeals, appeal proceedings.
− *de conciliation*: divorce proceedings in the reconciliation stage.
− *pendante*: pending suit.
demande introductive d'− : writ of summons.
en − : pendant, pendent, pending.
être en − *de divorce*: to be engaged in divorce proceedings.
exploit introductif d'− : first process.
former une − : to go to law, to institute an action.
introduire une − : to institute an action.
reprise d' − : revivor.
tribunal de première − : original jurisdiction, court of first instance (# county court).
acquittée en seconde − : acquitted on appeal.
vider une − : to fight out a case.

instant (a): urgent, pressing.

instigation (f): instigation, enticement, inducement.
agir à l' − *de qn*: to act on s.o.'s instigation.

instituer (v): *(une règle)* to institute, to set up, to found, to lay down, *(un juge, etc.)* to appoint.
− *une curatelle*: to establish a guardianship.
− *un héritier*: to appoint a heir.
− *des poursuites*: to institute proceedings.
institué (m): testamentary heir, legatee, devisee.

institut (m) : institute.
— *d'émission* : bank of issue, (U.S.) Fed Federal Reserve Board (system).
— *National des Statistiques et des Enquêtes Economiques* (I.N.S.E.E.) # [U.S.] National Bureau of Economic Research.

institution (f) : institution, body, agency.
— *(s) spécialisées des Nations Unies* : United Nations specialized agencies.
[J] — *contractuelle* : appointment of heir (spouse or future children) in prenuptial settlement.

instruction (f) : instruction, direction, training, briefing.
[J] preliminary investigation (of case).
code d' — *criminelle* (hist.) : code of criminal procedure.
— *écrite* : written statements of a case.
— *préalable* : preliminary investigation.
juge d' —, *juge instructeur* : examining magistrate.
ouvrir une — : to open a judicial enquiry.
instruire *une affaire* : to investigate a case.

instrument (m) : [J] legal instrument (deed, contract, writ, etc.).
— *authentique* : certified instrument.
— *de crédit* : bill.
— *diplomatique* : diplomatic instrument.
— *de preuve* : documentary evidence.
instrumenter : to draw up a document.
instrumenter contre qn : to order proceedings to be taken against s.o.
témoin **instrumentaire** : witness to a deed.

(à l')insu de : unknown of, without the knowledge of.

insuffisance (f) : insufficiency, deficiency.
— *du capital versé* : paid-up capital deficiency.
— *de moyens* : inadequacy of means.
— *de personnel* : shortage of hands.
[J] *clôture pour* — *d'actif* : closing of bankruptcy proceedings when assets are inadequate to defray legal expenses.

insuffisant (a) : inadequate.
évaluation — *(e)* : underestimation, undervaluation.

intangible (a) : intangible.

intégral (a) : complete.
[J] *restitution* — *(e)* : restitutio in integrum.
[C] *paiement* — : payment in full.
exigible **intégralement** : payable in full.

intégration (f) : integration, combination, [U.S.] trustification.
— *économique et monétaire* : Economic and Monetary Integration.
— *horizontale* : horizontal integration.
— *verticale (de la matière première à la vente au détail)* : vertical integration.

intégrité (f) : integrity, entirety.

intenter (v) : to bring, to enter.
— *une action* : to institute proceedings.
— *un procès* : to take legal action, to undertake proceedings, to sue.

intention (f) : intention, purpose, design.
[J] intent.
— *criminelle, délictueuse* : criminal, malicious, intent ; wrongful intention.
— *dolosive* : (civ.) intention to wrong s.o., (cr.) intention to injure interests protected by law.
— *d'exécuter l'obligation* : animus solvendi.
— *frauduleuse* : fraudulent intent.
— *malveillante, méchante, maligne* : evil, ill-willed, intent.
dans l' — *de nuire* : maliciously.
les — *(s) du législateur* : the aim of a bill, legislative intent.

intentionnel (a) : intentional.
délit — : deliberate offence (opp. *délit d'imprudence, délit contraventionnel*).
poser au jury la question — *(le)* : to put the question of intent to the jury.
causer **intentionnellement** *un dommage* : to inflict damage intentionally, on purpose.

intercéder (v) : to intercede.
[J] to go bail, either as joint debtor or as surety, or in providing real security.
intercession *de la femme en faveur du mari* : guaranty of wife in favour of husband.

interdiction (f) : interdiction, prohibition, forbidding, restraint.
[J] (civ.) state of minority declared by court in respect of a prodigal or of a lunatic, depriving him of the control over his property.
(cr.) disability inflicted by law to a convict, involving loss of civil rights.
— *des droits civiques* : suspension of civic rights.
— *de séjour* : banishment, prohibition to criminals to stay in France or in certain French departments.
mainlevée d' — : restoration of full rights.
aliéné **interdit** : certified lunatic.
faire **interdire** *qn* : to have s.o. declared incapable of managing his own affairs.

intéressé (a) : interested, concerned.
être — *dans une entreprise* : to have a vested interest in a concern.

les parties — *(es)* : the interested parties.
intéressement du personnel (sous forme d'actions de la société) : stock option, industrial co-partnership.

intérêt (m) : interest, share, stake ; advantage, benefit.
l'— commun : the common good.
l'— public : public interest.
« *il n'est pas de l'—* » *(du contribuable)* : it is not the taxpayer's interest.
[J] *—(s) civils :* damages awarded to private individual having instituted and won a civil action parallel to prosecution in a criminal case.
—(s) compensatoires : interest awarded by way of damages.
dommages- —(s) : damages.
accorder des dommages- —(s) : to give damages.
action en dommages- —(s) : action for damages.
[F] *— annuel :* yearly interest.
— du capital : interest on capital.
—(s) compensatoires : default interest.
— composé (anatocisme) : compound interest (anatocism).
— courant : current interest.
— couru : accrued interest.
— de droit, conventionnel : interest stipulated by contract.
— échu, exigible : outstanding interest, interest payable.
— à échoir : accruing interest.
— d'un investissement exprimé en pourcentage : rate of return.
— légal : legal rate of interest.
—(s) moratoires : interest on overdue payment.
—(s) sur prêts et dépôts : interest on loans and deposits.
—(s) du portefeuille : interest on investments.
—(s) prélevés sur le capital : interest paid out of capital.
—(s) à recevoir : interest receivable.
— simple : simple interest.
avoir des —(s) dans une affaire : to have a money interest in a venture.
hausse du taux d'— : rise in the rate of interest.
prêt à — : loan at interest.
porter, produire, rapport — : to bear interest.
taux de l'— : rate of interest.
[B] *— de report :* contango.
cotation d'actions sans —(s) (droit détaché) : quotation of shares ex-dividend.

intérieur (a et m) : internal.
commerce — : home, inland trade.
législation —(e) : municipal law.
le Ministère de l'— # the Home Office, [U.S.] Department of the Interior.

intérim (m) : interim, locum tenens.
assurer l'— : to carry on during absence.
bilan intérimaire : trial balance, provisional balance-sheet.
directeur intérimaire : acting manager.
[F] *dividende par — :* interim dividend.

interjeter (v) : to bring in.
[J] *— appel (d'un jugement) :* to give notice of appeal.

interligne(s) (et renvois) *d'un testament* (m) : marginal alterations of a will.

interlocutoire (a et m) : [J] (a) *décision — :* provisional order.
jugement — : interlocutory judgment.
(m) provisional order.
interloquer *une affaire :* to deliver an interlocutory judgment.

interlope (a) : suspect, shady.
commerce, maison — : dubious business.

intermédiaire (m) : agent, intermediary.
[C] middleman.
par l'— de : through the instrumentality of.
— dans des négociations : go-between *(quelquefois en mauvaise part).*
transaction sans — : direct deal.

intermédiation (f) **financière** : financial intermediation.

intermittent (a) : irregular.
main-d'œuvre d'emploi — : casual labour.

international (a) : international.
droit —, privé, public : international law, private, public.
Cour de justice —(e) : International Court of Justice.
mandat-poste — : foreign money order.

interne (a) : internal, domestic.
taux — de rentabilité : interne rate of return.

internement (m) : [J] *(étrangers)* internment, *(aliénés)* confinement.

interpellation (f) : interpellation.
[J] calling upon a minister in Parliament to account of his action; summoning s.o. to answer, putting a peremptory question.

interposition (f) : interposition, intervention.
[J] *— de personne :* putting forward of a third party not really concerned (mostly fraudulent).
personne interposée : nominee.

interprétation (f) : interpretation.
[J] construction.
— *d'après l'intention des parties* : construction falling in with the will of the parties.
— *de doctrine* : judicial construction in a specific case (binding only the parties concerned).
— *étroite, large, extensive* : narrow restrictive, liberal, broad construction.
— *par voie d'autorité* : authoritative interpretation (by the lawmaker).
fausse — : misconstruction.
texte sujet à — : unclear text.

interpréter (v) : *(une déclaration)* to construe, *(un texte)* to read.
il faut — *le texte comme* : the text should be read as.

interrogatoire (m) : [J] interrogatory, examination (of defendant), interrogation.
— *sur faits et articles* : (civ.) questions put by one party to the other, through a magistrate appointed to that effect (# discovery (oral)).
— *de clôture* : (cr.) final interrogation by the examining magistrate before decision, called *ordonnance de règlement*.
— *contradictoire* : cross-examination.
— *de fonds* : interrogation on the merits of a case.
— *de forme* : interrogation on civil status.
— *d'identité* : preliminary questions as to identity.
procéder à un — : to examine, to cross-examine.

interrompre *(activités)* (v) : to break off.

interruption (f) : [J] — *de la prescription* : interruption of the period of limitation, [U.S.] tolling of the statute of limitations.

intervenir *(dans)* (v) : *(sens général)* to interfere with, to intervene, *(dans une affaire, un acte...)* to be entered into.
partie **intervenante** *à un procès* : intervening party in a lawsuit.

intervention (f) : intervention, becoming a third party in an agreement, etc.
[J] — *forcée (appel en garantie)* : introduction of third parties (approximately an impleader).
tierce — : a third party intervening in a lawsuit.
[C] — *à protêt, acceptation par* —, *acte d'intervention* : acceptance supra protest, acceptance of protested bill for honour, act of honour.
paiement par — : payment on behalf of a third party.

intestat (a) : [J] intestate, intestacy.
héritier ab — : heir to an intestate estate.
mourir — : to die intestate.
succession ab — : intestate estate.

intimation (f) : notification.
[J] 1° notice of appeal handed to defendant.
2° — *de quitter les lieux* : formal notice to quit.
intimé : respondent (in appeal).

intime (conviction) (a) : deep-seated (conviction).

intimidation *(agir par)* (f) : (to act under) undue influence.

intitulé *(d'un acte)* (m) : abstract (of an act).

intra, ultra vires hereditatis : liability of heir.
intra vires : limited to assets, if the succession is accepted without liability beyond the assets descended *(acceptation sous bénéfice d'inventaire)*.
ultra vires : without restriction if acceptance is unconditional *(acceptation simple)*.

intransférable (a) : [J] untransferable (right, etc.).

intransmissible (a) : [J] unassignable (right).

intrants *(facteurs de production)* (m pl) : inputs.

intrinsèque (a) : intrinsic.

introduction (f) : introduction.
[J] — *d'instance* : writ of summons, first process.
[F] [B] — *d'actions* : bringing out of shares.
actions à l'— : shop shares.

intrusion (f) : intrusion.
[J] trespass.

invalidation (f) : [J] invalidation.

invalide (m et a) : disabled, incapacitated.
— *de guerre* : wounded soldier, disabled soldier.
ouvrier — : disabled workman.
[J] *mariage* — : marriage null and void.

invalider (v) : *(testament, élection)* to invalidate, to quash, *(testament)* to set aside.

invalidité (f) : infirmity.
[J] invalidity.
[A] disablement.

— *permanente* : permanent disablement.
pension d'— : disability pension.
[ASS] *assurance- —* : disablement insurance, workman's compensation.
évaluation, risque d'— : disablement assessment, risk.

invendus (m pl) : left-overs, returns.

inventaire (m) : inventory.
dresser, faire un —, **inventorier** : to draw up an inventory.
[J] *accepter une succession sous bénéfice d'—* : to accept an estate without liability to debts beyond the assets descended.
sous bénéfice d'— : conditionally, with reservations.
[C] stock-list, stock-taking.
dresser (faire) l'— : to take stock.
établissement, levée d'— : stock-taking.
livre d'— : balance-sheet book.

inventeur (m) : inventor.
[J] finder.

invention (f) : invention.
brevet d'— : patent.

investi (a) : invested, funded.

investigation (f) : investigation, inquiry.

investir (v) : to invest, to vest.
— qn d'une fonction : to invest, to vest, s.o. with an office.

investissement (m) : investment, investing.
— brut, courant, net, planifié, productif : gross, current, net, planned, productive investment.
—(s) compatibles : competing investments.
—(s) à l'étranger : investments abroad.
— « mise continue » : continuous output investment.
— ponctuel, « mise instantanée » : one-shot investment ; point input investment.
— de remplacement (modernisation) : obsolescence replacement.
— de maintenance (remplacement type pour type) : like for like replacement.
— stratégique : strategic planning.
déduction fiscale pour — : investment allowance.
fonds d'— : investment funds.
multiplicateur d'— : investment multiplier.
sociétés d'— à capital variable (S.I.C.A.V.) : [U.K.] Unit Trusts, [U.S.] Mutual Funds.
investisseur : investor.
investisseurs institutionnels : institutional investors.

invétéré *(délinquant)* (a) : confirmed, irreclaimable (offender).

inviolabilité (f) : inviolability.
[J] *— parlementaire* : immunity of Members of Parliament from arrest and prosecution, unless caught in flagrante delicto.

invisible(s) *(exportations et importations)* (a) : invisible (imports and exports).

involontaire (a) : involuntary.
délit — : unintentional offence.

invoquer (v) : to invoke.
— un motif : to put forward a motive.
— le témoignage de qn : to cal upon a witness.

invraisemblance (f) : unlikeliness, improbability.

irrationnel(le) *(gestion)* (a) : irrational management.

irréalisable *(valeur)* (a) : unrealizable (security).

irrecevable (a) : *(moyen, pourvoi, preuve)* barred, inadmissible, *(théorie)* unacceptable, *(preuve)* incompetent, irrelevant, immaterial.

irrécouvrable (a) : irrecoverable.
[J] *créance —* : bad debt.

irrécusable (a) : unimpeachable, unexceptionable, irrecusable.

irréformable (a) : unreformable, uncorrigible.
[J] irrevocable *(jugement, ordonnance)*.

irréfutable (a) : irrefutable, indisputable.
des arguments —(s) : an unanswerable plea.

irrégularité (f) : *(de la gestion)* irregularity, *(d'un employé)* unpunctuality.

irrégulier (a) : irregular, disorderly, loose (life).
procédure — : irregular procedure.
[B] *tendance —* : irregular trend.

irrémédiable (a) : [J] *vice de contrat —* : irremediable defect in contract (making it void).
vice de forme — : flaw.

irréparable (a) : *(tort)* irreparable, *(perte, erreur)* irretrievable.

irresponsable (a) : irresponsible.
[J] mentally defective, non compos (mentis).
la société n'est pas responsable de : the company is not liable for.

irrévocable (a) : irrevocable, final, indefeasible.
   [J] *jugement* – : decree absolute.
   obligation – : binding agreement.
   [F] *lettre de crédit* – : irrevocable letter of credit.

issu (a) : born from.
   cousin – *de germain* : second cousin.

item (m) : item, article in account.

itératif (a) : [J] reiterated, repeated (prohibition, etc.).
   itérativement : once again.

itinérant (a) : itinerant.

ivresse (f) : intoxication.
   [J] *en état d'– publique* : drunk and disorderly.

NOTES

NOTES

J-K

jacent (a) : ownerless.
[J] *biens* —(s) : estate, land in abeyance.
hoirie —(e) *ou vacante* : haereditas jacens, unclaimed estate.

jauge (f) : gauge, standard of measure.
— *brute, nette de registre* : gross, net, registered tonnage of ship.
le navire — *(200 tonneaux)* : the ship is of (200 tons) burden.

jauger *(un navire)* : to measure a ship.

jet (m) : [J] jetsam.

jeter *(des marchandises sur le marché)* (v) : to throw (goods on the market).
— *le discrédit (sur)* : to bring into disrepute.

jetons de présence (m pl) : tallies, attendance fees (allowances).
— *des administrateurs* : director's fees.

jeu (m) : game, gaming, gambling speculation, transactions.
intérêts en —. : at issue, at stake, involved.
—*(x) d'entreprise* : business games.
— *de bourse* : Stock Exchange transactions.
— *de hasard* : gambling.
— *d'imprimés* : full set of printed forms.
concession des —(x) : licence for a gaming-house, club.
dette de — : gambling debt.
exception de — : plea of gambling debts (unrecoverable in law).
libre — *de la concurrence* : free play of competition.
cacher son — : to plan an underhand game.
mettre en — : to call into play.

jeune (m et a) : young.
[J] — *délinquant* : juvenile offender.

joindre (v) : *(lettre)* to attach, to enclose, *(document)* to annex.
— *l'intérêt au capital* : to add the interest to the capital.
— *qqn (téléphone)* : to get in touch with.
ci-joint : hereto (annexed), herewith.
compte joint : joint account.
les documents (pièces) ci-joint : the enclosed (attached) documents.
« *pièces jointes* » : enclosures.

jonction (f) : junction.
[J] — *de causes, d'instances, de procédures* : joinder, consolidation.

jouer (v) : to play, to gamble, to speculate.
— *à la Bourse* : to gamble (to speculate) on the stock exchange.
— *à la baisse* : to operate for a fall, to go a bear, to bear the market.
— *à la hausse* : to operate for a rise, to go a bull, to bull the market, to play for a rise.
joueur : gambler, speculator.

jouir *(d'un droit)* (v) : to enjoy (a right).
— *des droits civiques* : to enjoy civil rights.

jouissance (f) : enjoyment, possession, tenure.
[J] — *légale* : parents' legal usufruct of their children's estate, husband's of wife's dowry.
— *de passage* : right of way.
droit de — : right of possession.
entrer en — : to enter into possession (of property, premises, etc.).
trouble de — : disturbance of possession.
maison à vendre avec — *immédiate* : house for sale with vacant possession.
[F] right to interest or dividend.
action de — : redeemed share that continues to bear dividends, junior stock.
date de — : date from which interest begins to run.

jour (m) : 1° day.
[J] [C] — *a quo, ad quem* : terminus a quo, ad quem, (mostly first and last day of grace).
— *d'audience* : day in court.
— *de caisse* : paying day (in business).
— *chômé, férié, de repos* : holiday.
— *civil* : 24 hours (day).
— *de congé* : day off.
— *fixe* : appointed day.
— *franc* : clear day (from midnight to midnight).
— *de grâce* : day of grace.
— *ouvrable* : working day.
— *de paie* : pay-day.
—(s) *de planche (staries)* : lay-days.
— *de scrutin* : polling day.
—(s) *de surestarie* : extra lay-days.
— *utile* : lawful day.
à — — : up to date.
à ce — : to date.
au — *le* — : day to day, daily.
argent au — *le* — : call money, overnight

— 149 —

money.
ce – d'hui = *aujourd'hui* : this day.
par – : per diem.
[B] *– de liquidation* : account day, settling day.
– du règlement mensuel : make-up day.
– des reports : contango day.
[F] *intérêts à ce –* : interest to date.
livres à – : books kept up to date.
mettre le grand livre à – : to post up the ledger.
2° aperture, opening.
[J] *– de coutume* : aperture made in the non-party wall, adjoining the next house (see *héberge*).
– de servitude : aperture in the party-wall or the neighbour's wall existing in virtue of an agreement, title or prescription.
– de souffrance, de tolérance : aperture for day-light only, on sufferance by the neighbour (see also *servitude de vue*).

journal (m) : diary, record, newspaper.
– parlé : broadcast news.
– télévisé : T.V. news.
papier – : newsprint.
[A] *– de navigation* : log-book.
– de navigation timbré : official log-book.
– de bord : a) mate's log-book, b) log-book in harbour.
[J] «*le – officiel*» (*lois et décrets, débats, documents parlementaires*) # «the London Gazette», (*pour les débats du Parlement*), «Hansard», (*textes législatifs*) [U.S.] «Statutes at large», (*décrets*) «Federal Register», (*débats du Congrès*) «Congressional Record».
[C] [F] day book, journal.
– des achats : purchases day book.
– originaire : book of original entry.
– des transferts : transfer register.
– des ventes : sales day book.

journalier (a et m) : (a) daily.
(m) day-labourer, journeyman.

journaliser (*une opération*) (v) : to journalize.

judicature (f) : judicature, judgeship, the Bench.

judiciaire (a) : judicial, judiciary, legal.
administrateur – : official receiver, [U.S.] trustee in bankruptcy, (*en matière successorale*) executor.
appareil – : the judicial system, the judiciary.
assistance – : (in forma pauperis) legal aid.
aveu – : cognovit actionem, admission, acknowledgment by record, confession of defence.
casier – : criminal record.

cautionnement – : (caution judicatum solvi) security for costs.
conseil – : guardian to spendthrift.
débats – (s) : hearing.
enquête – : judicial enquiry.
enquête – après mort d'homme : inquest post mortem.
erreur – : miscarriage of justice.
expertise – : report from experts appointed by court.
frais, droits – (s), frais de justice : court-costs, legal charges.
garde – : (in custodia legis) judicial custody.
hypothèque – : mortgage ordered by court.
liquidation – : winding up under court supervision.
nouvelles – (s) : law reports.
ordre – : the judicature.
pièce – : document in a case.
police – : criminal police section entrusted with judiciary matters.
poursuites – (s) : legal proceedings.
le pouvoir – : the Bench, the judicial power.
procédure – : rules of procedure.
service de l'identité – : criminal records office.
transaction – : composition sanctioned by court.
vente – : sale by order of court.
voie – : recourse to law.

juge (m) : judge, justice.
– d'appel : judge in appeal.
– assesseur : associate judge.
– de carrière : professional judge.
– de commerce, consulaire : tradesman acting as judge in a commercial court.
– -commissaire : official receiver.
– compétent : judge entertaining jurisdiction.
– délégué : deputy of the presiding judge.
– de l'enfance, des mineurs : judge sitting in juvenile court.
– d'instruction : examining magistrate.
– naturel : lawful judge.
– de paix (hist.) : justice of the peace, conciliation magistrate in commercial cases and police-court magistrate.
– -président : presiding judge.
– -rapporteur : judge in charge of legal enquiry.
– récusé : challenged judge.
– des référés : judge sitting in chambers to deal with matters of special urgency.
– requis : commissioned judge (by letters rogatory, etc.).
– taxateur : taxing master.
– tutélaire : judge supervising a guardianship.
pouvoir discrétionnaire du – : full authority of judge in court-room.
règlement des – (s) : referal of a case by higher court to one of several competent lower ones.

jugé (a) : judged.
au — : guessed.
[J] « *bien* —, *mal appelé, mal* —, *bien appelé* » : « well judged, wrongly appealed ; wrongly judged, well appealed » (formula in decrees of appelate jurisdictions in confirming or quashing judgments of the lower instances).
exception de chose — *(e)* : plea of res judicata.
jugement passé en force de chose — *(e)* : enforceable judgment, judgment-at-law.
un mal- — : challengeable judgment.

jugement (m) : [J] judgment, adjudication ; trial.
(— is generally translated by the generic term « jugment », the relevant A.A. technical terms such as « decree », « order », « sentence », not being applicable for obvious reasons to French judicial decisions).
— : judicial decision of an inferior court (opp. *arrêt* of the superior courts).
— *d'accord, convenu, d'expédient* : a) terms of judgment agreed upon by the contending parties, submitted to and approved by the court, judgment by consent.
b) interlocutory judgment approved by the parties, to allow further enquiries (expert's report, etc.).
— *d'acquittement* : acquittal.
— *d'adjudication* : adjudication of forced sale.
— *d'adoption* : probate of adoption.
— *d'annulation* : annulment, reversal, rescissory judgment.
— *attributif, constitutif* : declaration of a new legal status (opp. *jugement déclaratoire*).
— *avant dire, faire droit* : interlocutory judgment.
— *sur aveu* : judgment by confession.
— *civil* : judgment in civil matters.
— *comminatoire* : comminatory decree.
— *commun* : judgment affecting a third party.
— *de communication de pièces* : order of discovery.
— *de condamnation* : (civ.) condemnation, (cr.) sentence.
— *conditionnel* : suspended judgment.
— *confirmatif* : affirmative judgment, probate.
— *contentieux* : contentious judgment, jugdment in disputed matters.
— *contradictoire* : judgment after trial.
— *de, par contumace, par défaut* : judgment in contumacy, in absence, by default.
— *criminel, pénal* : sentence.
— *sans débat, sur pièces* : judgment on documentary evidence.
— *de débouté* : nonsuit.
— *déclaratoire* : adjudicative, declaratory judgment (opp. *jugement attributif, constitutif*).
— *déclaratif de décès* : finding of presumed death.
— *déclaratif de faillite* : adjudication order.
— *de défaut-congé* : judgment given against defaulting plaintiff.
— *définitif* : decree absolute, final recovery (opp. *jugement avant faire droit*).
— *de délibéré* : judgment adjourned for further consultation of judges.
— *sur désistement* : judgment upon withdrawal of suit.
— *de doctrine, de principe* : judgment involving an important decision on matters of principle.
— *de donner acte* : judgment of record.
— *d'espèce* : judgment based on practical motives pertaining to a specifice case, rather than on legal grounds.
— *étranger* : foreign judgment.
— *exceptionnel* : decision as to the admissibility of a demurrer.
— *exécutoire* : enforceable judgment.
— *exécutoire par provision* : judgment provisionally enforceable.
— *d'exequatur* : a) enforcement of award, b) grant of exequatur to a foreign judgment (extension of judgment).
— *d'expropriation* : expropriation order.
— *final* : final judgment.
— *au fond* : judgment on the merits.
— *de forclusion* : estoppel by judgment.
— *sur frais* : award of costs.
— *frappé d'appel* : judgment under appeal.
— *gracieux, sur requête* : voluntary judgment, judgment in undisputed matters.
— *d'homologation* : probate.
— *incident, interlocutoire* : interlocutory judgment.
— *d'irrecevabilité, de rejet* : dismissal, nonsuit.
— *irrévocable* : decree absolute.
— *de jonction* : joinder.
— *de mise hors de cause* : exonerating judgment.
— *par adoption de motifs* : judgment adopting the grounds of the lower court.
— *sur opposition* : judgment on request to stay execution by condemned defaulter.
— *susceptible d'opposition* : judgment liable to stay of execution.
— *de partage* : a) order to share out a succession, b) the judges being equally divided, a further judge is called in and a new trial begun.
— *passé en force de chose jugée* : judgment-at-law.
— *sur passé-expédient* : recognitory judgment upon waiver of claim or confession of defence.
— *en premier ressort* : appealable judgment.
— *en dernier ressort* : judgment by court of last resort.
— *en premier et dernier ressort* : judgment by court of first and last resort, if the case is within the jurisdiction of one court only.
— *préparatoire* : preparatory judgment (subject to appeal only in connection with the final judgment).

— *principal*: judgment on the main issue.
— *de principe*: a) declaratory judgment on an issue of fact in an affirmative action for a right (validity of contract, liability of a person, etc.) involving no condemnation for the time being, b) see *jugement de doctrine*.
— *provisionnel*: provisional order.
— *provisoire*: decree nisi.
— *sur rapport*: judgment upon report of the magistrate entrusted with the enquiry.
— *sur la recevabilité*: judgment on the admissibility (of action or appeal).
— *de référé (ordonnance sur référé)*: order in chambers in matters of special urgency.
— *de remise de cause, de sursis*: adjournment.
— *de reprise d'audience*: record of default.
— *avec réserves*: judgment with reservations rebus sic stantibus (e.g. for a disabled workman in case his disablement gets worse, etc.).
— *de séparation*: separation order.
— *sur le siège*: judgment delivered from the bench, without leaving the court-room.
— *souverain*: judgment by the court of last resort.
— *translatif de propriété*: conveyance by order of court.
— *de validité (de main-vidange)*: order to a debtor to pay over money in hand to s.o. appointed by court (mostly the judgment creditor in attachment of debts).
annuler un — : to repeal, to rescind, to quash a judgment.
confirmer un — : to confirm, to ratify a judgment.
considérants, motifs du — : grounds of a judgment.
en jugement: under consideration.
enregistrer un — : to docket a judgment.
expédition du — : copy of the judgment.
ester en — : to have capacity to appear.
exécuter un — : to enforce a judgment.
exequatur d'un — : recognition to a foreign judgment.
grosse du — : first authentic copy of the judgment (bearing the executory formula).
interprétation du — : construction of the judgment.
lever un — : to obtain a copy of the judgment.
mettre en — : to commit for trial.
minute du — : original draft of the judgment (signed).
notifier un — : to notify a judgment.
prononcer, rendre le — : to pronounce, to pass, to deliver, to give the judgment.
publication du — : publication of the judgment.
rapporter un — : a) to bring a judgment to the public knowledge by reading the text in the court-room, b) to quash a judgment.
réformer un — : to reverse a judgment.
rendre un — : to decide a case.
réviser un — : to review a judgment.

signifier un — : to serve a notice.
suspendre un — : to suspend a judgment, to adjourn a case.

juger (v): to judge, to try.
— *un accusé*: to pass sentence, to sit in judgment on a prisoner, to try a prisoner.
— *un procès*: to try a case.
— *une réclamation*: to adjudicate, to adjuge a claim.
[J] — *ultra petita*: to adjudge more than asked.

juguler (v) *(inflation)*: to curb (inflation).

juratoire (a): [J] *caution* — : guarantee given by oath.

juré (a et m): (a) expert- — : sworn expert.
traducteur — : sworn translator.
(m) juror, [U.S.] juryman.
les —(s): the jury.
liste des —(s): jury-panel.
liste des candidats- —(s): panel of veniremen.
premier — : foreman of the jury.

juridiction (f): jurisdiction, province.
— *administrative*: administrative jurisdiction.
— *arbitrale*: arbitration.
— *civile*: jurisdiction in civil matters.
— *consulaire*: a) consular jurisdiction (esp. under the Capitulations), b) commercial jurisdiction (also *juridiction commerciale*).
— *contentieuse*: contentious jurisdiction, jurisdiction in disputed matters.
— *correctionnelle, — disciplinaire*: summary jurisdiction.
— *criminelle, pénale*: criminal jurisdiction.
— *ordinaire de droit commun*: ordinary jurisdiction.
— *exceptionnelle*: special jurisdiction.
— *gracieuse, non-contentieuse*: voluntary jurisdiction, jurisdiction in undisputed matters.
— *de jugement*: tribunal entertaining jurisdiction.
— *des référés*: summary jurisdiction in matters of special urgency.
— *de renvoi*: tribunal to which a case is referred after review.
— *de travail*: jurisdiction in industrial disputes.
clause de — : competence clause.
conflit de — : conflict, concurrence of jurisdictions, adversity.
immunité de — : immunity from jurisdiction.
ordre de — : hierarchy of courts.
privilège de — : attachment of privilege.
ce n'est pas dans (ma) — : it is not within (my) province.

juridique (a): *(obligations, rapports)* juridical, judicial; legal.

conseil — : consulting lawyer.
conseiller — : legal adviser.
titre — : legal claim.

jurisconsulte (m) : jurisconsult, jurist, legal expert.

jurisprudence (f) : (the course of decision in the courts as distinguished from legislation and doctrine), case-law, the precedents of a case, holding of the courts on a case, leading cases and decisions, statute law.
— *constante* : unbroken line of precedents.
— *flottante* : uncertain line of precedents.

juriste (m) : jurist, legal writer.

jury (m) : [J] jury.
— *d'expropriation* : valuation board in expropriation proceedings.
dresser la liste du — : to empanel the jury.
verdict du — : the verdict.
membre du — : juror, juryman.
— *d'examen* : examining board.

juste (a) : accurate.

justice (f) : justice, law, legal proceedings.
— *commutative* : commutative justice, calling for equivalent performances by the parties.
— *distributive* : punishing and rewarding justice.
— *de paix* (hist.) : police court and court of conciliation in commercial matters.
— *prud'homale* : conciliation board in industrial disputes.
— *sommaire* # Jedburgh justice, Lynch law.
action en — : action at law.
actionner, appeler, citer, déférer, poursuivre, traduire en — : (civ.) to go to law, to sue s.o., to institute, to open legal proceedings, (cr.) to prosecute s.o.
conseil de — : court of justice held aboard ships at sea.
demande en — : claim, action.
déni de — : miscarriage of justice.
descente de — : visit of experts, officials, etc., to the scene of the occurrence.
en toute — : by rights.
faire — : a) to deliver a just sentence, b) to carry out death sentence.
gens de — : lower law officials.
Cour de — *des Communautés Européennes (Luxembourg)* : European Court of Justice (Luxembourg).
Haute Cour (de —*)* : political court elected by the legislative bodies entertaining jurisdiction in impeachment cases (similar to the British and American impeachment procedure).
Cour Internationale de — *(O.N.U., La Haye)* : International Court of Justice (U.N.O., The Hague).
palais de — : Law Courts.
poursuivre en — : to prosecute, to sue.
repris de — : habitual criminal, recidivist, «old lag» («*cheval de retour*»).
se faire — : a) to commit suicide, b) to take the law in one's own hands.

justiciable (a, m et f) : (a) under the jurisdiction of a court.
(m et f) everybody to whom the law applies.
— *d'un tribunal* : justiciable to (in) a court.

justificateur (a) : justifying, justificatory.

justifiable (a) : warrantable.

justificatif (a et m) : (a) justificatory.
pièce **justificative**, (m) — : relevant paper.
[J] document in proof.
[C] voucher.

justification (f) : justification, proof, vindication, warrant.

justifier (v) : to justify, to prove.
— *de sa bonne foi* : to vindicate one's good faith.
— *de son identité* : to prove one's identity.
— *de ses mouvements* : to give a satisfactory account of one's movements.
— *de sa solvabilité avant de fournir caution* : to justify bail.
se — : to clear oneself, to justify oneself, to vindicate ones' character.
— *qqn de (laver)* : to clear s.o. from.
[J] *préjudice* **justifié** : proved damage.
[F] *coût justifié* : proved cost.

négociations Kennedy : Kennedy round.

kidnapper (v) : to kidnap.

kilométrage (m) : distance in kilometres.

kleptomanie (f) : kleptomania.

krach (m) : financial crash, smash (of a bank).

NOTES

L

label (m) : label, trade-union mark.

laboratoire (m) d'idées : think tank.

laborieux (a) : laborious.
« *les classes laborieuses* » : the working classes.

lacune (f) : blank.
— *dans la législation fiscale* : leak in the tax law.
— *permettant d'échapper à cette législation* : loophole.

courbe de **Laffer** (f) : Laffer curve.

lais (m pl) : *(les lais et relais de la mer)* foreshore.

laisser (v) : to leave, to allow, to let.
— *pour compte (marchandises)* : to leave on hand (goods).
— *faire (économie)* : non interference, « laissez-faire » (economy).
laissez-passer : pass, permit (customs), transire, cart note.
laissez-suivre : sea-letter.

lancement (m) : launching, promoting, tossing.
— *d'une entreprise* : launching of an enterprise.
— *d'une émission* : floating, flotation (floatation) of an issue.

lancer (v) : *(une entreprise, un article, un emprunt)* to launch an enterprise, to put an article on the market, to float a loan.
— *un produit* : to launch a product.
— *une société* : to promote a company.
— *une souscription* : to start a fund.
se — *dans une affaire* : to launch forth (out) on an enterprise.
se — *dans (le commerce d'importation)* : to go in for (import trade).

languissant *(marché, affaires)* (a) : slack, flat (market), slow (business).

larcin littéraire (m) : plagiarism.

large (a et m) : (a) large.
au sens — : extended meaning.
(m) *au* — : off shore.

(se) laver *(d'une accusation)* (v) : to clear oneself of a charge.

lecture *(d'un bilan)* (f) : reading (of a balance-sheet).
à (première...) — : at the (first...) reading.

légal (a) : legal, statutory.
assassinat — : legal murder (the legal form being complied with, but the sentence being iniquitous).
disposition — *(e)* : statutory provision.
domicile — : legal domicile.
hypothèque — *(e)* : legal mortgage, statutory lien.
incapacité — *(e)* : legal incapacity.
intérêt — : official rate of interest.
jouissance — *(e)* : legal usufruct.
médecine — *(e)* : state, legal, forensic medicine, medical jurisprudence.
monnaie ayant cours — : legal tender, currency.
mesure — *(es)* : [U.S.] statute measures.
possession — *(e)* : lawful possession.
protection — *(e)* : protecting by law.
représentant — : legal representative.
réserve — *(e)* : portion that must devolve upon heirs.
réserves — *(s)* : legal reserves, statutory reserves.
sans motif — : unlawfully.
voie — *(e)* : recourse to law.

légilisation (f) : authentication, acknowledgment, certification, exemplification.

légaliser (v) : to legalize, to authenticate, to certify.
signature **légalisée** : certified signature.
— *une situation de fait* : to pass from a de facto situation into a de jure one (e.g. to marry one's mistress).

légalité (f) : legality, lawfulness.
rester dans la — : to keep within the law.
la — *républicaine* : legislation or action in conformity with the democratic principles of the Republic.

légataire (m et f) : heir.
[J] devisee (— *de biens immobiliers*), legatee (— *de biens mobiliers*).
— *appelé* : substitutional heir, reversioner, heir in remainder.
— *à titre particulier* : specific, particular devi-

see and (or) legatee.
— *à titre universel*: heir to a quota in an estate, either realty or personalty, or to a fixed share of each or of both = residuary devisee and legatee.
— *universel*: heir, general devisee and legatee (see also *léguer*).

légende (f): (journ.) caption (of illustration).

légiférer (v): to legislate.

législateur (m): legislator, law giver.
élection **législative**: parliamentary election.
fonction législative: legislative function.
pouvoir **législatif**: legislative power.

législation (f): 1° legislation, 2° set of laws pertaining to a particuler subject, [U.S.] enactments.
— *anti-trust*: anti-trust legislation.
— *comparée*: comparative legislation.
— *financière*: legal texts on financial matters.
— *fiscale*: taxation law.
— *industrielle*: (the) Factory Act.
— *nationale*: domestic law.
— *en vigueur*: laws in force.

législature (f): 1° legislature, legislative body, 2° duration of parliament.

légiste (m): legist, jurist.
médecin- — : medical expert commissioned by court.

légitimation (f): legitimation, official recognition of quality, submission of credentials, legitimation (affiliation) of child.
titre de — : identity papers.

légitime (a): legitimable, rightful.
— *défense*: self-defence.
enfant — : legitimate child, child born in wedlock.
héritier — : heir-at-law, rightful heir.
propriétaire — : rightful owner.
suspicion — : well-founded suspicion that fair trial will not be given (involving transfer of case to another court).
part **légitimaire**: portion in parents' estate secured by law to each child, [J] distributive share, (Scot.) legitim.

legs (m): (— *immobilier*) devise, (— *mobilier*) legacy, *(les biens mobiliers* **légués** *constituent* the bequest).
— *conditionnel*: contingent devise, bequest, legacy.
faire un — *à qn*: to leave a (particular) legacy to s.o. (see *légataire*).
recevoir un — : to come into a legacy.

léguer (v): [J] to devise, to bequeath, to leave.

les **lenteurs** (f pl) *de la loi*: the Law's delays.

léonin (a): leonine, lionlike.
[J] *contrat* — : leonine convention, unconscionable bargain, oppressive agreement.
[C] *par* — *(e)*: lion's share.

léser (v): to wrong, to trespass.
— *les droits de tiers*: to trespass, to encroach upon, to prejudice, the rights of a third party.
la partie **lésée**: the injured party.

lésion (f): injury, wrong.
— *(s) corporelles*: bodily injuries.
[J] *contrat où il y a* — : burdensome contract.

lettre (f): letter.
— *anonyme*: anonymous letter.
— *d'avis*: delivery note, advice note.
— *de change*: bill of exchange.
— *chargée, recommandée*: registered letter.
— *(police) de chargement*: consignment note.
— *de confort*: comfort letter.
— *de créance*: letter of credence, credentials.
— *de crédit*: letter of credit.
— *de crédit bancaire* (caution bancaire): standby letter of credit.
— *de crédit collective*: general letter of credit.
— *de crédit irrévocable garantie* (par deux banques, l'une du pays de l'exportateur, l'autre du pays de l'importateur): irrevocable confirmed letter of credit.
— *d'envoi*: covering note, letter of advice.
— *de gage*: mortgage, security bond.
— *de garantie*: guaranty given by shipper to the sea-carrier against any claims, in order to obtain a clear bill of lading.
— *à la grosse aventure*: bottomry contract.
— *d'injure*: libel.
— *de menaces*: threatening, intimidating letter.
— *de mer (congé)*: sea-letter, sea brief.
— *missive*: epistle, ordinary letter.
— *ouverte*: open letter.
— *de procuration*: letter of attorney, proxy.
— *de rappel*: reminder.
— *(s) de rappel*: letters of recall (of an ambassador).
— *de rebut*: dead, unclaimed letter.
— *de retrait*: letter of withdrawal.
— *de retour de souscription*: letter of regret.
— *de santé*: bill, certificate of health.
— *de service*: commission.
— *de souscription*: letter of intent.
— *de voiture*: way-bill, consignment note.
en toutes — *(s)*: in words at length.
selon la — *de la loi*: according to the letter of the law (opp. *esprit*).

lettre de change (f) : bill of exchange, (*désignée ci-après comme « b »*), note, letter.
 — *en blanc :* blank b.
 — *de complaisance :* accommodation b.
 — *à certain délai de note :* b. maturing n days after date.
 — *à un certain délai de vue :* b. maturing n days after presentation.
 — *distincte (« seule de change ») :* solo b.
 — *domiciliée, à domicile :* domiciliated b.
 — *fictive :* fictitious b. (a misdemeanour).
 — *à jour fixe, à terme fixe :* b. maturing at date.
 — *payable à l'ordre du tireur :* b. to drawer's order.
 — *payable à première réquisition, présentation, en tout temps, à vue :* b. on sight.
 — *(retour) sans frais, sans protêt :* « sans frais », « no expenses ».
 — *sans garantie, sans obligation :* unsecured, unbinding b.
 — *non à ordre :* b. not to order.
 — *sur moi-même :* promissory note.
 acceptation de la — : acceptance of b.
 acceptation en blanc : blank acceptance.
 acceptation par honneur, par intervention : acceptance of (protested) b. for honour.
 allonge de la — : allonge, rider.
 annulation d'une — (en cas de perte) : annulment of a (lost) b.
 aval d'une — : backing of a b.
 création d'une — : drawing up of a b.
 échéance de la — : maturity.
 émission d'une — : drawing of a b.
 endossataire, endossé (tiers porteur) d'une — : endorsee.
 endossataire-mandataire : endorsee by proxy.
 endos : endorsement.
 endos d'une — pour encaissement : endorsement for collection.
 endosseur : endorser.
 protêt en matière de — : protest.
 tiré : drawee.
 tireur : drawer.

levée (f) : raising, lifting, removal.
 — *d'un acte chez un notaire :* execution and authentification of a deed by a notary.
 — *d'arrêts :* cancellation of arrest.
 — *d'écrou :* discharge from prison.
 — *d'une interdiction :* removal of prohibition.
 — *d'une saisie :* replevin.

lever (v) : to levy, to lift, to raise.
 — *des actions :* to take up stock.
 — *l'embargo :* to raise the embargo.
 — *une difficulté :* to remove a difficulty.
 — *un impôt :* to levy a tax.
 — *la main :* to swear (oath).
 — *l'opposition à une poursuite :* to withdraw stay on proceedings.
 — *une option :* to declare an option.
 — *un plan :* to effect a survey.
 — *les scellés :* to break, to remove the seals.
 — *la séance :* to adjourn, to close, the meeting.
 — *la tutelle :* to remove the guardianship.

levier (m) *(effet, phénomène de)* : gearing, leverage.

liaison *(d'affaires)* (f) : (business) connection.

liasse *(d'actions)* (f) : bundle (of shares).
 — *de billets de banque :* [U.S.] roll.

libelle (m) : lampoon, libel.

libellé (m) : wording, particulars.
 — *d'une écriture :* particulars of an item.
 — *d'une loi :* text of a law.
 libeller : to draw up, to word (document, etc.), to sign and date, to draft.
 libeller un chèque : to make out a cheque.

libéral (a et m) : liberal.
 les **libéraux** : the liberal elements.
 interprétation — (e) : liberal interpretation, broad construction.
 les professions — (es) : the (learned) professions.
 un homme de profession — (e) : a professional man.

libéralisme *(économique)* (m) : (economic) liberalism.

libéralité (f) : liberality, act of liberality, gift.
 [J] — *à cause de mort :* gift post mortem.
 — *déguisée :* concealed liberality.
 — *entre vifs :* gift inter vivos.
 — *rapportable :* revocable act of liberality.
 faire des — (s) : to give freely (liberally).

libération (f) : liberation.
 [J] (civ.) discharge.
 — *de biens :* release of property.
 — *d'une hypothèque :* redemption of mortgage.
 — *judiciaire d'une hypothèque :* removal of mortgage by court.
 action, jugement en — de dette : action, judgment for discharge of debt.
 — *conditionnelle, sous surveillance :* release of prisoner on licence (ticket of leave), on probation.
 — *sous caution :* release on bail.
 — *provisoire :* temporary release.
 — *définitive :* final discharge of prisoner.
 mouvement de — de la femme (M.L.F.) : « Women's lib ».
 [A] — *des contraintes étatiques (néo-libéralisme) :* deregulation.

libératoire (a) : discharging.
effet — : release from a liability.
exception — : demurrer.
monnaie — : legal tender, acceptability of money.
moyen — : peremptory plea.
paiement — : final payment, full discharge.
prélèvement — : once and for all levy.

libérer (v) : to free, to liberate (cr.), to release.
— *un garant* : to discharge a surety.
se — *d'une dette* : to pay, to redeem debt.
se — *d'une obligation envers qn* : to discharge a liability to s.o.
libéré d'hypothèque : free of mortgage.
(revenu) libéré d'impôt : tax-paid (income).
prisonnier libéré sur parole : parolee, prisoner put on parole.
[F] *action libérée* : fully paid-up share.
action non-libérée : partly paid-up share.
titre de 1 000 F libéré de 750 F : 1 000 F share, 750 F paid-up.

liberté (f) : liberty, freedom.
[J] (civ.) — *civile* : civil liberty, freedom to do everything that is not prohibited by law.
— *des changes* : exchange freedom.
— *du commerce et de l'industrie* : right of free enterprise.
les —(s) *constitutionnelles* : the constitutional (civic) liberties.
atteinte à la — *du commerce* : restraint of trade.
— *individuelle* # right to habeas corpus.
— *surveillée* : probation.
(cr.) *mise en* — *provisoire, sous caution* : release on bail.
peine privative de — : punishment involving personal restraint.
mettre en — *sous caution* : to admit to bail.

libre (a) : free, open.
— *arbitre* : free will.
— *concurrence* : free competition.
— *échange* : free trade.
— *entreprise* : free enterprise.
— *pratique (exercice)* : free exercise.
— *service* : self-service.
papier — : unstamped paper.
union — : living together of unmarried couple, [U.S.] companionate marriage.
zone — : bonded area (esp. in port).

licence (f) : 1° licence, 2° university degree.
[A] — *de débitant* : liquor licence.
— *de fabrication* : licence to manufacture patented goods, manufacturing licence.
[E] — *d'exportation (d'importation)* : export (import) licence, permit.

licenciement (m) : dismissal, discharge.
— *abusif* : unfair dismissal.
— *à la demande de l'employé* : constructive dismissal.
indemnité de — : dismissal payment.
préavis de — : term of notice.

licencier (v) : 1° to grant a licence of manufacturing.
2° to discharge, to disband.
employé **licencié** : dismissed, laid off, redundant employee.
— *un employé* (fam.) : to sack, to lay off, to disband an employee.

licitation (f) : [J] sale by auction of one lot held indivisum.
— *amiable, volontaire, contrat* **licitatoire** : agreement between joint owners to sell property held indivisum.
— *judiciaire* : sale by auction of property held indivisum, ordered by court.
liciter *une maison indivise* : to sell a house by auction by agreement between joint owners.

licite (a) : licit, lawful, permissible.
reprise — : recaption.

lien (m) : tie, bond.
[J] privity.
— *causal* : causal connection.
— *conjugal, du mariage* : the conjugal bond, bonds of matrimony.
— *de droit* : privity.
— *de parenté* : blood relationship.
— *du sang* : near in blood.
avoir un — *de dépendance avec une société* : not to deal at arm's length (with a corporation).
avoir un — *de parenté (avec)* : to be related (to).
(héritiers) sans — *de parenté* : unrelated (heirs).

lieu (m) : place, locality, spot.
— *d'asile* : sanctuary.
— *de constitution d'une société* : place of incorporation of a company.
— *de jugement, juridiction* : venue.
— *du principal établissement* : regular and established place of business.
— *public* : public place.
— *de séjour* : residence, place of abode.
— *de la situation d'une chose* : location, site.
— *de stationnement* : parking place.
au — *et place de* : in lieu of.
descente, transport sur les lieux : visit of experts, officials, etc., to the scene of the occurrence.
état des —(x) : inventory of fixtures as between landlord and tenant.

ordonnance de non- — *:* nonsuit.
sur les — *(x):* to vacate the premisses.
le juge ordonne de faire vider la salle: the judge orders the court to be cleared.

lieudit (m): place, known as...

ligne (f): line, issue.
— *d'activité:* strategy.
— *ascendante:* line of ascent.
— *collatérale:* collatera line.
— *de crédit en garantie:* backup line of credit.
— *descendante:* line of descent.
— *directe:* direct line.
— *indirecte:* indirect line.
— *maternelle:* parentage on the mother's side.
— *de parenté:* relationship.
— *paternelle:* parentage on the father's side.
— *de démarcation:* dividing line.
— *de partage des eaux:* watershed, [U.S.] divide.
— *de substitution:* back up line.
« *au-dessous de la* — » *:* below the line.
« *au-dessus de la* — » *:* above the line.
en — *directe:* lineal ascent, descent.

ligue des consommateurs (f): consumerism, consumers' league.

limitatif (a): restrictive.
article — *:* limiting clause.

limitation (f): limitation, restriction.
— *des coûts (de production et de commercialisation):* cost containment.
— *du droit de propriété:* limitation of right of ownership.
— *des naissances:* family planning.
sans — *de temps:* without any time limit.

limite (f): limit, cut-off.
— *à l'action d'une administration:* limitation of an administration.
(la) — *d'âge:* the age limit.
cas — *:* border-line case.
date — *:* deadline.
— *de la baisse (baisse maximum):* limit down.
— *du crédit accordé (par une banque):* line of credit, credit line.
— *d'endettement:* debt capacity.
— *journalière de fluctuation (d'un prix):* day limit.
— *du territoire:* (border) frontier line.
vitesse — *:* maximum speed.

limiter (v): to limit, to restrict.
— *la portée d'une loi:* to restrain the scope of a law.
responsabilité **limitée**: limited liability.

(pays) limitrophe (a): borderland.

linéaire (a): linear, straight-line.
amortissement — *:* straight line depreciation.
programmation — *:* linear programming.
système — *:* straight line method (system).

lingot (m): ingot, gold bar.
étalon — *-or:* Gold Bullion Standard.
or et argent en — *(s):* bullion.

liquidateur (m): liquidator.
— *judiciaire:* referee.
[B] — *en bourse:* official assignor.

liquidation (f): liquidation, settlement, winding up, clearing of accounts, squaring.
— *de biens* # liquidation of an insolvent debtor's property.
[J] — *courante:* current settlement.
— *des dépens:* taxation of court-costs.
— *de la faillite:* settlement in bankruptcy proceedings.
— *d'une indivision:* sharing out of an indivisum.
— *judiciaire:* winding-up by decision of court.
— *du régime matrimonial:* settlement of accounts as between husband and wife.
— *des reprises:* ascertainment of property belonging either to husband or to wife (in view of partition).
— *d'une société:* winding up of a company.
— *d'une succession:* settlement of a succession.
— *volontaire:* voluntary winding up (liquidation).
bilan de — *:* statement of affairs.
société en — *:* company in liquidation.
[C] clearing of accounts.
— *de dette:* settlement of conditions for repayment.
— *du stock:* clearance sale, selling off.
[F] *chambre de* — *:* (bankers') clearing house.
[B] settlement.
jour de — *:* settlement day.
entrer en — *:* to go into liquidation, to wind-up.

liquider: (b) to close out.
— *les intérêts:* to determine rate of interest.
— *des marchandises:* to clear out.
— *des stocks:* to off-load stocks.
dommages **liquidés**: liquidated damages.

liquide (a): liquid.
actif — *:* available assets.
argent — *:* ready money, cash.
dette — *:* liquid debt.
fonds — *(s):* available funds.

liquidité (f): 1° liquid position (of bank, company).
2° (pl), [C] [F] liquid assets, available funds.
— *(s) de caisse:* cash in hand.
préférence pour les — *(s):* liquidity preference.

liste (f) : list, register, roll, roster.
— *d'actionnaires* : stock-ledger, register of members.
— *d'audience* : cause list.
— *civile* : civil list.
— *(s) électorales* : register of voters.
— *d'émargement* : pay-sheet.
— *du jury* : panel of jury.
— *de paie* : pay-sheet, roll.
— *de présence* : time-sheet.
— *de souscripteurs* : list of applicants (subscribers).
— *officielle de taux* : schedule of charges.
dresser, faire une — : to draw up a list.

lit (m) : bed, marriage.
enfants du même — : full brothers and sisters.
enfant du second — : child of the second marriage.
enfant d'un autre — : step-child.
aveu fait au — de mort : confession in articulo mortis, death-bed confession.

litige (m) : litigation, dispute at law, suit.
cas en — : case at issue.
dénonciation de — : (litis denonciatio) instituting proceedings.
matière à — : issuable matter.
litigant : litigant, one of the contending parties.
litigieux : litigious, disputable at law.
un cas litigieux : a debatable cause.
créance litigieuse : litigious claim.

litispendance (f) : [J] lis (alibi) pendens (that there is another action pending between the same parties for the same cause).
exception de — : plea of lis pendens.

littéral (a) : literal.
interprétation —(e) : strict, close construction.
[J] *preuve —(e)* : documentary evidence, proof in writing.

livrable (a) : deliverable, ready for delivery.
cours du — : forward price.
— *sur* : in futures on.

livraison (f) : delivery (of goods, shares, etc.).
[C] — *franco* : delivered free.
défaut de — : non-delivery.
payable à la — : payable on delivery.
prendre — : to take delivery, to collect.
[B] — *à terme* : futures.

livre (m) : book.
— *d'achats* : purchases book, bought book.
— *blanc* = White Paper.
— *de bord* : mate's log-book.
— *(s) de bord* : ship's books.
— *de caisse* : cash-book.
— *de comptabilité, des comptes* : accountbook.
— *d'échéance (échéancier)* : bill-book.
— *d'écrou* : prison calendar.
— *des effets à payer* : bills payable book.
— *des effets à recevoir* : bills receivable book.
— *des entrées et des sorties* : in-and outclearing book.
— *foncier* : land register, terrier.
— *des inventaires* : stock-taking ledger.
— *journal* : book of original entries, daybook, journal.
— *de magasin* : warehouse book.
— *(s) obligatoires* : books and documents that a merchant is bound to keep (day-book, stock-taking ledger, correspondence received and copies of his own letters).
— *de paie* : pay-book.
— *des recettes et dépenses* : incomings and outgoings, receipts and expenses book.
— *de réclamations* : claims book.
— *des transferts* : transfer register.
grand livre : ledger.
le grand — de la Dette publique : the National Debt Register.
teneur des —(s) (comptables) : book-keeper.

livre (f) : pound, i.e. 500 *grammes* (A.A. pound : 453 *grammes*).
— *sterling* : pound sterling.

livrer (v) : to deliver.
vente à — : time-bargain.
[J] *se — à des voies de fait envers qn* : to commit acts of violence, assault and battery.

livret (m) : booklet.
— *de banque* : pass-book.
— *de (caisse) d'épargne* : savingsbank book.
— *(carnet) de chèques* : cheque-book.
— *de famille* : family book.

local (a et m) : (a) *loi locale* : by(e)-law, [U.S.] municipal ordinance.
(m) premises, building.
— *d'habitation* : dwelling-place.
— *commercial, d'affaires* : business premises.
— *professionnel* : office of professional man (lawyer's chambers, etc.).

location (f) : letting, renting, hiring, tenancy; *(places en chemin de fer, au théâtre, etc.)* booking.
— *avec option d'achat (LOA)* : leasing.
— *emphytéotique* : long lease.
— *vente* : hire-purchase.
agent de — : house agent.
bureau de — : box-office.
prix de — : rent.
sous- — : sub-letting, underletting, [J] sublease.
locataire : tenant, occupier of property, *(en meublé)* lodger, [J] lessee, lease-holder.
sous-locataire : subtenant, under-tenant [J]

sub-lessee.
protection des locataires : rent-control.
immeuble **locatif** : mansions, tenement house.
réparations locatives, risques locatifs : tenantable repairs.
revenu locatif : rental.
valeur locative : rental (value).
valeur locative d'un logement dont le propriétaire se réserve la jouissance : imputed income, presumptive income.

logement (m) : lodging(s), housing, housing unit.
— *à loyer modéré* : # council house.
— *garni* : furnished apartment(s).
indemnité de — : living-out allowance.
subventions au — : housing subsidies.

loger (v) : to accommodate.

loi (f) : law ; act (of Parliament, Congress), law, enactment, statute.
— *agraire* : Land Act.
— *d'amnistie* : act of oblivion.
— *anti-trust* : anti-trust legislation.
— *-cadre* : skeleton-law, outline law.
— *(constitutionnelle) organique* : organic law.
— *d'exception* : emergency legislation.
— *de finances* : Finance Act.
projet de — *de finances* : appropriation bill.
— *martiale*, [J] *état de siège* : martial law, articles of war.
— *sur les mises à la retraite* : superannuation act.
— *municipale* : by(e)-law, [U.S.] municipal ordinance.
— *de l'offre et de la demande* : the law of supply and demand.
— *sur les sociétés* : [U.K.] companies act.
— *en vigueur* : law in force.
abroger, rapporter une — : to abrogate, to rescind, to repeal, a law.
adopter, voter une — : to pass, to carry, a bill.
amender une — : to amend a bill.
appliquer la — : to put the law in force, to enforce the law.
article de — : lawful.
article d'une — : section of an act.
conflit de — (s) : conflict, concurrence of legal provisions.
décret- — : [U.K.] Order in Council, [U.S.] executive order.
disposition de la — : legal provision.
exposé des motifs d'une — : explanatory statement for a bill.
faire — : provision considered as law.
homme de — : lawyer.
hors-la- — : outlaw.
lecture d'une — : reading of a bill (in Parliament).
nul n'est censé ignorer la — : nemo censitur ignorare legem) ignorance If law is no excuse.
passer en force de — : to become operative enforceable.
projet de — : Government bill.
proposition de — : private Member's bill.
promulguer une — : to promulgate a law.
rapporter une — : to revoke a law.
tomber sous le coup de la — : to come under law.
tourner la — : to cheat, to get around the law.
transgresser la — : to transgress, to contravene, to break, to infringe the law.
violation de la — : violation, breach, infringement, of law.
voter une — : to pass a law.

loisible (a) : optional, permissible.
il est loisible à qn de faire : it is open to s.o. to do.

long (a) : long.
à — *terme* : long term.
bail à — (ue) *échéance* : long lease.
— *cours* : foreign trade.
capitaine au — *cours* : master mariner.
voyage de — *cours* : ocean voyage.
papier à — (ue) *échéance* : long-dated bill.
position — (ue) : (B) long position.

lorsque : *traduit le plus souvent par* « where » *dans les textes juridiques et fiscaux.*

lot (m) : share of estate, portion, lot ; prize (at a lottery).
— *disparate ou incomplet* : broken lot.
— *de marchandises* : batch.
[F] *emprunt à* — (s) : lottery loan.
tirages à — (s) : prize-drawing.
obligation à — (s) : lottery loan bond.

loterie (f) : lottery.

lotir (v) : to allot, to apportion, to parcel out.
— *une propriété* : to parcel out an estate.

lotissement (m) : dividing into lots, development of building land, allotment, apportionment, parcelling out.

louage (m) : [J] (locatio rei) hiring, letting, contract of hire, lease, renting.
— *de capitaux* : loan on interest.
— *de chose* : lease of chattels or real property.
— *de services* : (locatio operarum) engagement of workmen, servants).
contrat de — *d'ouvrage* : locatio operis) work by contract agreement.
— *de terres* : farming lease.

louer (v) : *(locataire)* to rent, to hire ; *(propriétaire)* to let.
   sous- — : to under-rent.
   loueur : hirer out, letter, renter out.

lourd (a) : heavy.
   marché — : stale market.
   lourdement : heavily.
   être **lourdement** *taxé, imposé :* to be heavily taxed.

loyal (a) : fair, honest, straightforward.
   [J] *— (e) échute :* right whereby the rightful heir takes a succession forgone by a testamentary heir.
   frais et **loyaux** *coûts :* costs and notary's fee for drawing up a deed.
   bon et — inventaire : lawful inventory.
   [C] *marchandise — (e) :* merchantable goods.

loyer (m) : rent, hire.
   arriéré de — : rent in arrear.
   bail à — : (house) lease.
   contrôle des — (s) : rent control.
   [F] *— de l'argent :* prevailing rate of interest.
   — d'un emprunt : interest paid on a loan.

« **lu et approuvé** » : « read and approved ».

lucratif (a) : lucrative, profitable, profit-making.
   association sans but — : non-profit association.
   dans un but — : for pecuniary gain, profit-seeking.

lutte des classes (f) : (the) class struggle (war).

luxe (m) : luxury, wealth.
   articles de — : luxuries, luxury articles.
   taxe de — : luxury tax.

NOTES

NOTES

M

machination (f) : plot.

machine (f) : engine, machine.
— *à calculer* : calculating machine, calculator.
— *à copier* : copier, duplicating machine.
— *à écrire* : typewriter, typewriting machine.
— *-outil* : machine-tool.
— *(s)* : machinery.

magasin (m) : (large) shop, [U.S.] store.
grand — : emporium, department store.
— *(s) généraux* : bonded warehouse.
livre de — : stock-book.
— *à succursales multiples* : chain store, multiple store.
— *« à prix unique »* : [U.S.] oneprice store.
magasinage : warehousing, storage of goods.
droits de magasinage : warehouse dues, storage, (chemin de fer) demurrage.
magasinier : a) warehouse-man, store-keeper, b) stock-book.

magistrat (m) : magistrate, justice, judge.
— *de carrière* : professional magistrate.
— *consulaire* : tradesman acting as judge in a commercial court.
— *debout* : public prosecutor.
— *de fait (juré)* : juror, juryman.
— *municipal* : town counsellor.
— *du siège (assis)* : judge.

magistrature (f) : magistrature, magistrateship, magistracy.
— *assise, du siège* : the judges, the Bench.
— *debout, du parquet* : the body of public prosecutors, the law-officers of the State.
entrer dans la — : to be appointed judge or public prosecutor.
exercer une — : to assume an office (mayor, etc.).

magouille (f) *(fam.)* : monkey business.

main (f) : hand.
— *courante de dépenses* : paid cash book.
— *courante des recettes* : received cash book.
changer de —*(s)* : change hands.
à —*(s) levées* : by show of hands.
[J] *en* — *propre* : in own hands.
en — *de tiers* : in hands of a third party.
entre les —*(s) de* : in the hands of.
fermer la — : to levy a distress as a precaution.
vider ses —*(s),* — *-vidange* : to pay over money in hand to s.o. appointed by court (mostly the judgment creditor in attachment of debts).

main-d'œuvre : labour, man-power, cost of labour, [U.S.] labor, manpower.
main-d'œuvre qualifiée : skilled labour.
main-d'œuvre non spécialisée : unskilled labour.
main-d'œuvre spécialisée : semi-skilled labour.
mobilité de la main-d'œuvre : labour mobility.
pénurie de main-d'œuvre : shortage of labour.
main-forte : help, assistance (to or of authority).
prêter main-forte à la justice : to support law and order.

mainlevée (f) : withdrawal.
[J] — *d'une inscription hypothécaire* : release of mortgage.
— *d'interdiction* : restoration of full rights (of persons disqualified by law or justice).
— *de l'opposition au mariage* : withdrawal of a caveat to marriage.
— *de saisie* : replevin, restoration of goods taken in distraint, cancellation of garnishee order.
— *de la tutelle* : removal of guardianship.
donner — *d'opposition, de saisie* : to withdraw one's opposition, to grant replevin.

mainmise (f) : seizure of, distraint upon property.
— *sur des biens* : distraint upon property.

mainmorte (f) : [J] mortmain, deadhand.
biens de — : property in mortmain.

maintenir (v) : to maintain, to keep.
— *le cours du change* : to peg the exchange.
— *le cours des prix* : to keep prices up.
— *un mot rayé par erreur dans un document* : to stet.
se maintenir : to be maintained, kept.

maintenue (f) : [J] confirmation of possession.

maintien (m) : maintenance, keeping.
— *de l'activité économique* : maintenance of economic activity.
— *de l'ordre* : keeping of order, policing (of a town).

maire (m) : mayor.

mairie (f) : town hall, municipal buildings.

maison (f) : house, mansion.
- *d'aliénés* : lunatic asylum.
- *d'arrêt* : lock-up, gaol, jail.
- *centrale* : prison, [U.S.] penitentiary.
- *civile, militaire* : the secretariat, the military household of the Head of the State.
- *de commerce* : business firm.
- *commune, de ville* : town hall.
- *de correction* : house of correction, bridewell, reformatory.
- *d'éducation surveillée* : borstal institution, reformatory scholl, approved school.
- *d'expédition* : forwarding firm.
- *de gros* : wholesale firm.
- *d'une honorabilité reconnue* : firm of recognized standing.
- *de jeu* : gaming house.
- *mère* : head office, parent establishment.
- *de rapport* : revenue-earning house.
- *de réescompte* : discount house.
- *de retraite* : old people's home.
- *de santé* : nursing house.
la - *blanche* : [U.S.] the White House.
gens de - : servants.

maître (m) : master.
- *artisan* : master-craftsman.
- *chanteur* : arrant knave.
- *de la chose* : owner.
- *de l'ouvrage* : promoter.
chose sans - : derelict.
terres sans - : land in abeyance.
[J] title by courtesy given to members of the legal professions (magistrates excepted) and spelled mostly in the abridged form *Me*.
maistrance : the body of petty officers of the navy.

maîtrise (f) : mastery (in a profession).
personnel de maîtrise : skilled personnel.

maîtriser (v) : to control.
- *l'inflation* : to get inflation under control.

majeur (a) : [J] of (full) age.
cas de force - : case of absolute necessity, of force majeure, act of God.

majorat (m) : entailed estate.

majoration (f) : grossing up, increase, overestimate.
- *exorbitante des prix* : ramp.
- *fiscale* : overvaluation of assets for tax purposes.
- *d'impôt* : surcharge.

majorer (v) : to increase (invoice), to overcharge.

majoritaire (a) : majority.
participation - : majority holding.

majorité (f) : 1° [J] majority, coming of age.
- *électorale* : age of franchise.
- *matrimoniale* : legal age of marriage.
- *pénale* : age at which a person ceases to be a minor in criminal proceedings.
atteindre la - : to come of age.
déclaration de - : emancipation.
2° majority of votes.
- *absolue* : half of the votes plus one.
- *qualifiée* : specified majority.
- *relative, simple* : more votes than any other.
[J] - *de faveur (opp. minorité de faveur)* : unqualified majority of a jury, insufficient for conviction.
emporter la - : to carry a vote, to secure a majority.

mal (adv) : wrong, badly, ill.
- *acquis* : ill-acquired.
- *fondé* : ill-founded, groundless.

maladie (f) : sickness, illness.
- *professionnelle* : occupational, industrial disease.
assurance - : sickness insurance.
congé de - : sick leave.
prestation- - : sickness-benefit.
par suite de - : through illness.

malfaçon (f) : bad work, bad workmanship.

malfaisance (f) : [J] malfeasance.

malfaiteur, malfaisant (m) : malefactor, wrong-doer, evil-doer.
association de - (s) : conspiracy.
[J] malfeasant.

malhonnête (a) : dishonest.

malice (f) : malice.
avec intention **malicieuse** : with malice aforethought.

maljugé (m) : [J] miscarriage of justice (error in judgment only).

malversation (f) : malversation, embezzlement, malpractice.
- *de fonds publics* : fraudulent conversion of public moneys.
[J] positive misprision.

mandant (m) : mandator.
[J] principal (in transaction), employer.

mandat (m) : 1° mandate, commission.
(civ.) *et* (cr.) : warrant, order.
- *d'amener* : order to offender or witness

to appear enforceable through arrest = writ of capias.
— *d'arrêt*: warrant for arrest = writ of capias.
— *de comparution*: summons.
— *de dépôt*: committal order.
— *d'internement*: order to intern alien, to confine madman.
— *de perquisition*: search warrant.
décerner, lancer un —: to issue a warrant.
signifier un —: to serve, to notify, a warrant.
(civ.) — *ad litem*: proxy to appear in court.
— *général*: full power of attorney.
— *légal*: legal representation (of minor, etc.).
— *spécial*: act of specific agency.
— *parlementaire*: Member's (electoral) mandate.
2° [F] money-order, draft.
— *de banque*: order on a bank.
— *international*: foreign money-order.
— *poste*: postal money-order.
— *télégraphique*: telegraphic money-order.
— *du Trésor*: Treasury warrant.
— *de virement*: transfer order.

mandataire (m): mandator, assign, *(des électeurs)* mandatory *ou* mandatary, *(à une assemblée, réunion)* proxy, representative.
[J] authorized agent, trustee, attorney-in-fact, *(administrateur-séquestre)* assignee.
[C] commission agent.
— *chargé des achats*: purchasing agent.

mandater (v): to commission.
— *(des frais, etc.)*: to pay (expenses, etc.) by draft.

mandement (m): [J] executory formula in judgment.
mander qn: to summon s.o. to attend, to send for a subordinate.

manière (f): way.
la — de remplir un formulaire: the way of filling a form, how to fill a form.

manifeste (m): [J] ship's manifest.

manifestement (adv): [J] overtly.

manœuvre(s) (f pl): scheming, working, handling, [U.S.] manœuvrer.
— *(s) abortives*: procuring of abortion.
— *(s) de bourse*: manœuvres in Stock Exchange quotations.
[J] — *(s) frauduleuses*: (civ.) misrepresentation, (cr.) fraudulent representation, cheating, swindling.
un manœuvre: a labourer.

manquant (a): [D] ullage.
[C] missing, out of stock, lacking.

manque (m): lack, scarcity, shortage of.
— *à gagner*: loss of profit, lost profit.
manquer *(d'un article)*: to be out of stock (for an article).
manquer de personnel: to be understaffed.

manquement (m): lack, failure.

manuel (a et m): (a) manual.
travailleur —: labourer.
(m): handbook.

manufacturé (f): management, administration; handling of stores, materials, etc.

maquette (f): mock-up.

maquis (m): bush.
le — de la procédure: the junglegrowth of legal procedure.

marasme (m): slackness, slump, dullness, stagnation.
les affaires sont dans le —: business is slack, is in the doldrums, stagnates.

marc (m): mark (ancient measure).
[J] *au — le franc*: pro-rate repartition of assets.

marchand (m et a): (m) merchant, tradesman, trader, dealer, shopkeeper.
— *ambulant*: pedlar, itinerant merchant.
— *de biens*: estate-agent, [U.S.] realtor.
— *en détail*: retailer.
— *forain*: stall-keeper.
— *de grains*: cornhandler.
— *en gros*: wholesale dealer, wholesaler.
— *des quatre saisons*: costermonger, hawker (of fruit and vegetables).
(a) *marine —(e)*: mercantile marine, merchant service.
navire —: merchant-man, tramp, freighter, merchant ship, trading vessel.
place —(e): shopping centre.
prix —: wholesale price, trade price.
qualité loyale et —(e): merchantable goods, fair merchandise.
valeur —(e): market-value.
ville —(e): commercial town.

marchandage (m):
1° jobbing a contract, sub-contracting a job.
[J] work by contract.
2° bargaining.
marchander *qch*: to haggle over the price with s.o.

marchandisage (m): merchandising.

marchandiseur (m): merchandiser.

marchandise (f) : goods, wares and merchandises ; stock-in-trade.
une — : a commodity.
[J] *titre représentatif de* — *(warrant)* : warehouse-dock, warrant.
droits sur les —*(s) acquittés* : duty paid goods.
[C] —*(s) acheminées par air* : Air cargo.
— *de bon aloi* : merchantable goods.
—*(s) en commission* : goods on sale.
— *de contrebande* : contraband, smuggled goods.
— *échangeable (fongible)* : fungible commodity.
— *d'exportation* : export goods.
— *flottante ou roulante* : goods rolling or afloat.
—*(s) livrées en pièces détachées* : completely knocked down goods.
— *en magasin* : stock-in-hand.
— *de premier choix* : best quality.
— *de rebut* : rejects, rubbishy goods, trash.
— *de traite* : trade-goods.
—*(s) de vente courante* : convenience goods.
avance sur —*(s)* : advance loan on goods.
bourse de —*(s) (de commerce)* : Commodities Exchange (# Royal Exchange).
courtier en —*(s)* : produce broker.
dédouaner des —*(s)* : to clear goods.
dépôt, entrepôt de —*(s)* : warehouse.
warrant en —*(s)* : produce warrant.
train de —*(s)* : goods train, [U.S.] freight train.
wagon de —*(s)* : truck, [U.S.] box car.

marché (m) : 1° market overt, 2° contract, deal, sale, 3° market of a commodity or in a commercial centre.
[A] [C] — *sur adjudication* : allocation of contract.
— *clandestin* : clandestine, illicit market.
— *clef en main* : contractor's undertaking to deliver a house ready to move in.
— *au comptant* : cash transaction.
— *sur concours* : contract concluded by a public authority after free choice among competitive tenders.
— *sur devis* : contract base on specifications.
— *extérieur* : foreign market.
— *fait* : fixed price.
— *à forfait* : lump-sum contract.
— *de fournitures* : contract of supply.
— *de gré à gré* : transaction by mutual agreement.
— *hétérogène* : fragmented market.
— *hypothécaire* : mortgage market.
— *intérieur* : home, domestic market.
— *noir* : black market.
— *public* : public procurement contract.
— *public de fournitures* : government procurement.
— *à tempérament* : hire-purchase.
bon — : cheap.
conclure un — : to strike a bargain.
jeter sur le — : to launch, to throw on the market.
par-dessus le — : into the bargain.
[B] — *de l'argent* : money market, loaning.
— *baissier, à la baisse* : bearish market.
— *des changes* : exchange market.
double — *des changes* : dual exchange market.
— *au comptant* : spot market.
— *de contrat à terme* : futures market.
— *de couverture* : covering order.
— *à découvert* : deal on differences in quotations.
— *d'escompte avec faculté d'anticipation* : discount transaction whereby a party is entitled to call for settlement before time.
— *faible* : few transactions.
— *ferme* : steady market.
— *forfaitaire* : selling of futures.
— *haussier, à la hausse* : the market is all bulls, bullish market.
— *hors cote (« pieds humides »)* : curb market, outside brokers, unlisted security market.
— *irrégulier* : unsteady market.
— *monétaire* : monetary market.
— *officiel en Bourse* = the Ring.
— *à prime* : put, call, option market.
— *à double prime (stellage)* : double option, put and call market, [U.S.] straddle, spread eagle.
— *à terme* : forward market.
— *à terme d'instruments financiers (MATIF)* : financial futures market.
— *à terme sur les matières premières* : commodity futures trading (market).
consolider un — *à primes* : to take up an option.
orientation du — : market trend, tendency.
résistance du — : firmness of the market.
tenue du — : tone of the market, market trend.
[CEE] — *intérieur, sans frontières, unique* : [EEC] internal, frontier-free, single, market.

marchéage (m) : [C] marketing, marketing mix.

marcher (v) : to go, to run, to travel.
affaire qui **marche** *bien* : going concern.
ses affaires marchent bien : he is doing well.
(les affaires) marchent : business is brisk.

marge (f) : margin, cover.
[F] spread.
— *de bénéfice* : profit, the mark-up.
— *brute d'autofinancement* (M.B.A.) : cash flow.
— *de découvert réciproque* : swing.
— *de garantie* : surplus value of pledge over the loan it secures.
— *de sécurité* : safety margin.
[B] *appel de* — : request for additional cover

in forward deals.

marginal (a): marginal.
avantages **marginaux**: fringe benefits.
bénéfices marginaux: marginal profits.
coût(s) — (marginaux): marginal cost(s).
entreprise —(e): marginal firm.

mari (m): [J] husband.
le — est le chef de la communauté: the husband is the head of the community.
le — exerce les actions de la femme: the husband represents his wife at law.
femme en puissance de — (hist.): feme covert *(sp. eu égard à ses incapacités légales)*.
autorisation **maritale**: husband's authorization.
lieu marital: legal domicile of married couple (the husband's).

mariage (m): marriage, matrimony, wedding, nuptials.
— blanc: unconsummated marriage.
— in extremis: marriage on death-bed.
— légitime: legal marriage.
— nul: marriage null and void.
— par procuration: marriage by proxy (esp. of soldiers in the field).
— putatif: putative marriage.
acte de —: wedding, marriage certificate.
action en nullité de —: action for avoidance of marriage.
âge requis pour contracter —: marriage majority.
consommer le —: to consummate the marriage.
contracter —: to marry.
contrat de —: antenuptial settlement for the purpose of regulating the enjoyment and devolution of real and personal property.
enfant né hors —: child born out of wedlock.
foi du —: mutual faithfulness of married couple.
lien du —: marriage bond, tie.
opposition au —: caveat to a marriage.
promesse de —: promise to marry.
rupture de promesse de —: breach of promise.
marié: married.

marin (m): seafaring man, mariner, sailor, seaman.

marine (f): the sea service.
la — marchande: the mercantile marine, the merchant service.
la — nationale: the Navy.
officier de —: naval officer.

maritime (a): marine, maritime.
agent —: shipping agent.
assurance —: marine insurance.
code, droit —: maritime law, admiralty law,
navigation laws.
commerce —: seaborne trade.
congé —: sea-letter, -brief.
courtier —: ship-broker.
droit —: maritime law, law of shipping.
gare —: harbour station.
hypothèque —: hypothecation.
inscription —: marine registry.
messageries —(s): sea transport.
mouvement —: shipping intelligence.
préfet —: port-admiral.
route —: sea route.
tribunal —: court of Admiralty, naval court, marine court.

marque (f): make, [J] trade mark, service mark, collective mark, certification mark, brand.
— déposée: registered trade mark.
— distinctive: ear mark.
— de la douane: customs stamp.
— d'un revendeur (grossiste ou détaillant qui n'est pas celle du fabriquant du produit): own brand, own label.
image de —: brand image.
au prix **marqué**: at marked price.

marron (a): (a person) carrying on a trade without qualification (physician, broker, unlicensed trader, etc.).
courtier —: outside broker.

martiale *(loi)* (a): martial (law).

masse (f): [J] fund, stock.
— active, passive: assets, liabilities.
— des biens de la faillite: bankrupt's total estate.
— des biens de la succession: gross estate (of a succession).
— des créanciers: general body of the creditors (in bankruptcy).
— monétaire: monetary supply.
liquidation de la —: settlement (in bankruptcy).

massif (a): heavy.
retraits —(s) des dépôts en banque: run on banks.

matériel (a et m): (a) material.
besoins —(s): bodily needs.
dommages —(s): damage to property.
valeurs —(les): tangible assets.
(m): material, equipment, plant, stock.
— roulant: rolling-stock.
— pour le traitement de l'information: hardware.
— d'une usine: plant, working stock.

matière (f): material, matter, substance, topic.
— première: raw material.

[J] – *d'un délit, d'un crime :* gravamen of a charge.
– *à procès :* grounds for litigation.
[F] – *imposable :* the subject-matter of taxation.
comptabilité – (s) : store accounting, [U.S.] materials accounting.

matrice (f) : matrix, womb.
[A] – *du rôle des impôts :* original of assessment roll.
– *cadastrale :* alphabetical register of landowners.
– *de décision rectangulaire :* pay-off matrix.

matricide (a, m et f) : (a) matricidal, (m) matricide.
[J] the crime of matricide ; the murderer, the murderess.

matricule (m) : roll, register, list ; inscription, registration, enrolment ; registration certificate.

matrimonial (a) : matrimonial.
agence – (e) : matrimonial agency.
capacité – (e) : legal capacity to marry.
droits **matrimoniaux** : rights on property acquired by married couple.
régime – : choice of one of the antenuptial settlements provided by law (see *régime*), [U.S.] regime.

mauvais (a) : bad, ill, wrong.
– *(e) créance :* bad debt.
en – état : in a bad state, damaged, in bad repair.
de – foi : mala fide.
– *(e) gestion :* maladministration.
– *marché :* losing market.
– *papier :* unrecoverable bills.
– *(e) réputation :* ill fame, ill repute, disrepute, bad name.
[ASS] *mauvais risque :* bad risks.

maximisation *(des profits)* (f) : maximizing (profits).

maximum (a et m) : (a) maximum, highest, top.
au – : at most, not exceeding.
baisse – : limit down.
hausse – : limit up, limit gains.
taux – : top rate.
(m) maximum.

mécanisation (f) : mechanization.

mécanisme (m) de la prise de décision : decision making process.

mécanographie (f) : data processing, use of computers.

traitement **mécanographique** *des éléments d'une déclaration fiscale :* automatic processing of the data contained in a tax return.

mécénat (m) (opp. parrainage) : patronage (opp. sponsoring).

mèche (f) : wick (of candle).
vendre la – : to let the cat out of the bag.

médecin (m) : medical man, doctor, physician.
– *de caisse :* impanelled doctor.
– *légiste :* medical expert commissioned by court.
– *sanitaire :* medical officer.
médecine *légale :* state, legal, forensic medicine, medical jurisprudence.
médecine du travail : industrial medicine.
exercice illégal de la médecine : illegal practice of medicine.
expertise **médico**-*légale :* medico-legal report.

médiateur (m) : ombudsman.

médical (a) : medical.
certificat – : medical certificate.
commission – (e) : medical board.
frais **médicaux** : medical expenses.

mélioration (f) : [J] improvement of land.

membre (m) : member.
– *de droit :* ex-officio member.
– *fondateur :* founder member.

mémoire (m et f) : (f) *(sens général)* memory, *(électronique)* storage.
(m) memorial, dissertation, thesis, memorandum, written report.
– *d'entrepreneur :* contractor's account.
[J] – *de demande, de défense :* memorandum of law, (written) statement of case.
– *de dépens, – taxé :* memorandum, taxed bill of costs.
– *descriptif d'une invention :* specification of patent.
arrêter un – : to draw up an account.
pour – : as a reminder.
régler un – : to settle an account.

memorandum (m) : memorandum, (diplomatic) note, exposé.

menace (f) : threat.
[J] intimidation, duress per minas.
– *(s) et voies de fait :* assault and battery.

ménage (m) : household.
consommation des – (s) : private consumption.
dépenses des – (s) : household expenditures.

ménagère (f) : housewife.
panier de la — : basket of commodities.

mener (v) une étude : to carry out a survey (a study).

mensualisation (f) : payment by monthly instalments.
mensualiser *l'impôt* : to collect (to pay) taxes by monthly instalments (payments).

mensualité (f) : monthly payment, instalment.
mensuel : monthly.

(aliénation) **mentale** (a) : insanity.

mention *(marginale)* (f) : (marginal) reference.
— *de service* : service instructions.

menu (a) : small, petty.
— *(s) frais* : petty expenses.
— *(e) monnaie* : loose cash.

mépris (m) : defiance.
au — *des lois* : in defiance of the law.

mer (f) : sea.
haute — : high seas.
lettre de — *(congé)* : sea-letter, -brief.
— *patrimoniale* : patrimonial sea.
— *territoriale* : territorial sea.
rapport de — : ship's protest.
[ASS] *fortune de* — : perils of the sea.

mercaticien (m) : marketing consultant.

mercatique (f) : marketing.

mercuriale (f) : [C] market price ; list of commodities.

mère (f) : mother.
[C] *maison* — : head office, parent establishment, house.
société — : parent company.

mésestimer (v) : *(mal évaluer)* to underrate, to underestimate, to undervalue.

messageries (f pl) : carrying trade, parcels office.
service de — : parcel post.

mesurable *(quantité)* (a) : measurable (quantity).

mesure (f) : measure, gauge, standard.
[J] — *(s) conservatoires* : measures of conservation, protective measures, measures of urgency.
— *(s) légales* : statute measures.
— *(s) provisionnelles* : provisional order.
— *(s) d'urgence* : emergency measures, stopgap measures.
dans la — *où* : to the extent that.
falsification des poids et — *(s)* : tampering with weights and measures.
par — *de* : as a measure of.
prendre des — *(s)* : to take measures (steps), to take action.
prendre des — *(s) contre (qch.)* : to make provisions against (sth.).

métal (m) : metal.
— *-étalon* : standard metal.

métallique (a) : metallic.
circulation, monnaie — : metallic currency.
réserves — *(s)* : metallic (bullion) reserve.

métaux (m pl) non ferreux : base metals.

métayage (m) : [J] farming leasehold whereby the farmer shares the produce of the farm with the landlord, [U.S.] share-crop system.
métairie : farm (as above).
métayer : the farmer, [U.S.] sharecropper (syn. *colonage partiaire, bail à mi-fruit*).

méthode (f) : method, practice, [U.S.] procedure.
— *(s) basées sur l'actualisation* : time-adjusted methods.
— *de l'annuité* : annual capital charge method.
— *du bénéfice brut actualisé* : present value of earnings method.
— *expérimentale* : experimental method.
— *hambourgeoise (ou par solde)* : balance method, steps method.
— *de l'indice de rentabilité interne* : discounted cash flow rate method.
— *des nombres* : product method.
— *d'amortissement d'après la valeur du moment* : appraisal method of depreciation.
— *d'amortissement dégressif* : declining (reducing) method.
— *« d'augmentation » pour le calcul des revenus* : accrual basis method.
— *de comptabilité de caisse* : cash method, cash basis method.
— *de l'imputation* : credit (tax credit) method.
— *d'incitation fiscale* : tax incentive method.
— *de paiement direct* : direct payment method.
— *d'évaluation des titres et des stocks* : stocks and shares, goods appraisement method.
— *de référence* : benchmark method.
— *(s) du taux interne de rentabilité* : 1) compound discount method, 2) earning power method ; 3) financial method ; 4) investor's method.

— *de la valeur actuelle en capital*: venture worth method.

métier (m) : trade, profession, craft, occupation.
— *manuel*: handicraft.
arts et — (s): arts and crafts.
chambre des — (s): chamber of trade.
corps de —: corporation, guild, trade association.

mettre (v) : to put, to lay, to set *(voir aussi mise)*.
— *au courant*: to inform.
— *à découvert*: to overdraw.
— *en dépôt*: to bond, to deposit.
— *en distribution*: to distribute.
— *aux enchères*: to put up for auction.
— *à exécution*: to implement.
— *en exploitation*: to exploit.
— *en faillite*: to bankrupt.
— *au point (un projet)*: to devise, to work out (a scheme).
— *au point (un produit, une invention)*: to perfect.
— *en pratique (système)*: to apply, to implement (system).
— *en rapport*: to get into touch.
— *en réserve*: to set by.
— *en valeur*: to develop.
se mettre en grève: to come out on strike, to go on strike.

meuble(s) (m) : movable(s).
biens —: personal estate, personalty.
[J] *biens — corporels*: tangible personal property, tangible assets, chattels personal.
biens — incorporels, biens meubles par détermination: (res incorporales) intangible property; intangible assets, choses in action, chattels real.
— *meublants*: furniture, movables (as opposed to fixtures).
« *en fait de —, possession vaut titre* » : « possession of chattels amounts to title ».

meublé (a et m) : (a) furnished, (m) furnished room, lodgings, furnished flat, [U.S.] apartment.

meurtre (m) : murder (see *homicide*).

meurtrier (m) : murderer.
[J] person guilty of murder.

mévendre (v) : to sell at a loss (at a sacrifice).

milieu (m) : background, environment, social class, surroundings.
« *le —* » : prostitutes' bullies.
les — (x) d'affaires: the business circles.

militant (m), **les militants** (m pl) : advocate, fighter for, the fighting wing.

milliard (m) : milliard, [U.S.] billion.

mince (a) *(revenu)* : scanty (income).

mine (f) : mine.
droit d'exploitation d'une —: right of working a mine.
concession **minière** : [U.S.] claim.
industrie minière: mining industry.

minerai (m) : ore.

mineur (m) : minor.
[J] infant, under age.
délinquant —: juvenile offender.
excitation de — à la débauche: enticement of minor to dissolute living.
traite des — (s) et des femmes: white slave traffic.
tribunal des — (s): juvenile court.

minima (pl of minimum) : [J] *appel à —*: public prosecutor's appeal againts too mild a sentence.
valeur **minimale** : minimal, minimum value.

minimarge *(magasin à)* (f) : discounthouse.

minimisation (f) : minimisation, minimizing.
— *des coûts*: minimizing cost.

minimum (m et a) : minimum.
— *vital*: living wage.

ministère (m) : 1° the cabinet, the Government.
2° [A] Ministry, [U.S.] Department ; seat, offices, building of a ministry.
— *des Affaires étrangères* # Foreign Office, [U.S.] Department of State.
— *de l'Agriculture*: Ministry of Agriculture, [U.S.] Department of Agriculture.
— *du Commerce*: [G.B.] Department of Trade and Industry.
— *de la Défense nationale*: Ministry of Defence, [U.S.] Department of Defense.
— *de l'Economie et des Finances* # The Exchequer, [U.S.] The Department of the Treasury.
— *de l'Intérieur* # the Home Office, [U.S.] Department of the Interior.
— *de la Justice* # Lord High Chancellor's Office, [U.S.] Department of Justice.
— *des postes et télécommunications* # Postmaster General's Office, [U.S.] Post Office Department.
— *de la Santé*: Ministry of Health.
— *du Travail*: Department of Employment.

— *de l'équipement* # Board of Works, [U.S.] Federal Works Agency.
3° [J] *le Ministère public* : the Department of the Public Prosecutor, the prosecuting magistrate.
par — *d'huissier* : served by a bailiff.

ministre (m) : minister.
le Premier — # Prime Minister.
— *plénipotentiaire* : minister plenipotentiary.
officiers **ministériels** : law officials *(avoués, huissiers, notaires)*, [U.S.] ministerial officers.
papier — : official foolscap.

minoration (f) : undervaluation.

minorité (f) : minority.
[J] minority, infancy, non-age.
— *de faveur* : qualified minority of a jury, sufficient for acquittal.
participation **minoritaire** : minority interest.

minus habens (m inv) : mental defective.

minute (f) : [J] minute, draft, record (of deed or judgment).
minuter *un acte* : to draw up a deed.
minutier : lawyer's minute-book or filing cabinet.

mise (f) : placing, putting of sth. in a place.
— *en accusation* : arraignment (in criminal procedure).
— *en cause* : to implicate s.o.
— *hors de cause* : to exonerate s.o.
— *en circulation de fausse monnaie* : passing counterfeit money.
— *en commun* : pooling.
— *hors cours* : to withdraw (currency) from circulation.
— *en délibéré* : adjourning (judgment) for further consultation of judges.
— *en demeure* : formal notice, summons to do sth.
— *en demeure de payer (avant action en justice)* : final demand.
— *en disponibilité* : to be placed on (half-pay) list.
— *à la disposition* : placing of s.o. or of sth. at the disposal of s.o.
— *aux enchères* : sale by auction.
— *dans les enchères* : bid.
— *en équilibre* : balancing.
— *en état d'une cause* : joinder of issue.
— *en faillite* : adjudication of bankruptcy.
— *de fonds* : putting up money.
— *en gage* : pledging.
— *à jour* : bringing up to date, loose leaf.
— *en jugement* : committing for trial.
— *en liberté* : release, setting free of prisoner.
— *en liberté provisoire* : release on bail.
— *en liquidation* : winding up, putting into liquidation.
— *hors la loi* : outlawing.
— *en possession* : vesting order, writ of possession.
— *en prévention* : imprisonment on suspicion, being taken into custody under remand.
— *à prix* : upset price.
— *au rebut* : scrapping.
— *en recouvrement* : notice to pay given to a taxpayer (advising him of the amount of his tax and of the basis of his liability).
— *à la retraite* : pensioning, *(à la limite d'âge)* superannuation, *(milit.)* placing on retired list.
— *au rôle d'un tribunal* : enrolling, inscription on cause-list.
— *au secret* : solitary confinement.
— *sous scellés* : imprint, affixation of official seals.
— *sous séquestre* : sequestration *(biens)*, embargo *(navires)*.
— *sous tutelle* : appointment of guardian.
— *en vente* : putting on sale.
— *en vigueur* : putting into force, enforcing.
miser *aux enchères* : to bid.

mission (f) : mission.

mi-temps (f) : half-time.
travailleur à — : half-timer.

mitoyen (a) : intermediate.
cloison —*(ne)* : dividing wall between two rooms.
mur — : party wall.
puits — : well common to two habitations.
[J] **mitoyenneté** : joint ownership (of party wall, hedge, etc.).

mixte (a) : mixed.
commission — : joint commission.
[J] *action* — : mixed action (real and personal).
contrat — : mixed contract (public and private).
[ASS] *assurance* — : endowment insurance.

mobile (a et m) : (a) mobile, movable.
[F] *capital* — : revenue assets.
échelle — *des salaires* : sliding wage scale.
(m) — : mobile incitement, motive.
— *déterminant* : prime motive.

mobilier (a et m) : (a) movable, personal.
action —*(e)* : personal action.
assurance —*(e)* : furniture insurance.
biens —*(s)* : personal property, chattels.
contribution —*(e)* (hist.) : occupancy tax.
gage — : pledge of chattels.
héritier — : distributee, legatee, heir to personal estate.
hypothèque —*(e)* : chattel mortgage.

propriété — *(e)* : personal property.
saisie — *(e)* : distraint upon furniture, seizure of movable property.
valeurs — *(es)* : transferable securities, stocks and shares.
vente — *(e)* : sale of chattels.
[J] *biens, droits* — *(s)* : see *meuble*. (m) furniture.

mobilisation (f) : mobilization.
[J] mortgaging real estate, representation of an accruing liability by negotiable instrument.
[F] liquidation, liberation of capital.
— *de fonds* : raising of funds.

modalité (f et f pl) : method, terms and conditions, clauses.
— *(s) d'un accord* : lines on which an agreement is reached.
— *(s) d'application* : mode of application.
— *(s) de paiement* : methods of payment.
[F] — *(s) d'une émission* : terms and conditions of an issue.

mode (f et m) : (f) 1° fashion, style.
2° method, mode.
haute — : fashion trade.
à la — : fashionable.
— *de vie* : way of life.
3° (m) — *d'emploi* : direction for use.
— *de règlement* : method of payment.

modèle (m) : design, model pattern.
— *(s) analogiques, iconiques, symboliques (par ex. simulations sur maquettes)* : analogical, iconic, symbolic models.
— *(s) économiques* : economic models.
— *déposé* : registered pattern.
— *de revenus* : time pattern.
— *de signature* : specimen signature.

modération (f) : moderation.
— *des revendications salariales* : wage restraint.
[J] — *de peine* : mitigation of penalty.
[C] — *de prix* : reduction in price.
[F] *demande en* — *d'impôt* : request for an abatement of taxes, for tax relief.
prix **modéré** : moderate price.

modernisation (f) : modernization.

modification (f) : rectification, change.
— *du risque* : variation of risk.
— *des statuts* : rectification in the articles.

modifier (v) : *(un article de loi)* to amend an act, *(une déclaration)* to modify a statement.

mœurs (f pl) : morals, manners, customs.
[J] *attentat aux* — : immoral offence.
[A] *certificat de bonne vie et* — : certificate of good character.
brigade des — : vice-squad.

moindre (a) : lesser.
le — *des deux montants* : the lesser of two amounts.

moins (adv) : minus, less.
à — *que* : unless.
de — *en* — : less and less.

moins-perçu (m) : amount not drawn.

moins-value (f) : depreciation, diminution, drop in value, capital loss.
titres qui enregistrent une — : stock that is dropping, falling.
— *(de titres)* : drop in value, depreciation.

mois civil (m) : (calendar) month.
— *en cours* : current month.
— *légal* : thirty days.

monétaire (a) : monetary.
circulation — : flow of money.
fonds — *international* : International Monetary Fund.
marché — : money market.
stabilisation — : currency stabilization.
stock — : money supply.
système — : monetary system.
unité — : monetary (money) unit, currency unit.
valeur — : money value.

monnaie (f) : money, currency.
(Hôtel de) la — : the Mint.
— *d'appoint divisionnaire* : small change.
— *ayant cours, légale* : currency, legal tender.
— *de compte* : money of account (in international dealings).
— *d'échange* : money of exchange.
— *faible, forte* : light (soft), hard currency.
— *fiduciaire* : fiduciary currency, paper money.
— *métallique* : hard cash.
— *-or* : gold currency.
— *-papier* : paper money.
— *de réserve* : reserve currency.
— *saine* : sound currency.
— *scripturale* : representative money.
crime de fausse — : coinage offence.
faire de la — : to get change.
fausse — : counterfeit coinage.
petite — : (small) change.
monnayage : minting, coining.

monopole : monopoly.
— *(s) d'Etat* : State monopolies.
— *de fait* : actual monopoly, de facto monopoly.
droit de — : franchise tax.

monopoliser : to monopolise.
monopoliste : monopolist.

monopolistique (a) : monopolistic.
comportement — : monopolistic behaviour.
contrôle — : monopoly control.

mont-de-piété *(now Crédit municipal).*
(m) : Municipal Pawn-Office.

montant (m) : amount, proceeds, total.
— *brut* : gross amount, sum total.
— *net* : net amount.
— *global des salaires* : payroll.
(C.E.E.) —(s) *compensatoires monétaires* : (E.E.C.) monetary compensation amounts.

monter (v) : to rise, to increase.
les prix **montent** *en flèche* : prices are rocketing.
se — *à* : to amount to.
montée *en flèche des prix et des salaires* : wage-price spiral.
montée soudaine des prix : surge of prices.

morale (a) : moral.
personne — : corporation, corporate body, legal entity.

moralité (f) : morality, morals.
de — *douteuse* : of doubtful honesty.
d'une — *irréprochable* : beyond reproach.
certificat de — : good conduct certificate.

moratoire (a et m) : (a) moratory (agreement, etc.), (payment) delayed by agreement.
(m) [J] moratorium, stay law.
intérêts —(s) : interest on overdue payments.
sentence — : judgment allowing respite.

morcellement (m) : breaking, cutting up.
— *de la propriété foncière* : parcelling out (of estate).

morgue (now *Institut médico-légal*) (f) : mortuary.

mort (f) : death.
— *accidentelle* : accidental death.
— *apparente* : apparent death.
— *civile* : (hist.) attainder.
— *d'homme* : killing of a human being.
— *naturelle* : natural death.
— *par pendaison* : death by hanging.
— *par strangulation* : death by strangulation.
[J] death by strangling, throttling.
— *subite* : sudden, unexpected death.
— *violente* : violent death.
« *le* — *saisit le vif, le vif chasse le* — » : « the estate is vested in the heir the very moment the woner dies ».
arrêt de — : death sentence.
cheptel — : farm implements and buildings leased.
peine de — : death penalty.

mortalité (f) : death-rate.
tables de — : mortality tables, expectation of mortality tables.

mortel *(accident)* (a) : fatal (accident).

morte-saison (f) : [C] off season.

mort-gage (m) : [J] chattel mortgage.

moteur (a) : motive, mover.

motif (m) : motive, cause, reason.
[J] ground.
—(s) *d'un jugement* : grounds of judgment.
défaut de — : omission (in judgment) to deal with one or several counts of indictment or complaint.
exposé des —(s) : explanatory statement (to a bill), preamble.
jugement par adoption de —(s) : judgment in appeal adopting the grounds of a lower court.
juste — : peremptory reason justifying termination of contract without notice.
avis **motivé** : (well-grounded) counsel's opinion.
décision motivée : well-founded (justifiable) opinion, decision.
clause **motivale** : clause expressing the reasons for a decision.

motion (f) : motion, proposal.
présenter une — : to move a motion (a proposal).
— *de synthèse* : composite motion.

motivation (f) : motivation.

mouillage (m) : anchorage.
[A] *droits de* — : keelage, berthage.

mouvement (m) : movement, motion, flow, fluctuation, trend.
— *de capitaux* : movement of money.
— *du marché* : fluctuations of the market.
— *des navires* : ship news.
[B] —(s) *d'accélération et de retardement sur le marché des changes* (quand une dévaluation est pressentie) : leads and lags.

moyen (a et m) : (a) middle.
(m) means.
[J] ground.
les —(s) *de droit, de fait* : legal, practical grounds put forward.
— *frauduleux* : fraudulent mean.
— *libératoire* : peremptory ground for nonsuit.
— *de nullité* : grounds for avoidance.
— *d'opposition* : ground to move for injunction.

– *de preuve* : element of proof.
– *de recours* : appeal, remedy at law.
– *subsidiaire* : auxiliary plea.
les voies et les –*(s)* : ways and means.
[F] *cours* – : average (middle) price.
coût – : average cost.
– *terme* : intermediate, medium-term.
[C] –*(s) de livraison des marchandises* (du fabricant au consommateur) : physical distribution.
–*(s) de paiement* : means of payment.
–*(s) de production* : means of production, production facilities.

moyennant (prép.) : on a (certain) condition, in consideration of, at a charge of.
– *finances* : for a consideration.

moyenne (f) : average, mean.
– *arithmétique* : arithmetic mean.
– *à la baisse* : average down.
– *pondérée* : weighted mean, weighted average.
– *des ventes* : average sales.
[B] *faire la* – : to average.
prendre la – : to take the average.
tendance à la – : central tendency.

emprunts (m pl) **multidevises** (a) : multicurrency loans.

multilatéral (a) : multilateral.
accords **multilatéraux** : multilateral agreements.

multiple (m et a) : multiple.
taux internes –*(s)* : multiple rates of return.

multiplicateur (a et m) : multiplying.
(m) multiplier.
– *du crédit, de l'emploi* : credit, employment multiplier.
effet – *(du multiplicateur)* : multiplier effect.
multiplier : to multiply.

municipal (a) : municipal.
conseil – : town council.
arrêté – : by(e)-law, [U.S.] municipal ordinance.
police –*(e)* : constabulary.
taxes –*(es)* : (municipal) rates.

municipalité (f) : 1° municipality, 2° municipal, territorial, corporation, incorporated town, 3° town council, 4° town hall.

mur (m) : wall.
– *d'appui* : low wall.
– *de clôture* : enclosing wall.
– *mitoyen* : party wall.
– *orbe* : blind wall.
– *de refend, de séparation* : partitionwall.
gros –*(s)* : main walls.
mettre qn au pied du – : to corner, to drive s.o. into a corner.

mûr (a) : mature.
âge – : middle age.

mutable (a) : alienable.

mutation (f) : change, alteration.
[J] change of ownership, transfer (of property), conveyance.
– *entre vifs* : conveyance of property inter vivos.
– *par décès* : transfer by death.
– *à titre gratuit* : donation, gift.
–*(s) imposables* : taxable transfer of capital.
– *à titre onéreux* : conveyance for valuable consideration, (Scot.) onerous conveyance.
droits de – : transfer taxes (estate duty, inheritance tax, succession duty, gift tax).

mutilé (a et m) : (a) disabled.
(m) – *de guerre* : disabled exserviceman.

mutualité (f) : mutuality, reciprocity.

mutuel (a) : mutual.
accord – : mutual agreement.
assurance –*(le)* : mutual insurance (company).
concessions –*(les)* : give-and-take.
pari mutuel : totalizator system (racing).
société de cautionnement – : mutual guarantee society.
société de crédit – : mutual loan society.
société de secours –*(s)* : friendly society, mutual benefit society.

mystification (f) : hoax.

mystique (a) : mystic.
[J] *testament* – (syn. *testament secret*) : will written or dictated by testator and sealed, and handed to the notary in the presence of two witnesses.

NOTES

NOTES

N

naissance (f) : birth.
- *à terme :* normal birth.
- *après terme :* delayed birth.
- *avant terme :* premature birth.
- *posthume :* afterbirth.
acte, extrait de − *:* birth certificate.
lieu de − *:* birth-place.
limitation des −*(s) :* family planning.
régulation des −*(s) :* birth-control.
industrie **naissante** *:* infant industry.
enfant à **naître** *:* future child.

nantir (v) : to secure, to pledge.
- *des valeurs :* to pledge securities.
biens **nantis** *:* pledged chattels.
créancier nanti : secured creditor.

nantissement (m) : [J] hypothecation, pledging, bailment ; pledge, collateral security, cover.
déposer des valeurs en − *:* to lodge stocks as security.
droit de − *:* lien on goods.
- *de créance :* perfected security.
titres déposés en − *:* stock lodged as security.
prêt sur − *:* secured loan (see *antichrèse, droit de gage*).

natalité (f) : birth-rate.
taux de − *:* birth-rate.

nation (f) : nation.
clause de la − *la plus favorisée :* most favoured nation clause.
comptes de la − *:* national (social) accounting.
Organisation des −*(s) Unies (O.N.U.) :* the United Nations Organization (U.N.O.).
Société des −*(s) :* (hist.) League of Nations.

national (a et m) : (a) national.
revenu − *:* national income.
(m) national (of a country), subject, citizen.

nationalisation (f) : nationalization.
le secteur **nationalisé** *:* the nationalized sector.

nationalité (f) : nationality, nation, national status.
acquisition de la − *:* acquisition of nationality.
déchéance de − *:* loss of nationality.
réintégration dans la − *:* restoration of nationality.
renonciation à la − *:* renunciation of nationality.
retrait de la − *:* withdrawal of nationality.

sans − *(apatride) :* stateless (person).
[J] *acte de* − *:* ship's certificate of registry.

naturalisation (f) : naturalization.
décret de − *:* certificate of naturalization.
demande de − # [U.S.] declaration of intention.

nature (f) : kind, nature.
- *d'une entreprise :* kind of a business.
avantages, paiements, prestations en − *:* benefits, payment, allowances, in kind.
exécution en − *:* specific performance.
de quelque − *que ce soit :* of any kind whatever.

naturel (a) : natural.
cause −*(le) :* Act of God.
droit − *:* natural law (as the emanation of the Divine Providence).

naufrage (m) : shipwreck.
[J] *droit de* − *(d'épave) :* escheat.

naval (a) : naval.
chantier − *:* shipyard, shipbuilding yard.
construction −*(e) :* shipbuilding.

navicert (m) : navycert.

navigabilité (f) : [A] *certificat de* − *: (navires)* certificate of seaworthiness, *(avions)* of airworthiness.

navigation (f) : navigation, sailing, shipping.
- *aérienne :* aerial navigation, flying.
- *au cabotage, côtière :* coastal trade.
- *au long cours :* ocean sailing.
- *fluviale :* inland water transport, river shipping.
certificat, permis de − *:* ship's passport, sea letter.
droits de − *:* shipping dues.
société de − *:* shipping company.
naviguer *au commerce :* to be in the merchant service.

néant (m) : nothingness, nought, naught.
[J] *mettre un jugement, un appel à* − *:* to quash a sentence, to dismiss an appeal.
[A] « − », *dans une déclaration d'impôt sur le revenu :* « none ».
dans un questionnaire : « nil », « nothing to report ».

nécessaire (a) : necessary, needful.

nécessité (f) : necessity.
denrées de première − : essential foodstuffs.

négatif (-tive) (a) : negative.
réponse − : negative answer.
se tenir sur la − : to maintain a negative attitude.

négation (f) : negation.

négatoire (a) : denying.
[J] *action* − : negatory action (to establish the non-encumbrance of an estate).

négligeable (a) : negligible, unimportant.

négligence : carelessness.
[J] *(terme générique)* negligence, *(dans un cas concret)* neglect.
− *simple* : levissima culpa, slight neglect (a nonfeasance).
− *lourde* : levis culpa, ordinary neglect (a misfeasance).
− *criminelle* : lata culpa, gross neglect (a malfeasance).
clause de − : [ASS] negligence clause.
par − : through an oversight.

négoce (m) : business, trade, commerce, traffic.

négociable (a) : *(instruments)* negotiable, *(instruments et biens mobiliers)* assignable, transferable, marketable.
− *en banque* : bankable paper.
valeur − : marketable share.

négociant (m) : trader, wholesale merchant, dealer.

négociation (f) : dealing, negotiation, transaction.
− *(s) en bourse* : Stock Exchange transactions.
− *au comptant* : dealing for money.
− *d'un effet* : negotiation of a bill.
− *(s) employés-employeur dans le cadre de l'entreprise* : plant bargaining.
− *salariale* : wage bargaining.
− *(s) Kennedy* : Kennedy Round.
− *(s) à terme* : dealings for the account.

négocier (v) : to deal, to treat, to negotiate.
− *un emprunt* : to place a loan.
− *un effet, un traité* : to negotiate a bill, a treaty.
− *des valeurs* : to trade.
être **négocié** : to be traded.
l'obligation x a été négociée hier à 95 dollars : the X bond was traded at US $. 95 yesterday.

« **nègre** » (m) d'un écrivain : ghost writer.

net (a) : net.
− *d'impôt* : free of tax.
bénéfice − : net (clear) profit.
poids − : net weight.
prix − : net price.
recettes − *(tes)* : net receipts.
solde, − : final balance.
ventes − *(tes)* : net sales.
[B] *couverture* − *(te)* : net margin.

neutralité (f) : neutrality.
neutre : neutral.

neveu (m), **nièce** (f) : nephew, niece.
petit- − : grand-nephew.

nice (a) : simple.
[J] *action* − : claim based on a simple promise.
promesse − : simple promise.

niveau (m) : level, standard.
− *des prix* : level of prices.
− *de renouvellement des stocks* : reorder level.
− *des salaires* : wage level.
− *de vie* : standard of living (*l'expression* : « level of living » *s'emploie aussi parfois aux U.S. et au Canada*).

niveler *(les revenus)* (v) : to equalize, to level (income).

nœud (m) : fork, node.

noir (a) : black.
caisse − *(e)* : bribery fund, [U.S.] boodle, slush fund.
marché − : black market.
travail − : moonlight work.

nolis (m) : 1° freighting of ship.
2° cost of freight.
[J] *acte de* **nolisement** : charter-party.
nolisateur : freighter, charterer.
noliser : to freight, to charter.

nom (m) : name.
− *de baptême, petit* − : Christian name.
− *commercial* : trade-name.
− *d'emprunt* : assumed name.
− *déposé* : registered name.
− *de famille, patronymique* : surname.
− *de jeune fille* : maiden name.
− *générique* : generic term.
− *supposé* : assumed, false, fictitious name.
− *de terre* : name of nobility drawn from landed property.
décliner ses − *(s) et qualités* : to state one's full name and standing.
être connu sous le − *de* : to go by the name of.

en son propre – : for oneself.
prête- – : dummy.
voyager sous un faux – : to travel under an alias.
[J] *erreur de* – : misnomer.
société en – *collectif* : private company, general partnership, copartnership.

nombre (m) : number, figure.
méthode des –(s) : product method.
le – *minimum d'actionnaires* : the quorum at a shareholders' meeting.
– *de chômeurs* : unemployment figure(s), (U.S.) unemployment rate.

nombreux (a) : large.
famille nombreuse : large family.

nomenclature (f) : list, nomenclature.

nominal (a) : by name.
appel – : roll-call, call-over.
autorité – : nominal authority.
faire l'appel – : to call over (assembly).
revenu – : money-income.
salaire – : nominal wage.
[J] *faire l'appel* – *du jury* : to array the jury.
[F] *valeur* –(e) : face value.

nominatif (a) : by name.
effet – : registered security.
état – : list of names, nominal roll.
liste nominative : nominal list.
livret – : depositor's book.
titre – : registered stock.

nomination (f) : appointment.

nommer (v) : to name, to appoint.
[J] *le nommé Untel* : a) a man named So-and-so, b) the man So-and-so.

non-acceptation (f) : [J] non acceptance (of bill).
[C] refusal (of goods).

non-accomplissement (f) : non fulfilment, non completion.

non-activité (f) : *mettre un officier en* – : to put an officier on half pay.

non-affectation *(de recettes au fonds de réserve)* (f) : non-allocation (of returns to reserve funds).

non amorti, non amortissable (a) : unredeemed, unredeemable.

non avenu (nul et) (a) : invalid, null and void.

non-casse (f) : [C] *prime de* – : no-accident bonus.

non-comparution (f) : non appearance, default.

non compensé (a) *(chèque)* : uncleared (cheque).

non comptabilisé (a) : unaccounted.

non-concurrence *(clause de)* (f) : non competition (clause).

non-culpabilité (f) : non guiltiness.

non-déclaration (f) : failure to make a statement.

non-dénonciation de trahison *et par extension,* **de crime** (f) : misprision of felony.

non disponible (a) : not available.

non distribuable (a) : non apportionable.

non encaissé (a) : uncollected.

non endommagé (a) : sound.

non-exécution (f) : non-fulfilment (of agreement, etc.), non-performance.

non fondé (a) : unfounded, groundless.
une demande non –(e) : an unsubstantiated claim.

non garanti (a) : unsecured.

non-lieu (m) : no ground for prosecution, no true bill.
[J] *ordonnance de* – : nonsuit, nolle prosequi.
rendre une ordonnance de – : to direct a nonsuit.

non-livraison, non-réception (f) : [C] non-delivery.

non négociable (a) : not negotiable (bill, etc.).

nonobstant (prép) : notwithstanding.
[J] – *toute clause contraire* : notwithstanding any clause to the contrary.

non officiel(le) (a) *(grève)* : unofficial.

non-paiement (m) : non payment.
non payé : unpaid.

non perçu (a) : uncollected.

non recevable (a) : [J] inadmissible (excuse, etc.).
demandeur – dans son action : petitioner declared to have no cause for action. [J] nonsuited.

non-recevoir (v) : [J] *opposer une fin de – :* to put in a plea in bar, to traverse. (see *fins de –*).

non reconnu (a) : unacknowledged.

non rentable (a) : uneconomic.

non-rétroactivité (f) : non-retroactivity.
[J] *– des lois :* laws have no ex post facto effect.

non-révocabilité (f) : irremovability (of judges), office « during good behaviour ».

non taxé (a) : duty-free.

non-valeurs (f pl) : bad debts.
[F] revenue budgeted but not forthcoming.

non vérifié (a) : unchecked.

normal (a) : normal, standard.
usage – : normal, regular use.
usure – (e) : fair wear and tear.

normalisation (f) : standardization, return to normal conditions.

norme(s) *(industrielles, de sécurité)* (f pl) : (industrial, safety, security, standards).
– comptables : accounting standards.
conforme aux – (s) : up to standard.
– d'endettement des industries : external financing limit (E.F.L.).

notaire (m) : notary (in France a notary exercises many of the functions of a solicitor, including conveyancing. He authenticates deeds, deals with successions, antenuptial settlements, etc.), [U.S.] contract lawyer.
chambre des – (s) : elected board of the profession.
étude de – : notary's office.
par devant – : before a notary.
acte **notarié**, *attestation notariée :* authentic deed, certificate.

notation (f): [F] rating.

note (f) : note, memorandum, memo, invoice, bill.
– (s) d'audience : summary report by the clerk of the court of a sitting on a criminal case.
– de couverture : [ASS] cover-note, note of the insurer to the effect that the insurance will operate even before signing of the policy.
– diplomatique : diplomatic note.
– d'expédition : consignment note.
– de frais : note of expenses.
régler une – : to settle an account.

notification (f) : notification, notice, intimation, service, signification.

notoire (a) : notorious, manifest.
« *soit – que...* » : « be it known that... ».
dépenses ostensibles ou – (s) : open or well-known expenses.
débiteur **notoirement** *insolvable :* notoriously insolvent debtor.
fait – : well-known fact.
injustice – : manifest injustice.

notoriété (f) : *(d'un fait)* notoriety, notoriousness, *(d'une personne)* repute.
[J] *– de droit :* proof by documentary evidence.
– de fait : proof by the evidence of witnesses, common knowledge.
acte de – : identity certificate made out by a justice of the peace, in presence of three attesting witnesses, attested affidavit.
de – publique : matter of common knowledge.

nouveau, nouvelle (a) (adv) : (a) new, fresh, further.
jusqu'à – avis : until further advice.
(une) – opération : further transaction.
(adv) : forward.
« *à –* » *(commande renouvelée) :* repeat order.
report à – : amount carried forward.
solde à – : balance brought down, carried forward.

novation (f) : renewal.
[J] novation, accord, substitution of a new obligation to an old one.
– de créance : substitution of debt.

noyaux (m pl) **(industriels)** : (industrial) cores.

nubilité (f) : age of consent.

nue propriété (f) : ownership without usufruct or use, bare ownership.

nu propriétaire (m) : bare owner.

nuire (v) : to injure, to hurt.

nuisance (f) : nuisance.

nul (a) : void, invalid, null (and void).
– et non avenu : null and void.
croissance – (le) : nul growth.

solde — : null balance.

nullité (f) : nullity, invalidity.
— *absolue, radicale* : absolute nullity.
— *de droit* : nullity in law.
— *de fait* : actual nullity.
— *au fond* : substantive nullity.
— *de forme* : nullity of form.
— *de plein droit* : nullity as of right.
— *de procédure* : nullity of procedure.
— *expresse* : nullity expressly prescribed by law.
— *virtuelle* : construed nullity.
action en — : action for avoidance of contract.
clause frappée de — : clause voided.
frapper de — : to render void.
demande en — : plea in abatement.
recours en — : appeal on grounds of nullity.
sous peine de — : under pain of being declared void.

numéraire (m) : metallic currency.
payer en — : to pay in cash.
[F] *action de* — : share paid in money (opp. *part de fondateur* : founder's initial, deferred share).

numération *(décimale)* (f) : (decimal) notation.

numéro (m) : number.

numérotage (m) : numbering.

numéroter (v) : to number.
actions non **numérotées** : unnumbered shares.

nuncupation (f) : [J] nuncupation, oral declaration of will, deed, etc.
testament **nuncupatif** : nuncupated will.

nuptialité (f) : marriage.
taux de — : marriage rate.

NOTES

O

obéissance *(à la loi)* (f) : submission (to the law).

obérer (v) : to involve s.o. in debt, to encumber, to burden (sth.) with debt.
   être **obéré** *de dettes* : to be heavily in debt.
   — *les finances* : to weigh heavily on the finances.
   finances obérées : encumbered finances.

objecter (v) : to object.

objecteur de conscience (m) : conscientious objector.

objectif (a) : objective.
   exposé — : objective account.

objectif (m) : aim.
   direction par — : target management.
   —(s) *à long terme* : corporate planning.
   —(s) *économiques nationaux* : National Economic Objectives.

objection (f) : objection.
   lever, réfuter une — : to dispose of an objection.
   — *préalable sur la façon dont seront menés les débats d'une assemblée* : point of order.

objet (m) : 1° object, thing.
   [J] — *immobilier, mobilier* : realty, personalty.
   — *(postal) recommandé* : registered (postal) article, packet.
   — *de valeur* : valuable article (good).
   2° subject, subject-matter.
   [J] — *d'un litige* : subject of an action.
   3° object, aim, purpose.
   [J] — *d'un contrat* : purpose of a contract.
   remplir son — : to attain one's end.
   sans — : aimless, aimlessly.
   cette réunion a pour — : the purpose of this meeting is to determine.
   l' — *de notre association est de* : the objects of our association (on which our association is established) are.
   [C] — *donné en prime* : give-away.

obligataire (a et m) : (a) bonded.
   (m) [F] bondholder, debenture-holder, holder of redeemable stock.
   obligee (whose bill has been backed, etc.).

obligation (f) : (moral) obligation, duty, loan stock, loan capital.

[J] privity, recognizance, bond, liability, legal obligation.
   — *alimentaire, d'entretien* : maintenance obligation.
   — *chirographaire (opp. obligation hypothécaire* : naked, simple debenture (as opposed to mortgage debenture).
   — *contractuelle* : privity in deed, in contract.
   — *de faire* : obligation to do a particular thing. [J] mandatory injunction.
   — *de ne pas faire* : obligation to refrain from doing a particular thing. [J] restrictive injunction.
   — *fiscale (limitée, illimitée)* : (remittance, arising) basis.
   — *hypothécaire* : mortgage debenture.
   — *inconditionnelle* : absolute liability.
   — *irrévocable* : binding agreement.
   — *d'agir en bon père de famille* : obligation to administer (an estate) with due diligence.
   — *légale* : privity in law.
   — *morale* : moral obligation (not enforceable in law).
   — *de témoigner* : obligation to witness.
   cause d'une — : cause of a valid contract.
   droit des —(s) : law of contract.
   conflit d' —(s) : clash of obligations.
   contracter une — : to contract an obligation (to enter into an agreement).
   modalités de l' — : terms of an agreement.
   [F] debenture, bond, redeemable stock.
   — *amortissable* : redeemable stock.
   — *émise depuis plus de 3 mois* : seasoned bond.
   —(s) *émises pour le compte d'une société commerciale* : corporate debt securities.
   — *d'emprunt* : loan-bond.
   —(s) *d'Etat* : gilts.
   — *foncière* : debenture secured on landed property.
   — *funding* : funding debenture.
   —(s) *garanties par des actifs* : Asset Backet Obligations (A.B.O.).
   — *à lots* : premium bond.
   — *nominative* : registered stock.
   — *-or* : gold bonds.
   — *au porteur* : bearer-bond.
   — *remboursable* : redeemable bond.
   — *à la souche* : unissued debenture.
   —(s) *à taux fixe* : fixed rate bond.
   emprunt par —(s) : loan floated by issuance of bonds.
   porteur d' — : bondholer.
   souscrire une — : to subscribe, to sign, to enter into a bond.

obligatoire (a) : *(assurance)* compulsory, obligatory, *(accord, traité)* binding.

obligé (a et m) : (a) obliged, compelled, bound to.
(m) obligee.

(s')obliger (v) : *(pour qn)* to engage oneself, to stand surety for s.o.

oblitérer (v) *(un timbre)* : to cancel a stamp.
timbre **oblitéré** : used stamp.

(publications) **obscènes** : obscene (literature).

observateur (m) : observer.

observation (f) : 1° *(remarque)* comment, observation, remark.
2° *(le fait d'observer)* observance.

observer *(les règlements)* (v) : to observe, to comply with (the regulations).
faire – la loi : to enforce the law.

obsolescence *(de l'équipement)* (f) : obsolescence (of plant).
– créée délibérément : built-in (planned) obsolescence.

obstacle (a) (m) : check, hindrance, obstacle (to).
faire – à : to object to, to oppose.

obstruction (f) : obstruction.
faire de l' – : to practise obstruction [U.S., pol.] to filibuster.

obtempérer (v) : (judiciary and police term) to obey.
– à une sommation : to obey a summons.
– à une requête : to accede to a request.
– à un ordre : to comply with an order.

obtenir *(crédits)* (v) : to get, to obtain (credit).
– (qqch) par des moyens frauduleux : to obtain (sthg) by (under) false pretences.

obtention (f) : obtaining, obtainment, recovery (of damages).

occasion (f) : occasion, opportunity.
[C] bargain.
marchandise d' – : job-lot, second-hand goods.
vente d' – : bargain sale.

occasionnel (a) : occasional, casual.
opérations effectuées à titre purement – : purely occasional transactions.
main-d'œuvre – (le) : casual labour.

occulte (a) : secret, hidden.
rémunération – : secret (undisclosed) payment, payment to an undisclosed recipient.

occupant (m) : occupier.
[J] *avocat, avoué, juge – :* barrister, solicitor, judge of record.
– sans titre et de mauvaise foi : mala fide occupier.
possession à titre de premier – : occupancy.
– d'une maison (locataire ou propriétaire) : householder (owner or tenant).

occupation (f) : 1° occupation.
2° business, work, employment, profession.
– accessoire : accessory job.
– principale : main employment, occupation.
sans – : out of work.
3° [J] occupancy, possession (of real property) ; temporary occupation of private property by administrative authorities for public purposes (works, etc.), against compensation.

occuper (v) : 1° to occupy.
2° *(– des ouvriers, du personnel)* to employ workmen, a staff.
« occupé » *(téléph.)* : « engaged ».

octroi (m) : 1° town dues, 2° tollhouse.
– de mer : duties levied by certain seaboard townships.

octroyer (v) : to grant, to concede, to allow.
– un délai (de) : to grant, to allow, a time expansion (of).

œuvre (f) : work, working ; institution ; structure.
[J] *dénonciation de nouvel – :* see *dénonciation*.
– de bienfaisance : charitable corporation or foundation, non-profit organization.
mettre en – : to implement, to carry out, to carry into effect.

offense (f) : offence, transgression, sin, trespass.
[J] *– à la cour (outrages à magistrat) :* contumacy, contempt of court, positive misprision.

offenser (v) : to give offence.

offenseur (m) : offender.

office (m) : 1° office, function, duty.
d' – : as a matter of routine, automatically, officially.
imposition d' – : arbitrary, official assessment.
[J] *avocat d' – :* counsel in forma pauperis (mostly ex officio) appointed by the *bâtonnier*.
poursuite (pénale) d' – : prosecution ex officio (opp. *poursuite sur plainte*).

être mis à la retraite d'— : to be compulsory retired, pensioned off.
2° bureau, office, official agency.
— *des changes :* foreign exchange office.
— *de compensation :* clearing-house.
— *du tourisme :* tourist board.

officiel (a) : official, formal.
à titre — : officially, formally.
« *Journal — » :* see *journal.*
cote — (le) : quoted list, official list.
le marché — (Bourse) : the Ring, the official market (stock exchange).

officiellement (adv) : officially.

officier (m) : officer, civil and military.
1° *— de l'état civil :* registrar, municipal magistrate in charge of registers of birth, marriage and death.
— *de justice :* law-officer.
— *ministériel :* law official *(notaire, avoué, huissier),* [U.S.] ministerial officer.
— *de paix, de police :* police official (police officer : *gardien de la paix).*
2° (commissioned) officer.
— *général :* officer of the rank of general *(armée),* flag officer *(marine).*
— *supérieur :* field-officer.
— *subalterne :* officer of subaltern's or of captain's rank.
— *de marine :* naval officer.

officieux (a) : semi-official.
avertissement à titre — : inofficial warning.

offrant (m) : offerer.

offre (f) : 1° *(sens général)* bid, offer, proposal.
2° *(de contrat)* tender for contract.
3° *(à une vente aux enchères)* bid (at auction sale).
4° *(loi de l'— et de la demande)* law of supply and demand.
— *d'emploi :* situation vacant.
— *sans engagement :* offer without commitment.
— *globale :* aggregate supply.
— *d'une prime pour un achat :* premium offer.
— *de prix :* quotation.
— *publique d'achat (O.P.A.) :* take-over bid.
— *publique d'échange (O.P.E.) :* take-over bid for shares.
(l')offre supérieure : (the) highest bid.
prix d'— (de l'—) : supply price.
régulation d'— : supply control.
faire une — de vente : to tender for (sthg).
faire des —(s) : to make offers, to solicit orders.
[J] *— réelle :* cash offer, tender and payment in court.

offrir (v) : to offer, to bid, to supply.
— *(une certaine somme) pour (un objet) :* to bid (so much) for (an object).
adjugé au plus offrant et dernier enchérisseur : adjudicated to the highest and last bidder.

(capital) **oisif** : idle (uninvested) capital.

oléoduc (m) : pipe-line.

oligarchie financière (f) : financial oligarchy.

oligopole (m) : oligopoly.

olographe *(testament)* (a) : holograph (will).

omettre (v) : to omit.
— *(de faire) :* to fail (to do-).
— *de faire une déclaration d'impôts :* to fail to file a return.
— *de déclarer un dividende :* to pass a dividend.

omission volontaire (f) : wilful failure.

omnium (m) : holding company, omnium.

oncle (m) : uncle.

onéreux (a) : onerous, burdensome *(impôt),* heavy *(dépense).*
[J] *à titre — :* for valuable consideration.

opérateur (m), **opératrice** (f) : [B] hedger.

opération (f) : operation, working process, commercial transaction, deal, speculation.
[C] — *commerciale :* business deal.
— *au comptant :* cash transaction.
— *sur marchandises disponibles (loco) :* spot deal.
— *sur marchandises roulantes ou flottantes :* transaction in goods rolling or afloat.
[F] — *de banque :* bank transaction.
— *(s) de banque :* banking business.
— *de change :* foreign exchange transaction.
— *d'escompte :* discounting.
[B] — *d'achat à prime :* giving for the call.
— *à la baisse :* bear, short transaction.
— *de bourse :* stock exchange transaction.
— *à cheval :* straddle.
— *au comptant :* cash deal.
— *à double prime :* double option bargain.
— *d'escompte :* call for delivery of securities before settlement.
— *ferme, forfaitaire :* buying and selling at a date future and certain.
— *à la hausse :* bull, long transaction.
— *au multiple, à répétition :* call of more.
— *(s) à prime :* option dealings.
— *à prime simple :* option bargain.
— *à terme :* forward deal, dealings for the settlement.

— *de vente à prime :* taking for the put.
abandonner une — *à prime :* to relinquish the forfeit.
écart des primes : difference between the prices for firm and option stock.
heure de la réponse des primes : declaration time (on the day before contango day in Paris).
jour de la réponse des primes dans une — *à prime :* declaration day.

opérer (v) : to carry out, to perform, to effect.
[J] — *une descente sur les lieux :* visit of experts, officials, etc., to the scene of occurrence.
— *un paiement :* to make a payment.
— *une réforme :* to carry out a reform.
— *une saisie :* to attach, to distrain, to levy a distress.

opinion (f) : opinion.
— *préconçue :* preconceived opinion.
— *publique :* public opinion.
partager l'— *de qn :* to concur with s.o.

opposable (a) : demurrable.

opposante *(la partie)* (a) : the opponent.

opposition (f) : opposition, objection.
[J] attachment (also called *saisie-arrêt*).
— *sur titres :* attachment against securities.
— *susceptible d'*— *:* judgment liable to stay of execution.
former, mettre — *:* to ask for an injunction against sth.
mettre — *à un mariage :* to enter a caveat to a marriage.
[C] *frapper d'*— *:* to stop payment (cheque, etc.).
[Pol] l'— *:* the opposition, the parties in opposition.

opter (v) : to elect, to choose, to opt for.
si le contribuable opte (pour) : if the taxpayer elects (to).

optimal (a) : optimal, maximum.
production — *(e) :* maximum output (production).

option (f) : option, choice.
[J] — *légale :* right of a heir to accept or to forgo a succession.
[B] — *d'achat :* call option.
— *de vente :* put option.
jour d'— *:* option day.
— *sur contrats à terme :* futures option.
lever une — *:* to declare an option.
prendre une — *:* to take an option.
souscrire des valeurs à — *:* to buy an option on stock.

optionnaire (m) : *(acheteur à prime)* giver, *(vendeur à prime)* taker, of an option.

or (m) : gold.
encaisse — *:* gold holdings.
étalon — *:* gold standard.
point d'— *:* gold-point.
titre de l'— *:* fineness of gold.

ordinaire (a) : ordinary, usual, common, customary, average.
actions — *(s) :* ordinary shares, ordinaries.
budget — *:* ordinary budget.
juges, juridictions, tribunaux, — *(s) :* ordinary courts.
procédure — *:* normal procedure (opp. *procédure accélérée* and *procédure sommaire*).
réserves — *(s) :* ordinary reserve (of a company).
voies de recours — *(s) :* common remedies at law.
[J] *régler une affaire à l'*— *:* to transfer a case from a criminal to a civil court.

ordinateur (m) : computer.
jeu sur — *:* computer game.

ordonnance (f) : order, enactment.
[J] judgment delivered by presiding judge sitting alone, judge's order, decision or ruling.
— *de classement :* nolle prosequi.
— *de clôture :* closure of proceedings.
— *de comparution :* subpoena, summons to appear.
— *d'enquête :* opening of an enquiry.
— *d'exécution :* writ of execution.
— *d'exequatur :* enforcement of an award.
— *de faire, de ne pas faire :* mandatory, restrictive, injunction.
— *des frais :* award of costs.
— *de mise en accusation :* arraignment.
— *de non-lieu :* nonsuit.
— *de paiement :* order to pay.
— *de police :* police regulations.
— *de prise de corps :* writ of capias.
— *provisionnelle :* decree nisi.
— *de référé :* summary order injunction, delivered by the *juge des référés*.
— *de règlement :* final decision of examining magistrate.
— *de renvoi :* committal for trial.
— *de saisie :* writ of execution, warrant for attachment, garnishee order, charging order.
— *de saisie conservatoire :* cautionary judgment.
— *de soit communiqué :* (civ.) presiding judge's order to contending parties to discover all documents in hand to the Public Prosecutor, (cr.) order of the investigating magistrate to discover the brief to the Public Prosecutor.
— *de surseoir, avant faire droit, de sursis :*

injunction.
– *de visite domiciliaire*: search warrant.
annuler une – : to quash an order.
rendre une – : to make an order, to issue a warrant.
rendre une – *de non-lieu*: to direct a nonsuit.
[A] ordinance (declaration of the government lacking the authority of Parliament).

ordonnancement (m): money-order.
[A] written order to pay.

ordonnancer (v): [A] [F] to pass account for payment, to sanction expenditure, to initial an account.

ordonnateur (m): person entitled to make a payment.

ordonner (v) *(à qn de faire)*: to order, to direct (s.o. to do).
– *une grève*: to call a strike.

ordre (m): order, command, warrant.
[J] – *amiable*: agreement out of court between mortgagees and chargees with regard to the apportioning of proceeds of sale of the mortgaged property.
– *d'arrestation*: warrant for arrest.
– *des avocats*: the Bar.
– *de comparution*: summons.
– *conventionnel, consensuel*: agreement out of court between debtor and mortgagees and chargees with regard to the apportioning of proceeds of sale of the mortgaged property.
– *des créanciers*: ranking of creditors.
– *d'écrou*: committal to gaol.
– *d'exécution*: death warrant.
– *d'expulsion*: eviction order.
– *du jour*: agenda, *(milit.)* order of the day.
– *judiciaire*: the judiciary.
– *(s) de juridiction*: the jurisdictions (civil, criminal, administrative).
– *de justice*: judge's order, decision, ruling.
– *de mise en liberté, de relaxe*: release from prison.
– *public*: law and order.
troubler l'– *public*: to make a disturbance.
– *de service*: a) commission, b) instructions.
– *de succession*: a) classification, rank, b) canons of inheritance, c) order of succession to the throne.
délit contre l'ordre public: breach of the peac.
[C] [F] – *de virement*: transfer order.
assignation à – : transfer to order.
billet à – : promissory note, bill payable to order.
clause à – : clause to order.
– *de priorité des objectifs* (« *de haut en bas* »): hierarchy of objectives.
– *de commande venant de l'étranger*: indent.
compte d'– : suspense account.

[B] – *d'achat*: order to buy.
– *d'appréciation, ordre au mieux*: discretionary order.
– *de banque*: banker's order to banker.
– *de bourse*: Stock Exchange order.
– *au comptant*: cash order.
– *au cours limité*: limited price order.
– *au cours moyen*: average, middle price order.
– *au dernier cours*: closing price order.
– *lié*: straddle.
– *de livrer*: order for delivery.
– *au premier cours*: opening price order.
– *à prime*: option order.
– *à révocation*: revocable order.
– *à terme*: forward order, order for settlement.
– *à terme ferme*: order to buy or to sell at a date future and certain.
– *de vente*: order to sell.
cité à l'– *du jour*: mentioned in despatches.
passer à l'– *du jour*: to proceed with the business of the day, to set aside a motion.

organes de publicité (m pl): adversting media.

organigramme (m): organization chart, flow-chart.

organisateur (m): organizer.

organisation (f): organization.
– *des Nations unies*: United Nations (organization), *Organisations internationales*: International organizations, *Institutions spécialisées des N.U.*: specialized agencies (of the UN), *Union postale universelle*: Universal Postal Union *(U.P.U.)*, – *internationale du Travail*: International Labour Organization *(O.I.T., ILO)*, – *des Nations unies pour l'Alimentation et l'Agriculture*: Food and Agriculture Organization of the United Nations *(F.A.O.)*, – *des Nations unies pour l'Education, la Science et la Culture*: United Nations Education, Science and Culture Organization *(UNESCO)*, – *Mondiale de la Santé*: World Health Organization *(O.M.S., WHO)*, *Union internationale des Télécommunications*: International Telecommunication Union *(U.I.T., ITU)*, – *Météorologique Organization (O.M.M., WMO)*, – *de l'Aviation civile internationale*: International Civil Aviation Organization *(O.A.C.I., ICAO)*, *Banque internationale pour la Reconstruction et le Développement*: International Bank for Reconstruction and Development *(B.I.R.D., IBRD)*, *Fonds monétaire international*: International Monetary Fund *(F.M.I., IMF)*, *Agence Internationale du Développement*: International Development Agency *(A.I.D., IDA)*, *Société Financière Internationale*: Inter-

national Finance Corporation (*S.F.I.*, IFC), *Agence Internationale à l'Energie Atomique:* International Atomic Energy Agency (*A.I.E.A.*, IAEA).
– *judiciaire:* the French judiciary system.
conseil en – : management consultant.

organiser (v): to organize, to arrange.
– *un référendum:* to hold a referendum.

organisme (m): agency, body, public body.
– *de gestion:* managing agency.
– *international d'exploitation:* international operating agency.
– *jouissant de la personnalité morale:* incorporated agency.

orientation (f): trend, tendency.
[C] orientation (*en anglais: une philosophie de la gestion qui fait passer les besoins du consommateur avant ceux de la production*).
– *professionnelle:* vocational guidance, occupational guidance.
[B] – *à la baisse:* downward tendency (movement).
– *à la hausse:* upward movement.

orienter (*les investissements*): [C] to trim investments.

original (a) (*capital, facture*): original (capital, invoice).
document – : script.

origine (f): origin, source, nationality.
[J] – *de propriété:* vendor's title to property (must appear on the bill of sale).
[D] *certificat d'*– : certificate of origin.
[C] *marchandise d'*– : genuine article.
d' – *étrangère:* foreign.

oscillation (f): oscillation, fluctuation.
– *du marché:* fluctuation, swings of the market.

ostentatoire (*consommation*) (a): ostentatious (consumption).

otage (m): hostage.
en – : as (a) hostage.

ouir (v): to hear (obsolete).
[J] *ouï les témoins...:* the witnesses having deposed...

outil (m): tool, implement.

outillage (m): equipment, machinery, plant, set of tools.
l' – *national:* national capital equipment.

outrage (m): outrage, flagrant insult.
[J] – *à magistrat:* contempt of court, contumacy, positive misprision.
– *aux mœurs:* indecent offence.
– *public à la pudeur:* indecent exposure.
faire subir les derniers – *(s):* to rape a woman.

outre: besides, in addition to.

outre-mer: overseas.
commerce d'– : overseas trade.

outrepasser (v): to go beyond (*les droits, etc.*), to exceed (les ordres).
– *ses pouvoirs:* to override one's commission.
[J] *délit d'***outrepassé**: offence by contractor in overstepping the limits set for his cuttings in woods.

ouvert (*bureau, compte*) (a): open (office, account).

ouverture (f): opening.
– *de crédit:* opening up of credit.
– *d'un compte:* opening up of an account.
– *d'un testament:* reading of a will.
cours d'– : opening prices (quotation).
heures d'– : business hours.

ouvrier (m): worker, workman, [U.S.] operative, operator.
– *agricole:* farm labourer, farm hand.
– *d'usine:* factory hand (worker).
– *à domicile:* home worker.
– *à la journée:* journeyman, day-labourer.
– *à la pièce:* piece worker.
– *qualifié:* skilled worker.
– *non qualifié:* unskilled worker, labourer.
– *spécialisé:* semi-skilled worker.
participation – *(e) aux bénéfices:* industrial partnership.
(la) classe – *(e):* the working class.
législation – *(e):* labour legislation.

ouvrir (*compte, etc.*) (v): to open (an account etc.).
– *des négociations:* to set negotiations on foot.

NOTES

NOTES

P

pacage (m) : pasturage.
[J] *droit de* − : jus pascendi, grazing rights.

pacifique (a) : pacific.
[J] *possesseur* − : uncontested owner.
règlement − *d'un différend* : peaceful settlement of a dispute.

pacotille (f) : shoddy goods ; mariner's venture, [U.S.] crummy goods.

pacte (m) : agreement.
[J] − *commissoire* : (commissoria lex) resolutive clause in a contract of sale in case of non-payment within a stipulated time.
− *d'honoraires d'avocat* : (pactum de quota litis) champerty.
− *léonin* : leonine convention, unconscionable bargain, oppressive agreement.
− *de préférence* : preferential agreement.
− *de réméré* : option of repurchase.
− *social* : articles of association, bye-laws.
− *tacite* : tacit agreement.

pactiser avec (v) : to come to terms with.

paie (f) : wages, pays.
feuille de − : pay-sheet, -roll.
jour de − : pay-day.
livret de − : wages-book.

paiement (m) : payment, settlement of debt, of account, discharge.
− *à compte* : part payment in advance.
− *d'avance, anticipé* : pre-payment.
cessation de − : suspension of payments.
− *par compensation* : settlement « per contra ».
conditions de − : terms of payment.
− *différentiel* : deficiency payment.
− *échelonné* : instalment, spread out payments.
− *comptant en espèces, en numéraire* : cash payment.
délai de − : term of payment, respite.
facilités de − : easy terms.
− *de faveur* : ex-gratia payment.
− *des heures d'absence* : time off with pay.
imputation de − : appropriation of moneys.
− *de l'indu* : payment not due.
− *par intervention* : payment on behalf of a third party (bill).
− *à la livraison, contre remboursement* : cash on delivery (C.O.D.).
mode de − : how to pay.

− *pour solde* : payment of balance, final instalment.
− *à tempérament* : payment by instalments.
défaut de − : non-payment.
différer le − : to put off, to postpone payment.
parfaire le − : to complete payment.
suspendre les − *(s)* : to stop payment.
[J] *dation en* − : datio in solutum.

(homme de) paille : man of straw.

pair (a et m) : (a) equal, even (number), par. (m) par.
au − : at par.
change au − : par of exchange, title.
valeur au − : par value.
au-dessous du − : below par.
au-dessus du − : above par.

paix (f) : peace.
gardien de la − : (police) officer.
juge de − *(hist.)* : conciliation and police court magistrate = Justice of the Peace.
troubler la − *publique* : to break the peace.

palais (m) : palace.
[J] (abbreviation for *Palais de justice*) : the Law Courts.
gens de − : members of the legal profession.
jour de − : day in court.

palier (m) : range, stage.

palliatif (m) : palliative.

pamphlet (m) : lampoon, pamphlet.

pamphlétaire (m) : lampooner.

panage (m) : pannage, dues therefore.

panier (m) : basket.
− *de devises* : basket of currencies.
− *de la ménagère* : basket of commodities.

panique (f) : panic.
ne pas céder à la − : to keep one's hair on.
mesures dictées par la − : panic measures.

(être en) panne *(négociations)* : to be at a standstill (negociations).

panonceau (m) : escutcheon, sign over office of *avoué, huissier, notaire*.

paperasserie (f) : red-tape.

papier (m) : paper.
[A] papers (passport, identity card etc.).
– *(s) de bord* : ship's papers.
– *libre, timbré* : unstamped, stamped paper.
[C] – *bancable* : bills that may be rediscounted with the Bank of France.
– *de commerce* : commercial papers, bills, trade bills.
– *de complaisance* : accommodation bills.
– *court* : short-dated bills.
– *(s) domestiques* : private papers.
– *fait* : backed bills.
– *(s) de famille* : family papers.
– *long* : long-dated bills.
– *monnaie* : banknotes, [U.S.] bills.
– *négociable* : negotiable instruments.
– *à ordre* : bills to order.
– *au porteur* : bearer bill.
– *à vue* : sight bills.
– *journal* : newsprint.
[C] – *d'emballage* : wrapping paper.
– *de presse (subsides)* : handout.

paquet d'action (m) : block of shares.

par-devant *(notaire)* : in the presence of, before (a notary).

par *(jour, mois, année)* : per (day, month, year or annum).

(de) par : in the name of, by order of.

paraphe (m) : paraph, initials of one's name.

parapher (v) *un document* : to initial a document.

parafiscalité (f) : parafiscality.

paragraphe (m) : paragraph, subsection.

parallèle *(marché)* (a) : unofficial (market).

paralysie *(du marché)* (f) : market seize-up.
paralysé par la grève : strikebound.

paraphernal (a) : paraphernal, separate.
[J] *biens* **paraphernaux** : wife's separate property.

parc (m) *(d'automobiles, de véhicules)* : fleet (of vehicles).
– *de stationnement* : off-street car park.

parcelle (f) : parcel, patch of land, small fragment.

(cadastre) parcellaire : detailed survey of a commune.

parcomètre (m) : parking meter.

parcours (m) : route, course, distance covered.
[J] *droit de* – : grazing rights, jus pascendi.

pardon (m) : pardon, forgiveness (of an offence).
[J] remission of a sentence.

parenté (f) : kinship, consanguinity.
– *par alliance* : affinity, relation by marriage.
degré de – : degree of relationship.
lien de – : family relationship, blood relation.

parents (m pl) : 1° parents (father and mother), 2° relatives, connections, kinsmen and kinswomen.

parer (v) : to prepare.
[J] *titre paré* : process bearing the executory formula = writ of execution.

pari (m) : bet, betting, stake, wager.
– *mutuel* : totalizator system.
– *tiercé* : three-horse parlay.
taxe sur les –*(s)* : betting tax.

paritaire (a) : joint.
réunion – : round-table conference (meeting).

parité (f) : parity.
[F] – *des changes* : equivalence of exchange.
change à la – : exchange at par (of different stocks).
–*(s) croisées entre deux monnaies* : exchange cross-rate.
à – : at the money.
[ASS] *clause de* – *des primes en cas d'assurances multiples* : clause of equivalence of premiums in multiple insurance policies.

« **parlant à** » : « speaking to », mention by bailiff *(huissier)* of person on whom the process has been served, and whose name is inscribed thereon.

parlement (m) : Parliament, the legislative bodies of the Republic.

parlementaire (m) : member of the Parliament (M.P.).

parole (f) : word.
demander la – : to request leave to speak.
donner la – *à qn* : to call upon s.o. to speak.
donner sa – : to give (pledge) one's word.
manquer à sa – : to break one's word, to

fail to keep one's word.

parquet (m) : [J] 1° prosecution department, 2° well of the court, public prosecutor's room.
— *général, parquet du procureur général* : public prosecutor and his deputies.
[B] — *des agents de change* : the Ring, [U.S.] the Pit.

parrainage (m) (*opp. à mécénat*) : [F] sponsoring (contrary to patronage).

parricide (a et m) : parricidal, parricide.
[J] crime of parricide.

part (m) : [J] new-born child.
célation de — : concealment of birth.
confusion de — : confusion of children : a) exchange of two children, b) mother having had intercourse with several men at about the same time : both cases making affiliation doubtful or impossible.
exposition d'un — : abandonment of newborn child.
substitution de — : substitution of one newborn child for another.
supposition de — : personation of a child (mostly to displace the real heir).
suppression de — : concealment of birth.

part (f) : share, part, portion, participation.
[J] — *de collocation* : dividend (in bankruptcy).
— *de communauté* : share in common estate.
— *de copartageant* : share in partition.
— *de copropriété* : share in co-ownership.
— *d'enfant, d'héritage* : distributive share, due portion of inheritance.
— (s) *indivises* : shares in co-ownership before partition (opp. *parts divises*).
— (s) *d'intérêts* : share of a partner in the capital of a general partnership.
— *de prise* : prize-money.
— *de profit* : portion of earnings.
— *sociale* : share in the capital of a company.
— *virile* : lawful share of succession.
[F] *part d'association, bénéficiaire* : partnership share.
— *de fondateur* : founder's share (merely profit sharing rights).
— *privilégiée* : preference share.
compte à — : separate account.
être de — *à demi* : to go halves.
quote- — (*des gains*) : proportion (of the profits).

partage (m) : 1° allotment, apportionment, division ; lot, portion, share.
[J] partition (of real property).
— *amiable* : amicable, private partition.
— *des biens indivis* : partition of joint real property.

— *judiciaire* : partition by court.
— *par souche* : partition per stirpes.
— *successoral* : sharing out a succession.
— *par tête* : partition per capita.
— *par tirage au sort* : partition by drawing lots.
— *entre vifs* : partition intervivos.
action en — : action for partition.
conversion de — : arrangement for partition.
jugement de — : order to share out a succession.
— *des bénéfices* : splitting of profits.
2° division of opinion.
[J] *jugement de* — : the judges being equally divide, a further judge is called in and a new trial begun.

partageant (m) : [J] sharer.

partager (v) : to divide, to share, to split.
— *un risque* : to underwrite a risk.

partenaire (m et f) : partner.

parti (m) : 1° decision, choice, course ; advantage, profit.
prendre un — : to make up one's mind.
prendre — : to take sides.
tirer — : to take advantage.
2° (political) party.

(colonat) partiaire : [J] farming leasehold, whereby the farmer shares the produce of the farm with the landlord, [U.S.] sharecrop system.

participation (f) : participation, share, interest, holding.
— *aux bénéfices* : profit-sharing.
— *génératrice de dividendes* : holding giving rise to the dividends.
association en — : sleeping partnership.
compte en — : joint account.
— *majoritaire* : majority holding (interest).
— *minoritaire* : minority holding (interest).
produit des — (s) : investments income.
— *électorale* : turn-out.

participer à (v) : to participate in, to take part in.

particulier(e) (a et m) : (a) (*auto, maison*) particular, private (car, house).
à titre — : as a private individual, in a private capacity.
(m) individual.

partie (f) : part, party, parcel.
[J] party (to dispute).
— *en cause* : party to the case.
— *civile* : plaintiff claiming damages in a criminal case (see *conclusions civiles*).

— *gagnante*: the winning party.
— *lésée*: the injured party.
« — *(s) ouïes* » : « having heard the parties ».
— *opposante*: demurring party.
— *opposée*: the other, the opposing party.
— *perdante*: the losing party.
entendre les avocats des deux — *(s)* : to hear counsel on both sides.
se porter — *civile*: to sue for civil injury.
prendre qn à — : to call s.o. to account.
[A] — *prenante*: creditor of the state.
[C] — *de marchandises*: lot of goods.
comptabilité en — *simple, double*: single, double entry book-keeping.
ce n'est pas (ma) — : it is not (my) line of business.
les hautes — *(s) contractantes*: the high Contracting Parties.

parvenir à (v) : to reach.
— *à un accord*: to come to an agreement.

pas de porte (m) : [C] 1° the door-step of a shop, i.e. its opening into a thoroughfare which is taken into account in appraising the goodwill of a business.
2° key-money, lease-premium.

(salle des) pas perdus : hall (of law courts, etc.).

passage (m) : passage.
[J] *droit de — (servitude)*: right of way (as a covenant running with the land), right of passage, [U.S.] right of way.
[A] *droits de —*: ferry dues, toll traverse.
« — *à tabac* » : « third degree ».
« — *interdit* », « *défense de passer* » : « trespassers will be prosecuted ».

passager (m) **clandestin** : (Eco) free rider.

passation (f) : [J] drawing up, signing (of a contract, deed, etc.), placing.
[C] — *d'écritures*: posting an entry.
— *de commande*: ordering.

passavant, passe-debout (m) : [A] [D] transire.

passe-droit (m) : injustice, illegitimate favour.

passé-expédient (m) : [J] abandonment of action, discontinuance.

passeport (m) : passport.
— *diplomatique*: diplomatic passport.
— *de mer*: sea-letter, sea-brief.
— *sanitaire*: bill of health.

passer (v) : to pass, to proceed.
— *un acte*: to draw up a deed.
— *un accord*: to conclude an agreement.
(faire) — *une annonce*: to put (run) an ad in a newspaper.
— *une commande*: to give, to place an order.
— *au compte de profits et pertes*: to post to the profit and loss account.
— *en compte*: to put on account.
— *condamnation*: to accept a judgment.
— *un contrat*: to enter into, to sign a contract.
— *des écritures*: to book, to post an entry.
— *une écriture en compte*: to make an entry, to post an entry.
— *en force de chose jugée*: to be res judicata, to be enforceable, to be the law of the case.
— *en force de loi*: to be operative, lawful.
— *en jugement*: to come up for judgment.
— *une loi*: to pass, to carry a law.
— *un marché*: to enter into a bargain.
— *à l'ordre du jour*: to proceed with the business of the day, to set aside a motion.
— *outre à la loi*: to set the law at naught, at defiance.
— *outre à une objection*: to disregard, to take no notice of, to overrule an objection.
— *par profits et pertes*: to write-off a bad debt.
l'affaire **passera** *demain*: the case will be heard tomorrow.
« *je vais vous —...* » *(téléphone)*: I'll put you through to...

passible (a) : liable to.
— *d'une amende*: liable to a fine.
— *des droits de douane*: subject to custom duties.
jugement — *d'opposition*: judgment subject to stay of execution.

passif (m et a) : (m) liabilities, debt.
— *exigible*: arrears.
— *exigible à court terme*: current liabilities.
— *exigible à long terme*: long-term liabilities.
actif et —: credit and debit, assets and liabilities.
dettes **passives**: accounts payable.
(a) [A] *commerce —*: import trade.
[B] *rester —*: to hold over (in time bargain).

passionnel *(crime)* (a) : (crime) due to jealousy.

patente (f) : licence to exercice a trade or profession.
[F] (hist.) business licence tax.
payer —: to be duly licensed.
[A] — *de santé*: bill of health.

paternité (f) : paternity, fatherhood.
[J] *recherche de (la) —*: affiliation.

action en recherche de — : action by bastard for affiliation.
désaveu de (la) — : bastardy procedure, repudiation of offspring.
présomption de — : putative fatherhood.
reconnaissance de — : acknowledgment, declaration of paternity.
puissance **paternelle** : authority of father.

patrimoine (m) : patrimony, heritage.
[J] estate.

patrimonial (a) : patrimonial.

patron (m) : 1° employer, head of a firm, (fam.) boss, owner, proprietor ; shipmaster, skipper.
2° pattern, model.

patronage (m) : patronage.
sous le — *de* : sponsored by.

(chambre) patronale (a) : chamber of employers (of a given trade).
cotisation — : employer's share.

patronat (m) : body of employers (as a social group).

patronner (v) : to patronize, to support, to sponsor.

patronyme (m) : family name, surname.

pâturage (m) : pasture.
[J] *droit de* — : right of common, commonage.
bail de — : lease of grazing rights.

pâture (f) : fodder, pasture.
[J] *vaine* — : right of common, commonage.

paupérisation (f) : pauperization, immiserization.

paupérisme (m) : pauperism.

pause (f) : break.

pauvre (m) : poor (now «*économiquement faible*»).
[A] pauper, poor person.

pavillon (m) : flag, colours.
— *de complaisance* : flag of convenience (convenience flag).
— *couplé* : waft.
— *de départ* : blue peter.
— *de poupe* : ensign.
— *de détresse* : flag of distress.
battre — : to fly (to carry) a flag.
« *le* — *couvre la marchandise* » : the flag covers the cargo.

payable (a) : payable.
— *à ordre* : payable to order.
— *à vue* : payable at sight, at call, payable on demand.
— *d'avance* : prepayable, payable in advance.
— *à la commande* : cash with order.
— *à tant de jours* : payable at (...) days.

payant (a) : paying.
tiers — (m) : paying third party.

payer (v) : to pay.
—, *refuser de payer un effet* : to honour, to dishonour a bill.
— *à guichets ouverts* : all comers paid.
— *en main brève* : to pay over money in hand to s.o. appointed by court (mostly the judgment creditor in attachment of debts).
— *d'avance* : to pay beforehand.
— *au comptant* : to pay cash.
— *à l'échéance* : to pay at due date, when due, at maturity.
— *à la livraison* : to pay on delivery.
— *de la main à la main* : to hand over the money without receipt.
— *à la réception* : to pay on receipt.
— *à tempérament* : to pay by instalments.

payer-prendre (m) : cash and carry.

payeur (m) : payer.
[A] *trésorier-* — : disbursing official.
[F] bank-teller.

pays (m) : country, land.
— *d'asile* : sanctuary.
— *de coutume, de droit coutumier* : (hist.) provinces to the north of the river Loire where common law was in force.
— *de droit écrit* : (hist.) provinces to the south of the river Loire, where written law (roman) was in force.
— *d'origine* : country of origin.
— *développé* : developped country.
— *en voie de développement* : developing country.
— *limitrophe* : borderland.

péage (m) : toll, toll-house.
autoroute à — : toll motorway.
barrière de — : turnpike, [A] toll-bar.
pont à — : toll-bridge.
[F] *droit de* — : toll tax.

pêche (f) : fishing.

pêcherie (f) : fisheries.

péculat (m) : peculation, embezzlement (esp. of officials).

pécule (m) : savings, lump payment on discharge.
[J] (civ.) portion of earnings of a minor saved for his coming of age.
(cr.) *– de réserve :* portion of convict's earnings accumulated until his discharge (opp. *– disponible :* free portion).
[A] soldier's gratuity on discharge.

pécuniaire (a) : pecuniary.
avantages – (s) : pecuniary advantages, financial fringe benefits.
intérêt – : insurable interest.
intérêts – (s) : interest (on capital).
peine – : fine.
situation – : financial standing.
valeur – : money interest.

pécuniairement (adv) : pecuniarily.

peine (f) : punishment, penalty.
[J] (civ.) *– compromissoire :* penalty under referee's award.
– contractuelle, conventionnelle : penalty clause (for non-performance of contract).
– compromissoire, libératoire : penalty clause involving release from liability after payment.
– de retard : penalty for delay.
– statutaire : penalty provided in articles of partnership.
(cr.) *– accessoire :* accessory penalty (automatic, e.g. prohibition to pursue a profession or to ply a trade).
– afflictive, corporelle : punishment involving death, personal restraint or penal servitude.
– complémentaire : additional penalty.
– infamante : penalty involving loss of civil rights.
– de mort : death sentence.
– pécuniaire : fine.
– principale : principal penalty (opp. *peine accessoire*).
– privative de liberté : penalty involving personnal restraint.
– de simple police : penalty of one to tow months imprisonment or a small fine.
adoucissement, atténuation, réduction de la – : mitigation of penalty.
aggravation de – : increase of penalty.
commutation de – : commutation of penalty.
conversion de – : change of penalty (mostly mitigation).
cumul de – (s) : accumulative sentence, sentences running concurrently (but *cumul juridique :* sentences runnings consecutively).
purger une – : to serve one's sentence.
remise de la – : remission.
subir sa – : to undergo one's punishment.
sursis à l'exécution de la – : reprieve.
sous – de : under penalty of.
sous les – (s) de droit : under penalties prescribed by law.

homme de – : journeyman.

pénal (a) : criminal.
code – : criminal code.
clause – (e) : penalty clause (in contract). (see *peine contractuelle*).

pénalisation (f) : penal system, penalty.

pendant (adv.) : during.
– que : while.

pendant (a) :
fruits – (s) : standing crops.
question – (e) : question in abeyance, in suspense.

pénétration (f) *(du marché)* : breakthrough, market penetration.
pénétrer *un marché :* to penetrate, to break through a market.

pénitencier (m) : reformatory, convictstation.

pénitentiaire (a) : penitentiary.
système – : penitentiary system.

pension (f) : pension, allowance.
– alimentaire : alimony, allowance for necessaries.
– d'ancien combattant : veteran's allowance.
– complète : board and lodging.
– de guerre : war allowance, service pension allowance.
– d'invalidité : disablement pension.
– militaire : retired pay.
– pour cause de limite d'âge : superannuation pension.
– de retraite : retirement pension, retiring pension (pay, income), superannuation benefit.
– de réversion : reversion pension.
– viagère : life annuity.
– de vieillesse : old-age pension.
fonds de retraite, de – (s) : superannuation fund, pension scheme.

pensionner (v) : to pension off.

pente (f) : slope.
– fiscale : fiscal tip, tipping.

pénurie (f) : scarcity, shortage, dearth, lack.
– d'argent : lack of money.
– de dollars : dollar gap.
– de main-d'œuvre : labour shortage.

percepteur (m) : [A] tax-collector, tax gatherer.

perception (f) : collection, levying *(de droits, impôts, etc.)*, pernancy *(de loyers, intérêts, etc.)*, receipt.
bureau de − : Revenue office.
« taxe **perçue** *»* : postage paid.

percevoir (v) : to collect, to gather, to be derived from.
salaire **perçu** *par des personnes domiciliées en France* : salary derived by persons domiciled in France.
à percevoir : receivable.
cotisations à − : contributions still due.
effets à − *(recevoir)* : bills receivable.

perdre *(un procès, de la valeur)* (v) : to lose (a lawsuit, value...).

perdre (v) *(des points)* : to clip, to chip.
bâtiment **perdu** *corps et biens* : vessel lost with all hands.

père (m) : father.
(X) − : (So and so) senior.
gérer en bon − *de famille* : to administer (an estate) with due diligence.
valeurs de − *de famille* : gilt-edged securities.
de − *en fils* : for generations.

péremption (f) : time limitation in a suit, abatement.
− *d'instance* : extinction of an action, no steps having been taken within the period of limitation.
dévolu par − : lapsed.

péremptoire (a) : peremptory.
argument − : decisive argument.
délai − : strict time-limit.
exception − : peremptory plea, demurrer.
preuve − : conclusive evidence.

péréquation (f) : equalization.
− *des impôts, des salaires* : equalization of taxes, of wages.
− *des recettes fiscales* : tax revenue sharing.

perfectionnement (m) : improving, improvement, advanced training.
brevet de − : patent relating to improvements.
[D] − *passif* : outward processing.

perforée *(carte)* : punched card.

performant (a) : highly efficient.

péricliter (v) : to be in jeopardy.
la maison X **périclite** : the firm So-and-so is in a bad way.

péril (m) : danger.
− *en la demeure* : imminent danger.
à ses risques et − *(s)* : at his own risks.
mettre en − : to endanger.
[J] [ASS] − *de mer* : perils of the sea.

périmer (v) : to lapse, to become out of date.
[J] **périmé** : barred by limitation.
laisser périmer un droit : to forfeit a right.
billet périmé : ticket no longer valid, out of date.
effet périmé : expired, lapsed bill.
instance périmée : expired action.
traite périmée : lapsed money order.

période (f) : period, term, time.
courte (longue) − : short (long) period.
− *d'activité* : working life.
− *de récupération du capital* : pay back period, pay cash period.
− *de tirage (bons)* : draw-down period.

périssables *(denrées)* (a) : perishable (goods).

permanence (f) : permanence.
assemblée en − : (parliamentary) assembly sitting without interruption (esp. in time of stress).
[A] − *de police* : police station open day and night.

permanent (a) : permanent.
commission − *(e)* : standing commision.
revenu − : permanent income.

permis (m) : permit, permission.
− *de charger* : loading permit.
− *d'assigner en justice* : permission by court to enter a case for divorce (if reconciliation failed or, in serious circumstances, even before).
− *de conduire* : driving licence.
− *de construire* : building permit, licence to build, planning permission.
− *de chasse* : game, shooting licence.
− *de circulation* : car licence, free railway transport.
− *d'établissement* : permission to reside permanently.
− *d'exhumation* : exhumation permit.
− *d'exploitation minière* : working permit.
− *d'exportation* : export licence.
− *d'importation* : import licence.
− *d'inhumation* : burial permit.
− *de pêche* : fishing licence.
− *de port d'armes* : licence to carry fire-arms.
− *de séjour* : permission to reside.
accorder, délivrer un − : to grant permission, to deliver a permit.

permission (f) : permission, leave.

permutation (f) : exchange of posts.

permuter (v) : to exchange posts.

perpétrer (v) : to perpetrate.

perpétuel (a) : perpetual.
  rente — *(le)* : perpetual rent, consolidated stocks, « consols », government stock in perpetuity.
  servitude — *(le)* : easement, covenant running with the land.

perpétuité (f) : perpetuity.
  [J] *travaux forcés à* — : penal servitude for life.
  [A] *concession à* — : perpetual grant (of land, grave, etc.).

perquisition (f) : [J] thorough search or enquiry.
  — *à domicile* : domiciliary visit, house-search.
  mandat de — : search warrant.
  perquisitionner : to make, to conduct a search (of premises, etc.).

personnalité (f) : personality.
  [J] — *morale* : incorporation (legal status of an artificial person).

personne (f) : person.
  [J] — *morale* : artificial person, body corporate deemed fictitiously a natural person and permitted to go to law, legal person, legal entity.
  — *physique* : natural person.
  — *à charge* : dependent, dependant, dependent person.
  — *interposée* : intermediary, nominee.
  tierce — : third person, third party.
  sans acceptation de — : without respect of persons.

personnel (a) : personal.
  [J] *action* — *(le)* : personal action at law.
  abattement (d'impôt) — : personal allowance.
  biens à usage — : personal-use property.
  [F] *impôt* —, *contribution personnelle* : per capita levy.
  fortune — *(le)* : private means.
  objets — *(s)* : personal belongings.

personnel (m) : staff, personnel, hands, labour, servants.
  — *de bureau* : clerical staff, office staff.
  — *dirigeant* : management staff.
  — *d'encadrement* : executives, officers.
  — *enseignant* : teaching staff.
  — *d'exécution* : employees.
  délégué (syndical) du — : shop steward.
  avoir trop de — : to be overstaffed.

personnellement *(responsable)* (adv) : personally (liable, responsible).

perspectives (f pl) : prospects.

perte (f) : ruin, destruction, loss, leakage.
  — *brute* : trading loss.
  — *de l'exercice* : loss for the year.
  — *déductible* : deductible loss.
  — *sèche* : dead loss.
  profits et — *(s)* : profit and loss.
  passer une créance par profits et — *(s)* : to write off books.

pertinent (a) : pertinent, relevant, apposite.

perturber *(l'ordre public)* (v) : to disturb (the peace).

perversion (f) : perversion.

pervertir (v) : to corrupt, to pervert.

petit (a) : small, minor, little.
  — *(e) caisse* : petty cash.
  — *commerce* : small-scale retail trade.
  — *(e) industrie* : small-scale industry.
  — *(es) annonces* : small ads (advertisements).
  — *(s) travaux* : odd jobs.

petit-fils (m), **petite-fille** (f) : grand-son, grand-daughter.

pétition (f) : petition, memorial.
  [J] *action en* — *d'hérédité* : claim to an inheritance held by a third party.
  obtenir la grâce par — : to sue out a pardon.
  faire une — *de principe* : to beg the question.

pétitoire (a) : [J] *action pétitoire* : claim of ownership.

pétrodollars : petrodollars.

pétrole (m) : oil.
  nappe de — *polluante* : oil slick.
  industrie **pétrolière** : the mineral oil industry.
  trouver du — : to strike oil.

peu (de) : little, few.
  à — *chose près* : substantially.

phase (f) : stage, phase.
  — *de fabrication* : processing stage.
  — *(s) du développement économique* : stages (phases) of (the) economic development.

photocopie (f) : photocopy, photostat.

physiocrate (m et f) : physiocrat.

physionomie générale du marché (f) : the general tone of the market.

pièce (f) : piece, unit, fragment.
[J] document.
— *adirée* : act gone astray.
— *à l'appui* : proof in support of a case.
— *arguée de faux, de nullité* : a deed asserted to be forged, void.
— *assujettie au timbre* : act subject to stamp duty.
— *(s) de bord* : ship's papers.
— *(s) de caisse, comptable* : formal, accountable receipt, voucher.
— *communiquée* : discovered document.
— *à conviction* : object produced in evidence, exhibit.
— *détachée* : component part.
— *fausse* : forged document.
— *d'identité, de légitimation* : identity papers.
— *(s) en instance* : documents pertaining to the case.
— *judiciaire, pièce d'un procès* : document in a case.
— *justificative* : document in proof, voucher.
— *officielle* : official paper.
— *pertinente* : relevant document.
— *vue* : vised paper.
— *de monnaie* : coin.
— *jointe* : enclosure.
marchandises à la — : piece-goods.
travail à la — : piece-work, [U.S.] job work.
travail rémunéré aux — (s) : piece-work, task work.

pied (m) : foot, basis.
être en — : to be officially in charge (as an ambassador, etc.).
être mis à — : to be temporarily suspended.
[B] — *de la prime* : option price less option rate.
« *marché des* — (s) *humides* » : curb market, outside brokers.
mettre au — *du mur* : to corner.

pignoration (f) : pledging, pawning.

pilotage (m) : *(droits de)* pilotage (dues).

piraterie (f) : piracy.
— *(esp. aérienne)* : hijacking.

place (f) : place, town, market.
— *exterritoriale* : off-shore place.
— *marchande* : market town, trading town.
faire la — : to canvas(s) the town.

placement (m) : investment, investing (of money).
— *d'un emprunt* : floating, placing of a loan.
— *de père de famille* : safe investment.
— *pierre* : investment in building.

la pierre est le meilleur — : as safe as houses.
agence, bureau de — : employment bureau, agency.
fonds commun de — : mutual fund.
société de — : investment company.
syndicat de — : investment pool.

placer (v) : to invest, to place.
— *des actions* : to place shares.
— *des capitaux, de l'argent* : to put out, to invest capital, money.

placier (m) : [C] town-traveller, agent, canvasser, [U.S.] drummer, solicitor.

plafond (m) : limit, maximum attainable (permissible), ceiling.
— *des cotisations* : ceiling (limit) of assessment.
fixer un prix — : to fix a maximum price.

plafonner (v) : to reach the ceiling.

plagiat (m) : plagiarism.
faire un — *à un auteur* : to lift a passage from an author.
plagiaire : plagiarist.

plaid (m) : [J] plea, sitting of court.

plaidant (a) : [J] *avocat plaidant* : barrister appearing in court (opp. *avocat consultant*).
parties — (es) : the litigants.

plaider (v) : [J] to plead, to argue in court, to allege sth. in a plea.
— *l'alibi* : to plead absence from the scene of occurrence.
— *une cause* : to plead a cause.
— *la cause de qn* : to defend s.o.'s interest (as counsel).
— *les circonstances atténuantes* : to plead extenuating circumstances.
— *coupable* : to plead guilty.
— *en divorce* : to take divorce proceedings.
— *au fond* : to address the court.
— *l'incompétence* : to put in a declinatory plea.
— *un incident* : to put in an incidental plea.
— *innocent, non-coupable* : to plead the general issue, to plead not guilty.
— *par procuration* : to plead as attorney in fact.

plaideur (m) : litigant.

plaidoirie (f) : counsel's speech, pleading.

plaidoyer (m) : [J] address to the court, esp. speech for the defence.

— 201 —

plaindre (v) (se) : to complain.

plaignant (m) : plaintiff, complainant.
(also : *partie plaignante*).

plainte (f) : plaint, indictment, complaint.
[J] statement of claim *(droit moderne)*, declaration *(action en C.L.)*, bill *(action en* Eq., esp. devant la Chancery Division), libel *(en Cour d'Amirauté)*.
— *assortie de constitution de partie civile* : see *conclusions civiles*.
— *en diffamation* : action for libel or slander.
classer, repousser une — : to dismiss a complaint.
déposer une —, porter — contre qn : to lodge a complaint against s.o. *(auprès de* : with), to bring an action against s.o.
retirer une — : to withdraw a complaint.

plaisance (f) :
bateau de — : pleasure-boat, yacht.
maison de — : country seat.

plan (m) : draft, desing, plan, program(me), scheme, survey, [U.S.] schedule.
— *d'amortissement financier* : redemption table.
— *cadastral* : cadastral survey.
— *comptable général* : general accounting plan.
— *de développement* : development scheme.
— *de développement à long terme* : corporate planning.
— *quinquennal (décennal)* : five-(ten-) year plan.
— *d'urbanisme* : town-(city-) planning.
sur le — de... : from the point of view of...

(jours de) planche *(staries)* : lay-days.

plancher *(prix)* (m) : lowest price.

planificateur (m) : planner.

planification (f) : planning, [U.S.] scheduling.
— *à long terme* : (voir « plan »).
— *prévisionnelle destinée à parer aux cas imprévus* : contingency planning.
— *des ressources humaines* : manpower planning.

planifier (v) : to plan.
économie **planifiée** : planned economy.

plein (a) : full, whole.
— *consentement* : full consent.
de — droit : by right, with good reason.
— *emploi* : full employment.
de (son) — gré : of (one)'s free will.
— *(s) pouvoirs* : full power (of attorney).

donner —(s) pouvoirs (à qn) : to empower (s.o.).
— *tarif* : full rate, full tariff.

pléthore *(de capitaux, de marchandises)* (f) : glut (of capital, of goods).

pli (m) : cover, envelope, letter, note.
— *cacheté* : sealed letter, orders.
— *chargé, — avec valeur déclarée* : registered letter.
sous — séparé : under separate cover.
sous ce — : herewith.

plomber (v) : to lead.
[D] to seal packages, to affix leads to goods, waggons.

plumitif (m) : [J] minute-book of clerk to the court.

pluralité *(de cautions, de gérants)* (f) : plurality (of securities, of managers).

plus ample informé *(pour)* : until further information is available.

plus-value (f) : increment value, appreciated surplus, betterment, unearned increment.
impôt sur la — : a) betterment tax, b) tax on unearned increment.
— *(s) (en capital)* : capital gains, [U.S.] capital profit.
— *(s) à court (long) terme* : short-(long-) term capital gains.
impôt sur les —(s) : capital gains tax.
— *d'actif* : appreciation of assets.

poids (m) : weight, load, burden.
— *brut, mort, utile, net* : gross, dead, live, net weight.
[A] *le — public* : weigh bridge or Weigh-House.
— *de la fiscalité* : tax burden, weight of taxation.
vendre au — : to sell by weight.

poinçon (m) : punch, die, stamp.
[A] *poinçon de garantie, de contrôle* : hallmark.

point (m) : point, spot, position.
— *d'entrée (de sortie) de l'or* : import (export) gold-point.
— *d'équilibre (des profits et pertes)* : break-even point.
— *-événement* : chance event, mode.
— *d'intervention (sur le marché des changes)* : intervention point, support point (on the exchange market).
— *mort* : break-even point.
— *de référence* : reference position.
— *de rupture* : breaking point.

– *sur la situation de l'entreprise* : review.
– *de vente* : point of sale, outlet store.
baisser d'un – : to lose (decline) one point.
hausser d'un – : to gain (rise) one point.
mettre au – *des accords* : to finalize agreements.
perdre des – *(s)* : to chip, to clip.
reculer d'un – : to drop one point.
– *de droit* : issue of law.

pointage (m) : *(jour de)* declaration (day).

pointe (f pl) *(heures de)* : peak (rush) hours.
en dehors des heures de – : during off-peak hours.

pointer (v) : to check, to tick off, to prick off (names on a list), to scrutinize (votes, etc.).

police (f) : police.
tribunal de simple – : police-court.
[A] 1° state or municipal administration for maintaining public order. 2° regulations for maintainging public order.
– *fluviale* : river brigade.
– *des garnis* : hotel control brigade.
– *judiciaire (as well as la Sureté)* # Criminal Investigation Department, [U.S.] Federal Brueau of Investigation.
– *des mœurs* : vice squad.
– *municipale* : constabulary.
– *des chemins de fer, du roulage, sanitaire, de la voirie* : police regulations pertaining to railways, traffic and driving, health, and maintenance of streets and roads.
agent de – *(gardien de la paix)* : police officer.
commissaire de – : # police superintendent.
indicateur de – : informer.
officier de – : chief constable.
3° [E] – *d'affrètement* : charter-party.
police de chargement : bill of lading.
[ASS] – *d'abonnement, flottante* : floating policy.
– *d'assurance* : insurance policy.
– *générale, ouverte, à obligations non évaluées* : open policy.
– *maritime* : marine insurance policy.
– *à ordre* : policy to order.
– *au porteur* : policy to bearer.
– *à terme, à forfait* : time policy.
– *type* : standard policy.
porteur de – : policy-holder.
prendre une – *d'assurance* : to take out an insurance policy.

politique (a et f) : (a) politic, political.
économie – : economics.
(f) 1° policy, 2° politics.
– *d'aide aux « canards boîteux »* : lame duck policy.
– *d'arrêt et d'accélération (alternativement) de l'économie* : stop-go policy.
– *continue* : settled policy.
– *fiscale* : fiscal policy.
– *monétaire* : monetary policy.
– *des prix* : pricing policy.
– *des revenus* : incomes policy.
– *des salaires* : wage(s) policy.
– *de rechange* : alternative policy.
– *étrangère, intérieure* : foreign, internal politics.

polluer (v) : to pollute.

polyculture (f) : mixed farming.

polyvalent (a) : multipurpose (agent).

ponction *(sur les revenus)* (f) : drain (on incomes).

pondéré (a) : *(indice)* weighted (index).
coût moyen – : weighted average cost.

population (f) : population, people.
– *(laborieuse)* : working population, gainfully employed population.
– *effectivement au travail (entre 16 et 65 ans)* : total in civil employment (between 16 and 65 years of age).

port (m) : 1° port, harbour.
– *aérien* : air-port, flying field.
– *d'armement* : port of registry of merchant ships.
– *d'attache* : home port.
– *de commerce* : commercial port.
– *d'escale, de relâche* : port of call.
– *fluvial* : river port.
– *franc, libre* : free port.
– *de guerre* : naval port, base, harbour.
– *de mer* : seaport.
– *de transbordement* : transhipment port.
capitaine de – : harbour-master.
[F] *droits de* – : harbour dues.
2° act of carrying.
– *d'armes* : carrying of arms.
– *illégal d'uniforme* : illegal wearing of military uniform.
– *en lourd* : dead weight of a vessel.
permis de – *d'armes* : licence to carry firearms.
3° cost of transport.
(marchandises) porterage, carriage, *(lettres, colis)* postage.
– *payé, perçu, franc de* – : carriage paid.
en – *dû* : carriage forward.

portable (a) : portable.
dette, prime, rente, – : debt, premium, annuity, payable at the address of payee.

portage (m) : transport of goods.
frais de – : porterage.

porte (f) : door.
(fam) *mettre à la* — : to chuck out.

porte-à-porte (m) : door-to-door selling.
faire du — : to canvass.
— *« sauvage »* : cold canvassing.

portée (f) : [U.S.] coverage.
portée d'un traité : scope of a treaty.
— *restreinte d'une disposition* : limited application of a provision.

portefeuille (m) : portfolio, wallet.
[A] *le* — *des finances, de l'agriculture, etc.* : the portfolio, the office of minister of Finance, of Agriculture, etc.
clientèle en — : investing public.
— *effets* : holdings.
— *d'entreprise* : business account.
gestion de — : management of securities.
— *dont la gestion est confiée à un agent de change* : discretionary portfolio.
— *titres* : securities in hand.
service du — : bills department.

porter (v) : to bear, to bring, to carry.
— *atteinte (aux intérêts de)* : to interfere (with the interests of).
— *à un compte* : to enter in an account.
— *au compte (de qn)* : to charge to (s.o.'s) interest.
— *au crédit* : to credit, to enter on the credit, to pass to the credit.
— *au débit* : to debit, to enter to the debit.
— *une écriture* : to enter an item, to post an entry.
— *intérêt* : to bear interest.
— *un jugement* : to pass judgment.
— *préjudice (à qqn)* : to inflict injury, loss (on s.o.).
— *à la réserve* : to pass to the credit.

porteur (m) : holder, carrier, bearer, porter.
[A] — *de contrainte* : bailiff serving a contrainte (see *contrainte*).
[C] [F] — *de bonne foi* : holder in due course.
— *d'actions* : shareholder.
— *de chèque* : bearer of a cheque.
— *de créance* : creditor.
— *de créance hypothécaire* : mortgagee.
— *d'un effet* : holder of a bill of exchange.
— *de mauvaise foi* : holder mala fide.
— *d'obligations* : bondholder.
— *de police* : holder, beneficiary of an insurance policy.
— *de titres* : stockholder.
effets au — : bearer stock.
payable au — : payable to bearer.
titre au — : negotiable instrument.

portion (f) : portion, share, part.
[J] — *afférente à* : portion accruing to.

— *compétente* : rightful share.
— *contingente* : due portion.
— *(quotité) disponible* : disposable portion of property (esp. for testamentary purposes).
— *héréditaire* : portion.
— *légitimaire* : distributive share, (Scot.) legitim.
— *revenant à chaque héritier* : portion accruing to each heir.
— *virile* : lawful share (of succession).

portionnaire (m) : sharer in an estate.

positif (a) : positive.
droit — : positive law.

position (f) : position, situation, standing, status.
— *à la baisse* : bear position.
— *bancaire* : customer's position in a bank.
— *sociale* : social standing, status.
— *de trésorerie* : financial standing.

position être en (v) *(d'acheter ou de vendre à terme)* : to carry a position.

possédant (m) : owner.
les classes —*(es)* : the moneyed classes.

posséder (v) : to own.

possesseur (m) : owner.

possession (f) : possession, property, estate.
[J] — *d'état* : facts in proof of the civil status of s.o.
— *de fait* : adverse possession.
— *légitime* : lawful possession.
— *non équivoque* : possession sure and certain.
— *précaire* : temporary possession, precarious tenure.
— *en propre* : possession in own right.
en fait de meuble, — *vaut titre* : possession amounts to title (in respect of movables) *(pincipe inconnu du droit A.A.)*.
envoi en — : vesting order, writ of possession (hist.) livery of seisin.
titre de — : title.
transfert de la — : conveyance.
trouble de la — : disturbance of possession.
entrer, venir en — : to enter into possession.

possessoire (a et m) : [J] (a) *action* — : possessory action (see a) *complainte, dénonciation de nouvel œuvre,* b) *réintégrande*.
constitut — : constitutum possessorum.
(m) possessory right in real estate.
plaider le — : to sue for possession.

possible (a) : possible.
client — : prospective customer, [U.S.] prospect

poste (f) : the postal service.
P.T.T. # general post-office.
— *téléphonique (bureau)* : extension.

poste (m) : post, place, appointment, station.
— *à pourvoir* : vacancy.
— *de police* : police-station.
— *de travail* : work station.
être en — *à Londres* : to hold a post in London.
[C] entry in books, item.
— *(s) intermittents (exportations ou importations de caractère exceptionnel)* : erratic items.

postérieur (a) : subsequent.
à une date —*(e)* : at a later time.

postérité (f) : descendants.
mourir sans laisser de — : to die without issue.

posthume (a) : posthumous (child, etc.).

postulant (m) : applicant for post.
[J] attorney in fact in court (privilege of *avoué* in court of appeal).

pot-de-vin (m) : bribe, illicit commission.

potence (f) : gallows.
gibier de — : gallows-bird.

potentiel (a) : potential.

potestatif (a) : [J] *condition* **potestative** : condition depending upon the will of a party to a contract.

pour (prép) : *(au nom de)* on behalf of.

« **pour acquit** » : « received » (with thanks).

pourboire (m) : gratuity, tip.

pour-cent (m) : rate, per cent.

pourcentage (m) : rate of interest, percentage of commission.

« **pour copie conforme** » (**p.c.c.**) : [J] « certified true copy ».

« **pour le compte de** » : « for the account of ».

pourparlers (m pl) : negotiations, pourparlers.
engager des — : to enter into negotiations.

« **pour solde de tout compte** » : « in full settlement ».

« **pour son propre compte** » : « for his own account ».

poursuites (f) (mostly used in pl.) : [J] lawsuit, action, prosecution.
— *civiles* : taking proceedings against s.o., suing *(un débiteur)*.
— *(s) du ministère public* : public prosecution.
— *(s) en expropriation* : action for expropriation.
abandon des —*(s)* : nolle prosequi, abandonment of action, discontinuance, voluntary nonsuit.
commencer, engager, entamer, exercer, intenter des —*(s)* : to institute, to take proceedings.

poursuivant (m) : [J] prosecutor, plaintiff.

poursuivre (v) : [J] — *qn en justice, devant les tribunaux* : to undertake, to institute proceedings against s.o., to proceed against s.o., to sue *(un débiteur)*.
il n'y a pas lieu de — : there is no case.
— *des études* : to pursue studies.

pourvoi (m) : [J] appeal (esp. to the *Cour de cassation* to have the decision set aside and a new trial ordered).
— *en grâce* : petition for mercy.
— *dans l'intérêt de la loi* : appeal ex officio on a point of law.
— *en révision* : appeal for reconsideration.
— *pour vice de forme* : appeal for flaw.
se pourvoir *(en cassation)* : to lodge an appeal (with the *Cour de cassation*).
se pourvoir en cour de Rome : to petition the Holy See (esp. for annulment of religious marriage).

poussée (f) : push.
inflation due à la — *des coûts* : cost-push inflation.
— *de (la) droite, de (la) gauche* : Right, Left prize.

pousser (v) : to push.
— *les enchères* : to run up the bidding at auction.

pouvoir (m) : power, authority, influence.
abus de — : misuse of authority, ultra vires.
— *d'achat* : spending power, purchasing, buying power.
— *d'appréciation du juge* : the judge's discretion, comment, summing up.
— *en bonne et due forme* : credentials in order.
— *de compensation* : countervailing power.
les —*(s) constitués* : the powers that be, the officers properly appointed under the Constitution for the government of the people.
en dehors des —*(s) (de)* : not within the

competence (of).
— *discrétionnaire* : full powers to act, discretionary power.
— *discrétionnaire des juges de fond* : exclusive competency of courts of first instance and courts of appeals to appreciate facts (while the competency of the *Cour de cassation* is limited to points of law).
— *discrétionnaire du président* : full authority of presiding judge in courtroom.
commettre un excès de — : to exceed one's powers.
— *de marchandage* : bargaining power.
— *réglementaire* : right of public authorities to issue regulations and rules within their powers.
vérification de — *(s)* : checking of credentials.
commission de la vérification des — *(s)* : committee on credentials.
[J] power of attorney, procuration, credentials, proxy.
être muni de, recevoir, avoir pleins — *(s)* : to have full powers, to be fully empowered to act.
présenter ses — *(s)* : to show one's credentials.
fondé de — : agent (holding power of attorney).
[C] manager, managing director, signing clerk.

pouvoir (v) : *(dans les textes juridiques et fiscaux)*.
aucune déduction ne **peut** *être effectuée au titre de* : no deduction *shall* be made as to.

praticien (m) : practising, practician.

pratique (a et f) : (a) practical.
(f) (usual) practice, application.
[C] — = *clientèle* : customer.
donner sa — *(à qqn)* : to give (s.o.) one's custom.

(libre) pratique (f) : [J] pratique, permission to ship to enter port and disembark passengers and cargo (esp. after quarantine).

pratiqué (a) : done, ruling.
les cours — *(s)* : the ruling prices.

préalable (a et m) : (a) previous, prior, preliminary.
accord — : preliminary agreement.
formalités — *(s)* : formalities preceding a debate.
au — : as a preliminary, beforehand.
(m) prerequisite.

préambule (m) : preamble.

préavis (m) : notice.
— *de congé* : notice of discharge.

prébende (f) : prebend.

précaire (a) : precarious (tenure, holding).

précaution (f) : precaution, caution.
mesures de — : precautionary measures.

précéder (v) : to precede.
ce qui **précède** *(s'applique à...)* : the foregoing (applies to...).

précédent (m) : precedent (in law).
créer un — : to create, to set a precedent.
fait sans — *(s)* : unprecedented occurrence.

précédent *(le jour)* : (the day) before.

précieux *(métal)* : precious (metal).

préciput (m) : [J] portion taken in advance before apportioning an estate.
— *conventionnel* : estate set aside in the antenuptial settlement in favour of the surviving spouse (see dowry).
— *successoral* : portion of an inheritance set aside for one of the coheirs and devolving upon him in addition to his portion.

précis (a et m) : (a) accurate, precise, definite. (m) abstract, precis.

précision (f) : particulars.
pour plus de — : for greater certainty.

précompte (m) : [F] previous deduction from an account.
— *de cotisation* : previous deduction.
— *mobilier* : distributions prepayment.

prédécesseur (m) : predecessor.

prédiales *(servitudes)* (a) : predial, praedial (servitudes).

préemption (f) : pre-emption.
droit de — *de l'Etat* : Government's right of pre-emption.

préfecture (f) : [A] prefecture, public authority under the central Government which administers each of the *départements* of France.
la — *de police* : the headquarters of the police, in Paris and some provincial towns.
— *maritime* : port-admiral's headquarters.

préférence (f) : preference, priority, choice.
[J] — *d'un créancier* : priority of a creditor.
droits de —, **préférentiels** : priority rights.
[D] *tarif préférentiel* : preferential tariff.
[F] *action de* — : preferred share.
— *pour la liquidité* : liquidity preference.
[C] *fonction de* — *étatique* : state preference

function.

préfet (m): prefect, head of a *préfecture*.
— *maritime*: port-admiral.
— *des études*: vice-principal (in catholic schools).

préjudice (m): detriment, wrong, damage, moral injury, prejudice.
[J] tort.
porter, faire — à qn: to inflict injury, loss on s.o.
action en dommages-intérêts pour — moral: heart-balm action.
indemnité pour — moral: smartmoney, exemplary, retributory, vindictive damages.
— *moral*: mental distress.
sans — de: without prejudice to.

préjudiciable (a): damaging, detrimental, prejudicial.
action —: tortious action.

préjudiciaux (a): [J] *frais —*: security for costs before appeal.

préjudiciel (a): [J] *question, motion — (le)*: interlocutory question, motion.

préjugé (m): 1° prepossession, 2° precedent (in law).

préjuger (v): to prejudge, to prejudice.
autant qu'on puisse —: as far as one can judge beforehand.

prélegs (m): [J] preference legacy.

prélèvement (m): deduction in advance, sample, appropriation, levy, drawing, withdrawal.
[F] — *sur le capital, la fortune*: capital levy.
— *libératoire*: once and for all levy.

prélever (v): to draw, to set apart, to charge.
— *une commission*: to charge a commission.
somme **prélevée** *(sur)*: amount appropriated (from).

préliminaire (a): *(condition)* preliminary (condition).

préméditation (f): premeditation.
avec —: deliberately.
[J] with malice aforethought, with malice prepense.

premier (a): first.
[J] — *(e) instance*: first instance.
— *intéressé*: chargee.
— *juge*: court of original jurisdiction.
— *lit, premières noces*: first marriage.

— *né*: first-born.
— *ressort*: first resort (possibility of appeal).
— *et dernier ressort*: first and last resort (without appeal).
[C] — *(e) de change*: first of exchange.
de — choix: first choice, of finest quality.
— *(s) cours*: opening prices.
denrées de — (e) nécessité: staple products, staples, essential products.
frais de — établissement: first, initial outlay.
matières — (es): raw material.

premier entré, premier sorti (PEPS):
[F] first in, first out (FIFO).

prenant (a): [F] *partie prenante*: recipient, payee.

prendre (v): to take.
— *acte*: to take cognizance of.
— *en considération*: to take into account (consideration).
— *effet*: to become operative, to take effect.
— *sur le fait*: to catch in the act (red-handed).
— *qn en otage*: to take (s.o.) as hostage.

preneur (m): taker.
[J] lessee, lease holder, [C] buyer, purchaser, [F] payee of cheque, [ASS] holder of a policy, (Lloyd's) underwriter.

prénom (m): first name, Christian name.

(le) pré-nommé: (the) aforesaid.

prénuptial (a): antenuptial.

prépondérant (a): preponderant.
voix — (e): casting vote.

préposé (m): official in charge, servant, employee.
[A] — *à la caisse des dépôts et consignations*: official receiver.
— *des P.T.T.*: postman.
[D] — *des douanes*: custom-house official.
[C] *commettant et —*: principal and agent.

préposer (v): to appoint (to an office).

prescriptible (a): prescriptible.

prescription (f): prescription, regulations, directions, stipulations.
[J] barring by limitation.
— *acquisitive*: acquisitive, positive prescription, adverse possession.
délai de —: term of limitation.
— *de droit commun*: prescription at the end of thirty years.
— *d'exécution*: (cr.) prescription of enfor-

cement of a judgment.
– *extinctive, libératoire* : extinctive, negative prescription.
invoquer la – : to raise a defence under the statute of limitations.
[A] – *(s) légales* : official regulations.

prescrire *(de faire)* (v) : to direct (to do).
un délit se **prescrit** *par trois ans* : an action on a misdemeanour is barred at the end of three years.

prescrit (a) : prescribed.
dans les délais – *(s)* : within the required time.
arrérages – *(s)* : statuate-barred interest.
chèque – : stale cheque.

présélectionner (v) : to short-list.

présent (a) : 1º present, current, 2º « hereby ».
par le – *acte, le conseil déclare* : the council hereby declare.
par les – *(es)* : hereby.

présentation (f) : 1º presentation, appearance, introduction.
2º *(d'une lettre de change)* sighting of a bill.
– *d'un chèque à l'encaissement* : compensation of a cheque.
3º *(de marchandises)* packaging, [U.S.] get-up.
paiement sur – : payable on demand, at sight.

présenter (v) : to present, to offer, to show, to display.
– *une requête* : to lodge a request.
[J] *se* – *contre qn* : to appear against s.o.
se – *pour qn* : to act as attorney in fact.
– *à l'acceptation* : to present for acceptance.
– *un bilan* : to draw a balancesheet.

présidence (f) : chairmanship, presidency.

président (m) : president, chairman, managing director, [U.S.] chairman and president.
– *du conseil d'administration* : chairman of the board of directors.
le – *de la cour* : the presiding judge.
être élu – : to be elected chairman.

présider (v) *(réunion)* : to chair, to preside over (a meeting).

présomptif *(héritier)* (a) : presumptive (heir).

présomption (f) : presumption.
[J] – *d'absence* : presumption of absence.
– *absolue, de droit, juridique légale* : presumption juris et de jure, legal presumption, intendment of the law (no evidence to the contrary being admitted, e.g. filiation of child born in wedlock).
– *d'acquêts* : presumption that property was acquired in common (by man and wife).
– *de la bonne foi* : presumption of action bona fide.
– *de décès* : presumption of life or death.
– *de fait* : presumption of fact.
– *irréfragable* : irrebutable presumption.
– *de survie* : presumption of survivorship (esp. of heirs of different ages, disappearing simultaneously, see *comourants*).
preuve par – : circumstantial evidence.
dans le doute la – *est en faveur de l'accusé* : (in dubio pro reo), benefit of doubt.

(la) presse (f) : (the) press, « the fourth estate ».
agence de – : news agency.

(être) pressé *(par la nécessité)* : to be pressed (by necessity).

pressentir (v) (qqn) : to approach (s.o.).

pression (f) : pressure.
– *fiscale* : burden of taxation.
groupe de – : pressure group, lobby.
faire – *sur* : to bring pressure to bear on, to lobby with.

prestataire *(de service)* (m) : supplier (of services).

prestation (f) : prestation, provision, benefit, loaning.
– *en nature* : allowance in kind.
– *familiale* : child bounty, family allowance.
– *(s) locatives* : rental.
– *maladie* : sickness benefit.
– *(s) de caractère social* : social benefits.
taxe sur les – *(s) de service* : tax on services.
– *de sûretés* : going bail for s.o.
[J] – *de serment* : taking the oath.

présuccession (f) : [J] anticipated succession to one's estate.

présumer (v) : to presume, to deem.
le meurtrier **présumé** : the alleged murderer.
revenu présumé : estimated (presumed) income.
il est à – *que* : the presumption is that.

prêt (m) : loan, advance, pay.
– *-bail* : leasing, lease-lend.
– *consenti, en cours, non remboursé* : current loan.
– *à court terme* : short loan.
– *à court terme pour permettre à l'emprunteur de trouver d'autres fonds* : accommodation bill.
– *à découvert* : loan on overdraft.

– *dénonçable en tout temps*: loan payable on demand.
– *à fonds perdus*: loan without security.
– *sur gage, gagé*: pledged loan, loan against security.
– *garanti*: secured loan.
– *à la grosse (aventure)*: bottomry, respondentia (loan).
– *d'honneur*: loan on trust.
– *hypothécaire*: mortgage loan.
– *à intérêts*: loan at interest.
– *au jour le jour*: money at call, call money.
– *à la petite semaine*: loan by the week.
– *à taux variable*: adjustable rate loan.
– *à terme*: loan at notice.
– *à long terme*: long-term loan.
– *sur titres*: advance on securities, loan on stock.
– *à usage*: (Scot.) commodatum.
– *usuraire*: usurious loan.
caisse de – *(s)*: loan bank.

prêtable (a): lendable, loanable.

prétendre (à) (v): to claim.

prête-nom (m): man of straw, figurehead.

prétention (f): claim.

prêter *(de l'argent, à intérêt)* (v): to lend, [U.S.] to loan (money, at interest).

prêteur (m): lender, loaner.
– *sur gages*: pledgee, pawn broker.
[J] bailor.

prétoire (m): [J] floor of the court.

preuve (f): proof, evidence, test.
– *à l'appui d'une demande*: evidence in support of an application.
– *authentique*: duly certified documentary evidence.
– *par l'aveu de la partie adverse*: (nolo contendere) evidence by record.
– *à charge*: evidence for the prosecution.
charge de la –: burden of proof.
commencement de (la) –: prima facie evidence.
– *par commune renommée*: hearsay evidence, common report, knowledge.
– *concluante*: conclusive evidence.
– *contraire*: evidence to the contrary.
– *de culpabilité*: evidence of guilt.
– *à décharge*: evidence for the defence.
– *directe*: direct evidence.
– *par indices*: evidence of proof.
– *indirecte (par présomption)*: circumstancial evidence.
– *irrecevable*: incompetent evidence.
– *libératoire*: peremptory evidence.
– *littérale*: documentary evidence.
– *patente*: proof positive.
– *recevable*: competent evidence.
– *testimoniale*: proof by witnesses.
administrer une –: to submit convincing evidence.

prévaloir (v): to prevail.
faire – *son droit*: to make good one's right.
se – *d'un droit*: to exercise a right.
se – *de qch.*: to avail oneself, to take advantage of sth.
se –: to presume on.

prévarication (f): prevarication, maladministration of justice, breach of trust, jobbery.
juge **prévaricateur**: unjust judge.

prévenir (v): to forestall, to stave off, to inform, to give notice to.

prévention (f): 1° prejudice, bias.
[J] imprisonment on suspicion.
être en état de –: to be in custody, committed for trial.
mise en –: charge, indictment, committal for trial.
détention **préventive**: detention on suspicion, detention awaiting trial.
2° prevention, forestalling.
– *de la criminalité*: prevention of crime.
– *routière*: road safety.

prévenu (a et m): (a) prejudiced.
[J] – *de vol*: charged with, accused of theft.
(m, f) *le* –, *la prévenue*: the prisoner, the accused.

prévision (f): forecast, forecasting, estimate, prevision, provision, expectations, schedule.
– *(s) budgétaires*: budget estimates.
– *(s) à court (long) terme*: short-(long-)term expectations.
– *(s) de dépenses*: estimate of expenses.
– *économique*: business forecasting.
en – *de*: in (the) anticipation of.
selon les – *(s)*: according to schedule.
dépasser les – *(s)*: to exceed expectations.

prévisionnel (a): estimated.

prévoir (v): to anticipate, to forecast, to provide for.
marchandises dont la livraison est **prévue** *pour le*: goods that it is anticipated will be delivered on.
la période prévue par le contrat: the period provided for by the contract.

prévôt (m): provost.

prévôté (f) : military police establishment.

prévoyance (f) : foresight, precaution.
caisse de — : provident fund.
— *sociale* : state insurance.
fonds de — : reserve fund.
réserve de — : contingency reserve.
société de — : provident society.

primage (m) : [J] primage, hat-money.

prime (f) : premium.
faire — to be at premium, to be above par.
[A] bounty, subsidy, bonus.
— *d'ancienneté* : seniority premium (pay).
— *à la construction* : building subsidy.
— *de conversion* : retraining award.
— *d'intéressement (dans un système de participation aux bénéfices)* : share of the profits.
— *de licenciement* : redundancy payment, severance pay.
— *de rendement* : output, efficiency bonus.
— *de risque* : bonus for risk, danger money.
— *de risque ajoutée (au coût du capital)* : risk-adjusted rate of return.
— *de transport* : allowance for transportation.
travail « à la — *»* : work on the bonus system.
— *d'engagement* : voluntary enlistment in the armed forces bonus.
— *(s) d'exportation* : export subsidies, bounties on export.
— *de réexportation* : drawback.
[C] [F] interest, compensation.
— *d'émission* : agio on issue.
— *de grosse (aventure)* : interest on bottomry loan.
— *publicitaire* : free gift.
— *de remboursement* : premium on redemption.
— *pour résiliation de contrat* : compensation for cancelling an agreement.
[B] option money.
marché à — : option bargain, put, call, option market.
ordre à — : option order.
valeur à — : option stock.
— *contre ferme* : premium for transforming an option bargain into a firm deal.
— *contre* — : discharge of liability out of an option bargain with another option bargain.
— *pour lever* : call option.
— *pour livrer* : put option.
abandon de — : relinquishing the forfeit.
achat à — : buyer's option, giving for the call.
acheteur à — : giver.
cours de la réponse des — *(s)* : declaration day price.
double — : double option, straddle, put and call option.
écart des — *(s)* : difference between the prices for firm and option stock.
heure de la réponse des — *(s)* : declaration time.
jour de la réponse des — *(s)* : declaration day.
pied de la — : option price less option rate.
vendeur à — : taker.
vente à — : seller's option, taking for the put.
faire des opérations à — : to deal in options.
[ASS] insurance rate, premium.

primer (v) : to take precedence, to rank first.
[J] — *qn en hypothèque* : to take priority in mortgage.
« *la force* **prime** *le droit* » : « might is right ».

primitif *(texte)* (a) : original (text).

primordial (a et m) : (a) primary, original, overriding.
les fins — *(es) d'une société* : the original aims of an association.
(m) original document.

principal (a et m) : (a) principal, chief, leading.
[J] — *locataire* : head lessee.
auteur — *d'un crime* : principal of a crime in the first degree.
associé — : senior partner.
(m) principal, chief, headmaster *(d'une école)*, chief partner, senior partner *(d'une firme)*, leading shareholder.
[J] the main issue.
l'accessoire suit le — : the decision on the main issue applies to accessory matters.
les frais suivent le — : costs abide the event.
[F] capital sum.
le — *d'une obligation* : the principal amount of a debenture.
la — *(e) source de revenus* : the chief source of income.
intérêts et — : interest and principal.

principe (m) : principle, law, rule.
les — *(s) de l'imposition (de A. Smith)* : the canons of taxation (of A. Smith).

prioritaire (a) : prior, taking precedence.

priorité (f) : priority.
[J] priority of claim.
droits de — : priority rights.
[F] *actions de* — : preference shares.

prise (f) : hold, grasp, grip.
— *en charge* : taking over.
— *de contrôle majoritaire* : see « *contrôle* ».
— *de décision* : decision making.
— *d'inventaire* : drawing-up an inventory.
— *de participation majoritaire* : take over.
— *de possession* : entering into, taking pos-

session of *(biens immobiliers)*, perception *(biens mobiliers)*.
[J] 1° taking, capture.
— *de corps*: arrest.
— *à partie*: lodging claim for damages against a judge for miscarriage of justice in civil or criminal matters.
ordonnance de — de corps: writ of capias.
2° prize.
[F] — *ferme*: subscription (by banking interests) to a loan before public issue, bought deal.

prisée (f): [J] *prisée et estimation*: appraisal, valuation before auction.

priser (v): to appraise, to value goods.

priseur (m): *commissaire-priseur*: valuer and auctioneer.

prison (f): prison, goal, jail, [U.S.] penitentiary.

prisonnier (m): prisoner.
se constituer —: to give oneself up.

privation (f): [J] deprivation.
— *des droits civiques*: attainder.
peine privative de liberté: penalty involving personal restraint.

privé (a): private, individual.
droit, entreprise, propriété, secteur —(e): private law, enterprise, property, sector.

priver (v): to deny.
[F] — *une personne du bénéfice d'un dégrèvement*: to deny the relief to an individual.

privilège (m): privilege, licence, grant, lien, right of priority.
[J] preferential right.
— *de créancier*: creditor's preferential claim.
— *d'émission (billets de banque)*: right of issuing (bank notes).
— *général*: general lien.
— *d'hypothèque*: mortgage charge.
— *de juridiction*: attachment of privilege.
— *de souscription*: right of priority in subscription.
— *du Trésor*: preference of Treasury.
créance privilégiée: preferred debt.
créancier privilégié: chargee.
traitement privilégié: preferential treatment.
[F] *action privilégiée*: preference share.
banque privilégiée: chartered bank.

prix (m): cost, value, worth, consideration, charge.
[C] — *d'achat, d'acquisition*: purchase price.
— *d'adjudication*: knocking-down price.
— *annoncé (par un vendeur)*: asked, offered price.
— *d'attaque*: penetration price (pricing).
— *de barème*: scheduled price.
— *de base*: basic price.
— *brut*: gross value, all-in price.
— *C.A.F.*: C.I.F. price.
— *au comptant*: cash price.
— *courant*: market price.
— *coûtant, de revient*: cost price.
— *de détail*: retail price.
— *d'enchères*: auction price.
— *sans engagement*: price without engagement.
— *en entrepôt (en douane)*: in-bond price, ex-warehouse price.
— *(très) étudiés*: keenest prices.
— *de façon*: fashioning price.
— *fait, à forfait, global*: outright price.
— *fictif*: shadow price.
— *F.O.B.*: F.O.B. price.
— *de gros*: wholesale price.
— *initial*: prime cost.
— *net*: trade price.
à bas —: at a low price.
— *le plus bas*: bottom price.
— *réglementés*: administered prices.
— *de revient moyen*: average cost.
— *de tâche*: jobbing price.
— *de vente*: selling price.
hausse illicite des —: illicit rise in prices.
à — coûtant: at cost price.
à juste —: at a fair price.
à un — raisonnable: on fair terms.
à tout —: at all costs.
les — restent élevés: the prices rule high.
faire payer un — trop bas: to undercharge.
mise à —: upset price.
[F] — *du change*: exchange premium.
— *de souscription*: subscription rate.
[B] — *du report*: contango rate.

prix-courant (m): [C] price-list, catalogue, price current.

probabilité (f): probability, likelihood, *(de vie)* expectation (of life).

probant (a): probant, convincing, cogent.
document en forme —(e): duly certified document.
argument —: conclusive, cogent argument.

problème (m): problem, issue.

procédé (m): process, method.
— *de fabrication*: know-how.
— *(s) empiriques, —(s) de répartition des revenus du commerce et de l'industrie entre ceux qui sont de source française d'une part, étrangère d'autre part*: empirical methods, methods of allocating business income between those

of French source on the one hand and foreign source on the other.

procéder (v) : to proceed.
– *au civil, au criminel* : to institute proceeding before a civil, a criminal court.
– *contre qn* : to take proceedings against s.o.
– *à une enquête* : to institute an enquiry.
– *au vote* : to take a vote.

procédure (f) : [J] procedure, proceedings, practice.
– *amiable* : mutual agreement.
– *contentieuse* : ordinary proceedings in court.
– *gracieuse* : voluntary proceedings, proceedings in non-contentious business.
– *sommaire* : summary procedure.
acte de – : writ, process, summons.
mode, règles de – : rules, order of procedures = General Orders of the Supreme Court (code of procedure).
terme de – : law-term.
vice de – : faulty procedure.

procédurier (m) : pettifogger.

procès (m) : proceedings, action at law, case, cause, trial.
– *civil* : lawsuit.
– *criminel* : (criminal) trial.
abandonner un – : to withdraw an action.
être en – *avec qn* : to be at law with s.o.
faire – *à qn* : to prosecute s.o.
faire un – *à qn* : to go to law with, to sue s.o., to institute proceedings against s.o.
faire le – *de qn* : to criticize s.o.
intenter un – *en divorce* : to institute divorce proceedings, to file a petition, to ask for a divorce.
gagner son – : to win one's lawsuit.
perdre un – : to lose, to fail in a suit.

processif (a) : litigious.
formes **processives** : forms of legal procedure.

processus (m) : process, method.
– *de rendement* : production process.

procès-verbal (m) : (official) report, proceedings, minute(s), record (of evidence, etc.), policeman's report.
– *d'amende* : order to pay a fine.
– *des avaries d'un bateau* : protest.
– *de carence* : record of insolvency (in execution proceedings).
– *de constat* : establishment of fact.
– *de constatation* : acknowledgement of sth. as a fact.
– *de faillite* : report of bankruptcy.
– *de séance* : minutes of a meeting.

– *de vente* : record of forced sale.
consigner au – : to note in a report.
rédiger, dresser, tenir un – : to draw up a report, minutes, to report.
rédacteur de – *(de séance)* : minute-, preciswriter.

prochain (a) : nearest, *(à venir)* forthcoming.
[C] *fin* – : at the end of next month.

proche (a) : near, close.
au franc le plus – : to the nearest franc.
les – *(s)* : near relations.

proclamer (v) : *(élection)* to declare, *(loi)* to publish.

procuration (f) : procuration, power of attorney, proxy.
– *ad litem* : proxy for appearing in court.
– *collective* : joint power.
– *générale* : full power of attorney, general power.
donner la – *à qn* : to confer powers of attorney to s.o.

procureur (m) : proxy, attorney at law.
[J] – *général* : head of the Prosecution Department at the courts of appeals (# Director of Public Prosecution).
– *de la République* : head of the Prosecution Department at courts of first instance, [U.S.] district attorney.

prodigue (a et m) : (a) lavish.
(m) spendthrift.

producteur (a et m) : (a) producing.
capital – *d'intérêts* : interest-bearing capital.
(m) producer.

productif (a) : productive.
action **productive** *d'un dividende de...* : share yielding a dividend of...

production (f) : production, product, yield, processing.
biens de – : capital goods.
capacité de – : capacity of output.
– *continue* : continuous processing.
coût de – : production cost.
étude de – : production engineering.
– *jointe* : joint production.
moyens de – : means of production.
– *en grande série* : mass-production.
sous- – : underproduction.
taux de la – : rate of production.
[J] – *de créance* : producing a claim.
– *des pièces* : exhibition of documents.
– *de preuves* : producing, bringing, evidence.
– *d'un témoin* : bringing forward a witness.
– *tardive d'une déclaration fiscale* : late filing

of a return.

productivité (f) : productivity, output, yield.
campagne de — : productivity drive.

produire (v) : 1° to produce, 2° *(rapporter des intérêts, etc.)* to yield (interest, etc.), to earn, 3° *(un témoignage)* to adduce (evidence), 4° *(à une liquidation, faillite)* to prove claims (in a liquidation, a bankruptcy).

produit (m) : product, produce, yield, return.
— *des actions* : dividends proper.
— *agricole* : agricultural produce.
— *brut* : gross proceeds.
— *d'un capital* : yield of a capital sum.
— *(s) et charges* : revenues and charges.
— *(s) chimiques* : chemicals, chemical products.
— *fini* : finished product.
— *(s) immatériels* : services.
— *manufacturé* : manufactured article.
— *national brut (P.N.B.)* : gross national (domestic) product.
— *naturel* : natural produce.
— *net* : net proceeds.
— *nouveau* : 1° new earnings, 2° new product.
— *de première nécessité* : essentials, essential foodstuffs (products).
— *pharmaceutique* : drug.
— *de rejet* : waste product.
— *secondaire* : by-product.
sous- — : by-production.
— *d'une vente* : proceeds of a sale.
[C] *le* — *de la journée* : the day's takings, receipts.

profane (m) : layman.

profession (f) : occupation, trade, business, *(libérale)* profession.
— *indépendante* : independent profession.
les — *(s) libérales* : the professional classes.
— *de foi* : profession of faith.

professionnel (a et m) : (a) professional, vocational.
activité — *(le)* : personal services.
frais — *(s)* : expenses against earnings.
maladie — *(le)* : professional, vocational, industrial disease.
(m) professional.
— *du spectacle* : public entertainer.

profil (m) : profile.
le — *du marché* : market trends.

profit (m) : profit, benefit, earnings, gain, increment, return, [U.S.] avails.
sans — *(occupation)* : unprofitable, profitless (work).
au — *de* : for the benefit of, in favour of.

tirer — *(de)* : to derive (draw) profit (from).
[J] — *du défaut* : benefit of the other party's failure to appear.
[C] — *aventureux, maritime* : bonus over the official rate of interest paid in bottomry on ship not insured against sea and war risks.
[F] *compte de* — *(s) et pertes* : profit and loss account.
— *(s) illicites* : illicit profits.
maximation des — *(s)* : maximizing of profits.
— *net* : goodwill.
passer par -*(s) et pertes* : to write off bad debts.
— *(s) de l'exercice* : year's earnings.
— *(s) théoriques (fictifs)* : paper profits.

profiter (v) : to benefit (profit) by, to take advantage of.

profiteur (m) : profiteer.

progéniture (f) : offspring.

programmateur (m) : programmer, scheduler.

programmation (f) : programming.
— *linéaire* : linear programmation.

programme (m) : program, programme, schedule.
— *d'approvisionnement en capital* : capital appropriation program.
— *de fabrication, de vente* : manufacturing, sales schedule.
— *économique, financier* : economic, financial programme.
— *d'un parti politique* : political platform.
être en avance sur le — : to be ahead of schedule.
être en retard sur le — : to be behind of schedule.

programmer (v) : to program(me).

progressif (a) : 1° *(barème)* graduated (scale). 2° *(impôt)* progressive, graded (tax).
méthode **progressive** : forward method.
surtaxe progressive : progressive surtax.

progression (f) : progression, series increase.
recettes en — : receipts on the increase.

progressiste (a) : progressive.

progressivité (f) : progressiveness, progression.

prohibé (a) : prohibited.

prohibitif (a) : *(prix, etc.)* prohibitive (prices, etc.).

projet (m) : project, scheme, plan, draft.
— *de budget :* budget estimates.
— *de contrat, de convention :* draft contract, agreement.
en — : planned, scheduled.
— *de loi :* government bill, draft bill, proposal.
groupe de — : Task Force.

projeter (v) : to plan, to project.

prolétariat (m) : (the) proletariat(e).

prolongation (f) : prolongation, extension, lengthening.
demande de — *du délai d'opposition :* application to extend the time for objecting.
[B] *dernier jour de* — : declaration day (in time bargain).

prolongements *(d'une affaire)* (m pl) : the aftermath (of an affair).

prolonger (v) : to renew, to prolong.
— *une lettre de change :* to renew a bill.

promesse (f) : promise, assurance ; promissory note.
— *d'achat :* undertaking to purchase.
— *d'actions :* scrip (certificate).
— *de mariage :* promise of marriage.
— *de porte-fort :* going bail for s.o.
— *de vente :* undertaking to sell.

promissoire (a) : promissory.
[J] *serment* — : oath the execute an undertaking.

promoteur (m) : promoter, originator.

promotion (f) : 1° *(des ventes)* sales promotion.
2° *(à l'ancienneté)* promotion by seniority.
3° *(sociale)* social advancement, promotion.

promulgation (f) : promulgation, proclamation.
promulguer une loi : to promulgate a law.
promulguer un décret : to issue, to publish a decree.

prononcé (m) : [J] decision, terms of decision.
— *de jugement :* verdict.

prononcer (v) : to pronounce.
— *un discours :* to make, to deliver a speech.
[J] — *l'acquittement :* to discharge, to acquit, to dismiss (prisoner).
— *la faillite de qn :* to adjudge s.o. bankrupt.
— *un hors de cour :* to dismiss s.o.'s case, [U.S.] to discontinue a case.

— *un non-lieu :* to nonsuit s.o.
— *une peine :* to inflict a penalty upon, to impose a penalty on s.o.
— *une sentence :* to pass, to deliver a sentence, to pronounce sentence on, to sentence s.o.
se — *contre :* to pronounce against.
se — *sur :* to come to a decision on.

propension (f) : *(à consommer, à épargner, à investir)* propensity (to consume, to save, to invest, etc.).

proportion (f) : proportion, ratio.
en — *directe (inverse) :* in direct (inverse) ratio.

proportionnalité (f) : *(de l'impôt)* proportionnality (of taxation).

proportionnel (a) : proportional.
représentation — *(le) :* proportional representation.
taxe — *(le) :* proportional tax.

proportionnellement à (adv) : in proportion to.

proposition (f) : proposal, proposition.
— *de loi :* private Member's bill (opp. *projet de loi*).

propre (a et m) : (a) 1° proper, clean, inherent.
2° one's own.
pour son — *compte :* on one's own account.
fonds — *(s) :* capital stock, ownership.
en mains — *(s) :* in (s.o.'s) own hands.
(m) [J] — *d'une femme mariée :* separate property of a married woman.
propres (m pl) : [J] inheritance.

propriétaire (m et f) : proprietor, owner, holder, owner of a house, landlord.
— *d'actions :* shareholder.
— *commun, indivis :* joint owner.
— *foncier :* landowner.
nu — : bare owner.
— *indivis :* joint owner.
petit — : small farmer, holder.

propriété (f) : proprietorship, ownership, property, estate.
[J] — *artistique et littéraire :* copyright.
— *bâtie :* structures.
— *commerciale (droit au bail) :* right of a tradesman to receive a compensation for goodwill if a prolongation of lease is refused without sufficient grounds.
— *commune :* joint ownership.
— *fiduciaire :* trust.
— *foncière :* landed estate.

petite — foncière: small holding.
— immobilière: realty.
— industrielle: patent rights.
— mobilière: chattels.
— privée: private property.
— non bâtie: land plots.
nue —: ownership without usufruct.
pleine — (foncière): freehold.
titres de —: title-deeds.
translation de —: conveyance.

prorata (m): proportional part.
au —: in proportion to.
paiement au —: payment prorata.

prorogation (f): extension of time, etc., prorogation of Parliament.
— de bail: renewal of lease.
[J] *— d'enquête:* leave to protract an enquiry.
— de juridiction (ratione personae ou ratione materiae): extension of the scope of jurisdiction.
— de terme: days of grace.

proroger (v): 1° *(échéance)* to extend (the time limit).
2° *(billet)* to prolong (a bill).

proscription (f): proscription, banishment, outlawry.
[J] *— de biens:* selling of property of an absconding debtor.

prospecter (v): to prospect, to canvass.

prospective (f): forecasting, prospect.

prospectus (m): handbill, prospectus, leaflet.
— d'émission: prospectus, [U.S.] dodger.

prospère (a): flourishing, prosperous, thriving.
affaire(s) —(s): thriving business.
commerce —: flourishing trade.

prospérer (v): to flourish, to prosper, to thrive.

prospérité (f): prosperity, [U.S.] bonanza.
vague de —: boom.

prostitution (f): prostitution.
— clandestine: clandestine prostitution.
— réglementée: prostitution tolerated (in brothels and medically supervised).

protecteur (m et a): protector.
[B] *régime douanier —:* protectionist customs tariff.
droits —(s): protective duties.

protection (f): 1° *(par opposition à « libre échange »)* protection (as opposed to « free trade »).
2° *(contre un danger)* safeguard.

protectionnisme (m): protection(ism).

protectionniste (a): protectionist.

protéger (v): to safeguard, to shelter.

protester (v): to protest.
— de sa bonne foi: to plead bona fide.
— un effet de change: to give notice of a protest (a bill).
— d'incompétence: to challenge the competence of a court.
— d'innocence: to assert one's innocence.
laisser — une traite: to dishonour a draft.
— de nullité: to assert nullity of proceedings.
— de violence: to act under protest.

protêt (m): [J] [C] protest.
— faute d'acceptation: protest on non-acceptance.
— faute de paiement: non-payment and protest.
dresser, faire, lever —: to make a protest.
lever — d'un effet: to protest a bill.
notifier, signifier un —: to give notice of a protest.
« retour sans — », — « sans frais »: « no expenses », « retour sans protêt », « retour sans frais ».

protocole (m): protocol, ceremonial, correct form of procedure; etiquette; minutes (of a meeting).
[A] *chef du —:* head of the Protocol Section of the Foreign Office.

prouver (v): to prove.
[J] *— le bien fondé d'une réclamation:* to substantiate a claim.

provenance (f): origin, source.
de — étrangère: of foreign origin.

(revenu) provenant de...: (income) derived from...

provenir (v): to arise from, to be derived from.

provision (f): provision, stock, store, supply, funds, reserve.
[J] 1° sum paid into court.
2° amount provisionally allocated by a court before final judgment.
— alimentaire: provisional allowance for necessaries.
3° *— ad litem:* security for costs (esp. wife's

in divorce proceedings).
– *(versée à un avocat)* : retainer.
[C] [F] funds, cover, reserve, margin.
– *pour amortissement* : depreciation allowance.
– *pour créances douteuses* : bad debts reserve.
– *pour dépréciation des stocks* : reserves for inventory losses.
– *pour fluctuations du taux de change* : provision for exchange rate fluctuations.
– *pour impôts* : reserve for taxation.
– *d'une lettre de change* : consideration for a bill of exchange.
faire – pour une lettre de change : to protect a bill.
insuffisance de – : insufficient funds (to meet cheque, etc.).
manque de – (s) : no funds.
– *pour risques* : reserves for contingencies.
chèque sans – : worthless cheque, [U.S.] bouncing check.
provision de courtage : commission, brokerage.
verser des – (s) : to pay a deposit.

provisionner (v) : [C] [F] to give consideration to a bill, to pay-in a sum into one's account.

provisoire (a) : provisional, acting (manager, etc.), temporary.
[J] *sentence – :* provisional judgment.
être en liberté – : to be on bail.
[J] *facture – :* pro forma invoice.
[F] *dividende – :* interim dividend.

provocation (f) : provocation, instigation.
[J] – *au crime* : inciting to crime.
excuse absolutoire de – : excuse of provocation, involving acquittal.
excuse atténuante de – : excuse of provocation, allowing for extenuating circumstances.
agent **provocateur** : instigator.

provoquer (v) : to cause, to incite, to induce.

proxénète (m et f) : procurer, procuress ; pander.

proximité (f) : proximity, closeness.

prud'homme (m) : man of experience and integrity.
conseil des – (s), juridiction prud'homale : conciliation board of employers and wage-earners in industrial disputes.

public (a et m) : (a) public, open (meeting).
agent de la force **publique** : police, constabulary officer.
audience publique : open court.
charge publique, emploi public : office.
la chose publique : the public welfare, the commonweal.
cri public : public opinion.
la dette publique : the National Debt.
domaine – : public domain, property.
droit – : public law.
l'école publique : state schools.
fille publique : prostitute.
finances publiques : public finance.
fonctions publiques : public office.
fonds – (s) : public funds, government stock.
force publique : police, constabulary, armed forces.
homme – : politician.
marché – : a) market overt, b) adjudication (of contracts of supply, etc.), c) [EEC] public procurement contract.
ministère – : Public Prosecutor and his deputies.
ordre – : law and order.
rumeur publique : hearsay.
service – : public utility.
travaux – (s) : public works.
trésor – : public moneys.
le **public** (m) : the public, the people.

publication (f) : publication, issue, published work.
– *des bans de mariage* : publication of banns.
– *de la faillite* : adjudication of bankruptcy.
– *de vente aux enchères* : notice of sale by auction.
– *pour enfants* : children's periodical.

publicitaire (a) : advertising.
annonce – : adverstisement.
moyens – (s) (de masse), supports – (s) : advertising (mass) media.
objets – (s) : gifts for advertising purposes.

publicité (f) : publicity, advertising, [U.S.] advertizing.
[J] – *des débats judiciaires (huis ouvert)* : proceedings in open court (opp. *huis-clos*).
– *formelle en droit commercial* : formal publicity of important legal acts and commercial transactions.
– *matérielle des droits réels* : free access to registers, records, etc., pertaining to real property.
[C] *agent de – :* advertising agent.
budget de – : advertising account.
campagne de – : advertising campaign.
chef de la – : advertising manager.
exemplaires de – : press copies.
– *fallacieuse, mensongère* : deceptive advertising (publicity).
– *au point de vente* : in-store promotion.
– *tapageuse* : display advertising.

pudeur (f) : sense of decency, modesty.
[J] *attentat à la – :* indecent assault.
outrage public à la – : indecent exposure.

puiné (a, m et f) : (a) younger, born after the first-born.
(m) post natus, younger brother.
(f) *– (e)* : younger sister.

puissance (f) : power, force, authority.
[J] *– maritale* : husband's authority over wife.
– paternelle : authority of father (or of mother, if the father is dead).
les grandes –(s) : the great powers.
acheteur en – : potential buyer.

punition (f) : punishment.
– corporelle : restraint.
– disciplinaire : disciplinary punishment.
en – de : as a punishment for.
punir *qn de prison* : to punish s.o. with imprisonment.

pupille (m et f) : ward.
[A] *– de la nation* : ward of the nation, of the State (orphans of soldiers fallen in wars).
deniers **pupillaires** : ward's patrimony.
placement pupillaire : safe investment.
valeurs pupillaires : gilt-edged stock.

pur (a) : pure, mere.
concurrence – (e) : pure competition.
donation – (e) et simple : free gift, outright gift.
(c'est une) – (e) formalité : (it's a) matter of form.
en – (e) perte : uselessly, wastefully.
théorie – (e) : pure theory.

purement (adv) : purely, merely.

purge (f) : [J] satisfaction of mortgage.

purger (v) : to purge, to clean, to cleanse, to clear.
[J] *– l'accusation* : to submit the indictment to the jury.
– la condamnation, une peine : to serve one's sentence.
– la contumace : to surrender to law, after being sentenced in absence.
– le défaut : to cure a default.
– une hypothèque : to redeem, to pay off a mortgage.
se – d'une accusation : to prove one's innocence.

putatif (a) : putative, presumed, reputed.
[J] *mariage, père –* : putative marriage, reputed father.

pyramide (f) *des objectifs* : hierarchy of objectives.

NOTES

Q

quadriennal (a) *(plan)* : quadrennial (plan).

quai (m) : quay, wharf, pier, embankment.
 − *d'embarquement, de déchargement* : loading platform.
 à − : alongside the quay.
 à − *dédouané (nom du port)* : ex quay (name of the harbour) duty paid.
 à − *non dédouané...* : ex quay ... duties on buyers' account.
 droits de − : wharfage.
 se ranger à − : to berth.
 « *le* − *d'Orsay* » : the (French) Foreign Office.

qualifié (a) : qualified, skilled.
 acte qualifié de crime, de délit : action termed a crime, a misdemeanour.
 majorité, minorité −(e) : specified majority, minority.
 main-d'œuvre −(e) : skilled labour.
 ouvrier −, *semi-* −, *non-* − : skilled, semi-skilled, unskilled worker.
 le service − : the competent service.
 [J] *crime* − : aggravated crime.

qualifier (v) : to style, to call, to qualify.
 se qualifier pour : to qualify for.

qualité (f) : quality, qualification, capacity, title-brand, class.
 [J] − *pour agir (au procès)* : right to sue s.o.
 − *pour défendre (au procès)* : right to plead.
 − *substantielle d'un crime* : essence of crime.
 −(s) *d'un jugement* : record of proceedings before judgment.
 agir en − *de* : to act in one's capacity as a.
 avoir − *pour agir* : to be qualified, entitled to act, to have authority to act.
 marchandises de première − : first grade, first-quality goods.
 (de) − *supérieure* : first-rate, top-rate quality.
 (f pl) [J] bill of particulars, [U.S.] brief.

quant à... : with regard (respect) to...

quantième (m) : day of the month.

quantitatif (a) : quantitative.
 théorie **quantitative** *de la monnaie* : quantity theory of money.

quantité (f) : quantity, amount.
 une grande − *de* : a great deal of.
 indice de − : quantity index.
 − *optimum d'une denrée ou d'un produit à acheter sur commande* : Economic Order Quantity (E.O.Q.).

quantum (m) : proportion, amount, percentage, ratio.
 − *des dommages-intérêts* : amount of damages.

quarantaine (f) : quarantine.

quartier (m) général : head office, head quarters.

quasi (adv) : quasi, almost.
 [J] −-*contrat* : implied contract.
 − -*délit* : technical offence.
 − -*possession* : right to an easement.
 − -*usufruit* : usufruct of fungibles.

que... ou non : whether or not.
 − *le bien ait été* − *acquis par échange, achat, don ou héritage* : whether the property was acquired by exchange purchase, gift or legacy.

quel que soit *le montant* : irrespective of (the amount), whatever (the amount) may be.

questeur (m) : treasurer of parliamentary assemblies.

question (f) : question, query.
 [J] point at issue.
 − *d'actualité* : topic of the day.
 − *d'affaires* : matter of business.
 − *de droit, de fait* : issue of law, of fact.
 − *préalable, préjudicielle, préliminaire* : preliminary, previous question.
 − *tendancieuse* : leading question.
 en − : at issue.
 demander la − *préalable* : to move the previous question.

questionnaire (m) : questionnaire, list, set of questions.

queue (f) : queue, queueing.
 faire la − : to queue (up).

qui... : *(fréquemment traduit par* as, « such » *étant alors sous-entendu).*
 − *de droit* : those whom it may concern.

quidam (m) : person, name unknown.

quinquennal (a) : quinquennial.
plan — : five-year plan.

quirat (m) : [J] joint ownership in a ship.

quirataire (m) : joint owner of a ship.

quittance (f) : receipt, discharge, acquittance, replease.
— *comptable :* formal receipt.
— *de paiement :* receipt for payment.
— *pour solde de tout compte :* full discharge.

quitte *(de)* (a) : discharged of.

quitus (m) : 1° auditor's full discharge, receipt in full.
2° dismissal from office or employment.

quote-part (f) : share, portion, quota ; contribution prorata, proportion.
recevoir une — des bénéfices : to receive a portion of the profits.

quotidien (a) : daily.
un — (m) *:* daily newspaper.
— (s) à grand tirage : big circulation dailies.

quotient (m) : quotient, ratio.
— familial : family parts (splitting of the family income for taxation purposes).

quotité (f) : quota, share, amount, portion.
[J] *— disponible :* share of estate at the free disposal of the testator, disposable portion of an estate.
— insaisissable : undistrainable portion of an estate or sum (e.g. of a salary).
[A] *impôt de — :* tax calculated by application of a flat rate to all the property taxable (the total product of the tax is not stated in advance, unlike the *impôt de répartition*).
la — de dégrèvement fiscal : the extent of taxation relief.
— imposable : taxable quota.

NOTES

NOTES

R

rabais (m): rebate, allowance, discount, reduction in price.
[C] — *pour paiement au comptant*: discount for cash.
adjudication au — : adjudication to the lowest bidder (in Dutch auction).
vente au — : sale at reduced prices.
— de prime: rebate of premium.

rabatteur (m): [C] tout.

rabattre (v): to fold sth. back, to bring sth, to pull down, to reduce, to knock off.
[J] *— un défaut*: to cancel a sentence in absence.
[C] *— des clients*: to beat up customers.
— du prix: to make a reduction on price, to deduct from the price, to lower the price.

raccrochage (m): [J] accosting.

rachat (m): buying back, [C] repurchase, [F] redemption, [ASS] surrender (of insurance policy).
valeur de — : surrender value.
faire une offre de — de valeurs: to bid for a company's stock.
avec faculté de — : with option of repurchase, redemption.
[J] *— des bans de mariage*: marriage licence.
— d'une servitude: commutation of an easement, of a right of user.
[C] *accord de — à un pays étranger de biens produits dans ce pays*: buy-back agreement.
— des vendeurs à découvert: bear closing, bear covering.

racheter (v): 1° to buy back, to take over, 2° *(des obligations)* to redeem (bonds), 3° *(une police)* to surrender (a policy).

racolage (m): [J] *— sur la voie publique*: soliciting in a public place for the purpose of prostitution.

radiation (f): striking out, crossing out, cancellation.
[J] *— du barreau*: disbarring.
— d'une dette: cancellation of a debt.
— d'une hypothèque: entry of satisfaction of mortgage.
— d'instance judiciaire, du rôle: striking off the roll.

radical (a): radical (does not always mean politically extreme).

radier (v): to delete, to strike off.

radio-diffusion (f): broadcasting.

(se) raffermir (v): *(cours, prix)* to firm up, to harden, to steady (quotations, prices).

rafle (f): clean sweep, looting raid, « smash and grab it » *(par des malfaiteurs)*, sudden descent of police etc., upon suspected premises or illicit goods, raid, round-up, comb-out *(par la police)*.

raison (f): reason, motive, ground.
— commerciale: trade mark.
à — de: at the rate of.
en — directe de: directly proportional to.
— majeure: imperative reason.
— probante: evidence.
— sociale: name, style of a firm.
se faire rendre — soi-même: to take the law into one's own hands.
[J] *« pour valoir ce que de — »*: to be used as may be thought proper.

raisonnable (a) *(prix)*: fair (price).

rajuster (v): *(le taux)* to adjust (the rate).

ralentir (v) *(activité)*: to slack up, to slacken, to reduce.

ralentissement (m): slackening, slacking, slowing down, business slowdown.
— de l'économie: downturn in the economy.

rançon (f): ransom, penalty (of fame).

rang (m): rank, status, relative position.
— hypothécaire: mortgage priority.
— privilégié: priority.
par — d'ancienneté: according to seniority, length of service.
avoir — de: to hold the rank of.
— social: social status.

ranimer (v): *(l'économie)* to reflate (the economy).
se — (le marché): to rally (the market).

rapine (f): rapine, pillage, depredation.

rappel (m) : recall, calling in (of sum advanced).
[J] repeal *(d'une ordonnance, etc.)*.
– *d'impôt* : calling in additional or outstanding tax.
– *à l'ordre* : call to order.
– *de salaire* : deffered payment.
– *de traitement* : back pay.
lettre de – : reminder.
lettres de – : letters of recall, letters avocatory.

rapport (m) : 1° report, statement, account, 2° yield, profit, return, 3° relations, connection, ratio, proportion, 4° restitution, restoration.
– *(s) d'affaires* : business connections.
– *expliquant pourquoi l'entreprise a perdu un client (ou un contrat)* : lost business report.
– *annuel, de gestion* : annual report of a company.
– *en argent* : restitution in cash, settlement in money.
– *d'avaries* : damage report.
– *bénéfices-actifs utilisés* : productivity factor.
– *des dettes* : settlement of debts, even if not accrued, into the hands of the body of creditors before distribution.
– *d'un dividende en pourcentage* : dividend yield.
– *d'expert, d'expertise* : expert advice, appraisement, opinion, survey, testimony, valuation.
– *financier* : statement, treasurer's report.
– *fonds de couverture-engagements de capitaux* : capital over, capital ratio.
– *(s) d'héritiers* : settlement amongst heirs.
– *juridique* : legal position.
– *(s) juridiques* : legal relationship.
– *à la masse* : restoration to the body of creditors.
– *à la masse d'une avance d'hoirie* : (collatio bonorum) hotchpot.
– *de mer* : ship's protest.
– *moral* : secretary's report.
– *en nature* : restitution in kind.
– *(s) pécuniaires* : financial relationship.
– *de police* : police report.
– *sur la situation de l'entreprise* : situation report.
– *à succession* : restoration of property to a succession, hotchpot.
maison de – : mansions, tenement house.
terres de – : artificial soil.
terre de bon – : land yielding a good return.

rapportable (a) : [J] *bien* – *(s)* : property that must be restored to a succession.

rapporter (v) : 1° to bring back, to restore, 2° to bring in, to bear, to yield, to produce, 3° to relate, to report, to refer, 4° to ascribe sth. to a cause, 5° to post an item *(en comptabilité)*, 6° to rescind, to revoke *(une ordonnance,*
un décret, etc.), to withdraw *(un ordre)*, to call off *(une grève)*, to re-open *(une faillite)*.
s'en – *à la justice* : to leave the decision to the discretion of the court.
– *des bénéfices* : to yield profit.
– *des intérêts* : to return interest.
les documents se **rapportant** *à l'affaire* : the relevant documents.

rapporteur (m) : reporter, recorder, rapporteur.
[J] *juge* – : judge in charge of legal enquiry.

rapprochement *des législations* (CEE) : (EEC) approximation of laws.

rapt (m) : [J] abduction by force, menace or fraud, [U.S.] kidnapping.

rare (a) : *(argent)* scarce, tight (money).

rareté (f) : scarcity, rarity.

ratification (f) : ratification, confirmation, approval.
échange de – *(s)* : exchange of (diplomatic) instruments of ratification.

ratifier (v) : to confirm, to ratify.

rationalisation (f) : rationalization, rationalizing.
[F] – *des choix budgétaires* (R.C.B.) Planing, Programing and Budgeting System (P.P.B.S.).
rationaliser *(production)* : to rationalise.

rationalité (f) *limitée* : bounded rationality.

rationnement (m) : rationing.

rattachement (m) : linking up.
[J] *règle de* – : applicability of national or foreign law in a given case.

rattraper (v) : to catch up with.

rature (f) : erasure.

ravalement (m) : resurfacing, plastering, redressing (a wall).
les dépenses de – *peuvent être déduites* : resurfacing expenses can be deducted.

ravisseur (m) : kidnapper.

ravitaillement (m) : provisioning, food supplies.

rayon (m) : ray, territory.
– *d'action* : scope of activity.
[C] department *(d'un magasin)*.
– *de livraison* : cartage limit.

chef de — : head of a department.

réaction (f) : reaction.
les 4 —(s) *de l'acheteur qu'un vendeur doit savoir provoquer* : AIDA (attention, interest, desire, action).

réactionner (v) : to actuate again.
[J] to sue again.
[B] to react.

réaffecter (v) *(fonds)* : to reallocate.

réagir (v) : to react.

réalisable *(actif)* (a) : available, realizable (assets).

réalisation (f) : realization, carrying out, into effect ; selling out of shares.
— *de l'actif* : realization of assets.
— *(dans la faillite)* : selling up assets (in bankruptcy proceedings).
— *d'un droit* : exercice of a right.
— *forcée* : forced sale.
— *du gage* : sale of pledge.

réaliser (v) : to realize, to carry out, to achieve, to bring into being.
— *des actions* : to sell out shares.
— *sa fortune* : to convert one's property into cash.
— *un investissement* : to realize an investment.
— *un plan* : to carry out a plan.

réapprovisionnement (m) : re-stocking, revictualling, resupply.

(se) réapprovisionner (v) : to restock, to resupply, to revictual.

réassignation (f) : [J] fresh summons.

réassurance (f) : [ASS] reinsurance.
effectuer une — : to lay a risk.

rébellion (f) : rebellion.
faire — *à la justice* : to resist the authority, the law.
[J] coutumacy, contempt of court.

reboisement (m) : afforestation.

rebut (m) : *(marchandises de)* rebbishy goods, trash, waste product, garbage, scrapping.

récapitulation (f) : recapitulation, summary, résumé.
[J] summing up.
— *des témoignages* : summing up evidence.

recel (m) : [J] 1° receiving and concealing of stolen goods.
2° concealment *(d'enfant, d'un criminel, d'une part d'héritage)*.
receleur : receiver of stolen goods, « fence ».

recensement (m) : counting, return.
[A] — *de la population* : census.
— *des suffrages* : count of votes.
[C] — *des comptes* : checking off of accounts.
— *des marchandises* : new inventory, checking of goods.
recenseur : recording official, census-taker, enumerator, teller of votes.

recenser (v) : 1° *(des marchandises)* to check off (goods).
2° *(des voix, votes)* to count (votes).
3° *(population)* to take the census.

récépissé (m) : (written) acknowledgment of receipt.
[J] acknowledgement of complaint.
[D] docket.

réception (f) : acceptance, receipt, reception, taking delivery, taking over ; welcome.
accuser — : to acknowledge receipt.
accusé, avis de — : advice of delivery, acknowledgment of receipt.
dès — : on receipt.
essais de — : acceptance tests.
payable à la — : payable on receipt.
[A] *frais de* — : expenses of official entertainment, table-money.

réceptionnaire (m) : consignee, receiver of goods.
[C] receiving clerk.

récession (f) : recession.

recette (f) : incomings, receipts, returns, takings ; receiving of stores; prescription recipe.
garçon de — : bank-messenger.
[A] — *des finances* : collectorship (of rates and taxes), collector's office.
[F] —(s) *fiscales* : inland revenue receipts, revenue derived from taxes, [U.S.] internal revenue.
—(s) *publiques* : tax revenue.
excédent des —(s) *(sur)* : excess of receipts (over).
[D] — *des douanes* : receiver's office for the customs.

recevabilité (f) : [J] admissibility.
— *d'un recours* : admissibility of an appeal.

recevable (a) : admissible, allowable.
excuse non — : inadmissible excuse.
preuve non — : inadmissible, incompetent

evidence.
preuve — : competent evidence.

receveur (m) : receiver, addressee ; conductor (of a bus).
[A] — *des finances:* district tax-collector.
— *des contributions indirectes:* collector of excise.
— *de l'entregistrement:* receiver of registry fees and stamp duty.
—, **receveuse** *des postes:* postmaster, postmistress.

recevoir (v) : to receive, to get.
à — : receivable.
fin de non- — : plea in bar.
— *une déposition:* to take (s.o.'s) evidence.

rechange (m) : [C] redraft.

recherche (f) : pursuit, quest, search ; research.
— *de la filiation:* search for affiliation.
— *opérationnelle:* operational research.
— *de la paternité:* action (by bastard) for affiliation.
— *de police:* police inquiry.
droits de —, *de visite:* right of visit and search.
frais de — : research expenditure.
— *du profit:* profit seeking.
—(s) *minières:* prospecting.
— *scientifique:* scientific research.
—(s) *du troisième cycle:* postgraduate research.
être à la — *d'un emploi:* to be in search of an employment.

rechercher *(qn en justice)* (v) : to sue (s.o.).

récidive (m) : [J] repetition of an offence, relapse (into crime).
récidiviste : recidivist, habitual criminal, « old lag » *(« cheval de retour »)*.

réciprocité (f) : reciprocity.

réciproque (a) : reciprocal, mutual.

réclamation (f) : complaint, objection, protest, request.
cahier des — : request book.
lettre de — : collection letter, dunning letter.
service des —(s) : complaints department.
[J] claim, demand.
— *en dommages-intérêts:* claim for damages.
action en — *d'état:* action of legitimate child to claim his status.

réclamer : to claim, to complain.
réclamer contre une décision: to appeal against a decision.

réclamer son droit: to claim one's right.
réclamant : claimant.
[F] *dividende non-réclamé:* unclaimed dividend.

réclame (f) : advertising, [U.S.] advertizing.
article en — : article sold at a low price (as an advertissement), leading article.
vente- — : bargain-sale.

reclassement (m) : regrading, rehabilitation.

reclasser *(personnel)* : to resettle.

réclusion (f) : seclusion, reclusion.
[J] solitary confinement.
— *perpétuelle:* solitary confinement for life.

recognition (f) : recognition.
[J] *acte recognitif et confirmatif:* act of ratification and acknowledgment.

récolement (m) : [J] verification.
— *des comptes:* re-examining of accounts.
— *des dépositions:* reading of their depositions to the witnesses.
— *d'un inventaire:* checking of an inventory.
— *des meubles et effets saisis:* checking of attached chattels.

récolte (f) : crop, harvest, vintage.
— *sur pied:* standing crop.
— *exceptionnelle:* bumper crop.

recommandable (a) : advisable, recommendable.

recommandataire au besoin (m) : [C] referee in case of need (mentioned on a bill of exchange).

recommandation (f) : recommendation, injunction, advice ; registration of letter, of parcel.
lettre de — : letter of introduction, of reference.
[J] writ of detainer.

(lettre) recommandée : registered letter.

recomparaître (v) : [J] to appear again.

récompense (f) : recompense, reward.
[J] compensation.
— *à la communauté:* compensation to (matrimonial) joint estate.
— *entre époux:* claim for compensation by spouse.

réconciliation (f) : reconciliation.
[J] — *des époux:* condonation of matrimonial infidelity.
— *entre bénéfices comptables et fiscaux:* recon-

ciliation between book and taxable income.

reconduction *(d'un bail)* (f) : [J] reconduction, renewal of lease.
tacite — : renewal by tacit agreement.

reconnaissance (f) : recognizance, recognition, acknowledgment, admission ; gratefulness.
— *de la banque :* bank receipt.
— *de dette :* bill of debt, I.O.U. (I owe you), [U.S.] due bill.
— *d'enfant, de paternité :* affiliation of bastard.
— *et exécution d'actes judiciaires :* recognition and enforcement of judicial decisions.
— *d'une faute :* avowal, admission of a lapse.
— *de légitimité :* acknowledgment of legitimate status.
— *de marchandises :* verification of goods.
— *de mont-de-piété :* pawn-ticket.
— *d'une promesse :* admission of a promise.
— *sanitaire :* inspection of a ship by health authorities.
— *d'utilité publique :* official recognition (of an institution) as serving the public interest.

reconnaître (v) : to acknowledge, to recognize (a government, a right).
se — *coupable :* to admit one's guilt.
— *(qqch) :* to make an acknowledgment (of sthg).

reconstituer (v) : *(des réserves)* to reconstitute (reserves).

reconstitution (f) : *(de gisements)* reconstitution, restoration (of coal-, oil-fields).

reconvention (f) : [J] set-off, recoupment.
demande **reconventionnelle** : counter-claim, cross-action.

reconversion (f) : *(de l'économie)* reconversion, re-organization (of the economy).

recors (m) : [J] bailiff's aid and witness of his official acts.

recoupement (m) : cross-checking.

recours (m) : recourse, resort, resource, appeal.
[J] — *en annulation :* action for cancellation.
— *en cassation* # appeal (see *Cour de cassation*).
— *à défaut d'acceptation :* recourse for non-acceptance.
— *faute de paiement :* recourse for non-payment.
— *en grâce :* petition for a reprieve.
— *irrecevable :* inadmissible claim.
— *en nullité :* action for avoidance (of contract).

— *en revision :* petition for review.
— *contre un tiers :* third party complaint, introduction of a third party.
en dernier — : as a last resort.
voie de — : relief, remedy at law.
recourir à la violence : to resort to violence.

recouvrable (a) : (money, sum) recoverable, (debt) collectable.

recouvrement (m) : recovery, collection of bills, debts, taxes, etc.
— *de créance :* debt collection.
— *par la poste :* collection through the post.
[C] — *(s) :* outstanding debts.
en — : for recollection.

recouvrer (v) : to collect, to recover.
— *des impôts :* to collect taxes.

recrutement (m) *cabinet de (de cadres supérieurs doués)* : head-hunter.

rectificatif (m) : corrigendum.
[F] *loi des finances* **rectificative** : amending finance act.

rectification (f) : righting.
[J] — *d'acte d'état civil :* righting of material errors in civil status register by judgment of court.
[C] — *des comptes :* amending accounts, rectification of errors.

rectifier (v) : to correct, to rectify.
— *la comptabilité :* to rewrite the accounts.

recto (m) : face.

reçu (a et m) : (a) received.
(m) receipt, voucher (for goods or money).
— *libératoire pour solde de compte :* receipt for balance.

recueil (m) : collection.
[J] — *des lois :* compilation of laws.
— *des arrêts :* case-book.

recueillir un héritage (v) : to come into an inheritance.

recul (m) : fall (in prices), recession, set-back, downturn.

(servitude de) reculement : easement.

reculer (v) : 1° *(perdre de sa valeur)* to drop, to relapse.
2° *(retarder une échéance)* to defer a payment.

récupération (f) : recuperation, recapture, (of debt) recovery.

valeur de — : salvage value.
récupérable *(somme)* : cash recovery.

récupérer (v) : to recoup, to recover, to salvage.
— *du matériel* : to salvage material.
— *une perte* : to recoup a loss.

récusant (m) : challenger.

récusation (f) : [J] challenge, objection, exception (to).
— *d'arbitre* : objection to a referee.
— *de juge, de jurés* : challenge.
— *pour cause de suspicion légitime* : challenging the judge or the jury under wellfounded suspicion that fair trial will not be given (« bias and prejudice »).
— *de témoignage* : impugnment of evidence.
— *de témoin* : exception to a witness.

(se) récuser (v) : to decline to express an opinion.
[J] to disclaim competence.
— *un juré* : to challenge.

recyclage (m) : retraining, reschooling.
recycler *(main-d'œuvre)* : to retrain.

rédaction (f) : *(d'un contrat, d'un jugement)* drawing up (a contract, a judgment), wording.
— *des actes translatifs de propriété* : conveyancing.

reddition (f) : surrender.
— *de comptes* : rendering of accounts.
[J] *action en* — *de compte* : action for an account.

redéploiement (m) : redeployment (of workers).
[F] — *interne des crédits disponibles* : reappropriation of funds (contrary to supplementary estimates).

redevable (a et m) : (a) accountable.
être — *de* : to be accountable, liable for, to owe s.o. a sum of money.
[F] (m) debtor, taxpayer.

redevance (f) : royalty, dues, rent, rental fee.
[J] — *emphytéotique* : long lease rent.
droit de possession moyennant — : right of property on payment of royalty.
— *(s) d'auteur* : author's royalties.
— *minière* : mining royalties.
moyennant — : for a money consideration, for a fee.
[A] tax on telephone lines, wireless sets, etc.

rédhibitoire (a) : [J] *vice* — : latent defect that makes a contract void.

rédiger *(un document)* (v) : to draw up (a document), to draft.
— *un réquisitoire* : to draw up an indictment.

redressement (m) : *(économique, des prix)* (economic) recovery (of prices).
— *fiscal* : adjustment of tax.

redresser *(un abus)* (v) : to redress (an abuse).
— *une erreur* : to rectify a mistake.
— *un tort* : to right a grievance.

réduction (f) : reduction, cutting down, abatement.
[J] — *de dons et legs* : abatement of gifts and legacies.
— *de peine* : mitigation of penalty.
action en — : action in abatement (by heirs).
[F] — *des impôts* : abatement of taxes, tax relief, tax cuts.
— *de capital* : writing down of capital.
— *de prix* : reduction in price.
— *du taux de l'escompte* : lowering of the bank-rate.
— *des salaires* : wage-cuts.

réduire (v) : to reduce, to diminish, to cut, to restrict.
— *les dépenses* : to curtail, to cut down expenses, to axe expenditure.
— *les stocks* : to run down.
— *fortement (investissements, coûts)* : to chop (investments, costs).

(taux) réduit (a) : restricted (rate).

rééducation professionnelle (f) : vocational rehabilitation.

réel (a) : real, actual.
[J] of real estate.
action — *(le)* : action in rem.
droits — *(s)* : chattels real.
garantie — *(le)* : material pledge, security.
offre — *(le)* : cash offer, payment in court.
revenu — : actual, real income.
saisie — *(le)* : attachment of real property.
subrogation — *(le)* : substitution of things.

réescompte (m) : rediscount.

réestimation (f) : revaluation.
— *de bilan* : revaluation of balance-sheet (in case of devaluation of currency).

réévaluation (f) : *(des stocks)* (stock) revaluation, reassessment.
— *de bilan* : recopier.
(see *réestimation de bilan*).
— *monétaire* : (fam.) rejig.

réévaluer (v) : to reassess, to recompute.
réévalué (a) : reassessed, recomputed.

réexpédition (f) : reshipment, retransmission, sending on, sending back, return.

réexportation (f) : re-exportation, re-export.
prime de − : drawback.

refaction (f) : [F] tret.
[D] − des droits de douane : reduction of custom duties.
[C] allowance, rebate, reduction.

réfection (m) : repair.

référé (m) : [J] summary jurisdiction and procedure in maters of special urgency.
jugement, ordonnance de − : injunction order in chambers.
juger en − : to try a case in chambers.

référence (f) : reference, referring, background.
− de banquier : banker's reference.
− (s) commerciales : trade reference.
− de fournisseur : trade reference.
position de − : reference position.
prix de − : marker price.
taux de − : base rate.
− (pour un taux d'intérêt) : peg.
par − à (qch.) : with regard to (sth.).
« − à rappeler » : « for reference please quote... ».
brut de − (pétrole) : marker crude.

référendaire (m) : chief clerk (of commercial court).

référer (m) : to refer, to ascribe.
− à qn d'une question : to refer a matter to s.o.
en − à la cour : to submit the case to the court.
[J] − un serment décisoire : to tender back a decisive oath.
se − à : to refer to, (U.S., rare) to reference to.

reflux (m) : ebb.
flux et − de capitaux : ebb and flow of capital.

réforme (f) : (fiscale) (tax) reform.

réformer (v) : to reform, to amend.
[J] − un jugement : to reverse a decision (by a court of appeals).
− une disposition : to overrule a provision.
[A] to discharge soldiers, to invalid out.

refouler (v) : to drive back.
[A] mesure de **refoulement** : expelling (an undesirable foreigner).

réfractaire (m) : absentee conscript or reservist.

refuge (m) : shelter, haven, hedge, refuge.
− fiscal : tax haven.
société − : tax haven company.
− contre l'inflation : hedge against inflation.
droit de − : right of sanctuary.

refus (m) : refusal.
− d'acceptation : refusal to accept.
− de faire des heures supplémentaires : overtime ban.
[J] − d'entretien : non-support.
− d'obéissance : contempt in facie curiae, out of court, contumacy.
− d'obtempérer : rebellion against a police officer.
− de paiement : refusal to pay, dishonour (by non payment).

refuser (v) : to refuse.
− d'accepter ou de payer un effet : to dishonour a bill.

réfutation (f) : rebuttal, refutal.

réfuter (v) : to rebut.

(droit) régalien (a) : sovereignty rights.

régent (m) : member of the Board of the Bank of France.

régie (f) : administration, control stewardship of property.
− des contributions indirectes : excise administration.
− des dépenses : advance payment of public expenses.
− du dépôt légal : copyright department.
− directe : state owned industry.
− intéressée : bonus to administrator on revenue from public property.
− des tabacs : tobacco monopoly.
entreprise en − : State controlled industry.
succession en − : succession in hands of the Public Trustee.

régime (m) : 1° government, form of government or administration, regime, governing laws. 2° system, scheme.
− (s) de communauté : antenuptial settlements based on communal estate.
− dotal (hist.) # marriage settlement in trust for the married woman.
− des eaux : waterways and water supply legislation.
− financier : financial system.
− matrimonial : type of antenuptial settlement.

– *de la séparation des biens :* antenuptial settlement maintaining separate the estates of husband and wife.
– *d'assurance :* system of insurance, insurance scheme.
– *de retraites :* graduated pension scheme.
– *de retraites vieillesse :* old-age pension scheme.
– *de faveur (accordé à certaines importations) :* preference (granted to certain imports), preference duties.
le – du travail : working conditions.

région (f) : region, area, district.

régional (a) : regional.

régir (v) : to administer, to manage, to direct (undertaking).

régisseur (m) : manager agent, steward.
régisseur de domaine : land-agent.

registre (m) : register, record, account-book.
– *des actionnaires :* stock-book, registers of members.
– *des bateaux :* Lloyd's Register.
– *du commerce :* Trade Register.
– *des délibérations (des procès-verbaux) :* minute-book.
– *d'écrou :* prison calendar.
– *(s) de l'état civil :* the registers of births, marriages and deaths.
– *foncier :* Land Register, terrier.
– *des jugements rendus :* docket.
– *de présence :* record of attendances, attendance book.
– *des réclamations :* claims book.
– *(s) sociaux :* corporation's book.
– *des transferts :* transfer register.

règle (f) : rule, law, principle.
– *(s) de procédure :* adjective law.
– *(s) relatives au calcul du revenu :* rules relating to computation of income.
(être) de – : (to be) the rule.
– *(s) prudentielles :* prudential control.

règlement (m) : 1° *(d'un compte, d'une contestation, d'un différend)* settlement (of an account, of a dispute), adjustment (of a difference). 2° *(paiement)* paying, paying off, settlement. 3° *(ordonnance)* regulations, rules.
– *administratif :* by(e)-law.
– *amiable :* amicable arrangement.
– *d'application :* decree stating measures for the enforcement of a law.
– *d'atelier :* shop rules.
– *(s) boursiers, douaniers :* stock exchange, customs regulations.
– *à la commande :* cash with order (C.W.O.).
– *comptant :* cash payment.
– *d'un compte, de dette :* settling of an account, a debt.
– *en espèces :* payment in cash.
– *forfaitaire (global) :* lump-sum settlement.
– *intérieur :* General Orders, standing orders.
– *judiciaire :* a) rule of court, b) administration of an insolvent debtor's affairs under the supervision of a court.
– *des juges :* referal of a case by a higher court to one of several competent lower ones.
– *en nature :* settlement in kind.
– *de partage :* sharing out.
– *du passif :* paying off, settlement of the liabilities.
– *de police :* police regulations.
– *de qualités :* record of proceedings before judgment.
– *de service :* book of standing instructions.
observer le – : to comply with the regulations.
[B] *jour du – :* settling day.
[CEE] *règlement du Conseil ou de la Commission :* (EEC) regulation of the Council or of the Commission.

(pouvoir) réglementaire : [J] right of public authorities to issue regulations and rules within their competency.

réglementation (f) : (bringing under) regulation, regulating.
– *des changes :* control of exchange (money).
– *des prix :* price regulation.

réglementer (v) : to regulate.

régler (v) : to regulate, to settle, to compose, to adjust, to rule, to dispose off.
– *une dette :* to discharge a debt, to square.
[C] – *les livres :* to balance the books.
– *sa dépense :* to restrict one's expenses.
– *un litige :* to settle a dispute.
– *un sinistre :* to settle a claim.
le cas doit être réglé par référence à : the case is to be dealt with by reference to.

régressif (a) : *(impôt)* regressive (tax).

régression (f) : regress, regression.

régularisation (f) : regularization.
[F] – *des dividendes :* equalization of dividends.
fonds de – : equalization fund.
[ASS] *clause de – :* clause in policy to the effect that insurance starts after payment of first premium.
régulariser *sa situation :* to pass from a de facto to a de jure situation.

régulier (a) : regular, proper, due.
document, reçu — : document, receipt in due form.

régulièrement (adv) : regularly, duly.
caisses — autorisées : approved funds.

réhabilitation (f) : rehabilitation.
[J] recovery of civil rights, discharge of a bankrupt.
réhabiliter qn : to reinstate s.o. in his rights.
réhabiliter un failli : to discharge a bankrupt.
se réhabiliter : to re-establish one's good name.

réimplanter (v) : to relocate.

réimporter (v) : to reimport.

réintégrande (f) : [J] action for recovery of real estate (i.e. action for ejectment).

réintégration (f) : reinstatement, restoration.
— de domicile : resumption of residence.
— du domicile conjugal : resumption of conjugal life (esp. wife's return home).

réintégrer (v) : to re-engage (a civil servant, an employee).

réinvestir (v) : to reinvest, to plough back.

réinvestissement (m) : reinvestment.

réitération (f) : feedback.

rejet (m) : rejection, disallowance.
taux de — : hurdle rate, rejection rate.

rejeter (v) : 1° *(une dépense)* to disallow (an expense).
2° *(un appel)* to dismiss (an appeal).
3° *(un projet de loi)* to throw out (a bill).

relâchement (m) *(dans la gestion)* : slack.

relâcher (v) : to release.
— un prisonnier : to set a prisoner free.
— sous caution : to let out on bail.

relais (m) : relay, [J] derelict land.
crédit — : bridging loan.
travail par — : work in shifts.

relance (f) : reflation, pump-priming *(de « priming »* : *amorçage d'une pompe).*
relancer l'économie : to reflate, to boost the economy.
relancer l'inflation : to refuel.

relatif (a) : relative, comparative.
— à : re, in respect of, accruing to.

relations d'affaires (f pl) : business connections.

relations (f pl) *extérieures* : (U.S.) external affairs.

relations publiques (f pl) : public relations.

relativité (f) : relativity.

relaxe (f) : [J] discharge of prisoner, order of nolle prosequi, by a court of summary jurisdiction or police court.
relaxer l'accusé des fins de toute poursuite : to discharge the accused on every count.

relégation (f) : [J] transportation for life.

relevé (m) : statement, account.
— de caisse : cash balance.
— de compte : statement of account.
— (s) journaliers : daily returns.

relevée (f) : afternoon.
audience de — : court-sitting p.m.

relèvement (m) : rise, raising.
— du taux d'escompte : raising of the bank rate.

relever (v) : to raise, to lift, to set (sth.) up again.
— un compte : to make out an account.
— le taux : to raise the rate.
— qn d'un contrat : to release s.o. from a contract.
— qn de ses fonctions : to relieve s.o. of his office.
— qn de son serment : to release s.o. from his oath.
— d'un tribunal : to fall within the competence of a court.

relief (m) : [J] *demande de —* : opposition in legal form to a judgment in absence and request for a new trial.

reliquat (m) : remainder.
— d'un compte : balance of an account.
— d'impôts : outstanding taxes.

remaniement (m) : change.
— de capital : reorganization of capital.

remanier (v) : to reshuffle.

rembours (m) : drawback.

remboursable (a) : redeemable, refundable, reimbursable, repayable.

remboursement (m) : reimbursement, refunding *(dettes, dépenses, etc.)* ; repayment, redemption *(bons, obligations, rentes)*, return *(emprunt)*.
[C] – *d'un effet :* retirement of a bill.
– *accéléré :* accelerated redemption.
livraison contre – *:* cash on delivery.
– *in fine :* bullet.

rembourser (v) : to repay, to pay off, to refund.
[F] *registre des chèques à* – *:* in-book.

remembrement rural (m) : rural consolidation.
– *des terres :* re-allocation, re-grouping of land.

réméré (m) : [J] *faculté de réméré :* option of repurchase.
vente à – *:* sale subject to right of vendor to repurchase.

remettre (v) : to deliver, to hand in (over), to remit.
– *une affaire :* to adjourn, to remand a case.
– *une lettre :* to deliver a letter.
– *(faire une remise de) 5 % :* to allow a (5 %) discount.
– *une dette :* to release, to cancel, to remit a debt.
– *(à une date ultérieure) :* to postpone, to put off, to adjourn.
– *en vigueur :* to reenact.

remise (f) : putting back, deferment.
[J] remission of penalty, tax, etc.
– *de cause, des débats :* adjournment, ampliation.
[C] [F] remittance, commission, discount, allowance, rebate, poundage.
– *sur marchandises :* trade discount.
– *de 10 % :* discount of 10 %.
– *d'impôt :* remission of tax.
– *gracieuse d'impôt :* forgiveness of tax.
contre – *(d'un document) :* on presentation (of a document).
– *de pouvoirs :* handing over powers.

remisier (m) : [B] intermediate broker.

remplacer (v) *(qqn)* : to deputize for (s.o.).

remplir (v) : to fill, to fill in, [U.S.] to fill out.
– *les conditions (requises) :* to fulfil the (required) conditions.
– *une déclaration d'impôt :* to fill in a tax return.

– *des engagements :* to meet one's commitments.
– *une formalité :* to comply with a formality.

remploi (m) : [J] reinvestment (in real estate or gilt-edged securities of proceeds of sale of wife's property).

rémunérateur (a) : remunerative, profitable, paying, rewarding.
emploi – *:* profitable (paying) employment.

rémunération (f) : consideration, payment, reward.

rémunératoire (a) : *intérêt* – *:* interest on anticipated payment (of taxes, etc.) (opp. *intérêt moratoire*).
legs – *:* legacy in consideration of services rendered.

rémunéré (a) : *(travail)* remunerated, paid (work).

rémunérer des services (v) : to pay for services.

renchérir (v) : to go up in price, to make dearer, to outbid s.o.

renchérissement *(de prix, du coût de la vie)* (m) : increase (in price, of the cost of living).

rendement (m) : yield, return, productivity, efficiency, output (of work), (agricultural) produce.
– *apparent de l'action :* dividend yield.
– *du capital :* return, yield of capital.
– *(s) d'échelle croissants :* increasing returns to scale.
– *des impôts :* yield of taxes.
– *(rentabilité) d'un investissement :* return on investment.
prime de – *:* output bonus, [U.S.] merit bonus.
– *réel de l'action :* earnings yield.
taux de – *:* rate of return.

rendre (v) : to give back, to pay back, to return.
– *compte :* to report.
– *la justice :* to dispence justice.
– *un jugement :* to pass judgment.
– *témoignage :* to bear witness, to give evidence, to testify.
– *un verdict :* to return a verdict.
prendre un **rendez-vous** : to make an appointment.

rendu (m) : [C] returned article.
faire un – *:* to return an article.
– *(s) sur ventes :* sales returns.

renflouer (v) : *(une entreprise)* to refloat (an enterprise).

renommée (f) : renown, fame, good name.
[J] *commune* – : common report.
preuve par commune – : hearsay evidence.

renoncer (v) : to renounce.
– *à un droit* : to waive a right.
– *à une prétention* : to renounce, to waive a claim.
– *à un projet* : to give up a project.
– *à une succession* : to renounce a succession.
– *par contrat* : to contract out.

renonciataire (m) : [J] releasee.

renonciateur (m) : [J] releaser.

renonciation (f) : renunciation.
[J] abnegation, waiver (of a right), disclaimer.
la – à un droit ne se présume pas : waiving of rights must be explicit.

renouveler (v) : to renew.
– *un bail* : to renew a lease.
[C] – *une commande* : to repeat an order.

renouvellement (m) : renewal.
– *des achats* : repeat purchasing.

rénovation (f) : [J] renewal of title.

renseignement(s) (m) : information, enquiry.
– *(s) à porter sur une déclaration d'impôts* : information to be reported on a tax return.
demande de – *(s) complémentaires* : request for further information.
fournir des – *(s)* : to supply particulars.
prendre des – *(s) sur* : to make enquiries about.
– *(s) pris* : upon enquiry.

renseigner (v) : to inform, to give information.

rentabilité (f) : profitability, profit-earning capacity, [U.S.] pay-off (of an investment), return.
seuil de – : profitless point.

rentable (a) : worthwhile, profit-earning, profitable.

rente (f) : revenue, rent ; annuity, pension, private income, allowance ; unearned income.
– *-accident* : invalidity pension.
– *amortissable* : redeemable annuity.
– *(consolidée) sur l'Etat* : (consolidated) Government stock (« consols »).
– *foncière* : ground rent.
– *d'invalidité* : disablement, sickness pension, benefit.
– *nominative* : registered Government stock certificates.
– *viagère* : life annuity.
– *viagère (constituée) à titre onéreux* : purchased annuity.
– *viagère avec réversion* : survivorship annuity, survivor annuity.
– *reversible* : two-life annuity.
– *de vieillesse* : old-age pension.
vivre de ses – *(s)* : to live on one's income.

rentier (m) : 1° *(portefeuilliste)* investor, stockholder ; 2° *(viager)* annuitant.
petit – : small investor.

rentrée (f) : receipt of money, collection of taxes, tax levies.
– *(s) fiscales* : revenue receipts.
– *de fonds* : coming in of money.
– *des impôts* : collection, receipt of taxes.
– *(s) et sorties de caisse* : cash receipts and payments.
– *(s) nettes de trésorerie* : cash receipts.

rentrer dans ses fonds (v) : to get one's money back.
– *(un article) sur un compte* : to reenter (an article) in an account.

renvoi (m) : reference (of a matter to some authority).
[J] transfer of a case to another court.
– *devant les assises* : to refer a case to the assize court.
– *pour complément d'information* : to adjourn the hearing of a case requiring a fuller investigation.
– *des débats* : adjournment, continuance.
– *des fins de la demande* : nonsuiting the plaintiff.
– *devant le juge compétent* : transfer of case to the competent court.
– *à huitaine* : adjournment for a week.
– *à une loi étrangère* : see *rattachement*.
– *en marge* : marginal alteration.
– *au principal* : joining a request for an interlocutory injunction to judgment on main issue.
– *d'un employé* : dismissal of an employee.

renvoyer (v) : to send back, to refer.
[J] *renvoyer un accusé des fins de la plainte* : to discharge a defendant.
– *une affaire devant une autre cour* : to change the venue of a trial.
– *le prévenu à une autre audience* : to remand the prisoner.
– *les parties dos à dos* : to dismiss both parties unsuited.

– *les parties à se pourvoir (devant le juge compétent)* : to disclaim competence.
– *le plaideur à sa demande* : to non-suit the plaintiff.
– *un employé* : to discharge, to dismiss an employee.
– *à une date ultérieure* : to postpone, to put off.
– *(à un autre article)* : to refer to (another article).

réorganisation (f) : reorganisation.

réparation (f) : reparation, redress, amends.
– *civile* : compensation.
– *de dommages* : damages.
– *(s) d'entretien* : keeping in repair.
– *légale* : legal redress.
– *(s) locatives* : tenantable, tenant's repairs.
– *des accidents de travail et maladies professionnelles* : workmen's compensation.
– *d'un préjudice* : reparation for an injury.

réparer (v) : to repair.
– *une omission* : to rectify an omission.

répartir (v) : to distribute, to apportion, (shares) to allot, to assess, to appropriate, to spread.
– *les dividendes* : to distribute dividends.
– *un marché* : to bottom out.
– *les pertes sur une certaine période* : to spread losses over a certain period.

répartiteur (m) : distributor.
[A] *commissaire-* – : assessor of taxes.
[ASS] adjuster, stater, of averages (also *dispacheur*).
– *des impôts* : assessor of taxes.

répartition (f) : dispatching.
[J] distribution of available assets, adjudication of bankrupt's debts.
[F] *lettre d'avis de* – : notice of allotment of shares.
libération à la – : payment in full on allotment.
– *des actions* : allotment of shares.
– *des bénéfices* : sharing out of profits.
– *des charges* : breakdown (of expenses).
– *des moyens de production* : allocation of resources.
– *de la population* : breakdown of population.
– *des impôts* : assessment of tax.

répercussion (f) : *(de la charge fiscale)* consequential effects, incidence (of the tax burden).

repère (m) *(économique)* : bench mark.
– *de référence* : marker.

répertoire (m) : index, table, catalogue, repertory.
– *d'adresses* : directory.
– *de jurisprudence* : summary of leading cases and decisions.
répertorier : to make a reference table, to index.

répétition (f) : repetition.
[J] claiming-back.
– *de l'indu* : recovery of payment made by mistake.
[B] *opération de* – : repeated bargain.

replacement de fonds (m) : reinvestment of funds.

répit (m) : respite.
jours de – : days of grace.

(se) replier (v) : to fall back.
[B] *l'action s'est repliée de ... à ...* : the share fell back from ... to ....

réplique (f) : retort, rejoinder, [J] (plaintiff's) replication.

répondant *(pour qn)* (m) : security, surety (for s.o.).

répondre (v) : to answer, to reply, to answer for, to guarantee, to be liable.
– *pour qn* : to answer for s.o., to be security for s.o.
– *aux conditions requises* : to meet the requirements.

réponse (f) : reply.
[J] – *au fond* : (defendant's) plea.
droit de – : right to reply in the public press to a statement which appeared in the paper concerned.
[B] – *des primes* : declaration of options.
jour de la – *des primes* : declaration day.

report (m) : [J] antedate of a bankruptcy, etc.
[C] [B] amount carried forward ; carrying forward, carry-over, carry-out, bringing forward, extension, contango, contango rate, continuation.
– *à nouveau* : balance carried down ; posting of the journal entries to the ledger accounts.
– *antérieur* : balance brought forward from last account.
– *déficitaire* : carry-forward of losses, [U.S.] deferral.
– *en arrière* (de déficit) : (loss) carry back.
taux de – : contango rate.
[ASS] – *de primes* : carry-over of rates.
[F] – *d'impôt* : tax carry-over.

reporter (v) : 1° to carry (forward, out, over), to bring forward, to extend, 2° (date) to defer, to postpone.
bénéfices **reportés** : profits carried forward.
stocks reportés : carry over stocks.
« à — » : balance brought forward.

reporteur (m) : receiver (of contango), taker (of stock).

repos (m) : rest.
de tout — : reliable.
valeur de tout — : safe investment, gilt-edged security.

repousser (v) : *(une offre, un projet de loi)* to throw out, to reject (a proposal, a bill), *(une affirmation)* to rebut (an assertion).

répréhensible (a) : objectionable, reprehensible.

reprendre (v) : 1° *(sa parole, une promesse)* to take back (one's word, a promise), 2° *(recommencer le travail)* to resume (work), 3° *(les affaires)* to improve, to look up, to revive, to rally. 4° *(monnaie)* to bounce.
— des marchandises : to reclaim goods.
les affaires **reprennent** : business in looking up.
les valeurs (minières) reprennent (ont repris) : (mining) shares rallied.

représentant (m) : representative, agent.
[J] representative heir.
— légal : legal representative.
[C] *— de commerce* : business agent, commercial traveller, salesman, representative.
— attitré : accredited representative.
chambre des —(s) : [U.S.] House of Representatives.

représentation (f) : representation.
[J] production, exhibition of documents.
délit de — d'enfant : abduction of minor.
— proportionnelle : proportional representation.
— successorale : inheritance by right of representation.
droits de représentation : dramatic fees.
[F] *frais de —* : entertainment expenses (costs).
[C] agency.
— exclusive : sole agency.

représenter (v) : to present again, to produce, to represent (a firm), to appear (for s.o. in court).

répressif (a) : repressive.
loi répressive : criminal law.
mesures répressives : repressive, coercive, deterrent measures.

réprimande (f) : [J] censure.

repris de justice (m) : [J] habitual criminal, old offender, « old lag ».

reprise (f) : retaking.
— de l'actif et du passif d'une entreprise : taking over a business with all its assets and liabilities.
— (d'activité) : renewal, resumption (of activity).
— des affaires : recovery, revival, upward trend of business.
— boursière (des cours) : rally (in price).
— à l'économie : trade, (industrial) recovery.
— d'instance : revival, adjourned term.
— d'un article défectueux par le fabricant : product recall.
— des invendus : taking back of unsold goods or copies.
— (s) matrimoniales : retaking of personalty not included in communal estate.
— du travail : resumption of work.
— de la vie commune : resumption of conjugal life (esp. wife's return home), restitution of conjugal rights.
exercice des —(s) par la femme du failli (hist.) : wife's right to recover personal property out of bankrupt's total estate.
— (dans transaction d'achat ou de location) : premium.
droit de — d'un local commercial (par le propriétaire) : right to recover possession, right of resumption of possession (by the owner).
valeur de — : surrender value.
[C] [F] *— d'une entreprise par ses salariés (R.E.S.)* : leverage management buy-out (L.M.B.O.).

reprochable (a) : reproachable.
[J] *témoin —* : exceptionable witness.

reproche (m) : [J] taking exception to.
—(s) de droits : impugnment of a statement (made by witness).
—(s) de fait : exception to witness.
témoin sans — : unexceptionable witness.
reprocher *un témoin, un témoignage* : to take exception to a witness, to impugn evidence.

reproduction (f) : reproduction.
[J] *droit de —* : copyright.

répudiation (f) : [J] *— de femme, de dette* : repudiation.
— d'héritage : relinquishment, renunciation.

réputation (f) : reputation, repute.

— 235 —

réputé (a) : considered as.
les déductions suivantes sont — (es) applicables : the following deductions are deemed applicable.

requérant (a et m) : (a) *partie — (e) :* claimant ; (m) plaintiff, petitioner, applicant.

requérir (v) : to ask for.
[J] to claim.
— *aide et assistance :* to demand assistance.
— *l'application de la loi :* to claim the enforcement of law.
— *la force publique :* to call out the military.

requête (f) : request, suit, petition.
[J] — *civile :* extraordinary procedure against a judgment (in case of a serious miscarriage of justice).
— *en défense :* defendant's plea.
— *de faillite :* petition in bankruptcy.
— *d'intervention :* third person's request to enter a suit as party.
— *de mesures provisionnelles :* petition for an interlocutory injunction.
— *en reprise d'instance :* petition for resumption of proceedings, revivor.
« *à la — de... »* : « at the suit of... ».

requis (a) : required, due.
les conditions — (es) : the required conditions, the requirements.

réquisition (f) : requisition, levy ; claim, demand.
[J] — *d'expropriation totale :* demand of owner for complete expropriation (the unsurrendered property being useless).
— *de mainlevée :* motion for grant replevin.
— *(s) du ministère public :* address of the public prosecutor to the court.
— *de taxe :* request by the ministerial officer to court for taxation of costs.
à la — de : on s.o.'s requisition.

réquisitionner (v) : to requisition.

réquisitoire (m) : [J] public prosecutor's charge (also *plaidoyer réquisitorial*).
— *à fin d'informer, introductif d'instance :* public prosecutor's demand to examining magistrate to make an enquiry about reported facts (first process).

rescision (f) : [J] rescission, annulment ; avoiding of contract (owing to mistake or misrepresentation).
action **rescisoire** (or (m) *rescisoire*) : action for annulment, rescissory action.

réseau (m) : *(routier, ferroviaire, de distribution)* (road, railway, distributing) network, system.

réservataire (a et m) : [J] *héritier — :* heir who cannot be totally disinherited, [U.S., Louisiana] forced heir.

réserve (f) : preserve, reservation, reserve, surplus, supply.
[J] 1° portion of inheritance that must devolve upon the heirs, (Scot.) legitim (of free movables), (also *réserve légale*). 2° protest in writing.
biens **réservés** *des époux :* separate estates of husband and wife.
à la — de... : saving..., with the reservation of.
sans — : unreservedly, unconditionally.
sous — : without prejudice.
sous toutes — (s) : with all (proper) reserves.
— *(s) de devises :* foreign exchange reserves.
fonds de — : reserve fund, segregated fund.
impôt sur les — (s) : accumulated earning tax.
incorporation des — (s) au capital : incorporation of reserves.
— *latente :* hidden reserve.
— *métallique :* gold cover (of the Bank of France).
— *(s) obligatoires :* required reserves, reserve asset, special deposit.
— *(s) pour risques en cours :* reserve to meet pending claims.
somme prélevée sur les — (s) : sum appropriated from the reserve.
— *pour pertes :* del credere account.
mettre en — : to put in reserve, to set by.
— *fédérale :* [U.S.] Federal Reserve.

réserver (v) : to reserve, to book (a seat, etc.).

résidence (f) : *(habituelle, principale, secondaire, effective, etc.)* (customary, principal, secondary, actual) residence.

résident (m) : resident.

résidu (m) : fraction, residue.
— *de compte :* amount still owing.

résiduel (a) : residual.
valeur — (le) : residual value.

résiliation (f) : cancellation ex nunc ; annulment, termination (of contract).

résilier (v) : to cancel.

résipiscence (f) : resipiscence.
venir à — : to show repentance, to return to a better frame of mind.

résistant (a) : strong.
valeurs — (es) : strong shares.

résolution (f) : [J] cancellation ex tunc ; avoidance of agreement owing to breach, cancellation of sale.
action en — : rescissory action.
clause **résolutoire** : defeasance, amendment, avoidance, resolutive clause.
condition résolutoire : resolutory condition.

résorber (v) : to resorb, to absorb.

respecter (v) *(un délai)* : to meet (a deadline).
— *les objectifs* : to keep in line with the targets.

responsabilité (f) : responsibility, liability.
[J] — *aquilienne* : liability with respect to wrongful damage done to property.
— *atténuée* : mitigated responsibility.
— *civile* : civil, vicarious liability (for damage caused by an agent).
— *envers la communauté (environnement)* : Public responsability.
— *contractuelle* : liability out of contract.
— *délictuelle* : liability for damage due to misfeasance or nonfeasance.
— *de l'employeur* : employer's liability.
— (s) *liées à une fonction* : functional responsibilities.
— *illimitée* : unlimited liability.
— *restreinte* : (civ.) restricted liability, (cr.) restricted responsibility.
— *au tiers* : liability to third person.
— *aux personnes transportées* : passenger liability.
poste de — : responsible position.
société à — *limitée* : limited liability company (Ltd).
avoir la — *(de)* : to be responsible (for).

responsable (a) : responsible.

responsable (m) : official, person in charge, supervisor.
— *des relations publiques* : Public Relations Officer (P.R.O.).
— *du service des sinistres* : claims adjuster.

resserrement (m) *du crédit* : squeeze, credit crunch.

resserrer (v) : *(le crédit)* to squeeze (credit).

ressort (m) : [J] competence, scope, province (extent of) jurisdiction ; (territorial) venue.
jugement en dernier —, *en premier et dernier* — : judgment without appeal, judgment by a court of first and last resort.
jugement en premier — : appealable judgment.
affaire **ressortissant** *à la juridiction consulaire* : case belonging to a commercial court.

ressortissant (m) : national (of a country).

ressource (f) : resource, commodity, means, supply.
la — *principale d'un pays* : the chief resource, the staple commodity of a country.
— (s) *existantes* : supplies in hand.
— (s) *exceptionnelles* : non recurring income.
— (s) *humaines* : human capital.
— (s) *non renouvelables* : exhaustible resources.

restant (a et m) : (m) (the) remainder, (the) rest.
— *d'un compte* : balance of an account.
(a) *l'héritier* — : the remaining heir.
« *poste* — (e) : « to be called for », [U.S.] « general delivery ».

reste (m) : remainder, rest, residue.

restitution (f) : restitution.
[J] reinstatement, rehabilitation, restoration *(de biens)*, refund *(d'argent)*.
— *d'indu* : return of payment made in error.
— (s) *civiles* : reinstatement, compensation for wrongful damage.
— *d'impôts* : return of taxes.

restreindre (v) : *(les exportations)* to limit, to restrain, to restrict (imports), to curtail.

restreint (a) : *(crédit, sens)* restricted (credit, meaning).

restrictif (a) : [J] *clause* **restrictive** : limitative clause.

restriction (f) : limitation, restraint, restriction.
— *du crédit* : credit squeeze.

restructuration (f) : restructuration, reshaping.

restructurer (v) : to reshape.

résultat (m) : outcome, result, issue.
— (s) : performance, findings.
— (s) *nets* : bottom line.
— (s) *statistiques* : statistical returns.

résulter de (v) : to arise from, to result from, to follow.

résumé (m) *de la séance* : summary of the proceedings.

résumer (v) : to summarize.
[J] **résumé** *des débats* : summing up, charging the jury.

rétablir (v) : *(l'ordre public, l'équilibre)* to restore (public order, equilibrium).
— *dans ses droits, réintégrer :* to reinstate.
— *les faits :* to set the facts.

retard (m) : *(dans la livraison)* delayed delivery.

retarder (v) : *(un paiement)* to delay, to defer, to put off (a payment).

retenir (v) : 1° *(une place)* to book (a seat...). 2° *(déduire)* to withhold, to retain, to stop.
impôt sur le revenu retenu à la source : income tax withheld at the source.

rétention (f) : [J] retaining (of pledge).
droit de — : possessory lien.

retenue (f) : withholding, deduction, docking (of pay), stoppage.
retraite soumise à — : superannuation subject to contributions.
faire une — sur salaires : to stop from wages.
impôt retenu à la source : withholding tax.
méthode (britannique) de — à la source en matière de salaires : P.A.Y.E. (pay-as-you-earn).

réticence (f) : [J] [ASS] non-disclosure, concealment.
avec — : half-heartedly, grudgingly.

retirer (v) *de l'argent :* to withdraw money.
— *le permis de conduire :* to disqualify s.o. from driving.
se — des affaires : to retire from business.
se — du marché : to pull out of the market.

retombées (f pl) *économiques :* spin-off effects.

rétorsion (f) : [J] *mesures de — :* retaliatory measures.

retour (m) : [J] reversion (of an estate).
— *à l'expéditeur :* return to sender.
[C] — « *sans frais* » : « no expenses ».
« — *sans protêt, sans frais* » : no protest note (on bill).
prêt à — de voyage : bottomry loan ; return of goods, of dishonoured bill, etc.
par — : by return.
— *au tireur :* refer to drawer (R.D.).

rétracter (v) : to retract, to recant.
[J] — *un arrêt :* to rescind, to revoke a decree.
se — : to withdraw a charge.

retrait (m) : 1° [J] redemption, repurchase. 2° withdrawal, repurchase. 3° cancelling.
— *d'une plainte, de fonds :* withdrawal of a complaint, of capital.
— *d'un permis :* cancelling of a licence.
— *du permis de conduire :* disqualification from driving.
— *d'un ordre de grève :* calling off a strike.
[F] *lettre de — :* letter of withdrawal.

retraite (f) : [A] retirement, pension, superannuation, [C] redraft, counterdraft.
— *anticipée :* early retirement.
pension de — : retiring allowance, old age pension.
pension de — militaire : retired pay.
prendre sa — à la limite d'âge : to retire (on a pension) on account of age.
— *d'office :* compulsory retirement.
régime de — : superannuation plan.
retenue pour — : superannuation contribution.

retraité (m) : pensioner, [U.S.] retiree.

retrayant (m) : repurchaser.

rétribuer (v) : to remunerate, to pay (a salary), to reward.

rétroactif (a) : retroactive.
lois rétroactives : ex post facto laws.

rétroaction (f) : feedback.

rétroactivité (f) : retroactivity.
la — d'un jugement : ex post facto effect of a judgment.
la loi n'est pas rétroactive : the law has no retrospective effect (unless expressly provided).

rétrocession (f) : [J] retrocession, reconveyance, redemise.
rétrocessionnaire : assignee.

rétrograder (v) : to demote (e.g. a civil servant).

retrouver (s'y) (v) : to break even.

réunion (f) : 1° reunion, connecting, coming together, meeting. 2° *(assemblage)* combination, lumping.
— *électorale :* gathering of voters.
— *plénière :* plenary sitting.
— *publique :* public meeting.
[J] *droit de — :* right of public meeting.

réunir (v) : to gather, to combine.
— *une assemblée :* to convene an assembly.
se — : to meet.

revalorisation (f) : revalorization.

revaloriser (v) : *(une monnaie)* to revalorize (a currency).

révélation (f) : revelation, disclosure.
[J] breach of secrecy.

revenant-bon (m) : [F] perquisites, [C] bonus.

revendeur (m) : reseller, jobber.

revendication (f) : claim, claiming, demand, vindication, (pl.) grievances.
[J] *action en* – : action for recovery of property.
action en – *immobilière* : action for declaration of title to land.
revendiquer ses droits : to vindicate, to assert one's rights.

revendre (v) : to sell again, to resell.

revenir (v) : to return, to come back, to recover, to cost.
– *sur un contract* : to renege.
– *à qqn (des intérêts, une somme)* : to accrue.

revente (f) : re-selling, resale, selling out.
– *d'un fonds de commerce* : resale of a business.
[F] – *de titres* : selling out of stock.

revenu (m) : income, revenue, increment.
– *accumulé* : accrual property.
– *(s) annexes* : supplementary income.
– *annuel* : yearly income.
– *brut* : gross income.
– *du capital* : unearned income, capital yield.
– *(s) des capitaux mobiliers* : income from securities.
– *casuel* : fortuitous income, perquisites.
– *disponible* : disposable personal income.
– *de l'Etat* : the public revenue.
– *exonéré de l'impôt* : untaxed income.
– *(s) fonciers* : income from real property.
– *gagné, non gagné* : earned, unearned income.
– *imposable* : taxable income.
– *d'intérêt de placements* : income from capital.
– *net (brut) global* : total net (gross) income.
– *locatif* : rental.
– *professionnel* : professional earnings.
– *provenant d'une occupation* : earned income.
– *sur revenu* : income frome income.
– *des sociétés* : partnership income.
– *du sol* : ground rent.
– *du travail* : earnings, earned income.
valeurs à – *fixe* : securities bearing fixed interest, bonds.
actions à – *variable* : equity shares.

revers (m) : [J] protective letter.

reversement à un compte (m) : transfer back to an account.

reversibilité (f) : [J] reversibility (of succession).

reversible (a) : reversible, revertible.

reversion (f) : [J] reversion, remainder, substitution.

revêtir *(d'une signature)* (v) : to sign.

(prix de) revient : cost price, prime cost.

réviser (v) : to revise.
– *en baisse* : to revise downwards.
– *en hausse* : to revise upwards.

révision (f) : revision, inspection.
[J] reconsideration of sentence, review of lawsuit.
conseil de – : military appeal court (also recruiting board).
pourvoi en – : appeal.
[C] audit of accounts, overhaul, review.

révocable (a) : revocable.

révocation (f) : [J] 1° removal, dismissal of an official.
2° rescinding.
– *d'acte administratif* : cancellation, countermanding of an administrative decision.
– *d'un décret* : revocation of an edict.
– *d'un sursis* : repeal of probation.
– *d'un testament* : revocation of will.

révolu (a) : completed.

révoquer (v) : *(un choix)* to revoke (an election).
– *une sentence* : to reserve.

richesse (f) : wealth.
[F] *signes extérieurs de* – : external signs of wealth.
« *la* – *des Nations* » *(Smith)* : « the Wealth of Nations ».
– *(s)* : riches.

risque (m) : risk, contingencies, hazards.
analyse du – : risk analysis.
– *assurable* : insurable risk.
– *(s) de guerre* : war-risks.
– *locatif* : tenant's third party risk.
– *de mer (fortune de mer)* : perils of the sea.
– *pour la santé lié à la nature du travail* : health hazard.
– *de vol* : theft risk.
– *professionnel* : professional risk.

gestion des — *(s)* : risk management.
[ASS] *police tous* — *(s)* : all-in policy (see also *assurance*).
(Ass. mar.) — *à l'escale* : calls risk.
à (ses) — *(s) et périls* : at (his) own risks.
aux — *(s) de l'expéditeur* : at sender's risks.
protection contre le — *de remboursement anticipé (d'une obligation, etc., en période de taux d'intérêt élevé)* : call protection.

ristourne (f) : [C] 1° refund, rebate, discount, 2° transfer of item to another book-keeping account.
— *d'une somme payée en trop* : return of an amount overpaid.
[ASS] annulment of marine insurance policy.

ristourner (v) : to refund, to return.

riverain (a et m) : (a) riparian (owner, property, etc.) ; (m) [J] adjacent owner, abutter.

rixe (f) : brawl, scuffle, affray.

robe (f) : gown.
[J] *gens de* — : Bar and Bench, the Robe.

portrait-**robot** (m) : composite mind picture.

rogatoire (a) : see *commission*.

rôle (m) : register, list, bill.
[J] roll (of court), cause-list.
— *cadastral* : register of landowners in the terrier.
— *des créances* : list of claims.
— *de l'équipage* : muster-roll, list of the crew.
affaire sortie du — : case designed to come up for judgment shortly.
— *des salaires* : list of salaries.
— *d'équipage* : crew list, ship's articles.

— *des cotisations établi par le contrôleur des impôts* : assessment book made out by the tax inspector.
à tour de — : in turn, by turns.

rompre un engagement (v) : to break an agreement.

(en chiffres) ronds : in round figures.

rotation de capitaux (f) : capital turnover.
— *des stocks* : turnover of stocks.

rouages (m pl) *de l'administration* : wheels of government.

roulement (de fonds) (m) : circulation (of capital).
fonds de — : working capital, trading capital, cash reserve.

roulement (m) *(du personnel)* : turnover (of staff).

route (f) : *(code de la)* highway (code).
frais de — : travelling expenses.

routiers (a) : *(transports)* road (transport).

rubrique (f) : heading.
— (f) *spécialisée (journal)* : special feature.

(concurrence) ruineuse : cut-throat competition.

rumeur (f) : *(publique)* [J] common report, hearsay.

rupture (f) : breach, break.
— *de contrat* : breach of contract.

rurale (a) : *(économie)* rural (economy).

NOTES

NOTES

S

sabotage (m) : 1° willful damage, malicious destruction, sabotage.
2° (work) scamping, botching, bungling.

saboter (v) : to scamp, to botch, to bungle, to sabotage.

sacrifier des titres (v) : to sacrifice stocks, to sell stocks at a big loss.
article **sacrifié** : article sold at a sacrifice, [U.S.] lossleader.

sain (a) : healthy.
[J] — *d'esprit* : compos mentis, of sound mind.
— *et sauf* : safe and sound.

saisie (f) : execution.
[J] attachment *(immeubles, navires)*, distraint *(meubles)*.
[A] embargo *(navires)*, seizure *(contrebande, pièces à conviction, etc.)*.
— *-arrêt* : attachment, garnishment.
— *-brandon* : distraint by seizure of crops.
— *-conservatoire* : arrestation, sequester of property.
— *-exécution* : distress, execution by sale of debtor's chattels.
— *foraine* : distraint upon the goods of a person living in furnished rooms, foreign attachment.
— *-gagerie* : writ of execution on tenant's furniture and chattels.
— *d'une hypothèque* : foreclosure of a mortgage.
— *immobilière* : attachment of real property.
— *judiciaire* : seizure under legal process.
— *pour loyer* : distress.
— *mobilière* : distraint.
— *-revendication* : seizure under a prior claim.
opérer une — : to levy a distress.
ordonnance de — : garnishee order, warrant for attachment, writ of execution.
saisi : distrainee.

saisine (f) : [J] seisin.

saisir (v) : to catch, to seize, to grab, to grasp, to lay hold, to take hold of, to submit.
[J] to seize, to attach *(immeubles)*, to distrain upon *(meubles)*, to attach *(navires)* ; to vest.
— *qn au corps* : to attach s.o. for debts.
— *qn d'un héritage* : to vest s.o., with an inheritance.
— *la justice* : to go to law.
— *un tribunal d'une affaire* : to refer a matter to a court.
se — *de qch* : to possess oneself of sth., to seize upon sth., to attend to sth. (see also *mort*).

saison (f) : season.
haute — : peak season.
morte — : slack time, dull period.
baisse **saisonnière** : seasonal drop.
emploi, chômage **saisonnier** : seasonal employment, unemployment.

salaire (m) : wages, pay (of manual worker) ; retribution.
— *de base* : basic salary, basic pay.
— *de départ (débutant)* : starting salary.
— *à la pièce* : piece-work salary.
— *minimum garanti (de croissance)* : minimum guaranteed wage, [U.S.] guaranteed annual income.
— *net* : take-home money.
— *au rendement* : efficiency wages, [U.S.] incentive wages.
— *unique* : see *allocation*.
blocage des —(s) : wage freeze.
échelle mobile des —(s) : sliding wage scale, [U.S.] wage escalation.
hausse des —(s) : wage increase.
politique des —(s) : wage(s) policy.
zone des —(s) : wage zone.

salarial (a) : wage-, expenditure.
masse —(e) : wages bill.
revenus **salariaux** : earned income.

salariat (m) : 1° the wage-earning classes ; 2° the social condition of the working classes.

salarié (a et m) : (a) salaried, wage-earning. (m) wage-earner, [U.S.] wage worker.

salle (f) : room, hall.
— *d'audience* : court-room.
— *des ventes* : auction room.

salon (m) *(de l'auto, etc.)* : show.

salubre (a) : healthy, healthful.

salubrité (f) : *(des ateliers)* salubrity, sanitation (of workshops).

sanction (f) : 1° approbation, assent.
2° sanction.
—(s) *civiles* : consequences in law.

— *disciplinaire*: summary punishment.
— *fiscale*: tax penalty.
— *légale*: sanction of the law.
— *pécuniaire*: fine.
— *pénale*: penalty, coercive weapon.
— *(s) pénales*: vindicatory, punitive sanctions.
— *rémunératoire*: remuneratory sanction.

(les liens du) sang: the ties of kindred.

sanitaire (a): sanitary.
règlements — *(s)*: health regulations.

sans: no.
action — *valeur nominale*: no par stock.
— *garantie*: unsecured.
lettre — *date*: undated letter.
— *préavis*: without notice.

santé (f): health.
demande de — : health demand.

donner (v) **satisfaction**: to meet the requirements, to come up to (s.o.'s) expectations.

saturé (a): saturated, overstocked, glutted.
le marché est — : the market is overstocked, glutted, has reached saturation point.

sauf: except, excepted, unless.
— *avis contraire*: unless (I) hear to the contrary.
— *dispositions contraires*: unless contrary dispositions can be applied.
— *erreur ou omission*: errors and omissions except.

sauf-conduit (m): pass, safe-conduct.

sauter (v) *sur une offre*: to leap at an offer.

sauvage (a): wild.
grève — : wildcat strike.

sauvegarde (f): safe-guard.
[J] *clause de* — : saving clause.

sauvegarder (v): *(des intérêts)* to safeguard, to protect (interests).

savoir-faire (m): ability.
— *technique*: know-how.

sceau (m): seal.
— *de l'Etat*: State Seal.
le Garde des — *(x)*: the Minister of Justice.
[A] *les* — *(x)* # the Great Seal.
droit de — : seal duties.

scellé (a et m): (a) sealed, under seal.
(m) imprint of official seal.
apposer, lever des — *(s)*: to affix, to remove the seals.
[J] *bris de* — *(s)*: breaking of seals (a circumstance aggravating an offence).

(faire des) scènes à...: to pick quarrels with...

sciemment (adv): knowingly.

scinder (v): to divide.
[F] *actions* **scindées**: split stocks.
— *une société*: to spin off a company.

scission (f): scission.
faire — : to secede (from).

script (m): script.

scriptural (a): fiduciary, representative.
monnaie — *(e)*: bank money, representative money.

scrutin (m): poll; voting ballot.

secourir (v): to help, to aid, to relieve.
— *une entreprise*: to back up an undertaking.

secours (m): help, aid.
— *pour charges de famille*: child bounty, family allowance.
— *à domicile*: outdoor relief.
fonds de — : emergency fund.
— *de grossesse*: allowance to pregnant women.
société de — *mutuels*: benefit society, friendly society.

secret (a et m): (a) secret, (m) secrecy.
comité secret: private meeting (of Parliament).
fonds — *(s)*: appropriation at the discretion of the Government.
— *bancaire*: bank secrecy.
— *postal*: secrecy of correspondence.
— *professionnel*: professional secrecy, privileged communications.
— *du vote*: secrecy of the polls.
mettre un prisonnier au — : to put a prisoner in solitary confinement.

secrétaire (m): secretary.
— *général de ministère*: permanent secretary.
— *général de société*: company secretary.
— *de mairie*: town clerk.
— *particulier*: private secretary, confidential clerk.

secrétariat (m): secretariat, secretary's office, typing pool.
travail de — : secretarial work.

secteur (m) : *(de l'économie)* sector (of the economy), area.
— *primaire* : primary sector.
— *privé* : private (personal) sector.
— *public* : public sector, publiclyowned enterprise.
— *tertiaire* : service industries, tertiary industrial activity.
— *de vente* : sales area, trading area.

section *(administrative)* (f) : branch of a department.

sécurité (f) : safety, security.
— *publique* : public safety.
— *routière* : road safety.
— *sociale* : national insurance, [U.S.] social security.
— *sociale privée* : (U.S.) blue cross.
régime de — *sociale* : social security scheme.
société de — : guarantee society.
marge de — : safety margin.

sédition (f) : mutiny.

séduction (f) : seduction, enticement.
[J] — *dolosive* : deceitful enticement with intention to injure interests protected by law or to wrong s.o.
— *de témoins* : subornation of witnesses.
rapt par — : abduction with consent.

ségrégation (f) : segregation.

seing (m) : sign manual.
[J] *acte sous* — *privé* : private deed, simple contract, private agreement, signed but not sealed or witnessed.
blanc- — : signature to a blank document.

séjour (m) : stay.
[J] *interdiction de* — : local banishment.
— *habituel* : (permanent) abode.
durée de — : period of stay.
lieu de — : place of abode.
[A] *autorisation, permis de* — : permission to reside.

sélectif (a) : selective.

sélectionner (v) : *(des placements)* to select (investments).

selon : according to.
— *le cas* : as the case may be, depending on.
— *les dispositions du paragraphe* : under the provisions of paragraph.

semaine de travail normale : standard working week.

semestriel (a) : half-yearly.

(démence) sénile : insanity.

(au) sens de : *(l'article...)* within the meaning assigned by (section...).

sensible (a) : appreciable, marked.
augmentation — : appreciable rise.
amélioration — : marked improvement.

sentence (f) : sentence, judgment.
— *arbitrale* : award, settlement by arbitration.
— *capitale, de mort* : death sentence.
— *criminelle* : penalty.
— *par défaut* : sentence in absence, by default, contumacy.
prononcer une — : to pass a sentence.
rendre une — *arbitrale* : to make an award.

séparation (f) : separation.
[J] — *amiable* : separation agreement, voluntary separation (of married couple).
— *de biens* : 1° separate estates by antenuptial settlement, 2° separation of estate, which may be :
a) — *de biens judiciaire* : judicial separation.
b) — *de biens légale* : legal separation, resulting ipso jure from separation from bed and board.
— *de corps* : a mensa et thoro separatio, separation from bed and board, limited divorce.
— *des patrimoines* : separation of inherited property from the former estate of the heir (at the request of the creditors of the deceased, thus getting precedence over those of the heir).
— *des pouvoirs (hist.)* : principle of three separate powers of government : the legislative, the judiciary, the executive (described by Montesquieu).

séquestration (f) : 1° [J] sequestration of goods, 2° illegal restraint, duress of imprisonment.

séquestre (m) : 1° embargo ; 2° [J] (civ.) sequestration of goods (as a deposit, or while waiting for judicial determination of ownership).
(cr.) — *des pièces à conviction* : seizure of exhibits (as a protective measure).
[A] — *douanier* : seizure by customs.
mettre un bien sous — : to sequester, to sequestrate property.
administrateur- — : administrator, trustee of sequestrated property; depositary, receiver, sequestrator.

série (f) : series, set, succession.
— *d'articles* : line of goods.

fabrication en — : mass production, standard production, wholesale manufacture.
fin de — *(s)* : remnant, oddments.
hors — : especially manufactured.
(article) de — : standardized, [U.S.] run-of-the-mill (article).
— *(s) chronologiques* : time series.

serment (m) : oath.
[J] — *affirmatif, assertoire* : assertory oath.
— *de crédibilité, de crédulité* : oath administered to the widow and heirs of a debtor, to ascertain if to their knowledge a claim is still justified.
— *déclaratoire de manifestation révélatoire* : oath of insolvency.
— *décisoire* : decisive oath, sworn at the demand of the other party, upon which the decision of the court will be based.
— *de fidélité* : loyalty oath.
— *in litem, supplétif, supplétoire* : oath administered to parties in case of insufficient evidence.
— *promissoire* : promissory oath.
affirmer, certifier, sous la foi du — : to declare on oath, to make an affidavit.
assermenter : to administer, to tender the oath.
déférer le — *à qn* : a) *(sp. aux témoins)* to swear s.o., b) *(sp. au jury)* to swear s.o. in.
faire un faux — : to commit perjury.
prêter — : to take an oath.
déclaration sous — : sworn statement, affidavit.
fonctionnaire **assermenté** : sworn official.
[F] solemn confirmation of return of certain taxes.

serpent monétaire (C.E.E.) : (E.C.C.) monetary snake.

serré(a) *(scrutin)* : close (vote).

service (m) : service, department, administrative authority.
— *des achats* : purchasing department.
— *actif* : on the active list.
— *armé* : fighting services.
— *auxiliaire* : subsidiary troops.
— *des coffres-forts* : safekeeping department.
— *commandé* : on duty.
— *commandes clients* : [U.S.] sales order department.
— *commercial* : commercial, customer service.
— *de la comptabilité* : accounts, accounting department.
— *(s) concédés* : services under contract.
— *du contentieux* : legal department.
— *des domaines* : administration of state property.
— *des douanes* : board of customs and excise.
— *des eaux* : water supply.

— *d'un emprunt* : paying of interest on a loan.
— *(s) fonciers* : charges on real estate.
— *(s) des impôts, fiscaux* : board of inland revenue, tax authorities.
— *du personnel* : personnel (staff) department.
— *de presse* : press copies.
— *(s) publics* : public utilities, [U.S.] utilities.
— *des renseignements* : Intelligence Service, [U.S.] Central Intelligence Agency (C.I.A.).
— *des sinistres* : claims adjustment department.
— *social* : welfare department.
— *après vente* : after-sale service, finished goods and service departments.
le — *de la voirie* # the Highways Department.
chef de — : departmental head.
contrôle de — : duty roster.
louage de — *(s)* : (locatio operarum) engagement (of workmen, servants).
règlement de — : standing orders.
être de — : to be in attendance.
servir *une rente* : to pay an annuity.

serviteur (m) : servant.

servitude (f) : [J] easement, encumbrance, charge on real estate, covenant running with the land, servitude.
(may be affirmative, when it permits an otherwise unpermitted act by the owner of it, or negative, when it imposes on the owner of the servient tenement forbearance of an otherwise permissible action).
a) *(espèces de* — *(s)* : kinds of easements).
— *apparente* : apparent, patent, conspicuous easement (with structures, outward works, etc.).
— *continue* : permanent charge (e.g. the obligation non aedificandi).
— *conventionnelle* : agreed easement.
— *discontinue* : easement to be taken advantage of by act of man (e.g. the right of way).
— *légale* : legal curtailment of ownership.
— *naturelle* : charge inherent to a site (e.g. the right of way).
— *non-apparente* : non-apparent charge (e.g. the obligation non aedificandi).
— *réelle* : praedial encumbrance.
— *rurale* : rural encumbrance.
— *urbaine* : urban encumbrance.
b) *(diverses* — *(s)* : some easements).
— *d'abreuvoir* : freedom of watering-place.
— *d'affouage* : common of estovers.
— *du chemin de halage* : freedom of tow-path.
— *de drainage* : acquae-ductus.
— *d'écoulement des eaux usées* : right to an unhampered outflow of water.
— *d'égout des toits* : stillicidii recipiendi.
— *d'irrigation* : right to irrigation (passing through another's property).

— *de marchepied* : right of way along river banks.
— *de mitoyenneté* : obligations resulting from joint ownership (wall, hedge, etc.).
— *non aedificandi* : prohibition to build.
— *altius non tollendi* : level not to be exceeded by structures.
— *oneris ferendi* : right to erect an abutting wall.
— *de pacage* : jus pascendi, grazing rights.
— *de passage* : right of way.
— *de parcours et vaine pâture* : right of common.
— *de reculement* : obligation to fall into the building line.
— *de voirie* : limitations imposed by the Highways Department.
— *de vue* : ne luminibus officiatur, right to have windows not shut off from light.
assiette de la — : the place to which an easement applies.
extinction d'une — *par le non-usage* : usucapio libertatis, extinguishment of an easement by non-use.

session (f) : session, sitting.
[J] term at law-courts.
— *de relevée* : court-sitting p.m.
— *du tribunal d'instance* : petty sessions.

seuil (m) : lower limit.
— *de rentabilité* : break-even point.

seul *responsable* (m) : solely responsible.

sévices (m pl) : ill-treatment.
[J] cruelty (esp. cruelty towards dependents).

si : — *perte il y a* : loss, if any.

sicav (voir : « *société* »).

sidérurgie (f) : iron and steel metallurgy.

siège (m) : [J] the judge's bench, the seat of a court.
magistrat du — *(assis)* : judge.
magistrature du — *(assise)* : the judges, the Bench.
le — *du tribunal est fait* : the court has formed an opinion.
jugement rendu sur le — : judgment delievered from the bench without leaving the court-room.
[C] — *principal* : head office.
— *de la direction d'une société* : place of management of a company.
— *social* : registered office (of company).
le Saint- — : the Holy See.

sieur (m) : [J] *le* — *Untel* : Mr. So-and-so.
[C] *notre* — *Untel* : Our Mr. So-and-so.

sigle (m) : acronym.

signalement (m) : description *(d'une personne)*, particulars *(d'une voiture)*.
donner le — *de qn* : police description of a person wanted.

(fiche) signalétique : descriptive form.

signataire (m) : signer, subscriber.

signature (f) : signature, sign-manual.
— *par procuration* : power to sign.
— *sociale* : signature committing the company.
apposer sa — *à un acte* : to set one's hand to a deed.
attester, certifier, légaliser une — : to authenticate a signature.
avaliser la — : to guarantee an endorsement.
avoir la — : to be empowered, to be authorized to sign.
conférer, donner la — : to give a proxy.
jeton de — : signing fee.
signataire : signatory.

signe (m) : sign.
— *(s) distinctifs* : special particularities.
— *(s) extérieurs de richesse* : external criteria, indicia, signs of wealth.

signer (v) : to firm, to sign.
— *définitivement un contrat* : to firm up a contract.

significatif (a) *(qui ne peut être expliqué par le hasard)* : significant.

signification (f) : signification, meaning, sense, import.
[J] notification, service, serving of writ.
— *par avis public* : notification by poster, notice in the press, etc.
— *des défenses* : discovery of the defendant's plea.
— *à domicile* : service at place of abode.
— *de jugement* : notification of judgment.
— *à personne* : personal service.
acte de — : writ, process.
signifier *un acte d'occuper* : to intimate to the other party one's power to act as attorney in fact (or barrister, solicitor, counsel of record).
signifier un arrêt : to serve a notice.
signifier un avis d'opposition : to serve a notice of objection.
signifier un congé : to give notice to quit.

simple (a) : mere.
avaries — *(s)* : particular average.

simplification (f) : streamlining.

(déclaration) simplifiée : simplified tax return.

simulation (f) : simulatio, feint, *(milit.)* malingering.
— *d'apport en nature* : simulation of contribution in kind.
[J] — *bilatérale* : agreed simulation, collusion.
— *simple, absolue* : sham transaction (and corresponding contract, deed, etc.).
— *unilatérale* : mental reservation.
exception de — : plea of simulation.
nullité pour cause de — *bilatérale* : voidance for agreed simulation.

simulé (a) : bogus, sham.
vente — *(e)* : bogus sale.
[C] *facture* — *(e)* : pro forma invoice.

simultané (a) : simultaneous.

sinistre (m) : disaster, catastrophe, calamity (esp. fire, earthquake, shipwreck), damage, loss.
[ASS] the contingency insured against.
— *majeur* : very serious disaster possibly entailing abandonment (e.g. a shipwreck).

sinistré (a et m) : (a) damaged, wrecked.
(m) the victim of a disaster.

site (m) : site.
protection des — *(s)* : beauty spot protection.

situation (f) : 1° situation, state, condition, report ; 2° *(emplacement)* location, site.
— *de caisse* : cash position.
— *dépendante* : dependent condition ;
— *difficile* : bind condition, (to be) in a bind.
— *de famille* : family, marital status, circumstances.
— *de fin de mois* : monthly report.
— *(solvabilité) financière d'une entreprise* : financial standing of a firm.
— *de fortune* : financial standing.
— *géographique* : location.
— *hebdomadaire (de la Banque de France)* : weekly report (of the Bank of France).
— *indépendante* : independent position.
— *juridique* : legal status.
— *du marché* : market report.
— *personnelle* : personal data or history.
— *de place* : Stock Exchange report.
— *sociale* : social status, station in life.
— *de trésorerie* : cash position, statement of finances.
rapport de — : statement, business survey, written statement.

social (a) : social.
actif, avoir — : company's assets.

année — *(e)* : (company's) trading year.
apport — : initial share, capital.
assistance, assurance, Sécurité — *(s)* : Social Security.
assistante — *(e)* : welfare worker.
capital — : registered capital, joint stock, capital stock, capital assets.
domicile, siège — : registered office.
nom social, raison — *(e)* : name, style of a firm.
signature — *(e)* : signature committing the company.

société (f) : company, firm, partnership, society, corporation.
— *par actions, anonyme* : joint-stock company.
— *des auteurs* : author's union, society.
— *de bienfaisance* : charity, relief committee.
— *à capital variable* : company with variable capital.
— *en commandite simple, en participation* : sleeping partnership.
— *en commandite par actions* : partnership limited by shares.
— *commerciale* : commercial company.
— *concessionnaire* : statutory company.
— *contrôlée par le gouvernement ou les municipalités* : [U.S.] public corporations.
— *cotée en bourse* : listed company.
— *de crédit* : loan society (bank).
— *d'entreposage* : warehouse company.
— *fantôme* : bogus company.
— *fermière* : company to which state property is farmed out.
— *fiduciaire* # trust company.
— *foncière* : estate-agency, [U.S.] realtors.
— *immobilière (de prêts à la construction)* : building society.
— *d'investissement à capital variable (SICAV)* : unit trust, mutual fund, open-end investment fund.
— *d'investissement* : investment trust.
— *mère* : parent establishment.
— *minière* : mining company.
— *nationalisée* : [U.K.] public corporation.
— *de navigation maritime, aérienne* : shipping company, air transport company.
— *en nom collectif* : private company.
— *de participations, de portefeuille* : holding company.
— *à participation salariale* : co-partnership.
— *en partie possédée par une autre (généralement de 20 à 49 % des actions)* : associated company.
— *de prêts* : (friendly) loan society.
— *de prévoyance* : provident society, association.
— *de réassurance* : reinsurance company.
— *relais* : base company.
— *à responsabilité limitée* : limited liability company (Ltd.).
— *sans but lucratif* : non-profit association.

— *de secours mutuels*: benefit, friendly society.
— *secrète*: secret society, organization.
— *sœur*: sister company.
— *sportive*: sporting union.
— *reconnue d'utilité publique*: institution officially recognized as serving the public interest.
acte de — : deed of partnership, memorandum of association.
constituer une — : to form, to incorporate a company.
dissoudre, liquider une — : to dissolve, to liquidate a company.
part de — : share in the capital of a company.
personnalité juridique des —(s) : legal status of companies.

socio-professionnel (a) : occupational, social and economic.

sœur
— *par adoption*: adoptive sister.
— *aînée*: elder, eldest sister.
— *cadette*: younger, youngest sister.
— *consanguine*: half-sister on the father's side.
— *légitime*: legitimate sister.
— *naturelle*: half-sister born out of parental wedlock.
— *puînée*: younger sister, sister(s) born after the first-born child.
— *utérine*: half-sister on the mother's side.
belle- — : sister-in-law.
demi- — : half-sister.
— *de lait*: foster-sister.

soit-communiqué (ordonnance de): [J] order of discovery.

solde (m) : [C] balance, remainder.
— *actif, en bénéfice, bénéficiaire*: positive, credit balance.
— *ancien*: old balance.
— *en banque*: bank credit.
— *budgétaire de plein emploi*: full employment budget surplus.
— *de caisse*: cash balance.
— *de compte*: balance of account.
— *créditeur*: credit balance.
— *débiteur*: debit balance, balance due.
— *déficitaire*: debit balance.
— *de dividende*: final dividend.
— *d'édition*: remainders, remainder line in books.
— *de marchandises*: surplus stock, remnant.
— *à nouveau, reporté*: balance carried, brought down, carried forward.
— *passif*: negative debit balance.
« *en* — » : « to clear ».
paiement pour — : payment of balance, final instalment.
prix de — : bargain prices.
vente de —(s) : clearance sale.
[B] — *acheteur*: buyer's balance.
— *vendeur*: seller's balance.

solde (f) : military pay.
—(s) *et indemnités*: ordinary pay and allowances.
— *de non-activité*: unemployed pay.
— *de transaction*: transaction balance.
officer en demi- — : officer on half pay.

solder (v) : 1° to pay.
2° [C] a) to settle, to discharge, to pay (off) (an account), b) to sell off surplus stock, c) to remainder (books).
— *un découvert*: to pay off an overdraft.

solidaire (a) : joint and several, liable, responsible.
cautionnement — : joint guaranty bond.
cautions conjointes et —(s) : sureties liable jointly and severally.
engagement — : joint covenant.
obligation — : joint obligation.
responsabilité conjointe et — : joint and several liability.

solidairement (adv) : jointly and severally.

solidarité (f) : [J] joint liability.
— *active*: plurality of creditors, any one being entitled to claim full payment.
— *légale*: joint liability prescribed by law.
— *passive*: plurality of debtors, any one being liable to the extent of the debt (several covenant).

solliciter (v) : *(des commandes)* to solicit (orders).

solution (f) : *(de continuité)* solution, break (of continuity).
— *d'un différend*: settlement of dispute.

solvabilité (f) : ability to pay, solvability, solvency.

solvable (a) : solvent.

sommaire (a) : summary.
[J] *jugement, procédure* — : summary judgment, proceedings.
justice — # Jedburgh justice, Lynch law.

sommation (f) : [J] summons *(de faire qch.)*, notice *(d'exécuter un contrat)*.
faire les trois —(s) *légales* # to read the Riot Act.
[F] — *de payer*: process served after two reminders to recalcitrant taxpayer by the Inland Revenue, followed by immediate exe-

cution notwithstanding opposition.

somme (f): amount, sum.
− *déductible de l'impôt sur le revenu*: tax write-off.
− *forfaitaire*: lump sum.
− *totale*: aggregate amount, total amount, sum total.

somptuaire (a): (hist.) [J] *loi somptuaire*: sumptuary law.
dépenses −*(s)*: sumptuary expenses.

sondage (m): test.
enquête par −: sample survey, (gallup) poll, opinion poll.
sonder: to poll.

sonnant (a): resounding.
espèces −*(es) et trébuchantes*: hard cash.

sophistication (f): [J] adulteration of foodstuffs (esp. of wine).

sortant *(administrateur)* (a): retiring (director).

sortie (f): exit, going out.
[J] − *du rôle*: case designed to come up for judgment shortly.
[D] *droits de* −: export duty.
[C] exportation (of goods).
−*(s) de caisse*: expenses, outgoings.
− *de fonds*: cash expenses, payments; outgoings.

sortir (v): to go out, to leave, to retire.
− *de la question*: to depart from the subject.

soubresauts (m pl) *du marché*: ups and downs.

souche (f): lineage, lineal descent.
[J] *partage, succession par* −: sharing out succession per stirpes.
[C] conterfoil, [U.S.] stub *(de chèque, etc.)*.
carnet, livret à −: counterfoil book, [U.S.] stub book.
faire −: to found a family.

(faire la) soudure: to bridge the gap.

souffrance (f): suffering.
[J] tacit permission, sufferance.
jour, vue de −: window or light overlooking neighbour's property, on sufferance (but mostly a legal right, see *servitude de vue*).
indemnité pour −*(s) endurées*: pretio doloris.
[C] suspense, abeyance, demurrage.
délai, jours de −: days of grace.
dette en −: outstanding debt.
chèque, facture, lettre de change demeurés en
−: unpaid invoice, cheque, refused bill.
colis en −: parcels hung up in transit or awaiting delivery.
envoi, marchandises en −: shipment in abeyance.
travail en −: work in abeyance.

soulte (f): balance, balance in cash, the difference in value to be paid in cash in an exchange, « boot », cash distribution (in the case of an exchange of shares).

soumettre (v): *(à l'arbitrage, à l'examen)* to subject (to arbitration, to an examination).
− *une demande*: to lay a request (before...).
(être) **soumis** *à l'impôt (à l'impôt sur le revenu)*: (to be) subject to taxation, liable (to income tax).
soumis aux lois: law-abiding.

soumission (f): submission (of rebels, etc.).
[J] [A] undertaking, bond.
− *de juridiction*: agreement of parties to submit the dispute to a tribunal not entertaining jurisdiction.
acte de −: a) guaranty given (in lieu of bail) for an individual, b) admission by a taxpayer of an infringement in excise matters.
[C] tender (for public works).
− *cachetée*: sealed tender.
offre de −: call for tenders.
soumissionner: a) to send in a tender, b) [F] to underwrite.
soumissionner à un emprunt: to tender for a loan.

soumissionnaire (m): party tendering for work on contract, tenderer.
[F] underwriter.

sourçage (m): sourcing.

source (f): *(de revenu)* source (of income).
retenir un impôt à la −: to withhold a tax at the source.
retenue à la −: withholding tax.
− *minérale, thermale, de pétrole*: mineral, hot, oil-spring.

sourceur (m), **sourceuse** (f): sourcing expert.

sous: under(neath), below, within (the time of).
− *l'inculpation de*: on a charge of.
− *peine de*: on pain (penalty) of.

sous −:
− *-affrètement* (m): sub-chartering.
− *-agent* (m): sub-agent.
− *-commission* (f): sub-committee.
− *-développée*: underdeveloped (area).
− *-estimation (sous-évaluation)* (f): underestimation (undervaluation).
− *-estimer (sous-évaluer)* (v): to underestimate (to undervalue).

— *-ferme* (f) : under-lease (of land).
— *-locataire* (m) : sub-tenant.
— *-location* (f) : sub-tenancy, subletting (underletting).
— *-louer* (v) : to sublet (to underlet).
en — *-main* : under-hand.
— *-ordre* (m) : subordinate, underling.
— *-production* (f) : under-production.
— *-produit* (m) : by-product.
— *-secrétaire* (m) : under-secretary.
— *-seing* (m) : private agreement, contract.
— *-titre* (m) : sub-title, caption.
— *-traitance* (f) : sub-contracting.
— *-traitant* (m) : sub-contractor.
— *-traiter* (v) : to sub-contract.

sous clef : under lock and key.

souscripteur (m) : [F] — *d'actions* : subscriber, applicant.
— *d'un chèque, d'un effet de change* : drawer.
— *à un emprunt* : subscriber to a loan.

souscription (f) : [J] execution, signing (*d'actes*).
[F] subscription, application (*à des actions* : for shares).
appel à — : prospectus.
— *en titres* : subscription by conversion of securities.
bulletin de — : allotment letter.
droit de — : warrant.
droit préférentiel, privilège, de — : preferential allotment of new stock.
lettre de — *éventuelle à forfait* : underwriting contract.

souscrire (v) : [J] *souscrire un acte* : to sign, to execute a deed.
— *un cautionnement* : to subscribe, to sign a bond.
[F] — *à des actions* : to apply for, to subscribe shares.
— *le capital* : to subscribe, to apply for the capital.
— *un chèque (au porteur), un effet de change* : to draw a cheque (to bearer), a bill.
— *à une émission, un emprunt* : to apply for, to subscribe to an issue, a loan.
— *à titre irréductible* : to apply as of right for new shares.
— *à titre réductible* : to apply for excess shares.
capital souscrit : subscribed capital.
— *à un abonnement* : to take out a subscription.
— *à une opinion* : to endorse, to subscribe, to agree to an opinion.
— *un risque* : to underwrite a risk.

sousdit (a et m) : below-mentionned, under-mentioned.

sous le nom de : (known) as, alias.

(le) soussigné (m) : the undersigned, the subscriber.

soustraction (f) : removal, abstraction, taking away.
[J] *acte de* — : purloining.
— *frauduleuse* : abstraction of documents.
— *d'impôt* : tax evasion.
— *d'une personne à une poursuite pénale* : knowingly to receive, comfort and assist an absconder.

soustraire (v) : to abstract, to take away from, to withdraw.
— *un document* : to purloin a document.
se — *à l'impôt* : to avoid (to evade) paying taxes.
se — *à la justice* : to abscond.

soutènement (m) : supporting.
[C] — *de compte* : vouchers in support of an account.
mur de — : retaining wall.

souteneur (m) : bully.

soutenir (v) : 1° *(les cours, en achetant)* to support prices (by buying).
2° *(une motion)* to second (a motion).
— *une entreprise* : to bolster up.
— *l'économie* : to prop.
— *sa famille* : to keep, to maintain one's parents.
— *financièrement* : to back s.o. financially.
marché soutenu : steady, buoyant market.

soutien (m) : [J] — *de famille* : bread-winner.

souverain (a) : sovereign.
[J] *cour* —*(e)* : final court of appeals, supreme court.
jugement — : judgment of the final court of appeal, final judgment.
« *le peuple* — » : « the sovereignty lies with the people ».

souveraineté (f) : 1° [J] sovereignty.
2° supremacy (of the law).
— *nationale* : the will of the « nation » as the supreme authority of the Republic.
droits de — : sovereign rights.

spécial (a) : special, particular.
affaire —*(e)* : particular business.
impôts spéciaux : specific taxes.

spécialisation (f) : specialization.
— *d'une hypothèque* : specialization of a mortgage.

spécialisé(e) (a) : *(production)* specialized (production).
ouvrier − : skilled worker.

spécialité (f) : speciality, special line of business.
− pharmaceutique : patent medicine.

spécification (f) : specification.

spécifier (v) : to specify, [U.S.] to itemize.

spectacle (m) : entertainment.
professionnel du − : public entertainer.
taxe sur les −(s) : entertainment tax.

spéculateur (m) : speculator, gambler.
− à la baisse, à la hausse : bear, bull.
− qui souscrit aux nouvelles émissions pour revendre avec prime : stag.

spéculatif (a) : speculative.
valeurs spéculatives : speculative stocks.

spéculation (f) : speculation, gamble, gambling.
− à la baisse, à la hausse : bear, bull operation.

spéculer (v) : to speculate, to gamble, [U.S.] to play the stock-market.
− à la baisse, à la hausse : to go a bear, to go a bull.

sphère (f) : *(d'influence)* field, sphere (of influence).

spirale *(des prix et des salaires)* (f) : (wage-price) spiral.

spoliateur (a et m) : (a) despoiling, spoliatory.
(m) despoiler.

stabilisation (f) *(de la monnaie, des prix)* : stabilization (of the currency, of prices).
fonds de − des changes : exchange stabilization fund.

stabilisateurs automatiques (m pl) : *(de l'économie)* built-in stabilizers.

(se) stabiliser (v) *(ex. ventes)* : to flatten.

stabilité (f) : stability, steadiness.
− de l'emploi : security (fixity) of employment, of tenure, job-security.
− des prix : stability in price, price stability.

stable (a) : *(monnaie)* stable (currency).

stage (m) : probation period.
− en usine : industrial traineeship.
− de formation pendant les horaires de travail : off-the-job training programme.

stagiaire (m) : trainee, articled clerk.

stagnation (f) : *(des affaires)* stagnant state (of business), stagnation, dullness.
− du marché : market standstill, dullness of the market.
− accompagnée d'inflation : stagflation.

standardiser (v) : to standardize.

standardiste *(téléphone) :* switch board operator.

staries (f pl) (also *jours de planche*) : laydays.

station (f) : station.
− touristique : (mountain, sea-side) resort, spa.

stationnaire (a) : *(cours, économie)* stationary (prices, economy).

stationnement (m) : parking.
droit de − : parking due.
« *− interdit* » : « no parking ».

statistique (a et m) : (a) statistical.
échantillonnage − : lot-plot method.
(m) statistics.
les −(s) hebdomadaires : the weekly returns.

statuer (v) : to decree, to enact, to ordain, to rule.
[J] *− sans appel :* to give a final decision.
− au fond, au principal : to decide on the merits of a case.
− à nouveau : to review a judgment.
− de nouveau : to take a case up again.
− en premier ressort : to pronounce a judgment open to appeal.
− des prescriptions : to enact rules.
− sur une affaire : to deal with a case.
− sur un appel : to dispose of an appeal.
− sur un litige : to settle a dispute.
− sur une question : to determine a question.
− sur les reproches : to rule on impugnment of witnesses, etc.

statu quo (m) : status quo.

statut (m) : statute, ordinance, articles, rule, regulation, status.
− juridique : legal position.
− des fonctionnaires : the civil servant's statute.
− légal : legal status.
− local : by(e)-law.

— *personnel*: personal status.
— *réel*: legal status of s.o.'s real property.
— *organique*: constitution, status of a country, port, etc.

statutaire (a): statutory, statutable.
actions — (s): qualifying shares.
apport, réserve — : initial share, reserve provided by the articles.
dispositions — (s): articles of association.
gérant — : manager appointed according to the articles.

statuts (d'une société) (m pl): Memorandum and Articles of Association (of a company), [U.S.] bye-laws, charter and bye-laws.

stellage (m): [B] double option, put and call deal, [U.S.] straddle, spread eagle.

stellionat (m): [J] swindle, fraud in real estate deals (relating to ownership, mortgages, etc.).

stérilité (f): sterility.
— *masculine*: impotentia procreandi.
— *féminine*: impotentia concipiendi vel generandi.

stimulant (m): *(fiscal, de la production)* (tax, production) incentive, stimulus, inducement.

stimuler (v): to foster, to give a stimulus to, to incite (investments).
mesures destinées à — l'économie: economic pump priming.

stipulation (f): stipulation, provision.
[J] *— (s) d'un contrat*: articles, clauses of a contract, conditions laid down in an agreement, specification of a contract.
— *particulière*: special provision.
— *pour autrui*: provision in favour of a third party.
stipulant: stipulator.

stipuler (v): to lay down, to provide that.

stock (m): [C] stock (of goods).
— (s) bas: lean stocks.
— (s) reportés: opening stocks.
— en magasin: stock in hand.
— d'or d'une Banque d'Etat: the gold reserve of a Bank of State.
évaluation des — (s): appraisement of goods.
épuisement des — (s): stock depletion.
liquidation du — : stock clearance.
renouvellement des stocks: restocking.
réserve de — : stock pile.
rotation de — : stock turnover.
rupture de — : understocking.

— *final*: clearing inventory.
— *initial*: beginning inventory.

stockage (m): stocking, building up of stocks.

stocker (v): to stock, [U.S.] to stockpile.

stratégie (f): strategy.

strict (a): stringent.

stupéfiant (m): narcotic, dangerous drug.

(effets) structurants: structuring effects.

structure (f): set-up, structure.
— *linéaire de l'entreprise*: line organisation.

studio: (U.K.) apartment.

subalterne (a): subordinate, minor.

subdiviser (v): to subdivide.

subdivision (f): subdivision.

subhastation (f): [J] forced sale.

subir (v): *(une perte)* to bear, to sustain (a loss).

subordonner (v): *(son acceptation à)* to subordinate (one's acceptance to).

subornation (f): subornation.
[J] — *d'un juré*: embracery.
— *des témoins*: tampering with, intimidation or bribing of witnesses.

subreption (f): [J] subreption.

subrogation (f): [J] 1° subrogation, substitution.
2° delegation (of powers, rights).

subrogatoire (a): [J] *acte — :* act of subrogation, of substitution (of guardian, etc.).

subrogé (a): surrogated.
[J] — *-tuteur*: deputy, surrogate guardian.
demeurer — aux droits d'un créancier: to enter into the rights of a creditor.

subséquent (a): ensuing, subsequent, later.
testament — : later will.

subside (m): subsidy.

subsidiaire (a): subsidiary.
[J] *conclusions — (s), demande —* : accessory claims, demand.
moyen — : auxiliary plea.

subsistance (f) : subsistence, keep, maintenance.
frais de — : living expenses.
moyens de — : means of subsistence.

subsister (v) : 1° *(vivre de)* : to live (on), to subsist.
2° *(rester)* : to remain, to be left.

substituer (à) (v) : to substitute (for).
— *un héritage* : to entail an estate.

substitut (m) : alternate, assistant, deputy (to official).
[J] assistant public prosecutor.
des — *(s)* : substitutes, adjuncts.

substitution (f) : [J] 1° substitution ; 2° entail, remainder, reversion.
— *d'enfant* : setting up of a child (to displace the real heir).
— *de part* : substitution of one new-born child for another.
enfant **substitué** (or *supposé*) : suppositious child.
— *vulgaire* : appointment of heir in succession to another or failing another.
bien **substitué** : entailed estate, estate in reversion, remainder.
héritier **substitué** (also called *l'appelé*) : substitutional heir, reversioner, remainderman.
entrer en possession d'un bien par — : to come into a reversion.
[F] — *fiscale* : substitution of taxpayer.

subterfuge (m) : subterfuge, makeshift.
user de — : to resort to subterfuge.
— *(s) fiscaux* : tax gimmicks.

subvenir (v) *(aux besoins)* : to supply, to provide for (the needs), to support s.o.
— *aux frais* : to defray, to meet the expenses.

subvention (f) : subsidy, subvention, grant, bounty.
— *(s) à l'agriculture* : deficiency payment to farmers.
— *d'équipement* : investment grant.

subventionner (v) : to subsidize.
subventionné par l'Etat : state-aided.

subversif *(action, propos)* (a) : subversive.

succédané (m) : substitute.

succéder (à qn) (v) : to succeed to (s.o.).
— *à un domaine* : to inherit an estate.

successeur *(de)* (m) : successor (to, of).

successible (a) : [J] entitled to inherit, to succeed.
parenté au degré — : degree of relationship carrying title to share in intestate estate.

successif (a) : successive.
[J] *délit* — : repeated, identical or similar offence.
droit — : law of succession, canons of inheritance.
droits — *(s)* : right to succeed, right of succession.
[C] *endossements* — *(s)* : an uninterrupted sequence of endorsements.

succession (f) : succession.
[J] 1° inheritance, inheriting, deceased estate, coming into property.
— *ab intestat* : intestate estate, succession.
actif brut d'une — : gross estate.
administrateur d'une — : administrator of an estate.
— *bénéficiaire* : (beneficio inventarii), estate accepted without liability to debts beyond the assets descended.
— *collatérale* : succession distributed to collaterals.
— *déférée aux ascendants* : succession distributed in the line of ascent.
— *déférée aux descendants* : succession distributed in the line of descent.
— *en deshérence* : estate in escheat.
— *indivise* : inheritance in indivisum.
— *jacente* : unclaimed estate.
— *légale, légitime* : legal succession, i.e. distributed in the statutory order provided for intestacy (opp. — *testamentaire*).
— *en ligne directe* : lineal inheritance.
— *linéale* : succession per stirpes.
réserve légale d'une — : legal share in an estate.
— *testamentaire* : succession bestowed by will (opp. *succession ab intestat*).
— *vacante* : estate in abeyance, without a claimant.
2° estate.
laisser une — *considérable* : to leave a large estate.
droits de — *(droits de mutation après décès)* : estate duty, probate duty, death duties.
droits de — *sur parts héréditaires* : inheritance tax.
ordre de — : canons of inheritance.
[F] — *fiscale* : substitution of taxpayer.

successoral (a) : successional.
loi — *(e)* : law on inheritance.
taxe — *(e)* : death duties.

succursale (f) : branch (office), subsidiary.
magasin à — *(s) multiples* : multiple store, [U.S.] chain store.

suffire (v) : to suffice, to be sufficient, to be adequate, to be enough.

suffrage (m) : suffrage, vote.
– *direct, secret et universel* : direct, secret and universal franchise.

suicide (m) : suicide.
[J] felo de se.
assistance au – : help toward suicide.
commettre un – : to commit suicide.
tentative de – : attempted suicide.

suite (f) : continuation.
donner – à : to give effect to.
comme – à : in further reference to.
par la – : hereafter, subsequently.
prendre la – d'une affaire : to succeed to a business.

suivi (m) (**des produits**) : follow-up (of products).

sujet (a et m) : (a) *(à des droits)* subject to, liable to (duties).
(m) *(d'un Etat)* subject (of a State).

(au) sujet de : re ; in re (about).

sujétion (f) : subjection, constraint.

superbénéfice (m) : excess (surplus) profit.
impôts sur les –(s) : excess profit taxes.

supercherie (f) : deceit, fraud, hoax.

superdividende (m) : surplus dividend.

supérieur (a) : higher, upper, top-senior.
cadre – : senior executive (officer).
enseignement – : higher education.
offre –(e) : higher bid.

superimpôt (m) : surtax.

supermarché (m) : supermarket.

superposer (v) : to superimpose.

(impôt) de superposition : superimposed tax.

suppléant (a et m) : (a) acting pro tem., temporary, substitute for, (m) deputy, locum tenens.

supplément (m) : addition, excess, excess charge, extra charge, supplement, supplementary charge.
– *d'honoraires (à avocat)* : refresher.
– *d'imposition* : additional tax.
– *d'information* : further information (investigations).
– *de salaire* : extra pay.
payer le – : to pay the difference.

supplémentaire (a) : supplementary, additional, extra, further.
délai – : days of grace.
heures –(s) (de travail) : overtime.
juré – : extra juryman (tales).

supplétif (or **supplétoire**) (a) : suppletory.
[J] *serment –* : suppletory oath.

supplique (f) : petition (for reprieve, for relief, etc.).

supporter (v) : 1° *(une perte, la charge fiscale)* : to bear (a loss, the burden of taxation).
2° *(des dépenses)* : to incur (expenses).

supports (m pl) *(publicitaires, etc.)* : (advertising) media.

supposition (f) : 1° supposition ; 2° assumption.
[J] putting forward (sth.) as genuine.
– *d'un contrat* : (im)personation of party to contract.
– *d'enfant, de part* : setting-up a child, displacing the real heir.
– *de nom* : giving a false name.
– *de personne* : (im)personation.
– *de pièce* : presenting a forged document.
– *de testament* : producing a forged will.
enfant supposé (or **substitué**) : supposititious child.

suppression (f) : 1° suppression ; 2° removal, abolition.
[J] – *de part ou d'enfant* : concealment of birth, offence by a woman concealing her pregnancy and making away with the child in order to suppress his claim to an inheritance.
– *d'état civil* : destroying the proofs of s.o.'s civil status.
– *de pièce, de titre* : concealment or destruction of a document.
– *de borne* : removal of a boundary stone.
– *de barrières douanières* : removal of tariff walls.
– *de solde* : stoppage of pay.

supprimer (v) : to cancel.

sur : out of.
dividende payable – : dividend payable out of.

sûr (a) : safe, reliable.
placement – : safe investment.

sur-arbitre (m) (also **tiers arbitre**) : umpire (deciding a tie between arbitrators).

surcharge (f) : overload.
[J] [C] writing on or over an existing text.

surcoût (m) : overcost.

suremploi (m) : over-employment.

surenchère (f) : higher bid.
surenchérisseur : outbidder.
surenchérir : to outbid.

surérogation (f) : supererogation.

surestarie(s) (f) : [A] demurrage.
jours de – : extra lay-days.

surestimation (f), **surévaluation** (f) : over-estimate, overvaluation.

sûreté (f) : safety, security, safe-keeping.
[J] – *personnelle* : bail-bond, collateral security, joint and several guaranty.
– *réelle* : secured debt.
transfert de propriété à fin de – : pledge.
[A] *la* – *nationale* # the Criminal Investigation Department [C.I.D.], [U.S.] the Federal Bureau of Investigation [F.B.I.].

surface (f) *de vente* : shopping area.

surimposer (v) : [F] to overtax.

surinvestissement (m) : overinvestment.

surnom (m) : appellation, nickname.

surnombre (m) : *(d'ouvriers)* redundancy.
en – : redundant.
compensation accordée aux ouvriers en – : redundancy payments.

surnuméraire (m) : supernumerary (esp. official).

surplus (m) : surplus, balance, [U.S.] overage.
– *non distribué* : unappropriated surplus.
méthode des – : surplus method.

surprendre (v) : to surprise.
– *la bonne foi de qn* : to misuse s.o.'s good faith.
– *qn en flagrant délit* : to catch s.o. in flagrante delicto, red-handed, in the act.

sursalaire (m) : bonus, extra pay.

surseoir (v) : [J] – *à l'exécution* : to stay the execution of a sentence.
– *à une inhumation* : to postpone burial.

– *à un jugement* : to delay, to put off, to stay a judgment.
– *à des poursuites* : (civ.) to stay proceedings, (cr.) to suspend prosecution.
ordre de – : stay of execution.

sursis (m) : delay.
[J] stay of proceedings, respite, reprieve (from execution), arrest of judgment.
– *concordataire* : stay of bankruptcy, proceedings to allow time for composition.
– *conditionnel à l'exécution des peines* : respite for a probationary period to prisoner convicted for the first time, verdict to be executed in case of second offence.
– *à exécution* : cesset executio, stay of execution.
– *à statuer* : putting off of judgment.
[A] (milit.) *sursis d'appel, d'incorporation* : deferment.
– *de paiement* : delay for payment.
– *de paiement d'impôt* : stay of collection.
mettre un homme en – : to defer call-up.

surtare (f) : supertare.

surtaux (m) : [A] over-assessment.

surtaxe (f) : surtax, [U.S.] additional tax.
– *d'une lettre* : extra postage, surcharge on letter.
– *progressive sur le revenu* : supertax.

surveillance (f) : supervision, watching, superintendence, surveillance.
[B] *commission de* – *(des opérations de Bourse)* : surveillance department.
– *des mineurs* : protection of minors.
– *de police* : (police), probation.
– *des prix* : price control.
conseil de – : inspection committee, supervisory board.
exercer la – *(sur un équipement)* : to monitor.

surveillant (m) : supervisor, superintendent.

surveiller (v) : to watch over, to superintend.
le commissaire aux comptes **surveille** *la comptabilité* : the auditor watches over the bookkeeping.

survie (f) : survivorship.
[J] *droits de* – : advantages stipulated in a contract (or antenuptial agreement) in favour of the surviving party.
présomption de – : presumption of survivorship (see *comourants*).
tables de – : expectation of life tables, survival tables.

survivance (f) : outliving.
[J] (hist.) reversion of estate or office.

survivant (a) *(conjoint, parent)* : surviving (spouse, relation).

survivant (m) : survivor.
donation au dernier — : mutual testament.
[ASS] *assurance vieillesse et* —*(s)* : old age and survivors insurance.

(être en) sus de

suscription (f) : superscription.
[J] name and particulars of the person concerned, inscribed on a document.

(de la manière) susdite : as above mentioned, as aforesaid.

susnommé (a et m) : aforenamed, abovenamed.
entre les **susdénommés**, *les* — *(s)* : between the above-named.

suspendre (v) : to suspend.
— *l'audience, les débats* : to adjourn the sitting, the hearing.
— *l'application d'un texte* : to leave a text in abeyance.
— *un fonctionnaire* : to suspend an official.
— *ses paiements* : to stop payment.
— *une séance* : to suspend, to adjourn a meeting.
— *la vie commune* : to separate from bed and board (see also *surseoir*).

(en) suspens : abide, in suspense, in abeyance.
la prescription est en — : the prescription is interrupted.
questions en — : outstanding questions.

suspension (f) : suspension.
— *d'armes* : armistice, ceasefire, truce.
— *de paiement* : stoppage (suspension) of payment.
[A] *arrêt de* — : injunction.

suspicion (f) : suspicion.
être en — : to be suspected.
[J] — *légitime* : well-founded suspicion that fair trial will not be given, involving transfer of case to another court.

synallagmatique (a) : [J] *contrat* — : synallagmatical, bilateral contract, indenture.

syndic (m) : syndic.
[J] (in bankruptcy proceedings) — *des créanciers, de faillite* : assignee of the body of creditors.
— *définitif* : official receiver, trustee in bankruptcy.
— *provisoire* : provisional receiver appointed by court on adjudication of bankruptcy, to take protective measures.
— *de l'union* : receiver appointed after refusal of certificate to bankrupt or after legal settlement by cession.
[B] — *des agents de change* : president of the Chamber of stock-brokers.

syndicat (m) : syndicate.
— *agricole* : union of agriculturists.
— *de banques* : banking syndicate.
— *d'émission et de placement* : issue and investment syndicate.
— *financier* : financial syndicate.
— *de garantie* : underwriting syndicate.
— *industriel* : pool.
— *ouvrier* : trade-union, [U.S.] labor union.
— *patronal* : employers' association, federation.
— *de placement d'actions* : pool.
— *de prise ferme* : [B] pool, underwriting group.
— *de producteurs* : producers' association.
— *professionnel* : trade association, syndicate.
— *d'initiative* : association for the encouragement of touring.

(se) syndiquer (v) : to syndicate, to form an union, a syndicate.

système (m) : system, scheme, method.
— *d'amortissement dégressif* : declining (reducing) balance method.
— *décimal* : decimal system.
— *dégressif* : regressive tax system, diminishing instalment system.
— *fiscal* : tax system.
— *interagent de marché* (SIAM) : interdealer broker system (IDBS).
— *linéaire* : fixed instalment system.
— *de l'imputation* : tax credit method.
— *monétaire* : monetary system.
— *de participation aux bénéfices* : profitsharing scheme.
— *de primes* : bonus system.
—*(s) des points de vente en chaîne* : on line point of sale systems.

NOTES

T

tabellion (m) : [J] [A] tabellio, scrivener.

table (f) : table.
[ASS] *— (s) d'actualisation :* present value tables.
— (s) d'espérance de vie : « expectation of life » tables.
— (s) de mortalité : mortality tables.
— (s) de renvoi : cross-reference table.
— ronde : round table.

tableau (m) : board, list, table, schedule, panel.
— d'affichage : board.
— d'amortissement : redemption table.
— d'avancement : list of officers marked of promotion.
— des avocats : roll of lawyers.
— des créances de faillite : list of claims in bankruptcy.
— de distribution, de répartition : plan for the division of a bankrupt's property among creditors.
— des durées d'utilisation des biens : depreciation guideline.
— d'échanges inter-industriels : input-output tables.
— synoptique : conspectus.
— des traitements : salary scale.

tâche (f) : task, job, work.
travail à la — : task-work, job work, piecework.
travailleur (ouvrier) à la —, tâcheron : jobbing workman, piece-worker, jobber.

tacite (a) : tacit, implied, understood, implicit.
[J] *— reconduction :* tacit reconduction, renewal (of contract) by tacit agreement (esp. tacit relocation).

taille (f) : (hist.) [F] per capital levy.
taillable *et corvéable à merci :* talliable and liable to forced labour at pleasure.

taille : size.
de — moyenne : medium-size(d).

talion (m) : talion, retaliation.
la loi du — : lex talionis, the law of retaliation.

talon (m) : [C] *— de souche :* counterfoil, [U.S.] stub.

tangible (a) : tangible.
biens — (s) : tangible goods.
valeurs — (s) : tangible assets.

tante (f) : aunt.
grand- — : great-aunt.

tantième (m) : quota, share, percentage.
— d'action : subshare.
— des administrateurs : directors' fees, directors' percentage of profits.

tapage (m) : loud noise, din, uproar.
[J] *— nocturne :* brawling, disturbance of the peace by night, noctural disturbance.

tardif (a) : late.
dépôt — d'une déclaration d'impôt : late filing of a tax return.

tarif (m) : tariff, price-list.
— ad valorem : ad valorem (of taxes, in proportion to estimated value of goods).
— de base : open rate, basic rate.
— des chemins de fer : railway tariff.
— des courtages : scale of commissions (brokerage, factorage, agent's commission).
— dégressif : tapering charges, earned rate.
— d'entrée : import list.
— des dépens : scale of extra-judicial costs, costs de incremento.
— douanier : custom tariff.
— des émoluments : scale of charges.
— de fret : freight rate.
— d'impôt : rate of taxation.
— préférentiel (de faveur) : preferential rates, tariff.
— des salaires : scale of wages.
— de sortie : export list.
accord général sur les — (s) douaniers et le commerce : general agreement on tariffs and trade (G.A.T.T.).
article du — : section, item of tariff.

tarifaire (a) : tariff ; -rating.

tarifer (v) : to tariff, to rate.
prix **tarifé** : list price.

tarification (f) : rate-fixing.
— égale au coût marginal : marginal pricing.

tassement (m) : setback, consolidation.
— du marché : dullness.
— des prix : sagging of prices.

— 259 —

taux (m) : rate, interest ; established price (of commodities).
— *d'accroissement* : rate of growth.
— *d'amortissement* : rate of redemption, amortization quota.
— *d'assurance* : insurance rate.
— *des avances sur nantissement* : lombard rate.
— *de base* : base rate, standard rate.
— *de capitalisation* : capitalization rate.
— *de change* : rate of exchange.
— *de conversion* : rate of conversion.
— *de couverture* : reserve ratio.
— *de couverture du dividende* : cover.
— *de couverture des intérêts des emprunts* : interest cover.
— *de croissance* : growth rate.
— *de croissance mesuré sur une période d'un an* : year ou year rate of growth.
— *de distribution des bénéfices* : pay out ratio.
— *d'émission* : rate of issue.
— *d'escompte* : discount rate.
— *d'escompte hors banque* : open market discount rate.
— *d'escompte officiel* : bank rate, [U.S.] prime rate.
— *de flambage* : burning cost.
— *hors banque* : market rate.
— *de l'intérêt* : rate of interest.
— *global d'intérêt effectif* : effective interest.
— *hypothécaire* : rate of mortgage interest.
— *d'impôt* : rate of taxation.
— *interbancaire offert* (T.I.O.) : IBOR (Interbank offered rate).
— *interbancaire à Londres* : LIBOR (London Interbank Offered Rate).
— *interbancaire à Paris* (T.I.O.P.) : PIBOR (Paris Interbank Offered Rate).
— *d'intérêt légal* : official rate of interest.
— *interne de rentabilité* : internal rate of return, rate of return over cost, break-even rate.
— *interne de rentabilité intégré* : overall rate of return.
— *internes multiples* : multiple rates of return.
— *d'invalidité* : degree of disablement.
— *au jour le jour* : call money rate.
— *maximum* : top rate.
— *minimum de prêt* (surtout par la Banque d'Angleterre) : minimum lending rate.
— *de natalité, mortalité, nuptialité* : birth, death, marriage rate.
— *moyen* : average rate.
— *nominal* : coupon.
— *plein* : full rate.
— *prêteur* : lending rate.
— *de rendement* : rate of return.
— *usuraire* : usurious rate.
— *de rejet (d'actualisation)* : cut off rate, hurdle rate, rejection rate.
— *de rémunération* : wage rate.
— *de report* : rate of contango.
— *de responsabilité* : degree of responsibility.

— *des salaires* : rate of wages.
— *de sécurité* : permissible degree of error.
abaisser (relever) le — d'escompte de la Banque de France : to reduce, to lower (to raise) the Bank rate.

(juge) taxateur : taxing master.

taxation (f) : assessment, rating, taxation.
double — : double taxation.
— *d'office* : arbitrary, official assessment.
— *d'office d'après les dépenses ostensibles ou notoires* : taxation by reference to open or well-known personal expenditure.
— *forfaitaire d'après les éléments du train de vie* : notional assessment based on certain elements of the taxpayer's way of life.
— *des frais* : taxation of costs.

taxe (f) : tax, charge, duty, fee, rate.
1° fixed price (of certain foodstuffs, etc.), fixed rate (of wages).
vente à la — : sale at official price.
2° charge (for service).
— *d'abattage* : slaughter-house charge.
— *d'aéroport* : airport tax.
— *de débarquement* : unloading, landing charges.
— *de port* : harbour rates, wharfage.
— *postale* : postage.
— *de recommandation* : registration fee.
— *supplémentaire (postale)* : surcharge, late fee.
— *de voirie* : Road Fund tax.
3° tax, rates, taxation, duty.
— *d'abonnement au timbre* : composition for stamp duty.
— *sur les achats* : purchase tax.
— *d'apprentissage* : tax of apprenticeship, apprenticeship tax.
— *cadastrale* : cadastral assessment.
— *compensatrice* : surcharge.
— *sur le chiffre d'affaires* : turn-over tax, sales tax.
— *des dépens, frais* : taxation of costs.
— *d'habitation* : residence tax.
— *locale d'enlèvement des ordures ménagères* : local garbage levy.
— *locale d'équipement* : local equipment tax.
— *officielle* : assessment.
— *professionnelle* : business licence tax, [U.S.] small business tax.
— *proportionnelle* : proportional tax.
— *de séjour* : visitor's tax.
— *sur les spectacles* : entertainment tax.
— *de stationnement* : demurrage charge.
— *supplémentaire dissuasive sur les importations* : import surcharge.
— *d'utilisation* : charge, fee, rates (esp. for public utilities).
— *sur la valeur ajoutée (TVA)* : value-added tax (VAT).

hors — (s) : net of taxes.

(mémoire) taxé : taxed bill of costs.

taxer (v) : to assess, to tax.

taylorisme (m) : taylorism.

technicien (m) : technician.

technocratie (f) : technocracy.

technologie (f) : technology.

technologique (a) : *(chômage)* technological (unemployment).

téléimprimante (f) : ticker.

téléscripteur (m) : telex, ticker.

témoignage (m) : testimony, evidence.
[J] hearing (of witnesses).
appeler qn en — : to call s.o. in testimony.
faux — : false evidence, perjury.
invoquer le — de qn : to call s.o. to witness.
porter — : to certify, to bear witness, to give evidence.
recueillir des —(s) : to collect evidence.
récuser un — : to impugn evidence.
rendre — à qn : to testify in s.o.'s favour.
rendre — de qch : to give evidence about sth., to bear testimony to sth.
« *en — de quoi...* » *:* « in witness whereof... ».

témoin (m) : witness.
— *auriculaire :* ear-witness.
— *certificateur :* subscribing, attesting witness.
— *à charge :* witness for the prosecution.
— *à décharge :* witness for the defence.
— *défaillant :* defaulting witness.
— *digne de foi :* reliable witness.
— *direct :* direct witness.
— *de fait :* material witness.
faux — : false witness.
— *indirect :* indirect witness.
— *instrumentaire :* witness to a signature, a deed.
— *irréprochable :* unexceptionable witness.
— *judiciaire :* witness in court.
— *à un mariage :* witness to a wedding.
— *de moralité :* witness to the good character.
— *muet :* mute witness.
— *oculaire :* eye-witness.
— *patenté :* witness of well-established position.
— *reprochable :* exceptionable witness.
— *réticent :* reticent witness.
— *taxé :* witness receiving conduct money.
appel des —(s) : roll-call of witnesses.
appeler qn comme — : to call s.o. as witness.
assermenter un — : to swear in a witness.

assigner, citer un — : to subpoena a witness.
audition de —(s) : hearing of witnesses.
déposer comme — : to depose, to give evidence.
récuser, reprocher un — : to take exception to a witness.
suborner un — : to suborn, to bribe, to tamper with a witness.
témoigner : to testify, to bear witness.

tempérament (m) : [C] *à tempérament :* by instalments, [U.S.] on time, by easy payments.
commerce à — : tally trade, hire-purchase trade.
vente à — : sale on the deferred payment system. [F] on the tally system.

temporaire (a) : temporary, provisional.
incapacité — : temporary disablement.
personnel — : temporary staff.

temps (m) : time.
à — partiel (travail) : part-time (work).
en — utile : in good time.
à — voulu : in due time.

tenancier (m) : *(de terres)* holder, tenant-farmer ; *(de maison de jeu)* keeper ; *(de bar, casino, etc.)* lessee.

tenant (m) : *tout d'un tenant, d'un seul tenant :* all in one block (of landed property).
[J] *les —(s) et aboutissants :* abuttals, fronting and abutting parts (of estate).
les —(s) et les aboutissants d'une affaire : full details of an affair.

tendance (f) : tendency, inclination, propensity, trend, turn.
— *à la baisse (à la hausse) :* downward (upward) trend, bearish (bullish) tendency.
[B] — *boursière :* trend of business transacted.
— *générale du marché :* the general trend of the market.
—*(s) inflationnistes :* inflationary tendencies.

(question) tendancieuse (a) : leading (question).

tendu (a) : hard, stiff.
rapports —(s) : strained relations.

teneur (f) : 1° *(d'un contrat, d'un document)* terms of a contract, of a document.
2° *(industrie)* grade, content, percentage.
[B] — *de marché :* market maker.

tenir (v) : to hold, to keep.
— *audience :* to hear.
— *une audience :* to hold a sitting.
— *(une maison) à bail :* to hold (a house) under lease (on lease).

— *la caisse*: to have the care of the cash.
— *compte de*: to make allowance for, to take into account.
— *un emploi*: to occupy (to hold) a situation.
— *ses engagements*: to keep one's engagements, to meet one's committments.
— *à un fonds*: to abut on an estate.
— *les livres*: to keep the books.
— *le procès-verbal*: to write minutes.
— *une terre à ferme*: to hold a farming lease.
— *séance*: to hold a meeting.
se — *(assemblée)*: to be held (a meeting).
[B] *prix* tenus: firm, hard, steady prices.

tentative (f): attempt.
— *de crime, de vol*: attempted murder, robbery.

(être) tenu *(de faire)*: to be bound, obliged (to do).

tenue (f): 1° *(d'une réunion)* holding (of a meeting).
2° *(de la Bourse)* tone.
3° *(de la rente)* firmness.
4° *(de livres)* book-keeping (bookkeeping).

terme (m): 1° limit, boundary, end.
2° [J] [C] term.
a) « *à* — »: forward, future.
cours à — : futures position.
le — *d'un contrat*: the term, the duration of a contract.
— *de droit*: legal term (opp. *terme de grâce*).
— *(s) de l'échange (international)*: (international) terms of trade.
— *d'échéance*: appointed time of expiry, term falling due, maturity.
— *de grâce*: days of grace, time to pay.
— *de livraison*: time of delivery.
— *de rigueur*: latest due.
— *de la vie*: end of life.
argent à court — : money at call.
effets à court, à long — : short, long-dated bills.
— *(s) et délais*: to attermine.
payable à deux — *(s)*: payable in two instalments.
prêt à court (long) — : loan at short (long) notice.
placement à long — : long term investment.
« *qui a* —, *ne doit rien* »: « a debt cannot be claimed before it is due ».
règlement à — : credit settlement.
b) quarter (of rent) term, quarter's rent, quarter-day, time of payment.
3° [B] *le* — : settling day.
acheter, vendre à — : to buy, to sell for the account, on credit.
marché à — : time settlement, bargain for the account, forward market.
opérations à — : forward deals, dealings for the settlement, buying and selling at a date future and certain.
4° term, expression.
les — *(s) d'un contrat*: the terms of a contract.
— *de commerce*: commercial expression.
— *de droit*: legal term.
— *de métier*: technical term.

terminaux (m pl): terminals.

terminer (v): to finish.
l'action A. termine *à...*: the A. share finished at...

(se) terminer (v): to end.
exercice fiscal se terminant *(le 20...)*: fiscal period (year) ending on (the 20th).

terrain (m): land, ground, piece of ground.
— *à bâtir*: building site (plot).
— *d'entente (pour)*: common grounds (for).
— *(s) inexploités*: undeveloped land.
perdre du — : to lose ground.

terre (f): estate, property.
fonds de — : landed property, plot of land.

(propriétaire) terrien: landowner, landed proprietor.

territoire (m): territory, district, area or region under jurisdiction.
— *(s) non-autonomes*: non self-governing territories.
— *(s) sous tutelle*: trust territories.

territorial(e) (a): territorial.
eaux — *(s)*: territorial waters.
[J] *compétence* — : jurisdiction of a court *ratione loci* (also called *compétence du lieu, locale*).

territorialité *(de l'impôt)* (f): territoriality (of tax).

tertiaire (a): *(activités...)* tertiary (activities, etc.).

test (m): test, testing.
technique de commercialisation par — : test marketing.
— *objectif (une seule réponse exacte pour chaque question posée)*: objective test.

testament (v): will, testament.
[J] — *authentique, par acte public*: public will dictated by testator, executed by two notaries, or by one notary in the presence of two witnesses.
— *autographe, olographe*: holograph will.
— *mystique, secret*: will written or dictated by testator and sealed, and handed to the

notary in the presence of two witnesses.
— *nuncupatif, oral* : nuncupative will.
— *ordinaire* : ordinary will (made under normal conditions, in legal form, opp. *testament privilégié*).
— *privilégié* : privileged will (made under special circumstances provided by law, by certain individuals, e.g. soldiers, sailors, persons at sea, etc.).
capable de disposer par — : having capacity to make a will.
captation de — : obtaining succession by insidious means, captation.
disposer par — : to devise.
dresser un — : to draw up a will.
être couché sur le — *de qn* : to be a legatee.
être habile à recevoir par — : to be entitled to inherit by will.
faire un — : to make a will.
héritier par — : devisee.
homologuer un — : to prove a will.
mourir sans — : to die intestate.
ouverture d'un — : reading of a will.
révoquer un — : to revoke a will.
clause, disposition **testamentaire** : clause, disposition, provision of a will, devise.
exécuteur testamentaire : executor.
héritier testamentaire (institué) : testamentary heir, legatee, devisee.
témoin testamentaire : witness to a will.

testateur (m), **testatrice** (f) : testator, testatrix.
[J] devisor.

testimonial (a) : [J] by assertive testimony of witness.
lettre — *(e)* : testimonial, certificate.
preuve — *(e)* : proof by witnesses ; oral, parol evidence.

tête (f) : *à la tête de* : at the head of.
par — : per capita, per head.
viager sur la — *de* : (annuity) on the life of.
« chasseur de — *(s) »* : search consultant.

texte (m) : text, textual.
textes législatifs : enactments.

théorie (f) *(de l'impôt, de l'inflation)* : theory (of taxation, of inflation), principle.
— *des jeux de situation* : theory of games.
[F] — *métallique* : currency principle.

théorique (a) : theoretical.

thésauriser (v) : to hoard.

ticket (m) : ticket, numbered slip.
— *modérateur* : portion of the cost of medical treatment borne by the insured.
— -*restaurant* : meal voucher.

tiercé (m) : forecast, [U.S.] three horse parlay.

tiers (m et a), **tierce** (a) : third person, party, power, etc.
— -*acquéreur* : subsequent buyer.
[J] — *arbitre* : umpire (in case of division of opinion among arbitrators).
— *de bonne foi* : third party acting in good faith.
— *caution* : contingent liability, collateral security.
— *détenteur* : third party holding property claimed by a person other than the one from whom it has been received.
— -*expert* : super-expert appointed in case of a difference of opinion between two experts.
— -*monde* : third-world.
— *opposition* : opposition by a third person to a judgment in a suit to which he is not a party but by which he suffers a prejudice.
— -*opposant* : third party (in a suit such as above).
— *payant* : paying third.
— *porteur* : second endorser (of a bill), holder in due course.
— -*saisi* : garnishee.
— *provisionnel* : provisional third.
[ASS] *assurance au* — : third party insurance.
avoir recours à un — : to have recourse to a third person.

timbre (m) : stamp.
— *de dimension* : stamp (on posters, etc.) according to size.
droit de — : stamp duty, [U.S.] stamp taxes.
— *épargne* : savings-(bank) stamp.
— *fiscal* : revenue stamp.
— -*poste* : postage stamp.
— *prime* : trading stamp.
— *proportionnel* : stamp on letter of exchange according to amount payable (ad valorem).
— *quittance* : receipt stamp.
— *retraite* : old age pension stamp.
[A] *le* — : the Stamp Office.
abonnement au — : composition for stamp duty.
papier **timbré** : stamp-paper, stamped paper.

tirage (m) : pulling, stretching.
[C] drawing (of bill, cheque, etc.).
droits de — *spéciaux (D.T.S.)* : special drawing rights (S.D.R.).
— *de la loterie* : drawing of the lottery.
tirer *(à vue) sur qn* : to draw on, to value upon s.o. (on sight).
tirer un chèque : to make out a cheque.
tirer un revenu de : to derive gain, income from.
tirer au sort : to draw lots.
tiré : drawee.
tireur : drawer.
[F] *obligations amortissables par* — : lottery-

loan bonds.

titre (m) : title, claim, right, security.
1º title (of nobility).
2º official title, status ; diploma, certificate, qualification.
3º chapter, subdivision of a code.
4º title (of book, etc.), heading of chapter, caption.
5º [J] a) legal right, being entitled to sth., b) title-deed, voucher, conveyance, any instrument or document recording a transaction in real estate.
6º [C] [F] warrant, bond, certificate, (pl.) stocks and shares, securities.
7º title, titre of gold, grade, content of ore, titre of solution.
— *d'action* : scrip.
— *de circulation* : pass, passport.
— *de créance* : proof of debt, evidence of indebtedness.
— *de dette foncière* : certificate of debt secured on landed property.
— *d'un emprunt* : loan-bond.
— *d'Etat, de rente* : Government bond.
— *exécutoire* # writ of execution.
— *faux* : false document.
— *frappé d'opposition* : attached stock.
— *de gage* : security bond.
— *honorifique* : title of honour.
— *hypothécaire* : mortgage bond.
— *d'investiture, de nomination* : document vesting s.o. with an office, appointment letter.
— *de légitimation* : identity papers.
— *à lots* : lottery-loan bond.
— *négociable* : negotiable, assignable, transferable instrument.
— *nominatif* : registered security, scrip.
— *à ordre* : bill to order.
— *de paiement* : order to pay (see *ordonnancement*).
— *paré* : process bearing the executive formula # writ of execution.
— *de permission* : soldier's leave pass.
— *de placement* : safe investment.
— *au porteur* : bearer bond, negotiable instrument.
— *à prime* : option stock.
— *de procuration* : proxy.
— *de propriété* : title-deed, document of title.
— *(s) publics* : Government, public corporations stock.
— *putatif* : putative title.
— *de rachat* : certificate of redemption.
— *recognitif* : recognitory, confirmative title.
— *de rente foncière* : bond of groundrent.
— *de répartition* : notice of allotment (of shares, of quota of bankrupt's estate, etc.).
— *supposé* : put-up title.
— *de tout repos* : sound stock, « blue chip ».
— *de transport* : railway ticket, etc., [U.S.] transportation.
à — de... : as...
à — gratuit : gratuitously, without a consideration.
à — onéreux : for a (valuable) consideration.
cours des —(s) : quotations of stock and shares.
héritier à — particulier : specific, particular legatee.
héritier à — universel # residuary legatee (see *légataire*).
preuve par — : documentary evidence.
avoir des —(s) à : to be entitled to, to have the right to.

titrisation (f) *des créances bancaires* : [F] bank debt securitisation.

titulaire (m) : holder, titular (*d'un droit, titre, diplôme, certificat, etc.*), occupant (*d'un emploi, d'une fonction*).
— *d'une action* : a) person entitled to institute proceedings, b) holder of a registered share.
— *d'une créance* : creditor.
fonctionnaire — : established civil servant.
— *d'une option* : holder of an option.
[B] giver, taker of an option.
— *d'une pension, rente* : pensioner, annuitant.
— *d'une servitude* : beneficiary of an easement.

titulariser (v) : [A] to put s.o. on the establishment, to confirm s.o. in his post or appointment.

tolérance (f) : tolerance, toleration.
[J] *jour de —* : see *souffrance (jour de)*.
— *(douanière)* : allowance, quantity permitted.
— *de poids* : tolerance for error in weight.

tonnage (m) : tonnage.

tontine (f) : [F] [ASS] tontine.
tontinier : a party to a tontine.

tort (m) : wrong ; error, fault ; injury, harm, detriment, hurt.
aux —(s) partagés : contributory fault.
divorce prononcé aux — réciproques des époux : divorce pronounced against both parties.
réparer un — : to make amends for an injury.

total (a et m) : (a) aggregate.
(m) whole, total, aggregate, overall.
— *global* : sum total.
au — : as a whole, in the aggregate.

totalité (f) : whole, totality.
en — : as a whole, wholly.

toucher (*un chèque*) (v) : to cash (a cheque).
— *un salaire* : to receive a salary.

— *le cours le plus bas (haut)* : to record a low (high) price.

tour (f) **(immeuble)** : high-rise block.

tour (m) **de table** : [F] pool.

tout : all, whole, any.
dans — autre cas : in another case.
— *-compris :* all-in, all-inclusive.

tradition (f) : tradition, folklore.
[J] delivery, handing over (of property).

traduire (v) : to translate, to decode ; to interpret, to express, to explain *(les sentiments, les idées, etc.)*.
[J] — *qn en justice :* to sue, to prosecute, to indict, to arraign s.o.
— *qn en conseil de guerre :* to summon s.o. before a court-martial.

trafic (m) : traffic.
1° transport ; 2° trade ; 3° illicit trading, traffic.
— *aérien :* air transport.
— *des chemins de fer :* railway traffic.
— *fluvial :* inland shipping.
— *international :* international traffic.
— *maritime :* sea-borne shipping.
— *passagers :* passenger traffic.
— *routier :* road transport.
— *de compensation :* clearing.
— *frontalier :* local traffic and trade across the border.
— *d'armes :* smuggling of arms.
— *clandestin :* black market.
— *de devises :* illicit dealings in currency.
— *d'enfants et de femmes :* white slavery.
— *d'esclaves :* slave traffic.
— *illicite :* illicit trading.
— *d'influence :* trading on one's influence.
— *d'or :* smuggling of gold.
— *de stupéfiants :* drug traffic.
trafiquant : trader, *(péjoratif)* trafficker.

trahison (f) : betrayal.
[J] treason, leze-majesty.
haute — : high treason, *(cas moins grave)* treason-felony.

train (m) : train.
— *de mesures :* package.
— *de vie :* way of life, rate of living.

(avoir) trait à : to be relevant to.

traite (f) : 1° [C] bill of exchange ; 2° trade.
— *fictive :* fictitious bill.
— *bancaire :* banker's draft.
— *à échéance :* usance draft.
— *à courte échéance :* short bill.

— *documentaire :* bill with attached documents (bill of lading, invoice, etc.), documentary bill.
— *« en l'air » :* windmill.
— *libre :* clean bill.
— *à vue :* demand-bill, sight draft, draft at sight (see also *effet 2* and *lettre de change*).

traité (m) : treaty, compact, agreement ; treatise.
— *d'alliance :* treaty of alliance.
— *d'arbitrage :* arbitration treaty.
— *de commerce :* commercial treaty.

traitement (m) : 1° salary ; 2° treatment, process.
échelle des — (s) : scale of salaries.
échelon de — : class of salary.
personne employée sans — : unpaid person.
rappel de — : back-pay.
retenue sur le — : docking of pay.
— *discriminatoire :* discriminatory treatment.
— *industriel :* manufacturing treatment, process.
— *des données par procédés mécanographiques :* automatic, electronic data processing.
mauvais — : ill-usage.

traiter (v) : to treat, to process, to deal.
— *des affaires :* to transact business.
— *avec ses créanciers :* to negotiate with one's creditors.

tranche (f) : portion, instalment, slice, bracket, range, cross-section, group, tranche.
— *d'âge :* age bracket (range).
— *de revenu (imposable) :* income bracket.
— *des salaires moyens :* middle-income bracket.
progressivité par — (s) : bracket progression.

trancher un différend (v) : to settle a dispute.

transaction (f) : transaction.
[J] settlement arrived at by parties inter se.
— *judiciaire :* arrangement recorded by court.
[C] a) composition, arrangement, b) deal.
— *boursière :* bargain.
arriver à une solution **transactionnelle** : to effect a compromise.

transcription (f) : transcription.
[J] — *hypothécaire :* inscribing of mortgages, charges on real estate, etc. in the Land Register.

transférable (a) : transferable.

transfèrement (m) : [A] transfer of a prisoner from one place to another.

— *cellulaire*: transfer as above, in policevan («*panier à salade*»: « Black Maria »).

transfert (m): transference.
[J] making over, transfer, assignment *(de droits, créances, actions, etc.)*, demise, conveyance *(de biens)*.
acte de — : deed of assignment.
— *de biens (entre vifs, à un conjoint)*: (inter vivos) transfer of property (to spouse).
[C] — *d'un article de compte*: to post up.
— *de fonds*: funds transfer.
— *(s) sociaux*: welfare transfers, transfer payments.

transformation (f): *(industrie)* processing, transformation, change (into).
— *(s) (d'une maison)*: alterations.
industries de — : process industries.

transformer (v): to transform, to turn into, to process.

transgresser (v): to transgress, to contravene, to break, to infringe (the law, etc.).

transiger (v): to compromise, to compound (a debt).
— *avec ses créanciers*: to compound, to come to terms with one's creditors.
— *avant jugement*: to settle an affair out of court.

transit (m): [D] transit.
acquit de — : transit-permit, transire, excise bond, bond-note.
droit de — : transit dues.
entrepôt de — : bonded warehouse.
maison de — : forwarding agency.
marchandises en — : goods in transit.
marchandises de — : bonded, warehoused goods for transit.
transitaire: forwarding agent.

translation (f): transferring, conveyance.
[J] *acte* **translatif** *de propriété*: conveyance, deed.

transmettre (v): to transmit, to pass over, to convey *(message, ordre, maladie)*.
[J] to transfer, to convey, to make over *(biens, droits)*, to assign *(actions, brevet, etc.)*.
transmission d'un bien par succession: descent of an estate.
[A] *transmission des pouvoirs*: « handing over ».

transparence fiscale (f): tax transparency.

transpirer (v) (**renseignement**): to leak out (information).

transport (m): conveyance, carriage, [U.S.] transportation.
[J] — *-cession*: transfer, assignment, making over, conveyance (of property, rights).
— *sur les lieux*: visit of judges, experts, officials, etc., to the scene of the occurrence.
— *en droiture*: guaranty of direct shipping.
— *par air*: air transport.
— *par eau*: water carriage.
— *par mer*: affreightment.
— *maritime à la demande*: tramping.
— *routier*: road transport, [U.S.] trucking.

transporter (v): to transport, to convey.

transporteur (m): carrier.
— *routier*: (road) haulage contractor.

travail (m): work, labour.
accident de — : industrial injury.
arrêt de — : work interruption, [U.S.] tiein.
— *à la chaîne*: flow (line) production, work on the assembly line.
— *à domicile*: homework, outwork.
— *en équipe*: team work.
— *à façon*: jobbing.
— *à forfait*: contract work.
— *manuel*: manual work (labour).
— *à mi-temps*: part-time work.
— *à plein temps*: full-time job, wholetime job.
— *temporaire*: interim work.
organisation scientifique du — : industrial engineering.
séance de — : business meeting.
être sans — : to be unemployed.
travaux *en cours*: work in progress.
— *d'entretien*: maintenance (work).
— *préliminaires (avant réunion)*: spadework (before meeting, symposium, etc.).
— *publics*: public works, civil engineering.

travailler (v): to work.
— *la clientèle*: to work the town, to canvass.
[F] — : to produce interest.
faire — *son argent*: to put one's money out at interest, [U.S.] to put one's money to work.

travailleur (m): worker, workman, labourer, operative.
— *appointé*: salaried worker.
— *indépendant*: self-employed person.
— *intellectuel*: head worker.
— *manuel*: blue-collar worker.
— *à mi-temps*: part-time worker.
— *à plein temps*: full-time worker.
— *manuel*: manual (hand) labour.

tréfonds (m): subsoil, minerals, etc., lying below the ground.
vendre le fonds et le — : to sell soil and

— 266 —

subsoil.
tréfoncier : owner of the soil and subsoil.
redevance tréfoncière : mining royalties.

trentenaire (a) : lasting thirty years.
concession — : thirty year lease (esp. of grave).
obligation — : bond redeemable in thirty years.
possession — : possession for thirty years.
prescription — : prescription after thirty years.

trésor (m) : treasure.
le — *public* : the Treasury.
[J] — *(découvert par hasard)* : treasure-trove.
[F] *bons, valeurs du* — : Government bonds, stock, treasury bonds.

trésorerie (f) : available funds, liquid assets, of the Treasury or of an enterprise.
coefficient de — : cash ratio.
moyens de — : technical means applied by the Treasury to ensure fluidity.
situation de — : financial statement.
[A] — *générale* : office, functions or office of a *trésorier général*.
commis de — : clerk at such office.

trésorier-payeur général (m) : [A] chief Treasurer and Paymaster of a departement.

tribunal (m) : tribunal ; judge's seat, bench ; court of justice, law court ; the magistrates ; the court-house.
— *administratif* : administrative court.
— *arbitral, d'arbitrage* : court of arbitration.
— *d'instance ou de grande instance* : court of first instance (# country court), [U.S.] district court.
— *civil* : civil court.
— *de commerce, consulaire* : commercial court.
— *des conflits* : court arbitrating concurrence of jurisdiction between the administrative and judiciary courts (in France).
— *correctionnel* : court sitting in criminal matters either as original jurisdiction for misdemeanours, or as court of appeals for police offences.
— *disciplinaire* : summary jurisdiction.
— *de droit commun, ordinaire* : ordinary court.
— *pour enfants et adolescents* : juvenile court.
— *d'exception* : special jurisdiction.
— *maritime* : a) court of admiralty, b) naval court.
— *de (simple) police* : police court.
— *de police correctionnelle* : court of summary jurisdiction (= Petty Sessions or Magistrate's Courts).
— *de première instance* : court of first instance.
— *des prises* : prize-court.

— *répressif* : criminal court (opp. *tribunal civil*).
— *de tutelle* : court supervising a guardianship.
actionner qn devant le — : to sue s.o.
chambre d'un — : division of a court.
greffe d'un — : office of the clerk of the court.
citer qn devant un — : to summon s.o. to appear.
comparaître devant un — : to stand one's trial.
compétence d'un — : jurisdiction of a court.
gazette des **tribunaux** : law reports.
greffier du — : clerk of the court.
huissier du — : bailiff.
rôle du — : roll of court, cause-list.
salle du — : court-room.
(see also *conseil* [J] , *cour, organisation judiciaire*).

tribut (m) : tribute.

(être) tributaire de : to be dependent on.

trier (v) : to sort.

trimestre (m) : quarter.
un — *de loyer* : a quarter's rent.

trimestriel (a) : quarterly.

en **triple** exemplaire : triplicate.

triplicata (m) : triplicate, third copy.
[J] third exemplar of a deed which, unlike a *copie*, is accepted as an original draft.
[C] *(troisième de change)* : third of exchange.

triplique (f) : reply to the *duplique* # (plaintiff's) surrejoinder.

tripotage des comptes (m) : tampering with accounts.
— *financier* : financial juggle, jobbery, manipulation.

troc (m) : barter, exchange, swap, truck.

tromper (v) : to deceive.
— *la loi* : to elude the law.

tromperie *(sur la marchandise)* (f) : fraud (relating to goods).
déclarations **trompeuses** : deceptive statements.

trop : too many, too much.
— *perçu* : overassessment, overpayment.

troquer (v) : to barter, to exchange.

trouble (m) : confusion, disorder, perturbation.
[J] interference with s.o.'s rights, disturbance.
— *de droit* : action under pretence of having rights on s.o.'s property.
— *de fait* : taking the law in one's own hands.
— *de jouissance* : disturbance of possession.
troubler *l'ordre public* : to break the (Queen's) peace.

(objets) trouvés : lost property.

truc (m) : gimmick, trick.

truquer *des comptes* : (fam.) to doctor accounts.

trust (m) : trust, pool, private monopoly.
— *de placement* : investment trust, securities trust.
— *de valeurs* : holding company.
loi anti- — : anti-monopoly (anti-trust) law (acts).

turpitude (f) : turpitude, depravity, baseness ; scurvy trick, base deed, vile consideration.

tutelle (f) : [J] tutelage, guardianship, wardship.
— *dative* : tutelage established by the board of guardians.
enfant en — : child under guardianship.
— *légale, — de père et mère* : tutelage by right of surviving father or mother.
— *légitime* : guardianship in the line of ascent.
— *testamentaire* : guardianship established by will.
conseil de — : board of guardians entrusted with the tutelage.
mise sous — : a) putting a child in tutelage, b) declaration by court depriving a prodigal or lunatic of control over his property *(interdiction)* and establishing a guardianship *(curatelle)*.
rendre sa — : to give account of one's guardianship.

tutelle administrative (f) : [A] supervision by a higher authority, established compulsorily over a public body corporate in case of mismanagement.

tuteur (m), **tutrice** (f) : [J] tutor, guardian.
subrogé- — : deputy guardian.

tuyau (m) : dope.
(fam.) *donner un —* : to give a tip.

T.V.A. : V.A.T. (see *« taxe »*).

type (m) : type, standard.
écart, erreur — : standard deviation, error.

typique (a) : typical.

NOTES

NOTES

U

ultérieur (a) : further, subsequent.
ordres — (s) : further orders.

ultérieurement (adv) : subsequently, later on.

ultra petita : [J] *statuer — :* to adjudicate more than is asked for.

unanime (a) : *(consentement)* unanimous (consent).

unanimement (adv) *(à l'unanimité)* : unanimously.
élu à l'unanimité moins (n) voix : elected unanimously with (n) dissentient votes.

unification (f) : unification, standardization.

unifier (v) : to unify, to standardize.
dette **unifiée** : unified debt.

uniforme (a) : uniform, flat, unvarying.
organisation — : uniform organization.
taux d'imposition, d'intérêt — : flat (unvarying) rate of taxation, of interest.

unilatéral (a) : unilateral, one-sided.
contrat — : unilateral (one-sided) contract.
stationnement — : parking on one side.

union (f) : union.
[J] *— des biens :* community regime (in matrimony).
— des créanciers : body of creditors (in bankruptcy).
— douanière : customs union.
— monétaire : monetary union.
— professionnelle : professional syndicate, union.
contrat d'— : agreement on the part of creditors in bankruptcy to take concerted action.
syndic d'— : assignee of the body of creditors in bankruptcy.

uniprix (a) : one-price.
magasin — : [U.S.] one-price shop.

unique (a) : only, sole, single.
fils — : only son.
impôt — : single tax.
propriétaire — : sole owner, proprietor.
taxes — (s) : single taxes.

unitaire (a) : unit, unitary.
prix de revient — : unit cost.

unité (f) : 1° unit ; 2° *(abstrait)* unity.
— de compte : accounting unit, unit of account.
— monétaire : monetary unit.
— monétaire composite : composite currency units.
— (groupe) de prise de décision : Decision Making Unit (D.M.U.).
prix de l'— (unitaire) : unit-price, price of one article.
— de production : production unit.
— de réserve : reserve unit.
— budgétaire, nationale : budgetary, national unity.
« *une —* » : ten thousand francs.
— de taxe (téléph.) : unit charge.

universel (a) : universal.
[J] *héritier — :* heir, general devisee and legatee.
légataire à titre — : residuary devisee and legatee (see *légataire*).

université (f) : university.
[A] *l'— (en France) :* the entire body of State university (in France).

urbain (a) *(centre, population)* : urban (centre, population).

urbanisation (f) : urbanization.

urbanisme (m) : town-planning.

urbaniste (m) : town-planner.

urgence (f) : emergency, urgency.
en — : urgently.
[J] *clause d'— :* emergency clause.
mesures d'— : emergency measures.
réparations d'— : tenantable repairs.
convoquer d'— les actionnaires : to call an extraordinary meeting of the shareholders.

us (et coutumes) (m pl) : ways and customs.

usage (m) : use, using, employment ; usage, custom, practice.
[J] 1° *droit d'— continu :* (right of) user.
2° a kind of usufruct, personal right to make use of sth. belonging to another.

3° common of estovers.
— *abusif du droit*: misuse of law.
— *(s) forestiers*: common of estovers and grazing rights.
— *immémorial*: custom for time out of mind.
— *indu*: illicit practice.
— *(s) locaux*: local customs.
article d'— courant: article for everyday use.
à — personnel: for personal use.
biens à — personnel: personal use property.
les —(s) (d'une profession): the (professional) practices.
valeur d'—: value in use.
frais pour droits d'—: stand-by charge.
il est d'— de: it is customary to, that.
comme d'—: as is customary, usual.

usager (a et m): (a) [D] *effets usagers*: articles for personal use.
(m) user (of sth.).
les —(s) de la route: road-users.

usance (f): [C] usance (of 30 days).
lettre de change à une —, à deux —(s): bill of exchange payable in one, in two months.

user (*d'un droit*) (v): to exercise (a right).
— *d'une possibilité*: to avail oneself of a possibility.

usine (f): factory, works, mill, [U.S.] plant, manufactory.
— *hydraulique*: waterworks.
— *métallurgique*: iron-, steel-, works.
— *pilote*: pilot plant.
— *textile*: mill.
ouvrier(ère) d'—: factory-hand, factory worker.

usucapion (f): [J] acquisitive prescription.

usufruit (m): [J] usufruct, life estate, interest, life use.

usufruitier (m): usufructuary, tenant for life (unless a shorter time is expressed).

usuraire (a): *(taux)* usurious (rate).

usure (f): 1° usury.
2° wear and tear.
[J] — *naturelle, normale*: fair wear and tear.

usurpation (f): usurpation.
— *d'état civil, d'identité, de pouvoir*: usurpation of civil status, of identity, of powers.

usurper (v): *sur les droits de qn*: to encroach, to usurp (up) on s.o.'s rights.

utérin (a): [J] *frère —, sœur —(e)*: frater uterinus, half-brother, half-sister on the mother's side.

utile (a): useful.
renseignements —(s): relevant information.
en temps —: in due time, within the prescribed time.

utilitaire (a): utilitarism.
véhicule —: commercial vehicle.

utilité (f): utility, useful purpose, usefulness.
échelle d'—: utility scale.
— *marginale*: marginal utility.
[J] *expropriation pour cause d'— publique*: expropriation for a public purpose, compulsory purchase of ownership (CPO).
reconnaissance d'— publique: official recognition of an institution as serving the public interest.

NOTES

NOTES

V-W-Z

vacance (f): vacancy, abeyance.
— *accidentelle*: casual vacancy.
— *(s)*: holidays.

vacant (a): vacant.
succession — *(e)*: estate in abeyance, without a claimant.

vacation (f): 1° attendance, sitting of officials.
2° day's sale at auction.
3° (pl) fees of a lawyer.
[J] a) *(d'une succession, de droits)* abeyance, b) *(des tribunaux)* vacation, recess.
chambre des — *(s)*: vacation court.

vagabond (m): rogue and vagabond, [U.S.] « hobo ».

vagabondage (m): vagrancy, truancy.
[J] — *spécial*: living on a prostitute's earnings (an offence).

vague (f): *(de spéculation, ...)*: wave (of speculation, ...).

vain (a): vain.
— *droit*: sham, unreal, empty title.
terres — *(es) et vagues*: waste land.
— *(e) pâture*: common land.
— *(es) promesses*: hollow promises.
[J] *droits de* — *(e) pâture*: right of common, commonage.

valable (a): available, valid, good.
le billet n'est plus — : the ticket is no longer available.
quittance — : valid receipt.

valeur (f): value, worth.
[F] asset, (pl.) bills, shares, securities.
— *d'achat, en fabrique*: cost price.
— *qu'auraient les actifs d'une société si elle cessait ses activités*: break-up value.
— *acquise*: future worth.
— *(s) actives*: assets.
— *actualisée*: discounted present value.
— *actuelle*: present value.
— *(s) adirées*: securities gone astray.
— *(s) d'apport*: vendor's shares.
— *assurée*: insured value.
— *(s) aurifères*: golds.
— *(s) en baisse*: light stock.
— *de bon père de famille, pupillaire*: safe investment.

— *(s) de bourse*: stocks and shares.
— *en bourse*: quotation.
— *comptable*: book-value, written down value.
— *au comptant, en espèces*: cash value.
— *en compte*: (value) for the account.
— *(s) cotées officiellement (à la cote officielle)*: quoted securities, securities quoted in the official list.
— *(s) qui seront cotées au moment de l'émission*: « when issued » securities.
— *d'échange*: value in exchange, purchasing power.
— *aux échéances*: cash at maturity.
— *effective (réelle)*: real value.
— *d'émission*: subscription price.
— *(s) immobilisées*: fixed stock.
— *intrinsèque*: intrinsic value.
— *d'inventaire*: stock-taking value.
— *de liquidation*: realization value.
— *locative*: rental value, letting value.
— *locative imposable*: rateable value.
— *à lots, à primes*: lottery bond, prize bond.
— *marchande*: market value, sale value.
— *(s) minières*: mining stock.
— *(s) mobilières*: transferable securities, stocks and shares.
— *moyenne*: average value.
— *(s) négociables*: marketable securities.
— *(s) non cotées*: unlisted shares.
— *nominale*: face value, [U.S.] par value.
— *nominative*: registered stock.
— *à ordre*: bill to order.
— *au pair*: par value.
— *(s) passives*: liabilities.
— *(s) de placement*: investment securities.
— *au porteur*: bearer bill.
— *de rachat, de remboursement*: redemption price, [U.S.] cash surrender.
— *découlant de la rareté*: scarcity value.
— *(s) réalisables*: stock that can be sold out.
« — *reçue* »: « for value received ».
« — *reçue comptant* »: « value received in cash ».
— *de récupération*: salvage value.
— *probable de récupération*: cash recovery.
— *résiduelle*: net worth, abandonment value, residual value.
— *(s) refuge*: gilt-edged securities.
— *(s) à revenu fixe*: bonds, fixed yield investment.
— *(s) à revenu variable*: shares.
— *(s) de roulement*: floating assets.
— *saisonnière*: seasonal swing.
— *substantielle*: book-value.

— 275 —

— *(s) sûres* : gilt-edged securities, blue chips.
— *(s) à terme* : bills to mature.
— *unitaire* : unit value.
— *vedette* : leaders, leading shares, [U.S.] floaters.
colis, paquet, avec — déclarée : registered parcel.
centre- — : exchange value.
droits sur la, — : ad valorem duty.
bourse des —(s) : stock exchange.
mettre en — : to reclaim, to develop (land).
mise, remise en — : development, restoration.
de — : valuable, precious.

validation (f) : *(d'une élection, d'un mariage)* validation, *(d'un testament)* probate, *(d'une loi)* ratification.

valide (a) : *(testament)* valid (will).

validité (f) : validity, availability.
[J] *jugement de —, de main-vidange* : order to a debtor to pay over money in hand to s.o. appointed by court (mostly the judgment creditor in attachment of debts).
— *d'un billet de chemin de fer* : availability of a railway ticket.

valoir (v) : to be worth.
à — (sur une somme) : on account (towards a sum), against.
à — sur qqn : for the account of s.o.
faire — qch. : to turn sth. to account, to set off sth. to advantage.
faire — un droit en justice : to put in a claim, to have a right enforced by court.
faire — ses droits : to press a claim.

valorisation (f) : [C] [F] appreciation, valorization, stabilization.

valoriser (v) : to valorize.

(moins-)value (f) : decrease in value, depreciation.
— *en capital* : capital loss.

(plus-)value (f) : betterment, increase in value, appreciation.
— *en capital* : capital gain.

vaquer (v) : to be vacant.
les assemblées, les tribunaux **vaquent** : the legislative bodies, the law courts are in vacation, are not sitting.

variable (a) : variable, changeable.
actions à revenu — : equities, variable yield securities.
taux de change — : fluctuating exchange rate.
taux — (d'un prêt) : adjustable rate.

variation *(des cours)* (f) : fluctuation (of), shift (in) quotations.
— *(s) saisonnières* : seasonal swings.

varier (v) : to fluctuate, to vary.
— *légèrement (monter ou baisser)* : to edge ahead.

(être en) vedette (v) : : to be prominent.

véhicule (m) : vehicle, carriage.

vénal (a) : purchasable, venal, marketable.
valeur —(e) : market(able) value.

vendable (a) : saleable.

vendeur (m) : seller, salesman, [U.S.] sales clerk, vendor, counter hand.
[B] — *à découvert* : short seller, bear seller.

vendre (v) : to sell.
— *à couvert* : to sell for delivery.
— *à crédit* : to sell on credit.
— *aux enchères* : to auction.
— *à perte* : to sell under cost price, to undersell.
— *à terme* : 1° to sell on credit ; 2° to sell for the account (for the settlement) ; 3° to sell forward.
« *à —* » : to be sold, for sale.

(se) vendre (v) : 1° to be sold ; 2° to sell.
cet article se vend dans les grands magasins : this article is sold in large stores.
cet article se vend bien : this article sells well.

venir (v) *à échéance* : to fall due.

venir (v) *à maturité* : to come to maturity.

vente (f) : sale.
— *par acomptes, à tempérament* : sale on the deferred payment, instalment scheme.
— *par autorité de justice, judiciaire, forcée* : sale by order of the court, forced sale.
— *au comptant* : sale for cash.
— *à la consommation* : sale for consumption.
— *par correspondance* : mail order sale.
— *à l'acquitté* : sale with customs duties paid.
— *à crédit, à terme* : sale on credit.
— *à cri public, aux enchères* : sale by auction.
— *à découvert (à terme)* : short sale.
— *au détail* : retail trade.
— *au disponible* : sale for immediate delivery.
— *sur l'échantillon* : sale on sample.
— *à l'encan* : public sale of movables.
— *aux enchères* : auction.
— *à l'essai (à condition)* : sale on approval.
— *exclusive* : sole agency.
— *ferme* : definite sale.
— *fictive* : fictitious sale.

– *fiduciaire* # sale in trust.
– *par filière*: sale by trace.
– *sur folle enchère*: resale at an auction when the purchaser or highest bidder has either been unable to pay for it or otherwise failed to fulfil the conditions.
– *forcée (le vendeur compte sur « l'inertie » de l'acheteur)*: inertia selling.
– *de gré à gré*: transaction by mutual agreement.
– *en gros*: wholesafe trade.
– *d'immeubles*: sale of real property.
– *intensives*: intensive selling.
– *judiciaire*: sale by order of the court.
– *par autorité de justice*: judiciary sale.
– *de liquidation*: selling out.
– *à livrer, à terme*: forward deal.
– *-location*: hire-purchase.
– *mobilière*: sale of chattels.
– *(s) nettes (le total des ventes moins les invendus et « la casse »)*: net sales.
prix de – : selling price, consideration for sale.
– *publicitaire*: promotional sale.
– *à un prix inférieur à celui habituellement pratiqué*: price cutting.
– *publique*: public sale, auction sale.
– *avec faculté de rachat, à réméré*: sale with option of repurchase.
– *en reprise*: trading-in.
– *par téléphone*: telephone selling.
[B] – *à terme*: sale for the account, forward sale.
– *d'une terre*: sale of an estate.
– *sur la voie publique*: sale by streetvendors.
acte de – : bill of sale.
agent de – : sales agent.
salle de – : sales room.
salle des – *(s)*: auction mart, room.
mettre en – : to put up for sale, to offer for sale.
retirer de la – : to withdraw from sale.
n'avoir pas la – *(d'un article)*: to have no sale (for an article).

ventilation (f): [J] separate valuation (of chattels or parts of estate).
[C] dispatching.
– *des coûts*: absorption costing.
– *des dépenses et des recettes*: apportionment (allocation) of expenses and receipts.

ventiler (v): to apportion.

ventre (m): abdomen, womb.
[J] *curateur au* – : guardian to child unborn.

verbal (a): verbal, by word of mouth.
[J] *convention* – *(e)*: simple, parol, contract.
procès- – : (q.v.).
verbalisateur: an official who took down the particulars.

verbalisation (f): official entry, taking down name and address (by policeman, etc.) of (motoring, etc.) offence.

verbaliser (v): to charge for an offence.

verdict (m): [J] finding of the jury, verdict.
– *d'acquittement*: verdict of not guilty.
– *de culpabilité*: verdict of guilty.
prononcer, rendre un – : to return, to bring in, a verdict *(en faveur)* for, *(contre)* against, to find for, against, s.o.

véreux (a): shady, dishonest, bad.
financier – : shady financier.
affaire **véreuse**: bubble scheme, fishy business.
créance véreuse: bad debt.
société véreuse: bogus company.

vérificateur (m): examiner, auditor.
– *des comptes*: auditor.
– *des poids et mesures*: inspector of weights and measures.

vérification (f): verification, inspection, examination, test, checking.
– *des comptes, des écritures*: auditing of accounts.
– *des comptes d'un ou plusieurs services d'une entreprise*: internal audit.
– *des créances*: listing of claims (in bankruptcy proceedings).
– *des denrées alimentaires*: inspection of food.
– *d'écriture*: identification of handwriting.
– *fiscale*: tax audit.
– *de l'identité*: personal identification.
– *d'inventaire*: checking of inventory.
– *de pièces justificatives*: checking vouchers.
– *des pouvoirs*: examination of credentials.
– *des suffrages*: scrutiny of a vote.
– *d'un testament*: probate.

vérifier (v): to check, to confirm.
– *des comptes, une déclaration de revenus*: to audit accounts, a tax return.
– *un fait*: to verify a fact.

véritable (a): *(article)* genuine (article).

(sous les) verrous: in safe custody.

versé (a): *(capital)* paid-in, paid-up, (capital).

versement (m): payment, paying in, instalment, remittance, call.
– *anticipé*: payment in advance.
– *d'appel de fonds*: payment of calls.
– *à un compte*: payment-in, payment into an account.
payer par – *(s) échelonnés*: to pay by (in)

instalments.
– *forfaitaire* : contractual payment.
– *fictif* : sham payment.
– *global* : lump sum.
– *libératoire* : final instalment.
– *partiel* : instalment.
– *de souscription d'actions* : application money.

verser (v) : to pay (in, up), to deposit.
– *une caution* : to leave a deposit.
– *des fonds à un compte* : to make a remittance of funds (into an account), to pay money (into an account).
– *des fonds à la Caisse d'épargne* : to deposit money in the savings bank.

verso (m) : back (of a sheet), overleaf.

(en) vertu de : by virtue of, pursuant to, under, whereby.
– *d'un accord antérieur* : under a previous agreement.

veto (m) : veto.
– *suspensif* : suspensory veto.
mettre son – : to veto.

veuf (m), **veuve** (f) : widower, widow.

veuillez *(répéter)* : please (repeat).

viabilisé (a) : developed.

viabilité (f) : practicability, traffic condition.

viable (a) : *enfant né* – : viable infant, capable of living.

viager (a et m) : (a) for life, during one's life time.
bien – : life estate.
rente **viagère** : life annuity, life interest.
rentier – : annuitant.
(m) life interest.
placer son argent en – : to invest one's money at life interest, in a life annuity, to buy an annuity.

vice (m) : vice, depravity, corruption ; fault, defect.
– *apparent* : conspicuous defect.
– *caché* : concealed defect.
– *congénital* : congenital defect.
– *de consentement* : lack of consent.
– *de construction* : constructional defect, faulty workmanship.
– *dirimant* : nullifying defect.
– *de droit* : legal fault.
– *essentiel* : fundamental defect.
– *de forme* : flaw, faulty drafting (of a deed, etc.).

(ASS.) – *inhérent* : inherent vice.
– *latent, redhibitoire* : latent defect (that makes a sale void).
– *propre, inhérent* : inherent defect (of goods).

vicier (v) : [J] to vitiate, to invalidate (deed, contract).

victime (f) : victim, casualty.
– *d'un accident* : injured in an accident.
(les) – (s) *(d'accidents)* : the injured, the casualties.

vide (a), **à vide** : empty.

vider (v) : to empty.
– *un délibéré* : (of judges) to give a verdict after consultation.
– *un différend* : to settle a dispute.
– *les lieux* : to vacate premises.
– *ses mains* : to pay over money in hand to s.o. appointed by court (mostly the judgment creditor in attachment of debts).
– *un procès* : a) to fight it out, b) to settle a difference.

viduité (f) : widowhood.
[J] *délai de* – : period after decease of husband during which a widow is not allowed to marry again (300 days). •

vie (f) : life, living.
assurance sur la – : life insurance.
coût de la – : cost of living.
espérance de – : expectation of life, life expenctancy.
niveau de – : standard of living, [U.S.] level of living.
train de – : rate of living.
gagner sa – : to earn one's living (livehihood).
à – : for life.
pension à – : life pension.

vieillard (m) : old person.
les -(s) : the aged, old people.
assistance aux –(s) : old age relief.

vieillesse (f) : old age.
assurance – : old age insurance.
pension – : old age pension.

vieillissement (m) : ageing.
– *calculé* : planned obsolescence.

vif (a et m) : (a) alive.
(m) [J] living person.
acte de donation entre –(s) : deed of gift inter vivos.
« *le mort saisit le* –, *le* – *chasse le mort* » : « the estate is vested in the heir the very

moment the owner dies ».

vignette automobile (f) : vehicle tax licence.
— *(à coller sur le pare-brise)* : sticker.

vigueur (f) : vigour, strength.
en — : in force.
être en — : to be operative.
entrer en — : to come into force, into effect, into operation.
mettre en — : to put into effect, (force).
mettre une loi en — : to enforce a law.
cesser d'être en — : to lapse.

vil (a) : cheap, low-priced.
vendre à — prix : to sell at a low price, to sell at a knockdown (knock out) price.

ville *(commerçante, industrielle)* (f) : (trading, manufacturing) town.

villégiature (f) : holiday resort.

viol (m) : rape, criminal assault.

violation (f) : violation, infringement, breach, trespass.
— de clôture : trespass quod clausum fregit, breach of close.
— de la Constitution : violation of the Constitution.
— de contrat : breach of contract.
— de dépôt : breach of trust.
— de domicile : breach of domicile, forcible entry.
— des droits : infringement of rights.
— de frontière : trespass of frontier.
— de garantie : breach of warranty.
— de la loi : a) breach of the law, b) *(par un juge)* miscarriage of justice.
— d'une loi : infringement of a law.
— de la paix publique : breach of the peace.
— de propriété (sur un bien foncier) : trespass on land.
— du secret de fonction : misuse of official information.
— du secret de lettres : breach of the secrecy of correspondence.
— du secret professionnel : breach of professional secrecy, standards.
— de sépulture : desecration of a grave.
— d'un traité : violation of a treaty.

violence (f) : violence, force.
[J] duress.

violenter (v) : to do violence (to s.o.).

violer *(la loi)* (v) : to violate, to transgress (the law).
— un secret : to commit a breach of confidence.

virement (m) : [A] transfer of appropriations to another budget estimate.
[F] transfer, remittance.
— bancaire : bank transfer.
— (s) de compte à compte (système de) : giro.
— de parties : balancing on account per contra.
banque de — : clearing bank.
chèque de — : transfer cheque.
comptoir général de — (« le clearing ») : banker's clearing house.
mandat de — : order to transfer.

virer *(une somme à)* (v) : to transfer (an amount to).

viril (a) : manly.
[J] part, portion — (e) : lawful share of succession.

visa (m) : visa, certification.
[C] — d'une lettre de change : sighting of a bill.

viser (v) : 1° to visa, to visé, to certify, to mark, to stamp, to check.
— un passeport : to visa, to visé, to stamp, a passport.
chèque visé : certified cheque, marked cheque.
2° to affect, to describe, to provide for.
les denrées alimentaires ne sont pas visées par ce décret : articles of food are not affected by this order.
l'exception visée à l'alinéa 2 : the exception described at (provided for by) paragraph 2.
— à : to relate to ; to aim at.

visite (f) : visit.
— des bagages de la douane : customs examination.
— domiciliaire : domiciliary visit, housesearch.
— des lieux : see *descente sur les lieux*.
— médicale : medical examination.
— de personnes : personal search.
droit de —, de recherche : right of visit and search.
droit de — (sur le plan fiscal) : right of inspection.

visiteur (m) : 1° visitor ; 2° inspector.

vitesse (f) : speed, velocity.
— de rotation (de la monnaie, des stocks) : rate, speed, velocity (of money, of stock).
— de transformation de la monnaie en revenu : income-velocity of money.
commettre un excès de — : to exceed the speed limit.

viticulture (f) : winegrowing.

(de son) vivant: during (his) lifetime.

vocation (f): vocation.
[J] – *successorale*: title to inheritance.

voie (f): way, highway.
– *administrative, hiérarchique*: the official channels, chain of command.
– *d'appel, de cassation*: lodging of an appeal.
– *civile*: suing s.o.
– *de conciliation*: settling amicably.
– *diplomatique*: diplomatic channels.
– *de droit*: recourse to legal proceedings.
– *d'exécution*: measures of execution.
– *(s) de fait*: acts of violence, assault and battery.
– *judiciaire*: going to the law.
– *pénale*: prosecution.
– *privée*: private road.
– *publique*: highway.
– *de recours*: remedy at law.
par – *de règlement*: by (through) regulation.

voies et moyens: ways and means, supply.

voirie (f): the highways.
la grande – : the high roads.
la police de la – : the road police.
le service de la – : the Highways Department.

voisinage (m): vicinity, neighbourhood,.
bon – : neighbourliness.

voiture (f): vehicle, carriage, motor car.
– *cellulaire*: police-van (« *panier à salade* »: « Black Maria »).
– *de fonction*: company car.
– *de tourisme*: private car.
[A] conveyance, transportation.
[E] *lettre de* – : way-bill, consignment note, [U.S.] bill of lading.

voiturier (m): carter, carrier.
[J] – *public*: common carrier.

voix (f): voice; vote.
– *consultative*: consultative voice.
avoir – *consultative*: to be present in an advisory capacity.
– *prépondérante*: casting vote.
mettre une résolution aux – : to move a resolution.

vol (m): theft, stealing, robbery.
[J] – *à l'américaine*: confidence trick.
– *avec effraction*: burglary.
– *à l'entolâge*: inveigling and robbing by a prostitute.
– *à l'étalage*: shop-lifting.
– *de grand chemin*: highway robbery.
– *à main armée*: armed robbery, robbery under arms.
– *qualifié*: aggravated theft, larceny, compound robbery.
– *régulier*: scheduled flight.
– *simple*: simple, petty, larceny.
– *à la tire*: pocket-picking.
– *d'usage*: « borrowing » a thing without the owner's knowledge, for a short employment (e.g. taking a car in a parking for a ride and leaving it).
receleur d'un – : receiver.

volant (*d'un carnet de chèque*) (m): leaf (of a cheque book), detachable slip.
– *de sortie*: voucher.
– *de trésorerie*: floating cash reserve.

voler (v): to steal, to rob.

voleur (m): thief, robber, (*à l'étalage*) shoplifter.

volontaire (a): voluntary.
mutilation – : self-mutilation.

volontairement (adv): voluntarily, wilfully.

volonté (f): will.
– *déclarée*: avowed will.
– *unilatérale*: unilateral will.
les dernières – (s): the last will.

volume (m): volume, bulk.
le – *des affaires*: the volume of business.
– *des transactions*: turnover.

votant (m): voter.

vote (m): vote, ballot, poll.
– *d'une loi*: passing, carrying of a bill.
bulletin de – : voting-paper.
déclarer le résultat du – : to declare the poll.
droit de – : franchise, right to –.
droit de – des actionnaires: voting rights.
– *à bulletins secrets*: secret ballot.
– *à mains levées*: show of hands.
– *par procuration*: vote by proxy.
section de – : polling district, station, [U.S.] precinct.

voter (v): to vote, (*au Parlement*) to come to a division.

(dans les délais) voulus: within the required time.

voyage (m): travel, journey, voyage.
agence de – (s): travel agency.
chèque de – : traveller's cheque.
– *à forfait*: all-inclusive tour (through bookings).
frais de – : travelling expenses.

voyageur *de commerce*: commercial traveller,

travelling salesman.

(en) vrac: in bulk.

vu que: considering that; whereas...

(le) vu d'un arrêt: the preamble of a decree.

vue (f): [J] *droit* *−(s)*: ancient lights.
 — *de servitude*: see *servitude de vue*.
 [C] *dépôt à* *−*: sight deposit.
 payable à *−*: payable at sight, on demand, at call.
 retrait à *−*: sight with drawal.
 à sept jours de *−*: seven days fater sight.

vulgarisation (f): popularization.

vulgariser (v): to popularize.

wagon (m): wag(g)on, carriage, truck.
 — *-citerne*: tank wagon.
 — *de marchandises*: goods van.

warrant (m): warrant, deposit, note of hand.
 — *agricole*: farm produce warrant.

warrantage (m): securing of goods by warrant.

warranter (v): to secure goods.

zéro (m): cipher, nought.
 partir de *−*: to start from scratch.

zone (f): area, zone.
 — *bleue*: pink area (zone).
 — *de développement*: development area.
 — *franche*: bonded area, sufferance quay.
 — *frontière*: border area.
 — *d'influence*: controlled area.
 — *de libre-échange*: free trade area.
 — *de silence*: silence zone (around hospitals).
 — *suburbaine*: suburban area.

NOTES

ANGLAIS-FRANÇAIS

ABBREVIATIONS

A.	Administration	Administration
a.	adjective	adjectif
A.A.	Anglo-american	Anglo-américain
adv.	adverb	adverbe
ASS.	Insurance	Assurance
B.	Stock Exchange	Bourse
C.	Commerce, commercial law	Commerce, droit commercial
C.E.E.	European Economic Community	Communauté Économique Européenne
cf.	confer	confer
civ.	civil	civil
C.L.	Common Law	Common Law
conj.	conjunction	conjonction
cr.	criminal	criminel
D.	Customs	Douanes
Eco.	Economy	Économie
E.	Export	Exportation
e.g.	exempli gratia	par exemple
Engl.	England	Angleterre
Eq.	Equity	Equity
esp.	especially	spécialement
etc.	et cetera	et caetera
F.	Finance, taxation	Finance, fiscalité
f.	feminine noun	substantif féminin
Fam.	colloquial	Familier
fig.	figuratively	au figuré
hist.	historic	historique
i.e.	id est	par exemple
inform.	data processing	informatique
inv.	invariable	invariable
journ.	journalism	journalisme
J.	Juridical	Juridique
m.	masculine noun	substantif masculin
milit.	military	militaire
M.P.	Member of Parliament	Membre du Parlement
n.b.	nota bene	nota bene
N.Y.	New York	New York
opp.	opposed	opposé
part.	participle	participe
pej.	pejorative	péjoratif
p.ex.	for example	par exemple
pol.	political	politique
pl.	plural	pluriel
pr.	procedure	procédure
prep.	preposition	préposition
qch.	something	quelque chose
qfs.	sometimes	quelquefois
qn.	some one	quelqu'un
q.v.	see (this word)	se reporter à (ce mot)
r.	relative	relatif
s.	substantive	substantif
Scot.	Scotland	Ecosse
sg.	singular	singulier
s.o.	some one	quelqu'un
sp.	especially	spécialement
sth.	something	quelque chose
syn.	synonymous	synonyme
U.K.	United Kingdom	Royaume-Uni
U.S.	United States	États-Unis
v.	verb	verbe

The symbol = means equal to.
The symbol # shows the nearest meaning of a term or notion in the other language.

Le signe = veut dire égal à.
Le signe # indique la plus proche correspondance d'un terme ou d'une notion dans l'autre langue.

A

« a » shares *(non voting shares)* : actions (f) prioritaires ne donnant pas à leurs détenteurs le droit de voter aux Assemblées Générales.

aaa bonds : [F] bons de première qualité.

a fortiori : a fortiori.

a mensa et thoro : (séparation) de table et de lit (de corps et de biens).

a posteriori : a posteriori.

a priori : a priori.

A.R. (Anno Regni) : de l'année du règne.

a verbis legis non recedendum est :on ne doit pas s'écarter de la lettre de la Loi (quand il s'agit de l'interpréter).

a vinculo matrimonii : du (des) lien(s) du mariage.

ab antiquo : depuis l'antiquité, les temps anciens.

ab initio : depuis le commencement.

ab intestato : (succession) ab intestat.

to abandon : abandonner, renoncer, se désister, se démettre.
— *one's domicile* : abandonner son domicile.
— *prosecution* : renoncer aux poursuites.
[B] — *an option* : abandonner une prime.

abandonnee : abandonnataire (m).

abandonment : abandon (m).
[J] *(of family, mortgage, property, ship)*, délaissement (m), *(of claim, patent, easement)* renoncement (m), *(of action)* passé-expédient (m).
— *decision* : décision (f) d'abandon, de désinvestir, de se désengager ; désinvestissement.
— *of property* : cession (f) de biens.
— *value* : valeur (f) résiduelle.

to abate : abolir, annuler, diminuer.

abatement : diminution (f), affaiblissement (m), réduction (f), abattement (m), dégrèvement (m), réfaction (f).
[J] [C.L.] suspension ou arrêt de poursuites en raison de l'incapacité de l'une des parties (décès, mariage, faillite) ou d'une erreur de procédure *(defect in the writ)*.
— *of legacies* : réduction (f) des dispositions du défunt.
— *of nuisance* : suppression (f) d'un abus.
[F] — *of taxes* : défalcation (f) de l'impôt, dégrèvement (m).
basic — : abattement (m) à la base.
[C] rabais (m), remise (f) sur le prix.

abdication : abdication (f).
to abdicate *a right, an office* : renoncer à un droit, se démettre d'une charge.

abduction : enlèvement (m).

to abet : provoquer, encourager, soutenir.
whoever aids or **abets** *such person* : quiconque aide cette personne ou se fait son complice.

abetment : incitation au crime ou délit.
[J] *aiding and* **abetting** : complicité (f).
abettor of a crime : complice (m).
abettor of disorders : fauteur de désordres.

abeyance : *(of a law)* suspension (f), *(of rights, of an office)* vacation (f), interruption (f), cessation (f).
cases held in — : causes en suspens.
decision in — : question pendante, litispendance.
[J] *estate, inheritance, in* — : succession vacante, deshérence (f).
land in — : biens jacents.
law in — : loi inappliquée.
to fall in — : tomber en désuétude.
to hold a decision in — : se prononcer ultérieurement, remettre la décision, le jugement.

to abide : demeurer, rester en suspens ; se conformer, s'incliner, se soumettre.
[J] *costs* **abide** *the event* : les frais suivent le principal.
— *by* : respecter.
— *by a decision* : se soumettre à un jugement.
*law-***abiding** *citizen* : citoyen respectueux des lois.
— *by the testimony of* : s'en rapporter au témoignage de.
we abide by the treaty : nous nous en tenons à la stricte exécution du traité.

ability: capacité (f), pouvoir (m) (de faire qch.), compétence (f), aptitude (f), efficience (f).
[J] *(to inherit, to devise property)* habilité (f), *(to make a will)* capacité (f) légale de tester.
– *to pay*: solvabilité, faculté contributive.
– *to succeed*: capacité à succéder.
– *taxes*: impôt-facultés contributives, impôt-ressources.
[C] **abilities**: disponibilités (f pl), ressources nécessaires pour satisfaire aux obligations.

able: capable.
– *in body and mind*: sain de corps et d'esprit.
– *in law*: versé dans les questions juridiques.
a debtor – to pay: débiteur solvable.

abnegation: 1° désaveu (m), 2° renonciation (f) (voir *disclaimer, waiver*).

abode: demeure (f), habitation (f), résidence (f).
[J] *place of –*: domicile (m) ou résidence (f).
of, with, no fixed –: sans domicile fixe.
at his usual place of –: au lieu ordinaire de son domicile.
to take up one's –: élire domicile.
[F] séjour habituel.

to abolish: abolir, supprimer.
[J] annuler, abroger.
abolishment, abolition: abolition, suppression, abrogation (f).

abortion: [J] avortement provoqué (opp. *miscarriage*).
procuring of –: manœuvres abortives.

abortive: manqué, avorté.
– *law*: loi inopérante.
– *trial*: audience (f) remise pour faute de procédure.
to render –: faire avorter (un projet).

abos *(Asset Backed Obligations)*: obligations (f) garanties par des valeurs (des actifs).

above: au-dessus de, ci-dessus.
[B] – *par*: au-dessus du pair.
the – circumstances: les circonstances susmentionnées.
[F] – *the line expenditures*: dépenses inscrites au budget ordinaire.
– *the line advertising expenditure*: budget (m) ordinaire de publicité.

abridgment: *(of authority)* diminution (f), *(of rights)* restriction (f).

abroad: à l'étranger.

abrogation: abrogation (f).

to abscond: [J] se soustraire à la justice, fuir.
– *with*: lever le pied avec.
absconding *witness*: témoin défaillant.
absconder: contumax, défaillant.

absence: absence (f).
[J] a) défaut (m); b) présomption de décès après une absence de sept ans.
– *of consideration*: absence de contrepartie (dans un contrat).
– *without pay*: congé sans solde.
sentence in –: condamnation (f) par défaut, par contumace.
in the – of express language to this effect: faute d'une stipulation à cet effet.
in the – of evidence to the contrary: jusqu'à preuve du contraire.
in the – of other arrangements: sauf arrangements contraires.
leave of –: congé (m).
to absent *oneself*: refuser de comparaître.
absentee: absentéiste.

absolute: absolu, irrévocable, péremptoire.
[J] (ordonnance, jugement, etc.) en état et immédiatement applicable.
– *acceptance*: acceptation pure et simple.
decree –: jugement définitif.
– *interest*: propriété incommutable.
– *liability*: obligation inconditionnelle.
– *magnitude*: valeur absolue.
– *owner*: propriétaire incommutable.
– *right*: droit irréfragable.
– *title*: titre de propriété inscrit au registre foncier, garanti par l'Etat.
absolutely *void*: radicalement nul.
case of – necessity: cas de force majeure.

absolution: acquittement (m).

to absolve: absoudre, acquitter.
– *from a penalty*: remettre une pénalité.

to absorb: absorber, résorber.
– *a surplus*: résorber un surplus.
marginal propensity –: capacité d'absorption marginale.

absorption: fusion, absorption, concentration (f).
– *casting*: évaluation (f) des coûts par absorption, ventilation (f) des coûts.

abstention: abstention (f).
[J] renonciation tacite à une succession.

abstract: résumé (m), abrégé (m), sommaire (m), précis (m), extrait (m), analyse (f).
[J] — *of title*: extrait du répertoire des mutations de propriété.
— *case*: cas hypothétique.
— *statement*: état récapitulatif.

to abstract: distraire, soustraire, détourner.
abstraction *of funds*: détournement de fonds.
[J] *abstraction of documents*: soustraction frauduleuse.

abundans cautela non nocet: excès de précaution ne nuit pas.

abundant: abondant.
[J] *over-* — : surabondant.

abuse: abus (m).
[J] viol (si dit aussi *rape, criminal attempt*).
— *of discretion*: excès de pouvoir.
— *of distress*: faire abus de quelque chose, mésuser de quelqu'un, outrepasser son droit.
— *of law, of rights*: abus (m) du droit.
— *of process*: abus (m) de procédure, chicane (f).
—, abusive *language*: emploi de termes injurieux.
glaring — : abus scandaleux.
to point out —(s) : signaler les abus.
[F] *the rule lent itself to an* — *whereby...* : la règle offrait des possibilités d'évasion puisque...

to abut: confiner.
[J] *abutting parts of an estate*, **abuttals**: les (tenants et) aboutissants.
abutter: propriétaire bordier, limitrophe, riverain.

to accede: accéder à, entrer en possession.

accelerated: accéléré (a).
[F] — *amortization, depreciation*: amortissement accéléré.
— *cost recovery system*: (U.S.) système (m) fiscal d'amortissement dégressif, accéléré, exceptionnel.
— *redemption*: remboursement (m) anticipé.

acceleration: accélération (f), réduction (f) (du délai d'exécution).
[J] prise de possession anticipée.
[C] — *of maturity*: avancement d'une échéance (d'exécution de contrat, d'une traite, etc.).
— *clause*: stipulation à cet effet (p. ex. en cas de non-paiement d'intérêts, etc.).
— *(accelerator) principle (theory)*: principe (m) de l'accélération, théorie (f) de l'accélérateur (Keynes).

to accept: accepter, approuver, agréer.
— *a bill of exchange*: accepter une lettre de change.
— *goods*: prendre livraison de marchandise.
refusal — : refus d'acceptation.

acceptable quality level: quantité (f) maximale d'unités défectueuses tolérées par le chef de fabrication.

acceptance: acceptation (f), consentement (m), approbation (f), agrément (m).
[J] — *of a judgment*: acquiescement (m) à un jugement.
[C] réception (f) (d'un article commandé).
— *for honour, supra protest*: acceptation (f) d'un effet, par honneur, par intervention après protêt.
[F] — *house*: banque d'escompte (des effets étrangers).
— *of persons*: partialité (f).
— *company*: société de financement.
— *of bribe*: acceptation de pots-de-vin.
clean — : acceptation sans réserve.
collateral — : acceptation par intervention.
for non — : faute d'acceptation.
— *paper*: billet à ordre.
qualified — : acceptation conditionnelle.
to present for — : présenter à l'acceptation.

acceptor: [C] tiré (m), accepteur (m) (d'une lettre de change).
— *for honour,* — *supra protest*: intervenant (m), avaliste (m), donneur d'aval.

access: [J] exercice des droits conjugaux; présomption de relations sexuelles.
non- — : a) refus du devoir conjugal (cause de divorce); b) impossibilité d'avoir eu des rapports conjugaux (motif de désaveu de paternité).
right of — : droit de passage.
to have — *to record*: avoir accès aux documents.

accession: [J] a) droit d'accession; b) avènement (m) au trône; c) assentiment (m).
— *to the EEC*: adhésion à la CEE.
— *to an estate*: entrée (f) en possession, en jouissance.
— *to income*: augmentation (f) de revenus.
— *to office*: entrée (f) en fonction.
— *to a treaty*: accession (f), adhésion (f) à un traité.
— *number*: numéro (m) matricule.
instrument of — : instrument d'admission.

accessory: [J] complice (m).
— *after the fact*: complice après coup.
— *before the fact*: complice (m) par instigation.
— *expenses*: frais accessoires.

to be — to: concourir à.

accident: accident (m).
[J] cas fortuit.
personal — insurance: assurance (f) individuelle contre les accidents.
—(s) at sea: fortune (f) de mer.
— to third party: accident causé aux tiers.

to accite: citer à comparaître.

accomenda: [J] (droit maritime) partage (m) des bénéfices faits sur la vente, entre le capitaine et le propriétaire de la cargaison.

to accommodate: adapter, approprier, convenir, loger, accueillir.
— a dispute: régler un différend.

accommodation: facilité (f), compromis (m), accommodement (m), commodité (f), logement (m), installation (f).
[C] *— bill:* traite de complaisance, (fam.) cavalerie, prêt (m) à court terme pour permettre à un emprunteur de trouver d'autres fonds (par ex. en s'adressant à une banque).
friendly —: arrangement à l'amiable.
for the — of the public: pour l'usage du public.
object of general —: objet à l'usage du public.
— land: terrain acquis en vue d'améliorer le terrain contigu.
residential —: immeuble d'habitation.

accomplice: complice (m), (fam.) acolyte (m).
to be — in a crime: tremper dans un crime.

accord: accord, règlement transactionnel, consentement.
[J] *executory —:* novation (f).
— and satisfaction: novation exécutée.
in — with: conformément à.
to accord *a request:* faire droit à une requête.

accordance: accord (m), conformité (f).
in — with: d'accord avec, conformément à, en exécution de, en vertu de.
in — with the foregoing: comme il est dit ci-dessus.
in — with the provisions of article 1: aux termes de l'article 1.
in — with the stipulations of: par application des dispositions de.

according to: conformément à, suivant, en fonction de, selon.
— circumstances: au gré des circonstances.
— custom: suivant l'usage.
accordingly: en conséquence, à l'avenant.
to act accordingly: agir en conséquence.

account: compte (m).
[J] compte de tutelle, de *trust* ; action (f) en reddition de compte.
involuntary —: action en reddition de compte (en Eq.) par le bénéficiaire d'un *trust* (mineur à sa majorité, héritier, etc.).
voluntary —: action (en Eq.) du *trustee* pour obtenir son quitus.
[F] 1° *abstract of —:* relevé de compte.
— agreed upon: arrêté de compte.
— book: livre de compte.
— of assets and liabilities: état de l'actif et du passif.
— day: jour de liquidation.
— market: marché à terme.
amount paid on —: acompte versé.
—(s) payable: dettes (f) passives.
—(s) receivable: dettes (f) actives.
« *— (s) payee only* »: formule (f) que l'on écrit sur la face d'un chèque et qui équivaut à le barrer.
appropriation —: compte d'affectation.
balance of an —: solde, balance d'un compte.
to balance an —: balancer, solder un compte.
balance on current —: solde d'un compte courant.
balancing property of the —(s): équilibre obligatoire des comptes.
bank —: compte en banque.
bargain for —: marché, négociation à terme ; marché à livrer.
bear —: position à la baisse ; découvert.
bull —: position à la hausse.
business —: portefeuille (m) d'entreprises, registre des relations d'entreprises.
to buy on one's own —: acheter pour son propre compte.
capital —: compte capital.
capital expenditure —: compte immobilisations.
cash- —: compte de caisse.
cash management —: compte courant portant intérêt placé chez un agent de change.
charge- —: [U.S.] compte crédit d'achats.
to charge an expense on, to, an —: imputer une dépense à un compte.
clean —: compte en règle.
clearing —: compte de virement.
closed —: compte inactif.
combined —(s): comptes additionnés.
committee on public —(s): [U.S.] Cour des comptes.
consolidated —(s): comptes consolidés.
contingent —: compte d'éventualité.
contra —: compte contrepartie ; jumelage.
to cover a short —: couvrir un découvert.
to credit an —: créditer un compte.
creditor —: compte créditeur.
current —: compte courant.
dealing for the —: négociations à terme.
debtor —: compte débiteur.
deposit —: compte de dépôt.

detailed — : compte spécifié.
drawing — : compte de dépôt à vue.
drawings on current — : prélèvements sur compte courant.
exchange equalization — : fonds de stabilisation des changes.
external — : compte transférable.
fixed-deposit — : compte de dépôt à échéance.
following — : liquidation suivante.
to give an — *of* : rendre compte de.
impersonal — : compte anonyme.
interest — : compte d'intérêts.
itemized — : compte détaillé.
joint — : compte joint.
loan — : compte de prêt ; compte d'avances.
to look over an — *(again)* : réviser un compte.
loss and profit — : compte de pertes et profits.
management — : compte de gestion.
money of — : monnaie de compte.
money as a unit of — : monnaie en tant qu'unité de compte.
name of an — : intitulé d'un compte.
next — : liquidation prochaine.
office — : compte professionnel.
open — : compte ouvert.
outstanding — : compte arriéré.
overdrawn — : compte découvert, désapprovisionné.
particulars of an — : détails d'un compte.
partner in joint — : coparticipant.
to pay on — : verser un acompte.
payment on — : acompte.
personal — : compte personnel.
placing money on current — : dépôt à vue.
price for the — : cours à terme.
private — : compte « particulier ».
property — : compte de valeurs.
property — *(s)* : comptes de l'exploitation.
proprietary — *(s)* : comptes de résultats.
provisional — : compte provisoire.
purchases — : compte d'achat.
real — *(s)* : comptes de l'exploitation.
receipt on — : reçu à valoir.
running — : compte courant.
sale for the — : vente à terme.
sales — : compte de vente(s).
securities dealt in for the — : valeurs à terme.
settlement — : compte de liquidation.
settlement of — : arrêté de compte.
short — : découvert.
statement of — : relevé de compte.
stock- — : compte de capital.
subsidiary — : sous-compte.
succeeding — : liquidation suivante.
summary — : compte récapitulatif.
sundries — : compte de divers.
suspense — : compte d'ordre.
to swell an — : gonfler un compte.
to tick off items in an — : pointer les articles d'un compte.
total — : compte collectif.
trading — : compte d'exploitation.

transaction for the — : opération, négociation à terme.
underwriting — : compte d'assurance maritime.
in full discharge of all — *(s)* : pour solde de tout compte.
2° — *(s)* : comptabilité, écritures comptables.
to agree the — *(s)* : faire accorder les livres (comptables).
to audit the — *(s)* : vérifier et certifier les comptes.
chart of — *(s)* : [U.S.] cadre comptable (d'une entreprise).
— *(s) closing* : arrêté (m) des comptes.
earmarking — *(s)* : comptes d'affectation.
external — *(s)* : comptes extérieurs.
externalities — *(s)* : comptabilité des externalités.
falsification of — *(s)* : faux en écritures comptables.
to keep the — *(s)* : tenir les livres, la comptabilité.
national — *(s)* : comptabilité nationale.
satellite — *(s)* : comptes satellites (ils isolent, en comptabilité nationale, des fonctions particulières : éducation, santé...).
systems of — *(s)* : la comptabilité.
to cook the — *(s)* : falsifier les écritures.
to draw up — *(s)* : arrêter un exercice.
to rewrite the — *(s)* : rectifier la comptabilité.

accountability : responsabilité (f).

accountable (for) : redevable, comptable, responsable.
— *receipts* : pièces comptables.

accountableness : responsabilité (f).

accountancy : comptabilité (f).
following — *rules* : conformément aux règles comptables.

accountant : [J] défendeur dans une action en reddition de compte.
[A] — *-general (Clerk of the Crown)* : dépositaire (m) des fonds consignés en justice.
[C] agent comptable.
[U.K.] *chartered* — (C.A.), [U.S.] *certified public* — (C.P.A.) : expert comptable.
chief — : chef comptable.
the — *('s) department* : service de la comptabilité.

accounting : comptabilité (f).
[C] *accrual* — : comptabilité d'engagement.
accounting department : service de comptabilité.
— *for (taxes, etc.)* : comptabilisation (des impôts, etc...).
— *period* : exercice comptable, financier.
— *procedure* : organisation comptable.

– *profit and its make-up* : bénéfice comptable et renseignements s'y rapportant.
– *records* : pièces (f) comptables.
cash – : comptabilité de caisse.
cost – : comptabilité de prix de revient.
national – : comptabilité nationale, comptes de la nation.
separate – : comptabilité distincte.

accreditation : accréditement (m) (d'un agent diplomatique).
accredited *representative* : représentant attitré.

accretion : [J] 1° accroissement (m) organique (alluvionnement, etc.) ; 2° majoration (f) d'héritage (voir *to lapse, lapsed legacy*).

accrual :
[J] – *of a cause of action* : date de survenance d'une cause d'action en justice.
– *of a right* : date de naissance d'un droit.
clause of – : clause d'accroissement (dans un testament ou une donation).
[F] – *of dividend* : échéance de dividende.
– *basis method* : système de comptabilisation tenant compte des créances acquises et des dépenses engagées.
on the – *basis* : suivant la comptabilité de l'exercice.

to accrue : provenir, dériver, s'ajouter, s'accumuler, revenir à (qqn).
accrued *dividends* : dividendes accumulés.
accrued interest : intérêt accumulé, couru.
accrued rents, liabilities : loyers, engagements exigibles.

accruing (to) : afférent (à).
income accruing to the taxpayer : revenus réalisés par le contribuable.
accruing interest : intérêts à échoir.
portion accruing to each heir : portion (f) revenant à chaque héritier.
profits accruing to a company : bénéfices réalisés par une société.

accumulation : cumul (m), épargne (f).
accumulated *earning tax* : impôt sur les réserves, (U.S.) impôt (m) sur les bénéfices non distribués.

accumulative : accumulé, cumulatif.
[J] – *sentence* : jugement ordonnant le cumul des peines.
[F] – *dividends* : dividendes cumulatifs.

accusation : accusation (f).
[J] a) incrimination (f), b) dénonciation (f) d'un acte délictueux.
a ground of – : un chef d'accusation.
to bring an – : proférer une accusation.
to substantiate an – : établir une accusation.

under the – *of* : accusé de.

to accuse : accuser, incriminer.
the **accused** : [J] *(in all cases)* le, la prévenu(e), *(of a misdemeanour)* l'inculpé(e), *(of a crime)* l'accusé(e).

acknowledgment : constatation (f), reconnaissance (f) (d'un fait, d'une obligation).
to make an – *of (sthg)* : reconnaître (qqch).
[J] certification (f) d'un acte (sp. sous forme d'un *affidavit*, correspond à l'acte notarié), aveu.
– *by record* : aveu (m) judiciaire.
– *of debt* : reconnaissance (f) (d'une dette).
written acknowledgment : reconnaissance écrite.
[A] – *of complaint* : récépissé d'une réclamation.
[C] reçu (m), quittance (f).
– *of deposit* : récépissé de dépôt.
– *of receipt* : accusé (m) de réception.
acknowledgment(s) : remerciements.

acquaintance : connaissance (f), relations (f pl) (d'affaires).
wide **acquaintanceship** : (des) relations étendues.

acquest : [J] biens acquis par acte entre vifs.

acquiescence : acquiescement (m).
[J] assentiment (m), consentement (m) exprès ou tacite, ratification.
to acquiesce *in a decision* : laisser un jugement passer en force de chose jugée.

to acquire : acquérir, entrer en possession.
after **acquired** *clause* : clause gageant des obligations nouvelles sur une hypothèse ancienne.
property acquired for valuable consideration : propriété acquise à titre onéreux.

acquisition : acquisition (f).
compulsory – *of property* : expropriation pour cause d'intérêt public.

the **acquisitive society** : la société d'acquisition (f) (les gens veulent toujours acheter les tout derniers articles sur le marché).

acquittal : [J] acquittement (m), décharge (f), d'un accusé, d'une dette, d'une obligation, accomplissement (m), quitus (m).

acquittance : [J] [C] acquittement (m) (d'une dette).
[C] [A] quittance (f), décharge (f).
to give an – : donner acquis.

acronym : sigle (m).
across-the-board diversification : diversification (f) maximum.
across-the-board increase *(e.g. of wages)* : augmentation (f) générale (ex. des salaires).
act : acte (m), action (f), mesure (f), loi (f).
[J] 1° – *of Parliament, Congress, Legislature* : loi.
– *of state* : acte de gouvernement.
to pass an – : adopter une loi.
2° act (m), document (m), contrat (m).
– *of bankruptcy* : tout acte d'un débiteur justifiant sa mise en faillite.
– *of confession* : aveu.
– *of God* : cas de force majeure.
criminal – : acte relevant du droit pénal.
outward – : tout fait de l'homme.
overt – : (cr.) commencement d'exécution.
– *of petition* : référé.
– *of sale* : acte de vente.
– *of substitution* : acte subrogatoire.
caught in the very – : pris sur le fait.
Single European – *(SEA)* : acte unique européen (A.U.E.).
[C] – *of honour* : intervention (f) après protêt.
[U.S.] *Antimonopoly* – : législation anti-trust.
Companies – : législation sur les sociétés.
[U.K.] *Factory* – : législation industrielle.
Finance – : loi de finances.
Land – : loi agraire.
Navigation – : législation maritime.

to act : agir, intervenir, mettre à exécution.
– *for* : faire fonction de, remplacer, suppléer, agir à titre de.
– *upon* : donner suite à.
the court acted favourably on the petition : le tribunal a donné suite à la requête.
acting mayor : maire par intérim.
acting manager : gérant, administrateur provisoire.
acting order : délégation de pouvoir.

actio personalis moritur cum persona : une action personnelle s'éteint avec la personne.

action : action (f).
[J] 1° – *at law* : action en justice.
– *for an account* : action en reddition de compte.
court – : décision judiciaire.
– *for damages* : demande de dommages-intérêts.
– *in expropriation of real property* : procédure d'expropriation.
feigned – : cause fictive.

– *on a foreign judgment* : demande d'exequatur.
for – : pour exécution.
– *for infringement of patent* : assignation en contrefaçon.
– *for libel* : plainte en diffamation écrite.
local – : action qui doit être intentée au lieu où le droit a pris naissance, notamment la réintégrande (– *for recovery of land*), ou au domicile du débiteur.
– *for payment* : action en paiement.
penal voir *popular* –.
– *for penalties* : action en recouvrement d'amendes.
pending – : affaire en cours.
petitory – : action pétitoire.
– *respecting copyright* : action en réclamation des droits d'auteur.
transitory – : a) action qui peut être intentée en tout lieu, notamment action en exécution de contrat ou de demande de dommages-intérêts (opp. *local action*), b) revendication qui doit être jugée selon la loi étrangère.
right of – : plainte recevable, droit d'ester en justice.
to bring an – *against s.o.* : intenter un procès à, contre qn.
to bring the law into – : mettre la justice en action.
to bring a civil – *against* : se porter partie civile (contre).
to institute an – : introduire une instance en justice.
to take – : attaquer, citer, poursuivre en justice.
actionable *fraud, negligence* : fraude (f), négligence (f) passible de poursuites.
2° *choses in* – : droits incorporels.
[A] *official* – : acte d'administration.
to take – : prendre des mesures.

active : actif, agissant, énergique, productif (a).
– *balance* : solde créditeur.
– *chairman* : président en exercice.
– *debt* : dette active.
in – *employment* : en activité.
– *loans* : prêts productifs.
– *market* : marché animé.
– *money* : espèces.
– *partner* : associé actif.

activity : activité (f), occupation (f).
– *chart* : diagramme (m) de production (indiquant quelle partie du travail doit être exécutée et quand le travail doit être terminé).
legal **activities** : œuvre juridique.
activities multipliers : multiplicateurs d'activités.
operational activities : programme d'action à exécuter.
political activities : visées politiques.

— *sampling*: échantillonnage (m) estimatif du temps passé à produire un article.
specialized field of activities: domaine d'activités spécialisé.

actual: réel, véritable, effectif (a).
[J] — *case*: cas concret, — *knowledge*: connaissance directe (opp. *constructive knowledge*).
— *notice*: signification à personne.
— *possession*: possession effective.
the — *provisions*: les dispositions expresses.
[C] — *cost*: prix d'achat.
— *disbursements*: paiements effectivement opérés.
— *earnings*: gains effectifs.
— *price*: prix réel.
— *value*: valeur marchande.
in — *employment*: en activité.
[F] — *basis of assessment*: imposition « au réel ».
— *tax*: impôt réel.
— *yield*: rendement effectif.

actuality: fait accompli, état de chose.

actually: réellement, véritablement, effectivement.
profits — *realized*: gains effectivement réalisés.

actuarial: actuariel.
on — *basis*: d'après les calculs actuariels.
— *tables*: tables actuarielles.

actuary: [ASS] actuaire.
actuaries' *tables*: tables de mortalité (se dit aussi *survival tables, life expectancy tables*).

acumen: finesse (f) d'esprit, clairvoyance (f).
business — : sens (m) des affaires.

acute: aigu, pénétrant, vif, violent.
— *competition*: concurrence acharnée.
— *depression*: marasme.

ad: annonce (f) (dans un journal).
to put (to run) an — *in a newspaper*: faire passer une annonce dans un journal.

adman: publiciste (m).

to add: ajouter, additionner, accroître, augmenter.
— *back*: réintégrer.
— *documents to a file*: joindre des pièces au dossier.
— *the interest to the capital*: ajouter l'intérêt au capital.
— *the signature*: apposer la signature.
— *one's income*: accroître son revenu.
over **added**, *under* **added**: additionné en plus, en moins.
— *up*: additionner, totaliser.
value **added** *tax* (V.A.T.): taxe sur la valeur ajoutée (T.V.A.).

addition: addition (f), adjonction (f), augmentation (f), annexe (f).
[J] — *to a law*: loi complémentaire.
[F] — *to the stock*: augmentation du capital par incorporation de réserves.
— *(s) to tax*: pénalités (f) fiscales.
[U.S.] — *to surplus*: addition à la réserve générale.
in — : en outre, par surcroît.
name and — : nom et qualité.

additional: additionnel, complémentaire.
— *assessment*: imposition supplémentaire.
[A] — *income*: revenu supplémentaire.
— *postage*: surtaxe postale.
[C] — *charges*: frais supplémentaires.
[E] — *freight*: surfret.
— *pay*: supplément de salaire.
— *security*: garantie accessoire, nantissement, sûreté.
[J] — *clause*: additif, avenant.

address: adresse (f), allocution (f), apostrophe (f).
[J] supplique (f), requête (f), pétition (f).
— *for service*: domicile élu.
counsel's opening — : exposé des faits = requête introductive d'instance.
— *to the court*: plaidoirie.

to adduce: apporter, offrir.
[J] alléguer.
— *an argument*: invoquer une raison.
— *authorities*: citer les bons auteurs.
— *evidence*: fournir une preuve.
— *grounds*: exposer les motifs.
— *a witness*: produire un témoin.
the evidence **adduced** *in support*: la preuve à charge.

adduction: allégation (f) (de faits), production (f) (de preuves).

ademption: [J] ademption (f) (révocation implicite d'une disposition testamentaire).

adequacy: compétence (f) (d'un tribunal).

adequate: suffisant (a).
— *security*: des garanties (f pl) suffisantes.

to adhere: adhérer.
— *to a proposal*: donner son accord à une proposition.

adherence: adhésion, observance, obéissance.

— 292 —

ad hoc: spécial, approprié, à cet effet, ad hoc.
— *bodies*: organes spéciaux.
— *committee*: commission spéciale.
expert appointed — : expert désigné selon les besoins.
on — *bases*: selon des méthodes appropriées.

ad idem: sur la même chose (pour qu'un contrat soit valable il faut qu'il y ait accord « sur la même chose »).

ad interim: par intérim, intérimaire.
judgment — : sentence provisoire.

ad litem: pour le procès (tuteur, représentant d'un enfant en bas âge nommé par le tribunal).

ad medium filum aquae: à partir de la ligne médiane de l'eau.

ad medium filum viae: à partir de la ligne médiane de la voie.

ad valorem: selon la valeur.

ad vitam aut culpam: pour la vie ou tant qu'il n'y aura pas eu faute.

adjacent: adjacent (a).
[J] — *lands*: les tenants et aboutissants.
— *owner*: propriétaire limitrophe, riverain.

adjective: adjectif (a).
[J] — *law*: procédure (f) (opp. *substantive law*).

to adjourn: ajourner, différer, remettre, renvoyer, suspendre.
— *a session*: clore les débats, lever la séance.
the committee stands **adjourned**: la séance est levée.
upon such adjourned hearing: à la reprise de l'audience ajournée.

adjournment: ajournement (m), interruption (f), renvoi (m), remise (f), suspension (f).
— *for a week*: remise à huitaine.
— *of debate*: renvoi de la suite de la discussion.
to move the — : proposer l'ajournement.

to adjudge: [J] adjuger, déclarer, prononcer sur.
— *damages*: accorder des dommages-intérêts.
— *So-and-so guilty*: déclarer Untel coupable.
— *the prize to the captor*: adjuger la prise au capteur.
adjudged *and ordered*: prononcé.
adjudging *costs*: adjuger les dépenses.

adjudgment: jugement (m), arrêt (m), décision (f).

to adjudicate: juger, décider judiciairement, rendre un arrêt, une sentence arbitrale, statuer.
— *s.o. bankrupt*: mettre qn en faillite.
— *a claim*: juger une réclamation.
magistrate entitled — : juge compétent.

adjudication: [J] jugement, décision, prononcé d'un jugement.
[A] adjudication, marché public.
— *of bankruptcy*: jugement déclaratif de faillite (règlement judiciaire ou liquidation de biens).
— *of a bankrupt's debts*: répartition des dettes d'un failli.
— *of marital status*: décision au sujet de la validité d'un mariage.
— *on questions of law*: décision sur des questions de droit.
adjudicative *decree*: jugement déclaratif.
adjudicator: juge.

adjunction: adjonction (f).
[J] accession (f).

adjuration: adjuration (f).
[J] affirmation (f), engagement (m) sous serment.

to adjust: régler, accommoder (un différend), arranger (une affaire), rectifier (des comptes), régulariser (un acte).
[ASS] — *an average*: répartir une avarie.
— *claims*: régler des créances.
adjustable *rate*: taux (m) variable (d'un prêt).
adjusted *balance*: bilan rectifié.
adjusted *net book value*: actif (m) net rectifié.
seasonally adjusted (v. « *seasonally* »).
adjusting *entry*: inscription (f) rectificative.

adjuster: liquidateur (m), répartiteur (m), arbitre (m) (en assurances).

adjustment: ajustement (m), arrangement (m), régularisation (f), règlement (m), redressement (m), remaniement (m), accord (m).
[ASS] — *of average*: règlement (m), répartition (f) d'avaries, dispache (f).
— *of quotas*: ajustement (m) des quotes-parts.
— *of claims*: règlement des indemnités.
— *of conditions of industrial labour*: réglementation du travail.
— *bonds*: obligations de redressement.
— *of customs tariffs*: ajustement des tarifs douaniers.
— *of taxes*: péréquation de l'impôt.
balancing — : ajustement de solde.
annual — : régularisation annuelle.

– *of exchange rates*: alignement monétaire.
– *of wages*: révision des salaires.
– *payments*: paiements rectificatifs.
financial – : redressement financier.
period of – : période d'adaptation.
– *threshold*: seuil d'ajustement.
to bring about an – : amener un redressement.
– *(s) to the taxpayer's liability*: redressement du revenu imposable.

admanuensis: a) secrétaire à la main ; b) serment (la main) sur la Bible.

admeasurement: partage (m), attribution (f) de part.

adminicle: [J] adminicule (preuve corroborante).

to administer: *(a country, an estate, a business)* administrer, gérer, *(the law)* appliquer.
– *justice*: rendre la justice.
– *on oath*: déférer le serment.
– *to a will*: exécuter les clauses d'un testament.
– *upon an estate*: gérer une succession.
– *a portfolio*: gérer un portefeuille.
administrative *law*: droit administratif.

administration: administration (f), gestion (f), régie (f).
[U.S.] *the* – *in Washington*: le gouvernement fédéral.
tax – : administration fiscale, services fiscaux.
[J] *(of a minor's estate)* curatelle (f), *(of an intestate estate)* administration judiciaire.
– *ad colligendum*: administration provisoire d'une succession.
– *cum testamento annexo*: administration d'une succession testamentaire dont l'exécuteur ne peut assumer l'administration ou n'a pas été nommé.
– *de bonis non cum testamento annexo*: administration d'une succession dont l'exécuteur est décédé avant la liquidation.
– *durante minori aetate or absentia*: administration d'une succession dont l'exécuteur est mineur ou se trouve à l'étranger.
– *pendente lite*: administration provisoire d'une succession testamentaire faisant l'objet d'un litige.
ancillary – : administration locale des éléments d'une succession, subordonnée à l'administration principale, située au lieu du dernier domicile du de cujus.
– *order, letters of* – : ordonnance (f) instituant l'administrateur judiciaire d'une succession ab intestat.
– *of assets*: gestion de patrimoine.
– *of an act*: application d'une loi.
– *of an oath*: prestation de serment.

administrative: administratif.
– *body*: organe administratif.
– *expenses*: frais (m) d'administration et gestion, frais généraux.
– *staff*: personnel administratif.
public – *regulation*: règlement d'administration publique (R.A.P.).

administrator (m), **administratrix** (f):
administrateur (m), administratrice (f), gérant (m), gérante (f), gestionnaire (m et f).
[J] *(of an intestate estate)* administrateur (m), administratrice (f) judiciaire, *(of a minor's estate)* curateur (m), curatrice (f), *(of a spendthrift's estate)* conseil judiciaire.
– *to child unborn*: curateur au ventre.
administratorship: curatelle, gérance (f).

admissible: recevable, acceptable.
– *appeal, evidence*: pourvoi (m), preuve (f) recevable.

admission: admission (f), accès (m), acceptation (f), aveu (m), confession (f).
[J] *(of an offence)* confession (f), *(of an alleged fact)* reconnaissance (f).
– *to the bar* # inscription au barreau.
special – *(for purposes limited to a particular case)*: autorisation accordée à un avocat étranger de plaider (dans une affaire déterminée).
– *on record*: aveu judiciaire.
– *requirements*: conditions d'admission.
to make – *(s)*: admettre certains faits.
to make full – *(s)*: faire des aveux complets.
on his own – : de son propre aveu.
[D] *temporary* – : admission temporaire (des marchandises).

to admit: admettre, laisser passer, accepter, concéder, avouer.
– *a claim*: reconnaître une prétention, admettre un recours.
admitted *custom*: usage (m) admis.
admitted *in evidence*: admettre comme preuve.

admittance: admission (f), concession (f), accès (m).
[J] remise en possession d'un bien foncier.
– *of attorney*: désignation d'un avocat.
– *of a partner*: entrée d'un nouvel associé dans une affaire.
to gain – *to*: obtenir l'accès auprès de.

admonishment, admonotion: blâme (m), réprimande (f).
[A] avertissement (m).

adoption: adoption (f).
[J] **adopter**: adoptant(e).
adoptee: adopté(e).

adopted *child*: enfant adoptif.
adopted view: opinion partagée.
adoptive *act*: loi applicable seulement après son adoption.
[C] *adopted trade-mark*: marque de fabrique utilisée.

adult: adulte (m et f).
[J] majeur.

adulteration: altération (f).
(of food) fraude (f) alimentaire, altération (f), *(of texts)* corruption (f), *(of currency, documents)* falsification (f), *(of wines and spirits)* frelatage (m), sophistication (f).

adultery: adultère (m).
adulterer (m), **adulteress** (f) : adultère.
adulterine *child*: enfant adultérin.

advance: 1° anticipé (a), d'avance, à valoir.
— *charges*: débours.
— *corporation tax-act*: précompte mobilier.
— *money*: avance monétaire.
— *order*: souscription.
— *payment*: paiement anticipé.
— *report*: rapport préliminaire.
2° avance (f), avancement (m), prêt (m), essor (m), progrès (m), hausse (f), renchérissement (m).
[A] — *in seniority*: majoration d'ancienneté.
— *ruling*: (U.S.) rescrit (m) (consultation préalable de l'administration).
[C] [F] avance de fonds.
— *against collateral*: prêt sur titres.
— *factory* (U.K.): usine implantée dans une certaine région avant que le besoin s'en soit fait sentir dans l'espoir qu'un (ou des) entrepreneur(s) l'achèteront ou la loueront, créant ainsi des emplois.
— *in prices*: hausse (f) des prix.
— *on securities*: avance sur titres.
by way of —: à titre d'avance.
cash —: avance à découvert.
payment in — *to suppliers*: arrhes.

to advance *(s.o.) money*: avancer de l'argent (à qqn).
to advance (prices): augmenter (les prix).
[B] hausse des cours.

advanced: avancé, développé, évolué.
an — *liberal*: un libéral avancé.
— *cost of living*: augmentation du coût de la vie.
sums —: avances (f pl).

advancement: [J] avance (f) d'hoirie.

advantage: avantage (m), utilité (f), profit (m).
general —: utilité publique.
to good —: à un prix avantageux.
to our best —: au mieux de nos intérêts.
to take — *of*: profiter de, tirer parti.
to take an unfair — *of*: abuser de.

adventitious: adventice, fortuit, accidentel (a).
[J] — *property*: biens adventices.

adventure: risque (m), aventure (f).
[C] a) vente aux risques et profits de l'armateur ou de l'expéditeur, d'un navire ou de marchandises embarquées ;
b) [U.K.] — *in the nature of a trade*: transaction isolée qui n'est pas de nature commerciale.

adverse: adverse, opposé (a).
[J] — *enjoyment, user*: exercice non dissimulé d'un droit de servitude pouvant donner lieu à la prescription acquisitive.
— *holding on prescription*: prescription acquisitive.
— *party*: la partie opposée.
— *possession*: possession de fait susceptible de prescription acquisitive.
— *price movements*: fluctuations (f pl) défavorables des prix.
[E] — *trade balance*: balance commerciale déficitaire.

adversity: adversité.
[J] conflit (m) des lois.

advertisement: avis (m), avertissement (m), annonce (f), publicité (f).
— *required by law*: annonce légale.

advertising: publicité (f).
— *account*: budget publicitaire.
[C] — *agency*: agence de publicité.
deceptive —: publicité mensongère.
— *give-aways*: cadeaux publicitaires.
— *manager*: chef de publicité.
— *media*: organes (m pl) de publicité.
— *rate*: tarif publicitaire.
— *spot*: 1) courte annonce publicitaire, 2) « clin d'œil » (m) publicitaire.
— *strategy*: ligne d'action publicitaire.
— *space*: emplacement réservé à la publicité.
— *theme*: slogan (m) publicitaire.

advice: conseil (m).
[J] — *of counsel*: avis du défenseur.
piece of —: avis.
as per — *from*: suivant avis de.
with the — *and assent*: de l'avis et du consentement de.
legal —: avis d'un homme de loi.
until further —: jusqu'à nouvel avis.
— *note*: lettre (f) d'avis.
[B] — *of deal*: avis d'opérer.

— *of delivery:* avis de réception.

advisable : utile, avantageux, judicieux, approprié.
in case where he deems it — : dans tous les cas où il le jugera utile.

to advise : conseiller, recommander, avertir, instruire, aviser de.
as **advised** *:* selon l'avis.
unless advised to the contrary : sauf avis contraire.

advisee : destinataire (m).

adviser : conseiller (m), conseil (m).
legal, taxation — : conseil juridique, fiscal.

advisibility at the market : [B] au mieux, au cours du marché.

advisory : consultatif.
— *board :* commission, comité consultatif.
— *capacity :* voix consultative.
— *committee :* comité (m) consultatif, comité de restructuration.
— *functions :* attributions consultatives.
— *opinion :* avis consultatif.

advocacy : plaidoyer (m), plaidoirie (f).
to speak in — of : se faire l'avocat de.

advocate : avocat (m).
[J] *judge- — =* commissaire du Gouvernement (auprès d'un conseil de guerre).
judge- — general : chef de la justice militaire.
(Scot.) *the Lord — =* le Procureur général.
—(s)-General (EEC) : Avocats généraux (CEE).

affair : affaire (f), occupation (f), transaction (f).
to manage —(s) : gérer des affaires.
mercantile —(s) : affaires commerciales.
statement of —(s) : arrêté des comptes.

to affect : affecter, concerner, atteindre, se rapporter à, caractériser.
[U.S.] *business* **affected** *with a public interest (public utility) :* service public ou d'intérêt public exploité par une compagnie privée, concession de service public.
fact **affecting** *the findings :* fait qui n'est pas sans portée sur les conclusions.
— *a right :* porter atteinte à un droit.
— *the result :* influer sur le résultat.
leases affecting 10 acres of land : baux affermant 10 acres de terre.
affected interest : intérêt lésé.
persons hereby affected : personnes tombant sous l'application des présentes dispositions.
The firm is affected by a fall of prices : L'entreprise est touchée par une chute des prix.

affection : [J] affectation (f) hypothécaire.

affianced : le, la fiancé(e).
the — couple : les fiancés.
affiance : fiançailles.
[C] promesse mutuelle de mariage.

affiant : [J] auteur d'un *affidavit*.

affidavit : attestation (f) par écrit.
[J] a) affirmation, déclaration (par écrit et sous serment prêté devant une personne qualifiée pour le recevoir, ou enregistrée sur acte timbré) ; b) déposition de témoin sous serment.
(L'emploi de l'— est très fréquent dans la pratique judiciaire et administrative A.A. En cours d'instruction, tout fait qui n'a pas directement trait au fond de l'affaire, peut faire l'objet d'un —, cette affirmation étant admise d'emblée, sauf inscription en faux. Grosso mode, l'— participe à la fois de l'acte notarié, des déclarations de tiers et des attestations officielles du droit français.
— *of debt and danger : —* pour obtenir une ordonnance de saisie conservatoire contre un redevable.
— *of finding : —* exécuté lorsqu'un testament a été perdu et retrouvé.
— *of increase : —* concernant les frais de procédure supplémentaires.
— *of means : —* pour déclarer qu'une personne qui demande à ne pas payer une dette adjugée, a les moyens de le faire.
— *of plight and condition : —* déclarant qu'un testament est toujours dans l'état où il a été trouvé ou exécuté.
— *of service : —* infirmant, notification à personne d'un acte.
[U.S.] — *in support :* garantie fournie par un citoyen américain *(the sponsor)* qu'un immigrant ne tombera pas à la charge de l'Assistance.
evidence taken on — : dépositions recueillies sous serment.
to swear an — : faire une déclaration sous serment.
to take an — : recevoir une déclaration sous serment (juge, notaire).

affiliation : [J] a) légitimation (f), reconnaissance (f) d'un enfant ; b) adoption (f) d'un enfant.
action by bastard for — : action en recherche de la paternité.
— *order :* assignation d'enfant à un père putatif (procédure au criminel, l'acte charnel hors mariage étant illicite, voir *bastard, illegitimate*).
[C] affiliation.

affiliated *corporation, firm :* société affiliée, filiale.
[U.S.] *political* — *(s) :* attaches politiques.

affinity : parenté (f) par alliance.

affirmance *(of a conviction) :* confirmation d'une condamnation, d'un jugement.

affirmanti non neganti incumbit probatio : la charge de la preuve incombe à qui allègue, non à qui nie.

affirmation : affirmation (f).
[J] a) affirmation solennelle tenant lieu de serment (en cas d'objection de conscience) ; b) confirmation (f), homologation (f) d'un jugement ; c) ratification (f) d'une obligation contre laquelle la loi admet l'action en nullité ou rescision.
to prove the — *of :* prouver l'existence de.

affirmative : affirmatif.
— *action :* action pétitoire.
— *defence :* moyen de défense nouveau détruisant la thèse du demandeur, même si elle était justifiée au moment où la plainte a été déposée.
— *negligence :* faute par abstention.
— *pregnant :* allégation produite dans un plaidoyer admettant certains moyens de l'adversaire et, de ce fait, inopérante.
— *relief :* conclusions de la défense admises sur les points pouvant donner lieu à une demande reconventionnelle.
— *statute :* loi prescrivant l'accomplissement d'un acte (opp. *negative statute*).

to affix : attacher, apposer, ajouter.
[J] — *a seal :* sceller (un document).
— *seals :* placer sous scellés.
[C] *the* **affixed** *document :* la pièce ci-contre.
— *the signature :* apposer une signature.
— *a notice in all public places :* afficher dans tous les lieux publics.
in witness whereof I have hereunto affixed my name : en foi de quoi j'ai signé.

affluence : affluence.
affluent *society :* société d'abondance.

to afforce : employer des moyens coercitifs.

to afford : fournir, procurer, avoir les moyens (pécuniaires) de faire (qqch).

afforestation : reboisement (m).

affreightment : affrètement (m), nolis (m).

afloat : à flot.
[E] *always* — (A.A.) : toujours à flot.
vessels must discharge — (D/A *clause*) : les navires doivent décharger leur cargaison étant à flot.
[F] *to keep* — : demeurer solvable.

aforegoing : précédent (a).

aforementioned : susmentionné (a).

aforesaid : susdit, susmentionné, précité.
[J] *as* — : ainsi qu'il a été spécifié plus haut.

aforethought : préméditation (f).
[J] *with malice* — : avec intention criminelle.

after : subséquent, postérieur, d'après, suivant, à dater, à compter de.
— *a pattern :* suivant modèle.
— *the date of this present :* à dater de ce jour.
— *the period :* passé le délai.
— *the rate of :* au taux de.
— *-account :* compte ultérieur.
— *-acquired property :* acquêts (biens matrimoniaux).
— *-birth :* naissance postérieure au testament.
— *-care (of prisoners) :* assistance aux détenus libérés.
— *-edition :* édition subséquente.
[B] — *-hour :* après-bourse.
— *-management :* administration subséquente.
— *-mentioned :* mentionné ci-après.
aftermath : contrecoup, répercussion, suites (d'un événement).
— *-sales service :* service après vente.
— *-tax profits :* bénéfices impôts déduits, hors impôts, nets d'impôt.
— *tax earnings :* bénéfices après impôts.
— *-thought :* arrière-pensée.

against : opposé, à l'encontre de, imputable sur, en fonction de.
— *collection :* contre encaissement.
as — : en regard de, à l'encontre de.
offence — *this act :* acte prévu par la présente loi.
the amount paid — *the full amount due :* la somme versée à valoir sur le montant total dû.
the balance can be checked — : le solde peut être vérifié à l'aide de.
there is no rule — *that :* rien ne s'y oppose.

âge : âge (m).
[J] — *, full* —, *of* — : majorité (f).
under — : minorité (f).
to come of — : atteindre la majorité.
[A] *promotion in order of* — : avancement à l'ancienneté.
— *activity rate :* taux d'activité par âge.
— *-bracket (-range) :* tranche (f) d'âge.
— *of discretion :* âge de raison.

— *distribution*: répartition par classes d'âge.
— *-life method of depreciation*: méthode d'amortissement linéaire.
old- — *pension*: pension de vieillesse.
old- — *pension fund*: caisse de retraite.
old- — *pension scheme*: régime de retraite.

agency: agence (f), action (f), opération (f).
[J] mandat (m), pouvoir (m).
free — : libre arbitre.
[A] service gouvernemental, bureau (m).
administrative — : une administration (p. ex.
[U.S.] : — *of Works* # ministère des travaux publics).
[C] agence, représentation commerciale, comptoir (m).
— *-office*: bureau d'affaires.
employment — : bureau de placement, agence pour l'emploi.
estate- —, *land* — : agence, société immobilière, gérance d'immeubles.
— *fee*: commission de gestion.
incorporated — : organisme jouissant de la personnalité morale.
literary — : agence littéraire.
managing — : organisme de gestion.
news — : agence d'informations.
operating — : organisme d'exploitation.
shipping — : agence maritime.
sole — : représentation exclusive.
travel — : agence, bureau de voyages.
[F] succursale (f), agence de banque.
— *commissions*: profits des intermédiaires.
—*fee*: commission de gestion.
agencies *accounts*: comptes des administrations (comptabilité nationale).
[D] *customs* — : commissionnaire en douane.
through (his) — : par son intermédiaire.

agenda: l'ordre du jour, liste des questions à débattre.
the next item on our — *is*: l'ordre du jour appelle la discussion de...
to place a question on the — : inscrire une question à l'ordre du jour.

agent: agent (m), représentant (m), préposé (m).
[J] mandataire (m), fondé de pouvoirs.
«*principal and* — » : « commettant et mandataire ».
[A] agent politique ou diplomatique (sp. le représentant du Gouvernement britannique dans les Etats indigènes).
— *general*: représentant à Londres de chacun des territoires ou provinces de l'Australie et du Canada.
collecting — : agent de recouvrement.
secret — : agent du service des renseignements.
[C] agent commercial, représentant de commerce.

commission —, *mercantile* — : commissionnaire en marchandises.
— *('s) commission*: commission d'un agent (en pourcentage).
estate —, *land* — : marchand de biens, gérant de propriétés, d'immeubles.
forwarding — : commissionnaire-expéditeur (transport).
general — : homme d'affaires.
house- — : agent de location, courtier immobilier.
literary — : agent littéraire.
local — : agent sur place.
press — : agent de presse.
shipping — : courtier maritime.
sole — : dépositaire exclusif.
[U.S.] *station* — : chef de gare.
[F] directeur d'une agence ou succursale de banque.
— *(s) accounts*: comptes des agents (comptabilité nationale).
[ASS] *insurance* — : agent d'assurances.

to aggravate: aggraver, accroître.
aggravated *assault*: voie de fait.
aggravated larceny: vol qualifié.
aggravating *circumstances*, **aggravation** : circonstances aggravantes.

aggregate: global (a), collectif (a), total (a) ; total (m), ensemble (m), totalité (f).
— *amount*: montant global.
— *book*: livre général.
— *demand*: demande globale.
— *new issues ratio* (ANIR) : coefficient global de nouvelles émissions d'actifs financiers.
— *quotas*: ensemble des quotes-parts.
in the — : dans l'ensemble.
periods amounting in the — *to six months*: [F] periodes dont la durée totale atteint six mois.

aggregation: agrégation (f), accumulation (f).

to aggrieve: chagriner, blesser.
[J] *the* **aggrieved** *party*: la partie perdante (par une décision judiciaire).

agio: [F] agio (m), prix du change.
— *account*: compte d'agio.
agiotage: agiotage (m).

agist: [J] bail à cheptel.

agitation: agitation, discussion, débat, controverse.
the project now in — : le projet en discussion.

agnate: agnat (m).

agnomen: surnom (m).

agrarian: agraire (a) (loi, mesure).

to agree: consentir, accepter, se mettre d'accord.
— *the books, the accounts*: conformer les écritures.
agreed action: action concertée.
agreed consideration: prix convenu.
agreed procedure: accord sur la procédure de conciliation.
as agreed: comme convenu.
conditions agreed upon: conditions acceptées de part et d'autre.
penalty agreed beforehand: clause pénale (dans un contrat).
the terms are agreed: les conditions sont arrêtées.
unless otherwise agreed: sauf stipulation contraire.
who have agreed as follows: lesquels sont convenus des dispositions suivantes.

agreeable *(to)*: concordant, conforme (à).
this arrangement is — to the assembly: cette proposition a l'assentiment de l'assemblée.

agreement: [J] accord (m), convention (f), traité (m), engagement (m), règlement (m), contrat (m), acte (m), conciliation (f).
— *(s) and concentrations (EEC)*: ententes et concentrations (CEE).
— *arrived at by the parties*: accord conclu entre les parties.
— *for sale*: acte de vente.
amalgamation — : accord de fusion.
antenuptial — : contrat de mariage.
as per — : comme convenu.
binding — : convention liant les parties.
collective — : convention collective.
Economic Group Partnership — : Groupement d'Intérêts Economiques (G.I.E.).
double taxation — : convention relative aux doubles impositions.
formal — : accord en due forme.
general — *to borrow* (GAB): accords généraux d'emprunts.
marketing — : accord de commercialisation.
master — : accord type.
mutual — : accord de gré à gré.
by mutual — : d'un commun accord.
partnership — : contrat d'association.
pocket — : contre-lettre (f).
private — : acte sous seing privé.
real — : bail (m).
secret — : accord occulte.
special — : a) compromis arbitral, b) protocole de soumission à une juridiction internationale d'un litige entre Etats.
stand-by — *(s)*: accord de confirmation (voir *stand-by*).
stated parole — : convention verbale irrévocable.
swap — *(s)*: accords d'échange (voir *swap*).
to bring the parties to an — : concilier les parties.
to come to an — : se mettre d'accord.
to enter into an — : passer contrat.
to live up to an — : remplir les conditions d'un contrat.
to withdraw from an — : dénoncer un accord.
wages — : accord sur les salaires.
working — : modus vivendi.
written — : convention couchée par écrit.
[A] police d'abonnement aux services publics (eau, gaz, électricité), *all-in-* — : force et lumière (abonnement à l'électricité).
[C] entente industrielle, entre producteurs, *(in a disparaging sense)* collusion (f).

agribusiness (the): agro-alimentaire (l').

agrofoods: agro-alimentaire.

ahead: en avance, en avant.
the market finished well — : le marché a terminé largement en hausse.
to edge — : être en hausse légère.
the market is nervous — *of next week's figures*: le marché montre de la nervosité par anticipation sur les chiffres de la semaine prochaine.

aid: aide (f), assistance (f), secours (m).
action in — *of attachment*: demande d'une ordonnance de saisie.
bilateral or multilateral — : aide bilatérale ou multilatérale.
grant in — : subvention (f).
in — *of*: au bénéfice de.
legal — : aide judiciaire.
mutual- — *society*: société de secours mutuels.
tied — : aide liée.
Government **aided**: subventionné par l'Etat.

aida *(attention, interest, desire, action)*: Les quatre réactions de l'acheteur que le vendeur doit provoquer (l'attention (f), l'intérêt (m), le désir (m), l'action (f)).

aider: aide (m et f).
[J] — *by verdict*: conséquence découlant d'un verdict de couvrir les erreurs ou omissions de la procédure antérieure et de rendre inopérante toute opposition de ce chef.
— *and abettor*: complice (m).

ailing: défaillant.
— *firm*: entreprise en difficulté.

aim: but (m).
— *(s)*: objectif.

AIR
ALL

[J] *the — of a bill:* les intentions (f pl) du législateur.
with this — in view: à cet effet.

air: air (m), aérien (a), par avion.
— *cargo:* marchandises acheminées par air.
— *consignment,* — *waybill:* bordereau descriptif.

to air: rendre public, divulguer, publier.
— *grievances:* exposer ses doléances.

alderman: magistrat (m), conseiller (m), municipal.

aleatory: aléatoire (a).
[J] — *contract:* contrat aléatoire.

algorithm *(informatics)*: algorithme (m).

alibi: alibi, [U.S.] excuse.
to establish an — : prouver son alibi.
to plead, fall back on, set up, an — : invoquer un alibi, plaider l'alibi.
to produce an — : produire, fournir un alibi.

alien: étranger (m).
[J] ressortissant (m) étranger.
[U.S.] *non resident — :* étranger de passage, visiteur.
[U.S.] *resident — :* étranger immigré.
undesirable — : étranger indésirable.
custodian of — property: administrateur-sequestre de biens.

alienage: extranéité (f).

to alienate: aliéner, céder, transférer, détourner.
no right may be in any manner whatsoever **alienated** *(to):* les droits ne pourront en aucune manière être transférés (à).

alienation: aliénation.
[J] aliénation de biens.
— *of affection:* détournement de l'affection d'un époux, des enfants (cause de divorce et d'une action en dommages-intérêts pour préjudice moral, voir *heart-balm actions*).
mental — : aliénation mentale.

alienator: cédant (m).

alimony: [J] pension alimentaire versée par le mari à la femme séparée ou divorcée (se dit aussi, lorsque servie volontairement, *allowance for necessaries,* **alimentary** *endowment, support, maintenance*).
claim of — : demande d'aliments.
obligation to pay (to support) — : obligation alimentaire.

alio intuiti: avec une autre intention (que celle que l'on affiche).

aliud est celare, aliud tacere: silence n'équivaut pas à dissimulation.

aliunde: d'une autre source, d'autre façon.

all: tout.
— *fours:* analogie entre deux cas.
decision on — fours with that of another case: décision analogue à celle prise dans un autre cas.
— *-in policy:* assurance tous risques.
— *-in price:* prix tout compris.
— *-inclusive:* tout compris.
— *time high (low):* hausse (baisse) sans précédent.
— *rights reserved:* tous droits réservés.

allegation: [J] a) allégation (f), articulation des faits ; b) chef d'accusation, moyen de défense.

to allege: alléguer, exciper de, prétendre.
— *a charge:* porter une accusation.
— *one's good faith:* exciper de sa bonne foi.
— *self-defence:* plaider la légitime défense.
alleged: présumé, allégué.
alleged offence: infraction imputée.
alleged to be lost: présumé perdu.

allegiance: allégeance.
[J] (U.K.) *to pledge one's — to the Queen:* prêter serment d'obéissance à la Reine.
[U.S.] *oath of — :* serment de fidélité prêté sur le drapeau par les naturalisés.

to alleviate: alléger, atténuer (une peine).

allied: connexe, allié.
— *companies:* sociétés associées.
— *industries:* industries connexes.

to allocate: affecter, attribuer.
— *a sum to:* affecter une somme à.
— *a payment to a previous year:* affecter un paiement à une année fiscale antérieure.

allocation: allocation (f), assignation (f), ventilation (f), répartition (f).
[A] ordonnancement sur le Trésor.
— *of contract:* adjudication (f) (de fournitures, etc.).
— *to the highest bidder:* adjudication à la surenchère.
— *to the lowest bidder:* adjudication au moins disant.
[F] [C] — *of assets and liabilities:* ventilation de l'actif et du passif.
— *of capital:* affectation des investissements.
— *of funds:* affectation de fonds.

— *of income*: ventilation des revenus.
— *of overheads*: répartition des frais (entre les divers services).
— *of profits, of earnings*: répartition des bénéfices.
— *of shares*: attribution d'actions.
— *of business profits*: ventilation des bénéfices industriels et commerciaux.
scale of — : barème de répartition.

allocatur: état certifié des frais (après taxation).

to allot: a) attribuer, répartir ; b) lotir.

allotment: a) attribution (f), affectation (f), répartition (f); b) portion (f), part (f).
[F] attribution d'actions.
letter of — : avis de répartition, bulletin de souscription.
— *of property*: lotissement (m).
appropriation — : attribution de crédits.
payment in full on — : libération des actions à la souscription.

allottee: attributaire (m), souscripteur (m).

to allow: allouer, accorder, attribuer, admettre, recevoir, consentir.
— *a debtor time to pay*: accorder un délai à un débiteur.
— *a discount*: consentir une remise.
— *a request*: faire droit à une requête.
[J] *allowed challenges*: récusations permises.
allowed motion: requête accordée.
allowed time: temps accordé au personnel pour certaines activités en dehors du travail (repas, etc.).

allowable: admissible, permis, déductible.
allowable expenses: frais déductibles.
— *range*: fourchette significative.
allowable for tax: déductible du montant imposable.

allowance: allocation (f), gratification (f), rabais (m), ristourne (f).
[J] pension (f), rente (f), indemnité (f).
[F] déduction (f), abattement (m).
acting — : indemnité (f) de fonctions.
— *to cashier for errors*: passé de caisse.
— *for bad debts*: provision pour créances douteuses.
— *for decline in foreign exchange value*: provision pour perte de change.
— *for depreciation*: dotation aux amortissements.
— *for expenses*: déduction pour frais.
— *of items in an account*: allocation d'articles dans un compte.
— *in kind, in money*: prestations en nature, en deniers.

— *for loss*: réfaction.
— *for necessaries*: pension alimentaire servie volontairement (de même : *maintenance, support, alimentary endowment*, opp. *alimony*).
— *for special work*: indemnité de fonction.
— *for tare*: défalcation de tare.
— *to be made*: supplément à accorder.
annual — : amortissement linéaire.
capital — : déduction pour amortissement.
daily subsistence — : prime journalière fixe.
dismissal — : indemnité de licenciement.
entertainment — : frais de représentation.
family — : allocation familiale, réductions pour charges de famille.
first year — : annuité d'amortissement déductible au titre de l'exercice d'acquisition du bien.
initial — : déduction spéciale d'amortissement (pratiquée, le cas échéant, avant l'amortissement normal).
investment — : déduction d'investissement.
living — : indemnité pour augmentation du coût de la vie.
to make — *for his youth*: tenir compte de la jeunesse (du prévenu).
needs — : abattement pour les personnes de condition modeste.
office — : frais de bureau.
quick succession — [U.K.] : réduction de droits en cas de successions rapprochées.
rental — : indemnité de loyer.
retiring — : allocation de retraite.
round sum expense — : allocation forfaitaire pour frais.
(salary) — : appointements non fixes.
superannuation — : pension de retraite.
transitional — : allocation temporaire.
travelling and expense — : allocation pour frais professionnels.
veteran's — : pension d'ancien combattant.
wear and tear — : provision pour amortissement.
writing down — : déduction pour amortissement.
— *shall be made...* : il sera tenu compte...

alluvion: alluvion (m).
[J] *accretion by alluvion*, [U.S.] *bottomlands*: alluvionnement.

alteration: altération (f), modification (f), changement (m), remaniement (m).
[J] altération, falsification d'un document.
— *in articles*: modification des statuts.
marginal — : renvoi (m) en marge.
— *(s) and extensions*: modifications et ajouts.
closed for alteration(s): fermé pour transformations.

altercation: altercation (f), dispute (f).
[J] contestation (f).

alternate : substitut (m).
— *juror* : juré suppléant.
[U.S.] — *valuation* : possibilité pour les tribunaux d'admettre une valeur supérieure à celle donnée par les parties.

alternation : plaidoirie contradictoire *(the parties plead alternately)*.

alternative : alternatif, subsidiaire.
[U.K.] — *basis of charge*, [U.S.] — *tax* : possibilité offerte au contribuable d'opter pour le mode de taxation le plus avantageux (en matière de plus-values).
— *beneficiaries* : bénéficiaires subrogés.
— *benefits* : prestations de remplacement.
— *draft* : contre projet.
— *policy* : politique de rechange.
alternatively : toutefois, une seconde possibilité existe.

amalgamation : fusion (f).
[J] voir *merger*.

ambassador : ambassadeur (m).

ambiguity : ambiguïté (f).
latent — : ambiguïté, imprécision d'un texte légal, constatée après coup, dans un cas d'application concrète.
pertinent — : imprécision flagrante.

ambit : champ (m) d'application (d'une loi), portée (f) (d'une disposition).

amenable : responsable (a).
[J] relevant de, justiciable de, ressortissant à (une juridiction).
— *to a fine* : passible d'une amende.
— *to law* : soumis à la loi.
— *to process* : susceptible d'une action en justice.

to amend : amender, modifier, rectifier.
an act — : loi portant modification.
full **amends** : réparation complète.
to make amends to s.o. for sth. : dédommager qn de qch.
amendable *error* : erreur réparable.
amended *to provide* : modifié comme suit.
amending *process* : procédure de révision constitutionnelle.

amendment : modification (f), *(of a bill)* amendement (m), *(of a text)* correction (f), *(of a pleading, an account)* rectification (f).
— *negatived* : amendement rejeté.
— *to an* — : sous-amendement.
to move an — : proposer un amendement.
« *shall the* — *carry ?* » : « l'amendement est-il adopté ? »
wording of an — : libellé d'un amendement.

amentia : aliénation mentale.

amercement : [J] amende infligée par le jury.
— *to the Crown* : confiscation au profit de la Couronne (voir *fine*).

american deposit receipt (A.D.R.) : [F] titre américain émis en représentation d'une valeur étrangère (titre nominatif).

amicable : amiable (a).
[J] — *action* : instance en juridiction gracieuse en vue de la fixation d'un point de droit.
— *settlement* : arrangement à l'amiable.

amicus curiae : ami du tribunal (juriste qui donne son avis au juge lorsque ce dernier a des doutes sur un point de droit) ; tiers admis à faire valoir dans un procès l'intérêt public ou l'intérêt d'un groupe social important (autorisation de se porter partie civile).

amortization : amortissement (m).
[J] aliénation en main-morte.
[F] amortissement financier.
reducing balance — : amortissement dégressif.
straight line — : amortissement linéaire.

to amount to : s'élever à.
his attenuating circumstances — *a justification* : les circonstances atténuantes dont il excipe le justifient en fait.
transactions which — : transactions qui s'élèvent à.
an act **amounting** *to murder* : acte équivalent à un meurtre.

amount : somme (f), montant (m), quantité (f), valeur (f).
— *brought in* : report d'exercices antérieurs.
— *of business* : chiffre d'affaires.
— *carried forward* : report à nouveau.
— *in controversy* : montant de la demande fixant la juridiction compétente.
— *of expenses* : chiffre de dépenses.
— *invested* : mise de fonds.
— (s) *introduced* : suppléments d'apports.
— *of the issue* : montant de l'émission.
— *overpaid* : trop perçu.
— *paid on account* : acompte versé.
— *standing at your credit* : somme portée au crédit de votre compte.
— (s) *of stock negotiable* : quotités de titres négociables.
— (s) *withdrawn* : prélèvement sur apport.
— *written off* : sommes passées par pertes et profits.
to bring forward an — : reporter une somme.
gross — : montant brut.
net — : montant net.

to the — of : jusqu'à concurrence de.

ampliation : ampliation (f).
[J] a) (cr.) ajournement d'un procès pour complément d'enquête ; b) prorogation de délai.

analysis : analyse (f).
[C] — of an account : ventilation d'un compte.
— of time series : analyse de conjoncture.
[U.S.] cost-benefit — : analyse des coûts et des rendements.
[U.S.] cost effectiveness — : étude des coûts et d'efficacité.
operating costs — : comptabilité analytique d'exploitation.
analytically, the action is in Equity : il ressort clairement qu'il s'agit d'une demande relevant de l'Equity.

analyst : analyste (m).

ancestor : ancêtre (m), aïeul (m).
[J] a) ascendant en ligne directe ; b) de cujus successionis ; c) propriétaire antérieur.

ancient : ancien.
— lights : vues anciennes.
[J] servitude de vue acquise par prescription de vingt ans.
[J] — writings : écrits remontant à plus de trente ans, dont l'authenticité est présumée.

ancillary : subordonné (a) ; annexe à.
[J] — executor : exécuteur testamentaire (chargé de la liquidation d'une succession étrangère portant sur des biens sis à l'intérieur).
— occupations : professions connexes.
[C] — undertaking : filiale.

angary : angarie (f).

to animadvert : critiquer, censurer, blâmer.

animus (furandi, manendi) :
(l')intention (de voler, de demeurer).
animo furandi : avec l'intention de voler (élément constitutif du délit).

annotation : annotation (f).
[J] commentaire (m), note (f) sous une décision.
annotated text : texte commenté.

announcement : annonce (f).
[J] affiche judiciaire.
— of birth, marriage : faire-part de naissance, mariage.
— of death : avis mortuaire.

annual : annuel.
— capital charge method : méthode de l'annuité.
— depreciation : amortissement annuel.
— General Meeting : Assemblée Générale Annuelle.
— instalment : annuité.
— report : compte rendu annuel des activités (d'une société).
— tax concept : principe de l'annualité de l'impôt.
— value : annuité constante de capital.

annuity : annuité (f).
[J] [F] rente viagère.
— in redemption of debt : remboursement par annuités.
— bond : titre, obligation, de rente.
to buy an — : placer son argent en viager.
deferred — : rente à paiement différé.
Government — : rente sur l'Etat.
terminable — : rente à terme.
two-life —, — to the last survivor, reversionary — : rente réversible, rente sur deux têtes, rente au dernier survivant.
to pay an — : servir une rente.
perpetual, life, — : rente perpétuelle, viagère.
purchased — : rente viagère constituée à titre onéreux.
to settle an — on : constituer une rente au bénéfice de.
temporary — : rente temporaire, à terme.
annuitant : détenteur d'une rente, rentier viager, pensionné (de l'Etat).
life-annuitant : crédirentier.

annulment : annulation (f).
[J] (of a contract) résiliation, rescision, résolution, (of a will) cassation, (of marriage) dissolution, (of a law, a decree) abrogation, (of a treaty) dénonciation.
annulable contract : contrat résoluble.

answer : réponse (f), réplique (f).
[J] a) [U.S.] conclusions du défendeur ([U.K.] statement of defence, defendant's plea ; voir admission, demurrer, motion to dismiss, denial, defence].
b) déposition d'un témoin.
— to a charge : réfutation d'une accusation, réplique du défendeur.
full — : réponse satisfaisante.
no audible — : le témoin ne répond pas.
non-committal — : réponse diplomatique.
to answer : répondre, répliquer, être responsable.
to answer for costs : garantir les frais.
to be **answerable** for : être responsable de.
to be **answerable** to : être responsable envers.
answerer : répondant (m).

to antagonize: contrarier.
[U.S.] – *a bill*: s'opposer à un projet de loi.

antecedent: antécédent (m), précédent (m).
– *debt*: dette plus ancienne, prenant rang antérieur.

antedate: antidate (f).
to antedate a contract: antidater un contrat.

ante litem motam: avant l'introduction d'instance.

antenuptial: prénuptial.
[J] – *settlement, agreement*: contrat de mariage.

to anticipate: espérer, escompter, prévoir.
anticipated profit: bénéfice escompté.
anticipated return of capital: rendement escompté du capital.

anticipation: anticipation (f), expectative (f).
[J] exercice anticipé d'un droit.
restraint on – : limitation à l'avance d'hoirie.
anticipatory *breach* (non adempleti contractus): comportement d'une partie au contrat permettant de conclure qu'elle n'a pas l'intention de l'exécuter, d'où droit du co-contractant d'entamer une action en dommages-intérêts sans avoir à fournir la contre-partie au préalable.
[F] *price* – *(s)*: réaction des agents économiques en matière de prix.

anti-dumping: see « dumping ».

antiquated: suranné, désuet, archaïque.
antiquated law: loi tombée en désuétude.

anti-trust: see « trust ».

any: un quelconque, quiconque, tout.
increased to – *amount*: augmenté indéfiniment.
– *denominations of shares*: toute coupure d'actions.
subject to – *special agreement*: sous réserve d'accords spéciaux.
– *twelve jurors*: douze jurés quelconques.

apart from: en dehors de, indépendamment de, à part.

apartment: (U.S.), appartement (m) (U.K.)
– *studio* (m).

apology: excuses (f pl).
to make due – : faire amende honorable.

apparent: apparent, manifeste (a).
– *easement*: servitude apparente.
heir – : héritier présomptif.

appeal: [J] tout recours à une instance supérieure (appel et pourvoi en cassation).
Le recours, tant en *Eq.* qu'en *C.L.* se nomme –, aussi bien en deuxième qu'en troisième instance ainsi que tout moyen de droit invoqué. « Le fait nouveau » est décisif en la matière, de sorte qu'une faute ou erreur du tribunal inférieur est nécessaire pour que l'appel soit admis. L'arrêt de la cour supérieure peut prendre les formes suivantes :
judgment affirmed, decision set aside (vacated), new trial ordered (granted), case remanded, judgment modified (on the law and the facts) (voir ces termes).
Court of – *(Engl.), of* – *(s)* [U.S.] : cour d'appel.
Supreme Court of – *(s)* = Cour de cassation (voir *Court* (Engl.), [U.S.]).
notice of – : intimation d'appel.
without – : en dernier ressort.
– *(s) and prosecutions*: pourvois et poursuites.
– *to arbitration*: recours à l'arbitrage.
he has taken this case to – : il a porté cette affaire en appel.
the – *was dismissed*: le pourvoi a été rejeté.
to hear – *(s)*: juger en appel.
[C] – *for tenders*: appel d'offres.

to appeal, to lodge an appeal, to give notice of appeal: interjeter appel.
[J] a) faire appel (à un tribunal) d'une décision ; b) former un recours (opposition, etc.).
special leave to – *out of time*: autorisation spéciale de faire appel devant un tribunal constitué en session extraordinaire.
– *to the Supreme Court of Appeals* = se pourvoir en cassation (voir *appeal*).
[U.S.] – *a case*: interjeter appel.
– *from a judgment*: appeler d'un jugement.
– *to the chair*: en appeler au président.
appellant: appelant (m), **appellate** *jurisdiction procedure*: juridiction (f), procédure (f) d'appel.
appellee: intimé.
appellor: accusé qui récuse un ou plusieurs jurés.

to appear: paraître, apparaître, comparaître.
summons – : citation à comparaître.
– *in court*: ester en justice.
to fail – : faire défaut.
as it **appears** *from a judgment of the court*: ainsi qu'il appert du jugement du tribunal.
[ASS] *insurance for the benefit of all parties as their interest may* – : assurance au profit

— 304 —

de toute partie en cause, en cas de sinistre.

appearance : apparition (f), entrée (f).
[J] a) comparution (f) ; b) acte formel par lequel le défenseur signifie son intention de s'opposer à la demande.
failure of — : défaut de comparution.
(to put in a) general — : cf. b) ci-dessus, comportant la reconnaissance de la compétence du tribunal, même si ce dernier ne l'exerce pas ratione loci (« *the court acquires jurisdiction* »).
special — : comparution uniquement aux fins de contester la compétence du tribunal saisi.
the — *of a right* : un droit présumé.
[C] une bonne présentation.

to append one's signature to a document : apposer sa signature au bas d'un document.
— *a document* : annexer un document.

to appertain : appartenir à, relever de.
document appertaining *to this case* : document appartenant à cette affaire.

appertainment : privilège attaché.

appliance : appareil, instrument, dispositif, ressource.

applicant : demandeur, requérant, pétitionnaire, ayant droit, réclamant, intéressé (m).
— *for shares* : souscripteur (d'actions).

application : application (f), demande (f), requête (f), souscription (f), imputation (f).
[J] [C] — *of payments* : imputation de paiements.
[A] demande (f), requête (f), sollicitation (f).
— *form* : formulaire de demande.
— *for a patent* : demande de brevet.
— *for employment* : demande d'emploi.
— *for relief* : demande de dégrèvement.
— *for a survey* : demande d'expertise.
[F] — *form* : bulletin de souscription.
— *money* : somme versée avec la demande de titres.
preferential — *right* : droit de souscription préférentiel.
sample post free on — *(to)* : échantillon franco sur demande (à).
— *has been made to the court for an inquiry in the debtor's assets* : le tribunal est saisi d'une demande de discussion.

to apply : (s')appliquer (à), demander.
— *the deposit against the debt* : affecter le dépôt à l'acquittement de la dette.
— *a payment to a particular debt* : imputer un paiement à une dette spécifiée (droit strict du débiteur).
—, *to make application, for shares* : souscrire des actions.
— *for relief* : demander des secours.
[B] — *for stock-exchange quotation* : demander l'admission à la cote.
this rule does not — *in this case* : cette règle n'est pas applicable en l'espèce.
applied *Economies* : économie (f) appliquée.

to appoint : désigner, nommer, constituer, établir.
— *a day* : fixer un jour.
on the **appointed** *day* : au jour nommé.
appointed agent : agent attitré.
appointee : titulaire (m).

appointment : convocation (f), nomination (f), désignation (f), engagement (m), constitution (f).
[J] *power of* — : faculté de distribution de biens [conférée par testament ou mandat spécial *(trust deed)* par l'auteur d'une succession *(grantor, settlor, donor)* à une personne, en général un légataire *(grantee, donee)*, qui choisit librement les bénéficiaires *(the beneficiaries)*].
by — : sur assignation.
[U.S.] **appointive** *posts* : emplois administratifs pourvus par nomination (opp. *elective posts*).
— *(s) of an office* : émoluments.
by the Queen's — : d'ordre de la Reine.
by special — *to her Majesty* : fournisseur breveté de Sa Majesté.

to apportion : répartir, attribuer, ventiler, lotir.
— *a task* : assigner une tâche.
— *taxable and non-taxable profits* : déterminer les bénéfices imposables et non imposables.
apportionated *tax* : impôt de répartition.

apportionment : partage (m).
(of parts, shares) allocation (f), *(of food)* contingentement (m), *(of dividends)* distribution (f), *(of landed property)* lotissement (m), *(of taxes, expenses)* répartition (f), *(of costs, of assets and liabilities)* ventilation (f).
— *of overheads and running costs* : imputation des frais généraux et des frais d'exploitation.

appraisal : estimation (f), évaluation (f), appréciation (f).
— *before auction* : prisée (f).
— *interview* : entretien d'aptitude, probatoire.
— *method of depreciation* : méthode d'amortissement fondée sur la valeur du moment.
official — : expertise (f).

to appraise : estimer, évaluer, faire l'expertise.
appraised *value* : évaluation (après expertise).
appraisement : évaluation, estimation.

appraiser : commissaire priseur, expert.
customs appraiser : appréciateur des douanes.
maritime insurance appraiser : évaluateur en matière d'assurance maritime.

to appreciate : apprécier, estimer, évaluer, augmenter, s'améliorer, hausser la valeur de.
appreciated currency : monnaie réévaluée.
appreciated surplus : plus-value (f).

appreciation : appréciation (f), estimation (f), augmentation (f).
[C] [F] valorisation (f), hausse de valeur (f).
[B] plus-value monétaire.
– *of (in) prices :* amélioration des cours.
stocks showing an – : titres en hausse.

apprehension : appréhension (f), crainte (f), arrestation (f).
[J] prise de corps.

apprentice : apprenti (m).
apprenticeship tax : taxe d'apprentissage.

approach : approche(s) (f), accès (m), démarche (f).
to approach (s.o.) : pressentir, entrer en contact avec (qqn).

approbation : approbation (f), agrément (m), assentiment (m), autorisation (f).
full – : consentement entier.
in – : à l'essai, au choix.

appropriate : convenable, pertinent, approprié, qualifié (a).
– *authority :* autorité compétente.
– *form :* formule spéciale.
– *steps :* mesures idoines.
to take – action : prendre les mesures qui s'imposent.

to appropriate : approprier, affecter, allouer, répartir, doter, prélever.
– *funds (to) :* affecter des fonds (à).
how this sum has been **appropriated** *:* quel a été l'emploi de ces fonds...
sum appropriated from the reserve : somme prélevée sur la réserve.
appropriated earnings : bénéfices mis en réserve.

appropriation : appropriation (f), attribution (f), dotation (f), affectation (f), prélèvement (m).
[J] crédit budgétaire accordé (opp. *estimate*), ouverture de crédit.
– *account :* compte d'affectation.
– *bill :* loi de finances.
[C] – *ledgers :* grand livre des crédits.
allotment of – (s) : répartition des crédits entre les divers chapitres du budget.

[F] affectation de fonds.
– *of benefits :* affectation, répartition du bénéfice.
– *of funds :* détournement de fonds.
– *of moneys :* imputation de versement à un compte déterminé.
– *of a payment to the more burdensome debt :* imputation d'un paiement à la dette la plus criarde (voir *application*).
– *to the reserve :* affectation à la réserve.
overset of – : dépassement de crédit (budget).
to give effect to – : donner suite à l'affectation d'un crédit.
transfer between – (s) : virement budgétaire.

approval : approbation (f), agrément (m), assentiment (m), ratification (f), homologation (f).
[J] – *of a petition :* requête admise.
judicial – : autorisation en justice.
subject to the – of : sous réserve de l'agrément de.
to send on – : envoyer à l'approbation.
without – : sans avis favorable.
[A] agrément (m), ratification (f).
to stamp one's – on a document : homologuer, viser une pièce.
[C] *goods on – (« on appro »)* : marchandises à condition.
sale on – : vente à l'essai.
[F] *(special) ministerial – :* agrément ministériel.

to approve : approuver, agréer, acquiescer, ratifier, homologuer.
approved : agréé, approuvé.
approved endorsed note : billet avalisé.
approved financial institution : établissement financier agréé.
approved School : Maison d'Education Surveillée.
Approved Insurance Society : Compagnie d'Assurances agréée par l'Etat.
read and approved : lu et approuvé.

approver : [J] délinquant qui dénonce ses complices (plaidant coupable, il ne s'en assure pas moins l'impunité en tant que « *Queen's,* [U.S.] *State's evidence* » : principal et irréfutable témoin à charge).

approximation of laws (E.E.C.) : rapprochement des législations (C.E.E.).

appurtenances : accessoires (m pl), dépendances (f pl) d'un immeuble, apparaux (m pl) d'un navire, servitudes (f pl).
[J] a) droits accessoires réels (servitudes);
b) meubles à fixe demeure, immeubles par destination.

aptitude test: épreuve (f) de vérification des aptitudes.

arbiter: arbitre (m), médiateur (m).
[J] arbitre exerçant sa mission dans le cadre de la législation en vigueur (opp. *arbitrator*).

arbitrage, arbitrating: arbitrage (m).
— *in bills*: arbitrage sur les lettres de change.
— *shares with*: titres d'arbitrage avec.
— *transaction*: opération d'arbitrage.
arbitragist: arbitragiste.

arbitrary: arbitraire, d'office.
— *assessment*: taxation d'office.
— *deduction*: remise forfaitaire.
— *name*: nom de convention.

arbitration: arbitrage (m).
[J] — *agreement, treaty*: convention, traité d'arbitrage.
— *award*: sentence arbitrale.
— *board*: compromis d'arbitrage.
— *clause*: clause compromissoire.
— *court*: tribunal arbitral.
— *submission*: procédure arbitrale proposée dans un cas concret.
judgment by — : jugement, sentence arbitral(e).
procedure by — : procédure arbitrale.
to go to — : recourir à l'arbitrage.
[F] arbitrage (des changes).

arbitrator: arbitre (m).
[J] amiable compositeur (libre de se prononcer selon sa conscience et le bon sens), (opp. *arbiter*).
— *award*: sentence arbitrale.

area: aire (f), périmètre (m), surface (f), région (f), zone (f).
[J] étendue du débat, cadre de la discussion.
the — *of agreement*: les limites de l'accord.
judicial — *(s) of a district*: ressorts judiciaires d'une région.
customs area: territoire douanier.
[A] *postal* — : zone postale.
— *board*: centre d'administration et de distribution (eau, gaz...).
[C] — *of supply*: zone de consommation.
underdeveloped — : zone sous-développée, en voie de développement.
[F] *currency* — : zone monétaire.

to argue: discuter, débattre, soutenir, plaider.
— *away an objection*: réfuter une objection.
— *s.o. down*: réduire quelqu'un au silence.
— *innocence*: plaider non coupable.
— *out*: vider le débat.
arguable: discutable (a), soutenable (a) (point de vue etc.).

arguable position: opinion défendable.
if we assume **arguendo**: admettons pour les besoins du débat.

argument: discussion (f), dispute (f), débat (m), argument (m), thèse (f).
[J] plaidoirie (f).
— *on appeal*: débats en appel.
— *of a motion*: examen d'une requête.
counsel's — : plaidoyer.
factual — : exposé des faits.
forcible — : argument convaincant.
legal — : discussion juridique.
line of — : argumentation.
sound — : argument irréfutable.
tu quoque **argumentation**: argumentation ad hominem.
argumentative *denial*: extrapolation juridique des faits qu'il conviendrait de nier directement (souvent considérée comme un aveu ou une échappatoire).

to arise: survenir, se produire, se poser, provenir de, se rapporter à.
a case **arising** *under the Constitution*: un litige qui relève du droit constitutionnel.
all claims against arising: toutes réclamations contre.
all differences arising out of: tous différends portant sur.
disputes which may arise: les différends qui pourraient s'élever.
income arising to the taxpayer: revenu réalisé par le contribuable.
matter arising under: toute question se rapportant à.
obligations that arise under a clause: obligations qui découlent d'une clause.
should be occasion arise: le cas échéant.

arm's length: à des conditions normales, concurrentielles.
— *price*: prix de pleine concurrence.
[J] *to deal at* — : s'en tenir rigoureusement à la lettre du droit dans les transactions juridiques ou commerciales.

to arraign: traduire en justice, mettre en accusation.
arraigned *before the court*: traduit en justice.
arraigned on the indictment: inculpé, prévenu de.

arraignment: mise en accusation.
Le juge donne lecture à l'inculpé de l'acte d'accusation (*indictment*) et lui demande s'il se reconnaît coupable.

to arrange: arranger, régler, accommoder, mettre en règle.
— *for bail*: constituer une caution, consigner un cautionnement.

– *a matter:* accommoder une affaire.
– *a treaty:* préparer, conclure un traité.

arrangement : arrangement (m), accord (m), entente (f), accommodement (m).
[J] a) transaction (f), compromis (m) ; b) concordat (m) après faillite.
– *of all disputes:* accord général.
interim – : dispositions transitoires.
pooling – : apparentement.
price by – : prix à débattre.
private – : accord à l'amiable.
provisional – : mesure provisoire.
scheme of – : concordat.
testamentary – *(s):* dispositions testamentaires.
to appear by – : demander un acte de juridiction gracieuse.
to be party to an – : être partie à un accord.
to make an – : conclure un accord.
to make suitable – *(s):* prendre toutes dispositions utiles.

array : déploiement (m).
[J] tableau des jurés éventuels *(veniremen)*.
to array the jury: faire l'appel nominal des jurés.
to array a panel: dresser le tableau des jurés.
to challenge the – : récuser le jury au complet.

arrearage : retard, dettes, [U.S.] arriérés.

arrears : arriéré (m), arrérages (m pl).
– *of dividends:* arrérages de dividendes.
– *of interest:* intérêts moratoires, rappel d'intérêts.
in – *with:* en retard pour.
salary with – *as from:* traitement avec effet rétroactif à compter du.
tax – : arriérés d'impôt.

arrest : [J] a) (civ.) prise de corps, (cr.) arrestation ; b) (droit maritime et Scot.) saisie (f) (de navire, de biens mobiliers) ; c) – *for criminal contempt:* contrainte par corps pour outrages à magistrat (se dit aussi *attachment*) ; d) – *of judgment:* sursis à exécution.
close – : (milit.) arrêts de rigueur.
to effect an – : opérer une arrestation.
false – : arrestation arbitraire (voir habeas corpus).
to move in – *of judgment:* demander le sursis à exécution d'un jugement.
open – : (milit.) arrêts simples.
under – : en état d'arrestation, (milit.) aux arrêts.
warrant of – : mandat d'amener.
wholesale – *(s):* arrestations en masse.
(Scot.) **arrester** : saisissant.

to arrest : arrêter, mettre en état d'arrestation, suspendre.
– *for debt:* contraindre par corps.
– *judgment:* surseoir à l'exécution d'un jugement.

arrestable offence : délit (m) grave justifiant une arrestation sans mandat.

arrestation, arrestment : arrêt.
[J] a) saisie-arrêt ; b) saisie conservatoire ; c) opposition *(against salary, securities, etc.)*.

to arrive *(at a price)* : fixer (un prix).

arrogation : prétention injustifiée.

arson : [J] crime d'incendie volontaire.

art : art (m), métier (m), façon de faire.
[J] (droit des brevets) technique (f), méthode (f).
prior – : antériorité (f) (d'un procédé, d'une invention, etc.).
estate of the – : état actuel d'une matière à brevet.
useful – : procédé brevetable.
(cr.) *to have* – *and part in sth.:* être fauteur et complice de qch.

article(s) : article(s) (le plus souvent au pluriel), clause (f), stipulation (f), élément (m).
[J] a) (civ.) clause (f), (cr.) chef d'accusation ; b) plainte articulée devant un tribunal ecclésiastique.
– *of agreement:* projet d'une convention, d'un traité.
– *of apprenticeship:* contrat d'apprentissage.
– *of association:* statuts d'une société à responsabilité limitée.
– *of impeachment:* acte d'accusation de forfaiture (voir *impeachment*).
– *of incorporation:* statuts d'une société commerciale.
– *of marriage:* contrat de mariage.
– *of partnership:* acte de société.
– *of war:* code de justice militaire.
[A] *articles and conditions:* cahier des charges (se dit aussi *specifications*).
reserve provided by the – : réserve statutaire.
ship's – : a) conditions d'embarquement ; b) rôle de l'équipage.
spurious – : article contrefait.
[C] – *in a popular line:* articles bas de gamme.

to article : stipuler ; mettre en apprentissage.
articled *clerk:* stagiaire.
to be – : être stagiaire.

artificial: artificiel (a).
[J] – *person*: personne ou personnalité juridique, ou morale.

as: en qualité de, à titre de.
– *a lawyer*: en (ma) qualité d'avocat.
– *a reciprocal measure*: à titre de réciprocité.
– *at March 31 st*: arrêté au 31 mars.
– *aforesaid*: tel qu'il est stipulé ci-dessus.
– *from the coming into force of*: à partir de l'entrée en vigueur de.
– *of right*: de droit.
– *per agreement*: suivant l'accord.

ascendancy, ascent: ascendance (f).
[J] **ascendant** *line, line of* **ascent**: ligne ascendante de parenté.

to ascertain: constater, vérifier, déterminer.
– *damages*: constater les dégâts.
– *a taxpayer's income*: établir le revenu d'un contribuable.
ascertained *damages*: dommages liquidés.
it has been ascertained that: il a été constaté que.

ascertainment: constatation (f) (d'un fait).

asking of the banns: [A] publication des bans.

assault: assaut (m), attaque (f).
[J] tentative de voies de fait.
– *and battery*: coups (m pl) et blessures (f pl).
– *with intent*: voie de fait avec intention criminelle.
aggravated – : actes de violence caractérisés, coups et blessures.
common – : voie de fait simple.
criminal – : viol (m).
felonious – : guet-apens (m).
indecent – : attentat à la pudeur, outrage aux mœurs.

assay: a) essai d'un métal précieux; b) vérification des poids et mesures.

assembly: assemblée (f).
– *line*: chaîne de montage.
[U.S.] *General* – : délibération en séance commune du Sénat et de la Chambre des représentants.
General – *of the United Nations*: Assemblée générale des Nations Unies.
in open – : en séance publique.
right of – (« *right peacefully to assemble* »): droit de réunion.
unlawful – : attroupement dans une intention illicite.

assent: assentiment (m), approbation (f).
[J] agrément (m).
mutual – : commun accord.
royal – : sanction royale (# promulgation des lois).
verbal – : consentement verbal.

to assert: affirmer, revendiquer, alléguer.
– *one's claims*: faire valoir ses droits.
– *one's innocence*: protester de son innocence.
– *one's rights*: revendiquer ses droits.
assertion: revendication, assertion (f).
sweeping – : assertion péremptoire.
to make an – : affirmer qch.
unsupported – : affirmation sans (dénuée) fondement.
assertory *oath*: serment assertoire.

to assess: estimer, évaluer, fixer, cotiser, répartir, taxer, asseoir (l'impôt).
– *the amount of damages*: déterminer le montant des dommages-intérêts.
– *the damage*: évaluer les dégâts.
– *the fault*: fixer la responsabilité.
– *a fine*: infliger une amende.
assessed *taxes*: impôts directs.

assessment: répartition (f), assiette (f).
[F] *actual* – : imposition « au réel ».
additional – : imposition supplémentaire.
arbitrary – : évaluation d'office.
– *book*: (le) rôle.
– *of costs*: taxation des frais.
– *on landed property*: cote foncière.
– *on income*: cote mobilière, impôt sur le revenu.
– *role lists*: cote de l'impôt.
over- – : redressement (par voie d'évaluation d'office).
actual – : évaluation effective.
additional first – [U.K.]: majoration d'impôts.
administrative – : imposition d'office.
basis of – : base de l'évaluation.
direct – [U.K.]: imposition directe du revenu après déclaration.
discretionary – : taxation d'office.
empirical – : imposition forfaitaire.
– *by indices*: taxation indiciaire.
official – : taxation d'office.
[U.S.] *presumptive* – : imposition forfaitaire.
reduced – : dégrèvement partiel.
notice of – : avis d'imposition.
schedules of – *lists*: état des rôles.
taxes charged by direct – : impôts perçus par voie de rôle.
year of – : année d'imposition.
[ASS] évaluation de sinistre, d'avarie.

assessor: [J] juge assesseur; [A] répartiteur d'impôts, expert évaluateur.

— *of taxes*: contrôleur des contributions directes.

asset(s) : actif, avoir, biens, fonds, valeur, capital, actifs, masse active (d'une succession, etc.).
   appreciation of — : plus-value d'actif.
   — *brought in*: apports.
   — *coverage*: couverture par l'actif.
   — *and liabilities*: actif et passif.
   — *and securities*: valeurs et effets.
   — *in kind*: biens en nature.
   — *side*: côté actif (au bilan).
   — *taken over*: apports.
   — *transferred*: apports.
   — *value per share*: valeur de l'actif par action.
   available — : actif disponible.
   capital — : actif immobilisé.
   cash — : avoir en numéraire.
   company's (corporate) — : actif social.
   current — : actif réalisable, disponible, à court terme.
   doubtful — : actif douteux.
   earning — : capitaux qui rapportent.
   financial — : avoirs financiers, actifs financiers, produits financiers.
   fixed — : immobilisations.
   fixed — *disposal*: cession d'élément d'actif immobilisé.
   floating — : capitaux flottants.
   frozen — : fonds non disponibles.
   insufficiency of — : insuffisance d'actif.
   liquid — : disponibilités.
   monetary — : actifs monétaires.
   movable — : biens meubles.
   permanent — : capitaux fixes.
   personal — : biens meubles.
   pledged — : actif engagé.
   ready — : fonds disponibles.
   real — : biens immobiliers, actifs réels.
   — *stripping*: vente avec bénéfice des actifs d'une société que l'on a rachetée.
   wasting — : actif défectible.
   write-down of — : amortissement d'actif.

assign: ayant droit (m).
   heirs and —(s): héritiers et ayants droit.

to assign: donner en partage, assigner, imposer, déléguer, céder, transmettre, faire cession.
   assigned *property*: cession de biens.
   functions assigned to: fonctions dévolues à.
   rank assigned to a debt: rang assigné à une créance.
   [J] — *a day for trial*: fixer le jour d'audience.

assignation: affectation (f), attribution (f), cession (f), transfert (m).
   — *of a claim*: transport d'une créance.
   — *of shares*: transmission d'action.
   deed of — : acte de transport.

assignee: cessionnaire (m et f).
   [J] administrateur-séquestre, syndic.
   — *in bankruptcy*: syndic de faillite.

assignment: assignation (f), affectation (f).
   [J] cession (f), transfert (m), attribution (f), transport (m), acte attributif *(of rights, property)*.
   — *for the benefit of creditors (deed of assignation)*: acte attributif des biens du failli au syndic de la masse.
   — *of choses in action*: cession-transport (de droits mobiliers).
   — *of a claim*: transport d'une créance.
   — *of counsel to defendant*: désignation d'un avocat d'office.
   — *of dower*: allocation à la veuve de sa part d'héritage.
   — *of error*: conclusions d'un pourvoi.
   — *of interest*: cession d'usufruit.
   — *of patent*: concession de brevet.
   — *of a patent*: cession d'un brevet.
   — *of rents*: cession des loyers (que peut impliquer une hypothèque).
   — *without recourse*: cession de créance sans garantie du cédant en cas d'insolvabilité du débiteur.
   — *of shares*: transmission d'actions.
   —(s): répartition des affaires entre les chambres d'une cour.
   outright — *of copyright*: cession définitive de droits d'auteur.

assignor: cédant (m).
   [B] *official* — : liquidateur officiel.

assise, assize: session (f), assises (f pl).
   [J] —(s): sessions périodiques des juges-délégués de la *High Court of Justice* dans les différents comtés d'Angleterre (civ. et cr.).
   — *of novel disseizin*: plainte en trouble de jouissance.
   (Scot.) *the* — : le jury.
   court of —(s): cour d'assises.
   [A] barème des prix de vente (du blé, du pain et de la bière).

assistance: assistance (f).
   [A] *mutual* — *in the collection of taxes*: assistance réciproque en matière de recouvrement des impôts.
   reciprocal administrative — : assistance administrative réciproque.

assistant: aide (m et f), auxiliaire (m et f).
   [J] substitut d'un magistrat.
   — *accountant*: aide comptable.
   — *director*: sous-directeur.
   — *inspector*: aide-inspecteur.
   — *registrar*: greffier adjoint.

associate: a) associé, adjoint ; b) greffier de tribunal.
– *in crime*: co-délinquant.
– *judge*: juge-assesseur.
associated *company*: société en partie possédée par une autre qui détient de 20 à 40 % des actions.
– *companies*: sociétés apparentées.

association: association, société, amicale.
in – *with*: en société avec.

to assume: assumer, souscrire (à), s'attribuer, s'arroger, prétendre (à), admettre (que).
– *a responsibility*: assumer un engagement.
– *duties*: assumer une charge.
– *ownership*: faire acte de propriétaire.
– *a right*: s'arroger un droit.
– *all risks*: [C] aux risques et périls (de l'expéditeur ou du destinataire).
assumed *bonds*: obligations prises en charge (par une société autre que la société émettrice).

assumpsit: (il a promis, il a entrepris, pris sur lui de faire...) engagement.
[J] actio indebitatus – (il était débiteur et a promis d'acquitter sa dette) action en reconnaissance de dette.

assumption: présomption (f), prise (f) en charge, supposition (f), hypothèse (f), prétention (f), attribution (f).
[J] – *agreement*: prise en charge d'une dette.
– *of name*: adoption d'un nom.
– *of obligation*: acceptation d'une obligation.
– *of ownership*: entrée en possession.
– *of risks*: risque professionnel (sp. d'ouvriers, sans protection autrefois, voir *fellow-servants rule*, mais couverts aujourd'hui par les *Workmen Compensation Laws*).
– *of succession*: immixtion dans une succession.
– *to office*: entrée en fonction.

assurance: assurance.
[J] *common* – *(of property)*: a) constitution du droit de propriété ; b) transfert du droit de propriété ; c) actes relatifs à a) et b).
written – : promesse par écrit.
[ASS] assurance (voir *insurance, assurance* est tombé en désuétude).

at :
– *a bargain*: à bon compte.
– *all events*: en tous cas.
– *a discount*: au-dessous du prix d'émission.
– *large*: in extenso ; en liberté.
[U.S.] *congressman at large*: membre du Congrès élu par l'ensemble des électeurs d'un Etat.
[U.S.] *statutes at large*: recueil annuel d'actes du Congrès.
– *a loss*: à perte.
– *par*: au pair.
– *sight*: à vue.
– *the rate of exchange*: au cours du change.
– *the market*: au cours du marché.
(B) – *the money*: à parité (option dont le prix d'exercice est le plus proche du cours du titre support).
– *the opening order*: ordre à l'ouverture.

to attach: attacher, impliquer, imputer, contraindre par corps, saisir, mettre opposition.
debtor **attached**: débiteur saisi.
attached hereto: annexé aux présentes.
attached to: afférent à.

attachment: attachement (m), fixation (f).
[J] a) saisie (saisie-arrêt d'immeubles ou de navires) ; b) *(against salary securities)* opposition ; c) mandat d'amener ; d) prise de corps ou arrêt, *(for contemps of court)* contrainte par corps, *(for debts)* saisie au corps.
– *for rent*: saisie-gagerie.
– *of privilege*: privilège de juridiction.
– *of real property*: saisie immobilière.
– *order*: ordonnance de saisie.
conservatory – : saisie conservatoire.
foreign – : saisie foraine (terme technique : *distraint upon the goods of a person living in furnished rooms*).
simple – : saisie-arrêt chirographaire.
to lay an – *on*: mettre opposition sur.
warrant for – : ordonnance de saisie (pour toutes autres formes de saisie voir *arrestation, distraint, embargo, execution, foreclosure, garnishment, seizure*).

attack: attaque.
[J] – *on honour*: atteinte à l'honneur.
– *on the rights of property*: lésion des droits de propriété.
collateral – : allégation de nullité radicale (d'un jugement, d'un acte de procédure).
to attack *a judgment*: attaquer un jugement.

attainder: [J] confiscation des biens et perte des droits civils consécutive à une condamnation à mort.
bill of – : décret à cet effet.
to attaint: condamner à la perte de (ses) droits, (hist.) frapper de mort civile.

attempt: essai (m), effort (m), attentat (m).
[J] (civ.) intention non réalisée, (cr.) tentative.
– *against the State*: attentat à la sûreté de l'Etat.
– *against liberty*: mesure attentatoire à la liberté.

– 311 –

to attempt : essayer, entreprendre, chercher à.
— *s.o.'s life* : attenter à la vie de qn.
attempted *murder, theft* : tentative d'assassinat, de vol.
attempted commission of an offence : tentative de perpétration d'un crime.

to attend : assister, être présent, *(to)*, s'occuper de, prendre soin de, veiller à.
— *a trial* : assister aux débats.
— *to a case* : s'occuper d'une affaire.
to be summoned — as a witness : être appelé à témoigner.

attendance : présence (f), assiduité (f), exécution (f), attention (f).
— *book* : registre de présence.
— *fees* : jetons de présence.
— *sheet* : feuille de présence.
hours of — : heures de bureau.
to order — : ordonner la comparution.

attendant : accompagnateur.
— *circumstances* : circonstances concomitantes.
[J] — *terms* : droit réel accessoire stipulant l'intégrité de la transmission héréditaire d'un bien-fonds.

attention : attention, soins, égards.
our best — : nos meilleurs soins.
best and prompt — : tous soins et diligence.

attenuation : atténuation (f).
[J] circonstances atténuantes (se dit aussi **attenuating** *circumstances*).

attermining : [J] [A] [C] atermoiement (m).
to attermine : accorder, octroyer, des termes et délais.

attestation : attestation (f), assermentation (f).
[J] a) témoignage (m), déposition (f) de témoin ; b) légalisation (f) de signature ; c) intervention (f) d'un témoin dans un acte ; d) administration (f) ou prestation (f) de serment.
— *clause* : clause de certification, attestation de témoins instrumentaires.
— *paper* : certificat d'attestation.
attestant : témoin, déposant.
attested *copy* : copie certifiée.
duly attested declaration : déclaration authentifiée.
attested signature : signature légalisée.
attesting *notary* : notaire instrumentaire.
attesting witness, **attestor** : témoin instrumentaire.

attitude survey : étude (f) de comportement (ce que les acheteurs pensent d'un produit, ce que les ouvriers pensent de leurs conditions de travail).

attorney : mandataire (m), représentant dûment désigné.
[J] — *-at-law* : [U.K.] a) avoué *(solicitor)* ; b) agréé (au tribunal de commerce), [U.S.] avocat (« *attorney and counselor at law* »).
— *-in-fact* : fondé de procuration spéciale et authentique pour un cas déterminé.
— *-general* : [U.K.] membre du Parlement dont les fonctions se rapprochent de celles du procureur général près la Cour de cassation française ; [U.S.] ministre de la Justice.
— *of record* : avocat occupant.
[U.S.] (juridiction fédérale) *district —* # procureur de la République.
letter, power, warrant, of — : procuration, mandat pouvoirs.
full power of — : procuration générale.
attorneyship : charge d'avoué.

attornment : (hist.) transfert de vassalité à un nouveau seigneur.
[J] **to attorn** *to the new owner* : reconduire le contrat de ferme ou de location au nom d'un nouveau propriétaire.

attractive : avantageux.
such election is — : une telle option est avantageuse.

attributable : imputable.

auction : vente (f) aux enchères, adjudication (f), vente publique, *(of movables)* vente à l'encan, *(of produce)* vente à la criée.
— *-room* : salle des ventes, *(for the sale of produce)* salle des criées.
— *of shares* : vente publique de titres.
candle- — (ou — *by inch of candle*) : adjudication à l'éteinte de chandelle.
Dutch — : enchère au rabais.
forced sale by — : vente aux enchères par autorité de justice.
auctioneer *(and valuer)* : commissaire-priseur.

audi alteram partem : entendre l'autre partie.

audience : audience (f).
— *chamber* : salle d'audience.
— *research* : étude d'écoute (ex. quels sont les téléspectateurs qui regardent tel ou tel programme).
open — : audience publique.
[J] droit d'un avocat de plaider devant une juridiction déterminée.

audit, auditing: vérification (f), apurement (m) des comptes.
 social — : bilan (m) social (d'une entreprise).
 tax — : vérification de comptabilité (par le fisc).
 to carry out a tax — : procéder à une vérification de comptabilité.
 commissioner of — # auditeur à la Cour des comptes.
 to audit: vérifier, apurer (des comptes).
 to audit a taxpayer return: vérifier une déclaration d'impôt.
 audited *statement*: bilan, comptes, vérifiés par expert-comptable.
 auditor: commissaire aux comptes, réviseur de comptes.
 auditor's final discharge: quitus donné au commissaire aux comptes.
 tax auditor: auditeur interne, réviseur.

auricular: auriculaire (a).
 [J] — *witness*: témoin auriculaire.

austerity policy: politique (f) d'austérité.

authentic: authentique, de bonne foi.
 — *deed, instrument*: acte authentique.
 both texts being equally — : les deux textes feront également foi.

to authenticate: authentifier, certifier, homologuer.
 authenticated *copies*: expéditions authentiques.
 authenticated documents: copies légalisées.

authentification: a) authentification (f), certification (f), homologation (f), légalisation (f), validation (f); b) reconnaissance de l'authenticité (d'un document, etc.).

authority: autorité (f), pouvoir (m), mandat (m), compétence (f).
 [J] *abuse of* — : abus de pouvoir.
 — *of father*: puissance paternelle.
 [A] *public* — : les pouvoirs publics.
 port of London — : direction du port de Londres.
 Tennessee Valley — : administration (autonome) de la Vallée du Tennessee.
 the **authorities**: l'administration.
 the health authorities: les services d'hygiène.
 the police authorities: la police.
 reserve authorities: Institut d'émission.
 the revenue authorities: (le) fisc.
 the taxation authorities: l'Administration fiscale.
 to act on the — *of*: agir par délégation de.
 to apply to the proper — : s'adresser à qui de droit.
 to be acting under authorities of: agir en vertu d'une autorisation.

to authorize: autoriser, permettre, consentir.
 authorized *agent*: mandataire.
 authorized capital: capital autorisé, déclaré.
 authorized by law: prévu par la loi.
 authorized subdivision: subdivision légale.
 authorized clerk: commis de bourse.
 when not so authorized: à défaut de cette autorisation.

automatic data processing: traitement mécanographique des données.

automatic vending machine: distributeur (m) automatique (cigarettes, boissons, etc.).

automation: automatisation (f).

(in) autre droit: [J] pour le compte d'un tiers.

autrefois acquit, autrefois attaint, autrefois convict: [J] de par l'autorité de la chose jugée (acquittement ou condamnation antérieur pour la même infraction).

autre vie: [J] pour la durée de la vie d'une autre personne.

auxiliaries: matières (f pl) adjuvantes.

auxiliary: auxiliaire, secondaire (a).

avail: profit, avantage, fruits, produit.

available: disponible, utilisable, accessible.
 — *funds*: disponibilités.
 capital that can be made — : capitaux mobilisables.
 losses — *for carry forward*: déficits pouvant bénéficier du report (déficitaire).
 provision — *optionally*: disposition applicable sur option.

average: moyenne (f).
 [ASS] avaries (f pl).
 averager, — *adjuster, stater*: répartiteur d'avaries, dispacheur.
 — *bond*: compromis d'avarie.
 — *clause*: franc d'avarie.
 — *cost price*: prix de revient moyen (d'une série d'articles...).
 — *fixed cost, average variable cost*: prix de revient moyen fixe, variable.
 adjustment of — : règlement d'avarie.
 adjustment of — : règlement dispache.
 general — : avaries communes, grosses avaries.
 particular — : avarie simple, particulière.
 weighted — : moyenne pondérée.
 [B] *averager*: faiseur de moyenne.

averment : affirmation (f).
[J] allégation d'un fait avec preuve à l'appui.
prefatory — : affirmation préliminaire.

to avoid : résoudre, résilier, annuler.
« *shall avoid* » : invalide, sans valeur.

avoidance : action d'éviter.
[J] *(of a contract)* résolution (f), résiliation (f), *(of a sentence, a will, of proceedings)* annulation (f).
— *of contract owing to mistake or misrepresentation (rescission)* : rescision.
— *clause* : clause résolutoire.
action for — *of contract* : action en nullité.
condition of — : clause résolutoire.
tax — : évasion fiscale.

avouchment : affirmation (f), déclaration (f), garantie (f).
to avouch *for sth.* : se porter garant de qch.
[J] **avoucher** : mise en demeure adressée au garant de s'exécuter.

avowal : aveu (m).

avowant : [J] déclarant.

avowry : [J] déclaration en justification d'une saisie.

avowterer : [J] complice d'une femme adultère (voir *co-respondent*).

avulsion : [J] avulsion (f).

to await : attendre.
[C] **awaiting** *delivery* : en souffrance.

award : décernement (m).
[J] a) jugement irrévocable ; b) sentence arbitrale ; c) adjudication ; d) dommages-intérêts.
— *of alimony* : allocation d'une pension alimentaire.
— *of costs* : adjudication des frais taxés.
conciliation — : procès-verbal de conciliation.

to award : adjuger, octroyer, attribuer.
— *a judgment* : prononcer une sentence.
— *damages* : accorder des dommages-intérêts.
awarded *costs* : frais adjugés.
awarder : adjudicateur.

axe (the) : coupe (f) sombre dans les prévisions budgétaires, diminution (f) de personnel.

to axe : faire des coupes sombres, mettre à pied.
— *expenditure* : réduire les dépenses.

ay : oui.
— *(es) and noes* : voix pour et contre, votes affirmatifs et négatifs.
the — *(es) have it* : les « oui » l'emportent.

NOTES

NOTES

B

baby : [B] action nouvelle.

bachelor : célibataire mâle (opp. *spinster*).

back : dos (m), verso (m), en arrière (adv.).
— *claim* : avantage de réversion.
— *duty* : arriéré d'impôt.
— *freight* : fret, imprévu.
— *interest, back payment* : arrérages.
feed — *effect* : effet de retour.
— *pay of tax* : remboursement d'impôt.
— *-to-* — *credit* : crédit accordé à un acheteur étranger par une banque britannique qui sert d'intermédiaire entre lui et un vendeur (anonyme) également étranger.
— *bencher (pol. U.K.)* : membre du Parlement (M.P.) sans portefeuille ministériel et siégeant sur les bancs « de derrière ».

to back : renforcer, épauler, approuver ; endosser, avaliser, contresigner.
— *(s.o.)* : financer (qqn).
— *a bill* : endosser un effet.
backed bill : effet avalisé, papier fait.
backed currency : monnaie (fiduciaire) garantie.
backed warrant : *(from court to court)* mandat judiciaire visé, *(foreign)* revêtu de l'exequatur.

to backdate : antidater.

backer : donneur d'aval, commanditaire, garant.
financial — : bailleur de fonds.

background : historique, motif réel (ou caché), donnée (f), aspect, antécédent (m), formation (f), références (f pl).
— *information* : documentation de base.

backing : appui financier (m), couverture (f), remboursement (m).
financial — : soutien financier.

backlash *(of a move)* : contrecoup (m), répercussion (f), choc (m) en retour.

backlog : [U.S.] réserve, arriéré.
— *of orders* : ordre en carnet, accumulation d'ordres.

backslider : récidiviste, relapse.

back up line : ligne (f) de substitution.

backward : arrière, rétrospectif, à rebours.
— *effect* : effet de polarisation amont.
— *integration* : intégration par absorption des fournisseurs (ex. une verrerie achète une fabrique d'emballages dont elle était la cliente).
— *shifting of a tax* : translation fiscale régressive.

backwardation : [B] déport.
— *rate* : cours de déport, taux de déport.
backwardised stock : titre déporté.

backwardness : retard (m) d'un secteur de l'économie.

bad : mauvais, faux (a).
— *claim* : réclamation mal fondée.
— *coin* : fausse monnaie.
— *debt* : créance irrécouvrable.
— *debts reserve* : provision pour créances douteuses.
— *faith* : mauvaise foi.
— *in law* : illégal.
— *name* : mauvaise réputation.
— *paper* : mauvais papier (créance douteuse).
— *plea* : argument non pertinent.
— *title* : titre de propriété non valable.
— *voting paper* : bulletin de vote nul.
— *money drives out good* : la mauvaise monnaie chasse la bonne.
to write off a — *debt* : passer une créance irrécouvrable par pertes et profits.

bag : serviette (f).
brief — : serviette d'avocat.
a mixed — : un mélange d'articles (bons et mauvais).

bail : garantie (f).
[J] 1° caution (f) ; garant (m), 2° a) cautionnement (m) ; b) somme consignée à ce titre, 3° mise en liberté sous caution.
— *-bond* : engagement signé par la caution que le prisonnier relaxé provisoirement comparaîtra à date voulue.
release on — : mise en liberté sous caution.
to refuse — : rejeter la demande de mise en liberté sous caution.
to admit to — : mettre en liberté provisoire moyennant caution.
to allow — : admettre à caution.
to find — : fournir caution.
to grant — : admettre une caution.
to post, to go — *for s.o.* : se porter fort, se

— 317 —

rendre garant de qn.
to jump one's — : se dérober à la justice.
to skip — : forfaire à un cautionnement.
to surrender to one's — : décharger ses cautions, comparaître en jugement.
to forfait — : ne pas comparaître en jugement.
to bail *s.o. out* : cautionner qn.
bailable *offence* : délit comportant l'élargissement provisoire du délinquant moyennant caution.
bailed : admis à caution.
bailer, bailsman : caution.

bailiff : huissier (m).
— *('s) man* : recors.
bum- — : assistant de l'huissier.

bailment : [J] a) dépôt, cautionnement ; b) mise en liberté provisoire sous caution ; c) contrat de gage.

balance : balance (f).
[C] [F] a) solde (m), reliquat (m), solde de compte, soulte (f) ; b) bilan (m).
active, adverse — : balance excédentaire, déficitaire.
annual — : bilan annuel.
— *of an account* : solde d'un compte.
— *book* : livre des soldes.
— *brought, carried forward (— c/fwd.)* : report, solde à nouveau.
— *of current accounts* : balance des opérations courantes.
— *due* : solde débiteur.
— *in hand* : encaisse.
— *of indebtness* : balance débitrice.
— *of payments* : balance des paiements.
— *of payments surplus/deficit* : balance des paiements excédentaire/déficitaire.
— *sheet (stating the assets and the liabilities)* : bilan d'inventaire (par doit et avoir).
— *to next account* : report à nouveau.
— *of trade* : balance du commerce extérieur.
— *on capital account* : balance des opérations en capital.
bank — : solde en banque.
carrying over of a — : report d'un solde.
cash — : encaisse, solde de caisse.
credit — : solde créditeur.
debit — : solde débiteur.
declining, reducing, — *method* : système d'amortissement dégressif.
to get out a — *sheet* : établir un bilan.
invisible items — : balance des invisibles.
monthly — : bilan mensuel.
outstanding — : solde à découvert.
passive — : solde débiteur.
trial — : balance de vérification.
true — : bilan sincère.
unexpensed — : reliquat sans emploi.
to balance : solder, balancer, arrêter un compte.

to balance the budget : équilibrer le budget.
to balance by counter entry : balancer par contre écriture.
the books and accounts shall be balanced : les écritures et les comptes seront arrêtés.
balanced *growth* : croissance équilibrée.
balancing : équilibre, solde (m).
balancing item (in an account) : article (rectificatif) d'erreur (dans un compte).

ballot : (boule de) scrutin, tour de scrutin.
single — : élection à un tour.
second — : deuxième tour.
— *box* : urne de scrutin.
— *paper* : bulletin de vote.
by — : au scrutin.
tied — : égalité des voix dans un vote.
balloting : élection au scrutin.
[C] ballot (m) (de marchandises).

ban, bans, banns : 1° [J] ban (m), proclamation (f).
— *of matrimony* : bans de mariage.
asking of, putting up, — : publication des bans.
to forbid the — : mettre opposition à un mariage (se dit aussi *caveat to marriage*).
2° interdiction (f), bannissement (m).
— *on ex-post facto legislation* : principe de la non-rétroactivité des lois.
overtime — : refus de faire des heures supplémentaires.
to ban *war* : mettre la guerre hors la loi.
play **banned** *by censor* : pièce de théâtre interdite par la censure.

banco : monnaie de banque.

to bang : claquer.
— *the market* : [B] casser les cours.
banger : [B] fauteur de panique.

banishment : proscription (f), exil (m).
[J] bannissement (m).
local — : interdiction de séjour.

bank : [C] [F] banque.
— *of England (The Bank)* : la Banque d'Angleterre.
[U.S.] *federal reserve* — *(s)* : banques fédérales de réserve.
— *-account* : compte en banque.
— *-bill* : effet de banque à banque.
— *-book* : livret (m), carnet (m) de banque.
— *branch* : succursale bancaire.
— *charges* : frais de banque.
— *cheque* : chèque bancaire.
— *clearings* : compensations entre banques.
— *-clerk* : employé de banque.
— *collection* : recouvrement bancaire.
— *cover* : couverture en banque.
— *credit* : crédit en banque.

— *deposit*: dépôt (m) en banque.
— *-discount*: escompte en dehors.
— *guarantee*: caution bancaire.
— *-holidays*: jours de fête en Angleterre où les banques n'ouvrent pas.
— *of issue*: banque d'émission, banque centrale.
— *of International Settlements (B.I.S.)*: Banque des règlements internationaux.
— *-messenger*: garçon de recette.
— *order*: mandat de banque.
— *overdraft*: avance bancaire à découvert.
— *-paper*: papier bancable.
penny- — : caisse d'épargne.
— *-rate*: taux officiel d'escompte.
— *return*: état de banque.
— *shares*: valeurs, actions de banque.
— *statement*: bordereau de situation, relevé de compte.
— *-transfer*: virement bancaire.
— *weekly statement*: bilan hebdomadaire (d'une banque centrale).
business — : banque d'affaires.
clearing — : banque de virements.
commercial — : banque commerciale.
deposit — : banque de dépôt.
investment — : [U.S.] banque d'affaires.
land — : crédit foncier.
merchant — : [U.K.] banque d'affaires.
parent — : maison mère.
Post Office Savings — : Caisse d'Epargne Postale.
bankable: bancable.
bankable bill: effet bancable.
banker: banquier.
— *('s) draft*: traite bancaire.
lending — : banquier prêteur.
paying — : banquier payeur.
syndicate of — *(s)*: consortium bancaire.
banking: affaires, opérations bancaires.
— *(s) and banking*: banques et opérations de banque.
banking company: société bancaire.
branch banking: système de banques à succursales (en opp. à *unit banking*).
central checking of banking risks: centralisation des risques bancaires.
to bank: déposer (de l'argent) en banque.
to bank on sthg: compter sur (qqch).

banknote: billet de banque.
— *with compulsory currency*: billet de banque à cours forcé.
irredeemable — : billet de banque inconvertible.

bankrupt: failli (a et m), banqueroutier (m).
— *('s) certificate*: concordat.
— *('s) estate*: masse des biens de la faillite.
certificated — : concordataire, failli réhabilité.
to adjudicate s.o. a — : déclarer qn en état de faillite, prononcer la faillite.
to become, to go, — : tomber en faillite, faire faillite.
surrender of a — *('s) property*: abandon des biens d'un failli à ses créanciers.
uncertificated, undischarged — : failli n'ayant pas obtenu de concordat, failli non réhabilité.

bankruptcy: faillite (f).
(Peut être prononcée indistinctement à l'égard de commerçants et de non-commerçants.)
[J] *acts of* — : indices patents d'insolvabilité (état de cessation de paiements).
the — *Act*: législation sur les faillites.
— *proceedings*: procédure de faillite ou de règlement judiciaire.
composition — : concordat préventif à la faillite.
decree, adjudication, of — : jugement déclaratif de faillite.
discharge in — : révocation de la faillite, réhabilitation d'un failli.
(equal) distribution, dividend, in — : dividende distribué entre les créanciers (au marc le franc).
— *filing*: dépôt de bilan.
fraudulent — : faillite frauduleuse, banqueroute.
judgment in — : jugement déclaratif de faillite.
opening of — *proceedings*: ouverture de la faillite.
petition in — : assignation des créanciers (pour demander la liquidation de biens).
reorganization in — : arrangement permettant au failli de poursuivre son activité sous contrôle.
trustee, referee, in — : [U.S.] syndic de la faillite (U.K. voir *official receiver*).
to file a petition in — : déposer son bilan, se mettre en faillite.
to prove claims in — : produire à la masse.

banner: (U.S.) exceptionnel (a).
— *year*: année exceptionnelle.
— *headlines*: (journ.) titres flamboyants, manchette.

bar: barre.
[J] 1° la barre du tribunal.
the case at — : l'affaire en instance.
the prisoner at the — : l'accusé.
trial at — : audience plénière (opp. *nisiprius*).
to appear at the — : comparaître.
2° le barreau.
[U.S.] — *Association*: ordre des avocats.
[U.K.] — *Council*: Conseil de l'Ordre.
member of the Bar (barrister): avocat à la Cour.
to be called to the — : être inscrit au barreau.
to be called within the — : être nommé avocat de la Couronne: *Queen's Counsel (Q.C.*, titre

honorifique).
3° a) fin de non-recevoir ; b) empêchement (m), prescription (f).
plea in — (ou *special plea*) : exception péremptoire (soulevée dans le cas d'une *affirmative defence* ou de *denial*, voir ces mots).
sentence acts as a — *:* empêchement de recommencer une instance après rejet (res judicata).
— *date :* dernière limite, jour ad quem.
— *to marriage :* empêchement au mariage.
— *period :* délai de forclusion.
— *to set-off :* obstacle à la compensation.
agreement to — *award of alimony :* accord excluant le versement d'une pension alimentaire.
— *of the statute of limitations :* prescription.
[F] *lingot.*
[C] — *chart :* diagramme comparatif des ventes mois par mois (sous forme de colonnes parallèles).

to bar : exclure, empêcher, opposer une fin de non-recevoir.
— *s.o. from a trial :* exclure une personne de l'enceinte du tribunal, mettre quelqu'un hors cour.
action **barred** *by the statute of limitations :* action prescrite.
action shall be absolutely barred : il y aura une fin de non-recevoir absolue contre toute action.
to be barred by limitation (by statute of limitation) : être prescrit.
to be statute-barred : se prescrire.

bare : nu (a).
[J] — ou *dry trustee :* fidéicommissaire dont les pouvoirs sont sur le point d'expirer, tenu à remettre les biens qu'il détient au bénéficiaire du trust *(cestui que trust).*
— *contract :* contrat à titre gratuit.
— *owner :* nu-propriétaire.
[F] — *living :* réduit au minimum vital d'existence (exonéré d'impôt).

bargain : marché (m), affaire, contrat, soldes (f pl).
[J] — *and sale :* contrat de vente exécutable sur le champ.
to conclude a — *:* arrêter un marché.
Dutch — *:* contrat léonin.
[C] *to enter into a* — *:* passer un marché.
to strike a — *:* conclure un marché.
at a — *:* à bon compte.
— *counter :* rayon des soldes.
— *-price :* prix de solde.
— *sale :* vente de soldes.
— *work :* travail à l'entreprise.
[B] — *for account :* marché à terme.
— *book :* carnet d'agent de change.
— *for cash :* marché au comptant.

— *(s) done :* cours faits.
— *with option :* marché à prime.
settlement, time, — *:* marché à terme, vente à découvert.
bargainee : acheteur, preneur.
bargainor : vendeur, bailleur.
bargaining : marchandage, discussion, négociation.
collective bargaining : négociation, convention collective.
bargaining learning process : processus continuel de discussion tenant compte des leçons du passé.
freedom of industrial bargaining : libres négociations entre employeurs et salariés.
[J] *plea bargaining :* négociation avec le juge sur les chefs d'accusation à retenir.

baronet : dignité personnelle ou héréditaire, mais non titre de noblesse.

barratry : [J] a) baraterie ; b) simonie, vénalité de juge ; c) délit d'incitation aux litiges, abus du droit de plaider.
barrator : capitaine fraudeur, juge vénal, personne qui pousse à la chicane.

barrier : barrière (f), entrave (f).
trade — *:* entrave au commerce international.

barrister, barristress : [J]
— *-at-law :* avocat à la Cour.
(L'un des deux types d'avocats anglais, l'autre étant le *solicitor.* Seul admis à plaider et à déposer des conclusions auprès des instances supérieures et habilité à commenter des points de droit, le — doit être obligatoirement consulté par le *solicitor.*
« *as a rule of professional etiquette* » le — reçoit pas de mandat ni d'instructions directement, mais par l'intermédiaire du *solicitor.*
Il en est de même des honoraires, qui ne sont pas recouvrables en droit mais compris dans les frais taxables de ce dernier.)

barter : troc (m), échange (m).
[C] — *goods :* marchandises de traite, pacotille (f).
[E] *gross* — *terms of trade :* termes de l'échange brut.
— *trade agreements :* contrats de compensation.

base : fondamental, bas (a).
[J] — *fee :* droit de propriété sur le point de s'éteindre (p. ex., dans le cas de biens substitués, faute d'héritier idoine).

base : base (f).
— *company :* société relais.
cost — *:* prix de base.
fixed — *:* base fixe.

— *rate*: taux de base (le plus bas offert par une banque de virement).
— *stock*: stock de base.
taxable — : base d'imposition.
— *year*: année de base.

to base: baser, fonder, asseoir, se fonder.
— *taxation on (income)*: asseoir l'impôt sur (le revenu).

basic: fondamental, à la base, de base.
— *abatement*: abattement à la base.
— *commodity*: denrée témoin.
— *fact*: fait essentiel.
— *income*: revenu direct.
— *investments*: investissements de base.
— *pay*: salaire de base.
— *rules*: règles fondamentales.

basis: base, fondement, régime, assiette.
[F] *actual* — *of assessment*: régime du bénéfice réel.
arising — : [U.K.] obligation fiscale illimitée.
— *of assessment*: assiette d'imposition, base de cotisation.
— *of a tax*: assiette d'un impôt.
— *of a mortgage*: assiette d'une hypothèque.
— *rate*: tarif de base.
current year — : [U.K.] revenus d'une année imposables au titre de cette même année.
impersonal — *of liability*: base réelle de l'assujettissement.
normal actual — : régime normal du bénéfice réel (en France).
national — *of assessment*: régime du forfait.
on an accrual — : en tenant compte des créances acquises et des dépenses engagées (système de comptabilisation).
on a cash — : en faisant état des sommes encaissées et payées.
on a national — : au forfait.
on the actual — : au réel.
on the same — *(as)*: selon les mêmes règles (que celles prévues pour).
personal — *of liability*: base personnelle de l'assujettissement.
preceding year — : [U.K.] revenus d'une année imposables au titre de l'année suivante.
presumptive — : base forfaitaire.
remittance — : [U.K.] obligation fiscale limitée (aux sommes transférées au Royaume-Uni).
simplified actual — : régime du réel simplifié (en France).
tax — : assiette de l'impôt.
to treat on such a — : traiter sur une telle base.

basket: panier (m).
— *clause, provision*: clause résiduelle, disposition « fourre-tout ».
— *of currencies*: un panier de devises.

— *tax credit*: [US] imputation des crédits d'impôt en fonction de la répartition des revenus catégoriels.

bastard: enfant naturel.
[J] *action of* — *for affiliation*: action en recherche de paternité.
bastardy *procedure case*: contestation de légitimité, action en désaveu de la paternité.
bastardy order: ordre au père putatif d'avoir à subvenir à l'entretien de l'enfant.
to bastardize: a) fait de déclarer par un tribunal qu'un enfant est illégitime, b) témoignage apporté à cet effet (voir *affiliation*, *illegitimate*, *legitimate*).

batch: lot (m) (de marchandises).
— *production*: production par phases successives de fabrication.

battery: [J] voies de fait (voir *assault*).
— *farming*: élevage intensif.

bawd: proxénète (m et f).
bawdy house: lupanar (m).

bear: [B] baissier, spéculateur à la baisse.
— *covering*: couverture de position à la baisse.
— *position*: position vendeur.
— *raid*: attaque des baissiers.
— *rumours*: bruits alarmants.
— *transaction*: opération à la baisse.
to go a — : spéculer à la baisse.
to raid the — *(s)*: pourchasser le découvert.
to sell a — , *to sell short*: vendre à découvert.
to — *the market*: vendre à découvert, peser sur les cours.
bearish *market*: marché à la baisse, marché baissier.
bearish tendency: tendance à la baisse.
[F] — *account*: compte à découvert.
to frighten the — *(s)*: faire courir le découvert.

to bear: porter, produire, rapporter, supporter.
— *the cost*: supporter les frais.
— *interest*: porter intérêt.
— *a tax*: supporter un impôt.
— *out*: confirmer, corroborer.
interest-**bearing** *capital*: capital productif d'intérêt.

bearer: porteur.
(Les titres au porteur sont d'un usage bien moins répandu en Grande-Bretagne et aux Etats-Unis qu'en France, il n'y existe notamment pas d'actions autres que nominatives.)
[J] [F] [C] — -*bond*, — -*security*, — -*shares*, — -*stock*: titre au porteur.
— *of a cheque*: porteur d'un chèque.
— *of a passport*: titulaire d'un passeport.

instruments payable to — *(bills of exchange, promissory notes, cheques)* : effets négociables (lettres de change, billets à ordre, chèques).

to beat : tricher, frauder, mystifier.
  beating *board bill :* grivèlerie.

bed : lit.
  [J] mariage.
  child of the second — : enfant du deuxième lit.
  separation from — *and board :* séparation de corps (voir cette expression).
  [F] « — *and breakfast* » : vente de titres en baisse en vue des déductions fiscales correspondantes quitte à les racheter le lendemain.

before : antérieurement à, devant.
  [J] *the case* — *the court :* l'affaire dont le tribunal est saisi.
  the case — *the jury :* le cas sur lequel il appartient au jury de se prononcer.
  — *a notary :* par devant notaire.
  — *the orders of the day are called :* avant de passer à l'ordre du jour.
  [F] *redemption* — *due date :* remboursement anticipé.
  — *-tax :* avant impôt, brut d'impôt.
  [B] — *hours :* avant-Bourse.
  — *maturity :* avant l'échéance.

beforehand : d'avance (adv).
  penalty agreed — : clause pénale (dans un contrat).

to beg : avoir l'honneur, l'avantage de.
  — *the question :* commettre une pétition de principe (dans une plaidoirie, etc.).

(on) behalf : au nom (de qn).
  to act on — *of s.o. :* agir pour le compte de qn.

behaviour : conduite, comportement.
  [A] « *for good* — » : « tant qu'ils auront une bonne conduite » : principe d'inamovibilité.
  [U.S.] *federal judges shall hold office for good* — : les juges fédéraux sont nommés à vie (sauf indignité).

behest : ordre.
  at the — *of s.o. :* sur l'ordre de qqn.

behind : derrière.
  — *closed doors :* à huis clos.

behindhand : en retard.

belief : croyance, conviction (f).
  [J] « *Upon information and* — » : « en vertu de renseignements que je tiens pour véridiques », formule rituelle des *affidavits* lorsque l'auteur n'a pas eu une connaissance directe des faits. *to my best knowledge and* — : pour autant que je sache.

belligerency : belligérance (f).
  belligerent : belligérant (m).

bell-shaped curve : courbe en cloche (statistique).

belong : appartenir à, être affilié.
  belonging *thereto :* qui s'y rapporte.

below : en dessous, en aval.
  as stated — : comme il est indiqué ci-dessous.
  — *par :* au-dessous du pair.
  [F] — *the line expenditures :* dépenses inscrites au budget extraordinaire, destinées à financer la publicité par des moyens autres que les moyens habituels offerts par les medias (ex. financer une manifestation sportive, etc.).

bench : banc (m).
  [J] a) *the* — : la magistrature (assise) ; b) le tribunal ; c) le siège (du juge).
  Bar and — : la robe.
  witnesses' — : banc des témoins.
  — *warrant :* mandat d'arrêt décerné sur le siège (pour outrages à magistrat, défaut de témoin injustifié, etc.).
  from the — : énonciations du juge au cours des débats.
  bencher : avocat membre du corps des doyens des *Inns of Court* (voir ce mot).
  (parlement) *the Treasury* — : banc des ministres.
  front **benches** *(benchers) :* banquettes au premier rang à droite du *speaker* de la Chambre des Communes, occupées par les ministres, à gauche, par le cabinet virtuel de l'opposition *(shadow cabinet).*
  back **benches** *(benchers) :* banquettes du « rank and file » des partis : les simples députés non « ministrables ».
  to assent to the — : entrer dans la magistrature.
  to be on — : siéger au tribunal.

benchmark : repère (m) (en économie).
  — *method :* méthode de référence.

beneficial : profitable, avantageux (a).
  — *association :* société de secours mutuels.
  [J] — *interest :* titre de droit en *Eq.*, d'où :
  — *ownership :* usufruit, le droit de propriété restant imparfait tant qu'il n'est pas formel, c'est-à-dire reconnu comme *title* en *C.L.* Le bien sur lequel porte le *beneficial ownership*, est un *beneficial interest.*
  [B] — *shareholder :* propriétaire réel (d'actions).

beneficiary: bénéficiaire, ayant droit.
[J] sp. *« cestui que trust »*: bénéficiaire d'un *trust* (voir ce mot).
gratuitary — : bénéficiaire à titre gratuit.
third party — : bénéficiaire d'un contrat au profit de tiers (tiers bénéficiaire).
[ASS] bénéficiaire.

benefit: avantage (m), bienfait (m).
— *of the doubt*: bénéfice du doute.
[J] *for the public* — : dans l'intérêt général.
allocation (f), indemnité (f), prestation (f).
age — : secours à la vieillesse.
family — *(s)*: allocations familiales.
medical — *(s)*: secours médicaux.
sickness — : prestation maladie.
social insurance — *(s)*: prévoyance sociale.
social security — *(s)*: prestations sociales.
special — *(s)*: prestations exceptionnelles.
superannuation — *(s)*: pensions de retraite.
— *society*: société de secours mutuel.
— *theory*: théorie de la jouissance.
unemployment — : indemnité de chômage.
indemnity — : prestation.
[F] bénéfice, profit, avantage (m).
— *(s) in kind*: avantages en nature.
fringe — *(s)*: [U.S.] avantages accessoires au salaire.
[C] rendement.
cost- — *analysis*: [U.S.] analyse des coûts et des rendements.

to benefit by: profiter, bénéficier de.

to bequeath: léguer.

bequest: [J] les biens mobiliers légués, legs (voir *legacy*).

(the) best evidence rule: [J] règle de *l'evidence law* selon laquelle les présomptions *(secondary evidence)* ne sont recevables qu'exceptionnellement, à défaut de preuve directe *(primary evidence)* (voir *evidence*).

to bet: parier.

betterment, bettering: amélioration.
— *of the worker's lot*: amélioration du sort des travailleurs.
[F] plus-value (sp. foncière, dans d'autres cas on dit plutôt *appreciated surplus*).
— *tax*: impôt sur la plus-value ou la valeur ajoutée (se dit aussi *tax on unearned increment*).

bettings: paris.
— *tax*: impôt sur les paris.

beverage tax: impôt sur les boissons.

to beware: prendre garde à.
« beware of substitutes »: se méfier des contrefaçons.

« beyond a reasonable doubt »: [J] quasi-certitude qui doit être celle d'un jury pour rendre un verdict de culpabilité.

B/f *(« brought forward »)*: à reporter.

bias: prévention, opinion préconçue.
[J] — *and prejudice*: suspicion des juges ou des jurés. Si légitime, elle peut donner lieu à récusation.

bid: enchère (f), offre (f), mise (f).
[A] [U.S.] soumission dans une adjudication.
open — : [U.S.] marché public.
[C] *higher* — : surenchère (f).
irresponsible — : folle enchère.
last — : dernière mise.
to make a — : faire une offre, mettre une enchère.
by- — : enchère fictive (faite pour pousser les enchères).
[B] *take-over* — : offre publique d'achat (O.P.A.).
take-over — *for shares*: offre publique d'échange (O.P.E.).
— *and asked quotation*: cours acheteur et vendeur.

to bid: enchérir, faire une offre.
— *for a corporation's stock*: faire une offre de rachat d'actions d'une société.
— *down (up)*: faire baisser (monter) les enchères.
— *open*: mettre enchères sur.
to overbid: surenchérir.

bidder: enchérisseur.
false — : fol enchérisseur.
to the highest — : au plus offrant, au dernier enchérisseur.

bidding: enchères.
the first — : la mise à prix.

bilateral: bilatéral.
— *contract*: contrat synallagmatique.
— *monopoly*: monopole bilatéral.

bill: 1° [U.S.] projet de loi, [U.K.] loi.
2° facture, note (à payer), traite.
3° portefeuille, valeur, effet (de commerce), lettre de change, [U.S.] billet de banque.
4° acte, contrat, déclaration, affiche.
5° document.
6° projet.
[J] [C.L.] — ou — *of indictment*: résumé des chefs d'accusation présenté au *grand jury*. Celui-ci peut soit *find a true* — : déclarer

fondés les chefs d'accusation, soit *ignore the* — : refuser la mise en accusation. Dans le premier cas l'affaire vient devant le *petit jury*, dans le second, elle est classée. A quelques exceptions près, cette procédure a été abolie en Angleterre par *the Administration of Justice Act 1933*. Elle subsiste aux Etats-Unis (voir *indictment, jury*).
— *of complaint* : demande introductive d'instance.
— *of divorcement* : jugement de divorce.
— *dropped* : projet abandonné.
— *of particulars* : énonciation détaillée des demandes ou des moyens de défense d'une partie à communiquer à l'adversaire, pour lui permettre d'exposer son cas = conclusions au fond ou signification des défenses.
— *rejected, voted down* : projet rejeté.
— *for a new trial* : pourvoi en révision.
(taxed) — *of costs* : mémoire (taxé).
— *of Rights* : [U.K.] déclaration des droits (loi de 1689, proclamant les droits des sujets face au monarque).
Government — : projet de loi.
Private — : proposition de loi d'intérêt local (ou projet).
Private Member's — : proposition de loi.
public — : projet ou proposition de loi d'intérêt général.
Committee stage of a — : discussion d'un projet en comité.
passing of a — : adoption d'un projet.
preamble of a — : exposé des motifs d'un projet de loi.
tabling of a — : dépôt d'un projet.
no — : ordonnance de non-lieu.
true — : accusation fondée.
[F] *appropriation* — : [U.K.] projet de loi de finances.
— *of supply* : collectif budgétaire, projet de loi de finances rectificative.
— *(s) issued by Government* : titres et obligations d'Etat.
deficiency — *(s)* : collectifs budgétaires, loi de finances rectificative.
Exchequer — : [U.K.] bons du trésor.
Finance — : [U.K.] projet de loi de finances.
tax — : avertissement.
Treasury — : [U.S.] bons du trésor.
[C] *to accept a* — : accepter un effet de commerce.
accommodation — : traite de complaisance, cavalerie.
address for payment of a — : domiciliation d'une traite.
back of a — : verso, dos, d'un effet.
to back a — : avaliser, endosser, un effet.
bank- — : effet (tiré par une Banque sur une autre) ; [U.S.] billet de banque.
bankable — *(s)* : papier bancable.
— *book* : échéancier.
— *of costs* : état des frais.

— *of debt* : reconnaissance de dette(s).
— *(s) for discount* : effets à l'escompte.
— *(s) and drafts* : valeurs à recouvrer.
— *(s) domiciliated (in)* : traite payable (à).
— *of exchange* : lettre de change.
— *(s) in hand* : effets en portefeuille.
— *-head* : en-tête de facture.
— *to mature* : effets à échéance.
— *to order* : billet à ordre.
— *(s) payable* : effets à payer.
— *(s)-payable book* : échéancier.
— *payable at 4 days' date* : effet payable à 4 jours de date.
— *payable at sight* : effet payable, exigible, à vue.
— *of quantities* : devis.
— *receivable* : effets à recevoir, à encaisser.
— *of sale* : contrat de vente.
— *standing over* : traite en souffrance.
— *sticking* : affichage.
to collect — : encaisser une traite.
day bill : effet à date fixe.
to dishonour a — : ne pas honorer une traite.
to draw a — : créer un effet.
due- — : [U.S.] reconnaissance de dette.
to endorse a — : endosser un effet.
expired — : effet périmé.
fallen — : effet échu.
foreign — *(s) and securities* : effets et titres étrangers.
forged — : fausse facture.
guarantee of a — *of exchange* : aval d'une lettre de change.
guaranteed — *(s)* : effets avalisés.
to honour a — *of exchange* : payer une lettre de change.
honoured — : traite acquittée.
home, inland — : effet sur l'intérieur.
long-dated — *(s)* : papiers à longue échéance, papiers longs.
long — : effet à longue échéance.
made — : billet endossé.
to meet a — *of exchange* : honorer une lettre de change.
to note protest of a — *of exchange* : faire le protêt d'une lettre de change.
ordinary — *(s)* : papier commercial.
pay-bill : feuille de paye, [A] feuille d'émargement, *(milit.)* état de solde.
to pay a — : régler une facture.
to pay a — *of exchange for honour* : payer une lettre de change par intervention.
to pay a — *of exchange at maturity* : payer une lettre de change à l'échéance.
payee of a — *of exchange* : bénéficiaire d'un effet de commerce.
to present a — *for acceptance* : présenter une traite à l'acceptation.
presenter of a : — présentateur d'un billet, d'une traite.
prime trade — *(s)* : papier hors banque ; papier de haut commerce.

to prolong a — : prolonger l'échéance d'un billet.
to protect a — *of exchange* : faire provision pour une lettre de change.
to protest a — : protester une lettre de change, lever protêt d'une lettre de change.
to provide a — *for acceptance* : présenter un effet à l'acceptation.
to provide for a — : faire provision pour une lettre de change.
rebate on —*(s) not due* : escompte d'effets.
to receipt a — : acquitter une facture.
recourse to the endorser of a — : recours contre l'endosseur ou l'accepteur d'un effet.
to redeem a — : honorer un effet.
to rediscount a — : réescompter un effet.
to rediscount other banks' — *(s)* : réescompter le portefeuille d'autres banques.
to remit —*(s) for collection* : remettre des effets en recouvrement, à l'encaissement.
remittance of a — *for collection* : remise d'un effet en recouvrement, à l'encaissement.
to renew a — : prolonger une lettre de change.
to represent a — *for acceptance* : représenter un effet à l'acceptation.
to retire a — : retirer, rembourser un effet.
to return a — *dishonoured* : retourner un effet impayé.
return of a — *to drawer* : contrepassation.
to return a — *to drawer* : contrepasser un effet.
to return a — *unpaid* : retourner une traite faute de paiement.
rider to a — *of exchange* : allonge d'une lettre de change.
to send a — *for acceptance* : envoyer une traite à l'acceptation.
short (dated) — : effet à courte échéance.
sights —*(s)* : papier à vue.
sighting of a — *of exchange* : présentation d'une lettre de change.
to sign a — : accepter une traite.
skeleton — : traite en blanc.
to take up a — : honorer un effet.
taker of a — : preneur d'une lettre de change.
tenor of the — *of exchange* : échéance de la lettre de change.
time — : effet à courte, longue échéance ; échéance à terme.
trade —*(s)* : papier de commerce ; papier commercial.
to transfer a — *by endorsement* : transférer, céder un billet par voie d'endossement.
transferee of a — *of exchange* : cessionnaire d'un effet de commerce.
transferor of a — : cédant d'un effet.
unaccepted — : effet non accepté.
to undertake the collection of —*(s) remitted* : se charger du recouvrement d'effets remis.
to undertake to pay the — : s'engager à payer une traite.

undiscountable — : billet, effet inescomptable.
unnegotiable — : effet non négociable.
unprotested — : effet non protesté.
unstamped — : effet non timbré.
very short — : effet à très courte échéance.
[E] — *of entry* : déclaration en douane, (U.K.) bordereau descriptif.
— *of health* : patente de santé, certificat de contrôle sanitaire (d'un équipage).
— *of lading* : connaissement, [U.S.] lettre de voiture.
— *of store* : passavant, reconnaissance de douane.
— *of sufferance* : lettre d'exemption de droit de douane d'un entrepôt portuaire à un autre.
clean — *of lading* : connaissement net (sans clause surajoutée).
customs — : acquit de sortie.
foul — *of lading* : connaissement avec clause surajoutée.
general — *of lading* : connaissement collectif.
inward, outward — *of lading* : connaissement d'entrée, de sortie.
straight — *of lading* : connaissement simple.
through — *of lading* : connaissement à forfait (direct).
way — : lettre de voiture.
[ASS] *average* — : rapport d'avarie.

to bill : facturer.

billion : milliard.

billing : facturation, bilan (m) d'activités (d'une agence de publicité).

bind : coincement (m), grippage (m).
to be in a — : être dans une situation (financière) difficile.

to bind : obliger, lier, engager, attacher, contraindre.
[J] — *a transaction* : rendre une convention obligatoire, parfaire un contrat (en versant des arrhes, etc.).
— *s.o. over* a) *to appear when called upon* : inviter qn à se tenir à la disposition de la justice, b) *to keep the peace* : exiger de qn sous caution de ne pas se livrer à des voies de fait.
— *oneself in writing* : s'engager par écrit.
to be **bound** *over* : être sommé par le magistrat d'observer une bonne conduite.
the court is bound by the issues joined : le tribunal doit s'en tenir au litige tel qu'il est déterminé (par les parties).
jointly bound : engagé solidairement.
to refuse to be bound over : refuser de se soumettre à une obligation.

binder: [J] [C] arrhes.
[ASS] police d'assurance provisoire.

binding: obligatoire, irrévocable, commissoire, liant.
  a condition requiring on – : stipulation qui engage ou qui oblige.
  – *agreement*: obligation irrévocable.
  – *decision*: décision obligatoire.
  obligation – *on all parties*: obligation solidaire.
  the decisions will be – *on the parties concerned*: les décisions seront obligatoires pour les parties intéressées.
  [B] – *transaction on the exchange*: opération ferme.

bipartite: biparti.
  [J] – *document*: document établi en double expédition.
  – *treaty*: traité bilatéral.

birth: naissance.
  afterbirth: naissance posthume.
  delayed – : naissance après terme.
  normal – : naissance à terme.
  premature – : naissance avant terme.
  – *certificate*: acte, extrait de naissance.
  – *control*: limitation des naissances.
  – *place*: lieu de naissance.
  – *premium*: prime à la naissance.
  – *rate*: natalité (f).
  fall in the – *rate*: dénatalité.
  birthright: droit de naissance (sp. droit d'aînesse), patrimoine.

bis (ou : biz) *(Bank for International Settlements)*: Banque des Règlements Internationaux.

black: noir (a).
  – *acre*: *(hist.)* pour la commodité de la discussion juridique un champ était dénommé « noir », pour le définir par rapport au champ contigu, *the white acre*: le champ « blanc ».
  – *Book of the Admiralty*: ouvrage fondamental en matière de droit maritime (commencé à l'époque d'Edouard II et tenu à jour depuis).
  – *cap*: bonnet noir dont se coiffe le juge en prononçant la peine de mort.
  – *economy*: activité économique secrète (pour échapper à l'impôt), travail « au noir ».
  – *knight*: [B] chevalier noir (intervention inamicale d'un tiers, opp. « *white knight* »)
  – *list*: liste noire.
  – *market*: marché noir.
  « *the black Maria* » : « le panier à salade ».
  – *unionism*: coalition clandestine.
  – *-ball*: vote défavorable.
  to be in the – : avoir un compte en banque positif.

to black: (pour des ouvriers, et pas seulement pendant une grève) : refuser de manutentionner certaines marchandises (parce qu'ils pensent que ce serait contraire à leurs intérêts ou à ceux de leurs camarades).

blacklegs: briseurs de grèves.

to blacklist: mettre sur la liste noire.

blackmail: chantage (m), extorsion (f) de fonds.
  blackmailer: maître chanteur.

Blank: blanc, formulaire, formule en blanc.
  – *acceptance*: acceptation en blanc, sans réserve.
  – *bill*: traite en blanc.
  – *cheque*: a) chèque en blanc ; b) formule de chèque ; c) (terme familier) carte blanche.
  – *credit*: crédit en blanc.
  – *endorsement*: endos en blanc.
  paper signed in blank: blanc-seing.
  – *spaces*: les blancs.
  – *transfer*: transfert à titre de garantie.
  – *voting-paper*: bulletin de vote blanc.

blanket: général, d'application générale.
  – *authority*: carte blanche.
  [J] – *mortgage*: hypothèque générale.
  – *bond*: garantie générale.
  [C] [F] – *order*: ordre d'une portée générale.
  – *agreement*: accord salarial national (pour toutes les branches d'une même industrie).
  – *rate*: taux de base.
  [ASS] – *policy*: police d'assurance générale (non spécifiée).

blind test: sondage (m) « à l'aveuglette ».

block: masse (f), paquet (m), [J] obstruction.
  – *of shares*: paquet d'actions.
  – *release*: période « bloquée » pendant laquelle des stagiaires sont autorisés à suivre des cours théoriques tout en percevant l'intégralité de leur salaire.
  to block: faire de l'obstruction, bloquer.
  blocked *account*: bloqué.
  blocked *currency*: monnaie inconvertible.

blockade: blocus (m).
  to raise the – : lever le blocus.
  to run the – : forcer le blocus.

blockbuster: (U.S.) article (m) de choc.

blood: sang (m), parenté (f).
  – *feud*: vendetta.
  – *money*: prix du sang.
  – *relationship*: liens du sang.

blotter: buvard (m).
[A] [U.S.] livre d'écrou, *police* — : cahier des délits et écrous d'un poste de police (U.K. *charge-sheet*).
[C] main-courante.

blue: bleu (a).
the (National Income and Expenditure) — Book: [U.K.] Rapport Annuel sur les Comptes de la Nation.
— *-collar worker*: travailleur manuel.
— *laws*: [U.S.] législation d'inspiration puritaine sur le repos dominical.
— *ribbon jury*: jury trié sur le volet pour des affaires particulièrement compliquées.
[B] — *chip (or: leader)*: valeur de premier ordre.
— *-sky laws*: [U.S.] législation sur les sociétés de placement destinée à protéger l'épargne.

board: table et, par extension, tout ce qui se réunit autour d'une table : commission, comité, conseil, administration, ministère.
[C] [J] *separation from bed and* — : séparation de corps.
adjustment — : conseil des prud'hommes.
advisory — : comité consultatif.
— *of directors*: conseil d'administration.
— *of inquiry*: commission d'enquête.
— *of management*: conseil de gérance.
— *meeting*: réunion en conseil.
— *minutes*: procès-verbaux des réunions du conseil.
— *of referees*: commission arbitrale.
— *room*: salle du conseil.
compensation — : commission des accidents du travail.
conciliation — : conseil des prud'hommes.
[A] — *of Customs*: Office des douanes.
— *of Trade*: [U.K.] ministère du Commerce, [U.S.] chambre de commerce.
— *of Works*: ministère des Travaux publics.
Dependents' Allowance — : Bureau des allocations familiales.
Federal Appeal — : [U.S.] Bureau fédéral d'appel.
Junior Trade — : Jeune Chambre Economique.
Tax Review — : Commission de révision de l'impôt.
[F] *audit* — : conseil de vérification.
— *and lodging*: pension complète. *with — and lodging*: nourri et logé.
— *wages*: indemnité de logement et nourriture.
to be on — *wages*: être nourri en rétribution de son travail.
[B] — *list*: cote officielle.
— *lot*: a) lot régulier d'actions ; b) unité de transaction.
— *of Governors of the Brokers' Association* # Chambre syndicale des agents de change.

— *room (in a broker's office)*: salle d'affichage des cours (chez un courtier).
the «Big — »: la Bourse de New York.
[E] *free on* — *(F.O.B.)*: franco bord.

to board: [J] arraisonner (un bâtiment).

body: corps.
1° corps humain.
— *execution*: contrainte par corps.
dead — : cadavre.
2° élément principal.
— *copy*: (la) substance du texte d'une annonce publicitaire.
— *of an instrument*: corps de l'acte.
— *of a ship*: corps et quille.
3° ensemble, groupe, groupement, organisme.
— *of case laws*: la jurisprudence, les précédents.
— *of creditors*: la masse.
— *of evidence*: faisceau, corps de preuves.
— *of the Law*: corpus juris, corps des lois.
— *of laws*: recueil des lois.
corporate — : corps constitué, personne morale.
electoral — : collège électoral.
examining — : jury d'examen.
fact finding — : commission d'enquête.
governing — : conseil d'administration.
legislative — : organe législatif.
— *politic*: corps social.
— *of persons*: groupement de personnes.
public **bodies**: collectivités publiques.
regulatory bodies: organismes investis du pouvoir réglementaire.
subsidiary — : organe subsidiaire.
bodily: corporel.
(ASS.) *bodily injury*: dommage corporel.

bogus: faux, simulé, de complaisance.
— *cheque*: « chèque en bois ».
— *company*: société fantôme, fictive, « boîte aux lettres ».
— *transaction*: transaction véreuse.

to bolster up: soutenir, étayer.

bona: biens (meubles ou immeubles).

bona fide: bonne foi.
s'emploie comme adjectif (comme substantif et adverbe on dit *« good faith »* bona fide *buyer, he acted in good faith*).
— *holder*: détenteur de bonne foi.
— *offer*: offre ferme.

bona vacantia: biens sans maître.

bona waviata: biens abandonnés (dont un voleur s'est débarrassé dans sa fuite).

bonanza year: année (f) d'abondance.

bond: attache (f), lien (m).
[J] a) obligation (f), engagement (m), caution (f); b) *(specialty)* reconnaissance de dette sous forme authentique.
admiralty – : caution en garantie de dommages-intérêts dans un procès devant un tribunal maritime.
attachment – : cautionnement pour obtenir une ordonnance provisoire (de saisie conservatoire, etc.).
bail – : engagement signé par la caution (voir bail), cautionnement.
concurrence – : sûreté collatérale.
conditional (double) – : promesse sous condition résolutoire.
enforcement of – (s) : exécution du cautionnement.
insurance – : cautionnement d'employés ou garantie.
mortgage – : titre hypothécaire, lettre de gage.
performance – : garantie de bonne exécution.
security – : nantissement.
subsidiary – : bon collatéral.
surety – : lettre de garantie.
terminale – : obligation rachetable.
[A] *official* – : cautionnement ou garantie de fonctionnaires, tuteurs, administrateurs judiciaires, etc.
duties secured by – (s) : droits garantis par des soumissions cautionnées.
[E] [D] entreposage.
average – : compromis d'avaries.
bottomry – : contrat à la grosse aventure.
goods in –, **bonded** *goods* : marchandises entreposées.
goods out of – : marchandises sorties de l'entrepôt, dédouanées.
– *note, excise* – : acquit-à-caution.
– *-store, bonded warehouse* : entrepôt en douane.
in – : en douane.
transportation – : expédition en douane.
to take out of – : dédouaner.
[F] [B] obligation, titre, effet, bon de caisse.
bearer – : bon au porteur.
– *with coupon attached (cum-dividend)* : titre muni de coupon.
– *dividend* : dividende sous forme d'obligation.
– *indenture* : acte de fiducie relatif à une émission d'obligations.
– *index* : indice des obligations.
– *loan* : emprunt obligataire.
– *market* : marché des obligations.
callable – : obligation remboursable par anticipation.
corporation – : effet émis par une société, bon de caisse.
debenture- – : titre, certificat, d'obligation.

deferred – : obligation non libérée.
to draw – (s) *for redemption* : tirer au sort les bons destinés à être remboursés.
Exchequer – [U.K.] : bon du Trésor.
to float – (s) : émettre des obligations.
foreign – : obligation étrangère.
gold- – : obligations-or.
government – : obligations d'Etat, rente d'Etat.
guaranteed – : obligation garantie.
irredeemable government – (s) : obligations d'Etat non amortissables.
joint – (s) : obligations émises par un groupe de sociétés.
joint and several – : obligation conjointe et solidaire.
junior – (s) : obligations de deuxième rang.
junk – (s) : obligations « pourries ».
lottery – (s) : obligations à lots.
matured – : obligation échue.
perpetual government – (s) : obligations d'Etat perpétuelles.
preference – : obligation privilégiée.
premium – (s) : obligations à prime.
priority – : obligation prioritaire.
prize – : obligation à lots.
public – (s) : effets publics.
to redeem a – : amortir, rembourser, une obligation.
redeemable – (s) : obligations amortissables, remboursables.
redemption of – (s) : remboursement d'obligations.
registered – : obligation nominative.
savings – (s) : bons d'épargne.
secured – (s) : obligations garanties.
to service the – (s) : servir les obligations.
shortly maturing – (s) : bons à échéance rapprochée.
to subscribe a – : souscrire une obligation.
treasury – (s) [U.S.] : bons du Trésor.
undated – (s) : obligations sans date d'échéance.
yields of – (s) : taux de rendement des obligations.
« *my word is my* – » *(the motto of the London Stock Exchange)* : dictum meum pactum (ma parole vaut ma signature = devise de la Bourse de Londres).
to bond : nantir, garantir par obligation, entreposer.
bonded *debt* : dette garantie par obligation.
bonded goods : marchandises non dédouanées.

bonder : a) entrepositaire *(warehouseman)*; b) entreposeur *(entrusted with the sale of commodities in Government monopoly)*.
bonding : entreposage garanti.
bonding charges : frais et droits d'entrepôt.
bonding of salesmen : pour un employeur, système d'assurance contre les pratiques malhonnêtes éventuelles de ses vendeurs.

to enter goods for bonding: faire la déclaration d'entrée des marchandises.
bondholder: obligataire, porteur de bons.
bondsman: garant, caution.

bonus: allocation spéciale, prime (f), gratification (f), boni (m), sursalaire (m).
efficiency — : prime de rendement.
[F] second dividende, part de bénéfice.
— *percentage of profits*: tantième.
— *on shares*: bonification sur actions, super-dividende.
— *share, capital* — : action donnée en prime, action gratuite.
cost-of-living — : indemnité de cherté de vie.
salaries and — *(es)*: appointements et gratifications.
work on the — *system*: travail à la prime de rendement.
[ASS] — *to policy-holders*: surprime, bénéfice additionnel alloué aux assurés.
— *system*: sursalaire.
no-claim — : bonification pour non-sinistre.

boodle: concussion (f), malversation (f).

book: livre, registre.
[J] *minute-* — : minutier.
— *oath*: serment sur la Bible.
[A] [U.S.] liste des fonctionnaires.
the white — = livre blanc.
[C] [F] registre (m).
book of original entries: livre-journal.
— *(s) and records*: livres et documents comptables.
account- — : livre des comptes.
attendance — : registre des présences.
bank- —, *pass-* — : livret, carnet de banque.
— *debt*: dette active.
corporation's — *(s)*: livres sociaux (d'une société).
cash — : livre de caisse.
coupon — : livret d'épargne.
counterfoil — : carnet à souche.
day- — : sommier.
— *income*: résultat comptable.
invoice — : livre d'achats.
letter- — : copies de lettres.
order — : carnet de commande.
register — : registre d'inscription maritime.
waste- —, *rough-* — : main courante, mémorial.
savings-bank — : livret de caisse d'épargne.
ship's — : livre de bord.
stock — : livre d'inventaire.
— *-value*: valeur comptable, prix d'inventaire, valeur intrinsèque, valeur substantielle, coût d'acquisition.
[B] — *stock*: action non transférable par endossement et livraison.
the **books**: la comptabilité, les livres, les comptes.

to agree the — *(s)*: faire concorder les livres.
to audit the — *(s)*: apurer les comptes.
to close the — *(s)*: arrêter les comptes.
to keep the — *(s)*: tenir les livres.
to post in the — *(s)*: passer en écriture.
— *(s) and records*: livres et tableaux comptables.

to book: inscrire, enregistrer, réserver, comptabiliser, passer des écritures.
[J] — *the prisoner for theft*: porter mention d'une arrestation pour vol au registre de police.
[C] — *an order*: enregistrer une commande.
booking: réservation, location.
through booking: transport à forfait.

book-keeper: comptable (teneur de livres).

book-keeping: comptabilité, comptabilisation, tenue des livres.
— *voucher*: pièce comptable.
double entry — : comptabilité à double entrée, à partie double.
for — *purposes*: pour les besoins de la comptabilité.

boom: [C] [F] hausse rapide, boom, vague de prospérité.
[B] — *and bust*: emballement et effondrement des cours.
to boom: monter en flèche, faire du battage (en faveur de qqch.).
booming: battage (m), florissant (a).

boot: [F] soulte.

border: frontière, bordure, limite (f).
— *worker*: travailleur frontalier.
[J] — *-line case*: cas difficile à classer, cas limite.

borough: a) ville possédant statut municipal; b) circonscription électorale urbaine.
[A] — *council*: conseil municipal de chacune des communes *(boroughs)* constituant l'agglomération londonienne autour de la Cité *(the Metropolitan area)*.
(hist.) *rotten* — *(s)*: les bourgs pourris.
[F] — *rates*: taxes municipales.

to borrow: emprunter.
— *from*: emprunter à qn.
— *long, short*: emprunter à long, à court terme.
[B] — *stock*: reporter.
borrower: emprunteur.
borrowing *rate*: taux emprunteur.

bottom: fond (m).
the — *has fallen out of the market*: le marché s'est effondré.

— *line* : bénéfice net.

bottom-lands : [U.S.] alluvionnement.

bottomless : [J] sans fondement.

bottomry : [J] prêt à la grosse aventure, hypothèque sur un navire (opp. *respondentia*, voir ce mot).
— *bond* : contrat à la grosse aventure.
— *interest* : profit maritime.
— *loan* : prêt à la grosse.
— *regulations* : règles du contrat à la grosse aventure.

to bounce : [F] être retourné pour non provision.
bouncing *cheque* : chèque sans provision.

bounds, boundary : limites (f pl), frontière (f), bornage (m).
action to fix — : action en bornage.
— *mark, stone* : pierre de bornage.
— *post* : poteau-frontière.
description of land by metes and — : levée géodésique d'un bien-fonds.

bounds : *prices are rising by leaps and* — : les prix montent en flèche.

bounty : libéralité, gratification, indemnité, prime, subvention.
[J] « *the* — *of the testator* » : « le vœu du testateur ».
[A] *child* — : allocation familiale.
(milit.) prime d'engagement.
[F] — *to members of the staff* : gratification accordée, aux membres du personnel.
— *on production* : prime à la production.
non-contractual pension paid out of — : pension (versée) constituant une libéralité sans engagement du débiteur.
[E] — *for fitting out* : prime d'armement.
— *on exports* : prime à l'exportation.
shipping — : prime à la navigation.

box : boîte (f), urne (f), case (f).
— *to be filled in* : case à remplir.
jury — : banc des jurés.
witness — : banc des témoins.
to box : déposer à la barre, verser une pièce aux débats.

boycott : boycottage.

bracket : accolade, catégorie, groupe, tranche (de revenu).
[F] [U.S.] — *progression* : catégorie d'imposition (progressivité par tranches, dans le cadre de l'impôt sur le revenu).
zero-amount — : [U.S.] tranche zéro.

brain : cerveau (m), intelligence (f).
— *drain* : fuite des « cerveaux ».
brainstorming : stimulation et confrontation des conceptions d'individus réunis en un groupe restreint afin de dégager des idées nouvelles.

to brake (*inflation*) : freiner (l'inflation).

branch : branche (f), service (m), succursale (f), agence (f).
[J] — *of Government* : l'un des pouvoirs d'Etat.
— *of the law* : domaine du droit.
the executive — : l'Exécutif.
[C] [F] filiale (f).
— *of an industrial activity* : branche d'une activité industrielle.
— *house* : office (m), agence (f), bureau (m) de quartier, succursale (f).
country — : agence (en province).
main — : établissement principal, maison mère.
— *office* : agence (de quartier).

brand : marque (sp. au fer chaud).
[C] marque (f) de fabrique.
branded *goods* : produits de marque.

brawl, brawling : bagarre, rixe.
[J] a) délit de trouble dans un lieu consacré au culte ; b) tapage, sp. tapage nocturne.

breach : infraction (f), rupture (f), violation (f, contravention (f), manquement (m), atteinte (f).
[J] presque toutes les actions (*actions-in-law*) du droit A.A. étant conçues comme des actions en dommages-intérêts, le concept de la rupture de contrat ou d'une atteinte aux droits prend une importance toute particulière. C'est ainsi qu'en principe toute *cause of action* présuppose un droit (*right*) dont la violation (—) entraîne un préjudice (*damage*), qu'il convient de compenser (*damages*).
— *of agreement* : rupture d'un engagement.
— *of close* (trespass quod clausum fregit) : bris de clôture, effraction, violation de propriété privée.
— *of contract* : inexécution, rupture de contrat.
— *of domicile* : violation de domicile, effraction.
— *of duty* : manquement au devoir, forfaiture.
— *of faith* : manque de foi, de parole.
— *of international obligation* : rupture d'un engagement international.
— *of the law* : violation de la loi.
— *of the peace* : atteinte à l'ordre public.
— *of police regulations* : contravention de simple police.

— *of privilege* : atteinte aux privilèges (de qn).
— *of promise* : a) manque de parole ; b) rupture de promesse de mariage.
— *of the regulations* ; infraction aux règlements.
— *of secrecy* : indiscrétion.
— *of professional secrecy* : violation du secret professionnel.
— *of rules* : infraction aux règles.
— *of trust* : a) abus de confiance ; b) *(officials)* prévarication, fait de charge ; c) violation des devoirs de *trustee*.
— *of warranty* : rupture de garantie.
action for — *of contract* : action contractuelle, action en rescision pour inexécution de contrat.
(hist.) — = *cause of action*.

break : rupture (f), interruption (f), effondrement (m), chute (f).
— *-down* : effondrement, subdivision, répartition.
— *-even point* : seuil de rentabilité, point d'équilibre des profits et des pertes, « point mort ».
— *-even rate of return method* : méthode du taux interne de rentabilité.
— *in prices* : effondrement des prix.
— *on stocks* : effondrement des cours.
— *-up* : décompte.
— *-up value* : valeur de liquidation, valeur qu'auraient les actifs d'une société si elle cessait ses activités.
tax — : allégement fiscal.

to break : casser, briser, rompre, enfreindre, violer, manquer (à).
— *away (prices)* : [B] effondrement des cours.
— *bounds* : violer la consigne, (milit.) être en rupture de ban.
— *bulk* : désarrimer.
— *a contract* : rompre un contrat.
— *even* : avoir un budget en équilibre, « s'y retrouver ».
— *gaol* : s'évader de prison.
— *the oath* : manquer au serment.
— *open* : fracturer (une porte, une serrure, etc.).
— *the peace* : troubler l'ordre public.
— *the regulations* : enfreindre les règlements.
— *the seals* : briser les scellés.
— *a strike* : briser une grève.
— *up* : dissoudre, rompre, disperser.
breaking *stress (or strain)* : tension de rupture.

breakage : casse (f), bris (m).
[J] remplacement de l'objet détruit.

breakdown : répartition (f) des charges.

breaking : rupture (f), violation (f).

[J] a) bris (m) (de glaces, de scellés, etc.) ; b) levée des scellés.
— *in,* — *and entering, house-* — : effraction (f).
constructive — : entrée dans une maison obtenue sous menaces ou prétextes, assimilée à une effraction.
— *of the close* : trouble de jouissance.
— *of diplomatic relations* : rupture des relations diplomatiques.
— *of the Sabbath* : violation du repos dominical (voir *blue laws*).
[C] faillite (f).

breakthrough : hausse (f) soudaine (des prix), percée (sur un marché).

brethren : [J] confrères (m pl).

brevet : (milit.) brevet (m).

bribe : pot-de-vin.
— *given under the counter* : dessous de table.
to bribe *s.o. to silence* : acheter le silence de qn.
to bribe a witness : suborner un témoin.
bribing *of voters* : corruption électorale.

bribery : corruption (f) (d'un fonctionnaire, etc.).

bridge-over credit, bridge-over loan : crédit (m) passerelle, crédit relais.

to bridge : joindre, faire le pont.
— *the gap* : joindre les deux bouts, faire la soudure.

brief : exposé (m).
[J] dossier d'une affaire, [U.S.] conclusions *(trial —)*.
[U.S.] — *on appeal* : pourvoi.
to hold a — : être chargé de défendre une cause.
to brief : donner des instructions.
to brief a barrister : engager un avocat (lui donner des instructions).
to brief a case : réunir le dossier d'une affaire.
to brief a question of law : fournir une consultation juridique (sp. en s'appuyant sur les précédents, voir *case law*).
— *(s.o.) on* : informer (qqn), fournir des renseignements (à qqn).
briefing *of a case* : constitution du dossier d'une affaire.
oral briefings : exposés oraux.

to bring : apporter, amener.
[J] — *an action, a procedure, proceedings, a suit, against s.o.* : intenter une action en justice, entamer une procédure, faire un procès à qn, attaquer qn en justice.

— *a bill* : déposer un projet, une proposition de loi.
— *a dispute before a court* : porter un différend devant un tribunal.
— *down* : introduire (une demande).
— *s.o. in guilty* : déclarer qn coupable.
— *into account* : faire entrer en ligne de compte.
— *s.o. to justice* : traduire qn en justice.
— *the parties together* : mettre les parties en présence.
— *the parties to an agreement* : concilier les parties.
— *pressure to bear on s.o.* : exercer une pression sur qn.
— *s.o. to trial* : faire passer qn en jugement.
— *up a subject* : soulever une question.
— *in a verdict* : rendre un verdict.
to be **brought** *before the Judge* : être déféré au Parquet.
estate brought in : biens d'apport (en mariage).
[C] [F] — *back* : réintégrer, rapporter.
to — *down* : abaisser (tarifs).
— *off a deal* : réussir une affaire.
— *sth. out* : lancer une nouveauté.
— *in interest* : porter intérêt.
— *forward* : reporter (une somme).
brought forward : à reporter.
balance brought down : solde à nouveau.

brinkmanship : (politique, diplomatie, etc.) « du bord du gouffre ».

brisk : actif (a), animé (a).
business is — : les affaires marchent.
— *demand* : demande continue.
— *market* : marché animé.
— *trade* : commerce actif.

British funds : [U.K.] Emprunt d'Etat.

broad : large, vaste, libéral.
— *evidence* : preuve évidente.
— *outlines* : grandes lignes (d'une affaire).

broken : ruiné (a).
a — *man* : un homme ruiné.

broken cross-rates : [F] taux de change croisés.

broker : courtier, agent de change.
[J] officier ministériel exerçant concurremment les fonctions similaires à celles d'un commissaire-priseur et d'un huissier.
[C] courtier de commerce *(wool* —, *sugar* —, *etc.).*
custom — : agent en douane.
real estate — : agent immobilier [U.S. *realtor*].
second-hand — : brocanteur.
ship — : courtier maritime.
[F] [B] *(stock-)* — : agent de change.

bill- — : courtier de change.
— *('s) blanket bond coverage* : assurance globale des courtiers.
— *('s) charges* : courtage (sur achat de valeurs mobilières).
— *('s) contract* : contrat d'intermédiaire.
certified — : courtier agréé.
curb — : coulissier.
customs — : commissionnaire en douane.
exchange — : cambiste.
insurance — : courtier d'assurance.
intermediate — : remisier.
investment — : courtier en placement.
money — : prêteur.
note — : courtier de change.
outside — : coulissier.
pawn- — : prêteur sur gages.
(outside —*(s)* : courtiers du « marché des pieds humides »).
registered — : courtier inscrit.
shipbroker : courtier maritime.
unlicensed — : intermédiaire non reconnu.
brokerage : courtage (m), commission (f).
brokerage fee : frais de courtage.
outside brokerage : affaires de banque.

brother : frère (m).
[J] confrère.
— *german, own, full, brother* : frère germain.
foster — : frère de lait, frère adoptif.
half- — *on the father's side* : frère consanguin.
half- — *on the mother's side* : frère utérin.
elder — : frère aîné.
younger — : frère puîné.
youngest — : frère cadet.
— *-in-law* : beau-frère.
[C] « *Brown Bros & Co.* » : « Brown frères & Cie ».

brotherhood : confrérie (f), confraternité (f), corporation (f).

bubble company : [C] société véreuse.

buck : [fam. U.S.] dollar.

bucket shop : [B] officine douteuse.
— *shop swindler* : courtier marron.

budget : budget (m).
[F] — *account* : compte budgétaire.
— *deficit* : déficit budgétaire.
— *estimates* : prévisions budgétaires.
— *revenue* : recettes budgétaires.
— *surplus* : excédent budgétaire.
full employment — *surplus* : solde budgétaire de plein emploi.
to balance the — : mettre le budget en équilibre.
distress — : budget comprimé.
to fix the — : arrêter le budget.
laid dawn in the — : prévu au budget.

operational — : budget de fonctionnement.
overall financial — *deficit* : impasse budgétaire.
state — : budget de la nation.
to introduce, to open the — : présenter le budget.
to pass the — : voter le budget.
to budget : budgétiser.
to budgetise : inscrire au budget.
Planning, Programming, **Budgeting** *System (P.P.B.S.)* # Rationalisation des Choix Budgétaires (R.C.B.). Budget à base zéro.
zero base budgeting (Z.B.B.) : (préparation budgétaire avec remise en cause de toutes les dépenses une fois tous les cinq ans).

buffer : tampon (m), amortisseur (m).
— *state* : état tampon.
— *stock* : stock de régularisation, stocks régulateurs.

building : construction (f), édifice (m), bâtiment (m), immeuble (m).
— *contractor* : entrepreneur de bâtiment.
— *estate* : terrain (m) à bâtir, lotissement (m).
— *land, site* : terrain à bâtir.
office — : immeuble à usage de bureaux.
[J] — *line* : alignement (m).
— *association* : société coopérative de construction.
— *lease* : bail emphytéotique.
— *licence* : permis (m) de construire.
— *permit* : permis de construire.
— *plot* : lotissement.
— *restrictions* : servitudes de construction, règlements municipaux à cet effet.
— *society* : société coopérative de financement immobilier.
— *subsidy* : prime à la construction.
the — *trade* : le bâtiment.
owner **built** : construit par le propriétaire lui-même.
built-in inflation : inflation structurelle.
built-in obsolescence : obsolescence créée délibérément.
built-in stabilizers : mécanismes de stabilisation automatique de l'économie sans intervention gouvernementale explicite.
[F] *gains on disposals of* — *land* : plus values de cession de terrain à bâtir.
taxes on land and — *(s)* : impôts fonciers bâti et non bâti.
to build up *reserves* : constituer des réserves.

bulk : masse (f).
[C] chargement arrimé.
goods in — : marchandises en vrac.
to break — : rompre charge.
— *sale* : vente en bloc.

bull :
[B] haussier.
— *account* : position à la hausse.
— *campaign* : campagne de hausse.
— *operation* : spéculation à la hausse.
— *purchase* : achat à découvert.
— *transaction* : opération à la hausse.
to go a —, *to* — *the market* : spéculer à la hausse.
the market is all — *(s)* : le marché est à la hausse.
[fam. U.S.] « flic ».
bullish *market* : marché haussier.
bullish tone, **bullishness** : tendance à la hausse.

bullet : remboursement (m) in fine.
— *issue* : obligation entièrement remboursable à échéance.

bulletin : bulletin, communiqué.
[D] *export* — : bulletin de sortie.

bullion : [F] matières, lingots d'or et d'argent.
— *reserve* : réserve métallique, encaisse métallique.
gold — *standard* : étalon lingot or.

bumper crop : récolte (f) magnifique.

buoyant market : [B] marché soutenu.

burden : fardeau (m).
[J] — *of proof (onus of proof)* : charge de la preuve. Le droit A.A. moderne, de plus en plus porté vers la codification, a abandonné les formules strictes des anciens *pleadings*, mais il incombe toujours au plaignant d'analyser sa demande et d'y énoncer les faits dont il entend se prévaloir au cours des débats, faits dont il doit apporter la preuve pour avoir gain de cause.
the — *of proof rests on* : la charge de la preuve incombe à.
— *of going forward with the evidence* : charge à la défense de produire ses contre-preuves.
the — *of establishing the facts justifying the assessment of the penalty is on the Authorities* : la charge d'établir les faits qui justifient l'application de la pénalité incombe à l'administration.
[F] *money* — : charge nominale.
real — : charge réelle.
shifting of the tax — : répercussion de la charge de l'impôt, translation fiscale.
tax — : charge fiscale, poids de l'impôt, pression fiscale, incidence fiscale.
to burden *a budget* : grever un budget.
burdened *estate* : domaine grevé d'hypothèques.

burdensome: onéreux, lourd.
 – *contract*: contrat où il y a lésion.

bureau: bureau (m), office (m).
 [J] [U.S.] département d'un ministère ou office autonome.
 – *of Fisheries*: Office des pêches.
 – *of Immigration*: Service de l'Immigration.
 Internal Revenue – : département des contributions directes et indirectes.

buggery: [J] sodomie (f).

burglary: cambriolage (m).
 [J] vol de nuit avec effraction dans une maison d'habitation, [U.S.] notion étendue au même délit commis de jour ou de nuit, dans toute sorte de maisons, qui est qualifié, *a statutory burglary* = vol qualifié.
 cast- – : vol de nuit à l'escalade.
 cat **burglar**: monte-en-l'air.
 [ASS] – *insurance*: assurance vol.

to burgle: (fam.) cambrioler.
 burgling: cambriolage (m).

burning cost: [ASS] taux de flambage (tarification d'un traité de réassurance).

burst: rafale de courtes annonces publicitaires.

business: a) tâche, besogne, affaire.
 Government – : affaires d'Etat.
 b) ordre du jour (ou point de l'ordre du jour) :
 the – *before the meeting*: la question dont l'assemblée est saisie.
 c) commerce (m), métier (m), les affaires (f pl), occupation (f), firme (f), activité (f), commercial (a).
 d) [B] cours.
 e) fonds de commerce ; *he sold his* – : il a vendu son fonds.
 f) chiffre d'affaires.
 – *agent*: représentant de commerce.
 – *card*: carte de représentant.
 – *cessation (closing down)*: fin d'exploitation (d'une entreprise).
 – *circles*: milieux d'affaires.
 – *conditions*: (la) conjoncture.
 – *connexions*: relations d'affaires.
 – *corporation*: [U.S.] société commerciale anonyme.
 in the course (or furtherance) of a – : dans le cadre (ou aux fins) d'une activité professionnelle.
 – *cycle*: cycle d'activité.
 – *cycles*: cycles courts.
 – *data processing*: informatique de gestion.
 – *day*: jour ouvrable.
 – *is dull*: les affaires ne marchent pas.

 – *earnings*: gains de l'entreprise.
 – *establishments*: entreprises commerciales et industrielles.
 – *expenses*: frais d'exploitation.
 – *forecasting*: prévision économique.
 – *games*: jeux d'entreprise.
 – *growth*: croissance de la firme.
 hobby – : activité de loisir présentée sous la forme d'une activité industrielle ou commerciale.
 – *hours (office, shop)*: heures d'ouverture (bureau, magasin).
 – *indicator*: indicateur économique.
 – *house*: maison de commerce.
 – *income*: bénéfice d'exploitation.
 – *in future*: marché à terme.
 – *licence tax*: patente, taxe professionnelle.
 – *management*: gestion de l'entreprise.
 – *manager*: gérant d'affaires.
 – *minded*: qui a « l'esprit d'entreprise ».
 – *name*: raison commerciale.
 – *premises*: locaux commerciaux.
 – *profit tax*: impôt sur les bénéfices commerciaux.
 – *property*: biens professionnels (inscrits au bilan).
 – *saving*: épargne de l'entreprise.
 – *slowdown*: ralentissement d'activité (des affaires).
 – *training*: pratique des affaires.
 – *year*: exercice financier.
 call – : marché à préavis.
 discontinuance of – : cessation d'activité.
 doubtful – : affaire véreuse.
 fixed place of – : établissement stable.
 general – : question(s) diverse(s).
 government – : mesures gouvernementales.
 in – : dans les affaires.
 income from – : bénéfices industriels et commerciaux.
 isolated private and isolated – *transactions*: opérations occasionnelles effectuées à titre privé ou à titre professionnel.
 line of – : genre d'activité.
 mail order – : vente par correspondance.
 manufacturing – : entreprise industrielle.
 option – : opération à prime.
 out of – : retiré des affaires.
 outstanding – : affaire pendante.
 part of a – : branche d'activité.
 piece of – : opération commerciale.
 retail – : commerce de détail.
 retirement from – : cessation d'activité (d'une personne).
 run of – : courant des affaires.
 shipping – : armement maritime.
 transfer of – : cession d'une affaire commerciale.
 to wind up one's – : liquider ses affaires.
 [ASS] *insurance against* – *interruption*: assurance « pertes d'exploitation ».
 business-like: sérieux, régulier en affaires.

bust: (fam.) faillite (f).
 to be — : (fam.) être en faillite.
 to go — : faire faillite.

busy: actif, affairé.
 — *shop*: maison bien achalandée.
 — *hours*: heures de pointe.

buy-out: rachat (m) intégral.
 leverage management — *(L.M.B.O.)* # rachat d'une entreprise par ses salariés (R.E.S.).

to buy: acheter.
 — *annuity*: acheter une rente viagère.
 — *back*: racheter.
 — *in bulk*: acheter en vrac.
 — *a bull*: acheter à découvert.
 — *for cash*: acheter comptant.
 — *in*: racheter au compte du vendeur (dans une vente aux enchères).
 — *in (to) against a client*: couvrir de force un client à découvert.
 — *on credit*: acheter à crédit.
 — *on a fall*: acheter à la baisse.
 — *on option*: acheter à prime.
 — *out*: désintéresser un associé.
 — *for a rise*: spéculer à la hausse.
 — *on terms*: acheter à terme.
 — *up*: accaparer, rafler.
 — *up a business*: racheter une entreprise.
 — *a witness*: suborner un témoin.
 buy-back price: prix de rétrocession.

buying *in*: achat en bourse.
 — *order*: ordre d'achat.
 — *out*: exclusion par rachat d'actions.
 — *power*: pouvoir d'achat.
 — *spree*: frénésie d'achats.

— *and selling rates*: cours d'achat et de vente.
 to cover (to hedge) by — *back*: se couvrir en rachetant.

buyer: acheteur, acquéreur, client (m).
 [B] — *('s) market*: marché favorable à l'acheteur, marché où l'offre l'emporte sur la demande.
 — *('s) risk*: aux risques de l'acheteur.
 « — *('s)* » : cours acheteur.
 — *(s) ahead*: demande réduite.
 — *(s) over*: excédent d'acheteurs, « la place est chargée ».
 likely, prospective — : acheteur éventuel.

buzz group *(brainstorming syndicate)* : « syndicat de grosses têtes ».

by: de, par, en, dans, sur, de côté.
 — *a company*: à la requête de la société.
 — *or on behalf of*: par ou pour le compte de.
 — *order*: d'ordre, de par.
 — *right*: de droit.
 — *these presents*: par les présentes.

by-election: élection partielle.

by(e)-law: [J] a) arrêté municipal ou communal (U.S. *municipal ordinance*) ; b) (pl) statuts d'une société (où sont développées en détail les indications générales consignées dans [U.K.] *the corporate charter*, [U.S.] *the certificate of incorporation*).

by-product: sous-produit, produit accessoire, dérivé (m).

by-profit: bénéfice accessoire.

NOTES

C

CAA: Civil Aviation Authority.

cabinet: cabinet (m).
[J] conseil des ministres.
[U.K.] le cabinet se compose du Premier Ministre *(Prime Minister)*, de secrétaires d'Etat et de certains hauts fonctionnaires ayant rang de ministre.
shadow — : cabinet fantôme, contre-gouvernement formé par le parti qui est dans l'opposition.
[U.S.] le cabinet américain n'est, lui, que *the* — *of the President*, c'est-à-dire une réunion de fondés de pouvoir, chargés, à titre consultatif, de diriger les services, sous la responsabilité exclusive du Président : *the Chief Executive*. Il s'ensuit qu'en Grande-Bretagne, un membre du cabinet est *cabinet minister* et aux Etats-Unis, — *member*.

cable casting: diffusion (f) par câble.

cadaster: cadastre (m) (également *land register, ordnance survey, terrier, cadastral survey*).

caducary: [J] susceptible (a) de tomber en déshérence (sp. une succession, voir *escheat*).

calculated: prémédité, délibéré (a).

calculator: machine (f) à calculer ; barème (m).

calendar: calendrier (m).
[U.S.] ordre (m) du jour.
[J] liste des accusés au criminel, rôle (m) des causes, rôle des assises.
prison — : livre (m) d'écrou.
[U.S.] — *practice*: si le jour de l'audience n'a pas été notifié aux parties, il incombe à ces dernières de suivre le rôle des causes publié dans la feuille officielle et d'être prêtes *(to be ready)* à comparaître sans autre avis, lorsque leur affaire est appelée *(is reached)*.
— *year*: année civile.

call: appel (m), convocation (f).
[J] appel d'une cause.
calendar — : voir *calendar practice*.
roll- — *of witnesses*: appel des témoins.
[C] 1° passage d'un représentant.
cold —, — *canvassing*: passage d'un démarcheur (d'un représentant) sans entente préalable, porte à porte « sauvage ».
2° expérience (professionnelle).
fifteen years' — : quinze ans d'expérience.
3° convocation.
— *of a directors', shareholders', meeting*: convocation (f) des membres d'un conseil d'administration, d'une assemblée d'actionnaires.
4° [F] appel.
— *of bonds*: remboursement (m) d'obligations, rachat (m) d'un emprunt.
— *card*: v. *business card*.
— *deposit account*: compte à vue.
— *loan, money*: prêt (m) au jour, argent à vue.
— *money market*: marché de l'argent au jour le jour.
— *for funds*: appel de fonds.
— *for payment on stocks*, — *to subscribers*: appel de versements sur actions non libérées, appel aux souscripteurs.
— *up of capital*: appel de fonds.
loan on — : prêt au jour le jour.
(payable) at — : sur demande, à présentation, à vue.
[B] option (f) d'achat dans une opération à prime (opp. *put*), levée (f) des primes.
— *for margin*: appel de marge.
— *on bonds*: rachat anticipé d'obligations.
— *of more*: faculté (f) du double, appel (m) de supplément.
— *of twice more*: achat du double à prime.
— *-day*: jour de réception de nouveaux étudiants aux *Inns of Court* à Londres.
— *option*: prime à la hausse, option d'achat.
— *price*: prix de rachat.
roll- — : appel nominal.
port of — : port d'escale.
(ASS. mar.) — *(s) risk*: risques à l'escale.

to call: appeler, citer à comparaître, assigner, mettre en discussion, rappeler, réclamer.
at call: sur présentation, sur demande.
— *the banns*: publier les bans.
— *to the Bar*: admettre (des stagiaires) au barreau.
— *a division*: passer un vote.
— *the jury*: tirer les jurés au sort.
— *a loan*: demander le remboursement d'un emprunt.
— *the meeting to order*: ouvrir la séance.
— *s.o. to witness*: invoquer le témoignage de qn.
on the order being **called**: l'ordre du jour appelle...
the chairman called clause one: le président met en discussion l'article un.

— 337 —

so-called: soi-disant, prétendu, réputé.
to call for: assigner, faire quérir.
to call for production of documents: exiger la communication des pièces.
to call in: faire rentrer (des fonds); retirer (par ex. papier-monnaie) de la circulation.
to call off: résilier, décommander, annuler, se dédire.
– *off a deal*: annuler (rompre) un marché.
– *off a strike*: rapporter un ordre de grève.
to call out *a strike*: proclamer une grève.
– *out the military*: requérir la force publique.
to call together: convoquer une assemblée.
to call upon: mettre en demeure.
I now call upon (Mr so-and-so): la parole est à M. (Untel).

callable: rachetable, remboursable (a).
– *bonds*: obligations rachetables.

calling: convocation (f), appel (m).
– *over*: appel nominal.

calumny: calomnie.
[J] fausse accusation, dans l'intention de nuire (voir *defamation*).

cambist: cambiste (m).

camera: [J] chambre du conseil, cabinet du juge.
in – : à huis clos.
to consider a case in – : mettre une affaire en délibéré.

to cancel: *(in general)*, annuler, *(a law, a decree)* abroger, rapporter, *(a contract)* rescinder, *(a deed, a will, an order)* révoquer, *(a sentence, a word)* rayer, biffer.

cancellation: annulation.
[J] *(of an order, a sale, a contract)* annulation (f), résiliation (f), *(of a sale)* résolution (f), radiation (f), retrait (m).
– *charges*: frais d'annulation.
– *clause*: clause de résiliation.
– *of a debt*: remise de dette.
– *of garnishee order*: mainlevée de saisie.
– *of a lease*: résiliation d'un bail.
– *of a licence*: retrait (m) d'une patente, d'un permis.
– *of a mortgage*: radiation (f) d'hypothèque.
– *of an order*: contre-ordre.
retrospective – : déchéance d'avantages déjà obtenus.

canny: rusé, malin (a).
ca'canny: hésitant.
ca'canny strike: grève perlée.

canon: chanoine (m), canon (m) (règle).
[J] – *(s) of inheritance*: ordre de succession.

– *law*: droit canon.
canonical *hours*: heures pendant lesquelles il est permis de célébrer un mariage en Angleterre.

canvass: démarchage (m).
canvasser: placier, démarcheur.
canvassing: visites électorales.

CAP (Common Agricultural Policy)
: Politique Agricole Commune (CEE).

capable: [J] capable, habile (à).

capacity: 1° capacité, [J] capacité légale ; 2° qualité.
– *to act*: (avoir) qualité pour agir.
– *to contract and convey*: capacité de s'obliger.
– *to sue*: a) capacité d'ester en justice ; b) avoir une cause légitime d'action en justice ; être un ayant droit.
testamentary – : capacité de tester.
to act in one's official – : agir ès-qualités, agir dans l'exercice de ses fonctions.
in his – *as guardian*: en tant que, en qualité de tuteur.
he sued in his individual – : il a engagé le procès à titre personnel.
idle – : capacité inemployée.
spending – : pouvoir d'achat.
profit-earning – : rentabilité.
yield – : productivité.
to work to full – : tourner à plein.

capias, writ of: mandat d'amener, assignation, mandat.

capias ad audiendum judicium:
mandat de comparution (d'un accusé déclaré coupable en son absence) pour entendre la sentence.

(per) capita: par tête (voir *capitation*).

capital: capital, capitaux, fonds, fortune (f) en capital.
[J] – *crime*: crime capital.
– *punishment*: peine capitale.
[F] *adjusted* – [U.S.] : capital social plus réserves.
alteration of – : modification du capital.
authorized – : biens de capital, capital social déclaré.
available – : capital disponible, mobilisable.
basic – : capital initial.
called-up – : capital appelé.
– *account*: compte capital.
– *allowance*: exonération d'impôt par déduction des dépenses sur immobilisations.
– *appropriation program*: programme d'approvisionnement en capital.

— *asset* : élément de l'actif immobilisé.
— *assets* : capitaux fixes.
— *bonus* : action donnée en prime.
— *budgeting* : budget d'investissement. Sens large : « ensemble des problèmes concernant la décision d'investir ».
— *charges* : charges de capital.
[F] — *charge* : intérêt, service des capitaux investis.
— *deepening* : intensification du caractère capitalistique du processus de production.
— *dividend* : dividende prélevé sur le capital.
— *duty* : droits de constitution (d'une société).
— *employed* : les immobilisations plus l'actif réalisable, moins le passif exigible à court terme.
— *equipment* : capital d'exploitation.
— *expenditures* : immobilisations.
— *flight* : fuite des capitaux.
— *flow* : mouvement du capital.
— *formation* : augmentation des immobilisations.
— *gains* : gains en capital, plus-value.
— *gains tax* : impôt sur les plus-values en capital.
— *goods* : biens d'équipement, d'investissement.
— *inflow* : afflux des capitaux.
— *intensive* : se dit d'une industrie qui utilise un nombre considérable de machines (par rapport au nombre d'ouvriers).
— *investment* : capital engagé.
— *levy* : prélèvement sur le capital.
— *loss* : moins-value.
— *market* : marché des capitaux.
— *outlay* : frais d'établissement.
— *recovery factor* : facteur de récupération.
— *shares* : actions de capital.
— *stocks* : capital-actions.
— *tax* : impôt sur le capital.
— *turnover* : roulement du capital.
— *value* : valeur en capital.
cash — : capital en numéraire.
circulating — : capital circulant.
contingent — : capital d'apport.
corporate — : actif social.
dead — : capital improductif.
debenture — : capital-obligations.
fixed — : capitaux fixes.
floating — : capital flottant.
idle — : capital dormant.
initial — : capital d'apport.
initial — *expenditure* : frais de premier établissement.
issued — : capital souscrit, versé.
loan — : capital d'emprunt.
lock up of — : immobilisation de capitaux.
loss of — : perte en capital.
opening — (*original capital*) : capital d'apport.
paid-in — : remise de fonds.
paid up — : capital versé, libéré.
partnership — : capital social.
registered — : capital autorisé.
requisite — : capital minimum.
rest — : fonds de réserve.
return on — : rémunération du capital.
right of — : droit de constitution de privilège.
risk — : capital spéculatif.
rolling — : fonds de roulement.
spare — : capital disponible.
taxation of — : imposition de la fortune.
tied up — : capital immobilisé.
unpaid — : capital non libéré.
working — : capital d'exploitation, fonds de roulement.

capitalization : 1° capitalisation, conversion en capital ; 2° composition du capital.
— *shares* : actions de capitalisation.

capitalized value : valeur de rendement.

capitation : capitation (f) (et impôt sur la personne), distribution (f) par tête.
[J] *distribution* **per capita** : partage (m) (d'une succession) par tête (opp. **per stirpes** : par souche).

captation : [J] captation (f) (d'héritage, etc.).

caption : en-tête (m), rubrique (f), légende (f).
[J] 1° prise de corps ; 2° indication en tête d'un acte de procédure du lieu, de la date et de son origine.

capture : capture (f).
[J] prise (f).
the law of warlike — : droit de prises.
captor *ship* : vaisseau capteur.
[C] **to capture** *a market* : s'emparer d'un marché.
to capture the market : accaparer la vente.

card : carte (f).
box : fichier (m).
index — : fiche.
— *index file* : fichier.
credit — : carte de crédit.
punched — : carte perforée.

care : soin (m), souci (m), conservation (f).
[J] diligence (f).
slight — (ou *carelessness*) : (diligentia quam in suis) négligence (f), ordinary — : (diligentia bonis patris familiae) diligence normale.
the — *must be commensurate with the risk* : la diligence a déployer doit correspondre au risque couru.

carelessness : inattention (f), insouciance (f).

cargo: cargaison (f).
[E] *full- — charter:* affrètement total.

carriage: transport (m).
— *and package free:* franco de port et d'emballage.
[E] — *forward:* port dû.
— *inwards:* frais de transport à la charge du destinataire.
— *outwards:* frais de transport à la charge de l'envoyeur.
— *free:* franco.
— *paid:* port payé.

carrier: transporteur (m).
[J] *common — :* 1° voiturier public ; 2° entrepreneur de messageries maritimes.

to carry: porter ; adopter, voter (un projet de loi).
— *conviction:* gagner l'approbation.
— *interest:* porter intérêt.
— *a motion:* faire passer une proposition.
— *a resolution:* adopter une proposition.
— *the point:* avoir gain de cause.
— *on a business:* exploiter une entreprise.
— *on an activity:* exercer une activité.
— *on business dealings:* effectuer des transactions commerciales.
— *out:* appliquer, mettre en œuvre, s'acquitter (de), transposer (une écriture).
— *out the law:* appliquer la loi.
— *over:* reporter.
— *over a balance:* transporter un solde.
— *through:* mener à bonne fin.
carry back: report sur les exercices antérieurs.
loss — : report en arrière (de déficit).
carry forward: report déficitaire, montant (m) reporté à nouveau.
carry over: report sur les exercices postérieurs.
carrying *business:* entreprise de transports.
carrying capacity: charge utile.
[J] *carrying of arms:* port d'armes.
[B] *carrying charges:* frais de compte sur marge.

cascade taxes: taxes en cascades.

to carve the melon: [B] « se partager le gâteau » (distribuer les bénéfices).

case: cas (m).
[J] *instance* (f) judiciaire, *cause* (f), *affaire* (f), *procès* (m).
as the — may be: selon le cas.
border-line — : cas limite, cas particulier, incertitude.
case coming for hearing: affaire venant à l'audience.
— *history:* cas concret.
— *study:* étude de cas de situation.
— *work:* service social personnel.
commercial — : affaire sommaire.
concrete —, — in point: cas d'espèce.
contentious — : matière contentieuse.
— *for the Crown,* [U.S.] *the State:* (cr.) l'accusation.
— *for, against:* arguments pour, contre.
divorce — : procès en divorce.
in — of default: en cas de défaillance.
in — of necessity: en tant que de besoin.
in either — : dans l'un et l'autre cas.
leading — : précédent important, jugement de principe.
no — : débouté.
— *remanded:* affaire renvoyée à l'instance primitive.
— *-book:* recueil de jurisprudence.
famous —(s): causes célèbres.
party to the — : partie en cause.
stated — : exposé motivé.
test — : cause décisoire.
to decide a — : rendre un jugement.
to get up a — : instruire une affaire.
to have a — : avoir un grief légitime ou un moyen de défense valable.
to make out a — : justifier sa plainte.
to put the — for the prisoner at bar: présenter la défense du prévenu.
to state the — : exposer les faits.
the plaintiff's — rests upon the contention that... : la défense du prévenu repose sur le fait qu'il soutient que...
to try a — [U.S.] faire juger une affaire par un jury.
to win one's — : avoir gain de cause.
to withdraw a — : se désister.
(hist.) *action on the —, trespass on the — :* (actio if factum concepta, utilis) action ancienne du C.L. en dommages-intérêts pour toute lésion autre que corporelle, qui est à l'origine de la théorie moderne exposée à l'article *breach.*
[F] —(s): [U.S.] catégories à l'intérieur des cédules définissant un type de revenu particulier.

case-law: droit jurisprudentiel (opp. *statutory — :* droit établi par législation), jurisprudence.
(Encore que ne liant pas formellement les tribunaux, les précédents exercent sur la jurisprudence A.A. une influence prépondérante et leur étude constitue l'une des principales disciplines de l'enseignement juridique. En droit pénal, les causes célèbres n'ont pas qu'une valeur historique, comme en France : leurs solutions restent toujours valables en pratique).

case-load: volume (m) de travail (demandé par un dossier).

cash : argent (m), numéraire (m), encaisse (f), espèces (f pl), liquidité (f), fonds (m pl), comptant (m).
  balance in — : soulte.
  — *account* : compte de caisse.
  — *balance effect* : effet d'encaisses monétaires.
  — *basis method* : système de comptabilisation tenant compte seulement des recettes effectivement encaissées et des dépenses effectivement payées.
  (ASS.) — *bonus* : ristourne payée à l'assuré (au lieu de la déduire de la prime).
  — *book* : livre de caisse.
  — *box* : tiroir-caisse.
  — *and carry* : paiement comptant des marchandises emportées, « payer-prendre ».
  — *-capital* : capital en numéraire.
  — *card* : carte magnétique.
  — *credit* : crédit de caisse.
  — *disbursements* : paiement par caisse.
  — *on delivery* : paiement à la livraison.
  — *discount* : escompte au comptant.
  — *dividend* : dividende en espèces.
  — *down* : argent sur table.
  — *expense* : sorties de fonds.
  — *flow* : (notion relative) bénéfice disponible, marge brute d'autofinancement, bénéfice net plus amortissements.
  cash in advance : paiement anticipé.
  — *in hand* : disponibilités en liquide.
  — *inflow* : encaissement.
  — *management* : gestion de trésorerie.
  — *market* : marché au comptant.
  — *offer* : offre réelle.
  — *outflow, cash outlay* : décaissement.
  — *price* : prix comptant.
  — *quotation* : cours au comptant.
  — *receipts* : rentrées nettes de trésorerie.
  — *recovery* : somme récupérable ; valeur probable de récupération.
  — *requirement* : prévision de caisse.
  — *shares* : actions en numéraire.
  — *shorts and overs* : déficits et excédent de caisse.
  — *statement* : bordereau de caisse.
  — *transaction* : opération au comptant.
  — *voucher* : pièce de caisse.
  counter — *book* : main courante de caisse.
  hard — : espèces sonnantes et trébuchantes.
  ready — : liquidités, disponibilités.
  securities dealt in for — : valeurs au comptant.
  spot — : comptant.
  to pay — *down* : payer comptant, argent sur table.
  vault — : réserve en espèces.
  to cash : *(a banknote)* changer, *(a bill, a coupon)* encaisser, *(a bill)* escompter, *(a cheque, a money-order)* toucher.
  to cash in : déposer une somme en banque ; se faire rembourser ; profiter pleinement de (qqch).

to cash a bill on its maturity : encaisser une traite à l'échéance.

cast-iron alibi : alibi (m) irréfutable.

to cast : jeter.
  [J] 1° débouter ; 2° a) condamner aux frais, b) condamner aux dommages-intérêts *(to be cast in costs, in damages)*.
  — *off a manuscript* : évaluer la longueur d'un texte imprimé d'après celle du manuscrit.
  casting vote : voix prépondérante.

catalog show-room : [US] grandes surfaces qui exposent et livrent immédiatement les biens achetés.

casual : occasionnel, fortuit (a).
  — *labor* : main-d'œuvre intermittente.
  — *revenue* : recettes imprévues.

casualty : 1° accident de personne ; 2° accidenté (m).
  [ASS] — *insurance* : assurance contre les accidents.
  (the) casualties : les victimes (accident), les pertes (militaires).

casus omissus : cas non prévu par la loi.

catalla : possessions (f pl).

to catch : attraper.
  — *up* : rattraper
  to be **caught** *short* : être à découvert.
  catch penny (item) : (article de) camelote.
  — *up effect* : effet de rattrapage.

catchy : facile à retenir, insidieux (ex. publicité).
  — *question* : question insidieuse.

cats and dogs : [U.S.] valeurs qui se vendent pour quelques cents.

caucus[US] : comité électoral.

causa causans (causa proxima) : la cause immédiate.

causation : causalité (f).

cause : cause (f), raison (f), motif (m).
  [J] (# *case*) cause, procès (m).
  — *of action* : droit positif qu'on entend faire valoir par une action en justice déterminée.
  — *beyond control* : force majeure.
  — *for complaint* : motif de plainte.
  — *-list* : feuille (f), rôle (m), tableau (m) d'audience.
  — *of a valid contract* : cause d'une obligation.
  to challenge for — : récuser (un juré) pour

un motif déterminé.
first – : cause originelle.
order to show – : ordre à la partie qui s'oppose à une mesure judiciaire d'exposer ses raisons, avant qu'elle ne devienne définitive.
causeless : sans motif.

caution : précaution (f), avis (m).
[J] (Scot.) caution (f), garant (m).
cautionary *judgment* : ordonnance de saisie conservatoire.
[F] – *monetary assets* : encaisses de précaution.

caveat : avertissement (« qu'il prenne garde »), [U.S.] revendication de brevet.
[J] avertissement d'un particulier à qui de droit, d'avoir à s'abstenir d'actes envisagés, susceptibles de porter atteinte à ses droits ou à l'ordre public.
– *emptor* : mise en garde de l'acheteur contre tout risque possible.
– *to marriage* : opposition au mariage.
caveator : opposant.
to enter a caveat to : faire opposition à.

to cease : cesser.
[J] [U.S.] – *and desist order* (Engl. *restrictive injunction*) = ordonnance de ne pas faire.
ceasing : cessation (f).

to cede : [J] céder (un bien immobilier, un territoire).

ceiling : prix plafond, limite d'émission des billets.

the Censorship : la censure.

censure : [J] réprimande.
vote of – : motion de censure.

census : recensement.
– *enumeration* : dénombrement.
– *of opinion* : consensus.
– *of production* : (U.K.) inventaire (m) annuel de l'activité industrielle.
– *returns* : résultats du recensement.
– *-taker (enumerator, vote-teller)* : recenseur.

cent : *amount per* – : pourcentage.

central : central, moyen.
– *bank* : banque centrale.
– *bank money* : v. money base.
– *value* : valeur moyenne.

centralization : centralisme.

centre, [U.S.] **center** : centre.
big – *(s)* : grandes agglomérations.

business – : centre commercial.

certainty equivalent : espérance (f) mathématique, valeur espérée.

certificate : certificat (m), attestation (f), acte (m).
[J] – *of acknowledgment* : certification des signatures (par notaire, etc.).
bankrupt's – : concordat entre le failli et ses créanciers.
certificated *bankrupt* : concordataire.
– *of reasonable doubt* (cesset executio) : sursis à exécution de la peine, en attendant le résultat de l'appel.
[A] *birth* – : acte de naissance.
copy of birth – : extrait de naissance.
– *of competency* : certificat d'aptitude.
coroner's death – : acte de décès, extrait mortuaire.
– *of exemption* : certificat de dispense.
– *of good character* : certificat de bonne vie et mœurs.
– *of incorporation* [U.S.] : acte d'association, acte constitutif d'une personne morale [U.K. *corporate charter*, voir *by(e)-laws*].
land – : extrait de registre foncier.
marriage – : acte de mariage.
[F] *loan* – : titre de prêt.
– *of necessity* : [U.S.] certificat obligatoire dans le cas d'amortissement accéléré.
share – : certificat provisoire.
tax reserve – : bons d'impôt (pour l'étalement de la charge fiscale sur toute l'année).
[E] – *of health* : billet de santé (voir *bill of health*).
clearance – : congé de navire, d'aéronef.
international load line – : certificat international de franc-bord.
master's – : brevet de capitaine au long cours.
tonnage measurement's – : lettres de jauge.
[D] – *of insurance, of origin* : attestation d'assurance ; certificat d'origine.
– *of deposit (CD)* : certificat de dépôt.
– *of origin* : certificat d'origine.
– *of registry* : certificat d'immatriculation, lettres de mer, acte de nationalité, de francisation.

certification : certification (f), délivrance (f) d'un certificat.

certified :
[J] – *copy* : copie légalisée.
– *lunatic* : aliéné interdit.
duly – *copies* : expéditions authentiques.
– *statement* : constat.
[F] [U.S.] – *public accountant* : expert comptable (voir [U.K.] *chartered accountant*).
– *broker* : courtier attitré.
– *cheque* : chèque visé.

— *transfer*: transfert déclaré.

to certify: certifier, déclarer, attester, authentifier, légaliser.
I certify this a true copy: pour copie conforme.

certiorari: pour être plus amplement informé (pour plus ample information).

cessation: cessation.
— *from work*: arrêt de travail.

cesser: [J] 1° cessation (f); 2° non-exécution (f).

cesset executio: sursis à exécution d'une obligation.

cessio bonorum: [J] cession de biens.

cession: cession (de droits, etc.).
[J] abandon d'actif (aux créanciers de la faillite).

cessionary: cessionnaire (m).
[J] ayant cause (m).

cestui que trust: [J] bénéficiaire d'un *trust* (voir ce mot).

cestui que use: [J] usufruitier (m).

chain of command: hiérarchie (f).
vertical — of command: chaîne hiérarchique verticale de direction.

chair: siège, sp. siège de juge, fauteuil du président *(chairman)*, chaire du professeur.
[J] [U.S.] banc des témoins.
to fill the — : présider.
from the — : ex praesidio, énonciations du président.
in the — : sous la présidence.
to leave, to vacate the — : lever la séance.
to be voted into the — : être élu à la présidence.
the — was maintained: la décision du président est maintenue.
the motion before the — : la décision dont la présidence est saisie.
to appeal to the — : en appeler au président.
to resume the — : reprendre la séance.
to support the — : se ranger à l'avis du président.
to take the — : ouvrir la séance.

chairman: président (m) (de séance, d'une réunion).
acting — : président par interim.
active — : président en exercice.
— of the board: Président du Conseil d'administration.
— and managing Director # Président Directeur Général (P.D.G.).
deputy — : vice-président.
Madam, Mr — : Madame la présidente, M. le président.

chairmanship: (la) présidence.

to chalk up: réaliser des bénéfices.
— improvements: afficher des résultats améliorés.

to challenge (s.o.) (pol.) défier, interpeller (qqn).

challenge: défi (m), objection (f), opposition (f).
[J] récusation (f).
— to the array: récusation du jury en bloc.
— for cause: récusation motivée.
— to the favour: récusation d'un juré supposé partial.
peremptory — : récusation pure et simple (les parties disposent d'un certain nombre de récusations de cette nature).
— to the polls: récusation de certains jurés.
word economic — (s): défis économiques mondiaux.

to challenge: défier, mettre en demeure, provoquer, s'inscrire en faux contre, contester, récuser.
— a statement: contester l'exactitude d'une assertion.
— one's right to: contester à qn le droit de.
— the government: poser la question de confiance.

challenged: juré récusé.

challenger: (J) récusant (m).

chamber: chambre (f), salle des séances.
— of commerce: chambre de commerce.
double — system: bicaméralisme.
— lawyer: juriste conseil.
— of trade: chambre des métiers.
upper —, lower — : chambre haute (Chambre des lords, [U.S.] Sénat) chambre basse (Chambre des communes, [U.S.] Chambre des représentants).
chambers: cabinet de juge, d'avocat, étude d'avoué.
judge in — (s): juge des référés.
to hear a case in —(s): juger une cause en chambre du conseil.
to try a case in — (s): juger en référé.

champerty: [J] (pactum de quotat litis) pacte d'honoraires d'avocat.

chance: chance (f), hasard (m), probabilité (f).

— *event*, — *node*: point-événement.
[J] *last clear* — : théorie de l'ultime chance de salut d'une personne en péril de mort, qui lui revient malgré sa faute (p. ex. si elle se place devant un train en marche, il incombe au mécanicien de faire tout son possible pour freiner à temps. S'il ne le fait pas, la victime n'aura pas eu son ultime chance et il en portera la responsabilité).
— *-medley*: homicide involontaire.
[F] — *gains*: gains au jeu.
— *of profit*: perspective de bénéfices.

chancellor: chancelier (d'une cathédrale, d'un ordre de chevalerie, d'une université).
[U.K.] (hist.): titre des juges des juridictions de *equitable law* (ou *chancery law*; voir *chancery*).
the Lord High — : le Grand Chancelier d'Angleterre. Il préside la Chambre des lords et exerce, en tant que représentant de la Reine, la haute autorité judiciaire # ministre de la Justice.
— *of the Exchequer* # ministre des Finances.
— *of the Duchy of Lancaster*: chancelier du Duché de Lancaster, ministre d'Etat, représentant direct de la Couronne au sein du cabinet.

chancery: chancellerie (f).
[J] *court of* — : tribunal jugeant en *Eq.* Ne subsistent plus, en tant que juridictions « équitables » autonomes que *the* — *Courts of the Counties Palatine of Durham and Lancaster* (voir *county: counties palatine*). Par ailleurs, la juridiction en *Eq.* est exercée par *the* — *Division* de *the High Court of Justice* (voir ce terme).

change: changement (m).
[J] — *of ownership*: mutation.
— *of venue*: renvoi d'une affaire à un autre tribunal (pour incompétence ratione loci).
[A] monnaie divisionnaire.
to give — *for*: rendre la monnaie sur.
small — : l'appoint.
[B] **to change** *one investment for another*: échanger une valeur contre une autre.
on change: à la Bourse.
[C] évolution (plus précisément, d'une situation dans l'entreprise par suite de pressions internes ou externes).

channel: canal (m), conduit (m), débouché (m).
— *(s) for trade*: débouchés commerciaux.
through official — *(s)*: par voie hiérarchique.
through the ordinary — *(s) of diplomacy*: par voie diplomatique.
to channel *investments into*: diriger des investissements vers.

character: caractère (m), réputation (f).
evidence of — : témoignage de moralité.
[J] — *witness*: témoin de moralité.
[A] *certificate of good* — : certificat de bonne vie et mœurs.
characteristic *signs*: signalement.
characteristics of creativity: facteurs de mise en valeur de la créativité.

charge: charge, frais, commission, garde.
[J] 1° a) acte d'accusation, inculpation, mise en prévention, *(by public prosecutor)* réquisitoire ; b) chef d'accusation.
counter — : contre-accusation.
the — *is murder*: l'inculpé est accusé de meurtre.
on a — *of murder*: sous l'inculpation de meurtre.
the defendant is **chargeable** *with knowledge*: l'inculpé a eu connaissance de.
to meet a — : répondre à une accusation.
2° obligation (f), devoir (m).
— *(s) of upkeep*: obligation alimentaire.
3° résumé des débats, fait par le juge à l'intention du jury.
4° servitude (f), charge (f), droit grevant.
— *(s) on an estate*: charges d'une succession.
mortgage — : affection hypothécaire, privilège d'hypothèque.
charging lien: droit de nantissement.
charging order: ordonnance de saisie.
property **charged** *as security for a debt*: immeuble affecté à la garantie d'une créance.
— *book*: rôle des accusations.
rent- — (— *on landed property*): voir *rent* [J].
— *-sheet* [U.S. *blotter*]: cahier des délits et écrous d'un poste de police.
to bring, lay, a — *against s.o.*: relever une charge, porter plainte contre qn.
to take s.o. in — : arrêter qn.
to give s.o. in — : faire arrêter qn.
on — *of having...*: sous l'inculpation d'avoir...
5° privilège (m), droit (m).
first — : privilège de premier rang.
subject to the — : grevé de privilège.
right of — : droit de constitution de privilège.
[A] *official in* — : gestionnaire d'un service.
person in — : administrateur, préposé.
officer in — : a) officier de semaine ; b) officier commandant.
public — : personne assistée.
[C] [F] commission (f), imputation (f), prix (m), droits (m pl), taxe (f), frais (m pl), frais accessoires.
additional — : taxe complémentaire.
— *(s)*: frais de compte.
— *account*: accord de paiement différé.
— *card*: carte de crédit.
custody — *(s)*: droit de dépôt.
extra — *(s)*: frais en sus.
fixed — *(s)*: frais fixes d'exploitation.

free of — : sans frais, gratis.
— *(s) forward*: frais à percevoir (à la livraison), port dû.
labour — *(s)* : charges salariales.
— *(s) upon vessels* : gages sur navires.
balancing — : charge compensatrice (c'est-à-dire plus-value retirée de la vente ou du dédommagement accordé pour outillage, considéré comme recette et entrant dans le revenu imposable).
occupational — *(s)* : frais professionnels.
overhead — *(s)* : frais généraux.
paid on — *(s)* : débours.
remission of — *(s)* : détaxe.
schedules of — *(s)* : tarif.
to take — : assumer la gestion.
[E] *lighterage* — *(s)* : frais d'allège.
salvage — *(s)* : frais de sauvetage.
wharfage — *(s)* : frais de mise à quai.
[B] — *for safe custody*: droits de garde des titres.

to charge : charger de, donner mission, adjurer, inscrire, imputer, taxer, prélever, percevoir.
— *the defendant with the obligation* : imposer au défendeur l'obligation de.
— *the jury* : résumer les débats à l'intention du jury.
— *a tax* : prélever un impôt.
charged against the account : porté au débit du compte.

chargee : [J] créancier (m) privilégié.

chargehand : chef (m) d'équipe.

charity : charité (f), société de bienfaisance, organisme philanthropique.
— *performance* : gala au profit d'une œuvre de bienfaisance.
[A] *The* — *Commissioners* : commission de surveillance des œuvres de bienfaisance.
[J] **charitable** *contract* : contrat de bienfaisance.
charitable trust : fondation d'utilité publique, de bienfaisance, caisse de secours.

chart : diagramme, graphique (m).
— *of accounts* : plan comptable.
operating, flow- — : organigramme.
the Stock Exchange — *(s)* : la charte, le règlement de la Bourse.

charter : *(of a city, a university)* charte (f), *(of a bank)* privilège (m), *(of a company, a corporation)* acte (m), statuts (m pl) d'association, *(of a ship)* affrètement (m), nolis (m).
[C] — *member* : [U.S.] membre fondateur (d'une société).
[E] — *party* : charte-partie entre le chargeur et l'armateur.
charterer, *time charterer* : affréteur, affréteur unique, chargeur.
principal charterer : affréteur principal.
round **chartering** : affrètement aller et retour.
time chartering : affrètement à temps.
trip chartering : affrètement au voyage.
to charter : affréter.
[F] **chartered** *accountant, CA* (voir [U.S.] *certified public accountant, CPA*) : expert comptable.
chartered bank : banque privilégiée.
chartered company : compagnie à charte.
chartist : prévisionniste (m).

chattels : possessions (f pl).
[J] biens et droits, meubles et immeubles autres que la propriété immobilière.
— *personal* : biens et droits mobiliers.
— *real* : immeubles par l'objet auquel ils s'appliquent (droits réels).
— *mortgage* : gage, nantissement (« hypothèque mobilière »).
goods and — : biens et effets.

cheap : bon marché.
[F] — *money policy* : politique d'argent à bon marché.
— *rate* : tarif réduit.
to cheapen : baisser les prix.

cheating : tromperie (f), escroquerie (f).
[J] fraude pénale.
to cheat : frauder, tricher.

check : contrôle, vérification, [U.S.] chèque.
— *analysis* : contre-analyse.
— *-book* : carnet de chèques.
— *-list* : [U.S.] liste de contrôle, bordereau de contrôle.
(hist.) « *the* — *(s) and balances* » : dispositions contenues dans la constitution des Etats-Unis qui tendent à assurer le jeu harmonieux des trois pouvoirs.
— *off* : précompte (salarial).
— *sample* : échantillon témoin.
[C] — *-out* : caisse (f) à la sortie (dans un supermarché etc.), contrôle à la caisse.
checker : employé (m) chargé du contrôle à la caisse.

to check : *(accounts)* apurer, vérifier, *(an experience, etc.)* contrôler, *(documents)* collationner, *(books)* pointer, vérifier, *(goods)* réceptionner, *(an inventory)* récoler, *(economic recovery)* freiner, enrayer.
cross-checking : recoupements.

cheptel : [J] cheptel (m).

cheque, [U.S.] **check** : chèque (m).
[F] *banker's* — : chèque de banque.
bearer — : chèque au porteur.
blank — : chèque en blanc.
cashed — : chèque encaissé.

certified — : chèque visé, certifié.
crossed — : chèque barré.
— *without cover, provision; worthless* —, [U.S.] *flash check:* chèque sans provision.
to fill up a — : remplir un chèque.
open, uncrossed, — : chèque non barré.
— *to order:* chèque à ordre.
stale — : chèque prescrit.
to stop payment of a — : faire opposition au paiement d'un chèque.
traveller's — : chèque de voyage.

chief : chef, supérieur hiérarchique (m), principal (a).
— *accountant:* chef comptable.
— *clerk:* greffier en chef.
— *creditor:* créancier principal.
— *executive:* [U.S.] le président des Etats-Unis, le gouverneur d'un Etat, le maire d'une ville.
— *executive:* directeur général de société.
— *justice:* [U.S.] premier président d'une cour (sp. *the* — *Justice of the U.S.:* le président de la Cour suprême).
— *town:* chef-lieu.

child, (pl) **children** : enfant, enfants.
— *bounty:* allocation familiale.
— *care expenses:* frais de garde d'enfant.
future — : nasciturus, enfant à venir.
— *murder:* infanticide.
neglected — : enfant délaissé, enfant moralement abandonné.
posthumous — : enfant posthume.
— *unborn,* [J] (hist.) *en ventre sa mere, person en venter, person unborn:* enfant conçu.
guardian to — *unborn:* curateur au ventre.
— *welfare:* protection de l'enfance.
children's court (ou *juvenile court*) : tribunal pour mineurs.
woman with — : femme enceinte.

to chip : (F) perdre des points.

chiselling : escroquerie, filouterie (f).

to chop : réduire fortement les investissements, les dépenses.

chose : objet (m).
[J] — *local:* objet immobilier.
— *transitory:* objet mobilier.
— *in action:* titre de créance, droit incorporel permettant une action en justice (à l'origine, revendication de l'objet même, de la chose sur laquelle se fonde le droit d'intenter une action).
— *in possession:* titre possessoire, droit corporel constituant un commencement de preuve de la propriété.
assignation of — *in action:* cession, transfert.

to chuck out (s.o.) : (Fam.) mettre qqn à la porte.

chucking out time : [UK] heure de fermeture des débits de boissons.

church : église (f), religion (f), une communauté de culte chrétien.
[J] l'Eglise (d'Angleterre), institution de droit public, douée de la personnalité morale.
— *Assembly:* assemblée nationale de l'église anglicane.
— *-rate:* dîme.
— *society:* association culturelle.

to churn : gonfler artificiellement (ex. des ventes afin de prendre des commissions plus élevées).

churning : [B] gonflement des opérations d'un compte.

C.I.F. *(cost, insurance, freight)* : C.A.F. (coût, assurance maritime, fret), clause de contrat de vente stipulant que le prix englobe ces trois prestations, la marchandise étant livrable au port de destination.

circuit : circuit (m).
[J] circonscription de tournée (ressort) d'un tribunal itinérant (Engl. huit circuits, U.S. neuf circuits).
— *judge:* juge en tournée ; juge itinérant.

circuit of action : [J] circuit d'actions.

circulation : circulation (f), cours, mouvement (de l'argent), tirage (journal).
credit — : circulation fiduciaire.
big — *dailies:* quotidiens à grand tirage.
for private — : hors commerce.
to circulate : mettre en circulation.

circumstance : circonstance (f).
as —(*s*) *may require:* selon les nécessités.
whatever the —(*s*) : en tout état de cause.
[J] *extenuating* —(*s*) : circonstances atténuantes.
family —(*s*) : situation de famille.
particulier —(*s*) *(of the case)* : faits en cause.
circumstantial *evidence:* présomptions, preuve indirecte.

circumstantibus : spectateurs (et témoins).

citation : [J] citation (voir *summons, subpoena*).
[U.S.] **cited** *for bravery:* cité (à l'ordre de la nation).

citizen : habitant d'une ville, citoyen, ressortissant, national (m).

— *rights* : droits civiques.
fellow- — : concitoyen.
law-abiding — : citoyen respectueux des lois.
citizenship : nationalité, citoyenneté.
good — : civisme.
right of — : droit de cité.
citizens' Band (CB) : bande de fréquence autorisée pour les particuliers.

city : grande ville.
[U.K.] désignation honorifique d'une ville *(township)* soit à titre historique, soit octroyée par la Couronne, [U.S.] ville possédant son statut particulier (opp. *town*) et jouissant de l'autonomie administrative.
The — : la Cité de Londres.
to be in the — : être dans les affaires.

civic : civique, municipal (a).
— *election* : élection municipale.

civil : civil (a).
[J] [A] — *action*, — *case* : action civile.
— *death (attainder)* : mort civile.
— *disability* : incapacité.
— *fruits* : fruits civils.
— *law* : a) le « jus civile » et le droit romain dans son ensemble, ainsi que toutes les législations qui en dérivent en tant qu'entité juridique distincte du *C.L.* ; b) le droit civil, en tant que branche du droit privé.
— *List* : liste civile.
— *List pension* : pension sur la cassette de la Reine.
— *marriage* : mariage civil.
— *partnership* : société civile.
— *procedure (rules)* : procédure civile.
— *proceedings* : procès civil.
— *practice* : pratique du Palais.
— *rights* : a) droits civils ; b) droits civiques.
— *servant* : fonctionnaire, [U.S.] fonctionnaire de carrière nommé sur concours *(appointive posts*, opp. fonctionnaires élus : *elective posts)*.
established — *servants* : fonctionnaires titulaires.
— *service* : [U.K.] le corps de la fonction publique.
— *status* : état civil (m).

civilization : [J] conversion d'une action pénale en action civile.

civilly : civilement (adv).

claim : créance (f), demande (f), prétention (f), revendication (f), réclamation (f).
[J] 1° droits de toute nature qu'on entend faire valoir en justice (notamment : *title* : droit de propriété, *choses in actions* : créances, *personal rights* : droits relatifs au statut personnel) ; 2° réclamation, requête (f) ; 3°

demande de brevet.
— *allowed* : réclamation acceptée.
— *for damages* : action en dommages-intérêts.
— *(s) heard* : dossier instruit.
— *on the administration* : recours contre l'administration.
— *secured by bond, secured preferential claim* : créance privilégiée.
— *secured by mortgage* : créance garantie par hypothèque.
the enforcibility of the — : exigibilité de la créance.
— *of ownership* : action pétitoire.
statement of — : a) demande introductive d'instance ; b) conclusions en matière de dommages-intérêts.
to have a — *to sth.* : avoir droit à qch.
to lay a — *to sth.* : a) prétendre à qch ; b) s'attribuer qch.
to prove — *(s) in bankruptcy* : produire sa créance à la masse.
to put in —, *to claim one's due* : faire valoir ses droits.
to set up a — : faire une réclamation.
mining — *(s)* [U.S.] : concession minière.
— *for refund* : demande de remboursement.
— *for discharge of taxation* : demande de dégrèvement d'impôt.
personal — *(s)* : créances mobilières.
— *for relief for expenditure* : demande pour l'octroi de déduction.
fares — : demande de remboursement de frais de déplacement.
[F] *Revenue* — *(s)* : créances fiscales.
claiming *back* : répétition des taxes, de l'impôt indu.
disputed — *(s) office* : service de contentieux.
tax — : demande de dégrèvement.
[ASS] demande de la prime d'assurance (après sinistre).
— *(s) paid* : sinistre réglé.
[B] *prior* — : titre antérieur, préférentiel.
junior — : titre en second.

to claim : [J] requérir.
— *against s.o.* : attaquer qn en justice.
— *sth. back from s.o.* : répéter quelque chose contre qn.
— *diplomatic status* : prétendre au statut diplomatique.
by **claiming** : en ayant le droit de pratiquer, en ayant la faculté de retenir.

claimant : demandeur (m).
[J] partie requérante (f).
estate without a — : succession jacente, vacante.
rightful — : ayant droit.
— *of a patent* : demandeur d'un brevet.

to clamp *(prices)* : bloquer (les prix...).

clarification : [F] *the inspector requests* – : l'inspecteur demande des éclaircissements.

clash : conflit (m) (de lois, d'intérêts, etc.).

class : classe (f), catégorie (f).
governing – : classe dirigeante.
propertied – : classe possédante.
working – : classe ouvrière.
upper, lower, middle – : haute, basse, moyenne classe.
[J] [U.S.] – *action* (U.K. *representative action*) : action en justice d'une portée générale, dont l'issue intéresse « *all persons similarly situated* », par exemple tous les autres actionnaires *(U.K. a* – *-action sharcholder suit:* procès intenté par un ou plusieurs actionnaires contre une société anonyme) ; action de groupe (consommateurs, etc.).
– *legislation* : mesures législatives en faveur de certaines catégories sociales.
to class *several items together:* joindre plusieurs éléments sous une seule rubrique (d'ordre juridique ou autre).
[A] **classified** *matter:* confidentiel.
[U.S.] *classified service:* la fonction publique.
[ASS] – *of a ship:* cote d'un navire au *Lloyd's Register.*

classification : classification (f), classement (m).
– *certificate:* certificat de cote.
– *of accounts:* classification des comptes.
– *of disputes:* qualification des litiges.

clause : clause (f), article (m), condition (f).
[J] *acceleration* – : clause autorisant la prise de possession par anticipation.
additional – *(rider):* clause additionnelle, avenant (m).
agreement – : clause conventionnelle.
arbitration – : clause compromissoire.
comminatory – : clause comminatoire.
competence – : clause attributive de juridiction.
customary – : clause d'usage.
defeasance, avoidance, resolutive, – : clause résolutoire.
derogatory – : clause dérogatoire.
enacting – *(s):* dispositions d'une loi.
escalator – : clause d'échelle mobile.
formal – : clause de style.
– *(s) of a law:* dispositions d'une loi.
hardship – : clause de sauvegarde, d'équité, de révision.
most favoured nation – : clause de la nation la plus favorisée.
– *to order:* clause à ordre.
optional – : disposition facultative.
penalty – : clause pénale.
rescinding – : clause abrogatoire.
resolutory – : pacte commissoire.
restrictive – *(s):* modalités.
– *(s) governing a sale:* conditions d'une vente.
safeguard, saving – : clause de sauvegarde.
– *of a will:* disposition testamentaire.
waiver – : clause de renonciation.
[ASS] avenant de police.
[E] *average* – : clause « franc d'avarie ».
D/A – *(vessels must discharge afloat):* les navires doivent décharger la cargaison étant à flot.
deviation – : clause de déroutement.
running down – : clause de surestaries.

clean : propre, net, sans réserves, clair (a).
[J] – *acceptance:* acceptation sans réserves.
– *hands:* obligation pour un demandeur en Eq. d'avoir eu, en la matière litigieuse, une attitude irréprochable.
– *record, sheet* # casier judiciaire vierge.
[C] – *bill:* effet libre.
– *collection:* encaissement simple.
– *payment:* payement contre reçu.
– *receipt:* reçu sans réserve.
[E] – *bill of health:* patente de santé nette.
– *bill of lading:* connaissement net sans clause surajoutée.

clear : clair, limpide (a).
[J] – *-cut majority:* majorité absolue.
– *day:* jour franc.
– *estate:* biens francs d'hypothèque.
– *title:* titre incontestable, droit irréfragable.
[C] – *accounts:* comptes en règle.
– *loss:* perte sèche.
– *profit:* bénéfice net.
– *certificate:* congé maritime ou aérien, lettre de mer ou de l'air.

to clear : éclaircir, mettre au point, se disculper, purger, expédier.
– *the court:* 1° faire évacuer la salle ; 2° ordonner le huis-clos.
– *a suspect:* innocenter un suspect, retirer une accusation, ordonner un non-lieu.
– *oneself of an accusation:* se disculper.
[C] « – » : en solde.
– *the accounts:* solder les comptes.
[D] – *goods:* passer des marchandises en douane.
– *outwards:* expédier un navire en douane.
– *a ship inwards:* faire l'entrée en douane d'un navire.

clearance : libération (f), décharge (f), compensation (f) d'un chèque, présentation (f) d'un chèque à l'encaissement.
[J] 1° acquittement d'une dette ; 2° purge d'hypothèque.
[C] – *sale:* vente de soldes.
[D] – *certificate:* lettre de mer.
– *inwards:* déclaration, permis d'entrée.
– *papers:* papiers d'expédition d'un navire.

— *outwards* : déclaration, permis de sortie.
to effect customs — : procéder aux formalités de douane.

clearing : compensation (f).
— *bank* : banque de virement.
— *house* : chambre de compensation, banque centrale de compensation.
to pass a check through the — *house* : compenser un chèque.
[E] accords commerciaux dans lesquels le produit des exportations est affecté au règlement des importations de manière à atteindre l'équilibre des échanges.

clemency : clémence (f), indulgence (f).
[J] [U.S.] — *hearing* : audience consacrée à l'examen d'un recours en grâce.
— *case* : recours en grâce.
to apply for — : demander (sa) grâce.
to grant — : accorder la grâce, gracier.

clerical : d'employé, de commis (a).
— *assistance* : secrétariat (m).
— *error* : erreur de plume.
— *staff* : personnel de bureau.

clerk : employé de bureau.
[J] *articled* — : clerc d'homme de loi faisant son apprentissage de *solicitor*, stagiaire.
chief, senior, head, managing — : premier clerc.
— *of the court* : greffier.
— *of the court's office* : greffe.
— *('s) fees* : honoraires du greffier.
— *to the Justices* : [UK] juriste qui conseille le 'Magistrate' sur des points de droit ou de procédure (dans les 'Magistrate's Courts').
[A] [U.S.] *county* — : greffier d'un tribunal de première instance et secrétaire d'administration de district *(county)*.
managing — : chef de bureau.
telegraph — : buraliste.
town- — : secrétaire de mairie.
[C] commis, [U.S.] vendeur de magasin.
bank — : employé de banque.
booking — : employé de guichet (chemin de fer, etc.).
entering — : commis aux écritures.
invoice — : facturier.
managing : commis principal.
time- — : pointeur (de présence).
— *in holy orders* : ecclésiastique, clerc.
[B] *admitted* —, *authorized* — : [U.K.] commis de bourse.
unauthorized —, [U.K.] « *blue button* — » : commis de bourse stagiaire.

client : client (*dans les professions libérales* : dans le commerce se dit plutôt : *customer*).

to clinch a deal : conclure un marché.

to clip : (F) perdre des points (v. to chip).

clipping agency : agence spécialisée qui recherche et fournit contre rémunération des extraits de Presse ou des annonces publicitaires sur des sujets donnés.

to clock in : « pointer » (ouvrier se présentant au travail).

close : fermé, clos (a).
[J] clôture, bien-fonds clôturé (effectivement ou théoriquement).
— *arrest* : (milit.) arrêts de rigueur.
breach of — : voir *breach*.
— *prisoner* : prisonnier mis au secret.
— *question* : cas limite.
— *to the wind* : à la limite de la légalité.
« *the vote was* — » : le scrutin a été serré.
[C] — *down* : fermeture définitive.
— *company*, — *corporation* : société familiale ou comportant un petit nombre de participants (# SNC, SARL de famille).

to close : fermer.
[C] — *the books* : balancer les comptes.
— *a deal* : conclure une transaction.
— *a file* : fermer un dossier.
— *down* : cesser complètement son activité.
the right to open and — : droit du demandeur de s'adresser le premier et le dernier au jury.
[B] — *a deal* : liquider une opération.
closed issue : émission limitée.
closed shop : établissement qui n'emploie pas de travailleurs non-syndiqués (opp. *open shop*).

close end : à capital fixe, limité.
[B] — *investment company* : société d'investissement à capital fixe.
— *fund* : fonds de placement à capital fixe.
— *mortgage* : hypothèque limitée.

closing : clôture, liquidation (f).
[B] signature d'un accord de souscription.
closings : cours de clôture.
— *bid* : dernière enchère.
— *date* : date de forclusion.
— *quotations* : cotes en clôture.
— *of title* : remise de l'acte translatif de propriété (voir *conveyance, deed, delivery*) après accomplissement par les parties de toutes les prestations prévues (notamment du paiement).
— *prices* : derniers cours.
sunday — : repos hebdomadaire.
— *time* : heure de la fermeture (« on ferme »).

closure: clôture (f).
to move the — of debate: proposer la clôture des débats.

cloud:
[J] *— on title*: incertitude apparente quant à la plénitude d'un droit de propriété.

Cluster analysis *(market research)*: analyse de comportement d'un groupe d'acheteurs éventuels (étude de marché).

C.M.E. *(Chicago Mercantile Exchange)*: Bourse de Commerce de Chicago.

co-:
— *-administrator*: cogérant.
— *-defendant*: coaccusé, codéfendeur.
— *-executor*: coexécuteur testamentaire.
— *-heir*: cohéritier.
— *-insurance*: coassurance.
— *-obligant*: cobligé.
— *-offender*: codélinquant.
— *-optation*: cooptation.
— *-ownership*: copropriété.
— *-partnership*: coassociation.
— *-respondent*: codéfendeur.
— *-surety*: cofidéjusseur.
— *-tenant*: colocataire.
— *-trustee*: coadministrateur.
— *-vendor*: colicitant.

European coal and steel community: Communauté Européenne du charbon et de l'acier (CECA).

coasting: côtier (a).
— *trade*: cabotage (m).

C.O.B.O.L. *(Common Business Oriented Language)*: langage informatique de programmation pour la gestion.

C.O.D. *(abr. cash on delivery)*: paiement à la livraison.

code: code (m).
[J] la codification transforme de plus en plus l'aspect du droit A.A. La plus importante en Angleterre a porté sur la procédure, elle a abrogé les dispositions traditionnelles du C.L.
[A] *Internal Revenue —*: code des impôts des Etats-Unis.

codicil: *(of a will)* codicille, *(of a treaty)* avenant (m).
[J] en tant que disposition additionnelle, le codicille présuppose l'existence d'un testament. De ce fait, ce dernier subit une novation: il est « *republished* », de sorte que les défauts dont il pouvait être frappé sont levés si le codicille est valable ; « *it revives a revoked will* ». Les règles de forme sont identiques pour le codicille et le testament.

coding desk: poste (m) de codage.

coercion: coercition (f), contrainte (f), [J] coaction (f).
actual —: (vis absoluta) contrainte physique.
implied —: (vis compulsiva) contrainte morale.
coercive relief: ordonnance de faire.
coercive weapon: sanction pénale.
— *act*: loi qui suspend les droits civils.

cogency: force d'un argument, urgence d'un cas (m).
[J] bien-fondé (d'une cause, etc.).

cogent argument: argument (m) incontestable.

cognate: [J] cognat (opp. *agnate*).
— *sections of an act*: articles d'une loi qui s'apparentent les uns aux autres.

cognati: parents du côté maternel.

cognizable: du ressort, de la compétence, sous le coup de.
— *by indictment*: qui doit être porté par voie d'accusation.

cognizance: connaissance, perception.
[J] 1° connaissance.
to take —: prendre connaissance, prendre acte.
2° compétence.
within the — of the court: du ressort, de la compétence du tribunal.
court cognizant of an offence: tribunal compétent pour juger un délit.

cohabitation: cohabitation (f).
[J] union libre, concubinage.

coin: pièce de monnaie métallique.
bad —: monnaie de mauvais aloi.
false —: fausse monnaie.
in —: en espèces (sonnantes et trébuchantes).
[J] **coinage** *offence*: crime de fausse monnaie.
right of coinage: droit de battre monnaie.

cold chain: chaîne (f) du froid.

collapse: *(of prices, quotations)* effondrement (m), chute (f), krach (m).

collapsible corporation: société évanescente (créée pour une opération ponctuelle, généralement immobilière et dissoute dès la réalisation de l'opération).

collateral : additionnel, auxiliaire, indirect ; nantissement (m) ; parent en ligne collatérale.
[J] [C] — *attack :* allégation de nullité radicale (d'un jugement, d'un acte de procédure).
assignment as — : garantie offerte (gage de biens ou de droits mobiliers, dépôt de titres en nantissement, etc.).
— *promise :* promesse subsidiaire.
— *estopped by judgment :* force de la chose jugée.
— *loan :* prêt accessoire, garantie.
— *security :* sûreté supplémentaire, garantie additionnelle, nantissement.
— *trust bonds :* obligations nanties.
to collaterize : garantir.

collatio bonorum *(hotchpot)* : [J] rapport à la masse d'une avance d'hoirie.

colleague : collègue (m) (entre fonctionnaires).

to collect : assembler, rechercher, encaisser, recouvrer, percevoir.
collecting *charges :* frais de recouvrement.

collection : *(of a bill, a cheque)* encaissement, *(of taxes)* levée, perception, rentrée, *(of dividends, of a fine, of interests)* perception, *(of persons, of things)* rassemblement, réunion, *(of taxes, of a debt)* recouvrement, *(of an amount of money)* récupération.
[A] — *process :* centralisation des documents.
[F] — *assistance :* assistance en matière de recouvrement.
cash — : entrée de caisse.
— *at the source :* stoppage à la source.
— *procedure :* procédure de mise en recouvrement.
for — : aux fins de recouvrement.

collective : collectif (a).
— *agreement :* convention collective.
— *capital investments :* équipements collectifs.
— *farm :* ferme collective.
— *liability :* responsabilité collective.
— *ownership :* propriété collective.

collector : encaisseur (d'un chèque).
[A] — *of Inland Revenue (of direct taxes) :* percepteur des contributions directes, *his office :* perception, *(of excise duties) :* receveur des contributions indirectes, *his office :* recette.

collision : collision (f).
[J] (en mer) *fortuitous* — : abordage fortuit.
(ASS. mar.) — *clause :* garanties au tiers contre les collisions.
wrongful — : abordage délictueux.
— *regulations :* règles d'abordage.

to collocate : colloquer (des créanciers).

collusion : collusion (f).
[J] 1° connivence pour léser, sous les apparences de la légalité, les intérêts d'un tiers ; 2° accord entre époux, pour exciper d'une cause de divorce inexistante.
to act in — *with s.o. :* agir de connivence avec qn.
collusive *agreement :* arrangement collusoire.

colour : couleur (f), prétexte (m), simulacre (m), déguisement (m), vraisemblance (f).
— *bar :* ségrégation raciale.
[J] droit apparent.
by — *of office :* usurpation de fonctions ou de titres.
claim under — *of title :* revendication immobilière appuyée sur un droit non vérifié.
under — *of law :* sous les apparences de la légalité.
to give — : admettre (posito sed non concesso) le droit de l'adversaire pour démontrer ensuite son inexistence.
without any — *of right :* sans la moindre apparence de droit.
colourable *imitation :* a) bonne imitation ; b) contrefaçon.
[J] [A] [U.S.] **colored** *persons :* personnes de race noire.
colouring : faux semblant.

combination : combinaison (f).
[J] *right of* — : droit syndical.
[U.S.] association de malfaiteurs.
— *in restraint of trade :* entente industrielle ou commerciale illicite.
business — : regroupement d'entreprises.
horizontal, vertical — : intégration horizontale, verticale.

combine : coalition (f), cartel (m), combinaison financière, entente (f) industrielle.

to come : venir.
[J] comparaître.
— *of age :* atteindre la majorité.
— *into force :* entrer en vigueur.
— *out on strike :* se mettre en grève.
— *to an understanding :* tomber d'accord.
— *up for discussion :* réclamer.
(pol.) — *up for reelection :* se représenter.
— *within scope of the statute :* tomber sous les coups de la loi.
these cases **come** *before a commercial court :* ces affaires ressortissent à la juridiction consulaire.
[C] *to come down :* baisser les prix.
[E] *to come on demurrage :* tomber en souf-

france.
[F] *to come off the gold standard* : abandonner l'étalon-or.
– *to maturity* : venir à échéance.

COMEX *(Commodities Mercantile Exchange, New York)* : Marché à terme de l'or, de l'argent et des métaux précieux, New York.

comfort : consolation (f), soulagement (m), réconfort (m).
[J] *aid and – to the enemy* : intelligence avec l'ennemi.
[C] – *letter* : lettre de confort.

comity : courtoisie (f).
– *of nations* : comitas gentium, courtoisie internationale.
En théorie A.A., l'application des jugements étrangers ou même nationaux, le droit des étrangers d'ester en justice *(« access to our courts »)* etc., ne résultent pas uniquement des stipulations des traités ou des dispositions du droit interne, on y voit surtout un acte de courtoisie internationale ou de déférence confraternelle, de nation à nation, de juge à juge.

command : commandement (m), ordre (m), possession (f).

to command : ordonner, commander.
« *we command you that...* » : formule rituelle d'une citation *(subpoena)*.
« *the statute commands the court to...* » : « aux termes de la loi, le tribunal doit... ».

commencement : commencement.
– *of proof in writing* : commencement de preuve par écrit.
[ASS] – *of a policy* : effet d'une police.
commencing *salary* : salaire de début.

comment : commentaire (m), remarque, critique (f).
adverse – : observation défavorable.

commerce : le commerce en général, les affaires (f pl).
[J] commerce charnel.

commercial : commercial (a).
(T.V.) – : émission (f) publicitaire.
[J] [C] *action of a – nature* : affaire relevant de la juridiction consulaire.
– *agency* : agence de renseignements commerciaux.
– *bank* : banque commerciale.
– *clause* : « clause commerciale » (Art. 1, par. 8 de la constitution des Etats-Unis, qui réserve au pouvoir fédéral l'ensemble de la législation commerciale *(« the Congress shall have Power to regulate Commerce with foreign Nations and among the several States and with the Indian Tribes »).* Cette disposition, interprétée très extensivement englobe dans le terme *« interstate commerce »* le processus entier de la production des biens).
– *court* : tribunal consulaire, de commerce.
– *credit* : délai de paiement.
[U.S.] *Department of Commerce* : ministère du Commerce [U.K. *Board of Trade*].
– *efficiency* : rendement économique (d'une machine, etc.).
– *laws* # code de commerce.
– *paper* : effet négociable, billet de trésorerie.
– *town* : place marchande.
– *traveller* : voyageur de commerce.
– *value* : valeur vénale.
– *world* : « le commerce », le monde des affaires.

commission : commission (f), mandat (m), délégation (f) de pouvoirs ; brevet (m) d'officier ; titre (m) nominatif ; armement (m) d'un navire.
[J] 1° – *of an offence* : consommation, perpétration d'un délit ; 2° *open* – : commission rogatoire en vertu de laquelle les avocats des parties interrogent les témoins, dont les réponses sont consignées par le *commissioner* (opp. *letters rogatory*, voir ce terme) ; 3° une commission, parlementaire ou autre.
the Ecclesiastical – : la Commission d'administration des biens de l'Eglise anglicane.
fact-finding – : commission d'enquête.
royal – : commission d'enquête parlementaire.
– *-day* : jour de l'ouverture des assises.
[A] [U.S.] instance administrative quasi-indépendante telle que *the Federal Trade* – – : commission de la lutte contre la concurrence illicite.
the Interstate Commerce – : commission de surveillance du commerce entre Etats (voir *commercial clause*).
[C] [F] commission (f), pourcentage (m), courtage (m), remise (f).
guarantee- – : ducroire.
illicit – : remise illicite, « pot de vin ».
– *merchant, agent* : commissionnaire en marchandises.
on – : à la commission.
to charge a – : prélever une commission.
[B] *half* – : remise (f).
securities and exchange – (SEC) # Commission des Opérations de Bourse (C.O.B.).

commissioner : commissaire (m).
[J] – *for oaths* : officier ministériel habilité à recevoir les déclarations sous serment.
[U.S.] – *of deeds* : notaire résidant dans un

Etat et habilité à dresser des actes valables dans un autre.
[A] – *of Audit* # conseiller référendaire à la Cour des comptes.
the Charity – *(s)* : la commission de surveillance des œuvres de bienfaisance.
the Civil Service – *(s)* : le corps chargé du recrutement des fonctionnaires par voie de concours.
the – *of Inland Revenue* # le fisc, les autorités fiscales.
– *of police* # préfet de police.
wreck – : commissaire des naufrages.
[U.S.] fonctionnaire de haut rang de l'Union, d'un Etat ou d'une ville, à la tête d'une grande administration, p. ex. :
Internal Revenue – : directeur des contributions au ministère des Finances.
– *of Customs* : directeur général des douanes.
– *of Patents* : directeur de l'Office de la propriété industrielle.

commissoria (lex) : [J] clause (f), pacte (m), commissoire.

to commit : commettre, confier, livrer, remettre, perpétrer, renvoyer à un comité.
[J] 1° *(a crime)* perpétrer, *(a crime, an offence)* commettre ; 2° *(– s.o.)* : délivrer un mandat de dépôt, d'écrou, **(committal** *order)* un ordre d'internement contre qn.
– *for trial* : 1° mettre en état de prévention ; 2° mettre en accusation.
– *a bill* : renvoyer un projet de loi à la commission (Parlement).
– *money to a bank* : faire un dépôt en banque.
– *oneself* : 1° prendre un engagement ; 2° se compromettre.

commitment : engagement (m), obligation (f), renvoi (m) à une commission, incarcération (f).
– *fee* : honoraires d'engagement, commission d'engagement.
to limit the amounts of one's – : limiter le montant de son engagement.
to meet one's – *(s)* : faire face à ses engagements.
warrant of – : mandat de dépôt.
water-tight – : engagement sans réserve et sans faille.

committal : délégation (f), renvoi (m), incarcération (f).
– *for trial* : renvoi devant la cour d'assises, mise en accusation.
– *order* : mandat de dépôt.

committee : comité (m), commission (f), conseil (m).

[J] curateur d'un aliéné (désignation faite par *the Lord Chancellor*).
advisory – : comité consultatif.
– *of coordination* : comité de coordination.
– *on credentials* : commission de vérification des pouvoirs.
– *of inspection* : délégation des créanciers, chargée de la surveillance dans une procédure de faillite.
– *of management* : conseil d'administration.
– *on rules and regulations* : commission du règlement.
– *of the whole* : comité plénier.
joint – : commission mixte.
joint production – : comité d'entreprise.
select – : commission d'enquête parlementaire.
standing – : comité de direction, *(Parliament)* réunion des présidents.
[U.S.] – *of ways and means, supply* – # commission des voies et moyens, commission des finances.
credentials – : comité de vérification des pouvoirs.
standing – : comité permanent.
steering – : comité de direction.
sub- – : sous-commission.
working – : comité restreint.
[B] *The Stock Exchange* – # la Direction de la Bourse.
The House resolves itself, goes, into – *(– of the whole House)* : la Chambre des communes se constitue en commission (sp. pour discuter le budget, afin de pouvoir appliquer le règlement intérieur, moins formel, des commissions parlementaires).

committal *proceedings* : audience préliminaire devant une 'Magistrate's Court' (afin d'établir si l'affaire doit être renvoyée devant une juridiction criminelle supérieure).

commodity : [C] marchandise, article, sp. denrée ou produit d'usage.
commodities : biens (tels que les entend l'économie politique).
Commodities Exchange (Royal Exchange) : Bourse de commerce.
[F] – *credits* : crédits commerciaux.
– *taxes* : impôt à la consommation.
[C] *basic* – : produit de base.
– *line markets* : [US] grandes surfaces spécialisées en libre service.
standard – : produit de référence.
staple – : produit de base.
[B] – *futures trading* : marché à terme sur les marchandises.
– *market* : bourse des marchandises.
commodities pool : groupement d'achat de matières premières (en vue de spéculer).
staple – *market* : marché de(s) matières premières.

common : commun (a).
- *average* : avarie simple.
- *bail* : caution légale.
- *gaol* : maison d'arrêt.
- *good* : intérêt général.
- *hangman* : bourreau.
- *informer (private prosecutor)* : délateur (voir *informer*).
- *jury (petty jury)* : jury de jugement (opp. *grand jury*).
- *knowledge* : fait notoire.
- *law* : voir l'article ci-après.
- *-lawyer* : jurisconsulte en droit coutumier.
- *market* : marché commun.
- *ownership* : copropriété en main commune.
- *plea* : (hist.) plaid commun.
- *policy* : police type d'assurance.
- *property* : copropriété.
- *report* : rumeur publique.
- *roll* : égalité civile.
[B] — *equity, share, stock* : action ordinaire.

common (s) : terrain communal (se dit aussi au pluriel —), droit banal.
[J] *(right of)* — : droit d'usage, sp. droit de vaine pâture (se dit aussi **commonage**).
- *of estovers* : (droit d') affouage.
- *of piscary* : droit de pêche.
- *of pasture* : droit de pacage.
- *of turbary* : droit à la tourbe.

commonage : communauté (f).

commoner : roturier, bourgeois ; se dit d'un membre de la Chambre des communes.
the First — # the speaker.

common law : droit coutumier et jurisprudentiel.
[J] 1° l'ensemble des institutions du droit A.A., en tant qu'entité distincte des systèmes juridiques issus du droit romain *(civil law)* ; 2° le droit historique, antérieur aux codifications modernes. Cependant, ce droit reste valable tant qu'il n'a pas été remplacé par une loi moderne *(statute)*, qui reste d'interprétation étroite. C'est là le point où le droit anglais et le droit américain ont, en se séparant, pris chacun sa voie, mais, lorsqu'il y a lieu de recourir au *C.L.*, l'application en est stricte de part et d'autre, sans aucune considération pour les cas d'espèce. C'est pourquoi on a constitué une juridiction de recours systématique : *the Equity*. A l'origine, les deux ordres de juridiction étaient distincts ; aujourd'hui, les mêmes tribunaux appliquent le *C.L.* et l'*Eq.*, pour autant qu'ils n'ont pas été fondus dans une nouvelle législation.
— *action* : plainte suivant la procédure ordinaire.
employer's — *liability* : responsabilité civile de l'employeur (indépendante des assurances sociales et de la législation sur les accidents de travail).
— *marriage* : (hist.) (consensus de presenti) mariage par consentement mutuel et consommation.

commonplace book : memorandum.

Commons (the) : [U.K.] La Chambre des Communes.

commonwealth : Etat, sp. l'ensemble des Etats monarchiques et républicains groupés sous l'égide de la dynastie dont le représentant régnant en Angleterre porte le titre de *Chief of the* —.

commorientes : comourants (m pl).
Aux termes du *C.L.*, le décès est présumé simultané.

commotion : insurrection (f).

communal : communal, banal (a).
communal forest : forêt communale.
[J] — *estate* : communauté de biens entre époux.
[U.S.] **community** *property*, — *tenure* : jouissance en commun.
inclusion of realty in the — *estate* : ameublissement d'immeubles.

commune : [A] commune [U.S. *township*].

communications mix : ensemble (m) des moyens publicitaires utilisés par une société (une entreprise).

community : collectivité (f), agglomération (f), collectivités publiques.
— *chest* : fonds civiques.
— *of property* : communauté des biens.
conventional — : communauté conventionnelle.
industrial **communities** : groupes industriels.
— *transit form* : carnet de passage en douane communautaire.

commutable : commuable (a).

commutation : commutation (f).
[J] — *of sentence* : communation de peine.
— *of an easement, of a right of user* : rachat d'une servitude.
pension — : liquidation d'une pension.
commutative *contract* : contrat commutatif.
to commute : commuer (une peine), racheter (une rente).
commuter : frontalier (m) ; banlieusard (m) (qui fait un long trajet aller et retour en chemin de fer pour se rendre à son travail

et rentrer chez lui).
commuting *expenses* : frais de transport domicile-travail.

compact : convention (f), pacte (m), contrat (m) (voir *covenant*).

companion laws : lois complémentaires.

companionate marriage : [U.S.] union libre (et stérile).

company : compagnie (f), personne morale, société commerciale ou industrielle.
ship's — : équipage.
[J] [C] société de capitaux. Les termes « — *limited by shares* », « *limited (liability)* — » désignent toujours des sociétés de capitaux ; mais comme il n'y a pas de correspondance exacte entre les diverses formes de sociétés en droit français et en droit A.A., il peut s'agir soit d'une société anonyme soit d'une société à responsabilité limitée, soit encore d'une société en commandite par actions.
affiliated — : filiale.
— *agreement* : accord salarial entre une seule société et un syndicat.
— *bargaining* : négociations entre la direction d'une société et un syndicat.
bogus — : société fictive.
— *car* : voiture de fonction.
chartered — : société exemptée de certaines obligations par accord spécial.
civil — : société civile.
(simple) commandite — : société en commandite simple.
— *deeds* : actes de société.
dormant — : société inactive agréée.
— *in commendam* : société en commandite simple.
— *limited by shares* : société en commandite par actions.
finance — : société de financement.
foreign — : société, collectivité étrangère.
holding — : société de participations financières.
(personal) holding — : [U.S.] société de portefeuille, société de contrôle en nom collectif.
(foreign personal) holding — : [U.S.] société étrangère de participations financières au capital privé.
incorporated — : société constituée, [U.S.] société anonyme.
joint stock — : société de capitaux, par actions.
(regulated) investment — : société mutuelle de placement.
limited liability (Ltd) — : société à responsabilité limitée (S.A.R.L.).
management — : [U.S.] société de placement à capital fixe.
no personal liability (N.P.L.) — : société sans responsabilité des actionnaires.
« *one man* » — : [U.K.] société dont le nombre de membres ne dépasse pas cinq.
parent — : société mère.
private, privately held — : société à responsabilité limitée.
public, publicly held — : société anonyme.
subsidiaries of foreign parent — : filiales d'une société mère étrangère.
promotary — : [U.S.] société de financement.
purchasing — : société preneuse.
— *secretary* : secrétaire général.
trust — : société de gestion de portefeuille.
— *union* : syndicat d'entreprise.
vendor — : société apporteuse.
wildcat — : société véreuse.
to form a — : constituer une compagnie.
to wind up a — : liquider une société.
[F] — *tax* : impôt sur les sociétés.

comparative : comparatif, relatif (a).
— *advantages* : avantages relatifs.
— *legislation* : droit comparé.
law of — *costs* : loi des coûts comparatifs.

compassionate allowance : secours de commisération.

compendium (of laws) : recueil (m) des lois.

to compensate : compenser, indemniser, dédommager.
— *s.o. for a loss* : dédommager qn d'une perte.

compensation : *(for loss injury)* dédommagement (m), *(for damage)* indemnité (f), *(for personal services)* rémunération (f), [U.S.] salaire (m).
by way of — : en dédommagement.
workmen's — : réparation des accidents de travail et maladies professionnelles.
[J] réparation civile, composition (f).
pecuniary — : réparation pécuniaire, rétribution (f).
war damages — : dommages (m pl) de guerre.
Workmen's — *Act* : loi sur les accidents du travail.

compensatory *damages* : compensation (f).

competence, competency : moyens d'existence suffisants, compétence en un sujet, aptitude.
[J] 1° compétence ; 2° capacité.
— *of evidence* : capacité nécessaire pour témoigner.
— *of persons* : capacité civile des personnes.
to be within, beyond, the — *of a court* : être, ne pas être du ressort d'un tribunal.
to disclaim — : se récuser.
to disclaim the — *of the court* : décliner la

compétence du tribunal.
[A] attributions (f pl).
usurpation by the administrative agency of power beyond its – : excès de pouvoir commis par l'administration.
within our – : dans nos attributions.
competent *advice :* avis qualifié.
competent *evidence :* preuve recevable (opp. *incompetent evidence*).
– *to make a will :* habile à tester.
court of – *jurisdiction :* tribunal compétent.

competing : concurrentiel, concurrent (a), en concurrence (avec).
– *investments :* investissements (m pl) compatibles.

competition : rivalité (f), concurrence (f), concours (m).
cut-throat – : concurrence sans merci.
fraudulent – : concurrence illicite.
keen – : concurrence acharnée.
to meet – : faire face à la concurrence.
[J] [C] *unfair* – : concurrence déloyale.

competitive : concurrent, concurrentiel (a).
– *bidding :* appel d'offres.
– *claims :* avantages offerts aux acheteurs par des compagnies concurrentes fabriquant des produits similaires (« surenchère concurrentielle »).
– *edge :* (mince) avantage sur les concurrents.
– *equality :* principe d'égalité en matière de concurrence.
– *goods, price, products :* articles, prix, produits concurrents.
– *markets :* marchés où s'exerce la concurrence.
– *tender :* soumission en vue d'adjudication.
on a – *basis :* par voie de concours.
competitor : concurrent.

compilation : *(of a dictionary)* compilation, *(of an inventory)* confection.
[J] recueil in extenso, de textes législatifs en vigueur (opp. *consolidation, codification*).

to compile : compiler, [U.S.] refondre (un texte) et expliciter à partir d'une compilation.

complainant, complainer : [U.K., U.S.] plaignant, [U.S.] demandeur.

complaint :
[J] [U.K., U.S.] plainte auprès de qui de droit (commissariat de police, parquet), [U.S.] demande introductive d'instance (voir *burden of proof, cause of action, pleading*).
– *dismissed with cost :* rejet de la plainte avec dépens.
– *fails :* la plainte est rejetée.

– *succeeds :* il est fait droit à la plainte.
to lay, lodge a – : porter plainte.
[F] réclamation (f).

to complete : compléter, remplir, achever.
completed *contract :* marché exécuté.

completion : achèvement (m), établissement (m).
[J] – *of contract :* signature du contrat.
– *of mandate :* terme de mandat.
[A] – *of formalities.*

compliance : acquiescement (m), soumission (f), consentement (m).
certificate of – : certificat de conformité.
– *costs :* coûts de soumission (coûts supportés par les agents économiques quand ils remplissent les obligations qui leur sont imposées par les dispositions légales et réglementaires, fiscales ou autres).
in – *with the law :* conformément à la loi.
want of – : non-conformité.

complicity : complicité (f).

compliment : compliment (m).
with the publisher's – *(s) :* « Hommage de l'Editeur ».
complimentary *copy :* exemplaire gratuit, à titre gracieux, spécimen (non payant).
– *ticket :* billet de faveur.

to comply : obéir, exécuter, se conformer.
– *with a clause in a treaty :* exécuter la clause d'un traité.
– *with a demand :* accéder à une demande.
– *with a reinvestment requirement :* effectuer un remploi obligatoire.
– *with a request :* faire droit à une requête.
– *with the allotments :* rester dans les limites des crédits alloués.
failure – *with these rules... :* le non-respect des règles...

component : constituant (a), composant (a), constitutif (a), composante (f).
– *companies :* compagnies subsidiaires.

compos mentis : dans son bon sens.

composition : composition (f), arrangement transactionnel, accommodement (m), concordat (m).
[J] concordat préventif à la faillite (par exemple par abandon d'actif : *cession*).
[A] forfait fiscal, transaction avec le fisc.
– *for stamp duty :* abonnement au timbre.
– *tax :* impôt forfaitaire.
– *of ten shillings in the pound :* décharge de 50 %.
[D] – *for dues :* transaction avec la douane.

[C] arrangement (m), atermoiement (m), compromis (m).
to come to a — : parvenir à un compromis.
composite *demand* : demande composite (un même produit utilisé à des fins différentes).
composite motion : motion de synthèse.

compound : composé (a).
[F] — *interest* : intérêts composés, anatocisme.
— *discount method* : méthode du taux interne de rentabilité.
— *sum* : valeur acquise.
compound entry : article récapitulatif.

to compound : composer, s'arranger, établir un concordat.
— *a debt* : transiger sur une dette.
— *a felony* : fermer les yeux sur un crime contre rémunération (délit).
— *for a tax* : 1° payer un impôt à forfait ; 2° transiger avec le fisc.
— *with creditors* : s'arranger avec ses créanciers.
compoundable *debt* : dette sur laquelle il est possible de transiger.
power of **compounding** : pouvoir de transiger.
compounding factor : facteur d'accumulation.
compounder : amiable compositeur.

comprehensive : bienveillant, large, vaste, étendu (a).
— *guarantee* : garantie étendue.
— *inquiry* : enquête étendue.
— *planning* : see corporate planning.
— *settlement* : réglementation d'ensemble.
[ASS] — *insurance* : assurance tous-risques.

compromise : compromis (m), transaction (f).
[J] compromis d'arbitrage.
to agree for a — : accepter une transaction.
to arrive to a — : transiger ; parvenir à un compromis.

comptroller : contrôleur (m).
[A] [U.S.] chef d'un service de contrôle des comptes d'Etat ou de municipalité.
[F] vérificateur des comptes, commissaire aux comptes.
comptrollership : commissariat aux comptes.

compulsion : contrainte, violence.
[J] voir *coercion*.
to be under — *to do sth.* : être astreint à faire qch.
to pay under — : effectuer un paiement sous contrainte.

compulsory : obligatoire, forcé, coercitif (a).
— *acquisition of property by public bodies* : expropriation pour cause d'utilité publique.
— *feature* : élément contraignant.
— *insurance* : assurance obligatoire.
— *joinder* : jonction d'instances obligatoires.
— *jurisdiction* : compétence obligatoire.
— *liquidation* : liquidation judiciaire.
— *loan* : emprunt forcé.
[U.S.] *compulsory prostitution* : vagabondage spécial.
— *registration* : enregistrement obligatoire.
— *retirement* : (mise à la) retraite d'office.
— *sale* : vente par autorité de justice.
— *quotation* : cours forcé.

compurgation : [J] témoignage justificatif.

computation : compte (m), calcul (m), décompte (m).
[J] *civil* — *of time* : le premier jour est compris dans la computation d'un délai.
[F] — *of net asset value* : calcul de la valeur de l'actif net.
detailed — : déclaration détaillée.
salary — : méthode de calcul des traitements et salaires.
tax — # : passage du résultat comptable au résultat fiscal, recalcul des résultats sociaux en vue de leur imposition.
computed *interest* : intérêt capitalisé.
computer *aided design (C.A.D.)* : conception assistée par ordinateur (C.A.O.).
computer processing : traitement sur ordinateur.
to computerize : informatiser.

to conceal : dissimuler, cacher.
concealed assets : actif incorporel.
concealed unemployment : chômage déguisé.

concealment : dissimulation (f), déguisement (m), réticence (f).
[J] 1° recel (d'objet volé, de malfaiteur, d'enfant) ; 2° dissimulation (par exemple d'un fait tel que le défaut d'une marchandise qui, connu, aurait empêché la conclusion du contrat et qui en justifie la rescision.
— *of birth* : suppression de part.
— *of evidence* : dissimulation de preuves.
— *of profits* : dissimulation de bénéfices.
[ASS] *material* — : dissimulation d'un fait pertinent pouvant donner lieu à l'annulation de la police (voir *contract* ASS, *representation* ASS).

concept : [J] principe fondamental.
[B] — *stock* : action d'innovation.

concern : affaire, intérêt, entreprise.
going — : entreprise « qui marche ».
artificial — : compagnie fictive.

to concern : concerner, regarder, intéresser.
the department **concerned** : le service compé-

tent.
the parties concerned: les intéressés.
to whom it may concern: à qui de droit.

concession: concession (f) (de terrain, d'opinion, d'un service, d'un kiosque, etc.).
mining – : concession minière.
[F] *tax* – *(s)*: dégrèvements fiscaux.
by – : dans un souci d'allègement.

concession(n)aire: concessionnaire (m) (sens restreint en anglais: personne exerçant des activités commerciales ou industrielles dans des locaux appartenant à une autre personne).

conciliation: conciliation, arbitrage, réconciliation.
– *award*: procès-verbal de conciliation.
– *board (in industrial disputes)*: conseil d'arbitrage (des conflits du travail), conseil des prud'hommes.

to conclude: achever, terminer, arrêter (un marché), passer (un contrat), clôturer (une session).
– *an agreement, a transaction*: conclure un accord, une transaction.
– *an option*: exercer une option.
the plaintiff is **concluded** *by this pleading*: les faits articulés dans ses conclusions rendent irrecevable la (nouvelle) déclaration du demandeur.

conclusion: conclusion (f).
[J] conséquence.
– *of fact*: argument basé sur des faits vérifiés.
– *by judgment*: décision judiciaire, chose jugée.
– *of law, legal* – : conséquences juridiques de l'état de fait allégué, qu'il est interdit d'exposer dans un *affidavit* ou dans les conclusions préalables *(pleadings)*.
conclusive argument: argument probant.
conclusive evidence: preuve péremptoire.
the findings of the jury are conclusive upon the court: le verdict du jury lie le tribunal.
conclusive presumption: présomption irréfragable.
conclusory pleading: conclusions simplement théoriques, omettant le nécessaire exposé des faits *(evidentiary facts)* sur lesquelles elles s'appuient.

concordance: concordance (f).
– *of the evidence*: concordance des témoignages.

concourse: [U.S.] hall (m) d'accueil (gare, aéroport).

concrete: concret, réel, objectif, particulier (a).
[J] – *case*: cas d'espèce.
– *instance*: cas patent.

concubinage: concubinage.
concubins: concubins.
concubinary: concubinaire.
concubine: concubine.

to concur: approuver, adopter, adhérer.
– *in a request*: accéder à une requête.
report **concurred** *in by all members*: rapport adopté à l'unanimité des membres.

concurrence: (a) approbation (f), assentiment (m), accord (m).
[J] conflit de droits, concurrence de droits.
– *of sentences*: confusion des peines (opp. *cumulative sentence*).
to move – *in a report*: proposer l'adoption d'un rapport.
with the – *of*: avec l'assentiment de, sur avis conforme de.

concurrent: (a) concurrent, contribuant, simultané, concomitant, coexistant.
– *bond*: sûreté collatérale.
– *cause*: cause contribuante.
– *jurisdiction*: compétence simultanée de plusieurs tribunaux (au choix du demandeur).
– *lease*: bail sujet à la servitude d'une autre fin de bail à courir.
– *opinion*: avis concordant.
– *powers*: pouvoirs communs, correspondants, parallèles.
– *writ*: assignation lancée en plusieurs exemplaires (p. ex. en raison de la pluralité de défendeurs, de résidences, etc.).
performance and payment are – *conditions*: la prestation et le paiement doivent se suivre immédiatement.
[ASS] – *fire-insurance*: assurance-incendie répartie à conditions identiques entre plusieurs assureurs.

to concuss: ébranler, secouer.
[J] intimider qn.

condemnation: condamnation (f), blâme (m), réforme (f).
[J] 1° condamnation d'un coupable ; 2° expropriation pour cause d'utilité publique ; 3° (droit maritime) a) déclaration de bonne prise, b) retrait du certificat de navigabilité.
– *to costs*: condamnation aux dépens.

condition: condition (f), état d'une personne.
[J] condition (f), stipulation (f).
[D] *according to their* – *(s)*: selon leur conditionnement.
– *(s) laid down in a contract*: conditions d'un

contrat.
— *(s) of the contract* : cahier des charges.
— *(s) of payment* : modes de paiement.
— *precedent* : condition suspensive.
— *subsequent* : condition résolutoire.
express — : condition expresse.
implied — : condition tacite.
loan made on — : prêt conditionnel.
on — : sous réserve.
on terms and — *(s)* : selon les modalités.

conditional : conditionnel (a), sous condition.
— *acceptance* : acceptation sous réserve.
— *agreement* : contrat sous condition.
— *clause* : clause conditionnelle.
— *fee* # succession substituée (voir *reversion*).
— *limitation* : héritage dévolu sous condition résolutoire.
— *on the exportation* : à la condition de réexporter.
— *promise* : promesse sous certaines réserves.
— *release* : libération conditionnelle.
— *sale* : vente sous condition.

condominium : [J] copropriété immobilière.

condonation : pardon (m).
[J] — *of matrimonial infidelity* : pardon d'une infidélité entre époux, constituant renonciation à l'action en divorce. La réconciliation peut être tacite (par la reprise des rapports conjugaux) ou conditionnelle, sur promesse d'une conduite irréprochable à l'avenir.

conduct : conduite (f), marche des affaires, exécution (f).
— *of affairs* : gestion d'affaires.
— *-money* : frais de déplacement d'un témoin.
good- — *certificate* : certificat de moralité.
safe- — : sauf-conduit (m).

to conduct : mener, entamer, diriger, gérer.
— *an inquiry* : faire une enquête.
— *one's own case* : plaider personnellement sa cause.
the case shall be **conducted** *in English* : la procédure aura lieu en anglais.

conduit : canalisation (f), [J] homme de paille.

confederacy : confédération d'Etats.
[J] conspiration (f), complot (m) [U.S. *combination*], (*Eq.*) collusion.

confederate : complice (m).

Confederation of British Industries (C.B.I.) : Confédération Patronale Britannique.

to confer : conférer, accorder.
— *an advantage* : accorder une faveur.
— *a degree* : conférer un grade universitaire.
— *jurisdiction by consent* : attribution contractuelle de compétence.

conference : conférence (f), entretien (m).
[J] entretien avec un seul avocat (opp. *consultation*).
[U.S.] séance commune des commissions intéressées du Sénat et de la Chambre des représentants en vue de trancher un désaccord sur un projet de loi, (commission mixte paritaire).
round-table — : consultation paritaire.

to confess *(judgment)* : faire un aveu (en justice).

confession : confession (f), aveu (m).
[J] (civ.) reconnaissance des droits, (cr.) aveu judiciaire.
— *of defence, of plea* : désistement.
— *and avoidance* : reconnaissance des faits matériels allégués par l'adversaire, tout en excipant d'autres faits qui en infirment les conséquences juridiques.
judgment by — : jugement sur aveu.

confidence : confiance (f).
— *clerk* : homme de confiance.
— *crook (con man)* : escroc.
— *trick (con trick)* : vol à l'américaine.
— *vote* : vote de confiance.
motion of no — : motion de défiance.
told in strict — : strictement confidentiel.

confidential : confidentiel (a).
confidential clerk : homme de confiance.
[J] — *communications* : informations dont on n'a pas le droit de se décharger (secret professionnel, sceau de la confession, confidences entre époux, etc.).

to confine : détenir.
— *a boy in a reformatory* : envoyer un mineur dans une maison de correction.
he **confined** *himself to the statement* : il s'est borné à déclarer.
— *oneself to facts* : s'en tenir aux faits.

confinement : 1° emprisonnement ; 2° couches.
[J] réclusion.
close, solitary, — : emprisonnement cellulaire (au secret).

confirmation : confirmation (f), ratification (f).
[J] homologation (f), validation (f).
— *of bankruptcy composition* : homologation d'un concordat.

— *(of an expert's report, etc.) by Court:* entérinement (d'un rapport d'expert, etc.) par le tribunal.
to confirm : *(a decision)* adhérer à, *(a report)* adopter, *(a nomination)* approuver, *(a decree)* homologuer, *(an election)* valider.
the court confirms the referee's report : le tribunal adopte, fait siennes, les conclusions du juge rapporteur.
confirmed *irrevocable letter of credit :* lettre de crédit irrévocable garantie (par deux banques, l'une du pays de l'exportateur, l'autre du pays de l'importateur).
confirming *house :* (U.K.) maison qui travaille pour le compte d'un acheteur étranger et confirme les commandes passées par lui en Grande-Bretagne.

confiscation : confiscation (f).

conflict : conflit (m), dérogation (f), contradiction (f), antagonisme (m).
[J] — *of laws :* conflit de lois.
law of — *(s) :* droit international privé.
to come in — *with :* être en désaccord avec.

to conflict : être en conflit, en contradiction, en désaccord.
duties that conflict with each other : fonctions incompatibles.
conflicting *evidence :* témoignages contradictoires.

conformity : conformité, soumission (à).
in — *with mercantile usage :* conforme aux usages du commerce.
in — *with the usual rules and customs :* conformément aux règles et usages établis.

conglomerate : association (f) de compagnies aux activités multiples.

to confront : envisager, confronter, aborder de front.
— *the prisoner with the evidence :* mettre le prisonnier en présence des preuves.

confusion : confusion.
[J] fusion (voir *merger*).

congress : congrès (en matière autre que politique le terme est plutôt *convention*).
[U.S.] Le Congrès (pouvoir législatif de l'Union, composé du Sénat et de la Chambre des représentants. Cependant, le terme **congressman** ou **congresswoman** s'applique uniquement aux membres de la Chambre basse).
congressional *district :* district territorial représenté au Congrès.
congressional investigation : comité d'enquête parlementaire.

« *Congressional Record* » : compte rendu sténographique des débats du Congrès (le terme — est également employé pour désigner une session du Congrès).

conjugal rights : droits conjugaux, sp. le devoir conjugal.
[J] *decree of restitution of* — *:* injonction à réintégrer le domicile conjugal.

conjonction : conjonction (f).
in — *with s.o. :* de concert avec qqn.
in — *with sthg :* concurremment avec qqch.

connection : [C] clientèle (f), relation (f) d'affaires.
in — *with :* en raison de.
wide — *:* belle clientèle.
[J] **connected** : connexe.

connivance : connivence (f), collusion (f).
[J] 1° complicité dans un crime ou délit ; 2° tolérance par l'un des époux de l'adultère de l'autre.
to connive *with a criminal :* favoriser un criminel.

connubiality : état de mariage, exercice des droits conjugaux.
[J] capacité de mariage.

consanguinity : consanguinité (parenté dans la ligne paternelle).

consensual *(termination)* : (cessation) par consentement mutuel.

conscience : conscience (f).
— *clause :* article d'une loi réservant les droits de l'objection de conscience.
— *-money :* restitution anonyme d'une somme due au fisc.
conscientious *objector :* objecteur de conscience, réfractaire (en matière de service militaire, de vaccination, etc.).
class **consciousness** : conscience de classe.

consensus : consensus (m), opinion (f).
on the basis of the — *of opinion :* en se fondant sur l'accord général.
— *omnium :* assentiment universel.

consent : consentement (m), assentiment (m), approbation (f), acquiescement (m).
[J] *age of* — *:* âge nubile (requis : (civ.) pour le mariage, (cr.) pour éviter la qualification de crime en cas de rapports hors mariage).
— *decree :* jugement d'expédient en *Eq.*, sp. ordonnance de ne pas faire sur plainte de l'administration et promesse du défendeur de s'abstenir à l'avenir des actes incriminés.
mutual — *:* accord de gré à gré, *(divorce)*

consentement mutuel.
by mutual — : d'un commun accord.
with one — : à l'unanimité.

consequence : conséquence, suite (f).
in — *of such default* : en raison de cette inexécution.
in — *of the crisis* : par suite de la crise.

consequential : conséquent, consécutif (a).
[J] — *damage* : dommage indirect.
— *effects of an action* : répercussions d'une action.
— *relief* : ordonnance accordant une réparation supplémentaire.

conservancy : conservation (f).
— *measures* : mesures conservatoires.

(nature) conservation : protection (f) (de la nature).

conservationism : (pol.) conservatisme (m), mouvement (m) écologiste.

conservative : modéré, réservé (a).
— *estimate* : évaluation prudente.

conservatory *(attachment)* : (saisie) conservatoire.

to consider : considérer, regarder, estimer, examiner, envisager.
— *measures* : envisager des mesures.
— *the budget* : examiner le budget.
the business that be **considered** : les questions dont on doit délibérer.

considering... : vu que...

consideration : considération (f), examen (m), réflexion (f), délibération (f).
[J] chose appréciable ou somme d'argent. Contre-partie, qui, en vertu d'un principe fondamental du C.L., doit être fournie, pour assurer la validité d'un cotnrat. En effet, la cause gratuite du droit français n'existe pas en droit A.A. : « *consideration is a necessary requirement for a valid agreement* ».
for good — : 1° à titre onéreux ; 2° à titre amical.
for valuable — : à titre onéreux.
question under — : question à l'étude.
[C] [F] prix (m), provision (f), cause (f), indemnité (f), rémunération (f).
for a — : contre espèces.
— *for sale* : prix de vente.
— *given to a bill* : cause d'un billet.
to give — *for a bill* : provisionner une lettre de change.
trusting that you will be able to give favourable — *to my application* : en espérant que vous voudrez bien prendre ma demande en considération.

to consign *(goods)* : expédier (des marchandises).

consignation : consignation (f).
[J] (Scot.) offre réelle suivie de consignation entre mains de tiers.
[C] envoi en consignation.
[F] dépôt en banque.

consignee : destinataire (m).

consignment : expédition de marchandises.
[C] **consigned** *goods* : marchandises en commission.
— *note* : a) lettre de voiture, bordereau de consignation ; b) récépissé de chemin de fer.
— *price* : prix à la commission.
consignee : destinataire.
consignor : expéditeur.

consistency : consistance (f), conformité (f), cohérence (f).
inheritance **consisting** *of a house* : héritage en consistance d'une maison.

consistent : conforme, compatible (avec), constant, cohérent.
— *with the facts, with the law* : conforme aux faits, à la loi.
a — *trend in the cases decide* : une tendance uniforme dans les décisions prises.
these provisions are no longer — *with present conditions* : ces dispositions ne correspondent plus aux circonstances actuelles.
— *with* : eu égard à.

to consolidate : codifier, réunir, consolider (la dette publique).
[J] joindre des instances.
— *a floating debt* : convertir une dette flottante.

consolidated : consolidé, capitalisé, unifié (a).
— *annuities* : rentes consolidées.
— *balance sheet* : bilan consolidé, unifié.
— *profits* : bénéfice consolidé.
the — *fund* : Fonds d'amortissement de la dette publique, auquel sont affectés les revenus des douanes et divers droits (timbre, etc.).

consolidation : consolidation (f), unification (f), textes définitifs, fusion (f), centralisation (f), concentration (f).
[J] — *of actions* : jonction d'instances.
— *of rights* : confusion de droits (de créancier et de débiteur, des fonds servant et desservi, etc.).

— *of companies*: fusion de sociétés (voir *merger*).
— *of statutes*: refonte et unification de textes législatifs (opp. *codification, compilation*).
[F] [U.K.] consolidation de la dette publique par l'émission de **consols** *certificates*, titres consolidés établis par *the* **Consolidated** *Fund*.
[A] *land, rural* — : remembrement territorial.

consols : [J] [U.K.] fonds consolidés, rentes consolidées, perpétuelles (contraction de **conso-lidated** *funds, stocks*).
— *guaranteed by the government* : [U.K.] obligations du gouvernement.

consort : consort.
prince — : époux de la reine régnante.
queen — : épouse du roi (opp. *queen-regnant*).

consortium : [J] mariage légitime et devoir d'aide réciproque qui en découle.
loss of — : rupture de la communauté conjugale donnant lieu, le cas échéant, à des dommages-intérêts en cas d'adultère ou d'un détournement d'affection provoqué : *alienation of affection*.
[C] [F] consortium.

conspicuous *(consumption)* : (consommation) que l'on peut déterminer.

conspiracy : conspiration (f), conjuration (f), complot (m).
[J] (civ.) coalition, (cr.) association de malfaiteurs. (Au civ. le délit de coalition entraîne la responsabilité solidaire *(joint and several liability)* de tous les participants, au cr., l'entente n'a pas besoin de recevoir un commencement d'exécution pour être qualifiée de délictueuse et punie comme telle).

constable : gardien de la paix, agent de police, [U.K.] officier de police.
chief — : commissaire de police.
rural — : garde champêtre, [U.S.] magistrat municipal, chargé d'administrer la justice.
county **constabulary** # gendarmerie.

constituency : circonscription électorale (f).
— *poll* : scrutin d'arrondissement.

constituent : constituant (a), constitutif (a), commettant (m), électeur (m).
— *part* : partie constituante.

constitution : constitution.
[U.K.] la Constitution britannique repose essentiellement sur la coutume : « *an unwritten body of customs* ». Comme toutes les constitutions démocratiques, elle reconnaît la suprématie du législatif, mais ne contient aucun dispositif spécial pour procéder à des changements constitutionnels : un simple *Act of Parliament* suffit.
[U.S.] la constitution fédérale de 1787 est « *the Supreme Law of the Land* ». Elle soumet le législatif à la loi constitutionnelle dont l'application et l'interprétation sont confiées à la Cour Suprême. Un jeu de contrôle réciproque minutieux (« *the checks and balances* »), assure la sauvegarde des libertés individuelles.

constitutional : constitutionnel (a).
— *convention* : [U.S.] assemblée constituante ayant pouvoir d'amender la Constitution.
— *courts* : [U.S.] tribunaux créés par *the Judiciary Acts 1789* (voir *court* U.S.).
— *grounds* : motifs d'ordre constitutionnel.
— *law* : droit constitutionnel.
— *office* : [U.S.] une administration créée par la Constitution et non par le législatif.

constraint : contrainte (f), obligation (f).
[J] 1° contrainte par corps ; 2° privation de liberté (p. ex. internement d'un aliéné).

construction : explicitation (f), interprétation (f) logique et systématique des termes.
broad, liberal, — : interprétation large, extensive.
narrow, restrictive, — : interprétation étroite, littérale.
[J] — *contract* : contrat de longue durée.

constructive : 1° établi par déduction (— *possession, — promise, — treason, — trust, etc.*) ; 2° positif, constructif (— *criticism, — cooperation, — suggestion, etc.*).
— *dismissal* : licenciement à la demande de l'employé (s'oppose à « *unfair, wrongful, dismissal* » : licenciement abusif).
— *loss* : perte implicite.

to construe : *(a text)* interpréter, analyser.

consuetude : [J] *(Scot)* usage local.

consular : consulaire (a).
— *fees* : droits consulaires.
(C) — *invoice* : certificat consulaire de conformité (délivré à un exportateur).

consulate : [A] consulat.
The British — : le consulat de Grande-Bretagne.

to consult : consulter, prendre conseil.
— *with* : conférer avec qn.
consultant : conseil (m), expert (m).
consultation *committee* : comité consultatif.
consultative *arrangements* : accords en vue de consultation.
consulting *panel* : commission consultative.

consumables: denrées (f pl) comestibles.

consumer: consommateur, usager (m).
— *behaviour*: étude du comportement des consommateurs.
— *credit*: crédit à la consommation.
— *council*: [U.K.] comité consultatif des consommateurs.
— *of gas*: abonné au gaz.
— *goods*: biens de consommation.
— *panel*: jury de consommateurs.
— *price index-numbers*: indice des prix à la consommation.
— *research*: étude sur les besoins des consommateurs.
— *('s) risk*: risque pour le consommateur d'acquérir des marchandises défectueuses.
— *surplus* (the difference between the total amount of money an individual would be prepared to pay for some quantity of a good and the amount he actually has to pay): surplus du consommateur.
the — society: la société de consommation.
consuming *power*: possibilité d'absorption du marché.
consumerism: a) action des consommateurs pour la défense de leurs intérêts ; b) force de consommation.

consummation: consommation.
[J] — *of marriage*: consommation du mariage.
— *of the final steps*: dernières mesures d'exécution.

consumption: consommation (f).
— *goods*: biens de consommation.
— *function* (the relationship between total expenditure in the economy and total consumer's income): fonction de consommation.
over, under — : sur, sous-consommation.
private — : consommation des ménages.

container: conteneur (m).

contango: [B] intérêt de report.
— *-day*: l'avant-veille du jour de règlement.
— *market*: marché des reports.
payer of — : reporté.
— *rate*: taux de report.
contagoable: reportable.

contemner: [J] celui qui s'est rendu coupable d'un outrage à magistrat, contumax (« contempt of Court »).

contemplation: prévision (f).
in legal — : du point de vue juridique.

contempt: mépris, dédain (m), offense (f), outrage (m), manque (m) de respect.
— *of the chair*: manquement envers l'autorité du Président.

— *of court* (terme technique : *contumacy*) : outrages à magistrat, (civ.) refus d'obtempérer aux ordonnances du tribunal *(injunctions)*, une partie de l'amende est attribuée à l'adversaire, à titre de dommages-intérêts; (cr.) refus d'obéir aux ordres du tribunal : « *direct* — » à l'audience (p. ex. refus de répondre), « *indirect, constructive* — », en dehors de l'audience (p. ex. non-comparution).
— *of Parliament*: conduite pouvant discréditer le Parlement.
[U.S.] — *of Congress*: refus de comparaître devant les comités d'enquête parlementaire, passible de peines prononcées directement par le Congrès.

to contend: affirmer, prétendre, arguer.
contending *party*: partie contestante.

contender: compétiteur, rival (m).

content: consentement, vote favorable.
— *51, no* — *49*: ont voté pour : 51, contre : 49.

contention: contestation, dispute, controverse, discorde (f).
bone of — : pomme de discorde.

contentious: litigieux, contentieux (a).
— *business*: contentieux (m).
— *matters*: points litigieux.

contents: contenu (m), contenance, teneur (f).
— *of a law*: contenu d'une loi.
table of — : table des matières.

contest: controverse, conflit, débat.
beyond — : sans contestation possible.

to contest: contester, disputer.
[J] *(a will)* attaquer, *(a succession, a debt)* contester.
contested *case*: instance contradictoire.
contestant: opposant (m).
contestation: débat, contestation, litige.

context: contexte (m).
unless the — *otherwise requires*: à moins que le contexte ne s'y oppose.

contiguous: contigu (a, m) contiguë (a, f).
— *countries*: pays limitrophes.

contingency: contingence (f), événement incertain, éventualité (f), cas (m) imprévu.
— *planning*: planification prévisionnelle destinée à parer aux cas imprévus.
should a — *arise*: en cas d'imprévu.
[J] — *fee*: [U.S.] pactum de quota litis.

[C] **contingencies** : 1° faux frais divers ; 2° risques.
[ASS] *(assured against)* – : sinistre.
the remarriage – : possibilité de remariage.

contingent : éventuel, conditionnel, fortuit (a).
[J] – *annuity :* rente éventuelle.
– *case :* cas fortuit.
– *condition :* condition casuelle.
– *estate :* biens dont la dévolution dépend d'un événement futur incertain (p. ex. de la naissance d'un enfant).
– *fees :* honoraires éventuels (de quota litis).
– *remainder :* propriété sous condition suspensive.
[C] [F] – *account :* compte de frais divers.
– *expenses :* dépenses imprévues.
– *liability :* 1° engagements éventuels, passif éventuel exigible ; 2° tierce caution.
– *order :* ordre lié.
– *profit :* bénéfice, profit aléatoire.

continuance : continuation (f).
[J] ajournement (m).
– *of suit :* reprise d'instance.

continuation : continuation (f).
[B] report (m).
– *day :* jour des reports.
– *fee :* taux des reports.
– *on foreign exchanges :* reports sur devise.
– *rate :* prix du report.

to continue : continuer, conserver, perpétuer.
– *in force :* demeurer en vigueur.

continuous : continu, permanent, suivi (a).
– *input investment :* investissement mise continue.
– *output investment :* investissement produit continu ; exploitation étalée.

contra : contrepartie (f).
– *account :* compte contrepartie.
– *entry :* contre-écriture.
per – : en contrepartie.
to – *an item :* contrepasser une écriture.
[B] – *order :* ordre en contrepartie.

contraband : contrebande (f).

contract : contrat (m), convention (f), pacte (m).
[J] 1° (contrat en général).
as per – : au vu du contrat.
express – : contrat en bonne et due forme.
implied – : contrat tacite, de fait, quasi-contrat.
by private – : à l'amiable, de gré à gré.
– *of record :* contrat enregistré ou résultant d'une décision judiciaire.
– *under seal, speciality* – (ou *deed*) : contrat formel, sous seing privé.
– *of service :* contrat entre une société et un administrateur.
simple – : contrat de fait, convention verbale, tacite (dont la validité est conditionnée par l'existence d'un prix : *a consideration*), un contrat est *executed*, exécuté lorsque les parties ont accompli toutes les prestations prévues et lorsqu'un objet est vendu, livré et payé sur-le-champ. On dénomme *executory* un contrat certain, un contrat comportant promesse d'exécution ultérieure, *entire* – : un contrat bilatéral parfait (contractus bilateralis aequalis), *open* – : contrat dont les stipulations ne sont pas encore arrêtées, *severable* – : un contrat dont les conditions peuvent être ajustées aux prestations variables des parties, (contractus bilateralis inaeaqualis) *quasi-* – : un quasi-contrat, *benevolence* – : un contrat unilatéral désintéressé, *burdensome* – : contrat où il y a lésion. La validité d'un contrat dépend des conditions suivantes :
capacity to – : capacité de contracter, *intention to* – : intention de contracter, consensus ad idem, *valuable consideration :* prix, *legality of purpose :* conformité à l'ordre public, *sufficient certainty of terms :* précision suffisante du libellé.
2° acte de vente, contrat translatif de propriété.
– *of benevolence :* contrat unilatéral.
breach of – : rupture de contrat.
– *date :* date contractuelle.
– *law :* droit des obligations.
– *in proper form :* contrat en bonne et due forme.
draft – : projet de contrat.
– *in the lump :* contrat à forfait.
– *methods :* marchés.
– *null and void :* contrat nul.
– *of record :* contrat enregistré.
frustration of the – : disparition du contrat (par suite d'éléments extérieurs aux co-contractants).
penalty for non-fulfilment of – : peine contractuelle, clause pénale.
provisions of a – : stipulations contractuelles.
action for breach of – : action contractuelle, action en rescision pour inexécution de contrat.
action for specific performance of – : action en exécution de contrat.
two-sided – : contrat bilatéral.
[A] prix de série.
[A] [C] entreprise (f), soumission (f), adjudication (f), convention forfaitaire, marché (m).
– *labour :* main-d'œuvre contractuelle.
– *note :* bordereau d'achat ou de vente.

— *of partnership* : contrat de société.
— *price* : prix à forfait.
— *work* : travail à l'entreprise.
the conditions of a — : le cahier des charges.
[B] — *note* : avis d'opéré, bordereau d'exécution.
[ASS] le contrat d'assurance est un contractus uberrimae fidei : contrat qui impose la plus entière bonne foi aux parties, sous peine de nullité (voir *concealment* ASS, *representation* ASS).
to annul — : résilier un contrat.
to break a — : rompre un contrat.
to enforce a — : faire exécuter un contrat.
to enter into a — : passer un contrat.
to put up to — : mettre en adjudication.
to sell by private — : vendre de gré à gré.
to tender for — : soumissionner pour une adjudication.
to contract *in* : adhérer par contrat.
to contract out, away : renoncer par contrat, par une entente préalable, à certaines dispositions de la loi ou d'un traité.
contracting out *clause* : clause de renonciation.
contractable *obligation* : obligation contractable.
contractant : contractant (m).
contracting : contractant (a).
contracting party : contractant (m), partie contractante.
contractings : affermage.
contractor : adjudicataire, entrepreneur, contractant (m).
contractual : contractuel (a).

contradiction : [J] contredit (m).

contrary : contraire à, en opposé, à l'encontre de.
— *to the law* : contrairement aux prescriptions de la loi.
notwithstanding any provision to the — : nonobstant toute disposition contraire.
until the — *is proved* : jusqu'à preuve du contraire.

to contravene (*the regulations*) : enfreindre (les), contrevenir (aux) règlements.

contravention : contravention, infraction.
in — *of* : en violation de.

contravener : transgresseur.
[J] contrevenant.

to contribute : contribuer, collaborer, payer sa quote-part.

contribution : contribution (f), cotisation (f), quote-part (des Etats membres de l'O.N.U.).
— *analysis* : méthode d'analyse des prix de revient faisant apparaître les coûts variables.
— *pro rata* : quote-part.
[J] 1° part d'un légataire demandée pour acquitter les dettes d'une succession ; 2° apport des époux.
[C] *capital* — : versement à la masse sociale d'une compagnie.
— *pricing* : fixation du prix de vente en y incluant les coûts variables.
— *of property* (*to a partnership*) : apport de biens (dans une société).
[ASS] contribution d'un assureur, fixée par le règlement d'avance.
charitable — : dons de bienfaisance.
[F] *special* — : [U.K.] (hist.) impôt sur le capital perçu en 1947-48.
contributor : contribuant, cotisant.

contributory : contribuant, contributif (a).
— *cause* : cause accessoire.
— *pension* : pension financée par des contributions à part égale du travailleur et de son employeur.
— *negligence* : allégation d'un manque de précautions ou d'une imprudence de la part de l'accidenté, du sinistré ou de la victime, sans lesquels il n'y aurait pas eu dommage (voir *negligence*).

control : maîtrise, autorité, pouvoir, direction.
currency —, — *of exchanges* : contrôle réglementaire des changes.
rent — : protection des locataires.
case beyond — : cas de force majeure.
— *of credit* : réglementation du crédit.
— *survey* : expertise contradictoire.
price — : réglementation des prix.
state — : étatisme (m).
under government — : assujetti (a) au contrôle du gouvernement.
[B] participation déterminante.

to control : diriger, gouverner, avoir la maîtrise, réglementer.
controlled economy : économie dirigée.
controlled market : marché officiel.
controllable expenditures : dépenses facultatives.
controllable factors : facteurs de décision contrôlables.
controllership : [U.S.] commissariat aux comptes.
controlling *directors* : associés-dirigeants.

controversory : différend (m), litige (m).

contumacy : contumace, désobéissance aux ordres de la cour, défaut (voir *contempt of court*).

to convene : (*an Assembly*) réunir (une assemblée), convoquer les membres (d'une

assemblée), *(a conference)* assembler.
[J] — *someone before a court* : citer qn devant un tribunal.

convenience : facilité, convenance, commodité (f).
— *goods* : marchandises de vente courante.
with **convenient** *speed* : avec toute la diligence possible.

convention : accord international, convention.
The Hague — *(s)* : les Actes de La Haye.

conventional : conventionnel (a).
— *community* : communauté conventionnelle.
— *estate* : droit de propriété fondé sur l'accord des parties.

conversation : conversation (f), entretien (m), commerce (m), rapports sexuels.
[J] *criminal* — : adultère (sp. eu égard à l'action en dommages-intérêts pour préjudice moral, *heart balm actions*).

conversely : réciproquement, inversement (adv.).

conversion : conversion (f).
[J] 1° ameublissement et immobilisation (une — se produit dans les cas suivants : a) lorsque des biens-fonds tenus en commun sont ameublis ; b) par ordre de tribunal ; c) en vertu d'un *trust* ; d) lors de la vente de biens immobiliers *(equitable —)*. Ces derniers sont considérés comme convertis en argent dès la signature du contrat. C'est ainsi qu'en cas de décès du vendeur ou de l'acheteur, leurs testaments seront interprétés de manière que les héritiers du premier auront droit au prix et ceux du second, à l'immeuble.
2° *(fraudulent)* — *of public moneys* : malversation de fonds publics.
false, wrongful — : détournement de fonds.
[F] *(of Government stock)* conversion, *(of currencies)* change.
involuntary — : conversion forcée.
[B] — *loan* : emprunt de conversion.
— *terms* : conditions de conversion.
to convert *into* : convertir en.
to convert (property) fraudulently : carambouiller.
to convert funds to one's own use : détourner des fonds.
converted *share* : action convertie.

convertible : convertible (a).
— *bond into stock* : obligation convertible en action.
— *securities* : titres convertibles.

to convey : céder, transmettre, faire transport.

conveyance : transport (m), moyens de transport, transmission (f).
[J] 1° tout mode de transmission de biens (surtout immobiliers) autre que testamentaire *(Law of Property Act, 1925)*.
— *assignment* : translation.
— *of actual chattels* : apport effectif.
— *duty* : droit de mutation.
fraudulent — : cession de biens au détriment des créanciers, assimilée à un *act of bankruptcy* (voir ce terme).
— *of a patent* : transmission de propriété d'un brevet.
— *of real estate* : transport d'immeubles.
voluntary — : disposition de biens à titre gracieux (pour être valable, doit s'effectuer par acte formel sous seing privé).
2° acte, contrat translatif de propriété, acte de cession.
deed of — : acte de cession.
derivative — : avenant aux actes ci-dessus.
3° *public* — : voiture publique.
public means of — : les transports en commun.
[A] — *(s) and transfers duty*: [U.K.] droits sur les transferts de propriété des valeurs mobilières.

conveyancer, conveyancing lawyer :
solicitor (# *notaire*) qui se consacre spécialement à la rédaction d'actes translatifs de propriété immobilière.

conveyancing : (J) rédaction (f) des actes translatifs de propriété (f) immobilière.

convict : [J] individu déclaré coupable et condamné à mort ou aux travaux forcés pour crime ou trahison (forçat, déporté, bagnard), [U.S.] détenu d'un pénitencier.
a former — : repris de justice.
— *colony* : lieu de déportation.
— *prison* # maison centrale.
— *station* : pénitencier.
gang of —*(s)* : chiourme.
to convict : déclarer coupable, condamner.
convicted *person* : condamné (m).

conviction : [J] condamnation (f).
previous —*(s)* : dossier du prévenu.
summary — : condamnation par un juge de paix.

convenience store : bazarette (f).

to cook *(the accounts)* : trafiquer (les comptes).

— 366 —

cooling off: (J) période (f) de réflexion (f) pour les adversaires dans un conflit.

cooperative advertising: frais (m pl) de publicité partagés entre le fabricant et le distributeur.

cooperative society: société (f) coopérative (a), coopérative (f).

co-ownership: propriété (f) partagée (et non copropriété: joint ownership).

coparcenary, coparcener: [J] (hist.) biens dévolus aux filles comme cohéritières d'une succession immobilière ab intestat.
Quelquefois, terme improprement employé pour désigner une succession indivise et un indivisaire.

copartnership: association, actionnariat ouvrier (opp. *profit sharing*), société à participation salariale.

coppers: [B] valeurs cuprifères.

copy: copie (f), transcription (f), *(of a book)* exemplaire, *(of a newspaper)* numéro, manuscrit destiné à l'impression.
[J] expédition (f).
certified – : copie authentique, ampliation.
certified true – : « pour copie conforme ».
– *of a deed*: expédition d'un acte.
examined – : copie attestée sous serment par la personne qui a examiné l'original du document.
exemplified – : exemplification, copie officielle d'un document, sous le sceau d'un tribunal ou d'un fonctionnaire compétent.
fair – : copie au net.
first authentic – : première expédition, grosse exécutoire.
office – : copie dressée par un fonctionnaire désigné à cet effet, sous le sceau de son office.
« *true* – » : « pour ampliation ».
(hist.) extrait du rôle de la cour seigneuriale (tenant lieu du titre de la propriété terrienne, voir *Copyhold*).
[C] *traced* –, *tissue* – : calque.
– *test*: test d'appréciation de l'intérêt suscité par un texte publicitaire.
copying *clerk*: expéditionnaire.

copyright: droit d'auteur, propriété littéraire, [U.K.] protection cinquantenaire après la mort de l'auteur (– *Act*, 1956).
– *case, action for infringement of* – : procès en contrefaçon.
– *matter*: œuvre protégée par la loi sur les droits d'auteur.
out of – : tombé dans le domaine public (ouvrage).
– *reserved*: tous droits réservés.
– *royalties*: produits de droits d'auteur.
to copyright *a book*: effectuer le dépôt légal.
The International – *Union*: l'Union internationale de Berne pour la protection de la propriété artistique et littéraire.

core activities: activités (f pl) essentielles (d'une société).

co-respondent: (J) co-défenseur (m) (en adultère).

to corner: accaparer, monopoliser.
– *the market*: accaparer le marché.
cornerer: accapareur.
cornering: accaparement.

coroner (*custos placitorum coronæ*): [J] (Engl., U.S.) officier d'ordre judiciaire et administratif à la fois, chargé de faire une enquête (*inquest*) en cas de mort violente ou suspecte.

corporal: corporel (a) (ayant trait au corps, à ne pas confondre avec *corporeal*).
– *defect*: défectuosité physique.
– *oath*: serment prêté en plaçant la main sur un objet sacré d'une religion (p. ex. la Bible).
– *punishment*: peine corporelle.

corporate: formant un corps.
[J] relatif à une personne morale, sociale, jouissant de la personnalité morale.
– *assets*: actif social.
– *banking*: banque d'entreprise.
– *body*: corps constitué, personne morale.
– *identity, image*: réputation d'une société.
– *minimum tax* # imposition forfaitaire annuelle à la charge des sociétés (I.F.A.).
– *name*: raison sociale.
– *objectives*: objectifs à long terme (fixés par le Conseil d'Administration).
– *planning*: plan de développement à long terme.
– *seal*: sceau d'une société.
– *stock*: actions d'une société.
– *town*: ville dotée d'un statut municipal.
– *world*: monde des affaires.
– *year*: exercice social.
Status of body – : personnalité civile.

corporation: corporation, corps constitué [U.S.] société, (hist.) corps de métier.
[J] entité dotée de la personnalité morale.
– *aggregate*: personne morale formée de plusieurs individus (p. ex. une société enregistrée, un corps municipal).
– *sole*: personne morale composée de personnes se succédant dans certaines charges ou fonctions, chacune de ces personnes constituant à elle seule la personne morale

— 367 —

tant qu'elle reste en fonction (p. ex. le roi pour la couronne, un évêque pour son évêché).
[U.S.] société commerciale de capitaux (société anonyme ou société à responsabilité limitée, correspondant à la *company with limited liability* du droit anglais).
business — : société de commerce enregistrée.
charitable — : société de bienfaisance.
municipal — : municipalité, conseil municipal.
public — : [U.S.] entité de droit public.
small business — : société commerciale de faible dimension.
[F] — *tax*: impôt sur les sociétés.
— *duty*: impôt prélevé sur le revenu de toute personne morale autre qu'une société de commerce pour compenser les droits de mutation après décès.

corporeal : corporel, doté d'une existence physique (a).
[J] — *hereditaments*: biens corporels transmissibles par héritage.
— *property*: biens corporels.

corps : [A] corps (m).
the diplomatic — : le corps diplomatique.

corpus : le corps, le capital (d'une fondation).
[J] masse successorale.
— *delicti*: corps de délit.
[F] le capital, en tant que distinct des intérêts qu'il rapporte, capital érigé en *trust*.

to correct : rectifier.
— *a statement*: rectifier une déclaration.
corrected *invoice*: facture rectifiée.
correct up to: mis à jour jusqu'au.

correction : correction.
[J] rééducation, réhabilitation, réforme (f).
correctional *institution*: maison de correction.

correspondence : courrier, correspondance, concordance.
— *clerk*: correspondancier.
[B] **correspondent** *security firm*: correspondant (m) (en matière de valeurs).
[F] **corresponding** *entry*: écriture conforme.
factor analysis of — : analyse factorielle de correspondance (statistique).

corroboration : corroboration, confirmation.
[J] **corroborating** *evidence*: preuve corroborante (indispensable en procédure criminelle), malgré l'aveu de l'inculpé.

corruption : corruption (f), trafic (m), altération (f).
— *of witness*: subornation.

costs : coût, frais, dépense, prix de revient, charge.
[J] frais d'instance et dépens. Ils comprennent : 1° les émoluments du *solicitor*; 2° les sommes à recouvrer par la partie gagnante ; 3° le cas échéant, la somme adjugée au *solicitor*, pour l'indemniser de ses frais. [U.S.] L'adjudication des frais n'a qu'une existence théorique. La partie demanderesse préfère souvent un compromis plus ou moins favorable.
to allow — : accorder les frais et dépens.
bill of — : état de frais.
cost of **custodian** : frais du curateur.
court — : frais de justice.
order to pay — : exécutoire de dépens.
untaxable — : faux frais.
[C] *actual, first, net, prime,* — : prix d'achat, de revient, coûtant, initial.
replacement (reequipement) — : prix de remplacement (rééquipement).
— *and freight (CF)*: coût et fret (C et F).
—, *insurance, freight (C.I.F.)* : coût, assurance, fret (C.A.F.).
— *account*: compte de charges.
— *accounting*: comptabilité analytique.
— *allocation*: imputation des coûts.
— *-book*: livre de charges.
— *keeping*: comptabilité de prix coûtants.
— *of management*: frais de gérance.
additional — : frais accessoires.
free of — : sans frais.
historical — : coût d'acquisition.
— *of maintenance*: frais d'entretien.
laid-down — : prix livré.
entertainment — : frais de représentation.
operating — : frais d'exploitation.
opportunity — : coût d'opportunité.
capital — : frais de premier établissement.
— *plus fee*: [U.S.] prix de revient plus honoraires.
to defray one's — : se défrayer.
[F] — *of capital*: coût du capital, de l'équipement.
— *center*: groupement des coûts.
— *containment*: maintien des coûts dans des limites fixées.
financial — : frais d'exploitation exprimés en numéraire.
— *of a share*: valeur d'achat d'une action.
— *variance*: écart des prix.
— *-volume-profit analysis*: analyse du rapport coûts-volume des ventes-bénéfices.
— *of living adjustment*: [U.S.] échelle mobile des salaires.
— *of living*: coût de la vie.
— *of living bonus*: indemnité de cherté de vie.
— *control*: surveillance des prix.
— *-push inflation*: inflation créée et maintenue par l'accroissement des prix de revient à la production indépendamment de la

demande.
— *-benefit analysis*: [U.S.] analyse des coûts et des rendements, analyse du rapport coût-profits (en termes de monnaie), analyse coûts-avantages.
opportunity — : coût d'opportunité.
to cost *an article*: établir le prix de revient d'un article.
costing: évaluation des prix de revient.
full costing: évaluation des prix de revient tous frais confondus.

cottage industry: petit artisanat.

council: conseil (m), assemblée (f).
Army — : conseil supérieur de la guerre.
borough — : conseil municipal de chacune des communes formant l'agglomération londonienne ou le comté de Londres.
cabinet — : conseil de cabinet.
city, town, municipal — : conseil municipal.
— *chamber*: chambre du conseil.
county — : conseil de comté (# conseil général).
the Court of Common — : le Conseil municipal de la Cité de Londres.
the King (Queen, Crown) in —, *the Privy* — : le Conseil privé (de la Couronne).
order in — : décret en conseil.
security — (UNO) : conseil de sécurité (ONU).
work's — : conseil d'entreprise.
[J] — *of legal education*: commission d'examen pour les candidats au barreau.
councillor: conseiller.

Council for Mutual Economic Assistance (CMEA): COMECON.

counsel: avocat, conseil ; avis, consultation, conseil.
— *('s) advice*: consultation.
— *in chambers*: conseil juridique, avocat consultant.
— *for the defence*: défenseur, (civ.) avocat de la défense.
— *('s) opinion*: avis motivé.
Queen's — *(Q.C.)*: conseiller de la reine, titre conféré à des membres éminents du barreau.
to be represented by — # comparaître par avoué.
to take — *('s) opinion*: consulter un avocat.
counselling: [U.S.] orientation par entretien personnel.

counselor-at-law: [U.S.] avocat inscrit à un barreau.

count: titre étranger de comte (titre anglais — *earl*, mais son épouse est une *countess*).
[J] chef d'accusation.

— *out*: ajournement d'une réunion.

to count: compter, calculer, dénombrer.
— *in*: comprendre dans un total.
— *out*: 1° ne pas comprendre dans un total ; 2° ajourner la séance (faute de quorum).
counting from: à compter de.

to countenance: favoriser, encourager, approuver, sanctionner (un acte).

counter: contre.
[J] — *-bond*: contre-promesse.
— *-case*: contrepartie (dans un arbitrage).
— *-charge*: contre-accusation.
— *-claim* (ou *counterclaim*) : demande reconventionnelle.
— *-deed*: contre-lettre.
— *-entry*: contre-écriture.
— *-enquiry* (ou *inquiry*) : contre-enquête.
— *-evidence*: preuve contraire.
— *-hand*: vendeur.
— *-offer*: contre-offre.
— *-plea*: réplique.
— *-security*: contre-sûreté.
— *-statement*: contre-mémoire.
— *-surety*: contre-sûreté.
— *-trading*: troc de produits entre deux pays.
— *-valuation*: contre-expertise.
— *-value*: contre-valeur, valeur d'échange.
[A] — *-verification*: contre-épreuve des voix (à une élection).

counter: comptoir, caisse, guichet.
— *cash book*: main courante de caisse.
over the — : au guichet.
paying — : bureau payeur.
[B] *over the* — *market*: marché hors cote.

to counteract: neutraliser.
— *fraud*: lutter contre la fraude.

counterfeit: contrefaçon (f), faux (m).
— *coin, money*: fausse-monnaie.
counterfeiter: contrefacteur.
counterfeiting: contrefaçon.

counterfoil: talon (d'un chèque), souche, coupon.
— *and leaf*: talon et volant.
— *book*: carnet à souche.

countermand: contre-avis, contrordre (m).
to countermand: *(an order)* annuler, rappeler, révoquer, *(a strike, etc.)* contremander, décommander.

counterpart: contre-partie (f) (voir *indenture*).
[J] duplicata (m).
tally — : souche (d'un reçu).

countersign: contreseing (m), visa (m).

countervailing *(duties)* : [D] (droits) compensateurs.

to counterweight: contrebalancer, équilibrer.

country: pays, territoire, nation, peuple.
– *of origin*: pays de provenance.
participating – : pays contractant.
– *planning*: aménagement du territoire.
– *risk*: risques encourus par un prêteur en raison d'une situation financière inquiétante dans le pays emprunteur.
to go to the – : en appeler au pays (par un vote).
[F] [B] – *banks*: organismes parabancaires.

county: comté (m).
[J] [A] [U.K., U.S.] division administrative et judiciaire du territoire, pourvue d'une certaine autonomie *(local government)*.
– *borough*: commune, réputée comté pour les besoins d'une administration décentralisée.
– *corporate*: ville ou cité érigée en comté par charte royale.
– *council*: assemblée locale # conseil général.
– *court* # tribunal d'arrondissement de première instance.
counties *palatine*: (hist.) les comtés de Chester, Durham et Lancaster (les seuls où subsistent des tribunaux de « *equitable law* » autonomes).
– *sessions*: sessions trimestrielles des tribunaux criminels itinérants dans les comtés.
– *-seat town*: chef-lieu de comté.

coupon: [F] [B] coupon, taux nominal.
– *bond*: obligation au porteur avec coupon.
– *date*: échéance d'un coupon.
– *pack*: emballage sur lequel est collé un bon de réduction.
– *due payable*: coupon dû.
– *rate*: taux d'intérêt nominal du coupon.
– *registered bonds*: obligations nominatives munies de coupon.
– *yield*: rendement au taux du coupon.
cum- – : coupon attaché.
ex- – : coupon détaché.
couponing: couponnage (m).
cross – : couponnage croisé.

course: courant, cours.
by – *of law*: suivant la loi.
– *of business*: marche des affaires.
– *of exchange*: cours du change.
in – *of manufacture*: en cours de fabrication.
in the – *of the duty*: dans l'exécution de la fonction.

court: cour, cour royale.
[J] cour de justice, tribunal. Les différents ordres d'instances et de juridictions se classent comme suit (Engl. et U.S.) : a) *inferior* – *(s)*: tribunaux de première instance, *superior* – *(s)* ou – *(s) of appeal* (U.S. *appeals*) : cours d'appel, – *(s) of last resort*: cours souveraines, jugeant en dernier ressort ; b) *civil* – *(s)*: tribunaux civils (qui appliquent concurremment le *C.L.* et l'*Eq.*), *criminal* – *(s)*: tribunaux criminels ; c) – *(s) of law* qui appliquent le *C.L.*, – *(s) of equity* qui appliquent l'*Eq.* ; d) – *(s) of record*: tribunaux dont les actes font foi jusqu'à inscription de faux, – *(s) not of record*: tribunaux inférieurs dont les actes ne font foi que jusqu'à la preuve du contraire.
arbitration – : tribunal d'arbitrage.
commercial – : tribunal de commerce, juridiction consulaire.
circuit – : tribunal (criminel) itinérant.
county – # tribunal de première instance.
– *crior*: huissier « aboyeur ».
– *day*: jour d'audience.
– *fees*: frais de justice.
– *of inquiry*: (milit.) commission d'enquête.
juvenile – : tribunal pour mineurs.
Law – *(s)*, – *House*: Palais de Justice.
– *-martial*: conseil de guerre (juge le personnel militaire d'après le *military law*, tandis que les civils sont jugés par une *military commission* d'après le *martial law*).
police – : tribunal de simple police.
in open – : à huis ouvert, en audience publique.
– *records*: archives judiciaires.
– *room*: salle d'audience.
single – : tribunal d'exception.
(Engl.) La législation a été définitivement consolidée dans « *The Supreme* – *of Judicature (Consolidation) Act, 1925* » dénommé plus brièvement *the Judicature Act, 1925*. Voici les principaux tribunaux existants à l'heure actuelle :
The Supreme Court of Judicature, composée de deux tribunaux : **the High Court of Justice,** tribunal de première instance et **the Court of Appeal,** cour d'appel. **The High Court of Justice** comprend trois divisions : **the Chancery Division, the Queen's Bench Division** et **the Probate, Divorce and Admiralty Division.**
The Court of Arches : Cour d'appel ecclésiastique de Cantorbéry, **the Courts of Chancery** : tribunaux de droit équitable (exception, voir *Chancery* et *counties palatine*), **the Court of Criminal Appeal** : cour d'appel en matière pénale, **the Court of Passage** : tribunal de première instance, à Liverpool, **the Court of Pie Poudre** : tribunal « des pieds poussiéreux », compétent en matière de litiges survenant dans les marchés et foires à Bristol, **the Central Criminal Court** (« *The Old*

Bailey ») : tribunal criminel principal et cour d'assises de Londres.
(Scot.) **Court of Session** : Cour Suprême d'Ecosse (en matière civile).
[U.S.] L'organisation judiciaire des Etats-Unis est fonction du régime fédéral de gouvernement. Il s'ensuit qu'il existe deux systèmes judiciaires, celui des Etats, et celui des Etats-Unis. Le nombre de titres et d'appellations analogues à ceux d'Angleterre, mais correspondant à des fonctions différentes, les modes de penser et d'agir fort dissemblables sur l'immense territoire de l'Union, exigent une prudence très grande de la part du traducteur.
The Judiciary Acts du 24 septembre 1789 ont créé l'organisation judiciaire fédérale, telle qu'elle existe encore actuellement, avec de légères modifications.
Le Sénat des Etats-Unis, siégeant comme « **Court of Impeachment** », correspond à la Haute Cour de Justice. **The Supreme Court of the United States** est Cour de cassation et Cour d'appel pour toutes les causes dépendant de la juridiction fédérale, elle se prononce également sur la constitutionnalité des lois du Congrès et fonctionne comme tribunal de première instance dans les procès où les Etats, les ministres et les agents diplomatiques sont parties. La juridiction d'appel est assurée par des **Circuits Courts of Appeals**, cours d'appel itinérantes (créées par la loi du 3 mars 1891), tandis que les **District Courts** correspondent aux tribunaux d'arrondissement de première instance. **The Supreme Court and Court of Appeals of the District of Columbia**, est également un tribunal fédéral.
Enfin, il existe plusieurs tribunaux à compétence spéciale, tels que **the Court of Claims**, qui juge les réclamations contre le Gouvernement des Etats-Unis, **the Court of Custom and Patent Appeals** : cour d'appel en matière de propriété industrielle. L'organisation judiciaire des Etats suit, à peu près le modèle fédéral. Ainsi, à New York, **the Supreme Court** exerce la juridiction civile de première instance, l'appel est porté devant les **Appellate Divisions** et la troisième instance est constituée par **the Court of Appeals**. Ces tribunaux sont des *superior courts*, et lorsqu'ils jugent en première instance, ils exercent une « *general jurisdiction* », c'est-à-dire qu'ils sont compétents en toutes matières contentieuses et même, concurremment, pour celles qui ressortissent normalement aux *inferior courts* dont il existe un grand nombre : **Municipal Courts, Magistrate Courts, Justices of the Peace, City Courts** et **County Courts**, ces deux derniers tribunaux étant compétents en matière civile et pénale à la fois.
The International Court of Justice (I.C.J.) :
La Cour Internationale de Justice (C.I.J.) siégeant à La Haye.
to be summoned to — : être cité en justice.
to go to — : aller devant les tribunaux.
to hold in — : tenir audience.
to rule out of — : débouter.
to settle out of — : régler une affaire à l'amiable.

court-hand : (écriture en) grosse.

courtesy : courtoisie, bons procédés.
by — *(of)* : à titre gracieux (de la part de).

covenant : contrat (m), convention (f), pacte (m), engagement (m).
[J] convention accessoire d'une transaction immobilière ou d'un acte de location (p. ex. promesse par l'acheteur de n'édifier sur le terrain qu'un immeuble locatif).
action of — *(C.L.)* : action en dommages-intérêts pour inexécution de contrat.
joint — : solidarité active.
positive — : stipulation de faire qch. ou d'effectuer un paiement.
— *of quiet enjoyment* : garantie contre trouble de la possession.
restrictive, negative — : stipulation de ne pas faire qch.
— *running with the land* # servitude foncière.
several — : solidarité passive.
— *(s) for title* : stipulations accompagnant l'acte de vente d'un bien-fonds.
usual — *(s)* : conditions locatives coutumières.
(hist.) — *of the League of Nations* : Pacte de la Société des Nations.

covenantee : [J] créancier.

covenanter : partie contractante (f).

cover : couverture, garantie, provision, marge (f), taux de couverture du dividende.
call for additional — : appel de marge.
to lodge stock as — : déposer des titres en nantissement.
to operate with, without — : opérer avec couverture, à découvert.
under registered — : sous pli recommandé.
without — : sans couverture, à découvert.
[ASS] *full* — : garantie totale.
[B] *call for additional* — : appel de marge.

to cover : 1° couvrir, se couvrir ; 2° comprendre, englober ; 3° parer à une éventualité.
— *short sales, shorts* : se racheter, racheter des actions vendues à découvert.
covering deed : acte d'autorisation.
covering letter : lettre d'envoi, lettre de confirmation.
covering purchase : rachats.

— 371 —

covering note : garantie.
[F] *covering on the spot market* : couverture au comptant.

coverage : champ d'application.
news — : (journ.) l'ensemble des nouvelles.
[F] — *rate* : taux de couverture.

covert : couvert (a).
[J] (hist.) *feme* — (ou *under coverture*) : femme en puissance de mari.

CPA : 1° *Certified Public Accountant* : [US] expert-comptable.
2° *Critical Path Analysis* : analyse critique méthodique.

craft : métier (m) artisanal.

craftmanship : artisanat (m), savoir-faire artisanal.

crash : [B] krach (m), effondrement des cours.

crawling peg system : [F] système de parité à crémaillère.

creative department : (dans une agence publicitaire) équipe (f) de créateurs.

creative group : groupe (m) d'étude et de création (f) (organisation et recherche), « les créatifs ».

credentials : lettres de créance, certificat d'un domestique, papiers d'identité.
— *committee* : comité de vérification des pouvoirs.

credit : crédit (m), réputation de solvabilité, imputation (f).
[J] *cross-examination to* — : questions posées à un témoin pour éprouver sa véracité.
to pass a — *vote* : voter un douzième provisoire.
[C] [F] — *ability* : solvabilité.
— *account* : compte créditeur.
— *balance* : solde créditeur.
blank — : crédit à découvert.
— *circulation* : circulation fiduciaire.
control of — : réglementation du crédit.
— *currency* : crédit fiduciaire.
— *document* : titre de crédit.
— *note* : bordereau de crédit, facture d'avoir.
— *method* : système de l'imputation.
— *rating* : estimation du crédit que l'on peut accorder à un client.
— *side* : avoir.
— *slip* : bulletin de versement.
— *squeeze, stringency* : restriction, resserrement du crédit.
— *transfer* : virement de compte à compte.

— *worthiness* : solvabilité (f).
— *(s) against net income tax* : [U.S.] déductions groupées (voir *deduction, exemption*).
— *(s) for overpayment* : imputation de l'excédent de perception.
— *(s) provision for taxes paid abroad* : clause prévoyant déduction des impôts payés à l'étranger.
cross — *relief* : déduction réciproque.
documentary — : crédit, accréditif documentaire.
frozen — : crédit bloqué.
full — : imputation intégrale.
granting of — *(s) for taxes paid abroad* : déduction pour impôts payés à l'étranger.
letter of — : lettre de crédit, accréditif.
long — : crédit à long terme.
opening of a — : ouverture de crédit.
overdraft — : crédit à découvert.
real estate — : crédit foncier.
secured — : crédit garanti.
situs — *approach (or solution)* : emploi simultané du critère du situs et du principe de la déduction.
tax — : crédit d'impôt.
title to — : titre de créance.
transaction upon — : opération à terme.
to pass to the — : porter au crédit.
to give s.o. — : faire crédit à qn.
to enter a sum to s.o. — : porter une somme au crédit de qn.
to credit *an account* : créditer un compte.
crediting *all of the tax paid* : accorder un dégrèvement total.
crediting a proportionate part of the tax paid : accorder un dégrèvement partiel.
[B] — *on securities* : crédit sur titres.
[ASS] — *insurance* : assurance contre le défaut de paiement.

creditor : créancier, créditeur (m).
chief — : créancier principal.
bond — : créditeur obligataire.
composition with — *(s)* : concordat.
— *in bankruptcy* : créancier dans la masse.
— *of the general body of the creditors in bankruptcy* : créancier de la masse.
— *of a creditor* : créancier en sous-ordre.
privileged (preferential) — : créancier privilégié.
— *on mortgage* : créancier hypothécaire.
paying off — *(s)* : désintéressement des créanciers.
scheme of composition between debtor and — : concordat amiable.
secured — : créancier nanti.
simple — : créancier chirographaire.
[J] — *('s) bill* : (Engl.) requête des créanciers d'une personne décédée en vue de répartir l'actif de la succession au prorata des créances.
[U.S.] requête d'un créancier muni d'un juge-

ment exécutoire, tendant à faire exécuter ce jugement sur certains biens du débiteur.
— *('s) relief*: protection du gage commun.
— *('s) suit*: action en recouvrement de créances, visant des biens déterminés du débiteur.
[C] — *side (of balance)*: compte créditeur.

creeping *(inflation)*: (inflation) rampante.

crime: crime (m).
[J] les crimes sont répartis arbitrairement en trois catégories : *treasons*: crimes de trahison, *felonies*: crimes proprement dits, et *misdemeanours* # délits graves.
(milit.) manquement à la discipline.
— *-sheet*: feuille de punitions.

criminal: criminel (a et m).
— *act, behaviour*: action, conduite, criminelle.
— *action*: action au criminel.
— *assault*: viol.
— *code*: code pénal.
— *conversation*: adultère.
— *court*: tribunal criminel.
— *damage*: infraction ayant causé des dégâts matériels graves.
— *Investigation Department (C.I.D.)* # Sûreté nationale.
— *law*: droit pénal.
— *leanings*: penchants criminels.
— *offence*: infraction criminelle.
— *procedure*: procédure criminelle.
— *record*: casier judiciaire.
the — *Records Office*: le service de l'identité judiciaire.
habitual — («*old lag*»): repris de justice, récidiviste (« cheval de retour »).

critical: critique (a).
— *path analysis*: analyse critique méthodique.

crisis: crise (f).
cabinet — : crise ministérielle.
economic — : crise économique.
financial — : crise financière.

criterion (pl *criteria*): critère (m).

crook: [U.S.] (fam.) escroc.

crop: récolte (f), moisson (f).
[J] [U.S.] *share-* — : colonat partiaire.

cross: contre-, anti-.
blue — *security*: [U.S.] Sécurité Sociale privée.
— *-account*: compte de contrepartie.
— *-action, cross-complaint*: action reconventionnelle, opposition.
— *-appeal*: appel incident.

— *-bill demand*: demande incidente formée par le défendeur contre ses co-défendeurs ou contre le demandeur et les co-défendeurs.
— *-checking*: recoupement.
— *default*: défaut croisé.
— *-defendant*: défenseur reconventionnel.
— *-entry*: contre passement.
— *-examination*: (civ. et cr.) interrogatoire par les parties de l'adversaire et de ses témoins, (tendant à déprécier leurs dépositions et jeter le doute sur la véracité et les facultés d'observation des déposants. Le rôle du juge se borne à décider de l'admissibilité des questions faisant l'objet de protestations de l'adversaire : *objection*).
— *-motion*: contre-plainte.
— *-plaintiff*: demandeur reconventionnel.
— *-question*: question posée au cours d'une *cross-examination*.
— *rates*: parités croisées.
— *reference tables*: tables de renvoi.
— *-summons*: contre-citation, citation au contraire.
— *-tabulation*: tableau à double entrée (statistique).

crossing off (out): radiation (d'une inscription).

crowding out: éviction (f).

crown: la Couronne, # l'Etat.
— *agency*: organisme d'Etat.
— *asset*: biens de la Couronne.
— *case*: affaire criminelle.
— *-colony*: colonie d'administration (britannique) directe.
— *debt*: créance de l'Etat.
— *-lands, estates*: biens domaniaux.
— *-law*: droit pénal.
— *-lawyer*: avocat du Gouvernement.
— *-liability Act*: loi sur la responsabilité de la Couronne.
The — *-Office*: les services administratifs de la Couronne.
The — *in Parliament*: [UK] le (pouvoir) législatif.

crucial: définitif, capital (a).

crude: brut, à l'état brut (a).
— *(oil)*: (pétrole) brut.
— *rate*: taux brut.
— *statement of facts*: exposé brutal des faits.

cruelty: cruauté (f), mauvais traitements (m pl).
[J] sévices (m pl).
extreme — : sévices graves.
mental — : excès et injures graves.

to crumble: [B] s'effriter.

cujus est solum ejus est usque ad coelum et ad inferos : celui à qui appartient le sol, il lui appartient jusqu'au ciel et jusqu'au milieu de la terre.

culprit : coupable (m et f).
[J] accusé, prévenu.

cum : avec.
— *coupon* : avec coupon.
— *dividend* : dividende attaché.
— *rights* : avec les droits de souscription.

cumulative : cumulatif (a).
[J] — *evidence* : témoignages concordants.
— *sentence* : confusion des peines (voir *sentence*).
[F] — *cash surplus* : bénéfice actualisé net.
— *dividend* : dividende cumulatif afférent à des actions privilégiées cumulatives et prélevé sur les bénéfices futurs, si celui de l'exercice est insuffisant.
— *interest* : intérêt accumulé.
— *office* : cumul de fonctions.
— *preference, preferred, share, stock* : action privilégiée à dividende cumulatif.
— *present value cash surplus as percentage of initial investment* : bénéfice actualisé unitaire (d'un projet).
— *voting* : faculté de réunir sur un seul candidat à un conseil d'administration toutes les voix dont on dispose.
cumulating *taxes* : impôt « en cascade ».

C.U.P. method (*comparable uncontrolled price*) : [F] méthode comparable du marché de pleine concurrence.

cur. adv. vult (curia advisari vult) : le tribunal désire délibérer.

curator : [J] (Scot.) curateur d'un aliéné.
curatorship : curatelle.

curb : coulisse (f).
— (*stone*) *broker* : coulissier.
— (*stone*) *market* : marché hors cote.
(hist.) — *Exchange* : [U.S.] La Bourse de New York.

to cure : guérir.
[J] — *a default* : purger le défaut.
— *a defect* : guérir un vice de contrat.

currency : circulation (f), cours (m) (de l'argent).
[A] monnaie, unité monétaire (ayant cours légal), devise.
— *adjustment* : réajustement des devises.
counterfeit — : fausse monnaie.
forced — : cours forcé.
— *gain, loss* : gain, perte de change.

foreign — : monnaie, devise étrangère.
inflation of — : inflation monétaire.
legal — (*tender*) : monnaie libératoire.
paper- — : papier-monnaie, circulation fiduciaire.
soft, hard — : monnaie faible, forte.
— *regulations* : réglementation des changes.
— *principle* (c.p.) : [U.K.] théorie suivant laquelle chaque billet émis doit avoir une contrepartie en monnaie.
to debase a — : déprécier la monnaie.

current : courant, actuel, qui a cours, en cours.
— *account* : compte courant, balance des opérations courantes (d'un pays).
— *act* : loi actuelle.
— *assets* : actif réalisable.
— *exchange* : taux actuel du change.
— *interest* : intérêt en cours.
— *liabilities* : passif exigible à court terme.
— *prepayment* : acompte.
— *price* : prix du jour.
— *year* : année en cours.
— *yield* : mesure du dividende perçu pour une action par rapport à son prix d'achat.

to curtail : réduire, contingenter.
— *expenses* : restreindre les dépenses.
curtailed *credit* : crédit amputé.

curtilage : [J] enclos avec habitation.

custodian : garde, conservateur (de musée, etc.).
[J] — *of property* : administrateur-séquestre.

custody : garde (f).
[J] garde d'un enfant.
— *procedure* : attribution de la garde d'un enfant.
judicial — (*in custodia legis*) : garde judiciaire.
into — : en état d'arrestation.
in safe — : sous bonne garde.
[F] *safe-* — *receipt* : récépissé (m) de dépôt.

custom : coutume (f), usage (m), [C] clientèle (f).
[J] droit coutumier.
(la coutume : — *and usage* devient droit coutumier : *legal* —, lorsqu'elle est «*immemorial, continued, peaceable, reasonable, certain, compulsory and constant*»).
— (*s*) *of the port* : selon les usages du port.

customary : habituel, coutumier (a).
— *clause* : clause d'usage.
— *residence* : résidence habituelle.
— *right* : droit coutumier.

customary: coutumier (m), recueil des coutumes.

customer: [C] client (m).
[F] déposant (m).
— *of doubtful standing*: client douteux.
— *profile*: profil du client-type (pour un produit donné).

customs: [D] douanes (f pl).
— *-agent*: commissionnaire en douanes.
— *agreement*: accord douanier.
— *bill outward*: acquit de sortie.
— *-broker*: agent en douanes.
— *clearance*: expédition en douane.
— *declaration*: déclaration en douane.
— *duties*: droits de douane.
— *entry*: déclaration en douane.
— *examination, formalities*: visite de la douane.
— *house*: bureau, poste de douane.
— *-house officer*: douanier.
— *note*: bordereau de douane.
— *permit*: acquit-à-caution.
— *regime, tariff*: régime, tarif douanier.
— *registered number*: [U.K.] numéro d'identification douanière d'un exportateur (5 chiffres).
— *regulations*: règlements douaniers.
— *seizure*: saisie douanière.
— *tariff*: tarif douanier.
— *union*: union douanière.
— *value*: valeur douanière.
— *walls*: barrières douanières.
Board of — *and Excises*: [U.K.] administration des impôts indirects et des droits de douane.
Bureau of — : [U.S.] administration des douanes.

— *Cooperation Council (C.C.C.)*: Conseil de Coopération Douanière (fondé en 1952, Siège à Bruxelles; 87 pays membres; langues: français, anglais).
International — *Pass*: carnet de passage en douane.

cut: réduction (f), compression (de prix).
— *in wages*: réduction des salaires.
— *price*: prix inférieur à la moyenne.
tax — *(s)*: dégrèvements fiscaux.
cut off: limite.
— *rate*: taux de rejet.
a five year — : limitation à cinq ans.
a tax loss — : disparition du droit au report déficitaire.
to cut back: réduire (les coûts).

cutback: réduction des coûts imposée par une baisse des profits et/ou des commandes; compression (f) (du personnel).

cutdown: baisse, réduction (f).
a — *inproduction*: une baisse de production.
to cut down: réduire (la production), rogner (les dépenses).

staff-cutting: mesures (f pl) de réduction du personnel.

cut-throat competition: concurrence (f) féroce, impitoyable.

cycle: cycle (m).
complete commercial — : cycle complet d'opérations.
trade — : cycle économique.
cyclical *variations*: variations cycliques.
cyclical *unemployment*: chômage conjoncturel.

D

to dabble *(on the stock exchange)* : [B] boursicoter.

dabbler *(on the stock exchange)* : boursicotier, boursicoteur.

daily : quotidien, journalier, par jour.
— *living allowance* : indemnité journalière.
— *loans* : prêts au jour le jour.
— *quotation sheet* : cote officielle quotidienne.
— *statement* : extrait journalier.

damage : dommage (m), dégâts (m pl).
actual — : dommage réel.
— *in transit* : avarie en cours de route.
— *to reputation* : atteinte au bon renom.
to make good a — : réparer un dommage.
[J] *cattle* — *feasant* : bétail trouvé en dommage.
— *to property* : dommage matériel.
[ASS] — *survey* : expertise d'avarie.
[E] *fresh water* — : avarie par eau douce.
sea — : fortune de mer.
to damage : endommager, détériorer, porter atteinte.
damaged goods : marchandises avariées.
damaged property : biens endommagés.

damages : dommages-intérêts, indemnité (f).
[J] *action for* — : action en dommages et intérêts.
compensatory — : compensation.
criminal — : infraction ayant causé des dégâts matériels graves.
exemplary, punitive, vindictive, — (ou *smart-money*) : réparation d'un préjudice moral assortie d'une pénalité.
general — : dommages-intérêts dus pour tout préjudice.
liquidated — : dommages liquidés.
genuine pre-estimation of — : clause pénale ayant pour unique but de déterminer préventivement le montant des dommages.
nominal — : dommages-intérêts symboliques (« 1 franc »).
special — : indemnité réclamée dans un cas concret, avec justification à l'appui.
substantial — : réparation d'un préjudice réel.
speculative — : dommages-intérêts réclamés (mais en principe refusés) pour préjudice extrapolé, non chiffrable (par exemple un manque à gagner).
to assess the — : évaluer le montant des dommages-intérêts.
to award — : accorder des dommages et intérêts.
to sue s.o. for — : poursuivre qn en dommages et intérêts.

to damnify : [J] léser, causer un préjudice.

danger money : prime (f) de risque.

data : données (f pl), informations.
— *based information system* : système d'information basé sur l'utilisation de toutes les données disponibles dans l'entreprise à l'effet de résoudre des problèmes spécifiques.
business — *processing* : informatique de gestion.
factual — : données concrètes.
primary — : éléments de base.
raw — : données brutes.

date : date (f).
[J] *certified* — : date authentique.
[C] — *of a bill* : terme (m), échéance (f) d'un effet.
at long, short — : à longue, courte échéance.
at two months' — : à deux mois de date.
— *of maturity* : date d'échéance.
due — : jour de l'échéance.
latest — : terme de rigueur.
of even — : à la date de ce jour.
one year after — : un an de date à date.
out of — : périmé.
up-to-date : à jour ; au niveau des derniers progrès, « dans le train », au point.
to date : à ce jour.
to date back : anti-dater, remonter à (une date).
short-dated bill : « papier court ».
[Journ.] **dateline** : dernier délai (avant bouclage d'un numéro).

dation : [J] dation (m).
tutory **dative** : tutelle dative.

daughter : fille (par rapport à ses parents).
— *in-law* : belle-fille.

day : jour (m).
[J] — *in-court* : jour de palais, audience.
clear — : jour franc.
[B] [C] [F] *account* — : jour de liquidation.
— *book* : journal.
— *labour* : travail à la journée.
— (s) *of grace* : jours de grâce.
— *release* : jour de congé payé pour une formation hors de l'entreprise.

— *(s') sight* : jours de vue.
— *order* : ordre valable le jour même.
— *to — money* : argent au jour le jour.
— *trade (daylight trade)* : transaction du jour.
market — : jour de bourse.
option — : jour de la réponse des primes.
pay — : jour de liquidation.
price of the — : cours du jour.
working — : jour ouvrable.

dead : mort, improductif, fictif (a).
— *account* : compte dormant.
— *-hand* : mainmorte.
— *-house* : institut médico-légal.
— *law* : loi tombée en désuétude.
— *loan* : emprunt irrécouvrable.
— *loss* : perte sèche.
— *money* : argent qui dort.
— *season* : morte saison.
— *stock* : valeur improductive.
[E] — *freight* : faux fret.
— *weight charter* : affrètement en lourd.
— *weight tonnage* : chargement en lourd.
— *works* : œuvres mortes.

deadline : date (f) limite, clôture (f) (ex. des inscriptions, d'un emprunt), échéance (f).

deadlock : impasse (f).
to be in a — : être dans l'impasse (négociations...).

(in-substance) defeasance : défaisance (technique d'ingénierie financière qui permet à une entreprise d'extraire une dette de son bilan sans la rembourser elle-même mais en demeurant juridiquement tenue comme débitrice principale).

deal : [C] affaire (f), marché (m), accord (m), négociation (f), contrat (m).
[B] transaction (f), opération boursière.
cash — : opération au comptant.
— *on the stock exchange* : coup de bourse.
even — : opération blanche.
package — : accord en bloc, transaction globale.

to deal : traiter, faire du commerce, négocier des valeurs.
— *firm* : traiter ferme.
— *flat, net* : traiter sans intérêt.
— *with* : négocier avec, traiter de, concerner.
— *with disputes* : statuer sur les différends.
dealt *with, in* : visé par, mentionné dans.
to be dealt with in the accounts : être comptabilisé.

dealer : négociant, marchand, commerçant, [U.S.] courtier de change, cambiste, intermédiaire (m), (pej.) trafiquant (m) de stupéfiants.
— *markets* : marchés de contrepartie.
retail — : détaillant.

second-hand — : revendeur, marchand d'occasion.
wholesale — : grossiste.

dealing : négociation, opération, transaction (f).
— *for a fall, a rise* : opération à la baisse, à la hausse.
— *profits* : profits réalisés par les marchands de biens.
dealings : menées commerciales, transactions boursières.
dealings for the account : opérations à terme.
dealings for money : opérations au comptant.
forward exchange dealings : opérations de change à terme.

dealt : traité (a).

dear : cher (a).
— *money* : argent cher.
to get **dearer** : réenchérir.

dearth : pénurie (f).

death : mort (f), trépas (m).
[J] décès (m).
— *action* : action en dommages-intérêts pour homicide d'un parent du demandeur, aux termes du « Lord Campbell's Act », 1846. Des *death statutes* analogues existent dans divers Etats de l'Union américaine.
— *certificate* : a) acte de décès ; b) extrait mortuaire.
— *duties* : droits de succession.
finding of presumed — # déclaration judiciaire de décès.
— *notice* : avis mortuaire.
— *penalty sentence* : condamnation à mort.
— *rate* : mortalité (taux de).
— *warrant* : ordre d'exécution.
civil — : (hist.) mort civile.
in contemplation of — : en prévision du décès.
proof of — : constatation de décès.
register of —(s) : registre mortuaire.
[ASS] — *benefit* : indemnité versée en cas de décès.

to debar *(s.o. from sth.)* : exclure, priver qn de qch.
[J] *debarred from succeeding* : exclu d'une succession pour cause d'indignité.
— *s.o. a right* : refuser un droit à qn.

debasement *(of currency)* : dépréciation (f) (de la monnaie).

to debate : débattre, discuter.
debated question : question controversée.

de bene esse : pour ce qu'il vaut.

debenture : reconnaissance de dette.
[J] – *capital, stock* : capital-obligations d'une société.
[D] certificat (m) de remboursement à la sortie des droits perçus à l'entrée.
[F] # obligation (f) non cautionnée, sans garantie spécifique : (au Canada : débenture).
– *-bond* : titre d'obligation.
– *conversion* : conversion d'obligations en actions.
– *-holder* : obligataire.
– *loan* : emprunt obligataire.
– *-stock* : obligation sans garantie.
irredeemable – : obligation non amortissable, non rachetable.
mortgage – : obligation hypothécaire.
unissued – *(s)* : obligations à la souche.

debit : débit (m).
– *balance* : solde débiteur.
on the – *side* : au débit.
to charge a sum to the – *of an account* : passer une somme au débit d'un compte.

debt, indebtness : dette (f), créance (f).
[J] *Crown* – : créance de l'Etat.
– *of record* : créance reconnue ou adjugée.
– *-claim secured by mortgage, mortgage debt* : créance hypothécaire.
proof of – : titre de créance.
secured – : créance garantie.
simple contract – : dette, créance simple.
specialty – : dette en vertu d'un acte.
unsecured – : créance chirographaire.
preferential – : créance privilégiée.
[C] *accruing* – : dette non exigible.
active – : dette active.
attached – : créance saisie.
bad – : créance irrécouvrable.
bonded – : dette garantie.
claimable, due, outstanding, – : créance exigible.
doubtful – : créance douteuse.
floating – : dette flottante, non consolidée.
funded – : dette consolidée.
liquid – : dette échue.
outstanding – : dette à recouvrer.
pledged – : créance garantie par gage.
privileged – : créance privilégiée.
qualified – : créance conditionnelle.
redemption of – : remboursement d'une dette.
release of – : abandon de créance.
– *restructuring (rescheduling)* : réaménagement des échéances des dettes.
secured – : créance garantie.
substitution of – : cession de créance.
to incur – : contracter des dettes.
to run into – : s'endetter.
to compound a – : transiger sur le montant d'une dette.
to set off a – : compenser une dette.

to summon for a – : assigner en paiement de créance.
to write off a – : apurer une dette.
unsecured – : créance chirographaire.
– *owed by us (liability)* : dette passive.
– *owed to us* : (créance figurant à l'actif) dette active.
[F] *the consolidated, funded* – : fonds consolidés, dette inscrite, perpétuelle, rentes sur l'Etat.
– *capacity* : limite d'endettement.
public, national – : dette publique.
foreign-held public – : dette publique à l'étranger, porteurs étrangers de titres de la dette publique.
methods of public – *issue* : modalités de l'émission de la dette publique.
types of issue of public – : types d'émissions de la dette publique.
public – *outstanding* : emprunts publics émis ou non remboursés.
ownership of public – : porteurs de titres de la dette publique.
redemption of the public – : amortissement ou rachat de la dette publique.
– *restructuring* : rééchelonnnement de dette.
public – *service* : service de la dette (intérêt).
– *-collector* : agent de recouvrements.

debtor : débiteur.
[C] – *account* : compte (m) débiteur.
– *attached* : débiteur saisi.
– *and creditor account* : compte par doit et avoir.
– *side* : débit, doit.
– *(s)-to-sales ratio* : rapport débiteurs-ventes.

decease : mort (f).
[J] [A] décès (m).

deceased, [U.K.] **decedent** : personne décédée, le défunt.
[J] de cujus *(in succession matters)*.
– *estate* : succession.

deceit : tromperie (f), fourberie (f).
[J] dol (m), fraude (f).
« *fraud and* – » escroquerie qualifiée.

deceleration : décélération (f).

deceptive : trompeur, mensonger, déloyal.
– *advertising* : publicité mensongère.
– *statement* : fausse déclaration.

to decide : décider, trancher, juger.
– *a case* : rendre un jugement.
decided : résolu, absolu, sans réserve.

decision : décision (f), délibération (f) (d'une assemblée), résolution.
[J] (sens général) toute réponse de droit :

judgment, decree, order, writ, warrant, (sens strict) énonciation du juge *(Eq.)* qui correspond au verdict (dans une procédure sans jury), arrêt (m).
means of resisting a — : moyens de recours.
to give a — : rendre une décision.
to reach a — : se prononcer.
to reverse a — : réformer un jugement.
[C] — *maker* : décideur.
— *making* : prise de décision.
— *Making Unit (D.M.U.)* : unité de prise de décision, groupe de décideurs.
— *tree* : arbre décisionnel, arbre de décision, graphique des décisions.
decisive oath : serment décisoire.

declarant : [J] déclarant (m).

declaration : déclaration (f).
[J] 1° déclaration ; 2° décision judiciaire ; 3° *[C.L.]* a) exploit introductif d'instance, b) dispositif de jugement.
— *against interest* : énonciations proférées à l'encontre d'intérêts propres, admises exceptionnellement comme preuve indirecte (voir *hearsay rule*).
— *of intention* [U.S.] # demande de naturalisation (voir *naturalization*).
— *of the poll* : proclamation du résultat du scrutin.
dying — *(s)* : déclarations in articulo mortis, auxquelles il est accordé la même valeur qu'à une — *against interest* (voir ci-dessus).
statutory — : déclaration sous serment.
[A] — *of income* : déclaration de revenu.
— *of solvency* : déclaration de solvabilité (consécutive à une liquidation volontaire).
tax — : [U.S.] déclaration estimative de l'impôt présumé (opp. *tax return* : déclaration définitive).
failure to file — : absence de déclaration.
[D] *customs* — : déclaration en douane.
[F] — *of dividend* : déclaration de dividende.
[B] — *day* : jour de réponse des primes.
— *of options* : réponses des primes.
[ASS] — *policy* : police d'abonnement, police flottante, ouverte.
(hist.) — *of Rights* : voir *Bill of Rights*.
[U.S.] — *of Independence* : déclaration de l'indépendance des Etats-Unis.
declaratory *judgment* : jugement déclaratoire.
declaratory statute : loi précisant la législation existante.

to declare : déclarer, se prononcer, proclamer.
— *s.o. a lunatic* : interdire qn en démence.
— *a trust* : établir un *trust* (voir *trust*).
— *in debt [C.L.]* : introduire une action en reconnaissance de dette.
— *the principal due* : avancer l'échéance par décision judiciaire.

— *a strike* : déclencher une grève.
declared : déclaré, reconnu, qualifié.
declared capital gains or losses : plus ou moins-values constatées (en comptabilité).
offence declared : fait qualifié (délit).

decline : baisse.
[B] — *in prices* : fléchissement des cours.
— *of stocks* : effritement des actions.
declining *balance method* : [U.S.] système de l'amortissement dégressif.

to decoy : leurrer, attirer dans un piège.
[J] — *a girl under age* : dévoyer, séduire une mineure.

decrease : réduction, compression (f), fléchissement, abaissement, amoindrissement (m).
[F] allègement (m).
to decrease : décroître, fléchir (activité).

decree : décision d'ordre judiciaire ou administratif.
[J] jugement rendu par une « *Court of Equity* » ou une « *Court of Admiralty* » (opp. *judgment*, dans une procédure en *C.L.*).
— *absolute* : jugement définitif.
arbitral — : sentence arbitrale.
— *in bankruptcy* : jugement déclaratif (de faillite).
— *in equity* : arrêt d'équité.
final — : jugement définitif.
interlocutory — : jugement interlocutoire.
— *nisi* : a) jugement provisoire ; b) jugement interlocutoire en matière de divorce, transformable ultérieurement en — *absolute* : jugement définitif, si la partie défenderesse ne parvient pas à le faire annuler dans le délai imparti (généralement 6 semaines. Voir *adjudication, judgment, order, rule, sentence*).
preamble to a — : attendus (m pl) d'un arrêt.
[A] décret (m), arrêté (m), ordonnance (f).
— *-law* : décret-loi.
to issue a — : promulguer un décret.
to pass a — : prendre un arrêté.

dedication : dédicace (f).
[J] fait de consacrer un bien-fonds à l'usage public (notamment de rendre publique une voie privée).

to deduce : déduire, conclure.

to deduct : déduire, défalquer, retrancher, soustraire, imputer.
all charges **deducted** : tous frais déduits.
after **deducting** : déductions faites.

deduction : déduction (f), défalcation (f), précompte (m), retenue (f).
[A] abattement (m), dégrèvement (m).
automatic — : retenue de plein droit.

— *allowed in respect of*: déduction autorisée au titre de.
— *at the source*: retenue à la source.
— *from the basic taxable income*: abattement, dégrèvement à la base.
— *from payroll*: retenue sur feuille de paye.
— *from the salary*: prélèvement sur le salaire.
personal —: déduction personnelle.
standard —: déduction forfaitaire.
— *(of tax) at the source*: stoppage (m), perception de l'impôt à la source.

deed: ation (f), acte (m), instrument (m).
[J] acte notarié, sur papier timbré, signé par les parties (stricto sensu acte translatif de propriété. Cette translation s'opère par traditio symbolica: *closing of title*: remise du titre. Voir *contract, conveyance*).
— *of arrangement*: accord, compromis, (écrit et signé), protocole d'accord.
counter —: contre lettre.
— *of covenant*: contrat; engagement de payer une certaine somme fixe à une organisation pendant un nombre déterminé d'années.
— *of gift*: acte de donation entre vifs.
— *of giving in payment*: dation (f).
— *of settlement*: acte de constitution.
— *of transfer*: acte de transport.
— *indented*: contrat synallagmatique.
— (ou *articles*) *of partnership*: contrat, acte, de société, d'association.
— *-poll*: acte unilatéral, contrat à titre gratuit.
private —: actes sous seing privé.
purchase- —: acte d'achat.
title- —: titre (constitutif) de propriété.
to draw up a —: établir un acte.
trust- —: acte fiduciaire, acte de fidéicommis, acte de fiducie.

to deem: estimer, réputer, présumer, regarder comme.
— *it right to*: estimer qu'il convient de.
deemed *to be*: censé, réputé être.
offence deemed (to): infraction qualifiée (de).
the following deductions shall be deemed applicable: les déductions suivantes sont réputées applicables.
this Act shall be deemed to have had effect as from: la présente Loi sera réputée être entrée en vigueur à compter de.

de-emphasis: [C] abstention de promouvoir la vente de certains produits en magasin.

deep-sea: haute mer (f).
— *-sea animals*: espèces pélagiques.
— *-sea fishing*: pêche hauturière.
— *-sea navigation*: navigation au long cours.

to deface: *(a stamp)* oblitérer, *(an account)* effacer.
defacing *coin*: dépréciation de la monnaie.

defalcation: défalcation, déduction, déficit.
[J] détournement de fonds, malversation financière.

defamation: diffamation (f) (voir *libel*, diffamation écrite, et *slander*, diffamation verbale).
defamatory: diffamatoire.

default: manquement à un engagement, défaillance.
[J] défaut, (civ.) non comparution (f), (cr.) contumace (f).
— *of heirs*: deshérence.
— *summons*: procédure sommaire en vue de recouvrer une dette liquidée en justice.
in — *of agreement*: faute d'accord.
judgment by —, *to* —: jugement par défaut, défaut contre partie.
to cure a —: purger le défaut.
to put in —: mettre en demeure.
[C] état de cessation de paiement.
— *interest*: intérêts pour défaut de paiement.
[B] — *price*: cours de résiliation.
[ASS] *protracted* —: carence de paiement garantie par un système d'assurance-crédit.
to default: tomber en déconfiture, manquer à ses engagements.
defaulter: [J] contumax (m), défaillant (m).
[B] défaillant, retardataire, failli, agent en défaut.
defaulting *party*: partie défaillante.

defeasance: [J] 1° annulation, abrogation; 2° contre-lettre.
— *clause*: clause résolutoire.

defeat: [J] annulation (f).

to defeat: déjouer, défaire, frustrer, faire échouer.
— *one's creditors*: frustrer, léser ses créanciers.
— *the object of*: faire obstacle à.

defect: défaut (m), défectuosité (f), vice (m), lacune (f), manque (m).
concealed —: vice caché.
conspicuous —: défaut apparent.
latent —: vice rédhibitoire.
defective: défectueux, imparfait.
to render defective: rendre inopérant.

defence, [U.S.] **defense**: défense, justification (f).
[J] la défense.
counsel for the —: (civ.) avocat de la défense, (cr.) défenseur.
peremptory —: défense au fond.

statement of — : conclusions de la défense, signification des défenses.
witness for the — : témoin à décharge (voir aussi *affirmative defence*).
self- — : légitime défense.

defendant : [J] (civ.) défenseur, défenderesse, (cr.) accusé, accusée, *(on appeal)* intimé, intimée.
plea of the — : réponse au fond.

defender : défenseur.
— *of the Faith* : défenseur de la Foi.

to defer : différer, retarder, ajourner, atermoyer.
— *a payment* : différer un paiement.

deferment : (J) ajournement (m), remise (f) (d'une affaire).
[F] — *factor* : facteur d'escompte.

deferral : [F] report (m), [U.S.] report de l'imposition (du revenu des filiales étrangères de sociétés américaines) au moment de la distribution.

deferred : différé (a).
[A] — *pay* : rappel de traitement, (milit.) arriéré de solde (payable lors de la libération).
[C] [F] — *annuity* : rente à paiement différé, dont le premier versement sera différé.
— *charges* : frais différés.
— *tax charges* : fiscalité latente active (les impôts payés sont supérieurs à la charge fiscale comptabilisée).
— *credits* : crédits prorogés.
— *tax credits* : fiscalité latente passive (les impôts exigibles sont inférieurs à la charge fiscale comptabilisée).
— *dividend* : dividende différé.
— *income tax* : impôt sur le revenu reporté.
— *payment* : paiement par versements échelonnés.
— *shares, stock* : actions différées.
[J] — *creditor* : créancier (m) d'un failli (m) dont la dette ne pourra être honorée qu'après que les autres créanciers auront été remboursés.

defiance : défi provocation.
in — *(of)* : au mépris (de).

deficiency : insuffisance (f), manque (m), défaut (m), déficit (m), découvert (m), pertes (f pl).
[J] — *judgment* : jugement condamnant le débiteur hypothécaire ou gagiste, à acquitter la différence entre le montant de sa dette et le produit du bien réalisé.
mental — : déficience mentale.

[A] *to assess a* — : établir un impôt supplémentaire.
— *bills* : crédits additionnels, recettes additionnelles, collectifs budgétaires, pour couvrir un déficit budgétaire.
— *payment* : [U.K.] subvention à l'agriculture ; paiement différentiel.
[C] découvert (m).
— *payment* : paiement différentiel.
[F] *paid-up capital* — : insuffisance du capital versé.
— *in tax* : redressement fiscal.
to make up a — : combler un déficit.

deficit : déficit (m), moins-value (f).
[C] [F] [U.S.] *operating* — *(s)* : pertes d'exercice.
budget — : déficit budgétaire.
to cover a — : combler un déficit.

to define : définir, fixer, déterminer.
as **defined** : tel qu'il est défini.
taxation year defined : définition de l'exercice fiscal.

definite : précis, défini, délimité (a).
[J] — *certificate* : titre définitif.
[C] — *order* : commande ferme.

to deflate : amener la déflation (de la monnaie), ramener une série statistique exprimée en prix courants à des prix constants.

deflation : dégonflement (m), déflation (f).
— *policy* : politique déflationniste.

deforcement : [J] usurpation (f), détention illégale de personnes ou de biens.

to defraud : frauder.
— *the Revenue* : frauder le fisc.
defrauder : fraudeur, spoliateur.

to defray : défrayer, prendre à sa charge.
— *s.o.'s expenses* : défrayer qn.

degree : degré (m).
[J] — *of relationship* : degré de parenté.
[U.S.] *murder in the first* — : assassinat.
[U.S.] *murder in the second* — : meurtre, homicide par imprudence, etc.
[U.S.] « *third* — » # « chambre des aveux spontanés », « passage à tabac ».
[A] grade universitaire.

degression : [A] diminution progressive de l'impôt sur le revenu.
— *scales* : barèmes dégressifs.

degressive : dégressif (a).
— *taxation* : impôt dégressif.

to delate: dénoncer, accuser.

delay: retard (m), délai (m), prorogation (f), sursis de paiement (m).
deliberate — : retard intentionnel.
penalty of so much per day of — : pénalité de tant par jour de retard.
« *the law's* —(s) » : les lenteurs (f) de la loi.
to delay a payment: différer un paiement.
delaying: dilatoire.

del credere: [C] ducroire.

delegata potestas non potest delegari: une autorité déléguée ne peut être déléguée.

delegate: délégué, [B] commis de Bourse (m).

to delegate: déléguer.
delegated legislation: disposition réglementaire prise en application d'une loi, # règlement d'application.
delegatee: délégataire (m).

delegation: délégation (f), subrogation (f).
— *of power*: délégation de pouvoir.
trade — : délégation commerciale.

to delete: effacer, rayer, supprimer, radier, retrancher, annuler.
deletion: suppression (f).

deliberate: délibéré, intentionnel, prémédité (a).

to deliberate: délibérer (sur), débattre (de).

deliberation: délibération (f), débat (m), prudence (f), circonspection (f).
deliberative assembly: assemblée délibérante.

delict: [J] délit (m).

delinquency: délinquence (f), culpabilité (f), délit (m), faute (f), créance douteuse (f).
[J] *juvenile* — : enfance délinquante.

delinquent: coupable, fautif (m).
[A] [U.S.] — *return*: déclaration tardive.
— *taxes*: majorations pour retard dans le paiement de l'impôt.

to deliver: livrer, transmettre.
[J] signifier, notifier, prononcer.
— *a contract*: conclure un marché.
— *in trust*: déposer, mettre en dépôt.
— *free of payment*: livrer franco.
delivered: rendu, livré.
[J] *the judgment shall be delivered in English*: le jugement sera rendu en anglais.

[C] *to be delivered*: livrable à domicile.
[E] *goods delivered free on board*: marchandises rendues franco bord.

deliverance: déclaration, expression d'opinion, libération.
[J] 1° prononcé, jugement ; 2° verdict rendu par le jury.
second — : nouvelle ordonnance de mainlevée à la suite d'un désistement d'instance.

delivery: livraison (f).
[J] 1° *(of property, of goods)* tradition, transfert, *(of a legacy)* délivrance, *(of a deed)* signification ; 2° accouchement.
— *of deed*: voir *closing of title*.
— *of a writ*: signification d'un acte.
actual — : tradition effective.
conditional constructive, symbolical, — : tradition théorique (l'accord des volontés « *that title passes* » est suffisant pour légaliser le transfert. Voir *escrow*.
writ of — : exécutoire pour reprise de tous biens autres que terres ou argent.
[C] *cash on* — : payable à réception.
certificate of — : vu-arriver.
— *date*: date de livraison.
free — : livraison franco.
for — : bon de réception.
— *order*: bon de réception.
future — : livraison à terme.
payment on — : livraison contre remboursement.
short — : manque à la livraison.
— *terms*: conditions de livraison.
[F] transmission de titres au porteur.
[B] — *of stocks*: cession de titres.
to sell for — : vendre à couvert.
non- — : défaut de livraison.
[A] *General* — : [U.S.] poste restante.

delusional insanity: [J] folie sensorielle.

dem: [B] excès de la demande.

demand: demande (f), réclamation (f), revendication (f), prétention (f).
— *analysis*: analyse (des éléments) de la demande.
— *curve, demand schedule*: courbe prévisionnelle de la demande.
supply and — : l'offre et la demande (en économie).
on — : sur demande, à la demande.
overall — : demande globale.
effective — : demande « effective » (expression keynésienne qui doit être comprise dans le sens de : demande attendue résultant de l'ajustement entre offre et demande globales).
— *-pull inflation*: inflation créée et maintenue par une demande supérieure à la capacité de production.

[J] 1° sommation (f), mise en demeure ; 2° requête (f).
cross — : demande reconventionnelle.
[F] — *deposit* : dépôt à vue.
— *note*, — *for the tax* : avertissement (m) du fisc, sommation (f).
[C] — *bill* : traite (f) à vue.
— *loan* : prêt à demande.
— *note, payable on* — : billet, billet à ordre, payable à vue.
in full of all — *(s)* : pour solde de tous comptes.
[A] — *of returns* : demande de communication.
[B] — *rate* : cours à vue.

to demand : demander, solliciter, exiger, réclamer.
— *against s.o.* : requérir contre qn.
— *damages* : réclamer des dommages et intérêts.

demandant, demander : [J] demandeur dans une action réelle.

demarcation : classification (f).
— *problem* : problème de classification du personnel.

demesne : [J] possession (en toute propriété).
— *of the Crown* : domaine de la Couronne.
— *lands* : terres domaniales.

demisable : [J] cessible.

demise : [J] 1° cession à bail ; 2° *(of lands)* affermage, *(by will)* legs, transmission, *(of title)* transfert, transmission ; 3° décès (sp. d'un monarque).
— *of the Crown* : succession au trône.

to demise : léguer, faire transport, céder, affermer, donner à bail.

demonetization : démonétisation (f).

demonstration : manifestation politique, populaire.
demonstrator : manifestant (m).

to demote : rétrograder (par suite d'une sanction disciplinaire).

demotion : [U.S.] rétrogradation (f).

demur : hésitation, objection (f), scrupule (m).
[J] **to demur** : produire une exception.
demurrable : opposable.

demurrage : [A] 1° a) surestaries, b) droits de surestarie ; 2° (chemins de fer) a) magasinage, b) droits de magasinage.
on — : en souffrance.

demurrer : [J] [C.L.] exception péremptoire, fin de non-recevoir.
(en Angleterre, maintenue en procédure criminelle, au civil, remplacée par « *raising a point of law* », aux Etats-Unis, par « *motion to dismiss for failure to state a cause of action* »).
(Engl.) — *book* : dossier d'une procédure.

denial : dénégation (f), déni (m).
[J] — *of justice* : déni et justice.
formal — : démenti formel.
general — : dénégation absolue (d'un crime ou délit, d'une accusation).
special — : dénégation sur un point de l'accusation.

denizen : indigène, habitant.
[J] (Engl.) étranger ayant obtenu la « petite naturalisation » par lettres patentes royales (*letters of* **denization**), qui lui confèrent la qualité de sujet britannique, sans lui en donner tous les droits.

denomination : coupure (f), titre (m).
[B] 1° coupure d'obligation ; 2° nombre d'actions d'un certificat.
small — *(s)* : petites coupures.

to denounce : dénoncer.
denouncer : dénonciateur.
[J] **denounciative** : comminatoire.

denunciation : [J] accusation publique, dénonciation.
right of — *of a treaty* : faculté de dénonciation d'un traité.

to deny : nier, contester, priver.
— *aid* : refuser de porter secours.
to be **denied** *a right* : être frustré d'un droit.

department : département, service (m).
[J] [U.S.] — *trial* : poursuites disciplinaires.
[A] [U.S.] — ministère.
— *of State* : Ministère des Affaires Etrangères.
[C] [U.S.] — *store* : grand magasin.
departmental *committee* : comité ministériel.
departmental *order* : arrêté ministériel.
departmental *store* : grand magasin.

departure : départ (m), écart (m).
[J] changement d'argumentation en cours de procédure.
— *from the provisions of an act* : dérogation aux dispositions de la loi.
— *from the standards* : procédés contraires aux règles.
[ASS] déroutement intentionnel de navire (entraînant annulation de la police d'assurance et de la charte-partie).

to depend: dépendre de, être subordonné à, [J] être pendant.
  dependable: digne de foi, bien fondé, fiable.
  depending on *the method*: selon la méthode.

dependant: pensionnaire (m), protégé (m).

dependence, dependency: protectorat (m), fait d'être à la charge de qn.
  [F] *load of* — : nombre de personnes à charge.
  [J] *to be in* — : être pendant.

dependent: 1° personne à charge (f).
  dependents: charges de famille.
  dependents' allowance: allocations familiales.
  — *spouse*: conjoint à charge.
  2° à charge (a).
  — *child*: enfant à charge.
  — *relative relief*: déduction, dégrèvement pour parents ou alliés à charge.
  relative — *on the taxpayer*: personne à la charge du contribuable.

depletion: épuisement (m), raréfaction (f).
  — *allowance*: provision pour reconstitution de gisement.
  — *cost method*: [U.S.] méthode de calcul de la déduction pour épuisement d'un bien naturel.
  percentage — *method*: méthode de calcul de la déduction pour épuisement d'un bien naturel en pourcentage du revenu brut :
  — *unit*: unité de dépréciation servant de base à la déduction pour épuisement d'un bien naturel.

deponent: [J] 1° signataire d'un affidavit ; 2° témoin déposant (voir *deposition*).

(rural) depopulation: exode (m) rural.

deportation: [J] [A] expulsion d'étranger.
  — *order*, [U.S.] *warrant of deportation*: arrêté d'expulsion.

deposal: destitution (f), déposition (f).

to depose: [J] déposer.

deposit: dépôt (m), dépôt de garantie.
  [J] consignation (f) *(pledge)*, cautionnement *(security)*, arrhes (f pl) *(earnest money)*.
  — *and Consignment Office*: Caisse des dépôts et consignations.
  to pay a — : verser un cautionnement.
  [D] **to deposit** *a customs duty*: payer un cautionnement (remboursable) sur droits de douane.
  [F] — *account, time* — : compte de dépôt à terme.
  — *on current account*: dépôt en compte courant.
  — *on fixed accounts, for a fixed period*: dépôt à échéance fixe.
  bank, general, — : dépôt en banque.
  sight — : dépôt à vue.
  cash — : dépôt en espèces.
  demand — : dépôt à vue.
  — *slip*: bordereau de versement.
  fixed — : dépôt à échéance fixe.
  S.A.Y.E. (save as you earn) — : plan d'épargne individuel.
  (sum) on — : (somme) en dépôt.
  depositary: dépositaire (m), consignation (m).
  depositary institution: établissement financier qui accepte des dépôts publics.
  [J] (administrateur) : séquestre.
  depositing *of documents*: apport de pièces.
  deposition: déposition (f), destitution (f).
  [J] 1° déclaration sous serment d'un témoin ; 2° témoignage en justice consigné par écrit ; 3° # affidavit.
  depositor: déposant (m).
  depositor's book: livret d'épargne.

to depreciate: déprécier, amortir.
  countries of **depreciated** *currency*: pays à monnaie faible.

depreciation: dépréciation (f).
  [C] [F] amortissement (m), moins value résultant de l'usure (voir *obsolescence*).
  accelerated, declining balance, straight-line — : amortissement accéléré, dégressif, linéaire.
  annual — : amortissement annuel.
  basis for — : taux d'amortissement.
  — *allowance, deduction*: annuité d'amortissement.
  fixed — : amortissement constant.
  — *on diminishing values*: amortissement dégressif.
  additional first year, bonus — : déduction supplémentaire d'amortissement.
  — *guideline*: tableau des durées d'utilisation des biens.
  free — : amortissement libre.
  depreciable *assets*: biens amortissables.

depressed *(market)* : [B] (marché) languissant (a).

depression: [C] crise (f), dépression (économique), marasme (m) (des affaires).

deprivation: privation, révocation, destitution (f).
  — *of civil rights*: déchéance des droits civiques.
  — *of office*: révocation d'emploi.

depth interview *(market research)*: entretien (m) approfondi avec un client (étude de marché).

deputation : les députés, la représentation nationale.

deputy : représentant (de qn), adjoint, député français, *(of an official)* délégué, *(of a judge)* substitut, suppléant, *(of a managing director)* sous-directeur, *(of a chairman)* vice-président.
— *chief clerk* : sous-chef (de bureau).
to deputize *(for s.o.)* : remplacer (qqn).

to derate : dégrever.
derating : dégrèvement.
derating *scheme* : programme de dégrèvement fiscal.

to deregulate : assouplir (les réglementations).

deregulation : déréglementation (f), libération (f) des contraintes étatiques, libéralisation (f).
financial — : libéralisation financière.

derelict : épave (f).
[J] bien sans maître, sp. navire abandonné en mer.
— *land* : lais et relais.

dereliction : délaissement (m).
[J] 1° abandon de biens mobiliers ; 2° recul de la mer (voir *derelict land*).
— *of duty* : manquement au devoir.

derivable : dérivable (a).
income — *(from)* : revenu envisageable (provenant de).

derivative : dérivé (a).
[J] — *action* : voir *class action*.
— *conveyance* : avenant à un acte translatif de propriété.
— *title* : droit (de propriété) acquis indirectement.

to derive : provenir.
earnings **derived** *from* : salaire provenant de.
salaries **derived** *by persons domiciled in France* : salaires perçus par des personnes domiciliées en France.

to derogate : déroger, porter atteinte à.
« *No one can* **derogate** *from his own grant* » # « foi sacrée des contrats ».

derogation : dérogation, atteinte, diminution (f).

derogatory : dérogatoire (a).
[J] — *clause* : clause testamentaire autorisant sous réserves les changements que les circonstances pourraient imposer. D'une manière générale, les tribunaux y passent outre.

descent : descendance.
[J] transmission de biens par voie de succession ab intestat (voir *intestate succession*).
property **descended** : biens transmis par succession.

to describe : décrire, viser, signaler.
described *in paragraph* : visé à l'alinéa.
property that was **described** *in an inventory* : biens qui figuraient dans un inventaire.

description : description (f), libellé (m).
[A] signalement.
[C] désignation (de marchandises).
descriptive *return* : état signalétique.

desertion : désertion, *(of wife, etc.)* abandon, (milit.) désertion.
[U.S.] *obstinate* — : abandon de domicile conjugal sans esprit de retour.

design : dessein (m), intention (f), projet (m), conception (f).
[J] [C] modèle (m).
[U.K.] *copyright in a* —, [U.S.] — *patent* : propriété industrielle.
industrial — : création de modèle industriel.

to design : concevoir.

designer : créateur (m) d'un projet, concepteur (m).

to designate *(as)* : désigner, qualifier (de).
designated *surplus* : surplus désigné.

desk : bureau, caisse (dans un magasin).
— *audit* : vérification sur pièces.
— *-banging* : claquement de pupitres (au Parlement).
— *drawer company* : société inactive.
[C] — *research* : étude du marché d'après des documents de seconde main.

destitute : privé de ressources, dans le dénuement, enfant pauvre.
destitution : misère (f).

detachment : détachement.
on — : détaché.

detail : détail (m), particularité (f), précision (f).
for further — *(s)* : pour plus ample informé.

to detain : retenir, détenir, garder.
detaining *Power* : puissance détentrice.
detainee : détenu.

detainer : [J] *forcible detainer:* prise de possession (d'un immeuble) sans autorisation.
unlawful — : détention illégale d'un bien.
writ of — : mandat de dépôt confirmant l'incarcération d'un individu déjà détenu pour un autre motif.

detaxation : reduction de la fiscalité.

detention : [J] *(in prison, of money due, etc.)* détention (f), *(of a ship)* arrêt.
— *on suspicion,* — *awaiting trial:* détention préventive.
house of — : maison d'arrêt.
[A] — *camp:* camp d'internement.
(milit.) — *allowance:* indemnité journalière.
— *barracks:* locaux disciplinaires.
[D] — *of goods:* retenue de marchandises.

deterioration : détérioration (f), perte de valeur.

determinable : déterminable (a), soumis à une condition résolutoire.
[J] — *contract:* contrat résoluble.
— *life estates:* usufruit à vie (sp. en faveur de la veuve, voir *dower*).

determination : détermination.
[J] 1° a) décision judiciaire dans une affaire donnée ; b) arrêt, sentence.
2° *(of a contract)* a) résolution, résiliation ; b) expiration.
— *clause:* clause résolutoire.
— *of compensation:* détermination de l'indemnité compensatoire.
notice of — : dénonciation (d'un contrat, d'une association, etc.).

to determine : déterminer, décider, régler.
[J] mettre fin à, résoudre, résilier.

detriment : détriment (m), préjudice (m), perte (f).
without **detriment (to)** : sans préjudice (de).
detrimental to : préjudiciable à.

devaluation : dévaluation.

devastavit : « il a gaspillé ».
[J] manquement d'un administrateur ou exécuteur aux devoirs de sa charge, qui le rend personnellement responsable à l'égard des créanciers ou successeurs.

to develop : 1° développer, mettre en valeur, aménager.
— *a district:* [U.S.] mettre en valeur une région.
2° lotir.
developer : lotisseur.
the **developing** *countries:* pays en voie de développement.

development : aménagement, expansion, progrès (m), accroissement, création (f), perfectionnement (m), élaboration, réforme, augmentation (f).
— *areas:* (politique des) zones à développer.
— *companies:* sociétés d'exploitation.
— *of building land:* viabilisation de terrain à bâtir, lotissement d'un terrain.
— *licence:* permis de mise en valeur.
— *planning:* see « corporate planning ».
policy of — : politique d'expansion économique.
under — : en cours d'exploitation.

deviation : déviation (f), biais (m), dérogation (f), écart (m).
— *clause:* clause « changement de route ».
standard — : écart-type (statistique).

device : moyen (m), invention (f), mécanisme (m), stratagème (m).
[J] *(copyright in design)* dispositif (m), arrangement (m).
gambling — : appareil de jeu truqué.

devise : [J] disposition testamentaire de biens immobiliers, soit à titre universel *(residuary —)*, soit comme legs *(specific —)*.
executory — : disposition testamentaire comme ci-dessus indiquée, valable sous condition suspensive (p. ex. : à la majorité, au moment du mariage, etc.).

devisee : [J] institué, héritier testamentaire, légataire.

devisor : [J] testateur.

devolution : dévolution, transmission (f).
to devolve upon : incomber à, échoir à.

diary method : (C) méthode (f) du calendrier (m) (étude portant sur un échantillon de consommateurs et sur les objets ou produits qu'ils achètent au jour le jour).

dictum : [J] opinion incidente du juge contenue dans les attendus, sans portée directe sur le litige, qui ne peut être invoquée comme précédent (se dit aussi : obiter dictum).

to die intestate : décéder intestat.

dies : jour (m).
[J] terme (m).
— *non:* fête légale.
sine die: (ajournement) pour un temps indéfini, sans indication de terme.

difference : différence (f), contestation (f), désaccord (m).
  to pay the — : faire l'appoint, payer le supplément.
  to reconcile the — *(s)* : mettre d'accord.
  [B] — *between cash and settlement prices (contango)* : report (m).

differential : différentiel, particulier (a).
  — *compensation* : sursalaire de nuit.
  — *rate* : tarif différentiel.
  — *resources* : ressources particulières.
  [A] — *income tax* : taux différentiel en matière d'impôt sur le revenu.
  — *taxation on property* : taux différentiel en matière d'impôt sur le capital.
  [C] — *advantage* : élément d'un produit qui le fait préférer à un autre.

differentiation : [F] discrimination (fiscale).

digamy : [J] second mariage après la mort de la première femme.

digest : [J] digeste (m), recueil de lois et de décisions jurisprudentielles (annoté).
  (hist.) *the* — : le Digeste (de Justinien).
  [B] **digested** *issue* : émission bien placée.

digit : chiffre (m).
  two — *inflation* : inflation à deux chiffres.

dignity : dignité (f).
  [J] titre héréditaire (transmissible en tant que bien incorporel).

dilapidations : [J] réparations locatives nécessaires à l'expiration d'un bail.
  [F] — *payment* : frais de remise en état.

dilatory : dilatoire (a).
  [J] [C.L.] — *pleas* : exceptions dilatoires visant l'incapacité des parties ou l'incompétence du tribunal (voir *abatement*).
  — *methods* : moyens dilatoires.

diligence : diligence (f), application (f).
  [J] *due* — : diligentia bonis patris familiæ.
  — *search* : recherches minutieuses.

to dilute equity : [F] diluer l'intérêt des valeurs.

to dip : [C] s'infléchir ; [B] baisser.

diplomatic bag, [U.S.] **pouch** : valise diplomatique.

direct : direct, immédiat, sans intermédiaire, catégorique (a).
  [J] — *cause* : cause immédiate.
  — *contract* : contrat sans intermédiaire.

— *examination* : interrogatoire du témoin par la partie qui l'a cité.
— *expenses* : frais spéciaux (opp. *overhead expenses*).
— *evidence* : preuve directe.
[F] — *taxation* : imposition directe.
[C] — *costing* : approche par les coûts directs.
— *mail* : vente par correspondance.
— *selling* : vente sans passer par un intermédiaire (détaillant).
— *trade* : commerce de gros.

direct : directement (adv).
  to hand over the money — : payer de la main à la main.

to direct : diriger, ordonner, prescrire, enjoindre, conseiller, guider.
  as **directed** : conformément aux instructions.
  — *the attention to* : attirer l'attention sur.
  — *the jury* : instruire le jury (sur un point de droit).

direction : direction, administration (f), ordre, prescription (f).
  [J] exposé de la législation fait au jury par le juge lorsque le verdict dépend d'un point de droit *(directed verdict)*.
  [A] **directions** : directives, instructions.

director : administrateur d'une société, gérant d'une S.A.R.L.
  [J] — *of Public Prosecution (D.P.P.)* # Procureur Général.
  [F] [C] *board of* — *(s)* : conseil d'administration.
  — *(s') fees* : jetons de présence des administrateurs, rémunérations des dirigeants de sociétés.
  — *(s') percentage of profits* : tantième des administrateurs.
  — *(s') report* : compte rendu annuel du Conseil d'Administration à l'A.G. des actionnaires.
  managing — : administrateur délégué.
  majority managing — : gérant majoritaire.
directorate : directoire.

directory : annuaire, répertoire.
  [J] [U.S.] conseil d'administration d'une société.
  [D] bulletin des douanes.
  shipping — : répertoire maritime.
  trade — : annuaire commercial.

disability : [J] incapacité (juridique ou physique), *(of persons)* incapacité légale, *(imposed on property)* servitude.
  — *of coverture* : incapacité de puissance de mari.
  under — *of infancy* : incapacité pour cause de minorité.

[A] invalidité.
partial (short term) – : incapacité temporaire.
permanent, total, – : invalidité permanente.
– *pension* : pension d'invalidité.
[ASS] – *clause* : clause de police d'assurance-vie stipulant une pension ou l'arrêt de paiement de primes en cas d'invalidité.

to disable : rendre incapable.
[J] frapper d'incapacité.
badly **disabled** *serviceman* (B.D.S.) : grand invalide de guerre (G.I.G.).
50 per cent disabled : invalide à 50 %.
disablement *benefit* : prestation d'invalidité.
disabling *statute* : loi restreignant la portée d'une autre loi.

disadvantage : préjudice, désavantage.
to sell at – : vendre à perte.

to disagree : être en désaccord.
motion **disagreed** *to* : motion rejetée.

disagreement : désaccord (m).
[J] défaut d'unanimité du jury.
(en droit A.A. l'unanimité du jury où, dans certains cas, une majorité de 5/6, est nécessaire pour rendre un verdict valable. Faute de quoi *(mistrial)*, le juge peut ordonner un nouveau procès, avec un autre jury).

to disallow : ne pas admettre.
[J] rejeter, rebuter *(a testimony)*.
[F] ne pas admettre en déduction.
when the director's remuneration is excessive, the excess is **disallowed** : quand la rémunération des dirigeants est exagérée, l'excédent est réintégré dans les bénéfices imposables.
disallowance *of plea, of costs* : rejet d'une défense, de frais.
disallowance *of expenses* : réfaction pour frais et charges.

disaster area : zone (f) sinistrée.

disbarment, disbarring : radiation d'un avocat du barreau (Engl., par le *Inn of Court* de l'intéressé, [U.S.] par la cour d'appel).

disbursements : [J] frais exposés, [C] débours.
actual – : paiement effectivement opéré.

disc *(domestic international sales corporation)* : [U.S.] : société ayant pour objet la commercialisation des exportations américaines.

discharge : libération (f).
[J] [A] [C] *(of an accused)* acquittement, *(of an attachment)* mainlevée de saisie, *(of a bankrupt)* réhabilitation, *(of a debtor)* décharge, *(of an employee)* licenciement, renvoi, congé, *(of a loan)* acquittement, *(of a mortgage)* purge d'hypothèque, *(of a prisoner)* libération, mise en liberté, relaxe, élargissement, *(of a soldier)* libération, renvoi dans les foyers, *(of a soldier, for unfitness)* réforme, *(of a workman)* licenciement.
conditional – : condamnation avec sursis.
– *from prison* : levée d'écrou.
– *of obligation* : exécution des engagements.
dishonourable – : *(of an official)* révocation, destitution, *(of an officer)* cassation.
final – : quitus.
honourable – : mise à la retraite.
« *in full* – » : pour acquit.
receipt in – : paiement libératoire.

to discharge : s'acquitter, licencier, décharger, annuler, réhabiliter.
– *a debt* : donner quittance d'une dette.
– *the prisoner on every count* : relaxer le prévenu des fins de toute poursuite, ordonner le non-lieu.
– *the duties of an office* : remplir les fonctions de.
– *the jury* : congédier les jurés.
– *one's duties, liabilities, obligations* : s'acquitter de ses devoirs, dettes, obligations.
– *an order of the court* : réformer un arrêt.
– *a surety* : libérer un garant.
discharged *bankrupt* : failli réhabilité.

to disclaim : rejeter.
[J] se désister de, renoncer à.
– *a right* : renoncer à un droit.
– *all responsibility* : décliner toute responsabilité.

disclaimer : [J] renonciation explicite à un droit (en général sous forme d'un *deed*), refus d'une charge (de *trustee*, d'exécuteur testamentaire, etc., voir *renunciation*).
– *in bankruptcy* : refus de syndic de faillite d'inclure des créances dans la masse.

disclosure (of) : [C] information à fournir (aux actionnaires, etc...) (sur).

discontiguous : discontinu (a).
[J] – *estate* : propriété foncière en plusieurs parcelles.

discontinuance : cessation (f), abandon (m).
[J] désistement d'action.
– *of proceedings* : désistement d'instance.
voluntary – : abandon des poursuites par le plaignant, sous réserve d'une reprise, avec l'autorisation du tribunal.
involuntary – : rejet de la plainte pour abus de procédure ou délais injustifiés à procéder. L'action peut être reprise avec l'autorisation du tribunal.
[C] – *of business* : cessation d'exploitation,

d'entreprise, abandon de l'activité.
(J) **to discontinue** *an action* : abandonner les poursuites.

discount : escompte (m).
[C] remise (f), rabais (m), ristourne (f).
– *for cash* : escompte de caisse.
– *stores* : commerces vendant au rabais.
trade – : remise (f) sur marchandises.
to allow a – : consentir un rabais.
to stand at a – : accuser une perte.
to discount : escompter, rabattre, remettre.
[F] *bank* – : escompte de banque, escompte en dehors.
Bank (of England) rate (of –*)* : le taux d'escompte (escompte officiel).
– *houses* : maison d'escompte, courtiers en escompte.
less – : déduction faite de l'escompte.
– *market* : marché du réescompte.
– *rate* : taux d'escompte.
to issue shares at – : émission d'actions en dessous du pair.
true – : escompte en dedans.
discounted *cash flow* : prévision du rapport à terme d'un investissement.
discounted cash flow rate method : méthode de l'indice de rentabilité interne.
discounting *factor* : facteur d'escompte.
discounting rate : taux d'actualisation.

discovert : [J] femme célibataire ou veuve.

discovery : divulgation.
[J] signification des défenses, communication de pièces et interrogatoire sur faits et articles.
– *proceeding* : 1° serment révélatoire ; 2° procédure en vue d'identifier les actifs d'une succession.

discredit : déconsidération, discrédit.
to throw – *upon a statement* : mettre en doute une déclaration.
to discredit *s.o.'s evidence* : contester la véracité d'un témoignage.

discrepancy : désaccord, écart (m), divergence, contradiction, différence (f).
[A] – *report* : avis d'irrégularité.

discretion : discrétion (f).
[J] pouvoir d'appréciation du juge.
abuse of – : abus de pouvoir.
administrative – : pouvoir réglementaire de l'administration.
in exercising – : dans l'exercice du pouvoir discrétionnaire.
discretionary *portfolio* : portefeuille dont la gestion est confiée à un agent de change.
discretionary powers : pouvoir discrétionnaire (du juge).
discretionary statement : aveu d'adultère dans une instance en divorce, la partie coupable invoquant néanmoins la bienveillance du tribunal pour obtenir un jugement de divorce (en doctrine A.A., le divorce est considéré comme une faveur accordée à la partie lésée).
[B] *discretionary order* : ordre à appréciation.
discretionary account : compte « carte blanche ».

to discriminate : pratiquer la discrimination.

discrimination : discrimination, différence de traitement, distinction (f).
without – : à la légère.
– *duties* : droits différentiels.

discriminatory : discriminatoire (a).
– *legislation* : législation d'exception.
– *measure* : mesure discriminatoire.
– *policy* : politique de favoritisme.

discussion : discussion, examen, débat, délibération, pourparler.
– *followed* : la discussion s'engage, le comité délibère.
under – : à l'étude.

diseconomy : déséconomie (f).

to disencumber : dégrever.
– *a property* : purger l'hypothèque sur un bien immobilier.
disencumbered : libre de toute hypothèse.

to disfranchise : priver d'un droit, sp. du droit électoral.

disfranchisement : [J] déchéance des droits civiques.

dishoarding : [F] « déthésauriser ».

to dishonour : déshonorer.
[C] – *a bill* : refuser l'acceptation ou le paiement d'une traite, laisser protester un effet.
dishonoured *cheque* : chèque impayé.
[A] **dishonourable** *discharge* : *(of an official)* révocation (f), destitution (f), *(of an officer)* cassation.

disinheritance : [J] exhérédation (f).

disincentive : décourageant ; effet décourageant.
heavy taxation may have – *effects* : une forte fiscalité peut avoir un effet décourageant.

disinflation : désinflation (f) (pouvoir d'achat réduit mais taux de chômage en baisse).

to dismiss: renvoyer, congédier, destituer, dissoudre, rejeter.
[J] – *a charge*: rendre une ordonnance de non-lieu.
– *s.o.'s appeal*: débouter qn de son appel.
[A] – *summarily*: renvoyer sans préavis.
to be dismissed: être relevé de ses fonctions.

dismissal: renvoi (m), licenciement (m), congédiement (m), fin de non-recevoir (f).
[J] (civ.) rejet (m) d'une demande, (cr.) ordonnance (f) d'acquit, acquittement (m) d'un inculpé.
– *of action*: classement d'une affaire (sp. en cas de défaut ou de négligence du demandeur).
certificate of – : certificat de non-lieu.
– *by default*: congédiement par suite d'absence.
– *payment*: indemnité de licenciement.
order of – : ordonnance de non-lieu.
wrongful – : licenciement abusif.

disorderly: désordonné (a).
[J] – *conduct* = *breach of the peace* (voir ce terme).
– *house*: maison mal famée.
drunk and – : en état d'ivresse publique.

to disown: désavouer, refuser de reconnaître.
– *one's signature*: renier sa signature.

dispatch: expédition (f), envoi (m), diligence (f), promptitude (f), dépêche (f).
[E] jours sauvés.
– *bag*: valise diplomatique.
– *clerk*: expéditionnaire.
– *list*: feuille d'envoi.
– *money*: prime de rapidité pour le déchargement d'un navire, rachat de planches.
– *note*: déclaration d'expédition.
with – : avec diligence.
dispatcher: expéditeur, distributeur.
dispatching: expédition, répartition, ventilation.
to dispatch: expédier.

to dispauper: [J] rayer un demandeur de la liste des personnes ayant droit à l'aide judiciaire.

dispensation: dispense (f).
– *with a witness*: suppression de témoin.

to displace: déplacer, apporter la preuve contraire.
[J] **displaced** *heir*: héritier évincé.
[A] *displaced person*: personne déplacée.
[F] *displaced share*: action déclassée.

displacement: *(of funds)* déplacement.
[B] déclassement.
[E] – *ton*: tonneau-poids.
light – : déplacement du navire à lège.
load – : déplacement du navire en charge.

display: étalage (m), exposition (f).
– *advertising*: publicité tapageuse.
– *window*: vitrine.

disposable: disponible (a).
– *personal income*: revenu disponible.

disposal: vente, distribution, cession, résolution, affectation, destination (f).
[F] – *of household refuse tax*: taxe sur l'enlèvement des ordures ménagères.
fixed asset –(*s*): cession d'éléments d'actif immobilisé.
[J] – *of property*: aliénation de biens.
to have entire – *of sth.*: avoir la libre disposition de qch.

to dispose (of): vendre, céder, aliéner, régler, liquider, disposer, se dessaisir, trancher.
right of **disposing** *of oneself*: droit de libre disposition.
property **disposed of**: biens aliénés.
the board has disposed of the appeal: la commission a statué sur l'appel.

disposition: [J] disposition testamentaire, cession (f) (de biens).
for – : à vendre.

to dispossess: dessaisir.

dispossession: dépossession (f).
[J] 1° dessaisissement ; 2° expropriation.

disputants: [J] parties en litige.

dispute: différend (m), conflit (m), controverse (f).
[J] litige (m).
fact beyond – : fait sans contredit.
case under – : affaire en litige.
– *as to*: contestation sur le point de.
– *at law*: litige.
in the event of a – : en cas de contestation.
industrial –(*s*): conflits du travail.
party to a – : partie à un différend.
points in – : points litigieux.
territory in – : territoire contesté.
[F] **to dispute** *the assessment*: contester l'imposition.
disputed *question*: question litigieuse.
disputed *claims office*: contentieux (m).

disqualification: incapacité (f).
[J] – *to act*: incapacité d'ester en justice.

to disqualify: frapper d'incapacité.
  disqualified: frappé d'incapacité civique.
  disqualified from making a will: inhabile à tester.
  to be disqualified from driving: avoir son permis de conduire suspendu.

disregard: négligence (f), désobéissance (f).
  – *of the law*: inobservation de la loi.

to disregard: ne pas faire cas de, méconnaître.
  – *an order*: enfreindre un ordre.
  – *the authority*: désobéir à l'autorité.

disrepute: discrédit (m), déconsidération (f).
  to bring into – : jeter le discrédit sur.

dissaving: [F] « désépargne ».

disseisin: (hist.) dessaisissement.
  [J] éviction, dépossession (illégale).

to dissent: différer d'opinion, être en désaccord.
  dissenting *judge*: juge dissident.
  dissenting opinion (minority opinion): [U.S.] avis de minorité des juges à l'encontre de celui de la majorité (*majority* ou *prevailing opinion*) qui détermine la décision. L'avis de la minorité est rendu public et a quelquefois des effets jurisprudentiels importants.

dissentient: dissident (m).

dissolution: dissolution (f) (du mariage, d'une société, du parlement, etc.).
  to dissolve *an injunction*: annuler une ordonnance provisoire.

distiller: distillateur (m).
  – *of moonshine*: bouilleur de cru.

distinct decline: [B] baisse sensible.

distinction: distinction, démarcation (f).

to distrain: [J] saisir, opérer une saisie.
  distrainer, distrainor: saisissant.

distraint: [J] 1° saisie-exécution ; 2° l'objet saisi.
  – *of property*: discussion de biens.

distress: [J] saisie en cas de non paiement du loyer.
  – *sale*: vente publique de biens saisis.
  – *warrant*: mandat de saisie.

to distress: [J] saisir des biens (pour obliger qn à remplir ses obligations).

to distribute: vendre (en qualité de concessionnaire).

distribution: distribution (f), répartition (f), partage (m).
  [J] *the statutory order of* – (*canons of inheritance*): règles de partage d'une succession ab intestat.
  [F] – *of income*: répartition des revenus.
  – *of profits*: répartition des bénéfices.
  – *(s) prepayment*: précompte mobilier.
  hidden – *(s)*: distributions occultes.
  [C] *wholesale and retail* – : commerce de gros et de détail.
  distributee: répartiteur (m).
  distributive *justice*: justice distributive.
  distributive share: part légitimaire.
  distributor: concessionnaire (m) (d'une marque d'automobile).
  sole distributor: agent, concessionnaire exclusif.

district: district (m), quartier (m).
  (Engl.) – *auditor*: contrôleur aux comptes des autorités locales.
  – *council*: conseil de district (urbain ou rural).
  – *Registry*: greffe local de *the Supreme Court of Judicature* (voir *Court*, Engl.).
  electoral – : circonscription électorale.
  [U.S.] – *attorney* # procureur de la République.
  – *of Columbia*: district fédéral.
  – *court*: tribunal fédéral de 1re instance.
  congressional – : circonscription électorale pour le Congrès.
  judicial – : ressort territorial d'un tribunal.

to disturb: déranger, troubler.
  [B] **disturbed** *market*: marché perturbé.

disturbance: dérangement (m), perturbation (f).
  [J] – *of possession*: trouble de jouissance (sp. en matière de droits incorporels).
  – *of the peace* # *breach of the peace* (voir ce terme).

disuse: désuétude, non-usage.

disutility: désutilité (f).
  marginal – : désutilité marginale.

ditto: dito, idem.

divergence: divergence (f).
  – *indicator*: (système monétaire européen) indicateur des divergences des monnaies nationales par rapport à l'ECU.
  – *limit*: limite de divergence (à partir de laquelle il est nécessaire d'intervenir).

to diversify: diversifier (investissements, etc.), répartir (risques, etc.).

diversion: diversion (f), *(of funds)* distraction (f), détour (m).
[J] [A] — *of profits*: transfert illicite de bénéfices.
intermediate output — *(s)*: détours de production.

diversity: diversité.
[J] (cr.) moyen de défense d'un détenu plaidant sa non identité avec la personne visée par l'accusation.
[U.S.] — *of citizenship*: domiciliation des plaideurs dans des Etats différents de l'Union. Dans ce cas, la compétence revient aux tribunaux fédéraux.

to divert: *(money)* distraire, détourner.

to divest, devest: divertir, détourner, priver.
(of a right) dessaisir, *(of an estate)* déposséder.
this statute **divests** *preexisting rights*: cette loi porte abrogation des droits antérieurs.
— *oneself of a privilege*: renoncer à un privilège.

divestment: cession (f) d'actifs, transfert (m) de droits de propriété.

to divide: diviser, répartir, partager.
— *a profit*: répartir le bénéfice.
— *the House*: (pol.) aller aux voix (Parlement).

dividend: dividende (m).
[J] dividende concordataire.
[B] [F] *accrued* — : dividende proportionnel.
cum —, [U.S.] — *on*: coupon attaché.
— *announcement*: déclaration de dividende.
— *cover*: taux de couverture du dividende, méthode d'évaluation de ce taux.
— *coverage*: couverture du dividende par le bénéfice.
— *credit*: dividende crédité.
— *disbursing agent*: agent payeur des dividendes.
— *paid out of capital*: dividende prélevé sur le capital.
— *payable: first jan.*: dividende jouissance : 1er jan.
— *payment*: versement du dividende.
— *payout*: pourcentage du bénéfice net distribué en dividende.
— *plan*: plan de participation.
— *ploughed back into capital*: dividende réincorporé au capital.
— *policy*: ligne de conduite en matière de dividende.
— *share*: action de jouissance, de bénéficiaire.
— *on shares*: dividende d'actions.
— *statement*: bordereau des dividendes.
— *warrant*: 1° ordonnance de paiement (ou *dividend mandate*); 2° chèque-dividende (ou *dividend check*); 3° certificat de dividende.
— *yield*: rapport d'un dividende en pourcentage.
ex —, [U.S.] *dividend off*: coupon détaché.
extra — : surdividende.
fictitious — : dividende fictif.
final — : solde de dividende.
first and final — : première et dernière répartition.
interim — : dividende provisoire.
overdue — : dividende arriéré.
passing of the — : passation du dividende.
preferred — : dividende privilégié.
sham — : dividende fictif.
stock — : action(s) gratuite(s).
superdividend: second dividende.
uncalled, unclaimed, unpaid — : dividende non réclamé, arriéré.

divisible: répartissable, divisible (a).
— *surplus*: bénéfice de participation.

division: 1° division (f), partage (m), répartition (f), morcellement (m); 2° discorde (f), désunion (f), scission (f); 3° vote (m), scrutin (m), vote par division; 4° [A] direction.
— *of labour*: division du travail.
on a — : à la majorité des voix.
taking a — : enregistrement des votes.
territorial — : circonscription territoriale.
to carry a — : obtenir la majorité.
to challenge a — : (pol.) provoquer un vote.
without a — : (pol.) (U.K. Parliament) sans scrutin (adopté, refusé...).
[F] — *of the assets*: partage de l'actif social.
[A] *the Budget* — : la Direction du Budget.

divisional: divisionnaire (a).
[B] — *bond*: obligation garantie par une hypothèque spéciale ne portant que sur une partie des biens d'une société.
[J] — *Court*: (Engl.) cour supérieure composée de deux juges au moins de *the High Court of Justice* statuant en appel des décisions des tribunaux inférieurs (sp. des *Quarter* et *Petty Sessions*).

divorce: divorce (m).
to sue for — : demander le divorce.
to take — *proceedings*: intenter une action en divorce.
[J] (Engl.) Le divorce est généralement prononcé provisoirement (*decree nisi*) et confirmé après six semaines environ (*decree absolute*), si la partie perdante ne parvient pas, entretemps, à faire annuler la décision provisoire (voir *decree nisi*).

[U.S.] les causes de divorce varient d'Etat à Etat.

divvy : [J] collusion (f) en vue d'un partage (secret) des profits au détriment d'un tiers.

dock : [J] banc des accusés.
— *-defence* ou *dock-brief* : défense d'un indigent assumée directement à l'audience par un avocat, sans l'intervention préalable d'un *solicitor*.
the prisoner in — : le prévenu.
[A] [C] dock (m), bassin de port.
— *-dues* : droits de bassin.
— *strike* : grève des dockers.
— *warehouse* : entrepôt des docks.
— *warrant* : warrant.
loading — : embarcadère.
unloading — : débarcadère.
dockage : droits de bassin.

docket : extrait (m), fiche (f), note (f).
[J] 1° résumé ou extrait de jugement. 2° bordereau d'un dossier de procédure. 3° [U.S.] registre des jugements rendus (« to docket *a judgment* »).
[D] récépissé (m) de douane.
[C] *wages-* — : feuille de paye.

doctor's commons : [J] (Engl.) (hist.) : collège des docteurs en droit civil.

to doctor : altérer, falsifier, truquer.

document : document (m).
[J] — *(s) pertaining to the case before the Court* : dossier d'une affaire.
(negotiable) — *of title* : titre de propriété (tel que connaissement, warrant).
legal — : acte authentique.
negotiable — : instrument négociable.
banker's credit for payment against — *(s)* : crédit documentaire.
credit — : titre de crédit.
— *(s) in support* : pièces à l'appui.
legal — : acte authentique.
official — : document de service.
public — : document officiel.
ship's — : papier de bord.
[C] — *against acceptance (abr. D/A)* : (lettre de change destinée à un acheteur étranger) sous réserve d'acceptation.
— *against payment (abr. D/A)* : sous réserve de paiement immédiat.

documentary : documentaire, justificatif, authentique (a).
[C] — *bill (draft with documents attached)* : traite documentaire (c'est-à-dire accompagnée du connaissement, de la police d'assurance et de la facture).
— *credit* : crédit, accréditif documentaire.

— *evidence* : preuve littérale.

dodger : 1° rusé, fraudeur ; 2° [U.S.] prospectus.
tax — : fraudeur fiscal.

doldrums : marasme (m).

dole : lot échu en partage.
[A] secours (aux indigents).
unemployment — : allocation de chômage.

doli capax (incapax) : capable (incapable) de crime (étant donné son âge).
doli capax : capable de discernement, c'est-à-dire responsable en cas de crime ou délit.
[J] adolescent de 14 à 21 ans.
doli incapax : incapable de discernement, c'est-à-dire irresponsable en cas de crime et délit.
[J] enfant de 8 à 14 ans.
Cette présomption peut être écartée par la preuve du contraire, en vertu du principe **malitia supplet aetatem**, mais elle demeure irréfragable en ce qui concerne un garçon de moins de 14 ans, accusé de viol.

dollar : dollar (m).
— *area* : zone dollar.
— *balances* : balances dollar.
— *country* : pays de la zone dollar.
— *cost averaging* : 1° achats périodiques par sommes fixes ; 2° coût moyen des actions achetées par sommes fixes.
— *exchange* : cours du dollar.
— *gap* : pénurie de dollars.
— *glut* : surabondance de dollars.
— *transaction* : opération en dollars.

domain : domaine (m), biens-fonds (m), terres seigneuriales.
[J] propriété pleine et entière de biens immobiliers (peu usité, si dit plutôt *ownership*).
eminent — : (Engl.) principe de droit selon lequel toutes les terres relèvent, en dernière analyse, de la Couronne, d'où *to take land by the power of eminent* — : exproprier.
(in the) public — : (dans le) domaine public.

domesday book : (Engl.) (hist.) cadastre du royaume, établi en 1086 sur l'ordre de Guillaume le Conquérant.

domestic : interne, familial, intérieur, national (a).
— *corporation* : société nationale (britannique, américaine, etc.).
— *hoarding* : thésaurisation intérieure.
— *law* : droit interne.
— *relations* : droit familial.
— *trade* : commerce intérieur.
gross — *product* : produit national brut

(P.N.B.).
— *Relations Court*: [U.S.] tribunal inférieur connaissant des affaires de famille et des questions relatives aux patrimoines.
— *mail*: [U.S.] courrier à destination de l'intérieur.
domestics: [U.S.] articles ménagers.

domicile: [J] domicile (m).
(Alors qu'en droit français le domicile est le lieu du principal établissement et que le statut civil des personnes est régi par leur droit national, en droit A.A. c'est la résidence permanente qui fournit le critère décisif de la notion du domicile).
breach of — : 1° violation de domicile ; 2° effraction.
— *of choice*: domicile d'élection.
— *of origin*: domicile d'origine.
legal — : domicile légal.
to domicile, domiciliate: domicilier.
domiciled: domicilié, établi.
domiciliary *clause*: clause attributive de juridiction.
[C] **domiciliation**: domiciliation (d'un effet).

dominant tenement: fonds dominant.

dominion: [J].
(hist.) *the British* —(s): ancienne dénomination de divers royaumes et pays reconnaissant le souverain de la Dynastie de Windsor, régnant sur la Grande-Bretagne et l'Irlande du Nord, comme chef du *Commonwealth*.
(Canada) — *Parliament*: Parlement fédéral.
the — *of Canada*: la Confédération canadienne (composée de Provinces).

dominium: [J] 1° *ownership* (voir ce terme) ; 2° nue-propriété ; 3° droit de disposition (par exemple en vertu d'un pouvoir).

donatio mortis causa: [J] donation pour cause de mort.

donation: [J] donation (f).
charitable — : acte de bienfaisance.
— *inter vivos*: donation entre vifs.

to donate: (J) faire donation (f) de.

done: fait, pratiqué (a).
— *and signed*: fait et signé.
— *at*: fait à.
[B] *bargains* — : cours faits.
business — *for cash*: cours pratiqués au comptant.
work — *on commission*: travail sur commande.

donee: donataire (m), bénéficiaire (m).

donor: donateur (m), donneur (m).

door-to-door selling: see « canvassing ».

dope: (fam.) renseignements, « tuyaux ».

dormant: endormi (a).
[J] (droit) non exercé.
— *claim*: droit en expectative.
— *judgment*: jugement périmé.
— *law*: loi inappliquée.
— *partnership* # commandite.
— *title*: titre tombé en désuétude.
— *warrant*: mandat en blanc.
[C] — *account*: compte dormant.
— *balance*: solde inactif.

double: double (a).
— -*chamber system*: bicamérisme, bicaméralisme.
— *dealing*: duplicité.
— *endowment*: assurance mixte.
— *entry bookkeeping*: comptabilité en partie double.
[B] — *option*: stellage.
[F] — *taxation agreement*: convention relative aux doubles impositions.
to double cross: duper.

doubt: doute (m).
[J] « *beyond a reasonable* — » : quasi-certitude qui doit être celle d'un jury pour rendre un verdict de culpabilité.
[F] **doubtful** *debt*: créance douteuse.

dower: dot (f).
[J] *[C.L.]* douaire (m), part de la succession immobilière du mari, en général un tiers, constitué en usufruit pour la veuve. Ne subsiste plus que dans quelques Etats des U.S. (cf. préciput conventionnel du droit français).

Dow Jones Index: [B] indice « Dow Jones ». (Indice des valeurs industrielles obtenu en faisant la moyenne des quotations de 30 actions à la Bourse de New York).
« — *theory* » : théorie d'analyse du marché fondée sur le rendement obtenu à partir de l'indice « Dow Jones ».

to be down: être en baisse.

to be down graded (*offer*): être rabaissée (offre).

to go down market: produire et vendre des biens ou des services d'une qualité inférieure à ce qu'elle était.

down-payment: acompte (m) versé à la signature d'un accord de vente à crédit ou de reconnaissance d'hypothèque.

down revision: dégrèvement (m), minoration (f).

downturn (in the economy): ralentissement (de l'économie).

downswings: [B] tendance à la baisse.

down tick (minus tick): [B] négociation à un cours inférieur à la précédente (opp. *up tick, plus tick*).

down time: période (f) où des machines restent inutilisées.

downturn: [B] repli (m).

downward movement: [B] tendance à la baisse.

dowry: [J] dot (f).

draft: [J] projet d'acte, [U.S.] (milit.) conscription (f).
[C] 1° tirage (m), disposition (f) sur qn ; 2° effet (m) de commerce, traite (f), lettre (f) de change, chèque (m).
alternative — : contre projet.
— agreement : projet de convention.
— at sight : effet à vue.
— bill : avant projet de loi.
— drawn on : traite tirée sur.
— regulation : avant projet d'ordonnance.
running — : traite en circulation.
to meet a — : honorer une traite.
to pass a — : céder une traite.
to draft: rédiger un projet, ébaucher.
drafting *panels from the jury list* : appel des jurés d'après les listes.
drafting committee : comité de rédaction.

drain: [F] drainage (m), saignée (f), épuisement (m).
« *brain —* » : « exode des cerveaux ».

drastic: rigoureux, draconien (a).
— cuts : coupes sombres.
— diversification : diversification brutale (par des productions sans rapport avec les fabrications en cours).
— provision : clause draconienne.

to draw: rédiger, formuler, dresser, souscrire.
[B] racheter, rembourser, par voie de tirage au sort.
— a bill : émettre une traite.
— up : lever, arrêter, dresser, établir.
— up a deed : rédiger un acte.
— up accounts : arrêter un exercice comptable, établir un bilan.
— up a balance sheet : établir un bilan.
— up the minutes : dresser un procès-verbal.

drawback: désavantage (m), inconvénient (m), déduction (f), remise (f), rembours (m).
[D] remboursement à l'exportation des droits d'entrée.
[E] prime à l'exportation.

draw-down in money: [F] moins-value en espèces.
— period : période (f) de tirage (m).

drawee: [C] le tiré (d'un effet), acceptant, payeur (d'une lettre de change).

drawer: [C] le tireur, le souscripteur (d'un effet).
— bond : obligation sortie au tirage.
drawing : tirage, tirage au sort.
drawing of bonds : tirage au sort d'obligation.
drawing right : droit de tirage.
special drawing rights (I.M.F.) : droits de tirage spéciaux (F.M.I.).
drawn *bond* : obligations sorties au tirage.

to dress the window: see « *window-dressing* ».

drift: courant (m), mouvement (m), portée (f), tendance (f), évolution (f).
— from the land : exode (m) rural.
— policy : politique de laisser-aller.
[B] **to drift** *downward* : s'effriter, se replier.

drilling offshore: forage en haute mer.

drinking and driving: conduite (f) en état d'ivresse.

to drive: conduire.
bad money **drives** *out good* : la mauvaise monnaie chasse la bonne (loi de Gresham).
driving licence : permis de conduire.
driving spirit : cheville ouvrière.
driving industries : industries motrices.
driving test : examen pour l'obtention du permis de conduire.

droits of admiralty: [J] [U.K.] droit en vertu duquel les biens ennemis saisis dans les ports du royaume sont acquis à la Couronne.

to droop: fléchir (les cours, etc.).

drop: baisse, chute, régression (f).
— in prices : baisse des prix.
— in value : 1° moins-value ; 2° chute des cours, 3° dépréciation.

heavy — : débâcle.

to drop : baisser, diminuer, renoncer, cesser, rayer, retirer.
   dropped *amendment* : amendement retiré.
   stocks dropped a point : les actions ont reculé d'un point.
   dropping : radiation (f).

drought : sécheresse.
   drought tax : « impôt-sécheresse ».

to drum up : battre le rappel (de ses relations...).

drunk and disorderly : [J] en état d'ivresse publique.

dry : sec (a).
   — *money* : argent liquide.

dual : double.
   — *economies* : dualisme économique.
   — *licensing* : cumul de permis, de licences.
   — *ownerships* : bi-propriété.

duces tecum, subpoena : amène avec toi. [J] ordre de soit-communiqué.

dud cheque (check) : chèque « en bois ».

due : dû, juste, convenable, opportun, suffisant (a).
   [J] légitime.
   [U.S.] — *process of law* : clauses de sauvegarde de la liberté individuelle consignées aux amendements 5 et 14 de la Constitution, qui doivent être observées au cours de la procédure, sous peine de nullité (notamment : l'égalité devant la loi, l'audition des deux parties, la non-rétroactivité des lois).
   — *care* : diligence normale, soins appropriés.
   — *consideration* : réflexion voulue.
   in — *form* : en bonne et due forme.
   [C] [F] exigible, échéant, échu, payable.
   balance — : solde dû.
   debts — *to the firm* : dettes actives, créances de l'entreprise.
   debts — *by the firm* : dettes passives.
   — *-bill* : [U.S.] reconnaissance de dette (non endossable).
   — *date* : échéance.
   interests falling — : intérêts à échoir.
   to fall — : venir à échéance.
   when — : à l'échéance.

dues : dû (m).
   [J] [A] droits (m pl), frais (m pl), taxes (f pl), redevance (f).
   clerk of the Court's — : droits de greffe.
   dock- — : droits de bassin.
   ferry — : droits de passage.

   legal — : droits judiciaires.
   market — : hallage.
   pier — : droits de quai.
   port — : droits de port.
   registration — : droits d'enregistrement.
   town — : octroi.
   tax and — : impôts et taxes.
   union — : contributions, cotisations syndicales.
   warehouse — : magasinage.

dull *(market)* : [B] (marché) sans animation, tendant à la baisse.

dullness : stagnation (f) (du marché), marasme (m), tassement (m).

duly : dûment (adv.), exactement, en bonne et due forme.
   — *authorized* : dûment autorisé, accrédité.
   — *collected* : régulièrement encaissé.
   — *licensed* : dûment patenté.
   — *paid* : payé en son temps.

dumb bidding : prix maximum fixé secrètement par avance (aux enchères).

dum bene se gesserit : « tant qu'il aura une bonne conduite », formule indiquant l'inamovibilité dans la nomination d'un juge (« *for good behaviour* »).

dummy : simulacre (m), prête-nom (m), homme de paille, maquette (f) (publicitaire), factice (a).
   — *company* : société prête-nom.
   « *dummies* » : papiers « en blanc » (factices).

dumping : 1° vente, écoulement à perte ; 2° pratique d'abaissement volontaire des prix dans le cadre de la libre concurrence ; 3° vente à perte sur les marchés extérieurs d'un produit se vendant au prix courant dans le pays d'origine.
   anti- — *duty* : impôt sur certaines marchandises importées pour empêcher qu'elles soient vendues à des prix trop bas (= « impôt anti-dumping »).

duopoly : duopole (m).

duplicate : duplicata (m), double (m), copie (f), ampliation (f).
   [J] — *document* : document ampliatif.
   — *receipt* : reçu en duplicata.
   in — : en double expédition.
   done in — : fait en double exemplaire.
   [C] deuxième de change.

duplication : double emploi (m).
   — *of payments* : doubles paiements.

durable *(goods)* : (denrées) non périssables.
consumer **durables** : biens de consommation durable.

durante lite (pendente lite) : pendant le cours du procès.

duration *(of conversion)* : [B] durée (de conversion).
— *of a lease* : durée d'un bail.

duress : violence (f).
[J] contrainte (f).
(— est seulement un aspect de la violence. Deux théories A.A., la notion de *duress [C.L.]* et celle de *undue influence (Eq.)*, correspondent à la théorie française unique de la violence comme vice du consentement dans les actes juridiques).
— *of imprisonment* : séquestration (f).
— *per minas* : menaces proférées pour forcer qn à donner un consentement contre son gré.
to be under — : agir à son corps défendant.

dutch auction : enchères (f pl) au rabais.

dutch bargain : profit unilatéral.

dutiable : taxable, passible (a) de droits.
— *goods* : marchandises passibles de droits.

duty : obligation (f), devoir (m), fonction (f), attributions (f pl).
bounder — : obligation stricte.
his **duties** *shall consist of* : ses attributions consisteront à.
it will be the — *of* : il appartiendra à.
to be off — : ne pas être en service.
to be on — : être de service (opp. *on leave*).
to consider it one's — *to* : croire de son devoir de.
to report for — : se présenter pour occuper un emploi.
under legal — : légalement tenu.
[J] — *of case* : devoir de chercher à éviter tout préjudice (ce qui limite l'étendue de la responsabilité civile).
[E] [F] [D] pl. impôts, taxes, droits.
ad valorem *duties* : droits ad valorem.
consumption duties : droits de consommation.
conveyance — : droit de succession.
corporations — : impôt sur les sociétés.
countervailing — : droit compensateur.
customs — : droits de douane.
death — : [U.K.] droits de succession.
discriminating — : droit différentiel.
— *free* : exempt de droits.
— *paid goods* : marchandises acquittées.
entertainment — : [U.K.] taxe sur les spectacles, droit des pauvres.
estate — : [U.K.] droits de succession sur l'ensemble de l'héritage.
excess profits — : taxe sur l'enrichissement (bénéfices de guerre).
excise — : impôts indirects, droits d'accise.
exemption from — : exonération de l'impôt.
extra — : droits supplémentaires.
fixed — : droits fixes.
free of — : en franchise de droits.
increment value — : [U.K.] taxe sur les plus-values immobilières.
inheritance — : droit de succession.
legacy and succession — : [U.K.] droits de mutation mortis causa (par décès).
liable to duty or duties : passible de droits.
mineral rights — : [U.K.] taxe sur les droits miniers.
probate — : droits d'homologation (succession).
protective — : droits protecteurs.
rebate of — : remise des droits.
registration — : droits d'enregistrement.
relief from — : exonération d'impôts.
to remit — : exonérer du paiement des droits.
return of — : détaxe.
stamp duties : droits de timbre.
succession — : taxe successorale, droits de succession (voir *tax*).
transfer — : droit de mutation inter vivos (entre vifs).
transit — : droit de transit.
underpaid customs — : droits perçus en moins.
value for — : valeur imposable.

dwelling : séjour (m), résidence (f), logement (m).
— *house* : maison d'habitation.

dwindling : déperdition (f), dépérissement (m).
— *of assets* : dépérissement de capital, diminution de l'actif.

dynamic peg : « cran dynamique » (ajustement progressif des changes).

NOTES

NOTES

E

each : chacun, « la pièce ».
[C] *these articles cost a shilling* — : ces articles coûtent un shilling la pièce.

eager : ardent, passionné (a).
[C] *an* — *buyer (seller)* : un acheteur (vendeur) empressé.
— *for gain* : âpre au gain.

eagle : [U.S.] pièce d'or de dix dollars.

early : précoce, rapproché (a).
at an — *date* : à une date prochaine, sous peu.
[C] — *closing day* : jour où les magasins ferment l'après-midi.
at your **earliest** *convenience* : le plus tôt qu'il vous sera possible.
— *recovery* : reprise rapide.
— *shift* : équipe de jour (industrie).

to earmark, to ear-mark : affecter, destiner, assigner.
[F] — *a certain amount for a purpose* : donner une affectation à une (certaine) somme.
— *funds for* : spécialiser des fonds, affecter des fonds à.
earmarked *property* : biens réservés, de même nature, identifiables ou distincts.
earmarked taxes : impôts affectés.
earmarking : affectation (de recettes).

to earn (money, a salary) : gagner (de l'argent, un salaire).
[F] — *one's living* : gagner sa vie.
pay-as-you-earn (P.A.Y.E.) : [U.K.] « payez au fur et à mesure que vous gagnez » ; système de retenue à la source de l'impôt sur les traitements et les salaires.
earned *income* : revenu provenant du travail.
profit earned on a sale : bénéfice acquis sur une vente.
earnest *money* : arrhes (f pl), dépôt de garantie.
earning : profitable, qui rapporte (a).
earning capacity : rapport, productivité financière.
earning power : capacité bénéficiaire.
earning power method : méthode du taux interne de rentabilité.
profit-earning : rentable.
profit-earning capacity : rentabilité (f).
earning(s) : fruit (m) du travail, salaire (m), bénéfices (m pl) (d'une entreprise), réserves.
accumulated earnings tax : (U.S.) impôt sur les réserves accumulées (par les sociétés).
corporation earnings : bénéfices des sociétés.
earnings per share (E.P.S.) : bénéfice par action (B.P.A.).
earnings yield : bénéfice par action hors impôt.
gross (net) earnings : bénéfice brut (net).
monopoly earnings : bénéfices de monopole.
operating earnings (income) : marge brute d'exploitation.
professional earnings : gain des professions libérales.

ear-witness : témoin auriculaire.

ease : aisance (f), facilité (f) (pour).
(B) faiblesse (f) des cours.

to ease (shares) : faiblir, mollir (actions).
— *off* : se relâcher, se détendre.

easement : servitude (f), droit (m) d'usage.
[J] *affirmative* — : servitude active.
— *appurtenance* : servitude, charge foncière, service foncier.
commutation of an — : rachat d'une servitude.
gross — : droit d'usage.
negative — : servitude passive.
quasi- — : droit à une servitude résultant d'une quasi-possession.

easiness : aisance (f), facilité (f), mollesse (f) (de la Bourse).
[F] *monetary* — : aisance monétaire.

easing (off) : détente (f) sur le marché.

easy : facile, aisé, calme (a).
[C] — *market* : marché calme.
— *money* : argent facilement gagné, argent abondant.
— *payments* : facilités de paiement.
— *prices* : des prix qui fléchissent.
to buy on — *terms* : acheter en profitant de facilités de paiement.
in — *circumstances* : à l'aise financièrement.

eatables : (denrées) comestibles.

econometrics : économétrie (f).

economic (activity, etc.) : (activité, etc.) économique (a).
— *adviser* : conseiller économique.
— *argument* : raisonnement économique.

– *flow* : flux économique.
– *growth* : croissance économique.
– *issue* : problème économique.
– *order quantity (E.O.Q.)* : quantité optimale d'une denrée ou d'un produit à acheter sur commande.
– *planning* : planification de l'économie.
– *recession* : marasme économique.
– *rent* : loyer qui rapporte.
– *stabilizers* : stabilisateurs économiques.
– *trend* : tendances de l'économie.
– *warfare* : guerre économique.
– *welfare* : bien-être économique.
National Bureau of – Research : [U.S.] Office National de la Recherche Economique.
economics : économie politique.

economies of scale : économies (f pl) d'échelle.

economist : économiste (m).
(classical, neo-classical, keynesian) – (s) : économistes (classiques, néo-classiques, keynésiens, etc.).

economy : économie (f).
advanced – : économie développée.
closed, open – : économie fermée, ouverte.
controlled – : économie dirigée.
planned – : économie planifiée, dirigiste.
market – : économie de marché.
motion – : économie des mouvements.

edge : bord (m), arête (f), tranche (f), avantage (m).
to give an – in world markets : rendre compétitif sur les marchés mondiaux.
gilt-edged : voir ce mot.

to edge down : baisser faiblement (ex. les prix).

to edge up : augmenter faiblement (ex. le chômage).

edibles : denrées comestibles.

educational guidance : orientation (f) pédagogique.

E.E.C. *(European Economic Community)* : C.E.E. (Communauté Economique Européenne, « Les Communautés »).

effect : effet (m).
feed-back – : effet de retour, rétroaction (f).
financial – : incidence financière.
leverage (or gearing) – : effet de levier.
multiplier – : effet de multiplicateur.
of no – : nul et non avenu.
« no – (s) » : défaut de provision.
ratchet – : effet de cliquet.

to the same – : dans le même sens.
to carry into – : mettre à exécution.
to come into – : entrer en vigueur.
[J] *effets* (m pl), *biens* (m pl) mobiliers.
movable – (s) : biens mobiliers.
personal – (s) : effets, biens personnels.
[F] *tax –* : incidence fiscale.

to effect : effectuer, réaliser.
to come into –, to take –, to become **effective** : entrer en vigueur.
– a compromise : en venir à un compromis.
– a payment : effectuer un paiement.
to be **effected** : s'opérer.

effective : effectif, réel (a).
– date : date d'entrée en vigueur.
– demand : demande « effective » (voir *demand*).
– interest : taux global d'intérêt effectif.
– money : monnaie réelle.
– rate : taux effectif (taux d'imposition correspondant au revenu global du contribuable, y compris ses revenus non imposables dans l'Etat du domicile fiscal).
– value : valeur réelle (actuelle).
– yield : rendement effectif.

effectiveness : efficacité (f), rendement (m) (d'une machine).

effectual *(contrat, rule)* : valide (a) (pour un contrat), en vigueur (pour un règlement).

efficiency : efficacité (f), rendement (m), capacité (f), compétence (f).
economic – : efficacité économique.
highest – : rendement maximum.
marginal – (of capital, of labour) : efficacité marginale (du travail, de la main-d'œuvre).
to achieve maximum – : parvenir au maximum d'efficacité.

efficient : efficace, fructueux, capable, compétent (a).
highly – : performant.
– labour : main-d'œuvre compétente.

effluent : rejet (m), liquide (industriel).

efflux : sortie (f), flux (m).
[F] *– of capital, of gold* : sortie de capitaux, d'or.

ejectment : [J] procédure d'éviction, action en revendication de biens.
ejection : éviction (f), expulsion (f).

elaborate (work) : (travail) fini, soigné, minutieux.
to **elaborate** *(a theory)* : élaborer (une théorie).
elaboration *(of a plan)* : élaboration d'un

– 402 –

plan.

elastic (demand, supply): (demande, offre) élastique (a).
elasticity *(of demand, of expectations, of supply)*: élasticité (f) (de la demande, des prévisions, de l'offre).
price elasticity: élasticité des prix.

to elect: choisir, élire.
[J] *to elect domicile*: élire domicile.
election: élection (f); option (f), choix (m).
by-election ([U.S.] *special élection*): élection partielle.
election of domicile: élection de domicile.
general elections, parliamentary: élections générales.
election petition(s): action(s) en vue de faire invalider une élection.

electioneering: propagande électorale.

electoral: électoral (a).
— *body*: corps électoral.
— *campaign*: campagne électorale.
— *franchise*: droit de vote.
— *platform*: programme électoral, politique.

eleemosynary corporation: association de bienfaisance.

elegit: « il a choisi ».
[J] ordonnance autorisant le créancier à prendre provisoirement possession des biens immobiliers d'un débiteur.

element: élément (m), principe (a) constitutif.
[C] *the* — *(s) of cost*: les éléments du prix de revient.
the personal — : le facteur humain.

to elicit: déduire, découvrir.
— *the facts*: tirer les faits au clair.

eligible: susceptible de, qui a droit à, avantageux (a), acceptable, (pol.) éligible.
[F] — *bank bill*: effet de commerce accepté par une banque et que la Banque Centrale peut réescompter.
— *investment*: placement avantageux.
— *paper*: effet bancable.
to be — *for an occupation*: être apte à occuper un emploi.
to be — *for the office of*: être qualifié pour remplir les fonctions de.
to be — *for retirement*: admis à faire valoir ses droits à la retraite.
eligibility: admission (f) (à une caisse de retraite par exemple).

elimination: élimination (f).
— *of waste*: lutte contre le gaspillage.

elopement: fuite (du domicile conjugal, de la maison paternelle), enlèvement (consenti).

to elucidate (a situation): mettre au net, tirer au clair (une situation).
elucidation: éclaircissement (m).

embargo: embargo (m), saisie (f) provisoire (de navires).
[J] *to be under an* — : être séquestré (navire).
to lay an — *on*: mettre l'embargo sur.
to raise, to take off the — : lever l'embargo.

(port of) embarkation: port d'embarquement.

embarrassed estate: [J] propriété grevée d'hypothèques.

embezzlement: détournement (m) de fonds, abus (m) de confiance, malversation (f).
embezzler: déprédateur (m), concussionnaire (m).

to embezzle funds: détourner des fonds.

emblements: [J] fruits naturels annuels du travail agricole, fruit civil.

to embody: inclure, incorporer, insérer.
— *an article in a bill*: incorporer un article dans un projet.
— *a clause in a contract*: incorporer une clause dans un contrat.
embossed stamp: timbre sec.

embracery: [J] subornation (f) de juré.

to emerge: se dresser, surgir (une difficulté, etc.).
it **emerges** *therefrom that*: il ressort de là que.

emergency: situation critique, exceptionnelle, cas d'urgence, cas imprévu.
in case of — : en cas d'urgence.
— *fund*: caisse de secours.
— *legislation*: mesures d'exception.
— *means*: moyens de fortune.
— *measures*: mesures d'exception, d'urgence.
— *repairs*: réparations d'urgence.
— *sitting, session*: séance, session extraordinaire, exceptionnelle.
state of — : état d'urgence.
to provide for **emergencies**: parer à l'imprévu.
to rise to the — : se montrer à la hauteur de la situation.
[F] — *tax*: impôt exceptionnel, extraordinaire, impôt de crise.

emigrant: émigrant (m).
  to **emigrate**: émigrer.
  emigration: émigration (f).
  emigration officer: fonctionnaire des services d'émigration.

to empanel a jury: [J] dresser le tableau des jurés.

emphatic: catégorique, énergique (a).
  – *denial*: démenti catégorique.
  to deny **emphatically**: nier énergiquement.

emphytheosis: emphytéose (f).

empiricism: empirisme (m).

employ: emploi (m).
  to be in s.o.'s – : être au service de qn.
  to **employ**: employer ; faire valoir, placer.
  to employ one's money: placer son argent.
  to employ resources: utiliser des ressources.
  to employ s.o. in doing something: occuper qn à une tâche.
  to employ workmen: employer des ouvriers.
  employed: a) employé (a) ; b) employé (m).
  a firm with five hundred employed: une entreprise qui emploie cinq cents personnes, qui occupe cinq cents employés.
  quantity of labour employed: quantité de travail employée.

employee: employé (m), salarié (m).
  – *benefits*: avantages accordés à un employé.
  – *compensation*: avantages globaux consentis aux employés.
  – *investment*: actionnariat ouvrier.
  a salaried – : un salarié.
  to dismiss, to engage an – : congédier, engager un employé.

employer: employeur (m), patron (m).
  –*(s') association, federation, union*: syndicat patronal.
  –*(s') liability*: responsabilité des patrons.
  –*(s') liability insurance*: assurance patronale contre les accidents du travail.
  –*(s') return (salary tax)*: déclaration patronale.
  –*(s') share*: cotisation patronale.

employment: emploi (m), occupation (f), situation (f), activité (f) salariée.
  – *agency, bureau, exchange*: bureau, office de placement ; agence pour l'emploi.
  – *of capital in production*: emploi de capitaux dans la production.
  elasticity of – : élasticité de l'emploi.
  full – : plein emploi.
  full – *policy*: politique de plein emploi.
  full-time – : emploi à temps plein.
  overfull – : suremploi.

part-time – : emploi à temps partiel.
  – *seeker*: demandeur d'emploi.
  to apply for, to seek – : chercher de l'emploi (un emploi).

to empower s.o. (to do...): donner pouvoir, procuration à qn (pour faire...), habiliter qn (à faire).
  to be empowered *(to do)*: être habilité (à faire), avoir pleins pouvoirs (pour faire).

empty journey: voyage à vide.
  [C] **empties**: emballages vides.

to enable s.o. to do sth.: habiliter qn à faire qch., donner pouvoir à qn de faire qch.
  enabling *power*: capacité légale.
  [J] *enabling statute*: loi d'habilitation, légalisant un état de choses de fait ou illégal.

to enact: décréter, promulguer, ordonner, arrêter, rendre (un arrêt).
  [J] *the* **enacting** *clauses of an act*: le dispositif d'une loi.
  « *be it* **enacted** *that* » : [U.S.] « qu'il soit statué » : formule de promulgation d'une loi.

enactment: loi (f), ordonnance (f), décret (m).
  enactment(s): textes législatifs.

to encash (a cheque): encaisser (un chèque).
  [C] **encashable**: encaissable.
  encashment: recette (f), rentrée (f), encaissement (m).

enclosed: ci-inclus.
  – *herewith (therewith)*: ci-inclus, sous ce pli.

enclosure: pièce annexée, document ci-joint.

to encroach (upon): empiéter (sur), anticiper (sur).
  – *upon one's capital*: entamer son capital.
  [J] – *upon s.o.'s rights*: empiéter sur, usurper les droits de qn.
  encroachment *(upon s.o.'s rights)*: usurpation (de droits), empiètement sur la propriété d'autrui.

to encumber: gêner, grever.
  [J] **encumbered** *assets*: actifs gagés.
  encumbered estate: propriété grevée de dettes ou d'hypothèques.
  encumbrance: embarras, charge grevant une succession ou un bien mobilier ou immobilier, servitude, hypothèque.
  search of encumbrances: relevé d'hypothèques.
  encumbrancer: créancier hypothécaire.

to encumber with mortgage: [J] grever d'une hypothèque.

end: fin (f), terme (m), but (m), objet (m).
[C] *at the − of the financial year*: en fin d'exercice.
− account # liquidation.
(payment) at the − of the present month: (paiement) fin courant.
− product: produit fini.
− user: utilisateur final.
− of a risk: extinction d'un risque.
for (to) this −: dans ce but.
to end: (se) terminer, clôturer.
[F] *the fiscal year ending on (December 31st)*: l'exercice (l'année) budgétaire finissant le (31 décembre).

endorsable (cheque): (chèque) endossable (a).
to endorse: endosser, adopter, viser (un passeport), souscrire à (une résolution).
[A] *to endorse a driving licence*: mentionner les détails d'un délit au verso d'un permis de conduire.
to endorse a document with sth.: mentionner qch au dos d'un document.
[C] *to endorse a bill*: avaliser un effet.
to endorse a bill of lading: endosser un connaissement.
to endorse back a bill to drawer: contrepasser un effet au tireur.
endorsement: adhésion (f), appui (m), approbation (f) (d'un appel), visa (m) (d'un passeport), aval.
accommodation endorsement: aval de complaisance.
blank endorsement: endos en blanc.
endorsement on a passport: mention spéciale sur un passeport.
qualified endorsement: endos conditionnel.
restrictive endorsement: endos restreint.
endorsement without recourse: endossement à forfait.
endorser: endosseur, concessionnaire, avaliste.
second endorser: tiers porteur.

to endow (with means...): doter (de moyens...).
endowment: dotation ; droit d'une femme à une dot ; assignation de fonds à une œuvre d'utilité publique.
− insurance: assurance à dotation fixe (à terme fixe), assurance à capital différé.
[F] *− contracts*: contrat de capitalisation.
educational −: dotation pour études.

energy: énergie (f).
Atomic − Commission: [U.S.] Commission de l'Energie Atomique.
European Atomic − Community: Communauté Européenne de l'Energie Atomique.
− supplies: ressources énergétiques.

to enforce: appliquer, mettre en vigueur, faire exécuter.
[J] *− a contract*: faire exécuter un contrat.
− the law: appliquer la loi.
− obedience: se faire obéir.
− one's rights: faire valoir ses droits.
− a rule: faire respecter le règlement.
enforceable: exécutoire.
enforcement: exécution, mise en vigueur, recouvrement.
enforcement of a foreign judgment: exécution d'un jugement étranger.
enforcement by legal process: exécution par la voie légale.
for enforcement: aux fins de recouvrement.
law enforcement: application (f) de la loi.

to enfranchise: affranchir, dégrever, accorder le droit de vote.

to engage: (s')engager, embaucher.
− in business, in politics: se lancer dans les affaires, la politique.
− capital: engager des capitaux.
− workers: embaucher des ouvriers.
to be engaged in...: se livrer à..., exercer (une activité).
(telephone) « line engaged » −: (téléphone) « ligne occupée ».

engagement: engagement (m), obligation (f) ; poste (m), situation (f).
to enter into an −: contracter une obligation.
to meet one's −(s): faire face à ses engagements.

engineer: ingénieur (m), mécanicien (m).
civil −: ingénieur civil.
sales −: ingénieur commercial.
engineering: science de l'ingénieur, technique, organisation, génie.
agricultural, civil engineering: génie agricole, civil.
engineering consultant: ingénieur-conseil.
engineering department (office): bureau d'études.
industrial engineering: organisation rationnelle (scientifique) du travail, de l'activité industrielle.
production engineering: technique de production.
[C] *sales engineering*: technique(s) de vente.

to engross: accaparer (des denrées).
[J] **engrossment**: copie (f), grosse (f) (d'un acte).

to enhance: accroître, augmenter, mettre en valeur, rehausser.

— *the value of*: augmenter (rehausser) la valeur de.

to enjoin: enjoindre, ordonner, prescrire, interdire.

enjoyment: jouissance (f), exercice (m) d'un droit.
[J] *covenant of quiet* — : garantie contre trouble de la possession.
prevention of — : trouble de jouissance.

to enlarge: étendre les délais légaux ; [U.S.] élargir, relâcher un prisonnier.
[J] — *bail, a recognizance*: proroger une caution, un engagement.
enlarged *powers*: pouvoirs élargis.

to enquire, to inquire: (se) renseigner, demander, faire des recherches.
[J] — *(into)*: se renseigner, enquêter (sur).
enquiry: enquête, investigation, renseignement(s), instruction (d'une affaire).
board of enquiry: commission d'enquête.
exhaustive enquiry: enquête approfondie.
enquiry office: bureau de renseignements.
public enquiry: enquête de commodo et incommodo.
to conduct (to hold) an enquiry: procéder à une enquête.
to make enquiries after s.o.: s'enquérir de qn.
to remand a case for further enquiry: renvoyer une affaire pour plus ample informé.

to enrich: enrichir.
enrichment: enrichissement (m).
[J] *unjust enrichment*: enrichissement sans cause.

enrolment: enrôlement (m), enregistrement (m).
[J] inscription d'un acte juridique sur registre officiel.
— *of workers*: embauche d'ouvriers.

to ensue: s'ensuivre.
[B] **ensuing** *account (settlement)*: liquidation suivante.

entail: [J] substitution d'héritiers ; bien substitué.
to entail: entraîner, occasionner ; transmettre (à titre inaliénable).
to entail expenses: entraîner des frais.
to entail an estate: substituer un bien au profit d'un tiers.
entailed *estate*: majorat.

to enter: entrer, enregistrer, inscrire, passer une écriture.
— *an action against s.o.*: intenter un procès à qn.
— *one's appearance*: comparaître.
— *a deed, a judgment*: enregistrer, minuter un acte, un jugement.
— *a deposition on the record*: consigner un témoignage au procès-verbal.
— *goods*: déclarer des marchandises à la douane.
— *an item in the books*: porter un article sur les livres, à un compte.
— *possession of premises*: emménager dans un local.
— *into an agreement (with)*: conclure un accord.
— *into a bargain*: passer un marché.
— *into a contract*: conclure un contrat.
— *into the rights of a creditor*: demeurer subrogé aux droits d'un créancier.
— *on negotiations*: entamer des négociations.
— *upon a property*: prendre possession d'un bien.
agreement to be **entered** *into*: accord à intervenir.
commitments **entered** *into*: engagements contractés.
transactions **entered** *from day to day*: opérations enregistrées au jour le jour.
breaking and **entering**: (vol) avec effraction.
entering up: inscription.

enterprise: esprit d'entreprise, entreprise (f), affaire (f), établissement (m).
[C] *associated* — *(s)*: entreprises ayant des liens entre elles (sociétés mères et filiales, société placées sous contrôle commun).
free — : libre entreprise.
nationalized, private — : entreprise nationalisée, privée.
parent — : maison mère.

to entertain: recevoir, concevoir, admettre.
— *a claim*: admettre une réclamation.
— *doubts*: concevoir des doutes.
— *a proposal*: faire bon accueil à une proposition.
entertainment: accueil (m), réception (f).
entertainment allowance (expenses), extrapay for entertainment: frais de représentation et de réception.
the World of Entertainment: le monde du spectacle.
[F] *entertainment tax*: taxe sur les spectacles.
entertainer: hôte.
public entertainer: professionnel du spectacle.

enticement: séduction (f).

entirety: intégralité (f), totalité (f).
[J] *in its* — : intégralement.
entire *contract*: contrat (m) indivisible (opp. *severable or apportionate contract*).

to entitle : donner le droit de, donner qualité pour.
    entitled *to :* autorisé à, fondé à, habilité à.
    entitlement : droit (de faire qch).

entity : entité (f).
    [J] *legal* — *:* personne morale, civique, juridique.

entrance : entrée (f) ; prise (f) de possession.
    — *fee :* cotisation d'admission, droit d'entrée.

entrenched : établi de façon durable (pour un texte constitutionnel dont la révision est soumise à une procédure lourde).

entrepreneur : entrepreneur (m) (propriétaire-gérant).
    entrepreneurial : d'entrepreneur, qui concerne l'entrepreneur.
    the entrepreneurial function : le rôle de l'entrepreneur.

to entrust s.o. with sth. : confier qch. à qn.
    — *a sum to s.o. :* remettre une somme à qn en toute confiance.
    to be **entrusted** *with :* être chargé de.

entrepot port : [C] port franc.

entry : enregistrement (m), déclaration (f), passation (f) d'écriture; poste (m), rubrique (f), article (m), débuts (m) (dans un domaine d'activité, en politique).
    [D] *customs* — *:* déclaration en douane.
    — *ex-warehouse :* déclaration de sortie d'entrepôt.
    — *into force :* entrée en vigueur.
    — *form :* formulaire d'inscription ou d'enregistrement.
    — *for home use :* déclaration de mise en consommation.
    — *inwards (outwards) :* déclaration (en douane) d'entrée (de sortie).
    port of — *:* port d'entrée.
    preliminary — *:* déclaration préalable.
    right of — *:* droit de prendre possession.
    right of free — *:* droit de passer librement la frontière.
    — *of satisfaction of mortgage :* radiation d'hypothèque.
    single, double- — *book-keeping :* comptabilité en partie simple, double.
    unlawful — *:* prise de possession illégale d'une terre.
    — *under bond :* acquit-à-caution, passavant.
    wrong — *:* faux emploi.
    to make an — *:* passer une écriture.

to enure : [J] entrer en vigueur, prendre effet.

the promise **enured** *to his benefit :* la promesse s'est réalisée à son avantage.

environment : environnement (m).
    — *lobby :* (pol.) groupe de pression écologiste.

envoy extraordinary : Ministre Plénipotentiaire.

eo nomine : en ce nom.

epoch-making : qui fait époque, mémorable.

equal : égal (a).
    [F] — *distribution of taxes :* péréquation des impôts.
    equalizing *exchange funds :* fonds de stabilisation des changes.
    — *distribution line :* ligne d'équirépartition.
    — *partners :* associés à part égale.
    on — *terms :* à conditions égales.
    — *voting :* partage des voix.
    creditors that rank — *:* créanciers qui viennent en concurrence.

equality : égalité (f).
    [F] — *before the law :* égalité devant la loi, égalité juridique.
    — *between creditors :* droits égaux des créanciers.
    — *of votes :* partage des voix, voix égales.

equalization : égalisation (f), compensation (f), péréquation (f).
    [F] *exchange* — *account :* fonds de stabilisation des changes.
    — *of rates :* péréquation des taux.
    — *tax :* taxe de compensation.
    — *of taxes :* répartition égale, péréquation des impôts.

to equate : identifier à.

equilibrium : équilibre (m).
    [C] — *of exchange :* équilibre des échanges.
    — *distribution :* répartition équilibrée.
    — *(market) price :* prix d'équilibre (du marché).
    — *rate of exchange :* taux équilibré des échanges (monétaires).
    to restore the — *:* rétablir l'équilibre.
    to upset the — *:* rompre l'équilibre.

to equip : équiper.
    equipment : matériel d'équipement, outillage.
    capital **equipment** *:* biens d'équipement.
    equipment *expenditure :* frais d'équipement.
    farm, medical, office **equipment** *:* matériel agricole, sanitaire, de bureau.

equitable : équitable (a).
[J] – *assets* : avoirs applicables au paiement de dettes.
– *assignment* : cession de créance.
– *charge* : nantissement.
– *claim* : réclamation en accord avec les principes de l'équité.
– *easement* : servitude tolérée.
– *interests* : droits équitables prenant le pas sur le droit formel de propriété.
– *lien* : privilège indépendant de la possession (par ex. privilège du vendeur sur le produit de sa vente).

equity : équité (f).
[J] recours aux principes mêmes de la justice, lorsque celle-ci se trouve en conflit avec le droit formel.
The – *(Eq.)* repose sur les 20 maximes suivantes :
1. *Eq. acts* in personam : l'*Eq.* porte sur le droit des personnes.
2. *Eq. acts on the conscience* : l'*Eq.* s'inspire des impératifs de la conscience.
3. *Eq. will not suffer a wrong to be without a remedy* : l'*Eq.* ne laisse passer aucune injustice.
4. *Eq. follows the law* : l'*Eq.* respecte la loi.
5. *Eq. looks to the intent rather than the form* : l'*Eq.* se préoccupe de l'intention plutôt que de la forme.
6. *Eq. looks on that as done which ought to be done* : l'*Eq.* considère que ce qui aurait dû être fait, l'a été effectivement.
7. *Eq. imputes an intent to fulfil an obligation* : l'*Eq.* présume l'intention de remplir une obligation.
8. *Equitable remedies are discretionary* : les moyens de l'*Eq.* sont à la discrétion du juge.
9. *Delay defeats* **equities** : le retard (injustifié) forclos l'appel à l'*Eq.*
10. *He who comes into Eq. must come with clean hands* : celui qui invoque l'*Eq.* doit être sans reproche lui-même.
11. *He who seeks – must do –* : celui qui recherche l'équité, doit agir avec équité.
12. *Eq. regards the balance of convenience* : l'*Eq.* tient compte des avantages réciproques.
13. *Where there are equal equities, the law prevails* : lorsque les droits en présence sont à égalité, le droit strict est applicable.
14. *Where there are equal equities, the first in time prevails* : lorsque les droits en présence sont également fondés, le plus ancien prévaut.
15. *Eq., like nature, does nothing in vain* : l'*Eq.* comme la nature, ne fait rien sans but.
16. *Eq. never wants a trustee* : l'*Eq.* trouve toujours un *trustee* (voir ce mot).
17. *Eq. aids the vigilant* : l'*Eq.* vient au secours du diligent.
18. *Equality is –* : l'*Eq.*, c'est l'égalité.
19. *Eq. will not assist a volunteer* : l'*Eq.* ne vient pas à l'aide de celui qui offre volontairement ses services.
20. *Eq. will not permit a statute to be a cloak for fraud* : l'*Eq.* ne permet pas la fraude sous le couvert du droit.
[F] – *capital* : capital effectif, fonds propres.
government (surplus) – : excédent d'exercice.
– *financing* : financement par augmentation de capital.
– *interest* : participation.
– *investment* : [U.S.] investissement en valeurs mobilières à revenu variable.
proprietorship – : part sociale, d'associé.
– *securities* : [U.K.] actions ordinaires, [U.S.] actions (de toute nature).
tax – : masse fiscale.

equities : [F] actions ordinaires. Dans une société en liquidation, la masse de l'actif qui reste à répartir entre les détenteurs d'actions ordinaires d'où le terme d'« equities » populairement employé pour désigner ces actions.

ergonomics : ergonomie (f).

(the) erosion of the purchasing power : l'érosion du pouvoir d'achat.

erratic items : postes (m) intermittents (exportations ou importations de caractère exceptionnel ; auto blindée, sous-marin d'exploration, etc.).

error : erreur (f), méprise (f).
[J] erreur de fait ou mal-jugé.
– *and omission(s) excepted (E and OE)* : sauf erreur et omission.
to commit an – : commettre une erreur.
[C] –*(s) in posting* : erreurs de report.
goods sent in – : marchandises expédiées par erreur.

escalation of prices : escalade des prix ; ajustement des prix.
escalator : échelle mobile.
escalator clause : clause d'échelle mobile.

escape : fuite (f), évasion (f), échappatoire (f).
– *clause* : clause de sauvegarde.
– *period* : délai de réflexion.
to escape *payment of a sum* : se dispenser de payer une somme.
escapee : évadé.

escheat : déshérence (f), bien tombé en déshérence.
[J] *right of –* : droit d'aubaine, droit de bris.

escrow : [J] engagement sous seing privé confié à un tiers pour être livré au destinataire sous certaines conditions spécifiées.

essence : essence (f), fond (m).
[J] — *of the contract* : condition en stipulation essentielle d'un contrat.
the — of the matter : le fond de l'affaire.
(cr.) *the — of a crime* : l'élément constitutif d'un crime.

essential : essentiel, indispensable (a).
— *foodstuffs, products, —(s)* : denrées, produits de première nécessité.

to establish : établir, fonder, affermir, constater.
— *a business* : fonder une maison, une affaire.
— *oneself in business* : s'établir (en affaires).
— *a file* : constituer un dossier.
— *an industry* : créer une industrie.
— *a reputation (for)* : se faire une réputation (de).
— *one's right* : faire apparoir son droit.
an **established** *fact* : un fait (bien) établi, avéré.
established business : maison solide.
established institutions : les autorités constituées.
established rule : règle établie.
old-established : établi de longue date.
a well-established business : une maison solide.
witness of well-established position : témoin patenté, caution bourgeoise.

establishment : établissement (m), installation (f), constatation (f), fondation (f), création (f) (d'une maison de commerce), assiette (f) (d'un impôt).
banking establishment : établissement bancaire.
business establishment : maison de commerce.
establishment charges : frais de premier établissement ; frais généraux.
government-owned establishments : établissements publics.
indoor establishment : service sédentaire.
permanent establishment : lieu du principal établissement.
to be on the establishment : faire partie du personnel.
the Establishment : les classes dirigeantes.

estate : 1° état (m), condition (f) (d'une personne) ; 2° mode (m) légal de possession ; 3° biens (m pl) immeubles ; 4° patrimoine (m) ; 5° masse (f) des biens.
[J] — *in abeyance* : succession vacante.
absolute — : droit inconditionnel et perpétuel de propriété immobilière.
— *agent* : agent immobilier.
bankrupt's — : masse (des biens) de la faillite.
burdened — : domaine grevé d'hypothèques.
clear — : bien libre d'hypothèque.
conditional — : droit conditionnel de propriété (par ex. le droit d'hériter).
determinable — : droit dont la naissance dépend d'un événement futur.
deceased — ([U.S.] *decedent's estate*) : succession (f).
distribution of an — : partage d'une succession.
— *duty (tax)* : droit de succession.
family — : patrimoine.
— *free of encumbrance (unencumbered estate)* : immeubles francs de toutes charges.
gross — : actif brut d'une succession.
housing — : lotissement (m).
— *income* : revenus provenant d'investissements en biens immobiliers.
joint — : communauté, biens en commun.
landed — : propriété foncière.
life — : biens en viager.
personal — : biens mobiliers.
real — : biens immobiliers.
real — agent : agent immobilier.
separate — : biens propres (d'une femme mariée).
taxable — : biens imposables.
the third — : le tiers état.

estimate : estimation (f), appréciation (f), évaluation (f), devis (m) estimatif, projet (m) (de budget).
[F] *additional —(s)* : crédits supplémentaires.
approximate (rough) — : devis approximatif.
budget —(s) (ou *—(s)*) : prévisions budgétaires.
building — : devis de construction.
conservatrice (sober) — : évaluation prudente.
— *of expenditure* : prévision de dépenses, chiffre prévu pour les dépenses.
— *of the losses* : évaluation des pertes.
monthly —(s) : évaluations mensuelles.
over- — : surévaluation.
provisional —(s) : prévisions approximatives.
— *of risk* : appréciation du risque.
under- — : sous-évaluation.
at the lowest — : au bas mot.
to make an — : établir un devis.
to put in an — : soumissionner.
to estimate : estimer, apprécier, évaluer.
estimated amount : montant prévu, estimatif.
estimated charges : imputations estimatives.
estimated cost : coût estimatif.
estimated tax : [U.S.] forme de paiement anticipé de l'impôt sur le revenu.
estimated value : valeur forfaitaire, d'estimation.

estimation : estimation, appréciation, jugement.
by official estimation : à dire d'expert.
in my estimation : à mon avis.

estoppage : [J] exclusion (f), empêchement (m).

estoppel : non-recevabilité.
[J] *promissory* — : force obligatoire d'une promesse.

estovers : [J] *common of estovers* : droit d'affouage.

estrays : [J] bétail égaré dont le maître reste inconnu.

estreat : [J] extrait des minutes d'un tribunal concernant les amendes, les reconnaissances et les confiscations.

etiquette : convenances (f pl), étiquette (f).
[J] *the — of the Bar* : les règles du Barreau.
breach of professional — : faute professionnelle.

euro-issuings : [F] euro-émissions.

european : européen (a).
European Atomic Energy Community : Communauté Européenne de l'Energie Atomique.
European Coal and Steel Community : Communauté Européenne du Charbon et de l'Acier.
European economic community (E.E.C.) : Communauté Economique Européenne (C.E.E.).
european plan : [U.S.] chambre d'hôtel sans pension.
european snake : serpent monétaire européen.

to evade : éluder, esquiver, se soustraire à, tromper.
[C] — *one's creditors* : esquiver ses créanciers.
— *the issue* : éluder la question.
[F] — *payment of a tax* : se soustraire à l'impôt.
— *taxes* : frauder le fisc.

tax evader : fraudeur (m) (fiscal).

evasion : moyen d'éviter, évasion (f), échappatoire (f), fraude (f).
[F] — *of tax, tax* —, [U.S.] *fiscal* — : fraude fiscale.
to use — (*s*) : user d'échappatoires.

even : uni, égal, uniforme (a).
— *chances* : chances égales.
of — *date* : de même date.
— *money* : compte rond.
— *numbers* : nombres pairs.
[B] *the contango is* — : le report est au pair.

event : cas (m), événement (m), occurrence (f).
[J] *fortuitous* — : cas fortuit.
costs abide the — (*s*) : les frais suivent le principal.
current — (*s*) : l'actualité.
in the course of — (*s*) : par la suite.
unforeseen — : occurrence imprévue.
[F] — *of default* : déchéance du terme.

eventual : final, éventuel (a).

eviction : [J] éviction (f), expulsion (f) d'un locataire; dépossession (f) judiciaire d'un bien immobilier; rentrée légale en possession.
active — : éviction effective.
constructive — : atteinte aux droits du locataire.
— *order* : ordre d'expulsion.
evicted *tenant* : locataire évincé.
to evict *property, title of property, of, from s.o.* : récupérer légalement une propriété, un titre de propriété, des mains de qn.
evictor : expulseur (m).

evidence : preuve testimoniale, témoignage (m), témoin(s).
[J] *all* — *available* : toutes les pièces justificatives.
circumstancial — : preuve indirecte, par présomption.
competent — : preuve recevable.
conclusive — : preuve concluante.
— *of debt* : titre de créance.
— *for the defence* : témoin à décharge.
derivative — : preuve dont la force probante a sa source ailleurs.
direct — : preuve directe.
documentary — : preuve authentique, littérale, notoriété de droit.
extrinsic — : preuve extrinsèque.
false — (*perjury*) : faux témoignage.
— *of guilt* : preuve de culpabilité.
hearsay — : preuve par commune renommée.
incompetent — : preuve non recevable.
— *of indebtedness* : titre de créance.
indirect — : preuve indirecte.
internal — : preuves intrinsèques.
the laws of — : la théorie des preuves.
oral — : témoignage, déposition orale.
original — : preuve ayant une force probante propre.
parol — : témoignage oral, extrinsèque.
peremptory — : preuve libératoire.
presumptive — : preuve par présomption.
prima facie — : commencement de preuve.
primary — : preuve qui s'impose comme la meilleure.
— *for the prosecution* : témoin à charge.
real — : preuve matérielle.
— *by record* : preuve par l'aveu de la partie adverse.
secondary — : preuve qui laisse supposer l'existence d'une preuve meilleure.
— *in support (of an application)* : preuve à l'appui (d'une demande).

unchallengeable — : preuve irrécusable.
— *in writing* : preuve littérale.
written — : preuve écrite.
to collect — : recueillir des témoignages.
to furnish — : fournir la preuve.
to give — : porter témoignage.
to give — *about sth.* : rendre témoignage de qch.
to impugn — : récuser un témoignage.
to take — : recueillir des témoignages.
to turn Queen's, [U.S.] *State's,* — : témoigner contre ses complices (sous promesse de pardon).

ex allotment (of new shares) : ex-répartition (d'actions nouvelles).

ex ante demand : demande prévue (ou souhaitée).

(goods sold) ex bond : (marchandises vendues) à l'acquitté.

ex-bonus : ex-bonus, ex-répartition.

(actions) ex contractu, ex delicto, ex maleficio : actions en rupture de contrat, fondées sur des griefs autres que la rupture de contrat.

ex-directory telephone number : numéro de téléphone sur « liste rouge ».

ex dividend : (coupon) sans dividende.

ex-gratia payment : paiement de faveur.

ex interest : sans intérêt.

ex investment : investissement projeté.

ex-officio member : membre de droit.

ex post facto (law) : (loi) ayant une application rétroactive.

ex proprio motu : spontanément, de sa propre initiative.

ex quay, duty on buyer's account : à quai non dédouané.

ex quay, duty paid : à quai — dédouané.

ex repayment : ex remboursement.

ex rights : ex droit, droit détaché, actions ou valeurs sans droits à dividendes et sans droits de souscription.

ex ship : au débarquement, à bord.

ex store : disponible.

ex wharf : franco à quai.

ex-work : ex-fabrique (f), ex-usine (f), départ usine.

exaction : exaction (f).
[J] délit d'extorsion de fonds par un fonctionnaire pour des services qui devraient être gratuits.

examination : examen (m), étude (f), inspection (f), visite (f).
[J] interrogatoire (m) d'une partie par l'avocat de l'adversaire (suivi fréquemment d'un compromis).
— *of the bill of health* : arraisonnement de la patente de santé.
cross- — : contre-interrogatoire.
medical — : visite médicale.
post-mortem — : autopsie (f).
— *of scene of crime* : descente sur les lieux.
under — : à l'étude.
— *of a witness* : audition d'un témoin.
to examine *(a witness, an account)* : examiner ; entendre (un témoin), vérifier (un compte).
examiner : examinateur, inspecteur, juge d'instruction.
examining *magistrate* : magistrat instructeur.
[D] *customs* — : visite (inspection douanière).

to exceed : excéder, dépasser.
when the supply **exceeds** *the demand* : quand l'offre est supérieure à la demande.
— *the instructions received* : aller au-delà des instructions reçues.
— *one's powers* : sortir de sa compétence.
— *the speed limit* : ne pas observer la limitation de vitesse.
not **exceeding** *(the market value)* : jusqu'à concurrence de (la valeur marchande).

except : excepté, sauf.
— *by agreement (between...)* : sauf accord (entre...).
— *as otherwise provided* : sauf dispositions contraires.
to except : excepter, exclure.
[J] *to except the jurisdiction of a court* : décliner la compétence d'un tribunal.
to except a witness : récuser un témoin.
errors and omissions excepted : sauf erreur ou omission.
exception : exception (f) ; fin de non-recevoir ; clause d'un acte exceptant une chose de la stipulation générale ; dérogation (f) (en matière d'impôt).
bill of exception : récusation (f).
exception rei judicatae : exception de la chose jugée.

to take exception to a witness: récuser un témoin.

excess: excès (m), excédent (m).
— *capacity*: capacité excédentaire.
— *fare*: supplément (d'un billet de chemin de fer, etc.).
— *luggage*: excédent de bagage.
— *weight*: excédent de poids.
[F] — *demand inflation*: inflation résultant d'une demande excessive.
— *expenditure*: frais supplémentaires.
— *over the original contribution*: boni de liquidation.
— *price*: excédent de prix.
— *profit*: bénéfice actualisé net.
— *profits*: superbénéfices.
— *profits tax*: impôt sur les bénéfices exceptionnels.
— *supply*: offre excédentaire.
to apply for — *shares*: souscrire des actions à titre réductible.

excessive: excessif, exagéré (a).
— *claims*: prétentions exagérées.
[F] — *duties taxes*: droits, impôts excessifs ;

exchange: échange (m), transmission (f) réciproque de biens, troc (m); Bourse (f).
[F] *Baltic* — : Bourse du commerce étranger des houilles, des bois, des huiles et des céréales, à Londres.
bank of — : maison de change.
bill of — : lettre de change.
— *broker*: courtier (agent) de change.
— *brokerage*: courtage de change.
— *control*: contrôle des changes.
— *cross rate*: parités croisées entre deux monnaies.
— *fluctuations*: fluctuations du change.
— *Stabilisation Fund*: Fonds de Stabilisation des Changes.
first (second, third) of — : première (seconde, troisième) de change.
foreign — *broker (dealer)*: cambiste (m).
foreign — : devises étrangères ; effets sur l'étranger.
foreign — *office*: bureau de change.
— *for forward delivery*: opérations de change à terme.
— *gain*: gain de chance.
— *holdings*: avoirs en devises.
labour — : Bourse du travail.
letter of — : lettre de change.
— *list*: bulletin des changes.
— *loss*: perte de change.
long (short) — : papier long (court).
medium of — : moyen d'échange.
par of — : change au pair.
purchase (sale) of — *(s)*: achat (vente) de devises.
— *rate(s) (rate of* —*)*: taux du change, cours

des changes.
at the current rate of — : au change du jour.
ratio of — : taux d'échange.
— *report*: compte rendu de Bourse.
Royal — : Bourse du Commerce (à Londres).
— *for spot delivery*: opérations de change au comptant.
the Stock — : la Bourse (des valeurs).
to gamble on the Stock — : jouer en Bourse.
— *value*: valeur d'échange.
— *value of a currency*: cours d'une monnaie.
value- — : contre-valeur.
to peg the — : maintenir le cours du change.
to exchange: échanger.

the Exchequer: [A] le Trésorier, le Ministre des finances, le fisc.
the Chancellor of — : le Chancelier de l'Echiquier (le Ministre des finances).
[F] *exchequer bills (bonds)*: bons du trésor.

excise: impôt indirect, contributions indirectes.
[F] — *duty*: droits indirects (sur les alcools, etc.).
the — *office*: le service des Contributions indirectes.
— *officer*: agent (receveur) des contributions indirectes.
— *-bond*: acquit à caution.
— *tax*: [U.S.] impôt indirect, droit de licence.
The Board of Customs and — : [U.K.] l'Administration des Douanes et des Contributions indirectes.

to exclude: exclure.
[ASS] (a) *policy which excludes risks*: (une) police qui exclut certains risques.
excluding: à l'exclusion de.

exclusion: [F] [U.S.] somme qui sur le plan fiscal n'est pas considérée comme un revenu.
— *clause*: clause d'exclusion, refus (m) d'admission.

exclusive: exclusif, unique ; fermé (a) (cercle, profession).
[C] — *agency agreement*: contrat d'exclusivité.
— *agent*: agent, dépositaire exclusif.
— *right*: droit exclusif.
— *(of)*: à l'exception de.
— *of charges*: frais non compris.
« — *of wine* » : « vin non compris ».

to execute: exécuter, effectuer.
[J] — *a deed*: passer, souscrire un acte.
— *a judgment*: exécuter un jugement.
— *a plan*: réaliser un plan, un projet.
— *a will*: faire un testament.

execution: exécution (f), mesure (f) exécutoire, accomplissement (m).

[J] — *of a deed*: souscription d'un acte.
— *of an order*: exécution d'une commande.
stay of —: ordonnance de surseoir (à un jugement).
— *of a will*: exécution d'un testament.
in the — of one's duties: dans l'exercice de ses fonctions.

executive: a) (a) exécutif; b) le pouvoir exécutif (l'Exécutif), cadre (m), membre du personnel dirigeant.
— *branch*: le pouvoir exécutif.
— *board (of an association)*: bureau (d'une association, d'une société).
— *committee*: comité exclusif.
— *director*: administrateur à temps plein.
— *functions*: fonctions exécutives.
— *order*: [U.S.] décret-loi.
— *secretary*: secrétaire administratif.
— *session*: [U.S.] séance à huis clos.
— *staff*: personnel administratif.
— *retirement plan*: [U.S.] retraite des cadres.
sales —: directeur commercial.
a senior —: un cadre supérieur.

executor, executrix: exécuteur (m), exécutrice (f).
[J] exécuteur, exécutrice testamentaire.
literary —: exécuteur littéraire.

executory: [J] exécutoire (a) (jugement, etc.).
— *consideration*: contrepartie d'une obligation.
— *contract*: contrat certain comportant promesse d'exécution ultérieure.
— *details*: détails d'exécution.
— *devise, right*: legs, droit dépendant d'un événement futur.
— *law, order*: loi, ordonnance en vigueur.
— *regulations*: règlements d'exécution.
— *sale*: vente forcée.

exemplary damages: [J] dommages-intérêts pour préjudice moral.

exemplification: [J] expédition (f), ampliation (f), copie (f) authentique (certifiée conforme).

exempt (from): exempt (de), franc (de).
to exempt: affranchir, exempter, exonérer.
to exempt s.o. from liability: exonérer qn de (ses) responsabilités.
[F] *to exempt from tax*: exonérer d'impôt.
exemption: exonération (f), exemption (f), dispense (f), affranchissement (m), dégrèvement (m), abattement (m).
basic exemptions: exemptions de base.
exemption clause: clause d'exonération.
exemption from duties: franc de droits.
personal exemption: [U.S.] abattement, déduction pour charges de famille.
reciprocal exemption: exemption réciproque (résultant de traités entre Etats).
exemption from tax: exonération d'impôt.

exequatur: [J] exequatur (accordé aux consuls).

exercise: exercice (m).
[C] — *price*: cours de base.
in the — of one's duties: dans l'exercice de ses fonctions.
to exercise: exercer.
to exercice an option for: exercer sa faculté (de), opter (pour).
[B] lever une prime, consolider un marché à prime.
to exercice a profession: exercer une profession.
to exercice a right: exercer un droit.

to exhaust: épuiser.
exhaustion: épuisement.

exhaustive: complet, approfondi (a).
[J] — *inquiry, investigation*: enquête approfondie.
[C] — *market-survey*: étude de marché approfondie.

exheredition: [J] exhérédation (f), déshéritement (m).

exhibit: [J] pièce à l'appui, pièce à conviction.
to exhibit: exhiber, produire, faire apparaître.
to exhibit documents: produire des pièces.
to exhibit profits (losses): faire apparaître des bénéfices (des pertes).
to exhibit proceedings: intenter.

exhibition: exposition (f).
[C] *Ideal home —*: Salon des arts ménagers.
Motor —: Salon de l'automobile.

exhibitor: exposant (m).
— *'s pass*: carte d'exposant.

(to be in) existence *(this firm has been in — for fifty years)*: cette maison existe depuis cinquante ans.

exitus: enfants et descendance; produit annuel de terres ou locations; mise en état de la cause ou conclusion d'un plaidoyer.

exodus of capital: [F] exode (m), fuite (f) de capitaux.

to exonerate (from): exonérer, dispenser (de).
[J] — *s.o. from blame*: disculper qn.

— *oneself from one's liabilities* : s'exonérer de ses responsabilités.
exonerating *evidence* : preuve libératoire, témoignage à décharge.
exoneration : exonération, décharge, dispense, extinction d'une dette.
exoneration from blame : disculpation (f).
exoneration clause : clause d'exonération.

to expand : (s')étendre, (se) développer.
(artificially) **expanded** *date* : données gonflées, chiffres gonflés (artificiellement).
[C] **expanding** *market* : marché en expansion.

expansion : expansion (f), développement (m), augmentation (f).
[F] *currency* — : expansion monétaire.
— *of the deficit* : augmentation du déficit.
rate of — : taux d'expansion.

to expect : s'attendre à, compter sur, prévoir.
the **expected** *profits* : les bénéfices escomptés.
expected value : espérance mathématique.

expectancy : attente (f), expectative (f).
[J] *estate, heir in* — : propriété dont la jouissance dépend d'un événement futur ; héritier présomptif.
expectant *heir* : héritier en expectative, présomptif.
[ASS] *life* — *(expectancy of life)* : espérance de vie.
— *of life tables* : tables de survie.

expectation : attente (f), prévision (f), probabilité (f).
elasticity of —*(s)* : élasticité des prévisions.
life —*(s)* (—*(s) of life)* : espérances de vie.
long (medium, short) term —*(s)* : prévisions à long (moyen, court) terme.
price —*(s)* : prévisions de prix.
— *of profits* : prévision de bénéfices.
— *value* : valeur probable.

expediency : convenance (f), opportunité (f) (d'une mesure).
on grounds of — : pour des raisons de convenance.

expenditure : dépense(s) (f).
actual — : dépenses effectuées.
additional — : frais supplémentaires.
[F] *budgetary* — : dépenses budgétaires.
capital —*(s)* : dépenses en capital, immobilisations, dépenses d'équipement.
the national — : les dépenses de l'Etat.
public — : dépenses publiques.
welfare — : dépenses sociales.
[C] *initial capital* — : frais de premier établissement.
operating — : dépenses d'exploitation.
to restrict one's — : réduire ses dépenses.

expense(s) : frais (m), dépenses (f pl), sorties (f pl).
[J] *legal* —*(s)* : débours, frais et dépens.
[C] [F] — *account* : indemnité pour frais professionnels.
allowance —*(s)* : dépenses déductibles.
carriage —*(s)* : frais de transport.
casual —*(s), contingent expenses* : frais imprévus.
deduction for —*(s)* : déduction avant impôt pour frais professionnels.
extra —*(s)* : frais supplémentaires.
household —*(s)* : budget domestique.
incidental —*(s)* : faux frais.
the —*(s) involved* : les dépenses à prévoir.
— *item* : chef de dépense.
maintenance —*(s)* : frais d'entretien.
management (managing) —*(s)* : frais de gérance, d'administration.
moving —*(s)* : frais de déménagement.
office —*(s)* : frais de bureau.
operating —*(s)* : dépenses d'exploitation.
overhead —*(s) (general expenses)* : frais généraux.
organization —*(s)* : frais de premier établissement.
petty —*(s)* : menus frais, faux frais.
— *preference* : dépenses préférentielles ; frais généraux discrétionnaires.
preliminary —*(s)* : frais de constitution (d'une société).
reconditioning —*(s)* : frais de remise en état.
regardless of —*(s)* : sans se préoccuper de la dépense.
relief for —*(s)* : déduction pour dépenses.
repair —*(s)* : frais de répartition.
return of —*(s)* : état de frais.
running —*(s)* : dépenses d'utilisation, dépenses courantes.
standing —*(s)* : frais généraux.
statement of —*(s)* : état de frais.
sundry —*(s)* : frais divers.
travelling —*(s)* : frais de déplacement.
upkeep —*(s)* : frais d'entretien.
working —*(s)* : dépenses d'exploitation.
to balance one's —*(s)* : équilibrer son budget.
to defray one's —*(s)* : couvrir ses frais.
to meet one's —*(s)* : faire face à ses dépenses.
expensiveness : cherté (f).

experience : expérience (f) professionnelle ; habitude (f) ; contre-temps (m).
to lack — : manquer de pratique.
(previous) work — : antécédents professionnels.
to experience : éprouver, expérimenter.
to experience a loss : éprouver une perte.
experienced *in business* : rompu aux affaires.
experiment : expérience (essai).

expert : expert (m).
(according to) — *advice* : (à) dire d'expert.

— 414 —

— *opinion, report*: expertise, rapport (écrit) d'expert.
— *testimony*: exposé (oral) d'expert.
[J] — *witness*: expert cité comme témoin.
— *workmanship*: travail de spécialiste.

expiration, expiry: expiration (f), cessation (f), échéance (f).
— *of a concession*: expiration d'une concession.
— *of a lease*: expiration d'un bail.
on — : à échéance.
to expire: expirer, échoir.
expired *bill*: billet échu, périmé.
expiring *contract*: contrat qui arrive à expiration.
— *(of a term of payment)*: expiration (d'un délai pour payer).
expiry notice: avis d'échéance.

explanatory: explicatif, interprétatif (a).
— *note*: note explicative.
— *statement*: rapport explicatif, éclaircissement.

to explode: démontrer la fausseté de, discréditer.
exploded *theory*: théorie discréditée.

to exploit: exploiter, mettre en exploitation.
[C] *(monopolistic etc.)* **exploitation**: exploitation (monopolistique etc.).

export: exportation (f).
[E] [F] — *agent*: représentant à l'étranger.
— *bonus*: prime à l'exportation.
— *duty*: droit de sortie, d'exportation.
— *gold point (specie point)*: point de sortie de l'or.
— *goods*: articles, marchandises d'exportation.
— *house*: maison d'exportation.
invisible (visible) — *(s)*: exportations invisibles (visibles).
— *licence*: licence d'exportation.
— *market*: marché d'exportation.
— *orders*: commandes d'exportation.
— *price*: prix d'exportation.
— *prohibition*: prohibition de sortie.
— *quotas*: contingents d'exportation.
— *specification*: déclaration d'exportation.
— *taxes*: taxes à l'exportation.
— *trade*: commerce d'exploitation.
to subsidize — *(s)*: accorder (des subventions) des primes à l'exportation.
to export: exporter.
exportable *(commodities)*: (denrées) exportables.
exportation: exportation (f).
exporter: exportateur (m).

to expose: exposer, dévoiler, démasquer.
[C] — *goods for sale*: exposer des marchandises pour la vente.
exposure: abandon (m) (d'enfant); dénonciation (f); dévoilement (m) (d'un crime); exposition de marchandises pour la vente, risque (m).
[J] *indecent exposure*: outrage public à la pudeur.
for fear of exposure: par crainte du scandale.

expresio unius est exclusio alterius
(the express mention of one thing excludes another): la mention expresse d'un élément écarte tout autre.

express: exprès, formel (a).
— *agreement*: convention expresse.
— *condition*: condition expresse.
— *delivery, letter, etc.*: livraison, lettre (par) exprès.
expressly: expressément.

to expropriate: exproprier, déposséder.
[A] **expropriation** *for public purposes*: expropriation pour cause d'utilité publique.

expulsion: expulsion (f).
[A] — *order*: décret d'expulsion, interdiction de séjour.

to expunge: rayer, effacer, réfuter.
[J] — *a proof*: réfuter une preuve.
[B] — *stock from the list*: rayer une valeur de la cote.

ex quay, duty on buyer's account: à quai, non dédouané.

ex quay, duty paid: à quai, dédouané.

ex-serviceman: [A] ancien combattant.

ex ship: à bord.

to extend: étendre, prolonger, proroger.
— *a lease*: prolonger la durée d'un bail.
extended *meaning*: sens large.
— *a payment (the time of payment)*: reculer la date d'un paiement, proroger un paiement.
— *a statutory provision*: interpréter un texte législatif de façon large.

extension: extension (f), « poste » (m) (téléphone intérieur, numéro d'un service).
[C] — *of business*: extension du commerce.
— *of patent*: prolongation de la durée d'un brevet.
— *of payment, of time*: prorogation de délai de paiement, atermoiement.
[F] — *for returns*: prorogation des délais pour produire les déclarations (d'impôt).

extent : étendue (f), limite (f).
[J] ordonnance d'exécution visant le recouvrement d'une dette fiscale.
— *-in-chief* : saisie des biens d'un redevable fiscal.
immediate — : exécution d'urgence.
— *of cover* : étendue de garantie.
— *of taxation relief* : quotité d'un dégrèvement fiscal.
to the — *of* : jusqu'à concurrence de ; dans la mesure où.

to extenuate : atténuer, minimiser.
exténuation : affaiblissement (m).
[J] *extenuation, extenuating circumstances* : circonstances atténuantes.

external : extérieur, externe (a).
— *Affairs* : (pol.) (U.S.) Relations Extérieures.
— *assets* : avoirs à l'étranger.
— *criteria (signs)* : signes extérieurs.
— *economies or diseconomies* : économies ou déséconomies externes.
— *environment* : environnement extérieur (qu'une entreprise ou une société ne peuvent contrôler mais qui affecte leurs plans — ex. situation politique...).
— *exchange* : change extérieur.
— *trade* : commerce extérieur.
externalities : externalités (f pl).

extinction of an action : [J] péremption (f) d'instance.
— *of a debt* : extinction d'une dette.

extinguishment : [J] extinction d'un droit ou d'une obligation.

extortion : extorsion (f) (de fonds).
to extort *money, a promise, etc.* : extorquer de l'argent, une promesse, etc.
extortionate *price* : prix exorbitant.

extra : supplémentaire, en plus (a).
[C] — *costs* : frais extraordinaires.
— *expenses* : frais accessoires.
— *fare* : supplément.
— *pay* : supplément de salaire, sur-salaire.
— *premium* : surprime (f).
— *profit* : bénéfice supplémentaire, profit additionnel.
— *work* : travaux supplémentaires.
—*(s)* : dépenses supplémentaires.

extract of an entry : extrait d'une inscription.

extradition : extradition (f).

to extradite : extrader.

extrajudicial : (procédure) extrajudiciaire.

extraordinary : extraordinaire (a).
— *budget* : budget extraordinaire.
— *general meeting* : assemblée générale extraordinaire.
— *remedies* : moyens de droit extraordinaires.
— *extraordinary resolution* : question à l'ordre du jour d'une Assemblée Générale extraordinaire.

extraterritorial(ity) : extraterritorial(ité).

extreme : extrême, outrancier (a).
[J] — *cruelty* : injures graves.
— *interpretation* : interprétation poussée.
— *measures* : mesures extrêmes.
to drive s.o. to the — *(s)* : pousser qn à bout.
extremity : extrémité, danger de mort immédiat.

extrinsic : extrinsèque (a).
[J] — *evidence* : toute preuve autre que le document lui-même dans un litige portant sur ce dernier.
— *fraud* : tromperie sur les circonstances dans lesquelles une personne a été amenée à conclure ou à ne pas conclure un contrat.
— *value* : valeur extrinsèque.

ex works : départ usine.

eye-witness : témoin oculaire.

NOTES

NOTES

F

fabric (*of a system etc.*) : structure (f) (d'un système etc.).

face : face, apparence, présence, façade (f).
 the − *of a cheque, of a document :* le recto d'un chèque, d'un document.
 − *amount :* montant prévu au contrat (à l'exclusion des intérêts).
 − *judgment :* montant de la somme allouée par jugement.
 − *value :* valeur nominale.
 in the − *of :* en face de, au vu de, en dépit de.
 on the − *of things :* à première vue, manifestement.

to face : affronter, faire face, confronter, envisager.
 to be **faced** *with* (*difficulties a problem*) : (devoir) affronter (des difficultés, un problème).
 to be faced with bankruptcy : être acculé à la faillite.
 − *up to* (*the facts*) : envisager (la situation).

facing : frontal (m).

facility (facilities) : facilités (f pl), avantages ; service (m), institution (f) ; [U.S.] installations, construction (f).
 business **facilities** : installations commerciales.
 [F] *credit facilities :* facilités de crédit.
 full facilities : toutes facilités.
 overdraft facilities : facilités de caisse.
 facilities for payment : facilités de caisse.
 port (*harbour*) *facilities :* installations portuaires.

fac-simile : fac-similé (m), copie figurée (d'un testament...).
 − *signature :* signature autographiée.

fact : fait (m), réalité (f).
 [J] *accessory after the* − : complice par assistance.
 accessory before the − : complice par instigation.
 ascertainment of −(*s*) : constatation des faits.
 evidentiary − : fait brut.
 issue of − : point de fait.
 material − : fait pertinent, contre-part de contrat.
 to accept a statement as − : ajouter foi à une déclaration.
 to set forth the −(*s*) : articuler les faits.
 to state −(*s*) : articuler les faits.
 to stick to the −(*s*) : s'en tenir aux faits.
 taken in the − : pris sur le fait, en flagrant délit.

factor : a) facteur (m), élément (m) ; b) agent (m), intermédiaire (m), mandataire (m), dépositaire (m).
 − *agreement :* accord entre la direction et le personnel d'une seule entreprise.
 − *analysis of correspondence :* analyse factorielle de correspondance (statistique).
 − *cost :* coût de facteur.
 − *for goods :* commissionnaire.
 − *of production :* facteur de production.
 random −(*s*) : facteurs aléatoires.
 scaling − : facteur, jauge d'échelle.
 to be a − *in :* entrer en ligne de compte dans.

factorage : droits de commission, courtage en marchandises.

factored trade bills : [F] lettre de change-relevé (L.C.R.).

factoring : [F] service d'affacturage, facture protestable, [C] achat (m) ferme de créances (f pl).

factory : manufacture (f), usine (f).
 − *act :* loi sur les accidents du travail.
 − *costs :* ensemble des coûts de production.
 − *hand :* ouvrier (ouvrière) d'usine.
 − *inspector :* inspecteur du travail.
 − *outlet :* magasin d'usine.
 − *outlet center :* centre de magasins d'usines.
 − *price :* prix de fabrique.

factual : positif, effectif.
 − *data :* données de fait.
 − *knowledge :* connaissance des faits.

faculty : faculté, liberté, droit de faire qch. qui serait interdit dans d'autres circonstances.
 − *theory :* [U.S.] théorie de la capacité contributive.
 in possession of all his **faculties** : jouissant de toutes ses facultés.

to fail : manquer, échouer, faire défaut.
 − *in one's duty :* manquer à son devoir.
 [J] − *for a million :* faire une faillite d'un million.
 − *in a suit :* perdre un procès.

failing ; *failing which :* à défaut de ; faute de quoi.
 failing payment : faute de paiement.

− 419 −

failure: manque (m), manquement (m), défaut (m), insuffisance (f), marasme (m); déconfiture (f), faillite (f), (voir ce mot dans la partie français-anglais du dictionnaire).
[J] — *of consideration*: défaut de provision.
— *of justice*: déni de justice.
— *of proof*: preuve non pertinente.
random — : défaillance imprévisible.
— *to accept a bill*: défaut d'acceptation d'un effet.
— *to appear*: non-comparution.
bank —*(s)*: [U.S.] krach bancaire.
[F] — *to collect*: non-encaissement.
— *to comply*: non-observation.
— *to keep a promise*: manquement à une promesse.
— *to make a return*: défaut de déclaration d'impôt.
— *to observe a regulation*: inobservation d'un règlement.
— *to pay a bill*: défaut de paiement d'un effet.
— *to reach an agreement*: impossibilité de parvenir à un accord.

fair: foire (f), exposition (f); équitable, juste, loyal, impartial (a).
— *average quality*: qualité courante, qualité loyale et marchande.
a — *chance of success*: une bonne chance de réussite.
— *copy*: transcription au net.
— *deal*: marché loyal, marché équilibré.
— *demand*: demande moyenne, raisonnablement satisfaisante.
— *market value*: juste valeur marchande.
— *means*: moyens, voies honnêtes.
— *presentation*: image fidèle.
— *price*: prix raisonnable.
— *report*: compte rendu loyal.
— *trade*: libre échange dans des conditions de réciprocité loyale.
— *Trading Act*: (U.K.) Loi destinée à protéger le public contre les agissements déloyaux éventuels, notamment des monopoles.
— *trial*: procès équitable.
— *value*: juste valeur.
— *wage(s)*: salaire équitable.
— *wear and tear*: usure normale.
to play — : jouer franc jeu.

fairly: raisonnablement, équitablement, impartialement.
in all **fairness**: en toute impartialité.

faith: confiance (f), foi (f).
to break — *with s.o.*: manquer à sa parole envers qn.
purchaser in good — : acheteur de bonne foi.

fake, faking: trucage (m).
to fake a balance-sheet: truquer un bilan.

fall: baisse (f), chute (f).
— *-back pay*: somme fixée d'avance qui sera payée à des ouvriers empêchés de faire leur travail contre leur gré (ex. à cause des intempéries...).
[F] — *clause*: clause de parité.
— *in price*: baisse de prix.
— *in value*: perte de valeur, dévalorisation.
to buy on a — : acheter à la baisse.
to deal for a — : opérer à la baisse.
to operate for a — *(to speculate)*: jouer à la baisse.
to fall: tomber, baisser, être en baisse, incomber, échoir, relever de.
— *into arrears*: prendre du retard (pour s'acquitter d'une obligation).
— *outside the competence (of s.o.)*: sortir des attributions de qn, échapper à la compétence de qn.
— *within article (20)*: relever de l'article (20).
— *away*: faire défection.
— *within the competence of*: relever de la compétence de.
— *back*: se replier, reculer, rétrograder.
X shares fall back a point: les actions X ont perdu un point.
— *due*: arriver à l'échéance (une créance), devenir exigible.
— *with a plan*: cadrer avec un plan.
— *with a proposal*: accepter une proposition.
— *off*: diminuer, décliner, se ralentir.
— *under suspicion*: devenir suspect.
employment has been **falling** *off*: l'emploi a décliné, la situation de l'emploi s'est dégradée.
the bottom has **fallen** *out of the market*: le marché s'est effondré.
the responsability **falls** *on*: la responsabilité incombe à.
the price of wheat has **fallen**: le prix du blé a baissé.
to buy on a **falling** *market*: acheter à la baisse.

fallacious: trompeur, erroné.

fallacy: faux raisonnement, erreur.
current — : erreur courante.

false: erroné, faux, trompeur.
[J] — *accusation*: dénonciation calomnieuse.
— *arrest*: arrestation illégale.
— *imprisonment*: séquestration.
— *representation (misrepresentation)*: déclaration mensongère, fraude civile.
— *statement*: faux rapport, fausse déclaration.
— *witness*: faux témoin.
to bear — *witness*: rendre faux témoignage.

to interpret sth. — : interpréter qch. à faux.
to obtain sthg on (under, by) — pretences: obtenir qqch par des moyens frauduleux.
[C] *— balance sheet:* faux bilan.
— entry: faux en écritures.
— price: prix erroné.
falsification *of accounts:* faux en écritures comptables.
to falsify *a balance sheet:* fausser un bilan.
to falsify the facts: dénaturer les faits.

family: famille.
[A] *— allowances:* allocations familiales, indemnités pour charges de famille.
— allowance fund: caisse d'allocations familiales.
— benefits: prestations familiales.
— circumstances: situation de famille.
— estate: bien de famille.
— income: revenu familial.
— life-cycle: théorie suivant laquelle la demande pour certains produits varie selon les différents stades de la vie familiale.
— planning: limitation des naissances, « planning » familial.
— quotient: quotient familial.
— welfare: protection de la famille.

famine prices salary: prix de famine, salaire de famine.

fancy goods: nouveautés.

far: loin, lointain.
— -reaching: d'une grande portée, de grande envergure.
in so — as: dans la mesure où.

fare: prix du transport, prix d'une place, tarif.
full —, half — : place entière, demi-place.
passenger — (s): prix du transport des voyageurs.

farm: ferme, exploitation agricole.
— credit, — loan: crédit agricole.
— equipment: matériel agricole.
— -hand, -labourer: ouvrier agricole.
— incomes: revenus agricoles.
— lease: bail à ferme.
— management: économie rurale.
— products: produits de la ferme.
— property: biens agricoles.
— subsidies: subventions aux agriculteurs.
subsistence — : [U.S.] exploitation qui assure seulement la subsistance d'une famille.
stock **farmer**: éleveur.
farmer's tax: impôt sur les bénéfices agricoles.
tenant farmer: cultivateur à bail.
to farm *out:* donner à ferme, faire valoir (une propriété).
farming: exploitation (d'un domaine), location d'une propriété.

farming business: entreprise agricole.
farming lease: bail à ferme.
mixed farming: polyculture.
large scale farming: exploitation de grande envergure.

fashion-house: [C] maison de haute couture.
the fashion trade: la haute mode.

fast moving consumer goods: biens (m pl) de consommation courante.

fat salary: (fam.) gros appointements.

fatal: fatal, mortel; inévitable.
— accident: accident mortel.
— injury: blessures ayant entraîné la mort.

fault: faute (f), négligence (f), défaut (m), imperfection (f).
[J] *latent — :* défaut, (vice) caché.
to be at — (in —): être fautif, être coupable.

faulty workmanship: vice (m) de construction.

favour: faveur (f), grâce (f), « honorée » (lettre).
[C] *your — of the... :* votre honorée du...
to favour: favoriser, approuver.
to favour s.o. with an interview: accorder une entrevue à qn.
to be favoured with an order: être honoré d'une commande.
[F] *the most favoured nation clause:* la clause de la nation la plus favorisée.
favourable: favorable.
favourable balance of payments: balance des paiements favorable.
favourable exchange rate: change favorable.
especially favourable rate: taux de faveur.

feasibility study: étude débouchant sur une solution techniquement possible et applicable.

featherbedding: (U.S.) a) gonflement des besoins en main-d'œuvre; b) subventions abusives.

feature: trait (m), caractéristique (f).
[F] *the — (s) of the budget estimates:* les éléments de prévision budgétaire.
— a piece of news: (journ.) mettre une nouvelle en manchette.

federal: fédéral.
[A] *— Bureau of Investigations* (F.B.I.) : [U.S.] Sûreté Nationale.
[F] *— Reserve Board* (F.E.D.) : [U.S.] Conseil Fédéral de Réserve.

— *reserve system* : [U.S.] système de réserve fédérale.

fee : 1° [F] honoraires, cachet, vacation, émoluments, cotisation, taxe.
2° [J] à l'origine fief héréditaire, actuellement terre ou droit réel transmissible.
[F] *attendance* — *(s)* : jetons de présence.
author's — : droit d'exécution.
consular — *(s)* : droits de chancellerie.
counsel's — *(s)* : honoraires d'avocat.
director's — *(s)* : jetons de présence des administrateurs.
front end — : honoraires précomptés.
judicial and administrative — *(s)* : droits judiciaires et administratifs.
late — : taxe supplémentaire.
medical — *(s)* : honoraires médicaux.
registration — *(s)* : droits d'enregistrement.
retaining — : provision (versée à un avocat).
— *(s) for the right to post bills* : droits d'affichage.
school — *(s), tuition* — *(s)* : frais de scolarité.
transfer — *(s)* : droits de mutation.
witness — *(s)* : indemnité versée aux témoins.
— *simple* : propriété inconditionnelle.
— *-tail* : bien substitué.

to feed : nourrir.
[F] **feed** *the cold theory* : théorie d'expansion par inflation.

feedback : rétroaction (f), réitération (f).
— *effect* : effet de retour ou de rétroaction.

feigned action (issue) : cause fictive.

fellow : collègue, compagnon, complice.
[J] — *convict* : codétenu.
— *delinquent* : coinculpé.
— *partner* : coassocié.
— *servants rule* : règle en vertu de laquelle, sauf accord contraire, l'employeur n'est pas responsable en cas d'accident de travail causé par un camarade.
— *-worker* : compagnon de travail, collaborateur.

felo de se (pl) **felones de se** : coupable de suicide ou de tentative de suicide.

felon : (J) criminel (m).

felonious act : acte délictuel grave.
loitering with — *intent* : vagabondage délictueux.

felony : infraction majeure.

female labour : main-d'œuvre féminine.
[J] **feme** *covert* : femme mariée.
feme sole : femme non mariée.
[C] *feme sole merchant (trade)* : commerçante.

feoffee-in-trust : [J] héritier fidéicommissaire.

ferry dues : [J] droits de passage.

feud : inimitié (entre familles, clans, etc.).
family — *(s)* : dissensions domestiques.
family blood — : vendetta (f.).

fiat : consentement (m), autorisation (f), décret (m).
[F] — *money* : monnaie fiduciaire fictive, sans couverture.

F.I.C.A. *(Federal Insurance Contribution Act)* : (U.S.) loi instituant une couverture obligatoire de sécurité sociale.
fica taxes : charges sociales.

fiction : fiction (f), chose imaginée.
legal — : fiction légale.

fictitious : fictif, simulé.
[F] — *accounts* : comptes de résultats.
— *assets* : actif fictif.
— *bill* : traite en l'air.
— *contract, dividend* : contrat, dividende fictif.
— *credit* : crédit fictif.
— *payee* : bénéficiaire fictif.

fiddling : fraude (m).

fidejussor : caution.

fidelity bond : assurance patronale contre la négligence ou la malhonnêteté éventuelle d'employés.

fiduciary : fiduciaire, scriptural (a) ; fiduciaire (m), dépositaire (m).
— *account* : compte fiduciaire (géré).
— *capacity* : qualité d'une personne agissant pour le compte d'un autre.
— *currency* : circulation fiduciaire.
— *issue* : émission fiduciaire.
— *relation* : rapports de confiance.

field : champ, domaine, sphère ; marché.
— *of activity* : champ d'activité.
oil — : champ pétrolifère.
in the social — : sur le plan social.
— *study, survey* : étude sur place, enquête sur les lieux.
there is a great — *for* : il y a un grand marché pour.

F.I.F.O. *(first in, first out)* : méthode d'évaluation des stocks « premier entré, premier sorti » (P.E.P.S.).

to fight *(an action at law)* : se défendre dans un procès.

figure(s) : chiffre (m), calcul (m), donnée(s) (f pl).
— *aggregate* — *(s)* : chiffres globaux, données globales.
— *benchmark* — *(s)* : chiffres repère.
— *code* : écriture chiffrée, message chiffré.
— *rounded* — : chiffre arrondi.
in round — *(s)* : en chiffres ronds.
sales — : chiffre d'affaires.
— *-head* : prête-nom.

file : collection (f), archives (f pl), dossier (m).
— *tape* : document, image d'archives.
[J] *master* — : fichier principal.
to file : verser au dossier, classer.
to file a petition : déposer (ou enregistrer) une requête.
to file a petition in bankruptcy : déposer son bilan.
to file an application for a patent : déposer une demande de brevet.
[F] *to file a return* : produire, faire parvenir une déclaration (de revenus).
statement to be **filed** : état à produire.
filing *cabinet* : fichier, classeur.
late filing : production tardive (d'une déclaration).

filiation : filiation (f).

filibustering : [U.S.] (pol.) obstruction, prise de parole destinée à retarder un débat.

to fill : remplir, exécuter, suppléer à.
— *in a form* : remplir une commande.
— *an order* : exécuter une commande.
— *the requirements* : répondre aux besoins (ou aux conditions).
— *up a cheque* : remplir, renseigner un chèque.
— *up a vacancy* : pourvoir à une vacance, nommer à un poste.
well-filled *order book* : carnet de commandes bien rempli.

final : final, dernier, définitif, concluant.
[C] [F] *final account* : compte définitif.
— *costs* : prix de revient final.
— *dividend* : solde de dividende.
— *invoice* : facture définitive.
[J] — *demand* : mise en demeure de payer avant action en Justice.
— *evidence* : témoignages concluants.
— *instalment* : dernier versement.
— *judgment (order)* : jugement définitif, sans appel.
— *process* : exécution.

finality : irrévocabilité ; prescription.

finance : finance(s), fonds.
[F] — *act* : loi de finances
— *bill* : effet de finance.
business — : gestion financière (des entreprises).
— *company* : société financière.
— *market* : marché financier.
public — : finances publiques.
— *statement* : état de finances.
— *syndicate* : syndicat de finance.
to finance : financer, commanditer.
to finance an undertaking : financer une entreprise.
financial : financier.
— *adjustment* : redressement financier.
— *aid* : secours ; assistance financière.
— *assets* : actifs financiers.
— *crisis* : crise monétaire.
— *difficulties, embarrassment* : embarras de trésorerie.
— *futures* : contrats à terme d'instruments financiers.
— *futures market* : marché à terme de valeurs, d'instruments financiers (MATIF).
— *interrelations ratio* : coefficient d'interrelations financières.
— *method* : see « compound discount method ».
— *pressure* : gêne pécuniaire.
— *standing of a firm* : situation financière d'une entreprise.
— *statement* : bilan, état des finances.
Financial Times Industrial Ordinary Share Index : indices boursiers du journal britannique « Financial Times », l'équivalent anglais du Dow Jones américain.
— *year* : exercice financier, année budgétaire.
financially *(sound, etc.)* : financièrement (sain, etc.).
financier : financier, homme de confiance, bailleur de fonds.
financing : financement.
— *capacity and requirements* : capacité et besoins de financement.
— *company* : compagnie de financement.
— *expenses* : charges financières.
internal — : autofinancement (m).
self- — : autofinancement (m).

to find : trouver, découvrir, se rendre compte, rendre, prononcer (un verdict).
[J] — *for s.o.* : rendre un verdict en faveur de qn.
— *s.o. guilty* : déclarer qn coupable.
— *an indictment* : prononcer une mise en accusation.
[F] — *money for* : (se) procurer des fonds pour.

finder *(of lost object)*: inventeur (d'un objet trouvé).
finder of a waif: inventeur d'une épave.
finding: découverte, trouvaille, objet trouvé, constatation.
statistical findings: données statistiques.

fine: fin, bon, beau (a), amende (f), peine (f).
[A] *liable to a* — : passible d'une amende.
to fine: condamner à une amende.
[C] *to cut prices too* — : trop baisser les prix.
to cut profits too — : trop réduire les profits.
— *trade bill*: papier de haut commerce, de 1re catégorie.
— *tuning*: réglage très fin (de l'économie).
of the **finest** *quality*: de première qualité.
fine-drawn *arguments*: arguments subtils.
fineness: qualité supérieure, titre (d'une monnaie).

to fingerprint: relever les empreintes digitales.

finish: finesse de l'exécution d'un travail, clôture.
[B] [F] *quotations at the* — *(— quotations)*: cours de clôture.
to finish *(shares)*: finir à (actions).

fire insurance policy: police d'assurance incendie.
— *risk*, — *hazard*: risque d'incendie.

firm: ferme (a), entreprise (f), établissement (m), société en nom collectif.
[C] *affiliated* — : filiale (f).
— *('s) capital*: capital social.
legal — *(law firm)*: cabinet d'avocats.
marginal — : entreprise marginale.
multiple — : maison à succursales multiples.
— *name*: raison sociale.
— *earning profits*: entreprise bénéficiaire.
— *showing losses*: entreprise déficitaire.
[B] — *bargain (deal)*: marché ferme.
— *buyer, seller*: acheteur, vendeur ferme.
the shares remained — : les actions se sont maintenues.
to firm: se raffermir.
to firm up a contract: signer définitivement un contrat.

first: originel, premier, premièrement.
the — *comer*: le premier arrivé.
[J] — *impression*: point de droit sans précédent, qu'un tribunal doit trancher pour la première fois.
— *process*: exploit introductif d'instance.
— *mortgage bond*: obligation portant première hypothèque.
[F] — *debentures*: obligations de premier rang.
— *and final dividend*: première et unique répartition.
— *grade paper*: effet de première catégorie.
— *of exchange*: première de change.
— *-hand information*: renseignement de première main.
— *in*, — *out (F.I.F.O.)*: premier entré, premier sorti (P.E.P.S.) (gestion des stocks).
— *outlay*: frais de premier établissement.
— *trial balance*: balance avant inventaire.

fiscal: fiscal, budgétaire.
[F] — *burden*: charge fiscale.
— *drag*: frein fiscal.
— *handles*: leviers fiscaux.
— *incentives*: incitations fiscales.
— *law*: loi fiscale, législation fiscale, fiscalité.
— *period, year*: exercice fiscal.
— *policy*: politique budgétaire.
— *stun*: tension croissante entre l'évolution des dépenses et celle des recettes.
— *year*: année fiscale.

fish royal: poissons appartenant au souverain lorsqu'ils sont pris dans les eaux territoriales ou rejetés au rivage.
fishing: pêche (f).
deep-sea, high-sea fishing: grande pêche.
fishing licence: permis de pêche.

to fit up *(premises)*: agencer (un local).
— *with*: cadrer avec.
fittings: installations.
statistical fitting: ajustement statistiques.

to fix *(the budget, a price etc.)*: fixer, établir (le budget, un prix, etc.).
[F] **fixed** *assets*: immobilisations.
fixed capital: capitaux immobilisés, valeurs immobilisées.
fixed charged, fixed expanses: frais généraux incompressibles.
fixed consideration: prix forfaitaire.
fixed costs: coûts fixes.
on the date fixed: à la date prescrite.
fixed deposit: dépôt à terme fixe, à échéance fixe.
fixed depreciation: amortissement fixe.
fixed exchange rate: taux de change fixe.
fixed interest security: valeur à revenu fixe.
fixed investment, yield investment: placement à revenu fixe.
fixed plant: installations fixes.
fixed price: prix fixe.
fixed property: (biens) immeubles.
fixed rate bond: obligation à taux fixe.

fixing: cotation (f), fixage (m).
(gold) fixing: fixation du cours de l'or.

fixtures: [J] immeuble par destination.
inventory of — : état des lieux.

flag: drapeau, pavillon.
[C] *convenience* — *(flag of convenience)*: pavillon de complaisance.
trade follows the — : le commerce suit le pavillon.
[A] — *Day*: [U.S.] le 14 juin, fête anniversaire de l'adoption du drapeau national.

flagrante delicto: en flagrant délit.

flash: éclair ; vil, de mauvais aloi.
[F] — *cheque*: chèque sans provision.
[C] — *pack*: emballage publicitaire.

flat: plat, uniforme, invariable (a), appartement (m).
— *denial*: démenti catégorique.
[F] *business is* — : les affaires sont calmes.
— *cost*: prix de revient, uniforme, inchangé.
— *fee*: honoraires à forfait, commission immédiate.
— *market*: marché calme.
— *quotation*: [U.S.] cotation sans intérêt.
— *rate of pay*: taux uniforme des salaires.
— *rate of tax*: impôt de quotité.
— *sales*: ventes languissantes.
— *yield*: see current yield.
to flatten: se stabiliser.

flaw: défaut, vice de forme (entraînant la nullité).

flexibility: flexibilité, souplesse.
[C] *price* — : flexibilité des prix.
flexible *prices*: prix flexibles.
[F] *flexible, variable, exchange rate*: taux de change flexible.

flight: fuite (f).
[J] *capital* — : fuite des capitaux.

to float: flotter, lancer (une affaire, un emprunt), porter un intérêt à taux variable, fonder (une compagnie), émettre (un emprunt).

float: flottant (banque et bourse).
[B] *dirty* — : flottement impur.
[F] — *bonds*: émettre des obligations.
— *a company*: créer une société.
— *a loan*: lancer un emprunt.
to let a currency float: laisser flotter une devise.
floating *assets, capital*: capitaux flottants, mobiles.
floating currency rate: taux de change flottant.
floating debt: dette non consolidée.
floating exchange rate: taux de change flottant.
floating policy: police flottante, ajustable.
floating population: population flottante.
floating cargo: cargaison en mer.
floats: [U.S.] épave (f).
floatsam: choses de mer.

flo(a)tation: lancement (m), émission (f) (d'un emprunt...).

floor: plancher (m).
[J] *the* — *of the court*: l'espace qui sépare le siège du juge du banc de la défense.
[F] — *price*: prix plancher.
price — : plancher des prix.
— *quotation*: cours plancher.

« **The Floor** »: le Parquet, le Prétoire ; (pol.) l'Hémicycle.
to have (to take) the — : (U.S.) prendre la parole (Parlement, A.G.,...).

flow: flux (m), mouvement (m).
[F] *cash* — : voir *cash*.
economic — : flux économique.
monetary — : flux monétaire.
— *-chart (diagram)*: graphique (m) de progessivité.

to fluctuate: fluctuer, osciller.
[F] **fluctuating** *exchange rates*: taux de change variables.
fluctuating prices: prix variables.
narrowing **fluctuation** *margins*: rétrécissement des marges de fluctuation.

fluid market: marché changeant.

fly-by-night: (pej.) personne d'une moralité (f) douteuse en affaires.

folder: prospectus (m), dépliant (m).

to follow: suivre, poursuivre, s'ensuivre.
following *my decision*: conformément, suite à ma décision.
— *up an advantage*: poursuivre un avantage.
— *up a clue*: suivre une piste.
follow-up: suivi (m) (de l'investissement).
— *of products*: suivi des produits.
a — *letter*: une lettre de rappel.

fondamentalist: prévisionniste (m).

food: nourriture, aliments, vivres.
[C] — *products, foodstuffs*: denrées alimentaires.
the — *processing industry*: l'industrie alimentaire.

foot: pied (m).
to set negotiations on — : ouvrir des négociations.
to foot up: additionner.
to foot up the account, the bill: faire l'addition, payer l'addition.
on an equal **footing**: sur un pied d'égalité.
on the footing that: à la condition que.
statutory footing: base légale.

to gain a foothold: prendre pied, s'implanter (sur un marché).

force: force, vigueur ; effectif.
(owing to) the — of circumstances: (par) la force des choses.
economic, social, etc., —(s): forces économiques, sociales, etc.
the labour —: la force de travail.
in —: en vigueur, applicable.
the methods in —: les méthodes appliquées.
to come into —: entrer en application, en vigueur.
forced bill: [U.S.] mesure coercitive.
forced construction: interprétation tirée par les cheveux.
forced currency: cours forcé.
forced loan: emprunt forcé.
forced sale, saving: vente, épargne forcée.
to force *sth. from s.o.*: arracher, extorquer à qn.
to force up prices: faire monter les prix.

forcible: violent, vigoureux ; de force.
[J] *— detainer*: possession illégale (obtenue par violence).
— entry: prise de possession illégale (par violence).
— entry and detainer: procédure sommaire permettant de rentrer en possession des lieux dont on a été évincé par la violence, illégalement.
forcibly: par force.

to forecast: prévoir, pronostiquer.
forecast, forecasting: prévision.
betting forecast: pronostic.
long-term, short-term business forecast: prévision économique à court-terme, à long terme.

to foreclose: forclore saisir, mettre fin à un prêt.
[J] *— the mortgage*: saisir l'immeuble hypothéqué.
foreclosure: forclusion, saisie d'une hypothèque.

to foredate: antidater.

foregift: prime payée pour obtenir un bail, « pas-de-porte ».

(the) foregoing: ce qui précède.

foreign: extérieur, étranger (terme juridique visant tous pays hors de la juridiction des tribunaux anglais, par ex. l'Ecosse).
[F] *— affiliate company*: société étrangère affiliée.
— bill: (U.K.) lettre de change non payable en Grande-Bretagne.

— bonds: obligations étrangères.
— broker: courtier de change étranger.
— commodities (goods): marchandises de provenance étrangère.
— currency: monnaie, devise étrangère.
— exchange: change extérieur.
— exchange dealer: cambiste.
— exchange gap: déficit en devises étrangères.
— exchange market: marché des changes.
— exchange mismatching: encaisse en devises insuffisante pour couvrir les emprunts.
— exploration expenses: frais d'exploration engagés à l'étranger.
— income: revenus de provenance étrangère.
— labour: main-d'œuvre étrangère.
— loan, market: emprunt, marché extérieur.
— money order: mandat international.
— national: ressortissant étranger.
the — Office, Secretary: Ministère, Ministre des Affaires Etrangères.
— owned: sous contrôle étranger.
— plea: exception d'incompétence.
— reserves: réserves en devises.
— resources: avoirs à l'étranger.
— stock: valeurs étrangères.
— tax: impôt étranger.
— tax credit: crédit pour impôt acquitté à l'étranger.
— trade: commerce extérieur.
— trade turnover: volume total des opérations commerciales extérieures (importations plus exportations).

foreman: contremaître (m).
[J] *jury —*: premier juré.

forensic medicine: médecine légale.
— scientist: expert légiste.

foreseeable: prévisible.
— (recovery, slump etc.): reprise, crise, etc. prévisible.

to forestall: anticiper.
[C] *— a competitor*: devancer un concurrent.
— the market: accaparer le marché.

forestry: exploitation forestière.

forfaiting: [F] affacturage à forfait.

forfeit: amende, délit, pénalité.
[J] *— clause*: clause de dédit.
to forfeit: perdre par confiscation, être déchu de.
— a deposit: perdre une caution.
— a right: être déchu d'un droit.
forfeited security: cautionnement perdu.
[F] *to relinquish the —*: abandonner la prime.
forfeited shares: actions périmées.
[ASS] *to forfeit an insurance*: laisser périmer

une assurance.

forfeiture: perte de biens par confiscation, déchéance d'un droit, mort civile.
[J] – *of a driving licence*: retrait d'un permis de conduire.
action for – of patent: acion en déchéance de brevet.
[ASS] – *of an insurance policy*: déchéance d'une police d'assurance.

to forge: forger, falsifier, contrefaire.
[J] **forged** *bank note*: billet de banque contrefait.
forged cheque: faux chèque.
to produce a forged will: supposer un testament.
production of forged documents: supposition.
forger: faussaire, contrefacteur.
forgery: faux, contrefaçon, falsification, supposition.
plea of forgery: inscription de (en) faux.
to put in a plea of forgery: arguer une pièce de faux.
forgery of a will: supposition de testament.
to commit forgery: se rendre coupable de faux.

forgiveness *(of tax)*: [F] remise (gracieuse) d'impôt.

form: forme (f), formalité (f) ; formule (f), imprimé (m).
application –: formulaire de demande, de candidature.
in due –: en bonne et due forme.
in the – of (declaration, etc.): sous forme de (déclaration, etc.).
a matter of –: une formalité.
for –('s) sake, as a matter of form: pour la forme.
– of proxy: formule de mandat, de pouvoir.
order –: bulletin de commande.
– of receipt: formule d'acquit.
– of return: formulaire de déclaration de revenu.
the – and the substance: la forme et le fond.
in written –: par écrit.
to fill in a –: remplir une formule, un bulletin.
to form: former, constituer, instituer, concevoir.
to form an association: constituer une société.
to form into a committee: se constituer en comité (en commission).
to form an opinion of: se faire une opinion sur (de).
*to be **formed***: se former, se constituer.

formal: régulier, conventionnel, absolu, formel.
– *agreement*: accord formel.
– *contract*: contrat en bonne et due forme.
– *denial*: démenti catégorique.
– *meeting*: réunion régulière.
– *notice*: mise en demeure.
– *receipt*: quittance comptable.
– *summons*: citation dans les formes.

formality: formalité.
[D] *customs* **formalities**: formalités douanières.
to fulfil the formalities required: accomplir les formalités prescrites.

formation: formation, constitution.
[F] – *expenses*: frais de constitution.
– *of prices*: formation des prix.
– *of a reserve fund*: formation d'un fonds de réserve.

formula: formule.

forthcoming: prochain, à venir.

forthwith: sur le champ, incontinent (dans un délai de vingt-quatre heures).

fortuitous event: cas fortuit.

forum: tribunal compétent et siège de celui-ci, le pays où s'exerce la juridiction pour une affaire donnée dont les deux parties sont des nationaux de pays différents.

forum originis: le tribunal du pays où un homme a son domicile de naissance.

forward: en avant, antérieur ; à terme.
[F] *to bring –, to carry –*: reporter.
– *contract*: engagement d'acheter ou vendre à un prix fixé, à une date ultérieure.
– *cover*: couverture à terme.
– *dealings*: opérations (de change) à terme.
– *delivery*: livraison à terme.
– *integration*: prise en charge des ventes jusqu'alors confiées à des détaillants.
– *linkage*: polarisation aval.
– *market*: marché à terme.
– *method*: méthode progressive, directe.
– *premium*: report ou déport (m).
– *rates*: cours à terme.
– *sale*: vente à livrer, vente à terme.
to sell –: vendre à terme.
amount carried –: report à nouveau.
[C] **to forward**: envoyer, expédier, transmettre, faire suivre.
to forward goods: acheminer des marchandises.
forwarding agent: transitaire, expéditionnaire.
forwarding charges (expenses): frais d'expédition.

forwarding station: gare expéditive.
« please — », « to be forwarded »: prière faire suivre.

to foster: élever, nourrir ; développer, stimuler.
foster brother, foster sister: frère adoptif, sœur adoptive.
[A] *foster care (fosterage):* placement familial.
foster-child: enfant placé dans une famille.
foster-home: foyer de placement familial.
foster-mother: gardien, mère adoptive.

foul: malpropre, déloyal (a).
[C] *— bill of lading:* connaissement avec des réserves.
— dealing: agissements malhonnêtes.
— play: jeu déloyal, malveillance.
[J] *to fall — of the law:* tomber sous le coup de la loi.

to found *(a company etc.):* fonder (une société, etc.).
ill, well-founded: mal, bien fondé.

foundation: fondation, institution, fondement.
devoid of —: dépourvu de fondement.
founder: fondateur.
[F] *founder's shares:* parts de fondateur.

foundling home: hospice pour enfants trouvés.

(the) four seas: l'Atlantique, la mer du Nord, la Manche et la mer d'Irlande, qui entourent la Grande-Bretagne.

(« the old) four »: [F] « les quatre vieilles » (taxes).

(the) fourth estate: le journalisme (m).

fraction: fraction (f), résidu (m).
[F] *shares which have lost a —:* actions qui ont perdu une fraction de point.
(B) *to add a —:* enregistrer de légers gains.
fractional money: monnaie divisionnaire.

fragmented market: marché (m) hétérogène.

to frame: former, concevoir, inventer.
— an accusation against: monter une accusation contre.
within the framework of: dans le cadre de.

franchise: liberté, privilège, concession de service public ; droit électoral ; minimum d'avaries au-dessous duquel l'assureur n'assume pas de responsabilités.
[F] *— tax:* droit de monopole.

franchising: franchisage (contrat qui permet au franchisé, en contrepartie d'une redevance, de présenter sous sa marque les produits ou les services concédés par le franchiseur).

franked *investment income:* crédit d'impôt attaché aux dividendes reçus.
— payment: dividendes distribués.
surplus — investment income: crédit d'impôt reportable.

franking machine: machine à affranchir.

frater consanguineus, uterinus: frère consanguin, utérin.

fraud: fraude, tromperie, abus de confiance.
[J] [F] *constructive —:* fraude par déduction.
— on the court: tentative de tromper le tribunal, outrages à magistrat.
— relating to goods: tromperie sur la marchandise.
tax —: fraude fiscale.
fraudulence: caractère frauduleux, infidélité (d'un dépositaire, d'un agent).
fraudulent: frauduleux, trompeur.
fraudulent balance-sheet: faux bilan.
fraudulent bankruptcy: banqueroute frauduleuse.
fraudulent clause: clause dolosive.
fraudulent concealment: fait de cacher un défaut de l'objet vendu.
fraudulent conveyance: transfert frauduleux de biens, au détriment des créanciers.
fraudulent declaration: déclaration frauduleuse.
fraudulent entry: fausse écriture.
fraudulent misuse of funds: détournement de fonds.
fraudulent transaction: transaction entachée de fraude.

free: libre, en franchise, exempt (a).
[C] [D] *admission —:* entrée (accès) libre.
— allowance of luggage: franchise de poids.
— alongside ship (F.A.S.): franco quai.
— on board (F.O.B.): franco bord.
— on rail (FOR): franco wagon.
— on truck (FOT): franco camion.
carriage —: franco.
— of charge: sans frais.
— of all claims: franc de tout recours.
— competition: libre concurrence.
— currency: devise qui s'échange librement.
— of all debts: franc de toutes dettes.
— delivery (delivery —): livraison franco.
duty — area: zone franche.
— enterprise: libre entreprise.
— hand: main(s) libre(s), carte blanche.
— in and out (FIO): bord à bord (BAB).
to give s.o. a — hand: donner carte blanche

à qn.
to have a — hand: avoir carte blanche.
— *market:* marché libre (ouvert).
— *offer:* offre spontanée.
— *port:* port libre.
port —: franco de port.
— *on rail:* franco train.
— *sample:* échantillon gratuit.
— *trade:* libre-échange.
— *trader:* libre-échangiste.
— *trial:* essai gratuit.
— *zone:* zone franche.
to free *oneself from one's commitments:* se délier de ses engagements.
[J] *to free from mortgage:* déshypothéquer.
freedom: liberté, franchise, immunité.
freedom from arrest and distress: immunité d'arrestation ou de saisie de biens.
freedom of information, of the press: liberté de l'information, de la presse.
[F] *exchange freedom:* liberté des changes, des échanges.
freedom from tax: exemption, immunité d'impôt.
— *of tax (of duty):* exempt d'impôt (de droits).
— *of income tax:* exempt d'impôt sur le revenu.
— *list:* liste d'exemptions.

freehold: [J] tenure en propriété perpétuelle et libre.
freeholder: propriétaire foncier.

freely: librement, largement.
— *offered (goods, stock):* largement offerte(s) (marchandises, valeur).
to circulate —: circuler librement, sans entraves.

freeman: homme libre, citoyen d'honneur.

freeze: gel (m), blocage (m).
[F] *price, wage — (freezing):* blocage des prix, des salaires.
to freeze: geler, bloquer.
to freeze wages: bloquer les salaires.
frozen account: compte gelé, bloqué, non productif.
frozen assets: fonds bloqués.

freight: fret, cargaison, nolis d'un navire, transport de marchandises, frais de transport.
air —: transport par avion.
— *charges:* frais d'expédition.
— *forward:* frais de transport à la charge du destinataire.
— *inward:* frais de transport des marchandises livrées à l'entreprise.
[E] *cost, insurance and — (C.I.F.):* coût, assurance et fret (C.A.F.).
dead —: faux fret; dédit pour défaut de chargement.
lump-sum —: fret à forfait.
freighting *(on weight, etc.):* fret, affrètement (au poids, etc.).
freighter: affréteur; navire marchand, [U.S.] wagon de marchandises.

frequency: fréquence, périodicité.
— *curve:* courbe de fréquences (statistique).
frequent *practice:* usage courant.

fresh: frais, nouveau.
— *arrival:* nouvel arrivage.
[J] — *evidence:* de nouvelles preuves.
[F] — *money:* argent frais.

friendly arbitrator: amiable compositeur.
— *society:* amicale, société de secours mutuel.

to frighten: effrayer.
[F] — *the bears:* faire courir le découvert.

fringe: accessoire.
[F] — *benefits:* [U.S.] avantages offerts par un employeur à un salarié en plus de ses appointements proprement dits.
— *expenses:* frais accessoires, faux frais.

frivolous: frivole (a).
— *pleading:* argument futile, non pertinent.

frontage: 1° terrain en bordure d'une route, d'un cours d'eau.
2° [J] droit de façade; part proportionnelle des riverains à l'entretien et à la canalisation.

front bench: [UK] = les ministres membres du Gouvernement (face au « Shadow Cabinet » et devant les « Backbenchers »).

fronting and abutting parts: [J] les tenants et les aboutissants.

front-line management: see « first-line management ».

to frustrate: faire échouer.
frustration: frustration (f), anéantissement (m); [J] impossibilité d'exécuter un contrat.

fuel oil, oil fuel: mazout (m), fioul.
to add — to the fire: mettre de l'huile sur le feu.

fugitive: fugitif (m), prisonnier évadé.
[J] — *from justice:* fugitif recherché par la justice.

to fulfil: accomplir, remplir, satisfaire à, exécuter.
— *a duty:* s'acquitter d'un devoir.

the conditions to be **fulfilled** : les conditions requises.
fulfilment *of an obligation* : exécution d'un engagement.

full : plein, entier, complet, intégral (a).
— *age* : majorité (d'âge).
of — *age* : majeur(e).
— *cargo* : cargaison complète.
— *cost* : coût total.
— *discharge* : congé définitif.
payment in — *discharge* : paiement libératoire.
— *disclosure* : divulgation complète.
— *duty* : droit plein.
— *employment* : plein emploi.
— *exemption* : exemption intégrale.
— *fare* : plein tarif.
— *-line stores* : [U.S.] grands magasins non spécialisés (de type traditionnel).
— *name* : nom et prénoms.
— *page spread* : annonce pleine page.
— *particulars* : détails complets, tous les détails.
— *payment* : paiement intégral.
— *premium* : prime entière.
— *price* : prix fort.
— *rate* : plein tarif, taux plein.
— *refund, full repayment* : remboursement intégral.
— *report* : rapport détaillé, complet.
in — *settlement* : pour solde de tout compte.
— *statement* : exposé complet.
— *text* : texte intégral.
— *time* : à temps plein.
to work — *time* : travailler à temps plein.
— *trial balance* : balance préparatoire d'inventaire.
— *value* : valeur entière.
— *weight* : poids juste.
until **fuller** *information is available* : jusqu'à plus ample informé.
in full : en entier, intégralement.
account given in full : compte rendu intégral.
name in full : nom en toutes lettres.
(capital) paid in full : capital entièrement versé.
receipt in full discharge : quittance, reçu libératoire.
to work — *out* : travailler à plein rendement.
to the — : complètement.
fully *paid shares* : actions entièrement libérées.
fully secured creditor : créancier entièrement nanti.

function : fonction (f), charge (f), emploi (m), rôle (m).
advisory — *(s)* : fonctions, attributions consultatives.
aggregate demand (supply) — : fonction de la demande (de l'offre) globale.
governmental — *(s)* : fonctions publiques.

utility — : fonction d'utilité.
to discharge one's — *(s)* : s'acquitter de ses fonctions.
to resign one's — *(s)* : se démettre de ses fonctions.
as a — *of* : en fonction de.
in (my) — *of* : en (ma) qualité de.
functional : fonctionnel.
functional responsibilities : responsabilités liées à une fonction.

fund : fonds (m), caisse (f), provision (f).
(plur.) — *(s)* : argent au jour le jour.
[F] *the* — *(s) (funded debt)* : la dette publique.
available — *(s)* : disponibilités, fonds liquides.
charity — : caisse de secours.
— *(s) of a company* : fonds social.
contingency — : fonds de prévoyance.
death — : caisse de secours en cas de décès.
depreciation — : provision pour dépréciation.
emergency — : fonds de secours.
exchange equalization — : fonds d'égalisation des changes.
extended — *facility* : mécanisme élargi de crédit.
— *(s) flow* : flux de fonds.
— *(s) flow analysis* : étude des mouvements de fonds.
— *flow statement* : tableau de financement.
International Monetary — *(I.M.F.)* : Fonds Monétaire International (F.M.I.).
misappropriation of — *(s)* : détournement de fonds.
mutual — *(s)* : fonds commun de placements, [U.S.] Société d'investissement à capital variable.
« *no* — *(s)* » : « défaut de provision ».
(old age, etc.) pension fund : caisse de retraite (pour la vieillesse...).
public — *(s)* : fonds publics.
reserve — *(s)* : fonds de réserve.
sinking — : fonds d'amortissement.
— *(s) transfer* : transfert de fonds.
unemployment — : caisse d'assurance chômage.
without sufficient — *(s)* : sans provision suffisante.
to have — *(s) with a banker* : avoir une provision en banque (chez un banquier).
to make a call for — *(s)* : faire un appel de fonds.
to misappropriate public — *(s)* : détourner des fonds publics.
to start a — : lancer une souscription.
superannuation — : caisse de retraite.
supplementary — *(s)* : budget annexe.
working capital — *(s)* : fonds de roulement.
to fund : consolider, placer de l'argent, fonder.
funded *capital* : capitaux investis.
funded debt : dette fondée, consolidée.
funded property : biens en rentes.

long-term funded property : capitaux consolidés à long terme.
to fund interest : consolider des arrérages.
to fund money : placer de l'argent en fonds publics.
funding *loan* : emprunt de consolidation.

fundamental : fondamental.
— *qualities* : qualités foncières.
— *question* : question de fond.
the — *of a system* : le principe essentiel d'un système.

furandi animus : (l')intention de voler.

to furnish : fournir, pourvoir, alléguer, meubler.
— *evidence that* : fournir la preuve que.
— *funds* : fournir des fonds.
— *information* : fournir des renseignements.
furnished *flat* : appartement meublé ; garni.

further : supplémentaire, ultérieur (a) ; de plus, au-delà (adv).
[J] *(until)* — *advice* : (jusqu'à) nouvel avis.
— *consideration* : mise en délibéré.
for — *enquiry (inquiry)* : pour plus ample informé.
to remand a case for — *inquiry* : remettre une affaire pour plus ample informé.
upon — *consideration* : après mûre réflexion.
— *information* : renseignements complémentaires.
[C] — *cover (margin)* : marge supplémentaire.
— *orders* : commandes ultérieures.
« *awaiting your* — *orders* » : « dans l'attente de vos nouvelles commandes ».
— *particulars* : de plus amples détails.
a — *transaction* : une nouvelle transaction.
to ask for — *credit* : demander un crédit supplémentaire.

to further : favoriser, faire avancer.
— *cooperation between nations* : développer la coopération entre nations.
furtherance : avancement, progrès ; appui.
(for) the furtherance of trade : (pour) développer le commerce.

fusion : fusion (de partis), fusionnement (de banques).

F.U.T.A. *(Federal Unemployment Tax Act)* : (U.S.) loi instituant l'assurance chômage.
— *taxes* : cotisations d'assurance chômage.

future : futur ; à terme.
[J] — *estates* : biens à venir.
[C] — *delivery* : livraison à terme.
for — *delivery* : livrable à terme.
— *orders* : commandes à venir.
— *prospects (prospects for the future)* : perspectives d'avenir.
— *tradings* : marché à terme.
in the near — : dans le proche avenir.
[B] **futures** : opérations, livraisons à terme, cotation à terme.
futures contract : commande à terme.
financial future(s) : contrat à terme d'instruments financiers.
financial future(s) market # marché à terme d'instruments financiers (MATIF).
futures market : marché à (du) terme, de contrats à terme.
future(s) option : options sur contrats à terme.
future(s) position : cours à terme.
future worth : valeur acquise.
to sell futures : vendre à découvert.

NOTES

G

gain : gain (m), profit (m), bénéfice (m).
[F] *(net long-term) capital* − : [U.S.] gain net de capital à long terme.
(net short-term) capital − : gain net de capital à court terme.
capital − *(s)* : plus-values.
capital − *tax* : impôt sur les plus-values en capital.
chance, contingent − : gain aléatoire.
− *in utility* : augmentation d'utilité.
limit − *(s)* : hausse maximum.
to make a − : réaliser un bénéfice.
to gain : gagner, tirer profit de.
to gain time : gagner du temps.
to gain wealth : gagner des richesses.
[B] **gainer** : qui gagne du terrain (valeur etc.).

gainful : rémunérateur, lucratif.
gainfully *employed* : qui exerce un emploi rémunéré, lucratif.
the gainfully employed population : la population active.

gale : [J] loyer (m).
hanging − : arrérages de loyer.

gallon : gallon ([U.K.] 4 litres 54, [U.S.] 3 litres 78).

galloping inflation : inflation galopante.

gamble : spéculation (f).
to gamble : jouer (de l'argent).
to gamble on a rise : jouer à la hausse.
to gamble on the Stock Exchange : jouer en Bourse, agioter.
to gamble away one's fortune : dilapider sa fortune (au jeu).

gambling, gaming : jeu de hasard.
− *debts* : dettes de jeu.
− *den, house* ; [U.S.] − *joint* : tripot, maison de jeu.
gambler : spéculateur (m).

game : jeu (m).
business − *(s)* : jeux d'entreprise.
− *of chance* : jeu de hasard.
− *theory (or theory of* − *(s))* : théorie des jeux.
− *tree* : arbre (m) de décision.
to play the − : jouer franc jeu.

gang *(fam.)* : [U.S.] bande organisée de malfaiteurs ; convoi de prisonniers.

gaol : prison, maison d'arrêt (f).

gap : intervalle (m), écart (m), fossé (m), disparité (f), déficit (m), lacune (f), décalage (m).
brain and know-how − : disparité sur le plan de la matière grise et du savoir.
deflationary (inflationary) − : écart déflationniste (inflationniste).
gold − : pénurie d'or.
management − : disparité sur le plan des méthodes de gestion des entreprises.
technological − : disparité sur le plan technologique.
trade − : déficit commercial.
to bridge the − : combler l'écart, faire la soudure.
to reduce the − : réduire l'écart.

garbage levy : [F] taxe locale d'enlèvement des ordures ménagères.

garnishee : tiers saisi.
[J] − *order* : ordonnance de saisissement.
garnisher : créancier saisissant.
garnishment : [U.S.] saisie-arrêt, opposition.

gas industry : industrie gazière (f).

to gather : rassembler, recueillir, réunir, percevoir.
− *informations* : recueillir, réunir des informations.
[F] − *taxes* : percevoir des impôts.
tax-gatherer : percepteur des contributions.

gatt : see « *General Agreement on Tariffs and Trade* »

gavel : marteau (d'un commissaire-priseur, du président d'une assemblée).

GDP (Gross Domestic Product) : #
P.I.B. (Production intérieure brute).

to gear : (s')embrayer, enclencher.
geared : indexé (a) (salaire etc.).
gearing : levier (m), effet phénomène (m) de levier ; endettement.

general : général.
− *acceptance* : acceptation sans réserves.
− *accounting plan* : plan comptable général.

— 433 —

– *Agreement to Borrow (G.A.B.) or* – *Loan Agreements*: Accords généraux d'emprunt.
– *Agreement on Tariffs and Trade (G.A.T.T.)*: Accord Général sur les Tarifs Douaniers et le Commerce (AGETAC).
– *audit*: see « audit ».
– *average*: avaries communes.
– *balance-sheet*: bilan d'ensemble.
– *bill of lading*: connaissement collectif.
– *cargo*: charge à la cueillette.
– *damages*: dommages-intérêt qui découlent naturellement de la plainte et qui n'ont pas besoin d'être spécifiés.
– *demurrer*: fin de non-recevoir.
– *denial*: dénégation absolue (d'une accusation, d'un crime, etc.).
– *expenses*: frais généraux.
– *income tax*: impôt général sur le revenu.
– *issue*: fond (d'un procès).
– *letter of credit*: lettre de crédit collective.
– *level of prices, of wages*: niveau général des prix, des salaires.
– *manager*: [U.S.] directeur général, administrateur-délégué.
– *meeting*: assemblée générale.
– *mortgage*: hypothèque générale.
– *orders*: règles de procédure.
– *partnership*: société en nom collectif.
– *reserve*: réserve générale.
– *strike*: grève générale.
The – *Tax Division*: (France) Direction Générale des Impôts (D.G.I.).
« *The* – *theory of employment, interest and money* » : « La théorie générale de l'emploi, de l'intérêt et de la monnaie ».
– *ticket*: scrutin de liste.
– *trial balance*: balance générale.

generalia verba: termes généraux.

generation of income: [F] génération des revenus.

genocide: génocide (m).

gentleman's agreement: convention verbale ne reposant que sur la loyauté réciproque des deux parties.
a gentleman of independent means: homme sans profession, qui vit de ses rentes.

(the landed) gentry: aristocratie terrienne.

genuine: authentique, d'origine.
– *article*: article garanti d'origine.
– *purchaser*: acheteur sérieux.
– *saving*: épargne authentique.

german: germain, apparenté au premier degré.
[J] *The court comments were* – *to the deci-sion*: les commentaires du tribunal se rapportaient directement à la décision.

gerrymander: [U.S.] (pol.) découpage électoral partial et prémédité.

get-up-and go: (fam.) énergie ; dynamisme (d'un entrepreneur, etc.).

to get: obtenir.
– *an advance*: se faire faire une avance.
[C] – *down to brass tacks*: (fam.) discuter sérieusement d'une affaire.
[F] – *into arrears*: s'arriérer.
– *into debt*: s'endetter.
– *one's living*: gagner sa vie.
– *one's money back*: récupérer son argent, rentrer dans son argent.
– *money in*: faire entrer des fonds.
– *orders*: recueillir des commandes.
– *out a balance-sheet*: établir un bilan.
– *(so much) out of a property*: retirer (tant) d'un bien.
– *value for one's money*: en avoir pour son argent.

gift: don (m), donation (f).
[J] *deed of* – : acte de donation (entre vifs).
– *inter vivos*: donation entre vifs.
– « *mortis causa* » : donation faite au moment d'un danger mortel imminent ou sur le lit de mort, annulable en cas de sauvetage ou de guérison.
outright – : don pur et simple.

gilt-edged investments: [F] placements sûrs, de tout repos.
– *-edged securities, stock* – *(s)*: valeurs de père de famille, « dorées sur tranche », pupillaires, obligations d'Etat.

gimmicks: « trucs » (m pl).
[F] *tax* – : subterfuges fiscaux.

(factory) girl, (work) girl: ouvrière d'usine.

giro: système de virement de compte à compte.
– *account*: CCP, compte chèque postal.
– *service*: les Chèques postaux.

to give: donner.
– *an account (of)*: rendre compte (de).
– *bail*: fournir caution.
– *for the call*: acheter la prime à livrer.
– *credit*: faire crédit.
– *evidence*: déposer, témoigner.
– *notice*: donner préavis.
– *an order*: passer un ordre.
– *for the put*: acheter la prime à recevoir.
– *a rise*: accorder une augmentation (de

salaire).
— *security*: fournir caution.
— *time*: accorder un délai.
— *and bequeath*: léguer.
at a **given** *price*: à un prix donné.
in a given time: dans un délai.
to give on: faire reporter (des titres).
to give up: livrer qn à la justice, faire arrêter qn, (B) céder des points.
to give up one's property: céder ses biens.
to give up on's security: se dénantir.
— *way*: céder, laisser passer (un navire), fléchir (des actions, des prix).
(C) **give-away**: objet donné en prime, cadeau publicitaire.
give-and-take *policy*: politique de concessions mutuelles.
giver *for a put and call*: preneur d'action.
giver of an option: optionnaire.
giver of the rate: payeur de la prime.
giver of stock: reporté.
giver of a trade order: auteur d'une commande.
giving: adjudication de dommages-intérêts.
giving of an option: achat d'une prime.
giving orders: passation de commandes.
giving up: remise (d'un document).
giving way (of shares): fléchissement (des actions).

glamours: (B) actions de prestige.

glut: encombrement (m), pléthore (f).
[F] — *of money*: capitaux trop abondants.
to glut: encombrer.
glutted *market*: marché encombré.

« **The Gnomes of Zurich** » : [B] (fam.) « Les Gnomes de Zurich », ces mystérieux banquiers suisses qui sont réputés faire la pluie et le beau temps en finance internationale.

goal: objectif (m).
— *programming*: programmation des objectifs.

to go bail for: se porter garant pour.
[F] — *a bear, a bull*: jouer à la baisse, à la hausse.
— *down (shares)*: baisser (des actions).
— *in for (e.g. import trade)*: se lancer dans (par ex. le commerce d'importation).
— *a fall, a rise*: être à la baisse, à la hausse.
— *into business*: se mettre dans les affaires.
— *into liquidation*: se mettre en liquidation.
— *out of business*: cesser les activités.
go-go: [U.S.] qui va de l'avant.
— *investments*: investissements à forte rentabilité mais à hauts risques.
go-slow *strike*: grève perlée.
stop-go *policy*: politique de coups de frein et d'accélération.

(act of) God: [J] cas de force majeure.

going concern: entreprise prospère.

going wage(s): salaire(s) courant(s).

going to law: recours à la justice.

on going business: entreprise déjà installée.

gold: or (m).
— *(s)*: valeurs aurifères.
[F] — *bonds*: obligations-or.
— *bullion standard*: étalon lingot-or.
— *currency*: monnaie-or.
— *drain*: fuites d'or.
— *exchange standard*: étalon de change or.
— *holdings*: réserves d'or.
import and export — *point*: point d'entrée et de sortie de l'or.
— *specie*: or monnayé.
— *standard*: étalon or.
standard — : or standard (au titre).
two tier — *market*: double marché de l'or.
[B] **Golden** *Boys*: (U.S.) jeunes spéculateurs sur le marché à options (stratégie basée sur la hausse).
golden handshake: grosse somme d'argent donnée à un Administrateur qui prend sa retraite.
golden rule: règle d'or (théorie économique).

good: bon (a).
— *bargain*: marché avantageux.
— *brand*: bonne marque.
[J] — *conduct certificate*: certificat de bonne vie et mœurs.
in — *faith*: de bonne foi.
— *receipt*: quittance valable.
— *title*: titre de propriété irréfragable.
to make — : indemniser.
[F] *bad money drives out* — : la mauvaise monnaie chasse la bonne (loi de Gresham).

goods: marchandises (f pl), articles (m pl).
[J] « — *and chattels* » : biens mobiliers (en matière de succession).
[C] [D] — *accounts*: compte de marchandises.
bonded — : marchandises entreposées en douane.
branded — : articles de marque.
capital — : biens d'équipement.
clearance — : marchandises en solde.
clearing of — : solde, liquidation (f).
consumer — *(consumption goods)*: biens de consommation.
durable — : biens durables.

dutiable — : marchandises sujettes à des droits.
duty-free — : marchandises exemptes de droits.
duty-paid — : marchandises dédouanées, acquittées.
export — *(exports)* : marchandises (articles) d'exportation.
fancy — : nouveautés.
free — : marchandises en franchise, exemptes de droits.
— *for home use* : marchandises pour la consommation intérieure.
manufactured — : produits manufacturés.
marketable — : marchandises disponibles pour la vente, destinées à la vente.
perishable — : denrées périssables.
private — : biens privatifs.
public — : biens collectifs.
— *rated* : marchandises tarifées.
— *rates* : tarifs marchandises.
refuse — : marchandises de rebut.
sale — : soldes (f pl).
staple — : produits de base.
tinned — : conserves alimentaires.
— *traffic* : trafic (des) marchandises.
warehoused — : marchandises entreposées.
to dispose of — : écouler des marchandises.
to seize — : saisir, confisquer des marchandises.
to value — : inventorier des marchandises.

goodwill : le terme a un sens différent selon qu'il s'agit de gestion commerciale ou de décision d'investir (f).
[C] achalandage, fonds de commerce (m) ; « image de marque, notoriété (f) de l'entreprise ou du produit », valeur de la clientèle.
[F] bénéfice actualisé net, profit net : dans une entreprise, le « — » (notion proche de : éléments incorporels) est apprécié en capitalisant le supplément de valeur pouvant exister entre la rentabilité future d'un capital et sa rémunération aux conditions normales de placement (opp. « *badwill* »).

gossip writer : chroniqueur mondain.

to govern : diriger, gouverner, régir.
prices are governed by : les prix sont régis par.
[F] *the amount of the allowance for dependents is governed by the age of the children* : le montant du dégrèvement pour charges de famille est défini par l'âge des enfants.
governing body : organismes directeurs.
the governing classes : les classes dirigeantes.
self-governing : autonome.

government : gouvernement, gouvernemental.
constitutional, democratic, federal... — : gouvernement constitutionnel, démocratique, fédéral...
— *agency* : agence, institution gouvernementale.
[A] — *annuity* : pension d'Etat, rente sur l'Etat.
— *aid* : aide gouvernementale, officielle.
— *bank* : banque d'Etat.
— *bonds* : obligations de l'Etat, titres de rente.
— *Borrowing Requirement (G.B.R.)* : (U.K.) Besoins d'emprunt du gouvernement.
— *controlled* : étatisé, sous le contrôle de l'Etat.
— *employees* : fonctionnaires.
— *loan* : emprunt d'Etat, emprunt public.
— *monopoly* : monopole d'Etat.
— *officials* : hauts fonctionnaires.
— *owned enterprises* : entreprises nationalisées, entreprises de l'Etat.
— *policy* : ligne de conduite du gouvernement.
— *revenue* : revenus publics.
— *securities, stock* : fonds, titres d'Etat.
self- — : autonomie politique.
— *taxes* : impôts d'Etat.
governmental : gouvernemental.
governmental accounting : comptabilité publique.

governor : gouverneur (m).
bank — : gouverneur de banque.

gown : robe des avocats, des magistrats.

grace : grâce (f), pardon (m).
[J] *act of* — : loi d'amnistie.
days of — *(grace period)* : délai de grâce, de franchise.
measure of — : mesure gracieuse.
petition of — : recours en grâce.

grade : grade (m), degré (m), qualité (f).
high, low — : de qualité supérieure, inférieure.
to be on the up — : (fam.) monter, tendre à la hausse (prix) ; reprendre (affaires).
to grade : classer, trier, graduer.
[F] **graded** *rates* : tarifs dégressifs.
graded tax : impôt progressif (le plus souvent) mais aussi (parfois) impôt dégressif.
gradual : graduel, progressif.
gradual extinction of a debt : extinction graduelle d'une dette.
graduated : gradué.
graduated duty : droit gradué.
graduated income tax, graduated according to income : impôt progressif, proportionnel au revenu du contribuable.
graduated pension scheme : régime des retraites complémentaires.
graduated rent : loyer s'élevant par paliers.

graduated tax brackets: barème d'impôt progressif par tranches.
graduation : gradation (des paiements).

graft: [U.S.] concussion (f), corruption (f) de fonctionnaires.

grain exchange: bourse des grains.
— *market*: marché aux grains.

grand: [U.S.] mille dollars (argot).

« grandfather » clause: [J] clause des droits acquis.

grand jury: jury d'accusation.

grant: concession (f), subvention (f), octroi (m).
— *-in-aid*: subvention (d'Etat), aide pécuniaire.
capital — *(s)*: subventions en argent.
death — : capital-décès.
exceptional — *(s)*: crédits exceptionnels.
— *of a patent*: délivrance d'un brevet.
— *of land (land grant)*: concession de terrain.
investment — : subvention pour investissement.
to grant: accorder, octroyer, consentir.
to grant a bail: mettre en liberté sous caution.
to grant a certificate: délivrer un certificat.
to grant a monopoly: concéder un monopole.
to grant an overdraft: consentir un découvert.
to grant a pardon: grâcier.
to grant a subsidy: accorder une subvention.
grantee: concessionnaire (m).
granting *(of a licence, of a loan, etc.)*: concession (d'une licence, d'un prêt, etc.).
grantor: concédant (m), donateur (m).

« grape-vine »: vigne (f).
to hear on the — : (fam.) nouvelle que l'on apprend par ouï-dire.

graph: graphe (m).

the grass-roots: « la base ».

gratuitously: à titre gratuit.

gratuity: gratification, libéralité, pourboire, pot-de-vin.

great seal: le Grand Sceau apposé sur les documents officiels [U.K. et U.S.].
(article) in — *request (demand)*: article très demandé.

greenback: (U.S.) billet d'un dollar.

greenmail: (B) pratique (f) qui consiste à acquérir une part importante du capital d'une société dans l'espoir d'effrayer la direction et de l'inciter à la racheter à un cours supérieur. Il s'agit en somme d'un « chantage aux actions » envers une société qui se sait vulnérable.

greenmailer: spéculateur pratiquant le chantage aux actions.

grid scores: degrés d'évaluation (en vue d'une promotion).

grievance: grief (m), injustice (f).
— *(s)*: revendications.
[J] — *committee*: commission du contentieux administratif.
— *committee of a bar association*: commission de discipline du barreau.
— *procedure*: procédure de règlement des différends.
to redress a — : redresser un tort.

gross: gros, grossier, trop fort, brut (a).
— *abuse*: abus choquant.
— *amount*: montant brut.
— *average*: avarie grosse.
— *carelessness*: négligence flagrante.
— *crime*: crime énorme.
— *displacement*: déplacement global.
— *Domestic Product (GDP)*: # Production intérieure brute (P.I.B.).
— *earnings*: revenu brut.
— *income*: revenu brut.
— *leasing areas, GLA*: [US] surface construite locative.
— *margin*: pourcentage ajouté au prix de revient.
— *miscarriage of justice*: déni de justice flagrant.
— *national (domestic) product*: produit national brut (P.N.B.).
— *negligence*: faute lourde.
— *price*: prix brut.
— *proceeds*: produit (rendement) brut.
— *profit method*: méthode du bénéfice brut.
— *receipts*: recettes brutes.
— *returns*: recettes brutes.
— *sales*: ventes brutes (l'ensemble des ventes compte non tenu des déductions diverses : rabais etc.).
— *tonnage*: jauge brute.
— *value*: valeur brute.
— *weight*: poids brut.

grossing up ratio: coefficient de majoration.

ground: terrain, raison, cause.
[J] *building* — : terrain(s) à bâtir.
— *for complaint, for exemption*: motif de plainte, d'exemption.
— *(s) of expediency*: raisons de convenance.
— *(s) of judgment*: considérants.

legal *—(s)* : raisons de droit.
—(s) for litigation : sujet de litige, matière à procès.
— rent : redevance foncière, rente foncière.
on the —(s) (that) : pour la raison (que), en raison de (ce que).
—(s) underneath a building : tréfonds d'un immeuble.
to lose — (shares) : perdre du terrain (actions).
groundless : sans fondement.

group : groupe, groupement, catégorie, collectivité.
financial, industrial — : groupe financier, industriel.
— dynamics : dynamique de groupe.
— insurance : assurance collective.
pressure — : groupe de pression, groupement de propagande.
— of shareholders : groupement d'actionnaires.
social — : milieu social.
— work : travail en équipe.
age grouping (of the population) : répartition (de la population) par groupes d'âge.

to grow : pousser, croître, augmenter.
growing *debt* : dette croissante.
growing *economy* : économie en expansion.
growing *tendency* : tendance croissante, de plus en plus accentuée.
grossing-up : *(U.K.)* # imposition selon la méthode du bénéfice mondial.

grower : cultivateur (m).

grown-up : adulte (m).
this firm has **grown** *considerably* : cette entreprise a pris une extension considérable.
home-grown product : produit indigène.

growth : croissance, développement, expansion, progrès.
balanced — : croissance équilibrée.
— chart : graphique de croissance.
economic — : croissance économique.
— path : sentier de croissance.
rate of — : taux de croissance.
— theory : théorie de la croissance.
sustainable — : croissance durable.

guaranty, guarantee : garantie (f), caution (f), cautionnement (m), aval (m).
[J] [C] *bank —* : caution, garantie bancaire.
collateral (subsidiary) — : garantie collatérale.
— commission : ducroire, commission de garantie.
— company : société de cautionnement ou de sécurité.
— fund : fonds de garantie, fonds de réserve.
— given (in lieu of bail) for an individual : acte de soumission.
— insurance : assurance de cautionnement.
joint — : cautionnement solidaire.
— (given) on oath : caution juratoire.
— society : association de cautionnement.
to go — (guarantee) for s.o. : se porter garant pour qn.
to guarantee : garantir, cautionner, donner son aval (à).
to guarantee (a person) : cautionner (une personne).
to guarantee a payment : répondre d'un paiement.
to guarantee a bill : avaliser un effet.
guaranteed *bond* : obligation garantie.
guaranteed *stock(s)* : titre(s), fonds garanti(s).
guaranteed *vintage* : appellation contrôlée.
guaranteed *wage* : salaire garanti.
guarantee : garanti, créancier à qui il est donné caution.
guarantor : garant, caution, répondant, avaliste.

guardian : tuteur (m), curateur (m), conseil (m) judiciaire (d'un prodigue).
[J] le droit A.A. distingue quatre catégories de tutelle (guardianship) : 1. la tutelle naturelle exercée par le père ; 2. la tutelle exercée par la personne désignée par le mineur ; 3. la tutelle dative, par testament ou par le tribunal ; 4. tutelle ad litem, exercée par une personne au nom d'un mineur, d'un interdit ou d'un absent.
Les fonctions de *— of the person* et du *— of the property* sont, en général, exercées par la même personne, mais il convient de noter que la tutelle paternelle ne porte que sur la personne, et si le mineur en est en possession de biens, un *— of the property* doit être désigné. Le plus souvent, d'ailleurs, c'est le père.
(Note : en droit moderne, le curateur d'un aliéné interdit est désigné sous le nom de : *committee for a lunatic*.)
acting — : protecteur.
board of —(s) : conseil de famille.
deputy — : subrogé tuteur.
joint — : cotuteur.
testamentary — : tuteur constitué par un testament.
guardianship : garde, curatelle, tutelle.
child under guardianship : enfant en tutelle.

guess, guessing : conjecture (f).

guesstimate : prévision (f) « à vue de nez ».

guidance : direction, conseils, orientation.
educational guidance : orientation scolaire.
vocational guidance : orientation professionnelle.

to guide : guider, diriger.
   guideline : [U.S.] tableau des durées d'utilisation des biens, en matière d'amortissement.
   guide-lines : directives, [U.S.] directives internes prises par une administration fédérale.
   growth guideline : ligne directive.
   guiding *idea, guiding principle* : idée directrice, principe directeur.

guild : association (f), corporation (f), cercle (m).
   trade — : corps de métier.

guilt : culpabilité (f).
   [J] **guilty** : coupable.
   — *in fact and law* : atteint et convaincu.
   to find s.o. — : déclarer qn coupable.
   to have a — *conscience* : avoir mauvaise conscience.
   to plead — : plaider coupable.

gun licence : [J] permis de port d'armes.
   gunman : [U.S.] tueur (à gages), voleur armé.

to gyrate : être soumis à de brusques fluctuations.

gyration : brusques fluctuations (f) (du marché).

NOTES

H

habeas corpus (*ad subjiciendum*) : « que tu aies le corps pour l'amener » (devant la cour), formule juridique exprimant qu'un prévenu doit comparaître devant le magistrat afin qu'il soit statué sur la validité de son arrestation.
writ of — : ordonnance d'habeas corpus.

habit : habitude (f).
[J] — *and custom* : comportement habituel.

habitable : habitable.
to keep one's tenant's house in — *repair* : tenir son locataire clos et couvert.

habitual : habituel.
— *criminal* : récidiviste, repris de justice.
— *drunkard* : ivrogne invétéré.
— *offender* : récidiviste.

hack : manœuvre (m), homme de peine.
— *reporter* : journaliste chargé de la rubrique « des chiens écrasés ».

to haggle, to higgle : marchander.
— *about, over the price* : débattre le prix, chicaner sur le prix.

The Hague : La Haye.
— *Conventions* : les Conventions de La Haye.
— *tribunal* : le tribunal de La Haye.

hail insurance : assurance contre la grêle.

half : demi (a).
[J] — *brother, half sister* : frère ou sœur, consanguins ou utérins.
— *day work* : travail à mi-temps.
[B] — *commission* : remise.
— *commission man* : remisier.
[C] — *measure* : demi-mesure.
— *pay* : demi-salaire.
— *price* : à moitié prix.
— *profits* : de compte à demi.
— *rate* : demi-tarif.
— *-yearly* : semestriel.
— *-yearly dividend* : dividende semestriel.
to work — *-time* : travailler à mi-temps.
to go **halves** : être de compte à demi.

(city) hall, (town) hall : [A] hôtel de ville.

hallmark : poinçon (m), cachet (m), contrôle (m).
to hallmark : poinçonner.

halo effect : « effet (m) d'auréole (f) » (impression très favorable que fait un candidat à un emploi à cause de qualités qui n'ont cependant pas directement à voir avec cet emploi).

halt : arrêt (m).
[F] *to bring (inflation) to a* — : mettre fin à l'inflation, donner un coup d'arrêt à l'inflation.
to come to a — : s'arrêter.
to halt : (s')arrêter, bloquer, mettre un terme à, contenir, enrayer.
to halt inflation : contenir, enrayer l'inflation.
to halt the rise in prices : mettre un terme à la hausse des prix.

hammer : marteau (m).
to come under the — : être vendu aux enchères.
to hammer : marteler.
to hammer prices : faire baisser les prix.
[B] *to hammer a defaulter* : exécuter un agent de change.

hand : main (f), ouvrage (m), talent (m) ; méthode (f) ; intermédiaire (m) ; entremise (f).
at — : sous la main.
by — : à la main, par messager, par express.
in — : en main, en caisse, en magasin.
on — : en main, à sa charge.
at first — : de première main.
balance in — : solde en caisse.
cash in — : encaisse.
clean — (s) : mains nettes (conduite irréprochable dont doit faire preuve le demandeur dans un procès en « *equity* »).
factory — : ouvrier d'usine.
farm — : ouvrier agricole.
jobbing — : tâcheron, ouvrier à la tâche.
— *labour* : travail manuel, main-d'œuvre.
— *made* : fait à la main.
note of — : reconnaissance de dette.
from — *to mouth (to live)* : vivre au jour le jour.
second- — : d'occasion, de seconde main.
second- — *dealer* : revendeur, brocanteur.
stock in — : marchandises en magasin.
« *hands wanted* » : « on demande de la main-d'œuvre ».
to be short of — (s) : manquer de main-d'œuvre.
to have money at — : avoir de l'argent sous la main.
to have a free — : avoir pleine liberté d'agir,

carte blanche.
goods left on — : marchandises laissées pour compte.
to make money — *over first :* (fam.) gagner de l'argent facilement, faire des affaires d'or.
to take in — : prendre en main.
to take the law into one's own — *(s) :* se faire justice à soi-même.
« given under my — *and seal » :* « signé ».
handbill : prospectus (m).
hanceuffs : menottes (f pl).
handout : subsides (m pl), papier de presse.
handsale : vente conclue par un « tope-là ».
handsel : étrenne (première vente de la journée), arrhes, avant-goût.
underhand : clandestin, subreptice(ment).

to hand : remettre, transmettre, léguer.
[J] — *over one's authority :* remettre ses pouvoirs.
— *over (s.o.) to justice :* remettre (qn) aux mains de la justice.
— *over money personally :* remettre de l'argent en mains propres.
— *over one's property to s.o. :* céder son bien à qn.

handicap : handicap (m), inaptitude (f).
occupational — : inaptitude à occuper un emploi.
physical — : déficience physique.
the industrial(ly) **handicapped** : les invalides du travail.

handicraft : métier, travail manuel, main-d'œuvre (artisanale).
—*(s) :* produits de l'industrie artisanale.
local —*(s) :* artisanat local.

handing over : a) remise de qch. entre les mains de qn ; b) *(of property)* cession, délivrance, *(of powers)* transmission, *(of benefit, etc.)* résignation.

to handle : manier, manipuler, exercer, pratiquer.
— *business :* brasser des affaires.
— *goods :* manutentionner des marchandises.
handling *charges :* frais de manutention.
handling *costs :* coût de la manutention.

handsome : beau, généreux, intéressant (a).
a — *price :* un bon prix.
— *profits :* de jolis bénéfices.

to hang : pendre, suspendre, accrocher.
[J] — *jury :* [U.S.] faire avorter les délibérations d'un jury (en refusant de se conformer à l'opinion émise par la majorité).
— *the landlady :* [U.S.] partir sans payer son loyer.
[C] — *out one's shingle :* [U.S.] ouvrir un magasin (un cabinet).
— *together :* s'accorder (déclaration).

hangman : [J] bourreau (m).

hangover : [U.S.] reliquat (m).

« hansard » : compte rendu officiel des débats parlementaires (longtemps rédigés par M. Hansard).

harbour : havre (m), port (m), gîte (m), abri (m).
— *craft :* bâtiment de servitude.
— *development :* aménagement d'un port.
— *dues :* droit de port.
home — : port d'attache.
— *master :* capitaine de port.
to harbour : donner asile à.
to harbour a criminal : donner asile à un malfaiteur.

hard : dur, pénible, difficile (a) ; (adv) dur, difficilement, avec peine, en hausse (valeurs).
[J] — *and fast rule :* règle de droit infrangible, règle stricte.
— *labour :* réclusion avec travail disciplinaire.
[F] — *cash :* espèces sonnantes, argent liquide.
— *currency :* (devise) monnaie forte.
—*-earned :* péniblement gagné.
— *money :* espèces sonnantes.
— *price of stocks :* cours tendu, soutenu, ferme.
— *work :* travail assidu.
— *to sell :* difficile à vendre.
a **hardboiled** *businessman :* un homme d'affaires tenace.
to harden *(up) (prices) :* (se) raffermir (les prix ou les cours).
a **hardened** *criminal :* un criminel endurci.
hardening *of prices :* fermeté des prix (des cours).
hardness : raffermissement (des cours), tension (du marché).
hardness of contangoes : tension des reports.
hardware : matériel de traitement de l'information.

harm : mal (m), tort (m), préjudice (m).
bodily — : lésion corporelle.
to do s.o. — : nuire à qn.

(fiscal) harmonization : harmonisation fiscale.
tax — *(in a customs or economic union) :* harmonisation des fiscalités.
to harmonize *interests :* concilier des intérêts.

harvest : moisson (f), récolte (f).

hatchet man: personne chargée de tâches impopulaires dans l'entreprise (ex. annoncer un licenciement).

hat-money: [J] primage (m).

haul: a) transport (m), traction (f), remorquage (m); b) changement (m), cargaison (f); c) prise (f), pêche (f), coup de filet (m).
  to make a good — : donner un fructueux coup de filet, faire un gain important.
  haulage: transport, charroi.
  haulage contractor: entrepreneur de transports.
  road-haulage: transport routier.

haven: refuge.
  [F] *tax* — : refuge fiscal (et non « paradis fiscal »).
  tax — *company*: société refuge.
  tax hell: pays à fiscalité forte (sans doute par opp. à tax « heaven »).

haves: nantis.
  — *and have-nots*: (pays) riches et pauvres.

having countries: nations nanties.
  — *-not countries*: nations défavorisées.

hazard: a) jeu (m) de hasard; b) danger (m).
  [C] [ASS] risque (m).

head: a) tête (f); b) chef de bureau, etc.; c) chef d'accusation; d) chapitre (m), rubrique (f), article (m).
  — *accountant*: chef comptable.
  — *(s) of an agreement*: principes d'un accord.
  — *(s) of a charge*: chefs d'accusation.
  — *clerk*: premier commis.
  — *of a department*: chef de service.
  — *of a family*: chef de famille.
  — *lessee*: locataire principal.
  — *office*: siège central (d'une société, etc.).
  — *partner*: associé principal.
  (so much) per — : (tant) par tête.
  — *post office*: bureau de poste central (principal).
  — *of state*: chef d'Etat.
  — *worker*: travailleur intellectuel.
  under separate — *(s)*: sous des rubriques différentes.
  to head: être à la tête de, conduire.
  to head a delegation: conduire une délégation.
  heading: en-tête, intitulé, rubrique, chapitre.
  heading of expenditure: chapitre (rubrique) des dépenses.

headhunter: « chasseur de têtes », recruteur de cadres spécialement compétents.

headquarters: administration centrale, siège d'une société; (milit.) quartier général.

headway: avancement, progrès.
  [F] *to make* — : avancer, faire des progrès.
  the Franc is making a little — *against the dollar*: le franc gagne un peu sur le dollar.

health: santé, hygiène (f).
  [A] *(clean, foul) bill of* — : patente de santé (nette, suspecte).
  the Board of — : la commission d'hygiène.
  — *center*: dispensaire, centre d'hygiène.
  — *certificate*: certificat médical.
  — *department*: service de santé.
  — *insurance*: assurance maladie.
  — *officer*: médecin sanitaire, médecin du service d'hygiène, fonctionnaire de la santé publique.
  public — : santé publique.
  — *record*: fiche médicale.
  school — : hygiène scolaire.
  — *visitor*: infirmière visiteuse.
  — *and welfare activities*: action sanitaire et sociale.
  World — *Organisation (W.H.O.)*: Organisation Mondiale de la Santé (O.M.S.).
  [J] — *hazard*: risque pour la santé lié à la nature du travail (Médecine du travail).

to hear: entendre, écouter, instruire (une affaire).
  [J] — *a case*: instruire une affaire, un procès.
  the case will be **heard**... : l'affaire passera...
  hearing: a) audience d'un tribunal, débats; b) interrogatoire d'un accusé, témoignages.
  hearing of a case: audition d'une affaire.
  full hearing: interrogatoire contradictoire.
  full hearing of witnesses: audition des témoins.
  resumption of the hearing: réouverture des débats.
  the case will come up for hearing... : la cause sera entendue...

hearsay: ouï-dire, rumeur.
  [J] — *evidence*: a) déposition sur la foi d'autrui; b) commune renommée. La preuve par ouï-dire n'est pas admise (« — *rule* ») pour éviter d'influencer les jurés, mais de nombreuses exceptions ont dû être faites et constituent la majeure partie du *« law of evidence »*.

heart: cœur (m), centre (m).
  the — *of the matter*: le vif du sujet.
  — *-balm action*: action en dommages-intérêts pour préjudice moral.

hearth: foyer (m).
  without — *or home*: sans feu ni lieu.

heavy : lourd, massif, pesant, onéreux, pénible (a).
[C] [F] — *charges are involved in (it)* : (cela) entraînera de gros frais.
contangoes are — : les reports sont chers.
— *day :* journée chargée.
— *debts :* de lourdes dettes.
— *deliveries :* livraisons massives.
— *expenses (expenditure) :* dépenses élevées.
— *industry :* industrie lourde.
— *fall (of quotations, etc.) :* forte baisse (des cours, etc.).
— *fine :* lourde peine d'amende.
— *freight :* fret lourd, coûteux.
— *losses :* de lourdes pertes.
— *penalty (penalties) :* lourde(s), grave(s) sanction(s).
— *sugar :* [U.S.] (fam.) grosse somme d'argent.
— *taxes :* de lourds impôts.

hedge : couverture, arbitrage, (péj.) interlope.
[J] — *clause :* [U.S.] clause de sauvegarde (dans un contrat).
— *lawyer :* avocat marron.
to hedge : se mettre à couvert ; chercher des échappatoires.
[F] *to hedge by buying at long date :* se couvrir en achetant à long terme.
hedger : opérateur(-trice) en couverture.
hedging : couverture, arbitrage, [U.S.] contrepartie.
hedging for the settlement : arbitrage à terme.

heir, heiress : héritier (ière).
[J] — *-at-law, rightful heir :* héritier légitime.
— *apparent :* héritier présomptif (personne qui succèdera à son ascendant si elle lui survit).
— *presumptive :* héritier présomptif (qui pourrait se trouver disqualifié par la naissance d'un héritier plus direct).
joint — *(s) :* cohéritiers.
last — *:* dernier héritier (appelé à hériter en cas de déshérence).
representative — *:* représentant de la succession.
testamentary — *:* héritier désigné par disposition testamentaire.
to be — *to an estate :* être l'héritier d'une propriété.

heirloom : meubles ou bijoux de famille ; apanage.

held *(part. passé de to hold) :* détenu.
goods — *at the customs :* marchandises en consigne (en souffrance) à la douane.
securities — *in pledge :* valeurs détenues en gage.

help : assistance, secours ; [U.S.] femme de ménage.

« — *wanted » :* offres d'emploi.

hereafter : ci-après ; ultérieurement.

hereby : par là, par les présentes, par le présent acte.
the council — *resolve that... :* le conseil déclare par le présent acte que...
notice is — *given :* il est fait connaître par les présentes.

hereditament : tout bien immeuble transmissible par héritage.
[J] *corporeal* —*(s) :* biens corporels (terres, bâtiments, etc.).
incorporeal —*(s) :* biens réels incorporels (servitudes, profits à prendre, etc.).

herein : en ceci, en cela, ci-inclus(e).
the letter — *enclosed :* la lettre ci-incluse.

hereto (annexed document) : document ci-joint (ci-annexé).

hereunder : ci-dessous, ci-après.

herewith : avec ceci, sous ce pli.
I am sending you — *:* veuillez trouver ci-joint, je vous envoie sous ce pli.

heritable : [J] héréditaire, héritable (bien...), capable d'hériter, apte à hériter.
heritably : par voie de succession.

heritage : héritage (m), patrimoine (m).
[J] (Scot.) biens immobiliers.

hiccup : (B) (F) accident de parcours (dans le déroulement normal des opérations du marché).

hidden : caché, secret.
— *defect :* vice caché.
— *hand :* influence occulte.
[F] *hidden reserve :* réserve latente, réserve occulte.

hierarchy of objectives : hiérarchie (f), pyramide (f) des objets, ordre de priorité (de haut en bas) des objectifs.

high : élevé, haut, important.
— *class :* de grande classe, de première qualité.
— *cost firms :* entreprises à prix de revient élevé.
— *cost of living :* cherté de la vie.
— *Court of Justice :* Haute Cour de Justice.
— *duty goods :* marchandises fortement tarifées (taxées).
the Lord — *Chancellor :* le Grand Chancelier d'Angleterre (qui exerce la haute autorité).

(a) − *executive*: (un) cadre supérieur.
− *finance*: haute finance.
− *grade*: de grande qualité, à haute teneur (minerai).
in a − *-handed way*: d'une manière arbitraire, tyrannique.
− *-handedly*: arbitrairement.
− *income taxpayers*: gros contribuables.
to be − *in office*: occuper un poste important.
to borrow at − *interest*: emprunter à intérêt élevé.
− *money*: argent emprunté à taux élevé.
− *official*: haut fonctionnaire.
− *percentage*: fort pourcentage.
− *-pressure sale*: vente à main forcée.
− *-pressure salesman*: vendeur dynamique.
− *price*: prix élevé.
to fetch a − *price*: se vendre cher.
prices are ruling − : les prix restent élevés.
− *-priced*: cher, coûteux.
to make − *profits*: réaliser de gros bénéfices.
− *-rise block*: tour (immeuble).
− *-salaried*: qui reçoit de forts appointements.
− *seas*: mer au-delà de la limite des eaux territoriales, haute mer.
− *Street Bank*: banque de dépôts.
− *tech*: industrie de pointe.
− *treason*: haute trahison.
− *wages*: salaire élevé.
higher *bid*: surenchère.
the **highest** *bidder*: le plus offrant, le plus fort enchérisseur.
the highest efficiency: le rendement maximum.
the highest price: le cours le plus haut.
the highest and lowest prices: les cours extrêmes.
highbinder: [U.S.] filou, escroc, politicien corrompu.
the **highlights** *(of a political platform)*: les grandes lignes, les points saillants (d'un programme politique).
highly *taxed (product)*: (produit) fortement taxé.
highness *(of prices)*: élévation (des prix).

highway: [J] route ou passage ouvert au public, même si le sol est propriété privée.
the − *code*: le code de la route.

hijacking: détournement (m) (d'un avion, etc.).

to hike: augmenter subitement (volume des affaires etc.).

hilary term: [J] Session de la Saint-Hilaire (commençant le 11 janvier et se terminant le mercredi avant Pâques).

to hinder (an enquiry): [J] entraver (une enquête).

hindrance: obstacle (m), empêchement (m).

hire: loyer, louage; [U.S.] a) embauchage de main-d'œuvre; b) gages, salaire.
for − : à louer.
− *of money*: loyer de l'argent.
− *-purchase*: vente à tempérament.
− *-purchase credit*: crédit remboursable à tempérament.
to hire: louer (des services ou une chose mobilière).
hired *labour*: main-d'œuvre salariée.
hirer: locataire.

histogram: histogramme (m) (statistique).

historical cost: coût primitif d'acquisition.

history: antécédents (m pl), passé (m).
previous − : antécédents.
work − : états de service.
to look into the − *of an applicant for a post*: se renseigner sur les antécédents d'un candidat à un emploi.

to hit: atteindre, frapper.
[F] *tax which* **hits** *all incomes*: impôt qui frappe tous les revenus.
the strike hits the steel industry: la grève affecte la sidérurgie.

to hoard: accumuler (des réserves), thésauriser.
[F] *propensity* − : propension à thésauriser.
hoarded *cash*: encaisse thésaurisée.
hoarder: spéculateur, thésaurisateur.
hoarding: panneau publicitaire.
hoarding (up): thésaurisation, accumulation de réserves.

hobby: occupation d'agrément.
− *losses*: déficit sur occupation d'agrément.

hock: *(argot)* [U.S.] gage.
to be in − *to s.o.*: être endetté envers qn.

to hold: tenir, détenir; posséder ou occuper de plein droit; être investi (d'une fonction); conclure, juger; tenir (une audience, une séance, etc.); obliger (en matière de contrats).
− *the affirmative*: être tenu de fournir la preuve (dans un procès).
− *court*: statuer, décider.
− *an inquiry*: procéder à une enquête.
− *a meeting*: tenir une réunion.
− *oneself liable for*: se porter garant de.
− *pleas*: entendre et juger un procès.
− *prices*: tenir les prix.
− *responsible*: tenir pour responsable, rendre responsable.
the rise (in x shares) was not **held**: l'avance (des valeurs x) n'a pas duré.

— *back (off)* : montrer peu d'empressement, hésiter, se tenir sur la réserve.
— *down (prices)* : empêcher de monter (les prix).
— *on a lease* : tenir à bail.
— *over* : a) (pour un locataire) ne pas évacuer les lieux malgré la fin du bail ; b) (pour un fonctionnaire déplacé) continuer à expédier les affaires courantes en attendant l'arrivée de son successeur désigné.
— *over a payment* : différer un paiement.
— *up* : arrêter, retarder, résister (les prix).

holder : détenteur (m) (d'un permis), porteur (m).
— *of an account* : titulaire d'un compte.
bond — : porteur d'obligations.
[J] — *of debt claims* : créancier.
— *in due course* : porteur (d'effet négociable) de bonne foi.
joint — : coporteur.
— *(of land)* : propriétaire (de terres).
licence — : concessionnaire.
loan — : créancier hypothécaire.
— *(of a passport, of a permit...)* : détenteur, titulaire (d'un passeport, d'un permis).
— *of shares (shareholder)* : actionnaire.
small — : petit propriétaire.
third — : tiers détenteur (de biens hypothéqués).
— *on trust* : dépositaire (de valeurs de qn).

holding : tenue (d'une réunion) ; portefeuille, valeurs en portefeuille, disponibilités ; ferme, tenure.
[J] — *(s) of the courts (on a question)* : jurisprudence (d'un cas de droit).
[F] — *company* : « holding », société de portefeuille, trust de valeurs, société de contrôle.
personal — *company* : [U.S.] société holding dans laquelle 50 % au moins des actions sont détenues directement ou indirectement par cinq personnes au maximum.
gold — *(s)* : encaisse or, réserves d'or.
majority (minority) holding : participation majoritaire (minoritaire).
paper — *(s)* : papiers-valeurs.
small — *system* : régime de la petite propriété.
substantial — : participation importante dans une société de capitaux.

holiday : jour férié, congé.
legal (statutory) — : jour chômé, fête légale.
— *(s) with pay (paid holidays)* : congés payés.

holograph : olographe (a).

home : a) foyer (m), logis (m), terre natale (f) ; b) domestique, intérieur (a) ; c) (adv) en plein, à fond.
— *for the aged* : maison de retraite, asile de vieillards.
— *-aid* : [U.S.] auxiliaire familiale.
— *banking* : banque à domicile.
— *for the blind* : hospice d'aveugles.
— *-bound* : retournant au pays.
homecraft ([U.S.] *home economics*) : enseignement ménager.
— *center* : maisonnerie.
— *consumption* : consommation intérieure.
— *freight* : fret de retour.
— *industries* : industries à domicile.
— *manufactures* : produits indigènes.
— *market* : marché intérieur.
permanent — : foyer permanent d'habitation (pour les besoins fiscaux).
— *produce (products)* : produits indigènes.
— *port* : port d'attache.
tax — : domicile fiscal.
— *trade* : commerce intérieur.
— *(trade) bill* : effet sur l'intérieur.
for — *use* : à (pour) usage domestique.
— *use entry* : sortie de l'entrepôt (de la douane) pour consommation intérieure.
— *worker* : travailleur à domicile.
to bring a charge — *to s.o.* : prouver une accusation contre qn.
[A] — *Office* : Ministère de l'Intérieur.
— *Secretary* : Ministre de l'Intérieur.

homestead : exploitation rurale.

homeward bill of lading : [D] connaissement d'entrée.
— *freight* : fret de retour.

homicide : homicide (m).
[J] *felonious* — ([U.S.] *murder in the first degree*) : homicide intentionnel, prémédité, volontaire, (assassinat).
excusable — ([U.S.] *murder in the second degree, manslaughter*) : homicide excusable (ex. en cas de légitime défense).
justifiable — : homicide justifiable (ex. commis dans l'exercice de ses fonctions).
— *squaden* : brigade criminelle.

honest dealings : affaires de bonne foi.
— *means* : moyens légitimes.

honour : honneur (m).
in an **honorary** *capacity* : à titre bénévole.
honorary duties : fonctions bénévoles, honorifiques.
[C] *acceptance for* — : acceptation sous protêt.
acceptor for — : avaliste.
(to feel) in — *bound* : (se sentir) engagé d'honneur.
to honour : honorer, faire honneur à.
to honour a bill : faire bon accueil à une traite.
to honour a draft : honorer une traite.
honourable *(the most, the right...)* : honorable

(le très honorable...).

horizontal : horizontal (a).
— *increase in salaries* : augmentation uniforme des traitements.
— *integration* : intégration (f) horizontale (association de deux ou plusieurs sociétés appartenant à la même industrie).
— *trust* : trust horizontal.

to horn a prospect : vendre des valeurs (minières) véreuses.

hornbook : manuel élémentaire.
— *law* : rudiments du droit.

host country : pays (m) d'accueil.

hostage taking : prise (f) d'otage.

hot : chaud, à chaud, brûlant (a).
[F] — *bills* : effets brûlants, valeurs brûlantes.
— *money* : capitaux spéculatifs, capitaux errants, capitaux flottants.
(news) — *from the press* : nouvelles qui sortent tout droit de la presse.
— *tip* : (fam.) tuyau sûr (bourse, courses, etc.).
[J] — *pursuit* : droit de suite (en haute mer).

hotchpotch, hodge podge : (un pudding composé d'un grand nombre d'ingrédients) masse successorale.
[J] *bringing into* — : rapport à la masse successorale.

hour : heure (f), moment (m); circonstances (f pl).
after —*(s)* : après l'heure de fermeture.
at the — *stated* : à l'heure dite, convenue.
—*(s) of attendance* : heures de présence; heures de bureau.
business —*(s) (hours of business)* : heures ouvrables.
busy —*(s)* : heures d'affluence.
(to pay s.o.) by the — : (payer qn) à l'heure.
—*(s) of delivery* : heures de distribution (du courrier, etc.).
per (man-) — : par heure (d'ouvrier).
office —*(s)* : heures de bureau.
output per — : rendement par heure, horaire.
over- —*(s) (supplementary hours)* : heures supplémentaires.
peak- —*(s), rush-* —*(s), throng-* —*(s)* : heures de pointe, heures d'affluence.
slack —*(s)* : heures creuses.
stock-exchange —*(s)* : heures de bourse.
working —*(s)* : heures de travail.
to work long —*(s)* : faire de longues journées de travail.
hourly : à l'heure, horaire.
hourly wage : salaire horaire.

house : habitation (f), maison (f); maison de commerce, de banque, etc., corps législatif.
[J] — *of Commons (of Lords)* : Chambre des Communes (des Lords).
— *agency (agent)* : agence immobilière (agent immobilier).
to be under — *arrest* : être en résidence surveillée.
— *bills* : effets creux, papiers creux.
business — : établissement commercial.
[F] *clearing* — : chambre de compensation, banque de virement.
— *duty* : [U.S.] taxe d'habitation.
to pass a cheque through the clearing — : compenser un chèque.
clearing — *bill* : lettre de change creuse.
financial — : établissement de crédit.
[E] *export-(import)* — : maison d'exportation (d'importation).
— *flag* : pavillon d'une compagnie maritime.
[C] — *-letting* : baux à loyer.
— *-to-house selling* : porte-à-porte.
mail-order — : maison de vente par correspondance.
packing — : conserverie.
parent — : maison mère.
[B] — *price* : cours en bourse.
(land and) — *property* : biens immobiliers, biens fonds.
revenue-earning — : immeuble de rapport.
to take a — *on lease* : prendre une maison à bail.
to house : héberger.

housebreaking : violation (f) de domicile, effraction (f), cambriolage (m).

household : maison (f), ménage (m), famille (f); de ménage, domestique (a).
— *budgets* : budgets des ménages.
— *expenditures, (expenses)* : budget(s), dépenses des ménages, budget(s) domestique(s).
— *goods* : meubles.
head of — : chef de famille.
income of —*(s)* : revenus des ménages.
householder : a) chef de famille; b) personne qui occupe une maison à titre de locataire ou de propriétaire.

housekeeper : femme (f) de ménage.

housekeeping : économie (f) domestique.

housing : logement (m); emmagasinage (m); installation (f).
[A] *the* — *problem (question)* : le problème (la crise) du logement.
— *ramp* : majoration exorbitante des loyers, le scandale des loyers.
— *subsidies* : subventions au logement.

hub: centre (m) d'activité.
the — of the business world: le centre du monde des affaires.

hue and cry: clameur publique ; tollé général.

hull insurance: assurance (f) d'un navire hors cargaison.

human: humain (a).
— *capital*: ressources humaines.
— *engineering*: organisation rationnelle, scientifique du travail.
— *labour*: travail humain.
— *relations*: relations humaines.
Universal Declaration of — Rights: Déclaration Universelle des Droits de l'Homme.
— *(measures)*: (mesures) humanitaire.
humanitarian: humanitaire.

hunger-strike: grève (f) de la faim.

to hunt: chasser.
bargain hunting: chasse aux soldes.
hunting licence: permis de chasse.

hurdle rate: taux (m) de rejet, d'actualisation.

husband and wife: les conjoints.

to husband: cultiver, ménager.
— *one's resources*: bien gouverner ses ressources.
husbandry: gestion, administration, exploitation.
bad, good husbandry: mauvaise, bonne gestion.

hush-money: [J] argent donné à qn pour prix de son silence, pour éviter de témoigner, etc.
extorter of — : maître-chanteur.
extortion of — : chantage.

hyperinflation: hyperinflation (f).

hypothecary: hypothécaire (a).
[J] — *claim*: créance hypothécaire.
to hypothecate: hypothéquer, gagner, nantir.
hypothecation: a) engagement du navire ou de la cargaison contre prêt consenti au patron ; b) affectation hypothécaire de biens meubles ou immeubles dont la propriété demeure acquise au débiteur.
hypothecation certificate: acte de nantissement.
letter of hypothecation: lettre hypothécaire.
hypothecator: gageur (m).

hypothesis: hypothèse (f).

hypothetical: hypothétique (a).

NOTES

NOTES

I

I.B.O.R. *(Interbank offered rate)* : taux interbancaire offert.

ideal efficiency : rendement idéal, rendement théorique.

ideal home exhibition : salon des arts ménagers.

identification : identification (f), vérification (f).
 [J] — *card* : carte d'identité.
 — *certificate* : acte de notoriété.
 — *department* : service de l'identité judiciaire.
 — *papers* : papiers (carte) d'identité.
 — *parade* : confrontation d'un témoin avec un groupe de personnes parmi lesquelles se trouve un suspect.

to identify : identifier, reconnaître, s'identifier à.
 — *oneself* : se présenter.
 — *oneself with an enterprise* : prendre une part active à une entreprise.
 [J] **identity** : identité (f) ; identité personnelle ; similitude (f) de deux inventions (droits de brevet).
 certificate of identity : pièce d'identité.
 identity certificate : acte de notoriété, titre d'identité.
 identity of cost : parallélisme dans les prix.
 mistaken identity : erreur sur la personne.
 to prove one's identity : prouver (établir) son identité.

idiocy : idiotie congénitale.

idle : oisif, désœuvré, en chômage, inemployé (a).
 — *capacity* : potentiel non utilisé.
 [F] — *capital* : capital improductif, oisif, non utilisé.
 — *cash* : argent oisif.
 — *funds money* : fonds inemployés.
 — *period (time)* : temps mort, période creuse.
 — *plant* : outillage inactif.
 — *rumours* : rumeurs sans fondement.
 to lie (to stand) — *(a factory)* : chômer (une usine).

ignorance : ignorance.
 ignorant : ignorant.
 [J] *to be ignorant of a fact* : être ignorant d'un fait.
 « — *of law is no excuse* » : « nul n'est censé ignorer la loi ».
 to plead — : plaider l'ignorance.
 to ignore *the facts* : méconnaître les faits.
 to ignore an objection : passer outre à une objection.

ignorantia juris (legis) neminem excusat : l'ignorance de la loi n'excuse personne (nul n'est censé ignorer la loi).

ill : mauvais, mal (a et adv).
 — *-advised* : peu judicieux, peu sage.
 — *-balanced* : mal équilibré.
 — *-fame* : mauvaise réputation.
 on account of — *-health* : pour raison de santé.
 — *-planned* : mal conçu.
 — *-qualified* : incompétent.
 of — *-repute* : de mauvais renom.
 an — *-timed measure* : une mesure inopportune.
 — *-treatment* : mauvais traitement.
 — *-will* : mauvaise volonté, malveillance, rancune.
 to ill-use : maltraiter (un enfant).

illegal : illégal, illicite (a).
 [J] — *acts* : actes illégaux.
 — *practice* : actes illicites (en matière électorale).
 — *proceeding* : procédure illégale.
 illegality : illégalité.
 plea of illegality : exception d'illégalité.

illegible : illisible (a).

illegitimate (child) : [J] (enfant) illégitime.

illicit : illégal, illicite (a).
 — *bettings* : paris clandestins.
 — *commission* : pot-de-vin.
 — *profits* : bénéfices illicites.
 — *trade (trading)* : commerce illicite ; trafic prohibé (de stupéfiants, etc.).

illiquid : [U.S.] à court de capitaux liquides.
 illiquidity : non-liquidité.

illiteracy, illiterate : analphabétisme, analphabète.

illusory profits : bénéfices mensongers.

image : image (f), conception (f).
brand – : image (f) de marque.

imbalance : déséquilibre (m), déficit (m).
– *of external payments* : déséquilibre des paiements.

imbecile : faible d'esprit.

imitation : imitation (f), factice (a).
– *jewels* : bijoux faux, bijoux en toc.

immaterial : sans importance ; sans rapport avec la question, non pertinent.
[J] – *evidence* : témoignage non pertinent.
– *issue* : détail secondaire.
« –, *incompetent and irrelevant* » : locution couramment employée (par la partie adverse) pour formuler une objection à une preuve ou prétendue telle.

immeasurability : incommensurabilité.
immeasurable : incommensurable.

immediate : immédiat, direct, pressant (a).
– *cause* : cause immédiate.
[C] *(for) immediate delivery* : à livrer sans délai, d'urgence.
– *possession* : jouissance immédiate.
– *wages* : salaire de début.

immemorial : immémorial (a).

immersed in debts : accablé de dettes.

immigration : immigration (f).
– *policy* : politique d'immigration.
– *quotas* : contingents d'immigration.

to immobilize capital : immobiliser des capitaux.

immoral : immoral (a).
[J] – *classes* : « le milieu ».
– *contract* : contrat contraire aux bonnes mœurs.
– *offence* : attentat aux mœurs.

immovable : immobilier (a).
[J] – *property* : biens immeubles, (immobiliers).
– *(s)* : biens immobiliers.

immune : inaccessible, dispensé, exonéré (a).
[F] – *from tax* : exonéré d'impôt.
immunity : immunité, exemption, exonération (f).
immunity from distraint, seizure : insaisissabilité.
immunity from taxes, taxation : exemption, exonération d'impôts, immunité fiscale.
[J] *(parliamentary, diplomatic) immunity* : immunité parlementaire, diplomatique.

impact (of taxation) : incidence, répercussion (f) (de la fiscalité).
[F] *the point of – of the burden of taxation* : le point d'impact de la charge fiscale.

to impair : affaiblir, compromettre, porter atteinte ou préjudice (à).
physically or mentally **impaired** : diminué physiquement ou mentalement.
impairment : affaiblissement (m), altération (f), diminution (f).
[J] *impairment of a law* : dérogation à une loi.
physical impairment : infirmité.

to impanel : dresser la liste du jury.

to impeach : mettre en accusation, récuser (un témoignage), sp. mettre en accusation un ministre, un haut fonctionnaire (devant une Cour spéciale).
[J] – *defendant's title* : contester le droit de propriété du défendeur.
– *a testimony* : mettre en doute un témoignage.
– *a witness* : récuser un témoin.
impeachment : mise en accusation (devant la haute cour de justice), récusation.
bill of impeachment : mise en accusation (d'un ministre, d'un haut fonctionnaire) devant la haute cour de justice.
impeachment of a witness : récusation d'un témoin.
patent impeachment : poursuite en contrefaçon (d'un brevet).

impecunious : impécunieux, insolvable.

to impede : empêcher, entraver.

impediment : entrave (f), obstacle (m) ; cause d'incapacité de contracter (minorité, etc.).
[J] *dirimant –* : empêchement dirimant au mariage.

imperative : impérieux, urgent, absolu (a).
under – circumstances : en raison de circonstances impérieuses.

imperfect : imparfait, défectueux (a).
– *competition* : concurrence imparfaite.
– *market* : marché imparfait.
[J] – *obligations* : obligation morale ne comportant pas de sanction.
– *title* : droit de propriété ou d'acquisition de propriété insuffisamment établi.

(economic) imperialism : impérialisme économique.

impersonal account: [F] compte anonyme, fictif.
- *accounts*: comptes de résultat.
- *basis*: base réelle (d'assujettissement).

impersonation: personnification (f), [J] supposition (f) de personne.

impertinent: non pertinent, hors de propos (a).
[J] – *allegations*: allégations inutiles ou sans rapport avec la question.

(to give) impetus to sales: [C] donner de l'impulsion (aux ventes).

impleader: [J] appel en garantie, intervention forcée.

to implement: mettre à exécution, appliquer, mettre en application, mettre en œuvre.
- *a decision*: donner suite à une décision.
- *an obligation*: s'acquitter d'une obligation.
- *a policy*: mettre en œuvre une politique.
- *one's promise*: tenir sa promesse.
implementation: mise en œuvre, en application, exécution.
implementation of an agreement, of a contract: exécution d'un accord, d'un contrat.
implementation of a policy: mise en œuvre d'une politique.
regulation in – of the Treaty establishing the EEC: règlement pris en exécution du Traité instituant la C.E.E.

implication: incidence, répercussion; [J] intention ou état de fait présumé par la loi en se fondant sur des faits ou actes établis.
the financial – (s) of a program: les incidences financières d'un programme.
by –: implicitement.
implicit: implicite, tacite, absolu.
[J] – *agreement, consent*: accord, consentement tacite.
- *costs*: coûts supplétifs.
- *terms*: termes (conditions) implicites.
implicit trust: confiance sans réserve.
to imply: impliquer, comprendre, faire supposer.
implied *acceptance, condition*: acceptation, condition tacite.
implied contract: quasi contrat.
implied in law: conséquences juridiques inéluctables, indépendantes de la volonté des parties.
implied promise: promesse implicite.
implied warranty: garantie implicite.
it is to be implied (from-that): il résulte (de, que).

import: a) signification, importance; b) importation.

of general –: de portée générale.
[E] – *business*: commerce d'importation.
- *deposit*: cautionnement exigé (ou exigible) pour autorisation d'importer.
- *duty*: droit d'entrée, d'importation.
goods liable to – duty: marchandises soumises à un droit d'entrée.
- *entry*: déclaration d'entrée en douane.
- *-export coverage*: taux de couverture des importations par les exportations.
- *gold point (specie point)*: point d'entrée de l'or.
- *licence, permit*: licence (f) d'importation.
- *premium*: prime (f) d'importation.
- *price index*: indice des prix d'importation.
- *quotas*: contingents d'importation.
- *restrictions*: restrictions à l'importation.
- *surcharge*: taxe supplémentaire (dissuasive) à l'importation.
- *tariff, trade*: tarif, commerce d'importation.
to import: importer.
propensity to –: propension (f) à importer.
imported *duty free*: admis en franchise.
importation: importation (f), entrée (f).
importation bounty: prime (f) d'importation.
list of importations: tarif (m) d'entrée.
importer: importateur (m).
importing country: pays importateur.

importance *(descending order of)*: (ordre décroissant d') importance.

to impose a tax (on): taxer.
[F] *imposition*: impôt (m), taxe (f).

impossible contract: [J] contrat inexécutable.

impost: [F] droit d'entrée.

impotence: impotence, impuissance (f).

to impound: a) saisir, confisquer (des marchandises); b) capter, endiguer des eaux.
[J] – *documents*: déposer des documents (au greffe).

impoundment: (U.S.) (pol.) refus du Président d'ordonnancer des dépenses votées par le Congrès.

impoverishment: appauvrissement (m).

imprescriptible rights: [J] droits imprescriptibles.

impression: impression (f).
[J] *case of first –*: cas sans précédent.

imprest: [A] avance de fonds (par l'Etat, à un fournisseur pour frais de déplacement).

imprint: empreinte.
finger — : empreinte digitale.

imprisonment: emprisonnement, peine de prison pour délits.
[J] — *in the first division, ordinary division*: emprisonnement de police.
false — : séquestration, détention, arbitraire, illégale.
precautionary — : internement d'élimination.
rigorous — : réclusion, emprisonnement correctionnel.

improper: impropre, incorrect, inavouable, irrégulier (a).
— *use*: usage abusif.
improperly: incorrectement, d'une manière inconvenane ou déplacée.

impropriety: inopportunité, inexactitude (f).

to improve: (s')améliorer, mettre à profit, mettre en pratique, faire valoir.
[F] *his financial position has* **improved**: sa situation financière s'améliore.
the lot is improved with a one storey structure: le terrain est mis en valeur avec un bâtiment d'un étage.
— *on s.o.'s offer*: enchérir sur l'offre de qn, surenchérir.
improvement: aménagement (m), amélioration (f), augmentation (f), gain (m).
land improvements: améliorations foncières.
the latest improvements: les derniers perfectionnements.
improvement lease: bail qui impose l'obligation (pour le preneur) d'effectuer des améliorations.
improvement loan: prêt destiné à la modernisation.
improvement in pay: amélioration des salaires.
improvement of prices: amélioration des cours.
to make improvements: apporter des améliorations, faire des embellissements, faire des progrès.

to impugn: discuter, mettre en doute.
[J] — *a contract*: attaquer un contrat.
— *the opponents' good faith*: mettre en doute la bonne foi des adversaires.
— *a piece of evidence*: récuser un témoignage.
— *the character of a witness*: attaquer la moralité d'un témoin.
impugnment (*of a testimony, of a witness*): récusation (d'un témoignage, d'un témoin).

impulse shopping: achat(s) (m) sur impulsion.

in alieno solo: sur un terrain qui appartient à un tiers.

in custodia legis: (biens) sous la garde de la loi.

in extremis (in articulo mortis): à l'article de la mort.

in re: en matière de, pour ce qui est de.

(action) in rem: action visant à satisfaire une prétention (à un droit) sans intention de faire condamner la partie adverse à une peine de quelque nature qu'elle soit.

in tenorem: dans un but d'intimidation.

in (en) ventre sa mère: enfant conçu.

inability: incapacité, impuissance (f).

inaccuracy: inexactitude, imprécision (f).

inaction: immobilisme (m).

inadequacy: insuffisance (f).
inadequate: insuffisant, disproportionné.
inadequate arrangements: défauts d'organisation.
inadequate information: renseignements incomplets.
inadequate means: moyens insuffisants.

inadmissible: inadmissible, illicite, irrecevable (a).

inalianable right: [J] droit inaliénable.

inasmuch as: attendu que, vu que.

to inaugurate (a policy): [U.S.] mettre en vigueur, appliquer (une politique).

incapable: incapable, peu susceptible de, incompétent.
— *of being elected*: inéligible.
— *of making a will*: inhabile à tester.

to incapacitate: interdire, frapper d'incapacité (légale).
incapacitation from work: incapacité de travail.
permanent incapacitation: incapacité permanente.
incapacity: incapacité (f), incompétence (f), inaptitude (f), inhabilité (f).
[J] *legal incapacity*: incapacité légale.
incapacity to inherit: inhabilité à succéder.

incendiarism: crime d'incendie.

incentive: stimulant (m), incitation (f), encouragement (m), mobile (m), prime (f).
[E] *export* – *(s)*: encouragements à l'exportation.
[F] *fiscal (tax)* – *(s)*: encouragements fiscaux, incitations à investir par des mesures fiscales.
tax – *method*: méthode d'incitation fiscale.
monetary – *(s)*: incitations monétaires.
– *payments*: prime d'encouragement à la production (individuelle).
production – *(s)*: stimulants de la production.
– *scheme*: plan d'encouragement à la vente au moyen de primes.
– *tour*: voyage de stimulation.
– *wage*: prime au rendement.
wage – *(s)*: intéressement du personnel au rendement.

inception: [C] commencement (m) d'activité d'une entreprise.

incest: [J] inceste (m).

inchoate: en puissance, incomplet (a).
[J] – *agreement*: contrat que toutes les parties n'ont pas signé.
– *crime*: crime non parfait.
– *lien*: privilège qui ne se matérialisera que plus tard.
– *nationality*: [U.S.] nationalité américaine latente d'un candidat à la naturalisation.

incidence: incidence (f).
[J] – *of a tax (tax incidence)*: incidence d'un impôt (de l'impôt).
[F] *the person of* – : la personne obligée en droit.

incident: a) incident (m) ; servitude (f) ; privilège (m) ; b) fortuit (a); qui appartient (à).
(expenses) – *to...*: (frais) entraînés par...
incidental: fortuit, accidentel, éventuel, accessoire.
incidental expenses, incidentals: faux frais.
incidental intention: mobile secondaire.
incidental motion: motion incidente.
incidental plea of defence: exception.
incidental point (question): question incidente.
incidental result: conséquence secondaire.

incipient: naissant, qui débute.
– *inflation*: inflation à ses débuts.

incitement: [J] incitation (f), encouragement (m), instigation (f), provocation (f), au crime ou délit.

(to be) inclined to fall (prices): avoir tendance à baisser (prix).

to include: comprendre, inclure.
there shall be **included** *among...*: est (sont) à inclure parmi...
including *expenses*: y compris les dépenses.
inclusion: inclusion (f), insertion (f).
inclusion of a clause: insertion d'un article.
inclusion of a question: inscription d'une question (dans un ordre du jour).
inclusions: éléments à inclure.
inclusive: inclus, inclusivement.
– *price*: prix net.
– *sum*: somme globale.
all-inclusive: tout compris, forfaitaire (prix).

income: revenu (m), recettes (f pl).
[F] *actual* – : revenu réel (effectif).
adjusted – *tax*: crédit d'impôt déduit.
adjusted gross – : (U.S.) revenu brut ajusté (après déduction des dépenses professionnelles).
agreed – : forfait (m).
aggregate – : revenu global.
– *aggregation*: forfait (m).
allocation of – : ventilation des revenus.
assessable – : revenu imposable.
– *bracket*: tranche de revenu.
– *from business*: bénéfices industriels et commerciaux.
net business – : revenu commercial net.
corporate – : revenu des sociétés.
corporate – *retention*: autofinancement (m).
corporation – *tax*: impôt sur le revenu des personnes morales.
disposable – : revenu disponible.
earned – : revenus gagnés (par le travail).
fully-earned – : revenu entièrement gagné.
– *effect*: effet de revenu.
estimated – : forfait, revenu présumé.
– *estimates*: prévisions de recettes.
– *and expenditure account*: compte de pertes et de profits, compte justificatif des recettes et des dépenses.
family – : revenus familiaux.
– *from farming (farm income)*: bénéfices agricoles.
financial – : produits financiers.
– *from foreign sources*: revenu de source étrangère.
graduated – *tax*: impôt progressif.
gross – : revenu brut.
– *of households*: revenus des ménages.
– *from immovable property*: revenus fonciers.
– *from* – : revenu sur revenu.
– *on investments*: revenus de portefeuille-titres.
« *franked investment* – »: revenu de placements francs d'impôts.
– *items*: catégories de revenus.
– *from (occupation of) land*: revenu provenant de l'occupation du terrain.
life – *(income for life)*: revenu viager.
mixed – : revenu mixte.

money — : revenu nominal.
national — : revenu national.
net — : revenu net.
net — for the period: bénéfice net de l'exercice.
total net — : revenu net global.
— *from non commercial activities*: revenus des professions non commerciales.
non-recurring — : ressources exceptionnelles.
operating — : bénéfice d'exploitation.
part-earned — : revenu mixte.
private — : fortune personnelle.
presumptive — *(imputed* —*)*: valeur locative d'un logement dont le propriétaire se réserve la jouissance ; valeur des produits prélevés en nature par un exploitant.
— *producing expenses*: dépenses pour l'acquisition du revenu.
professional — : bénéfices non commerciaux.
— *from the ownership of the property*: revenu perçu à titre de propriétaire du terrain.
real — : revenu réel.
— *from real property*: revenus fonciers.
relevant — : partie imposable au nom des participants dans les « close companies ».
— *from sales*: produit(s) des ventes.
— *from securities and similar*: revenus des capitaux mobiliers.
— *from shares*: dividendes d'actions.
— *splitting system*: système du quotient familial.
social — : revenu national.
supplementary — : revenus annexes.
(general) — *tax*: impôt sur le revenu.
— *relief*: somme à déduire du revenu imposable.
— *tax return (form)*: (imprimé de) déclaration des revenus.
— *spreading*: étalement des revenus.
— *statement*: compte de résultat.
taxable — : revenu imposable.
tax-free — : revenu exonéré d'impôt.
— *derived from trade and manufacture*: bénéfices industriels et commerciaux.
unearned — : revenu ne provenant pas du travail.
undistributed — : bénéfices non répartis.
— *velocity of money*: vitesse de transformation de la monnaie en revenu.
— *from wages, salaries, pensions and annuities*: revenus des traitements, salaires, pensions et rentes viagères.
to draw an — *(from)*: tirer un revenu (de).

incoming: a) entrée (f) ; b) entrant (a).
— *mail*: courrier à l'arrivée.
— *profit*: profits réalisés (à réaliser), accrus.
— *(s)*: recettes, rentrées d'argent.

incommunicado: au secret.
[J] *the prisoner is held* — : le prisonnier est gardé au secret.

incommensurate: disproportionné (a).

in — **company training**: formation à l'intérieur de l'entreprise.

incompatibility: incompatibilité (f), inconciliabilité (f).
— *of temper*: incompatibilité d'humeur.
incompatible *(with)*: incompatible, inconciliable.
functions incompatible with...: des fonctions incompatibles avec...
incompatible interests: intérêts inconciliables.

incompetence, incompetency: incompétence, inhabilité, incapacité (f).
incompetent: incompétent, inhabile, non qualifié (pour).
[J] *incompetent evidence*: preuve irrecevable.
incompetent judge: juge récusable (ou récusé).
incompetent person: incapable, interdit (aliéné, etc.).
incompetent to make a will: inhabile à tester.
incompetent witness: témoin non qualifié, récusé.

inconclusive test: épreuve non concluante.

inconsistency: inconsistance, incompatibilité, contradiction, incohérence (f).
inconsistent: incompatible, contradictoire, incohérent, illogique (a).
(an) inconsistent argument: (un) argument inconséquent.
inconsistent reasoning: raisonnement illogique.
inconsistent with: inconciliable avec.
wholly inconsistent: plein de contradictions.
inconsistently: d'une manière illogique, inconséquente.

inconvenience: incommodité, gêne (f).
inconvenient: gênant, inopportun (a).

inconvertible currency, money: [F] devise (f), monnaie (f) inconvertible.

to incorporate (a company): incorporer, organiser, constituer (une société).
[J] **incorporated** *company* ([U.S.] *inco*) : société constituée, autorisée, enregistrée (pas forcément anonyme).
incorporated Law Society: compagnie d'avoués ([U.S.] association d'avocats).
incorporation: incorporation (de réserves, etc.) ; introduction (d'une clause), fusion de plusieurs éléments en une entité, octroi de la personnalité morale à un groupe d'individus (constitution d'une société), érection d'une agglomération en municipalité.
certificate of incorporation: certificat de constitution.

charter of incorporation : statut de constitution de société.
place of incorporation : lieu de constitution d'une société.
incorporation of reserves : incorporation de(s) réserve(s).

incorporeal : incorporel (a).
[J] — *hereditaments* : héritage incorporel.

incorrect : inexact, défectueux.
— *valuation* : évaluation inexacte.

incoterms : termes utilisés dans le commerce international, proposés par la Chambre de Commerce Internationale et sur lesquels la plupart des pays sont tombés d'accord.

increase : augmentation (f), majoration (f), accroissement (m), surcroît (m).
— *of capital* : augmentation de capital.
— *of customs duties* : relèvement des droits de douane.
— *in demand* : accroissement de la demande.
(an) — *in exports* : (une) progression des exportations.
— *in the paid-up capital* : augmentation de capital.
(an) — *in prices* : (une) hausse des prix.
tax — : augmentation de la pression fiscale.
(an) — *in taxation* : (une) majoration des impôts.
— *of taxation* : augmentation d'impôt.
— *in value* : plus-value.
— *in wages (pay increase)* : augmentation de salaire(s).
on the — *(unemployment)* : (chômage) en augmentation.
without any — : sans aucune majoration.
to increase : augmenter, majorer, relever, progresser.
to increase discount rates : relever le taux de l'escompte.
to increase in price : renchérir.
to increase (the) taxes : majorer les impôts.
increased cost of living : renchérissement du coût de la vie.
increased consumption : augmentation de la consommation.
increased productivity : accroissement de la productivité.
(an) **increasing** *competition* : une concurrence de plus en plus forte, accrue.
increasing returns : rendements croissants.
increasible : susceptible d'augmenter.

increment : accroissement (m), augmentation (f), profit (m), coût différentiel.
annual increment : augmentation annuelle.
increment per cent : taux d'accroissement, coût marginal.
salary increments : augmentations de traitement.
unearned increment : plus-value (non gagnée par le travail).
incremental cost : coût d'accroissement.
incremental capital-output radio (I.C.O.R.) : coefficient marginal de capital.

incriminating documents : [J] pièces à conviction.

incrimination : [J] accusation.

incumbent (on, upon) : incombant (à), dévolu (à).

incumbent : titulaire (n) d'un poste.

incumbrance : charge (grevant un immeuble), dette, hypothèque, servitude (f).

to incur : encourir, subir.
— *a fine, a liability, a penalty* : encourir une amende, une responsabilité, une peine.
— *debts* : contracter des dettes.
— *expenses* : engager des frais.
— *losses* : subir des pertes.
the expenses **incurred** : les dépenses effectuées.
expenses to be incurred (in) : dépenses afférentes (à).

indebted (**to** : à, envers ; *for* : de) : redevable, débiteur.
[C] *to be indebted for (so much) to...* : être endetté de (tant) envers...
indebtness : dette (f), endettement (m), emprunt (m), créance (f).
evidence of indebtness : titre de créance.
note of indebtness : bon de caisse.
over-indebtness : excédent du passif.
preferential indebtness : créance privilégiée.
unsecured indebtness : créance chirographaire.

indecency : indécence (f).
gross — : crime impliquant un contact sexuel illégal.
[J] **indecent** *assault* : viol, attentat aux mœurs.
indecent exposure : exhibition, outrage public à la pudeur.
indecent publication : publication pornographique.

indefeasibility : irrévocabilité, inaliénabilité (f).
indefeasible : imprescriptible, irrévocable (a).

indefinite payment : paiement effectué sans que son affectation soit précisée.

indemnification : indemnisation (f), dédommagement (m).
to indemnity : indemniser, dédommager.

indemnity: garantie (f), indemnité (f), dédommagement (m), compensation (f), dommages-intérêts (m pl).
[J] *indemnity bond*: décharge, lettre de garantie, d'indemnité, cautionnement.
contract of indemnity: contrat d'assurance.
indemnity for expropriation: indemnité pour cause d'expropriation.
war indemnity: indemnité de guerre.
as an indemnity: à titre d'indemnité.
act of indemnity: loi amnistiant les auteurs d'actes illégaux, mais commis pour le bien public en temps de guerre.

indent: acte, contrat (m).
[J] **to indent**: obliger par contrat; mettre en apprentissage (*to*: chez).
— *for*: passer une commande (de tel produit).
deed **indented, indenture**: contrat synallagmatique, engagement contractuel.
indentures, indenture of apprenticeship: contrat d'apprentissage.
to indenture: lier par contrat.
indentured *labour*: main-d'œuvre engagée à long terme (par contrat).
[C] *indentured order*: commande passée par un acheteur d'Outre-Mer à une maison d'exportation.

independent: indépendant, qui vit de ses rentes.
— *income*: fortune personnelle.

index: a) table (f) des matières; b) indice (m), coefficient (m).
card- — : fichier (m).
— *linkage*: indexation (f).
— *-linked stocks*: valeurs indexées.
cost of living — : indice du coût de la vie.
— *-number*: indice (m).
consumer price — *-numbers*: indice des prix à la consommation.
overall — : indice global.
production, trade — : indice de la production, de commerce.
stock — : [U.S.] indice des valeurs.
weighted — : indice pondéré.
overall **indexation**: indexation généralisée.

indexed: indexé
— *on the cost of living*: indexé sur le coût de la vie.
tax rates **indexing**: indexation du barème d'imposition.

indicative: indicatif.

indicator: indicateur (m) économique, indicateur (m), « clignotant » (m) (pour le seuil des prix, du chômage, etc.).
coincident — *(s)*: indicateurs des activités économiques au cours d'une courte période précédente.
lagging — *(s)*: indicateurs des activités économiques retardées.
leading — *(s)*: indicateurs des activités économiques avancées.
longer (shorter) — *(s)*: indicateurs à long (court) terme.

to indict: accuser, incriminer, inculper.
[J] — *s.o. for (a crime etc.)*: poursuivre qn pour (un crime etc.).
— *a statement as false*: s'inscrire en faux contre une déposition.
indictable: passible de poursuites.
— *offence*: délit (m), (UK) infraction (f) grave jugée devant la « Crown Court » (avec jury).
indicted *(for)*: inculpé (de).
indictment: acte d'accusation, inculpation, incrimination.
bill of — : acte d'accusation.
to dismiss (to quash) the — : refuser la mise en accusation.
to draw up an — : rédiger un réquisitoire.
to read the — : lire l'acte d'accusation.

indignity: indignité, cruauté morale (f).

indirect: indirect, impropre, déloyal (a).
[J] — *evidence*: preuve indirecte, présomption.
[C] — *bill*: traite domiciliée, effet domicilié.
— *cost*: élément indirect du prix de revient (ex. loyer, entretien des locaux...).
— *expenses (charges)*: frais indirects, frais généraux (fixes).
— *investment*: investissement indirect (ex. une compagnie d'assurances investit en partie les sommes versées sous forme de primes par les assurés).
— *labour cost*: élément direct du coût de la main-d'œuvre.
[F] — *taxation (taxes)*: fiscalité indirecte, impôts indirects.

individual: individuel, particulier (a), personne (f) physique, particulier (m).
— *firm*: entreprise individuelle.
private — : simple particulier.
to act as a private — : agir en qualité de simple particulier.
— *property*: propriété individuelle.
for tax purposes — *(s) may be divided into three categories: a)* — *(s) domiciled in France, b) etc.*: aux fins d'établissement de l'impôt les particuliers peuvent être répartis en trois catégories: a) les particuliers domiciliés en France; b) etc.

indivisible capital: [F] investissements indivisibles.

indivisium: [J] bien détenu par deux personnes dans l'indivis.

indorsement: voir: – *(of a deed)*.

to induce: persuader, inciter, provoquer.
[F] **induced** *investment*: investissement induit.
inducement: encouragement (m), incitation (f), motif (m), raison (f) déterminante.
inducement to saving: encouragement à épargner.

induction *(of facts)*: apport (m) (de preuves).

inductions training: formation (f) des ouvriers nouvellement recrutés.

indulgence: indulgence (f); [C] jour de grâce, délai de paiement (au règlement d'une lettre de change).

industrial: industriel (a).
– *accident*: accident du travail.
– *action*: actions entreprises par le personnel à la suite d'un conflit du travail non résolu.
– *bonds*: valeurs (obligations industrielles).
– *concern*: entreprise individuelle.
Congress of – *Organizations (C.I.O.)*: Congrès des organisations industrielles.
– *consultant*: expert en organisation industrielle.
– *development*: expansion industrielle.
– *co-partnership*: actionnariat ouvrier.
– *development bank*: banque pour l'expansion industrielle.
– *disease*: maladie professionnelle.
– *dispute*: conflit du travail.
– *espionage*: espionnage industriel.
– *estate*: zone d'industrialisation.
– *hazard*: risque professionnel.
– *insurance*: assurance ouvrière.
– *law (legislation)*: législation industrielle.
– *property*: propriété industrielle.
– *recovery*: reprise économique.
– *research*: recherche industrielle appliquée.
– *securities (stocks)*: valeurs industrielles.
– *unit*: usine (f).
– *unrest*: climat social agité.
industrialist: industriel (m).
industrializing *industries*: industries industrialisantes.
– *(s)*: valeurs industrielles.
to carry on an – *activity*: exercer une activité industrielle.
industry: industrie (f).
agricultural industries: industries agricoles.
basis industry: industrie de base, essentielle.
the car industry: l'industrie automobile, l'automobile.
cottage industry: industrie artisanale.

infant industry: industrie naissante.
key industry: industrie clef.
primary industry: industrie de base.
small-scale industry: petite industrie.
subsidized industry: industrie subventionnée.
industry-wide agreement: accord employeurs-syndicats pour une branche entière de l'industrie.

inefficiency: incapacité, inefficacité, incompétence (f).
inefficient: insuffisant, inefficace.

inelastic: inélastique (a).
– *demand (supply)*: demande (offre) inélastique.
inelasticity *of demand (supply)*: inélasticité de la demande (de l'offre).

ineligibility: inéligibilité (f), [J] insuffisance de capacités.
ineligible: inéligible, dépourvu des qualités requises, non admissible, inacceptable.

inequitable: inéquitable (a).
[F] – *distribution of taxation*: répartition inéquitable de la fiscalité.

inertia selling: (C) vente forcée (le vendeur compte sur l'inertie de l'acheteur).

inescapable: inévitable, inéluctable (a).
the conclusion is – : la conclusion s'impose.

infamy: infamie (f); [J] incapacité de témoigner encourue par un faussaire, parjure, etc.
infamous *crime*: crime abominable.
infamous person: [U.S.] personne privée des droits civils.

infancy: petite enfance, premier âge.
[J] – *proceedings*: procédure en matière de tutelle.
to plead – : plaider l'incapacité en tant que mineur.
infant: mineur (jusqu'à l'âge de deux ans).

infanticide: infanticide (m) (l'acte et la personne).

to infer: conclure, comporter.

inference: supposition, déduction, inférence (f).
inferential *evidence*: preuves indirectes.

inferior court: tribunal inférieur.
[J] tout tribunal autre que *the High Court, the Central Criminal Court* ou *the Chancery Courts of Lancaster and Durham* (voir *court*, Engl. et U.S.).

infirmity: nullité (d'un acte).

to inflate: recourir à l'inflation, laisser se développer l'inflation.
[F] **inflated** *currency*: circulation fiduciaire accrue créant l'inflation.

inflation: inflation (f).
controlled inflation: inflation dirigée.
cost-push inflation: inflation par poussée sur les coûts.
crawling or creeping inflation: inflation rampante.
inflation of currency: inflation fiduciaire.
excess-demand inflation: inflation par excès de la demande.
galloping (raging) inflation: inflation galopante.
imported inflation: inflation importée, inflation « par contagion ».
inflation policy: politique inflationniste.
price inflation: inflation des prix.
non accelerating — rate of unemployment (NAIRU): taux de chômage non inflationniste.
wage inflation: inflation salariale.
inflationary: inflationniste.
inflationary gap: écart inflationniste.
inflationary pressures: poussées inflationnistes.
inflationary spiral: spirale inflationniste.

inflexibility (of prices, etc.): fixité, rigidité (des prix, etc.).

to inflict (a fine, a penalty): infliger (une amende, une peine).

inflow: afflux (m), entrée (f), apport (m) (de capitaux).
[F] *the — and outflow of gold*: les entrées et les sorties d'or.
capital —: afflux de fonds.

influence: influence (f), effet (sur), ascendant (sur).
undue —: abus d'autorité.
to influence: exercer une influence sur.

influx: afflux (m), affluence (f), abondance (f).
(an) — of goods on a glutted market: abondance de marchandises sur un marché encombré.

informal: officieux, de caractère privé, irrégulier.
— discussions: discussions non officielles, « en coulisse ».
— meeting: réunion non officielle.
— step: démarche officieuse.

informant: dénonciateur, délateur.

informatics: informatique.

information: [J] information(s), renseignement(s), acte d'accusation émanant du ministère public ; information ouverte sur ordre d'informer; dénonciation, délation.
[A] échange de renseignements entre administrations fiscales nationales.
advance —: préavis.
(readily) available —: renseignements (aisément) accessibles.
specific case —: renseignements sur des cas d'espèce.
confidential —: renseignements confidentiels.
eliciting —: obtenir des renseignements.
exchange of —: échange de renseignements.
exchange of — in the ordinary course: échange de renseignements d'office.
first-hand —: renseignements de première main.
for further —: pour plus ample informé.
full —: documentation complète.
qualitative —: information descriptive.
quantitative —: information exprimée en dimensions spécifiques et précises.
reliable —: renseignements sûrs.
request for —: demande d'information.
routine —: renseignements de caractère courant.
second-hand —: renseignements de seconde main.
— slip: fiche individuelle.
upon —: en vertu de renseignements.
— to be reported on the tax return: renseignements à porter sur la déclaration d'impôts.
— to be supplied on request: renseignements à fournir sur demande.
informer: informateur, dénonciateur (m).
police informer: agent provocateur.
to turn informer: dénoncer ses complices.

infortunium: malchance, accident.

to infringe: enfreindre, violer, empiéter sur.
[J] *— upon s.o.'s rights*: empiéter sur les droits de qn.
infringement: infraction, violation (d'une loi), contrefaçon (en matière de brevets ou de droits d'auteur).
infringement of a contract: rupture de contrat.
infringement suit: poursuites en contrefaçon.

ingot of gold: lingot d'or.

ingress: entrée (f).
[J] *free — and regress*: (servitude du) droit de libre accès et de libre sortie.
— and regress: [U.S.] article de la constitution stipulant la libre circulation des

citoyens dans tous les Etats de l'Union.

inhabitancy : habitation, séjour (dans une maison).
[J] résidence pendant la période requise (pour devenir électeur, etc.).

inherent (in) : inhérent, propre (à), naturel.
(ASS) — *vice* : vice inhérent.

to inherit : hériter de.
[J] — *s.o.'s estate* : hériter de qqn.
inheritance : [J] succession, héritage, patrimoine de famille; procédure en matière de succession.
canons of inheritance : ordre de succession.
law of inheritance : droit successif.
lineal inheritance : succession en ligne directe.
right of inheritance : droit de succession.
to come into an inheritance : recueillir un héritage.
[F] *inheritance tax* : droit de mutation après décès, droit de succession sur les parts héréditaires.

inhibition : interdiction (f).
[J] défense expresse, prohibition (f).

initial : initial.
[C] — *capital* : capital d'apport.
— *(capital) expenditure* : frais d'installation, frais de premier établissement.
capital outlay (—) : première mise de fonds.
— *cost depreciation* : amortissement au coût historique.
— *margin (or deposit)* : dépôt de garantie.
— *salary* : traitement de début.

to initial : parapher (un traité), émarger.
initials : paraphe.

to initiate : commencer.
[J] — *proceedings* : entamer des poursuites.

initiation : instauration, mise au point.

initiatory steps : démarches préliminaires.

to inject *capital into (a business)* : injecter (mettre) des capitaux dans (une affaire).

injunction : injonction (f), ordre (m).
[J] arrêt de suspension, de sursis; jugement avant faire droit.
compulsive (mandatory) — : ordonnance de faire, commandement du tribunal.
restrictive (preventive) — : [U.S.] ordonnance de ne pas faire.
interlocutory (interim) — : ordonnance interlocutoire.
perpetual — : injonction dépositive.

to injure : porter préjudice à, léser; blesser, offenser.
— *s.o.'s reputation* : endommager, nuire à la réputation de qn.
the injured *party* : la partie lésée.
injurious : nuisible, dommageable, préjudiciable.
injury : tort, préjudice, dommage, lésion (d'un droit).
injury benefit : indemnité pour dommages corporels.
bodily injury : lésion corporelle.
injury to person (to property) : dommage à la personne (aux biens).
work injury : accident du travail.

injuria : tort (dont on peut demander réparation, passible de poursuites).

inland : intérieur, de l'intérieur, indigène.
— *bill* : lettre de change sur l'intérieur.
— *duties* : taxes intérieures.
— *navigation* : navigation intérieure.
— *produce* : produit indigène.
— *revenue (inland revenue receipts)* : recettes fiscales, rentrées fiscales.
— *system* : régime intérieur.
— *trade* : commerce intérieur.
— *waterways* : réseau intérieur de fleuves et canaux.

Inn of court : (UK) confrérie (une des quatre) de « barristers » (à Londres).

inner : intérieur, interne, latent.
[F] — *reserve* : réserve latente.

innings : [J] relais (m pl) de mer.

innocent : innocent (a) (le terme [J] pour se déclarer ou être déclaré innocent, est *not guilty*).
[J] — *purchase* : acquisition (f) de bonne foi.

innominate : [J] (contrat) innomé.

innovation : innovation (f).
— *cluster* : grappe d'innovations.
[J] (Scot.) novation.

inns of court : les quatre écoles de droit à Londres (« the judicial university ») créées au XIVe siècle.

innuendo : [J] insinuation (f), partie de la plainte en diffamation *(slander, libel)* qui explique la signification véritable des propos proférés (« *meaning thereby...* ») dans leur rapport avec la personne du demandeur, explication que ce dernier demande au tribunal d'adopter.

inofficious testament: [J] testament deshéritant des héritiers légitimes sans raison suffisante et, de ce fait, annulable.

inoperative clause: [J] clause inopérante.

input: mise de fonds, apport, facteur de production, intrant.
– *lag*: retard dans l'adaptation des facteurs.
– *-output*: entrée-sortie.
– *-output table*: tableau d'échanges interindustriels, tableau d'entrées-sorties.

inquest: enquête (f).
[J] *coroner's –, – post mortem*: enquête après mort d'homme menée par un coroner.
to inquire: enquêter, s'informer, faire des recherches.
authority to inquire: pouvoir d'enquête.
inquiry: enquête, recherche, investigation, demande de renseignements.
board (commission) of enquiry: commission d'enquête.
inquiry office: bureau de renseignements.
to open (to set up) an enquiry: ouvrir une enquête.

inquisition: investigation (f), enquête (f) abusive.
[J] perquisition (f).

insanity: aliénation mentale.

inscribed: enregistré.
– *securities (stock)*: valeurs (actions) inscrites.

to insert: insérer.
[J] – *a clause (in a contract)*: introduire une clause dans un contrat.
insertion: insertion d'une annonce, introduction.

inside job: [J] [U.S.] crime attribué à un familier de la victime.

insider dealings: [B] achat ou vente d'actions par des personnes qui ont eu connaissance d'un événement ignoré du public qui en affecte la valeur.
– *dealings offence*: délit d'initié.
– *'s profits*: profits d'initié.

to insist on: insister sur, demander avec insistance, revendiquer, exiger.
– *payment*: exiger le paiement.

insistent: instant, intense, importun.
– *demand*: réclamation instante.

insolvency: [J] insolvabilité, carence, mise en liquidation judiciaire.

insolvent: insolvable.
insolvent act: loi relative à la liquidation judiciaire.
insolvent debtor: débiteur insolvable.

inspection: inspection (f), vérification (f), examen (m), contrôle (m), visite (f).
right of –: droit de regard.
[D] *custom –*: visite douanière.
[J] *– of documents*: remise de documents à la partie adverse pour examen.
factory trade –: inspection du travail.
medical –: examen médical.
[F] **inspector** *of taxes*: inspecteur des impôts.

(monetary) instability: [F] instabilité monétaire.

instalment: acompte (m), versement (m) partiel.
[C] *annual –*: annuité.
– *base*: acompte provisionnel de base.
diminishing – system: système dégressif d'amortissement.
final –: paiement pour solde.
fixed – system: système linéaire d'amortissement.
monthly –: mensualité.
– *plan*: vente à tempérament.
to pay by –(s): échelonner les paiements.

instance: circonstance, preuve, instance (f).
[J] *appeal –*: instance d'appel.
« *in the present –* »: « dans les circonstances actuelles ».

instant: pressant, immédiat, imminent, en cours.
– *case*: la présente affaire.
– *month*: mois en cours.

institute: [J] héritier virtuel désigné par testament, à charge pour lui de transférer la succession à l'héritier effectif dénommé *substitute*.

to institute: [J] *(a law, an order)* instituer, établir, *(a company)* fonder, constituer.
– *an action*: introduire une instance.
– *an appeal*: interjeter appel.
– *an enquiry*: procéder à une enquête.
– *s.o. as heir*: instituer qn héritier.
– *legal proceedings*: entamer des poursuites, ester en justice.

institution: institution (f), établissement (m), constitution (f).
institutional: institutionnel; de prestige.
institutional advertising: publicité de prestige.
institutional investors: investisseurs institutionnels.

in - store promotion: publicité (f) au point de vente.

to instruct: instruire, donner mandat (à).
[J] *to instruct (to brief) counsel*: constituer avocat.
instruction: instruction(s), indication(s), directive(s).
to comply with instructions: se conformer aux directives.
to carry out instructions: exécuter les instructions.
to confine oneself to one's instructions: s'en tenir à ses instructions.
to go beyond one's instructions: outrepasser ses instructions.

instrument: instrument (m), acte (m) juridique, document (m) officiel, élément (m) de preuve écrite.
[J] — *of appeal*: acte d'appel.
— *of commerce, of credit*: instrument de commerce, de crédit.
— *of donation*: acte de donation.
negotiable — : effet négociable.
— *of title*: titre de propriété.
— *of transfer*: acte de cession, acte translatif de propriété.
— *in writing*: acte instrumentaire.
written — : acte écrit.
instrumental: instrumental; utile, actif.
instrumental capital: capital productif.
to be instrumental in: contribuer à.
through the **instrumentality** *of*: par l'intermédiaire (m) de.

insufficiency: insuffisance, défaut.
— *of assets*: insuffisance d'actif.
insufficient: insuffisant.
insufficient assets: insuffisance d'actif.
insufficient funds: insuffisance de provision.

insurance: assurance (f).
[ASS] *accident, casualty* — : assurance contre les accidents.
agricultural — : assurance agricole.
aircraft — : assurance avion.
all-in — : assurance tous risques.
automobile — : assurance automobile.
automobile all-in — : assurance automobile tous risques.
bail and credit — : assurance de cautionnement et crédit.
builder's risk — : assurance bâtiment.
burglary — : assurance contre le cambriolage.
— *in case of death of third party*: assurance en cas de décès de tiers.
cargo — : assurance sur faculté (de marchandises).
certificate of — : certificat d'assurance.
— *charges*: frais d'assurance.
commercial — : assurance commerciale.

commercial credit — : assurance crédit commercial.
— *company*: compagnie d'assurance.
complementary — : assurance complémentaire.
compulsory — : assurance obligatoire.
contributory — : assurance à cotisations.
crop — : assurance récoltes.
cumulative — : assurance cumulative.
deferred annuities — : assurance de rentes différées.
deferred capital — : assurance à capital différé.
disablement — : assurance invalidité.
disablement pension — : assurance de rente d'invalidité.
double — : assurance double cumulative.
dowry — : assurance dotale.
employers' liability —, *workmen compensation* — : assurance patronale contre les accidents de travail.
endowment — : assurance mixte.
equipment — : assurance machines.
fire — : assurance incendie.
foreign currency — *(indexed insurance)*: assurance en monnaie étrangère (assurance indexée).
freight — : assurance sur le fret.
— *fund*: caisse d'assurance.
group — : assurance collective.
hail — : assurance contre la grêle.
health, sickness — : assurance-maladie.
hull — : assurance sur corps (de navire).
joint — : assurance conjointe.
life — : assurance sur la vie.
life annuity — : assurance de rente viagère.
live-stock — : assurance bétail.
luggage — : assurance des bagages.
marine — : assurance maritime.
movable property — : assurance mobilière.
multiple — : assurance multiple.
mutual — : assurance mutuelle.
old age — : assurance vieillesse.
old age pension — : assurance de rente vieillesse.
paid-up — : assurance libérée.
plate glass — : assurance contre le bris de glaces.
professional risks — : assurance contre les risques professionnels.
— *with (without) profit-sharing*: assurance avec (sans) participation aux bénéfices.
property — : assurance immobilière.
provisions of an — *policy*: stipulations d'une police d'assurance.
— *with redeemable (or irredeemable) premiums*: assurance à primes (non) restituables.
revertible life annuity — : assurance de rente viagère reversible.
school children — : assurance des écoliers.
securities — : assurance des valeurs.

social — benefits: prestations d'assurances sociales.
social — fund: caisse d'assurances sociales.
survivors, two lives, —: assurance survivants.
temporary —: assurance temporaire.
terms of —: conditions d'assurance.
third party —: assurance contre les accidents causés à des tiers.
title —: assurance du droit de propriété.
transport —: assurance transports.
unemployment —: assurance chômage.
— value: valeur d'assurance.
vicarious liability —: assurance de la responsabilité civile.
voluntary —: assurance facultative.
water-damage —: assurance contre les dégâts d'eau.
— agent: agent d'assurances.
— branch: branche d'assurance.
— broker: courtier d'assurances.
carry-over of (—) rates: report des primes d'assurance.
— claim: droit à l'assurance.
— company: compagnie d'assurances.
— contract, policy: contrat d'assurance.
general conditions of —: conditions générales de l'assurance.
contributory — scheme: [U.K.] sécurité sociale.
(—) indemnity benefit: prestation d'assurance.
redemption of the (—) policy: rachat de l'assurance.
reinsurance: contre-assurance.
to have **insurable** *interest:* avoir des titres à l'assurance.
insured: assuré.
insured interest: intérêt (pécuniaire) assurable.
insured parcel: colis avec valeur déclarée.
insured value: valeur d'assurance.
insurer: assureur (en assurance maritime: *underwriter*).

intake: consommation (f).

intangible: intangible, impalpable (a).
[J] *— property (intangibles):* biens et droits incorporels.
[C] *— assets:* valeurs immatérielles, intangibles.
— factors: les impondérables.

integration: intégration (f), rétablissement (m).
economic —: intégration économique.
social —: intégration sociale.
integrated planning: see « corporate planning ».

integrity: intégrité, probité (f).
[C] *commercial —:* probité commerciale, loyauté commerciale.

intellectual property: propriété (f) intellectuelle (ex. brevet d'invention...).

intelligence: intelligence (f), renseignements (m pl).
— bureau: bureau (agence) de renseignements.
economic —: nouvelles économiques.

INTELSAT (*International Telecommunications Satellite Organisation*): Organisation Internationale des Télécommunications par Satellite.

to intend (for): avoir l'intention de, projeter, destiner à.
intended: projeté, proposé, intentionnel.
intended transaction: transaction projetée.
intending: en perspective, futur, éventuel.
intending buyer (purchaser): acheteur éventuel, en perspective.

intendment: intention véritable (d'un testateur, etc.), esprit, sens (d'un texte).
[J] *— of the law:* présomption légale, interprétation de la loi.

intensive: intensif (a).
capital —: qui exige l'engagement de capitaux importants.
— cultivation: culture intensive.
— selling: ventes (f) intensives.
labour —: qui exige beaucoup de main-d'œuvre.

intent, intention: intention (f), motif (m), but (m), dessein (m).
[J] *with criminal (malicious) —:* dans un but délictueux.
with — to...: en vue de...
with — to commit a crime (with murderous —): avec intention criminelle.
the legislative —: les intentions du législateur.
with no ill —: sans songer à mal.
a question of —: une question d'interprétation (de la volonté des parties...).
to the — that: à l'effet que.
to all —(s) and purposes: sous tous les rapports.
declaration of —: [U.S.] demande de naturalisation.
fraudulent —: intention frauduleuse.
with honourable —(s): pour des motifs honorables.
statement of —: déclaration d'intention.

intentional: prémédité.

interaction: action réciproque.

inter-bank deposit: [F] dépôt de banque à banque.

inter-bank rate: taux (m) interbancaire.
interchangeable (bond): [F] (obligation) échangeable, interchangeable.
inter-company, inter-firm comparison: comparaison (f) des résultats avec ceux d'une autre entreprise.
intercourse: rapport, relations, commerce charnel.
 [J] *adulterous* – : commerce adultère.
 business – : rapports de commerce.
interdealer-broker system (IDBS): [B] système interagent de marché (SIAM).
interdepartmental: inter-services, interministériel.
interdependent markets: marchés interdépendants.
interdiction, interdict: interdiction (f), défense (f).
 [J] *to remove an* – : lever un interdit (une interdiction).
 judicial – : interdiction judiciaire.
interest: a) intérêt (m), avantage (m), influence (f), participation (f); b) droit (m), titre (m); c) parti (m), groupe (m).
 accrued – : intérêts échus.
 accruing – : intérêts à échoir.
 agricultural –(s): les agriculteurs.
 back- – : arrérages.
 – *bearing*: qui porte intérêt.
 the big –(s): les (grands) capitalistes.
 brewing – : les brasseurs.
 capital –(s): immobilisations.
 controlling – : participation qui donne la prédominance financière dans une affaire.
 compound (simple) – : intérêts composés (simples).
 – *cover*: taux de couverture des intérêts des emprunts.
 cumulative – : intérêt cumulatif.
 –*-earning*: qui rapporte des intérêts (placement, etc.).
 –(s) *free of tax*: intérêts nets d'impôt.
 group of –(s): groupement d'intérêts.
 joint –(s): droits indivis.
 the landed –(s): les propriétaires fonciers.
 life –(s): usufruit à vie.
 – *on loan*: intérêts de prêt.
 majority (minority) – : participation majoritaire (minoritaire).
 moneyed – : les capitalistes.
 –(s) *in the profits*: participation aux bénéfices.
 (effective, legal) – *rate*: taux d'intérêt (réel, légal).
 – *rate differentials*: differentiel d'intérêt.
 – *rate futures*: contrats à terme de taux d'intérêt.
 – *receivable*: intérêt à recevoir.
 red –(s): intérêts rouges (débiteurs).
 reversionary –(s): rente viagère à paiement différé.
 speculative –(s): valeurs spéculatives.
 statutory –(s): intérêts légaux.
 – *table*: table des intérêts.
 vested – : droit acquis.
 – *warrant*: coupon d'intérêt.
 to bear – : rapporter des intérêts.
 to have an – *in the profits of an undertaking*: avoir une participation dans les bénéfices d'une entreprise.
 to yield – : produire, porter intérêt.
to interfere (with): intervenir, s'immiscer (dans), contrarier, contrecarrer.
 [J] – *with the course of justice*: entraver le cours de la justice.
 interference: intervention, ingérence, instruction.
 – *with conditions of compétition*: atteinte aux conditions de la concurrence.
 unwarrantable interference: immixtion.
 interfering *claims*: réclamations contradictoires, conflits de droits.
interim: provisoire, transitoire (a).
 – *arrangements*: dispositions transitoires.
 – *dividend (share)*: dividende (action) provisoire, acompte sur dividende.
 – *report*: compte-rendu provisoire.
 – *statement*: bilan intermédiaire.
interior waterways: voies fluviales intérieures.
interlocking: interdépendant.
 [F] – *investments*: participation entre des sociétés du même groupe.
interlocutory: interlocutoire.
 – *decision, decree, judgment*: décision (f), arrêt (m), jugement (m) interlocutoire.
intermediary: intermédiaire (m), [J] personne (f) interposée (par ex. dans le cas d'une donation illicite).
 intermediate: intermédiaire.
 [F] *intermediate broker*: remisier.
 intermediate financing diversions: détours de financement.
 intermediate loan: prêt à moyen terme.
 intermediate output diversions: détours de production.
 intermediate technology: stade intermédiaire de développement technologique (du Tiers Monde).
internal: interne, intérieur, intrinsèque.
 [F] – *audit*: vérification des comptes d'un ou plusieurs services d'une entreprise.

[F] – *debt:* dette intérieure.
– *loan:* emprunt intérieur.
– *revenue:* [U.S.] fisc, recettes fiscales.
– *revenue code* # [U.S.] code général des impôts.
– *revenue service (I.R.S.)* # [U.S.] administration fiscale.
– *trade:* commerce intérieur.

international: international.
– *agreement:* accord international.
– *Atomic Energy Agency (I.A.E.A.):* Agence Internationale pour l'Energie Atomique (A.I.E.A.).
– *balance of payments:* balance des comptes internationale.
– *Bank for Reconstruction and Development:* Banque Internationale pour la Reconstruction et le Développement.
– *Chamber of Commerce (I.C.C.):* Chambre de Commerce Internationale (C.C.I.).
– *Committee of the Red Cross:* Comité international de la Croix-Rouge.
– *Commodity Agreement:* Accord international sur les produits de base.
– *Court of Justice:* Cour Internationale de Justice.
– *Fund for Agricultural Development (I.F.A.D.):* Fonds International pour le Développement Agricole (F.I.D.A.).
– *Labour Office:* Organisation Internationale du Travail.
– *Monetary Fund:* Fonds Monétaire International.
– *law:* droit international (privé, public).
– *money market:* [U.S.] marché financier (devises) de Chicago.
– *trade:* commerce international.

interpellation: [J] interpellation, sommation.

interpleader: [J] action pétitoire, incidente intentée soit par le détenteur d'un bien, soit par le *« sheriff »*.

to interpret: interpréter.
interpretation: interprétation, traduction.
[J] *interpretation clause:* clause interprétative (dans une loi ou dans un acte).

interrogatory: interrogatoire (m).
[J] pl. questions écrites échangées entre les parties.

interruption: interruption (f).
[J] interruption de la prescription.

interstate commerce: [U.S.] commerce entre les Etats de l'Union.

intervener: intervenant.
[J] **intervening** *party:* partie intervenante.
intervention: intervention (f).
intervention by government: intervention de l'Etat.
[C] *intervention on protest:* intervention à protêt.

intervivos gift: [J] donation entre vifs.

intestacy: [J] fait de mourir intestat, sans testament.
partial – *:* fait par le de cujus de n'avoir disposé que d'une partie de ses biens.
intestate: sans testament.
– *estate, succession:* succession ab intestat.

intimacy: intimité (f), accointances (f pl).
[J] commerce charnel.

intimidation: intimidation (f), menaces (f pl).
[J] – *of witness:* subornation de témoins.

intoxicated: en état d'ébriété.
intoxicating *liquors:* boissons alcooliques ([J] seulement, en [A]: *alcoholic beverages*).
intoxication: ivresse; quelquefois empoisonnement.

intra vires: de (sa) compétence, en (son) pouvoir.

in-tray: plateau (m) sur lequel on a déposé des documents à l'attention d'un chef de service.
– *exercice:* méthode d'entraînement à la gestion par jeux d'entreprises.

intrinsic defect, value: vice (m), valeur (f) intrinsèque.

to introduce: introduire, présenter (un projet), faire adopter (un projet de loi).
– *a bill:* présenter un projet de loi.
introduction: introduction, présentation.
introduction of a bill: présentation d'un projet de loi.
letter of introduction: lettre de recommandation.
introductory: préliminaire.
introductory price: prix de lancement.

intromission: ingérence (f).

intrusion: intrusion (f), usurpation (f), empiètement (m).

to inure, to enure: accoutumer, aguerrir; entrer en vigueur (loi).

to invade: envahir, violer, empiéter, porter atteinte à.
[J] — *a right*: violer un droit.

invalid: sans effet légal, non valable.
[J] — *clause*: clause non-valable.
— *decision*: décision nulle et non-avenue.
— *marriage*: mariage invalide.
— *pension*: pension d'invalidité.
to invalidate: invalider, casser, infirmer, abroger.
[C] *to invalidate a bargain*: annuler un marché.

invasion of a right: [J] violation d'un droit.

invention: invention (f), chose inventée.
inventor: inventeur (m).

inventory: [C] inventaire (m), stock (m), [U.S.] bilan de faillite.
beginning — : stock initial.
book — : [U.S.] inventaire comptable.
change in — : variation de stocks.
closing — : stock final.
— *control*: contrôle des stocks.
ending — : stock final.
excessive **inventories**: stocks excédentaires.
— *of fixtures*: état des lieux.
— *profit*: profit sur stocks.
reserve for — *maintenance*: réserve pour reconstitution des stocks.
to draw up, to take an — : faire (dresser) un inventaire.

inverse: inverse (a).
in — *ratio (to)*: en raison inverse (de).
— *(inverted) yield curve*: courbe inversée des taux d'intérêt.

to invest: investir, placer de l'argent.
[F] — *capital*: placer des fonds.
— *the management of sth. (to s.o.)*: [U.S.] confier la direction de qch. (à qn).
capital **invested** *in a business*: capital investi dans une affaire.

to investigate: faire une enquête, vérifier.
[J] **investigating** *commission*: commission d'enquête.
investigating magistrate: magistrat instructeur.
investigation: enquête (f), investigation (f), recherches (f pl), approfondissement (m).
investigation of a case: examen d'un dossier ; instruction d'une affaire criminelle.
preliminary investigation: enquête préalable.
under investigation: à l'étude.

investment: investissement (m), placement (m) de fonds.
[F] — *allowance*: déduction d'investissement.

— *bank*: [U.S.] banque d'affaires.
close ([U.S.] *closed)-end investment trust*: société d'investissement « fermée », à capital fixe.
— *company*: société de placement (de portefeuille).
— *decision*: décision (f) d'investir.
depreciation of — *(s)*: moins-value du portefeuille.
direct — *(s)*: investissements directs.
equity — *(s)*: actions ordinaires, [U.S.] actions de toute nature.
fixed yield — *(s)*: valeurs à revenu fixe.
foreign — : placement à l'étranger.
good — : placement avantageux.
— *goods*: biens d'investissement.
— *grant*: subvention pour encourager l'investissement.
gross — *ratio*: taux brut d'investissement.
— *income*: revenus de placements.
international — *(s)*: placements internationaux.
open-end — *trust*: société d'investissements « ouverte », à capital variable.
— *policy*: politique d'investissement.
portfolio — *(s)* (« *investments* »): portefeuille titres, valeurs en portefeuille (d'une banque), investissements de portefeuille.
private — *company*: société privée d'investissement.
real property (real estate) — *trust*: société immobilière d'investissement.
safe — : placement de père de famille, valeur de tout repos.
— *shares (stock)*: valeurs d'investissement, valeurs classées.
short-term — : placement à court terme.
— *(s) tax credit (ITC)*: [U.S.] crédit d'impôt valant aide fiscale à l'investissement.
— *trust (C°)*: société d'investissement.
variable yield — *(s)*: placements à revenus variables.
investor: épargnant, rentier, actionnaire, capitaliste (m).
investor's method: see « compound discount method ».

invisible: invisible (a).
[E] — *exports, imports*: exportations, importations invisibles, les « invisibles » (ex. dépenses de tourisme des non-résidents).
— *loss*: coulage.

to invite: convier, inviter, faire appel (à).
— *tenders for*: solliciter des offres de soumission.
invitee: invité (autorisé à pénétrer dans un lieu ou à s'y trouver).

invoice: [C] facture (f).
as per — : d'après facture.
— *book*: copie des factures.

consular — : facture consulaire.
fraudulent — : facture frauduleuse.
proforma — : facture « pro forma », simulée.
provisional — : facture provisoire.
purchase — : facture d'achat.
sale — : facture de vente.
shipping — : facture d'expédition.
invoicing back price : cours de résiliation.
invoicing machine : machine à facturer.

involuntary : involontaire, obligatoire (a).
— *act, action :* acte (action) involontaire.
— *manslaughter :* meurtre accidentel, non prémédité.

to involve : impliquer, entraîner, toucher à, engager.
[C] *the expenses involved...* : les dépenses qu'occasionnera, les dépenses à prévoir...
[J] *to get involved in :* se trouver impliqué, mis en cause dans.

inward : intérieur.
— *bill of lading :* connaissement d'entrée.

iou (initiales de « I owe you ») : (« je vous dois »), reconnaissance de dette.

ipso facto : de ce fait (ipso facto).

iron and steel shares : [B] actions métallurgiques.

to iron out difficulties : aplanir des difficultés.

irrebutable : irréfragable.
[J] — *presumption :* présomption absolue.

irrecoverable : irréparable, non recouvrable (a).
[C] — *debt :* créance (dette) non recouvrable, irrécouvrable.

irrecusable (evidence) : [J] irrécusable (preuve, témoignage) (a).

irredeemable : irrachetable, non remboursable ; irrémédiable (a).
[F] — *bond :* obligation non amortissable.

irrefragable : irréfragable, irréfutable (a).
irrefragably : d'une manière irréfragable.

irregular : irrégulier (a), entaché d'un vice de forme.
[J] — *document :* document informe, instrument entaché d'un vice de forme.
[C] — *tendency of the market :* tendance irrégulière du marché.
irregularity : irrégularité, vice de forme.
to commit irregularities : commettre des irrégularités (dans les écritures comptables, etc.).

irrelevance, irrelevancy : impertinence (f), inconséquence (f), manque de rapport (avec).
irrelevant : sans rapport (avec), non pertinent, inapplicable, hors de cause.
irrelevant in point of law : sans effet juridique.

irrespective : indépendant, indépendamment.
— *of the amount... :* quel que soit le montant...

irresponsible : [J] irresponsable, [C] insolvable (a).

irrevocable : irrévocable (a).
— *letter of credit :* lettre de crédit non recouvrable.

I.R.S. agent : agent (m) du fisc.

issue : sortie (f), conséquence (f).
[A] [F] émission (f) ; produit (m), profit (m).
[J] descendance en ligne directe ; point en litige.
at — : en jeu, en discussion.
interests at — : intérêts en jeu.
matters at — : affaires (matières) en discussions.
banks of — : instituts d'émission.
new — *of capital :* augmentation de capital.
case at — : cas en litige.
economic — : problème économique.
fiduciary — : circulation fiduciaire.
— *(of law, of fact) :* question (de droit, de fait) ; conclusion.
main — : fond (d'un procès).
note — *ceiling :* plafond d'émission de papier-monnaie.
over- — : surémission.
— *of a prospectus :* lancement d'un prospectus.
— *of securities (of shares, etc.) :* émission de valeurs, etc.
restricted — : émission limitée.
side — : question secondaire.
under — : émission trop restreinte.
to bring to an — : faire aboutir.
to confuse the — : brouiller les cartes.
to die without — : mourir sans postérité.
to evade the — : user de subterfuge.
to join — : accepter un point de fait affirmé par l'adversaire.
the — *joined :* la cause en état.
to plead the general — : plaider non coupable.
to put a claim in — : contester une réclamation.
to state an — : poser une question (pour qu'il en soit débattu).
to take an — : soulever une controverse,

— 468 —

contester une affirmation.
to issue : émettre, faire une émission, mettre (des billets) en circulation, lancer (un mandat d'arrêt), publier (un communiqué).
to issue a certificate : délivrer un certificat.
to issue a decree : rendre un arrêt.
to issue a cheque : émettre un chèque.
to issue execution : délivrer un exécutoire.
to issue a loan : lancer un emprunt.
to issue shares (at par, at a premium, at discount) : émettre des actions (au pair, au-dessous du pair, au-dessus du pair).
shares issued to the public : actions émises dans le public.
to issue an order : donner un ordre.
to issue a subpoena : assigner (un témoin) à comparaître.
to issue a summons : lancer une citation, signifier un ajournement.
to issue a warrant for the arrest of s.o. : décerner un mandat d'arrêt contre qn.
to issue a writ : signifier une assignation, un exploit, une ordonnance.
bills **issued** *for value in goods* : billet causé en valeur reçue en marchandises.
issued capital : capital versé.
issued price : prix d'émission.
issuing, issuance : [U.S.] délivrance (d'un brevet ou d'un permis).
children issuing from... : enfants nés ou à naître...
issuing bank : banque d'émission.
issuing house : banque de placement, maison d'émission.
issuing office : bureau d'émission.

item : [C] [F] article (m), chapitre (m) (d'un budget), rubrique (f), poste (m), écriture (f).
(adv) item, idem, de même.
big ticket — *(s)* : articles coûteux.
— *on the agenda* : question à l'ordre du jour.
— *in an account* : article d'un compte.
balance-sheet — *(s)* : délais du bilan.
cost — : article de dépense.
deductible — : montant à déduire.
— *of expenditure* : poste de dépense.
expense — : chef de dépense.
(an) — *of income* : un élément du revenu.
income — *(s)* : catégories de revenus.
news — *(s)* : faits divers.
small — *(s)* : menus frais.
to item : noter, prendre note de.
to itemize : [U.S.] détailler, spécifier, ventiler (un compte).
itemized *account* : compte spécifié.
— *bill (invoice)* : facture détaillée.
— *déduction* : déduction justifiée, sur pièces justificatives.

itinerant : ambulant, itinérant.
[J] — *judge* : juge en tournée.
[C] — *merchant* : marchand ambulant.

NOTES

J

(the union) jack: le pavillon britannique.

to jack up prices: monter les prix (de : « *a jack* », un cric).

jack leg (lawyer, politician): [U.S.] (avocat, politicien) véreux.

(to hit the) jackpot: [U.S.] gagner le gros lot, tirer le bon numéro.

jaccitation, jactitation: [J] (le) fait pour l'une des parties de se vanter (latin : jactare) d'une chose que l'autre partie affirme être fausse. S'emploie surtout dans l'expression « — *of marriage* »: (le) fait de prétendre faussement que l'on est marié à une certaine personne.

jaded customers: clients (m pl) blasés.

jail: [J] prison, maison d'arrêt (f).
   to break — : s'évader.
   jailbreak: évasion.
   jailbreaker: évadé.
   jailor (jailer): gardien de prison.

jam: cohue (f), encombrement (m), [U.S.] brouillage d'une émission radiophonique.
   traffic- — : embarras de circulation.
   to be in a — : se trouver dans une situation délicate (difficile).

(lawyer's) jargon: [J] jargon d'homme de loi (du Palais).

to jar (with sthg): être en désaccord.
   jarring interests: intérêts incompatibles (discordants).

jawbone policies: lignes directrices.

J curve: courbe en forme de J marquant l'amélioration de la balance commerciale (après une dévaluation).

jedburgh justice: justice sommaire (du nom d'un village écossais où les voleurs étaient pendus sans autre forme de procès). Loi de Lynch.

jelly-fish policy: politique de demi-mesures.

jeofail: [J] vice de forme (négligence ou oubli).

to jeopardize: mettre en danger, compromettre.
   [C] *— one's business*: laisser péricliter ses affaires.
   — one's situation: compromettre sa situation.
jeopardy: danger, risque (m).
   (business) in jeopardy: (affaire) qui péricline.
   [J] *to be in (double) jeopardy*: être traduit en justice pour un crime ou délit dont on a déjà eu à répondre.
   [F] *jeopardy assessment*: taxation d'office.
   tax in jeopardy: danger de non-recouvrement d'impôt.

jerry-built: construit avec des matériaux de mauvaise qualité.

jetsam: marchandises jetées à la mer (pour alléger un navire en danger).
   — and flotsam: choses de flot et de mer.

jettison (of cargo): jet (de cargaison) à la mer, largage.
   to jettison (goods): jeter (des marchandises) à la mer.
   to jettison a bill: abandonner un projet de loi.
jetty: jetée.

job: emploi (m), occupation (f), poste (m), situation (f), tâche (f), travail (m).
   — aim: objectif professionnel.
   — analysis: analyse des emplois.
   — enrichment: nouvel arrangement (m) des méthodes de travail, enrichissement des tâches.
   — estimate: estimation des prix de revient d'une commande.
   — evaluation: évaluation des tâches.
   fat — : emploi grassement rémunéré.
   full-time — : emploi à temps plein.
   — goods: soldes, articles dépareillés.
   — guidance: orientation économique.
   — line, — lot: marchandises d'occasion, soldes, articles dépareillés.
   — mobility: mobilité (f) de la main-d'œuvre.
   — order record: fiche de prix de revient d'une commande.
   — production: production linéaire (de la matière première à l'objet fini).
   part-time — : emploi à temps partiel.
   — -related injury: accident du travail.
   — retraining: recyclage.
   — seeker: demandeur d'emploi.
   — time ticket: bon de travail.

— *wage*: salaire à la tâche.
— *work*: [U.S.] travail rémunéré à la pièce.
work by the — : travail à forfait.
— *worker*: tâcheron.
odd — *(s)*: bricolage.
to do odd — *(s)*: bricoler.
to be out of — : être sans travail, en chômage.
to look for a — : chercher du travail.
to throw up one's — : abandonner son emploi, se démettre de son emploi.
every man to his — : (à) chacun son métier.
[B] **to job** *in and out*: faire la navette, jouer les allées et venues.

jobber: 1° tâcheron, intermédiaire, sous-traitant.
[B] 2° remiseur, coulissier, agioteur.
stock- — : agioteur.
— *('s) turn*: bénéfice que fait un coulissier sur la vente des valeurs.
(political) **jobbery**: intrigues politiques.
(stock) jobbery: agiotage, spéculation boursière.
jobbing: qui travaille à la tâche ou à façon ; a) travail (m) à la tâche; b) commerce (m) d'intermédiaire, de demi-gros; c) [B] courtage (m), agiotage (m), spéculation (f), arbitrage (m).
jobbing contract: contrat à forfait.
jobbing in contangoes: arbitrage des reports.
jobbing-house: [U.S.] firme de courtage.
stock-jobbing: spéculation boursière.
jobbing work: travail à forfait.
jobless: sans travail, chômeur.
the jobless: les chômeurs.

to join: se joindre (à), s'unir (à), rejoindre, adhérer (à).
— *a party, a trade-union*: s'affilier à un parti, à un syndicat.
[J] — *issue*: accepter un arbitrage.
— *a lawsuit*: intervenir dans un procès.
joinder *(contrary: misjoinder, non-joinder)*: réunion (f), union (f).
joinder of actions, of causes, of action, of parties: jonction d'instances (des défendeurs et des demandeurs).
compulsory joinder: jonction d'instances obligatoire.
joinder in pleading: jonction de causes.

joint: associé, commun, conjoint, coordonné, à demi, joint, solidaire (a).
— *account*: compte joint, conjoint, à demi.
— *action*: action collective.
(to take) — *action*: (agir) en nom collectif.
— *application*: demande collective.
— *attorney*: commanditaire.
— *beneficiaries*: bénéficiaires joints, indivis.
— *board*: commission mixte, paritaire.
— *bond*: dettes ou cautionnements communs.

— *business*: exploitation en commun.
— *capital*: actif commun.
— *commission, committee*: commission mixte.
— *complaint*: plainte collective.
— *conference*: commission médiatrice (Cour internationale).
— *consultations*: délibérations communes (direction-personnel).
— *costs*: coûts joints (qu'entraîne la production de deux ou plusieurs produits mais qui ne peuvent être attribués à aucun en particulier).
— *covenant*: solidarité active (opp. *several covenant*: solidarité passive).
— *creditor*: cocréancier.
— *debtor*: codébiteur.
— *defendant*: codéfendeur.
— *demand*: demande liée, solidaire (de deux biens qui en raison de leur complémentarité d'usage ne peuvent être achetés séparément, comme par exemple l'un ou l'autre soulier d'une même paire).
— *estate*: communauté, copropriété.
— *float*: flottement concerté des monnaies.
— *founder*: cofondateur.
— *guardian*: cotuteur.
— *heir*: cohéritier, copartageant.
— *holder*: codétenteur, porteur indivis.
— *interest*: intérêt commun.
— *legatee*: colégataire.
— *liability*: responsabilité conjointe.
— *management*: codirection.
— *manager*: cogérant.
— *owner, ownership*: copropriétaire, copropriété.
— *partner, partnership*: coassocié, coassociation.
— *plaintiff*: codemandeur.
— *products*: produits liés (la production de l'un entraîne automatiquement la production de l'autre).
— *purchasers*: acquéreurs associés, coacquéreurs.
— *report*: rapport collectif.
— *responsibility*: responsabilité solidaire.
— *security, surety*: co-caution.
— *shares*: parts, actions indivises.
— *stock*: capital social, capital-actions.
— *stock bank*: société de dépôt.
— *stock company*: compagnie, société par actions, anonyme.
— *tenancy*: location (ou propriété) indivise.
— *tenant*: colocataire.
— *tortfeasors (wrongdoers)*: codélinquants.
— *undertaking*: entreprise en participation.
— *use*: mitoyenneté, co-jouissance.
— *venture*: coentreprise, association en participation, opération conjointe.
— *and several*: solidaire, conjoint.
— *and several liability, obligation*: responsabilité, obligation conjointe et solidaire.
jointly: 1° conjointement, solidairement, en

collaboration, de concert, par indivis, indivisément.
jointly and severally liable: solidairement et conjointement responsable.
to inherit jointly: être cohéritier.
to make, render s.o. jointly liable, responsible: rendre solidairement responsable, solidaire, solidariser.
to manage (a business) jointly: co-gérer (une entreprise).
2° contradictoirement (constater, examiner).

jointure: [J] a) douaire, disposition prématrimoniale en faveur de la future ; b) propriété indivise (entre deux conjoints), domaine indivis.

joker: [U.S.] clause ambiguë d'une loi.

to jot down (one's purchases etc.): [C] tenir registre (de ses achats etc.).

journal: [C] livre-journal.
economic, trade- — : revue économique.
law — : journal des tribunaux.
sales — : livre des ventes.
— *entry*: écriture (dans un livre-journal).
journalization: journalisation.
to journalize: journaliser.

journey: voyage, trajet (m).
home (ward) out (ward) — : voyage retour, voyage aller.
— *overland*: voyage par terre.
journeyman: ouvrier qualifié, compagnon.

judge: juge, magistrat (m).
[J] *circuit* — : juge en tournée.
— *of the court of appeal*: juge d'appel.
alternate, deputy — : juge suppléant.
— *in lunacy*: tribunal des tutelles.
—(s) *order*: mandat, ordonnance de juge.
presiding — : président du tribunal.

judgment: [J] jugement, décision judiciaire, arrêt.
— *in absence*: jugement par contumace.
— *absolute*: jugement irrévocable.
adjudicative — : jugement déclaratoire.
— *affirmed* — : jugement confirmé.
appeal — : jugement rendu en appel.
arrest of — : suspension de jugement.
cautionary — : ordonnance de saisie conservatoire.
conforming — : arrêt confirmatif.
considered — : jugement sur le fond.
contentious — : jugement contentieux.
copy of a — : expédition d'un jugement.
— *creditor*: plaignant qui a obtenu satisfaction.
— *debt*: somme attribuée par le tribunal à un plaignant qui a obtenu satisfaction.
— *by default*: jugement par défaut.

enforceable — : jugement exécutoire.
final — : jugement final, définitif.
grounds of a — : attendus, considérants.
interlocutory — : jugement interlocutoire.
— *-at-law*: jugement passé en force de chose jugée.
— *lien*: privilège judiciaire.
— *modified (on the law or on the facts)*: jugement révisé (sur des points de droit et de fait).
— *nisi*: jugement conditionnel.
— *over*: jugement commun.
— *in personam*: jugement visant une personne déterminée.
— *in rem*: jugement d'ordre général, opposable à quiconque.
— *of record*: jugement de donner acte.
— *summons*: mise en demeure par jugement de s'acquitter d'une dette.
— *after trial*: jugement contradictoire.
to abide by a — : s'en rapporter à un jugement.
to arrest a — : suspendre (l'exécution d') un jugement.
to attack a — : attaquer, se pourvoir contre un jugement.
to confirm, ratify a — : confirmer un jugement.
to construe a — : interpréter un jugement.
to deliver a — : rendre un jugement.
to docket a — : enregistrer un jugement.
to obtain a — *against*: obtenir un jugement contre.
to deliver, to give, to pass, to pronounce a — : rendre un jugement, un arrêt.
to quash, to repeal, to rescind a — : annuler, rapporter un jugement.
to reverse a — : réformer un jugement.
to review a — : réviser un jugement.
to suspend a — : suspendre un jugement.
to vacate a — : annuler, casser un jugement.
— *creditor*: créancier titulaire d'un jugement exécutoire pour le montant d'une créance.
— *debtor*: débiteur dont les biens peuvent être saisis à la demande du créancier, par suite d'un jugement.

judicature: [J] a) la magistrature ; b) période d'exercice d'un juge.
Supreme Court of — : Cour Suprême de Justice instituée en Grande-Bretagne par une loi de 1873 abrogée en 1925 et remplacée alors par d'autres dispositions.

judicial: judiciaire, juridique (a).
[J] — *assistance*: assistance judiciaire.
— *code*: code de procédure.
— *duties*: fonctions judiciaires.
— *enquiry*: enquête judiciaire.
— *investigation*: information judiciaire.
— *murder*: assassinat légal.
— *notice*: fait pour les tribunaux de reconnaître sans qu'il soit besoin d'une preuve

formelle que « les choses sont ce qu'elles sont ».
– *power :* pouvoir judiciaire.
– *proof :* preuve en justice.
– *record :* casier judiciaire.
– *sale :* vente judiciaire.
– *separation :* séparation de corps.
– *trustee :* administrateur judiciaire.
judicially : judiciairement.
judiciary : a) la magistrature (f) ; b) judiciaire (a).
judiciary police, power : police, pouvoir judiciaire.
judiciary sale(s) : vente(s) par autorité de justice.

to juggle (with figures) : jongler (avec les chiffres).
juggling *of figures :* manipulation de chiffres.
financial juggle (juggling) : tripotage financier.
jugglery : escamotage, fourberie, mauvaise foi.

jumble sale : vente (f) de charité.

jumbo loan : (F) prêt (m) géant consenti par un groupement de banques à un gouvernement ou à de grosses sociétés (de « Jumbo » : avion gros porteur).

jump : avance (f) rapide, bond (m).
(a) – *in prices :* (une) flambée des prix.
the expected – in (our) exports : le bond attendu de nos exportations.
to jump : faire un bond, monter en flèche.
to jump a bill : [U.S.] laisser une facture impayée.
to jump to conclusions : tirer des conclusions hâtives.
(the) **jumpiness** *(of the market) :* (l')instabilité, (la) nervosité du marché.

juncture : occurrence, circonstance (f) (souvent : critique).

junior : cadet, subalterne (a).
[F] – *bonds :* obligations de deuxième rang.
– *clerk :* petit commis, petit clerc.
– *officer :* officier subalterne.
– *partner :* dernier associé (et le moins influent).
– *position :* poste subalterne.
– *shares :* nouvelles actions.
juniority *(rare) :* s'oppose à *« seniority »,* infériorité d'âge ou de position.

junk : pacotille (f), [U.S.] drogue (f).
– *bonds :* obligations « pourries ».
– *dealer :* ferrailleur.
– *pusher :* [U.S.] trafiquant de drogue.

jural : légal (a).

jurat : [J] brève formule à la fin d'un affidavit indiquant où, quand et devant qui il a été reçu.

juration : [J] prestation de serment.

juridical : [J] judiciaire, juridique, légal, agissant pour l'administration de la justice.
– *day :* jour d'audience.
– *dissimulation :* dissimulation juridique.
– *position :* situation juridique.
– *system :* système juridique.

jurisdiction : a) juridiction (f), compétence (f), autorité (f) judiciaire ; b) jurisprudence (f).
[J] *appellate – :* juridiction d'appel.
– *clause :* clause attributive de compétence.
fiscal – : compétence fiscale.
court of general – : tribunal compétent en toutes matières contentieuses.
special – : juridiction d'exception.
court of summary – : tribunal de simple police.
to come within the – of : être de la compétence de.
to fall outside the – of : échapper à la compétence de.
the court entertains – : le tribunal est compétent.
want of – : incompétence.
jurisdictional : juridictionnel, exigé par la loi.

juris et de jure : [J] présomption irréfragable.

jurisprudence : [J] la science du droit et quelquefois aussi l'ensemble des décisions des tribunaux (cf. John B. Saunders : Mozley and Whitelaw's Law Dictionary, Butterworths, London 1970).
comparative – : droit comparé.
medical – : médecine légale.

jurist : [J] juriste (m), légiste (m), [U.S.] homme (m) de loi, avocat (m).

juror : [J] juré(e), membre du jury.
panel of – (s) : liste du jury.

jury : [J] jury (m).
common – : jury de jugement.
to empanel the – : constituer le jury, en faire l'appel.
grand – : jury d'accusation.
– *-box :* banc des jurés.
– *('s) findings :* verdict des jurés.
– *of matrons :* (hist.) jury de matrones.
– *process :* convocation des jurés.
trial by – : jugement par jury.
verdict of the – : verdict du jury.

juryman, jurywoman : juré(e).

jus : (le) droit, (la) loi.

jus ad rem (acquirendam) : le droit d'acquérir un bien.

jus disponendi : le droit de disposer d'un bien.

jus in re : plein droit.

jus tertii : droit d'un tiers.

just : juste, équitable, légitime (a), conforme à la loi.
[J] *a – cause* : une juste cause.
a – charge : une accusation fondée.
– price : juste prix.
a – and lawful decision, verdict : un bien-jugé.
– suspicion : soupçon légitime.

justice : [J] a) justice, équité (f) ; b) administration de la justice ; c) titre donné aux magistrats de rang aussi bien le plus élevé que le plus bas.
denial of – : déni de justice.
distributive – : justice distributive.
miscarriage of – : erreur judiciaire.
to bring s.o. to – : traduire qn en justice.
to dispute the – of a claim : contester le bien fondé d'une réclamation.
to pervert – : fausser la justice.
court of – : tribunal.
– of the Peace : Juge de Paix, [U.K.] juge non professionnel dans une "Magistrate's Court" (guidé par un "Clerk to the Justices").
the Lord Chief – : le Président du Tribunal du Banc du Roi, le Président d'une Cour Supérieure, [U.S.] d'une Cour Suprême.

justiciable : [J] justiciable (de).

justifiable : justifiable, légitime (a).
– refusal : refus légitime, motivé.

justification : a) justification (f) (de sa conduite...) ; b) moyens (m pl) de défense.
final – : raison dernière.
justificative, justificatory : justificatif (document).
to justify : justifier, légitimer, motiver.
to justify bail : justifier de sa solvabilité avant de fournir une caution.
a justified decision : une décision justifiée.
justly : à juste titre, équitablement.

juvenile : juvénile (a).
[J] *dependent –(s)* : mineurs à charges.
– court : tribunal pour enfants.
– delinquency : délinquance juvénile.
– delinquent, offender : jeune délinquant, accusé mineur.
– labour : travail des enfants (ou des adolescents).
– welfare : protection de l'enfance.

NOTES

K

kaffirs: [F] valeurs mobilières sud-africaines (mines d'or).

kangaroo: [J] droit du président de la chambre des communes constituée en commission générale *(Committee of the Whole House)* de choisir (de « sauter », d'où : « — ») les amendements qui seront discutés.
— *-court*: tribunal illégal, irrégulier (à l'origine, tribunal organisé par des détenus pour juger certains de leurs co-détenus qui auraient violé la « loi » de leur « milieu »).

K.D.: see « Knocked down ».

keelage: [A] droits de mouillage *(keel*: quille d'un navire).

keen: vif, perçant, mordant, acéré (a).
— *competition*: concurrence acharnée, sans merci.
— *demand*: demande active, forte demande.
— *prices*: prix très étudiés, compétitifs.

keep: entretien (d'une personne), frais de subsistance.
to earn one's — : gagner sa vie.
he earns (so much) a day and his — : il gagne (tant) par jour, logé et nourri.

to keep: garder, observer, tenir, conserver, mettre en réserve, maintenir, retenir.
— *the accounts*: tenir la comptabilité.
— *books of record*: avoir une comptabilité.
— *the cash*: tenir la caisse.
— *one's engagements*: tenir ses engagements.
— *going*: se maintenir en activité.
— *(an industry) going*: maintenir l'activité (d'une industrie).
— *one's hair on*: ne pas céder à la panique.
— *the minutes (of a meeting)*: tenir le procès-verbal (d'une réunion).
— *the order*: maintenir l'ordre.
— *the peace*: ne pas troubler l'ordre public.
— *a record*: tenir un registre.
— *(a building) in repair*: entretenir (un bâtiment).
— *in trust, safely*: garder en dépôt.
— *within the law*: se tenir dans la légalité.
— *back from, out of (an employee's pay)*: retenir sur (le salaire d'un employé).
— *prices down*: empêcher les prix de monter.
— *prices down to*: empêcher les prix de monter au-dessus de.
— *prices up*: maintenir les prix élevés.
— *under lock and key*: tenir sous clef.

keeper: garde (m), gardien (m), gérant (m), dépositaire (m), conservateur (m) (de musée).
[C] *hotel-* — : hôtelier, gérant d'hôtel.
[J] *Lord* — *of the Great Seal*: [U.K.] Garde du Grand Sceau.
— *of the records*: greffier (d'un tribunal).
keeping: garde, maintien (de l'ordre), observance, tenue.
to leave in the keeping of: laisser à la garde de.
keeping books (accounts): tenue des livres (des comptes).
in safe keeping: en lieu sûr, en mains sûres.

Kennedy round (of trade negotiations): [E] Négociations Kennedy (de 1964 à 1967 à Genève) qui aboutirent à des concessions tarifaires sur les importations consenties par un certain nombre d'Etats (dont Tchécoslovaquie et Yougoslavie).

kerb, kerb-stone: bord du trottoir.
[B] — *broker*: [U.S.] coulissier.
(the) — *market*: (le) marché hors côte, (la) coulisse.

key: clé (f), clef (f), indice (m).
code- — : chiffre d'un code.
— *currency*: monnaie, devise clef.
— *-industry*: industrie clef.
— *-man*: [U.S.] homme indispensable (à la marche d'une administration, d'une entreprise).
— *-money*: pas-de-porte, arrhes.
— *-position*: position clef.
— *-products*: produits-clefs.
— *-staff*: cadres (d'une entreprise).
— *-word*: mot-clef.
keyed *advertisement*: publicité confiée à un organe de presse déterminé et dont on peut mesurer l'efficacité grâce à une « clef ».

keyboard: clavier (de machine à écrire).

keynesian (model, etc.): (modèle, etc.) keynésien.

kick-back: [U.S.] ristourne, dichotomie, commission clandestine (f).

kicked-upstairs: (fam.) promotion-sanction (f) (on donne des avantages financiers à qqn dont on veut se débarrasser).

kicker : avantage (m) supplémentaire propre à allécher les investisseurs.

kidnapping : [J] rapt d'enfant.

to kill : tuer, barrer la route (à), [U.S.] rejeter un projet de loi.
[F] — *inflation :* donner un coup d'arrêt à l'inflation.

kilometer-ton : [C] tonne kilomètre, tonne kilométrique.

kin, kindred : parent (m), allié (m), parenté (f), souche (f).
(my, our...) kith and — : (mes, nos...) parents et amis, proches.
next of — : le parent (l'héritier) le plus proche.

kind : espèce, genre, manière, (en) nature.
all — *(s) of :* toutes sortes de.
allowances in — : prestations en nature.
indemnity, payment, remuneration, settlement in — : indemnité, paiement, rémunération, règlement en nature.
[F] *to levy taxes in* — : prélever des taxes en nature.
kindly : prière de..., vouloir bien...
kindly remit by cheque : veuillez nous couvrir par chèque.

king's bench : [U.K.] Cour du Banc du Roi, *(Queen's)* de la Reine.
[J] — *evidence (queen's, state) :* témoin dénonciateur de ses complices.
— *highway :* grande route.
[D] — *warehouse :* dépôt de douane.

kit : prêt à monter.

kite : a) usurier ; b) cerf-volant, traite en l'air, billet de complaisance.
[C] — *-flier :* tireur à découvert.
to kite *a cheque :* émettre un chèque sans provision.
to fly, to send up a kite : a) tirer à découvert ; b) « tâter le terrain ».

knight (of the garter, etc.) : chevalier (de la Jarretière, etc.).
[B] *black* — : « chevalier noir » *(see black).*
white — : « chevalier blanc » *(see white).*

knitted goods : bonneterie (f).

knock-down price : [C] prix minimum, prix de réclame, prix choc.
to knock-down *prices :* baisser considérablement les prix.

knock-for-knock agreement : (ASS) accord (m) entre deux compagnies pour dédommager séparément leurs clients respectifs.

knocked down (K.D.) (goods) : [C] (marchandises) expédiées en vrac.
completely — *delivered (goods) :* (marchandises) livrées en pièces détachées (meubles, autos...).

to knock sth. off (the price) : rabattre qch, (du prix).

knock-out : [C] entente illégale entre enréchisseurs.
— *price :* prix très bas, imbattable.

knocking : publicité qui tend à critiquer un produit concurrent.
— *off time :* (fam.) fin de la journée de travail.

knotty : noueux, embrouillé, épineux (a).
— *problem, question :* problème épineux, question épineuse.

to know : savoir, reconnaître.
[J] « *know all men by these present...* » : « faisons assavoir par ces présentes... ».
— *for a fact :* savoir de source certaine.
be it known... : il est fait assavoir...
know-how : savoir-faire (m), technique (f), procédé (m), formule (f) de fabrication (moyens brevetables ou non ayant le caractère de secret ou de nouveauté, du moins pour celui qui veut en obtenir la jouissance ou la propriété).
knowingly : sciemment.

knowledge : connaissance (f), science (f), savoir (m).
branch of — : branche du savoir.
expert — : connaissance(s) de spécialiste.
factual, full — : connaissance de cause.
to speak with full — : parler en connaissance de cause.
with inside — : de bonne source.
a matter of common — : un fait de notoriété publique.
lack of — : ignorance.
knowledgeable *investors :* des investisseurs bien informés.

known (fact) : (fait) connu, constaté.
a — *thief :* un voleur avéré.

NOTES

NOTES

L

« la reyne le veult » : promulgation par la reine d'une loi votée par le parlement.

« la reyne s'avisera » : refus de promulguer une loi (ce qui ne s'est pas produit depuis 1707).

label : étiquette (f), marque (de qualité...).
to label : étiqueter.

labor [U.S.], **labour** : travail (m), labeur (m), peine (f), main-d'œuvre (f), les salariés.
— *agreement* : convention collective.
allocation of — : répartition de la main-d'œuvre.
(the) American Federation of — : (la) Fédération Américaine du Travail.
capital and — : le capital et le travail.
casual — : main-d'œuvre temporaire.
contract — : main-d'œuvre contractuelle.
cost of — *(labour cost)* : coût de la main-d'œuvre.
demand for — : demande de main-d'œuvre.
the demands of — : les revendications des salariés.
— *disputes* : conflits du travail.
— *exchange* : bourse du travail, bureau de placement.
the division of — : la division du travail.
farm — : main-d'œuvre agricole.
— *force* : force de travail, main-d'œuvre globale, effectif de la main-d'œuvre.
foreign — : main-d'œuvre étrangère.
hired — *charges* : charges salariales.
indentured — : main-d'œuvre sous contrat d'apprentissage.
— *intensive process* : fabrication qui exige beaucoup de main-d'œuvre.
International — *Office* : Bureau International du Travail.
— *leaders* : dirigeants ouvriers, syndicaux.
— *legislation* : législation du travail.
manual — : travail manuel.
— -*market* : marché du travail, offre ouvrière.
material and — *(of a suit of clothes)* : tissu et façon (d'un complet).
mobility of — : mobilité de la main-d'œuvre.
regulation of — : réglementation du travail.
rights of — : droits du travail.
shortage of — *(— shortage)* : pénurie de main-d'œuvre.
skilled — : main-d'œuvre spécialisée.
specialization of — : spécialisation du travail.
— *standards* : normes de travail.
— *troubles* : conflits sociaux du travail.
— *turnover* : fluctuations du personnel (salarié).
unfair — *practices* : emploi illicite de la main-d'œuvre.
— *union* : syndicat.
— *unrest* : agitation ouvrière.
unskilled — : main-d'œuvre non spécialisée.
to live by one's — : vivre de son travail.
to save — : économiser du travail.
— *saving device* : appareil ménager.
hard — : réclusion criminelle.
The — *Party* : le Parti travailliste.
to labour : peiner, travailler.
to labour under difficulties : avoir à surmonter des difficultés.
the **labouring** *class* : la classe ouvrière.
labourer : travailleur, manœuvre, journalier (m).
agricultural (farm) labourer : ouvrier agricole.
casual labourer : travailleur occasionnel, temporaire.
day-labourer : journalier.
skilled labourer : ouvrier qualifié, spécialisé.

laches : [J] négligence (f), délai immotivé à faire valoir un droit.

lack : manque (m) de, pénurie (f), rareté (f).
[J] — *of jurisdiction* : incompétence.
[F] — *of capital (finance)* : manque de capitaux.
— *of funds* : insuffisance de fonds, de provision.
— *of money* : rareté de l'argent, manque de fonds, d'argent.
to lack : manquer de, faire défaut.
to lack ability (for business) : manquer de capacité pour les affaires.
to lack money : manquer d'argent.
evidence is **lacking** : les preuves manquent.

lading : chargement d'un navire.
bill of — : connaissement.
— *port* : port d'embarquement ; de chargement.

Laffer curve : courbe de Laffer (économiste américain) dont l'interprétation permet de soutenir que l'abaissement du taux des impôts aboutit en fin de compte à des recettes fiscales plus élevées.

lag : retard (sur), décalage (par rapport à).
input — : retard dans l'adaptation des facteurs de production.

technical — : retard sur le plan technique (technologique).
time — : décalage dans le temps.
an old — : un repris de justice, un récidiviste.
to lag *(behind)* : être en retard, retarder, se laisser distancer (par un concurrent).
laggard : « à la traîne », délaissée (valeur).
lagging : a) en retard, retardateur ; b) ralentissement (m).
lagging factor : élément retardateur, frein (m).
« *our country is now lagging far behind other european countries as regards touristic equipment* » : « notre pays vient maintenant loin derrière d'autres pays européens pour ce qui est de l'équipement touristique ».

laid down (to lay down) : imposé.
[C] — *cost* : prix livré, à la livraison.
— *price* : prix imposé.

laissez-faire economy : économie libérale du « laisser-faire ».

lame : boiteux.
— *duck* : affaire non rentable, « canard boiteux ».
— *(duck) policy* : politique d'aide aux canards boiteux de l'économie.

land : terre (f), terrain (m), propriété foncière (f), fonds (m) de terre, bien-fonds (m), pays (m), patrie (f).
« — *is the factor of production which obviously embraces all natural resources, the original raw material for production* » : « la terre est le facteur de production qui, de toute évidence, embrasse toutes les ressources naturelles, la matière première originelle de la production ».
[J] — *act* : loi agraire.
— *agency (agent)* : agence (agent) immobilière.
arable — : terre arable.
— *in abeyance* : biens jacents.
— *bank* : banque hypothécaire.
building — : terrain à bâtir.
crown — *(estates)* : terres domaniales.
— *development* : mise en valeur du territoire, d'un terrain.
entailed — : bien grevé.
grass- — *(grassland)* : prairie, herbage.
— *legislation* : législation foncière.
— *office* : [U.S.] administration des domaines.
— *patent* : [U.S.] titre d'une concession de terrains.
— *question* : problème agraire, question agraire.
reclaimed — : terrain gagné (sur l'eau, sur des marais...).
— *register (registry)* : conservation des hypothèques, de la propriété foncière ; cadastre.
— *survey* : arpentage.

— *surveyor and valuer* : géomètre expert, arpenteur.
(system of) — *tenure* : régime foncier.
— *uses* : utilisation des sols.
waste — : terrain inculte.
— *-worker* : travailleur agricole.
— *and house property* : biens-fonds.
to own — : être propriétaire terrien.
[F] — *rent* : revenu foncier.
— *tax* : impôt foncier.
to land : atterrir, débarquer, mettre à terre.
landed : foncier, immobilier.
landed aristocracy (gentry) : aristocratie terrienne.
landed estate : propriété foncière, biens-fonds.
the landed interest : les propriétaires fonciers.
landed property : propriété foncière, biens-fonds, biens immobiliers.
assessment on landed property : cote (f) foncière.
landed proprietor : propriétaire foncier.
[C] *landed terms* : condition de livraison de marchandises à l'exportation « rendues quai de débarquement ».
landlady : propriétaire, logeuse (f).
landlord : propriétaire, hôtelier, aubergiste (m).
landlord and tenant law : législation (f) des fermages et loyers.
landmark : limite (f), borne (f), repère (m).
landowner : propriétaire foncier, terrien (m).

landslide vote : majorité (f) écrasante, raz de marée (résultats électoraux).

lapse : défaillance, erreur, méprise, caducité, déchéance (d'un droit), extinction (f), laps (m) de temps.
— *of a patent* : déchéance d'un brevet.
— *from one's duty* : manquement à son devoir.
to lapse : *(rights, patents)* périmer, se périmer, tomber en désuétude, *(credits)* tomber en annulation, *(estate)* devenir disponible, *(legacy, insurance policy)* devenir caduc, *(benefit)* tomber en dévolu, *(law)* s'abroger, cesser d'être en vigueur.
to allow a patent — : laisser périmer un brevet.
lapsed : déchu, périmé, caduc.
right which has — : droit qui est devenu périmé.
— *bill, order* : effet, mandat périmé.
— *legacy* : disposition testamentaire caduque.
— *insurance policy* : police d'assurance périmée (résiliée).
lapsing : déchéance, caducité.
— *of a committee* : dissolution d'une commission.

larceny: vol (m).
[J] *aggravated, compound, mixed* — : vol qualifié.
grand — : vol important (au-dessus d'une certaine valeur).
petty — : larcin.
simple — : vol simple (non accompagné de circonstances aggravantes), détournement de fonds.

large: grand, gros, important, nombreux (a).
at — : en général, en détail.
to set a prisoner at — : relâcher un prisonnier.
— *expenditure* : fortes dépenses.
— *estate* : grand domaine.
— *family* : famille nombreuse.
in a — *mesure* : en grande partie.
(the law of) — *numbers* : la loi des grands nombres.
— *powers* : pouvoirs étendus.
— *-scale* : à grande échelle, de grande envergure.
— *scale industry* : la grande industrie.
— *scale production* : production sur une grande échelle.
— *size* : grand modèle.

laspeyres index: indice Laspeyres.

lassalle's iron law of wages: la loi d'airain des salaires (de Lassalle).

last: dernier, final (a).
[J] — *buyer, bidder* : dernier acheteur, enchérisseur.
— *chance* : dernière chance.
— *clear chance* : ultime chance de salut (d'une personne en péril de mort).
— *heir* : dernier héritier appelé à succéder, en cas de déshérance, c'est-à-dire l'Etat.
— *in first out (L.I.F.O.)* : dernier entré, premier sorti (D.E.P.S.) (gestion des stocks).
— *resort* : dernier ressort.
— *will* : dernières volontés.

to last: durer.

late: a) récent, tardif ; b) « feu... ».
a — *-comer* : un nouveau venu.
— *delivery* : livraison tardive.
— *events* : la suite des événements.
— *filing (of a return)* : production tardive (d'une déclaration de revenus).
— *intelligence (news)* : dernières nouvelles, nouvelles de dernière heure.
at the **latest** : au plus tard.
latest date : délai de rigueur.
of — : récemment, ces derniers temps.
the — *Mr Jones* : feu Mr Jones.
Jones — *Smith* : Jones, successeur de Smith.
« *Mr Smith,* — *of Edinburgh* » : « M. Smith dernièrement établi à Edimbourg ».

latent: latent, caché (a).
[J] — *defect, fault* : vice caché.
— *defect clause* : clause de vice caché.

to launch: lancer.
— *a product* : lancer un produit.
— *(out, forth) on an enterprise* : se lancer dans une entreprise.

to launder money: blanchir de l'argent.

law: droit.
[J] Alors que le terme français « droit », a un sens à la fois objectif et subjectif, la langue anglaise dispose de deux expressions qui permettent d'éviter les circonlocutions. Ainsi, le droit de propriété est *the* — *of property*, mais un droit de propriété est *a right of property*. Les termes de tous les idiomes continentaux pouvant produire la même confusion que le français : jus, Recht, diritto, derecho, pravo, etc., les juristes anglo-saxons ne sont pas peu fiers de la clarté de leur langage en la matière.
1° — : droit (m), législation (f), science (f) juridique.
administrative — : droit administratif.
air — : droit aérien.
— *of business corporations* : [U.S.] droit des sociétés commerciales.
case — : droit jurisprudentiel, fondé sur des précédents, jurisprudence.
civil — : droit civil.
commercial — : droit commercial.
comparative — : droit comparatif.
compared — : droit comparé.
constitutional — : droit constitutionnel.
— *of contract* : droit des obligations.
corporation — : droit des sociétés.
criminal — : droit criminel, pénal.
crown — : droit pénal.
customary — : droit coutumier.
domestic — : législation interne, nationale.
election (electoral) — : droit électoral.
fiscal — : droit fiscal.
ground — : droit foncier.
— *(s) of inheritance* : lois successorales.
(private) international — *(law of conflicts)* : droit international privé.
(public) international — *(law of nations)* : droit international public.
international tax — : droit fiscal international.
issue of — : question de droit.
maritime — : droit maritime.
martial — : loi martiale, état de siège.
mercantile —, — *merchant* : droit commercial.
military — : droit militaire.
navigation — *(s)* : droit maritime.
the — *of Peace and Development* : le droit de la Paix et du Développement.
penal — : droit pénal.
private — : droit privé.

public — : droit public.
Roman — : droit romain.
rural — : droit rural.
skeleton — *(outline law)* : loi-cadre.
statutory — : droit écrit.
— *student* : étudiant en droit.
substantive — : droit positif.
unwritten — : droit non écrit.
yielding — : droit dispositif.
war — : droit de la guerre.
written — : droit écrit.
to study — : faire son droit.
2° — : la loi, la justice (f).
to abide by the — : respecter, observer la loi.
a — *-abiding citizen* : un citoyen respectueux de la loi.
to administer the — : dispenser la justice, appliquer la loi.
to break the — : enfreindre, transgresser la loi.
— *-breaker* : transgresseur de la loi.
to come under the — : tomber sous le coup de la loi.
to enforce the — : faire respecter la loi.
to get round the — : tourner la loi.
to have the — *on s.o.* : citer, poursuivre en justice.
to keep the — : observer la loi.
to keep within the — : rester dans les limites de la loi, s'en tenir à la loi.
to repeal a — : abroger une loi.
to be at — : être en procès.
to go to — : aller devant les tribunaux.
to practise — : exercer une profession juridique.
abuse of — : abus du droit.
action at — : action en justice.
adjective — : règles de procédure.
— *-adviser* : conseiller juridique.
— *-case* : cause civile, affaire contentieuse.
— *of the case* : autorité de la chose jugée.
— *costs* : frais de procédure.
— *court* : tribunal.
— *day* : date d'échéance d'une dette hypothécaire.
— *department (of a firm)* : service juridique (d'une entreprise).
dispute at — : litige.
heir-at- — : héritier légitime.
judgment at — : jugement exécutoire.
labour — (s) : législation du travail.
— *-lord* : membre juriste de la Chambre des Lords.
— *-maker* : législateur.
— *-officer* : conseiller juridique (de la couronne).
motion denied on the — : requête mal fondée et rejetée comme telle.
officer of the — *([U.S.] law official)* : fonctionnaire de l'ordre judiciaire.
promise in — : promesse en bonne et due forme.

— *Society (England and Wales)* : Conseil de l'ordre des Juristes (habilite les « solicitors » en Angleterre et Pays de Galles).
— *-term* : a) terme de droit ; b) session des tribunaux.
— *and order* : ordre public.
3° — : formule générale (énonçant un rapport entre des phénomènes).
economic — : loi économique.
— *of consumers' demand* : loi de la demande des consommateurs.
— *of diminishing returns* : loi des rendements décroissants.
Say's — : loi de Say.

lawful : légal, permis, licite, légitime (a).
— *age* : majorité.
— *contract* : contrat valide.
— *currency* : [F] monnaie ayant cours légal.
— *interest* : intérêt légitime.
— *money* : monnaie légale.
— *representative* : [J] représentant légal.
— *share* : part virile d'un héritage.
— *trade* : commerce licite.
lawfully : légalement, légitimement.
lawfulness : légalité, légitimité.

lawgiver : législateur (m).

lawless : sans loi, sans frein, désordonné (a).
lawlessness : dérèglement, désordre.

lawsuit : procès (m).
[J] *to bring a* — *(against s.o.)* : intenter un procès (à qn).

lawyer : homme de loi, juriste, [U.S.] avocat (m).

lax : relâché, inexact, négligent (a).
— *attendance (of the meetings...)* : présence irrégulière (aux réunions...).
laxity : négligence, absence de précision.

lay : a) laïque, profane, non initié (a) ; b) pose (f), disposition (f).
— *day* : jour d'estarie (de starie), de planche.
extra — *days* : jours de surestarie.
— *lord* : membre non juriste de la Chambre des Lords.
layman : (un) profane, (un) non-initié.
— *people* : membres du jury.
— *-out* : [U.S.] bande de malfaiteurs.
— *of the land* : configuration du terrain.
— *-by* : économies, épargne.
— *-off* : [U.S.] chômage temporaire.
to lay : poser, placer, étendre, parier, imposer, soumettre (un cas...).
— *a complaint* : déposer une plainte.
— *an embargo (on...)* : mettre l'embargo (sur...).
— *the facts* : exposer les faits.

— *a matter before a court* : saisir un tribunal d'une affaire.
— *so much on (a horse...)* : parier tant sur (un cheval...).
— *a tax (on)* : frapper d'un impôt.
— *aside, to lay by* : mettre de côté, mettre en réserve.
— *down* : poser, imposer, fixer, stipuler.
— *down that* : stipuler que.
— *down conditions, prices...* : imposer des conditions, des prix...
— *off (workers)* : licencier (des ouvriers).
— *(sthg) on the line* : donner des instructions précises et strictes.
— *out* : étaler (des marchandises), arranger, disposer, dépenser.
— *out money* : débourser de l'argent.
layout : disposition (d'un chantier...), agencement, mise en page.
— *sheet-operation* : gammes d'opérations.
laying-off *(of workers)* : licenciement (d'ouvriers).
laying up : chômage, accumulation.

lead : plomb (m).
[D] *customs* — : plomb de la douane.

lead : conduite, avance, préséance (f).
to give the — : monter la voie.
— *(s) and lags* : avances et retards, (B) termaillage, mouvements d'accélération et de retardement sur le marché des changes quand une dévaluation est pressentie.
— *time* : délai de livraison.
— *story* : (journ.) gros titre, affaire à la une.

leader : dirigeant (m), chef (m), chef de file, [J] avocat principal (lorsqu'ils sont plusieurs à plaider une cause).
— *of the House of Commons* : chef de la majorité gouvernementale (à la Chambre des Communes).
the — *(s) of the market* : les chefs de file du marché.
party — : chef de parti.
strike — : meneur de grève.
[F] —, *equity* — : valeur vedette.
leadership : conduite, domination, fonctions de chef, direction.
under the leadership of : sous la direction de.
leading : a) conduite, direction (f) ; b) dominant, marquant, principal (a).
leading article (leader) : article de fond.
leading case : cas d'espèce faisant autorité.
leading growth sectors : secteurs de croissance dominants.
leading industry : industrie principale.
a leading man : un homme important, un notable.
leading partner : associé principal.
leading question : question tendancieuse, insidieuse suggérant une réponse.
leading share : valeur vedette.
leading shareholder : gros actionnaire.

league : ligue, société (f) (hist. *of Nations* : des nations), alliance.

leak : fuite, perte (f).
[F] — *in the tax system* : lacune dans le système fiscal.
to leak : couler, fuir, s'ébruiter.
— *out* : « transpirer » (information).
leakage : fuite, coulage, pertes.
— *of official secrets* : fuite de secrets officiels.

lean : maigre (a).
— *years* : années de vaches maigres, de disette.

leap : bond.
— *-frogging* : jouer à « saute-mouton », mais aussi : action entreprise par un groupe d'employés d'un secteur économique pour obtenir des salaires égaux à ceux d'un autre groupe.
— *-year* : année bissextile.
to rise by — *(s) and bounds (prices)* : monter (les prix) d'une manière vertigineuse.
to leap *at an offer* : sauter sur une offre.

to learn : apprendre.
learning *by doing* : perfectionnement par la pratique.

lease : bail (m) (baux), concession (f), contrat de bail.
[J] — *agreement* : contrat de bail.
— *-back* : cession-bail (crédit-bail réversible), contrat par lequel une entreprise vend un immeuble industriel à un établissement de crédit-bail, lequel lui concède immédiatement un contrat de crédit-bail sur ledit immeuble.
building — : bail emphytéotique (99 ans).
cancellation of a — : résiliation d'un bail.
dwelling — : bail à loyer.
farming — : bail à ferme.
— *of land* : bail à ferme.
— *-lend* : prêt-bail.
long — : bail à long terme.
perpetual — : bail à vie.
— *of power* : [U.S.] pleins pouvoirs.
— *premium* : droit d'entrée, « pas-de-porte ».
repairing — : bail qui engage le locataire à maintenir les locaux dans l'état où il les a reçus.
sub- — : sous-location.
term of a — : durée d'un bail.
to lease : affermer, donner à bail.
to let on lease, to lease out : louer à bail.
to sign a lease : passer un bail.
to take on lease : prendre à bail.
to transfer a lease : céder un bail.
leasehold : tenure à bail, bien-fonds loué à

bail.
leaseholder: locataire à bail.
leasing: affermage, location à bail, crédit-bail, location avec option d'achat (LOA).
leasing company: société fermière.
leasing package: location de longue durée.

least squares: moindres carrés (statistique).

to leave: laisser, quitter, disposer (par testament).
— *off (work)*: cesser le travail.
— *over*: remettre.
[C] **left over** *stock, left overs*: surplus (américains).
leave: congé (m), permission (f).
full-pay leave: congé à plein traitement.
sick-leave: congé de maladie.
leave without pay: congé sans traitement, pour convenances personnelles.
special leave, leave of court: autorisation du tribunal (par ex. pour entamer une action en vue de modifier un état de procédure).

ledger: grand livre (m).
[C] — *account*: compte de grand livre.
general — : grand livre des comptes généraux.
pay-roll — : grand livre de paie.
[F] *share* — : registre des actionnaires.

legacy: legs.
[J] a) legs d'un bien mobilier (opp. *devise*);
b) legs à titre universel.
specific — : legs d'une partie déterminée des biens mobiliers du testateur.
demonstrative — : legs d'une somme d'argent prélevée sur un fonds déterminé.
general — (Engl. *residuary* — *and devise*, [U.S.] *universal* —): legs à titre universel.
— *duties*: droits de mutation par décès.
specific — : legs à titre particulier.
to come into a — : recevoir un legs, faire un héritage.
to leave a — *to*: faire un legs à.

legal: légal, judiciaire, juridique, licite (a).
[J] — *aid (assistance)*: assistance judiciaire.
— *adviser*: conseil juridique.
— *charges*: frais de contentieux.
— *claim*: créance fondée en droit, titre juridique.
— *costs, expenses*: dépens, frais de justice.
— *crime*: assassinat légal.
— *department*: service juridique, contentieux.
— *document*: acte authentique.
— *estate*: bien légal, patrimoine existant ou pouvant être créé et transmis.
— *expert*: avocat conseil.
— *fare*: tarif autorisé.
— *fiction*: fiction légale.
— *fineness*: titre légal des monnaies.
— *holiday*: fête légale, chômée.
— *interests*: intérêts légaux.
— *investment*: placement pupillaire.
— *liability*: responsabilité légale.
— *matters*: questions de droit.
— *practitioner*: homme de loi.
— *proceedings*: poursuites judiciaires.
— *process*: voies légales, voies de droit.
— *redress, remedy*: recours à la justice.
— *representative*: représentant légal.
— *reserve*: réserve légale (banque).
— *science*: science du droit.
— *security*: caution judiciaire.
— *settlement*: concordat.
— *standard*: étalon légal.
— *status*: statut légal.
— *term*: terme de pratique.
— *tender*: (monnaie) ayant cours légal, pouvoir libératoire.
— *ties*: liens juridiques.
— *year*: année civile.
to go into the — *profession*: embrasser une (la) carrière juridique.
to take — *advice*: consulter un homme de loi.

to legalize: authentiquer, légaliser.
legalization: authentification, légalisation.

legally: légalement, juridiquement.
[J] — *binding*: tenu de par la loi.
— *responsible*: responsable en droit.

to legate: léguer.
[J] **legatee**: légataire (m).
general, residuary legatee: légataire universel.
sole legatee: légataire unique.
legator: testateur (m).

to legislate: légiférer.
legislation: législation (f).
delegated, secondary, subordinate — : dispositions réglementaires prises en application d'une loi.
legislative: législatif (a).
legislative assembly, body: assemblée législative, corps législatif.
legislative courts: [U.S.] tribunaux créés par le congrès (et non par la constitution).
legislative intent: les intentions du législateur.
legislative power: pouvoir législatif.
legislator: législateur.
Legislature: (pol.) Corps Législatif.

legitimacy: légitimité (f).
[J] **legitimate** *(child, heir, authority)*: légitime (enfant, héritier, autorité).
legitimate claim: prétention légitime, réclamation justifiée.
legitimate doubt: doute justifié.

leisure: loisirs (m pl).
a policy of – : une politique des loisirs.
the **leisured** *classes*: les classes oisives.

to lend: prêter.
[F] – *against security, on stock*: prêter sur titres.
– *at interest*: prêter à l'intérêt.
lender: prêteur (m).
lender of last resort (in Britain the Bank of England acts as a lender of last resort only to discount houses): prêteur en dernier ressort (en Grande-Bretagne la Banque d'Angleterre ne fait office de prêteur en dernier ressort qu'à l'égard des banques d'escompte).

lending: a) prêteur (a), de prêts ; b) prêt (m), placement (m), location (f).
[F] *a* – *bank, company*: une banque, une société de prêts.
borrowing and – : les emprunts et les prêts.
– *capital*: prestation de capitaux.
– *rate*: taux prêteur.
lend-lease *(agreements)*: (accords) prêt-bail.

length: longueur, distance (f).
to go to the – *of...*: aller jusqu'à...

to lengthen: allonger, se gonfler (les carnets de commandes).

less: moindre, moins.
[C] *purchase price* – *5 % discount*: prix d'achat sous déduction d'un escompte de 5 %.
[F] – *tax*: hors taxe, impôt déduit.
– *developed countries (L.D.Cs.)*: pays en voie de développement (P.V.D.).
the **lesser** *of the two amounts*: la moins élevée des deux sommes.

lessee: locataire, tenancier, concessionnaire (m).

to lessen: (s')amoindrir, diminuer, abaisser (tarifs).
[F] *the inflationary pressure appears to have* **lessened**: les pressions inflationnistes semblent s'être affaiblies, avoir diminué.

lessor: bailleur (m).

to let: laisser.
– *the cat out of the bag*: vendre la mèche (et faire échouer la transaction).
[J] [C] louer.
[A] adjuger un contrat de travaux publics.

letter: lettre (f).
– *of acceptance*: lettre d'adhésion.
– *of acknowledgment*: accusé de réception.
– *of advice*: lettre d'avis.

(J) – *of Administration*: décision d'un tribunal nommant un administrateur judiciaire.
– *of allotment (allotment letter)*: avis de répartition, d'attribution (d'actions).
– *of application*: bulletin de souscription.
– *of attorney*: procuration.
commendatory – : lettre de recommandation.
– *of confirmation*: lettre de confimation.
covering – : lettre d'envoi, annexe.
– *of credit*: lettre de crédit.
documentary – *of credit*: lettre de crédit accréditive.
– *of exchange*: traite, lettre de change.
– *of hypothecation*: lettre de nantissement.
– *of indemnity*: lettre de garantie.
irrevocable – *of credit*: lettre de crédit irrévocable (ne peut être modifiée sans l'accord du vendeur).
– *of licence*: accord entre un débiteur défaillant et ses créanciers lui permettant de continuer son commerce pendant un certain temps.
– *patent*: document homologuant un brevet.
registered – : lettre recommandée.
– *of regret*: avis de retour de souscription.
– *of request*: commission rogatoire adressée à l'étranger par voie diplomatique.
– *rogatory*: commission rogatoire.
sea- – : congé maritime.
– *testamentary*: nomination d'un exécuteur testamentaire.
[B] – *of intent*: lettre de souscription.

letting: location (f), louage (m).
– *value*: valeur locative.

level: a) niveau (m) ; b) de niveau, égal (a).
– *of employment, of prices*: niveau de l'emploi, des prix.
– *of living*: [U.S.] niveau de vie.
at ministerial – : à l'échelon ministériel.
on a national – : au plan (sur le plan) national.
on – *terms*: sur un pied d'égalité.
to level: aplanir, égaliser, niveler.
the market has **levelled** *off*: le marché s'est stabilisé.
levelling off *(in investment)*: tassement, ralentissement (des investissements).

leverage (gearing) effect: [F] effet de levier (analyse du comportement d'endettement des entreprises).

leverage management buy out (L.M.B.O.): rachat (m), reprise (f) d'une entreprise par un mécanisme financier avec effet de levier, # rachat d'une entreprise par ses salariés (R.E.S.).

levy: impôt, levée d'un impôt.
[F] *betterment* – : impôt sur les plus-values,

contribution, prélèvement.
local garbage **levies** : taxe locale d'enlèvement des ordures ménagères.
tax levies : rentrées fiscales.
to levy : prélever, imposer, frapper de, saisir.
to levy a duty, a tax (on) : lever, percevoir une taxe, un impôt sur.
to levy a distress, execution on : faire une saisie-exécution (sur).
to levy a fine : imposer une amende, frapper d'une amende.
to levy a fine by warrant of distress : prélever une amende par mandat de saisie-exécution.

lex loci solutionis : la loi du pays où un contrat doit être exécuté.

lex non scripta : la loi non écrite, le droit coutumier.

liability : a) obligation (f), engagement (m), responsabilité (f) ; b) passif (m) (au pluriel, **liabilities** : s'oppose à *assets* : actif, ensemble de dettes) ; c) assujettissement (m) (à l'impôt).
[J] [ASS] *absolute* ([U.S.] *strict*) – : responsabilité, obligation inconditionnelle.
contingent – : obligation future, éventuelle, dépenses (obligations) imprévues.
employer's – : responsabilité des employeurs.
employer's – insurance : assurance-responsabilité des employeurs (contre les accidents du travail).
joint – : obligation conjointe.
joint and several – : obligation conjointe et solidaire.
– *to a fine* : risque d'encourir une amende.
limited – : responsabilité limitée (d'une société).
public – insurance : assurance au tiers.
several – : obligation séparée, responsabilité séparée, responsabilité par faute d'autrui.
– *(passenger* –*) to third person* : responsabilité au tiers (aux personnes transportées).
vicarious – *(over)* : responsabilité civile.
to meet one's liabilities : faire face à ses engagements.
[C] *current liabilities* : exigibilités.
fixed liabilities : passif exigible à terme.
long-term liabilities : passif à long terme.
– *reserve* : provision pour dettes.
statement of assets and liabilities : relevé de l'actif et du passif.
total liabilities : total du passif.
[F] – *to tax* : assujettissement à l'impôt.

liable (to, for) : a) susceptible de, sujet à, passible de ; b) tenu (de faire), assujetti à, astreint à, redevable de ; c) responsable (de).
a plan which is – *to modifications* : un plan qui est susceptible de modifications.
[D] *(goods)* – *customs duties, to customs inspection* : (marchandises) soumises à des droits de douane, à la visite douanière.
– *to prosecution* : passible de poursuites.
[F] *(income)* – *to tax* : (revenu) soumis à l'impôt.
– *for damage* : responsable des avaries.
– *for damages* : passible de dommages-intérêts.
jointly – : solidairement responsable.
severally – : individuellement responsable.

to liaise : coordonner, assurer la liaison.

libel : libellé (m), écrit (m) diffamatoire.
[J] *public* – : écrits diffamatoires, obscènes ou séditieux.
– *in rem, action for* – : demande d'indemnité.

liberal : libéral, généreux (a).
liberalism : libéralisme.
liberation : libération.
[F] *liberation of capital* : mobilisation de capitaux.
to liberate : libérer, mettre en liberté.
to liberate capital : mobiliser des capitaux.

liberty : liberté (f), faculté (f) (de faire).
[J] *civil* **liberties** : libertés civiles.
– *of contract* : faculté de contracter librement.

libor *(London Interbank Offered Rate)* : taux interbancaire des devises européennes (taux de référence largement utilisé dans les emprunts internationaux).

licence, [U.S.] **license** : autorisation (f), licence (f), permis (m), concession (f), brevet (m).
[A] *automobile* –, *chauffeur's, driving* – : permis de conduire.
car – : carte grise.
– *to carry fire-arms* : permis de port d'arme.
liquor – : 1° *off* – ; 2° *on* – : licence d'exploitation d'un débit de boissons ; a) pour la vente exclusive de boissons alcooliques à emporter ; b) pour la consommation sur place.
marriage – : dispense de bans.
mining – : concession minière (permis d'exploiter).
– *number* : numéro matricule.
occupational number : permis de travail.
– *plate* : plaque d'immatriculation.
– *to practise (medicine etc.)* : autorisation d'exercer (la médecine etc.).
shooting – *(game* –*)* : permis de chasse.
tobacco – : autorisation d'exploiter un débit de tabac.
a trade which requires a – : métier dont l'exercice est soumis à autorisation préalable.
– *to use a patent* : licence d'exploitation d'un

brevet.
[F] *dog* — : taxe sur les chiens.
— *duty, fee* : taxe sur activité, patente.
[E] *export, import* — : licence (permis) d'exportation, d'importation.
to license : autoriser, accorder une licence, un permis, une autorisation.
licensed : autorisé, breveté, patenté.
licensed broker, dealer : courtier, commerçant patenté.
« *fully licensed* » *(house)* : (établissement) autorisé à servir toutes boissons alcooliques.
licensed trade : commerce des vins et spiritueux.
licensee : concessionnaire (d'une licence).
licensor : concédant (d'une licence).
licensing : autorisation, octroi (d'une licence).

licit : licite (a).
licitation *(forced, voluntary)* : licitation (forcée, volontaire).

lie : mensonge (m).
— *detector* : détecteur de mensonge.

to lie : être placé, se trouver dans une situation déterminée, résider, séjourner.
[F] — *at the bank* : être déposé en banque.
[J] — *under a charge* : être sous le coup d'une accusation.
— *idle* : être inactif.
— *in prison* : être en prison.
obstacles lie *in (our) way* : des obstacles se dressent sur (notre) chemin.
the fault lies *with (him)* : la faute en est à (lui).
the onus, burden of the proof lies with (him) : c'est à lui de faire la preuve.
the action lies : l'action est recevable.
no appeal lies against the action : l'action ne souffre pas d'appel.
— *under suspicion* : être soupçonné.

lien : privilège (m), droit (m) de rétention, nantissement (m), droit de suite, droit de gage.
[J] *(to have) a* — *on the property of a debtor* : avoir un privilège sur les meubles d'un débiteur.
first and paramount — : privilège et préférence.
general — : privilège général (qui protège toutes les créances du détenteur et non seulement celle qui porte sur l'objet en sa possession).
statutory — : hypothèque légale du trésor.
vendor's — : privilège du vendeur.

lienee, lienor : gageur (m), (créancier) gagiste (m).

(in) lieu of : au lieu et place de, à titre de.

life : vie (f), existence (f), manière (f) de vivre, terme (m), durée (f).
[ASS] — *assurance (insurance)* : assurance sur la vie.
— *expectancy* : espérance de vie.
expectation of — : probabilités de vie.
— *expectancy tables, expectation of* — *tables* : tables de mortalité, de survie.
[J] — *annuitant* : rentier viager.
— *annuity (pension)* : rente viagère.
— *estate* : biens en viager.
— *income* : revenu viager.
— *interest* : usufruit.
— *lease* : bail emphytéotique, à vie.
— *tenancy* : location à vie, usufruit.
— *tenant* : usufruitier.
— *use* : usufruit.
working — : période d'activité.
for — : à vie, viager.
imprisonment for — : emprisonnement à vie.
pension for — *(— pension)* : pension à vie, viagère.
product — *cycle* : cycle de vie d'un produit (de la conception à la finition).
station in — : position sociale.
on the — *of...* : sur la tête de...
[Pol.] — *of a Parliament* : législature (f).
— *Peer, Peeress* : pair (m), pairesse (f) à vie.

to lift : (re) lever, abolir, accroître.
[C] — *a discount bill* : honorer un effet escompté.
— *documents* : lever des documents.
— *productivity* : accroître la productivité.
— *restrictions* : abolir des restrictions.

L.I.F.O. (last in, first out) : [C] « dernier entré, premier sorti » méthode d'évaluation des stocks (D.E.P.S.).

light : a) léger, faible (a) ; b) lumière (f), jour donné par une ouverture, fenêtre (f).
[B] valeur en baisse.
[F] — *money* : monnaie faible, légère.
— *taxation* : faible imposition.
[J] *right of* — : droit de vue.
ancient — : ouvertures existant depuis plus de 20 ans couvertes par la prescription.

to lighten : alléger, réduire, mitiger.
[F] — *the burden of taxation* : alléger la charge fiscale, réduire la fiscalité.
lightening *(of taxation)* : allègement (de la fiscalité).

lighter : allège (f), péniche (f).

lighterage : frais (m) de débarquement (par péniche).

lightning : foudre (f), éclair (m).
— *strike* : grève surprise, sans préavis.

— 489 —

likelihood : vraisemblance.
criterion of maximum — : critère du maximum de vraisemblance (statistique).
likely : probable, vraisemblable.

(differencial) limen : seuil (différentiel) (statistique).

limit : limite (f), borne (f), délai (m), seuil (m), plafond (m).
age — : limite d'âge.
— (s) of accuracy, of error : limite de précision, d'erreur.
price — (s) : limites de prix.
time — : durée, limite de temps, délai de paiement.
to exceed the speed — : commettre un excès de vitesse.
[B] *— down* : limite de la baisse, baisse maximum.
— up : hausse maximum.
to limit *(one's activities etc.)* : limiter (ses activités etc.).
limitation : limitation, restriction, prescription.
[J] *limitation of actions* : prescription d'action.
constitutional limitations : [U.S.] cadre constitutionnel du pouvoir législatif.
limitation of liability (limitative clause) : clause restrictive.
limitation of a lesser estate : bien-fonds grevé d'un usufruit.
limitation of a right : droit assujetti à une condition ou à un délai ou aux deux.
statutes of limitation : loi fixant les délais de prescription.
subject to limitations : soumis à des restrictions.
term of limitation : délai de prescription.
time of limitation : péremption (d'instance).
limited : limité, borné, étroit, restreint.
limited company, limited liability company, company limited by shares, public company, limited partnership, partnership limited by shares : société anonyme, société en commandite, société à responsabilité limitée, société par actions (toutes expressions qui ne correspondent que d'une manière générale aux expressions anglaises).
limited divorce : séparation de corps.
limited estate : bien-fonds grevé d'un usufruit.
limited liability : responsabilité limitée.
limited owner : usufruitier.
limited partner : commanditaire.
limited price : cours limité, marché étroit.
limitedness *of a market* : étroitesse d'un marché.
limiting *clause* : clause limitative (restrictive).

limping standard : étalon boiteux.

line : ligne (f), trait (m), branche (f) (d'affaires), sphère (f) (d'activité), profession (f), ligne (f) (de chemins de fer).
[F] *« above the — »* : « au-dessus de la ligne » :
a) expression employée pour indiquer les recettes et les dépenses budgétaires définitives autorisées par le parlement ;
b) dépenses de publicité « directe » à la télévision, dans les journaux, par voie d'affiches illustrées, etc. ;
c) balance commerciale et compte capital.
« below the — » : « au-dessous de la ligne » :
a) opérations budgétaires temporaires telles que les prêts accordés par l'Etat, les avances aux entreprises nationalisées ;
b) dépenses de publicité « indirecte », sous forme de cadeaux aux acheteurs, timbres à prime, offres spéciales, etc. ;
c) les postes de la balance des paiements autres que la balance commerciale et le compte capital.
— budgeting : budget de moyens.
— of credit : limite du crédit (accordé par une banque).
[C] *— of business* : branche (de commerce), spécialité.
— of goods : série d'articles.
leading — : article réclame.
— organisation : structure linéaire de l'entreprise (chaque chef de service ou d'atelier rend compte directement à son supérieur hiérarchique).
— production : production à la chaîne.
— of samples : assortiment d'échantillons.
straight- — depreciation method : méthode d'amortissement linéaire, système linéaire.
[J] *collateral —* : ligne collatérale, les collatéraux.
direct — : ligne directe.
marriage — (s) (fam.) : acte de mariage.
an unbroken line of authorities : une jurisprudence constante.
(gen) *— of argument* : raisonnement.
— of thought : suite d'idées.
to draw a — (between) : délimiter (des pouvoirs).
to keep in — with the targets : respecter les objectifs.
to take a — : adopter une ligne de conduite.
air, railway — : ligne aérienne, de chemins de fer.
lineal : linéal.
lineal descent, relatives, succession : descendants, succession en ligne directe.

linear : linéaire (a).
[F] *— increase of taxes* : augmentation linéaire des impôts.
— programming : programmation linéaire.

liner : paquebot, navire de ligne (régulière).

link: lien, maillon (m).
  to link: lier, relier.
linkage: liaison (f), lien (m), polarisation (f) (investissements).
  backward linkage: polarisation amont.
  forward linkage: polarisation aval.

liquid: disponible, liquide (a).
  [C] [F] — *assets*: actif disponible (liquide), disponibilités.
  — *capital, debt*: capital, dette liquide.
  to liquidate *(a company, debts etc.)*: liquider (une société, des dettes etc.).
  liquidated *debt*: dette certaine.
  liquidation *(of a debt, a society...)*: liquidation (d'une dette, d'une société), amortissement (de capital).
  compulsory, forced liquidation: liquidation forcée.
  liquidation decision: see « abandonment decision ».
  judicial, voluntary liquidation: liquidation judiciaire, volontaire.
  to go into liquidation: se mettre en liquidation.
  putting into liquidation: mise en liquidation.
  liquidation value: see « break-up value ».
  liquidating dividends: boni de liquidation.
  liquidator *(liquidating partner)*: liquidateur (d'une société).
  liquidity *(liquidness)*: disponibilité, liquidité.
  cash liquidities: liquidités.
  liquidity of assets: disponibilité de capitaux.
  liquidity preference: préférence pour les liquidités.
  liquidity ratio: taux de liquidité.
  liquidity strain: insuffisance de liquidité.
  liquidity trap: « trappe à monnaie » (mécanisme de la théorie keynésienne).

lis pendens: [J] affaire en instance.
  — *alibi* —: litispendance.

list: liste (f), état (m), nomenclature (f), catalogue (m), inventaire (m), rôle (m) d'un tribunal, cote (f) de la bourse.
  assessment —: rôle (des impôts).
  black —: liste noire.
  — *of bills for collection*: bordereau d'effets à l'encaissement.
  case —: rôle.
  civil —: liste civile.
  exchange —: bulletin des changes.
  free —: liste des marchandises admises en franchise (douanière).
  — *of honours*: liste des distinctions honorifiques décernées.
  — *of investments*: inventaire du portefeuille.
  — *of names*: liste nominative.
  official —: cote officielle.
  — *of prices*: prix courants.
  price- —: prix courant.
  quoted —: cote officielle.
  — *of salaries*: rôle d'appointements.
  share- —: cours de la Bourse.
  sick —: liste des malades.
  stock —: bulletin des cours de la Bourse.
  subscribers' —: liste des abonnés.
  subscription —: liste de souscription.
  waiting —: liste d'attente.
  to list: cataloguer, enregistrer, énumérer, désigner, coter en Bourse.
  the items **listed** *in §*: les articles énumérés au §.
  listed company: société dont les actions sont cotées en Bourse.
  listed securities, stock: valeurs cotées, inscrites à la cote officielle.
  listed personal property: biens personnels désignés.

listing: cotation (f).

lite pendente: l'affaire étant en instance.

literary copyright: droit d'auteur.
  — *property*: propriété littéraire.

litigant: plaideur (m).
  [J] *the litigant party*: parties en litige.
  to litigate: mettre en litige, contester.
  litigation: litige, procès.
  litigious: litigieux.
  litigious claim: créance litigieuse.
  litigious matter: objet de litige.

little business: [C] peu d'affaires.

live: vif, animé (a).
  [C] — *account*: acheteur, client régulier.
  — *animal*: animal sur pied.
  — *claims*: créances valables.
  — *stock*: cheptel.
  — *weight*: charge utile.
  liveliness *(of the stock market...)*: animation du marché.

lively (market): [B] (marché) animé.

livery: délivrance, investiture (f).

living: existence, vie, subsistance (f).
  cost of —: coût de la vie.
  cost of — *bonus*: indemnité de cherté de vie.
  — *conditions*: conditions de vie.
  — *expenses*: indemnité de subsistance.
  standard of — *(living standard)*: niveau de vie.
  — *wage*: minimum vital.
  to earn one's —, *to make a* —: gagner sa vie.

Lloyd's Register: Registre de la Lloyd (donne des renseignements détaillés sur tous les navires).

load, loading: chargement (m).
  to load: charger.
  to off-load stocks: liquider des stocks.

loan: prêt, emprunt (m).
  [F] – *account*: crédit, compte de prêt.
  active – : prêt productif.
  – *agreement*: accord de prêt, d'emprunt.
  – *bank (loan office, loan society)*: caisse de prêts, établissement de crédit.
  – *bond (certificate)*: titre d'un emprunt.
  bottomry – : prêt à la grosse aventure.
  – *at call*: prêt remboursable sur demande.
  – *capital*: capital d'emprunt.
  club – : prêt que seul un groupe restreint de banques consent à accorder.
  – *on collateral*: prêt sur nantissement.
  consumption – : prêt à la consommation.
  current – : prêt non remboursé, consenti, en cours.
  day to day – : prêt au jour le jour.
  – *department*: service du crédit.
  foreign – : emprunt extérieur.
  funded – : emprunt consolidé.
  funding – : emprunt de consolidation.
  government – : emprunt d'Etat.
  gratuitous – : commodat.
  – *-holder*: créancier hypothécaire.
  inland – : emprunt intérieur.
  – *at interest*: prêt à intérêt.
  irredeemable – : rente perpétuelle.
  – *(s) make deposits*: les prêts engendrent de nouveaux dépôts.
  marriage – : prêt au mariage.
  mortgaged – : emprunt hypothécaire.
  – *at notice*: prêt à terme.
  – *on collaterals*: avances sur garanties.
  – *on overdraft*: prêt à découvert.
  pledged – : prêt (ou emprunt) sur gage, sur titres.
  preferential – : emprunt de priorité.
  – *receipt*: reconnaissance de dette.
  – *repayable on demand*: prêt remboursable sur demande.
  secured – : prêt garanti.
  – *shark*: requin, usurier.
  short (long) terme – : emprunt à court (long) terme.
  – *stock*: obligation.
  tied – : emprunt à emploi spécifié.
  usurious – : prêt usuraire.
  – *by the week*: prêt à la petite semaine.
  weekly – : prêt à sept jours.
  – *without security*: prêt à fonds perdus.
  to issue, to float, to raise a – : émettre, lancer, contracter un emprunt.
  to make a – : faire un emprunt, un prêt.
  to sink a – : amortir un emprunt.
  to return a – : rembourser un emprunt.
  loanable *(funds)*: fonds disponibles (à prêter).
  loanable assets demand: demande de fonds prêtables.
  loanee, loaner: emprunteur, prêteur.
  loaning: prestation, prêt.

lobby: couloir (m), antichambre (f), groupe (m) de pression, salle (f) des pas perdus.
  division **lobbies**: [U.K.] les vestibules où pénètrent les députés en votant par « division » lorsqu'ils sont comptés au passage.
  to lobby: faire les couloirs (du Parlement), essayer d'influencer les députés par des conversations de couloir.
  to lobby a bill through: faire passer une loi grâce à des manœuvres de couloir.
  lobbying: manœuvres, intrigues, propagande en faveur de groupes d'intérêts particuliers (exercée auprès des membres du Congrès des Etats-Unis).
  lobbying expenses: dépenses de propagande.

local: local, régional, décentralisé (a).
  [J] – *action*: procès en matière immobilière qui ne peut être intenté que devant le tribunal du lieu.
  – *allegiance*: [U.K.] obligation pour un étranger d'observer les lois du royaume tant qu'il y demeure en échange de la protection accordée par la Couronne.
  – *authorities*: collectivités locales.
  – *bank*: banque régionale.
  – *bill*: effet sur place.
  – *conditions*: conditions sur place.
  – *equipment tax*: taxe locale d'équipement.
  – *government*: administration régionale, décentralisée.
  – *habitation*: lieu de résidence.
  – *information*: renseignements recueillis sur place.
  – *law* ([U.S.] *municipal ordinance*): règlements municipaux.
  – *rates, local taxes*: impôts locaux.
  – *road*: chemin vicinal.
  – *trade*: commerce local.
  – *train, railway*: train, voie ferrée d'intérêt local.

locale: [U.S.] théâtre des événements.

locality: localité (f).
  choice of – : [U.S.] élection de domicile.

to locate: localiser, déterminer.
  to be **located**: être situé.
  property located abroad: biens situés à l'étranger.
  location (locating): situation (f), emplacement (m), établissement (m), implantation (f) (d'industries), [U.S.] bornage (m).

locating, location of industry: implantation d'une industrie.
location theory: théorie de l'implantation (qui tente d'expliquer et de prévoir les décisions d'implantation des entreprises).

location: location.

to lock: enfermer, bloquer, engager, immobiliser (des capitaux).
— *out*: interdire l'accès (d'une usine en fermant la porte), lock-outer (des ouvriers).
lock-out: grève patronale, fermeture d'usine.
lock, stock and barrel: (fam.) tout, sans exception.
[F] *lock-up (of capital), locking-up*: immobilisation (de capitaux).

loco-price: prix sur place.

locum tenens: substitut (m), remplaçant (m).

locus sigilli (L.S.): la place du sceau.

to lodge: déposer, placer, remettre, confier (des valeurs).
[J] — *an appeal*: interjeter appel.
— *a complaint (against)*: déposer une plainte (contre).
— *money (with a bank)*: déposer de l'argent (dans une banque).
lodged: déposé, consigné.
stock lodged with (a solicitor) as a cover: titres déposés chez un notaire à titre de nantissement.

lodger: locataire (m et f) (en garni).
lodging: logement, hébergement, dépôt (m).
board and lodging: pension complète.
furnished lodgings: appartements meublés.
to let lodgings: louer des chambres.
lodging allowance: indemnité de logement.

log: loch (m).
— *book*: livre (journal) de bord, livre de loch.

Lombard street: [F] expression souvent employée pour désigner le marché monétaire (beaucoup d'institutions concernant ce marché sont situées dans cette rue de Londres ou à proximité).

London interbank offered rates: [F] taux interbancaires des eurobanques de Londres (taux LIBOR).

London Metal Exchange: Bourse des Métaux non-ferreux à Londres.

London stock exchange: la Bourse de Londres.

long: a) long, étendu, prolongé (a), à terme, à longue échéance ; b) longtemps (adv), à long terme.
[F] — *bill,* — *-dated bill*: effet à long terme.
— *credit*: crédit à long terme, long crédit.
— *exchange*: papier long.
— *lease*: bail à longue échéance.
— *period loan*: prêt à long terme.
[B] — *position*: position longue.
— *price*: prix élevé.
— *range*: (de, à) longue portée.
— *range plans, programme*: projets, programme à long terme.
— *run*: longue période (assez longue pour permettre à une entreprise de diversifier tous ses facteurs de production, et pas seulement certains d'entre eux).
— *-term capital, expectations*: capitaux, prévisions à long terme.
— *-term investment, market, liabilities*: placement, marché, passif à long terme.
— *-term prospects*: perspectives à long terme.
to borrow, to lend — : emprunter à longue échéance.

to look up (market): (marché) se ranimer.

loophole: échappatoire (m).
[F] lacune (f) permettant l'évasion fiscale.

loose: détendu, relâché, mobile (a).
— *cash*: menue monnaie.
— *leaf (sheet)*: feuille volante, supplément, mise à jour.
— *leaf ledger*: grand livre à feuilles mobiles.
— *plant*: matériel mobile.

Lord: [UK] Lord (titre).
— *(High) Chancellor*: Président de la Chambre des Lords, membre du Cabinet à la tête du pouvoir judiciaire (# ministre de la Justice).
— *(s) of Appeal in Ordinary* (Law Lords) : Lords membres des comités d'appel de la Chambre des Lords.
— *(s) Spiritual*: Lords spirituels, archevêques ou évêques qui siègent à la Chambre des Lords.
— *(s) Temporal*: Lords Temporels, membres laïcs de la Chambre des Lords (pairs héritiers, pairs à vie, etc.).

to lose: perdre.
— *ground*: perdre du terrain.
— *in value*: perdre de sa valeur.
losing bargain: mauvais marché.
losing number: numéro perdant.

loser: (B) valeur qui perd du terrain (contr. « gainer »).

loss: perte (f), déperdition (f), déficit (m), dommage (m), préjudice (m).
[J] – *of a right*: déchéance d'un droit.
[ASS] sinistre (m).
excess of – : excédent de sinistre.
incurred but not reported – *(es) (IBNR)*: sinistres inconnus.
maximum foreseeable – *(MFL)*: sinistre maximum prévisible (SMP).
stop – : excédent de pertes.
[C] *clear, dead* – : perte sèche.
– *of capital*: perte, déperdition de capital.
– *leader*: article promotionnel, vendu à perte.
net generating – : déficit net d'exploitation.
partial – : perte partielle.
– *of profit*: manque à gagner.
total – : perte totale.
constructive total – : perte censée totale.
– *for the year*: perte de l'exercice.
losses carry back: report sur les années antérieures.
losses carry forward: report sur les années futures.
losses carry over: report déficitaire.
operating, trading losses: pertes d'exploitation.
firms showing losses: entreprises déficitaires.
profit and – *account*: compte de profits et pertes.
to bear, to meet with, to incur, to sustain a – : subir une perte.
to cut one's losses: faire la part du feu.
to recoup a – : dédommager une perte.
to sell at a – : vendre à perte.

lost: perdu.
– *-business report*: rapport expliquant pourquoi l'entreprise a perdu un client ou un contrat.
– *profit*: manque à gagner.
to regain the money – : regagner l'argent perdu.
– *or not* – : [ASS] « que le bien soit assuré ou perdu » (clause rituelle de police d'assurance).
the motion was – : la motion a été rejetée.

lot: a) lot (m), paquet (m); b) sort (m), tirage au sort; c) parcelle, [U.S.] terrain à bâtir.
in one – : en bloc.
the –, *the whole* – : le tout.
[C] *job-* – : soldes, articles d'occasion.
odd – : articles soldés.
[F] *(debentures) redeemed by* – : obligations rachetées par tirage au sort.

lottery: loterie (f).
[F] – *bond, loan*: obligation, emprunt à lots.

low: bas, faible, réduit, bon marché (a).
– *consumption*: faible consommation.
– *-duty goods*: marchandises peu taxées.
– *cost firm*: entreprise à bas prix de revient.
– *rate of exchange*: taux de change peu élevé.
– *income*: faible revenu.
– *income groups*: groupes sociaux à faibles revenus.
– *-income housing* # habitation à loyer modéré (H.L.M.).
– *pressure selling*: vente pour laquelle on n'a pas forcé la main de l'acheteur.
– *standard of living*: niveau de vie bas.
– *stocks*: stocks dégarnis.
lower *chamber*: chambre basse, Chambre des Communes, tribunal de première instance.
lower *management*: cadres d'atelier, chefs de rayon, agents d'exécution.
to lower *(the bank rate, trade barriers etc.)*: abaisser, diminuer (le taux de l'escompte, les barrières douanières).
lowering: abaissement, diminution.
lowering of economic activity: ralentissement de l'activité économique.
lowering the fineness of the coinage: abaissement du titre des monnaies.
lowest *price*: prix le plus bas.
lowest *tenderer*: mieux-disant.
lowness: modicité, bon marché.

lucrative: lucratif (a).

lucri causa: par intérêt.

lump: masse (f), bloc (m).
[C] – *sum*: prix global, à forfait.
– *sum settlement*: règlement global, paiement forfaitaire.
in the – : en gros, en bloc, à forfait.

lunatic: dément (m), aliéné (m).
[J] le terme n'est appliqué qu'en matière criminelle : « *criminal* – ». Sinon : « *person unsound of mind* », « *patient* », etc.

luncheon voucher: ticket (m) de restaurant.

luxurious: luxueux (a).

luxury: luxe (m).
[C] – *trade*: commerce de luxe.
luxuries: articles de luxe.
[F] *taxes on luxuries*: impôts sur les produits de luxe.

lying: a) mensonger; b) couché, placé.

Lynch law: [U.S.] la loi de Lynch, justice sommaire.

NOTES

NOTES

M

M1 (U.K. & U.S.) : l'ensemble des disponibilités monétaires au sens étroit du terme (monnaie en circulation et dépôts à vue).

M3 (U.K. & U.S.) (« the broad monetary aggregate » selon définition du Financial Times) : l'ensemble des disponibilités monétaires au sens large (comprenant les dépôts en devises étrangères).

M4 (U.K. & U.S.) : disponibilités des ménages.

mace : sceptre (m).
[J] masse, symbole du pouvoir législatif des deux chambres du Parlement britannique et de la Chambre des représentants des Etats-Unis, placée sur une table devant le président.

macer : [J] huissier (m).

machination : machination, intrigue (f).

machine : machine (f) (sens propre et sens figuré), appareil (m), organisation (f).
calculating — : machine à calculer.
machine down time : équipement non utilisé (par suite d'une défaillance).
the — *of government* : la machine gouvernementale.
— *idle time* : équipement non utilisé (faute de commandes, matières premières etc.).
— *loading* : plan d'utilisation de l'équipement.
— *made* : usiné, fait à la machine.
(the) party — : l'appareil du parti.
— *production* : production mécanisée, en (grande) série.
— *shop* : atelier.
— *ticket* : [U.S.] programme d'un parti politique.

machinery : machinerie, machines, outillage, rouages, fonctionnement.
administrative machinery : procédure administrative.
the machinery of business : les rouages de l'économie (des affaires).
obsolescence of machinery : obsolescence de l'équipement.
productive machinery : équipement productif.
the machinery of the State : les mécanismes, les rouages de l'Etat.
time-saving machinery : organisation permettant d'économiser le temps.
wage-fixing machinery : méthode de fixation des salaires.
machining : usinage.

macro-distribution : macro-distribution (f).

macro-économics : macro-économie (f).

made : fabriqué, confectionné, pratiqué (a).
[C] *foreign* — : de fabrication étrangère.
hand- — : fait à la main.
home- — : fait à la maison, de fabrication artisanale.
home- — *bread* : pain de ménage.
— *to order* : fait (fabriqué) sur mesure.
ready- — *(clothes)* : (vêtements) de confection.

magisterial : judiciaire (a).
[J] — *inquiry* : enquête judiciaire.

magistracy : [J] (la) magistrature (f).

magistrate : [J] magistrat (fonctionnaire de l'ordre administratif et politique).

magna charta : la Grande Charte octroyée par le roi Jean à ses barons le 15 juin 1215, fondement des libertés anglaises.

magnate (of industry) : magnat (m) (d'industrie).

magnetic tape : bande (f) magnétique.

magnitude : grandeur, importance (f).

maid : jeune fille, servante (f).
maiden : vierge (a).
[J] *maiden assize* : session d'assises où il n'y a pas de cause de juger.
maiden name : nom de jeune fille.
maiden speech : premier discours d'un député au parlement.
maiden trip (voyage) : premier voyage d'un navire.

mail : poste (f), courrier (m), service (m) postal.
the Royal — : le service (britannique) des postes.
incoming — : courrier à l'arrivée.
[C] — *credit* : crédit de courrier.
— *-order business, sales* : ventes par correspondance.

outgoing — : courrier à expédier.
registered — : lettres recommandées.
to mail : (surtout [U.S.]) envoyer par la poste.
mailing : prospection, démarchage, vente par voie postale, publipostage.
mailing date : date d'envoi par la poste.
mailing list : liste d'adresses, de diffusion.

to maim : [J] (cr.) estropier, mutiler qn.

main : principal (a).
— *condition* : condition principale.
— *office* : bureau principal.
— *road* : grand-route.
[C] — *supplier* : fournisseur principal.

to maintain : maintenir, conserver, entretenir.
— *economic growth, prices* : maintenir la croissance économique, les prix.
— *a residence (in France)* : entretenir, disposer d'une résidence (en France).
— *one's rights* : défendre ses droits.
maintenance : maintien, entretien, soutien, conservation, défense (de ses droits), pension alimentaire.
maintenance charges : frais d'entretien.
maintenance grant : bourse d'études.
maintenance of law and order : maintien de l'ordre public.
maintenance order : obligation alimentaire.
resale price maintenance : prix de vente imposée (par le fabricant).
separate maintenance : pension alimentaire.
maintenance shift : équipe d'entretien.
deduction of the cost of repair and maintenance : déduction des frais d'entretien et de réparation.
reserve for inventory maintenance : reconstitution des stocks.
stoppages on wages for the maintenance of relief or provident funds : retenues sur les salaires pour la constitution et l'alimentation de caisses de secours ou de prévoyance.

major : a) personne (f) majeure ; b) majeur, important, essentiel, aîné (a).
— *casualty* : sinistre majeur.
— *crisis* : crise d'envergure.
— *industries* : industries essentielles.
— *shareholder* : (l')actionnaire le plus important.

majority : a) majorité (f) ; b) majoritaire (a).
[J] *absolute, relative* — : majorité absolue, relative.
[F] — *interest* : participation majoritaire.
— *verdict* : verdict non-unanime.

make : marque, fabrication (f).
[C] [F] *a car of French* — : une auto de marque française.

— *-up day* : jour du règlement mensuel (banque).
to make : faire, fabriquer.
« — *or buy* » : « fabriquer ou acheter » (les pièces détachées).
— *a bargain* : faire, passer un marché.
— *a bid for* : mettre une enchère sur.
— *a bill, a cheque* : libeller un effet, un chèque.
— *a call* : a) faire une visite ; b) faire escale.
— *a complaint* : porter plainte.
— *good* : compenser.
— *an investment* : faire un placement.
— *a killing* : faire un bénéfice sensationnel.
— *a loan* : faire un emprunt, un prêt.
— *an order* : rendre une ordonnance.
— *profits* : réaliser des bénéfices.
— *a tender* : soumissionner.
— *out an account, a cheque* : relever un compte, tirer un chèque.
— *out a case* : see « case ».
— *out an invoice* : dresser une facture.
— *use of* : se servir de.
— *up* : régler, établir, dresser (*a list* : une liste).
— *up an account* : arrêter un compte.
— *up for* : compenser, indemniser, réparer.
— *up for damages* : réparer des dégâts.
— *up for a loss* : compenser une perte.
— *up for the want of* : suppléer au manque de.
— *up on a competitor* : l'emporter sur un concurrent.
— *up the even money* : faire l'appoint.
maker : constructeur, fabricant, souscripteur.
market — : (marchand etc.) qui « fait » le marché.
making : construction, fabrication, confection.
decision- — : prise de décision.
a profit- — *concern* : une entreprise payante, qui réalise des profits.
— *out a statement of account* : relèvement d'un compte.
— *over a debt* : revirement de fonds.
— *up* : confection, conditionnement, formation, compensation.
— *up price* : cours de liquidation (bourse).
— *up the balance sheet* : confection du bilan.
— *up the cash* : arrêté de la caisse.

maladministration : mauvaise administration, mauvaise gestion (en général, des affaires publiques).
[J] forfaiture (f).
— *of justice* : prévarication.

mala fide (purchaser) : (acheteur) de mauvaise foi.

mala fides : mauvaise foi.

mala in se: actes mauvais en eux-mêmes (interdits ou non par les lois humaines).

male: mâle (m).
— *line of descent*: ligne masculine.

malefactor: malfaiteur (m).

malfeasance: [J] méfait (m), prévarication (f), acte (m) illégal.

malice: malice, malveillance (f).
[J] — *aforethought (with aforethought malice)*: préméditation (d'un crime).
malicious: malveillant ; fait avec intention de nuire, criminelle.
malicious injury to property: sabotage.
malicious injury: attentat à l'intégrité physique.
malicious intent: intention de nuire, délictueuse, criminelle.
malicious prosecution: poursuites abusives.

malingerer: simulateur (de maladie).
malingering: simulation (de maladie), absentéisme.

malinvestment: [F] mauvais investissement.

malnutrition: sous-alimentation, malnutrition.

malpractice: faute, négligence professionnelle (spécialement d'un médecin).

malthusian, malthusianism: malthusien, malthusianisme.

malversation: a) malversation (f) ; b) mauvaise gestion (f).

man (business man): homme (d'affaires).
— *-day (hour)*: journée ou heure individuelle de travail.
— *of law*: homme de loi.
— *of straw*: homme de paille.
— *-power*: main-d'œuvre, effectifs.
— *-power training*: formation de la main-d'œuvre.
payments in respect of — -power training are exempt from income: les paiements relatifs à la formation de la main-d'œuvre sont des revenus exonérés.
— *-servant*: domestique.
the employers and the **men**: les patrons et les ouvriers.

to manage: manier, conduire, diriger, gérer, mener, s'y prendre pour, arriver à.
— *(one's) affairs, a business, a household*: gérer (ses) affaires, une entreprise, une maison.
managed *economy*: économie dirigée.

management: ensemble des techniques d'organisation et de gestion de l'entreprise, maniement, gestion, direction, gérance, exploitation.
[C] *business* — : gestion des affaires, de l'entreprise.
— *account*: compte gestionnaire.
— *charges, expenses*: frais de gestion.
— *committee*: comité de direction.
— *consultant*: conseil en organisation.
— *control system*: contrôle de gestion.
— *by crisis*: gestion au jour le jour.
cutback — : gestion de l'austérité.
— *development*: formation des cadres de direction.
— *fee*: indemnité de direction, commission de chef de file.
— *of funds*: gestion de fonds.
— *games*: jeux d'entreprise.
leverage — *buy out (L.M.B.O.)* # reprise d'entreprise par les salariés (R.E.S.).
risk — : politique de l'entreprise à l'égard des risques.
— *by objectives (M.B.O.)*: gestion par objectifs.
— *planning*: gestion prévisionnelle.
scientific — : rationalisation, gestion scientifique.
science of —, — *science*: sciences (et techniques) de gestion.
— *services*: services auxiliaires de direction.
place of effective — *of a company*: siège de la direction effective d'une société.
manager: directeur, gérant, administrateur, gestionnaire, liquidateur (d'une entreprise).
acting manager: directeur intérimaire.
assistant-, deputy-manager: directeur adjoint.
business manager: directeur commercial.
departmental manager: chef de service.
district manager: directeur régional.
receiver and manager: syndic de faillite.
sales manager: directeur commercial.
staff manager: chef du personnel.
works manager: directeur d'usine.
managerial: directorial, technocratique.
managerial duties: fonctions directoriales.
managerial revolution: révolution technocratique.
managing: directeur, gérant, gestionnaire.
managing agent: agent gérant.
managing clerk: maître clerc, commis principal, chef de bureau.
managing director: administrateur délégué, administrateur gérant.
managing expenses: frais de gestion.

manchester school (of economics), manchesterism: école de Manchester, doctrine libre-échangiste de l'école de Manchester qui de 1820 à 1850 inspira les adversaires de la loi sur le blé *(corn law)*.

mandamus : « nous ordonnons ».

mandatary (mandatory) of a company : mandataire (m) d'une société.
– : impératif, obligatoire (a).
[J] – *injunction :* commandement d'un tribunal.
– *rule (writ) :* acte ou action obligatoire.

mandate : mandat (m), procuration (f).

manifest : manifeste (m) (d'un navire).
outward – : manifeste de sortie.
to manifest *(a cargo) :* manifester (une cargaison).

to manipulate (accounts) : manipuler, tripoter des comptes.
manipulation *(of accounts, of the market) :* tripotage de comptes, en bourse.

manning : effectifs (m pl), armement (m) (d'un navire).
– *arrangments :* gestion du personnel.
– *problem :* problème de main-d'œuvre.

manœuvre, [U.S.] **maneuver** : manœuvre (f), menées, intrigues (f pl).

manpower : (le) personnel, effectifs (m pl), main-d'œuvre (f).
– *planning :* prévision d'emploi du personnel, planification des ressources humaines.

mansion : immeuble de rapport (divisé en appartements).

manslaughter (with, without malice aforethought) : [J] homicide (m) (sans, avec préméditation).

manual : a) manuel (a) ; b) manuel (m) (livre d'études).
– *labour, work :* travail manuel.

manufacture : construction (f), fabrication (f), manufacture (f), produit (m) manufacturé.
[C] *of British* – : de fabrication britannique.
the cotton, woollen – : l'industrie cotonnière, lainière.
to manufacture : manufacturer, fabriquer, confectionner.
manufactured *goods, products :* marchandises (articles), produits manufacturés.
manufacturer : fabricant, industriel.
manufacturer's agent, representative : représentant régional d'une entreprise.
manufacturer's price : prix de fabrique.

manufacturing : a) industriel, manufacturier (a) ; b) fabrication (f).
manufacturing licence : licence de fabrication.
manufacturing town : ville industrielle.

to map out a policy : déterminer une politique, tracer une ligne de conduite.

margin : marge (f).
[C] [F] marge, limite (f), écart (m), provision (f), couverture (f).
[B] acompte versé au courtier, marge.
– *of consumption and production :* marge de consommation et de production.
fixed – : limite fixe.
gross – : marge brute.
– *of profit :* marge bénéficiaire.
safety – : marge de sécurité.
to allow a – *of error :* accorder, admettre une marge d'erreur.
to require a – *(of...) in cash :* exiger une couverture (de...) en espèces.
marginal : marginal.
– *analysis :* analyse marginale.
– *borrower* (contraire : *marginal lender*) : emprunteur marginal (qui n'empruntera pas si un taux déterminé d'intérêt est dépassé).
– *buyer* (contraire : *marginal seller*) : acheteur marginal.
– *case :* cas limite.
– *cost :* coût marginal.
– *efficiency of capital, of investment, of labour :* efficacité marginale du capital, de l'investissement, du travail.
– *firm :* entreprise marginale.
– *notes :* notes marginales.
– *pricing :* tarification égale au coût marginal.
– *product, productivity :* produit marginal, productivité marginale.
– *productivity theory of wages :* théorie des salaires fondée sur la productivité marginale.
– *propensity to consume, to save :* propension marginale à consommer, à épargner.
– *relief :* décote (f).
– *return :* rendement marginal.
– *revenue :* recette marginale.
– *unemployment :* chômage marginal.
– *utility :* utilité marginale.

marine : marin, maritime, marine.
– *court :* tribunal maritime.
– *insurance :* assurance maritime.
mercantile (merchant) – : marine marchande.
– *risk :* risque de mer.
(ASS. mar.) – *survey :* expertise maritime.

marital : marital, matrimonial (a).
[J] – *status :* état matrimonial, situation de famille.

maritime : maritime.
— *law* : droit maritime.

mark : marque (f), but (m), signe (m), preuve (f), témoignage (m), croix (f) (signature d'un illettré).
— *of fraud* : preuve de la fraude.
hall — : poinçon de contrôle (sur les objets d'orfèvrerie).
post- — : cachet de la poste.
trade- — : marque de fabrique.
the — *-up* : marge bénéficiaire.
to mark : marquer, indiquer (le prix), coter, estampiller.
— *a price* : coter un cours.
— *down* : baisser (le prix), s'inscrire en baisse, dévaloriser.
— *out* : délimiter, borner, aborner.
— *-up* : hausser (le prix), majorer, s'inscrire en hausse.
marked : marqué.
— *cheque* : chèque visé.
— *price* : prix marqué.
— *recovery* : reprise marquée.

marker : repère, témoin.
— *crude (oil)* : brut de référence (pétrole).
— *price* : prix de référence.

market : marché (m), Bourse (f), débouché (m), cours (m), clientèle (f).
[B] [C] *active* — : marché actif.
black — : marché noir.
brisk — : marché animé.
bull — : marché orienté à la baisse.
capital — : marché financier.
— *capitalisation of the equity of a company* : valeur en bourse des actions d'une société.
commodity — : marché des matières premières.
common — : marché commun.
— *coverage* : nombre de clients éventuels touchés par une publicité.
depressed — : marché déprimé.
discount — : marché de l'escompte.
dull — : marché terne.
— *economy* : économie de marché, économie libérale.
employment — : marché du travail.
(foreign) exchange — : marché des changes.
— *failure* : défaillance du marché.
falling — : marché en recul.
firm — : marché ferme.
flat — : marché languissant.
foreign — : marché extérieur.
futures — : marché du terme.
grey — : marché gris (ensemble des transactions portant sur des valeurs mobilières en cours d'émission et intervenant avant leur cotation officielle).
glutted — : marché encombré.
home — : marché intérieur.
— *jobbery* : agiotage, tripotage de bourse.

labour — : marché du travail.
lively — : marché animé.
— *maker* : teneur (m) de marché.
on normal open — *commercial terms* : aux conditions commerciales normales du marché libre.
outside — : la coulisse.
overseas — : marché d'outre-mer.
pegged — : marché stationnaire, cours stationnaire.
— *price* : cours, prix du marché.
— *rate* : cours du marché, hors banque.
— *report* : compte rendu de bourse.
a rising — : des cours en hausse.
— *research* : étude de marché.
slack — : marché calme.
spot — : marché du comptant, du disponible.
— *standing* : position d'une maison sur le marché.
stock — : marché des valeurs.
— *survey* : étude de marché.
tone of the — : dispositions du marché.
— *transactions* : opérations de bourse.
trends (tendencies) of the — : tendances du marché, valeur boursière.
— *value* : valeur vénale, marchande.
to be on the — : être en vente.
to bull the — : acheter à découvert.
to come into the — : être mis en vente dans le commerce.
to find a — *for* : trouver un débouché pour.
to find a ready — : se vendre facilement.
to market : faire son marché, trouver des débouchés, lancer un produit.

marketable : vendable, d'un débit facile.
[C] — *value* : valeur marchande.

marketing : (techniques de) commercialisation, organisation des marchés, distribution, mercatique (f).
— *concept (philosophy)* : façon de concevoir un marché après étude.
— *consultant* : mercaticien.
[C] — *board* : office commercial, office de régularisation des ventes.
— *costs, policy* : frais, politique de commercialisation.
— *mix* : ensemble des moyens mis en œuvre pour trouver des débouchés, marchéage (m).

marriage : mariage (m).
[J] — *articles* : contrat de mariage.
caveat to — : opposition au mariage.
— *certificate* : acte de mariage.
— *guidance* : consultation prénuptiale.
— *impediment* : empêchement au mariage.
— *licence* : dispense de bans.
— *portion* : dot.

to marshal : ranger, mettre en ordre.
— *assets, liens, securities* : ordonner les divers

éléments d'une succession, d'une faillite.
— *facts :* rassembler des faits et les présenter ordonnés.

mart : centre de commerce, [U.S.] marché.
[F] *money* — : [U.S.] marché monétaire.
[C] *trade* — : expomarché.

(court-)martial : [J] conseil de guerre.
— *-law :* loi martiale.

marxian, marxist, marxism : marxiste, marxisme.

mass : masse (f), bloc (m), grand nombre (m).
the — *of creditors :* la masse des créditeurs.
— *of labour :* somme de travail.
the — *media :* les moyens d'information de masse.
— *production :* production en masse, en grande série.
economy of — *production :* économies d'échelles.

master : maître (m), chef (m), patron (m), capitaine (m) (d'un bateau).
— *budget :* marché prévisionnel principal (d'une entreprise).
— *file :* fichier central.
harbour- — : capitaine de port.
— *porter :* entrepreneur de chargement et de déchargement (de navires).

to match : égaler, assortir.
matched sample : échantillon de population absolument identique à un autre (afin de comparer les réactions de ces acheteurs-témoins).
matching : assortiment (m).
(C) alignement (sur les conditions de la concurrence en matière de crédit).
(F) *matching credit :* bonification du crédit d'impôt accordé par l'Etat du siège à une société ayant une activité dans un pays en développement.

mate : camarade (m), compagnon (m), compagne (f) (de vie), officier en second (dans la marine marchande).
[C] — *('s) receipt :* reçu provisoire des marchandises reçues à bord.

material : a) matériel, important (a) ; b) matière (f), matériaux (m), fournitures (f pl).
— *damage :* dégâts matériels.
— *evidence :* preuve matérielle.
— *fact :* fait essentiel.
— *needs :* besoins matériels.
building — *(s) :* matériaux de construction.
— *and labour :* fournitures et main-d'œuvre, façon.
raw — *(s) :* matière première.

to materialize : se réaliser, aboutir.

maternity allowance, benefit : [A] prime (f), prestation (f) de maternité, allocation (f).

mathematical programming : programmation (f) mathématique.

mathematical reserves : [ASS] provisions mathématiques.

matricide : matricide (m).

matrimonial causes : [J] nom générique donné aux affaires touchant l'état conjugal.

matrix : matrice (f).

matter : matière, substance (f).
business — *(s) :* affaires.
— *of form :* formalité.
legal — *(s) :* questions juridiques.
money — *(s) :* affaires d'intérêt.
— *in suspense :* affaire en suspens.

mature : mûr (a), venu à échéance.
[C] [F] **to mature** : échoir, venir à échéance.
matured bill : effet déchu.
matured bond : obligation échue.
maturity : échéance (f).
date of maturity : date d'échéance.
maturity mismatching : financement d'emprunts à long terme par des dépôts à court terme.
payable at maturity : payable à l'échéance.

maximization : maximation, maximisation (f).
to maximize : porter à son maximum, maximiser.
maximum load : charge limite.
maximum price : prix plafond.
maximum rate : taux limite.

mayor : maire (m).

meal voucher : ticket restaurant.

mean : a) moyen intermédiaire (a) ; b) moyen (m), milieu (m), moyenne (f).
— *cost :* coût moyen.
— *deviation :* écart moyen.
— *time :* temps moyen.
— *value :* valeur moyenne.
[F] — *(s) of payment :* moyens de paiement.

meaning : sens (m).
« *within the* — *assigned by section 4...* » : au sens de l'article 4...

means: moyens (m pl), façons (f pl), ressources (f pl).
− *of conveyance*: moyens de transport.
− *of exchange*: moyens d'échange.
fair − : moyens honnêtes, façons loyales.
financial − : moyens financiers.
lawful − : moyens légaux, licites.
private − : fortune personnelle.
− *of subsistence*: moyens de subsistance.
− *test*: enquête sur les ressources, sur la situation de fortune (de qn).
to have ample − *at one's disposal*: disposer de capitaux considérables.
to live beyond one's − : vivre au-dessus de ses moyens.

measure: mesure (f), démarche (f).
austerity, emergency, exceptional −*(s)*: mesures d'austérité, d'urgence, exceptionnelles.
[J] −*(s) of conciliation*: voies d'accommodement.
precautionary − : mesure de précaution, de conservation.
measurement: mesure, dimension, cubage.
− *ton*: tonneau (m) de capacité, d'encombrement.
measuring *apparatus, tool*: appareil, outil de mesure.

meat-packing industry: [C] industrie, de la conserve de la viande.

mechanical civilisation: civilisation mécanique.
− *engineering*: construction, industrie mécanique.

mechanic's lien: [J] privilège du constructeur.

mechanism: mécanisme (m), rouages (m pl).

media *(sing. medium)*: moyens (m) de communication de masse.
advertizing − : organes de publicité, supports publicitaires.
− *analysis*: analyse (f) de la valeur comparative de la publicité selon les media.
− *buyer*: personne qui achète de la publicité sur les recommandations d'un conseiller en publicité.
− *owner*: propriétaire (m) de chaînes publicitaires.
− *planner*: conseiller (m) en publicité.

median values: valeurs médianes.

mediation: médiation (f), intervention amicale.
[J] procédure de conciliation, juridiction gracieuse (opp. *arbitration*, procédure judiciaire comportant l'application obligatoire de la sentence arbitrale, syn. [U.S.] *pre-trial practice*).

medical: médical (a).
− *board*: commission médicale.
− *certificate*: certificat médical.
− *department*: service de santé.
− *evidence*: expertise médicale.
− *expenses*: frais médicaux.
− *fees*: honoraires médicaux.
− *jurisprudence*: médecine légale.
− *profession*: corps médical.
− *record*: fiche médicale, feuille de maladie.

medium: a) moyen (a); b) milieu (m), moyen (m), intermédiaire (m).
− *of exchange*: moyen d'échange.
through the − *of*: par l'intermédiaire de.
− *-sized enterprise, firm*: entreprise moyenne.
− *-term forecasting*: prévisions à moyen terme.
− *-term loan*: emprunts (ou prêts) à moyen terme.

medley: confusion (f).
[J] *chance-* − : rixe.

to meet: (se) rencontrer, satisfaire à, répondre à (un besoin), faire face à (des exigences), (se) réunir, se joindre à.
[C] − *a bill*: honorer une lettre de change, faire face à une échéance.
− *a demand*: faire face à une demande.
− *a draft*: honorer une traite.
− *expenses*: faire face à des dépenses.
− *expenditure from taxation*: financer des dépenses grâce au produit des impôts.
− *the needs (the requirements)*: satisfaire aux besoins.
− *with a refusal*: essuyer un refus.
meeting: rencontre, réunion, assemblée (f).
meeting of the Board of directors (Board meeting): réunion du Conseil d'administration.
general meeting: assemblée générale.
plenary meeting: assemblée plénière.
private meeting: réunion à huis clos.
special meeting: assemblée extraordinaire.
to call a meeting: convoquer une assemblée.
to hold a meeting: tenir une réunion, une assemblée.

melon: bénéfice à distribuer.

member: membre, adhérent (m).
active, associate − : membre actif, correspondant.
[F] − *bank*: banque affiliée ([U.S.] faisant partie du *Federal Reserve System*).
− *of a company*: membre d'une société, sociétaire.

— 503 —

[B] – *firm :* firme d'agent de change, membre de la Bourse des valeurs.
– *of a mutual insurance company :* mutualiste.
– *of Parliament,* [U.S.] *of Congress :* membre de la Chambre des Communes, [U.S.] membre de la Chambre des représentants.
– *States :* Etats membres.
membership : qualité de membre, adhésion ; charge, office ; nombre des adhérents.
to acquire membership : acquérir la qualité de membre.
membership dues : cotisation (de membre d'une association).
membership form : bulletin d'adhésion.

memorandum (en abrégé : **memo**) : (mémoire) mémorandum (m), note (f), bordereau (m).
[J] – *of agreement :* convention.
– *of association :* charte constitutive d'une société à responsabilité limitée.
– *and articles of association :* statuts.
– *books :* registres d'ordre, agenda.
– *of insurance :* arrêté (provisoire) d'assurance.
as a – : pour mémoire.
[C] *sale on memorandum :* vente à condition.

memory : mémoire (m).
living – : période pendant laquelle un témoignage peut être fourni par le témoin en vie le plus âgé.

menace (of dismissal...) : menace (f), (de licenciement...).

mend : amélioration, reprise (f).
trade is on the – : les affaires s'améliorent, reprennent.

mens rea : [J] intention délictueuse, criminelle.

mensurable, mensuration : mesurable (a), mensuration (f), mesure (f), cubage (m).

mental : mental (a).
– *anguish :* souffrance morale (élément d'évaluation des dommages-intérêts alloués à la victime d'un accident).
– *capacity :* discernement.
– *cruelty :* sévices et injures graves.
– *defectiveness :* débilité mentale (comportant l'irresponsabilité pénale).
– *element :* élément moral constitutif d'un délit.
– *hospital, home :* asile psychiatrique.
– *reservation :* restriction mentale.

mercantile : mercantile, marchand (a).
– *agency :* agence de renseignements commerciaux.
[C] – *business :* opérations commerciales.
– *law :* droit commercial.
– *marine :* marine marchande.
– *nation :* nation commerçante.
– *paper (bill) :* papier commercial.
the – *system, theory :* le système, la théorie mercantile.
mercantilism : mercantilisme (m).

merchandise : marchandises (f pl).

to merchandise : commercialiser.

merchandiser : marchandiseur (m).

merchandising : marchandisage (m), commercialisation (f).

merchant : a) marchand (a), de commerce ; b) commerçant (m), marchand (m), négociant (m).
[F] – *banks :* banques d'escompte d'effets étrangers, banques pour le commerce international, aussi : « trusts de placement » (Bannock, Baxter et Rees).
[C] – *fleet :* flotte marchande.
itinerant – : marchand ambulant.
law – : droit commercial.
– *marine,* – *service,* – *navy :* marine de commerce, marchande.
– *ship, vessel :* navire de commerce.

mercy : merci (f), miséricorde (f), grâce (f), clémence (f).
– *killing :* euthanasie.
[J] *petition for* – : pourvoi (m), recours en grâce.
plea of – : recours en grâce.
prerogative of – : droit de grâce.
works of – : œuvres de bienfaisance.

to merge : fusionner, s'amalgamer.
merger : fusion (f), unification (f), [J] extinction (f) d'un droit, absorbé par un droit supérieur, acquis par la même personne ; confusion (f) (de droits, de peines).
– *acquisition :* fusion-absorption (f).
– *of banks :* fusion de banques.
– *of corporations :* fusion de sociétés.
industrial – : concentration industrielle.
partial – : fusion partielle.
merging : fusion, fusionnement.

merit : mérite (m) ; [J] le fond (m), la substance (f).
– *bonus :* [U.S.] prime de rendement.
– *goods :* # biens sous tutelle.
– *payment :* prime (f) de responsabilité ou de spécialité.
– *rating :* jugement de valeur (sur un employé).

– *system*: avancement fondé sur le mérite.
complaint dismissed on the – *(s)*: plainte rejetée comme non fondée.
defence, judgment upon the – *(s)*: plaidoyer, jugement au fond.
the case is at issue upon its – *(s)*: le fond de la cause est en état.
to go into the – *(s) of*: discuter le pour et le contre de.
meritorious: méritant ; valable.
meritorious cause of action: motif valable (d'un dépôt de plainte).
meritorious consideration: intérêt moral dans une transaction.

mesne: intermédiaire (a).
[J] – *assignments*: cession intermédiaire (dans une suite ininterrompue, par ex. des endos).
– *conveyance*: transfert effectué entretemps.
– *process*: instance en cours.
– *profits*: bénéfices prélevés pendant la durée de la possession illégitime d'un bien.

messuage: [J] maison (f), dépendances et terres (f pl).

(coined) metal: numéraire (m).
the – *industries*: les industries métallurgiques.
[F] – *reserve (metallic reserve)*: réserves métalliques.

to mete out (punishment, rewards): assigner (des punitions), décerner (des récompenses).

meter: compteur (m).

method: méthode (f), procédé (m), système (m).
[F] – *(s) of depreciation*:
-annuity – : méthode d'amortissement par annuités.
-appraisal – : méthode d'amortissement basée sur l'estimation (l'évaluation) du moment.
-declining –, *diminishing instalment* –, *double declining* – : système dégressif.
-fractional apportionment – : méthode de la ventilation fractionnée.
-gross profit – : méthode basée sur les bénéfices bruts.
-net profit – : méthode basée sur les bénéfices nets.
-reducing balance – : méthode d'amortissement décroissant, système dégressif.
-straight line – : système linéaire.
cash – : (système de la) comptabilité de caisse.
completed job – : méthode spéciale de comptabilité dite: méthode de l'ouvrage achevé.
cost – : méthode comptable d'évaluation des stocks marchandises dite: méthode du coût.
cost or market – : méthode comptable d'évaluation des stocks marchandises dite: méthode du chiffre le plus faible du coût et du prix du marché.
machine hour – : méthode d'amortissement dite: « l'heure de machine ».
– *of payment*: modalités de paiement.
– *study*: étude critique des méthodes de travail.
– *of taxation*: mode de taxation.
percentage of completion – : méthode spéciale de comptabilité fiscale: méthode du pourcentage d'achèvement.
retail – : méthode comptable de définition de coûts dite: méthode du prix de détail.

methodology: méthodologie (f).

metre, [U.S.] **meter, metric**: mètre, métrique.

micro economic, micro economics: micro-économique, micro-économie.

mid-term review (GATT): réunion ministérielle du GATT (AGETAC) examinant les résultats des négociations précédentes.

middle: milieu, moyen.
the – *class*: la bourgeoisie.
– *course*: moyen terme.
– *management*: cadres intermédiaires de direction.
– *price*: prix, cours moyen.

middleman: [C] intermédiaire (m), revendeur (m).

mileage: parcours (m), distance (f), kilométrage (m), indemnité (f) kilométrique de déplacement.
– *allowance*: indemnité pour frais de transport.
– *rate*: tarif au mille, kilométrique.

military law: code de justice militaire (mais non « loi martiale » : *martial law*).

to milk: argot [U.S.] « plumer », dépouiller, intercepter (une communication).

milk products: produits laitiers.

mill: moulin (m), fabrique (f), usine (f) (sauf pour industries chimiques et métallurgiques).
cotton- – : filature de coton.
oil- – : huilerie.
paper- – : papeterie.
saw- – : scierie.

silk- — : filature de soie.
spinning- — : filature.
sugar- — : raffinerie de sucre.

(of sound) mind : (sain d') esprit.

mine : mine (f).
to mine : creuser, extraire (le charbon), exploiter.
mineral *rights :* droits miniers.
mining : a) minier (a); b) exploitation (f) minière.
coal-mining : charbonnage.
mining company : société (compagnie) minière.
mining concession : concession minière.
the mining industry : l'industrie minière.
[J] *mining law :* droit minier.
mining licence : acte de concession de mine.
mining regulations : règlements miniers.
[F] *mining royalties :* redevance tréfoncière.
mining shares : valeurs minières.

minimal value : valeur minimale.

to minimize : minimiser, limiter, atténuer, réduire au minimum.
[C] *— losses :* limiter les pertes.
minimum : minimal, minimum.
minimum cost : coût minimum.
minimum interest : intérêt minimum, intérêts minima.
Mininum Lending Rate (M.L.R.) : (U.K.) taux minimum de prêt par la Banque d'Angleterre.
minimum price : prix minimum.
(guaranteed) minimum wages : salaire minimum garanti.

minister, ministry : ministre (m), ministère (m).
ministerial : ministériel.
[J] *ministerial act :* acte d'exercice du pouvoir exécutif.
ministerial officer : [U.S.] fonctionnaire de l'ordre judiciaire.

minor : a) mineur (a); b) mineur (m).
— changes : changements de peu d'importance.
— coin : appoint, monnaie divisionnaire.
[J] *— defects :* vices de forme n'entrant pas en ligne de compte.
— expenses : menus frais.
— interests : droits et facultés qui ne peuvent faire l'objet de dispositions formelles et pouvant être écartées.
— repairs : petites réparations.
— violations : contraventions.
minority : minorité, minoritaire (par le nombre, d'âge).
minority holding (interest) : participation minoritaire.

mint : la Monnaie (f).
*the Royal — * (U.K.) # Direction des Monnaies et Médailles (France).
[F] **to mint :** battre monnaie.
— par, — par of exchange : pair du change, pair intrinsèque.
in a — condition, state : à l'état neuf (a).
minted money : argent monnayé, monnaie métallique.

minus : (en) moins, moindre.

minute : menu, minutieux, circonstancié (a).
— investigation : enquête minutieuse.

minute(s) of a meeting : procès-verbal d'une réunion.
[J] *— -book :* registre des délibérations, minutier, plumitif.

misadjustment : mauvaise adaptation.

misapplication (of funds) : détournement (m) (de fonds).
to misapply : détourner (des fonds).

misapprehension (of facts) : fausse interprétation (des faits).

to misappropriate : distraire, détourner (des fonds).
[J] **misappropriation :** distraction de biens, abus de confiance.
misappropriation of public funds : concussion (f).

miscalculation : faux calcul, mécompte.

miscarriage : échec, avortement (m).
[J] *— of justice :* erreur judiciaire, déni de justice.

miscellaneous : divers, mêlé, mélangé.
— provisions : dispositions diverses.
— taxes : impôts divers.
— unclassified material : divers papiers et documents non classés.

mischief : dégâts (m pl), dommage (m), méfait (m).
[J] *public — :* attentat aux mœurs.

misconception : malentendu, idée fausse.

misconduct : mauvaise administration, mauvaise gestion, inconduite.
[J] adultère.
official, professional — : faute commise dans l'exercice de ses fonctions, de sa profession.

to misconstrue : mal interpréter.

misdemeanour : délit (m), infraction (f) (grave).

misdrescription : [J] erreur (f), faute (f), fausse indication dans la description de biens immobiliers, fausse désignation d'un article de commerce.

misdirection : renseignement inexact, fausse adresse.

misfeasance : accomplissement incorrect d'un acte licite.

misfit : laissé pour compte, marchandise refusée.
 the social misfits : les inadaptés.

to mishandle : [C] mal conduire (ses affaires).

misinformation : faux renseignements.

misjoinder : [J] fausse constitution des parties, jonction injustifiée d'instances.

to mismanage : mal gérer.
 [C] **mismanagement** : mauvaise gestion.

mismatching : see « foreign exchange mismatching ».

misnomer : [J] erreur sur le nom d'une partie.

misprision : forfaiture (f).
 [J] — *of felony* : non-dénonciation de crime, recel de malfaiteurs ;

misrepresentation : déclaration ou conduite tendant à induire en erreur.
 [J] *false (wilful)* — : fraude civile.
 fraudulent — : fraude pénale.

to miss (an opportunity, a market) : manquer (une occasion, un marché).
 [J]« *Have you seen this missing child ?* » # avis de recherche d'enfant disparu.

misstatement : déclaration, inexacte, fausse déclaration.

mistake : erreur (f), faute (f), méprise (f), inadvertance (f).
 — *in calculation* : erreur de calcul.
 mistaken *identity* : erreur sur la personne.
 mistaken opinion : opinion erronée.
 mistaken statement : déclaration mal comprise, erronée.

mistrial : [J] erreur (f) judiciaire.

misunderstanding : malentendu.

misuse : mauvais usage, abus.
 — *of authority* : abus de pouvoir.
 (fraudulent) — *of funds* : détournement de fonds.

to mitigate : atténuer.

mitigation, mitigating : adoucissement (m).
 [J] — *of damages* : réduction des dommages-intérêts.
 [F] — *of taxes* : atténuation d'impôt.
 mitigating *circumstances* : circonstances atténuantes.

mixed : mixte, mélangé, mêlé, douteux (a).
 — *action* : action mixte (réelle et personnelle).
 — *economy* : économie mixte.
 — *farming* : polyculture.
 — *fund* : fonds constitué par le produit de biens mobiliers et immobiliers.
 — *income* : revenu composé en partie de rentes.
 — *larceny* : vol qualifié.
 — *property* : patrimoine composé de biens mobiliers et immobiliers.

mixture : mélange (m).

mobile, mobility : mobile (a) ; mobilité (f).
 — *shop* : atelier mobile.
 — *of capital, of labour* : mobilité du capital, de la main-d'œuvre.

mobilization : [F] mobilisation (f).

mock : d'imitation, contrefait (a), faux (a), pour rire.
 — *auction* : fausse vente aux enchères.
 — *court* : cour de justice fictive (exercice d'entraînement pour les étudiants).
 — *trial* : simulacre de procès.
 — *-up* : maquette.

model value : valeur modale.

model : a) modèle (a) ; b) modèle (m).
 analogue, ironic, symbolic — : modèle analogique (ex. faire des vagues dans un bassin et étudier le comportement d'un navire modèle réduit à l'échelle du navire en construction).
 econometric, economic, keynesian —, *etc.* : modèle économétrique, économique, keynésien, etc.
 — *farm* : ferme modèle.

moderate : modéré, moyen, raisonnable (a).
 – *income* : revenus modiques.
 – *price* : prix raisonnable.
 – *-rent housing cooperatives* : sociétés H.L.M.
 – *sale* : vente au ralenti.
 – *size* : dimension, taille moyenne.

modern : moderne (a).
 modernism, modernity : modernisme (m).
 modernity-snobbery : le snobisme de la nouveauté, du modernisme.

modification (of the terms of a contract) : modification (f) (des clauses d'un contrat).
 to modify : modifier.

module : module (m).

M.o.F. (ministry of Finance) : ministre des Finances.

(to gather) momentum : (sens figuré) s'accélérer (l'inflation, la hausse des prix).

monetary : monétaire (a).
 [F] – *aggregates* : agrégats monétaires (constituant les disponibilités monétaires).
 – *base* : argent déposé dans une Banque Centrale par des banques commerciales.
 – *compensation amounts (E.E.C.)* : montants compensatoires monétaires (C.E.E.).
 – *inflation, policy, reform, standard, etc.* : inflation monétaire, politique, réforme, étalon, etc.
 monetization : monétisation.
 to monetize : monétiser.

money : argent (m), fonds (m), monnaie (f), numéraire (m).
 [J] *action for – had and received* : action pour enrichissement sans cause.
 hush – : prix du silence, achat des consciences.
 (B) *in the –* : dans les cours (option dont le prix d'exercice est inférieur au cours du titre support dans le cas d'une option d'achat, ou : option dont le prix d'exercice est supérieur au cours du titre support dans le cas d'une option de vente).
 [F] – *of account* : monnaie de compte.
 at the – : à parité.
 bad (base) – : fausse monnaie.
 « *bad – drives out good* » (*Gresham's Law*) : « la mauvaise monnaie chasse la bonne » (Loi de Gresham).
 bank – (written –) : monnaie scripturale.
 – *bill* : loi de finances.
 – *-broker* : courtier de change.
 call –, – at call : dépôt à vue, prêts remboursables sur demande ([U.S.] argent comptant).
 caution –, command – : cautionnement.
 counterfeit, forged – : fausse monnaie.
 earnest – : arrhes.
 fiat – : monnaie fiduciaire, monnaie à cours forcé.
 – *in hand* : argent disponible.
 hot – : capitaux « brûlants », errants, spéculatifs.
 idle –, – lying, idle, inactive : argent qui dort, monnaie oisive.
 – *illusion* : illusion sur la valeur de la monnaie.
 – *interest* : intérêt pécuniaire.
 – *for jam, for old rope* : (fam.) argent facilement gagné.
 lawful – : [U.S.] monnaie légale ([U.K.] *legal tender*).
 – *lender* : bailleur de fonds, prêteur d'argent.
 – *market ([U.S.] mart)* : marché financier, monétaire.
 – *market fund* : fond de placement sur le marché monétaire.
 – *-off item, pack* : article, paquet publicitaire (avec bon de réduction).
 – *order* : mandat-poste.
 – *payment* : paiement en numéraire.
 out of the – : hors du cours.
 public – : fonds public.
 purchase – : prix d'achat.
 – *rates* : taux de l'argent.
 ready – : argent comptant.
 sale for – : vente au comptant.
 scarce – : argent rare.
 soft – : [U.S.] papier monnaie.
 standard – : monnaie-étalon.
 – *stock* : disponibilités monétaires.
 – *supply* : masse monétaire.
 – *supply target* : objectif de croissance de la masse monétaire.
 tight – : argent rare.
 tightening of – : resserrement du crédit.
 token – : monnaie fiduciaire.
 – *wages* : salaires nominaux.
 to bring in – : rapporter de l'argent.
 to come into – : faire un héritage.
 to get one's – worth : rentrer dans ses fonds.
 to have one's – worth : en avoir pour son argent.
 to make – : gagner de l'argent.
 to be pushed for – : être à court d'argent.
 to raise – : se procurer de l'argent, des capitaux (par voie d'emprunt, etc.).
 to recover one's – : récupérer (son) argent, regagner l'argent perdu.
 to refund – : rembourser, restituer de l'argent.
 to want – : avoir besoin d'argent.
 to waste – : gaspiller l'argent.
 to withdraw – from the bank : retirer de l'argent de la banque.
moneyed (*monied*) : riche, qui a de l'argent.
 the moneyed classes : les classes possédantes.

moneyed corporation (using money to make money): société financière (qui se sert de l'argent pour gagner de l'argent).
moneyed interest: les capitalistes.
(the public) **moneys** *(monies)*: les deniers (publics), le trésor public.
– *(s) owing to*: créances envers.
– *(s) paid in*: recettes effectuées.
– *(s) paid out*: versements opérés, effectués.
moneyless: dépourvu d'argent, insolvable.

monition: avertissement (m), [J] citation (f) à comparaître.

to monitor *(equipment)*: exercer une surveillance (sur l'équipement).

monkey business: (fam.) [U.S.] affaire (f) malhonnête, « magouille ».

monometallic, monometallism: monométallique, monométallisme.

monopoly: monopole (m).
discrimination – : monopole qui pratique des tarifs discriminatoires.
government (state) – : monopole d'Etat.
– *price* – : prix de monopole.
selling – : monopole de vente.
monopolist, monopolistic: monopoliste, monopolistique.

monopsony: situation (f) du marché dans laquelle il y a un seul acheteur pour plusieurs vendeurs (« Monopsonie »).

month, calendar month: [J] mois civil.
[C] *paper at (six)* –(s), *(six)* –(s') *paper*: papier à six mois d'échéance.
– *requirements*: échéances mensuelles.
monthly: mensuel.
monthly allowance: allocation mensuelle.
monthly instalment: mensualité.
monthly statement: relevé de fin de mois.

moonlight work: travail (m) noir, clandestin.

moot: discutable (a).
[J] – *case*: litige fictif soumis à la justice afin de créer un précédent.
– *point*: point litigieux (de caractère académique).

to mop up (profits): absorber (les bénéfices).

moratium, moratory: [J] [F] moratoire.
– *loan*: emprunt moratoire.

mortality: mortalité (f).
(infant, etc.) – *rate*: taux de mortalité (infantile, etc.).
– *tables*: tables de mortalité.

mortgage: hypothèque (f).
[J] *blanket* – : hypothèque générale.
– *bond*: titre hypothécaire.
– *charge*: privilège d'hypothèque.
credit on – : crédit hypothécaire.
creditor on – *(– creditor)*: créancier hypothécaire.
debt on – *(– debt)*: créance hypothécaire.
– *debtor*: débiteur hypothécaire.
– *deed*: contrat d'hypothèque.
first, second... – : première, deuxième... hypothèque.
first – *debentures (bonds)*: obligations de première hypothèque.
– *foreclosure*: saisie d'hypothèque.
free of – : libre d'hypothèque.
legal – : hypothèque légale.
– *loan (loan on mortgage)*: prêt hypothécaire.
– *market*: marché hypothécaire.
open-ended – : créance hypothécaire dont le taux d'intérêt peut être modifié.
registrar of – : conservateur des hypothèques.
– *registry*: bureau des hypothèques.
redemption of – *by mortgagee*: purge d'hypothèque.
redemption of – *by mortgagor*: extinction d'hypothèque.
release of – : mainlevée d'hypothèque.
– *security*: garantie hypothécaire.
satisfaction of – : extinction d'une hypothèque.
transfer of – : transfert d'hypothèque.
to be bound by – : être obligé hypothécairement.
to borrow on – : emprunter sur hypothèque.
to pay off a – : lever (purger) une hypothèque.
to raise a – : prendre une hypothèque.
to redeem a – : purger une hypothèque.
to secure a debt by – : hypothéquer une créance.
to take a – *on...*: prendre une hypothèque sur...
to mortgage *(a house, etc;)*: hypothéquer (une maison, etc.).
mortgaged *estate*: domaine grevé d'hypothèques.
mortgageable *(property)*: (biens) hypothéquable(s).
mortgagee: créancier hypothécaire.
mortgagor: débiteur hypothécaire.

mortmain: mainmorte (f).

mortuary: [J] Institut médico-légal.

most-favoured nation clause, treatment: [E] clause, traitement de la nation la plus favorisée.

mother country: mère (f) patrie.

(foster-) mother: mère (f) nourricière.

motion: mouvement (m), motion (m), proposition (f).
[J] demande (f), requête (f).
— *to dismiss*: requête en référé de la défense, tendant à faire débouter le demandeur.
— *for judgment*: requête au tribunal de prononcer le jugement si la défense fait défaut.
— *to set aside judgment*: demande d'annulation présentée à la Cour d'appel en alléguant une erreur dans le verdict ou la sentence.
— *economy*: économie des mouvements.
— *study*: étude des mouvements (d'un ouvrier effectuant un travail déterminé).
to carry a —: faire adopter une motion, une proposition.
to do (sth.) out of one's own —: faire (qch.) de sa propre initiative.
to propose (to bring forward) a —: présenter une motion, faire une proposition.
to second, to support a —: soutenir une motion.

motivation: motivation (f).

motive: motif (m), mobile (m), raison (f), « ressort » (m).
profit-making is one of the —(s) of business: le profit est un des ressorts des affaires (de l'économie).
saving, speculative —: motif d'épargne de spéculation.

to mount (up): monter (les prix), croître.
mounting *expenditures*: dépenses en augmentation.

(to live from hand to) mouth: vivre au jour le jour.

movable: mobile, mobilier, meuble (a).
[B] — *assets*: valeurs mobilières.
— *effects (property)*: effets mobiliers.
to quote — exchange: coter l'incertain.

movables: biens mobiliers.

move: mouvement (m), démarche (f), décision (f).
what is the next — ?: que faut-il faire maintenant ? quelle doit-être la prochaine démarche ?
false —: faux pas, fausse manœuvre.
to move: se déplacer, proposer.

to move an amendment: proposer un amendement.
to move a resolution: présenter une résolution.
the shares **move** *round...*: les actions oscillent autour de...
this article is not **moving**: cet article ne se vend pas.
to move for papers: demander la publication des pièces.
Sterling **moved** *ahead in terms of the D.M.*: la Livre s'est relevée par rapport au Deutsch Mark.
to move down (prices): baisser (les prix).
to move forward: avancer, progresser, continuer.
to move up: monter, se relever.
Sterling **moved** *up at the close*: la Livre s'est relevée en fin de séance.
movement *of capital (capital movement)*: mouvement de capitaux.
downward, upward movements of stocks: mouvements de baisse, de hausse des valeurs.
free movement of goods: libre circulation des marchandises.
political movement: mouvement politique.

moving: a) mobile (a); b) déménagement (m).
— *averages*: moyennes mobiles (statistique).
— *expenses*: frais de déménagement.

mulier: fils, fille, frère et sœur légitimes en tant qu'opposés aux naturels.

multicurrency: multidevise (f).
— *loan*: emprunt multidevises.

multilateral agreement: accord, multilatéral, convention multilatérale.
— *settlements*: règlements plurilatéraux.
— *trade treaty*: commerce, traité multilatéral.

multimarket corporation: société (f) (ou groupe de sociétés) aux activités diversifiées.

multinational corporation: société multinationale.

multiple: multiple (a).
[C] — *firm*: maison à succursales multiples.
—*(s), — shops, stores*: magasins à succursales multiples.
— *rates of return*: taux internes multiples.
— *territory big unit*: grande unité interterritoriale.
[B] — *shares*: actions multiples.
[F] — *currency standard*: étalon de change multiple.
[F] — *taxation*: impositions multiples.

multiplication, to multiply: multiplication (f), multiplier.
   multiplier: multiplicateur (m).
   activity multipliers: multiplicateurs d'activité.
   multiplier-accelerator model: modèle du multiplicateur-accélérateur.
   multiplier effect: effet de multiplicateur.
   employment multiplier: multiplicateur d'emploi.
   foreign trade multiplier: multiplicateur du commerce extérieur.
   national income multiplier: multiplicateur du revenu (national).

multiplicity of actions: [B] multiplicité d'actions.

multiproduct firm: [C] entreprise qui fabrique plusieurs productions.

multipurpose: à buts (à fins) multiples.

municipal corporation: [A] municipalité (f), conseil (m) municipal.
   – *law*: droit interne.
   – *ordinance*: [U.S.] arrêté municipal.

muniments: [J] titres et autres documents relatifs à la propriété d'un bien-fonds.

murder: meurtre (m).
   [J] crime d'homicide illicite avec préméditation : « *killing of a human being with malice aforethought* », la préméditation étant entendue dans un sens très large : soit l'intention de donner la mort (dolus directus), soit l'intention de commettre une *felony* susceptible d'entraîner mort d'homme *(felony* – *)*, en tant que conséquence de versari in re illicita.
   [U.S.] selon leur gravité, les législations des divers Etats distinguent jusqu'à 5 catégories *(degrees)* de l'homicide, mais, en général, on se contente de deux : – *in the first degree* : assassinat assorti de circonstances aggravantes, telles que l'empoisonnement et le guet-apens, ou *felony* – commis dans les mêmes circonstances, p. ex. au cours d'un incendie provoqué *(arson)*, d'un vol avec effraction *(burglary)*, d'un viol *(rape)*, et – *in the second degree* : homicide involontaire (voir *manslaughter*).

mute: muet (a).
   [J] « *to stand* – » : refuser de répondre aux questions du tribunal qu'il s'agisse de – *of malice* : cas de refus délibéré, ou de – *by visitation of God* : d'un sourd, d'un muet ou d'un sourd-muet.

mutiny: mutinerie (f).

mutual: mutuel (a).
   – *assent*: accord des parties.
   – *assurance*: coassurance.
   – *benefit society*: société de secours mutuels.
   member of – *benefit society*: mutualiste.
   – *claims, credits*: créances réciproques donnant légalement lieu à compensation.
   – *contract*: contrat synallagmatique.
   – *insurance company*: société d'assurances mutuelles.
   – *promises*: engagements réciproques.
   – *terms*: stipulation de réciprocité.
   – *testament*: donation au dernier survivant.

NOTES

N

nail: ongle (m).
to pay on the — : payer rubis sur l'ongle.

naked: nu, évident, pur (a).
[J] dépourvu de qualités essentielles.
— *bond*: engagement unilatéral, sans garantie.
— *contract*: contrat sans garantie non exécutable, à titre gratuit.
— *debenture*: obligation chirographaire, non valable.
— *possession*: possession ne reposant sur aucun titre, de fait (et non de droit).

name: nom (m), marque (f), intitulé (m), raison (f) sociale, réputation (f).
— *of an account*: intitulé d'un compte.
assumed — : nom d'emprunt.
— *of bearer*: nom du porteur.
brand — : marque de fabrique.
— *of a company*: raison sociale, dénomination d'une société.
cable — : adresse télégraphique.
corporate — : nom social, raison sociale.
[B] — *day (ticket day)*: deuxième jour de liquidation (où l'on donne les noms des acheteurs aux fins de règlement).
fictitious — : nom supposé.
— *of a firm*: raison sociale.
full — : nom et prénoms (en toutes lettres).
maiden — : nom de jeune fille.
registered — *(trade name)*: nom déposé, marque déposée.
the — *of the game*: (fam.) la règle du jeu.
to have a bad — *(in business)*: avoir mauvaise réputation (en affaires).
to go by the — *of*: être connu sous le nom de.
to name: nommer, dénommer, mentionner, accréditer.
the party (the person) **named**: la personne accréditée.
named policy: police (d'assurances) nommée.
named port, ship: port, navire désigné.
naming: attribution, désignation, nomination (f).

narcotic drugs, narcotics: stupéfiants (m pl).
commission on — (s): commission des stupéfiants.
— (s) *Bureau*: (Bureau) section de lutte anti-drogue.

narratio: déclaration, relation (de faits).

narrow: étroit, limité, minutieux (a).
(in) — *circumstances*: dans la gêne.
— *examination*: examen minutieux.
— *majority*: faible majorité.
— *margin*: marge étroite.
— *means*: moyens (financiers) limités.
« *the narrow seas* » : la Manche et la Mer d'Irlande.
to narrow: rétrécir, réduire, restreindre.
to narrow the gap: réduire l'écart, rattraper le retard.
narrowing *fluctuation margins*: [F] rétrécissement des marges de fluctuations.
narrowness: étroitesse (de vues).

natality: natalité (f).
— *tables*: tables de natalité.

nation: nation (f).
créditor — : nation créditrice.
debtor — : nation débitrice.
[J] *(the) law of* —(s): droit international, (le) droit des gens.
most favoured — *clause*: clause de la nation la plus favorisée.

national: a) national, public (a); b) ressortissant (m) (d'un pays).
— *accounting*: comptabilité nationale.
— *advertising*: publicité qui touche tout un pays.
— *assistance*: assistance publique.
— *bank*: banque nationale.
— *claim*: revendications communes à l'échelle nationale.
— *Coal Board*: Charbonnages de Grande-Bretagne.
— *currency*: monnaie nationale.
— *debt*: dette publique.
— *development bonds*: [U.K.] bons (à cinq ans) du développement national.
— *dividend*: dividende (revenu) national.
— *Economic Development Office (N.E.D.O.)*: Institut National de la Statistique et des Etudes Economiques (I.N.S.E.E.) (France).
— *Entreprise Board (N.E.B.)*: [U.K.] Conseil d'Aide aux Entreprises.
— *expenditure*: dépenses publiques.
— *flag*: pavillon national.
— *gouvernement*: [U.S.] gouvernement fédéral.
— *health services*: services de la santé publique.
— *income*: revenu national.

— 513 —

– *insurance* : sécurité sociale.
– *loan* : emprunt national.
(gross, net) – *product* : produit national (brut, net).
– *property* : domaine(s) de l'Etat.
– *Association of Manufactures* : Confédération Nationale des Industriels (britanniques).
– *Bureau of Economic Research* : [U.S.] Bureau national des recherches économiques.
– *Health System* : [U.K.] service national de santé.
– *Research and Development Corporation* : [U.K.] Société Nationale pour la Recherche et le Développement.
– *status* : nationalité, statut national.
– *treatment* : traitement des nationaux accordé aux étrangers.
nationality *(of a ship)* : nationalité (d'un navire).
nationalization *(of an industry...)* : nationalisation (d'une industrie...).
to nationalize : nationaliser, naturaliser (un étranger).
nationalized *(industry, etc.)* : (industrie, etc.) nationalisée.

native : indigène, originaire (m et f).
– *industry* : industrie du pays.
– *labour* : main-d'œuvre indigène.

natural : naturel (a).
– *assets* : richesses naturelles.
– *-born subjects* : sujets (britanniques) de naissance.
– *child* : enfant naturel.
to die a (from) – *death* : mourir de mort naturelle ; (fig.) tomber dans l'oubli, échouer (un projet).
– *heir* : héritier naturel.
– *increase* : accroissement naturel.
– *inheritance (of property)* : transmission héréditaire (de biens).
– *justice* : principes d'impartialité et de loyauté dont doivent s'inspirer tous ceux qui sont appelés à juger des droits d'autrui.
– *law* : droit naturel.
for his (her) – *life* : (condamnation) à vie.
– *obligation* : obligation naturelle.
– *person* : personne au sens ordinaire, personne physique.
– *rate of increase* : taux d'accroissement naturel.
– *resources* : ressources naturelles.
– *rights* : droits fondamentaux, communs à tous les peuples civilisés.
– *wastage* : déperdition, diminution naturelle de la main-d'œuvre, du nombre des salariés (par retraite, vieillesse, décès etc.).

naturalization : naturalisation (f).
certificate of – : décret de naturalisation.
to naturalize : naturaliser.

nature : nature (f), espèce (f), genre (m).
– *of business* : genre d'affaires.
of a private – *(information)* : de caractère privé (renseignement...).

nautical : nautique, naval, marin (a).
– *matters* : questions navales.
– *mile* : mille marin (1 854 m).

naval : naval (a).
– *agreement* : accord, traité naval.
– *law* : droit maritime.
– *port (base)* : base navale, port de guerre.

navigation : navigation (f).
coastal, coasting, coastwise – : cabotage, navigation côtière.
– *dues* : droits de navigation.
inland – : navigation fluviale.
the – *Laws* : le Code maritime.

(the) Navy : (la) marine de guerre.
mercantile, merchant – : marine marchande.
Secretary for the – : [U.S.] Ministre de la Marine.

near : proche, rapproché, exact, chiche (a).
a – *concern* : une affaire qui touche de près.
– *at hand* : à portée de la main.
– *cash ratio (or liquidity ratio)* : coefficient de trésorerie.
– *of kin* : proche parenté.
– *money* : quasi-monnaie.
a – *relation* : un proche parent.
– *position* : [B] le rapproché.
– *silk* : soie artificielle.
nearest *safe port* : port de relèvement.
nearness *of relationship* : proche parenté.

neat cattle : le cheptel bovin.

necessary : nécessaire (a).
[J] *(the)* **necessaries** *of life* : les besoins de chaque jour, les choses nécessaires à la vie, les denrées de première nécessité, la subsistance (pour un enfant en bas âge) ; les fournitures de navire indispensables achetées par le capitaine, et que l'armateur achèterait s'il était à sa place. Le capitaine peut, à cette fin, consentir une hypothèque sur son bâtiment.
to do the – : faire le nécessaire.
– *condition* : condition nécessaire.

necessity : nécessité (f).
case of absolute – : cas de force majeure.
port of – : port de relâche.

« **neddy** » : [U.K.] abréviation de *National Economic Development Council* : Conseil national du développement économique.

need : besoin (m), difficulté (f).
in case of — : en cas de besoin.
to be in — *of, to have* —, *to stand in* — *of* : avoir besoin de, manquer de.
— *(s)* : « besoins » (m pl) (le terme est souvent employé pour décrire les objectifs que des personnes ou des entreprises s'efforcent d'atteindre).

ne exeat regno ([U.S.] **republica**) : « Qu'il ne quitte pas le royaume », [J] interdiction à un débiteur poursuivi en justice de quitter le territoire de la Grande-Bretagne (ou des Etats-Unis).

negative : a) négatif (tive) (a) ; b) négative (f).
— *cash flow* : rentrée de liquidités inférieures aux sorties.
— *evidence* : preuve négative, par la négative.
— *income tax* : impôt négatif sur le revenu (système de subvention versée aux personnes les plus démunies qui, n'étant pas imposables, ne peuvent bénéficier des abattements fiscaux).
— *investment* : désinvestissement.
— *saving, value, etc.* : épargne, valeur négative.
(to answer) in the — : répondre par la négative.

neglect : négligence (f).
to neglect : négliger, délaisser.
[B] **neglected** *stocks* : valeurs négligées, délaissées.
negligence : négligence (f), incurie (f), omission (f) coupable (par opp. à *heedlessness* : inadvertance).
[A] inobservation (f) des règlements.
[J] *action for negligence* : demande de dommages-intérêts.
negligence clause : clause de négligence, négligence-clause.
contributory negligence : imprudence, part de responsabilité de la victime elle-même dans l'accident.
criminal negligence : négligence criminelle, faute grave, de caractère pénal.
gross (wanton) negligence : négligence, faute de nature délictuelle.
ordinary (slight) negligence : négligence simple, faute légère.
negligent : négligent, fautif.
negligent collision : abordage fautif.

negotiable : négociable (a).
[F] — *bill* : effet négociable.
— *instrument* : instrument négociable, valeur négociable.
— *paper* : papier négociable.
— *stocks on the Stock Exchange* : valeurs négociables en Bourse.
not- — : non négociable.
negotiability *(of a bill...)* : négociabilité, commerciabilité (d'un effet).
to negotiate : négocier, trafiquer, traiter.
to negotiate a bill : négocier un billet.
to negotiate a contract : passer un marché.
to negotiate a loan : négocier un emprunt.
to négotiate a treaty : conclure un traité.
negotiation : négociation, tractation, gré à gré.
negotiation of a bill : négociation d'un effet.
matter of negotiation : chose, affaire à débattre.
price a matter of negotiation : prix à débattre.
settlement by negotiation : règlement de gré à gré.
to enter into negotiations : entamer des pourparlers.
negotiator : négociateur (m).

(good-)neighbour (hood) policy : politique de bon voisinage.
neighbouring *country* : pays limitrophe.

nemine contradicente : personne ne contredisant.

nemo tenetur seipsum accusare : personne n'est forcé de s'accuser.

net : net (a), exempt de droits, de frais.
[C] — *amount* : montant net, somme nette.
— *assets*, — *current assets* : actif net.
— *assets* : valeur du moment (d'un effet), produit net.
« *terms strictly* — *cash* » : « payable au comptant », sans déduction.
— *cost* : prix de revient net.
— *income* : revenu net.
— *loss* : perte nette.
— *margin* : couverture nette.
— *out* : à déduire.
operating — : bénéfices nets d'exploitation.
— *premium* : prime nette.
— *present value (worth)* : bénéfice actualisé net.
— *price* : prix net.
— *proceeds (of a transaction...)* : produit net (d'une transaction).
— *receipts* : bénéfices nets, recettes nettes.
— *register tonnage* : (tonnage de) jauge nette.
— *result* : résultat net.
— *sales* : ventes nettes.
— *saving* : épargne nette.
— *surplus* : excédent net.
— *of taxes* : hors taxes.
— *weight* : poids net.
— *working capital* : fonds de roulement net global (actif circulant moins dettes à court terme).
— *worth* : fonds propres, capitaux propres.
— *worth ratio* : coefficient de valeur nette.

NET | NON

— *yield*: rendement net.

netting: compensation (f) monétaire de groupe.

network (of railways, etc.): réseau (m) (de chemins de fer, etc.).
distributing — : réseau de distribution.

neutral (flag, port, etc.): neutre (a) (pavillon, port, etc.).
neutrality: neutralité (f).

never: jamais.
to be on the never-never: (demander à) acheter à tempérament.

new: nouveau, neuf, récent, prochain (a).
— *capital (money)*: capitaux (argent) frais.
— *fashion*: mode nouvelle.
— *for old*: [ASS] maritime ; différence du vieux au neuf.
— *issue*: nouvelle émission de titres.
— *-made*: de facture récente.
— *money*: crédit de restructuration.
— *trial*: nouveau procès, pourvoi en cassation.

news: nouvelle(s), information(s), renseignement.
newsagency: agence d'information.
newsagent: dépositaire de journaux.
broadcast —, *news bulletin*, *newscast*: journal parlé.
— *conference*: conférence de presse.
— *editor*: rédacteur chargé des actualités.
— *film reel*: actualités cinématographiques.
financial — : chronique financière.
—, *press release*: communiqué de presse.
— *-print*: papier journal.
« *shipping* — »: « mouvement des navires ».
newspaper advertisement: annonce de journal.
newspaper cutting: découpure de journal.
newspaper heading: rubrique de journal.
newspaper rate: tarif postal des publications périodiques.
newsroom: salle de rédaction (d'un journal).

next: prochain, suivant (a).
[B] — *account*: liquidation prochaine.
— *-of-kin*: parents les plus proches.
(by) — *mail*, — *post*: (par le) plus prochain courrier.

nicety: précision, subtilité, délicatesse (f).
[J] *legal* — : subtilité juridique.

nickel: [U.S.] pièce de 5 cents.

night: nuit (f).
[J] période entre 21 h et 6 h pendant laquelle il ne peut être procédé à une arrestation, sauf en flagrant délit.
— *shift*: équipe de nuit.

nihil: rien.

nil: nul (a) ; néant (m), zéro (m).
[C] — *balance*: solde nul, balance nulle.
— *business*: affaires nulles.
— *growth*: croissance zéro.
— *profit*: bénéfice nul.

no abatement: [C] prix fixe.

no bid: [B] pas de demande.

no bill: [J] (ordonnance de) non-lieu.

no change: statu quo.

no dealings (in): pas de transactions (sur).

no funds: défaut de provision.

nolens volens: qu'(il) veuille ou non.

nominal: nominal, nominatif (a).
— *accounts*: comptes de résultats (enregistrant les gains et les pertes).
— *authority*: autorité nominale.
— *capital*: capital social.
— *damages*: dommages-intérêt symboliques.
— *exchange*: change nominal.
— *fine*: amende pour la forme.
— *head*: chef de nom seulement.
— *ledger*: grand livre des comptes.
— *partner*: prête-nom, associé fictif.
— *plaintiff*: demandeur qui a cédé son droit à un tiers, le demandeur réel.
— *price*: prix nominal, fictif.
— *rent*: loyer pour la forme, insignifiant, symbolique.
— *roll*: état nominatif.
— *salary (wage)*: salaire nominal.
— *transfer*: transfert gratuit (transfert d'ordre).
— *value*: valeur nominale.
[B] — *market*: marché quasi nul.

to nominate: nommer, désigner.
nomination: nomination, désignation (f).
nominee: personne désignée, candidat choisi.

non *(prefix)*: (préfixe) non-.
— *-ability*: incapacité (f).
— *-acceptance (of a bill)*: non-acceptation (d'un effet).
— *-access*: [J] impossibilité (f) légale de cohabitation entre époux (permettant le désaveu de paternité).
— *-accomplishment*: inaccomplissement (m).
— *-active assets*: valeurs improductives.

— 516 —

— -age : minorité (f) (légale).
— -alignment : neutralité (f).
— -assessment : non-imposition (f).
— -attendance : absence (f).
— -available : indisponible, non disponible.
— business day : jour chômé.
— -claim : défaut de porter plainte dans les délais.
— -committal (answer...) : (réponse...) qui n'engage pas.
— -completion : inachèvement, non-exécution (de contrat).
— -compliance : insoumission (f), refus de se conformer (à un règlement).
— constat : il n'apparaît pas (que).
— -contributory pension scheme : caisse de retraite sans versement de la part des bénéficiaires.
— culpabilis : non coupable.
— -cumulative (dividend) : (dividende) non cumulatif.
— -cupative will : testament non cupatif.
to — -concur : [U.S.] rejeter un amendement.
— -delivery : non-livraison (f).
— -disclosure : réticence (f) (en justice).
— durable goods : biens non durables.
— enforceable : non exécutoire.
— -executive director : administrateur temporaire à titre consultatif.
— existent : inexistant.
— -feasance : [J] délit d'abstention (lorsqu'il y a obligation d'agir).
— -joinder : omission (f) volontaire dans une demande (pour ne pas mettre en cause une personne qui aurait dû être impliquée).
— liability clause : clause de non-responsabilité.
— liquet : il n'est pas clair.
— -listed stock : valeurs non cotées.
— -member : non-membre, invité (à un club).
— -monetary : extra-monétaire, non monétaire.
— -payment : défaut de paiement.
— -performance : inexécution (f).
— -price competition : concurrence basée sur la qualité, non sur le prix de vente.
— -profit (association) : (association) sans but lucratif.
— quotation : absence de cotation.
— -recoverable : irrécupérable.
— -recurring (income) : ressource(s) exceptionnelle(s).
nonsense : absurdité (f).
— sequitur : il ne s'en suit pas.
— -striker : non gréviste.
nonsuit : [J] cessation de poursuites.
to direct a nonsuit : rendre une ordonnance de non-lieu.
to be nonsuited : être déclaré irrecevable dans sa demande.
— -support : [J] non-paiement de pension alimentaire.

— -tax revenue : recettes non fiscales.
— -taxable income : revenu non soumis à l'impôt.
— wasting (assets) : (actif) indéfectible.

no quotation : pas coté.

normal : normal, régulier (a).
— curve : graphique montrant les caractéristiques ordinaires normales d'une population.

no sale : non vente.

not guilty : non coupable.
[J] a) déclaration d'innocence faite par l'accusé ; b) verdict d'acquittement par le jury.

not negociable (cheque) : (chèque) non négociable.

notary public : [J] # notaire (m) (la notion de l'acte notarié n'existe pas en droit A.A.), personne qualifiée pour établir des certifications de signatures, de documents, etc.

notch : encoche (f), marque (f).
to notch : enregistrer.

note : note (f), observation (f), bordereau (m), bulletin (m), billet (m) (de banque, etc.), bon (m) de caisse, emprunt (m), obligation (f).
[D] custom-house — : bordereau de douane.
[C] advice — : lettre d'avis.
commission — : bon de commission.
consignment — : lettre de voiture, récépissé.
— of hand : reconnaissance de dette.
promissory — : billet à ordre.
[F] bank — : billet de banque.
— -broker : [U.S.] courtier de change.
circular — : lettre de crédit circulaire.
credit — : facture de crédit.
currency — : coupure (f).
demand — : feuille de contributions, avertissement, billet à ordre payable à vue.
discount — : bordereau d'escompte.
— of expenses, of fees : note de frais, d'honoraires.
forged (bank) — : billet (de banque) contrefait.
— of protest : note de protestation.
shipping — : permis d'embarquer.
treasury — : bon du Trésor.
to issue bank —(s) : émettre, (mettre en circulation) des billets de banque.
to note : noter, constater, relever.
noted bill of exchange : lettre de change protestée.

« **nothings** » : éléments incorporels.

notice : avis (m), préavis (m), notification (f), intimation (f), avertissement (m), indication (f), convocation (f), information (f), connaissance (f).

[F] — *of assessment (notice to pay)* : avertissement (des Contributions).
loan at — : prêt à terme.
[J] *actual* — : avis exprès.
— *to admit* : invitation à la partie adverse d'admettre un document ou fait important sous peine d'encourir les frais d'établissement de la preuve.
— *of appeal* : intimation d'appel.
— *board* : panneau d'affichage.
— *of sale by auction* : publication de vente aux enchères.
— *of defect* : dénonciation d'un vice de forme.
— *of delivery* : accusé de réception.
— *of distraint* : dénonciation de saisie.
formal — : mise en demeure.
judicial — : fait de notoriété publique.
— *of (general) meeting* : convocation en assemblée (générale).
— *of motion* : assignation en référé.
— *of objection* : avis d'opposition.
— *to pay* : avis d'échéance, intimation de payer.
peremptory — : mise en demeure.
— *to perform* : sommation d'exécuter (contrat).
— *to proceed* : préavis de reprise d'instance.
— *to produce* : sommation à la partie adverse.
public — : avis au public.
— *to quit (to vacate)* : (avis de) congé, intimation de vider les lieux.
— *of receipt* : accusé de réception.
— *of rescission* : notification de rescision.
at short — : à court terme.
— *to terminate* : dénonciation (de contract, de traité...).
— *of withdrawal (withdrawal notice)* : avis de retrait.
written — : avis par écrit.
to give — *(s.o. to do sth.)* : informer, donner avis, aviser (qn de faire qch.).
to give — *(a week) beforehand, to give a (seven days)* — : donner un préavis de (sept jours).
to give — *to an employee* : signifier son congé à un employé.
to give — *to an employer* : donner sa démission.
to receive — *to do sth.* : être mis en demeure de faire qch.
to serve a — *on s.o.* : signifier un arrêt à qqn.
to take — : prendre connaissance.
without further — : sans autre avis.

noticeable : perceptible (a).

notifiable (disease) : [A] (maladie) dont la déclaration est obligatoire.

notification : notification (f).

to notify : notifier, annoncer, signaler.
[A] — *the authorities of a fact* : saisir l'administration d'un fait.
[J] — *the parties* : faire des intimations aux parties.

noting : relevé (m), constatation (f).

notion : idée, conception (f).

notional : fictif (a).

notions : [U.S.] mercerie (f).

notorious : a) connu, reconnu ; b) peu recommandable.
it is — *that...* : il est de notoriété publique que...

(this) notwithstanding : [J] (ce) nonobstant, par dérogation.

novation : [J] novation.

novelty : chose nouvelle, innovation.
[J] nouveauté, élément essentiel pour rendre une invention brevetable.
[C] article de nouveauté.

nude contract : [J] contrat à titre gratuit.

nude ownership : [J] nue-propriété.

nuisance : acte (m) dommageable, dommage (m), désagrément (m).
[J] *attractive* — : source de danger (pour les enfants), qui engage la responsabilité du propriétaire.
private — : atteinte aux droits privés, trouble de jouissance.
public — : atteinte aux droits du public (par ex. : à la libre circulation).
to have a — *value* : servir à gêner autrui.

null and void : [J] nul et non avenu.

nulla bona : pas de biens.

nullification : [U.S.] déclaration de nullité.

to nullify : rendre nul, annuler.

nullity : nullité (f).
[J] — *of marriage* : nullité de mariage.

number : nombre (m), quantité (f), chiffre (m), numéro (m).
aggregate — : nombre total.
call — : numéro d'appel (téléphone).
code — : numéro de la déclaration (en douane).
(price) index — *(s)* : indice(s) (des prix).

manufacturing — (serial number) : numéro de série.
— *plate* : plaque d'immatriculation d'une automobile.
reference — : numéro de référence.
social security — : numéro de sécurité sociale.
telephone — : numéro de téléphone.
voucher — *(s)* : numéros des pièces justificatives.
weighted index- — *(s)* : indices pondérés.
winning — : numéro gagnant.
wrong — : faux numéro.
to number : numéroter, chiffrer.
numbered *account* : compte enregistré sous un numéro confidentiel (ex. en Suisse).
numbering : numérotage, dénombrement.
numeral, numerical : numéral, numérique.

to nurse : nourrir, soigner.
— *an account* : soigner un compte.
— *a business* : nourrir une affaire.

nursing staff : personnel hospitalier (infirmières).

nutritional standards : normes alimentaires.

nuts and bolts : (fam.) tous les détails pratiques.

NYMEX *(New York Mercantile Exchange)* : Marché à terme de produits pétroliers (et de platine), New York.

N.Y.S.E. *(New York Stock Exchange)* : Bourse de New York.

NOTES

O

oath: serment (m).
[J] — *of allegiance*: serment de fidélité, d'allégeance.
assertory — : serment affirmatif, assertoire.
false — : faux serment, parjure.
guarantee (guaranty) given (up) on — : caution juratoire.
legal — : serment judiciaire.
promissory — : serment promissoire.
by — : par serment.
to be bound by — : être lié par serment.
on — *(witness)*: (témoignage) sous la foi du serment, témoin assermenté.
under — : sous serment.
under the — *of secrecy*: sous le sceau du serment.
to administer the — *to s.o.*: déférer le serment à qn.
to break one's — : violer son serment, se parjurer.
to put s.o. on his — : faire prêter serment à qn.
to release s.o. from an — : délier qn d'un serment.
to take an — : prêter serment.
taking of an — : prestation de serment.
to tender the — *to s.o.*: faire prêter serment à qn.

O.A.U. *(Organisation of African Unity)*: (pol.) Organisation de l'Unité Africaine (O.U.A.).

(to enforce) obedience of the law: faire respecter la loi.

to obey a summons: répondre à une assignation.

obiter dictum: opinion d'un juge sur un point qui n'a pas de rapport direct avec l'affaire qui lui est soumise.

object: objet, but, objectif (m).
(the) — *of the company*: (l') objet social, (le) but de la société.
the — *(s) for which company is established*: le but que s'est assigné la société à sa fondation.
— *(s) of expenditure*: chefs de dépenses.
[J] **to object** *(to)*: objecter, élever des objections, récuser (un témoin).
objection: objection, opposition, réclamation, recours.
« *objection overruled* »: « objection rejetée ».
« *objection sustained* »: « objection admise ».
conscientious objection: objection de conscience.
objection (to a witness, an arbitrator): récusation (d'un témoin, d'un arbitre).
[B] *objection to mark*: opposition à la cote.

objectionable: répréhensible (a).

objective: objectif, but (m), objectif (a).
the — *(s) of a policy*: les objectifs d'une politique.
National Economic **Objectives**: (U.K.) Objectifs Economiques Nationaux (que le gouvernement fixe à la nation).
— *test*: test objectif (une seule réponse exacte par question).

(conscientious) objector: objecteur de conscience.

to obligate: lier, obliger à.
— *s.o. to do sth.*: imposer à qn l'obligation de faire qch.

obligation: obligation (f), dette (f), devoir (m).
[J] lien entre deux ou plusieurs individus leur imposant les devoirs légalement déterminés.
contractual — : engagement contractuel.
imperfect — *(natural, moral)*: obligation morale.
perfect — : obligation légale.
to be under an — *(to do...)*: être dans l'obligation (de faire...).
to implement an — : s'acquitter d'une obligation.
to lay (put) s.o. under an — *(to do)*: obliger qn (à faire).
to meet one's — *(s)*: honorer, faire honneur à ses engagements.
without — *(on the part of...)*: sans engagement (de la part de...).
obligatory: obligatoire.
obligee: obligataire, créancier (m).
obligor: obligé, débiteur (m).

oblique ways: moyens détournés.

to obliterate, obliteration (of marks): oblitérer, effacements (de marques).

obscene publication: publication pornographique.

observance of the law: respect de la loi.
[J] **to observe** *(a clause in a contract, the law, etc.)*: observer, respecter une clause dans un contrat, la loi etc.

obsolescence: désuétude (f), vieillissement (m), obsolescence (f).
[C] amortissement (m) industriel.
– *of plant*: obsolescence de l'équipement.
– *replacement*: investissement de modernisation, de rationalisation de la productivité.
obsolescent: obsolescent, désuet, caduc, hors d'usage.
[J] **obsolete** *(law, rule)*: désuet, tombé en désuétude (règlement, loi).

obstinate desertion: [J] [U.S.] abandon de domicile conjugal sans esprit de retour.

to obstruct: encombrer, gêner, entraver.
[J] – *a bill*: faire de l'obstruction (parlementaire).
– *process*: empêcher un huissier d'accomplir les devoirs de sa charge.
– *the traffic*: entraver la circulation.

obstruction of the highway: entrave (f) à la circulation.

to obtain: obtenir, avoir cours, être de règle.
– *credit*: obtenir du crédit.
– *security*: prendre des sûretés.
the practice now **obtaining**: l'usage actuellement de règle.

to obviate a difficulty: obvier à une difficulté.

obvious (mistake): (erreur) évidente.

occasion, occasional: occasion, occasionnel.
as – requires: à telles fins que de raison.
to go about one's lawful –(s): vaquer à ses affaires dans le cadre de la loi.
occasional *charges*: faux frais.

occupancy: occupation (f) (des lieux).
[J] a) prise de possession de chose sans maître ; b) droit de premier occupant.
[F] – *tax*: taxe d'habitation.

occupant: occupant (m), locataire (m), titulaire (m) (d'un poste).
[J] *beneficial –*: usufruitier.

occupation: occupation (f), profession (f), possession (f) effective (de terres).
out of –: oisif, en chômage.

occupational: professionnel (a).
– *accident*: accident du travail.
– *disease*: maladie professionnelle.
– *guidance*: orientation professionnelle.
– *hazards*: risques du métier.

occupier: occupant (m).
to occupy *(a situation)*: occuper, tenir un emploi.
occupied *population*: population active.

to occur: se produire, avoir lieu, arriver.

(should the case) occur: le cas échéant.

occurrence: événement (m), occurrence (f).
of frequent –: qui se produit fréquemment.

ocean carrying trade: grande navigation.

ocean freight: fret au long cours.

odd: impair, dépareillé, bizarre (a).
to do – jobs: bricoler.
[C] *to make up the odd money*: faire l'appoint.
– *lot*: solde, (B) quantité de valeurs (actions, etc.) ne correspondant pas à l'unité habituelle.
– *size*: dimension non courante, non conforme à la norme.
oddments: fins de série.

O.E.C.D. *(Organisation for Economic Cooperation Development)*: Organisation pour la Coopération et le Développement Economique (O.C.D.E.).

of course: évident.
[J] de plein droit. Se dit d'un acte de procédure qu'il n'est pas du pouvoir du tribunal d'interdire à condition que les formes soient respectées.

off: (au) loin, séparé, écarté, à déduire.
[B] *to be –*: être en baisse.
the deal is –: l'affaire est manquée, ne se fera pas.
– *the books*: « au noir », non déclaré (revenu).
– *day*: jour de liberté.
– *-the-job training*: formation professionnelle externe.
– *licence*: licence permettant seulement la vente des boissons (alcooliques) à emporter.
– *-peak hours*: heures creuses.
– *-peak tariff*: tarif de nuit.
– *prime*: au-dessous du taux d'intérêt préférentiel sur découvert en banque (prime rate).
– *the record*: officieusement (adv.).

— *season* : morte-saison.
— *-shore* : au large, en mer ; en provenance d'un pays étranger ; dans un pays étranger ; extraterritorial.
— *-shore Banking Unit (O.B.U.)* : Unité bancaire opérant outre-mer.
— *-shore company* : société n'ayant pas d'activité dans l'État du siège social.
— *-shore oil field* : gisement pétrolier sousmarin.
to be well — : être à l'aise (financièrement).
to be well — *for hands* : trouver facilement de la main-d'œuvre.

offence : offense (f), agression (f), faute (f), toute violation de la loi, crime ou délit, acte délictueux.
[J] *capital* — : crime capital.
cognizable — : délit qui tombe sous le coup de la loi.
continuing — : délit à l'état permanent.
indecence — : attentat aux mœurs.
indictable — : acte délictueux, crime ou délit.
minor, petty — : contravention.
perpetrated — : délit consommé.
second — : récidive.
serious — : faute grave.
the specific — : les faits en cause.
technical — : quasi-délit.
unnatural — : crime contre nature.
to commit an — : se rendre coupable d'une infraction.
to note an — : dresser une contravention.
— *triable either way* : infraction (f) au choix, procédure simplifiée devant la "Magistrate Court" ou procès devant la "Crown Court" avec jury (# correctionnalisation des crimes).

offender : contrevenant (m), délinquant (m), criminel (m).
[J] *abnormal* — : délinquant anormal.
first — : délinquant primaire.
habitual — : délinquant d'habitude, récidiviste.
hardened — *(old* —*)* : repris de justice, récidiviste.
joint — : complice.
juvenile (young) — : mineur délinquant (pl. enfance délinquante).
major — : auteur principal (du délit).
mentally defective — : délinquant atteint de déficience mentale.
partially responsible — : délinquant à responsabilité atténuée.
persistent — : multi-récidiviste.
primary — : délinquant primaire.
psychopatic — : délinquant psychopathe.
second — : récidiviste.
third — : récidiviste pour la deuxième fois.

offer : offre (f), proposition (f).
(firm, liberal etc.) — : offre (ferme, généreuse etc.).
[B] *tender* — : offre publique d'achat (ou d'échange).
tentative — : première offre (au début des négociations).
to close with an — : accepter une offre.
to make an — *(for sth.)* : faire une offre (pour qch.).
to offer : offrir, proposer, présenter.
to offer a document in evidence : fournir une preuve littérale.
to offer (goods) for sale : mettre en vente, offrir en vente (des marchandises).
to offer a plea : exciper d'une excuse.
to offer a thing at so much (to offer so much for a thing) : proposer tant pour un objet, faire un objet à tant.
prices **offered** : cours offerts (vendeurs).
offerer : offrant (n).
[B] **offering** : nouvelle émission.

office : office (m), fonctions (f pl), charge (f), bureau (m), ministère (m), siège (m) d'une administration, caisse (f), recette (f).
[A] *the directors in* — : les administrateurs en fonctions, en exercice.
— *-holder* : [U.S.] fonctionnaire.
public — *(s)* : administrations publiques.
to be in —, *to hold* — : (tenir) remplir un emploi, être au pouvoir.
to come into —, *to take* — : entrer en fonctions.
to leave — : se démettre de ses fonctions.
branch —, *sub-* — : succursale (f).
cash — : caisse (f).
— *-clerk* : employé de bureau.
— *of collector of customs* : recette des douanes.
complaints — : bureau des réclamations.
— *-copy* : expédition, copie légalisée.
district — : bureau régional.
exchange — : bureau de change.
— *expenses* : frais de bureau.
— *of Fair Trading* : see « Fair Trading Act ».
head — : siège central d'une société, siège social.
head post — : bureau central des postes.
inquiry — : bureau de renseignements.
— *of issue* : bureau d'émission.
— *manager* : chef d'un bureau.
— *of origin* : bureau d'origine.
pay- — : guichet (m), caisse (f).
paying- —, — *of payment* : bureau payeur.
— *of profit under the Crown* : poste ministériel incompatible avec la qualité de député.
registered — : siège social.
registry- — : bureau d'enregistrement, greffe, bureau de l'état-civil.
— *requisites* : fournitures de bureau.
revenue — : recette des impôts.
— *staff* : personnel de bureau.

tourist — : bureau de tourisme, syndicat d'initiative.
— *work* : travail de bureau.
Foreign —, *Home* — : Ministère des Affaires Etrangères, de l'Intérieur.

Officer : officier (m), fonctionnaire (m).
[C] — (s) *of a company (of a meeting)* : membres du bureau d'une société (d'une assemblée).
[A] *customs* — (— *of customs*) : douanier.
excise — : receveur des contributions indirectes.
health — *(medical officer)* : médecin sanitaire.
judicial — (— *of the law*) : fonctionnaire de l'ordre judiciaire.
police — : gardien de la paix.
public — : fonctionnaire.
rating — : répartiteur des contributions (directes).
tax — (— *of taxes*) : agent des contributions directes.
the — (s) *and crew* : les officiers et l'équipage.

official : a) officiel, d'office (a) ; b) fonctionnaire (m).
— *act* : acte officiel.
— *announcement (information)* : avis officiel.
— *appraisal, appraiser* : expertise, expert.
in (his) — *capacity* : ès-qualités.
— *document* : document officiel.
— *holding* : avoirs d'une institution publique.
— *letter* : pli officiel.
— *list (of quotations)* : cote officielle.
— *market* : marché officiel, parquet.
— *misconduct* : [U.S.] faute commise dans l'exercice de la fonction publique, forfaiture.
— *quotation* : cours officiel (authentique).
— *rate* : taux officiel d'escompte.
— *receiver* : administrateur (liquidateur) judiciaire.
— *statute of a company* : statuts officiels d'une société.
— *seal* : cachet réglementaire.
from an — *source* : de source officielle.
diplomatic and consular officials : fonctionnaires diplomatiques et consulaires.
high — : haut fonctionnaire.
officially : officiellement, d'office.

offset : contre-partie (f), dédommagement (m).
[C] compensation (f) (d'une écriture).
as an — *to the expenses we incurred* : en compensation des dépenses que nous avons encourues.
to offset : compenser, rattraper, faire contrepoids.
[F] **offsetting** : compensation (f), changement (m) de cap dans les opérations (f pl) du marché (ex. acheter au lieu de vendre).
offsetting assets and liabilities : compensation des créances et des dettes.
offsetting gains and losses : imputation des moins values sur les plus values.

offshore : see « off-shore ».

offspring : descendance (f).

oil : huile (f), pétrole (m).
— *company* : société pétrolière.
— *deposit*, — *field* : gisement pétrolifère.
— *distillery* : raffinerie de pétrole.
— *market* : [B] marché des pétrolifères.
— *port* : port pétrolier.
— *shares (oils)* : valeurs pétrolières (pétrolifères).
— *ship*, — *tanker* : pétrolier.
— *slick* : nappe de pétrole polluante (en mer).
— *trust* : trust de pétrole.
— *well* : puits de pétrole.
to strike — : trouver du pétrole (au cours d'un forage).

old : vieux, ancien (a).
— *age* : vieillesse (f).
[ASS] — *-age insurance, pension* : assurance vieillesse, pension vieillesse.
— *-age pension fund, security fund* : caisse des retraites, d'assurance vieillesse.
[C] — *balance* : solde ancien.
— *established (firm)* : (maison) établie depuis longtemps.
— *fashioned* : démodé, à l'ancienne mode.
— *shares* : actions anciennes.
debt of — *standing (old standing debt)* : dette ancienne.
firm of — *standing* : maison ancienne et de bonne réputation.
[F] « *the* — *four* » : « les quatre vieilles » (impositions).

oligopoly : oligopole (m).
oligopolistic *markets* : marchés oligopolistiques.

oligopsony : marché (m) dans lequel un petit nombre d'acheteurs achètent de grosses quantités d'un produit et peuvent ainsi influencer les prix (oligopsone).

ombudsman : (pol.) Médiateur (m) (chargé d'examiner les conflits entre les citoyens et les administrations et d'en faire rapport).

omission to discharge a legal duty : négligence à s'acquitter d'un devoir imposé par la loi.
errors and — (s) *excepted* : sauf erreurs ou omissions.

omnibus bill : projet de loi touchant des mesures d'ensemble.

omnium investment company: [F] omnium de valeurs.

on-costs (oncosts): [C] frais (généraux) indirects s'ajoutant aux « coûts directs » de production.

on-the-job training: formation (f) professionnelle interne.

to on-lend: re-prêter.

one-man business: entreprise (f) individuelle.

one-month stagger rule: [F] (règle du) décalage d'un mois (taxe à la valeur ajoutée).

one-off: exceptionnel (a).
— *arrangement*: disposition (f), mesure (f) exceptionnelle (ex. une société verse des indemnités exceptionnelles à des employés qu'elle a dû licencier, dans une région où le chômage est très élevé).

one-shot investment: investissement (m) ponctuel.

onerous contract: [J] contrat à titre onéreux.
— *title*: titre onéreux.

onus of proof: [J] charge de la preuve.

onus probandi: la charge de la preuve.

O.P.E.C. (*Organisation of Petrol Exporting Countries*): Organisation des Pays exportateurs de Pétrole (O.P.E.P.).

open: ouvert, public, libre, accessible (a).
[C] [F] — *account*: compte courant.
in — *assembly*: en séance publique.
— *bids*: [U.S.] marchés publics.
— *cheque*: chèque non barré.
— *contract*: contrat de vente contenant uniquement les noms des parties, la spécification des biens et le prix.
— *credit*: crédit à découvert.
— *discount market*: marché de l'escompte hors banque.
— *door policy*: politique de la porte ouverte.
— *-end investment trusts*: sociétés d'investissement à capital variable.
— *or well-known personal expenses*: dépenses personnelles ostensibles ou notoires.
— *market*: marché ouvert, libre.
— *market discount rate*: taux (d'escompte) hors banque.
— *market operations*: opérations sur le marché monétaire libre.
— *market policy*: politique d'intervention sur le marché monétaire par achat et vente de titres.
— *policy*: police (d'assurances) flottante, ouverte.
— *port*: port libre.
— *shop (contrary of closed shop)*: entreprise employant des ouvriers syndiqués et non syndiqués.
[J] — *court*: tribunal siégeant en audience publique.
in — *court*: au cours des débats, en plein tribunal.
open trial: jugement public.
to open: ouvrir.
to open an account: ouvrir un compte.
to open the case: exposer les faits de la cause.
to open a credit: ouvrir un credit.
to open a default: autoriser à purger le défaut.
to open the door: donner à l'adversaire l'occasion de faire quelque chose qu'autrement il n'aurait pas été autorisé à faire.
to open a, judgment: accorder la révision d'un jugement de première instance.
to open up a country to trade: ouvrir un pays au commerce.
to open up negotiations: ouvrir des négociations.

opening: ouverture (f).
[J] *the* — *of the courts*: la rentrée des tribunaux.
the — *of the case*: l'exposé des faits.
— *of an enquiry*: ouverture d'une enquête.
[C] — *balance sheet*: bilan d'entrée.
— *capital*: capital d'apport.
— *prices, quotations*: cours d'ouverture.
— *stocks*: stocks reportés.
— *(s) for employment*: débouchés (emplois).

to operate: opérer, fonctionner, gérer, exploiter.
[C] — *for a fall, for a rise*: opérer à la baisse, à la hausse.
— *an air-line system, a business*: exploiter un réseau aérien, une entreprise commerciale.

operating capital: fonds d'exploitation.
[c] — *budget*: budget d'exploitation.
— *costs (expenses, expenditure)*: frais d'exploitation, d'utilisation de l'équipement.
— *deficit*: déficit d'exercice.
— *expenses*: dépenses de fonctionnement.
— *income*: revenu d'exploitation.
— *profits (losses)*: bénéfices (pertes) d'exploitation.
— *staff*: personnel d'exploitation, « sur le tas ».
— *statement*: compte d'exploitation.

operation : exploitation (f), opération (f), fonctionnement (m).
[J] — *of law* : application, effet d'une loi.
[C] [F] *banking, financial* — : opération de banque, financière.
input, output — *(s)* : opérations d'entrée et de sortie.
— *and maintenance expenses* : dépenses de fonctionnement et d'entretien.
— *research (O.R.)* : étude scientifique des problèmes liés à l'exploitation, recherche opérationnelle interdisciplinaire.
to come into — : entrer en vigueur.
operational : opérationnel, d'exploitation.
operational methods : méthodes d'exploitation, de travail.
operational plannings : see « corporate planning ».

operative : a) effectif, efficace (a) ;
the — *phrase is "well-informed"* : pour être efficace, il faut être bien renseigné.
b) [U.S.] ouvrier (m), artisan (m).
— *facts* : état de fait.
— *part, words* : clauses essentielles d'un acte, dispositif.
the — *class* : la classe ouvrière.

operator : opérateur (m), spéculateur (m), joueur (m) (à la Bourse), exploitant (m).
— *for a fall, for a rise* : opérateur à la baisse, à la hausse, spéculateur.

ophelimity : ophélimité (terme suggéré par Pareto pour éviter des confusions sur le concept d'« utilité » : *utility*).

opinion : opinion (f), avis (m), consultation (f) (juridique).
biased — : opinion préconçue.
[J] *concurring* — : avis d'un ou de plusieurs juges qui se rallient à la sentence, tout en s'inspirant de motifs différents de ceux de la majorité.
counsel's — : avis motivé.
deliberate — : opinion réfléchie.
dissenting — : avis de la minorité.
expert's — : avis d'expert.
in expert's —, *in the* — *(s) of experts* : à dire d'expert, d'experts.
public — : l'opinion publique.
to be of — *that* : estimer que, être d'avis que.
to form an — *of...* : se faire une idée, une opinion sur, de...
to take counsel's — : consulter un homme de loi.
(EEC) — *on the proposal for a Council regulation* : (C.E.E.) avis sur une proposition de règlement du Conseil.
— -*shopping* : chalandage (m) d'opinion.

opportunity : occasion (f) (favorable), possibilités (f pl), faculté (f).
[F] — *cost* : coût d'opportunité, coût d'option optimale (rapprochée).
— *curve* : courbe d'opportunité, courbe d'option optimale.
job **opportunities** : possibilités de trouver des emplois.
(to have) full — *to...* : avoir pleine liberté, toute faculté pour...
productive opportunities : possibilités de production.

to oppose : s'opposer à.
[J] — *an action, a marriage* : mettre opposition à un acte, à un mariage.
— *a motion* : demander le rejet d'une requête.
the **opposing** *counsel* : l'avocat de la partie adverse.
the opposing party : la partie adverse.

opposite : opposé, vis-à-vis (a et adv.).

opposition : le camp adverse, les concurrents (m pl).
[J] opposition (f).
opposition proceedings : procédure d'opposition.
— *to judgment* : opposition à un jugement.
to start up (business) in — *to s.o.* : se lancer (dans une affaire) en concurrence avec qn.
the — *spokesman* : (pol.) le porte-parole de l'opposition.
(C) *to start up (a shop) in* — *to s.o.* : ouvrir un magasin en concurrence (avec qqn).

oppression : oppression (f), tyrannie (f), abus (m) d'autorité.

option : faculté (f), option (f), droit de souscription.
[B] — *bargain* : marché à prime, marché libre.
buy — : option d'achat.
— *dealings* : opérations à prime.
— *money* : montant de la prime.
— *price* : cours, base de la prime.
— *of purchase* : faculté de rachat, de réméré.
sell — : option de vente.
— *stock, stock in* — : valeurs à prime.
to exercise one's right of — : exercer son droit d'option.

to ordain that... : statuer que...

order : ordre (m), rang (m), suite (f), commande (f), ordonnance (f), arrêté (m), décret (m), mandat (m) ; pl. *orders* : instructions (f pl).
[J] *administrative* — : gestion ordonnée par le tribunal.

amnesty – : décret d'amnistie.
breach of – : infraction au règlement.
charging – : ordonnance de saisie-exécution.
– *of the court*: injonction.
departmental – : arrêté ministériel.
deportation – : arrêté d'expulsion.
formal – : injonction.
general – : arrêt (administration).
– *in council*: décret-loi, décret présidentiel.
judge's – : ordonnance.
– *for payment (to pay)*: ordonnance de paiement.
police – : arrêté de police.
provisional – ; ordonnance en référé.
traffic – : règlement de circulation.
– *to view a house*: permis de visiter une maison.
by – *of*: sur ordre de.
by – *of the court*: par autorité de justice.
[C] – *book*: carnet, livre de commandes, d'ordres.
– *cheque (cheque to* –*)*: chèque à ordre.
delivery – : ordre de livraison.
– *form*: bulletin de commande.
– *information*: condition de vente.
limit – : ordre d'achat ou de vente au prix fixé maximum.
(foreign, international) money – : mandat-poste (sur l'étranger, international).
– *number*: numéro de commande.
selling – : ordre de vente.
– *sheet*: feuille (bulletin) de commande.
standing –*(s)*: ordres permanents, règlements.
to call for –*(s)*: passer prendre des commandes.
to give an – *(to s.o.)*: a) commander qch (à qn); b) passer une commande à qn.
« *pay to the* – *of...* » : « payez à l'ordre de... ».
to place an – *with s.o.*: passer une commande à qn.
to put goods on – : mettre des marchandises en commande.
to withdraw an – : révoquer un ordre, annuler une commande.
to order: ordonner, commander, commissionner.
to order an enquiry: ordonner une enquête.
to be **ordered** *to pay costs*: être condamné aux frais (aux dépens).

order-call ratio: (C) rapport du nombre de visites d'un représentant sur le nombre de commandes.

ordinance: ordonnance (f), décret (m), règlement (m).
municipal (city) – : [U.S.] arrêté municipal.

ordinary: ordinaire (a).
[J] – *courts*: juridictions ordinaires.
– *judge*: juge titulaire.
[C] – *bill*: papier commercial.
– *creditor*: créance ordinaire, chirographaire.
– *general meeting*: assemblée générale ordinaire.
– *rate*: tarif ordinaire, normal.
– *repairs*: réparations courantes.
[B] *ordinary shares, stock,* **ordinaries** *actions*: actions ordinaires.
– *average*: avaries simples.
– *skill*: compétence professionnelle normale.
out of the – : exceptionnel.

(official) organ: organe (m) (officiel).

organic law: loi organique, [U.S.] constitution (f).

organization: organisation (f), institution (f), système (m).
charity (non-profit) – : institution charitable (sans but lucratif).
– *chart*: organigramme (m).
– *costs (expenses)*: frais de premier établissement.
food and agriculture – *(F.A.O.)*: Organisation pour l'Alimentation et l'Agriculture.
International Civil Aviation – : Organisation de l'Aviation Civile Internationale.
Monetary – : Système monétaire.
U.N.E.S.C.O. (United Nations Educational, Scientific and Cultural –*)*: Organisation des Nations Unies pour l'Education, la Science et la Culture.
– *and Methods (O.M.)*: organisation et méthodes.
profit-oriented – : entreprise à but lucratif.
organisational *structure*: organisation structurale.

to organize: organiser.
– *a corporation*: fonder une société.
organized *labour*: les syndicats ouvriers, les organisations ouvrières.
organizer: organisateur (m).

origin: origine (f).
[A] *certificate of* – : certificat d'origine.
country of – : pays d'origine, de provenance.
of foreign – *(goods)*: d'origine étrangère (marchandises).

original: 1° original, originaire, initial, primitif (a) ; 2° l'original (m).
– *acquisition*: droits acquis à l'origine.
– *bill*: a) [J] acte introductif d'instance (dans un procès) ; b) [C] [F] première d'une traite.
– *capital*: capital primitif.
– *cost*: frais d'achat, coût initial.
– *document*: a) [J] primordial ; b) [C] pièce comptable.
– *entry*: écriture originale.

— *invoice* : facture originale.
— *jurisdiction* : juridiction de première instance.
— *subscriber* : souscripteur primitif.
— *value* : valeur initiale.
— *writ* : acte introductif d'instance (en droit coutumier).
the — *idea (of a scheme)* : l'idée première, mère (d'un projet).

to originate : donner naissance à, tirer son origine de.
— *an industry, a project* : être le promoteur d'une industrie, à l'origine d'un projet.

origination : origine (f), création (f).
— *fee* : commission versée d'avance.

orphan : orphelin (m).

ostentations expenditures : consommations ostentatoires.

otherwise : autrement, par ailleurs.
except as — *provided* : sauf dispositions contraires.

ounce : once (f) (28, 35 g).

to oust : évincer.
[C] — *from the market* : éliminer du marché.
ouster : éviction illicite.

out (of date), out (of fashion) : périmé, désuet, démodé.
— *of pocket expenses* : débours (m).
— *of use* : hors d'usage.
— *of work* : en chômage.

to outbid : surenchérir, faire surenchère.
outbidder : enchérisseur (m).

outcome : résultat (m), issue (f).

outdoor staff : (personnel du) service actif.

outer barrister : [J] avocat qui n'est admis à plaider que « derrière la barre ».

outer harbour : avant-port (m).

outfit : équipement (m) ; (fam.) entreprise (f).

outflow (of capital, of gold) : sortie (f) (de capitaux, d'or).
capital — : fuite des capitaux.

outgoing : de (au) départ, de départ.
— *inventory* : inventaire de sortie (quand on quitte un logement).
— *mail* : courrier au départ.
— *ministry* : ministère démissionnaire.

[F] — *gold-point (specie point)* : point de sortie de l'or.
— *V.A.T.* : hors T.V.A.
— *(s)* : débours (m).

to outlaw : proscrire, [U.S.] prohiber.
[J] — *a claim* : refuser le droit d'action sur une créance.
— *cooperation (of-with)* : interdire les ententes (entre).

outlay : débours (m), frais (m), dépenses (f pl).
capital, first, initial — : frais de premier établissement, première mise de fonds.
wage — *(s)* : coûts de la main-d'œuvre.

outlet : sortie (f), débouché (m).
[C] — *(for trade)* : débouché (pour le commerce).

outline : contour (m), esquisse (f), grandes lignes (f pl).
broad, general, main — *(s) of a scheme* : grandes lignes d'un projet.
— *law* : loi-cadre.
[F] credit **outlining** : encadrement du crédit.

outlook : perspective(s) (f).

outlying : éloigné, isolé (a).

to outpace : gagner de vitesse, aller plus vite que, l'emporter sur.
prices have **outpaced** wages : les prix ont progressé plus vite que les salaires.

output : production (f), rendement (m).
aggregate — : production globale.
average — : production moyenne.
— *bonus* : prime de rendement.
capacity of — : capacité productive.
— *per hour, per week* : rendement à l'heure, à la semaine.
(input) - — *flows* : flux entrants et sortants (d'entrée-sortie).
scale of — : échelle de (la) production.
— *of the staff* : rendement du personnel.
to curtail the — : contingenter la production.

outright : pur et simple, à forfait.
[C] — *purchase, sale* : achat, vente à forfait, au comptant, sans réserve, ferme.

to outsell (s.o.) : vendre plus (que qqn).

outside : extérieur (m).
— *broker* : courtier marron.
— *market* : marché hors cote, coulisse.
— *prices* : prix maximum.
— *transactions* : transactions coulissières.
— *worker* : travailleur à domicile.

outstanding: a) saillant, marquant, éminent ; b) impayé, échu, en retard, en souffrance ; c) en circulation.
[J] — *legal estate*: titre de propriété d'un bien dont l'hypothèque a été remboursée mais dont la translation à l'ex-débiteur n'a pas encore été effectuée.
[C] [F] — *account*: compte en souffrance.
— *claim*: réclamation en instance.
— *coupons*: coupons en souffrance, arrérages.
— *debts*: dettes exigibles, créances à recouvrer.
— *expenses*: frais restant à payer.
— *interest*: intérêts échus.
— *matter*: affaire arriérée.
— *payment*: paiement arriéré.
— *premiums*: primes (d'assurance) échues.
— *securities, shares, stock*: actions émises, actions en circulation.

to outstrip: devancer, surpasser.

outward: extérieur, de sortie, d'aller.
— *bound (ship)*: (navire) en partance.
— *bill of lading*: connaissement de sortie.
— *dividends*: paiement de dividendes à la société mère.
— *journey, voyage*: voyage aller.
— *trade*: commerce extérieur d'exportation.

over: sur, dessus (prep.), par-dessus, en excès, par-delà.
overactivity: suractivité (f).
overassessment: trop perçu (impôt), surtaux (m), imposition (f) excessive.
overbid: suroffre (f).
overcapitalized: surcapitalisé.
overconsumption: surconsommation.
— *the counter*: hors bourse, hors cote, en coulisse, sur le marché libre.
overdevelopment: surdéveloppement (m).
overestimate: surestimation (f).
gift — : donation ou legs substitués.
— *-insurance*: assurance pour une somme excédant la valeur de la chose assurée.
— *-issue*: surémission (f).
judgment — : jugement commun.
left- — *(s)*: surplus, invendus, restes (m pl)
liability — : responsabilité civile.
shorts and — *(s)*: déficits et excédents.
overstaffed (firm): (entreprise) qui occupe de la main-d'œuvre en excès.
cash shorts and — : déficits et excédents de caisse.
(difference) — *or under*: différence en plus ou en moins.

over-all (overall): général, d'ensemble, total (a).
— *consumption*: consommation totale.
— *demand*: demande globale.
— *expenses*: dépenses globales, total des dépenses.
— *rate of return*: taux interne de rentabilité intégré.
— *settlement*: règlement général.

overbalance (of exports): [E] excédent (m) (des exportations).

to overbook: réserver en trop grand nombre.

to overcapitalize: investir au-delà de (ses) besoins.
overcapitalization: surcapitalisation.

overcharge: surcharge (f), prix (m) surfait, excessif, majoration (f) excessive (d'impôt).
fraudulent — : extorsion (f), duperie (f).
to overcharge *for, in*: surfaire, faire trop payer.
to overcharge in an invoice: majorer une facture.
to overcharge for goods: surfaire des marchandises.

overcost: surcoût (m).

overdraft: découvert (m), facilités (f pl) de caisse.
[F] *bank* — : avance (f) bancaire.
insecured — : découvert en blanc, sur notoriété.

to overdraw: mettre à découvert.
[F] — *an account*: mettre un compte à découvert.
overdrawn *account*: compte à découvert.

overdue: arriéré, échu, en souffrance, en retard.
[C] [F] — *bill*: effet échu, impayé.
interests on — *payments*: intérêts moratoires.
long — *measures*: (mesures) qui auraient dû être prises depuis longtemps.

overflow: surabondance (f).
— *meeting*: réunion supplémentaire.

overfull employment: suremploi (m).

to overhaul: examiner, amender.
overhaul *(of a social security scheme)*: refonte (d'un système de sécurité sociale).

overheads ; overhead charges, costs, expenses: frais généraux, frais fixes, faux frais.
manufacturing — : frais de fabrication.
— *absorption*: ventilation (f) des frais généraux.
— *allocation (allocation of overheads)*: répar-

tition des frais généraux.
— *expenses*: frais généraux.
fixed — *(s)*: frais (généraux) fixes.
— *price*: prix forfaitaire.
to divide the — : ventiler les frais généraux.
[F] *social* — *capital*: équipements collectifs.

overheating: surchauffe (f).

overland journey, travel: voyage par terre.

to overlap: chevaucher, faire double emploi.
overlapping: double emploi.
overlapping benefits: cumul de prestations.

to overload: surcharger (sens propre et sens figuré).
[C] **overloaded** *market*: marché alourdi.

overmanning: employer un personnel trop nombreux.

overnight carriers: messageries (f pl) qui acheminent les envois en 24 heures, messageries rapides.

to overpay: trop payer.
overpayment: trop perçu (m), surpaye (f).

overplus: excédent (m) de caisse.

overproduction: surproduction (f).

to overrate: surestimer, surévaluer.
[F] surtaxer.

to override: outrepasser, passer outre.
[J] — *a veto*: passer outre à un veto.
overriding *clause*: clause dérogatoire.
overriding commission: escompte (m) supérieur à la normale, commission supérieure à la normale payée à un représentant.
overriding interests: droits, charges, intérêts ou pouvoirs non immatriculés.
overriding principle: principe auquel il ne saurait être dérogé.
decision overriding a former decision: arrêt de cassation.

to overrule: décider contre.
[J] annuler (une décision), passer outre (à une objection).

overrun: excédent (m), surplus (m) de fabrication.
— *costs*: [U.S.] dépassement (m) des frais prévus.

oversea (s): (d') outre-mer.
— *investments*: investissements outre-mer.

— *markets*: marchés (d') outre-mer.

overset of appropriation: [F] dépassement de crédit.

to be overstaffed: employer du personnel en surnombre.

oversubscribed issue: [F] émission surpassée.

oversubscribed shares: [B] demande (f) d'actions (très) supérieure à l'offre.

to overstock the market: [C] encombrer le marché.

overt: patent, évident (a).
— *act*: acte manifeste.
market — : marché public.

to overtax: [F] surimposer, surtaxer.

overtime: heures supplémentaires, travail supplémentaire.
to work — : faire des heures supplémentaires.

over-trading: (F) opérations (f pl) financières excédant les capacités d'une entreprise.

overvaluation, to overvalue: sur-estimation (f), surestimer.

overweight: exédent (m) de poids.

to owe: devoir.
owing: dû, exigible, arriéré.
the money owing to: l'argent qui est dû à.
rent owing: loyer en retard, arriéré.

to own: posséder.
[J] *government*- —, *privately owned*: propriété de l'état, propriété privée.
— *up to having made a mistake*: reconnaître que l'on a fait une faute.
— *up to a crime*: reconnaître (avouer) un crime.
own: qui appartient en propre.
own brand, label: marque d'un revendeur qui n'est pas celle du fabricant.
to come into one's own: entrer en possession de son bien.

owner: propriétaire (m), armateur (m).
[J] *absolute ownership*: propriété incommutable.
bare —, *bare* **ownership**: nu propriétaire, nue propriété.
beneficial — : usufruitier.
equitable — : propriétaire en droit, propriétaire dont le titre de propriété prendra effet à la réalisation d'une condition.

joint —, part — : propriétaire indivis, copropriétaire.
landowner : propriétaire terrien (foncier).
lawful, legitimate — : propriétaire légitime.
reputed — : propriétaire apparent.
rightful — : possesseur légitime, ayant droit.
sole — : propriétaire unique (d'une entreprise).
at —(s) risk : aux risques et périls du propriétaire.
[C] *shipowner* : armateur.
— *-charterer* : armateur-affréteur.
at —(s) risk : aux risques et périls du propriétaire.
(F) *—(s) equity (investment)* : capitaux propres.

ownership : propriété (f), droit de propriété.
[J] *collective —* : propriété collective.
joint — (— in common) : co-propriété (f).
private — : propriété privée.
proof of — : preuve (f), titre (m) de propriété.
[F] *— of public debt* : porteurs de titre de la dette publique.
— of the controlling interest : [U.S.] contrôle financier d'une entreprise.

oyer : audition (f).

oyer and terminer : compétence ratione loci, territoriale.

NOTES

P

pace : allure (f), vitesse (f).
to keep — with : aller (marcher) de pair avec.

to pack : emballer, confectionner.
to — goods : emballer des marchandises.
to — a meeting : s'assurer une majorité de partisans dans une assemblée (ou une réunion).
packed *meeting* : assemblée (salle) acquise d'avance (à un orateur).

package : emballage (m), paquet (m), conditionnement (m), produit informatique (programme).
[C] *— deal* : [U.S.] marché (contrat global) ; ensemble (m) des questions à débattre.
« this is a — deal » : « c'est à prendre (en bloc) ou à laisser ».
salary package : enveloppe (f) des salaires.
— store : [U.S.] magasin vendant des boissons alcooliques à emporter.
package tour : voyage organisé.
to package : conditionner, préconditionner.
packaging : conditionnement (m), emballage (m).
[ASS] *package policies* : garanties multirisques.

packet : paquet (m), colis (m).
pay — : enveloppe de paie.
registered — : objet, colis recommandé.

packing : (frais d') emballage (m).
[C] *— charges* : frais d'emballage.
— industry (trade) : (la) conserverie, industrie (commerce) de la conserve.
— plant : (une) conserverie.
throwaway — : emballage (m) perdu.

launching pad : rampe (f) de lancement (s'emploie au figuré, par ex. the present rate of exchange offers a launching pad for exports (the Observer) : le taux de change actuel constitue une rampe de lancement des exportations).

page rate : prix (m) d'une page de publicité.

paid (p. passé de *« to pay »*) : payé.
[D] *duty- — (goods)* : (marchandises) dédouanés.
[F] *— -in capital* : capital versé.
(amount) — into an account : somme versée à un compte.
capital — in full : capital entièrement versé.
— cash book : main courante de dépenses (banque).
« — » *(on receipted bill)* : « pour acquit ».
— -on charges : débours.
— -up bonds : obligations payées.
— -up capital : capital effectif.
— -up shares : actions libérées.

pain : châtiment (m), peine (f), douleur (f).
[J] *— (s) and penalties* : châtiments et peines.
compensation (allowance, recovery) for — and suffering : « pretium doloris », indemnités pour blessures et souffrances du fait d'autrui.
on (under) — of death : sous peine de mort.
— of : sous peine de...

palpable : sensible, évident, manifeste (a).
— difference : différence sensible.

paltry : misérable, insignifiant, mesquin (a).
— sums : sommes insignifiantes.

(advertising) pamphlet : brochure (f) (publicitaire).

panel : panneau (m), groupe (m), comité (m), commission (f).
[J] *The —* : le Jury.
advisory (consulting) — : comité consultatif.
— -discussion : réunion-débat (de groupe).
— of experts : commission d'experts.

panic prices : [B] cours de panique.

paper : papier (m), journal (m), billet (m), effet (m).
[C] [F] *— assets* : valeurs en portefeuille.
commercial — (s) : papier(s) d'affaires, effet de commerce.
commodity — : effet de commerce.
convertible — : papier convertible.
paper currency (— -money) : papier-monnaie, monnaie fiduciaire.
— holdings : portefeuille-titres.
— loss : moins value (de titres), perte comptable.
negotiable — : papier négociable.
— profits : profits fictifs.
— securities : titres fiduciaires.
stamped — : papier timbré.
— standard : étalon-papier.
trade — : effet de commerce (commercial).
— value : valeur fictive.

par : pair (m).
above — : au-dessus du pair.

— 533 —

at – : au pair.
below – : au-dessous du pair.
issue – : prix d'émission.
exchange at – : change au pair.
– *of exchange* : parité de change.
– *of stocks* : pair des effets, des titres.
par value (value at –*)* : valeur nominale (au pair).
to issue (shares) at – : émettre (des actions) au pair.
to sell at – : vendre au pair.

parafiscal : parafiscal (a).

parallel import : importation (f) parallèle (par une méthode qui n'a pas l'assentiment de l'exportateur).

parameter : paramètre (m), limite (f) fixée.

paramount : éminent, supérieur (a), de première importance.
of – *importance* : d'une importance capitale.
(of) – *necessity* : (d'une) nécessité vitale.
– *title* : le titre de propriété le mieux établi.

parcel : colis (m), paquet (m), lot (m), parcelle (f), partie (f) qui suit les clauses essentielles d'un document.
– *of land* : pièce de terre.
– *of shares* : paquet d'actions.
– *(s) traffic* : messageries.
to parcel out *(land)* : morceler (des terres), partager (un héritage), lotir.
to parcel up : emballer.

pardon : grâce (f) (accordée par un chef d'Etat, etc.).
[J] *general* – : amnistie (f).
petition for – : recours en grâce.
the right of – : le droit de grâce.

parent(s) : parent(s) (m) (père, mère), ascendant(s) (m), origine (f).
[J] – *and relations* : les ascendants directs et les collatéraux.
foster – : père nourricier, mère nourricière.
[A] *pension to* – : pension d'ascendants (des militaires tombés au Champ d'Honneur).
[C] – *company* : société mère, maison mère.
– *establishment (house)* : maison mère.
– *office* : bureau central.
parental *authority (power)* : puissance paternelle.

pari passu (« *on an equal footing* ») : sur un pied d'égalité.
[J] sans préférence, proportionnellement (quand il s'agit de rembourser des créditeurs).

parish : paroisse (f).
– *council* : conseil communal (d'une paroisse comptant au moins 300 habitants).
civil – : commune.
– -*pump mentality, politics* : esprit, politique de clocher.

parity : parité (f), analogie (f).
above – : au-dessus du pair.
at – : au pair.
below – : au-dessous du pair.
– *of exchange* : rapport de parité.
gold – : parité-or.
by – *of reasoning* : par raisonnement analogique.
– *table* : table des parités.
[F] *exchange of* – : change au pair.
[B] – *price* : coût à la parité.

parking : parcage (m), stationnement (m).
[A] « *no* – » : défense de stationner.
– *lights* : feux de position.

parkometer : parcmètre (m).

parlance : langage (m), parler (m).
[J] *in legal* – : en termes juridiques, de pratique.

parliament : parlement (m).
act of – : loi (f).
in – : au parlement.
parliamentary *committee* : commissions parlementaires.
parliamentary franchise : droit de vote.
member of – *(M.P.)* : un parlementaire.
proceedings of – *(parliamentary proceedings)* : débats parlementaires.

parol : oral (a).
[J] – *contract, evidence, lease* : contrat, témoignage, bail verbal.

parole : [J] probation (f), [U.S.] libération conditionnelle surveillée.
(on) under – : en liberté surveillée.
parolee : [U.S.] délinquant en liberté conditionnelle et surveillée.

parricide : parricide (m et f).

part : partie (f), fraction (f), élément (m).
[J] un des deux originaux d'un contrat (« *part* » et « *counterpart* »).
... *of the one* –, *of the other* – *(in an agreement, a contract between two person)* : d'une part, d'autre part (termes d'un accord, d'un contrat, entre deux personnes).
– *cargo charter* : affrètement partiel.
– *exchange* : reprise (f).
operative – : dispositif (d'une loi).
– *owner* : copropriétaire (m).

— *payment* : acompte (m).
— *time* : à temps partiel, à mi-temps.
— *time employment, personnel, work* : emploi, personnel, travail à temps partiel, à mi-temps.
(to be) on — -time : être en chômage partiel.
(to be) — and parcel : faire partie intégrante.
to part *with (a right, a property)* : céder, aliéner (un droit, un bien).
partial : partiel, partial (a).
partial acceptance : acceptation partielle.
partial insanity : aliénation mentale avec intervalles de lucidité.
partial loss : sinistre partiel, perte partielle.
partial merger : fusion partielle (de sociétés).

particeps criminis : complice d'un crime.

to participate *(in profits and losses)* : participer (aux profits et pertes).

partial *loss,* **particular** *average loss* : (ASS. mar.) perte partielle, dommages causés dans des circonstances prévues et couvertes par l'assurance (ex. collision, tempête etc.).

participation : participation (f).
participation loan : prêt en participation (consenti par plusieurs banques conjointement).

particular : a) particulier, spécial, minutieux, détaillé, déterminé (a); b) détail (m), précision (f).
[J] *bill of — (s)* : énonciation détaillée des demandes ou des moyens de défense d'une partie à communiquer à l'adversaire pour lui permettre d'exposer son cas.
— *case* : cas d'espèce.
— *lien* : privilège spécial.
(a) — *object* : (un) objet déterminé.
— *partnership* : association en participation (limitée à une seule opération).
— *power* : procuration spéciale.
any — taxpayer : tout contribuable.
— *(s) of an account* : détails d'un compte.
— *(s) of charge* : chefs d'accusation.
full particulars : (toutes) précisions, détails.
for further — (s) : pour plus amples détails.
the — (s) of an item : le libellé d'un article.
[C] — *(s) of sale* : cahier des charges, conditions de vente.

partition : partage (m), démembrement (m).
[J] *action for —* : demande de partage pour sortir de l'indivis.
— *of an inheritance among co-heirs* : répartition d'un héritage entre les ayants droit.
— *of land* : morcellement (m).

partly paid shares : [F] actions non intégralement libérées.

partner : associé (m), commanditaire (m).
[J] *contracting —* : co-contractant (m).
[C] *active —* : associé commandité, associé en nom.
— *in a bank* : associé d'une maison de banque.
dormant — : bailleur de fonds.
general — : associé ordinaire.
joint — : coassocié (m).
— *in joint account* : coparticipant (m).
junior — : dernier associé.
latent, limited, secret, sleeping — : commanditaire (m).

partnership : association (f), société (f), société de personnes sans personnalité morale.
[F] — *capital (funds)* : capital d'une société, capital social, fonds social.
— *debt* : dette de société.
[J] — *deed* (plus rarement *articles*) *of —* : acte d'association, acte de société.
general — # société en nom collectif.
— *income* : revenu des sociétés.
industrial — : participation ouvrière aux bénéfices.
limited — # société en commandite simple.
limited liability — : société à responsabilité limitée.
— *limited by shares* : société en commandite par actions.
— *share* : part d'association.
to enter (to go) into — : s'associer.
to take (s.o.) into — : prendre (qn) comme associé.

party : parti (m) politique, groupe (m), ayant droit (m).
[J] partie (f).
to be — to a crime : être impliqué dans un crime.
to be — to a suit : être en cause.
the adverse — : la partie adverse.
[A] *contracting —* : partie adjudicataire.
the contracting **parties** : les parties contractantes.
— *entitled* : ayant droit.
the — at fault (in an accident) : l'auteur d'un accident.
the injured — : la partie lésée.
the interested parties : les ayants droit, les intéressés.
the — named : l'accrédité.
the — in opposition : le parti de l'opposition.
the — in power : le parti au pouvoir.
third — : tierce personne, tiers.
for account of a third — : pour le compte d'autrui.
payment on behalf of a third — : paiement par intervention.
[ASS] *third — insurance* : assurance au tiers.
third — risks : risques de préjudice au tiers.
— *wall* : mur mitoyen.

pass: laissez-passer (m), autorisation (f).
— -*book*: carnet (livret) de banque.
to pass: passer, voter, adopter, allouer.
— *a bill*: adopter un projet de loi.
— *a cheque through the clearing house*: compenser un chèque.
— *a dividend (of...)*: approuver un dividende (de...).
— *an enactment*: adopter un texte de loi.
— *an item of expenditure*: allouer une dépense.
— *a law*: voter une loi.
— *a resolution*: prendre (adopter) une résolution.
— *(a) sentence*: prononcer une condamnation.
— *(goods) in transit*: transiter (des marchandises).
— *on the department concerned*: transmettre au service compétent.

passage: passage (m), trajet (m) (par mer, air), adoption (f).
[J] — *of a bill*: adoption d'un projet de loi.
right of — : droit de passage.
[C] — *money*: prix du voyage.
passenger: passager (m), voyageur (m);
passenger contract: contrat de transport des passagers (des voyageurs).
passenger rates: tarif de voyageurs.
passing: passage (m), adoption (f).
passing of a dividend: passation (f) d'un dividende.
passing entries: passation d'écritures.
passing events: actualités (f pl).

passing off: [J] délit commis en vendant des marchandises, en traitant des affaires, etc. sous un nom, une firme, une description, etc., propres à faire croire qu'il s'agit d'un autre article ou d'une autre personne [U.S. « *palming off* »].

passion: passion, accès de colère.
[J] « *manslaughter in the heat of* — » : meurtre passionnel.

passive: passif (a).
[C] [F] — *balance*: balance déficitaire.
— *bond*: obligation ne portant pas intérêt.
— *debt*: dette passive.
[J] — *misrepresentation*: omission volontaire (dans un témoignage).

passport: passeport (m).

past: passé, antérieur (a).
— *year*: exercice écoulé.

pasture: pâturage (m).
[J] *common of* — : droit de parcours et vaine pâture.

patch: pièce (f), morceau (m), échappée (f) (de ciel).
the bright **patches**: les motifs de satisfaction (pour un chef d'entreprise).

patent: a) breveté, patent, évident (a); b) brevet (m) (d'invention).
— *offence*: délit manifeste, bien établi.
— *product*: produit breveté.
— *agent*: agent en brevets d'invention.
— *expenses*: redevances sur brevets.
forfeiture of a — : déchéance d'un brevet.
infringement of — : contrefaçon (f).
land- — : [U.S.] concession de terrains.
— *office*: office de la propriété industrielle, bureau des brevets.
— *rights*: propriété industrielle.
to claim for a — : demander un brevet.
to work a — : exploiter un brevet.
patentee: détenteur d'un brevet d'invention.

(growth) path: sentier de croissance.

patient: patient (m), terme qui désigne actuellement un aliéné, dénommé *a lunatic* avant 1930.

patrimonial assets: éléments de patrimoine.

patron: client (m), protecteur (m).
patronage: protection (f), patronage (m), appui (m), [U.S.] apport commercial, (opp. *sponsoring*) mécénat.

to patronize: favoriser, encourager, accorder sa clientèle à.

pattern: modèle (m), échantillon (m), type (m), structure (f).
— *book*: livre d'échantillons.
— *of employment*: structure de l'emploi.
— *of life*: mode de vie.
price — : structure des prix.
according to —, *as per* — : selon échantillon.

pauper: indigent (m) (*now* économiquement faible).
— *children*: enfants assistés.

pawn: gage (m), mise en gage, nantissement (m).
to put in — : mettre en gage.
— *-ticket*: reconnaissance de dépôt de gage.
to pawn: mettre en gage.
to pawn securities: gager, nantir des valeurs.
pawnbroker: prêteur sur gages.
pawnee: créancier sur gage.
pawner: emprunteur sur gage.
pawnshop, — -*office*: Mont-de-Piété (*now* Crédit municipal).

pay: paye (f), paie (f), salaire (m), traitement (m), gages (m pl).
[F] *back* – : rappel de traitement.
– *back period, pay cash period*: période de récupération du capital (de recouvrement, de remboursement).
base –, [U.S.] *basic* – : salaire de base.
– *bill (voucher)*: bon de paie.
– *bracket*: tranche d'imposition.
– *-day*: jour de paie ; [B] jour de liquidation.
– *differentials*: écarts des salaires.
– *envelope*: enveloppe de paie.
– *freeze*: blocage des salaires.
full – *leave*: congé à plein traitement.
holidays with – : congés payés.
– *-list*: feuille de paie, bordereau de salaires.
– *load*: charge utile.
– *off*: rentabilité (f).
– *off matrix*: matrice (f) de décision rectangulaire, tableau des conséquences.
– *off period*: durée de remboursement (critère d'investissement reposant sur la minimisation de la durée de remboursement du capital investi par les recettes nettes).
– *-office*: guichet (m), caisse (f).
– *-roll, -sheet*: feuille de paie, bulletin de salaire.
to be on the – *-roll*: être sur la liste du personnel.
– *-roll tax*: impôt sur les salaires.
employers – *-roll tax*: versement forfaitaire.
retired – : pension de retraite.
– *-in slip*: bordereau de versement.
– *out period, time*: see « pay back period ».
– *out ratio*: taux de distribution des bénéfices.
sick- – : indemnité de maladie.
stoppage of – : retenue sur le salaire.
strike – : allocation de grève.
unemployed – : solde de non-activité.
unemployement – : secours de chômage.
vacations with – : [U.S.] congés payés.
to pay: payer, verser, rémunérer.
ability to pay: solvabilité (f).
failure to pay: défaut de paiement.
to pay by instalments: payer par mensualités, échelonner les paiements.
to pay at maturity: payer à l'échéance.
order to pay: ordre de paiement, ordonnancement.
to pay money into an account: verser une somme à un compte.
to pay for services: rémunérer des services.
to pay spot cash (cash down): payer comptant.
to pay taxes: payer des contributions.
to pay its way: couvrir ses frais.
it does not – : ce n'est pas rentable.
– *(pay to)*: veuillez payer à, payez à.
– *bearer (to bearer)*: payez au porteur.
– *as you earn (P.A.Y.E.)*: [U.K.] système de retenue à la source de l'impôt sur les traitements et salaires (« payez au fur et à mesure que vous gagnez »).
– *as you go*: méthode de forfait avec rectification périodique.
– *to the order of*: payez à l'ordre de.
– *self (selves)*: payez à moi-même (à nous-mêmes).
to pay back: rembourser.
to pay down: payer comptant.
to pay in: verser.
to pay (a sum) into the bank: verser (une somme) en banque.
to pay off: acquitter.
to pay off a debt: éteindre, régler une dette.
to pay off an employee: congédier un employé.
to pay off a mortgage: purger une hypothèque.
the business paid off well: [U.S.] l'affaire s'avéra très rentable.
to pay out: débourser, décaisser.
to pay one's (own) way: rapporter, être rentable.
paying-out: décaissement (m).
to pay-up: verser, libérer, se libérer.
(fully) paid up capital: capital (entièrement) versé.
to pay up a share: libérer une action.
to pay up one's debts: se libérer de ses dettes.
to pay up in full: libérer, (se libérer) intégralement.
paid-up capital deficiency: insuffisance du capital versé.

payability: exigibilité (f).

payable: payable, exigible (a), à la charge de.
[F] *accounts* – : dettes passives.
– *to...*: à l'ordre de...
taxes – *by the tenant*: impôts à la charge du locataire.

payee: bénéficiaire (m), porteur (m) d'un effet.
« *name of the* – » : « nom du bénéficiaire ».

payer, payor: payeur, tiré (d'un effet).
rate- –, *tax-* – : contribuable (m).
– *for honour*: payeur par intervention.

paying: a) rémunérateur, payant (a) ; b) payeur (m), paiement (m).
a – *concern*: une entreprise payante.
a – *proposition*: une affaire intéressante, rentable.
– *third system*: système du tiers payant.
– *banker*: banquier payant.
– *guest*: hôte payant.

paying off: liquidation (f), règlement (m), extinction (f), amortissement (m), *(of a debt)* remboursement (m), *(of an employee)* congédiement (m), *(of a mortgage)* purge (f), *(of a sailor)* débarquement (m), *(of a ship)* désar-

mement (m), *(of troops)* licenciement (m).
paying office : bureau payeur.
– up – a share : libération d'une action.

paymaster : payeur, trésorier (m).

payment : paiement (m), rémunération (f), versement (m), exécution (f) d'une promesse ou d'une obligation, remboursement (m).
[J] *– into court :* consignation en justice.
[J] *– on account (account payment) :* paiement à valoir, acompte.
additional – : supplément.
advance – : paiement par anticipation, d'avance.
balance of – (s) : balance des paiements.
– bill : traite (f.).
– of calls : paiement libératoire (sur capital).
cash – : paiement comptant.
– against documents : paiement contre documents.
deferred – : paiement par versements (échelonnés).
deficiency – : subvention aux agriculteurs.
by easy – (s) : avec facilités de paiement.
exchange – (s) : paiement en devises.
extended – : délai supplémentaire de paiement.
– in full : paiement intégral, libération complète, parfait paiement.
– in full discharge : paiement libératoire.
golden handshake – : indemnité de départ.
incentive – : see « incentive ».
– instalment : versements échelonnés.
inward – : paiement reçu.
method of – : mode de règlement.
monthly – (s) : mensualités (f pl).
– by monthly instalments : mensualisation (f).
outward – : décaissement (m).
part – : acompte, paiement partiel.
« – received » : pour acquit.
– under protest : paiement sous protêt.
term of – : délai de paiement.
terms of – : conditions de paiement.
to hold over a – : différer un paiement.
to make a – : effectuer un paiement.
to stop – (s) : cesser les paiements.
[F] *– of interest :* service (d'intérêts).
to stop – of a cheque : frapper un chèque d'opposition.

payroll : montant (m) global des salaires, feuille (f) de salaires.
[F] *– déduction :* retenue à la source.
–, employment tax : (U.S.) impôt sur les salaires.

peace : paix (f).
industrial – : paix sociale.
– officer : gardien de la paix.
– and order : l'ordre public.

peak : pointe (f), sommet (m), point culminant.
– demand : demande maximum.
– hours, period : heures, période de pointe, d'affluence.
– output : production maximum (à son maximum).
– year : année record.
off- – hours, period : heures creuses, période creuse.

peasant : paysan (m).
the **peasantry** : le paysannat, la paysannerie.

peculation : péculat (m), malversation (f), appropriation (f) de fonds publics.
[J] prévarication (f).

peculiarity : trait distinctif.
[A] *special* **pecularities** : signes particuliers.

pecuniary : pécuniaire, financier (a).
– advantages : avantages matériels.
– difficulties : difficultés de trésorerie.
– loss : perte d'argent.
[F] *for – gain :* dans un but lucratif.
– offence : délit passible d'amende.

to peddle (paddle) : faire du colportage.
pedlar, peddler : colporteur.
peddling : colportage (m).

pedigree : arbre généalogique.

peer, peeress : pair (m), pairesse (f).
to be tried by one's – (s) : être jugé par (ses) pairs, par un jury.
– in her own right : pairesse héréditaire (de son propre chef).
life peeress : pairesse à vie.

peerage : pairie (f).
hereditary – : les Pairs du royaume (collectivement).

peg : référence (f) (ex. pour des taux d'intérêt).

to peg : maintenir, indexer, aligner (sur).
[F] *– the exchange :* maintenir, stabiliser le cours du change.
– the market : stabiliser le marché.
– prices : indexer les prix.

(crawlings) pegs : [F] (régime) des parités à crémaillères.

penal : pénal (pénaux) (a).
– action : action pénale, au criminel.
– law : droit pénal.
– legislation : législation pénale.
[F] *– tax :* amende fiscale.

penalty: pénalité (f), peine (f), amende (f), délit (m), forfait (m) d'indemnité.
[F] – *charges*: pénalisations (fiscales).
fiscal – : amende fiscale.
[J] – *clause*: clause pénale (sanction pécuniaire en cas d'inexécution d'un contrat).
death – : peine capitale.
on –, *under* – *of...*: sous peine de...
– *for non performance of an agreement*: délit en cas d'inexécution d'un accord (d'un contrat).
to be liable to **penalties**: être passible de pénalités.

pendant, pendent, pending: en instance, en cours.
the action is – : l'action est en cours.
– *the negociations*: en attendant l'issue des négociations.

penetration: pénétration (f).
– *pricing, prices*: prix de lancement.

penitentiary: a) pénitentiaire (a); b) pénitencier (m).

pension: pension (f), retraite (f).
[A] *disability (invalid)* – : pension d'invalidité.
– *fund*: caisse de retraite.
government – : pension de l'Etat.
graduated – *scheme*: [U.K.] régime obligatoire de retraites complémentaires.
– *for life (life* – *)*: pension à vie, rente (viagère).
old age – : pension de vieillesse, retraite vieillesse.
pension planning: constitution d'une pension.
retiring – : pension de retraite.
to be discharged with a – : être mis à la retraite.
to retire on a – : prendre sa retraite.
to pension: pensionner.
to pension (s.o.) off: mettre (qn) à la retraite.
pensionable: qui donne droit à une pension, qui a droit à la retraite.
pensionable injury: blessure qui donne droit à une pension.
pensionable age: âge de mise à la retraite.
pensionable emoluments: traitement soumis à retenue.
pensioner: retraité (m).

pent-up inflation: inflation contenue.

people: peuple (m), nation (f), [U.S.] le gouvernement dans un procès où l'Etat est mis en cause.
the – *at large*: le grand public.

pep talk: (fam.) paroles (f pl) paroles d'encouragement.

peppercorn rent: [J] loyer nominal.

per: par, selon, conformément à.
per annum: par an.

per (pur) autre vie: pendant la vie d'un autre.
per capita, per head: par tête.

per curiam: par le tribunal.

per cent: pour cent.

per diem: journalier.

per incuriam: par négligence.

per infortunium: par malchance.

per procurationem: par procuration.

per quod: en raison de quoi.

per se: de (en) lui-même.

percentage: pourcentage (m), tantième (m), quantum (m), proportion (f).
[F] *additional* – *(s)*: centimes additionnels.
– *depletion* # provision pour reconstitution de gisements.
[C] *commission* – *(on sales)*: guelte.
directors' – *of profits*: tantièmes des administrateurs.
– *distribution*: répartition en pourcentage.
– *of incapacity*: degré d'incapacité.

perception: perception (f), recouvrement (m).

peremptory: impératif, décisif, absolu (a).
– *argument*: argument décisif.
– *call*: mise en demeure formelle.
– *challenge*: exception péremptoire, récusation pure et simple de jurés.
– *defence*: défense au fond.
– *necessity*: nécessité absolue.
– *notice*: mise en demeure.
– *rule*: règle absolue.
– *writ*: ordre de comparaître en personne.

perfect competition: concurrence parfaite.
– *market*: marché parfait (des économistes classiques).

performance: accomplissement (m), exécution (f) (d'un accord), exercice d'une profession.
– *appraisal review*: évaluation des compétences des résultats.
best – : rendement maximum.
[A] – *rights*: droits d'exécution (musique)

ou de représentation (théâtre).
[J] *part* – *of an agreement*: exécution partielle d'un contrat.
– *bond*: garantie donnée par un tiers (ex. banque) à l'une des parties d'une transaction.
specific – : exécution intégrale d'un contrat ordonnée par un tribunal, exécution d'une obligation.
substantial – : exécution substantielle.
in the – *of (his) duties*: dans l'exercice de (ses) fonctions.

peril(s) of the sea: [ASS] fortune(s) de mer.

period: période (f), durée (f), délai (m).
within the agreed – : dans le délai fixé.
average – : durée moyenne.
– *of assessment (assessment period)*: période de l'imposition.
base (basic) – : époque (période) de référence.
fiscal – : exercice financier.
fixed – : période déterminée.
deposit for a fixed – : dépôt à terme fixe.
grace – : délai de grâce.
net income for the – : bénéfice net pour l'exercice.
intervening – : période intermédiaire, intervalle.
– *money*: dépôt à terme (pendant une période d'un mois minimum).
– *of prescription*: délai de (la) prescription.
probation (trial) – : période d'essai (d'épreuve).
– *running from... to...*: exercice s'étendant du... au...
in the short – : dans la courte période.
transitional (transitory) – : période transitoire.
the – *under review*: l'exercice écoulé.

periodical: a) périodique (a) ; b) (un) périodique (m), une publication périodique.

perishable goods: [C] marchandises (denrées) périssables.

perjury: parjure (m), fausse allégation, faux serment, faux témoignage.
[J] *subornation of* – : subornation de témoin.

perks: see « perquisites ».
(fam.) gratte.

permanent: permanent (a).
– *abode, address, dwelling*: résidence (f), domicile fixe.
– *appointment*: titularisation (f).
– *assets*: actif immobilisé, capital fixe, immobilisations.
– *employment*: emploi permanent.

– *establishment*: lieu d'établissement capital.
– *investment*: placement permanent.
– *residence*: résidence habituelle.
[F] – *income effect*: effet de revenu permanent.

permissible: permissible, tolérable (a).

permission to reside: [A] permis de séjour.

permissive: licite, facultatif (a).
permissible degree of error: taux de sécurité.
[J] – *legislation*: législation facultative, non impérative.
– *waste*: négligence, défaut d'entretien.

permit: autorisation (f), licence (f), permis (m).
[D] acquit-à-caution (m), passavant (m), passe-debout (m), congé (m).
customs – : permis de douane, acquit-à-caution.
export (import) – : autorisation d'exporter (d'importer).
building – : permis de construire.
labour – : permis de travail.
loading (discharging) – : permis de chargement (de déchargement).
– *of residence*: permis de séjour.
to take out a – : se faire délivrer un permis.

perpetual: perpétuel (a).
[J] – *injunction*: ordonnance d'un tribunal faisant à l'une des parties injonction définitive et permanente de s'abstenir d'un certain acte.
[F] – *loans*: emprunts perpétuels, rentes.

perpetuity: perpétuité (f) de la jouissance d'un bien, d'une rente, d'une peine.

« per procurationem » (P/P): see « appendice ».

perquisite: revenant-bon (d'une charge), profit éventuel, émolument (m).
– *(s)*: avantages accessoires, gratifications, petits profits.

perquisition: perquisition (f), descente de justice.

persistent demand: [C] demande soutenue.

person: personne (f), individu (m), gens (pl).
[J] *artificial, juridical, juristic* – : personne morale, civique, juridique.
– *liable (for tax)*: personne redevable (de l'impôt).
– *named*: accrédité.

natural – : personne physique, naturelle.
private – : (simple) particulier.
personal : personnel (a).
personal action : action mobilière.
personal allowance : déduction personnelle.
personal assistant (P.A.) : attaché de direction.
personal estate, property : biens meubles, biens mobiliers.
personal interview : entretien en tête-à-tête.
personal loan : prêt individuel personnalisé.
personal rights : droits civiques.
personal sale : vente directe.
[ASS] *personal accident assurance* : assurance contre les accidents corporels, assurance-accidents.
[F] *personal exemption* : [U.S.] abattement pour charges de famille.
personal income : revenus des particuliers.
personal tax : impôt personnel.
taxes both personal and impersonal : impôts à double base.
articles for personal use : effets personnels.

personality promotion : vente (f) d'un produit dont une « personnalité » (artiste, etc.) fait la publicité.

personalty : personnalité (f).
[J] biens meubles successibles.
pure – : biens meubles sans rapport avec des biens immeubles.
mixed – : biens meubles se rapportant à des biens immeubles (tels que baux).
conversion of realty into – : ameublissement.

to personate (s.o.) : usurper l'état-civil de qn.
[J] **personation** : personnification, usurpation de nom ou d'état-civil.
personator : imposteur (m).

personnel : (le) personnel (m).
– *department* : service du personnel.
– *management, manager* : organisation, chef du personnel.

P.E.R.T. *(Program Evaluation and Review Technique)* : méthode de révision et d'évaluation de programme.

to persuade : convaincre.
persuasive *precedent* : précédent (m) qui influence, qui fait jurisprudence.

pertinent : pertinent (a).
– *information* : renseignements utiles.
– *question* : question bien posée, opportune.

perverse : pervers, perverti, méchant (a).
[J] – *verdict* : verdict rendu à l'encontre des directives du juge portant sur un point de droit.

to pervert *the course of justice* : égarer la justice.

« Peter principle » : principe de Peter (théorie selon laquelle l'ancienneté finit par permettre la promotion de certains employés à des postes qu'ils sont incapables de tenir).

petit, petty : petit, peu important (a).
[C] – *cash* : petite caisse.
– *cash-book* : livre de petite caisse.
– *charges, expenses* : menus frais.
[J] – *jury* : jury de jugement.
– *larceny* : vol simple.
– *offence* : contravention.
– *session* : session des juges de première instance.
– *theft* : larcin (m).
petit treason : meurtre d'un mari par sa femme.

petition : pétition (f), requête (f), supplique (f).
[C] – *in bankruptcy* : dépôt de bilan, requête des créanciers.
to file one's – : déposer son bilan.
[J] – *for a divorce* : demande de divorce.
– *for a reprieve* : recours en grâce, pourvoi.
– *for review* : demande en révision.
– *of right* : action en recouvrement de propriété ou en exécution de contrat dirigée contre l'Etat (la Couronne).
to petition *the court (for sth.)* : réclamer (qch.) au tribunal.
petitioner : requérant.

petitory action (suit) : [J] [U.S.] action pétitoire.

pettyfoggery : chicane (f), avocasserie (f).

phases of the business cycle : phases du cycle économique.

Philadelphia lawyer : [U.S.] avocat retors.

physical : matériel (a), corporel (a).
– *assets* : biens matériels, corporels.
– *disability* : incapacité (f), invalidité (f) physique.
a **physically**-*handicapped person* : (une personne) invalide, diminué(e) physiquement.
– *distribution* : moyens de livraison des marchandises (du fabricant au consommateur).
– *impossibility* : impossibilité matérielle.
– *management* : service de livraison.
– *stock-taking* : inventaire détaillé.

(strike-) picket : piquet de grève.
picketting : constitution de piquets de grève.

pick-up » : [C] reprise.
to pick up : prendre (des passagers), ramasser, se ressaisir, reprendre, être en reprise.
[C] *to — sthg. cheap* : acheter qch. à bon marché.
[B] X *shares picked up* : les actions X reprennent.

pie : pâté (m).
— *chart* : graphique (m) sous de forme de cercle découpé en tranches comme un pâté et permettant de comparer immédiatement des résultats (« camembert »).

piece : pièce (f), morceau (m).
a — of business : une affaire.
— *of ground (of land)* : fonds de terre, terrain.
a — of news : une nouvelle.
— *rates* : rémunération aux pièces.
— *wage* : salaire aux pièces.
— *work* : travail à façon, à forfait, aux pièces.
to pay by the — : payer à la pièce.

pier : jetée (f), quai (m).
— *dues (pierage)* : [F] droits de quai, d'amarrage.

pilferage : chapardage (m), maraude (f), coulage (m).
to pilfer : chaparder, commettre de menus larcins.

pilfering : larcin (m).

pilot plant : usine (f) pilote.

pilotage dues : [F] taxes, droits (frais) de pilotage.
— *inwards* : permis d'entrée (au port).
— *outwards* : permis de sortie (du port).

pincer (or racking) effect : effet de tenaille.

pin money : argent de poche.
[J] somme prévue dans un contrat de mariage « à l'antique » pour les dépenses personnelles de la femme.

pioneer selling : vendre un produit pour la première fois.
to do — work in a subject : faire un travail de pionnier, défricher (un sujet).

pipe-line : oléoduc (m).
orders in the — : commandes en souffrance.

piracy : piraterie (f).
literary — : plagiat (m), contrefaçon (f).
to pirate : contrefaire, démarquer (ex. un livre).

pit : fosse (f), puits (m) (de mine) ; [U.S.] marché (m) (boursier), (B) corbeille (f).
pitfall : fosse (f), piège (m).
the pitfalls of the law : les traquenards de la procédure.

pitch : (C) (fam.) baratin (m) d'un vendeur.

place : lieu (m), endroit (m), emploi (m).
— *of abode, of residence* : résidence (f), domicile (m).
— *of business* : siège (m) (d'une société).
— *of delivery* : lieu de livraison.
— *of payment* : lieu du paiement.
to do the — : faire la place.
to place : placer des capitaux, prêter, donner, mettre, remettre.
to place a loan : négocier un emprunt.
to place an item on the agenda : inscrire un article à l'ordre du jour.
to place an order : passer un ordre.

placement : placement (m).

plaint : plainte (f).

plaintiff : [J] demandeur (demanderesse), plaignant(e), requérant(e).
— *in error* : demandeur en appel.

plan : dessein (m), plan (m), projet (m), procédé (m).
[C] *American —* : [U.S.] chambre d'hôtel sans pension.
European — : [U.S.] chambre d'hôtel avec pension.
five-year — : plan de cinq ans, quinquennal.
general — : plan d'ensemble.
instalment — : vente(s) à tempérament.
preliminary — : avant-projet.
[A] *superannuation —* : régime de retraite.
unemployment insurance — : régime d'assurance-chômage.
to change one's —(s) : adopter d'autres dispositions.
to put a — into operation : mettre un projet à exécution.
to upset —(s) : déranger les combinaisons de qn.
to plan : faire le plan de, projeter, combiner, planifier.
planned *economy* : économie dirigée, planifiée.
planned maintenance : entretien planifié.
(ill) well-planned : (mal) bien conçu, concerté.
planning : planification (f), organisation (f), aménagement (m).
country planning : aménagement du territoire.
economic planning : planification économique.
city-(town-) planning : urbanisme (m).
family planning : contrôle (limitation) des naissances.

planning horizon: horizon économique.
planning permission: permis de construire, autorisation préalable à l'élaboration d'un projet.
rural planning: aménagement des campagnes.
[F] *planning and programming, budgeting system (P.P.B.S.)*: rationalisation des choix budgétaires (R.C.B.).

plant: matériel (m), équipement (m), installations (f pl) (industrielles), [U.S.] usines (f).
— *bargaining*: négociations employés-employeur dans le cadre de l'entreprise.
— *capacity*: capacité de production.
fixed — : installations fixes.
power — : usine électrique.

(electoral) platform: programme politique (électoral).

(the free) play of competition: le libre jeu de la concurrence.

(to make a) play for sth.: mettre tout en œuvre pour obtenir qch.

to play the market: (B) jouer en Bourse.

plea: défense (f), moyens de défense, [U.S.] cause (f), procès (m).
[J] — *in abatement*: demande en nullité.
— *in bar (peremptory, special plea)*: exception péremptoire, fin de non-recevoir.
— *bargaining*: (US) négociation (f) avec le juge.
defendent's — : première exception, conclusion de la défense.
foreign — : exception d'incompétence, non-lieu.
— *of guilty*: aveu de culpabilité fait à l'audience.
incidental — : exception.
— *of incompetence*: exception déclinatoire, d'incompétence.
— *of insanity*: exception d'irresponsabilité pour cause d'aliénation mentale.
— *to the jurisdiction*: exception d'incompétence.
— *for mercy*: appel à la clémence, recours en grâce.
— *of necessity*: cas de force majeure invoqué par la défense.
sham — : moyens dilatoires, excuse, prétexte, justification.
to enter a — *(to put in a* —*)*: faire valoir une exception.
to offer a — : exciper d'une excuse.
to submit the — *that*: plaider que.
on the — *that*: sous prétexte que (de).

to plead (for-against): plaider (pour-contre), invoquer.

[J] — *(s.o.'s) cause (with s.o.)*: intercéder pour qn, auprès de qn.
— *duress*: alléguer la contrainte.
— *extenuating circumstances*: invoquer des circonstances atténuantes.
— *guilty (not guilty)*: plaider coupable (non coupable).
— *ignorance*: prétexter l'ignorance.
pleading: art de plaider, plaidoirie, plaidoyer, (les) débats.
common law pleading: procédure civile.
special pleading: plaidoyer spécieux ou fondé sur les particularités d'un cas.

« please forward »: prière de faire suivre.

pledge: nantissement (m), gage (m), engagement (m), vœu (m), promesse (f).
[J] *deposited as a* — : laissé en gage.
— *holder (holder of a* —*)*: créancier gagiste.
to hold (securities) in — : détenir (des titres) en gage.
to put (sth.) in — : mettre qch. en gage.
to take (sth.) out of — : dégager qch.
to pledge: gager, engager, mettre en gage.
to pledge one's property, one's word: engager son bien, sa parole.
to pledge securities: nantir des valeurs (des titres).
pledged chattels: biens nantis.
pledgee: créancier gagiste, prêteur sur gages.
pledger: emprunteur, débiteur sur gage(s), gageur.
pledging: engagement, mise en gage, nantissement.

plenary: complet, entier (a).
— *action, cause*: procès en bonne et due forme.
— *assembly (meeting)*: assemblée (réunion) plénière.
— *powers*: pleins pouvoirs.

plot: parcelle (f) (de terrain); intrigue (f), complot (m).
building — : terrain à bâtir.
plotting: levé d'un plan, machinations.

to plough back: réinvestir les bénéfices de l'entreprise.
[F] **ploughing back**: autofinancement (m).

plough-land: terre arable.

ploy: (Scot) démarche (f).
legal — : démarche auprès d'un homme de loi.

to plug: (fam.) faire de la publicité obsédante (ex. pour un film, un livre, en répétant constamment le titre).

plum: [F] [U.S.] superdividende (m).

plummet: sonde (f).
to plummet *(prices)*: plonger (les prix).

plurality: pluralité (f), [U.S.] majorité relative (des voix).
– *of offices*: cumul des fonctions.

poaching: braconnage (m).

pocket-money: argent de poche.
out-of-pocket expenses: menues dépenses.
unemployment pockets: foyers de chômage.

point: point (m) (d'indice, de pourcentage), lieu (m), sujet (m), question (f), seuil (m), dollar.
break- – : point de rupture.
break-even – : seuil de rentabilité.
bullion- – : point de sortie de l'or ou de l'argent.
a case in – : en cas d'espèce.
gold- – : point de sortie de l'or.
growth- – : seuil de croissance.
– *input investment*: investissement ponctuel.
– *output investment*: investissement produit instantané, exploitation ponctuelle.
the – *at issue*: la question en litige.
– *of law (legal point)*: point de droit.
– *of no return*: point de non retour.
[J] – *of order*: objection préalable sur la façon dont seront menés les débats.
profitless – : seuil de rentabilité.
[C] – *of purchase, of sale*: point d'achat, de vente.
saturation – : point de saturation.
to carry one's – : établir la validité de son argument.
to lose a –, *several* –(s): perdre un, plusieurs points.
to rise a –, *several* –(s): gagner un point, plusieurs points.
stock which has (lost, risen a –): valeur qui a perdu, gagné un point.
to maintain one's – : maintenir son point de vue.
to make a – : faire ressortir un argument.
to stress a – : faire ressortir un point, mettre en évidence un aspect de la question.

to poise: équilibrer.
the market appears to be **poised**: le marché semble équilibré.

police: police (f).
[A] *civil* – : force publique.
– *court*: tribunal de police.
– *force*: corps de police.
– *form*: fiche de police.
– *inspector*: inspecteur de police.
– *intelligence*: nouvelles judiciaires.
– *office*: commissariat (central) de police.
– *raid*: descente de police.
– *station*: poste de police.
(under) – *supervision*: en liberté surveillée.

policy: politique (f) générale, ligne (f) de conduite, principes (m pl) directeurs ; police (f) (d'assurance).
assurance – : police d'assurance.
– *to bearer*: police au porteur.
budgetary – : politique budgétaire.
commodity – : politique en matière de produits de base.
credit – : politique de crédit.
currency – : politique monétaire.
fiscal – *(customs* –): politique douanière.
floating – : police flottante, d'abonnement.
full-employment – : politique de plein emploi.
– *holder*: titulaire d'une police d'assurance.
life insurance – : police d'assurance sur la vie.
marine insurance – : police maritime.
open door – : principe de la porte ouverte.
open – *(blanket* –): police générale, ouverte, à obligations non évaluées.
– *to order*: police à ordre.
price – : politique des prix.
public – : l'intérêt public.
round – : police à l'aller et au retour (d'un voyage maritime).
– *slip*: [U.S.] billet de loterie publique (illégal).
standard – : police type.
agricultural support – : [U.S.] politique de soutien à l'agriculture.
time – : police à terme, à forfait.
valued – : police fixe.
wage(s) – : politique salariale.
to surrender a – : racheter une police.
to take out a – : prendre une police.

political body: organe politique.
– *economy*: économie politique.
– *jobbery (manœuvering)*: manœuvres politiques, politicailleries (f pl).
– *levy*: cotisation syndicale.
– *movement, party*: mouvement (m), parti (m) politique.

politics: la politique (f).
foreign, internal – : politique étrangère, intérieure.
parochial – : politique de clocher.

poll: tête (f), individu (m), scrutin (m) par tête, liste électorale (f), sondage (m), enquête (f).
[J] *challenge to the* –(s): récusation de certains jurés.
deed – : contrat à titre gratuit.
constituency – : scrutin d'arrondissement.
second – : scrutin de ballotage.
to poll: recueillir les votes ; donner son vote.

to poll a jury: demander aux jurés, un par un, quel était leur verdict.
polling *day:* jour du scrutin.

pollutants : matières polluantes, facteurs de pollution.
pollution : pollution (f).

pool : [C] [F] mise en commun de ressources, fonds commun, masse commune, équipe, syndicat de placement (de marchandises), syndicat de prix ferme, tour de table.
producers' — : syndicat de producteurs.
to pool : mettre en commun (les fonds, les commandes).
pooling of resources: mise en commun des ressources.
pooling agreement: convention régissant une exploitation en commun.

popular action : [J] action pénale en recouvrement d'amende par un particulier se substituant aux pouvoirs publics.

population : population (f).
active, gainfully employed — : population active.
decrease (increase) in — : décroissement (accroissement) démographique.
excess — : surpopulation.
— trends : tendances démographiques.

port : port (m).
— of call : port d'escale.
— dues (charges) : droits de port.
free — : port franc.
home — (port of commission) : port d'attache.
— of necessity (of refuge) : port de relâche.
— of registry : port d'attache (d'immatriculation).
— regulations : règlements portuaires.
— of shipment : port d'embarquement.
— of survey : port de visite.
transshipment — : port de transbordement.

porterage : factage (m), manutention (f).
— tax : taxe de factage.

portfolio : portefeuille (m) d'assurances.
[F] *securities in — :* valeurs en portefeuille.
— selection : choix des investissements entre portefeuilles.
[C] *— technique :* technique de permutation des facteurs de production d'une série de produits à une autre.

portion : portion (f), part (f), tranche (f), avance (f) d'hoirie.
— accruing to... : portion afférente à...
[F] *— of the income (of a tax payer) :* tranche de revenu (d'un contribuable).
— of shares : tranche d'actions.

[J] *— of inheritance :* part d'héritage.
marriage — : dot (f).
portioner : portionnaire (d'un héritage).
portionless : sans dot.

position : état (m), situation (f), poste (m), emploi (m).
(C) cours d'une marchandise livrable immédiatement.
cash — : situation de caisse.
customer's — at the bank : situation en banque du client.
financial — : moyens financiers.
market — (position of the market) : situation (position) de la place, état du marché.
to be in a — to : être en état de, à même de.
to occupy, (to hold) a — (of trust) : occuper un poste de (confiance).
to recover one's financial — : se remettre à flot.

positive : positif, affirmatif, explicite (a).
— cash-flow : rentrées de liquidités supérieures aux sorties.
— economics : économie positive.
— law : législation en vigueur.
— position : situation de caisse.
— prescription : prescription acquisitive.
— proof : preuve manifeste.
— proposal : proposition concrète.
— statement : déclaration formelle.
— yield : rendement positif.
— yield curve : courbe, graphique (m) des rendements positifs.

posse : (J) détachement d'hommes chargés de la police.

to possess : posséder.
possession : possession (f).
[J] *« possession is nine tenths (points) of the law » :* « possession est droit pour les neuf dixièmes », adage qui ne correspond pas tout à fait (en fait de meubles) « possession vaut titre », mais reconnaît que la possession constitue une présomption de droit à la propriété.
actual possession : possession effective.
adverse possession : possession de fait.
prevention of possession : trouble de jouissance.
right of possession : possessoire.
vacant possession : libre possession (d'un immeuble).
house to let with vacant possession : maison à louer, clefs en main.
to be in possession of : disposer de.
to take possession of : prendre possession, entrer en jouissance.
possessor : possesseur, détenteur (m).
possessory : possessoire (a).

possessory lien : droit de rétention.

(consumption, production) possibilities : possibilités de consommation, production.

post : a) préfixe (latin) ; après ; b) poste (f), courrier (m), emploi (m).
— *-entry :* [D] déclaration additionnelle (en douane).
[C] écriture postérieure.
post-completion audit : contrôle « a posteriori » de la rentabilité (des investissements).
— *-dated cheque :* chèque post-daté.
— *-mortem examination :* autopsie (f).
— *-obit bond :* contrat exécutoire, obligation réalisable après le décès d'un tiers.
— *-war :* d'après-guerre.
— *-free :* franc de port.
— *-graduate research :* recherches de troisième cycle (universitaire).
— *office order :* mandat poste.
— *office (postal) savings bank :* caisse d'épargne (postale).
by return of — : par retour du courrier.
to take up one's post : entrer en fonctions.
to post : a) poster, affranchir ; b) afficher ; c) porter, passer (une écriture) ; d) affecter.
to post (up) an account : reporter un compte.
to post the books : passer les écritures.
to post an entry : passer écriture.
to post a notice : afficher un avis.
to post up the ledger : mettre le grand livre à jour.
posted earnings : bénéfices (m pl) inscrits.
posted *prices :* prix affichés.

postage : affranchissement (m), port (m), taxe (f) (postale).
[F] — *due stamp :* timbre-taxe.
extra (additional) — : surtaxe postale.
— *paid :* port payé.
— *rates (postal rates) :* tarifs postaux.
to affix the proper — : affranchir comme il convient.

post-code : code (m) postal.

posting : a) dépôt (m), envoi (m) par la poste ; b) affichage (m) ; c) passation (f) (d'une écriture) ; d) affectation (f) (d'un fonctionnaire).

to postpone : ajourner, différer, remettre.
— *a payment, a settlement :* différer un paiement, un règlement.
postponement : renvoi, ajournement (m).

potential buyer (consumer) : acheteur, consommateur en puissance, éventuel.

potentialities : potentiel économique.

pound : a) livre (f) (sterling ou mesure de poids) ; b) fourrière (f), dépôt (m) de marchandises saisies (f pl).

poundage : droit (m), commission (f), remise (f) (de tant par livre sterling) ; frais (m pl) de fourrière.

poverty-line : [U.S.] minimum vital.

power : pouvoir (m), faculté (m), capacité (f), talent (m), vigueur (f), énergie (f), puissance (f), influence (f), autorité (f).
[J] — *of appointment :* pouvoir donné à un usufruitier de désigner celui qui bénéficiera d'un legs.
— *of attorney :* procuration (écrite), mandat (de faire).
general — : procuration générale.
judicial (executive, legislative) — : pouvoir judiciaire (exécutif, législatif).
private — (s) : droits conférés par un particulier à un autre.
public — (s) : droits conférés par l'Etat à ses fonctionnaires.
purchasing — : pouvoir d'achat.
special — (s) : droits conférés spécialement (par une procuration, etc.).
the — (s) that be : les Autorités constituées.
to act with full — (s) : agir de pleine autorité.
to exceed, to go beyond one's — (s) : sortir de sa compétence.
to restrict the — (s) : restreindre les pouvoirs.

PR (proportional representation) : RP (représentation à la proportionnelle).

practical example : cas concret.
— *owner :* propriétaire de fait.
— *trade experience :* expérience acquise dans l'exercice d'une profession.

practice : pratique (f), usage (m), méthode (f).
[J] procédure (f), [C] usance (f), clientèle (f).
administrative — (s) : usages administratifs.
civil — : procédure civile.
the — of the courts : la procédure.
illegal — (s) : manœuvres frauduleuses.
restrictive — (s) : manœuvres, pratiques restrictives d'un oligopole.
selling — (s) : méthodes de vente.
the — of law, of medicine : l'exercice du droit (de la profession d'avocat), de la médecine.
in — : en exercice.
to put into — : mettre en pratique.

to practise : pratiquer, exercer.
practising *barrister (barrister in practice) :* avocat en exercice.

(general) practitioner: médecin généraliste, avocat non spécialisé.

praecipe: commande.

praedial: prédial, réel, foncier(s) (a) (biens).

preamble: préambule (m).
[J] exposé des motifs d'une loi, attendus d'un arrêt.
the — (s) of a treaty: les préliminaires (d'un traité).

precarious right: [J] droit (de jouissance) accordé à titre précaire.

precatory words: termes exprimant un vœu (ou un espoir) du testateur.

precautionary measure: mesure de précaution, préventive.
— *motive, saving*: motif, épargne de précaution.

to precede: précéder.

precedence: préséance, priorité, droit de priorité.
to give — to: donner la priorité à.

precedent: a) précédent (a); b) précédent (m).
[J] décision judiciaire faisant jurisprudence.
to be a —: servir de précédent.
— (s) of a case: jurisprudence d'un cas de droit.
condition —: condition suspensive.

precept: précepte (m), mandat (m) (écrit) d'un magistrat.
[A] feuille de contributions.

precinct: enceinte (f).
[U.S.] circonscription électorale; division administrative d'une ville.

to preclude: empêcher, prévenir, exclure.

precognition: préconnaissance, connaissance antérieure.

preconceived intent: (J) intention préconçue.

pre-contract: contrat préalable, compromis, l'existence d'un tel contrat empêche les parties d'en conclure un autre de même nature.

to predate: antidater.

predatory (export) financing: concurrence déloyale à l'exportation, crédits déloyaux aux exportateurs (accordés aux exportateurs par un gouvernement pour leur permettre de conquérir un marché).

predecease: prédécès.
*the **predeceased** parent*: le parent (père ou mère) le premier décédé.

predecessor: prédécesseur (m).

predelinquency: pré-délinquance (f).

predetermined standard: see « standard ».

preemption: préemption (f).
[J] **preemptive** *right*: droit de préemption.
preemptor: [U.S.] acquéreur en vertu d'un droit de préemption.
to preempt: accaparer, acquérir en usant d'un droit de préemption.

pre-entry closed shop: adhésion (f) à un syndicat comme condition préalable à une embauche.

to prefer: préférer, accorder un traitement de faveur, privilégier, présenter.
the Government is **preferred** *over all creditors*: le Gouvernement passe avant (est préféré à) la masse des créanciers.
— *a complaint*: déposer une plainte.
— *an indictment*: porter une accusation.
— *a petition*: adresser une pétition.
preferred *position*: emplacement (dans un journal ou une revue) où l'on veut insérer une annonce publicitaire (contre paiement supplémentaire).
preferred stock: actions privilégiées, de priorité.

preference: préférence (f), droit de priorité.
[J] avantage particulier accordé par un débiteur insolvable à un de ses créanciers qu'il rembourse avant les autres; privilège d'un créancier lui permettant d'être payé avant les autres.
— *bonds*: obligations privilégiées.
— *fiscal claims*: privilège des créances fiscales.
— *legacy*: prélegs.
liquidity —: préférence pour la liquidité.
— *shares*: actions privilégiées, de priorité.
tax — (s): élément(s) du revenu soumis à un impôt spécial si le montant excède certaines limites.

preferential: préférentiel, privilégié, de faveur.
preferential agreements: accords préférentiels.
(creditor's) preferential claim: préférence du créancier.
preferential rates: tarifs préférentiels, spé-

ciaux, minimum.
preferential right: privilège (m), droit préférentiel.
preferential shares, stock: actions privilégiées, titres privilégiés.
preferential tariff: tarif (douanier) de faveur.

preferment: avancement (m), promotion (f).

prefinancing: préfinancement (m).

prejudice: préjudice (m), tort (m), dommage (m), préjugé (m), opinon (f) préconçue.
to the – of: au préjudice de.
[J] *without – :* sous toutes réserves, sans préjudice de.
without – to any claim: sous réserve de tous recours.
prejudicial *(to)*: nuisible, dommageable.
prejudicial error: procédure erronée.
prejudicial evidence: preuve manifestement inopérante.

preliminary: a) préliminaire, préalable (a) ; b) préliminaire (m).
[J] – *agreement, contract, condition*: contrat, convention, condition préalable.
– *entry*: déclaration préliminaire.
– *expenses*: frais de constitution.
– *injunction*: ordonnance interlocutoire.
– *investigation*: instruction (d'une affaire).
– *question*: question préjudicielle.
– *scheme*: avant-projet.
by way of – : à titre de mesure préventive.
the **preliminaries** *of a treaty*: les préliminaires d'un traité.

pre-marital agreement: [U.S.] contrat de mariage.

premeditation: préméditation (f).

premises: prémisses (f pl).
[J] – *of a deed*: intitulé d'un acte.
the – : les lieux, le local, l'immeuble.
on the – : sur les lieux, sur place.
to vacate the – : vider les lieux.
[C] *business – :* locaux commerciaux.
depreciation on – : amortissement sur immeubles.

premium: prime (f) (d'assurance), agio (m), indemnité (f), récompense (f), reprise (f), prix convenu, profit net, « au-dessus de la valeur nominale ».
[ASS] *additional (extra) – :* surprime (f).
insurance – : prime d'assurance.
loaded – : surprime.
low- – insurance: assurance à prime réduite.
[F] – *bonds*: obligations à lots, à prime.
exchange – (– on exchange): agio, prime de change.

– *offer*: offre d'une prime pour un achat.
– *on a lease*: redevance à payer au début d'un bail.
– *pay*: salaire supplémentaire.
– *prices*: prix élevés, sans remise.
redemption – : prime de remboursement.
– *reserve*: réserve prime d'émission.
stock sold at a – : titres vendus au-dessus du pair.
to stand (to be) at a – : faire prime.
– *to be arranged*: prime à débattre.
premises to let, small – : local à louer avec petite reprise.

to prepay: payer d'avance, par anticipation.
prepaid *(freight)*: (fret) payé d'avance.
prepaid expenses: frais payés d'avance.

prepayment: paiement anticipatif, affranchissement (d'une lettre, du port, etc.).
[J] – *clause*: clause d'un billet autorisant le débiteur à s'acquitter, en tout ou partie, avant l'échéance.
[D] – *of customs charges*: affranchissement des droits de douane.

prepense malice: acte criminel prémédité.

preponderance: [J] supériorité des preuves du demandeur, emportant la conviction du juge.

prepriced: dont le prix est payé d'avance.

prerequisite: condition préalable.

prerogative (of pardon): prérogative (f) (du droit de grâce).

to prescribe: prescrire, ordonner.
as expressly **prescribed**: selon les dispositions expresses.
in the prescribed time: dans les délais prescrits.

prescription: prescription (f).

prescriptive: prescriptif (a), entraînant obligation.

present: présent, actuel (a).
– *position*: fonction actuelle.
[C] – *capital*: capital appelé.
– *value*: valeur actuelle.
discounted – value: valeur actualisée.
– *value of earnings method*: méthode du revenu global actualisé, du revenu brut actualisé.
– *value tables*: tables d'actualisation.
– *value worth*: valeur actuelle.
[J] « *by these – (s)... »* : « par ces présentes... ».

presentation for acceptance (for payment) : présentation à l'acceptation (au paiement).
on — : à vue, sur demande.

presentment : [J] déclaration de mise en accusation ; déclaration émanant du jury.
— *of a bill* : présentation d'une traite.

presiding judge : président du tribunal.

press : la Presse (f).
— *release* : see « news release ».
— *conference* : conférence de presse.
— *cutting* : coupure de presse.

to press : insister (sur), réclamer, persister, requisitionner, enrôler de force.
— *a claim* : insister sur une demande.
[C] — *for a debt* : réclamer une dette.
to be **pressed** *by (one's) creditors* : être harcelé, pressé par (ses) créanciers.
to be pressed for funds (money) : manquer de disponibilités.
pressing debt : dette criarde.

pressure : pression, tension (f).
economic — : pression économique.
financial — : embarras financiers.
— *groups* : groupes de pression.
inflationary — : pression inflationniste.
under — : sous la contrainte.

prestige : prestige (m).
— *advertising* : publicité destinée à améliorer une image de marque.

presumption : présomption (f).
[J] — *of death* : présomption de décès.
— *of fact* : présomption de fait.
— *of law* : présomption légale.
rebuttable — : présomption réfutable.
— *of survival* : présomption de survie.
presumptive : présomptif (a).
presumptive evidence : preuve par déduction, par présomption.
presumptive heir : héritier présomptif.
[F] *presumptive assessment* : évaluation forfaitaire.
presumptive income : revenu présumé.
presumptive loss (of a ship) : présomption de perte (d'un navire).
presumptive method : méthode forfaitaire.
presumptive taxation : imposition forfaitaire.

pre-tax profits : bénéfices (m pl) hors taxes, hors impôts.

pretence : affectation (f), faux semblant, prétexte (m), simulation (f).
[J] *false* — : fausses allégations, moyens frauduleux.

to pretend : prétendre, feindre, faire semblant de.
[J] **pretended** *right or title* : droit ou titre dont se prévaut le demandeur dans une action possessoire.

pretest : essai préliminaire, vérification (f) préalable.

to prevail : prévaloir, prédominer.
prevailing : commun, général, régnant, actuel.
prevailing party : partie gagnante dans un procès.
the prevailing quotation : le cours actuel.
the (economic) prevailing conditions : les conditions (économiques) actuelles.
the prevailing tone of the market : l'ambiance générale du marché.

preventive maintenance : see « *planned maintenance* ».

previous : (a) précédent, antérieur.
— *close (closing)* : clôture précédente.
— *conviction* : condamnation antérieure.
— *notice* : préavis.
— *price* : cours précédent.
— *year* : année précédente, exercice précédent.
to call for the — *question* : (pol.) poser la question préalable.

price : prix (m), coût (m), cours (m), cote (f), taux (m).
[C] [F] *actual* — : prix réel.
administrated — : [U.S.] prix imposé.
advance in — : hausse, augmentation de prix.
agreed — : prix convenu.
auction — : prix d'adjudication.
base (basic) — : prix de base, de référence.
cash — (— *for cash*) : prix au comptant, cours au comptant.
catalogue — : prix marqué.
ceiling — : prix-plafond.
closing — : cours de clôture.
contract — : prix forfaitaire.
cost — : prix de revient.
— *control* : contrôle des prix.
— *current* : prix courant, tarif.
— *cutting* : vente au rabais.
— *differential spread* : ciseaux de prix (phénomènes de).
downward trend of —(*s*) : mouvement de baisse des prix.
— -*discrimination* : discrimination dans les prix.
— *earning ratio (PER)* : coefficient de capitalisation des résultats, (C.C.R.), rapport cours-bénéfices.
— *ex-works* : prix départ-usine.
fair — : juste prix.
fixed — : prix fixe.

full — : prix fort.
gross — : prix brut.
— *index* : indice des prix.
issue — : prix d'émission.
jobbing — : prix de tâche.
knock-down — : prix minimum, prix choc, prix d'adjudication.
laid-down — : prix imposé par le fabricant.
— *-leader* : entreprise sur les prix de laquelle les autres s'alignent, entreprise qui « fait » les prix.
— *leadership* : prix directeur.
— *-level financial statements* : comptes corrigés des variations monétaires.
list — : prix de nomenclature.
— *list* : tarif, barème des prix.
(the) lowest — : (le) dernier prix.
— *maker* : celui qui fixe le prix.
market — : prix courant.
— *of money* : taux de l'escompte.
net — : prix net.
pegged — : prix stable, prix de soutien.
— *of option* : cours de prime, (prix de) base de la prime.
— *of put and call* : prix de l'option.
purchase — : prix d'achat, d'acquisition.
put-up — : mise à prix (dans une adjudication).
range of — (s) : échelle des prix.
reduced — : prix au rabais, réduit.
retail — : prix de détail.
— *-ring* : coalition de vendeurs.
rise in — (s) : hausse des prix.
scheduled — (s) : prix de barème.
selling — (sale price) : prix de vente.
spot — : prix du disponible.
steady — : prix fermes, soutenus.
supply — : prix d'offre.
support — : prix de soutien.
top — : cours le plus haut.
trade — : prix marchand, sur place.
under — : au-dessous du cours (du prix).
upward trend of — (s) : mouvement de hausse des prix.
upset — : mise à prix, prix de départ.
wage- — *spiral* : spirale des prix et des salaires.
ex-warehouse (in-bond) — : prix en entrepôt (de douane).
wholesale — : prix de gros.
to reach a high — : atteindre un prix élevé.
to price : fixer un prix.
— *oneself out of the market* : perdre sa clientèle en demandant des prix trop élevés.
*high-***priced**, *low-priced (goods)* : (marchandises), chères, bon marché.
pricing : fixation (f) des prix, tarification (f).
common — : prix de cartel.
— *policy* : politique des prix.
[F] *transfer* — : technique d'évasion fiscale fondée sur la fixation des prix (entre sociétés apparentées, entre sociétés relevant de pays à fiscalité contrastée, etc.).

prima facie case : [J] affaire qui, de prime abord, paraît fondée.

prima facie evidence : [J] commencement de preuve.

primae impressionis : (affaire) de première impression (pour laquelle il n'existe pas de précédent).

primage : prime de chargement.

primary : primaire, primitif, primordial (a), de base.
— *cause* : cause première.
— *commodities (products)* : produits de base, matières premières.
— *data* : informations de première main.
— *election* : [U.S.] élection primaire (« *primaries* »).
— *industry* : industrie de base, secteur primaire.
— *legislation (opp. delegated)* : les lois (votées par le Parlement) (opp. règlements).
— *products* : produits bruts, de base.
— *purpose* : but direct.
— *right* : droit découlant directement d'un contrat.

prime : premier, principal, de qualité supérieure, taux de base.
— *cause* : cause première.
— *cost* : prix de revient, prix de fabrication.
of — *importance* : de (toute) première importance.
— *motive* : principal mobile.
— *necessity* : nécessité première.
[F] — *base lending* : prêts indexés sur le taux de base.
— *bill* : effet de première qualité.
— *bond* : obligation de premier ordre.
— *rate* : [U.S.] taux d'intérêt préférentiel sur découvert en banque.
— *time* : heures de plus grande écoute (radio, T.V.).
— *trade bills* : papiers hors banque, de haut commerce.

primogeniture : primogéniture (f).

principal : principal (a).
[J] auteur d'un crime ou délit, mandant, commettant, débiteur principal.
[C] [F] capital (m), principal (m) d'une dette.
the — *amount of an obligation* : le principal d'un titre.
— *assistant* : secrétaire de direction.
— *clerk* : premier commis.
— *contract* : contrat direct.

— *creditor (debtor)* : principal créancier (débiteur).
— *establishment (residence)* : domicile principal.
— *heir* : héritier principal.
— *in the first degree* : auteur principal d'un crime.
— *in the second degree (accessory)* : complice.
— *and agent* : mandant et mandataire.
— *of a business house* : patron d'une maison de commerce.
— *and interest* : capital et intérêts.
— *residence* : résidence principale.
(B) donneur d'ordres.
[A] Assistant Principal : sous-chef de bureau.

principle : principe (m), loi (f), règle (f).
the — *of an act* : le motif d'une loi.
economic — *(s)* : lois, principes économiques.
to lay down as a — : poser en principe.

printed from : formulaire (m).

prior : antérieur, prioritaire (a) ; avant (adv).
— *appropriation on the net profits* : prélèvement prioritaire sur les bénéfices nets.
— *charge* : garantie d'un emprunt (prioritaire).
(to have) a — *claim* : être le premier en date, avoir un titre de priorité.
— *contract* : contrat antérieur.
— *lien* : dette privilégiée.

priority : priorité (f), préférence (f), privilège (m), hypothèque (f).
priority bond : obligation de priorité.
priority-holder : prioritaire.
priority of invention : antériorité d'invention.
priority rights : droits de priorité.
priority share : action privilégiée.

prison : prison (f).
prison *editor* : homme de paille appartenant à la rédaction d'un journal et qu'on met en avant en cas de procès.
— *governor* : directeur de prison.
prisoner *at the bar* : prévenu, accusé présent à l'audience.
prisoner awaiting trial : accusé en détention.
to discharge a prisoner : élargir un prisonnier.

private : privé, particulier (a).
— *account* : compte particulier.
— *agreement* : acte sous seing privé.
— *arrangement* : accord à l'amiable.
— *attorney* : fondé de pouvoirs.
— *bill* : projet de loi d'intérêt local.
— *car* : voiture de tourisme.
— *company* : société privée (particulière), société à responsabilité limitée.
— *consumption* : consommation des ménages.
— *deed* : acte sous seing privé.
— *enterprise* : (l')entreprise privée.
— *income* : revenus personnels, fortune personnelle.
— *information* : renseignements de source privée.
— *international law* : droit international privé.
— *issue (of shares)* : émission privée d'action.
— *law* : droit privé.
— *means* : fortune personnelle, ressources personnelles.
— *ownership* : (l')entreprise privée (opposée à l'étatisation).
— *person* : simple particulier.
— *placement* : placement (m) privé.
— *property* : biens personnels.
— *rate (of discount)* : taux privé (de l'escompte), taux hors-banque.
— *sale* : vente de gré à gré.
— *seal* : sceau (seing) privé.
— *sector* : secteur privé.
[J] [A] — *sitting* : audience (f), séance (f) à huis clos.
for — *use* : à usage personnel.
to hear a case in — : juger une affaire à huis clos.
privately *owned* : qui appartient à un particulier.
privately sold : vendu à l'amiable.

privatisation : privatisation (f).

privilege : privilège (m), prérogative (f).
[J] *the* — : la prérogative royale.
— *of necessity, of self-defence* : droit de légitime défense.
parliamentary — : immunité parlementaire.
plea of — : invocation du secret professionnel.
professional — : secret professionnel.
special —*(s)* : droits particuliers.
privileged *claim (debt)* : créance, dette privilégiée.
privileged creditor : créancier privilégié.
privileged motion : motion (parlementaire) d'urgence.
privileged statement : déclaration diffamatoire dont l'auteur échappe aux conséquences, lorsqu'il la formule dans l'accomplissement de ses fonctions ou en déposant devant un tribunal.
to waive the — : relever du secret professionnel.

privity : [J] lien de droit, obligation, lien de sang.
— *in deed* : obligation contractuelle.
— *in law* : obligation de droit.
without — : sans lien de droit.

privy : a) privé (a) ; b) ayant cause, partie intéressée, contractant (m).
to be — *to (sthg)* : avoir connaissance de qch, tremper dans (un complot).

— 551 —

the – council: le Conseil privé (du souverain).
the – Seal: le Petit Sceau, dont l'apposition autorise le lord Chancelier à apposer le Sceau de l'Etat *(the Great Seal).*

prize: lot (m), prix (m).
[J] – *court:* conseil (tribunal) des prises.
[F] – *bond:* obligation à lots.
– *drawing:* tirage à lots.

pro: (devant une signature) « pour ».

pro forma: pour la forme.

pro hac vice: pour cette occasion.

pro indivisio: indivis (d'un terrain).

pro interesse suo: pour son propre intérêt.

probability: probabilité (f), vraisemblance (f).
– *sampling:* sondage probabiliste.

probate: preuve (f), en forme probante, validation (f), vérification (f), homologation (f) (d'un testament).
[J] – *court:* [U.S.] tribunal des successions et des tutelles.
– *duty:* droit de timbre appliqué à tout héritage supérieur à une certaine somme.
the – copy of a will: la copie homologuée d'un testament.

probation: [J] probation (f) (régime de la mise à l'épreuve); stage (m), essai (m).
(to be) on – : (être) à l'épreuve, à l'essai, faire un stage.
probationary *(clerk, teacher, etc.):* (commis, instituteur, etc.) stagiaire.
probationary period: (période de) stage.

probative: exploratoire (a).

probe: [U.S.] enquête (f).

to probe (the evidence): examiner de près, scruter (les témoignages).

problem cases: (affaires) cas exceptionnels.

(housing) problem: (la) crise du logement.

procedural: de procédure.
[J] – *law:* code de procédure.
– *matters:* affaires de procédure (ou courantes).
– *step:* acte de procédure.
procedure: procédure; façon de procéder.

civil, parliamentary procedure: procédure civile, parlementaire.
the correct procedure: la bonne méthode (pour, de).
order of procedure: règles de procédure.

to proceed: procéder, se mettre à (faire), poursuivre, continuer.
– *to blows:* en venir aux coups.
– *with the business of the day:* passer à l'ordre du jour.
[J] – *against (s.o.):* procéder contre, poursuivre, intenter un procès (à qn).
to pay as the work proceeds: payer au fur et à mesure des travaux.
proceeding: marche (f) à suivre, démarche (f), procédé (m); acte (m) de procédure, procès (m); délibérations (f pl).
arbitration proceedings: procédure d'arbitrage.
proceeding in bankruptcy: procédure en faillite.
civil proceedings: procédure civile, action civile.
collection proceedings: procédure en recouvrement.
criminal proceedings: poursuites au criminel.
divorce proceedings: instance en divorce.
illegal proceeding: abus de pouvoir.
legal proceedings: procès, procédure judiciaire, poursuites judiciaires.
the proceedings (of the Royal Society, in Parliament, etc.): les travaux, les délibérations, les débats, les procès-verbaux de séance (de la Société Royale, du Parlement, etc.).
stay of proceedings: sursis à statuer.
summary proceeding: procédure sommaire.
to initiate, to institute, to take proceedings against s.o.: intenter un procès, engager des poursuites contre qn, avoir recours aux moyens légaux.
to order proceedings to be taken against s.o.: instrumenter contre qn.
the proceedings will begin at...: la séance, la réunion commencera à...

proceeds: produit (m), montant (m), gains (m pl); (qfs contrepartie).
[F] *gross, net – :* bénéfice, produit brut, net.
– *from tax:* produit de l'impôt.

process: processus (m), procédé (m), méthode (f) de traitement industriel, évolution (f), développement (m), opération (f).
[J] ensemble des moyens de contrainte appliqués par un tribunal pour donner effet à ses décisions.
– *of adjustment (adjustment process):* mécanisme d'ajustement; processus de règlement.
– *chart:* diagramme descriptif des diverses phases d'une opération, d'une fabrication.
decision making – : mécanisme de prise de décision.

– 552 –

final − : ordonnance d'exécution, exécutoire.
first − *(original* −*)* : [U.S.] exploit introductif d'instance.
fitting − : ajustement statistique.
− *industry* : industrie de transformation.
judicial − : action en justice, procès.
jury − : convocation du jury.
− *of recovery* : opération de recouvrement.
− *-server* : huissier (m).
in − *of (development)* : en voie de (développement).
to process : traiter, transformer.
processed *(goods, products)* : (produits) ayant subi une transformation, un traitement.
processing : production (f), fabrication (f), traitement (m), transformation (f).
(automatic) data processing : traitement mécanographique des données de l'information.
processing and marketing : conditionnement et vente.
processing stages : phases de la fabrication.
[F] *processing tax* : [U.S.] impôt sur la transformation d'une denrée en produit industriel.

proclamation : proclamation, promulgation (f).

Queen's, King's proctor : procureur (m) de la reine, du roi (devant certaines juridictions).

procuration : procuration (f), acquisition (f), mandat (m).
[C] commission payée à un agent pour l'obtention d'un prêt.
act of − *(in purchase)* : commandement.
letter of − : mandat.
− *signature* : signature par procuration.
procurator : fondé de pouvoir.
to procure : jouer un rôle d'entremetteur (m).

procurement : obtention, acquisition (f), achat de fournitures, d'approvisionnements.
− *agency* : office de commissionnaire.
− *costs* : dépenses d'acquisition ; [U.S.] dépenses d'équipement, d'approvisionnement.

produce : produit(s), denrées (f pl), rendement (m).
[F] − *exchange* : bourse de marchandises.
[C] *farm* − : produits agricoles.
net − : produit net.
− *market* : marché commercial.
raw − : produits bruts, matières premières.

to produce : produire, rapporter, présenter.
[J] − *documents* : produire, présenter des pièces.
− *a witness* : produire un témoin.
[C] *capacity* − : capacité de production.
− *evidence* : fournir des preuves.
− *interest* : rapporter un intérêt.
producer : producteur (m).
− *good* : bien de production.
producing : producteur, productif (a).
producing industry : industrie productrice.

product : produit (m), denrée (f), résultat (m).
[C] *by-* − : sous-produit (m).
− *development* : amélioration apportée à une fabrication, à un produit.
− *differentiation* : différenciation d'un produit par rapport à d'autres de même usage (par la présentation etc.).
end- −, *finished* − : produit fini (m).
− *extension* : croissance circulaire (diversification par introduction de produits apparentés aux productions actuelles).
− *feature* : particularité d'un produit propre à le faire vendre.
gross, net national − : produit national brut, net.
− *liability insurance* : assurance contre les risques afférents à un défaut de fabrication.
− *life-cycle* : see « life ».
primary − *(s)* : produits de base, matières premières.
− *recall* : reprise, à l'échelle nationale d'un article défectueux pour vérification ou modification par le fabricant.
secondary − *(s)* : sous-produits.
− *test* : sondage pour savoir ce que les acheteurs pensent d'un produit.
standardized − *(s)* : produits normalisés.
waste − : produit de rejet.
production : production, fabrication, présentation.
belt system of production : travail, production à la chaîne.
certificate of production : certificat d'origine.
production capacity : capacité de production.
comparative efficiency of production : rendement comparatif de la production.
production control : contrôle de la production.
production cost : prix de revient de la production, coefficient d'exploitation.
cost of production : coût de production.
excess of production : surproduction.
flow-production : travail à la chaîne.
production incentives : stimulants de la production.
production lines : séries de fabrication.
production-oriented company : entreprise qui se préoccupe davantage de ses produits que des besoins des consommateurs.
production-oriented firm : entreprise qui se préoccupe plus de la fabrication de ses produits que des besoins des consommateurs.
line production : production à la chaîne.
mass production : production en série.
production process : procédé de fabrication.

— 553 —

standard production : production de série.
standardized production : production en série.
production targets : objectifs chiffrés de production.
uneconomic production : production contraire à une économie saine.
to freeze the existing pattern of production : figer la production dans son moule actuel.
[J] *production of documents, of titles of property :* production, communication de documents, de titres de propriété.
production of evidence : production de preuves.

productive : producteur, productif (a).
[C] *— capacity :* capacité de production.
— capital : capitaux en rapport.
— industry : industrie productrice.
[F] *— value :* valeur de rendement.

productivity : productivité (f).
— of an enterprise : rentabilité (productivité) d'une entreprise.
— factor : facteur (m) de productivité ; rapport bénéfices-actifs utilisés.
labour — : productivité du travail.
land in full — : terres en plein rapport.
marginal, net — : productivité marginale, nette.
to lift — : accroître la productivité.

profession : profession (f), métier (m).
the learned — (s) : les professions libérales.
the medical, teaching — : le corps médical, enseignant.
professional : professionnel.
professional advice : conseil(s) d'un spécialiste.
professional ethics : déontologie.
professional fees : honoraires.
professional man : homme exerçant une profession libérale.
professional privilege, secrecy : secret professionnel.
[F] *professional earnings :* bénéfices non commerciaux.

proficiency : compétence, capacité (f).

proficient : versé, compétent, capable (a).

customer profile : profil (m) du consommateur.

profit : a) profit (m), bénéfice (m), gain (m), plus-value (f) ; b) bénéficiaire (a).
[F] *— allowances :* tantièmes (m pl).
balance-sheet showing a — : bilan bénéficiaire.
apportionment of — (s) : répartition des bénéfices.
— balance : solde bénéficiaire.
book — (s) : bénéfices d'écriture, comptables.
business — (s) (trading — (s)) : bénéfices commerciaux.
casual — (s) : revenant-bon.
clear — : bénéfice net.
capital — : boni, plus-value.
— -center : groupe détude des prix de revient et des bénéfices.
concealment of — (s) : dissimulation de bénéfices.
distributed — (s) : bénéfices distribués.
distribution of — (s) : répartition, partage des bénéfices.
diversion of — (s) from one country to another : transfert illicite de bénéfices d'un pays à un autre.
pre-tax — (s) : bénéfices bruts d'impôt, avant impôt.
— -earning : rentable.
— -earning capacity : rentabilité.
excess — (s) : superbénéfices.
extra — : bénéfice (profit) additionnel (supplémentaire).
firm earning — (s) : entreprise bénéficiaire.
gross, net — : bénéfice brut, net.
incoming — : profit accru.
loss of —, missed — : manque à gagner.
margin of — (s) (— margin) : marge bénéficiaire.
motive — : see « objective profit ».
payments out of — (s) : versements sur bénéfices.
— and loss account : compte de profits et pertes.
non- — organization : organisation à but non-lucratif.
operating — (s) : bénéfices d'exploitation.
— -seeking : intéressé, à but lucratif.
— sharing : participation aux bénéfices.
— sharing allowances : tantièmes.
— sharing scheme : intéressement.
— taking : participation aux bénéfices, prise de bénéfice.
— -tax : impôt sur les bénéfices.
taxable — (s) : bénéfices imposables.
— (s) of (a) trade : bénéfices industriels et commerciaux.
undistributed (undivided) — (s) : bénéfices non distribués, non répartis.
windfall — (s) : profits de conjoncture (d'aubaine).
profitability : rentabilité (f).
profitability index (P.I.) : indice de rentabilité, d'enrichissement, coefficient de rentabilité, valeur présente du taux de profit.
profitable : profitable, rémunérateur.
profitable bargain : marché avantageux.
profitable employment : emploi lucratif.
profitably : profitablement.
profiteer : profiteur, accapareur (m).
profitless : non rentable (a).
profitless point : seuil de rentabilité.

profiteering: mercantilisme (m).

pro forma: fictif, simulé, pour la forme.
[C] — *invoice*: facture fictive, simulée, provisoire.
— *purchase, sale*: achat simulé, vente simulée.

programme, program: programme, plan (m).
— *evaluation and review technique*: méthode d'évaluation du temps nécessaire pour terminer des parties importantes d'un travail complexe (ex. construction d'un pont...); analyse critique méthodique (v. *critical path analysis*).
labour —, working programme: plan de travail.
programming: programmation (f) (cf. *planning*).

progress: progrès, avancement (m).
— *chaser (factory)*: technicien-surveillant.
economic —: essor économique.
negotiations in —: négociations en cours.
— *payment*: paiements d'un industriel effectués au fur et à mesure de l'avancement d'un travail.
— *report*: état périodique.
trial in —: procès en instance.
[F] — *tax*: impôt progressif.
progression: progression, progressivité (f).
bracket progression: progression par tranches.
scale of progression by increasing fractions of slices of income: barème de progressions par pourcentage de tranches croissantes.
progressive: progressif.
progressive scale: barème progressif.
by progressive stages: par degrés.
progressive tax: impôt progressif.

to prohibit: interdire.
prohibited *goods*: marchandises interdites, de contrebande.
the parties are prohibited from...: défense et inhibitions sont faites de...
prohibition: prohibition (f), défense (f), interdiction (f).
export, import prohibition: prohibition de sortie, d'entrée.
writ of prohibition: défense de statuer adressée par une cour supérieure à une inférieure ou une instance administrative.
prohibitive *duty*: droit prohibitif.

project: projet, plan (m).
project financing — financement de projets d'intérêt national.
project group — groupe constitué pour l'étude d'un projet déterminé.
pilot- —: expérience témoin.
— *method*: méthode des « projets » ou « centres d'intérêts ».
to project: projeter.
projection: conception (f) (d'un projet), prévision (f), anticipation (f).

to prolong a bill: proroger l'échéance d'un billet.

prolongation: prorogation (f).

promise: promesse (f).
[J] *an agreement consists of mutual — (s)*: un accord se présente comme un échange de promesses.
— *to pay*: promesse de payer.
— *of sale*: promesse de vente.
to promise: promettre, s'engager à.
promising: prometteur.
promissory: promissoire, de promesse.
promissory estoppel: force obligatoire d'une promesse (lorsque le détenteur de celle-ci s'y est fié pour agir).
promissory note: billet à ordre.
joint promissory note: billet solidaire.
promissory representation: déclaration comportant des promesses.

to promote: encourager, promouvoir, lancer; [U.S.] faire de la réclame (pour un article de commerce).
[C] — *a company*: lancer une société.
— *sales*: stimuler la vente.
— *s.o. to an office*: nommer qn à un poste.
promoter: organisateur, promoteur, instigateur.
company promoter: promoteur (fondateur) d'une société.
promoter's shares: part de fondateur.
promotion: promotion (f), avancement (m), lancement (m), encouragement (m).
promotion money: coût de premier établissement.
sales promotion: promotion des ventes.
promotion shares: actions de primes.
promotion of standards: établissement de normes.
[A] *promotion list (roster)*: tableau d'avancement.
promotional *mix*: ensemble des méthodes utilisées pour stimuler les ventes.
promotional sale: vente publicitaire.

prompt: prompt, rapide (a).
[C] — *cash*: argent comptant.
— *cotton*: coton livrable comptant et sur le champ.
— *delivery*: livraison immédiate.
— *forwarding (of goods)*: expédition à bref délai (de marchandises).
net — cash: comptant sans escompte.
— *payment*: paiement à court terme.
to pay **promptly**: payer comptant, ponctuellement, sans atermoiement.

promulgation: promulgation (f), diffusion (f) (de renseignements), proclamation (f).

to pronounce: déclarer.
[J] – *a decree* : rendre un arrêt.
– *a judgment, a sentence*: prononcer un jugement, une sentence.

proof: preuve (f), épreuve (monnaie de collection).
[J] – *is the effect or result of evidence*: un fait est considéré comme établi lorsque le tribunal se déclare satisfait des témoignages avancés et des preuves fournies.
the burden of – : la charge de la preuve.
clear – : preuve évidente.
– *of death*: constatation de décès.
– *by documentary evidence*: preuve authentique, notoriété de droit.
– *of identity*: justification d'identité.
– *of indebtedness*: titre de créance.
– *of loss*: justification de perte.
onus of – : charge de la preuve.
– *of origin*: justification d'origine.
– *of ownership*: titre de propriété.
– *by the evidence of witness*: notoriété de fait.
written – : preuve littérale.

to prop: étayer.
– *up the economy*: soutenir l'économie.

propensity: propension (f), penchant (m), tendance (f).
– *to consume*: propension à consommer.
– *to invest*: propension à investir.
– *to save*: propension à épargner.
– *to spend*: propension à dépenser.

proper: approprié, convenable, opportun, régulier (a).
[C] (agir) de bon droit.
in – *condition*: en bon état.
in – *form*: en bonne et due forme.
at the – *time*: en temps voulu.

properly: dûment, régulièrement (adv).

property: propriété (f), biens (m pl), avoirs (m pl), immeuble.
[J] [A] droit de propriété appliqué (cf. *ownership*).
acquired – : acquêt.
assessment of – *for taxation purposes*: évaluation d'une propriété aux fins d'imposition.
assignment of – : cession de biens.
business – : actif commercial.
capital – : biens en immobilisations.
common – : copropriété (f).
conveyance of – *(disposal of* –*)*: transmission de biens.
community – : [U.S.] biens de communauté.
damages to – : dommages matériels.
farm – : biens agricoles.
fixed – *(immovable* –*)*: biens immobiliers, immeubles.
inalienable – : biens inaliénables.
intangible – : biens incorporels.
intellectual – : propriété intellectuelle.
item of – : élément de la fortune.
landed – : propriété foncière, biens-fonds.
leasehold – : propriété louée à bail.
literary – : propriété littéraire.
movable – *(personal* –*)*: biens mobiliers, meubles.
movable, tangible – : meubles corporels.
income from the ownership of the – : revenu perçu à titre de propriétaire du terrain.
personal – *accessory to real* – : biens meubles accessoires à des biens immobiliers.
public – : domaine public.
real – : immeubles, biens immobiliers.
seizure of movable, real – : saisie mobilière, immobilière.
separate – : propres de la femme mariée.
tangible personal – : biens mobiliers corporels.
tax on real –, – *taxes on land*: impôt(s) foncier(s).
taxes on – *transfer*: droits de mutation.
wife separated as to – : femme séparée de biens.
– *for sale*: immeuble (maison) à vendre.
to redeem one's – : dégager son bien.
to take a mortgage on (s.o.'s) – : prendre une hypothèque sur les biens, la propriété de (qn).

proportion: proportion (f), quotepart (f), quotité (f), prorata.
– *of a benefit*: fraction d'une prestation.
in – *to*: au prorata de, proportionnellement.
out of – *(with, to)*: hors de proportion avec.
proportional: proportionel(le).
compensation proportional to the damage sustained: indemnisation proportionnelle au préjudice (dommage) subi.
inversely proportional (to): inversement proportionnel (à).
proportionate: proportionnel.
proportionate ownership: propriété détenue proportionnellement.

proposal: proposition (f), offre (f), projet (m).
to propose: proposer, mettre en délibération.
to propose an amendment: proposer un amendement.
motion **proposed** *from the chair*: motion mise en délibération.
proposer *of a bill*: auteur d'un projet de loi.

to propound a will: [J] demander l'homologation d'un testament.

proprietary: de propriété, de propriétaire.
— *accounts*: compte de(s) résultats.
— *article*: spécialité, article exclusif.
the — *classes*: les classes possédantes.
— *insurance company*: compagnie d'assurances à primes.
— *medicine (preparation)*: spécialité médicale.
— *rights*: droits de propriété.
proprietor: propriétaire (m).
co-proprietor, joint proprietor: copropriétaire (m).
landed proprietor: propriétaire foncier.
peasant proprietor: petit propriétaire.
proprietorship: possession, propriété, droit de propriété.
sole proprietorship: entreprise individuelle.

pro rata: au prorata, au marc le franc, proportionnel.

prorogation: prorogation (f), clôture (f) de la session parlementaire.

to prosecute: poursuivre en justice.
[J] — *a claim*: poursuivre une réclamation.
— *an action*: intenter une action.
« *trespassers will be* **prosecuted** »: « défense d'entrer (de passer) sous peine de poursuite ».
prosecution: poursuite(s), accusation, action publique, ministère public; le(s) plaignant(s).
counsel for the prosecution: avocat du plaignant.
criminal prosecution: poursuites pénales.
limitation of prosecutions: prescription des poursuites.
malicious prosecution: poursuites injustifiées.
public prosecution: le ministère public.
witness (evidence) for the prosecution: témoin à charge.
to abandon the prosecution: renoncer aux poursuites.
to start a prosecution (against s.o.): attaquer (qn) en justice, engager des poursuites contre (qn).
prosecutor: demandeur, plaignant, accusateur (m).
public prosecutor: ministère public.

prospect: perspective (f), possibilité (f); [U.S.] client éventuel.
employment — *(s)*: perspectives d'emploi.
— *(s) for the future (future* — *(s))*: perspectives d'avenir.
no — *of agreement*: aucune perspective d'accord, aucune chance de parvenir à un accord.
prospective: en perspective, éventuel.
a prospective buyer: un acheteur éventuel.
prospective yield: rendement prévu, escompté.

prospectus: [F] prospectus (d'émission), appel à souscription publique.
to issue a — : lancer un prospectus, une émission.

(economic) prosperity: prospérité (f) (économique).

prostitution: prostitution (f).

to protect: protéger, sauvegarder (les intérêts de qn).
protection: protection (f), protectionnisme (m).
the protection of a bill: la bonne fin d'un effet.
(a) *policy of protection*: une politique protectionniste.
[D] *tariff protection*: protection douanière.
[J] *protection racket*: chantage à la protection contre le gangstérisme.
protectionism, protectionist: protectionnisme, protectionniste.
protective *duties, tariff*: droits, tarif protecteur.
protective practice: accord entre deux sociétés pour réduire la concurrence et augmenter les bénéfices.

protest: contestation (f), protestation (f), réserve expresse dans un acte, protêt (m).
[J] [C] *bill* — : protestation de traite.
— *for non acceptance (for want of acceptance)*: protêt faute d'acceptation.
— *for non payment (for dishonour)*: protêt faute de paiement.
ship's — : déclaration d'avaries, rapport de mer.
to act under — : protester de violence, agir à son corps défendant.
to lodge, to make a — : lever protêt.
to note — *(of a bill of exchange)*: faire le protêt d'une lettre de change.
to raise a — : élever des protestations.
to accept (to sign) under — : accepter (signer) sous réserve.
to protest *a bill*: protester une lettre de change.
to protest a merchant: protester un négociant.

protestation: [J] affirmation solennelle (invoquant le témoignage divin).

protocol: protocole (m), étiquette (f), procès-verbal (m).
supplementary — : avenant (m) additionnel.

to prove: prouver, justifier, établir, vérifier, attester.
— *one's claim*: prouver le bien-fondé de sa réclamation.
proved *cost, damage*: coût, préjudice justifié.

the evidence goes — that: les témoignages concourent à établir que.
— *a loss:* faire la preuve d'un sinistre.
proved technique: technique éprouvée.

proven: prouvé, qui a fait ses preuves, attesté.

to provide: fournir, pourvoir, munir, prévoir, stipuler.
— *against (a fall, a rise):* se prémunir contre (la baisse, la hausse).
— *for a bill:* faire provision pour une lettre de change.
— *(s.o.) with sth.:* fournir qch. (à qn).
— *oneself with money:* se munir (se nantir) d'argent.
as **provided**: comme il est prévu, aux termes de, conformément à.
provided for all contingencies: préparé à faire face à l'imprévu.
except where otherwise provided: sauf disposition(s) contraire(s).
exception provided for by the law: exception prévue par la loi.
(the) period provided for by an insurance contract: (la) période prévue par un contrat d'assurance.
reserve provided by the articles: réserve statutaire.
provided that: pourvu que, à condition que.
provident *fund:* caisse de prévoyance.
provident scheme: œuvre, système de prévoyance.
provident society: société de prévoyance, de secours mutuel.
staff provident fund: caisse de prévoyance du personnel (d'entreprise).

province: province (f), juridiction (f), compétence (f) (d'un tribunal), ressort (m).
[F] **provincial** *bank:* banque de province.

provision: provision (f); disposition (f), article (m) (d'un traité), stipulation (f), clause (f).
the — (s) of an act: prescriptions, dispositions d'une loi.
— *for bad debts:* provision pour créances douteuses.
— *of capital:* prestation de capitaux.
constitutional — (s): dispositions de la constitution.
charging — : disposition spécifique.
— *for depreciation (of investments, of securities, etc.):* prévision pour moins-value (des investissements, du portefeuille-titres, etc.).
— *of the necessities of life:* satisfaction des besoins vitaux.
— *(s) for redemption of premises:* amortissement sur immeubles.
— *for rises in prices:* provision pour hausse des prix.
restrictive — : clause restrictive.
saving — : réserve.
statutory — (s): dispositions légales; [U.S.] dispositions statutaires.
subject to the aforesaid — (s): sous réserve des dispositions ci-dessus.
notwithstanding any — to the contrary: nonobstant toute clause contraire.
to come (to fall) within the — of the law: tomber sous le coup de la loi.
to make — against (sth.): prendre des mesures contre (qch.).
to make — for one's family: pourvoir aux besoins de sa famille.
to make a — for s.o.: assurer une pension à qn.

provisional: provisoire, temporaire, provisionnel (a), conservatoire (a).
[C] — *account:* compte provisoire.
[J] — *attachment:* saisie conservatoire.
— *certificate:* certificat, titre provisoire.
— *duties:* fonctions temporaires.
— *government:* gouvernement provisoire.
— *injunction:* ordonnance du référé interlocutoire.
— *insurance:* assurance provisoire.
— *judgment:* jugement par provision.
— *measures:* mesures conservatoires (temporaires).
— *receiver:* syndic provisoire (de faillite).
— *remedy:* ordonnance de référé, mesure provisoire.
[F] — *third:* tiers provisionnel.

proviso: clause conditionnelle d'un acte, dont dépend généralement sa validité.
under one — : avec une seule réserve.
with the — that: à condition que.

provocation: provocation (f).
[J] actes qui réduisent l'exercice de la raison et éliminent ainsi la notion de l'intention criminelle.

proximate: immédiat, proche (a).
proximate cause: cause immédiate (d'un accident, du dommage).
— *consequence:* conséquence directe.

proximo: du mois prochain.

proxy: [J] a) mandataire (m), fondé (m) de pouvoir(s); b) procuration (f), mandat (m).
personnally or by — : en personne ou par procuration.
— *contest, fight:* bataille de procurations.
form of — (— form): formule de procuration.
general — : pouvoir général, pleins pouvoirs.
— *signature:* signature par procuration.
to vote by — : voter par procuration.

prudential committee: [A] [U.S.] comité de surveillance (d'une société).
— *insurance*: assurance industrielle.
— *(s)*: questions d'administration locale.

public: 1° public (a); 2° le public (m), la clientèle (f), les administrés (m pl).
— *accounts*: comptabilité publique.
— *affairs*: affaires publiques.
— *agency*: agence gouvernementale.
— *announcement*: notification publique.
— *attorney*: [U.S.] avocat (m).
— *authorities*: pouvoirs publics.
— *bill*: projet de loi d'intérêt public.
— *body*: organisme public.
— *carrier*: transporteur public.
— *company*: société anonyme.
— *corporation*: société à participation étatique.
— *debt(s)*: dette publique.
— *department*: (une) administration publique.
— *expenditure*: dépenses publiques.
— *finance*: finances publiques.
— *funds*: fonds publics.
the *general* — : le grand public.
— *good*: bien collectif.
— *hearing*: audience publique.
— *holiday*: fête légale.
— *house*: débit de boissons.
— *indecency*: outrage public à la pudeur.
of — *interest*: d'intérêt public.
— *international law*: droit international public.
— *issue (of shares)*: émission publique (d'actions).
— *law*: droit public.
— *laws*: lois générales.
— *liability insurance*: assurance au tiers.
— *loan*: emprunt public.
— *means of conveyance*: transport en commun.
— *meeting*: réunion publique autorisée.
— *mischief*: délit d'entraver l'action de la justice ou de la police (au préjudice de la communauté).
— *money (purse)*: deniers publics.
— *Offices*: charges publiques.
— *officer*: a) fonctionnaire ; b) membre du conseil d'administration d'une société.
— *ownership*: régie publique (nationale).
— *policy*: ordre public.
— *policies*: programme d'action gouvernementale (communément appelés « politiques publiques »).
the — *purse*: les finances de l'Etat, le Trésor.
— *property*: propriété de l'Etat.
— *prosecutor*: ministère public.
— *Records*: Archives Nationales.
— *Relations*: Relations Publiques.
— *responsibility*: responsabilité envers la communauté (ne pas polluer, etc.).
— *revenue*: revenu de l'Etat.
— *sale*: vente publique.
— *sector*: secteur public.
— *Sector Borrowing Requirement (P.S.B.R.)*: besoins d'emprunt du secteur public non couverts par les rentrées fiscales.
— *servant*: fonctionnaire (m).
— *surplus*: solde budgétaire.
— *treasury*: trésor public.
— *trustee*: curateur de l'Etat aux successions, tuteur d'office, fidéicommissaire ordinaire ou datif.
— *utilities*: services publics concédés.
— *utility company (corporation)*: service public.
— *utility stocks*: valeurs de services publics.
the — *weal*: le bien public (commun).
— *welfare*: le bien public, l'assistance publique.
to go — # (d'une S.A.R.L.) se transformer en Société Anonyme faisant appel public à l'épargne.
to issue shares to the — : émettre des actions dans le public.
the general — : le grand public.

publication: publication (f).
service by — : signification par avis public.

publicity: publicité (f).
— *bureau*: agent de publicité.
— *campaign, expenses*: campagne, dépenses de publicité.
— *department*: service de la publicité, de presse.

publicness: [J] publicité d'une audience, des débats parlementaires, huis-ouvert.

publisher: éditeur (m).

publishing (company) house: maison d'édition (f).

puffer: compère aux enchères, faux enchérisseur.

puisne: puîné, postérieur, subalterne (a).
[J] — *judge*: juge puîné (assesseur).
— *mortgage*: toute hypothèque non appuyée par la production du titre de propriété.

pull: traction (f), tirage (m), force (f) d'attraction.
[F] *cost* — : pression inflationniste due à la hausse des prix de revient.
demand — : pression de la demande.
— *factors*: facteurs d'attraction.
to pull *out of the market*: se retirer du marché.

pum-priming: préfinancement (m).
[F] — *measures*: mesures de relance de l'économie (par les dépenses publiques).

punched card: carte perforée (f).

punctual, punctuality: ponctuel (a); ponctualité (f).

punishment: punition (f), châtiment (m), peine (f), sanction (f).
[J] *capital (death)* — : peine capitale.
liable to — : punissable, passible de peine.
maximum — : maximum de la peine.
mitigation of — : atténuation de la peine.
pecuniary — : peine d'amende.

punitive: punitif, répressif (a).
— *justice*: justice répressive.
— *measure*: mesure pénale.

to punt: boursicoter.

pupillage: [J] pupillarité, minorité (f), stage (m) (au cabinet d'un "barrister").
[C] *industry in its* — : industrie naissante.

purchase: achat (m), acquisition (f).
[C] — *(s) account*: compte d'achat.
— *book (journal)*: livre d'achat (des achats).
by — : à titre onéreux.
covering — *(s)*: rachats.
credit — : achat à crédit.
— *fund*: fonds d'amortissement.
hire- — *(agreement)*: (contrat de) location-vente.
— *invoice*: facture d'achat.
— *-money (purchase-price)*: prix d'achat.
— *officer*: chef du service des achats.
— *order*: commande.
— *returns*: rendus sur (sous) achats.
— *for settlement*: achat à terme.
sham — : achat fictif.
— *vouchers*: justification (produite à l'appui de dépenses).
at (so many years') — : moyennant (tant d'années) de loyer.
purchaser: acheteur, acquéreur.
bona fide purchaser (purchaser in good faith): acheteur de bonne foi.
mala fide purchaser (purchaser in bad faith): acheteur de mauvaise foi.
purchasing: 1° acquéreur, d'achat (a); 2° achat (m), acquisition (f).
purchasing agency: comptoir d'achat.
purchasing agent: mandataire chargé des achats.
purchasing company: société preneuse.
purchasing office: service des achats.
the purchasing party: l'acquéreur.
purchasing power: pouvoir d'achat.

pure: pur, net (a).
— *premium*: prime nette.
purely *occasional transactions*: opérations effectuées à titre purement occasionnel.

to purge: purger.
[J] se justifier, expier, purger.
— *an offence*: purger sa peine.
— *oneself of a charge*: se disculper.

purloining: détournement (m), vol (m).

purport: sens, portée, teneur (d'un document).
the — *of a statement*: la teneur d'une déclaration.

purpose: but, dessein, objet (m), affectation (f).
for the — *of*: aux fins de, en vue de.
for the — *of this convention*: pour l'application de la présente.
to all intents and — *(s)*: à tous égards.
[F] *for tax* — *(s)*: à des fins d'imposition.
for customs — *(s)*: conformément à la législation douanière.

purposeful: prémédité.

pursuance: action de poursuivre, exécution (d'un plan).
in — *of (your) instructions*: conformément à (vos) instructions.
in — *of article (section)...*: en exécution de l'article...
pursuant to: conformément à, en vertu de...
pursuant to (your) instructions: conformément à (vos) instructions.
to pursue: continuer, suivre, poursuivre (une enquête).
to pursue a line of conduct: suivre une ligne de conduite.
to pursue a profession: suivre, exercer un métier.
to pursue studies: poursuivre des études.

pursuit: poursuite (f), carrière (f), occupation.
commercial (mercantile) — : carrière commerciale.
to engage in (scientific) — *(s)*: s'adonner à des recherches (scientifiques...)

purveyance: fourniture (f) (de provisions), approvisionnement (m).
purveyor: fournisseur, pourvoyeur (m).

purview: corps (m), texte (m) (d'un statut), clause (f); limites (f pl), portée (f) (d'un projet).
to lie within the — *of (s.o.)*: être de la compétence, du ressort de (qn).

push : poussée, impulsion (f).
[F] *cost- — inflation* : inflation causée par la poussée sur les coûts.
— *factors* : facteurs de pulsion.
— *money* : commission donnée à un vendeur pour l'encourager à « pousser » certains produits.
to push *(shares)* : pousser (des actions).
share **pusher** : placier de valeurs peu sûres.

put (put option) : [B] prime pour livrer ou non, prime inverse, option de vente.
— *and call* : double option, doubles primes, stellage.
— *and take* : vente au comptant contre rachat à terme.

put-back : faculté (f) de remboursement anticipé.

to put : mettre, présenter (une motion), poser (une question), estimer.
— *a clause in a contract* : insérer une clause dans un contrat.
— *in for a job* : (fam.) poser sa candidature à un emploi.
— *(a law) into force* : mettre en vigueur (une loi).
— *a motion, a resolution to the meeting* : mettre une motion aux voix, présenter une résolution à l'assemblée.
— *money into* : placer de l'argent dans.
— *out* : produire (see « output »).
— *out at interest* : prêter avec intérêt.
— *the population of a town at* : estimer la population d'une ville à.
— *by (money)* : mettre de côté, économiser (de l'argent).
— *down* : déposer, inscrire.
— *down an amendment* : déposer un amendement (en vue du débat).
— *down to (s.o.'s) account* : inscrire au compte de (qn).
he won't be able — down the money : il ne pourra pas payer comptant.
— *off* : remettre (à plus tard), ajourner.
— *off a case for a week* : remettre une affaire à huitaine.
— *off the maturity* : proroger l'échéance (d'une lettre de change).
— *on the market* : lancer un article sur le marché.
— *on trial (to test)* : mettre à l'essai (à l'épreuve).
shares which **put** *on one point* : des actions qui ont gagné un point.
— *(profits) to reserve* : mettre (des bénéfices) en réserve.
putting in : a) inscription ; b) relâche (dans un port)
putting in force : mise en vigueur.
putting in liquidation, in possession : mise en liquidation, en possession.
putting off : renvoi (m).
putting up of money : mise de fonds.
putting up for sale : mise en vente.

putative(ly) : putatif (putativement).

to pyramid : [B] continuer à acheter une valeur quand elle est en hausse.
pyramiding : [U.S.] système d'opérations boursières consistant à employer les gains au fur et à mesure qu'ils sont réalisés, à l'achat de certains titres en nombre croissant, afin de peser sur les cours dans le sens désiré.
[F] *pyramiding taxes* : accumulation des impôts ; superposition des impôts ; impôt de superposition, qui fait boule de neige ; taxes en cascade.

NOTES

Q

q regulation : [f] [U.S.] réglementation Q (interdiction de rémunérer les dépôts (à moins de 30 jours) libellés en monnaie étrangère).

quadrennial (plan, report) : quadriennal (a) (plan, report).

quagmire : marécage (m).
to be in a — : être dans le marasme, être dans une impasse.
the negotiations are a — : les négociations s'enlisent.

qualification : 1° qualité (f) requise, compétence (f), qualification (f) ; 2° habilitation (f), habilité (f) (à exercer un droit) ; 3° restriction (f) (de portée), réserve (f) ; 4° cautionnement (m).
to have, to possess the necessary — *(s)* : remplir les conditions, avoir la compétence nécessaire.
— *(s) for an appointment, for membership* : titres à un emploi, d'éligibilité.
full — *(s)* : plein droit, pleine capacité.
proof of — : certificat de capacité.
— *(s) to exercise a right* : capacité, habilité à exercer un droit.
— *(s) of an official* : titres d'un fonctionnaire.
— *(s) record* : dossier professionnel.
subject to one —, *to many* — *(s)* : sous une seule réserve, sous bien des réserves.
to accept with (without) — *(s)* : accepter avec (sans) réserves.
— *shares* : actions de garantie, déposées en garantie, statutaires.
to qualify : a) avoir ou acquérir les qualités requises, devenir apte à, donner qualité ; b) limiter, restreindre (la portée), modérer ; c) faire des réserves.
— *as (a) doctor* : être reçu médecin.
— *for* : remplir les conditions, avoir droit à.
— *for a job* : se qualifier pour un emploi.
— *as a witness* : être admis comme témoin.
— *a statement* : limiter la portée d'une déclaration, faire des réserves sur une déclaration.
to be **qualified** : posséder les qualités requises.
— *acceptance (of a bill of exchange)* : acceptation (d'un effet) sous réserve conditionnelle.
— *accountant* : [U.S.] expert-comptable (m).
— *accounts* : comptes sur lesquels des réserves sont exprimées, comptes douteux.
— *endorsement* : endossement spécifiant les limites de la responsabilité de l'endosseur.
— *offer* : offre conditionnelle.
— *person* : personne compétente.
— *property* : droit du dépositaire (de biens sous contrat) ou emprunteur portant sur la possession des biens et droits annexes.
— *title* : droit conditionnel, relatif.
— *vote* : vote acquis à la majorité.
— *worker* : ouvrier qualifié.
fully — : pleinement (entièrement) qualifié.
to be (fully) — *to inherit* : être habile à succéder.
ill- — : incompétent.
qualifying : qui donne droit à ; modificateur ; conditionnel.
— *certificate* : certificat d'aptitude.
— *conditions* : conditions requises.
— *period* : période probatoire.
— *shares* : actions de garantie.

quality : qualité (f), qualité (pour faire...), statut (m), condition (f).
[C] *of the best* — : de première qualité.
fair average — : bonne qualité courante.
— *goods* : marchandises de qualité.
inferior, poor, prime — : qualité inférieure, médiocre, supérieure.
— *as per samples* : qualité conforme aux échantillons.
— *subject to approval* : qualité vue et agréée.
[J] — *of an estate* : la certitude de durée d'un droit réel.
as to — : qualitativement.
to act in the — *of* : agir en qualité de.

qualitative, quantitative information : information (f) qualitative, quantitative.

quandiu bene se gesserit : aussi longtemps qu'il se comportera bien.

quando acciderint : « quand ils se conformeront ».

quango : (U.K.) Commission consultative en matière d'économie et d'environnement.

quantitative restrictions : [D] contingentement (m).

quantity : quantité (f), quotité (f).
[J] — *of estate* : le temps de durée d'un droit réel.
[C] — *discount* : escompte (m), rabais (m) sur achats en grande quantité.

— 563 —

economic order — : quantité économique de commandes.
— *index* : indice de quantité.
— *of labour* : somme de travail.
marketable — *of shares* : quotité négociable de titres.
— *production* : production en série, en masse.
to buy (sell) in large **quantities** : acheter par quantités considérables, en gros.
wholesale dealing in small quantities : vente en demi-gros.
bill of quantities : devis (m).
[F] *the* — *theory of money* : la théorie quantitative de la monnaie.
[D] — *permitted* : quantité permise, tolérance.

quantum : quantum (m).
to assess the — *of damages* : fixer le quantum des dommages-intérêts.

quarantine : quarantaine (f).
— *dues* : droits de quarantaine.
to place a ship in — : mettre un navire en quarantaine.
to raise the — : lever la quarantaine.

quarter : quart (m), quartier (m) (d'une ville), trimestre (m), terme (m), milieu(x) (l).
[C] *business* — (s) : quartiers commerçants.
— *day* : jour du terme, terme.
— (s) *rent* : terme, trimestre de loyer.
from reliable — (s) : de source sûre.
in responsible — (s) : dans les milieux autorisés.
— *sessions* : assises trimestrielles.
quarterly : trimestriel, trimestriellement, par trimestre, (U.S.) dividende trimestriel.
quarterly instalment (payment) : versement, paiement trimestriel.
quarterly meeting : assemblée trimestrielle.
quarterly rent : loyer trimestriel.
quarterly salary : appointements trimestriels.
quarterly trade accounts : comptes trimestriels.
to be paid quarterly : être payé par trimestre.

to quash : casser, infirmer, annuler (une élection), une décision.
[J] — *an action (proceedings)* : arrêter les poursuites.
— *an indictment* : prononcer un non-lieu.
— *a judgment* : réformer un jugement.
motion — : demande en infirmation.
quashed : invalidé, annulé, infirmé.
quashing : cassation (f), annulation (f), infirmation (f), répression (f) (d'une révolte).

quasi *(prefix)* : quasi (préfixe).
[J] — *-contract* : quasi-contrat (m).
— *-delict (quasi-tort)* : quasi-délit (m).
— *-easement* : droit à une servitude résultant d'une quasi-possession.

— *-realty* : biens personnels par détermination de la loi.
— *-trustee* : personne qui agit en trustee sans y avoir été autorisée.

quay : quai (m).
— *berth* : place (poste) à quai.
— *handling charges* : frais de manutention à quai.
— *rates* : droits de quai.
— *-side worker* : docker (m).

queen : reine (f).
[J] *Court of* — (s) *Bench* : Cour du Banc de la Reine.
— (s) *Council (Q.C.)* : conseiller de la Reine (titre conféré à des membres éminents du barreau).
to turn — (s) *evidence* : (pour un prisonnier) dénoncer ses complices sous promesse de pardon.

queer : bizarre, suspect (a).
[F] — *money* : [U.S.] fausse monnaie (m).
to shove — *money* : (fam.) refiler de la fausse monnaie.
on the — : (fam.) par des moyens malhonnêtes.
to be in — *street* : (fam.) être dans une situation financière très peu brillante.

query : question (f), interrogation (f).
to query *(if, whether...)* : s'informer (pour savoir si...), mettre en doute (que).

question : question (f), demande (f), interrogatoire (m), mise aux voix, mise en doute.
beyond (past) — : incontestable, hors de doute.
catch — : question insidieuse.
contentious — : question litigieuse.
cross — : contre-interrogatoire (par la partie adverse).
labour — : question ouvrière.
land — : question agraire.
leading — : question tendancieuse (posée à un témoin, destinée à le « mettre sur la piste »).
misleading — : question trompeuse.
pending — : question pendante.
— *of procedure (of fact, of law)* : point de procédure (de fait, de droit).
the — *under consideration (investigation)* : la question à l'étude.
a vexed — : une question souvent débattue.
there is no — *that* : il est de fait que.
to come into — : venir en discussion.
to move the previous — : demander la question préalable.
to put the — : mettre la question aux voix.
to put to the — : (hist.) mettre à la question.
without — *put* : sans mise aux voix

(Parlement).
to question : interroger, mettre en doute.
to question (s.o.) closely: soumettre (qn) à un interrogatoire serré.
to question a statement (a motive) : contester, mettre en doute une affirmation (un mobile).
questionable : contestable, douteux, discutable.
questioning : interrogatoire (m).
questionnaire : questionnaire (m).

queue : file (f) d'attente, queue (f).

queueing theory : [U.S.] théorie du cycle d'approvisionnement (technique employée pour réduire le temps d'attente dans une file).

quibble : faux-fuyant (m), argutie (f).
to quibble : user de faux-foyant, ergoter.
quibbling : argutie, chicane de mots, « avocasserie ».

quick : rapide (a).
[C] *— ratio* : see « liquidity ratio ».
— recovery (of business) : reprise rapide (des affaires).
— return : rentrée de fonds rapide.
— sale : vente facile.

quickie : [U.S.] (fam.) grève décidée sur le champ, le plus souvent irrationnelle.

quid pro quo : compensation (f), contre-partie (f).

quiet : calme (a).
[J] *— enjoyment* : clause de paisible jouissance.
[B] *— market* : marché calme, peu animé.

quietus : quitus (m).
to give — : donner quitus.

to quit : cesser, quitter, vider les lieux.
— one's job : [U.S.] abandonner son emploi, démissionner.
to give notice to quit : donner congé.

quitclaim deed : [J] acte de transfert d'un droit ou d'un titre par voie de renonciation, mais sans garantie de validité.

quittance : quittance (f), acquit (m), quitus (m).
to give — : donner quitus.

quorum : quorum (m), quantum (m).
the — is (is not) : le quorum est (n'est pas) atteint.
to form a — : constituer un quorum.
to want a — : ne pas réunir un quorum, ne pas être en nombre.

quota : quota (m), contingent (m), quote-part (f), cote (f), cotisation (f).
[A] contingent (m) d'immigrants de chaque nationalité pouvant être admis annuellement aux Etats-Unis.
— sampling : échantillonnage de population par groupes homogènes (see « stratified sampling »).
electoral — : quotient électoral.
[E] *export (import) —* : contingent d'exportation (d'importation).
special — : contingent de faveur.
[F] *— of profits* : tantième de bénéfices.
to fix —(s) (for imports) : contingenter (des importations).
taxable — : quotité imposable.
to contribute (to pay) one's — : apporter (payer) sa quote-part.
quotable *security* : valeur cotable.

quotation : référence (à) ; cote (f), cotation (f), cours (m).
[B] *actual —* : cours effectif.
admission to — : admission à la cote.
bud — : soumission (f).
closing — : cours de clôture.
compulsory — : cours forcé.
enquiry for — : demande de prix.
latest — : dernier cours.
list of —(s) : bulletin de cours.
— in the list : inscription à la cote.
— of prices : cotation des cours.
spot — : cote (cours) du disponible.
wide — : cours faisant apparaître un écart considérable entre le prix d'achat et le prix de vente.
to quote : se référer à, rappeler (une référence), établir, fixer (un prix), coter (une valeur).
please quote this reference number : veuillez rappeler ce numéro de référence.
to quote a price : fixer un prix.
to quote terms : fixer (stipuler) des conditions.
quoted *list* : cote officielle.
quoted *price* : prix affiché.
quoted securities, securities quoted in the official list : valeurs inscrites à la cote officielle, valeurs (admises) de corbeille (de parquet).
quoted shares : actions cotées.
shares quoted at (so much) : actions qui se cotent à (tant).
quoting : quotation (f).

quotity : quotité (f).

NOTES

R

to rack: extorquer, pressurer (un locataire).
— *up*: enregistrer des profits très élevés.

racking effect: effet de tenaille.

rack jobber: fabricant (m) ou grossiste (m) qui confie à un magasin la vente de ses articles qui y sont exposés.

rack-rent: [J] loyer raisonnable (dans le langage courant, au contraire, loyer exorbitant).

radical: extrémiste (a).

raid: descente (f), rafle de police ; razzia (f) de bandits ; [B] chasse (f).
« *smash and grab it* » — : rafle de bijoux, etc., après bris de la devanture.
raider: corsaire, navire de course.
[B] attaquant (m) (voir : *black, white knight*).
to raid the bears: chasser le découvert.

railhead *(railways)*: tête de ligne (chemins de fer).

to raise: élever, dresser, produire, soulever, hausser.
— *a loan*: contracter, *(by the State)* émettre un emprunt.
— *money*: se procurer de l'argent.
— *money on an estate*: emprunter de l'argent sur une terre.
— *funds by subscription*: réunir des fonds par souscription.
— *taxes*: lever des impôts.
— *a dividend*: augmenter un dividende.

rake-off: (fam.) gratte (f), profit malhonnête.

rally: reprise (des cours, des affaires).

to rally *(market)*: reprendre, se redresser (pour un marché).

ramp: majoration (f) exorbitante des prix, des loyers.
housing — : loyers scandaleusement élevés.
rampant *inflation*: inflation rampante.

random: au hasard, aléatoire.
— *sampling*, **randomization**: [U.S.] échantillonnage au hasard.

range: gamme.
salary — : éventail des salaires.
— *of amount*: tranche de revenu.
to range: s'échelonner.

rank: rang, grade.
the — *and file*: « la base » (cf. the grass-roots).
[J] ordre de priorité.
— *of a mortgage*: rang d'une hypothèque.
to rank *(among)*: être classé (parmi).
shares that — *first in dividend rights*: actions qui priment en matière de dividende.
shares that will — *for this month dividend*: actions qui prendront part à la distribution de dividendes du mois.
to — *for*: être pris en considération.
the cost of construction of a farm-house may — *for an allowance*: le coût de la construction d'une ferme peut être pris en considération pour un dégrèvement.
ranking: classement.

ransom: rançon (f).
[J] — *of cargo*: rachat (m) de cargaison.

rape: rapt (m), enlèvement (m), [J] viol (m).
assault with intent to commit — : tentative de viol.

rash speculations: [B] spéculations téméraires.

rasure: rature (f) (voir : *alteration*).

rate race: foire (f) d'empoigne, curée (f) des places (dans une organisation).

ratchet: cliquet (m), encliquetage (m).
— *effect*: effet de cliquet.
to ratchet: être entraîné dans un mouvement de baisse ou de hausse sans possibilité de l'inverser.

rate: taux (m), cours (m), tarif (m), classe (f) (« *first* —, *second* — », etc.).
— *per cent*: pourcentage.
—(*s*) *and taxes*: [F] a) impôt, [U.K.] taxe locale, cotisation impôts et contributions ; b) taux de l'impôt.
blended — : taux mixte (de l'impôt) en fonction de la date de clôture de l'exercice.
differential — : taux différentiel.
fixed —(*s*) (*or* « *ceilings* ») : taux fixes (ou « plafonds »).
flat — : [U.S.] taux uniforme.
general — : [U.K.] impôt local unique, au

taux uniforme pour toute la circonscription.
graduated − *(rising in steps)* : tarif progressif par tranches (cf. *progressive scale*).
increased − : taux majoré.
minimum lending − : taux de prêt minimum (taux d'escompte).
proportional −*(s)* : taux proportionnels.
reduced − : tarif réduit.
− *of return* : intérêt (rapport) d'un investissement exprimé en pourcentage.
− *of return over cost* : taux-pivot, taux interne de rentabilité (Keynes).
tax − : taux de l'impôt.
usual − : taux habituel.
borough −*(s)* : centimes municipaux.
county −*(s)* : centimes départementaux.
harbour −*(s)* : droits de port.
to come upon the −*(s)* : tomber à la charge de l'Assistance publique.
to reduce the −*(s) on a building* : dégrever un immeuble.
rateable *value* (**ratal**) : valeur locative imposable (d'un immeuble), évaluation cadastrale (d'un terrain à bâtir).
rate-collector : percepteur.
rate-payer : contribuable.
birth-, death-, marriage-, sickness- − : (taux de) natalité, mortalité, nuptialité, morbidité.
crude birth − : taux brut de natalité.
gross reproduction − : taux brut de reproduction.
natural − *of increase* : taux d'accroissement naturel.
[C] *basic* − : salaire de base.
− *of fare* : tarif des transports.
freight − : fret maritime.
market −*(s)* : cours du marché.
− *of return* : taux de rendement.
− *of turnover* : vitesse de rotation des stocks.
− *of wages* : taux des salaires.
[F] *the Bank* −, *the discount* − : le taux de la Banque, le taux (officiel) de l'escompte.
prime − : [U.S.] taux (officiel) de l'escompte.
compound − : taux composé.
− *of conversion* : taux de conversion.
− *of exchange* : cours du change.
− *of interest, of discount* : taux de l'intérêt, de l'escompte.
gross − : taux brut.
higher − : taux supérieur (dans un barème progressif).
−*(s) for money on loan* : le loyer de l'argent.
lombard − : taux des avances sur nantissement.
marked − : taux (de l'escompte, de l'argent) hors banque, taux du cours libre (dit « parallèle » en France).
standard − : taux unique.
[B] − *of contango* : (taux du) report.
capitalization − : taux de capitalisation.
spot − : cours du comptant.
to give the − : faire un prêt d'actions.
to take the − : emprunter des actions.

ratification : ratification (f), entérinement (m).
[A] homologation (f).
[J] *act of* − *and acknowledgment* : acte recognitif et confirmatif.
to ratify : ratifier.

rating : estimation (f), évaluation (f) des capacités d'emprunt, notation (f).
−*(s)* : estimation (f) de l'importance de l'écoute (radio, T.V.).
− *system* # les impôts locaux.
zero − : [UK] taux zéro (en matière de TVA).

ratio : rapport (m), proportion (f), raison (f), quotient (m), coefficient (m).
in inverse (direct) − : en proportion, raison inverse (directe).
gross investment − : taux brut d'investissement.
incremental capital-output − : coefficient marginal de capital.
price earnings − : coefficient de capitalisation des résultats, rapport cours-bénéfices.
cash − : coefficient de liquidité.
containment − : coefficient de retenue.
debt-equity − : ratio d'autonomie financière.
liquidity − : coefficient de trésorerie.
− *of weight* : coefficient de pondération.

ratio decidendi : (le) fondement d'une décision.

rational expectations : anticipations (f) rationnelles.

rationalisation : rationalisation (f).

rationality : rationalité (f).
bounded − : rationalité limitée.

rationing : rationnement (m).

ravishment : rapt (m).

raw : cru, brut (a).
− *materials* : matières premières.

re : concernant, relatif à.
limitation − *employment expense deduction* : restriction concernant les réductions afférentes à un emploi.

to reach : parvenir, atteindre, toucher, prendre.
− *a decision* : prendre une décision.

to read : lire, interpréter.
− *an act* : interpréter une loi.

the text should be **read** *(as)*: le texte doit être interprété (comme...).
read and confirmed: lu et approuvé.
– *over*: collationner.
reading: interprétation.

readjustment: rectification (f).

ready: prêt (a).
ready money: argent comptant, argent liquide, disponibilités.

real: vrai, [J] réel (a).
– *action*: action réelle (mais le terme actio in rem est préférable).
[J] – *estate, property*: biens immobiliers.
– *estate developer*: promoteur immobilier.
– *estate loan*: prêt hypothécaire.
exchange of – *property*: mutation de biens immobiliers.
– *property company, trust*: société civile immobilière.
– *representative*: la personne immédiatement saisie d'un héritage, telle qu'un exécuteur testamentaire.
sale of – *property*: vente immobilière.
tangible – *property*, – *things*: immeuble par nature.
intangible – *property, chattels* – : immeuble par l'objet auquel il s'applique.
[A] – *centre of management*: direction effective.
– *income*: revenu réel.
[F] – *accounts*: comptes de valeur.
– *value*: valeur (f) effective.
« *in* – *terms* »: en monnaie constante.
– *securities*: valeurs foncières.
– *balance effect*: effet d'encaisses réelles.

realizable: réalisable.
– *assets*: actif réalisable.
realization: réalisation, liquidation, vente.
realization account: compte de liquidation.
to realize *one's assets*: réaliser sa fortune.

to re-allocate: réaffecter.

to re-appraise: réévaluer.

to re-assess: (F) réestimer, réévaluer (pour des raisons de fiscalité).

realty: abréviation pour *real estate* (voir supra).
[J] *interests in* – : droits réels.
[F] *tax on* – : impôt immobilier.
[U.S.] **realtor**: agent immobilier.

reappraisal: réévaluation (f).

reason: raison (f).
[J] – *(s) adduced*: les attendus.

reassessment: réévaluation (f).

rebate: rabais (m).
[F] (impôts) remise (f), abattement (m).
basic – : abattement à la base.
increase of – : majoration d'abattement.
[C] ristourne (f), remboursement (m), escompte (m), remise (f), bonification (f).
food, fuel – : réduction sur le prix des denrées alimentaires, sur le prix du combustible.

to rebut: rebuter, riposter.
[J] **rebutting** *evidence* (ou *evidence* in **rebuttal**): preuve contraire qui réfute la preuve prima facie (voir ce terme).
rebuttable *presumption*: présomption réfutable.
rebutter: duplique (f) (voir *pleading*).

to recall: rappeler.
[J] infirmer un jugement pour des motifs de fait (opp. *to reverse*).
[A] [U.S.] révoquer un fonctionnaire par un vote du corps électoral qui l'a élu.
letters of **recall**: lettres de rappel d'un représentant diplomatique.

to recant: se rétracter, rétracter.

receipt: reçu (m), entrées (f pl), encaissement (m), acquit (m), quittance (f), accusé (m) de réception.
tax – *(s)*: [F] perception (f) (d'impôts), rentrées fiscales.
[D] *custom-house* – : quittance des droits d'entrée.
[C] *certificate of* – : certificat de chargement.
– *(s) and expenses*: recettes et dépenses.
formal – : quittance comptable.
– *in full (discharge)*: quittance pour solde, quittance finale, libératoire.
– *for a loan*: reconnaissance.
official – *(for a parcel, etc.)*: récépissé (d'un colis, etc.).
to acknowledge – *(of)*: accuser réception (de).
to give a – *for*: donner acquit de.
to pay on – : payer à la réception.
receipt-book: quittancier.
receipt-form: quittance.
receipt-stamp: timbre d'acquit.
to receipt: acquitter, émarger.

receiver: personne qui reçoit (quelque chose), destinataire, liquidateur.
[J] 1° *official* – : a) séquestre, administrateur judiciaire ; b) préposé à la caisse des dépôts et consignations ; 2° liquidateur de sociétés; 3° receleur.
– *of wreck*: fonctionnaire chargé de préserver les navires ou épaves jetés à la côte.

— 569 —

receivable *evidence:* preuve recevable, plausible.
receivable: recevable.
[F] *accounts receivable:* sommes à encaisser («argent dehors»).
bills receivable: effets à recevoir.
receiving *order:* ordonnance de mise sous séquestre.
[A] receveur des finances.
receiver's office: recette (f).
receiving *home:* centre d'accueil.
to receive *(income):* recevoir, percevoir, encaisser.
income received in France: revenus encaissés en France.
[C] réceptionnaire (d'un envoi).
received with thanks: pour acquit.

reception order: [J] ordonnance autorisant un établissement psychiatrique à recevoir et détenir un aliéné reconnu *(certified lunatic).*

recess: vacances judiciaires, intersession parlementaire, suspension d'audience (ou de séance).

recession: [U.S.] suspension d'audience, de séance, recul (m); [J] retrocession.
[C] récession (dépression économique).

recidivism: récidive (f) (terme de criminologie, terme courant: *relapse).*

recipient: bénéficiaire (m), destinataire (m).

reciprocal: réciproque (a).
— *contract:* contrat bilatéral.
— *holdings:* participations croisées.
law of — *markets:* lois des débouchés.
— *trading:* commerce sur la base de la réciprocité.

to reciprocate: se rendre des services.
[C] — *an entry:* passer écriture conforme.

recitals: [J] dans un instrument juridique, partie introductive destinée à en expliquer le dispositif exposant d'une part *(narrative recitals)* les faits et, d'autre part *(introductory recitals),* les motifs à l'origine du document. Un *recital* commence toujours par «Whereas».
— *in the lease:* les conditions du bail.
the — *of legislative intent in the preamble:* exposé des intentions du législateur dans le préambule.
an unfounded — *in a foreign judgment:* un attendu mal fondé dans un jugement étranger.
(ASS.) — *clause:* liste (f) de garanties.

reckless driving: conduite dangereuse.

to reckon: compter, calculer.
— *in:* tenir compte de.
— *off:* décompter.
— *up:* évaluer, supporter.
reckoning *from today:* à compter d'aujourd'hui.

to reclaim: récupérer, défricher, mettre en valeur (terrain).
— *goods:* reprendre des marchandises.
[F] *the tax cannot be* **reclaimed:** l'impôt ne peut être récupéré.
reclamation: défrichement; récupération de sous-produits.

recognition: reconnaissance (f).
[J] a) reconnaissance d'un gouvernement (de jure, de facto); b) confirmation d'un acte accompli par une autre personne.
[F] *revenue* —: constatation des produits.
recognizable: vérifiable.
recognizable gain: bénéfice vérifiable.
recognizance: caution (f) juridique, somme fournie à titre de cautionnement.
to enter into recognizances: donner caution.
[U.S.] **to recognize** *s.o.:* donner la parole à qn.

recommendation: recommandation (f).
[J] — *to mercy:* avis émis par le jury en faveur d'une commutation de peine = signature du pourvoi en grâce par le jury.

recompense: récompense (f).
[J] dédommagement.

to recompute: réévaluer.

to reconcile: ajuster.
[J] — *an account:* apurer un compte.
reconciliation *account:* (comptabilité): compte collectif.

reconduction: reconduction (f).
tacit —: reconduction tacite.
to reconduct: reconduire.

reconstitution: reconstitution (f) (de gisement).

reconvention: reconvention (f), contre-accusation (f).
[J] action reconventionnelle, défense au contraire.

reconversion: [J] immobilisation ou ameublissement à nouveau (voir *conversion*).
[C] [U.S.] retour d'établissements industriels transformés en usines d'armements à leur destination première.

reconveyance: nouveau transport.
[J] rétrocession de la propriété d'un bien hypothéqué au débiteur, après paiement de la dette.

record: enregistrement (m), document (m), dossier (m), minutes (f pl), antécédents (m pl), archives (f pl).
off the — : confidentiel.
on — : de notoriété publique.
[A] *service* — : état des services.
[J] 1° a) rôle des minutes; b) dossier du tribunal contenant tous les actes de procédure d'un procès, y compris les feuilles d'audience *(court* —*(s))* qui font foi de leur authenticité (voir *courts of* —).
attorney of — : avocat occupant (opp. *counsel*).
conveyance by — : transfert le bien-fonds par voie judiciaire ou législative, établi par acte officiel *(record)* tel que la procédure fictive de compromis ou par la loi.
— *of evidence*: procès-verbal de témoignage.
keeper of the —*(s)*, **recorder**: greffier, archiviste, avocat nommé par la Couronne pour remplir certaines fonctions de juge.
— *office*: greffe.
to travel out of the — : statuer d'après un motif non articulé.
2° pl. archives (f pl).
criminal, police — : casier judiciaire.
the Criminal — *(s) Office*: le service de l'identité judiciaire.
matter of — : fait enregistré.
— *office*: bureau des archives.
Public —*(s)*: Archives Nationales.
vital —*(s)*: registre d'état civil.
to have a clean — : avoir un casier judiciaire vierge.
[C] *books and* —*(s)*: livres et papiers d'affaires.
official record(s): bulletin officiel (d'une société).
[F] *day of* — : date à laquelle il faut avoir été en possession d'une action, pour toucher le dividende.
to record: enregistrer.
to record an entry: passer une écriture (comptable).
to record a high (low): atteindre le cours le plus haut (bas).
recorded delivery: accusé de réception.
recording: enregistrement comptable.
recording Act: [J] [U.S.] méthode d'enregistrement des actes translatifs de biens immobiliers.
recording fees: droits d'enregistrement.

recoupment: dédommagement (m), défalcation (f), décompte.
— *doctrine*: théorie des corrections symétriques (écritures comptables).
to recoup: récupérer, dédommager, rattraper, défalquer, faire le décompte de, se rattraper de ses pertes.

recourse: recours (m).
[J] [C] *endorsement without* — : endossement à forfait.
to have — *to the law*: employer les voies judiciaires.

recovery: recouvrement (m), récupération (f).
[J] a) réintégrande ([U.S.] *action for ejectment*, voir *ejectment*); b) — *on judgment* « *ut recuperat* » (en latin de Palais) obtention d'une chose par jugement (par le demandeur); c) montant alloué par jugement.
— *of damages*: obtention de dommages-intérêts.
final — : jugement définitif.
rule against the — *of speculative damages*: interdiction, en principe, d'accorder des dommages-intérêts réclamés pour préjudice extrapolé, non chiffrable (p. ex.: un manque à gagner).
— *of payment made by mistake*: répétition de l'indu.
recoverable *tax*: impôt récupérable (sur l'acheteur).
[C] redressement économique, reprise des affaires.
to recover: recouvrer, récupérer, (B) se ranimer, se redresser.
to recover a debt: recouvrer une échéance.

recrimination: récrimination (f), contrepartie (f).

rectification: rectification, redressement.
to rectify: rectifier, redresser.
to rectify an entry: redresser une écriture.

to recruit: recruter.
recruitment: recrutement.

to recycle: recycler.

red: rouge (a).
— *clause*: clause rouge.
— *light district*: quartier réservé.
— *tape*: ruban rouge servant à ficeler les dossiers de l'administration, (fig.) bureaucratie, chinoiseries administratives.
to be taken — -*handed*: être pris sur le fait.
to be in the — : avoir une balance déficitaire.

red herring: [B] prospectus provisoire (préalable) avant une nouvelle émission (d'actions). (Bien que « a red herring » signifie un « hareng saur » ou encore en termes d'argot, surtout policier, un subterfuge pour engager sur une fausse piste, l'expression n'a ici rien de péjoratif: elle vient de ce que le prospectus porte un avertissement imprimé en rouge indiquant qu'il s'agit seulement d'un projet.)

reddendum : (clause d'un bail) qui précise les périodes auxquelles le loyer doit être payé.

redeemable : rachetable, remboursable (a).
 to **redeem** : racheter, rembourser.
 to redeem a loan : amortir un emprunt.

redemise : [J] rétrocession (f).

redemption : rachat (m).
 [J] 1° *— of a mortgage.*
 a) *by mortgagor (extinguishment) :* extinction d'une hypothèque.
 b) *by mortgage (satisfaction) :* purge d'une hypothèque.
 2° faculté de réméré.
 covenant of — : pacte de rachat.
 sale with power, option, of — : vente à réméré.
 [F] remboursement (m).
 (of a bond) amortissement (m), *(of a pledge, a collateral security)* dégagement (m), *(of a loan)* rachat (m).
 — allowance : amortissement autorisé, taux d'amortissement autorisé (voir *« depreciation »*).
 — fund (sinking fund) : caisse d'amortissement.
 — table : plan d'amortissement.
 — before due date : remboursement anticipé.
 — bond : obligation de conversion.
 — rate : taux de remboursement.
 — value : valeur de rachat, de remboursement.
 debt — : amortissement de la dette publique.

to **re-deploy** : redéployer.
 redeployment : redéploiement (m) (de la main-d'œuvre).

redhibition : [J] rédhibition (f).

to **rediscount** : réescompter.

redraft : nouvelle rédaction (d'un document, etc.), [C] traite par contre.

redress : redressement, secours porté (à), *(of a corrupt practice)* réforme, *(of a distress)* soulagement, *(of a tort)* réparation.
 [J] *legal — :* réparation légale (en C.L. le terme technique est *remedy*, en Eq. *relief*).

to **reduce** : abaisser, réduire.
 — the par value : abaisser la parité.
 — the share capital : réduire le capital-actions.
 reducing *balance method :* système d'amortissement dégressif.

reduction : réduction (f), diminution (f), *(of salaries, prices)* baisse (f), *(of a claim)* amputation (f).
 [J] 1° (civ.) a) conversion, p. ex. *— of possession :* convertir, en l'exerçant, un droit résultant d'une créance ; *chose in action,* en une chose en possession. De même une dette est convertie en possession par le paiement (voir *« chose in action »*) ; b) réduction, p. ex. *— of capital :* réduction de capital d'une société anonyme.
 2° (cr.) relaxation.
 the claim has been **reduced** *to judgment :* le montant de la revendication a été fixé par jugement.
 to **reduce** *an oral agreement into writing :* coucher sur papier un accord verbal.
 the sheriff must **reduce** *the property in his custody :* le shériff doit prendre effectivement possession des biens confiés à sa garde.
 [F] *tax — (s) :* réductions d'impôt.
 — of taxation : allègement des impôts.
 [C] rabais (m).

redundancy : surplus, excédent, surnombre, [J] # licenciement économique.
 — compensation : allocation de chômage partiel.
 — payments : compensation accordée aux ouvriers en surnombre, prime de licenciement.
 redundant : ouvrier (m) en surnombre.

to **re-elect** : (pol.) : réélire.
 to come up for **reelection** : se représenter.

re-enactment : (civ.) remise en vigueur d'une loi ; (cr.) reconstitution (f) d'un crime.

to **re-enact** : remettre en vigueur.

re-entry : voir *entry,* ré-importation.
 — permit : [A] [U.S.] visa aller-retour d'un étranger.

re-examination : nouvel examen.
 [J] nouvel interrogatoire du témoin par la partie qui l'a cité, au cours de l'interrogatoire contradictoire (voir *« examination »*).
 [D] contre-visite.

re-exchange : nouvel échange.
 [C] rechange (d'une lettre de change).

re-export : réexportation (f).
 [C] *— trade :* commerce intermédiaire.

re-extent : [J] [A] deuxième ordonnance d'exécution pour une même créance fiscale, la première étant restée sans résultat (voir : *« extent »*).

to **refer** : référer de qch. (à une autorité).
 — to a document as a proof : invoquer un

document.
[J] renvoyer (une affaire devant un tribunal).
– *the matter to arbitration*: soumettre la question à arbitrage.
[C] *to refer a cheque to drawer*: refuser d'honorer un chèque faute de provision.
R.D. (**refer to drawer**) : retour au tireur.
referred *to drawer*: « voir le tireur ».
the gains referred to: les gains visés.

referee: arbitre, arbitre expert, amiable compositeur.
[J] [C] 1° – *in bankruptcy*: [U.S.] administrateur séquestre, liquidateur judiciaire.
– *in case of need*: donneur d'aval, besoin, avaliste, garant.
official – : juge rapporteur.
special – : arbitre désigné par les parties.
– *between arbitrators (umpire)*: tiers-arbitre.
board of – *(s)*: commission arbitrale (voir : *arbiter, arbitrator*).
2° – *on private bill*: membre désigné par la Chambre des Communes pour rapporter sur les questions de locus standi, c'est-à-dire de l'habilité des personnes qui demandent à être entendues sur les projets de loi d'intérêt local.

reference: référence (f), renvoi (m), attribution (f), mention (f), (lettre de) recommandation (f).
by – *to*: en fonction de.
without – *to*: faisant abstraction de.
the – *(s) to expenditures which occur in subsection...*: les mentions des dépenses qui figurent au paragraphe..:
[J] 1° a) nomination d'un arbitre ; b) solution arbitrale ; 2° renvoi d'une affaire : a) devant arbitre ; b) devant la cour de chancellerie ; 3° compétence d'un tribunal ; 4° clause compromissoire ; 5° répondant.
– *book*: ouvrage à consulter, de référence.
– *terms*: mandat (m), attributions (f pl), délimitation des pouvoirs.
terms of – : cahier des charges.
cross- – : renvoi (m), appel (m).
incorporation by – : dans un document, renvoi à un autre document, qui, de ce fait, est intégré dans le premier.

referendum: referendum (m), plébiscite (m).

refinancing: refinancement (m).

refinement: perfectionnement (m).

reflation: augmentation (f) de la masse monétaire en vue de relancer l'économie.

reformation: réforme, [J] terme [U.S.] pour « *rectification* » (voir ce mot).

reformatory: prison pour jeunes détenus.
– *school*: établissement d'éducation surveillée.

refresher: rafraîchissement (m).
[J] honoraires supplémentaires versés à l'avocat au cas où un procès se prolonge outre mesure.
– *course*: cours de perfectionnement.

refreshing memory: [J] un témoin peut au cours de la déposition rafraîchir sa mémoire en consultant ses notes ou des documents, qui ne sont pas cependant admis comme éléments de preuve. Des documents peuvent lui être également soumis : « *does this* **refresh** *you recollection ?* ».

to refuel: réalimenter (en combustible), relancer (ex. l'inflation).

refugee: réfugié, [A] personne déplacée, « D.P. » *(displaced person)*.

refund: remboursement (m), restitution (f), ristourne (f).
[F] **refundable** *tax*: impôt remboursable.
[J] **refunding** *clause*: clause de remboursement.
to refund: rembourser.

refusal: refus (m).
[F] – *to register*: refus d'enregistrement.
[J] – *of justice*: déni de justice.
[C] non-acceptation (de marchandises).
to have the first – *of sthg*: (C) avoir la première offre de qqch..

regalia: [J] a) les droits et privilèges du souverain ; b) les joyaux de la Couronne.
The Coronation – : les honneurs.

regard: considération (f).
having – *to*: compte tenu de.
without – *to*: indépendamment de.
to regard: considérer.
regarded *as*: considéré comme.

regime: régime (m), forme (f) de gouvernement.
[J] [U.S.] régime matrimonial.
the community property – : le régime de la communauté universelle.

regina: reine.
[J] – *([U.S.] the People) versus Smith*: « la Reine ([U.S.] le Peuple) en cause avec Smith » ; formule des procès de l'Etat contre les particuliers.

regional employment premium: (U.K.) prime (f) (de fonctionnement) à l'emploi régional.

register : registre public ; [U.S.] fonctionnaire chargé de la tenue d'un registre (U.K. *registrar*) ; lettre de mer, acte de nationalité ([U.S.] *protection*), *(French ships)* acte de francisation.
— *(s) of births, marriages and deaths* : actes d'état-civil.
commercial, trade — : registre de commerce.
— *of deaths* : registre mortuaire.
— *of directors* : (U.K.) registre des Membres du Conseil d'Administration (inscription obligatoire).
land — : voir *land, land registry*.
Lloyd's — : la classification de navires marchands (# le « Veritas »).
— -*office* : greffe, bureau de l'état-civil.
police — : listes de contrôle de la police.
public — : actes publics.
ship's — : livre de bord.
transfer- — : journal des transferts.
— *of voters, parliamentary* — : liste électorale.
— *of writs* : collection des originaux des ordonnances.
— -*House* : Archives nationales d'Ecosse, à Edimbourg.
[D] — *of goods in bond* : sommier d'entrepôt.
to register *a birth* : déclarer une naissance.
to register a company : faire enregistrer une société.
to register a divorce : transcrire un divorce.
to register (oneself) with the police : s'inscrire à la police.
to register a trade-mark : opérer le dépôt d'une marque.
registered : enregistré, inscrit, immatriculé ; agréé, diplômé d'Etat.
registered authorized capital : capital social, nominal, déclaré.
registered letter : lettre recommandée, chargée.
by registered mail : sous pli recommandé.
registered office : siège social.
registered parcel : colis avec valeur déclarée.
securities registered for tax : titres abonnés (voir : « *tax subscription* »).
registered shareholder : actionnaire inscrit au registre des actionnaires (*stock-book* ; en Grande-Bretagne et aux Etats-Unis il n'existe d'actions que nominatives).
registered stock : effets nominatifs.
registered tonnage : tonnage enregistré, net, jauge de registre, nette de douane.
registered trade-mark : marque déposée.

registrar, [U.S.] **register** : teneur de registres; greffier, archiviste, officier de l'état-civil, etc. ; secrétaire-archiviste d'une université.
[A] — *of companies* : directeur de l'enregistrement de sociétés.
— *of mortgages* : conservateur des hypothèques.
the — *General's Office (of births, deaths and marriages)* : archives de l'état-civil.
— *of transfers* : agent comptable des transferts.
to get married before a — : se marier civilement.

registration : enregistrement (m), inscription (f), immatriculation (f), transcription (f).
certificate of — : matricule, (*of alien*) permis de séjour.
— *deadline* : clôture des inscriptions.
— *duties* : droits d'enregistrement.
— *and transfer taxes* : taxes d'enregistrement et de mutation.
— *fee* : taxe de recommandation.
hotel — *form* : fiche de police.
— *of land* (ou *title to land*) : voir « *land register* » et « *Recording Act* ».
— *of mortgages* : inscription hypothécaire.
— *number* : numéro matricule.
— *of trade-mark* : dépôt d'une marque de fabrique.
[A] *place of* — *of the mortgage* : bureau de conservation des hypothèques.

registry : enregistrement (m).
[J] *Land* — : voir *land*.
[A] a) bureau d'enregistrement, greffe ; b) bureau de l'état-civil.
certificate of — : lettre de mer, certificat d'inscription ou d'immatriculation, acte de nationalité, ([U.S.] *protection*), *(French ships)* acte de francisation.
(port of) — *of a ship or aircraft* : port d'attache d'un navire ou d'un aéronef.
— *marriage* : mariage civil.
[C] — *books* : livres d'ordre, de statistiques.

regress : rentrée (f).
[J] [U.S.] rentrée en possession d'un bien-fonds.
regression *analysis* : analyse prévisionnelle par analogie avec une situation passée.
regressive *taxation* : see « *taxation* ».

regular : régulier, normal (a).
— *agent* : agent attitré.
— *model* : modèle courant.
— *partnership* : société en nom collectif.

regulations : règlement (m), instruction (f) administrative.
— *of the Council or of the Commission (EEC)* : règlements du Conseil ou de la Commission (C.E.E.).
by — : par voie de règlement.
[A] *collision* — : règles d'abordage.
hospital — : régime des hôpitaux.
road — : police de la voirie, du roulage.
safety — : prescriptions relatives à la sécurité.
[D] *the customs* — : les règlements de la douane.
to regulate : régler, calculer, réglementer. (J)

— 574 —

Fixer les règles d'une procédure.

rehabilitation: redressement (m).
[J] réhabilitation (f), rétablissement (m) dans ses droits d'une personne précédemment déchue par une condamnation judiciaire.
[A] réadaptation sociale.
social – : reclassement social.
vocational – : reclassement professionnel.
rehabilitative *aid*: secours par le travail.
[F] assainissement (m).
– *plan*: plan de réorganisation.
financial – : assainissement monétaire.

rehearing: nouvelle audition.
[J] réouverture des débats devant le même tribunal, après le prononcé du jugement.

reimbursement: remboursement (m).

reinstatement: a) réintégration (f) ; b) rétablissement.
the third instance **reinstated** *the verdict returned in the first instance*: la troisième instance a rétabli le jugement rendu en première.
to reinstate (*s.o.*): réintégrer, rétablir (qqn) dans ses droits.

reinsurance: réassurance (f), contre-assurance (f).
[ASS] *excess-* – : réassurance excédentaire.
treaty – : réassurance générale.

reinvestment: [F] nouveau placement, réinvestissement.

to reissue: [F] émettre de nouveau, réémettre.

rejection: rejet (m).
– *rate*: taux de rejet.

rejoinder: répartie (f).

related party: [C] parties liées.

relating to: correspondant à, afférent à.

relation: relation (f), récit (m), rapport (m), parent (m), parenté (f).
[J] a) dénonciation (f).
– *back*: théorie de la rétroactivité.
b) *affin*: agnat ou cognat.

relationship: rapport (m), degré de parenté.
blood – : proximité (f) de sang.

release: délivrance (f), libération (f).
[J] 1º cession du droit de propriété d'un bien-fonds à l'usufruitier ou à la personne en possession ; 2º abandon d'un droit, libération d'une obligation (considération nécessaire) ; 3º décharge donnée à un tuteur, un trustee ou un exécuteur testamentaire par le pupille ; 4º relaxe (f), relaxation (f) ; 5ª cession, transfert (de terrains) ; 6º mise en vente ; 7º libération (de capitaux).
– *on bail*: mise en liberté provisoire, sous caution.
– *in or on licence, on ticket of leave*: libération conditionnelle.
order of – : (ordre de) levée d'écrou.
– *procedure*: procédure de libération.
pre- – *programme*: programme de préparation à la libération.
to release: décharger (d'une obligation), libérer (un prisonnier), délier (qqn de sa promesse), rendre sa parole à qqn, renoncer (à un droit).
releasee: renonciataire, cessionnaire, abandonataire.
releasor: renonciateur, cédant.
[D] – *from bond*: congé (m).
– *of goods against payment*: libération de marchandises.
[C] acquit (m), quittance (f), reçu (m).

relegation: [J] a) renvoi (m) ; b) (hist.) relégation (f).
to relegate *the plaintiff to another cause of action*: inviter le plaignant à invoquer une autre *cause of action* (voir ce terme).
to relegate the plaintiff to the Surrogate's Court: inviter le plaignant à se pourvoir devant la *Surrogate's Court*.

relevant: pertinent, applicable, approprié (a).
all – *information*: tous renseignements utiles.
the – *authority*: l'autorité compétente.
the – *documents*: les pièces justificatives à l'appui.
to be – *to*: se rapporter à.

reliable: digne de confiance.
reliability: fiabilité.

relict: [J] veuve (f).

relief: secours (m), aide (f), soulagement (m), allègement (m).
[J] Eq. *(of a grievance)* réparation (f), *(of a tort)* redressement (m).
affirmative – : conclusions de la défense admises sur les points pouvant donner lieu à une demande reconventionnelle.
coercitive – : ordonnance de faire.
declarative – : jugement déclaratif.
he could get no – : il ne put obtenir justice.
[A] *(Poor-)* – : Assistance publique, aide aux économiquement faibles.
– *in cash*: secours en espèces.
direct – : secours pur et simple (opp. *rehabilitative aid*).

indoor – : assistance aux pauvres hospitalisés.
– *in kind* : secours en nature.
medical home – : soins médicaux à domicile.
parish – : secours du bureau de bienfaisance.
– *ticket* : bon de secours.
child in receipt of – : enfant assisté.
[F] dégrèvement fiscal.
application for – : demande de dégrèvement (voir « *credit* »).
basic – *(s) (and exemptions)* : dégrèvements et exemptions de base.
cross-credit – : déduction réciproque.
earned income – : dégrèvement des revenus du travail.
group – : transfert de charges dans un groupe de sociétés.
– *for increase in stock-value* : [UK] déduction fiscale par accroissement de la valeur des stocks.
marginal – : dégrèvement marginal.
tax – : allègement fiscal.

relinquishment : *(of one's property)* abandon, *(of a right)* renonciation, *(of a property)* dessaisissement.
[J] – *of a succession* : répudiation d'un héritage.
[B] **to relinquish** *the forfeit* : abandonner la prime.

to relocate : réimplanter.
relocation : réimplantation.

remainder : [J] (C.L.) substitution des biens.
contingent – : substitution sous condition suspensive.
vested – : substitution immédiate à l'expiration du droit de propriété antérieur.
heir in –, – -*man* : héritier appelé, substitué (voir « *entail* », « *reversion* »).
[C] pl. solde (m) d'édition, fin (f) de série, reliquat (m), bouillon (m).

remand : [J] a) ajournement (m), renvoi d'un prévenu à une autre audience ; b) renvoi de la cause à l'instance inférieure.
– *on bail* : mise en liberté sous caution.
detention under – : détention préventive.
to remand *a prisoner in custody* : renvoyer à huitaine la comparution de l'inculpé, avec détention provisoire.

remedy : remède (m).
[J] C.L. moyen de droit, recours ; réparation, dédommagement.
provisional **remedies** : voir « *provisional* ».
remedial *statutes* : [U.S.] lois destinées à combler les lacunes du C.L., notamment en matière de procédure.
the institute of prescription is rather remedial than concerning the substantive law : la prescription a un caractère formel plutôt que celui d'une loi positive.
[A] *remedial exercise clinic* : centre de réadaptation physique.

remembrancer : mémento (m), agenda (m).
[A] *City* – : représentant de la Cité de Londres devant les commissions parlementaires.

reminder : mémento (m), rappel « pour mémoire ».
[C] rappel d'échéance.

remise, release and quittance : clause de style dans les contrats de transfert de propriété.

remission, remittal : rémission (f).
[J] a) renvoi à une instance inférieure ; b) remise d'une dette ; c) remise de la peine.
[A] – *of a tax* : exonération d'impôt.
– *of charges* : détaxe.

to remit : envoyer des fonds ; (J) renvoyer à une autre juridiction.
– *a debt* : remettre une dette.
– *a sum to s.o.* : remettre une somme à qn.

remittance : [C] envoi de fonds, remise, virement, versement (par extension : traite ou chèque).
[F] – *basis* : [UK] partie des revenus transférée au Royaume-Uni (seule imposable).

remittee : destinataire (m) d'un envoi de fonds.

remitter : [J] remplacement d'un titre de propriété valable par un autre, également valable mais plus ancien et jugé meilleur de ce fait.

remnant : coupon (m).
[C] –(s) : soldes, fins de série.

remoteness : éloignement (m).
[J] nullité d'une disposition de biens devant entrer en vigueur au-delà de la période fixée par « *the rule against perpetuity* ».
– *of damage* : dommage indirect, sans lien entre la cause et l'effet, qui ne peut donner lieu à des dommages-intérêts.
remote *cause* : la cause supra.
remote *possibility* : éventualité peu probable.

removal : déplacement (m), suppression (f), enlèvement (m).
[J] renvoi d'une cause par un tribunal à un autre (p. ex. pour être jugée simultanément avec une autre, connexe, qui y est pendante).
– *jurisdiction* : [U.S.] compétence d'un tri-

bunal fédéral, déterminée par une déclaration unilatérale du défendeur à cet effet, lorsque les parties relèvent des juridictions de deux Etats différents *(diversity jurisdiction)*, toutes deux compétentes in abstracto.
[A] *(of an official)* révocation, *(of an officer)* destitution.
first cousin once **removed** : cousin issu de germain (parent au 5e degré).
cousin twice removed : cousin issu de fils de germain (7e degré).
[C] — *expenses* : frais de déménagement.
to remove *controls on* : lever les restrictions sur.

remuneration : rémunération (f).
— *of controlling directors* : rémunération des dirigeants.

to render : rendre.
[J] abandonner ou payer.
— *an account, a bill* : remettre un compte.
— *judgment* : prononcer le jugement.

renewal : renouvellement (m).
[J] reconduction (f), *(of title)* rénovation (f).
— *clause* : clause de reconduction pour un laps de temps déterminé, sauf dénonciation.
— *of lease (by tacit agreement)* : renouvellement d'un bail (par tacite reconduction).
[C] — *bill* : retraite (f).
— *of a bill* : atermoiement (m), prolongation (f) d'une lettre de change.
[B] — *of the coupon sheets* : recouponnement (m).
to renew : renouveler, prolonger, proroger.

renouncement : renonciation (f).
[J] — *of one's property* : dépouillement volontaire de ses biens.
— *of a succession* : répudiation d'un héritage.
to renounce *an agreement, a claim, an office, one's office, a right* : se désintéresser d'un contrat, abandonner une revendication, se démettre d'une fonction (démissionner), se désapproprier, renoncer à un droit.
[B] **to renounce** *an allotment letter* : abandonner un droit de souscription.

rent *(of a house, etc.)* : loyer (m), prix (m) de location, prix locatif, *(of land)* fermage (m), affermage (m), rente (f).
[J] — *-charge (charge of landed property)* : servitude de rente grevant un bien-fonds.
— *control* : réglementation des loyers (cf. *Rent Restriction Act, 1920 et 1939)*.
ground- — : redevance emphytéotique.
land- — : rente foncière.
peppercorn — : loyer nominal.
quarter's — : terme.
rack- — : loyer raisonnable (voir ce terme).
— *rebate scheme, plan* : barème de loyers

dégressifs.
— *-collector* : receveur de loyers.
— *-day* : jour du terme.
— *-free* : à titre gracieux.
— *-restriction* : blocage des loyers.
— *-roll* : montant des loyers (d'une maison de rapport, etc.).
— *-roll of an estate* : état des fermages d'une propriété.
[F] — *-a-star company* : société qui loue les services d'une vedette (qui est souvent le véritable propriétaire de la société).

rental : loyer (m), locative (a).
— *value* : valeur locative (montant du loyer).
— *value of premises* : valeur locative des locaux.
yearly — : redevance annuelle.
films — : [U.K.] redevance pour location de films.

renting : location.

renunciation : renoncement (m), période d'exonération de droits d'enregistrement.
[J] délaissement par l'exécuteur testamentaire désigné de la charge que lui a destinée le testateur (voir *disclaimer*), répudiation d'une succession.
— *on oath* : abjuration (voir aussi *renoncement*).

renvoi : [J] doctrine de droit international concernant le choix de la loi internationale applicable dans les circonstances où intervient la question du domicile à l'étranger.

reorganization : réorganisation (f), réforme (f), *(of a bank)* assainissement (m).
corporate — : restructuration d'entreprise.
« — *plans* » : [U.S.] espèces de concordats pour sociétés (om p. ex. les actionnaires cèdent une partie de leurs actions aux créanciers pour permettre à la société de subsister, tandis que ces derniers abandonnent une partie de leurs créances, surtout des obligations, pour réduire le passif et donner à la société la possibilité de reprendre son activité).

repair : réparation (f).
keeping in — : réparations d'entretien.
tenantable — *(s)* : réparations locatives.
[J] **repairing** *lease* : bail qui engage le locataire à maintenir les locaux dans l'état où il les a reçus.

reparation : réparation (f).

reparcelling out : remembrement (m).

(prorata) repartition of assets: au marc le franc.

repatriation: [J] réintégration (f) dans la nationalité.
[A] a) rapatriement (m); b) *(of a foreigner)* refoulement (m).

repayment: remboursement.
[A] *– of income tax*: [U.K.] remboursement de trop-perçu.
[F] *bond due for –*: obligation amortie.
– (s) by repurchase: remboursement par rachat.

repeal: *(of a law)* abrogation (f), *(of a decree)* révocation (f), *(of an order)* rappel (m), annulation (f).
[J] *express –*: abrogation d'une loi ou d'une partie de celle-ci par une disposition législative subséquente.
implied –: se dit d'une loi tombée en désuétude.

to repeat *(an order)*: (C) renouveler (une commande).
repeat order: commande renouvelée, « à nouveau ».
repeat purchasing: renouvellement des achats.

replacement: remplacement (m).
– demand: demande (prévue) d'articles neufs en remplacement d'articles usagés.
– of assets: renouvellement des immobilisations.
[ASS] *– value*: valeur de remplacement.

repleader: jugement ordonnant la reprise de la procédure ab ovo.

replevin: [J] a) mainlevée (f) de saisie; b) ordonnance à cet effet.
to grant –: donner mainlevée.
to replevy: a) obtenir mainlevée; b) admettre à donner caution (n.b. la mainlevée n'est donnée que sur caution).

reply, replication: (voir *« pleading »*).
– -paid: réponse payée.

report: rapport (m), compte-rendu (m), procès-verbal (m), exposé (m), réputation (f), rumeur (f).
[J] 1° a) rapport officiel; b) dénonciation (f), plainte (f); c) rapport du juge rapporteur, comportant généralement les procès verbaux et un projet de sentence *« to confirm the – »* (voir *« referee »*).
2° *(Law –(s))* recueil de jurisprudence (dont on ne saurait exagérer l'importance en pays de C.L.).
3° *(common –)* commune renommée, rumeur publique, notoriété (f).
[ASS] *damage –*: rapport d'avaries.
annual – (of a company): rapport de gestion.
policeman's –: procès-verbal.
secretary's – (of an association): rapport moral.
survey –: rapport d'expertise.
treasurer's –: rapport financier.
to report: rapporter, déclarer.
to report a bill: présenter un projet de loi.
to move to report progress: (pol. Parl.) demander la clôture des débats.
to report to the court: en référer au tribunal.
to report damage: signaler des avaries.
to report (s.o.) to the police: dénoncer (qqn) à la police.
to report to the port authorities: arraisonner avec les autorités du port.
[D] *to report a vessel*: faire la déclaration d'entrée.

reporter (in): (journ.) envoyé (m) spécial (à).

reporting: [F] système de comptes rendus.
– dealer: correspondant (m) en valeurs du Trésor (CVT).

representation: représentation.
[J] a) venir par représentation à une succession; b) exposé par un contractant des faits pouvant être déterminants pour la décision de son contractant (voir: *false –, misrepresentation*).
[ASS] déclaration par l'assuré de toutes les circonstances de nature à permettre à l'assureur d'apprécier les risques qu'il assume.
[A] *– allowances*: allocations de représentation.
representative; [U.S.] député, représentant du peuple.
the House of Representatives: [U.S.] la Chambre des représentants.
lawful representative: représentant légal.
legal representative: mandataire.
personal representative: exécuteur testamentaire, administrateur judiciaire en matière de succession.
real representative: le précédent *(personal representative)* pour les biens immobiliers que comporte la succession.
representative action: (voir: *class action*).
commercial representative: représentant de commerce.
in a representative capacity: pour compte d'autrui.
representative government: régime parlementaire.
representative heir: héritier par représentation.
representative money: monnaie scripturale.
representative sample: échantillon type.

reprieve: [J] (cr.) a) sursis (m); b) commutation (f) de la peine capitale; c) lettres (f pl)

de grâce.
[C] répit (m), délai (m).

reprimand: réprimande (f).
[J] [A] blâme (m).

reprisal: représaille (f).
[J] a) reprise licite ; b) représailles, toutes mesures hormis la guerre, adoptées par un Etat pour obtenir réparation d'un autre Etat, y compris l'embargo et la rétorsion ; c) en temps de guerre, réponse à une violation des lois de la guerre par une autre violation.

reprises: [A] déductions (f pl) à faire sur un revenu foncier.
revenue above, beyond — : revenu net.

republican party: [U.S.] le parti républicain, « *the Grand Old Party* » *(GOP)*, l'un des deux grands partis américains, l'autre étant le parti démocrate.

republication: [J] a) renouvellement d'un testament révoqué de fait ou explicitement (voir « *codicil* ») ; b) nouvelle publication du texte d'une loi...

to repudiate: renoncer.

repudiation: refus (m).
(of wife, of contract, of debts by a government) répudiation (f), *(of a child)* désaveu (m), *(of one's obligations, debts)* reniement (m), *(of an accusation)* rejet (m).

repugnant: contraire à, qui répugne à.
— *conduct*: conduite répréhensible.
— *to constitutional principles*: incompatible avec les principes de la constitution.
— *provisions*: dispositions contradictoires.

repurchase: rachat (m).
[J] réméré (m).
with option to — : avec faculté de réméré.
sale with privilege of — : vente à réméré.
[F] — *agreement*: contrat de report.

reputation: [J] a) réputation (f) ; b) commune renommée. (Dans les questions d'intérêt public, telles que les limites des communes, les droits de passage, de vaine pâture, etc., la preuve peut être établie par « *the general reputation* » la notoriété de la chose.)
[A] *of bad, good* — : mal, bien noté.

reputed: réputé, censé, supposé.
[J] — *father*: père putatif.
— *ownership*: propriété présumée (cas intéressant surtout le règlement des faillites).

request: demande (f), prière (f).
at the — *of*: sur les instances de.
on — : sur demande.
[J] a) sommation (f), mise en demeure ; b) requête (f), demande (f).
the payment was refused though duly on — : le paiement a été refusé, malgré la sommation.
refund will be made upon — *only*: le remboursement n'aura lieu que sur demande.
[C] *article in great* — : article très demandé.

requirement: besoin (m), exigence (f), condition requise ; pl. [U.S.] cahier des charges.
monthly — *(s)*: échéances mensuelles.
to require: exiger.
in the **required** *time*: en temps voulu.
to be required: être astreint.
required reserves: réserves obligatoires.

requisition: demande, requête ; réquisition (de vivres, etc.).
[J] demande formelle adressée à un gouvernement étranger, p. ex. requisition for extradition — demande d'extradition.
— *(s) on title*: demande par écrit adressée par un acheteur de biens immobiliers au vendeur d'avoir à rectifier les défauts ou indications douteuses concernant le droit de propriété de ce dernier qui figurent sur l'acte de vente.
[A] demande de prestation adressée par un service administratif à un autre.

res gestae: les faits matériels d'une affaire.

res judicata: (une) affaire jugée.

res nullius: (une chose) qui n'appartient à personne.

resale: revente (f).
— *price maintenance*: see « maintenance ».

to reschedule: réaménager (des échéances).

rescission: [ ] rescision (f), abrogation.
— *for breach of warranty*: actio redhibitoria, suivie éventuellement de *action for damages for breach of warranty*: actio quanti minoris.
to rescind: *(a deed)* rescinder, *(an agreement, a vote, a decision)* annuler, *(a law, a statute)* abroger, *(a judgment)* casser, *(a contract)* résilier, résoudre, *(a decree)* révoquer, retirer.

rescue: délivrance (f).
[J] a) délivrance (illégale) d'un prisonnier ; b) reprise (f) par la force des biens saisis (licite, si la saisie n'est pas en forme légale ; c) rescousse (f) (reprise d'un navire capturé par l'ennemi).

— *cases*: litiges résultant de risques volontairement assumés.

re-search: [J] nouvelle perquisition. [D] revisite (f) (d'un navire).

research: recherche (f).
— *and development*: recherche et développement.
— *expenses*: frais de recherche.
— *in the field*: recherche opérationnelle.
market — : étude exploratoire de marché.
— *project office*: bureau d'études.

reservation: réserve (f), restriction (f).
[J] clause d'un contrat par laquelle le cédant, donateur, loueur, etc. se réserve une chose, un avantage, etc. sur l'ensemble de la cession, donation, location, etc., stipulée.
— *(s) and safeguards*: réserves et garanties.
with — *(s)*: sous toutes réserves.
without — : sans condition.

reserve: réserve (f).
— *assets*: réserves obligatoires (v. required reserves).
— *authorities*: see « authorities ».
federal — *system*: (voir: « *federal* »).
foreign exchange — : réserve en devises, réserves de change.
gold and foreign exchange — *(s)*: avoirs en or et en devises.
optional — *(s)*: réserves facultatives.
— *currency*: monnaie de réserve.
— *for depreciation*: provision pour dépréciation.
— *for doubtful debts*: provision pour créances douteuses.
— *for inventory maintenance*: provision pour reconstitution des stocks.
— *for loss investments*: provision pour fluctuation des cours.
— *price (Scot. et U.S.: Upset price)*: prix le plus bas qu'une personne ayant mis un objet en vente aux enchères est décidée à accepter.
— *for taxation*: provision pour impôts.
— *fund*: fonds de réserve.
— *requirement*: réserve obligatoire.
— *(s) to meet pending claims*: réserves pour risques en cours.
reserved *dividends*: dividendes différés.
— *powers*: [U.S.] droits réservés, pouvoirs des Etats qui n'ont pas été cédés à l'Union.
— *share*: part réservataire.

to resettle: réaffecter, reclasser (du personnel).

to reshuffle: remanier (personnel).
cabinet **reshuffle**: (pol. fam.) remaniement ministériel.

residence: résidence (f).
[J] (voir: *domicile*).
[A] — *for tax purposes*: résidence fiscale.
— *tax*: taxe d'habitation.

residue: résidu (m).
[J] **residuary** *estate*: montant (m) de la succession après déduction des charges.
residuary account: décompte de l'actif net d'une succession aux fins de la computation de la taxe successorale.
residuary beneficiary: ayant cause à titre universel.
residuary clause: legs (m) à titre universel.
residuary devisee: légataire de biens immobiliers à titre universel.
residuary legatee: légataire universel (voir *heir*).
[F] **residual** *equity*: part (f) en actions.
residual value: valeur résiduelle.

resignation: résignation (f), soumission (f).
[A] démission (f).

resilience: élasticité (f) (du marché).

to resist: résister.
[J] — *the authority of the court*: faire rébellion à la justice (outrage à magistrat).
— *authority*: résister à l'autorité.
— *a motion*: s'opposer à une motion.

to resize: remettre à la bonne dimension.
[F] *next President must cut the deficit and resize taxes*: le nouveau Président devra réduire le déficit (budgétaire) et ajuster les impôts en conséquence.

resolution: résolution (f), délibération (f), proposition (f), vœu (m), ordre (m) du jour.
[J] *joint* — : [U.S.] projet de loi adopté par les deux Chambres du Congrès, en état pour recevoir la sanction présidentielle.
corporative — : résolution du conseil d'administration ou de l'assemblée générale d'une société anonyme.
resolutive *(avoidance, defeasance) clause*: clause résolutoire (d'un contrat).

resort: recours (m).
[J] *court of last* — : tribunal statuant en dernier ressort.
to resort *to*: avoir recours à.

resource(s): ressources (f), moyens de production et de création de services.

respect: rapport (m), égard (m).
in other — *(s)*: à d'autres égards.
in — *of*: relatif à, au titre de.
with — *to*: quant à, en ce qui concerne.

respite: délai (m).
[J] sursis (m).
[C] atermoiement (m).

to respond: [J] être responsable.
— *in damages*: être tenu à des dommages-intérêts.

response: réaction (f) (ex. de la clientèle).

respondeat superior: que le supérieur soit tenu pour responsable.

respondent: répondant (m), personne (f) interrogée (sondage).
[J] a) intimé ; b) défendeur en Eq., sp. dans une instance en divorce.
co- — : co-défendeur, complice d'adultère.

respondentia: [J] prêt sur la cargaison d'un navire.

responsibility: responsabilité (f).

responsible: a) responsable, solidaire ; b) compétent.
to be — *for*: avoir à charge.
the — *quarters*: les milieux autorisés.

rest: reste (m).
[F] réserve (f).
[C] arrêté de compte (m).
— *account*: compte de réserve.

restitution: restitution (f), réparation (f), dommages-intérêts (m pl).
[J] a) restitution de biens enlevés en exécution d'un jugement cassé par la suite ; b) réparation du dommage souffert par le propriétaire des marchandises jetées à la mer par voie de contribution des autres propriétaires de la cargaison ; c) restitution des biens représentant un enrichissement sans cause ; d) — *of conjugal rights*: ordre du tribunal *(Probate, Divorce and Admiralty, Division of the High Court)* à l'époux fugitif d'avoir à réintégrer le domicile conjugal dans un délai prescrit.

restocking: réapprovisionnement, reconstitution des stocks.

restoration: restitution.
[J] — *of goods taken in distraint*: a) mainlevée de saisie ; b) restauration ; c) reconstitution (de gisement).

to restore: rétablir, rééquilibrer.
— *the balance sheet*: rééquilibrer le bilan.

restraint: contrainte (f), restriction (f), entrave (m), frein (m), empêchement (m),
détention (f) de qn.
[J] contrainte par corps, interdiction d'un aliéné, emprisonnement (m), séquestration (f).
— *on alienation*: interdiction à une femme mariée d'aliéner des biens paraphernaux donnés à elle sous cette condition.
— *on anticipation*: (voir *anticipation*).
— *of marriage*: un contrat ou une disposition tendant à empêcher quelqu'un de se marier ou de n'épouser qu'une personne déterminée (contraire à l'ordre public).
— *of trade*: a) en principe, toute disposition contractuelle portant atteinte à la liberté du commerce contraire à l'ordre public ; b) clause licite spécifiant que le vendeur d'un fonds de commerce ne pourra pas se réinstaller dans un périmètre donné.
contracts and combinations in — *of trade*: [U.S.] (voir : *Anti-trust Acts*).

restraining *order*: ordonnance de ne pas faire (« prohibitions et défenses sont faites... »).

restraining *statute*: loi apportant une restriction aux effets du C.L. dans un domaine déterminé.

restricted: restreint, limité, borné (a).
[A] — *area*: zone où la vitesse des automobiles est limitée.
— *district*: quartier soumis à des servitudes de construction, quartier résidentiel.
[B] — *securities*: valeurs sujettes à restriction.

restrictive: restrictif (a).
[J] — *covenant*: (voir *covenant*).
[C] — *indorsement*: endossement restrictif de tout endossement ultérieur (p. ex. la mention « payer à X exclusivement »).

to result: résulter.
[J] faire retour.

resulting *trust*: trust par déduction, dont le titre *(beneficial interest)* revient, dans certains cas, à celui qui l'a créé (n.b. analogue au constructive trust mais non identique).

resumption: reprise (f) (de négociations, etc.).
[J] reprise des terres louées par leur propriétaire.
— *of residence*: réintégration de domicile.
to resume *work*: reprendre le travail.
[F] **resumed** *dividends*: reprise du paiement des dividendes.

retail: [C] détail (m), vente (f) au détail.
— *audit*: [C] enquête auprès d'un échantillon de détaillants pour s'informer sur les prix, les ventes etc.
— *bank*: see « *commercial bank* ».
— *banking*: banque de détail.
— *outlet*: Centre de ventes au détail (super-

marché, etc.).
- *price*: prix de détail.
recommended – price: prix au détail recommandé par le fabricant, prix conseillé.
- *Price Index (R.P.I.)*: indice des prix de détail.
- *trade*: petit commerce.
- *trader*: détaillant.
to retail: vendre au détail.

to retain: retenir, arrêter.
[F] **retained** *earnings, income*: bénéfices non répartis, non réinvestis (see « undistributed profits »).

retainer: arrhes (f pl).
[J] a) droit d'un exécuteur testamentaire ou administrateur judiciaire d'une succession de prélever sur l'actif de celle-ci le montant de leurs créances sur le de cujus, par privilège sur les autres créanciers venant au même rang; b) mandat donné à un avocat; c) honoraires, provision constituée pour retenir les services d'un avocat *(general retainer)*.

retaliation, retorsion: revanche (f), représailles (f pl).
[J] (mesures de) rétorsion *(between States, as applied to their respective nationals)*.
[C] (of a bill) remboursement (d'un effet); retrait.

retirement: [A] retraite (f).
- *on account of age*: retraite par limite d'âge.
compulsory – : retraite d'office.
executive – plans: [U.S.] retraites des cadres.
optional – : retraite sur demande.
- *savings plan*: plan d'épargne, retraite.
retiring *allowance*: indemnité de départ à la retraite.
retiring fund: caisse des retraites.
retiring pension: pension de retraite.
[C] **to retire** *(a bill)*: honorer (une traite), rembourser (un effet), retirer.

retour sans protet: (expression française employée comme telle).

retraction: rétractation (f).
[J] rétractation d'une renonciation: (voir : « renouncement »).
retractable: retractable.
retractable bond, debt: obligation (f), dette (f) que l'on peut rembourser avant échéance.

to retrain: recycler (main-d'œuvre).
retraining: recyclage(m).

to retreat: se retirer.
[J] « *– to the wall* »: nécessité pour plaider la légitime défense d'avoir fait tout le possible avant de recourir à la violence.
[B] reculer.

retrieval: récupération (f), réparation (f) (d'une erreur).

retrospective: rétroactif (a).
- *effect*: effet rétroactif.

return: retour (m).
[J] 1° mandat de renvoi, rapport qu'adresse le sheriff au tribunal au sujet d'une exécution: *he* **returns** *a warrant, a writ, – day*: jour fixé à cet effet dans l'ordonnance (« *writ* **returnable** *on May 1* »); 2° *(annual –)* : rapport annuel obligatoire d'une société anonyme au directeur de l'enregistrement des sociétés *(Registar of Companies)*.
the – of the writ: appel d'un particulier à la justice pour l'application d'un *writ*, sp. de celui de habeas corpus.
to return *a verdict*: prononcer, rendre un verdict.
the prisoner was **returned** *guilty*: l'accusé fut déclaré coupable.
[A] résultats chiffrés d'un dénombrement, statistique.
- *(s) of a census*: résultats d'un recensement.
counting of the – (s): comptage (m).
false – (s) (or double counting): fait de compter deux fois la même personne ou le même objet.
official – (s): relevés officiels.
published – (s): résultats publiés.
Board of Trade – (s): statistiques de commerce.
[F] déclaration (d'impôts).
- *of collections*: états des recouvrements, rentrées d'impôts.
compulsory – : déclaration obligatoire.
delinquent – : [U.S.] déclaration tardive.
- *of charges, of duties*: détaxe.
- *(s) of income*: déclaration de revenu.
joint – : déclaration conjointe (en matière de droits de succession).
- *on real property*: revenus d'immeubles.
tax – : [U.S.] déclaration définitive. (opp. *tax declaration*: première déclaration de l'impôt présumé).
[C] a) pl. recettes, rendement.
gross – (s): recettes brutes.
quick – (s): vente rapide.
law of diminishing – (s): loi des rendements décroissants.
b) revenu, gain, profit.
c) renvoi, retour, réexpédition (de marchandises avariées, etc.).
- *on capital*: rémunération, rendement du capital.
gross – : rendement brut.
by – of post: par retour du courrier.
- *address*: adresse (f) de l'expéditeur.

— *commission*: ristourne (f).
— *of an amount overpaid*: ristourne d'une somme payée en trop.
— *of bill to drawer*: contre-passation (f).
— *on investment (R.O.I.)*: taux de rendement comptable, rendement des actifs.
on sale or —: marchandises en commission.
— *of capital sum*: remboursement de capital.
Bank —: situation de la Banque.
weekly Bank —: bilan hebdomadaire de la Banque.
quarterly —: rapport trimestriel.
returned *article*: laissé pour compte.
returning *officer*: fonctionnaire chargé d'une élection: *he returns the result of the poll*: il fait rapport sur les résultats du scrutin.

revalorization: revalorisation (f).

revaluation: réévaluation (f), réestimation (f).
— *of the assets*: réévaluation des éléments d'actif.

revenue: revenu (m), rentes (f pl), rapport (d'une terre, etc.).
[F] fisc.
— *accounts*: compte des recettes et des dépenses, compte de produits.
— *authorities*: autorités fiscales, agents du fisc.
Board of Inland —: [U.K.] administration des impôts sur le revenu et la fortune.
Board of Internal —: [U.S.] administration du revenu intérieur.
excise —: contributions indirectes.
— *expenditure*: frais de gestion.
Internal — *Code*: code fiscal des Etats-Unis.
— *office*: recette.
— *claims (for collection)*: créances fiscales (à recouvrer).
priority status of — *claims*: priorité des créances fiscales.
— *duties*: droits fiscaux.
government —: recettes budgétaires.
— *laws*: législation fiscale.
— *receipts*: rentrées fiscales.
— *stamp*: timbre fiscal.
tax —: recettes fiscales.
revenuer: [U.S.] agent du fisc.
[C] — *assets*: valeurs de roulement.
[D] — *cutter*: cotre de la douane.
— *officer*: douanier.

reversal: [J] réforme d'un jugement en appel, arrêt d'annulation.
reversible *error*: erreur justifiant l'annulation d'un jugement.

reverse: inverse.
[C] — *stock split*: consolidation de capital.
[J] **to reverse**: réformer, révoquer (une sentence).
reversed *take-over*: contre-O.P.A.

reversion: retour (m).
[J] 1° a) réversion (f) ; b) substitution (f).
estate in —: bien grevé : d'une réversion ; de substitution.
— *of an estate to an ascendant*: retour d'un héritage à un ascendant.
right of —: droit de retour (d'une donation).
reversionary *annuity*: annuité réversible (après la mort du titulaire).
reversionary *interest*: tous droits de jouissance futurs en vertu d'une —, d'un *remainder* ou de droits mobiliers analogues.
2° survivance (f).

reverter: réversion (f) (voir supra).

review: revue (f), examen (m) à nouveau.
[C] point (périodique, semestriel, etc.) de situation de l'entreprise.
[J] a) révision (f) *(review on appeal)*.
court of —: (se dit d'une) cour d'appel, de cassation.
— *of taxation*: révision des frais fixés par le juge taxateur.
b) vérification des actes des administrations publiques par les tribunaux ordinaires.
[C] *the year under* —: l'exercice écoulé.

to revise: réviser, modifier, distribuer.
— *downwards*: baisser, diminuer, réduire, réviser en baisse.
— *upwards*: hausser, élever, accroître, réviser en hausse.

revival: renaissance (f).
[J] remise en vigueur.
to revive *an action*: reprendre une instance.
to revive a debt: faire une nouvelle reconnaissance d'une dette éteinte par prescription.
to revive a judgment: donner une nouvelle force exécutoire à un jugement périmé.
to revive a law: remettre en vigueur une loi.
to revive a testament: renouveler un testament (voir *republication*).

revocation: révocation (f).
[J] révocation (f), abrogation (f).
[A] retrait (m), *(of an official)* révocation.
— *of election*: révocation du choix.
revocable: révocable.

to revoke: [A] rapporter (décret), révoquer.
— *a driving licence*: retirer un permis de conduire.

revolving: rotatif (a).
[B] — *credit*: crédit par acceptation renouvelable.

[C] – *fund*: fonds de roulement, crédit renouvelé à intervalles réguliers.

reward: récompense (f), rémunération.
[J] prime de l'inventeur.

to rezone: réaménager.

rider: cavalier (m), ajouté (m).
[J] avenant à un verdict, p. ex. recours en grâce signé par les jurés *(recommendation)*, *(to a law, an insurance policy)* avenant, *(to a document)* papillon, annexe, *(to a contract)* clause additionnelle, *(to a treaty)* annexe, protocole additionnel, *(to a formula)* correctif, rectificatif.
[F] – *(in the Federal Budget)*: « cavalier budgétaire » (disposition non financière figurant à tort dans une loi de finances).
[Eco] *free* – : passager clandestin.
to ride out *(a crisis)*: surmonter (une crise).

to rig: [B] tripoter.
– *the market*: provoquer une hausse factice.
– *up prices, rates*: faire monter les prix, les taux artificiellement.
rigging: agiotage.

right: le droit, la justice, le bien.
[J] un droit, un titre, un privilège.
Le terme « droit » est sous-entendu par ex. dans :
accretion: droit d'accroissement.
appurtenances: droits accessoires.
escheat: droit de bris, déshérence.
severance: droit de distraction.
Dans d'autres cas le terme est inclus dans un mot composé, p. ex. dans :
birthright: droit d'aînesse.
copyright: droit d'auteur.
Enfin, dans les cas suivants, le terme est spécifié :
– *of (or: in) action*: droit d'ester en jugement (plainte recevable, syn. « *chose in action* »).
– *to begin*: (civ.) droit de l'avocat de la partie à qui il incombe de faire la preuve de plaider en premier, (cr.) le réquisitoire qui précède les plaidoiries.
– *of common*: droit d'usage.
– *of entry*: (voir : « *entry* » [J]).
– *of search*: droit de visite.
– *of way*: droit de passage.
– *of withdrawal*: droit de désengagement, droit de retrait.
civic – *(s)*: droits politiques.
civil – *(s)*: droits civils.
human – *(s)*: droits de l'homme.
intangible – *(s)*: propriété intellectuelle.
to act by – : agir de plein droit.
petitioner declared to have no – *of action*: demandeur non recevable dans son action.
– *of sanctuary*: droit d'asile.
with – *of transfer*: avec faculté de transfert.
to vindicate one's – : faire valoir son bon droit.
[F] *application* – *(s)*: droit(s) de souscription.
[B] – *(s) issue*: faculté pour des actionnaires d'acheter de nouvelles actions à un prix inférieur à leur valeur d'émission (souvent porportionnellement au nombre de celles qu'ils détiennent).

rightful: légitime, équitable (a).
[J] – *claimant*: « ayant droit ».

ring: [B] parquet (m), marché officiel (m).
[F] – *fence*: [UK] « enclos fiscal », règles fiscales spécifiques d'imposition du secteur pétrolier de la Mer du Nord.

riot: émeutes (f), sédition (f).
[J] (cr.) attentat à l'ordre public.

riparian: riverain (a).
[J] – *owner*: propriétaire riverain, bordier.
– *rights*: droits des riverains.

rise: hausse (f), augmentation (f).
– *in price*: renchérissement.
to rise: monter, s'élever.
to rise a point: monter d'un point.

risk: risque (m), aléa (m), hasard (m), péril (m).
[J] *the buyer's* – : le risque de l'acheteur (l'achat d'une marchandise transfère les risques qu'elle peut courir à la charge du nouveau propriétaire. La livraison effective n'est pas nécessaire).
– *note*: [U.K.] accord entre une compagnie de chemins de fer et un consignataire dégageant la compagnie de sa responsabilité de voiturier, celle-ci ne restant engagée que pour les pertes résultant des fautes graves de la compagnie ou de ses employés.
[ASS] le risque chiffré, (langage courant) la personne, l'objet assurés.
– *adjusted rate of return*: prime de risque ajoutée (au coût du capital).
– *analysis*: analyse des risques.
fire- – : risque d'incendie.
insurable – : risque assurable.
professional – : risque professionnel.
– *capital*: capital à risques.
– *premium*: prime nette.
– *management*: contrôle des pertes, gestion des risques.
– *profile*: densité (distribution) de probabilités.
sea – *(s)*: fortune de mer.
war – *(s)*: risques de guerre.
to lay off a – : effectuer une réassurance.
to be attended with – *(s)*: comporter des

risques.

robbery: [J] vol qualifié.
armed – : vol à main armée.
highway – : brigandage.

(the) robe: la robe, les gens de justice.

rock-bottom: niveau le plus bas.

roll: rouleau (m).
[J] a) rôle (m); b) liste (f) des membres du barreau.
judgment – *(s)*: dossiers complets des affaires jugées.
Parliament – *(s)*: procès-verbaux des séances du Parlement.
[A] rôle, contrôle (m), liste.
assessment – : rôle de l'impôt.
muster- – : rôle de l'équipage.
nominative- – : contrôle, état nominatif.
payroll: feuille d'émargement, feuille de paie.
– *-back*: baisse des prix imposée.
– *-call*: appel nominatif.
– *-forward*: majoration imposée des prix.
[F] – *over credits*: billets de mobilisation.
rollover credit: crédit à taux révisable.
rollover credit facilities: crédit à taux variable (suivant les changements intervenant sur le marché, tirages courts successifs).
to roll over: renouveler.
rolling-rate note: obligation à taux variable.
rolling readjustment: réajustement graduel.
rolling stock: matériel roulant.

rough: grossier (a).
[C] – *book*: brouillard (comptabilité).
– *estimate*: estimation approximative, devis approximatif.

round: rond (a).
in – *figures*: en chiffres ronds.
– *lot*: quotité.
to round *down*: arrondir au chiffre inférieur.
to round off (up) a sum to the next highest franc: arrondir une somme au franc supérieur.

roundtripping: (B) opération (f) qui consiste à retirer de l'argent d'une banque à découvert pour le prêter sur le marché monétaire.

rout: bande (f).
[J] attroupement illégal dans une intention délictueuse, intermédiaire entre une réunion illégale *(unlawful assembly)* et un attroupement séditieux.

route: itinéraire (m).
– *sheet*: [U.S.] gamme de fabrication.

royal assent: [Pol] sanction royale (dernière étape du processus législatif).

royalty: royauté, princes du sang; pl. redevance, sp. redevance tréfoncière *(mining royalties)*.
royalties on copyright (and other intellectual properties): redevances sur le droit de reproduction *(copyright)* et autres droits de propriété intellectuelle.
royalties on patents: redevances sur les brevets.
royalties on the use of patents: redevances pour concession de l'exploitation de brevets.
royalties on natural resources: redevances afférentes à l'exploitation de ressources naturelles.

rubber: caoutchouc (m).
[F] – *cheque*: chèque sans provision.
[B] – *(s)*: les caoutchoucs.

rubbing unemployment: chômage frictionnel.

rule: règle (f), disposition générale.
[J] a) règles de procédure; b) ordonnance ou décision d'un tribunal au cours d'une instance; c) règle de droit immuable, telle que « the – *against perpetuity* » ou encore, exemple classique: « *the* – *in Shelley's case* ».
hospital – *(s)*: régime des hôpitaux.
– *of law*: état de droit.
– *(s) and regulations*: statuts et règlements.
– *(s) relating to computation of income*: règles relatives au calcul du revenu.
the – *(s) of the road*: le code de la route.
the – *(s) of a society*: les statuts d'une société.
standing – : règle permanente.
by – *of thumb*: méthode empirique.

to rule: (pol.) régir, gouverner.
(J) décider.
– *sthg out of order*: décider que qqch n'est pas en règle.
(C) clore, régler (affaire).

to rule off: [C] arrêter.
– *an account*: arrêter un compte.

to rule out: éliminer (une possibilité.

ruling: ordonnance (f), décision d'un juge sur un point de droit.
to give – *in favour of s.o.*: décider en faveur de qn.
[F] [U.S.] doctrine administrative exprimée par les Services fiscaux.
advanced – *(s)*: prise de position de l'Ad-

ministration fiscale sur demande de renseignements d'un contribuable.
[C] *(the)* — *prices*: (les) cours actuels.

run: parcours (m), [U.S.] lot de fabrication.
a — *on a bank*: des guichets (de banque) assiégés.
there is a — *on the franc, pound, etc.*: les gens se débarrassent de leurs francs, leurs livres, etc. (par manque de confiance).
the — *of the market*: les tendances du marché.
prices — *high*: les prix sont élevés.
— *down*: affaiblissement.
to run: a) exploiter, diriger ; b) couvrir, encourir.
to run a factory: diriger une usine.
interest which **runs**: les intérêts qui courent.
to run counter to the general trend: aller à l'encontre de la tendance générale.
to run down (stocks): réduire (des stocks).
to run into debt: s'endetter.
to run on: continuer.
to run out: être à cours de, prendre fin.
to run up: s'élever.

runaway: incontrôlable (a).
— *inflation*: inflation galopante.

running: courant, en cours (a).
— *account*: compte courant.
— *-in-period*: période de rodage.
— *costs*: frais d'exploitation.
— *with the land*: servitude foncière.
— *year*: exercice en cours.

rush: ruée (f), course (f).
[B] *a* — *on mining stocks*: une ruée sur les valeurs minières.

NOTES

NOTES

S

S. R. and O. *(Statutory Rules and Orders)*: voir ce terme.

sac: juridiction.

to sack: (fam.) mettre à la porte, licencier.

sacred interests: [F] intérêts intangibles.

sacrifice: sacrifice (m), [C] mévente (f).
— *-prices*: vente (f) à perte.

to saddle: grever.
[F] **saddled** *with a tax*: grevé d'un impôt.

SAE (stamped addressed envelope): enveloppe timbrée (à l'adresse du candidat).

safe: sain, sûr (a); coffre-fort (m).
— *investment*: placement de tout repos.
— *conduct*: sauf-conduit.
— *custody*: dépôt en garde.
— *-limit*: limite de sécurité.
— *deposit*: dépôt en coffre-fort.
— *deposit company*: banque de dépôt.
— *custody account*: compte de dépôt de titres.
as — *as houses*: placement pierre.

safeguard: sauvegarde (f).
— *index*: indicateur d'alerte.
safeguarding *account*: compte-titres en garde.
safeguarding *duties*: droits de sauvegarde.

safekeeping department: service (m) des coffres-forts.

safety: sûreté, sécurité, salut, garantie.
— *-first policy*: politique de prudence.
— *fund*: fonds de garantie.
— *margin*: marge de sécurité.
— *standards*: normes de sécurité.

to sag: s'affaisser, fléchir, s'effriter.
[B] *prices are* **sagging**: les cours fléchissent.
sagging *market*: marché creux.

said: susdit, susvisé, susnommé, susmentionné.
the — : ledit, ladite, lesdits, lesdites.

salary: traitement (m), appointement (m), émoluments (m) (ne pas traduire par salaire: *wages*).
deduction from the — : retenue sur le traitement.
leave without — : congé sans solde.
minister's — : appointement d'un ministre.
salaries *and wages lists*: état des traitements et salaires.
— *advances*: avances sur traitement.
— *bracket*: échelon de traitement.
— *cut*: réduction sur le traitement.
— *range*: échelle des traitements.
— *record*: état des rémunérations successives.
scale of — : barème, échelle des traitements.
starting — : traitement initial.
to draw a — : toucher un traitement.
monthly — : appointements mensuels.
salaried *worker*: salarié.

sale: vente (f), débouché (m), écoulement (m).
[J] *bill of* — : acte de vente.
compulsory — : vente par autorité de justice, adjudication forcée.
candle — : vente à l'éteinte de la chandelle.
deed of — : contrat (acte) de vente.
distress — : vente publique de biens saisis.
execution — : vente par exécution forcée.
goods under a bill of — : marchandises hypothéquées.
sheriff's — : vente par exécution forcée.
[F] *tax* — : vente forcée au profit du fisc.
—*(s) tax*: impôt sur le chiffre d'affaires.
[C] *auction* — : vente aux enchères, à cri public.
bargain — : vente au rabais, soldes.
—*(s) campaign*: campagne de ventes.
cash on delivery — : vente contre remboursement.
cash — : vente au comptant.
clearance — : réalisation du stock, vente en liquidation.
closing-down — : liquidation avant départ.
conditional — : vente conditionnelle.
credit — : vente à crédit.
day's — *(at auction)*: vacation.
—*(s) forecast*: prévision de ventes.
gross proceeds of —*(s)*: montant brut des ventes.
heavy —*(s)*: ventes importantes.
—*(s) incentives*: moyens d'encourager les ventes.
judicial — : vente judiciaire.
jumble — : déballage.
—*(s) manager*: chef du service des ventes.

memorandum — : vente à la commission.
missive of — : acte de vente.
outright — : vente à forfait, vente en bloc.
particulars of — : description de la propriété à vendre ; cahier des charges.
private — : vente de gré à gré.
pro forma — : vente simulée.
public — : vente publique, adjudication.
ready — : (marchandises) de bonne vente.
— *(s) account* : compte de vente.
— *and leaseback* : location-vente.
— *(s) book* : facturier.
— *(s) budget* : chiffre d'affaires.
— *(s) budget* : estimation prévisionnelle des ventes et des dépenses à envisager (publicité etc.) pour parvenir au résultat prévu ; budget prévisionnel du poste « ventes ».
— *by private contract* : vente à l'amiable, de gré à gré.
— *by sample, sample order* : vente sur échantillon.
— *by sealed tender* : vente par soumission cachetée.
— *(s) check* : [U.S.] facture.
— *ex bond* : vente à l'acquitté.
— *(s) figure* : [U.S.] chiffre d'affaires.
— *for consumption* : vente à la consommation.
— *for futures* : vente à découvert.
— *invoice* : facture.
— *(s) ledger* : grand livre des ventes.
— *of joint property* : vente sur licitation.
— *of standing trees* : vente sur pied.
— *on approval* : vente à l'essai.
— *on commission* : vente à la commission.
— *on instalments* : vente à tempérament.
— *on trial* : vente à l'essai.
— *on return* : vente à condition (marchandises en dépôt avec reprise des invendus).
— *price* : prix de vente, de solde.
— *(s) promotion* : promotion des ventes.
— *(s) prospect* : client.
— *and repurchase agreement* : accord de vente avec promesse de rachat.
— *(s) receipts, returns* : produits (recettes) des ventes.
— *(s) talk* : boniment du vendeur.
— *(s) to non-residents* : ventes à l'étranger.
— *value* : valeur marchande.
— *with all faults* : vente tel quel.
— *with option to repurchase* : vente à réméré.
short — : vente à terme, vente à découvert.
spot — : vente en disponible.
terms of — : conditions de vente.
white — : vente de blanc.
[B] *bear* — : vente à découvert.
— *(s)* : volume d'affaires, de transactions.
— *contract* : bordereau de vente.
— *for the account* : vente à terme.
— *of investments (or sales from the port-folio)* : ventes de valeurs en portefeuille.
wash — : vente fictive.

salesman : a) vendeur (m) ; b) voyageur de commerce (m) ; c) commis (m) voyageur.

salesmanship : art de vendre.

salvage : 1° [J] a) prime de sauvetage accordée aux personnes (**salvors**) ayant sauvé un navire, une cargaison ou la vie de personnes embarquées du danger ou de la perte en mer ; b) *(paid to salvagetug)* indemnité de remorquage.
— *agreement, bond* : contrat de sauvetage.
— *company* : société, corps de sauvetage.
— *dues* : droits de sauvetage.
— *money* : prime, indemnité de sauvetage.
— *plant* : appareil de renflouage.
— *value* : valeur de rebut, résiduelle, de récupération.
2° biens récupérés ou préservés par l'intermédiaire de l'avoué *(solicitor)* qui a mis la procédure en branle.

salvo jure : sans préjudice de.

sample : échantillon (m), spécimen (m).
[C] *free* — *(s)* : échantillons gratuits.
picked — : échantillon choisi.
probability — : échantillon aléatoire (v. « random sampling »).
reference — : contre-échantillon.
representative — : échantillon type.
— *market* : vente sur échantillon.
— *plot* : champ d'essai.
— *survey* : enquête par sondage.
up to sample, true to sample : conforme à l'échantillon.
random sampling : échantillonnage au hasard.

sanction : sanction, autorisation, approbation, consentement.
[J] *punitive, vindicatory* — : sanction pénale.
remuneratory — : sanction rémunératoire.

sandwich course : études (f) poursuivies hors de l'entreprise par un employé.

sans frais : expression française employée telle quelle.

sans jour : sine die.

sans nombre : expression française pour indiquer que le nombre des bêtes admises au pâturage en vertu d'un droit de pacage n'est pas limité.

sans recours : expression française employée comme telle.

satisfaction : satisfaction (f), consentement, réparation (f), *(of a debt)* acquittement, liqui-

dation, paiement, *(of a condition)* accomplissement, *(of a creditor)* désintéressement, *(of a mortgage)* purge, *(of a judgment, promise)* exécution.
[J] — *piece*: certificat remis à l'intéressé indiquant qu'il a satisfait au jugement en s'acquittant d'une obligation pécuniaire.
to enter — : enregistrement à l'effet du précédent au *judgment roll* (dossier d'une affaire).
until — *is made*: jusqu'à ce que la somme soit payée.

to satisfy *(a claim)* : faire droit (à une réclamation), remplir (une obligation).
— *the jury*: convaincre le jury.
to be **satisfied** *that*: être convaincu que.
— *one's creditors*: désintéresser ses créanciers.

to save: 1° sauver ; 2° [F] épargner.
save all: clause de sauvegarde générale (d'un contrat).
saver: sauveteur, [F] épargnant.
small saver: petit épargnant (n.m.).
saving: sauvetage, [F] économie, épargne.
[J] *saving clause*: réserve, clause restrictive, clause de sauvegarde, clause conditionnelle.
saving the statute of limitations: interruption de la prescription extinctive.
[F] *appreciable saving*: sérieuse économie.
labour saving: économie de travail.
labour-saving machinery: machine économisant la main-d'œuvre.
savings account: compte d'épargne.
savings bank, savings and loans association: institution (f) d'épargne.
savings bank book: livret de caisse d'épargne.
savings certificate: certificat d'épargne.
savings invested in securities: épargne mobilière.
to draw on one's savings: prendre sur ses économies.

scab: see « blackleg ».

scale: échelle (f), barème (m).
[J] *costs on the higher* — : le maximum de frais.
to turn the — : faire pencher la balance.
[F] barème.
degressive —(s) : barèmes dégressifs.
progressive —(s) : barèmes progressifs.
— *of salaries*: barème des traitements.
sliding wage — : échelle mobile des salaires.
[C] *large* — *industry*: industrie à grand rendement.
— *economies*: économies (f pl) d'échelle.
— *of charges*: tarif.
— *of commissions*: tarif des courtages.
to scale down: dégrever (le tarif douanier) ; diminuer, réduire (dans une proportion déterminée).
in time of depression firms are **scaling** *down their activities*: en temps de crise les entreprises réduisent leurs activités dans une certaine proportion.
to scale up: majorer, augmenter (dans une proportion déterminée).
to scale wages: majorer les salaires d'un certain pourcentage.

to scalp: [U.S.] a) vendre au-dessous du prix normal ; b) boursicoter.

scandal: scandale, honte.
[J] allégations injurieuses, sp. écarts de langage dans des conclusions ou au cours d'une plaidoirie, atteignant la dignité du tribunal, qui peut ordonner la suppression des passages incriminés.

scarcity: rareté (f), pénurie (f), insuffisance (f), manque (m), disette (f).
— *of capital*: pénurie de capitaux.
— *of raw materials*: pénurie de matières premières.
the growing — *of skilled labour*: la raréfaction de la main-d'œuvre qualifiée.
— *value*: valeur découlant de la rareté.

scare: peur (f), alarme (f), panique (f).
— *headline*: (journ.) manchette sensationnelle.
[B] — *on the stock exchange*: panique en bourse.

scatter coefficient: coefficient de dispersion, de distribution.
— *diagram*: graphique des données dispersées.

schedular: cédulaire (a).
— *system of taxes*: système d'imposition des revenus sur la base des cédules.

schedule: note explicative, tableau, [U.S.] prévisions, plan.
[J] a) annexe, avenant (à une loi, un instrument, à des statuts, etc.); b) bilan d'une faillite.
contract — : bordereau de prix annexé au contrat.
— *of cases*: rôle des causes.
— *of documents, investments*: bordereau de pièces, de portefeuille.
— *to a balance sheet*: annexes d'un bilan.
— *to a contract*: annexe à un contrat.
[F] cédule (f).
income tax —(s) : cédules des impôts sur les revenus.
individual —(s) : bordereaux individuels.
taxation — : tarif de l'impôt.
scheduled *taxes*: impôts cédulaires.

progressive scheduled surtax: barème de surtaxe progressive.
[ASS] — *bond:* police de garantie collective.
— *of property:* liste des choses assurées.
[C] *nomenclature* (f), *inventaire* (m) des machines, barème (des prix), [U.S.] horaire (m), emploi (m) du temps.
according to —: selon les prévisions, suivant l'horaire prévu.
ahead of, behind, —: en avance, en retard sur les prévisions, sur le programme.
production —(s): barèmes de production.
railroad —: [U.S.] indicateur des chemins de fer.
wages —: barème des salaires.
work —: horaires de travail.
to prepare a —: dresser un tableau.
to schedule: ajouter en annexe, inscrire sur une liste, établir un programme, un horaire.
scheduled flight: vol régulier.
scheduled prices: prix conformes au tarif.
scheduled territories: zone sterling.

scheme: arrangement (m), système (m), plan (m), projet (m), intrigue (f).
[J] [U.K.] distribution d'une succession ou d'un fonds.
— *of composition (between debtor and creditors):* concordat préventif de la liquidation de biens.
staff retirement —: régime des retraites du personnel.
bubble —: entreprise véreuse.
deep-laid —: intrigue habilement machinée.
financial —: plan, programme financier.
pension —: plan de retraite.
profit-sharing —: plan d'intéressement.
put-up —: affaire machinée à l'avance, coup monté.
shady —: combinaison louche.
to lay a —: ourdir une machination.

scholarship: érudition (f), savoir (m), science (f); bourse (f) d'études.
open —: bourse accessible à tous.
— *grantee:* boursier.
— *(s) and fellowships:* bourses d'études et de recherches, bourses universitaires.
travelling —: bourse de voyage.

science: science (f).
applied —: applications de la science à l'industrie.
forensic —: médecine légale.

scienter: (latin) en connaissance de cause, sciemment.
[J] *to prove a —:* prouver dans une conclusion qu'un acte a été commis ou permis à bon escient (indispensable dans une action pour présentation erronée des faits = *misrepresentation*).

scientific: scientifique (a).
— *adviser:* conseiller scientifique.
— *business administration:* gestion scientifique des affaires.
— *consultant:* expert conseil scientifique.
— *management:* see « operational research ».
— *property:* propriété scientifique.

scientist: homme de science, scientifique.
social —(s) and engineers: théoriciens et praticiens des sciences sociales.

scilicet, scil.: à savoir, c'est-à-dire.

scintilla: étincelle (f), parcelle (f).
[J] — *of evidence:* indice (m) infime, soupçon de preuve. C.L. du moment qu'il existe la plus faible présomption d'un fait, son existence est laissée à l'appréciation du jury.

scire facias: que tu lui fasses connaître (un « writ » scire facias peut en particulier être notifié à un actionnaire d'une société dans un jugement prononcé contre cette société).

scope: a) portée (f), champ (m) d'action; b) compétence.
[J] *the — of review:* limites de la compétence en appel.
matters within the — of... : questions qui sont du ressort de...
of limited —: dont le champ d'action est limité.
that is beyond (outside) his —: cela n'est pas de sa compétence.
the — of a tax: le champ (d'application) d'un impôt.
to enlarge the — of an inquiry: agrandir le champ d'une enquête.
to extend the — of the powers of a committee: élargir le cadre des attributions d'un comité.

score: a) sujet (m), point (m); b) cause (f), raison (f), motif (m), considération (f).
on that —: sur ce point, à cet égard, à ce sujet.
objection on the — of privilege: objection fondée sur la considération du privilège.
scoring: évaluation par score, scorage.

scots: écossais (utilisé en Ecosse de préférence à **Scottish** pour désigner la nationalité).
[J] — *Law:* droit écossais.

scrap: rebuts (m pl), déchets (m pl), riblons (m pl).
— *iron:* ferraille.
— *value:* valeur de rebut, valeur résiduelle.
to scrap: 1° mettre au rebut, hors service; 2° informer, éliminer.

scratch: improvisé, sommaire, provisoire (a).
— *vote*: vote par surprise.
— *majority*: majorité de rechange.
to scratch *out*: rayer, raturer.

to screen: interroger un suspect; faire un choix parmi des personnes ayant demandé une entrevue; rechercher s'il vaut la peine de continuer une fabrication.

scrip: [F] certificat (m) d'action provisoire, document (m), reçu (m).
debenture — : certificat d'obligations.
registered — : titre nominatif.
— *certificate*: titre, certificat provisoire.
— *dividend*: promesse écrite de dividende.
— *-holder*: détenteur de titres, détenteur de certificat d'action provisoire.
— *issue*: émissions d'actions.

script: écrit (m), [J] document original, [U.S.] concession de terrain.

scrivener: écrivain public, copiste; notaire *(notary public)*.

scrutiny: recherche minutieuse, investigation (f).
[J] vérification de la validité des votes émis au cours d'un scrutin (en cas de contestation).
to demand a — : demander la vérification du scrutin, contester la validité d'une élection.

scuttling: [J] [ASS] sabordage intentionnel d'un navire.
scuttler: assureur frauduleux.

sea: mer (f).
beyond the — *(s)*: au-delà des mers, outre-mer.
perils of the — : fortune de mer.
— *law*: droit maritime.
— *lawyer*: chicaneur, avocat « de haute mer », (coupeur de cheveux).
— *letter*: permis de navigation.
— *transport of goods*: messageries maritimes.
the four — *(s)*: les mers qui entourent la Grande-Bretagne.
the seven — *(s)*: toutes les mers du monde.
within the four — *(s)*: en Grande-Bretagne.
seaborne trade: commerce maritime.

seal: cachet (m), sceau (m).
[C] *quality* — : marque de qualité.
[J] l'apposition du sceau (sur cire) sur un document *(a sealed instrument)* avait la plus grande importance en C.L. On se contenta ensuite de le remplacer par les lettres L.S. (loco sigilli) et la formule : « *I have set my hand and* — ». Enfin, de nos jours, la signature est considérée, en Grande-Bretagne, comme un acte indiquant l'intention de sceller et suffisant de ce fait pour authentifier un document.
keeper of the Great — : Garde des Sceaux, Lord Chancelier.
official — : a) scellé ; b) cachet officiel.
to affix, to remove the — *(s)*: apposer, lever les scellés.
to break the — *(s)*: rompre les cachets.
to set one's — : apposer son cachet.
under private — : sous seing privé.
[D] *Custom-house* — : plomb de la Douane.
sealing: mise sous scellés.
sealing of the boundary line: fermeture hermétique de la frontière.
sealed: scellé (a).
sealed agreement: convention sous seing privé et scellée.
sealed letter: lettre close.
sealed tender: soumission cachetée.
sealed will: testament mystique.

seamen's wages: salaires, gages des gens de mer.

search: recherche (f), inspection (f).
— *consultant*: « chasseur de têtes » (see "headhunter").
[J] droit de visite, perquisition, fouille.
house- — : visite domiciliaire, perquisition à domicile.
illegal — *and seizure*: perquisition et saisie illégale.
right of — : droit de visite.
— *and seizure*: perquisition et saisie.
— *of encumbrances, title search*: relevé d'hypothèques.
— *warrant*: mandat de perquisition.
to search: chercher, examiner, enquêter.
[J] perquisitionner, fouiller.
to search the record: vérifier le dossier d'une affaire (outre l'examen d'office de chaque conclusion au fur et à mesure qu'elles sont déposées ; voir *pleading*). Le tribunal peut être obligé de revenir sur les conclusions antérieures déjà formellement admises, à la suite d'une exception à cet effet *(demurrer* ou *motion)*. Il se peut donc qu'en concluant au rejet *(motion to dismiss)* de la réplique *(answer)* de la défense, le demandeur court le risque, si ses arguments ne s'inspirent pas rigoureusement de sa demande première, de voir celle-ci rejetée elle-même, comme mal fondée.
to search goods: inquisitionner des marchandises.
searching: examen minutieux.
searching enquiry: enquête approfondie.
searching questions: questions allant au fond des choses.

season: saison (f).
close — : morte-saison, période creuse.
end of — *sale*: vente de fin de saison.
— *ticket*: carte d'abonnement, abonnement.
seasonal: saisonnier.
seasonal adjustment: rectification (f) saisonnière.
seasonal articles: articles de saison.
seasonal discount: escompte, rabais de basse saison.
seasonal drop: baisse saisonnière.
seasonal revival: reprise saisonnière.
seasonal swings: variations saisonnières.
seasonal unemployment: chômage saisonnier.
seasonally *adjusted*: rectifié pour éliminer les variations saisonnières.
seasoned bond: obligation émise depuis plus de trois mois.

seat: a) siège (m) (au Parlement, dans un conseil, en Bourse, d'un tribunal); b) mandat (m) (d'un député); c) siège social (d'une société); d) foyer (m) (d'une conspiration); e) place (f) (en voiture, au spectacle).
country — : maison de campagne.
county — : chef-lieu.
to resign one's — : donner sa démission.
seating *arrangement*: attribution des sièges.

seaworthiness: bon état de navigabilité d'un navire.

seck: sec.
[J] terme qualifiant un droit foncier autre que la tenure qui ne peut être sanctionné comme celle-ci par une saisie, p. ex. une servitude de rente grevant un bien-fonds *(rent-charge)*, laquelle, le cas échéant doit faire l'objet d'un procès en bonne et due forme.

second: second, deuxième (a).
— *best*: numéro deux (en théorie économique : « optimum second »).
[J] — *deliverance*: nouvelle ordonnance de main-levée, à la suite d'un désistement d'instance.
— *offender*: récidiviste.
— *timer*: récidiviste qui fait de la prison pour la deuxième fois.
[F] — *debentures*: obligations de deuxième rang.
— *endorser*: tiers porteur d'une traite.
— *mortgage*: deuxième hypothèque.
— *of exchange*: deuxième de change.
— *rate stock*: titre de second ordre.
— *trial balance*: balance d'inventaire.
[C] — *-hand*: d'occasion.
— *-hand dealer*: fripier, revendeur, brocanteur.
— *-hand goods*: objet de vente, friperie.
— *-hand market*: marché de revente.
— *-hand shop*: boutique d'occasions, de brocanteur.
— *rate goods*: marchandises de qualité inférieure, camelotte.
« — *(s)* » : articles de deuxième qualité.
to second: appuyer, soutenir, approuver, seconder.
to second a motion: appuyer une motion.

secondary: secondaire, accessoire (a).
— *evidence*: présomption (voir *best evidence rule, evidence*).
— *claim*: a) créance accessoire ; b) taxe accessoire.
— *income*: revenus accessoires.
— *legislation*: dispositions réglementaires prises en application d'une loi.
— *motive*: mobile secondaire.
— *matter*: affaire d'intérêt secondaire.
— *picket*: piquet de grève constitué par des travailleurs non directement concernés par le conflit.
— *production*: industrie, secteur secondaire.
— *residence*: résidence secondaire.

secrecy: secret (m).
[J] *breach of* — : indiscrétion, violation d'un secret.
official, professional — : secret professionnel.
under pledge of —, *under the seal of* — : sous le sceau du secret.

secret: secret, caché (a).
— *ballot*: vote à bulletins secrets.
— *partner*: bailleur de fonds.
— *payment*: rémunération occulte.
— *reserve*: fonds occultes.
— *traffic*: commerce clandestin.

secretary: secrétaire (m et f).
[J] [A] [U.K.] — *of State*: ministre-secrétaire d'Etat, [U.S.] ministre des Affaires étrangères. Les autres ministres américains portent le titre de — : — *of the Interior, of the Army*, etc., à l'exception du ministre de la Justice *(Attorney General)* et du ministre des P. et T. *(Postmaster General)*.
deputy — : secrétaire adjoint.
executive — : secrétaire de direction.
legation — : chancelier de légation.
— *private*: secrétaire particulier.
— *treasurer*: secrétaire trésorier, secrétaire financier.
union — : secrétaire syndical.

secretion: [J] recel, dissimulation.

section: section (d'un ouvrage).
[J] article (d'une loi).
in pursuance of — *(s)*: en vertu des articles.
— *of an Act*: article d'une loi.
[B] compartiment, groupe.

mining — : groupe de valeurs minières.

sectional : fractionnaire, de classe (a).
— *law* : loi d'exception.
— *ledger* : grand livre fractionnaire.
— *policy* : politique, esprit de classe ou de parti.
— *strife* : luttes régionalistes, querelles de clocher.

sector : secteur (m).

secure : sûr, de tout repos (a).
— *investments* : placements sûrs, de père de famille.
to secure : a) réussir à avoir, obtenir ; b) garantir, nantir.
to secure a debt by mortgage : garantir une créance par hypothèque.
to secure by warrant : warranter des marchandises.
to be secure on : être nanti sur, gagé sur, assis sur.
secured : assuré, garanti, gagé, nanti.
secured bonds : obligations garanties.
secured call loan : emprunt garanti par des valeurs sûres.
secured creditor : créancier nanti.
secured debt : créance garantie.
secured loan : emprunt (ou prêt) garanti.

securitisation : transformation (f) de créances en valeurs, « valeurisation » (f) *(the new business of turning debts into securities, a technique known as securitisation* (Financial Times) : la nouvelle pratique qui consiste à transformer des créances en valeurs, technique connue sous le nom de « valeurisation »), mobiliérisation (f) (traduction du Ministère français des Finances), titrisation (f).

security : securité (f), sûreté (f) ; garant (m).
job — : [U.S.] sécurité d'emploi.
— *of employment, of tenure* : stabilité d'emploi.
social — : sécurité sociale.
[J] a) répondant (m) ; b) caution (f), cautionnement (m), gage (m), garantie (f).
additional — : nantissement (m), contre-caution (f).
collateral — : nantissement.
— *for costs* : provision ad litem, cautio judicatum solvi, *(before appeal)* (frais) préjudiciaux.
— *for a debt* : garantie d'une créance.
landed — : gage hypothécaire.
personal — : garantie mobilière.
sufficient — : caution bonne et valable, caution bourgeoise.
— *of tenure* : garantie de l'emploi ou de la propriété.
to give a — : verser une caution.

to give sth. as a — : donner qch. en gage.
loan without — : prêt à fonds perdu.
loan on — *of goods* : prêt sur nantissement de marchandises.
to lend money on — : prêter de l'argent sur de bonnes sûretés.
to lend money without — : prêter de l'argent à découvert.
to lodge a — : effectuer un cautionnement.
to lodge stock as additional — : déposer des titres en nantissement.
to obtain — *before lending money* : prendre des sûretés avant de prêter de l'argent.
to stand — *for s.o.* : se porter caution, garant, se porter fort, pour qn.
to stand — *for a signature, a debt* : avaliser une signature, assurer une créance.
to pay in a sum as a — : verser une provision.
[F] **securities** : titres (m pl), valeurs (f pl), fonds (m pl).
— *analysis* : analyse des valeurs mobilières.
determinable interest — : valeurs à revenu variable.
forward — : titres à terme.
gilt-edged — : valeurs de tout repos.
government — : fonds, titres d'Etat, bons du trésor.
highgrade — : valeurs de premier plan.
listed — : valeurs cotées.
outstanding — : titres non amortis, en circulation.
paper — : titres fiduciaires.
public — : effets, fonds publics.
redemption of — : amortissement de titres.
registered — : titres nominatifs.
— *account* : compte de valeurs.
— *clerk* : caissier des titres.
— *dealings* : commerce de valeurs mobilières.
— *department* : service des titres (d'une banque).
— *Exchange Commission (S.E.C.)* : [U.S.] Commission de contrôle des opérations boursières.
— *held in safe custody in the bank* : titres en dépôt à la banque.
— *investment account* : compte de portefeuille.
— *ledger* : registre des valeurs.
— *long* : valeurs en compte.
marketable — : titres négociables.
— *market* : marché des valeurs, bourse.
— *portfolio* : valeurs en portefeuille.
— *registered for tax* : titres abonnés (voir *tax subscription*).
— *short* : valeurs à découvert.
— *survey* : bulletin d'information sur les valeurs.
— *to bearer* : titres au porteur.
— *trust* : trust de placement, société de

gérance.
transferable — : valeurs mobilières.

sedition : sédition (f).
— *offences* : séditions, actes séditieux.
seditious words : propos séditieux.

seduction : séduction (f), corruption (f).

seed money : [F] investissement initial.

to seesaw : [B] osciller.

segment : a) segment (m) ; b) branche (f) (d'une activité industrielle).
information by — : information sectorielle.

unperfect segmentation : cloisonnements (m) imparfaits.

segregation : ségrégation (f), séparation (f), isolement (m).

seisin : [J] envoi en possession, saisine.

to seize : saisir, confisquer, faire arrêt sur.
[J] — *s.o. with* : mettre qn en possession de.
[B] — *up* : se bloquer.

seizure : saisie (f).
[J] a) prise de corps ; b) *(attachment or execution)* saisie-arrêt ou saisie-exécution.
lifting of the — : levée de la saisie.
— *and forfeiture* : saisie et confiscation.
— *for security* : saisie conservatoire.
— *of exhibits* : séquestre (m) de pièces à conviction.
— *of chattels* : saisie des biens et effets.
— *of corps* : saisie brandon.
— *of movable property* : saisie mobilière.
— *of property* : mainmise sur les biens, confiscation.
— *of real estate* : saisie immobilière.
— *report* : procès-verbal de saisie.
— *under a prior claim* : saisie, revendication.
[D] — *of smuggled goods* : saisie de marchandises de contrebande.

select : choisi, spécial, élu (a).
[C] premier choix, qualité supérieure.
— *cases* : risques de choix.
— *committee* : commission d'enquête parlementaire.
to select a specimen at random : prélever un spécimen au hasard.

selection board : comité (m) de sélection.

selective : sélectif (a).
— *use of available resources* : utilisation judicieuse des ressources disponibles.
[F] — *employment tax* : [U.K.] impôt sélectif sur l'emploi (cf. *tax*).
[B] — *stocks* : valeurs de choix.
selectivity : sélectivité.
market selectivity : sélectivité boursière.

self : moi-même.
pay — : payez à moi-même.
— *-addressed enveloppe* : enveloppe-réponse.
— *-completion questionnaire* : questionnaire rempli par la personne interrogée (et non par l'enquêteur).
— *-consumption* : autoconsommation.
— *-defence* : légitime défense (voir *to retreat*).
— *-determination* : autodétermination.
— *-determination of peoples* : droit des peuples à disposer d'eux-mêmes.
— *-employed person* : travailleur indépendant.
— *-executing* : acte législatif ayant force exécutoire immédiatement.
— *-financing* : autofinancement.
— *-government* : autonomie locale, administration décentralisée.
— *-helpfulness (spirit of)* : (esprit de) coopération, (de) collaboration.
— *-incrimination* : incrimination de soi-même.
— *-liquidating projects* : entreprises rentables.
— *-regulating stabilizers* : stabilisateurs automatiques.
— *-service* : libre-service.
— *-service statement (or declaration)* : déclaration dans l'intérêt de celui qui la formule.
— *-sufficiency* : autarcie.
— *-supporting* : qui se suffit à soi-même, (entreprise) qui paie ses frais.

to sell : vendre, écouler.
— *at a high price* : vendre cher.
— *at a loss* : vendre à perte.
— *by auction* : vendre aux enchères.
— *on trust* : vendre à crédit.
— *privately* : vendre à l'amiable.
[B] — *a bear* : vendre à découvert.
— *for delivery* : vendre à couvert.
— *forward* : vendre à terme.
— *short* : vendre à découvert.
a flow of **selling** *orders* : une vague de liquidation.
— *off* : solder, liquider.
— *on* : [U.S.] convaincre.
— *out* : [F] réaliser (un portefeuille) ; [B] revendre.

sell-by date : date limite d'utilisation (d'un produit).

sell-off : dégagement, fortes ventes.

seller : vendeur (m).
[B] *bear* — : vendeur à découvert.
— *on advance* : vendeur à terme.
— *('s) market* : marché favorable aux vendeurs (« marché vendeur »).

– *('s) option* : livraison au gré du vendeur (dans un délai convenu).
– *('s) option to double* : faculté de livrer double, à la baisse.
– *(s) ahead* : [U.S.] nombreux vendeurs en perspective.
– *(s) over* : excès de vendeurs.

selling : vente (f).
– *cost* : frais de mise en vente (publicité etc.).
loss leader – : ventes à perte (pour attirer la clientèle).
– *off* : liquidation.
– *office* : comptoir de vente (d'un cartel).
– *on cost* : frais de vente.
[B] – *out* : revente, vente forcée.
– *group* : syndicat de vente.
– *order* : ordre de vente.
– *out against a buyer* : revente de titres impayés (par l'acheteur).
– *point* : argument de vente.
– *price* : cours de vente, cours vendeur, prix de vente.

semi-manufactured : demi-ouvré (a).
– *goods* : produits semi-ouvrés.

senate : Sénat.
[U.S.] Chambre haute représentant le principe fédéraliste, composée de deux représentants par Etat, élue pour six ans et renouvelable par tiers. La plupart des corps législatifs des Etats comportent également un Sénat élu au suffrage universel.
senator : sénateur, (Scot.) *Senator of the College of Justice* = juge.

to send : envoyer, expédier, adresser.
– *back* : renvoyer.
– *for* : faire quérir, faire venir (des témoins, des documents).
– *in* : remettre.
– *in one's resignation* : remettre sa démission.
– *on* : transmettre, faire suivre.
– *out a prospectus* : lancer un prospectus.

senior : aîné, doyen ; principal.
[J] – *judge* : le doyen des juges.
– *clerk* : chef de bureau, commis principal, *(in a lawyer's office)* premier clerc.
– *staff* : cadres supérieurs.
[C] – *debt* : créance prioritaire.
– *financing* : financement par émission d'actions privilégiées.
– *partner* : associé principal.
– *shares* : actions privilégiées.

seniority : priorité d'âge.
[A] – *list* : liste à l'ancienneté.
right of – : droit à l'ancienneté.
to be promoted by – : avancer à l'ancienneté.

sense : a) sens (m) ; b) sentiment (m), opinion (f), avis.
– *of justice* : sens de la justice.
to take – *of the House* : consulter, prendre l'avis de la Chambre.

sensitive : sensible (a).
[B] – *market* : marché prompt à réagir, instable.

sensitivity analysis : analyse (f) de sensibilité (f) (de la rentabilité d'un investissement aux changements de ses variables).

sentence : sentence (f), condamnation (f).
[J] jugement.
commutation of – : commutation de peine.
court – : condamnation judiciaire.
cumulative – : a) *concurrence of penalties* : cumul des peines ; b) –*(s) to run consecutively* : cumul juridique.
death – : arrêt de mort.
indefinite, indeterminate – : jugement fixant le minimum et le maximum de la peine, dont la durée précise est déterminée par l'autorité chargée de l'exécution (en général la direction de la prison), compte tenu de la conduite du condamné, de ses antécédents, etc.
mitigation of – : atténuation de peine.
remission of – : remise de peine.
– *in absence* : condamnation par défaut, par contumace.
– *of hard labour* : peine de travaux forcés.
– *with probation (suspended* –*)* : condamnation avec sursis.
stay of –, *suspended* – : jugement conditionnel : a) sursis à statuer sur l'application de la peine ; b) sursis à exécution.
suspension of – : sursis à statuer sur l'application de la peine.
to pass a – : prononcer une condamnation.
to quash a – : casser un jugement.
to serve one's – : purger sa peine (voir *adjudication, decree, judgment, order, rule*.
to sentence s.o. to 3 years imprisonment : condamner qn à 3 ans d'emprisonnement.

separation : séparation (f).
[J] séparation des époux. La séparation des époux suspend le droit et le devoir de cohabitation, elle laisse subsister l'obligation de la fidélité et l'impossibilité de contracter un nouveau mariage. La séparation peut être judiciaire *(judicial* –*)* ou volontaire *(voluntary* –*)* qui s'opère par un acte de séparation *(– deed)*. Ce dernier légalise l'existence séparée des époux et peut contenir des dispositions relatives aux aliments de la femme (support ou maintenance, opp. *alimony*, dans le cas d'une séparation judiciaire) et à la garde et l'entretien des enfants *(custody)*.

— *of powers*: doctrine de la séparation des pouvoirs.
— *as to bed and board*: séparation de corps.
— *as to property*: séparation de biens.
— *order*: ordonnance de séparation.
— *action*: action (en justice) distincte.
separate *estate*: a) propres de la femme, biens paraphernaux ; b) patrimoine privé, en tant que distinct des capitaux engagés dans une association *(partnership)*.
separate property: séparation de biens.
separate trial: procès distinct.
separate taxation: imposition distincte.

sequence: succession (f), suite (f).
cyclic — : succession cyclique.

sequential: continu (a).
— *sampling*: échantillonnage multiple, successif.

sequestration: séquestration (f).
[J] mise sous séquestre.
sequestrator: administrateur-séquestre (voir *writ of assistance, of sequestration*).

sergeant-at-law: docteur en droit civil.
common — : magistrat de la municipalité de Londres.

serial: en série ; feuilleton (télévisé, etc.).
[F] — *bonds*: obligations échéant en série, tirées au sort.
— *maturities*: échéances en série.

seriatim: séparément, individuellement.

series: série (f), gamme (f).
[F] *securities redeemable in* — : valeurs remboursables en série.

servant: a) employé ; b) domestique, serviteur.
administrative civil — : haut fonctionnaire.
civil — : fonctionnaire.

to serve: servir.
— *a point*: (J) présenter un argument (ex. par l'avocat de la défense).
— *one's sentence*: purger sa peine (f).
— *a summons on s.o.*: signifier une assignation à qn.

service: service (m).
[J] a) relations entre employeur et salarié ; b) signification d'un acte, assignation.
— *department*: service de l'après-vente.
direct — : signification à personne (en principe, seule admise pour la citation à comparaître).
oath — : serment professionnel.
— *by publication*: signification par avis public.

— *pension*: pension de guerre.
substituted — : signification indirecte (à un représentant, à domicile, par lettre recommandée à l'étranger, etc.).
address for — : domicile élu.
request for — : demande en vue de la signification des actes.
[C] — *industries*: secteur tertiaire.
to serve *the defendant*: assigner (qn).
to serve on a jury: faire partie d'un jury.
to serve a notice: signifier un arrêt.
to serve a prison term: purger sa peine.
the senior service: [U.K.] la marine.
servicing: assurer le service.
servicing of government debt: service (de l'intérêt) de la dette publique.

servient *(tenement)*: (fonds) servant.

servitude: servitude (f).
[J] (civ.) les servitudes du droit A.A. sont essentiellement celles du droit romain, donc analogues aux servitudes du droit français. Il vient s'y ajouter la rente foncière (voir *easement, rent-charge*).
penal — : (cr.) travaux forcés (transformés désormais en réclusion).
penal — *for life*: travaux forcés à perpétuité.
a term of penal — : travaux forcés à temps.

sess: a) taxe (f), impôt (m), cotisation (f) ; b) assiette (f) des taxes.

session: session (f), séance (f).
[J] a) audience du tribunal ; b) période s'écoulant entre l'ouverture et la clôture du Parlement. [B] séance.
closed — : audience à huis clos.
closing — : séance de clôture.
joint — : séance commune (notamment des deux chambres du Congrès américain).
opening — : session d'ouverture.
Petty —*(s)*: session du tribunal d'Instance.
—*(s) of the peace*: réunions des juges de paix *(justices of the peace)* pour l'exercice de leurs fonctions dénommées *general, petty, quarter ou special* —*(s)* (voir *quarter* —*(s), special* —*(s)*).
plenary — : séance plénière.
(Scot.) Court of — : la cour suprême civile.

set: ensemble (m), groupe.
bill drawn in a — *of three*: lettre de change tirée à trois exemplaires.
setback: recul, [F] [B] tassement, repli.
bull market interrupted by a few setbacks: mouvement de hausse entrecoupé de quelques tassements.
set *of exchange*: [C] jeu d'effets (première, deuxième de change, etc.).
set off: a) [J] demande reconventionnelle (en matière de dette), reconvention (ou *counter-*

claim, voir également *recoupement*) ; b) [C] écriture inverse.
as a set off against : en contrepartie de.
set up : structure (d'une organisation).
— -up cost : frais de mise en route.

to set : mettre, placer, poser.
— *against :* déduire.
— *apart :* mettre de côté, affecter.
— *apart funds for :* affecter des fonds à.
— *aside :* a) [J] casser, infirmer (sp. un verdict par le juge, lorsqu'il est manifeste que le jury a commis une grave erreur sur un point de droit ou de fait. Un nouveau procès s'ensuit *(new trial).*
— *aside an agreement :* annuler, résilier un contrat.
— *aside a request :* rejeter une demande.
— *aside :* b) [F] affecter, consacrer, prélever (une somme pour une fin déterminée).
— *aside a certain amount of money for capital expenditures :* affecter une certaine somme à des investissements.
— *objectives :* fixer des objectifs.
— *one's hand and sign :* apposer sa signature.
[A] *to set a tax rate :* déterminer un taux de taxe.
— *down :* consigner, fixer, [J] mettre (une affaire) au rôle.
— *forth, out :* énoncer, citer, *(facts)* articuler, entrer dans le détail, *(an argument)* développer, *(one's reasons)* exposer, faire valoir, *(a theory)* avancer, *(a reason)* invoquer, *(one's grievances)* formuler *(ses griefs).*
— *free :* [F] mobiliser, libérer.
capital set free : capital mobilisé.
— *in :* débuter, commencer, s'amorcer, apparaître.
— *off (a debt) :* compenser (une dette).
— *out :* exposer, montrer, présenter.
— *out the views of :* exposer les vues de.
— *together :* comparer.
— *up :* a) [J] exciper de (p. ex. *to set up the statutes of limitation).*
b) [J] intenter (p. ex — *up a counterclaim).*
c) établir, nommer, constituer, instituer, créer (p. ex. — *up a special committee).*
— *up a child to displace the real heir :* supposer un enfant.
— *up on his own account :* se mettre à son compte.
setting : mise, pose, disposition.
setting free : [F] mobilisation (de capitaux).
setting up : mise en place, implantation.
setting of standards : élaboration de normes.

to settle : régler.
— *for sth :* s'accorder sur qch.
[J] a) établir le libellé d'un document ; b) transiger, adopter une solution transactionnelle ; c) procéder à un *settlement.*
— *a lawsuit amicably :* arranger un procès.

(by arbitrator) — *a case :* arbitrer une affaire.
— *an affair out of court :* transiger avant jugement.
« **settled** *account* » : compte arrêté, excellent moyen de défense dans une action en reddition de compte, si accepté sans plus, à moins de faux (voir *account).*
— *law :* principes bien établis de la "Common Law".
— *policy :* politique continue.

settlement : *(of a dispute)* arrangement, solution, règlement, *(of a question)* résolution, décision, *(of a date, etc.)* détermination, fixation, *(of a treaty)* conclusion, *(between two powers)* accord.
[J] 1°) disposition de la propriété, d'un bien-fonds passant successivement à plusieurs personnes *(settled estate).*
compound — : ensemble d'actes entre vifs, de testaments, etc., dressés au cours d'une période au sujet des arrangements suivants :
marriage, antenuptial — = contrat de mariage (règle la jouissance et la dévolution des biens) ; *strict* — = institution de majorat, arrangement destiné à maintenir le bien-fonds dans la famille, au profit du fils aîné, en assurant divers avantages, en contrepartie à la femme (voir *jointure, pin-money)* et aux autres enfants (voir *portion).*
voluntary — : disposition à titre gracieux.
2°) le règlement des legs et dettes d'une succession préalable à la distribution finale.
3°) le domicile légal.
— *of a pauper :* domicile de secours, donnant droit à l'assistance publique.
— *of an annuity :* constitution de rente.
— *deed :* acte de disposition.
family — : pacte de famille.
— *before judgment,* — *arrived at by the parties inter se :* transaction (avant jugement).
marriage — *in trust :* régime dotal.
— *of portion by anticipation :* avancement d'hoirie.
to reach a — : arriver à un accord.
compromise and —, *legal* — : concordat.
in full — : pour règlement de tout compte, pour solde.
penal — : colonie pénitentiaire.
[F] — *estate duty :* impôt frappant une disposition.
[C] règlement (m), paiement (m), apurement (m), balancement (m) des comptes.
— *of account :* arrêté de compte, [B] liquidation.
— *discount :* see cash discount.
early — : règlement anticipé.
the — : le terme.
dealing for the — : opérations à terme.
— *day :* jour du règlement, de liquidation.
— *market :* marché à terme.
— *options :* modalités de règlement.

— *price*: cours à terme.
— *room clerk*: liquidateur.
time — : marché à terme.
yearly — : liquidation de fin d'année.

to sever *(diplomatic ties)*: (pol.) rompre (les relations diplomatiques).

settlor: fondateur (m), constituant (m).

several: séparé, différent ; respectif (a).
[J] *(property)* individuel, indivis, *(responsibility)* individuelle.
joind and — *bond*: obligation conjointe et solidaire.
— *covenant*: solidarité passive (opp. *joint covenant*: solidarité active).
joint and — *liability*: responsabilité conjointe et solidaire.
«*jointly and* **severally**» : conjointement et solidairement.

severalty: [J] co-propriété, non solidaire (opp. *joint ownership, coparcenary*).
land held in — : bien tenu individuellement, sans solidarité.
[J] disjonction (f) (de causes).

severance: a) séparation (f) ; b) [J] rupture (f) (de contrat).
motion for — : [U.S.] requête pour être jugé séparément (dans le cas où il y a plusieurs accusés).
— *of diplomatic relations*: rutpure des relations diplomatiques.
— *pay*: indemnité de rupture de contrat, de licenciement.

to shade: diminuer progressivement.
— *prices*: réduire légèrement le prix (particulièrement pour obtenir un effet psychologique, par ex. 1,99 $ au lieu de 2,00 $) ;
prices **shaded** *for bulk buying*: tarif dégressif pour achats en gros.
— *from... to...*: [B] passer de... à...

to shadow: filer, suivre (un suspect).

shadow cabinet: (Pol. UK) : # contre-gouvernement.

shadow *price*: prix virtuel.

shady: douteux, louche, suspect, véreux (a).
— *business*: affaire louche, commerce interlope.
there is something — *about this*: il y a du louche là-dessous.

to shake: nier de la tête.
shake-down : demande d'argent, extorsion.
shake-out: débandade de boursicoteurs, chute, chambardement ; (fam.) compression de personnel.
shake-up: remaniement, restructuration (d'un marché).

sham: faux, fictif, simulé, feint, d'emprunt (a).
[J] — *contract*: acte simulé.
— *plea*: moyens dilatoires.
— *sale*: vente fictive.
— *title*: titre d'emprunt.
[F] — *bid*: offre fictive, enchère fictive.
— *dividend*: dividende fictif.

to shape: former, façonner.
— *a policy*: déterminer le cours de la politique.

share: part (f), portion (f).
[J] *legal* — : part légitimaire.
proportionate — : contingent.
[F] action (f), part sociale.
«*A*» — *(s)*: actions prioritaires.
bearer, transferable — : action au porteur.
block of — *(s)*: paquet d'actions.
bonus, free, scrip, plough — : action gratuite.
company's — : part sociale, action de société.
dividend, junior —, *stock dividend*: action gratuite, de jouissance.
founder's — : part de fondateur.
joint — : action indivise.
listed — : action cotée.
unlisted — : action non cotée.
new — : action nouvelle.
ordinary — : action ordinaire.
paid up — : action libérée.
partly paid up — : action non entièrement libérée.
personal or registered — *(s)*: actions nominatives.
preference, senior — : action privilégiée.
promoter's — : part de fondateur.
qualification — : action de garantie, action statutaire.
registered — : action nominative.
— *broker*: courtier d'actions.
— *capital*: capital-actions.
— *certificate*: titre d'actions, certificat d'actions.
— *deposited as security*: action déposée en garantie.
— *dividend or interest*: dividende d'actions.
— *index*: indice des cours des actions.
— *in profits*: participation aux bénéfices.
— *interest*: participation dans le capital.
— *issued for cash*: action émise contre argent comptant.
— *list*: cours de la bourse.
— *premium*: prime d'émission.
— *pusher*: courtier marron.
— *qualification*: cautionnement en actions.
— *(s) on the market*: actions fluctuantes.

— -*split*: fractionnement d'actions.
— *(s) quoted ex dividend*: actions cotées sans droit au dividende.
— -*warrant*: titre au porteur.
— *with multiple votes (or with voting rights)*: action à vote plural.
shop — : action à l'introduction.
transferable — : action au porteur.
to issue — *(s) at par*: émettre des actions au pair.
to issue — *(s) at discount*: émettre des actions en dessous du pair.
to issue — *(s) at premium*: émettre des actions au-dessus du pair.
to sell out — *(s)*: réaliser.
shareholder: actionnaire.
shareholder's dividend: dividende d'actions.
shareholder's equity: a) avoir des actionnaires ; b) valeur nette (d'une société) ; c) valeur comptable (d'une société).

sharecrop system: [J] [U.S.] métayage (m).
sharecropper: métayer.

sharer (in an estate): portionnaire (m).

sharing: partage (m), participation (f).
profit — *scheme*: système d'intéressement aux bénéfices.
international production process — : segmentation internationale des processus de production.
time — : temps partagé (traduit souvent à tort par multipropriété), utilisation collective (d'un bien).

shark: requin (m), escroc (m). [U.S.] racoleur de main-d'œuvre.

sharp: a) astucieux, retors ; b) vif, net, prononcé (a).
— *changes*: brusques changements.
— *practices*: procédés peu scrupuleux.
— *protest*: protestation énergique.
— *rise*: très forte hausse.

shattering: dislocation (f).
the — *of world trade*: la dislocation des échanges internationaux.

to shave *the budget estimates*: rogner les prévisions budgétaires.

to shed: [B] céder (des points).

sheet: feuille (f).
[B] *clearing* — : feuille de liquidation.
pay — : feuille de paye.
[C] *balance* — : bilan.
order — : bulletin de commande.

shell company: société fictive.

to shell out: (fam.) débourser, payer la note.

Shelley's case [J] (« *the rule in* — ») : (célèbre interprétation donnée dans un cas survenu en 1581) une disposition en faveur de « A et ses héritiers » ne signifie pas usufruit pour A., avec substitution pour les héritiers, mais, simplement, propriété pleine et entière pour A.

tax shelters: pertes fiscales déductibles ; [U.S.] déductions fiscales liées à certaines formes d'investissements.

sheltered: protégé, abrité (a).
— *industry*: industrie protégée (contre la concurrence étrangère).

sheriff: (Scot.) [J] premier président d'un tribunal de comté.
— *('s) substitute*: (Scot.) juge de première instance d'un comté.
[A] (Engl.) : principal représentant de la Couronne, dans un comté. Il organise les élections parlementaires, veille à l'exécution des jugements, ordonnances et mandats au criminel et de la *High Court*, procède à la convocation des jurés et conduit les ventes judiciaires.
[U.S.] principal fonctionnaire administratif d'un comté, élu par la population. Ses fonctions sont analogues à celles d'un — anglais ; en outre, dans les districts ruraux, il assume les fonctions de chef de police.
deputy- — *(special constable)*: citoyen assermenté faisant fonction d'agent de la police.

shift: a) changement (m), déplacement (m) ; b) moyen (m), expédient (m), artifice (m) ; c) équipe (f), poste (m) (d'ouvriers).
changing in population — *(s)*: déplacement des courants migratoires.
— *in demand*: changements de la demande (des goûts de la clientèle).
night — : équipe de nuit.
overtime — *(s)*: postes supplémentaires.
— *system*: système dit « des trois huit » (trois équipes, travail continu, vingt-quatre heures sur vingt-quatre).
[B] — *of prices*: variation des cours.
to resort to dubious — *(s)*: avoir recours à des expédients douteux.
to work in — *(s)*: se relayer.
to shift: déplacer, transférer, désarrimer.
the retailer is attempting to shift the tax burden on to the consumer: le détaillant cherche à faire retomber l'impôt sur le consommateur.
shifting: déplacement (m), transfert (m), désarrimage (m), translation (f).
shifting of income: transfert de revenus.

shifting of the Corporation income tax : translation, répercussion de l'impôt sur le bénéfice des sociétés.
shifting the burden of proof : fait de déplacer la charge de la preuve.

ship : navire (m), vaisseau (m), bâtiment (m).
[ASS] *sister- — clause :* clause prévoyant la collision avec un navire appartenant au même propriétaire.
— *articles :* conditions d'engagement de l'équipage d'un navire.
merchant, trading — : navire marchand, cargo.
— *news :* mouvement des navires.
training — : vaisseau-école.
warship : bateau (m), bâtiment (m) de guerre.
— *-broker :* courtier maritime.
— *-building :* construction maritime.
— *-chandler :* fournisseur de navires.
— *-load :* cargaison, fret, chargement.
— *-owner :* propriétaire de navires, armateur, [J] l'armateur ou son représentant (y compris le capitaine).
— *('s) husband :* capitaine d'armement (agent d'affaires du navire au port d'attache).
— *('s) papers :* papiers de bord, lettre de mer.
— *('s) register, books :* journal, livres de bord.
to ship : charger, expédier, embarquer.
shipment : expédition, embarquement, mise à bord de marchandises ; cargaison, chargement ; [U.K.] transport de marchandises par voie maritime ; [U.S.] transport de marchandises.
shipment to collect : expédition, transport en plus.
shipowner : armateur (m).
shipowner's firm : maison d'armement.
shipper : chargeur (m), expéditeur (m).
shipping : chargement (m), expédition (f), embarquement (m), tonnage (m).
shipping agency : agence d'affrètement.
shipping clerk : employé chargé des expéditions.
Shipping Exchange : Bourse des frets.
shipping instructions : instructions concernant le mode d'envoi des marchandises.
Shipping Office : inscription maritime, bureau maritime.
shipping shares : valeurs maritimes.
shipping terms : conditions de transport (par mer).
shipwreck : naufrage (m).
shipyard : chantier de constructions navales.

shire : comté (en Grande-Bretagne) # département.
the —(s) : les comtés centraux d'Angleterre.
— *-reeve* ou *shire clerk* # *sheriff.*

shock insurance : [ASS] assurance contre les méfaits du hasard.

shoddy : camelote (f).

on a shoestring : à peu de frais.
to set up in a business — : se lancer dans les affaires avec de maigres capitaux.

shooting licence : permis de chasse.

to shoot up : [B] monter en flèche.

shop : magasin, *(small)* boutique, *(for wine, tobacco)* débit, atelier.
[J] — *book rule :* recevabilité en preuve des livres de commerce.
— *-lifting :* vol à l'étalage.
[C] — *books :* livres de commerce.
closed —, [U.S.] *Union — :* entreprise n'employant que du personnel syndiqué.
open — : entreprise employant des ouvriers syndiqués ou non.
— *bucket :* officine de contrepartie.
— *buying :* achats professionnels.
— *floor :* (les ouvriers et employés de) « la base ».
— *selling :* ventes professionnelles.
— *shares :* actions à l'introduction.
— *-assistant :* employé de magasin.
— *-lifter :* voleur à l'étalage.
— *-walker :* surveillant (dans un grand magasin).
shopping *center :* centre commercial.
shopper : acheteur (m).

short : a) court, abrégé, insuffisant, incomplet ; b) [F] à court terme ; c) [B] bourse à découvert.
[J] — *cause :* affaire plaidée sommairement.
to stop — of crime : s'arrêter au bord du crime.
[F] *money's to in — supply :* l'argent est rare.
[B] *selling — :* vente à découvert.
— *account :* compte à découvert.
— *bill :* effet à courte échéance.
— *covering :* rachat (pour couvrir un découvert), couverture de position.
— *credit :* crédit à court terme.
— *-dated :* à court terme.
— *-handed :* à court de main-d'œuvre.
— *paper :* traite à courte échéance.
— *pay off period :* see « pay back period ».
— *position :* situation à découvert.
— *-run effects :* répercussions de courte durée.
— *sale :* vente à découvert, à terme.
— *-seller :* vendeur à découvert.
— *-term investment :* placement à court terme.
— *-term planning :* planification à court terme.
the demand for labour is — of the supply : sur le marché de l'emploi, la demande est inférieure à l'offre.
— *(s) :* fonds d'Etat à court terme.
to be — of : être à court de, manquer de.
to be short *of change :* ne pas rendre assez de monnaie.

shortage: a) manque (m), insuffisance (f); b) pénurie (f); c) déficit (m).
housing – : crise du logement.
labour – : pénurie de main-d'œuvre.
[C] – *in the cash*: déficit de caisse.
– *of payment*: retard de paiement.

shortcoming: faute (f), faiblesse (f), point (m) faible.

shortfall: [F] déficit.

shortlist: liste des admissibles, des candidats retenus pour l'entretien définitif.
to – : présélectionner.

shot: action (f) publicitaire.

to show: montrer, accuser, faire apparaître, présenter.
[J] – *cause*: voir *cause*.
[B] *the stock market continues* – *strength*: le marché des valeurs continue à faire preuve de résistance.
[C] *the balance sheet of the company* **shows** *a profit of*: le bilan de la société fait ressortir un bénéfice de.
show card: carte d'échantillons.
– *a balance of*: présenter un solde, se solder par.
– *a debit balance*: présenter un solde débiteur.
– *the reserve among the liabilities*: porter la réserve au passif.
[F] – *an appreciation*: accuser une plus-value.
show: spectacle (m), exposition (f), étalage (m), salon.
motor show: salon de l'automobile.
show case: présentoir, vitrine.
show of hands: vote à mains levées.

to shrink: se resserrer, se rétrécir, s'effriter.
export markets are **shrinking**: les marchés d'exportation se rétrécissent.
the value of the currency **shrinks** *as prices rise*: le pouvoir d'achat de la monnaie s'effrite à mesure que les prix montent.
shrinkage: diminution, contraction.
the shrinkage of personal income: la contraction des revenus des particuliers.
shrinking capital: capital qui diminue.

to shunt: [B] faire l'arbitrage de place à place.
shunting stocks: arbitrage de valeurs.

shut down: [U.S.] immobilisation, fermeture.
line – *time*: durée d'immobilisation d'une chaîne de montage.

to shut out: exclure.

shyster: [U.S.] avocat marron.

si non omnes: si pas tous.

sick: de maladie.
– *allowance, benefit*: prestation maladie.
– *fund*: caisse de maladie.
– *leave*: congé de maladie.
– *pay*: indemnité de maladie.
sickness: maladie.
sickness insurance: assurance contre la maladie.

side: côté (m), paroi (f).
official – : patronat.
staff – : salariat.
[J] *on civil and criminal* – *(s)*: au civil et au criminel.
the other – : la partie adverse.
to hear both – *(s) of the question*: entendre les deux côtés.

to side-track: donner le change.

sideline: activité (f) annexe.

to sight: viser (une lettre de change).
sight: vue (f).
[F] *bill payable at sight*: effet payable à vue.
sight deposits: dépôts à vue.
sight quotation: quotation à vue.
sight withdrawal: retrait à vue.
[D] *sight-entry*: déclaration provisoire.

to sign: signer.
please **sign** *and return the enclosed acknowledgment*: prière de nous retourner l'accusé de réception ci-joint revêtu de votre signature.
sign (Hand and sign): signature.
sign manual: seing, signature, signature manu proprio du souverain (opp. *signet*: seing apporté par le principal secrétaire d'état).
under his sign manual: signe de sa main.
signs of wealth assessment: taxation d'après les éléments du train de vie.
signatory: signataire (m), souscripteur (m).

signature: signature (f). [A] visa (m).
stamped – : griffe (f).
[C] *joint* – : signature collective. La signature sociale s'opère par l'apposition du cachet officiel (*corporate seal*).
to match – *(s)*: comparer des signatures.
signing: signature (d'un document).
signing clerk: fondé de pouvoir.

significance: portée (f), importance (f), conséquence (f), gravité (f).
matter of great – : affaire de la plus haute

importance.
– *threshold* : seuil critique.

significant : significatif (a), important (a), (en statistique) significatif, qui ne peut être expliqué par le hasard.

signification : sens (m) (et rien d'autre).

silent : a) silencieux ; b) [F] occulte, commanditaire.
– *partner* : associé commanditaire.
– *partnership* : participation occulte.

silo : silo (m).

silver : argent (m).
– *standard* : étalon-argent.

similarity : similitude (f).
ratio of – : coefficient de similitude.

similiter : de même.

simple : simple (a).
[J] *verbal* – *contract* : convention verbale, tacite.
– *contract creditor* : créancier chirographaire.
– *tool doctrine* : [U.S.] principe selon lequel la responsabilité d'accidents résultant de l'état d'outils dits « simples », c'est-à-dire pouvant être inspectés à vue, incombe aux ouvriers qui s'en servent.
[C] – *debenture* : obligation chirographaire.
– *interest* : intérêts simples.

simpliciter : [J] (Scot.) universellement, absolument (adv).
to resign – : démissionner sans faire valoir aucun droit (à la retraite, etc.).

sine die : indéfiniment, (ajournement) pour un temps indéfini, sans indication de terme.

sine prole : sans descendance.

sine qua non : condition indispensable.

« to sing » : [U.S.] avouer, dans le langage de la pègre : « se mettre à table » et trahir ses complices : « les donner » (voir *evidence* : « *to turn Queen's, State's evidence* »).

single : a) séparé, seul ; b) célibataire.
ballot for – *member* : scrutin uninominal.
[J] – *court* : tribunal d'exception.
– *woman* : femme seule.
[C] – *entry bookkeeping* : comptabilité en partie simple.
– -*line store* : magasin spécialisé.
– *payment compound account factor* : facteur (m) d'accumulation.

– *payment present worth factor* : facteur d'escompte.
– *sum* : versement unique.
[F] – *premium* : prime unique.
– *tax system* : système de la taxe unique.
to profit by the – *commission* : profiter du franco.

to sink : a) baisser (cours) ; b) diminuer (prix) ; c) amortir (un emprunt) ; d) éteindre (une dette) ; e) engloutir (de l'argent).
[F] – *a debt* : amortir une dette.
– *money in an annuity* : placer de l'argent en viager.

sinking : amortissement (m), extinction (f), engloutissement (m).
[C] – *or falling costs* : prix de revient en baisse.
[F] – *fund* : caisse (f), fonds (m) d'amortissement.
– *fund bonds* : obligations amortissables.
– *fund instalment* : versement au fonds d'amortissement.
[ASS] *permanent* – : submersion (f) d'un navire sans possibilité de renflouement.

sister : sœur (f).
– *german, own, full* – : sœur germaine.
foster – : sœur de lait, sœur adoptive.
half- – (*on the father's side*) : sœur consanguine.
(*on the mother's side*) : sœur utérine.
older – : sœur aînée.
younger – : sœur puînée.
youngest – : sœur cadette.
– -*in-law* : belle-sœur.
[ASS] – -*ship clause* : clause prévoyant la collision avec un navire appartenant au même propriétaire.

to sit : a) siéger ; b) être en séance ; c) occuper un siège (dans une assemblée).
[J] – *in camera* : siéger à huis clos.
– *on a case* (*for a judge*) : juger une affaire (pour un juge).
– *in judgment* : se faire juge des actes d'autrui.
– *for a constituency* : représenter une circonscription électorale.
– *in Parliament* : siéger au Parlement.
– *on committee, the jury* : être du comité, du jury.
sit-down strike : grève avec occupation d'entreprise, grève sur le tas.
sitting : séance (f), tenue (d'une assemblée), audience ou session (d'un tribunal).
judje sitting on the trial : juge siégeant au procès.
the court is sitting : la cour est en jugement.
private sitting (*of judges*) : délibéré (m).
sitting of a court : audience (f).

sitting of a congress: assises (f pl).
the sittings: les quatre sessions de l'année judiciaire.
the Hilary Sittings: du 11 janvier au dernier mercredi avant Pâques; *the Easter Sittings*: du premier mardi après Pâques jusqu'au dernier dimanche avant la Pentecôte ; *the Trinity Sittings*: du premier mardi dans la semaine de la Pentecôte au 31 juillet ; *the Michaelmas Sittings*: commençant le jour fixé par un ordre en conseil et finissant le 21 décembre.

site : a) site (m), emplacement (m) ; b) terrain, lot (à bâtir).
building- — : lot, terrain à bâtir.
— *of work* : chantier.
— *value* : valeur d'aliénation.
original — *value* : valeur d'acquisition.

situation : a) emploi (m), poste (m), place (f) ; b) situation (f), emplacement (m).
« — *(s) vacant* » : « offres d'emploi ».
« — *(s) wanted* » : « demandes d'emploi ».
[A] *actual physical* — : emplacement matériel.
— *report* : rapport de situation (sur la situation de l'entreprise).
(property) situated actually at... : (biens) ayant leur assiette matérielle à...
(property) situated legally at... : (biens) ayant leur assiette juridique à...
(property) situated nominally, nationally at... : (biens) ayant leur assiette fictive à...

situs : situs (m).
legal situs : (O.N.U.) « situs » juridique.
decisive is the — *of the res* : le lieu de la situation de l'objet a une importance décisive (tant pour la compétence des tribunaux que pour l'assiette fiscale).

size : dimension (f), format (m), mesure (f), taille (f).
— *disparity problem* : problème (m) de la différence des montants investis.
— *stamp* : timbre de dimension.
— *-up* : [U.S.] évaluation, estimation.
the — *of the active population* : le chiffre de la population active.

sizeable : tangible, appréciable, sensible, considérable (a).
a — *improvement* : une sensible amélioration.

skeleton-law : loi-cadre.

skilled : habile, expérimenté, spécialisé, qualifié (a).
highly — *workers* : ouvriers hautement qualifiés.
semi- — *workers* : ouvriers semi-qualifiés.
— *workers* : ouvriers qualifiés.

unskilled workers : manœuvres.
— *witness* : témoin-expert ; [J] expert appelé à témoigner en raison de sa compétence et, contrairement aux autres témoins, à donner son opinion.

skills analysis : détermination (f) des compétences (dans le cadre d'une entreprise).
technical — : compétence technique.

skimming price : prix (m) exorbitant (que seuls des clients très riches peuvent payer).

to skip : [U.S.] faire défaut en justice.
[J] *to skip bail* : se dérober alors que l'on jouit de la liberté provisoire.

sky-high : astronomique (prix).

slabbing-mill : laminoir (m).

slack : relâchement (m) (dans la rigueur de la gestion).
lâche, relâché, ralenti (a).
business is —, *slow* : les affaires sont presque nulles, traînent.
organizational — : relâchement organisationnel.
— *demand* : faible demande.
— *money* : argent facile.
the — *season* : la morte saison.
to slacken : ralentir.
slackening : relâchement, ralentissement.
a slackening of the pressure of overall demand : un relâchement de la demande globale.
slackness : marasme, stagnation.

slander : [J] diffamation (f) verbale.
— *action* : procès en diffamation.
— *and libel* : diffamation verbale et écrite.
— *of goods* : dépréciation fausse et malveillante de la qualité des marchandises vendues par les plaignants.
— *of title* : déclaration malveillante, mettant faussement en doute un titre de propriété.

slash : réduction (f) (importante).

slash-price : [C] prix sacrifié.

slaughter : [C] mévente.
— *price* : prix sacrifié.

slave driver : employeur exigeant.

sleeping *(silent, secret, latent)* **partner** : [C] associé commanditaire, bailleur de fonds.
— *partnership* : société en commandite.

slender : modique (revenu) (a).

sliding: a) en légère baisse, en légère régression ; b) mobile.
- *prices*: prix en légère baisse.
- *scale*: échelle mobile.
- *wage scale*: échelle mobile des salaires.

slight: léger, faible, modeste, modéré (a).
- *increase*: légère hausse.

slip: (C) bordereau (m).
pay-in – : bordereau de versement à un compte.

slip (slip-rule): [J] erreurs de plume, omissions accidentelles, etc., pouvant être rectifiées par le tribunal en tout temps.
[ASS] mémorandum (m) contenant les termes convenus d'une police d'assurance maritime, parafé par les assureurs.
to slip back: [B] reculer, glisser.

slogan: (C) devise (f), phrase (f) publicitaire.

slow-down: ralentissement (m).
slow-down, go-slow, strike: grève perlée.

sluggish: inerte (a).
- *demand*: faible demande.
sluggishness: caractère terne (du marché).

slum: taudis (m).
- *clearance*: élimination des taudis.

slump: a) marasme (m) (économique), dépression (f) (économique) ; b) baisse (f) soudaine, effondrement (m) (des prix).
the – *in the security prices*: l'effondrement du cours des valeurs.
slumpflation: dépression économique avec continuation de l'inflation.

slush: fange (f), bourbe (f).
- *fund*: caisse noire.

small: petit, faible, léger, peu important (a).
[F] – *denominations*: petites coupures.
- *deposits*: menus dépôts.
- *holding*: petit avoir.
- *and medium-sized enterprises (SMEs)*: petites et moyennes entreprises (P.M.E.).
- *pieces*: obligations de petite épargne.
- *scale industry*: petite industrie.
- *supermarket*: superette.

smart-money: [J] dommages-intérêts punitifs.

smash: krach (m), débâcle (f), chute (f) (d'une banque).

smash-and-grab raid: rafle (f) de bijoux, etc. après bris de devanture.

smelting works: fonderie (f), usine métallurgique.

to smooth out: aplanir (des difficultés), atténuer (des fluctuations).

smuggling: contrebande, fraude douanière.
[D] fraude (f) aux droits de douane.

snap: inopiné, imprévu, brusque (a).
- *judgment*: jugement sans réflexion.
- *strike*: grève au pied levé.

snip: (fam.) affaire avantageuse.

so: ainsi (adv), de cette façon.
if the law – *directs*: si la loi l'ordonne.

to soar: grimper, bondir, monter en flèche (cours, prix).

social: social, mondain (a).
- *account*: comptabilité sociale.
- *accounting*: comptabilité des charges sociales, comptes publics.
- *administration*: les services sociaux.
- *development plan*: plan d'équipement social.
international – *service*: aide aux immigrants.
- *event*: événement mondain (et non social).
- *gathering (or function)*: réunion mondaine.
- *history taking*: relever les antécédents de qn.
- *insurances*: assurances sociales.
- *obligations (or duties)*: obligations mondaines.
- *organization*: groupements sociaux, association de bienfaisance, œuvre.
- *overhead investments*: investissements dans l'infrastructure économique et sociale.
- *policy*: politique sociale.
- *rising*: ascension sociale.
- *security number*: numéro d'immatriculation à la sécurité sociale.
- *security scheme*: régime de sécurité sociale.
- *status*: rang social, hiérarchie.
- *work*: assistance sociale (en tant que profession).
- *worker*: assistant social, assistante sociale.
[A] – *benefits*: prestations sociales.
- *security charge*: contribution au titre de la sécurité sociale.
- *security taxes*: cotisations au titre de la sécurité sociale.

society: société (f), association (f), ordre (m).
building – : société pour le financement de la construction.
charitable – : société de bienfaisance.
co-operative – : société coopérative.
friendly – : société de secours mutuel.
guarantee – : association de cautionnement

mutuel.
law — : association d'avocats, ordre des avocats.
loan — : société de crédit.
mutual benefit — : société de secours mutuel.

soft : mou (a), (B) en baisse.
[F] — *currency* : monnaie faible.
the — *money ousts the hard money* : la mauvaise monnaie chasse la bonne monnaie (loi de Gresham).
[B] — *spot in the market* : compartiment en baisse.
— *goods* : matières textiles ; biens non durables.
— *sale* : vente par des moyens discrets.
software : travail de préparation des données, conception des langages (en informatique).

soil : terre (f).
— *bank* : [U.S.] service gouvernemental pour la régularisation de la production agricole.

solatium : dommages-intérêts pour préjudice moral, accordés, le cas échéant, en sus des dommages-intérêts matériels.

sole : seul, unique.
[J] — *corporation* : voir *corporation*.
feme — : femme non mariée.
— *legatee* : légataire universel.
— *selling rights* : droits de vente exclusifs.
— *right* : droit exclusif.
[C] — *agent* : agent exclusif.
— *of exchange* : seule de change.
— *management (of)* : l'entière direction (de).
— *trader* : chef d'une entreprise individuelle.

solemn : solennel, sacré (a).
[J] — *contract (or agreement)* : contrat solennel.
solemnly *and sincerely, I believe that* : en mon âme et conscience, je suis convaincu que.

soliciting : racolage (m).

solicitor : [J] (sorte de conseiller juridique, qui joue également le rôle d'un avocat devant certains tribunaux).
— *(s) have the monopoly of conveyancing* : les « *solicitors* » ont le monopole de la rédaction des actes de cession.
— *('s) department* : service du contentieux.
— *('s) indemnity* : assurange-garantie des « avocats ».
— *-general* : [U.K.] conseiller juridique de la Couronne.
[U.S.] représentant du Gouvernement auprès de la Cour suprême.

(in) solidum : (être responsable) conjointement et solidairement.

solus position : emplacement (m) publicitaire privilégié.

solvent : [J] solvable (a).
security given by a — *man* : caution bourgeoise.

Somerset house : dépôt à Londres des registres de l'état-civil, de commerce, etc.

sophisticated : a) enveloppé d'arguments spécieux ; b) frelaté, falsifié (a).
[C] — *wines* : vins falsifiés.

to sort : trier.

sorting : triage (m), tri (m).

sound : sain, sûr, solide, systématique, judicieux ; légitime, bien fondé (a).
— *argument* : argument solide.
— *conclusion* : conclusion juste, logique.
— *currency* : monnaie saine.
— *export policy* : politique d'exportation systématique.
— *investment* : placement sûr.
— *management* : gestion rationnelle.
— *purchases* : achats judicieux.
[ASS] — *market value* — valeur marchande à l'état sain.
soundness : solidité (d'une entreprise, d'un argument).

sounding in damages : [J] demande spécifique de dommages-intérêts (opp. action en recouvrement de dette, etc.).

source : source (f), origine (f).
[A] *income tax collected at* — : impôt sur le revenu retenu à la source.
retention at the — : [U.K.] retenue à la source.
— *tax* : impôt à la source.
taxation at — : imposition à la source.
withholding at — : retenue à la source.
from whatever — *derived* : de quelque source que (le revenu) provienne.
[F] — *and disposition of funds* : état de provenance et d'utilisation des fonds.

sourcing : sourçage (f) (mise en relation de l'importateur et du fabricant étranger).
— *expert* : sourceur (m), sourceuse (f).

sovereignty : souveraineté (f).

space : espace (m), étendue (f), emplacement (m), intervalle (m) (de temps).
living — : espace vital.
office — : surface des locaux commerciaux.
— *writer* : journaliste payé à la ligne.
to space out : espacer, décaler, échelonner.

spade work : travaux préliminaires.

span : portée (f).
— *of control* : étendue du contrôle qui doit

s'exercer sur les divers secteurs de l'entreprise.
– *of life* : durée probable de la vie.

spare : de secours, de trop, mis de côté.
– *capital* : fonds disponibles.
– *parts* : pièces de rechange.
to spare : épargner.
tax **sparing** (see « *matching credit* »).

speaker : orateur (m).
[J] terme désignant les présidents de la Chambre des communes britanniques et de la Chambre des représentants du Congrès américain (et des assemblées législatives de divers états).

special : spécial (a).
– *features* : (journ.) rubrique spécialisée.
[J] – *bill* : projet de loi d'intérêt local *(private bill)*.
– *case* : jugement gracieux, sur requête.
– *damage* : dommages d'une nature qui n'est pas présumée par la loi et qui doivent être expressément prouvés (par ex. : frais médicaux à la suite d'un accident).
– *plea* : exception péremptoire.
– *pleader* : avocat consultant.
– *pleading* : défense fondée sur ce que la cause offre de spécial.
– *sessions* : réunion de juges de paix en dehors des *quarter-sessions*, à des fins spéciales.
[A] – *peculiarities* : signes particuliers (mentionnés dans un passeport, etc.).
[B] – *dividend* : dividende extraordinaire.
– *general meeting of shareholders* : assemblée générale extraordinaire des actionnaires.
[C] – *delivery* : envoi par exprès.
– *endorsement* : endossement complet.
– *-order work* : travail à façon.
– *partnership* : société en participation (opp. à société en nom collectif : *general partnership*).
– *price* : prix de faveur.
[F] – *advance tax* : précompte mobilier.
– *amending Act* : loi de finances rectificative.
– *deposits* : réserves obligatoires.
– *drawing rights (S.D.R.)* : droits de tirage spéciaux (D.T.S.).
– *tax* : taxe exceptionnelle, impôt supplémentaire, surtaxe.

specialty : [J] contrat formel, sous seing privé (voir *deed*).

specie : numéraire (m), espèces (f pl).
[F] – *point* : point de l'or, gold-point, point d'exportation en numéraire.

specific : déterminé, spécifique (a).
[J] – *exceptions* : exceptions expresses.

– *legatee* : légataire à titre particulier.
– *performance* : exécution pure et simple (d'un contrat).
– *request* : demande expresse.
[F] – *amount* : forfait.
– *taxes* : taxes spéciales.
[D] – *duty* : droit spécifique.
(to provide) **specifically** : expressément (stipuler).

specification : spécification (f), devis descriptif.
[J] – *of charge* : chef(s) d'accusation.
patent – : description de brevet.
[A] pl. : cahier des charges.
– *(s) of a contract* : stipulations d'un contrat.
[B] bordereau des espèces.
[D] déclaration d'embarquement.
to specify : spécifier, préciser.
specified : spécifié dans la sentence.
the specified persons : les personnes désignées.
unless otherwise specified : sauf indication (ou avis) contraire.

specimen : spécimen (m), modèle (m), exemplaire (m), échantillon (m).
– *signature* : modèle de signature (ex. pour authentifier un chèque).
[ASS] – *clauses* : clauses types.

spectacular : [U.S.] publicité lumineuse.

to speculate : spéculer, jouer (à la bourse).
[B] – *for (on) a fall* : spéculer à la baisse.

speculation : spéculation (f), méditation (f).
[B] *bear* – *(s)* : spéculation à la baisse.
bull – *(s)* : spéculation à la hausse.
– *of a fall* : spéculation à la baisse.
– *for a rise* : spéculation à la hausse.
[F] – *monetary assets* : encaisses de spéculation.

speculative : spéculatif (a).
– *interest* : achats spéculatifs.

speculator : spéculateur (m).

to speed up : accélérer, activer.
– *production* : accélérer la production.

spending : dépense.
[F] *déficit* – : impasse budgétaire.
– *capacity* : pouvoir d'achat.
– *department* : administration dépensière.
– *estimate* : estimation de frais.

spendthrift : prodigue (m et f).

to spin off : scinder (une société).

spin off effects: effets induits, retombées économiques.

to spin out: faire traîner (une affaire).

spiralling costs: coûts (m pl) qui augmentent très vite.

spiralling prices and wages: la course salaires-prix.

to splash a piece of news: mettre une nouvelle en manchette.

to split: partager, diviser, [B] fractionner (actions).
— *the fee*: dichotomie (f).
[J] **split** *service*: condamnation mitigée.
[B] *split-coupon bond*: obligation à coupon partagé.
split spread: marge (f) de fractionnement du crédit.
split-up of stock: fractionnement d'actions.
splitting: fractionnement (m), division (fractionnement d'une action par division de son nominal).
hair-splitting: finasserie (f).
income splitting: quotient familial.

splurchase: (néologisme formé de : to splurge + purchase) achat (m) dispendieux (a).

to splurge: dépenser sans compter.

spoil system: [US] système des dépouilles (changement des hauts fonctionnaires après une élection présidentielle).

spokesman: (pol.) porte-parole (par ex. du gouvernement, etc.).

spoliation: spoliation (f), pillage (m).
[J] destruction ou altération de documents probants.
spoil *system*: [U.S.] distribution de postes officiels aux amis du parti vainqueur aux élections.

sponsion: [J] garantie personnelle.

to sponsor: a) prendre en charge ; b) [J] être le garant de ; c) parrainer, patronner.
sponsor: a) parrain, commanditaire (m) ; b) [J] caution, garant, répondant ; c) [U.S.] caution personnelle d'un immigrant (au moyen d'un *affidavit*)..

sponsoring *(contrary to « patronage »)* : parrainage (m) (opp. à « mécénat »).

spoon-fed industry: industrie soutenue par des subventions d'Etat ou protégée par des tarifs douaniers.

spot: disponible (a), point (m), lieu (m), [C] le disponible, brève annonce publicitaire (à la télévision).
[B] *a few strong* — *(s)* : quelques îlots de résistance.
— *cash*: argent comptant.
— *contract*: marché au comptant (opp. à *future contract*).
— *credit*: crédit ponctuel.
— *delivery*: livraison immédiate.
— *exchange transaction*: opération de change au comptant.
— *market*: marché au comptant.
— *news*: (journ.) dernière heure.
— *price*: cours du comptant (devises), cours du disponible (marchandises).
[C] — *quotation*: cote disponible.

spouse: époux ou épouse.

spread: a) extension (f) ; b) [B] opération « à cheval » ; c) [U.S.] écart entre deux prix ; marge.
[F] *price differential* — : ciseaux de prix.
[ASS] *the* — *of risk*: la répartition des risques.

to spread: échelonner, s'étendre, se déployer, se disperser, propager.
[C] — *sales*: échelonner les ventes.
spreading: échelonnement, propagation, diffusion.
induced spreading effects: effets d'entraînement induits.
spreading back income: étalement rétroactif du revenu.
spreading forth effects: effets de propagation.

to spur: stimuler (l'économie).

spurious: faux, falsifié ; apocryphe (a).
— *coin*: pièce fausse.
spuriousness: fausseté, caractère apocryphe (d'un texte).

squander: gaspiller.

to square: régler, balancer (un compte).
square: a) carré ; b) square, place ; c) en bon ordre, en règle, honnête.

squatter: [J] celui qui s'établit sans droit sur le terrain d'autrui.

squeeze: a) compression (f), resserrement (m) ; b) accaparement (m), monopole (m).
[F] *credit* — : resserrement du crédit.
[B] — *by long buyers*: accaparement par les haussiers.
to squeeze the bears: acculer les vendeurs à

découvert.

stabilization: stabilisation (f).
[F] – *fund*: fond de stabilisation.
stabilized *bonds*: obligations indexées.

stable *(market, quotations)*: (B) (marché, cours) stable(s) (a).

staff: personnel (m).
clerical – : personnel administratif.
field – : personnel extérieur.
– *and line organization*: organisation mixte.
– *cards*: fiches du personnel.
– *changes*: mouvement du personnel.
– *participation*: participation du personnel à la gestion.
– *provident fund*: caisse de prévoyance du personnel.
– *regulations*: statut du personnel.
the senior – : les cadres supérieurs.
– *training division*: division de la formation du personnel.
– *turnover*: renouvellement du personnel.

stag: [B] loup (chasseur de prime).

to stage (an exhibition): organiser (une exposition).

stagflation: stagflation (f) (situation de stagnation de la production associé à un taux d'inflation).

staggering: décalage (m), [U.S.] étalement des vacances.

stagnation: stagnation (f), léthargie (f), immobilisme (m), marasme (m).

stake: mise (f), enjeu (m).
to have a – *in (a business)*: avoir des intérêts dans (une affaire).
to have a voting – : avoir une participation qui autorise à prendre part aux votes.

stakeholder: a) dépositaire de l'enjeu d'un pari; b) détenteur d'une somme d'argent ou d'un bien réclamés par d'autres auxquels il ne prétend pas et qu'il remettra conformément à une décision judiciaire.

stale: a) prescrit; b) lourd, plat (a).
[J] – *cheque*: chèque prescrit.
– *demand*: demande périmée.
– *pretentions*: prétentions surannées.
[F] – *market*: marché lourd.

to stall: immobiliser, arrêter.

stallage: redevance (f) pour l'occupation d'une place dans un marché.

stamp: timbre (m).
– *duties*: droits de timbre. Recettes budgétaires obtenues par l'apposition de timbres sur divers documents et écrits.
finance- – : timbre d'effets.
postage- – : timbre-poste.
postage-due- – : chiffre taxe.
revenue – : timbre fiscal.
ad valorem – : timbre proportionnel.
stamped paper: papier timbré.

stampede of bears: [B] panique des vendeurs à découvert.

stand: a) stand (m) (dans une exposition); b) halte (f), pause (f), arrêt (m).
[F] – *pat budget*: budget stationnaire.
[J] **to stand** *aside*: mise à l'écart.
right to stand aside: droit d'ordonner la mise à l'écart, de récuser provisoirement (opp. à *challenge* qui est le droit de récusation définitive).
to cause a juror to stand aside: faire mettre un juré à l'écart.
to stand by: soutenir.
to stand for: représenter.
to stand surety for: se porter garant de.
to stand over: rester en suspens.

standard: a) étalon (m); b) niveau (m); c) standard, type.
elements of the – *of living*: éléments du train de vie.
gold specie – : étalon de numéraire or.
monetary – : étalon monétaire.
rise in the – *of living*: élévation du niveau de vie.
salary – : barème de traitements.
– *allowance*: allocation forfaitaire.
– *charge*: taxe forfaitaire.
– *deduction*: déduction forfaitaire, abattement.
– *deviation*: écart-type.
– *of a coin*: titre d'une monnaie.
– *of wages*: taux des salaires.
– *population*: population-type.
predetermined – : norme de référence fixée d'avance (exprimée en objectifs).
– *price*: valeur forfaitaire.
– *rate*: taux (m) de base.
– *samples*: échantillons types.
– *weight*: taux étalon.
standardization: standardisation, normalisation.
standardization of prices: péréquation des prix.

standby: ressource (f).
[F] – *agreement*: convention portant sur la ligne de crédit accordée par le F.M.I.
– *amount*: ligne de crédit.
– *credit*: crédit de soutien, ligne de crédit

confirmée.
— *letter of credit*: caution bancaire.

standing: debout, établi, fixe, stable, permanent, invariable (a).
— *committee*: comité directeur, commission permanente.
— *crops*: récoltes sur pied.
— *custom*: coutume établie.
— *expenses (or charges)*: frais généraux.
— *order*: ordre permanent.
firm of recognized — : maison d'une honorabilité reconnue.
[A] *book of* — *instructions*: règlement.
[J] — *mute*: silence opposé à une accusation de haute trahison (réputé dénégation).
— *orders*: règlement intérieur des assemblées législatives.
— *rule*: règle fixe.

standstill: arrêt (m), immobilisation (f), point (m) mort; [C.E.E.] stabilisation, interdiction d'introduire des divergences supplémentaires.
— *agreement*: moratoire.
— *credit*: crédit moratoire.
— *in business*: stagnation des affaires.
to be at a — : marquer le pas, s'immobiliser, chômer.
wage — : blocage des salaires.

staple: principal (a), de base.
— *commodities, goods*: denrées de première nécessité.
— *industry*: industrie principale.
— *products*: produits de grande consommation, produits normalisés.

stare decisis *et non quia movere*: respecter les décisions rendues (principe de la "case law": un juge est tenu de suivre un jugement précédent).

to start: commencer (un travail), ouvrir (un magasin), lancer (une affaire).
[C] — *an entry*: ouvrir une écriture.
— *from scratch*: partir de zéro.

starting price: [B] prix initial.

start-up: démarrage (m).
— *costs of new plants*: frais encourus durant la période de démarrage des nouvelles usines.
— *expenditures*: frais de démarrage.

state: état (m); [J] [U.S.] un des Etats de l'Union.
— *Department*: [U.S.] ministère des Affaires Etrangères.
— *ownership*: étatisation.
— *subsidized*: subventionné par l'Etat.
whatever the — *of the case may be*: en tout état de cause.
— *-aided*: subventionné (a).
— *(s) of the world*: événements.

to state: déclarer, régler.
as stated above: ainsi qu'il est dit plus haut.
stating the fact: établissant le fait.
the reasons for a judgment must be stated: tout jugement doit être motivé.
stated: établi, régulier, déterminé, arrêté.
stated account: compte arrêté.
stated case: cas spécifique; exposé motivé;
[J] exposé de cause; consultation juridique.
stated salary: salaire arrêté; salaire fixe.
stated value: valeur attribuée (à une action).

statement: déclaration (f), exposé (m), exposition (f), rapport (m), relation (f).
certified — : constatation.
official — : communiqué.
[J] *agreed* — : faits sur lesquels les avocats des deux parties sont d'accord.
bare — *of the facts*: simple énoncé des faits.
opening — : exposé introductif.
— *of a venue*: lieu du procès.
— *of affairs*: bilan de liquidation.
— *of claim*: a) demande introductive d'instance; b) conclusions en matière de dommages-intérêts.
— *of costs*: état de frais.
— *of defence*: conclusions de la défense.
— *of facts*: exposé préparé pour un «*special case*» (voir ce terme).
income — : compte d'exploitation.
official — *of facts*: constat.
— *of grounds for an appeal*: grief.
— *of particulars*: exposé de la demande fait par le créancier d'une dette liquide; mémoire détaillé sur un point du litige.
— *of prosecution*: accusation, réquisitoire.
— *of witness*: déposition.
— *to be filed*: état à produire.
[C] *cash* — : état de caisse.
itemized — : relevé de compte.
monthly — : fin de mois.
— *analysis*: analyse d'une situation comptable.
— *of account*: relevé de compte.
— *of expenses*: montant des frais.
[F] *bank weekly* — : bilan hebdomadaire de la banque.
budget — : relevé de la situation budgétaire.
consolidated — *of condition*: [U.S.] bilan consolidé.
financial — : exposé financier, comptes de résultats.
monthly — *of budgetary expenditures*: état mensuel des dépenses budgétaires.
operating — : comptes d'exploitation.
— *for the year ending...*: compte rendu de l'exercice terminé le...
— *of application of funds*: mouvements de

trésorerie.
– *of assets and liabilities*: bilan.
– *of the value of properties*: inventaire de la valeur des propriétés.
to draw up a – of account: faire un relevé de compte.

standing: durée (f.)
a barrister of 20 years – : un avocat ayant exercé pendant 20 ans.

statistics: statistique(s) (f), renseignements (m pl).
financial – : renseignements d'ordre financier.
vital – : statistique démographique.
statistical *returns*: résultats statistiques.

status: [J] 1° statut légal. Les droits et obligations, les facultés et incapacités d'une personne sont fonction de son statut légal (de mineur, de femme mariée, de failli, etc.).
action of legitimate child to claim his – : action en réclamation d'état.
2° capacité juridique.
to acquire legal – : acquérir la personnalité morale.
[A] *civil –* : état-civil.
marital, legal – : état matrimonial, union légitime.
personal – : statut personnel.
[F] *financial –* : solvabilité.
account – : état de compte.
– *inquiry*: enquête de solvabilité.
– *symbol*: signes extérieurs de la réussite.

statute: [J] acte législatif, loi écrite (opp. C.L. droit coutumier).
Les lois (*Acts of Parliament*) sont classées comme suit, selon leur nature :
1° *declaratory*: déclaratoires, lorsqu'elles ne modifient pas la législation existante, mais y apportent simplement des éclaircissements.
2° *remedial*: réformatrices, lorsqu'elles apportent des changements au C.L.
3° *amending*: portant amendement, lorsqu'elles modifient la loi écrite.
4° *consolidating*: consolidatrices, lorsqu'elles fondent en une seule plusieurs lois antérieures portant sur le même sujet.
5° *disabling or restraining*: imposant une capacité ou restrictives, lorsqu'elles limitent le droit d'aliéner des biens.
6° *enabling*: habilitantes, lorsqu'elles lèvent une incapacité ou une restriction.
7° *penal*: pénales, lorsqu'elles imposent une pénalité ou confiscation.
– *of frauds and perjuries*: loi anglaise de 1677 subordonnant la validité de certains contrats à la rédaction d'un écrit ou la production d'un commencement de preuve par écrit.

– *(s) at large*: [U.S.] recueil des lois fédérales dans l'ordre chronologique.
– *(s) of limitation*: (Engl.) loi de prescription datant de 1623, [U.S.] les dettes légales se prescrivent par six ans dans l'ensemble des Etats, mais, par ailleurs, des différences subsistent.
personal – : statut personnel.
real – : statut réel.
– *-barred*: prescrit, caduc.
– *-book*: code, codification, recueil des lois.
– *-labour*: corvée, prestation en nature.
– *-law*: droit écrit ou jurisprudence.

statutory: réglé par un texte de loi, légal, réglementaire, statutaire, (*of offence*) prévu par la loi (a).
– *appropriations*: crédits statutaires, budgétaires.
– *bodies*: organismes officiels, structures institutionnalisées.
– *cash reserves*: réserves statutaires.
– *coefficients of ratios (of taxation)*: coefficients légaux.
– *company*: compagnie créée par législation spéciale pour assurer un service public ([U.S.] *utility company*).
– *crime*: crime par la définition de la loi.
– *declaration*: a) attestation (au lieu de serment); b) attestation par un homme de loi que certaines formalités ont été accomplies; c) acte de notoriété.
– *holiday*: fête légale.
– *income*: revenu statutaire.
– *limitation*: prescription légale.
– *notice*: délai de préavis.
– *meeting*: assemblée statutaire.
– *procedure*: procédure contractuelle.
– *provisions*: [U.K.] dispositions légales, [U.S.] dispositions statutaires.
– *reserve*: réserve légale, statutaire.
– *rules and orders*: règlements pris en vertu d'un *statutory*, instrument-délégation des pouvoirs (cf. décret-loi).

to stave off: prévenir, éviter, échapper à (faillite, saisie etc.).

stay: arrêt (m), entrave (f).
[J] – *of appeal*: suspension d'appel.
– *of execution*: sursis (m), ordonnance à surseoir (à un jugement).
– *of proceedings*: suspension (f) d'instance.
judgment liable to – of execution: jugement susceptible d'opposition.
an appeal is not a – : un appel n'est pas suspensif.
[A] – *of collection*: [U.K.] sursis de paiement (d'impôts).
period of – : durée de séjour.
to stay a judgment: surseoir à un jugement.
to stay the debate: arrêter, suspendre le débat.

— -in strike : grève sur le tas.

steady : ferme, stable, soutenu, constant (a).
[F] — *resources earmarking ratio :* coefficient d'emploi de ressources stables. Les Banques doivent couvrir l'ensemble des crédits qu'elles distribuent par une fraction stable de leurs ressources à long terme.
steadying : affermissement.
steadying factor : volant (de production).

stealing : [J] [U.S.] plagiat (m), filouterie (f) (= *embezzlement, larceny*).
— *by finding :* vol commis par l'appropriation d'un objet trouvé.

steel : acier (m).
— *(s) :* valeurs sidérurgiques.
— *works :* aciéries.

steep : raide (a).
— *price :* prix exorbitant.

to steer : dirigier, conduire.
steering *committee :* comité directeur, comité de restructuration.

step : pas (m), démarche (f), mesure (f), cadence (f), échelon (m), seuil (m).
advisory — : démarche conseillable.
rising in a series of — *(s) :* progression par tranches (de l'impôt).
— *(s) method :* méthode de cotation par échelons.
to take — *(s) :* faire des démarches.
to step *up :* augmenter (production).

to sterilize : stériliser, éponger.
— *excess liquidities :* éponger l'excès de liquidités.

sterling : sterling (m).
pound — : livre sterling.
— *area :* zone sterling.
— *balances :* soldes en sterling, balances « sterling ».
— *bonds :* obligations payables en sterling.

to stet : (J) (C) maintenir un mot (rayé par erreur) dans un document.

steward : économe, régisseur, intendant ; steward, garçon de cabine.
shop — : délégué syndical.

to stick : coller.
« stick *no bills* » : « défense d'afficher ».

sticker : vignette (f), autocollant (m).

stiff : tendu, exagéré (a).
— *price :* prix exagéré.

still-born : mort-né ou apparemment mort-né.
[A] — *-births :* la mortinatalité.

stimulus : stimulant (m), aiguillon (m), excitant (m).

stipend : traitement (m), rémunération (f).

stipendiary : appointé (a).
— *magistrate :* juge d'un tribunal de simple police à Londres et dans les grandes villes.

stipulation : [J] a) stipulation d'une condition ; b) accord des parties sur un ou plusieurs points de procédure.
severance pursuant to — : ajournement, désistement d'action, disjonction, convenus.
the facts have been **stipulated** : l'état de fait a été reconnu de part et d'autre, etc.
stipulated damage : dommages-intérêts liquidés.
stipulated jointure : douaire préfixe.

stirpes : groupe, famille, ligne ; [J] souche.
succession per — : descente par souche.

stock : stock (m), marchandises (f pl) ; matières premières.
live- —, *grazing* — : bétail, animaux sur pied.
lean — *(s) :* stocks bas.
[J] 1° une famille. 2° a) capital d'une société anonyme *(joint* —*)* ; b) capital divisible et détenu en fractions diverses : actions (surtout aux Etats-Unis (pl.), en Grande-Bretagne, plutôt *shares*). 3° actif d'un fonds de commerce. 4° cheptel.
[F] *bank* — : valeur de banque.
— *certificates or warrants :* titres au porteur.
— *company* ([U.S.] *corporation) :* société par actions, anonyme.
— *dividend :* actions de jouissance, gratuites.
Government — : fonds d'Etat étrangers.
fully paid — : titres libérés.
— *ledger :* registre des actionnaires.
outstanding — : [U.S.] capital souscrit.
(cumulative) preferred — : action de priorité (cumulative).
railway — : valeurs de chemin de fer.
— *and shares :* valeurs mobilières, valeurs de bourse, titres (rentes, actions et obligations) (voir aussi *shares*).
[B] *dividend* — : action à haut rendement.
growth — : valeur de croissance.
— *taken in, carried over :* titres en report.
— *-account :* compte de capital, compte titres.
— *bought in, sold out :* valeurs exécutées.
— *-broker :* agent de change, courtier en bourse.
— *options plan :* système d'intéressement des salariés par levée d'option en vue de souscrire des actions de leur société à un prix

déterminé.
outside – -broker : coulissier.
stock-exchange : Bourse des valeurs.
– *exchange committee :* chambre syndicale des agents de change.
stockholder : actionnaire.
stockholder *action :* voir *class action.*
stockholders' equity : capitaux propres.
– *average :* indice des valeurs en Bourse.
joint- – company : société de capitaux.
– *exchange intelligence :* informations boursières, bulletin de la Bourse.
– *(s) in pawn :* valeurs en pension.
– *jobber :* courtier intermédiaire de bourse ; joueur en bourse, agioteur.
– *jobbing :* agiotage.
– *-list :* a) inventaire ; b) bulletin de la cote.
– *-market :* a) marché financier ; b) marché aux bestiaux, commerce des bestiaux.
– *option allowance :* plan d'option sur titres (intéressement du personnel sous forme d'attribution d'actions).
– *of record :* actionnaires inscrits sur les registres.
– *-register :* grand-livre des titres.
surplus – : soldes.
– *switches :* changement de position.
– *-taking :* inventaire.
– *-turn :* see « turn over ».
– *-in-hand, – -in-trade :* marchandise en magasin.
– *yield :* rendement d'une action.

stop : arrêt, suspension.
– *-gap measures :* mesures « bouche-trou », d'urgence ; mesures provisoires.
– *-go policy :* politique de progression par à-coups.
[B] – *order :* ordre stop, opposition sur titre.
– *payment order :* ordre de suspendre les paiements.
stoppage : a) blocage (m) ; b) cessation (f).
stoppage in transit : [E] droit du vendeur non payé d'arrêter la marchandise vendue en cours de transit.
stoppage of payments : cessation de paiement.
stoppage of work : débrayage.
to stop *(a cheque) :* frapper d'opposition (un chèque).

store : a) approvisionnement (m), fourniture (f) ; b) magasin (m), dépôt (m), entrepôt (m), réserve (f).
– *accounting :* comptabilité-matières.

stowage : magasinage (m) ; [A] droit de magasinage.

straddle ([U.S.] *spread eagle*) : [B] stellage, marché à double prime, opération à cheval, ordre lié.

straight : droit (a).
– *bill of lading :* connaissement simple.
– *bond :* obligation à taux fixe.
– *grade :* de qualité régulière.
– *line amortization or depreciation :* amortissement linéaire.
– *salary :* salaire fixe.

strain : tension (f), embarras (m), difficulté (f).
liquidity – : insuffisance de liquidité.

to be in straits : être dans une situation quasi désespérée, aux abois.

stranger : étranger, inconnu (m).
[J] a) sans lien de parenté ; b) tiers, celui qui n'est pas partie ou ayant cause (opp. *privy*).

strangling : étranglement (m). [J] strangulation (f).

strategic : stratégique (a).
– *investment :* investissement stratégique.
– *stockpiling :* constitution de stocks stratégiques.

strategy (strategies) : cours (m) de l'action, ligne (f) d'action, activités (f pl).
– *games :* jeux de stratégie.

stratified sampling : see « quota sampling ».

stratum : strate (f) (d'échantillon).

straw : prête-nom.

stray : a) animal égaré, [J] bête épave ; b) succession en déshérence.
waifs and – (s) : enfants moralement abandonnés.

streamline economy : économie (f) réduite à l'essentiel.

stream-lined capitalism : capitalisme dynamique.

streamlining : simplification (f).

street : rue (f).
[B] – *market :* marché hors bourse.
– *name certificate :* certificat de courtier, titre au porteur.
– *price :* cours hors bourse.

strength : a) force (f), vigueur (f), solidité (f) ; b) [B] résistance.

stress: tension (f).
breaking – : tension de rupture.
– *of business*: poids des affaires.
– *interview*: entretien (m) éprouvant (a) (pour un postulant que l'on harcèle de propos délibéré pour juger de ses réactions).

stretch: a) étendue (f) (de terrain); b) excès (m), abus (m).
– *of power*: abus de pouvoir.

strict: rigoureux, rigide, strict.
– *economy*: économie rigoureuse.
[J] – *law*: loi sévère.
– *liability*: responsabilité sans faute.
– *time-limit*: délai péremptoire, terme de rigueur.
with – *justice*: en toute justice.

strike: grève (f).
canny – : grève perlée.
hunger – : grève de la faim.
lightning – : grève sans préavis, grève surprise.
rotating – : grève tournante.
sit-down – : grève avec occupation.
slow-down – : grève perlée.
stay-in – : grève sur le tas.
– *breaker*: briseur de grève, « jaune ».
sympathy – : grève de solidarité.
token – : grève symbolique.
warning – : grève d'avertissement.
wildcat – : grève sauvage, non contrôlée.
work-to-rule – : grève du zèle.
working – : grève perlée, de règlement.
to call a – : appeler à la grève.
to call off a – : annuler un mot d'ordre de grève.
to go on – : se mettre en grève.
to strike a jury: constituer un jury, après élimination des jurés récusés.
to strike a bargain: conclure un marché.
to strike off: a) rayer (une affaire) du rôle ; b) radier un avoué (du tableau).
[B] *to strike out a security from the list*: rayer un titre de la cote.
striking price: cours de base.

stringency: rigueur (f), sévérité (f).
[F] *new* – *on bank credit*: nouveau resserrement du crédit bancaire.
policy of monetary – : politique d'austérité monétaire.

stringent: strict (a), rigoureux (a).
– *market*: marché tendu.
[F] – *money*: argent serré.

stripping: démembrement (m).

strong: résistant (a), en hausse.
– *financial position*: situation financière forte.
a – *market*: un marché bien orienté.
– *room*: salle des coffres.

structural unemployment: chômage (m) structurel.

structure: structure (f), mode (m) d'organisation.
simple product – : industrie à production simple.
– *of the banking system*: organisation du système bancaire.
the capital – *of a company*: la composition du capital d'une société.
the social – : l'édifice (m) social.

struggle: lutte (f), combat (m).
class struggle: lutte des classes.
– *against inequalities*: lutte contre les inégalités.
struggling *industry*: industrie en butte à une sévère concurrence.

stub: talon (m) (de chèque).

study trip: voyage (m) d'étude(s).

style: titre (m), nom (m), raison sociale.

to subcontract: sous-traiter.

subcontractor: sous-traitant (m).

subdivision: lotissement (m).

to subduct: retirer.

subject to: a) sujet, soumis à ; b) assujetti ; c) sous réserve de ; d) redevable de (a).
– *to alterations*: sous réserve de modifications.
– *to contract*: sous réserve de passation de contrat.
– *to a mortgage*: grevé d'hypothèque.
– *to quota*: contingenté.
– *to taxation*: soumis à l'impôt.
– *to the terms of this agreement*: sous réserve du présent contrat.
– *-matter*: *(of an action)* objet du litige, *(of a contract)* objet.

sub judice: [J] affaire pendante.

sub modo: sous condition.

sub-lease: sous-location (f).
sub- – : a) sous-location ; b) amodiation (de droits d'exploitation minière).

submission: soumission (f).
[J] a) plaidoirie (f) ; b) compromis arbitral.

— *of proofs of identity*: présentation de pièces d'identité.
to submit: soumettre, avancer, alléguer, produire.
to submit the case of the court: en référer au tribunal.
I submit that there is no case: je plaide le non-lieu.
latest **submittal** *date*: date limite de dépôt.
the woman **submitted**: la femme était consentante (il n'y a pas eu viol).

sub-office: succursale (f).

subordinated: (F) subordonné (ou remboursement des dettes).

subordinate legislation: règlements pris en application des lois.

subornation of perjury: [J] incitation au faux témoignage, subornation de témoin.

subparagraph: sous-alinéa (m) (d'une loi).

subpoena: sous peine d'amende.
[J] citation à comparaître adressée à des témoins (par l'avoué de la partie demanderesse, au nom du tribunal).
— *ad testificandum*: convocation pour déposer.
duces tecum, — : ordre de soit-communiqué.
— *to show cause*: convocation d'un mineur atteignant sa majorité, pour exposer pourquoi un jugement rendu contre lui pendant sa minorité, ne doit pas être exécuté.

subreption: [J] subreption (f).

subrogation: [J] subrogation (f).
subrogation act: acte subrogatoire.

to subscribe: signer, *(to apply for shares)*, souscrire (= *to sign, to attest*).
*to over-***subscribe**: [F] dépasser une émission.
subscribed *capital*: capital souscrit.
entirely **subscribed** *issue*: émission entièrement souscrite.
subscribing *witness*: témoin instrumentaire.

subscription: a) abonnement (m); b) cotisation (f); c) souscription (f).
— *price*: prix de souscription.
— *rental*: redevance d'abonnement.
— *to a loan*: souscription à un emprunt.

subsection: paragraphe (m) (d'une loi), sous-division (f).

subsequent: subséquent (a).
[J] *condition* — : condition résolutoire (opp. *condition precedent*).

[C] — *period*: exercice suivant, période suivante.
subsequently: consécutif à, par la suite, postérieurement.

subsidiary: subsidiaire, auxiliaire (a).
— *account*: sous-compte.
— *coinage*: monnaie d'appoint.
— *company*: filiale, société annexe.(voir *holding company*).
— *payments*: subsides.
— *tax*: taxe accessoire.

to subsidise: subventionner.

subsidy: subvention (f), allocation (f).
after deduction of indirect taxes and adding of **subsidies**: après déduction des impôts indirects nets de subventions.

subsistence minimum: [U.S.] minimum vital.

substance: substance (f), essence (f).
form yields readily to — : le fond importe plus que la forme.
[F] — *over form* # abus de droit (en contentieux fiscal).

substantial: important (a), sérieux (a).
— *damages*: dommages-intérêts effectifs (opp. *nominal damages*).
— *evidence*: preuve suffisante.
— *performance*: voir *performance*.
— *rights*: droits matériels découlant du droit positif.
the present order book is — : pour le moment le carnet de commandes est bien garni.

to substantiate *(a charge)*: établir (une accusation).
— *a claim*: prouver le bien-fondé d'une réclamation.

substantive charge: chef d'accusation sur un fait matériel précis (opp. p. ex. *conspiracy charge*).
— *(substantial) justice*: justice inhérente.
— *law*: droit positif (opp. *adjective law*).

to substitute: (J) subroger.

substitution: remplacement (m).
[J] a) substitution (f); b) subrogation (f); c) *(of a debt)* novation (f) de créance.
— *effect*: effet de substitution (le consommateur accroît la consommation du produit dont le prix relatif diminue, qu'il substitue aux produits à prix stables ou élevés).

substitute: a) succédané ; b) [J] représentant ; c) contrefaçon.

beware of — (s): se méfier des contrefaçons.
to become a —: se transformer en produit de substitution.
to find a —: se faire suppléer.
substituted, substitutional, *legatee*: héritier substitué (se dit plutôt: *heir in remainder*).
substituted service: signification à domicile.
[F] **substitution** *of taxpayer*: succession fiscale.

subtenant: sous-locataire (m).

subtotal: somme partielle.

succeeding: suivant (a).
[B] — *account*: liquidation suivante.

successful: heureux, qui réussit, fructueux (a).
— *bids*: soumissions acceptées.
— *lines of products*: produits vendables.

succession: succession (f), suite (f); lignée (f), descendance (f).
[J] *stricto jure*: entrée en fonction du successeur au décès du titulaire d'une *corporation sole*.
de facto: succession, héritage (m). [J] hoirie (f), avènement (m) ou succession au trône, reconduction (f) (p. ex. *a succession of leases*).
artificial, perpetual —: succession en permanence, fiction destinée à justifier la continuité de la personne morale en tant qu'elle est constituée d'une somme de droits individuels changeants.
to forgo a —: s'abstenir d'une succession, répudier un héritage.
general —: succession universelle.
— *law*: droit successoral.
rights of —: droits successifs.
singular —: héritier unique.
title by —: titre (de propriété) par droit de succession.
[F] — *duties*: droits de succession.
quick — *allowance*: [U.K.] réduction de droits en cas de successions rapprochées.

sudden rise: [B] hausse (f) subite, montée (f) en flèche.
— *turn*: revirement (m), volte-face (f).

to sue: [J] — *s.o. at law*: intenter un procès à qn, poursuivre, appeler, traduire qn en justice, actionner qn, agir (civilement) contre qn, se porter partie civile contre qn, porter plainte, déposer plainte contre qn.
— *in a civil action*: ester en justice.
— *s.o. for civil injury*: se porter partie civile (dans une affaire au criminel).
— *s.o. for damages*: poursuivre qn en dommages-intérêts.
— *in forma pauperis*: intenter une action avec assistance judiciaire.
to petition for leave — *in forma pauperis*: demander l'assistance judiciaire.
— *s.o. for infringement of patent*: assigner qn en contre-façon.
— *for libel*: attaquer en diffamation.
— *out*: obtenir (p. ex. *to sue out a writ of habeas corpus*).
— *for separation*: plaider en séparation.
liable to be **sued**: assignable.
A **sues** *B for specific performances*: A assigne B en exécution intégrale du contrat.
— *for peace*: demander la paix.

to suffer: subir, éprouver, supporter.
a tax **suffered** *by*: un impôt supporté par.

sufferance: souffrance (f), douleur (f), souffrance de, tolérance (f), permission tacite.
[J] *window or light on* —: jour, vue, de souffrance.
by, on, —: à titre précaire.
[D] *bill of* —: lettre d'exemption des droits de douane d'un entrepôt à un autre (situé dans un autre port).
— *wharf*: quai de débarquement des marchandises passibles des droits d'entrée (quai de la Douane).

suggestion scheme: disposition (f) permettant à un employé de faire connaître ses idées sur la marche de l'entreprise.

suicide: suicide (m). [J] voir *felo de se*.
— *pact*: lorsque deux personnes conviennent de se suicider et qu'une seule accomplisse l'acte, le survivant est coupable de meurtre comme complice par instigation.

suijuris: pleinement capable.
[J] personne pouvant s'engager en droit et contracter valablement de son propre chef.

suit (*at law*): action civile.
[J] sp. procès en Eq. (*suit in chancery*) et instance de divorce.
to conduct the suit: occuper pour le demandeur.
criminal —, — *of the peace*: poursuites au criminel.
— *money*: somme d'argent à verser par le mari sur ordre du tribunal, pour couvrir les frais de l'instance de divorce engagée par la femme.
suitor: plaideur.

sum: somme (f), montant (m).
agreed —: somme forfaitaire, montant convenu.
exempted —: montant exonéré.
— *assured*: capital assuré.
— *at length*: somme en toutes lettres.

summary: sommaire (a et m).
[J] – *offence*: infraction (légère) jugée devant la "Magistrate Court".
– *procedure*: affaire sommaire, référé.
– *proceedings*: procédure sommaire (terminée par un *summary judgment*).
– *of the proceedings*: résumé (m) de la séance (f).
« – *of leading cases and decisions* »: recueil de jurisprudence.
[C] *annual* – : bilan annuel.

summing-up: [J] résumé par le juge à l'intention du jury des points saillants des témoignages produits.

summons: appel d'autorité, convocation urgente.
[J] acte introductif d'instance: citation à comparaître, assignation.
to summon a meeting: convoquer une réunion.

sumptuary: somptuaire (a).
– *expenses*: dépenses somptuaires.
– *tax*: impôt sur le luxe.

sundries: articles (m pl) divers, faux frais (m pl).
– *account*: compte de divers.

sunk cost: somme (f) déjà investie dans un projet qu'il sera difficile de récupérer si le projet est annulé, investissement risqué.

sunset legislation: (U.S.) législation « du coucher de soleil » (exprime l'idée que chaque programme gouvernemental doit s'achever automatiquement dans un délai déterminé et ne peut être poursuivi qu'après une procédure d'évaluation et un vote spécifique de l'organe législatif).

superannuation: [A] retraite par limite d'âge.
– *act*: (U.K.) loi sur les mises à la retraite.
– *benefits*: pensions de retraites.
– *contribution*: retenue pour retraite.
– *fund*: caisse de retraites.

supercargo: subrécargue.

superdividend: superdividende (m).

superficies solo cedit: ce qui est attaché au sol en fait partie; [J] immeubles, meubles à fixe demeure, immeubles par destination.

to superimpose: superposer.
[J] – *the punishment*: frapper d'une peine additionnelle pour bris de prison.
[F] **superimposed** *tax*: impôt de superposition.

series of superimposed taxes: impôt « en cascade » (cf. *cumulating taxes*).

superintendent: directeur, surveillant général, chef; chef d'une circonscription ecclésiastique protestante (luthérienne); régisseur, intendant; [U.S.] chef de département.
police – : officier de paix.
shop- – : chef d'atelier.

superior: supérieur (a).
– *estate*: fonds dominant.
– *force*: force majeure.
– *orders*: fait du prince.

supermarket: supermarché (m).

supersede: remplacer, supplanter.
*this notice **supersedes** the notices published under dates of...*: cet avis annule les avis publiés le...

supertax: [U.K.] super impôt (voir *tax*).

supervisor: a) surveillant (m), directeur (m); b) chef d'atelier, agent de maîtrise.
board of – (s): conseil de surveillance.

supplemental, supplementary: supplémentaire (a).
[J] – *affidavit*: affidavit complémentaire.
– *bill or pleading*: mémoire supplémentaire basé sur des faits nouveaux.
[F] **supplementary** *charge*: taxe supplémentaire.
– *estimates*: budget supplémentaire des dépenses; crédits supplémentaires.
– *funds*: budget annexe.
[B] *supplementary list*: index hors cote.

suppletory oath: [J] serment supplétoire.

supplier: fournisseur (m).
– *('s) credit*: crédit fournisseur.
– *('s) export credit*: crédit fournisseur consenti à une firme exportatrice.

supply: fourniture (f), approvisionnement (m), offre (f).
[J] pl. crédits budgétaires accordés (= *appropriations*).
bill of – : projet de crédit supplémentaire, loi de finances.
committee of – : commission du budget.
– *control*: régulation (f) d'offre.
– *curve*: courbe de la demande.
monthly – *vote*: douzièmes provisoires.
*to stop a prodigal's **supplies***: couper les vivres à un prodigue.
supply and demand: l'offre et la demande.
supply effect: effet d'approvisionnement.
– *side economics*: « économie de l'offre »

– 618 –

(théorie (f) économique qui préconise l'encouragement à la production plutôt que l'augmentation de la consommation par des réductions d'impôt).
supply siders : « économistes de l'offre ».
to supply : approvisionner, fournir.
to supply collateral : donner des titres en nantissement.
to supply a want : remédier à un besoin.
supplier *of services* : prestataire de services.

support : appui (m), soutien (m), subsistance (f).
[J] a) pension alimentaire servie volontairement (de même : *allowance for necessaries, maintenance,* opp. *alimony*) ; b) *non-* — = refus d'entretien.
documents in —, *supporting evidence* : pièces, preuve à l'appui.
man without visible means of — : individu sans moyens d'existence connus.
— *of family* : charge de famille.
— *payment* : pension alimentaire.
[B] *industrials attracted little* — : les (valeurs) industrielles ont été peu soutenues.
— *prices* : prix de soutien, d'intervention.
[F] — *buying* : achat de soutien (sur le marché des changes) d'une devise nationale par un gouvernement.
supporting *purchases* : achats de soutien.
supporting receipts : reçus à l'appui.

supreme : suprême (a).
[J] (Engl.) — *Court of Judicature* : Cour souveraine de justice.
[U.S.] 1° — *Court of the United States* : Cour suprême fédérale.
2° — *court* : a) juridiction d'appel dans la plupart des Etats ; b) un tribunal de première instance, de compétence universelle (voir *court,* [U.S.] *jurisdiction general*).
« *the* — *law of the land* » : par. 2 de l'art. 6 de la constitution des Etats-Unis, selon lequel la constitution et les droits fédéraux représentent la loi fondamentale du pays, et lient donc chaque juge et fonctionnaire des Etats particuliers.

surcharge : surcharge (f), droit supplémentaire.
[J] a) inexactitude dans un arrêté de compte, dans une action en reddition de compte signalée par la partie requérante ; b) somme omise dans les frais taxés.
[A] a) déboursement inadmissible porté à la charge du fonctionnaire responsable ; b) surtaxe, taxe compensatrice.
[C] prix excessif.
to surcharge : a) surtaxer (le contribuable, une lettre) ; b) majorer.

surety : sûreté (f), certitude (f).
[J] garantie (f), sûreté (f), cautionnement (m), caution (f), garant (m), répondant (m).
good — : caution solvable.
— *in cash* : garantie en numéraire.
— *for a* — : arrière-caution.
— *-bond, suretyship* : contrat de cautionnement (voir *bail*).
[C] avaliste, donneur d'aval.
[ASS] — *company* : compagnie d'assurances spécialisée dans les cautionnements.

surface : surface (f).
— *royalty* : redevance tréfoncière.

to surge : déferler.
surge *of prices* : montée soudaine des prix.

surname : nom de famille.

surplus : excédent (m), surplus (m), boni (m), plus-value (f).
[J] — *assets* : reliquat après liquidation du passif et remboursement du capital ordinaire et privilégié d'une société.
[A] [U.S.] — *property* : « stocks américains » liquidés par le Gouvernement des Etats-Unis après les deux dernières grandes guerres.
[F] *budget* — : excédent budgétaire.
— *dividend* : superdividende.
— *in taxes* : plus-value des contributions.
— *of a corporation* : actif net de la société, après déduction du passif.
— *of assets over liabilities* : excédent de l'actif sur le passif.
operating — : bénéfices d'exploitation.

surplusage : superfluité (f).
[J] a) redondance, allégations superfétatoires dans des conclusions, dont le tribunal peut ordonner la suppression ; b) disposition d'une loi ou clause d'un contrat qui demande à être interprétée pour ne pas constituer un non-sens.

surprise : surprise (f).
[J] C.L. situation d'une partie « surprise » à l'audience par des allégations et arguments inattendus produits par l'adversaire, l'obligeant à demander un ajournement pour préparer sa réponse.

surrebutter, surrejoinder : voir *pleading*.

surrender : *(of property, rights) (of title) (of the throne)* abandon (m), abandonnement (m), cession (f), restitution (f), abdication (f), *(milit.)* reddition (f).
[J] abandon anticipé du droit de jouissance par l'usufruitier en faveur du nu-propriétaire.
compulsory — : expropriation (f).

— *of a brankrupt's property*: abandon des biens d'un failli à ses créanciers.
— *of a defendant to his bail*: décharge de ses cautions par un accusé libéré sous caution.
to surrender *a charter*: renoncer à la personnalité morale.
to surrender a prisoner: remettre un accusé libéré sous caution aux autorités (pour se décharger).
[ASS] rachat (m).
— *value*: valeur de rachat.
[F] *upon — of*: contre remise de.

surreptitious: subreptice, furtif, clandestin (a).

surrogate: suppléant, substitut (a et m).
[J] subrogé ; [U.S.] juge qui a charge des successions et tutelles.
— *('s) court*: [U.S.] tribunal des successions et tutelles.
— *guardian*: subrogé tuteur (voir *probate*).

surtax: surtaxe (voir *tax*).

survey: aperçu (m), regard (m), vue (f), relevé (m), inspection (f), enquête (f).
cadastral, ordnance, —: cadastre (m) (aussi : *cadaster, land register, terrier*).
feasibility —: étude préalable.
market research —: étude de marché.
— *certificate*: procès-verbal d'expertise, certificat d'expertise.
— *fee*: a) droit de visite ; b) (pl) honoraires d'expertise.
— *of vessel*: description d'un navire.
« *a — of American law* »: « un aperçu du droit américain ».

surveyor: expert (m), inspecteur (m), contrôleur (m).
— *of taxes*: contrôleurs des contributions.
property —: géomètre.

survival survivorship: survie (f).
[J] *right of —* (*as between husband and wife*): gain de survie.
— *statutes*: législation moderne qui, en modification du C.L., admet le droit des héritiers aux dommages-intérêts dus au de cujus (*death action*).
— *rate*: taux de survie.
— *ratio*: coefficient de survie.
— *tables*: tables de survie.
survivor: survivant (m).
[ASS] *survivor annuity*: rente viagère avec réversion (f).

suspense: suspens (m), [J] surséance (f) d'un jugement.
[C] — *account*: compte d'ordre.
bills in —: effets en souffrance.

suspension: suspension (f).
[J] — *of judgment*: surséance de jugement.
— *of the Statutes of limitation*: interruption de prescription.
[A] — *of a licence*: retrait temporaire d'une patente, d'un permis.
to suspend *the execution of sentence*: prononcer un jugement conditionnel.
to suspend sentence: surseoir au jugement.
to suspend the Habeas Corpus Act: déclarer l'état d'exception.
to suspend payments: suspendre les paiements.
to suspend a public officer, an officer, a M.P.: suspendre un fonctionnaire, mettre un officier en non-activité, exclure temporairement un membre du parlement.
to suspend trading: cesser ses activités commerciales (temporairement ou définitivement).

suspicion: soupçon (m), [J] suspicion (f).
to arrest s.o. on —: arrêter qn pour cause de suspicion légitime.
detention on —: détention préventive.
evidence not beyond —: témoignages sujets à caution.
held on —: inculpé.

to sustain: soutenir, supporter, subir.
[J] « *objection* **sustained** »: formule d'acceptation par le juge de l'objection formulée par une partie contre une question posée au témoin par la partie adverse au cours d'un interrogatoire contradictoire.
amount necessary — juridiction: valeur qui détermine la compétence.
ruling of the trial court sustained on appeal: jugement de la première instance confirmé en appel.
— *the burden of proof*: apporter la preuve.
— *a person*: entretenir qn.
[F] — *a loss*: subir une perte.

swap: troc (m), échange de monnaies.
[F] **swaps**: crédits croisés (accords de troc de devises entre Banques Centrales pour équilibrer leur trésorerie en devises).
— *transactions*: opérations croisées d'échanges sur devises.
to swap: « swaper », échanger un produit financier contre une autre valeur (devises, etc.).

to swear: jurer.
— *s.o. in*: déférer le serment, assermenter.

sweating system: système de travail intensif.

to sweeten : rendre plus attrayant(e) (a) (ex. une offre, une opération...).

to swell : gonfler, grossir, enfler.
— *an account* : gonfler un compte.

swindler : escroc (m).

swindling : escroquerie (f), tromperie (f).
[J] manœuvres frauduleuses.

swing : fluctuation (f), oscillation (f), orientation (f), passage (m), glissement (m).
[B] *a steady tone with a light upward* — : une tendance soutenue avec une légère orientation à la hausse.
swing margins : limites de fluctuation.
swings and roundabouts : fluctuations des cours.
seasonal swings : variations saisonnières.
swing of trade : nouvelle orientation des échanges.

switch : a) aiguillage (m), permutation (f) ; b) [F] opération de courtage international avec arbitrage de devises.

to switch *from stocks to bonds* : abandonner ses actions pour des obligations.
switching : a) virement de portefeuille, changement de position ; b) arbitrage (sur le marché financier).

switchboard : standard (m) (téléphonique).

sworn : assermenté (a).
to be — *in* : prêter serment.
— *affidavit, statement* : déclaration sous serment.
— *broker, official* : courtier, fonctionnaire assermenté.
— *declaration* : déclaration sous serment.

to move in sympathy *(prices)* : (C) suivre l'évolution (des prix).

symposium, symposia(pl.) : 1° colloque(s) 2° recueil(s) d'articles.

synallagmatic : contrat (m) synallagmatique, contrat bilatéral.

syndic : [J] représentant d'une société mandaté pour une affaire déterminée.

syndicate : syndicat, consortium.
banking or financial — : syndicat de banque.
syndicated loan : prêt (m) accordé (a) par plusieurs banques, au même taux, à un emprunteur unique.
syndicated market research : étude de marché financée par un consortium.
— *of bankers* : consortium bancaire.
underwriting — : syndicat de garantie.

system : a) système, régime ; b) réseau ; c) méthode (f) de travail.

NOTES

T

table: table (f).
  actuarial —(s): tables actuarielles.
  amortization (or redemption) — : tableau ou plan d'amortissement.
  — *of par values*: table des parités.
  to table *a bill*: [U.K.] déposer un projet de loi sur le bureau; [U.S.] ajourner indéfiniment un projet de loi.

to tabulate: classer (des informations).

tabulation: classement (m), dépouillement (m), présentation (f) des données, mise en tableau.

tacit: tacite (plus usité; *implicity, by implication*).

to tack: annexer.
  tacking: a) adjonction; b) annexe à une loi de finance.

tactical: tactique (a).
  — *decisions*: décisions de routine, tactiques.

tag: étiquette (f).
  licence —: vignette fiscale, timbre fiscal.
  — *end*: reliquat.

tail: [J] clause de substitution (voir *entail, estate*).

tainted: corrompu, infecté, souillé (a).
  — *heredity*: hérédité chargée.
  [J] — *with fraud*: entaché de dol.

to take: prendre.
  [J] — *an oath*: prêter serment.
  — *evidence*: recueillir des témoignages.
  — *advice*: consulter un avocat.
  — *proceedings*: poursuivre en justice.
  — *down*: inscrire au procès-verbal.
  [B] [F] — *a loss*: vendre à perte.
  — *a profit*: réaliser un bénéfice.
  — *delivery of stock*: prendre livraison des titres.
  — *firm*: prendre ferme.
  — *private*: privatiser.
  — *stock*: dresser l'inventaire.
  — *the rate*: reporter.
  — *in*: reporter.
  — *off*: enlever, supprimer, ôter, abolir, retirer.
  take off: envol, décollage, « démarrage » d'une économie, d'une industrie.
  — *on*: a) entreprendre, se charger de, aborder; b) embaucher, engager.
  — *on lease*: prendre à bail.
  — *out*: a) retirer; b) obtenir.
  — *out a policy*: contracter une assurance.
  — *over*: prendre en charge, se charger de, assumer, prendre la suite (d'un commerce, etc.).
  — *over an issue*: absorber une émission.
  — *over the business of a company*: prendre la suite des affaires d'une compagnie.
  — *up*: a) lever; b) honorer; c) entreprendre, s'occuper.
  — *up a bill*: honorer un effet.
  — *up a matter*: s'occuper d'une affaire.
  — *up an option*: lever une option.
  — *up stocks*: lever des titres.
  take-over *bid*: offre publique d'achat.
  — *price*: prix de reprise.
  — *companies' shares*: actions de sociétés en plein essor.

take-home money: salaire (m) net.

take-home pay: [U.S.] salaire net.

take-or-pay commitment: engagement (m) d'acheter ou sinon, de payer une certaine somme.

taker: a) preneur (m) (d'un bail par ex.); b) acheteur; c) [B] reporteur.
  [B] — *for a call of more*: donneur de faculté de lever double.
  — *for a put and call*: donneur de stellage.
  — *in*: reporteur.

taking: prix (m), capture (f).
  — *charge*: prise en charge.
  — *in currencies*: prise en report de devises.
  — *for an option*: vente d'une prime.
  — *on probation*: embaucher à l'essai.
  — *out*: relevé (m), prise (f).
  — *over*: a) réception (f), acceptation (f); b) reprise (f), rachat (m).
  — *over certificate*: certificat de prise en charge.
  — *up*: levée (f) (de documents, de titres, d'une prime...).
  — *up a rights issue*: certificat de prise en charge.

to tamper with: altérer, falsifier (un document), essayer d'influencer (des témoins).

tangible: tangible, palpable, sensible ; réel.
[J] – *ground of complaint* : grief réel.
– *personal property* : biens mobiliers corporels.
– *property* : biens corporels.
[C] – *assets* : valeurs matérielles, actif matériel, biens réels.

think tank : laboratoire (m) d'idées, groupe de réflexion.

to tap : percer, capter, puiser à ; mettre à contribution.
– *a new market* : exploiter, attaquer (un nouveau marché).
– *funds* : drainer des capitaux.
– *resources* : exploiter des ressources.

tape : bande (f) d'enregistrement (m) des cours.
« – *quotation* » : cotation télégraphiée.

to taper away (off) : diminuer, décroître, s'effriter, s'effacer.

tapering rate : taux (m), tarif (m) dégressif (a).

tapering vote : vote (m) à la proportionnelle inverse (ex. les actionnaires qui possèdent 100 actions disposent d'une voix pour 10 actions, ceux qui en possèdent de 100 à 1 000 disposent d'une voix pour 50 actions etc.).

tare : [C] tare (f), poids à vide (m).
average – : tare commune.
customary – : tare d'usage.
extra – : surtare.
real, actual – : tare réelle.
allowance for – : a) tarage ; b) la tare ; c) poids net (des voitures automobiles).
to ascertain, to allow for – : faire la tare.

target-date : [U.S.] date limite prévue pour la livraison du travail.

target market : marché (m) pris pour cible (f).

target price : prix (m) de référence (f).

target range : fourchette (f) des fluctuations de la masse monétaire.

tariff : tarif (m), barème (m).
[D] *customs (or trade* –) : tarif douanier.
lowering of – : dégrèvement du tarif.
full – : plein tarif.
General Agreements on –(s) *and Trade* : Accord général sur les tarifs douaniers et le commerce.
reduced – : tarif réduit.

revenue – : tarif fiscal.
– *schedule* : barème (de l'impôt).
– *walls* : barrières douanières.

task force : groupe de projet (groupe d'experts pluridisciplinaire assurant une mission ponctuelle).

tax : contribution (f), impôt (m), taxe (f).
[J] **to tax** *costs* : taxer les dépens d'un procès.
taxed *bill of costs* : mémoire taxé.
taxing *master* : juge taxateur.
taxpayer's *suit, action* : [U.S.] a) plainte en forfaiture contre un agent du fisc déposée par un contribuable ; b) action du même, en contestation du caractère constitutionnel d'un impôt.
[F] impôt (m), contribution (f), taxe (f).
addition to – (*es*) : supplément d'impôt.
additional – : impôt complémentaire.
(*general*) *additional* – : impôt général de superposition.
tax *acts* : législation fiscale.
– *adjustments* : redressements d'impôt.
– *administration* : administration fiscale.
ad valorem graduated – : droit progressif ad valorem.
– *adviser* : conseiller fiscal.
international – *agreement* : convention fiscale internationale.
– *allowance (or relief)* : [U.K.] dégrèvement fiscal.
alternative – : [U.S.] impôt optionnel frappant à un taux uniforme la totalité des plus-values à long terme, pouvant être choisi par le contribuable de préférence à l'imposition de ces plus-values au titre de l'impôt sur le revenu.
alternative capital gain – : [U.S.] impôt optionnel sur les plus-values de sociétés.
alternative minimum – (*AMT*) : [US] imposition forfaitaire minimale annuelle (se substituant à l'impôt de droit commun si celui-ci est inférieur) # I.F.A., imposition forfaitaire annuelle (des sociétés passibles de l'impôt sur les sociétés).
alternative simplified – : [U.S.] barème simplifié.
– *appeal* : procédure de recours.
« *apportioned* – » : impôt de répartition.
a – *is assessed...* : un impôt frappe...
assessed (or direct) – (*es*) : impôts directs.
assessment of – (*es*) : assiette de l'impôt.
method of – *assessment* : méthode d'évaluation de la matière imposable.
presumptive or empirical – *assessment* : imposition forfaitaire.
– *avoidance (or loophole)* : évasion fiscale.
illegal avoidance of – : fraude fiscale.
– *barriers* : barrières fiscales.
– *base, basis* : assiette de l'impôt.

— *bearer* : « contribuable de fait ».
Boards of — appeals : [U.S.] Conseil des appels fiscaux.
— *burden* : charge fiscale.
apportionment of — burdens : répartitions des charges fiscales.
business — : taxe professionnelle.
capital gains — : impôt sur les plus-values de capitaux.
capital stock — : [U.S.] impôt sur le capital actions.
— *on capital* : impôt sur le capital.
— *(reserve) certificates* : [U.K.] bons d'impôts.
chargeable to — : imposable, soumis à l'impôt.
— *claims* : créances fiscales.
« *coefficient — (es)* » : impôt de quotité.
tax-collecting *intermediary* : intermédiaire de perception.
collection of — (es) : recouvrement des impôts.
mutual assistance in the collection of — (es) : assistance réciproque en matière de recouvrement des impôts.
collector of — (es) : inspecteur du trésor.
— *consultant* : conseil fiscal.
— *convention* : convention fiscale.
— *(es) on conveyances* : taxes sur les mutations.
corporation — : impôt sur les sociétés.
advance corporation — : [U.K.] impôt anticipé sur les sociétés (système proche de l'avoir fiscal français).
— *credits* : déductions fiscales, crédits d'impôts.
underlying — credit : [UK] crédit afférent à l'impôt ayant frappé à l'étranger les produits versés à des sociétés britanniques.
to be entitled to a — credit : avoir droit à un crédit d'impôt.
credits against — (es) : [U.S.] déduction pour impôts payés.
foreign — credits : déductions pour impôts payés à l'étranger.
cumulating — (es) : impôt « en cascade » (cf. *series of superimposed taxes*).
death — : [U.S.] droits successoraux ou droits de succession.
death — jurisdiction : droit d'imposer des droits successoraux.
— *deduction* : dégrèvement, abattement.
delinquent — (es) : [U.S.] impôts non payés à temps.
distributive — (cf. apportioned —) : impôt de répartition.
— *(es) on dividends* : impôts sur les dividendes.
enforcement of — (es) : recouvrement des impôts.
estate — : droits de succession, [U.S.] impôt sur la fortune (mortis causa) (cf. *estate duty*).
additional estate — : [U.S.] taxe successorale complémentaire (impôt fédéral).
basic estate — : [U.S.] droits de succession de base (au profit de l'Etat fédéral).
estate — statute : [U.S.] loi fédérale sur les successions.
— *evasion (or escape)* : fraude fiscale.
exchange — (es) (on capital transfers) : taxes de change sur les transferts de capitaux.
Excise — Act : [U.S.] loi sur les impôts indirects.
— *exempt bonds* : [U.S.] obligations à intérêt non imposable.
— *exemption* : [U.S.] dégrèvement fiscal.
— *expenditures (S. Surrey)* : « dépenses fiscales », mesures (fiscales) dérogatoires à la norme.
— *experts* : experts en matière fiscale.
foreign — (es) : impôts étrangers.
— *form* : feuille de déclaration d'impôts.
free of — (es) : exempt d'impôt.
gift — : droits sur les donations.
global — (on the total income) : impôt général sur le revenu.
— *haven* : refuge fiscal.
head — : impôt sur la personne.
— *heaven* : paradis fiscal.
— *immunities* : immunités fiscales.
impersonal — : impôt réel.
imposition of the — : établissement de l'impôt.
— *incentives* : incitations fiscales.
incidence of the — : incidence de l'impôt.
income — : impôt sur le revenu.
income — return : déclaration de l'impôt sur le revenu.
— *on income from movable capital* : impôt sur le revenu des capitaux mobiliers.
corporation income — : [U.S.] impôt sur le revenu des personnes morales.
domination income — relief : [U.K.] réduction du taux de l'impôt (par suite de double imposition).
general income — : impôt général sur le revenu.
graduated income — : [U.K.] nouvelle dénomination de l'*income tax* (depuis 1974).
individual income — : [U.S.] impôt sur le revenu des personnes physiques.
income liable to — : revenu passible de l'impôt.
normal income — : [U.S.] impôt proportionnel sur le revenu.
organization income — (es) : agencement des impôts sur le revenu.
— *on income from transferable securities* : impôt sur le revenu des valeurs mobilières (France).
personal — on total income : impôt personnel sur le revenu global.
— *on the total income (superimposed on schedular — (es))* : impôt sur le revenu global (superposé aux impôts cédulaires).
indiciary global — (es) : impôts sur le revenu global, déterminé soit d'après les signes extérieurs ou d'après le train de vie.

indirect — *(es)* : impôts indirects.
inheritance — *(es)* : [U.S.] droits de mutation (droits des Etats, frappant les parts héréditaires).
inheritance — : [U.S.] taxe successorale (locale).
— *inspector* : inspecteur des impôts.
— *jurisdiction* : juridiction fiscale.
land — : impôt foncier, taxe foncière des propriétés non bâties.
— *law* : loi fiscale.
legacy — : [U.S.] taxe successorale (locale).
ordinary legal — : impôt de droit commun.
the — *is levied on...* : (tel...) est assujetti à l'impôt ; l'impôt est perçu sur...
bases of — *liability* : bases d'assujettissement à l'impôt.
impersonal — *liability* : assujettissement à l'impôt réel.
limited — *liability* : assujettissement limité, assujettissement réel.
personal — *liability* : assujettissement personnel à l'impôt.
total — *liability* : total des obligations en matière d'impôt.
unlimited — *liability* : assujettissement illimité, assujettissement personnel.
persons liable to — : personnes imposables.
— *lien* : opposition (f) du fisc, # privilège (m) du Trésor.
— *load* : [U.S.] montant de l'impôt.
local — *(es)* : impôts locaux.
luxury — : taxe sur les produits de luxe.
— *matters* : contributions publiques.
— *mitigations* : atténuation d'impôts.
notice for the — : avis, avertissement.
— *obligations which cannot be collected from assets* : obligations en matière d'impôt qu'on ne pourrait pas faire exécuter par prélèvement sur les avoirs.
to give rise to a — *obligation* : donner lieu à imposition.
occupational (licence and franchise) — : [U.S.] taxe professionnelle.
optional — *table* : [U.S.] barème à option pour déductions du revenu brut ajusté.
— *overlap* : chevauchement d'impôts.
crediting all of the — *paid* : accorder un dégrèvement total.
crediting a proportionate part of the — *paid* : accorder un dégrèvement partiel.
pay as you earn — : impôt retenu à la source.
— *payer* : contribuable.
individual — *paying* : capacité contributive individuelle.
payroll, employment — : impôt que l'employeur doit déduire du salaire.
— *overpayment of the* — : [U.S.] excédent de perception.
penal — : (voir *penalty*).
additional percentages to state — *(es)* : centimes additionnels aux impôts d'Etat.

personal — : impôt personnel.
— *(es) both personal and impersonal* : impôts à double base.
— *planning* : planification de l'investissement et des placements en fonction de la fiscalité.
— *point* : fait générateur.
— *policies* : politiques fiscales.
poll — *(or capitation)* : [U.S.] impôt de capitation.
— *practice* : technique des impôts.
— *and price index* : indice (m) des prix compte tenu de l'impôt.
international — *problems* : problèmes fiscaux internationaux.
proceeds from the — : produit de l'impôt.
production — : taxe à la production.
profit — : impôt sur les bénéfices.
— *on agricultural profits* : impôt sur les bénéfices agricoles.
— *on business profits* : impôt sur les bénéfices industriels et commerciaux.
excess profit — : [U.K.] impôt sur les bénéfices extraordinaires, impôt sur les bénéfices excessifs.
excess profits — : [U.S.] impôt sur les excédents de bénéfices.
declared value excess profits — : [U.S.] impôt sur les excédents de bénéfices, calculés d'après la valeur déclarée du capital social.
— *on profits from non-commercial occupations* : impôts sur les bénéfices de professions non commerciales (France).
undistributed profits — : impôt sur les bénéfices non distribués.
property — : impôt sur la fortune.
property — *on building and on land* : taxe foncière sur les propriétés bâties et non bâties (France).
general property — : impôt général sur la fortune, [U.K.] prélèvement général sur la fortune.
general property — *(es)* : [U.S.] impôts assis sur la fortune mobilière et immobilière.
— *on movable property* : taxe d'habitation (France).
personal property — : taxe mobilière (Belgique).
special property — *(es)* : [U.S.] impôts spéciaux sur la fortune, qui frappent les sociétés.
proportional — : taxe proportionnelle.
proportionate — : impôt proportionnel.
purchase — : [U.K.] impôt unique sur les ventes (avant l'application de la T.V.A.).
— *rate* : taux de l'impôt.
apportionment of the rate of — : méthode de la répartition ou de la subdivision de l'impôt.
ceiling or fixed — *rates* : taux « plafond » ou fixes de l'impôt.
flat rate of — : impôt à un taux uniforme.
graduated — *rate, rising in steps* : impôt progressif, par tranches (France).
— *is recoverable from the purchaser* : l'impôt

est récupérable sur l'acheteur.
– *reductions* : réductions d'impôt.
– *refund* : [U.S.] remboursement d'impôts versés.
regular – : [U.S.] impôt normal sur les revenus autres que ceux pouvant bénéficier de l'« *alternative tax* » (impôt optionnel).
sales – : impôt sur les ventes.
retail sales – : impôt sur les ventes au détail.
schedular – *(es)* : impôts cédulaires.
selective employment tax : [U.K.] impôt sélectif sur l'emploi (supprimé depuis 1973).
– *shares* : répartition des ressources fiscales.
– *shelters* : abris fiscaux.
shifting of the – : répercussion de l'impôt.
social security – *(es)* : contributions au titre de la sécurité sociale.
source – : impôt à la source.
– *sparing* : technique qui consiste à accorder à une société un crédit d'impôt fictif sur le montant des dividendes versés par une filiale établie dans un pays qui a réduit volontairement le taux de la retenue à la source.
special advance – : précompte mobilier.
– *subscription* : abonnement aux taxes.
succession – : [U.S.] taxe successorale locale (*State tax*).
– *suit* : contentieux fiscal.
superimposed or superposed – : impôt superposé ou de superposition.
series of superimposed – *(es)* : impôts « en cascade » (cf. *cumulating taxes*).
sur- – *ou super-* – : [U.K.] impôt complémentaire sur le revenu des personnes physiques (supprimé en 1974).
sur- – *on improper accumulations* : [U.S.] surtaxe sur les réserves abusives.
additional surtax : surtaxe additionnelle.
progressive surtax : surtaxe progressive.
– *on* – : impôt additionnel calculé en fonction de l'impôt payable.
tentative – : [U.S.] taxe provisoire.
tentative normal or sur- – : [U.S.] taxe fictive (servant d'élément de calcul).
principle of the territoriality of the – : principe de la territorialité de l'impôt.
trading – : taxe professionnelle (Belgique).
– *treaty* : convention fiscale.
– *treatment of foreigners* : traitement fiscal appliqué aux étrangers.
turnover – : impôt ou taxe sur le chiffre d'affaires.
value added – : taxe à la valeur ajoutée.
visitor's, non-resident – : taxe de séjour.
– *voucher* : attestation de paiement d'impôt sur dividendes (envoyée à un actionnaire par une société).
withholding tax : [U.K.] impôt retenu à la source.

taxability : facultés contributives.

taxable : imposable (a).

taxation : imposition (f).
[J] – *of costs* : taxation (f), taxe (f), des frais (d'un procès).
[C] a) imposition (de la propriété, etc.) ; b) charges fiscales, prélèvement fiscal.
the – *authorities* : l'administration fiscale, le fisc.
administrative – : imposition d'office.
arbitrary – : imposition arbitraire.
basis of – : assiette de l'impôt.
commensurate – : équivalence des charges fiscales.
– *of costs* : taxation des frais.
discriminatory – *of foreigners* : imposition discriminatoire des étrangers.
domicile – : imposition d'après le domicile.
double – : double imposition.
double – *agreements* : conventions relatives aux doubles impositions.
avoidance of double – : fait d'éviter la double imposition.
double – *of estates and successions* : double imposition des successions.
double – *of income* : double imposition des revenus.
highest scale of – : maximum de perception.
increase of –, *supplementary* – : surimposition.
oppressive double – : double imposition oppressive.
outright double – : double imposition manifeste.
specific double – *problem* : problèmes spécifiques de double imposition.
extraterritorial – *of foreigners* : imposition extraterritoriale des étrangers.
– *on actual income* : imposition sur le revenu effectif.
– *method or method of* – : mode d'imposition.
multiple – : imposition multiple.
– *by origin* : taxation d'après l'origine.
presumptive – : imposition forfaitaire.
regressive – : fiscalité régressive (les contribuables dont les revenus sont les plus bas paient proportionnellement plus d'impôts que ceux dont les revenus sont les plus élevés).
– *on returns* : imposition sur déclaration.
– *rights* : droits en matière d'imposition.
– *schedule* : tarif de l'impôt.
system of – : régime fiscal.

technical : professionnel, technique (a).
[J] de pure forme.
[J] – *assault* : quasi-agression.
– *difficulty* : question de procédure.
– *experience (or know-how)* expérience industrielle.
– *offence* : quasi-délit.
quashed on – *point* : cassé pour vice de procédure ou de forme.

— *training* : instruction (formation) technique.
— *words, words of art* : termes techniques (du droit, etc.).
technicality : technicité (f), caractère technique, détail (m), terme technique.
without entering into technicalities and details : sans entrer dans des considérations techniques et dans les détails.
technology *assessment* : évaluation des options technologiques.

telegraphic transfer : virement télégraphique.

telephone selling : vente (f) par téléphone.

teleprocessing : télétraitement (m).

teller : caissier de banque ; scrutateur.

« temp » : (fam.) personne employée à titre temporaire.

template : gabarit (m).

(the) temple : anciennement maison des templiers à Londres, aujourd'hui, nom donné à deux *Inns of Court*.

temporal lords : pairs laïques.

temporary : provisoire, temporaire, momentané (a).
— *appointment* : engagement à titre temporaire.
[D] *passed for — importation* : admis en franchise temporaire.
[F] — *rediscount* : pension (mise en pension de titres).

tenancy : droit du tenant, qu'il soit propriétaire, sous une forme ou sous une autre, ou simple locataire.
— *for life* : usufruit perpétuel.
— *for years* : usufruit à temps.
— *from year to year (landlord tenant relationship)* : location.

tenant : locataire (m et f), tenancier (m).
— *by the courtesy* : (voir : *Courtesy of England*).
Landlord and — Act : loi sur les loyers.
— *in Chief* : tenancier de terres données par le Roi.
— *in possession* : occupant.
—*('s),* **tenantable** *repairs* : réparations locatives.
— *('s) risks* : risques locatifs.
— *at will* : locataire qui ne tient son droit que de la volonté du loueur.
— *-farmer* : cultivateur à bail.

game- — : locataire d'une chasse.
— *-right* : droit d'un tenancier dans les districts agricoles de réclamer une part de bénéfices recueillis après l'expiration de son bail.
taxes payable by the — : impôt à la charge du locataire.

tendency : tendance (f), orientation (f).
[B] *downward* — : tendance à la baisse.
hardening — : tendance ferme.
to show an upward — : avoir une tendance à la hausse.
law of the **tendencial** *decrease of profits* : loi de la baisse tendancielle des profits.

tender : [J] offre réelle.
[J] **to tender** *an issue* : dans une plaidoirie ou des conclusions, faire ressortir l'importance décisive d'un point de fait.
to tender an oath to s.o. : déférer le serment à qn.
to tender back an oath, a decisive oath : référer un serment (décisoire).
[A] soumission (f), [U.K.] appel d'offres.
by — : par voie d'adjudication.
allocation to lowest **tenderer** : adjudication au plus bas soumissionnaire (au mieux-disant).
sealed — : soumission cachetée.
tendering *by private contract* : adjudication de gré à gré.
to invite —(s) *for a piece of work* : mettre un travail en adjudication.
[C] offre (f), devis.
to tender for sth. : soumissionner (pour qch.), faire une offre de vente.
[F] instrument de paiement.
legal, common — : cours légal, monnaie libératoire.
— *offer bid (T.O.B.)* : Offre publique d'achat (O.P.A.).
treasury bill — *system* : mode de soumission pour les bons du trésor.

tenement : maison (f), sp. un immeuble locatif.
[J] chose qui fait l'objet d'une tenure, c'est-à-dire une terre (voir : *tenure*).

tenor : teneur (f) (d'un acte, etc.).
[J] copie, ou citation conforme.
[C] teneur, terme d'une lettre de change (selon l'échéance).

tentative : expérimental (a).
— *draft* : avant-projet.
— *offer* : offre faite pour entamer les négociations, ouverture.
to make a — *offer* : faire une ouverture.
— *tax* : [U.S.] taxe provisoire.

tenure : (hist.) tenure (féodale).
[J] période de jouissance ou d'occupation.
[A] *− of office* : a) stabilité d'emploi dans le cadre de la fonction publique ; b) période d'occupation d'un office ou d'un emploi.
communal − : jouissance en commun (d'un bien).
stability of − : a) bail assuré ; b) stabilité d'un emploi.
system of land − : régime foncier.

term : terme (m), fin (f), limite (f), période (f), expression (f).
banishment for a − of years : bannissement à temps.
− of copyright : délai de protection littéraire.
− of an estate : durée d'un usufruit.
« *keeping −* » : obligation de dîner dans le hall d'un *Inn of Court* (voir ce terme) le nombre requis de fois au cours des études pour l'admission au barreau.
− of lease, contract : durée d'un bail, contrat.
legal − : a) terme de droit, de pratique ; b) terme de droit (en tant qu'opposé au terme de grâce : *to serve his (legal) term*).
− of limitation : délai de prescription.
− of notice : délai de congé.
−(s) of reference : mandat, attributions, (N.Y.).
special − : audience des référés.
to come to −(s) : arriver à un accommodement (m).
[A] *− of office* : durée des fonctions.
[C] conditions (f pl), clauses (f pl), teneur (f) d'un contrat, prix (m).
full −(s) : totalité des conditions.
his −(s) are very high : ses prix sont très élevés.
on easy −(s) : pour un prix raisonnable, avec facilités de paiement.
on −(s) : à tempérament.
on −(s) and conditions : selon les modalités.
« *−(s) inclusive* » : « tout compris ».
−('s) rent : loyer d'un terme.
−(s) of payment : délai de paiement, conditions de paiement.
− of sale : conditions de vente.
−(s) of trade : termes de l'échange international.
gross barter −(s) of trade : termes de l'échange bruts.
net −(s) of trade : termes de l'échange nets.
[F] *long − funded capital* : capital consolidé à long terme.
−(s) of an issue : conditions d'une émission.
−(s) and conditions of an issue : modalités d'une émission.
− loan : (surtout U.S.) prêt à terme remboursable par mensualités.
short- −, long- − movements (of capital) : mouvements à courte, longue amplitude.
[B] *long- −, short- − transactions* : opérations à long, court terme.
[ASS] *− insurance* : assurance sur la vie, sans valeur de rachat, à forfait.
− policy : police d'assurance temporaire.
to keep one's −(s) (in universities) : prendre ses inscriptions.
−(s) under which a ship is chartered : conditions de l'affrètement.

terminable : [J] résiliable, résoluble (contrat) (a).
[F] *terminable annuity* : rente à terme, rente temporaire, annuité terminable.
− bond : obligation rachetable.

terminal : situé à l'extrémité.
[F] (terminal), terme livrable (a).
− market : marché à terme.
by − payments : par versements trimestriels.
− price : cours du livrable.

termination : terminaison (f), fin (f), cessation (f).
[J] extinction (f), résolution (f), résiliation (f).
notice of − : congé (m).
to terminate : terminer ; mettre fin ; délimiter (une région).
[J] dénoncer, résoudre, résilier (un contrat).
[ASS] *to terminate a policy* : résilier une police.

terminus a quo : point de départ.

terminus ad quem : point d'arrivée (final).

termor : [J] possesseur à terme ou en viager.

terrier : [J] registre foncier.

territory : territoire.
non-self governing **territories** : (O.N.U.) territoires non autonomes (sous tutelle).
territorial *limits of jurisdiction* : principe fondamental du droit A.A. selon lequel la justice coercitive, même lorsqu'il s'agit d'un national, ne peut s'exercer qu'à l'égard d'infractions commises à l'intérieur du pays, à l'exception (Engl.) de l'homicide et de la trahison.
territorial waters : eaux territoriales.

ter-tenant : [J] possesseur effectif d'un bien-fonds.

tertiary industrial activity : secteur (m) tertiaire (a).

test : épreuve (f), essai (m), examen (m), test (m).
[J] *− -case* : cas dont la solution fait jurisprudence.

to test: a) viser un document, (Scot) tester, faire son testament ; b) éprouver, mettre à l'essai.
testing *plant*: laboratoire d'essai.
achievement — : test de connaissance.
aptitude — : test d'aptitude.
attitude — : test affectif.
performance — : test d'intelligence pratique.
trade — : test professionnel.
[C] — *marketing*: technique (f) de commercialisation (f) par tests.
— *product*: produit à l'essai.

testacy: le fait de mourir en laissant un testament.

testament: [J] testament portant sur des biens mobiliers.
testamentary *capacity*: capacité de disposer par testament.
testamentary disposition: clause testamentaire.
to die **testate**: mourir en laissant un testament.
testator, testatrix: testateur, testatrice (voir *will*).
to testify: attester.

testator, testatrix: testateur (-trice).

testimony: témoignage.
[J] déposition d'un témoin, attestation.
to produce — *of, to a statement*: apporter des preuves testimoniales à l'appui d'une affirmation.
testimonial: attestation (f), certificat (m).
utterances used **testimonially**: déclarations extrajudiciaires faisant l'objet d'une enquête en vue de déterminer l'exactitude des dépositions faites en justice ; en elles-mêmes ; elles relèvent du *hearsay rule* (voir *hearsay*).

text: texte (m).
— *-book*: manuel (m).
— *-hand*: grosse (f).

thanks *(received with)*: « pour acquit ».

theft: vol (m) (voir *larceny*).
aggravated — : vol qualifié.
petty — : vol minime.
[ASS] — *risk*: risque de vol.

theory: théorie (f), thèse (f), hypothèse (f).
— *of games*: théorie des jeux de situation.
[J] *the* — *of the case*: la base juridique du procès.

there: là, y (adv).
there and then: séance tenante.
thereafter: après cela, par la suite.
thereby: de cette façon, de ce fait.
therefrom: de là, de cela, de ceci, « en ».

therein: là-dedans, sur ce point.
thereinafter: plus loin, plus bas, ci-dessous, ci-après.
thereof: dudit, de la dite.
theretofore: jusqu'alors, avant cela.
thereinunder: plus bas, ci-dessous, ci-après.
thereunto: y.
thereupon: là-dessus, ci-dessus, plus haut.

thin: mince, ténu, faible ; rare ; léger, transparent (a).
— *argument*: argument peu convaincant.
— *market*: marché étroit.

thing: affaire (f), chose (f), objet (m), article (m).
expensive —(s) : articles coûteux.
[J] —(s) *personal*: biens mobiliers.
—(s) *real*: biens immobiliers.

third: troisième (a).
[J] — *party, person*: tiers, tierce personne.
— *party beneficiary contract*: contrat au bénéfice d'une tierce personne.
The — *Estate*: le Tiers Etat.
— *degree*: « passage à tabac » (par la police).
— *holder*: tiers détenteur.
— *party order*: [U.S.] saisie-arrêt (voir *garnishment*).
[ASS] — *party accident insurance*: assurance accidents aux tiers.
— *party insurance*: assurance de responsabilité civile.

thorough: complet, absolu ; achevé ; approfondi (a).
— *enquiry*: enquête approfondie.
— *measures*: mesures radicales.

those whom it may concern: qui de droit.

thread: ligne imaginaire au milieu d'un cours d'eau, constituant la frontière entre les terrains riverains.

threats: menaces (f pl).
[J] intimidation.
threatening *language*: menaces verbales.
threatening letter: lettre comminatoire (voir *intimidation*).

three: trois (a).
— *-cornered elections*: élections triangulaires.
— *-course rotation*: assolement triennal.
— *-shift system*: système des trois équipes de huit heures.

threshold: seuil (m).
adjustment — : seuil d'ajustement.
— *agreement*: accord sur un seuil de salaires minimum.

probability — : seuil de probabilité.
significance — : seuil critique.
tax — : seuil d'exonération.
upsetting (or breaking up) — : seuil de rupture.

thrifty : a) économe ; b) [U.S.] prospère, florissant (a).

through : direct, ouvert, dégagé, libre.
[E] — *bill of lading* : connaissement direct, à forfait.
— *freight* : fret à forfait.
— *rates* : taux forfaitaires.
— *traffic* : trafic en transit.
throughout *the period* : pendant toute la période.
throughput : (néologisme formé de « through » : « de bout en bout » et « output » : « production ») production maximale.

to throw : rejeter, faire retomber la faute sur qn.
— *an amendment* : rejeter un amendement.
— *up* : renoncer, abandonner.

throwback income : revenu (m) réintégré (a).

thruster : (fam.) fonceur (m).

thruway : [U.S.] autoroute.

thumb : pouce (m).
by rule of — : d'une façon empirique.
— *print* : empreinte digitale.

tick : écart (m) maximum des cours du marché.

to tick off : pointer.

ticker : téléimprimante (f), téléscripteur (m).

ticket : billet (m), ticket (m), contravention (f).
[J] — *of leave* : [U.K.] mise en liberté provisoire d'un condamné par le ministre de l'Intérieur pour une période et à des conditions déterminées.
[U.S.] liste des candidats d'un parti aux élections.
[B] fiche (f).
— *day* : veille de la liquidation.
[F] *banker's* — : compte (m) de retour.

tickler : échéancier.
[F] *discount* — : échéancier des billets (escomptés ou recevables).
maturity — : échéancier des billets (payables ou acceptés).

tide : marée.
— *power (or tidal)* : énergie marémotrice.

tie : lien (m), attache (f).
[J] *marital* — : lien conjugal.
tie-in : [U.S.] conditionnel.
tie-up : a) entente, accord ; b) [U.S.] arrêt de travail.
to tie up : bloquer, immobiliser.
[C] **tied** *house* : débit de boissons astreint par bail à vendre la bière d'une certaine brasserie.
tied sales : ventes exclusives.
[F] *tied aid* : aide liée.
tied loan : emprunt à emploi spécifique.
tied orders : ordres liés (en bourse).
tied-up capital : capital immobilisé, immobilisations.

tier : étage (m).
[F] *currency two* — *market* : double marché des changes.
gold two — *market* : double marché de l'or.

tight : a) étanche, hermétique ; b) [F] serré, rare (argent) (a).
— *market* : marché serré, étroit.
— *money policy* : politique de resserrement de crédit, d'austérité monétaire.
— *supplies* : approvisionnements insuffisants.
to tighten *the budgetary policy* : pratiquer une politique de rigueur budgétaire.
to tighten the credit reins : freiner, mettre en frein (a) à l'expansion du crédit, de la masse monétaire.
tightening *(or raising) of reserve requirements* : relèvement des obligations de réserves (des banques).
tightness *of money* : rareté de l'argent.

till : tiroir-caisse (m).
— *money* : encaisse (disponibilités en monnaie métallique ou fiduciaire).

timber : tout bois de construction ; les arbres comme tenant au sol sont des biens immobiliers.
— *claim* : concession forestière.

time : temps (m).
[J] la date des actes judiciaires et légaux se réfère toujours au premier moment du jour désigné, les actes des parties doivent porter la mention de l'heure du jour à partir de laquelle ils sont valables.
period of — : délai.
— *limit* : délai, dernier délai, durée (d'un privilège, etc.).
— *of limitation* : péremption (d'instance), prescription.
to do — : faire de la prison.
[C] — *-bill* : échéance à terme.
— *-charter* : contrat d'affrètement maritime conclu pour une période déterminée.
— *off with pay* : paiement des heures d'ab-

sence (par ex. pour activités syndicales).
– *-limit date* : échéance.
– *sales* : ventes à crédit.
– *-table* : horaire, emploi du temps.
– *-work* : travail à l'heure.
full- – *salary* : salaire de plein emploi.
part- – *salary* : salaire d'emploi partiel.
– *-money* : prêts à terme.
– *tax deemed to have been paid* : date où l'impôt est censé avoir été payé.
[B] – *adjusted methods* : méthodes basées sur l'actualisation.
– *adjusted rate of return method* : méthode du taux interne de rentabilité.
– *bargain* : vente à découvert, marché à terme.
– *disparity problem* : problème de la différenciation des durées d'utilisation des montants investis.
– *interest earned* : coefficient de couverture de l'intérêt.
[ASS] – *policy* : police à terme, à forfait.
– *pattern* : modèle de revenus, profil de survenance des recettes dans le temps.
– *premium* : prime au temps.
– *rate* : rémunération à l'heure.
– *risk* : risque à terme.
– *sharing* : temps partagé (exploitation d'un ordinateur).

timeliness : opportunité.
the – *of a measure* : l'opportunité d'une mesure.

timing : échéancier (m), calendrier (m).

tin : étain (m), fer-blanc (m).
[J] – *-pot lawyer* : [U.S.] avocat de second ordre.
[F] – *shares* : valeurs d'étain, valeurs stannifères.

tip : a) pourboire (m), gratification (f), cadeau (m); b) « tuyau » (m), renseignement (m).

tip-in : encart (m).

tipstaff : [J] huissier-audiencier.

title : titre (m).
[J] a) droit de propriété ; b) appellation officielle ou titre nobiliaire ; c) description ou intitulé d'une action.
absolute – : titre de propriété inscrit au registre foncier, garanti par l'Etat.
abstract of – : document constatant l'origine de la propriété.
covenants for – : stipulations accompagnant l'acte de vente d'un bien-fonds.
clear, good – : titre incontestable.
cloud on – : incertitude apparente quant à la plénitude du droit de propriété.

confirmative – : titre recognitif.
full, short – : intitulé complet, abrégé (d'un acte).
– *insurance* : voir *insurance*.
putative – : titre putatif.
to quiet – : action négatoire.
– *search* : relevé d'hypothèques.
warranty of – : attestation du titre.
– *-deed* : titre constitutif de propriété.
[A] [F] *documentary* – : titre documentaire.

toadskins : [U.S.] billets de banque.

tobacconist : débitant (m) de tabac.
– *('s) shop* : bureau de tabac (France).

toft : [J] a) emplacement d'une maison tombée en ruine ; b) petite ferme.

token : symbolique, nominal, fictif (a), bon (m) d'achat.
– *money* : monnaie fictive, monnaie fiduciaire.
– *salary* : salaire nominal.
– *strike* : grève symbolique.

toll : péage (m).
[A] *miller's* – : droit de mouture.
road – : droit de passage.
the – *of the roads* : la mortalité sur les routes.
– *through* : droit de passage prélevé par une municipalité.
– *traverse* : droit de passage sur un terrain privé.
town – : droit d'octroi.
to toll : tinter, sonner (une cloche).
[J] *to toll the Statutes of limitation* : interrompre la prescription (se dit aussi *suspension of the Statutes*, etc.).

ton : tonne (f), tonneau (m), (jauge des navires).

tone : ton (m), tendance (f), physionomie (f), orientation (f).
[B] – *of the market* : tenue du marché.

tontine : tontine (f).

tool : outil (m), instrument (m).
[J] – *of trade* : instrument de travail, échappant à la saisie.
to tool up : [U.S.] équiper (une entreprise).

top : haut (m), partie (f) supérieure, sommet (m).
– *executive* : grand directeur.
– *-heavy price* : cours trop élevé.
– *price* : cours le plus haut.
– *secret* : ultra-secret (intéressant la défense nationale).

— *securities*: valeurs de premier ordre.

topic: a) sujet (m), thème (m) de discussion ; b) questions (f pl) d'actualités.

tort: préjudice (m), tort (m) (fait à qn).

tort: c'est une définition de l'O.N.U. qui semble le mieux répondre aux besoins de la traduction en présentant le tort comme un « acte dommageable extra-contractuel, entraînant la responsabilité civile de l'auteur ; répond aux « délits et quasi-délits » du droit civil français.
    tortfeasor: auteur d'un tort.
    joint tortfeasors: co-délinquants, co-auteurs d'un *« tort »*. Ils sont conjointement et solidairement responsables.
    tortious act: action préjudiciable à qn (sous-entendu : délictueuse).

torture: torture (f).

tory: tory, membre du parti conservateur.

total: total (a et m).
    [F] — *account*: compte collectif.
    — *assets*: avoir total, total de l'actif.
    — *claims*: total des dettes.
    — *cost*: coût total.
    — *receipts*: recette totale.
    [ASS] — *loss*: perte totale (d'un navire).

totalitarian: totalitaire (a).
    — *government*: régime totalitaire.

totidem verbis: en autant de mots.

toties quoties: autant de fois que ce sera nécessaire.

to touch: toucher.
    — *off*: déclencher.

tourist: touriste (m).
    — *agency*: agence de voyages.
    — *bureau*: office de tourisme.

tout, touter: a) rabatteur d'affaire, « racoleur » ; b) placier, démarcheur (m).

towage: remorquage (m), droit de remorquage.

town: ville, cité, [C] place.
    township: commune, [U.S.] subdivision cadastrale d'un comté (6 milles carrés).
    townlet: bourgade.
    town-clerk: secrétaire de mairie.
    corporate — : municipalité.
    — *cheque*: chèque sur place.
    — *-council*: conseil municipal.

— *-dues*: octroi.
— *-hall*: hôtel de ville.
— *-planning*: urbanisme.

trace: [B] filière (f).
to trace: a) calquer ; b) retrouver trace de.

track: piste (f), voie (f).
    — *record*: historique (m) d'une entreprise.
    trackage: a) halage ; b) frais de halage ; c) [U.S.] réseau ferré.
    trackage price: prix avant chargement (sur wagon).

trade: commerce (m), trafic (m), négoce (m), branche (f) de commerce ; métier manuel, emploi (m).
    [J] *trade fixtures*: objets mobiliers, installés en vue d'exercer un métier, un commerce ou une industrie. Leur qualification comme meubles à fixe demeure que le locataire n'a plus le droit d'enlever, dépend essentiellement de l'objet et des buts de leur installation.
    trade-mark: marque (f) de fabrique, estampille (f).
    registered trade-mark: marque déposée.
    [C] — *allowance*: remise (f), escompte (m).
    — *balance*: balance commerciale.
    — *barrier*: entrave au commerce international.
    — *bills*: effets de commerce.
    — *Board*: [U.K.] ministère des Affaires économiques, [U.S.] chambre de commerce.
    coasting — : cabotage.
    carrying — : long cours.
    — *contracts (or agreements)*: contrats commerciaux.
    — *creditors*: fournisseurs.
    — *cycle*: cycle du commerce.
    — *disease*: maladie professionnelle.
    — *diversion effect*: effet de détournement (dans les unions douanières).
    domestic — : commerce intérieur.
    — *expenses*: frais de bureau.
    foreign — : commerce extérieur.
    — *gap*: déséquilibre commercial.
    — *in*: reprise (f) (des affaires).
    — *mart*: expomarché.
    — *name*: nom commercial, raison commerciale.
    — *profit*: bénéfice d'exploitation.
    this month's — : le chiffre d'affaires de ce mois.
    — *reference*: références commerciales.
    restraint of — : voir : *restraint*.
    retail — : commerce de détail.
    — *show*: salons, congrès, exposition interprofessionnelle.
    — *sign*: enseigne (f).
    — *tariff*: tarif douanier.
    — *union*: syndicat ouvrier.

— *value*: valeur vénale.
to be in the publishing — : s'occuper de publicité.
to drive a good — : faire de bonnes affaires.
by way of — : commercialement.
— *weighted index*: indice de la valeur moyenne d'une monnaie par rapport à un panier d'autres devises.
wholesale — : commerce en gros.
to trade: faire le commerce de, trafiquer.
to — — : négocier des actions.
to trade in (e.g. a car): donner en reprise (ex. une auto).

trader: a) commerçant (m), négociant (m), trafiquant (m); b) navire (m) marchand; c) contractant (m).
  tradesman: marchand (m), fournisseur (m), (U.S. et Scot.) artisan (m).

trading: commercial, commerçant, marchand (a).
— *account*: compte d'exploitation.
— *assets*: actif engagé.
— *capital*: capital de roulement.
— *company*: société commerciale.
— *concern*: entreprise commerciale.
— *floor*: parquet (de la bourse).
— *in*: vente (de qqch) en reprise.
— *loss, profit*: perte (f) brute, profit brut.
— *on equity*: see « gearing », « leverage ».
— *partnership*: société en nom collectif.
— *results*: résultats de l'exercice.
— *session*: séance de bourse.
— *square*: section de parquet (de la bourse).
— *stamp*: timbre prime.
stock — : opérations boursières.
— *year*: exercice financier.

tradition: tradition (f).
[J] voir *delivery*.

traffic: trafic (m) (commerce ou transports) terme plutôt péjoratif lorsqu'il s'agit de commerce, p. ex. :
a) — *in arms, in drugs*: trafic (illicite) d'armes, de stupéfiants.
b) — *in votes*: trafic d'influence, manigances électorales.
c) *white slave* — : traite des blanches.
to traffic: trafiquer, commercer, négocier.
to traffic in benefices: simonie.
— *accident*: accident de circulation.
road — : roulage.
— *regulations*: police de la voirie.
(navigation) near, far — : petit, grand cabotage.
ocean — : navigation au long cours.
currency **trafficker**: trafiquant en devises.

train: train (m), convoyeur (m).
[D] *train customs officer*: douanier convoyeur.

trainee: collaborateur temporaire (m), [U.S.] stagiaire (m).
  traineeship: [U.S.] stage.

training: instruction (f), formation (f).
advance, further — : formation continue.
on-the-job — : formation pratique, « sur le tas ».
off-the-job — : formation pendant les heures de travail.
selection and — *of staff*: choix et formation du personnel.
— *department*: service de formation du personnel.
— *within industry (T.W.I.)*: [U.S.] formation accélérée dans l'entreprise.
vocational — : formation professionnelle.

traitor: traître (m) (voir *treason*).

tramp: chemineau, « clochard ».
[C] cargo en cueillette.
  tramping: transport maritime à la demande.

tranche *(e.g. a new issue of stock, the first tranche of which...)*: [B] tranche (f) (une nouvelle émission d'actions, dont la première tranche...).

to transact: négocier, traiter, conclure.
— *business*: faire des affaires.

transaction: transaction (f), gestion (f), conduite (f) d'une affaire, délibération (f) d'une assemblée.
[J] compromis (m), arrangement (m) (mais plutôt *composition, adjustment*), mouvement (m).
[F] *cash* — *(s)*: mouvements d'espèces.
— *(s) in securities*: mouvements de valeurs.
[B] opérations (f).
— *balance*: solde de transaction.
cash — : marché au comptant.
— *for forward delivery*: opération à terme.
— *(s) in securities*: opérations sur les valeurs.
— *on credit*: transaction à terme.

to transcribe: transcrire.

transcript: copie (f), transcription (f).
[J] copie conforme d'un acte judiciaire ; b) transcription en clair d'un sténogramme d'une audience.

transfer: transfert (m).
[J] *(of estate) (of property) (of a right)*: mutation (f), translation (f), transmission (f), transport (m), transfert (m), transmission (f).
— *of a case to another court*: renvoi (m) d'une affaire devant un autre tribunal.
— *by death*: mutation après décès.
— *of a debt*: cession, revirement d'une

créance.
deed of – : acte translatif de propriété.
– *duty, tax*: droit de mutation entre vifs.
transferable *property*: biens cessibles.
transferable right: droit communicable transférable.
[A] – *of personnel*: mutation (f) de personnel.
[C] *(of an entry)*: contre-passation (f).
(of an amount from one account to another): ristourne (f), transport (m).
– *entry*: article de contre-passement.
– *payments*: déplacement des coûts d'un service à un autre.
[F] virement (m).
bank – : virement bancaire.
– *expenditures*: dépenses de transfert.
financial – *(s)*: transferts financiers.
– *payments*: transferts sociaux (couverts par des fonds d'Etat).
transferable securities: valeurs mobilières.
transferable share: action au porteur.
to transfer *home the profits*: rapatrier les profits.
to transfer to reserve: virer à la réserve.
– *form*: [B] (feuille de) transfert, formule de transfert.
– *of shares*: assignation, transfert d'actions.
transferee: cessionnaire.
transferor: cédant, *(of a bill)* endosseur.

to transgress: transgresser.
– *a law*: enfreindre, violer une loi.
– *one's competence*: outrepasser ses attributions.

transhipment: transbordement (m), transfert (m).
– *bond*: acquit-à-caution.
– *bond note*: transfert douanier.

transire: laissez-passer (m).
[D] passavant (m), passe-debout (m), acquit-à-caution (m) (aussi : *transit-bill*).

transit: a) transit, passage ; b) route, trajet.
[D] *in* – : en transit.
damaged in – : endommagé en cours de route.
– *duty*: droit de transit.
– *entry*: déclaration de transit.
[D] – *-bill*: passavant (m).
– *-duty*: droit de transit.
[ASS] *damage in* – : avarie(s) (f) en cours de route.
– *pass*: acquit de transit.

transitad: [U.S.] publicité sur autobus.

transitory: passager, transitoire, fugitif (a).
[J] – *action*: voir « *action at law* ».
[C] – *items*: articles d'ordre.

to translate: traduire, [F] convertir des capitaux à l'étranger.

translation: conversion (f).
foreign currency – : conversion d'une monnaie étrangère en une autre.

transmission: transmission (f).
[J] – *on death*: mutation par décès.

transmutation: mutation.

transportation: [U.S.] transportation (f), transport (m) (de marchandises, etc.).

transporter: entrepreneur (m) de transports.

travel: voyage (m).
business – : voyage d'affaires.
– *requisites*: articles de voyage.
traveller's *cheques*: chèques de voyage.
travelling *expenses allowance*: allocations de déplacement.
travelling *salesman and representative*: voyageur, représentant, placier (V.R.P.).

treachery: traîtrise (f).

treason: trahison (f).
– *-felony*: [U.K.] attentat à la sûreté de l'Etat.

treasure-trove: découverte (f) de trésor.
[J] invention (f).

treasury: trésor (m).
[A] [U.K.] ministère des Finances.
First Lord of the – : en général le Premier Ministre (*the Chancellor of the Exchequer* est le ministre des Finances proprement dit).
[U.S.] – *Department*: ministère des Finances.
Secretary of the – : ministre des Finances.
[F] – *bill*: bon du trésor, effet public (à court terme).
– *note*: bon du trésor à moyen terme.
– *bond*: bon du trésor à long terme.
– *('s) bill cover (or floor)*: plancher d'effets publics (applicable aux banques françaises jusqu'en 1967).

treatment: traitement (m).
most-favoured nation – : traitement de la nation la plus favorisée.
treating: traiter, payer des tournées.

treaty: a) traité (m), pacte (m), convention (f), accord (m), contrat (m) ; b) (pl.) négociations (f pl) pourparlers (m pl).
[F] – *shopping*: abus des traités, utilisation abusive des traités (spécialement dans le

cadre des conventions fiscales), chalandage fiscal.
tax **treaties** : conventions fiscales.

trend : tendance (f), orientation (f), allure (f), mouvement (m), climat (m), conjoncture (f).
— *line* : graphique (m) des tendances.
quick turn of the market — : renversement rapide de la tendance du marché.
underlying — : tendance profonde.

tresspass : transgression (f), contravention (f).
[J] infraction à la loi, du caractère d'un *tort*, portant atteinte à des droits privés et donnant lieu à des dommages-intérêts. Dans le sens usuel : intrusion illicite sur le fonds d'autrui.
action for — : demande de dommages-intérêts pour trouble de jouissance.
— *to land* : violation de propriété.
tresspasser : a) violateur des droits d'autrui ; b) intrus.
« *Tresspassers will be prosecuted* » : « défense d'entrer sous peine d'amende », « propriété privée ».

tret : [C] réfaction (f).

trial : essai (m), épreuve (f).
on — : à l'essai.
[J] a) jugement (m) ; b) procès (m), notamment la procédure qui s'avère nécessaire, au civil, lorsqu'il y a lieu de déterminer des points de fait (« *if the pleadings resulted in an issue of fact* »), au criminel, lorsque l'accusé se déclare non coupable (« *pleads not guilty* »). Dans ce cas, c'est aux « *triers of the facts* », jury ou juge unique, selon le cas, à décider, après avoir entendu les avocats des parties et assisté à l'interrogatoire contradictoire *(cross-examination)*.
awaiting — : en instance de jugement.
civil — : action civile.
committal for — : mise en accusation.
criminal — : procès criminel.
— *court* : tribunal de première instance.
— *by court-martial* : renvoi devant le conseil de guerre.
famous — *(s)* : causes célèbres.
held for — : inculpé, prévenu.
— *judge* : juge du fond.
— *by jury* : renvoi devant les assises, jugement par jury (voir *mistrial*).
[F] — *balance* : balance de vérification, balance d'ordre.
— *balance after closing* : balance d'inventaire.

tribunal : tribunal (m), cour (f) de justice.
may it please the — : plaise à la cour.
to lodge with the — : porter devant le tribunal.
[F] *lands* — : [UK] tribunal fiscal foncier (pour les litiges relatifs aux impôts locaux).

tribute : tribut (m), hommage (m).

trick : ruse (f), artifice (m), stratagème (m).

trier : celui qui essaie.
[J] — *(s) of the case, of the facts* : a) juge et jurés ; b) arbitre(s) chargé(s) d'apprécier le bien-fondé des récusations des jurés.

to trigger (off) : déclencher.
[J] **trigger** *clauses* : [F] clauses sans échappatoire (assortissant les concours supplémentaires du F.M.I. après épuisement des droits de tirage normaux).
trigger price : prix d'intervention, prix plancher.

triplicate : triplicata (m).
[C] troisième de change.

trouble : peine (f), souci (m), dérangement (m).
labour — *(s)* : conflits sociaux.

truck : troc, échange [U.S. : *swap*].
[J] [U.K.] Truck Acts (1831, 1887, 1896, 1940) lois interdisant le paiement des ouvriers en nature.

true : vrai, exact (a).
— *bill* : voir *indictment*.
— *copy* : copie conforme.
certified — *copy* : pour copie conforme.
— *justice* : justice idéale, décision parfaitement juste.
in — *order* : réglementairement.
— *owner* : propriétaire légitime.
plea of **truth** : offre de justifier des allégations prétendues diffamatoires (voir *justification*).

to trump up : faire hausser, forcer (les prix).
[J] — *a charge* : forger une accusation, déposer une fausse plainte.

trust : garde (f), dépôt (m).
[O.N.U.] tutelle.
[J] fidéicommis (m) fiducie (f). En droit anglo-saxon, relation ou association entre une ou plusieurs personnes d'une part et une ou plusieurs personnes d'autre part, fondées sur la confiance, en vertu desquelles des biens sont assignés à la première ou aux premières au nom et au bénéfice de la seconde ou des secondes. Le détenteur des biens est le *trustee* (fidéicommissaire) et le bénéficiaire *(beneficial owner)* est « *cestui que trust* ». Le premier a un droit in rem sur les biens, le second simplement un droit in personam à l'égard du *trustee*.
charitable, public — : trust créé dans un but philanthropique.
complex — : trust constitué à cause de mort

(avec accumulation et distribution périodique des revenus).
constructive — : (Eq.) fiction imposant l'obligation de restituer en cas d'enrichissement sans cause.
— *corporation (Public Trustee)* : fidéicommissariat officiel, exerçant des fonctions d'administrateur judiciaire, de tuteur, de curateur aux successions, de syndic, etc., dans des cas déterminés ainsi que celles d'une caisse des dépôts et consignations.
— *deed* : acte fiduciaire.
family — : fondation privée.
holder on — : dépositaire (des valeurs de qn).
— *instrument* : instrument créateur d'un trust.
intervivos — : trust constitué entre vifs.
simple — : trust constitué à cause de mort (avec distribution des revenus au fur et à mesure de leur réalisation).
testamentary — : trust constitué à cause de mort.
trustee *in bankruptcy* : syndic de faillite.
judicial trustee : trustee datif.

[C] a) crédit ; b) trust, cartel (voir *monopoly*).
Anti- — *Act* : loi interdisant les coalitions économiques.
loan on — : prêt d'honneur.
to supply goods on — : fournir des marchandises à crédit.
board of trustees : conseil d'administration.
— *territory* : (pol.) territoire sous tutelle.
[U.S.] — *company* : société de gestion de portefeuille.
employee — : fonds de prévoyance d'entreprise.
investment — *(s)* : société d'investissements, trust de placement.
no load investment — : société d'investissement « entrée libre » (aucun droit d'entrée n'est exigé des nouveaux investisseurs).
trustee savings-banks : caisses d'épargne.
trustee stocks : [U.S.] valeurs de tout repos.
unit investments — *(s)* : sociétés qui constituent des fonds de trust ordinaires.
trustification : [U.S.] formation d'un trust.
vertical trustification : intégration.
to trustify : réunir un trust, intégrer.
trustworthy *firm* : maison de confiance.

to try : essayer, éprouver, expérimenter.
[J] — *(a case)* : juger, mettre en jugement.
counts not tried : chefs d'accusation non instruits.
— *an issue* : instruire un procès.
— *whether* : vérifier si.

to tumble : [F] dégringoler, s'écrouler.

tune : cadence (f).
tune-up *(or break-up or start-up) period* : période de mise au point, de démarrage (des installations d'une entreprise).
[F] *fine* **tuning** *policy* : politique de régulation affinée (recherche d'un équilibre économique par approximations successives).
tuning in effet : effet de résonance (en matière d'amplification de hausses de prix par exemple).

turn : [F] changement (m), revirement (m) du marché et bénéfice qui en résulte.
— *of the market* : revirement du marché.
to turn in : déposer, remettre, retourner.
shares **turned in** *(or tendered)* : actions déposées.
turning : tournant.
turning point : moment critique, point décisif.
turning to account : mise en valeur.
turn-out : a) grève ; b) rendement, production.

turnkey contract : contrat (m) de livraison clefs en mains.

turnover : [A] [C] a) chiffre d'affaires ; b) rotation des stocks, volume des transactions, roulement du personnel ; c) période s'écoulant entre le placement d'un capital dans une affaire et la rentrée des fonds ainsi engagés.
account without — : compte sans mouvement.
assessment according to — : imposition d'après le chiffre d'affaires.
labour — : fluctuation de la main-d'œuvre.
staff — : renouvellement du personnel.
— *tax* : impôt, taxe sur le chiffre d'affaires.

turnpike : a) [U.S.] autoroute (f) ; b) barrière de péage.
— *money* : droit de passage.

turpis causa : une cause immorale (pour cause d'illégalité ou d'immoralité).

tutor : tuteur (m), précepteur (m).
[J] *subrogate tutor* : subrogé tuteur.
tutorship : fonction d'un tuteur, tutelle.
tutrix : tutrice.

two : deux.
the — *chamber system* : le système bicaméral.
— *digit inflation* : inflation à deux chiffres.
— *-pay bonds* : obligations payables en deux monnaies.
— *-sided contract* : contrat bilatéral.
— *-sided market* : marché à double tendance.
currency — *tier market* : double marché des changes.

tying up : [F] immobilisation (de capitaux).

type : a) marque (f), signe (m), caractère (m) ; b) type, spécimen, modèle.

— *of expenditures* : catégories de dépenses.
— *of treatment* : mode de traitement.
— *sample* : échantillon type.

typing pool : le secrétariat (l'ensemble du personnel).

NOTES

NOTES

U

uberrima fides: la franchise la plus parfaite.

ubi jus, ibi remedium: là où il y a un droit.

ullage: (D) manquant (a).

(the) ultimate customer: (C) le dernier consommateur, le consommateur du bout de la chaîne (ex. une femme achète de la nourriture non pour elle, mais pour ses enfants, qui sont ainsi les « derniers consommateurs »).

ultimatum: ultimatum (m).
[J] principe définitif ou fondamental.
to deliver an — : signifier un ultimatum.

« ultimo »: le mois dernier (expression quelquefois employée dans une correspondance).

ultra vires: au-delà de (leurs) pouvoirs, hors de (leur) compétence, [J] acte allant au-delà de l'autorité conférée par la loi et, par conséquent sans valeur. Terme appliqué notamment aux actes effectués par une société de commerce en dehors de ses status *(beyond the corporate powers)*.
to act — : commettre un excès de pouvoir.

umpire: surarbitre (m).
— *('s) award*: sentence d'arbitrage.
to umpire *a dispute*: arbitrer un différend.
to umpire between two parties: servir d'arbitre entre deux parties.

unaccounted: non comptabilisé (a).
— *for in the balance sheet*: qui ne figurent pas au bilan.

unaccredited: non accrédité (a).

unacknowledged: non reconnu (a) (enfant).

unalienable: inaliénable (a).

unallotted: non réparti (a).

unaltered: inchangé (a).

unappropriated: indivis, non distribué, non réparti (a).
— *funds*: fonds sans affectation déterminée.
— *profits*: bénéfices non distribués.

unassailable: inattaquable (a).

unassessed: non évalué, non imposé (a).

unassignable: inaliénable (a).

unavailable item: article (m) épuisé (a).

unbalanced: déséquilibré, non soldé (a).
— *growth*: croissance déséquilibrée.

uncalled: non versé (a).
— *capital*: capital non appelé.

uncertainty: incertitude (f).
[J] obscurité de rédaction d'un jugement pouvant en provoquer l'annulation.

uncertified: [J] (failli) qui n'a pas obtenu de contrat.

unchastity: infidélité de l'épouse.

unchecked: non contrôlé, non vérifié (a).

unclaimed: non réclamé (a).
— *letter*: lettre au rebut.
— *right*: droit non revendiqué.

uncleared: non liquidé (a).
[D] non dédouané.

uncleaved *(cheque)*: non compensé (chèque).

uncollected: non encaissé (a), non perçu.

unconscionable: sans conscience, sans scrupule (a).
[J] — *bargain*: contrat léonin.
oppressive and — *conduct*: existence immorale, sans vergogne.
— *demand*: demande inadmissible.

unconstituional: anti-constitutionnel (a), non conforme (a), contraire (à la Constitution).

uncontrollable: non contrôlable (a).
— *costs*: coûts qui échappent au contrôle (ex. à cause d'un changement du taux d'escompte, de la politique gouvernementale...).
— *factors*: facteurs qui échappent au contrôle.

uncorrected: non redressé (a).

uncovered: à découvert (a).
— *amounts*: montant des découverts.
— *bear*: baissier à découvert.

undefended: sans défense (a).
[J] — *prisoner*: accusé comparaissant sans avocat.
— *action, suit*: défaut (m) du défendeur.

undepreciated: non amorti (a).

under: sous, en vertu de, aux termes de, d'après.
— *arrest*: en état d'arrestation.
— *registered cover*: sous pli recommandé.
— *arrangements*: en vertu d'arrangements.
— *subsection*: aux termes du paragraphe.
— *the ordinary rules*: d'après les règles ordinaires.
— *the terms of*: aux termes de, d'après, selon.

undercapitalized: qui souffre d'investissements insuffisants.

undercharge: imposition insuffisante (f).

underconsumption: sous-consommation (f).

to undercut: faire des soumissions plus avantageuses, (se) vendre moins cher que.

under-developed: sous-développé (a).

under-employment: sous-emploi (m).

underestimation: sous-estimation (f).

to undergo: subir (une perte).

underlease: sous-location.

underlying: fondamental (a).
[F] — *inflation*: inflation sous-jacente.
[J] — *mortgage*: hypothèque de priorité.

undermanned: à court de personnel (a).

under par: au-dessous du pair (a).

underpayment: insuffisance de paiement.

underpriced: au-dessous de la valeur (a).

underprivileged classes: classes peu fortunées, économiquement faibles.

under-production: sous-production (f).

underseal (document): (acte) sur papier timbré.

undersecretary: sous-secrétaire d'état, adjoint de ministre.

to undersell: vendre au-dessous du cours (pour éliminer des concurrents).

undersigned: soussigné.

understaffed: à court de personnel (a).
to be — : manquer de (être à court de) personnel.

understanding: accord (m), entente (f).

to understate: minimiser, sous-estimer.

undersubscribed: non couvert (a).
the loan was — : l'emprunt n'a pas été couvert.

undertaking: engagement (m), promesse (f).
[J] soumission (f).
[C] entreprise commerciale.

undertone: fond (m).
market — : tendance profonde du marché.

undervaluation: sous-évaluation (f).
[ASS] sous-estimation (police d'assurance).

underwriting: souscription (f).
[F] garantie d'émission.
— *contract, agreement, commitment*: contrat de garantie, acte syndical, lettre de souscription éventuelle à forfait (par laquelle on s'engage, moyennant commission, à prendre tout ou partie des actions qui ne seraient pas souscrites à l'émission).
— *commission*: commission syndicale.
— *discount*: escompte à la souscription.
— *fee*: commission de garantie, commission de placement.
— *group, pool*: syndicat de prise ferme.
— *share*: part syndicataire.
— *syndicate*: syndicat, groupe de garantie, de souscription.
— *syndicate*: [ASS] a) souscription d'une police d'assurance; b) assurance maritime.
to underwrite: garantir, souscrire (une émission), assurer.
underwriter: [F] membre d'un syndicat de garantie, soumissionnaire (de bons), pl. le syndicat de garantie.
[ASS] assureur, sp. assureur maritime (qn. *Lloyd's underwriters*).

undeveloped land: propriété non bâtie, terrains inexploités.

undischarged : non déchargé, inaccompli (a).
[J] non réhabilité.
— *debt* : dette non soldée.
— *of an obligation* : non libéré d'une obligation.

undisclosed : caché, occulte (a).
[J] — *principal* : commettant dont le nom ne doit pas être divulgué, bailleur de fonds (voir *sleeping partner*).
payment to an — *recipient* : rémunération occulte.

undistributed : non réparti (a).
— , *undisposed of, profits* : bénéfices non distribués.

undivided : non divisé, entier (a).
[J] — *property* : biens indivis.
— *share (of property)* : fraction théorique du droit de propriété appartenant à chaque copropriétaire d'un bien indivis (*tenancy in common* et *joint tenancy*, voir *tenant*).
[F] — *profits* : bénéfices non distribués.

undue : indu.
[J] illégitime.
[J] — *influence* : a) captation d'héritage ; b) intimidation (voir *intimidation*).
— *preference* : fait par un débiteur insolvable de désintéresser un créancier in toto, dans les trois mois qui précèdent la faillite, susceptible d'empêcher et de suspendre sa réhabilitation ultérieure.
use of — *(military or administrative) authority* : abus d'autorité, excès de pouvoir.
[C] — *bill* : effet non échu, à échoir.
— *payment* : paiement inexigible, indu.

unduly : à tort, sans raison.
[J] illégalement.

unearned : immérité ; non gagné par le travail (a).
[A] — *income* : rente, revenu du capital.
— *increment* : plus-value, valeur ajoutée.
[C] — *commission* : commission payée d'avance.

uneconomic : non rentable (a).

unemployment : chômage (involontaire).
[A] — *benefit* : allocation, secours de chômage.
— *compensation, insurance* : assurance-chômage.
— *figure, rate* : taux de chômage.
— *funds* : caisse de chômage.
unemployed : chômeur, sans travail.
unemployed capital, funds : capital inemployé, fonds improductifs.
unemployed official : fonctionnaire en inactivité.

unencumbered : [J] libre d'hypothèque (a).

unendorsed : non endossé (a).

unfair : inéquitable (a), déloyal (a).
— *competition* : concurrence déloyale.
— *dismissal* : licenciement (m) injustifié.
— *labour practices* : emploi illicite de la main-d'œuvre.
— *price* : prix exorbitant.
— *wages* : salaires inadéquats.

unfashionable : démodé (a).

unfavourable (*balance of trade, exchange*) : (balance du commerce, change) défavorable (a).

unfit : impropre (a), qui ne convient pas, incapable (a).
to be — *for driving* : ne pas être en état de conduire.

unforeseen : imprévu (a).
[J] — *circumstances* : force majeure.

unfunded debt : [F] dette flottante, non consolidée.

unified : unifié, consolidé (a).
[F] — *debt* : dette consolidée.

uniform annual cost method : méthode (f) de l'annuité.

uniformity : uniformité (f).
Uniform *Sales Act* : [U.S.] modèle de loi destiné à uniformiser la législation sur les ventes dans les divers Etats de l'Union, et adopté par la majorité de ceux-ci.
[F] — *in taxation* : imposition uniforme, équitable.

unilateral contract : « contrat » unilatéral (en général échange d'une prestation contre une promesse).

uninsurable losses : pertes qu'aucune assurance ne peut couvrir.

union : union (f).
customs — : union douanière.
trade — : syndicat (m).
— *regulations* : règles syndicales.
— *shop* : see « *closed shop* ».

unissued : non émis (a).
— *capital* : capital non émis.
— *shares* : actions à la souche.

unit : unité (f), installation (f).
- *cost* : prix de revient unitaire.
- *holder* : investisseur dans une S.I.C.A.V. (see « *Unit trust* »).
monetary – : unité monétaire.
plant – *(s)* : installations d'une usine.
- *trust* # Société d'investissement à taux variable (S.I.C.A.V.).

United Kingdom : Royaume-Uni, comprenant l'Angleterre, le Pays de Galles, l'Ecosse et l'Irlande du Nord, mais non les îles anglo-normandes et l'île de Man.

United Nations Conference on Trade and Development
(U.N.C.T.A.D.) : Commission des Nations Unis pour le Commerce et le Développement (C.N.U.C.E.D.).

United Nations Organization : Organisation des Nations Unies (établie par la charte de San Francisco le 26 juin 1946).

united security market : marché (m) hors cote.

United States of America : Etats-Unis d'Amérique (créés par la Déclaration de l'Indépendance à Philadelphie, le 4 juillet 1776).

unity : unité (f), union (f).
[J] *the four* **unities** : les quatre communautés qui caractérisent l'indivision : a) communauté de possession : chaque indivisaire doit avoir droit à la possession de la totalité du fonds ; b) communauté de droit : les droits des indivisaires doivent être égaux ; c) communauté de titre : les droits de chacun doivent prendre source dans le même instrument ; d) communauté de durée : les droits doivent s'étendre sur une même période.
- *of possession* : consolidation de la possession, extinction de servitude (par fusion).
- *of title and interest* = *the four unities*.

university courts : [J] tribunaux des universités d'Oxford et de Cambridge, existant en vertu d'un privilège de juridiction..

unlawful : contraire à la foi, frauduleux (a).
[J] – *assembly* : attroupement séditieux.
- *child* : enfant illégitime, naturel.
- *entry* : prise de possession illégitime d'une terre.
- *means* : moyens illicites.

unless : à moins que.
- *otherwise agreed* : sauf stipulation contraire.

unlimited liability : responsabilité (f) non limitée.

unliquidated : de montant incertain.
[J] – *damages* : dommages-intérêts non liquidés, dont le montant doit être fixé par le jury (opp. *liquidated damages* = clause pénale).

unlisted : hors cote (a).
[B] *unlisted securities* : valeurs non cotées.

to unload *(stock)* : réaliser (valeurs).

unmarketable : invendable (a).

unmatured : [F] non échu (a).

unofficial : [B] libre (a).
- *market* : marché hors cote.
- *strike* : grève non officielle, non déclenchée par les syndicats.

unpaid : impayé (a).

unprofitable : non rentable (a).

unquoted : non coté (a).

unrecoverable : irrécouvrable (a).

unredeemable : non rachetable, non remboursable (a).

unrelated : sans lien de parenté (a).

labour unrest : agitation (f) sociale.

unsafe investment : investissement (m) hasardeux, véreux (a).

unsecured : non garanti, sans garantie, à découvert, ordinaire (a).
- *advances* : avances à découvert.
- *creditors* : créanciers ordinaires.

unsettled *(bill)* : note (f) impayée, impayé (m).

unsound : malsain (a).
- *business* : affaire qui périclite.
[J] – *in mind, of* – *mind* : aliéné, débile mental.
« *while of* – *mind* » : « alors qu'il n'était pas dans son bon sens ».

unsubscribed *(capital)* : (capital) non souscrit (a).

unsubsidized : non subventionné, sans prime.

– 644 –

untapped *(market)* : (marché) encore inexploité (a).

untaxable : non imposable (a).
— *costs :* faux frais.

unwarrantable : injustifié (a).

unweighed : non pondéré (a).
— *index :* indice non pondéré.

to unwind : dérouler.
[B] dégager, vendre en masse (marché monétaire).
unwinding : dégagement (m).

unwritten law : loi non écrite.
[J] droit coutumier et jurisprudentiel.

to be up : être en hausse.

to update : mettre à jour.
— *equipment, plant :* moderniser un équipement.

upfront : payable d'avance.

to upgrade : valoriser, enrichir.

upheaval : bouleversement (m).

upkeep : entretien (m).
— *expenses :* dépenses d'entretien, impenses.

up lift : [F] sur déduction.

upmarket products : produits de grand luxe, très chers.

upon : sur.
— *application :* sur demande.

Upper House : (Pol.) Chambre haute (ex. Lords, Sénat).

upscale *(item)* : (C) haut de gamme (article).

to upset : désorganiser.
upset *price :* mise à prix.
upsetting : désorganisation.

upsurge : [B] hausse très marquée.

upswing, uptrend, upward trend : tendance à la hausse, redressement, reprise.

up tick : [B] transaction à un cours supérieur.

uptown : [U.S.] quartier résidentiel.

up-valuation : réévaluation (f).

urban : urbain (a).
— *economics :* recherches d'économie urbaine.
— *equipment grid :* grille d'équipement urbain.

urgency order : [J] ordonnance de référé pour l'internement d'un aliéné.

usage : usage (m).
[J] a) pratique consacrée, qui peut devenir une coutume ; b) droit de passage.

usance : [C] usance (f).
bill and double — : effet à double usance.
— *draft :* traite à échéance (f).
local — : l'usance de la place.

use : bénéfice (m), emploi (m), usage (m), utilité (f).
— *value :* valeur d'usage.
for public — : pour cause d'utilité publique.

user : usager (m).
[J] a) droit d'usage continu ; b) détenteur précaire, usufruitier.
land subject to a right of — : propriété grevée d'une servitude.

usher : huissier.
[J] *court-usher :* huissier-audiencier.

usual terms : conditions d'usage (m).

usucaption : (civ.) usucaption.

usufruct : (civ.) [J] usufruit.
ownership without — : nue-propriété.

usurpation : usurpation (f).

usury : usure (f).
to lend upon — : prêter à usure.
usurious *interest :* intérêt usuraire.

utility : utilité (f) ; service public.
[U.K.] *public* — *undertaking :* services publics privatisés.
— *bill :* note d'eau, de gaz, d'électricité etc.
utilities : services publics, entreprise assurant un service public.

utter (outer) barrister : [J] (Engl.) avocat qui n'a pas encore été admis au barreau, qui plaide « en deçà » de la barre.

uttering : [J] émission de fausse monnaie, faux et usage de faux.

NOTES

V

vacancy: vide (m), vacance (f) (d'un emploi, d'une fonction), poste à pourvoir.
[ASS] — *clause*: clause dans une police maintenant l'assurance, même si le local reste inoccupé.
vacant *possession*: jouissance immédiate (d'un bien).
vacant succession: succession vacante.

to vacate: quitter, laisser libre, *(an apartment, land)* déménager, évacuer, *(office)* démissionner, se démettre, *(the premises)* vider les lieux.
[J] *(an order, a warrant of dispossess, a decree of divorce, an award)*: annuler *(in the first instance as well as on appeal)*.
vacating *of office*: démission.

vacation: vacances (f pl).
[J] vacations (f pl), vacances judiciaires.
[F] *accrued — pay*: provision pour congés payés.

vagabond, vagrant: vagabond (m).

vagrancy: vagabondage (m).

valid: valide, régulier (a).
— *until cancelled*: valable jusqu'à révocation, annulation.

validity: validité (f).
[J] *to dispute the — of a document*: s'inscrire en faux contre un document.

valorization: valorisation (f), [U.S.] maintien des prix.
[F] = *securitisation*: « valeurisation », mobiliérisation.

valuation: évaluation (f), appréciation (f) ; inventaire (m).
[J] prisée et estimation, expertise.
[ASS] valeur actuelle d'une police d'assurance sur la vie.
at a —: à dire d'expert.
incorrect —: évaluation inexacte.
to set too high a —: surestimer, surimposer.
to set too low a —: sous-estimer, sous-imposer.
valuator, *official* **valuer**: expert commissaire-priseur.

value: valeur (f), prix (m).
[J] **valuable** *consideration*: contre-partie dans un contrat (voir « *consideration* »).
[A] [C] *annual —*: [U.K.] revenu annuel (d'un bien agricole), valeur locative (de terres).
asset —: [U.S.] valeur de l'entreprise.
book —: valeur comptable.
current —: valeur courante.
discovery —: [U.S.] valeur de découverte (d'un gisement).
face —: valeur nominale.
fair —: valeur ou prix loyal et marchand.
market —: valeur marchande, vénale.
average market —: valeur moyenne marchande.
par —: montant nominal, au pair.
rental —: valeur locative.
site- —: [U.K.] valeur actuelle du sol (lors de la vente), valeur d'aliénation.
original site- —: [U.K.] valeur du sol à une date antérieure, valeur d'acquisition.
written down —: [U.K.] méthode d'amortissement dite de la valeur comptable.
increase of —: plus-value.
decrease of —: moins-value.
for — received: valeur reçue.
to lose —: s'avilir.
[F] se dévaloriser.
appraised —: valeur estimative.
— at cost: valeur au prix d'achat, au prix coûtant.
redemption —: valeur de remboursement.
— added tax (V.A.T.): taxe sur la valeur ajoutée (T.V.A.).
break-up —: valeur d'inventaire.
exchange —: valeur d'échange.
fall in —: dévalorisation.
invoice —: valeur de facture.
nominal —: valeur nominale.
rateable, taxable —: base brute d'imposition (en matière d'impôts locaux), valeur locative.
surrender —: valeur de rachat.
taxable —: valeur imposable.
— in exchange: contre-valeur.
valueless: sans valeur.
to be good —: être avantageux.
to value: évaluer, valoriser.
to value a cheque on London: valoriser un chèque sur Londres.
[ASS] *salvage —*: valeur résiduelle.
valued *policy*: police d'assurance dans laquelle la valeur de l'objet assuré est exprimée (opp. *unvalued, open policy*).

vanilla deal *(= (U.S.) « with no frills »)*: [F] [B] transaction en toute clarté (« sans

— 647 —

fioritures »).

variable : variable (a).
— *costs* : frais, coûts variables.
— *-yield securities* : titres à revenu variable.
[B] *to quote — exchange* : coter l'incertain.
[F] — *rate mortgage* : prêt (m) sur hypothèque à taux variable.

variance : désaccord (m), différence (f), écart (m), variance (f).
to be at — with s.o. : être en désaccord avec qn.

variation : variation (f).
seasonal — (s) : variations saisonnières.

variety : diversité (f).
— *reduction* : réduction des différences dans la fabrication et la présentation (afin de diminuer le prix de revient). Homogénéisation partielle de la production.

to vary : changer, modifier.
at varying intervals : à des périodes variables.

vault : chambre forte (f).
vault cash : [U.S.] réserves en espèces.

velocity : vitesse (f).
money —, — of money turnover : vitesse de circulation de la monnaie.

vendee : acheteur (m).
[J] acquéreur de biens immobiliers.
vending *machine* : distributeur (m) automatique (par ex. de boissons).

vendor : vendeur (m), apporteur (m).
[J] vendeur de biens immobiliers.
— *('s) assets* : valeurs d'apport.
— *('s) lien* : privilège du vendeur.
— *('s) shares* : actions de fondation.

vendue : [U.S.] vente aux enchères publiques.

venire facias : que tu fasses venir.

venireman : [J] candidat inscrit sur la liste des jurés *(panel)*.

venter (= womb) : ventre (m).
child by the second — : enfant du deuxième lit.

venture : risque (m), aventure (f).
[C] entreprise (f), opération (f), spéculation (f).
chances of a — : aléas d'une entreprise.
joint — : association en participation.
— *money* : argent aventuré.
— *nurturing* : contrat d'association-gestion.

— *capital* : capitaux de risque.
— *capital companies* : « sociétés de capitaux risqués », dont la raison sociale est le financement des technologies nouvelles.
— *worth method* : méthode de la valeur actuelle, méthode de la valeur en capital.

venue : juridiction (f), lieu du jugement.
[J] *to change the —* : renvoyer l'affaire devant un autre tribunal.

verdict : verdict (m) (quelquefois jugement).
[J] *general —* : (civ.) verdict en faveur du demandeur ou du défendeur fixant, le cas échéant, le montant des dommages-intérêts, (cr.) verdict de culpabilité ou d'acquittement.
special — : verdict admettant l'existence de certains faits et laissant au juge le soin d'appliquer la loi à ce sujet.
directed —, — set aside : voir jury.
open — : jugement dans une enquête de coroner : a) qui ne formule aucune conclusion sur les circonstances dans lesquelles la mort est survenue; b) qui conclut au crime, sans désigner le coupable.

verge : [J] ressort d'une juridiction.

verification : vérification (f), contrôle (m), confirmation (f).

to verify : vérifier.

versus (VS.) : contre (dans un procès : « Plaintiff » VS. « Defendant »).

vertical integration : intégration (f) verticale (d'une entreprise : de la matière première à la vente au détail).

to vest : investir d'un droit.
[J] — *s.o. with an authority* : revêtir qn d'une autorité.
— *s.o. with a function* : investir qn d'une fonction.
— *s.o. with an inheritance* : saisir qn d'un héritage.
— *property in s.o.* : assigner des biens à qn.
vested estate, interest : droits acquis.
vested funds : capitaux engagés (dévolus à).
to have a vested interest in a concern : avoir des capitaux (être intéressé) dans une entreprise.
vested in interest : droits acquis de jouissance future (en expectative).
vested in possession : droits acquis de jouissance immédiate.
vested rights : droits acquis en vertu de la constitution.
rights vested in the Crown : droits dévolus à la Couronne.
vesting *order* : envoi en possession.

vesting date of an annuity: date à partir de laquelle une rente doit courir.

vestry: sacristie (f).
vestry-book: registre de l'état-civil d'une paroisse.

to vet: (fam.) « mettre sur le gril » un candidat à un poste pour vérifier ses capacités (vient de *« vet »* pour *« veterinary »* : vétérinaire, et du verbe *« — »* : faire examiner une bête).

veteran (war): ancien combattant (m).

veto: veto (m).
 to veto: interdire, opposer son veto à.
 vetoing *stock:* action donnant le droit de veto.

vexata quaestio: question beaucoup débattue et non réglée.

vexatious: vexatoire (a).
 [J] — *actions:* abus de procédures judiciaires

vicarious: pour un autre, substitué (a).
 [J] — *liability:* responsabilité civile (syn. *liability over*).

vice: vice (m).
 [A] — *-squad:* brigade des mœurs.
 [C] *(of an instrument, of goods, etc):* vice (m), défaut (m).

vice: vice- (au lieu de).
 — *-president:* vice-président.
 — *-chairman:* vice-président.
 — *-manager:* vice-gérant.

videlicet, viz.: à savoir.

videotown: [U.S.] la clientèle des téléspectateurs.

view, viewers: regard (m), inspection (f) ; vue (f), jour (m).
 [J] descente sur les lieux du jury ou de quelques jurés *(the viewers)* et du juge dans un procès en matière immobilière ou au criminel.

viewdata system: système d'informations visualisées (qui permet de demander à un service spécialisé de télécommunications des informations qui sont reçues sur un écran de T.V.).

vigilance: vigilance (f).

villein: serf (m).

vinculo matrimonii: par (les, des) liens du mariage.

to vindicate: soutenir, justifier.

vindictive damages: dommages-intérêts punitifs pour préjudice moral.

vine-growing: viticulture (f).

vintage: vendange (m), cru (m), année (f).
 guarantee — : appellation contrôlée.

violence: violence (f).
 [J] *to resort to* — : se livrer à des voies de fait.
 robbery with — : vol à main armée.
 violent *presumption:* forte présomption.

virtue: vertu (f), qualité (f).
 by — *of:* en vertu de.

visit: visite.
 [J] *right of* — *and search:* droit de visite.
 — *to the scene of the occurrence:* descente sur les lieux.
 to visit *a place:* perquisitionner.
 visitorial *power,* **visitation:** droit de l'Etat d'inspecter la comptabilité des personnes morales.
 visitor: inspecteur, visiteur.
 chancery visitor: visiteur en matière d'interdiction d'aliénés.
 visitor's tax: taxe de séjour.

vis major: force majeure.
 [ASS] cas d'un des périls irrésistibles exceptés dans une police d'assurance maritime : ouragan, tremblement de terre, violence par les armes, etc.

vital: vital, essentiel à la vie ; mortel, fatal (a).
 [A] — *data:* données de l'état-civil.
 — *rate:* taux démographique.
 — *records:* registre d'état-civil.
 — *registration:* tenue des registres d'état-civil.
 — *statistics:* statistiques démographiques.

to vitiate: gâter, corrompre.
 [J] vicier.
 act **vitiated** *by a fundamental flaw:* acte entaché d'un vice radical.
 — *a transaction:* rendre une opération nulle.

vivos (inter): entre vifs.
 inter vivos gifts: donations entre vifs.

vocational: professionnel (a).
 — *guidance:* orientation professionnelle.
 — *training:* formation professionnelle.

voice: voix (f).
advisory — : voix consultative.

void: [J] nul et de nul effet (a).
absolutely — : radicalement nul.
null and — : nul et non avenu.
to make a clause — : frapper une clause de nullité.
voidable: résoluble, annulable.
voidance: résiliation.
voidness: nullité.

voire dire: [J] examen préliminaire d'un témoin par le juge pour se rendre compte de ses facultés et de son utilité.

volenti: à (celui) qui consent.

volition: volonté (f).
act of — : acte délibéré.

volume: volume (m).
— : volume des transactions.
— *discount*: rabais sur achats importants.
sales — : volume des ventes.
— *trading*: opération sur des blocs d'actions.

voluntary: volontaire (a et m).
[J] 1° a) résultant de la volonté des parties, exprimées dans un acte à cet effet, p. ex.
— *trust* = « trust » expressément constitué (opp. *implied, constructive trust*);
b) coupable, p. ex. : — *ignorance* = fermer les yeux (sur un délit, etc.);
c) bénévole, p. ex. : — *conveyance* = cession à titre gratuit;
d) spontané, p. ex. : — *confession* = aveu spontané.
2° a) bénéficiaire d'une cession à titre gratuit;
b) celui qui fournit des services sans promesse explicite ou tacite de rémunération.
— *body*: organisation soutenue par des contributions volontaires.

— *group*: groupement d'achat de détaillants.
— *liquidation*: liquidation volontaire (v. « declaration of solvency »).
— *redundancy*: licenciement consenti (contre indemnité).

vote: vote (m), suffrage (m), scrutin (m), *(by white and black balls or second ballot, at parliamentary election)* ballotage.
— *of an assembly*: délibération d'une assemblée.
— *of confidence*: vote de confiance.
— *of no confidence*: vote de défiance, motion (f) de censure.
popular — : consultation du corps électoral.
casting — : voix prépondérante.
to put to the — : mettre aux voix.
to tally the —*(s)*: compter les voix, dépouiller le scrutin.
to vote: voter.
to vote down: repousser.
[F] **voting** *trust*: arrangement selon lequel un ou plusieurs actionnaires détiennent des actions d'autres porteurs et exercent ainsi, par un vote groupé, le contrôle d'une société, tous les autres droits restant acquis.
voting power: droit de vote.
voting rights (of the shareholders): droits de vote (des actionnaires).
voting share: action donnant droit de vote.

voucher: a) garant; b) pièce à l'appui, pièce comptable, justificatif; c) bon d'échange, coupon.
[J] — *to warranty*: appel en garantie.
[A] *issue* — : facture (f) de sortie.
[C] fiche (f), bon (m), reçu (m).
cash — : bon de caisse.
— *copy*: justificatif.
— *for receipt*: récépissé, quittance.
vouchee: caution (f), personne appelée en garantie.
to vouch: affirmer, garantir qch., répondre de qn.

NOTES

NOTES

W

wage(s) : salaire (m), paye (f).
  hierarchical — *sliding :* hiérarchie des qualifications.
  incentive — : salaire au rendement.
  job — : salaire à la tâche.
  living — : salaire minimum.
  money — : salaire nominal.
  piece work — : salaire aux pièces.
  sliding — *scale :* échelle mobile des salaires.
  time- — : salaire au temps.
  — *agreements :* accords salariaux.
  — *bill, wage costs, wage outlay :* dépenses salariales.
  — *(s) board :* commission de contrôle de l'échelle des salaires.
  — *differential(s) :* grille des salaires.
  — *drift :* glissement des salaires.
  — *earners :* travailleurs salariés.
  — *freeze, wage standstill, wage stop :* blocage des salaires.
  — *hike* [U.S.] , *wage increase :* hausse des salaires.
  — *lag :* décalage des salaires par rapport aux prix.
  — *(s) policy :* politique des salaires.
  — *-price spiral :* spirale des prix-salaires.
  — *rate :* taux de rémunération.
  — *restraint :* modération (f) des revendications syndicales sur les salaires.
  — *sheet :* feuille de paye.
  — *system :* mode de rémunération.
  — *taxes :* taxe sur les salaires.
  — *worker :* travailleur payé à la semaine.

wager : pari (m).

waif : enfant abandonné.
  [J] épave (f), (pl) *(bona vavieta)* objets volés, jetés par le voleur dans sa fuite.

wait : attente (f).
  — *days :* jours d'attente.
  [J] *lying in* — : guet-apens (m).
  to wait : attendre.
  [C] « *repairs while you wait* » : réparations à la minute.
  [ASS] **waiting** *period :* période entre la signature d'une police et l'entrée en vigueur de l'assurance.
  [C] *waiting time compensation :* indemnité pour retard (à s'acquitter d'un service convenu).

waiver : [J] renonciation (f) à un droit.
  — *clause :* clause d'abandon.
  — *of a claim :* désistement de revendication.
  — *of exemption :* clause de renonciation à une exonération de responsabilité insérée dans un effet de commerce.
  implied — : renonciation tacite.
  — *of privilege :* renonciation au droit de récusation.
  — *of protest :* dispense de protêt (« sans frais »).
  — *of the Statute of limitation :* renonciation à faire valoir une prescription acquise.
  to waive *a defect :* ne pas insister sur un défaut de procédure.
  to waive a jury : s'accorder (entre parties) à renoncer au jury et s'en remettre au juge unique.
  to waive an objection : renoncer à une objection.
  when the payment has been **waived** : quand on a renoncé au paiement.

to walk out : faire grève.
  to stage a **walk out** : « débrayer », organiser une grève, un « débrayage ».

wall : mur (m).
  blind — : mur orbe.
  bow — : mur d'appui.
  enclosing — : mur de clôture.
  partition — : mur de refend, de séparation.
  party — : mur mitoyen.
  main — *(s) :* gros murs, l'œuvre.
  [D] *customs-* — *(s) :* barrières douanières.

wall-streeter : [U.S.] boursier (m).

« **wanted** » : (« on recherche ») avis (m) de recherche (criminel fugitif).
  situations — : demandes d'emploi (dans la presse).

war : guerre (f).
  — *damages :* dommages de guerre.
  — *veteran :* ancien combattant.

ward : a) tutelle (f) ; b) pupille (m et f) ; c) service (m), salle d'hôpital.
  [J] — *in Chancery,* — *of Court :* pupille sous tutelle judiciaire.
  [A] arrondissement, quartier d'une ville.
  electoral — : circonscription électorale.

warden : gardien, *(of an institution, a prison)* directeur, *(of a museum)* conservateur, *(of a city)* gouverneur.

— *of the standards*: gardien des poids et mesures.

warder: gardien de prison.
female — *or* **wardress**: gardienne de prison.

wardmote: [A] conseil d'arrondissement de la Cité de Londres.

warehouse: entrepôt (m), magasin (m), dépôt (m) de marchandises.
[D] *bonded* — : entrepôt en douane, magasins généraux, docks.
— *charges*: frais : a) de magasinage (m) ; b) d'entreposage (m).
— *company*: société d'entreposage.
— *receipt*: warrant (m), récépissé d'entrepôt.
furniture — : garde-meuble (m).

wares: marchandises (f pl), produits manufacturés.

warning: préavis (m).
— *indicator*: indicateur d'alerte.

warrant: garant (m), garantie (f) ; autorisation (f), pouvoir (m) ; certificat (m), brevet (m), bon (m) de souscription (f).
[J] mandat (m), ordre (m).
— *of arrest*: mandat d'amener.
— *of attachment*: ordonnance de saisie.
— *of attorney*: autorisation écrite donnée à une personne *(the attorney)* de comparaître par procuration.
bench — : mandat d'arrêt lancé en cours d'audience.
death — : arrêt de mort.
deportation — : ordre de refoulement (d'un étranger indésirable).
— *of dispossess*: ordonnance d'expulsion (d'un local).
— *of extradition*: mandat d'extradition.
search, ancillary — : mandat de perquisition.
[A] — *for payment*: ordonnancement.
royal — : brevet de fournisseur de la Cour.
[B] *with* — *(s)*: avec droits d'achat de titres.
bearer —, *share* — (ou *stock certificate*) : titre au porteur.
[D] *dock, warehouse* — : warrant, bulletin de dépôt, certificat d'entrepôt.
[F] *dividend* — : coupon d'arrérages.
interest — : mandat d'intérêts.
equity — : autorisation (f) ou droit de souscription d'actions.

warranty: autorisation (f), justification (f).
[J] clause pénale du contrat.
breach of — : rupture de garantie.
action for breach of —, *of authority*: action pour abus de mandat.
— *with reference to goods*: garantie du vendeur.

implied — : garantie tacite (de poids, de mesure, etc.).
— *of quiet enjoyment*: clause de paisible jouissance.
personal — : cautionnement personnel.
— *of title*: attestation du titre.
[ASS] déclaration d'un assuré concernant un risque ou un danger ; (ass. maritime) la condition préalable : la garantie de navigabilité (voir *seaworthiness*).

wash sale: [U.S.] [A] vente fictive d'un bien pour échapper à l'impôt.
[B] — *(s) of stock*: opération à un cours fictif.
wastage: gaspillage (m) (v. « natural wastage »).

waste: dégâts (m pl), terre en friche, gaspillage (m).
[J] dégradation (d'un fonds d'usufruit ou qui survient pendant une location).
permissive — : négligence, détérioration faute d'entretien.
[J] délit d'omission.
voluntary — : abus de jouissance, dégâts commis intentionnellement.
[J] délit de commission.
— *making*: développement du gaspillage.
radio-active — : déchets radio-actifs.

watercourse: cours (m), conduite (f) d'eau.
[J] servitude de drainage.

watered capital: [B] capital dilué.

water-power: houille blanche, sources d'énergie hydroélectrique.

wave: vague (f).
— *of speculation*: vague de spéculation.
[B] — *of selling orders*: vague de dégagement.
[C] *long* — *(s)*: cycles longs.

waveson: voir *floatsam*.

way: voie (f), route (f), chemin (m) ; côté (m), direction (f), moyen (m), façon (f), manière (f), cours (m), course (f).
by — *of*: sous forme de.
[J] *right of* — : servitude de passage.
[A] priorité de passage à un croisement.
— *-bill*: [C] a) lettre de voiture ; b) liste des passagers.
— *-going crop*: récolte parvenue à maturité après la fin du bail.
— *(s) and means*: voies et moyens.
— *(s) and Means Committee*: [U.S.] Commission des Finances.

weak: faible (a), (valeur) en baisse.
to weaken *(market)*: fléchir (le marché).

— 654 —

weakness: faiblesse (f), baisse (f), effritement (m).

wealth: richesse (f).

wear and tear: détérioration (f).
[J] usure normale (d'une chose louée).
[C] dépréciation et usure du matériel.

wedlock: [J] mariage (m).
born in, out of — : né dans le mariage, hors du mariage.

weight: poids (m).
the — *of taxation*: le poids de la fiscalité.
— *(s) and measures*: poids et mesures.
coefficient of — : coefficient de pondération.
weighted *average cost*: coût moyen pondéré (évaluation des stocks).
weighting *allowance*: indemnité supplémentaire.
to welch (*to welsh*): (fam.) lever le pied (pour ne pas payer des dettes, surtout de jeu).

welfare: bien-être (m).
public — : prospérité sociale.
[A] *advisory social* — *services*: fonctions consultatives en matière de service social.
child — : protection de l'enfance, le service des enfants.
community — : protection de la collectivité.
community — *center*: centre social.
family — : protection de la famille.
industrial — : services sociaux dans l'industrie.
maternal — : protection de la maternité.
public — : assistance sociale publique, (par extension) services publics d'assistance.
rural social — : service social rural.
— *secretary*: conseiller de service social.
social — : service social, prévoyance sociale.
social — *administration*: administration du service social, les services sociaux.
social — *adviser*: conseiller de service social.
social — *official*: travailleur social, membre du personnel du service social.
social — *services*: services d'assistance et de protection sociales.
social — *work*: travail social.
social — *worker*: travailleur social, assistante sociale.
« *The* — *State* » : « l'Etat Providence ».
youth — : protection de la jeunesse.
— *activities, organisations*: associations de bienfaisance.

the Well of the Court: [J] le Parquet.

well being effect: effet euphorisant.

wharf: quai (m), embarcadère (m), débarcadère (m).
[D] *sufferance* — : voir *sufferance*.

wharfage: débarquement (m), embarquement (m) ou mise (f) en entrepôt (de marchandises).
[A] droits de bassin.

wharfinger: a) propriétaire d'un quai ; b) gardien du quai.

whatever: quelque... que.
of any kind — : de quelque nature que ce soit.

wheat: blé (m).
— *acreage*: emblavure.
wheel: roue (f).
the — *(s) of government*: les rouages de l'Administration.
wheeler-dealer: (fam.) commerçant, homme d'affaires de moralité douteuse.
« **when issued** » **securities**: valeurs qui seront cotées au moment de l'émission.

where: où (se traduit souvent dans les textes fiscaux par « lorsque », « quand » ou « au cas où »).
whereby: par où, par le fait que, en vertu de.
— *-got* (*or* **wheregone**): méthode d'analyse des mouvements dans la comptabilité de l'entreprise.

whereas: vu que... (conj.).
[J] attendu que..., considérant que...
« *the* — *clause* » : « considérant ou considérants, préambule au dispositif du jugement, débutant par : « *now therefore...* ».
wherefore: par conséquent, pourquoi (adv).
[J] « *the* — *clause* » : conclusion de l'exposé des faits contenus dans la plainte et les autres pièces produites : « —, *plaintiff demands judgment against the defendant for the sum of...* ».

whips: [U.K.] chefs de file des groupes parlementaires, députés chargés de la discipline de vote.
the Government have taken off the — : le Gouvernement laisse ses partisans libres de voter comme bon leur semblera.

white: (a) blanc.
— *acre, black acre*: [J] [U.K.] désignation imaginaire de terrains pour les besoins d'une démonstration (au lieu de dire : champ A, champ B).
— *collar worker*: employé de bureau.
— *crime*: criminalité (f) d'affaires.
— *goods*: (gros) appareils de ménage, linge

de ménage.
— *knight,* — *squire (rescue bid)* : (B) intervention amicale d'un tiers qui achète par avance un pourcentage appréciable (30 % au moins) du capital d'une société menacée d'une OPA totale (technique de sauvetage « chevalier blanc », « page blanc »), intervention « chevaleresque », désintéressée pour sauver une société d'une OPA (*Knight :* chevalier et *Squire :* écuyer, page).

white persons : [J] [A] [U.S.] personnes de race blanche (opp. *colored persons*).

white slavery : traite des blanches.
to whittle away, down : rogner (la pension de qqn), comprimer (les prix de revient).

whole : entier, complet (a).
as a — : en totalité, dans son ensemble.
— *amounts :* montants arrondis.
— *life assurance :* assurance en cas de décès.
wholly-*owned subsidiary :* filiale en propriété exclusive.
wholly *dependent :* entièrement à charge.
wholesale : vente en gros.
— *dealer (trader),* **wholesaler** : grossiste (m).
— *firm, warehouse :* maison de gros.
— *price index :* indice (m) des prix de gros.

wife : épouse (f).
[J] « — *and children* » : un legs fait à « la femme et aux enfants » est présumé fait à la femme en usufruit, et aux enfants communs en nue propriété.

wig-and-pen folk : (fam.) les juristes.

wildcat : louche, illégal (a).
— *scheme :* opération suspecte.
— *strike :* grève sauvage.

wilful : volontaire, destiné.
[J] prémédité (a).
— *damage :* bris, dommage délibéré.
— *and malicious injury :* préjudice causé intentionnellement.
— *mistake :* erreur commise de parti pris.
— *murder :* assassinat, homicide volontaire.

will : volonté.
[J] testament (m) ; anciennement, l'acte de dernière volonté, concernant les biens immobiliers, était nommée « will » (ou « devise »), et les mobiliers « testament ». Actuellement les deux termes sont équivalents, avec une préférence pour le premier.
to dispute a — : attaquer un testament.
to make one's — : faire son testament.
to mention s.o. in one's — : coucher qn sur son testament.
[A] — *and Probate (Department) :* l'Enregistrement.
— -*form :* formule de testament.

windfall gains, profit :[U.S.]« cadeaux » de l'Etat sous forme d'allègements fiscaux, « cadeaux » fiscaux, profit exceptionnel.

winding-up : cessation (f) de commerce.
[J] liquidation d'une société, suivie de la dissolution.
— *a company :* liquidation judiciaire.

window : vitrine (f), période d'ouverture d'un marché intermittent.
— -*dressing :* art de l'étalage, truquage, [F] habillage de bilan.
— -*dressing of the balance sheet :* truquage du bilan.
— -*guidance :* [U.S.] qualifie les techniques de politique économique à modulation fine permettant de « naviguer à vue ».

winegrowing : viticulture (f).

winner : [B] valeur en hausse, qui gagne du terrain.

to wipe off : apurer, liquider.

to wipe out : supprimer, éliminer, annuler.

with all due despatch : [A] avec toute la diligence possible.
to withdraw : retirer, se retirer.

withdrawal : retrait (m).
[J] voir *discontinuance*.
— *of a juror :* retrait d'un juré au cours d'une audience par consentement mutuel des parties, pour arrêter les débats, le jury n'étant ainsi plus au complet.
— *of a complaint :* retrait d'une plainte.
[F] — *of capital :* retrait de fonds.
money — : opération de démonétisation.
account — : retrait bancaire.

withholding : refus (m).
[J] détention (f), rétention (f).
— *of the truth :* dissimulation de la vérité.
[F] *payroll* —, — *of tax at source on wages :* retenue à la source de l'impôt sur les salaires.
— *at the source :* retenue à la source.
— *tax :* impôt retenu à la source.
to withhold *a document :* refuser de communiquer une pièce.
to withhold property : détenir un bien.
to withhold release of the property : s'abstenir de libérer un bien.

within : dans, au cours de.
— *a reasonable time :* dans un délai raisonnable.

- *the year*: au cours de l'année.
- *two months*: dans les deux mois.
- *the meaning assigned by section...*: au sens de l'article...
- *prescribed time*: dans les délais prescrits.

without: sans.
- *notice*: sans préavis, de bonne foi.
- *prejudice*: sans préjudice (voir : *prejudice*).
- *recourse to me*: sans retour (clause d'endos).
- *reference to*: en faisant abstraction de.
- *regard to*: sans considération de.

with-profits: participation proportionnelle aux bénéfices (see « endowment assurance »).

with respect to: [A] quant à, en ce qui concerne.

witness: témoignage (m), témoin (m et f) (d'un accident...).
- [J] — *in court*: témoin judiciaire, déposant.
- *adverse, hostile* — : témoin se révélant hostile à la partie qui l'interroge.
- *attesting, subscribing* —, — *to a deed, a document*: témoin instrumentaire, certificateur.
- *defaulting* — : témoin défaillant.
- — *for the defence*: témoin à décharge.
- *direct* — : témoin direct.
- *ear-* — : témoin auriculaire.
- *eye-* — : témoin oculaire.
- *exceptionable* — : témoin reprochable.
- *false* — : faux témoin.
- *indirect* — : témoin indirect.
- *material* — : témoin de fait (dont la comparution est nécessaire dans une action au criminel).
- *mute* — : témoin muet.
- *prosecuting* — : délateur (voir : *informer*).
- *reliable* — : témoin digne de foi.
- *reticent* — : témoin réticent.
- *unexceptionable* — : témoin irréprochable.
- — *to a will*: témoin testamentaire.
- *to bear* —, *to testify*: témoigner.
- *to bribe, to suborn, to tamper with a* — : suborner un témoin.
- *to call s.o. as* — : appeler qn comme témoin.
- *to take exception to a* — : reprocher, récuser un témoin.
- *hearing of* — *(es)*: audition des témoins.
- *the proof* — : la preuve testimoniale.
- *to subpoena a* — : citer, assigner un témoin.
- *in* — *whereof*: en témoignage de quoi.
- *to witness*: déposer.
- *-box*: barre des témoins.

witnessing: témoignage (m).
- [J] [A] attestation (f), certification (f), *(of a signature)* légalisation (f).

wording: formulation (f).

work: travail (m).
- *clerical* — : travail de bureau.
- —*(s) council* # comité d'entreprise.
- *job* — : travail à la pièce.
- *repetitive* — : [U.S.] travail en série.
- — *day*: jour ouvrable.
- *(the)* — *force*: les effectifs.
- —*-in strike*: occupation (d'une usine, par le personnel) avec poursuite du travail.
- — *group, work study*: groupe de travail, d'étude d'un projet.
- — *to rule strike*: grève du zèle.

to work: travailler, produire, exploiter.
- ... *works a forfeiture*: ...conduit à la déchéance.
- *to work a mine*: exploiter une mine.
- *acceptance of performance* **worked** *a waiver of...*: l'acceptation de s'exécuter a entraîné la renonciation à...

to work out: élaborer, étudier, calculer.
to work up: étendre, élargir, avancer.

worker: ouvrier (m).
- *semi-skilled* — : ouvrier spécialisé.
- *skilled* — : ouvrier qualifié.
- —*(s') director*: membre du Conseil d'Administration chargé des intérêts du personnel.

working: exploitation (f).
- — *account*: compte d'exploitation.
- — *balance, capital*: fonds de roulement.
- — *control*: contrôle effectif.
- — *expenses*: frais d'exploitation.
- — *interest*: participation directe.
- — *out the interest due*: décompte des intérêts dus.
- — *plant, stock*: matériel d'exploitation.
- — *week*: semaine de travail.

working agreement: modus vivendi.

workloads: carnets (m pl) de commandes.

workmanship: fini (m), finition (f).

workmen's compensation: réparation des accidents du travail et maladies professionnelles.

works: établissement industriel, ensemble des installations.

workshop: réunion (f) périodique.

world: monde (m).
- — *markets*: marchés internationaux.
- — *trade*: commerce international.
- — *trade center*: centre d'affaires international.

worldwide *and consolidated results*: bénéfice mondial et consolidé.

worsening: détérioration (f).
- — *of terms of trade*: détérioration des termes

de l'échange.

worth : valeur (f)
future — : valeur acquise.

worthless : sans valeur.
[F] sans provision.

wraps : couverture (f) (de voyage).
to keep under — : garder secret (un nouveau modèle), ne pas divulguer.

wreck : épave (f).
[J] épave de navire ainsi que les choses de jet et de flot, et les choses sans maître.
— *commissioners* : commissaires nommés pour enquêter sur les décès survenus au cours d'accidents ou de catastrophes maritimes.

wrecked : sinistré (a).

writ : écrit (m).
[J] exploit, ordonnance, acte judiciaire (sp. acte introductif d'instance).
Le — est une ordonnance établie sous le sceau de la Couronne, d'un tribunal ou d'un fonctionnaire d'autorité, enjoignant à qn de faire ou de ne pas faire qch. Les — sont de deux ordres :
A. *prerogative* — (s) : ordonnances émises en vertu de la prérogative royale et rendues par un tribunal supérieur à sa discrétion, sur un commencement de preuve (prima facie *case*) pour empêcher un abus de pouvoir ou de droit. Ce sont les *writs* suivants :
1) — *of* Habeas Corpus (ad subjiciendum) : « prend sa personne et amène-la moi ». Orgueil du droit A.A., garantie des libertés civiques, c'est le *writ* assignant à un fonctionnaire ayant un prisonnier sous sa garde, de l'amener devant le tribunal.
Ce principe, très ancien, qui protégeait déjà au moyen-âge les sujets contre les « lettres de cachet », s'applique en droit moderne dans trois directions : a) droit de tout prisonnier de comparaître devant son juge naturel, pour vérifier la légalité de son emprisonnement, b) vérification de la compétence du tribunal qui aurait ordonné une arrestation ou une peine privative de liberté (voir *collateral attack*), c) en droit civil, lorsque l'un des parents réclame la garde d'un enfant.
2) Certiorari : — ordonnant à un tribunal inférieur de soumettre le dossier d'une affaire au tribunal supérieur, aux fins de vérification (Engl. remplacé par un *order of* certiorari, moins formel).
3) *Prohibition* : défense de statuer (absolue, provisoire ou partielle) (Engl. remplacé par un *order of prohibition*, moins formel).
4) Mandamus : « nous ordonnons », injonction à une personne physique ou morale d'accomplir un acte de fonction publique, lorsque tous autres moyens se sont révélés inefficaces (Engl. remplacé par un *order of* mandamus, moins formel).
5) Quo warranto : « de quelle autorité », ordre de la Couronne, enjoignant à celui qui revendique ou usurpe une fonction, franchise ou droit, de faire connaître l'autorité dont il se prévaut (Engl. remplacé par une injonction).
6) Ne exeat Regno, [U.S.] Republica : interdiction signifiée à un débiteur poursuivi en justice, de quitter le territoire.
7) Procedendo : « à procéder », — a) enjoignant au juge du tribunal inférieur qui impose aux parties des délais excessifs, de rendre le jugement, b) renvoyant au tribunal inférieur une cause évoquée sans raison suffisante par un tribunal supérieur.
Ces sept — (s) relèvent de la juridiction de la Division du Banc de la Reine.
B. — (s) *of right* : ordonnances de plein droit, ex debito justitiæ, dont on distingue deux catégories :
1) *original* — (s) : les actes introductifs d'instance de jadis qui sont à l'origine du système d'actions multiformes du C.L., comportant chacune son — spécial qui correspond au fondement juridique particulier de chaque demande.
Ces — (s), établis au nom de la Couronne, ont été remplacés par le — *of summons* judiciaire : citation, assignation, ajournement.
2) *judicial* — (s) : ordonnances judiciaires de toute nature, introductives d'instance, interlocutoires et exécutoires. En voici les principales :
alternative — : ordonnance enjoignant au défendeur de donner satisfaction au demandeur ou d'exposer au tribunal les raisons qu'il croit avoir de s'y refuser.
— *of assistance* : ordre permettant de mettre le bénéficiaire d'un jugement en possession d'immeubles attribués.
— *of attachment* : ordonnance de saisie-arrêt.
— *of execution* : exploit de saisie-exécution.
— *of execution on furniture* : saisie-gagerie.
— *of sequestration* : séquestre judiciaire.
— *of summons* : assignation (f), citation (f).
— *-server* : porteur de contraintes, huissier.
to serve a — *upon s.o.* : signifier un exploit à qn.
to writ : assigner.

to write : écrire.
[J] *the* **written** *law* : la loi écrite (opp. *the common law*).
— *down* : consigner par écrit.
[C] — *back* : contrepasser, ristourner (un article).
— *off* : amortir, défalquer.

written off : amorti, annulé (a).
written instrument : acte écrit.
— *out* : tirer (un chèque).
[B] — *up* : révaluer.
[ASS] — *insurance* : souscrire une police d'assurance.
write-down *allowance* : déduction (f) fiscale pour actif défectible.
write-down, written down value : provision (f) pour créances douteuses.
write off : passation (f) d'une créance irrécupérable par profits et pertes.
write-up : « papier » (m), article (m) (de journal).

writing : écriture (f).
[ASS] souscription (f).
[B] *covered* — : vente d'option d'achat sur des valeurs déjà détenues par le vendeur.
evidence in — : preuve littérale.
to confirm in — : confirmer par écrit.

wrong : mal (m), tort (m) fait à qn, action injuste.
[J] violation d'un droit, infraction à la loi.
private — : atteinte aux droits d'un individu.
public — : atteinte aux droits de la collectivité.
wrongdoer : auteur (m) d'une injustice.
wrongful *dismissal* : see « dismissal ».

NOTES

X-Y-Z

xenophobe, xenophobia : xénophobe, xénophobie.

xerography : photocopie (f).
   to xerox : photocopier.

yard : chantier (m).
   ship- — : chantier de constructions navales.

year : année (f), exercice (m).
   calendar — : année civile.
   present business — : l'exercice en cours.
   [F] *financial* — : année budgétaire.
   fiscal — : année fiscale, exercice financier.
   taxable — : année d'imposition.
   [J] — *and day :* une année et un jour (délai prévu dans certains cas). Ainsi « *assault and battery* » : le délit de coups et blessures est considéré comme homicide, si la victime meurt dans ce délai.
   — *in,* — *out :* une année après l'autre.
   — *on* — *rate of growth :* temps de croissance mesuré sur une période d'un an.
   — *('s) purchase :* (calcul de) la durée d'amortissement (d'un achat, d'un investissement).
   — *book :* annuaire, (pl) anciens recueils de jurisprudence.
   yearly : annuel.
   yearly rental : redevance annuelle.

yield *(of a mine, etc.)* : production (f), produit (m), débit (m), *(of a fruit tree, a capital)* rapport (m), revenu (m), *(of a field)* récolte (f), rendement (m), *(of a machine, a forest)* rendement (m).
   [J] **to yield** *a right :* céder un droit.
   yielding *law :* droit dispositif.
   [F] — *of a tax :* rendement d'un impôt.
   — *of taxation :* rendement des impôts.
   [B] **to yield points :** céder des points sur le cours.
   — *capacity :* productivité.
   — *curve :* courbe des taux d'intérêt.
   — *differential :* différentiel de rendement.
   — *to maturity :* rendement à l'échéance.
   gross current — : taux actuariel brut.
   net — : revenu net.
   to lock in a — : garantir un rendement.

york-antwerp rules : (ASS. mar.) textes juridiques de référence en cas de demande d'indemnité pour fortune de mer.

Z chart : diagramme (m) indiquant la moyenne de la production ou des ventes d'un mois sur l'autre.

zero : zéro.
   — *-base budgeting* (ZBB) : méthode de préparation budgétaire remettant en cause toutes les dépenses.
   [F] — *coupon :* coupon zéro.
   — *growth :* croissance zéro, stagnation.
   — *-rated :* biens et services soumis à la T.V.A. mais (momentanément) au taux de 0 %.

zipcode : (U.S.) code (m) postal.

zoom : montée (f) en flèche.
   zooming *inflation :* inflation galopante.

zone : zone (f), district (m), quartier (m).
   [A] zone de construction selon le plan d'urbanisme d'une ville = *the* **zoning** *law,* [U.S.] *ordinance.*
   business — : centre des affaires.
   industrial zoning : zones industrielles.
   residential, restricted — : quartier résidentiel (construction soumise à des servitudes).
   unrestricted — : district des usines (construction libre).
   postal — : arrondissement des P. et T.
   [C] *free* —(s) : zones franches.

NOTES

NOTES

NOTES

NOTES

NOTES

NOTES

DANS LA MÊME COLLECTION

Dictionnaire juridique Français-Espagnol/Espagnol-Français
N. AMOROS RICA et O. MERLIN

Dictionnaire juridique Français-Allemand/Allemand-Français
R. DUMEY et W. PLASA

Achevé d'imprimer en janvier 1992
sur les presses de l'imprimerie Laballery
58500 Clamecy

Pour le compte des :
Editions Juridiques Associées
26, rue Vercingétorix
75014 - Paris

Dépôt légal : janvier 1992
Numéro d'impression : 110036